清华营销学系列英文版教材

消费者行为学

Consumer Behavior Tenth Edition

[美] 利昂·希夫曼 (Leon G. Schiffman)
莱斯利·拉扎尔·卡努克 (Leslie Lazar Kanuk) 著

第10版

清华大学出版社

北京

北京市版权局著作权合同登记号 图字：01-2016-3550

Original edition, entitled Consumer Behavior, 10th Edition, 9780135053013 by Leon G. Schiffman and Leslie lazar Kanuk, published by Pearson Education, Inc, publishing as Prentice Hall, Copyright ©2010.

图书在版编目（CIP）数据

消费者行为学 =Consumer Behavior：第 10 版：英文 /(美) 利昂・希夫曼 (Leon G. Schiffman), (美) 莱斯利・拉扎尔・卡努克 (Leslie Lazar Kanuk) 著. —北京：清华大学出版社，2017（2022.2重印）

(清华营销学系列英文版教材)

ISBN 978-7-302-44976-8

Ⅰ. ①消… Ⅱ. ①利… ②莱… Ⅲ. ①消费者行为论－教材－英文 Ⅳ. ①F713.55

中国版本图书馆 CIP 数据核字(2016)第 213963 号

责任编辑：王 青
封面设计：常雪影
责任印制：沈 露

出版发行：清华大学出版社
网 址：http://www.tup.com.cn，http://www.wqbook.com
地 址：北京清华大学学研大厦 A 座 **邮 编**：100084
社 总 机：010-62770175 **邮 购**：010-62786544
投稿与读者服务：010-62776969, c-service@tup.tsinghua.edu.cn
质量反馈：010-62772015, zhiliang@tup.tsinghua.edu.cn
印 装 者：北京同文印刷有限责任公司
经 销：全国新华书店
开 本：203mm×260mm **印 张**：37.5
版 次：2017 年 1 月第 1 次印刷 **印 次**：2022 年 2月第 3 次印刷
定 价：109.00 元

产品编号：067008-03

出版说明

为了适应经济全球化的发展趋势，满足国内广大读者了解、学习和借鉴国外先进的管理经验和掌握经济理论的前沿动态，清华大学出版社与国外著名出版公司合作影印出版一系列英文版经济管理方面的图书。我们所选择的图书，基本上是已再版多次、在国外深受欢迎，并被广泛采用的优秀教材，绝大部分是该领域中较具权威性的经典之作。

由于原作者所处国家的政治、经济和文化背景等与我国不同，对书中所持观点，敬请广大读者在阅读过程中注意加以分析和鉴别。

我们期望这套影印书的出版对我国经济科学的发展能有所帮助，对我国经济管理专业的教学能有所促进。

欢迎广大读者给我们提出宝贵的意见和建议；同时也欢迎有关的专业人士向我们推荐您所接触到的国外优秀图书。

清华大学出版社经管事业部

2016 年 11 月

总 序

世纪之交，中国与世界的发展呈现最显著的两大趋势棗以网络为代表的信息技术的突飞猛进，以及经济全球化的激烈挑战。无论是无远弗界的因特网，还是日益密切的政治、经济、文化等方面的国际合作，都标示着 21 世纪的中国是一个更加开放的中国，也面临着一个更加开放的世界。

教育，特别是管理教育总是扮演着学习与合作的先行者的角色。改革开放以来，尤其是 20 世纪 90 年代之后，为了探寻中国国情与国际上一切优秀的管理教育思想、方法和手段的完美结合，为了更好地培养高层次的“面向国际市场竞争、具备国际经营头脑”的管理者，我国的教育机构与美国、欧洲、澳洲以及亚洲一些国家和地区的大量的著名管理学院和顶尖跨国企业建立了长期密切的合作关系。以清华大学经济管理学院为例，2000 年，学院顾问委员会成立，并于 10 月举行了第一次会议，2001 年 4 月又举行了第二次会议。这个顾问委员会包括了世界上最大的一些跨国公司和中国几家顶尖企业的最高领导人，其阵容之大、层次之高，超过了世界上任何一所商学院。在这样高层次、多样化、重实效的管理教育国际合作中，教师和学生与国外的交流机会大幅度增加，越来越深刻地融入全球性的教育、文化和思想观念的时代变革中，我们的管理教育工作者和经济管理学习者，更加真切地体验到这个世界正发生着深刻的变化，也更主动地探寻和把握着世界经济发展和跨国企业运作的脉搏。

我国管理教育的发展，闭关锁国、闭门造车是绝对不行的，必须同国际接轨，按照国际一流的水准来要求自己。正如朱镕基同志在清华大学经济管理学院成立十周年时所发的贺信中指出的那样：“建设有中国特色的社会主义，需要一大批掌握市场经济的一般规律，熟悉其运行规则，而又了解中国企业实情的经济管理人才。清华大学经济管理学院就要敢于借鉴、引进世界上一切优秀的经济管理学院的教学内容、方法和手段，结合中国的国情，办成世界第一流的经管学院。”作为达到世界一流的一个重要基础，朱镕基同志多次建议清华的 MBA 教育要加强英语教学。我体会，这不仅因为英语是当今世界交往中重要的语言工具，是连接中国与世界的重要桥梁和媒介，而且更是中国经济管理人才参与国际竞争，加强国际合作，实现中国企业的国际战略的基石。推动和实行英文教学并不是目的，真正的目的在于培养学生棗 这些未来的企业家棗 能够具备同国际竞争对手、合作伙伴沟通和对抗的能力。按照这一要求，清华大学经济管理学院正在不断推动英语教学的步伐，使得英语不仅是一门需要学习的核心课程，而且渗透到各门专业课程的学习当中。

课堂讲授之外，课前课后的大量英文原版著作、案例的阅读对于提高学生的英文水平也是非常关键的。这不仅是积累相当的专业词汇的重要手段，而且是对学习者思维方式的有效训练。

我们知道，就阅读而言，学习和借鉴国外先进的管理经验和掌握经济理论动态，或是阅读翻译作品，或是阅读原著。前者属于间接阅读，后者属于直接阅读。直接阅读取决于读者的外文阅读能力，有较高外语水平的读者当然喜欢直接阅读原著，这样不仅可以避免因译者的疏忽或水平所限而造成的纰漏，同时也可以尽享原作者思想的真实表达。而对于那些有一定外语基础，但又不能完全独立阅读国外原著的读者来说，外文的阅读能力是需要加强培养和训练的，尤其是专业外语的阅读能力更是如此。如果一个人永远不接触专业外版图书，他在获得国外学术信息方面就永远会比别人差半年甚至一年的时间，他就会在无形中减弱自己的竞争能力。因此，我们认为，有一定外语基础的读者，都应该尝试一下阅读外文原版，只要努力并坚持，就一定能过了这道关，到那时就能体验到直接阅读的妙处了。

在掌握大量术语的同时，我们更看重读者在阅读英文原版著作时对于西方管理者或研究者的思维方式的学习和体会。我认为，原汁原味的世界级大师富有特色的表达方式背后，反映了思维习惯，反映了思想精髓，反映了文化特征，也反映了战略偏好。知己知彼，对于跨文化的管理思想、方法的学习，一定要熟悉这些思想、方法所孕育、成长的文化土壤，这样，有朝一日才能真正"具备国际战略头脑"。

以往，普通读者购买和阅读英文原版还有一个书价的障碍。一本外版书少则几十美元，多则上百美元，一般读者只能望书兴叹。随着全球经济合作步伐的加快，目前在出版行业有了一种新的合作出版的方式，即外文影印版，其价格几乎与国内同类图书持平。这样一来，读者可以不必再为书价发愁。清华大学出版社这些年在这方面一直以独特的优势领先于同行。早在 1997 年，清华大学出版社敢为人先，在国内最早推出一批优秀商学英文版教材，规模宏大，在企业界和管理教育界引起不小的轰动，更使国内莘莘学子受益良多。

为了配合清华大学经济管理学院推动英文授课的急需，也为了向全国更多的 MBA 试点院校和更多的经济管理学院的教师和学生提供学习上的支持，清华大学出版社再次隆重推出与世界著名出版集团合作的英文原版影印商学教科书，也使广大工商界人士、经济管理类学生享用到最新最好、质优价廉的国际教材。

祝愿我国的管理教育事业在社会各界的大力支持和关心下不断发展、日进日新；祝愿我国的经济建设在不断涌现的大批高层次的面向国际市场竞争、具备国际经营头脑的管理者的勉力经营下早日中兴。

赵纯均 教授

清华大学经济管理学院

简明目录

Brief Contents

Contents

PART TWO I THE CONSUMER AS AN INDIVIDUAL 104

Chapters 4 through **8** provide the reader with a comprehensive picture of consumer psychology. They describe the psychological concepts that account for individual behavior and demonstrate how these dimensions influence the individual's consumption-related behavior. **Chapter 9** shows how communication links consumers as individuals to the world and people around them.

4 Consumer Motivation 104

5 Personality and Consumer Behavior 134

6 Consumer Perception 172

PART THREE | CONSUMERS IN THEIR SOCIAL AND CULTURAL SETTINGS 318

Chapters 10 to 13 provide the reader with a detailed picture of the social and cultural dimensions of consumer behavior. They explain how these factors affect the attitudes and behavior of individuals in the United States and the world beyond, and demonstrate how an in-depth knowledge of social and behavioral concepts enable marketers to achieve their marketing objectives.

12 Subcultures and Consumer Behavior 390

13 Cross-Cultural Consumer Behavior: An International Perspective 424

PART FOUR | THE CONSUMER'S DECISION-MAKING PROCESS AND ETHICAL DIMENSIONS 448

Chapter 14 describes the diffusion of innovations. **Chapter 15** examines the model of consumer-decision making, which ties together the psychological, social, and cultural concepts examined throughout the book. It also examines various related aspects of consumption behavior (such as gift giving) and explores the outcomes of relationship marketing from the consumer's perspective. The book concludes with **Chapter 16**, which explores marketing ethics and social responsibility in the context of consumer behavior.

14 Consumers and the Diffusion of Innovations 448

15 Consumer Decision Making and Beyond 476

Preface

This is the tenth edition of the first strategically focused consumer behavior textbook ever published. Since its first edition (issued in 1978), this book has centered on the examination and application of consumer behavior to the planning, development, and implementation of marketing strategies, and we continue this managerial emphasis in the tenth edition of *Consumer Behavior*. This edition captures the impact of new media on consumer behavior and on marketers' ability to learn more about customers' purchases and target them more precisely. Recognizing that new technologies may produce socially undesirable practices and also acknowledging the urgency of environmentally friendly business strategies, we have written a new chapter on marketing ethics and social responsibility. As in the past, we have continued integrating research about the global population into the discussion of every aspect of consumer behavior.

In this new edition, we have intensified our emphasis on marketing strategy, incorporating strong theoretical and applications orientations. Following the revised definition of *marketing* (by the American Marketing Association), which emphasizes creating value for customers and society, we enhanced the discussion of customer retention and loyalty throughout the text. Always true believers in the marketing concept, we are confident that we fully meet the needs of our own consumers—students, professors of consumer behavior, and marketing practitioners—by providing a text that is highly readable and that clearly explains the relevant and timely concepts on which the discipline of consumer behavior is based.

The text includes numerous real-world examples that demonstrate how marketing practitioners have used the understanding of consumption patterns in solving marketing problems and developing effective marketing measures. We remain convinced that effective market segmentation and strategic targeting provide the structure and direction for successful market practice. To this end, we have refined the discussion of these concepts and applied them to new media and communication technologies.

What's New to the 10th Edition

The text has been thoroughly updated and revised to best describe the changing environment of consumption behavior. The new features and where they appear in the text are fully detailed in the table on the inside front cover. They include:

- New and extensive coverage of the use of new media in creating more effective targeting strategies and addressable and customized promotional messages.
- New discussion of the role of consumer behavior in advancing marketers' social responsibility and ethics.
- Greater emphasis on applying the knowledge of consumer behavior in the development of marketing strategies.
- Enhanced coverage of the global dimensions of consumer behavior throughout the book.
- Learning objectives are now stated at the beginning of each chapter and identified at the start of the corresponding sections in each chapter.
- Many of the cases in this edition are brand new, and two cases now appear at the end of each chapter.
- Revised exercises that focus on critical thinking and the application of the material to real-world situations. Many exercises now require online research.

Innovative Learning Tools for Our Students

As professors, we are keenly aware of what makes students stand out in class. Just like **positioning** products and **differentiating** them from the competition (these concepts are described throughout the text) are the keys to effective marketing, your ability to *position yourself* in your professor's mind and distinguish yourself among your classmates are the keys to doing well in this course. Furthermore, following the logic of a classic commercial that states "you never get a second chance to make a first impression," your positioning (or marketing) of yourself must start at the *very beginning* of the course. To this end, this text includes several new features especially designed to enable you to stand out during the course, as well as facilitate your learning and enhance your involvement with the fascinating field of consumer behavior:

- The titles of all figures featuring ads are **questions**. You will be able to answer each question after reading the material pertaining to that figure. We suggest that you read each chapter and write down short answers to these questions *before* the class covering that chapter, so that you can productively participate in class discussions.
- Each chapter begins with a list of **learning objectives,** and a learning objective also appears at the start of every main section in each chapter. These objectives provide you with a focus in reading each part of the book.
- The **exercises** and **cases** at the end of each chapter are aimed at enhancing your critical thinking skills and ability to apply the text's material to real-world marketing strategies.
- We revised the exercises and focused them on critical thinking and the application of the material to real-world situations. You should complete those exercises that ask you to find materials (e.g., print ads), apply them to the course's material, and present them to the class. Even if your professor doesn't require you to do so, completing these assignments will most likely result in your professor's recognition. All professors appreciate students who bring in examples related to the course to class because such initiatives favorably reflect their own ability to generate enthusiasm toward marketing and consumer behavior among their students.
- **www.pearsonglobaleditions.com/schiffman** contains valuable resources for both students and professors, including free access to an interactive student study guide.

The Text's Organization

This 10th edition of *Consumer Behavior* is divided into four parts and sixteen chapters.

Part 1 provides the background and tools for a comprehensive understanding of the consumer behavior principles examined throughout the rest of the book. Chapter 1, "Consumer Behavior: Meeting Changes and Challenges," sets the tone for the book. It introduces the reader to the study of consumer behavior and its evolution, examines how providing value is the foundation for creating and keeping satisfied and profitable customers, and describes the enormous impact of new technologies and media on studying and targeting consumers. The chapter also introduces a model of consumer decision making, providing a structural framework for the interrelationships among the consumer behavior principles examined throughout the book. Chapter 2, "The Consumer Research Process," is a greatly expanded overview of the process and the techniques used to study consumption patterns. Chapter 3, "Market Segmentation and Strategic Targeting," was rewritten and now describes a unique classification of the bases for segmenting consumers and innovative strategic targeting methods.

Part 2 discusses the consumer as an individual. Chapter 4, "Consumer Motivation," describes consumer needs and motivations, exploring the key concepts of human motivation and setting goals, as well as the rational and emotional bases of consumer actions. Chapter 5, "Personality and Consumer Behavior," describes the impact of personality theories on consumer behavior and explores, among other concepts, consumer materialism, fixated consumption, and compulsive consumption behavior, as well as the notions of self-image and virtual personality and self. Chapter 6, "Consumer Perception," examines the impact of consumer perception on marketing strategy and the importance of product positioning and repositioning. Chapter 7, "Consumer Learning," describes how consumers learn, and discusses behavioral and cognitive learning theories, limited and extensive information processing, and the applications of consumer involvement theory to marketing practice. Chapter 8, "Consumer Attitude Formation and Change," examines consumer attitudes. Chapter 9, "Communication and Consumer Behavior," which was rewritten, demonstrates that communication is the bridge between individuals and the world around them and includes a brand new discussion of persuasive promotion, traditional and new media, and measuring the effectiveness of advertising messages.

Part 3 focuses on the social and cultural dimensions of consumer behavior. Chapter 10, "The Family and Its Social Class Standing," describes the influence of the family and its social class on consumption (in previous editions these concepts were covered in separate chapters). Chapter 11, "Influence of Culture on Consumer Behavior," focuses on the influence of culture and our society's core values on buying activities. Chapter 12, "Subcultures and Consumer Behavior," investigates the impact of societal and subcultural values, beliefs, and customs on consumer behavior. Chapter 13, "Cross-Cultural Consumer Behavior: An International Perspective," concludes this part of the book with a discussion of cross-cultural marketing within an increasingly global marketplace.

Part 4 explores consumer decision making and marketing ethics. Chapter 14, "Consumers and the Diffusion of Innovations," now focuses on the strategic applications of the diffusion of innovations framework (the coverage of interpersonal influences that was part of this chapter now appears in Chapter 9). Chapter 15, "Consumer Decision Making and Beyond," describes how consumers make product decisions, expands on the increasingly important practice of relationship marketing, and ties together the psychological, social, and cultural concepts discussed throughout the book. Chapter 16, "Marketing Ethics and Social Responsibility," is new to the text and covers social responsibility, potentially unethical marketing strategies, and socially desirable marketing such as advocating social causes and green marketing.

Acknowledgments

First, we are especially grateful to our own consumers, the graduate and undergraduate students of consumer behavior and their professors, who have provided us with invaluable experiential feedback to our earlier editions.

We thank our colleagues and friends at the Tobin College of Business at St. John's University, in particular: Dean Steven D. Papamarcos and Associate Dean Victoria Shoaf; Dr. A. Noel Doherty and the entire St. John's Department of Marketing for providing a warm and friendly environment in which to conduct research and write. Special thanks to our friends and colleagues: Benny Barak, Barry Berman, Joel Evans, William James, Charles McMellon, Susan Caccavale, Richard Laskin, and Elaine Sherman of the Zarb School of Business at Hofstra University; Randi Priluck, Martin Topol, and Mary Long of the Lubin School at Pace University; Stephen Pirog, Dean Karen Boroff, and Alex Simonson of the Stillman School of Business at Seton Hall University; Fredrica Rudell of the Hagan School of Business at Iona College; Steve Gould and other colleagues at Baruch College–CUNY; Mark Kay of Montclair State University; and Deborah J. Cohn at Touro College Graduate School of Business.

We especially would like to thank the following people who reviewed the 10th edition and offered many thoughtful comments and suggestions: Dale F. Kehr, University of Memphis; David W. Crain, Whittier College; Doug Cords, California State University, Fresno; Mary Laforge, Clemson University; Ronald Clark, East Carolina University; and Denise Guastello, Carroll College.

Over the years, we have received many thoughtful suggestions, insights, and highly constructive comments from the following professors: Harold Kassarjian, UCLA; David Brinberg, Virginia Polytechnic Institute; John Holmes, Simmons College; Joel Saegert, The University of Texas at San Antonio; Lewis Hershey, Eastern Missouri State College; William R. Dillon, Southern Methodist University; Havva J. Meric, East Carolina University; Ron Goldsmith,

Florida State University; Richard Yalch, University of Washington; Mark Young, Winona State University; Michael Taylor, Marietta College; Daniel Johnson, Bradford University; Bob Settle, San Diego State University; Gerald Cavallo, Fairfield University; Kristina Cannon-Bonventre, Northeastern University; Kathy Petit, University of Idaho; Douglas W. Mellott, Jr., Radford University; Darvin R. Hoffman, Texas A&M University; David Sheperd, University of Tennessee at Chattanooga; John T. Shaw, Providence College; Janet G. Hibbard, Eastern Kentucky University; Ron Lennon, Barry University; Jeanne Mueller, Cornell University; Charles Gulas, Wright State University; James W. Cagley, University of Tulsa; Kenneth R. Lord, Niagara University; Paul Chao, University of Northern Iowa; John H. Holmes, Skidmore College; Sheri Zeigler, University of Hawaii; Christina Goulding, Wolverhampton University, United Kingdom; U. B. Bradley, London Guildhall University, United Kingdom; Adrienne Czerwin-Abbott, Dublin Institute of Technology, Ireland; and Bernard A. Delagneau, The University of Wales, Aberystwyth, United Kingdom.

We graciously acknowledge Alan Pollack, who has provided us with invaluable insights into the legal and ethical issues of intellectual property and the marketing process. We also acknowledge Horace Phillimore of Gardmat Electronics; Ken Weinstein of Honeywell International, Inc.; Hank Edelman and Kelley Smith of Patek Philippe; Don Siebert, an independent marketing consultant; Ross Copper of Gold n Fish Marketing Group; Lancy Herman of Mediamark Research; and Walter McCullough and Moya Amateau of Ipsos Mendelsohn Research. We are grateful to the executives and staff of the following research firms for their continuous flow of interesting illustrative materials: Claritas Corporation, Simmons Marketing Research Bureau, Donnelley Marketing Information Services, and SRI International.

Our sincerest thanks go to the many people at Pearson who aided and supported us in the editorial, design, and production processes of this tenth edition, specifically our editor, James Heine, who has provided us with invaluable direction and encouragement; Ana Jankowski, our highly focused, ever-diligent and supportive production project manager; and Ashley Santora, product development manager, whose responsiveness and attention to detail helped us stay on track throughout the revision process.

Finally, we would like to give very special recognition to Professor Stanley Garfunkel of CUNY for his untiring support, assistance, advice, encouragement, and, most of all, friendship.

Pearson would like to acknowledge and thank the following people for their work on the Global Edition:

Dr. Melodena Stephens Balakrishnan, University of Wollongong in Dubai, Dubai.

Dr. Jean Boisvert, PhD, American University of Sharjah, UAE.

Dr. Bernard Lee, City University of Hong Kong, Hong Kong.

Mosquito WK Leung, Community College of City University, Hong Kong.

Fiona Newton, Monash University, Australia.

Dr. Ian Michael, Professor of Marketing, Zayed University, Dubai.

Professor Mohammad Ibrahim Obeidat, University of Jordan Amman, Jordan.

Dr. Piyush Sharma, The Hong Kong Polytechnic University, Hong Kong.

John and Diane Sutherland.

Taki Tshivhase, Department of Industrial and Organizational Psychology, University of South Africa, South Africa.

Dr Leona Ungerer, Department of Industrial and Organizational Psychology, University of South Africa, South Africa.

Christine Yum, Hong Kong Institute of Vocational Education, Hong Kong.

1

Consumer Behavior: Meeting Changes and Challenges

WE LIVE in a world of rapidly expanding communications options and shifting consumer information preferences. Global consumers of all backgrounds, but especially younger consumers, are increasingly getting their news and information from online sources, messages to their cell phones, or other digital mobile devices. Also, they are increasingly turning to the Internet for consumption-related information and using more information from other consumers (received via web forums, blogs, and social networks) and less from traditional advertising in mass media. There has also been a growing interest among younger consumers in safeguarding the environment and various forms of green marketing. Figure 1.1 presents a Siemens ad that asks the question: "How can you power a planet hungry for electricity without damaging it?" The ad goes on to provide its answer to the question. Research also suggests that there is a segment of consumers who are environmentally concerned and who are especially likely to pay attention to such an ad. Later in this chapter and in Chapter 16, we will further examine this important consumer and marketing topic. For now, we will examine how changing consumer appetites for communications and information are impacting how products, services, and even political candidates are being marketed.

After the presidential election of 2008, many politicians and their marketing consultants, be they Democrats or Republicans, supporters of Obama or opposed to Obama, agreed on one thing: No recent political marketing campaign better provides a picture of how to effectively communicate with target consumers than Barack Obama's campaign to become the 44th President of the United States. To set the tone for this 10th edition of *Consumer Behavior,* and the study of consumer behavior, we explore the dynamics of consumer behavior and marketing through a brief examination of Barack Obama's successful marketing drive for the U.S. presidency.

Early on, during Obama's quest to become the Democratic Party's candidate for the 2008 presidential election, his organization already demonstrated how in touch it was with the American public's mind-set by using a wide range of marketing communications options and communicating

FIGURE 1.1

Source: Courtesy of Siemens Corporation.

QUESTION: *To Which Segment of Consumers Will This Ad Appeal?*

superbly with different groups of target voters. Obama's effective communication strategy is well reflected in this quote from a major news magazine during the primary leading up to the 2008 presidential election.[1]

> It is a buzz that Obama is finding new and creative ways . . . in which the concept of community has grown to include MySpace and Facebook. No campaign has been more aggressive in tapping into social networks and leveraging the financial power of hundreds of thousands of small donors. Nor has any other campaign found such innovative ways to extend its reach by using the Internet . . .

It was clear that candidate Obama and his advisers thought strategically and envisioned a political marketing program that fully appreciated the importance of understanding consumers' needs and wants (i.e., in this case the "consumers" are "voting citizens"). The effectiveness of this marketing campaign comes from the integration of all types of marketing messages, targeted to specific audiences, and from employing a wide range of media tools (i.e., from mass media advertising to highly targeted Internet e-mail messages). Thus, Obama's campaign illustrates how an understanding of citizen-voters' shifting information preferences can be applied to effectively reach targeted consumers and provide them with an inspiring "picture" of how the candidate proposes to solve a wide range of important problems that will make both individuals and their country better off.[2] Political marketing experts and campaign strategists widely acknowledged that the Obama campaign was the first major political marketing campaign to understand voters' changing media and information-seeking patterns. Clearly, such insights enabled the campaign to deliver a convincing message to enough citizens.[3] Thus, the Obama campaign decision to combine an extensive amount of new media (e.g., e-mail and text messaging, with a strong Web site and social networking presence) with traditional marketing communications vehicles (e.g., political rallies, TV debates, press releases, mass media interviews, and political advertising) was a highly effective strategy. From a consumer behavior viewpoint, using such a combination of new and traditional media reflected a realization by the Obama campaigners that consumers were expanding their choice of communications vehicles and the need to better meet the newly changed media preferences of different segments of voters. Being armed with such knowledge, the campaign strategists were able to target the media preferences of voters, financial contributors, and those who wished to volunteer their time and effort to support the Obama candidacy.

Once nominated by the Democratic Party, candidate Obama's campaign was highly successful at pinpointing and regularly communicating with highly supportive microsegments of voters.[4] Moreover, Obama's campaign advisers were also able to engage large numbers of previously unregistered voters and small-scale financial supporters (many of whom had never made a political contribution before). Because of its strategic use of new and traditional media, President Obama's campaign tactics are likely to become a "guidebook" for how to run a political marketing campaign in the future.

The Obama campaign demonstrates that marketers who are responsive to consumers' needs, as well as how they wish to be communicated with, will be more likely to be successful. For instance, marketers are increasingly redirecting consumers from their traditional corporate Web sites to more informal and "friendlier feeling" brand or product-specific blog sites. Table 1.1 contains a sample of corporate Web sites and corresponding examples of consumer-oriented brand or product sites maintained by the same company. As an example, Figure 1.2 presents an example drawn from Table 1.1 of one pair of P&G sites (i.e., the company's main site and a corresponding consumer brand-specific site). The opening page of the company's main Web site is on the top, and the corresponding consumer-oriented product or brand-specific site is on the bottom. There may be some differences that pop out at you. However, in order to get a sense of the differences between the two types of sites, go online and compare a number of company main sites and consumer-product specific sites. Still further, if the consumer-oriented brand or product site happens to contain a consumer discussion forum, examine it. See if it provides an opportunity for consumers to exchange ideas and experiences in a "relaxed and friendly" atmosphere. Remember, the company can also benefit from hosting a discussion forum. Most important it provides the brand or product's marketing team with an opportunity to regularly "look-in" and secure invaluable consumer feedback that will enable it to design better products, and to craft more responsive consumer messages (see Chapter 2 for a detailed examination of the "looking-in" research approach).[5]

Learning Objectives

1.1 *To Understand What Consumer Behavior Is and the Different Types of Consumers.*

1.2 *To Understand the Relationship Between Consumer Behavior and the Marketing Concept, the Societal Marketing Concept, as Well as Segmentation, Targeting, and Positioning.*

1.3 *To Understand the Relationship Between Consumer Behavior and Customer Value, Satisfaction, Trust, and Retention.*

1.4 *To Understand How New Technologies Are Enabling Marketers to Better Satisfy the Needs and Wants of Consumers.*

1.5 *To Understand How Marketers Are Increasingly Able to Reach Consumers Wherever Consumers Wish to Be Reached.*

1.6 *To Understand How the World's Economic Condition Is Leading to Consumption Instability and Change.*

1.7 *To Understand the Makeup and Composition of a Model of Consumer Behavior.*

1.8 *To Understand the Structure of This Book.*

What Is Consumer Behavior?

Learning Objective

1.1 *To Understand What Consumer Behavior Is and the Different Types of Consumers.*

We define **consumer behavior** as the behavior that consumers display in *searching for, purchasing, using, evaluating, and disposing of products and services that they expect will satisfy their needs*. Consumer behavior focuses on how individual consumers and families or households make decisions to spend their available resources (time, money, effort) on consumption-related items. That includes what they buy, why they buy it, when they buy it, where they buy it, how often they buy it, how often they use it, how they evaluate it after the purchase, the impact of such evaluations on future purchases, and how they dispose of it.

While all consumers are unique; nevertheless, one of the most important constants among all of us, despite our differences, is that we are all consumers. We use or consume on a regular basis food, clothing, shelter, transportation, education, equipment, vacations, necessities, luxuries, services, and even ideas. As consumers, we play a vital role in the health of the economy—local, national, and international. The purchase decisions we make affect the demand for basic raw materials, for transportation, for production, for banking; they affect the employment of workers and the deployment of resources, the success of some industries and the failure of others. In order to succeed in any business, and especially in today's dynamic and rapidly evolving marketplace, marketers need to know everything they can about consumers—what they want, what they think, how they work, and how they spend their leisure time. They need to understand the personal and group influences that affect consumer decisions and how these decisions are made. And, in these days of ever-widening media choices, they need to not only identify their target audiences, but they need to know where and how to reach them.

In its broadest sense, the term *consumer behavior* describes two different kinds of consuming entities: the personal consumer and the organizational consumer. The **personal consumer** buys goods and services for his or her own use, for the use of the household, or as a gift for a friend. In each of these contexts, the products are bought for final use by individuals, who are referred to as *end users* or ultimate consumers. The second category of consumer—the **organizational consumer**—includes profit and not-for-profit businesses, government agencies (local, provincial, and national), and institutions (e.g., schools, hospitals, and prisons), all of which must buy products, equipment, and services in order to run their organizations. Despite the importance of both categories of consumers—individuals and organizations—this book will focus on the individual consumer, who purchases for his or her own personal use or for household use. End-use consumption is perhaps the most pervasive of all types of consumer

TABLE 1.1 A List of Selected Companies' Main Web Sites and Brand-Specific Sites

COMPANY	COMPANY URL	BRAND	BRAND URL
Amazon	www.amazon.com	AmazonWire	www.amazon.com/gp/gss/detail/10840/103-5286678-4472616
BMW	www.bmwusa.com/Default.aspx	BMW TV	www.bmw-web.tv/en/channel/new
Boeing	www.boeing.com/commercial	N/A	http://boeingblogs.com/randy
Coca-Cola	www.cokecce.com/pages/homeContent.asp	Coke	www.mycokerewards.com
Dell	www.dell.com	Direct2Dell	http://en.community.dell.com/blogs/direct2dell
Ford	www.ford.com	N/A	http://blog.ford.com/index.cfm?resetcountry=false
General Mills	www.generalmills.com/corporate/index.aspx	Betty Crocker	http://image.e.bettycrocker.com/members/8293/dme_example.html
General Motors	www.gm.com	Chevrolet Malibu	www.chevrolet.com/2009malibu
General Motors	www.gm.com	N/A	http://fastlane.gmblogs.com
Google	www.google.com/corporate	N/A	http://googleblog.blogspot.com
Intuit	www.intuit.com	QuickBooks	http://community.intuit.com/quickbooks
Kellogg's	www.kelloggcompany.com	Cheez-It Crackers	www.cheezit.com
Nike	www.nike.com/nikeos/p/nike/en_US	NikeID	http://nikeid.nike.com/nikeid/?sitesrc=USLP
Pacific Sands Inc.	www.pacificsands.biz	EcoOne	www.ecoonespa.com
Procter & Gamble	http://pg.com/en_US/index.shtml	Tide	www.tide.com/en_US/index.jsp
Sara Lee	www.saralee.com	Jimmy Dean	www.jimmydean.com
Southwest Airlines	www.southwest.com	N/A	http://twitter.com/SouthwestAir
Starbucks	www.starbucks.com	N/A	http://twitter.com/Starbucks
The Clorox Company	www.thecloroxcompany.com	N/A	www.thecloroxcompany.com/company/students/index.html
Wal-Mart	http://walmartstores.com	N/A	http://checkoutblog.com
Whole Foods	www.wholefoodsmarket.com	N/A	www.wholefoodsmarket.com/forums/index.php
Yum! Brands	www.yum.com	KFC	www.kfc.com
Zappos	www.zappos.com	N/A	http://twitter.com/zappos

Source: Prepared by Theodore S. LaBarbera, Webmaster for American Association of Advertising Agencies, and MBA student at the Peter J. Tobin College of Business, St. John's University, December 18, 2008.

FIGURE 1.2
P&G's Main Web Site and Its Tide Web Site

Source: Courtesy of Procter and Gamble.

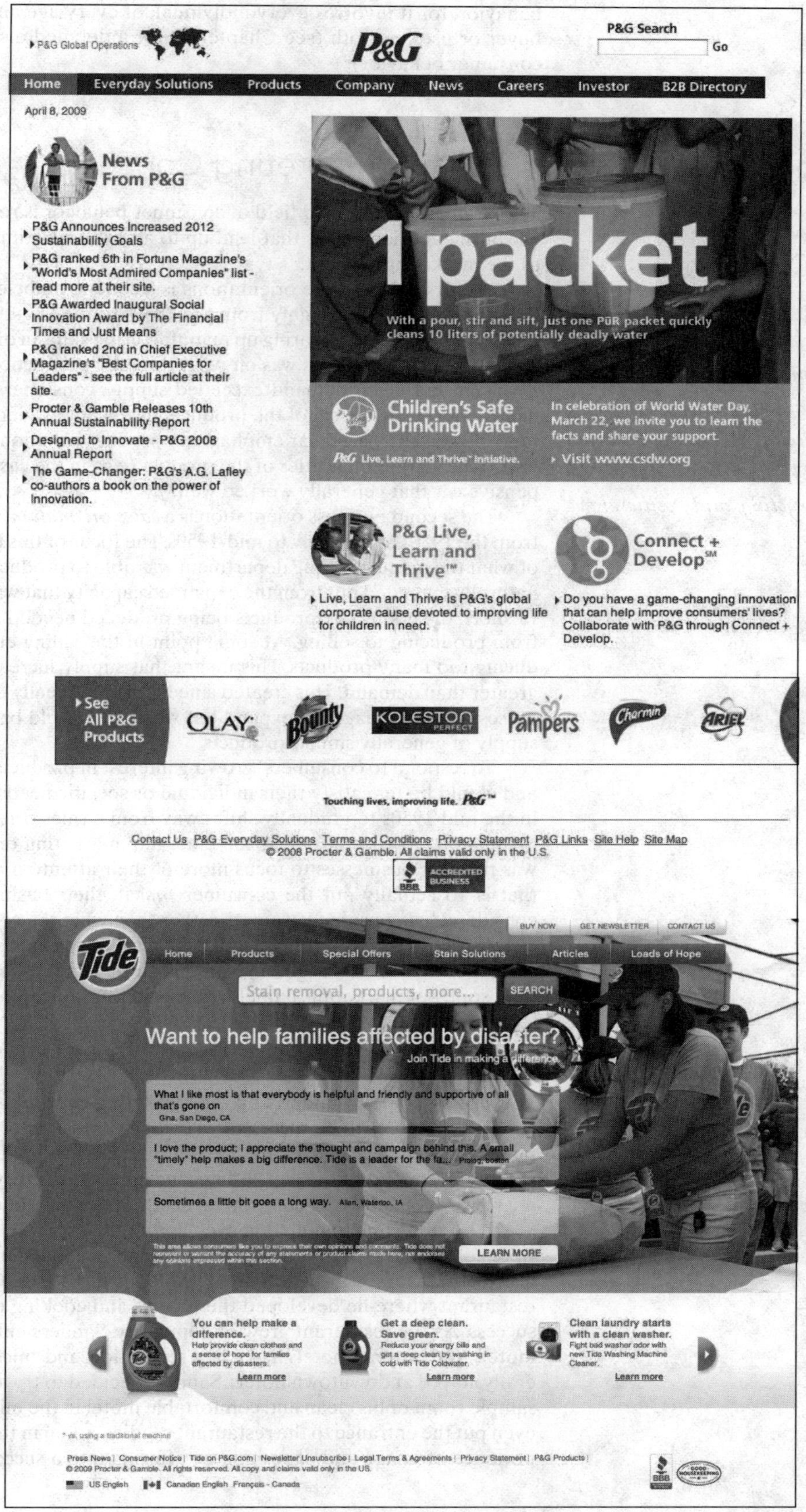

behavior, for it involves every individual, of every age and background, in the role of either buyer or user, or both (see Chapter 10 for a detailed discussion of the role of the family in consumer behavior).

Consumer Behavior and the Marketing Concept

LEARNING OBJECTIVE

1.2 *To Understand the Relationship Between Consumer Behavior and the Marketing Concept, the Societal Marketing Concept, as Well as Segmentation, Targeting, and Positioning.*

The strategic and applied field of consumer behavior is rooted in three philosophically different business orientations that lead up to an extremely important business orientation known as the marketing concept.

The first of the three orientations is frequently labeled the *production orientation*, with a time span extending roughly from the 1850s to the late-1920s.[6] As the term implies, the focus during this period was gearing up manufacturing skills in order to expand production—to make more products. The focus was on perfecting the production capabilities of the company. Since it was an era when demand exceeded supply, consumers were generally happy to get their hands on a generic form of the products they wanted. Neither the consumer nor the manufacturer placed any particular emphasis on product variation, but were rather satisfied to be able to produce larger quantities of the product (e.g., in the case of an automobile, "simply, an inexpensive car that generally worked well").

The second business orientation is a *sales orientation*, with a time frame extending roughly from the 1930s to the early to mid-1950s. The focus of this business orientation was to sell more of what the manufacturing department was able to produce. Thus, this second orientation quite naturally extended out from the expanded capacity that was created during the production era. In short, the additional products being produced needed to be sold; so the orientation shifted from producing to selling. At some point in the selling era, there were many companies producing too many products. This meant that supply increasingly reached a point where it was greater than demand. This created a need for some really different thinking on the part of businesses that were eager to expand but were being held back by what appeared to be an oversupply of generally similar products.

To respond to consumers' growing interest in products and services that were more unique and would better satisfy their individual or specific needs and preferences, companies started in the mid-1950s to gradually shift away from a sales orientation and to embrace a *marketing orientation.* At the "heart" of the emerging marketing orientation was the realization that it was time for businesses to focus more of their attention on consumers and their preferences; that is, to actually put the consumer *first* in their business thinking and planning. Thus, to consider what consumers wanted, rather than what the company finds easiest to make or least expensive to make, is in keeping with the marketing concept. Accepting a marketing orientation corresponded to the beginning of this third business orientation, which leads to the core philosophy of marketing, namely the marketing concept.

WHAT IS THE MARKETING CONCEPT?

The key assumption underlying the **marketing concept** is that in the mid-1950s and beyond, generally, in order to be successful, a company must determine the needs and wants of specific target markets and deliver the desired satisfactions better than the competition. Moreover, within the context of the marketing concept, a satisfactory profit is envisioned as an appropriate reward for satisfying consumers' needs, not as a right of simply being in business.

It is interesting to note that even before the establishment of the marketing concept, there were companies that intuitively realized that an understanding of consumer behavior was critical to their future growth. For example, in the 1930s, Colonel Sanders opened a roadside restaurant where he developed the recipes and cooking methods that were the key to KFC's success. As the restaurant grew in popularity, Sanders enlarged it and also opened a roadside motel. At that time, motels had a bad reputation, and "nice" people driving long distances generally stayed at downtown hotels. Sanders decided to try and overcome this image by putting a sample room of his clean and comfortable motel in the middle of his successful restaurant, and even put the entrance to the restaurant's ladies' room in that room. Sanders understood the importance of image and of turning an offering into a success by *repositioning*, long before this idea was articulated as a business objective. Later on, Sanders came up with the idea of franchising his cooking methods and chicken recipe, while keeping the ingredients of the recipe a secret, and founded KFC and a business model that has since been adopted by many other fast-food chains.[7] In the early 1950s, Ray Kroc, who purchased the idea of fast food from the McDonald brothers and established the McDonald's Corporation, selected locations for new outlets by flying over towns and looking for church steeples. He believed that where there were churches there were good American families—the kind of people he wanted as customers. Intuitively, Kroc understood and practiced *market targeting*.[8] Apparently, companies that continuously work at securing a current understanding of their customers' needs are the same ones that continue to grow, and remain leaders in their industries in spite of increased competition and changing business environments.

After more than 50 years, the marketing concept continues to thrive as a highly useful guideline and philosophy for managing a business because it has effectively served to remind businesses to keep the consumers' needs up-front when contemplating new products and services, crafting marketing communications, or planning other strategies. Nevertheless, there has been a particularly important proposed modification or extension to the marketing concept; that is called the **societal marketing concept**.[9] At its core, the societal marketing concept suggests that consumers may on occasion respond to their immediate needs or wants, while overlooking what is in effect in their own long-run best interest, or the best interest of their family and neighbors, the best interest of their country or region, or even the best interest of the entire planet. In such contexts, when we think of "societal marketing" we are thinking of the role of enlightened marketers; that is, management who takes it upon itself to remind consumers as to what is in consumers' long-run best interest, at the same time it sets out what its own company is doing in order to be a good corporate citizen. For instance, Figure 1.1 suggests that Siemens is committed to developing products that are not injurious to consumers, as well as not dangerous to the environment (for a more detailed exploration of this and related topics, see Chapter 16).

EMBRACING THE MARKETING CONCEPT

To identify both consumers' unsatisfied as well as their unrecognized needs, it is often important for companies to continuously conduct marketing research studies to monitor consumers' needs and preferences with respect to the products and services that they currently market, and those they possibly would wish to develop in the future. In doing so, marketers have tended to discover that consumers are highly complex individuals, subject to a variety of psychological and social needs quite apart from their more basic functional needs. They also discovered that the needs and priorities of different consumer segments differ dramatically, and the objectives of a company should be to target different products and services to different market segments in order to better satisfy their different needs. Again, to accomplish this task, the company must know in detail what products will satisfy different market segments. They have to study consumers and their consumption behavior in depth. In this context, the term **consumer research** represents the process and tools used to study consumer behavior. The adoption of the marketing concept underscores the importance of consumer research and provides the groundwork for the application of consumer behavior principles to marketing strategy. The tools and processes of consumer research are discussed in detail in Chapter 2.

SEGMENTATION, TARGETING, AND POSITIONING

The focus of the marketing concept is for marketers to know consumers' current needs, and to secure, as accurately as possible, a picture of their likely future needs. At the same time, recognizing the high degree of diversity among consumers, market and consumer researchers seek to identify the many similarities and differences that exist among the peoples of the world. For example, we all have the same kinds of biological needs, no matter where we are born—the needs for food, nourishment, water, air, and shelter from the elements. We also acquire needs after we are born. These needs are shaped by the environment and the culture in which we live, by our education, and by our experiences. The interesting thing about acquired needs is that there are usually many people who develop the same needs. This commonality of needs or interests constitutes many of the "ingredients" of a consumer market segment, and enables the marketer to target consumers with specifically designed products and/or promotional appeals that satisfy the segment's specific set of needs. The marketer must also adapt the image of its product (i.e., *position* it), so that each market segment perceives the product as better fulfilling its specific needs than competitive products. The three elements of this strategic framework are *market segmentation, targeting*, and *positioning*.

Market segmentation is the process of dividing a market into subsets of consumers with common needs or characteristics. The variables and methods used to form such subsets are discussed in Chapter 3. Because most companies have limited resources, few companies can pursue all the market segments identified. **Market targeting** is the selection of one or more of the segments identified for the company to pursue. To illustrate, Tab (a soft drink division of Coca-Cola) positions its new low-calorie energy drink to a sophisticated female audience concerned with watching their weight, being attractive, and being on the go. The criteria for selecting target markets are further explored in Chapter 3.

Positioning refers to the development of a distinct image for the product or service in the mind of the consumer, an image that will differentiate the offering from competing ones and faithfully communicate to the target audience that the particular product or service will fulfill their needs better than competing brands. Successful positioning centers around two key principles: first, communicating the *benefits* that the product will provide rather than the product's features. As one marketing sage puts it, "consumers do not buy drill bits—they buy ways to make holes." Also, because there are many similar products in almost any marketplace, an effective positioning strategy must develop and communicate a *unique selling proposition*—that is, a distinctive benefit or point of difference—for the product or service. In fact, most of the new products introduced by marketers (including new forms of existing products such as new flavors, sizes, etc.) fail to capture a significant market share and are discontinued because they are perceived by consumers as "me too" products lacking a unique image or benefit. The concepts and tools of positioning are explored in Chapter 6.

THE MARKETING MIX

The **marketing mix** consists of a company's service and/or product offerings to consumers and the methods and tools it selects to accomplish the exchange. The marketing mix consists of four elements (known as the *four Ps*): (1) the *product* (i.e., the features, designs, brands, and packaging of a good or service offering, along with postpurchase benefits such as warranties and return policies), (2) the *price* (the list price, including discounts, allowances, and payment methods), (3) the *place* (the distribution of the product or service through specific store and nonstore outlets), and (4) *promotion* (the advertising, sales promotion, public relations, and personal selling efforts designed to build awareness of and demand for the goods or service).

Customer Value, Satisfaction, Trust, and Retention

LEARNING OBJECTIVE

1.3 *To Understand the Relationship Between Consumer Behavior and Customer Value, Satisfaction, Trust, and Retention.*

Since its emergence in the 1950s, many companies have very successfully adopted the marketing concept. The result has been more products, in more sizes, models, versions, and packages, offered to more precisely targeted (and often smaller) target markets. This has resulted in an increasingly competitive marketplace. And, with the rapid and widespread acceptance of the Internet and other aspects of the digital revolution, marketers have been able to expand their offering of more products and services, and more options as to their distribution, while reducing the costs and barriers of entering many industries. This has accelerated the rate at which new competitors enter markets and has also speeded up the rate at which segmentation, targeting, and positioning approaches must be updated or changed, as they are imitated or made obsolete by the offerings of new business rivals. Most of all, these dramatic changes have overwhelmingly been very positive for consumers. Specifically, consumers have benefited from their ability to be proactive in seeking out online information, opinions, product availability, and price comparisons. Also, and very important, consumers have been able to use the Internet (i.e., discussion groups, forums, and consumer blogs) to easily find other consumers and read about their actual experiences and evaluations of the goods or services that they are contemplating purchasing. Within this context, interaction of the marketing concept and broad availability of the Internet serve the interests of consumers, and have led to an enhancement of consumers' quality of life.

Savvy marketers today realize that in order to outperform competitors they must achieve the full profit potential from each and every customer. They must make the customer the core of the company's organizational culture, across all departments and functions, and ensure that each and every employee views any exchange with a customer as part of a *customer relationship*, not as a *transaction*. Four drivers of successful relationships between marketers and customers are *customer value*, high levels of *customer satisfaction*, a strong sense of *customer trust*, and building a structure that ensures *customer retention*.

PROVIDING CUSTOMERS WITH VALUE

Customer value can be thought of as the *ratio between the customers' perceived benefits* (economic, functional, and psychological) and the *resources* (monetary, time, effort, psychological) *used to obtain those benefits*. Perceived value is relative and subjective. For example, diners at an exclusive French restaurant in Washington, D.C., where a meal with beverages may cost up to $300 per person, may expect unique and delicious food, immaculate service, and beautiful decor. Some diners may receive even more than they had expected and will leave the restaurant feeling that the experience was worth the money and other resources expended (such as a month-long wait for a reservation). Other diners may go with expectations so high that they leave the restaurant disappointed. On the other hand, many millions of customers each year visit thousands of McDonald's restaurants, in scores of countries around the globe, where they purchase standard, inexpensive meals from franchise owners and employees systematically trained by the McDonald's Corporation to deliver the company's four core standards: *quality, service, cleanliness*, and *value*. Customers flock to McDonald's outlets repeatedly because the restaurants are well maintained, customers know what to expect, and they feel that they are getting value for the resources they expend.

Developing a *value proposition* (a term rapidly replacing the popular business term *unique selling proposition*) and looking for the impact of emerging "megatrends" (e.g., individualism, choice overload, hiving, and geek chic) are influential factors in attaining successful positioning of a brand.[10] For example, Lexus claims to deliver to its customers *quality, zero defects in manufacturing*, and *superior, personal postpurchase service*. Dell's value proposition for personal computer users consists of *customized* PC systems *assembled speedily* and sold at *economical prices*. Apple provides users with many options to purchase, share, personalize, and listen to their favorite Apple products. The value propositions stated previously create customer expectations that these companies must continuously fulfill and even exceed as competitors try to win over their markets. Measures of customer satisfaction expectations and evaluations of products and services are discussed in Chapter 2, and the strategic applications of perceived customer value are explored in Chapter 6.

ENSURING CUSTOMER SATISFACTION

Customer satisfaction is the individual consumer's perception of the performance of the product or service in relation to his or her expectations. As noted earlier, customers will have drastically different expectations of an expensive French restaurant and a McDonald's, although both are members of the restaurant industry that tend to cater to segments of consumers, or sometimes the same consumers under different circumstances. The concept of customer satisfaction is a function of customer expectations. A customer whose experience falls below expectations (e.g., a limited wine list at an expensive restaurant or cold fries served at a McDonald's) will be dissatisfied. Diners whose experiences match expectations will be satisfied. And customers whose expectations are exceeded (e.g., by small samples of delicious food "from the chef" served between courses at the expensive restaurant, or a well-designed play area for children at a McDonald's outlet) will be very satisfied or even delighted. Indeed, both *customer satisfaction* and *customer delight* are fully consistent with the underlying principles of the marketing concept, and therefore they are worthy strategies for marketers to pursue.

With respect to satisfying consumers, a widely quoted study that linked levels of customer satisfaction with customer behavior identified several types of customers.[11] On the *positive side*, there are completely satisfied customers who are either *loyalists* who keep purchasing, or *apostles* whose experiences exceed their expectations and who provide very positive word-of-mouth about the company to others. In contrast, on the *negative side* there are *defectors* who feel neutral or merely satisfied and are just as likely to stop doing business with the company; consumer *terrorists* who have had negative experiences with the company and who spread negative word of mouth; and *hostages* who are unhappy customers who stay with the company because of a monopolistic environment or low prices and who are difficult and costly to deal with because of their frequent complaints. Finally, there are *mercenaries* who while being satisfied customers, really do not have any real loyalty to the company and may defect at any point for a lower price elsewhere or on impulse, defying the satisfaction—loyalty rationale. The researchers propose that companies should strive to create *apostles*, raise the satisfaction of *defectors* and turn them into *loyalists*, avoid having *terrorists* or *hostages*, and reduce the number of *mercenaries*.[12]

BUILDING CUSTOMER TRUST

Closely related to the challenge of satisfying consumers is the challenge of establishing and maintaining *consumer trust* in a company and its products. The challenge of securing consumer trust is not only of concern to product and service companies, but it is also of paramount importance to both online and off-line retailers, as well as online and off-line product- and service-rating establishments (e.g., see *Consumer Reports*, the magazine or its very popular Web site—**www.online.consumerreports.org**).[13] According to Nielsen's Customized Research Services, consumers' trust of a range of different consumer information sources reveals that word-of-mouth communications or recommendations from other consumers is in a league by itself in terms of being the most trusted source of consumer information (with 78 percent trusting such sources).[14] The research also indicates that newspapers, consumer opinions posted online, and brand Web sites are also relatively high scoring in terms of being trustworthy in the minds of consumers. Toward the bottom of this list are "ads before movies," "search engine ads," "online banner ads," and "text ads on mobile phones" (for a more detailed discussion of the influence of both new and traditional media, see Chapter 9).

Still further, trust is the foundation for maintaining a long-standing relationship with customers, and it helps to increase the chances that customers will remain loyal. Looking at a specific dimension of trust, *privacy*, Table 1.2 presents the results of a collaboration between the Ponemon Institute and TRUSTe to conduct a survey that identified the 20 most trusted U.S. companies in terms of privacy during the year 2008 (the numbers and words in parentheses reflect the change in each company's standing relative to its position in the 2007 survey).[15]

If for some reason a situation occurs where a customer's relationship is at risk in terms of trust, there is also the related concept of *delight*, in which a company seeks to recover in the eyes and minds of consumers by setting things right with the customer, and further demonstrates to that customer that he or she is valued as a customer. Such efforts to provide true *customer delight* in the face of an event that had extremely dissatisfied the customer can be turned around by the marketer, and represent a positive win-win outcome for both the consumer and the marketer.[16]

SECURING CUSTOMER RETENTION

The overall objective of providing value to customers continuously and more effectively than the competition is to have and to retain highly satisfied and trusting customers, and from time to time even surprise them by providing the element of delight to their dealings with the company. A strategy of **customer retention** is designed to make it in the best interest of customers to stay with a company rather than switch to another company. In almost all business situations, it is more expensive to secure new customers than to keep existing ones. Studies have shown that small reductions in customer defections produce significant increases in profits because (1) loyal customers buy more products; (2) loyal customers are less price sensitive and pay less attention to competitors' advertising; (3) servicing existing customers, who are familiar with the company's offerings and processes, is cheaper; and (4) loyal customers spread positive word of mouth and refer other customers. Furthermore, marketing efforts aimed at attracting new customers are expensive; indeed, in saturated markets, it may be impossible to find new customers.[17]

The Internet and the cell phone are extremely important "tools of interaction" for both marketers and consumers to communicate with each other. For instance, marketers can create

TABLE 1.2 Top 20 Ranked U.S. Companies in Terms of Consumers' Trust That the Companies Will Respect Consumers' Privacy

1. American Express (remained number one)	13. Intuit (+7)
2. eBay (+6)	14. WebMD (−1)
3. IBM (no change)	15. Yahoo! (new to the top 20)
4. Amazon (+1)	16. Facebook (new to the top 20)
5. Johnson & Johnson (+1)	17. Disney (−1)
6. Hewlett-Packard (+10)	18. AOL (−12)
7. U.S. Postal Service (+1)	19. Verizon (new to the top 20)
8. Procter & Gamble (+2)	20. FedEx (new to the top 20)
9. Apple (new to the top 20)	21. US Bank (−2)
10. Nationwide (remained the same)	22. Dell (−7)
11. Charles Schwab (−8)	23. eLoan (−9)
12. USAA (+4)	

Source: Study conducted by Ponemon Institute and TRUSTe, 2008, at www.marketwire.com/press-release/Trust-930017.html.

customized products and services, coupled with customized marketing messages that cater to the specific needs of consumers (often termed *one-to-one marketing*). In contrast, consumers can likewise use the same media tools (their Internet connection and/or cell phones) to express their feelings and provide invaluable feedback to marketers.

Marketers who designate customer retention as a strategic corporate goal must also recognize that all customers are not equal. Sophisticated marketers build *selective relationships* with customers, based on where customers rank in terms of profitability, rather than merely strive to retain customers. A customer retention-savvy company closely monitors its customers' consumption volume and patterns, establishes tiers of customers according to their profitability levels, and develops distinct strategies for each group of customers. For example, customers who have purchased and registered several of a company's products should receive extensive and expedited customer support. On the other hand, less profitable customers who, let's say, make a few minor purchases, should receive only limited communications. Still further, customers who are unlikely to purchase any more products or services are often ignored (i.e., receive no targeted communications of any form).

Classifying customers according to profitability levels goes beyond traditional segmentation methods that subdivide consumers on the basis of demographic, sociocultural, or behavioral characteristics. *Customer profitability-focused marketing* tracks costs and revenues of individual customers and then categorizes them into tiers based on consumption behaviors that are specific to the company's offerings. Such a strategy is a very effective way to utilize the knowledge of consumer behavior. For example, a recent study advocates using a "customer pyramid" where customers are grouped into four tiers: (1) The *platinum tier* includes heavy users who are not price sensitive and who are willing to try new offerings; (2) the *gold tier* consists of customers who are heavy users but not as profitable because they are more price sensitive than those in the higher tier, ask for more discounts, and are likely to buy from several providers; (3) the *iron tier* consists of customers whose spending volume and profitability do not merit special treatment from the company; and (4) the *lead tier* includes customers who actually cost the company money because they claim more attention than is merited by their spending, tie up company resources, and spread negative word of mouth. The authors of the study urge companies to develop distinct marketing responses for each customer group.[18]

A corporate philosophy centered on customer value, satisfaction, and retention evolves from the marketing concept and unfolds new dimensions of marketing. Table 1.3 compares traditional marketing with perceived value and retention marketing. Applications of consumer behavior concepts to value- and retention-focused marketing are discussed throughout the book.

TABLE 1.3 The Traditional Marketing Concept Versus Value- and Retention-Focused Marketing

THE TRADITIONAL MARKETING CONCEPT	VALUE- AND RETENTION-FOCUSED MARKETING
Make only what you can sell instead of trying to sell what you make.	Use technology that enables customers to customize what you make.
Do not focus on the product; focus on the need that it satisfies.	Focus on the product's perceived value, as well as the need that it satisfies.
Market products and services that match customers' needs better than competitors' offerings.	Utilize an understanding of customer needs to develop offerings that customers perceive as more valuable than competitors' offerings.
Research consumer needs and characteristics.	Research the levels of profit associated with various consumer needs and characteristics.
Understand the purchase behavior process and the influences on consumer behavior.	Understand consumer behavior in relation to the company's product.
Realize that each customer transaction is a discrete sale.	Make each customer transaction part of an ongoing relationship with the customer.
Segment the market based on customers' geographic, demographic, psychological, sociocultural, lifestyle, and product-usage related characteristics.	Use hybrid segmentation that combines the traditional segmentation bases with data on the customer's purchase levels and patterns of use of the company's products.
Target large groups of customers that share common characteristics with messages transmitted through mass media.	Invest in technologies that enable you to send one-to-one promotional messages via digital channels.
Use one-way promotions whose effectiveness is measured through sales data or marketing surveys.	Use interactive communications in which messages to customers are tailored according to their responses to previous communications.
Create loyalty programs based on the volume purchased.	Create customer tiers based on both volume and consumption patterns.
Encourage customers to stay with the company and buy more.	Make it very unattractive for your customers to switch to a competitor and encourage them to purchase "better"—in a manner that will raise the company's profitability levels.
Determine marketing budgets on the basis of the numbers of customers you are trying to reach.	Base your marketing budget on the "lifetime value" of typical customers in each of the targeted segments compared with the resources needed to acquire them as customers.
Conduct customer satisfaction surveys and present the results to management.	Conduct customer satisfaction surveys that include a component that studies the customer's word-of-mouth about the company, and use the results immediately to enhance customer relationships.
Create customer trust and loyalty to the company and high levels of customer satisfaction.	Create customer intimacy and bonds with completely satisfied, "delighted" customers.

Source: Joseph Wisenblit, "Beyond the Marketing Concept: From 'Make Only What You Can Sell' to 'Let Customers Customize What You Make,'" Working Paper, May 2002, the Stillman School of Business, Seton Hall University, South Orange, NJ.

The Impact of New Technologies on Marketing Strategies

LEARNING OBJECTIVE

1.4 *To Understand How New Technologies Are Enabling Marketers to Better Satisfy the Needs and Wants of Consumers.*

The opening discussion in this chapter of the groundbreaking 2008 Obama presidential campaign is insightful as to how people are securing information and taking action as consumers (or voters). As already indicated by this example, new technologies have enabled marketers to greatly customize their products, services, and promotional messages. These new technologies and new media have made it easier for marketers to adapt the elements of the marketing mix to specific consumers' needs and to more quickly and efficiently build and maintain relationships with customers. Marketers are also collecting and analyzing increasingly complex data on consumers' buying patterns and personal characteristics, and quickly analyzing and using this information to target smaller and more focused groups of consumers. On the other hand, the same technologies enable consumers to find more information about goods and services (including prices), and to more easily and efficiently, from the comfort of their own homes on their home computers, get the answers they need to make more informed decisions. Therefore, more than ever before, marketers must ensure that their products and services provide the right benefits and value and are positioned effectively to reach the right consumers.

As the following discussion reveals, online communication and emerging digital technologies have introduced several dramatic changes into the marketing environment:

CONSUMERS HAVE MORE POWER THAN EVER BEFORE

They can use "intelligent agents" to locate the best prices for products or services (i.e., "where to get the new car they desire, at a price they can afford"), bid on various marketing offerings ("eBay all the way"), bypass distribution outlets and middlemen, and shop for goods around the globe and around the clock from the convenience of their homes.[19] Therefore, marketers must offer more competitively priced products, with more options.

Moreover, some aspects of the digital age have enabled consumers to gain more power over what they see or hear in the marketplace. Specifically, devices like the TiVo digital recorder allow viewers to control what they watch on TV, when they watch it, and whether or not they wish to view the commercials for which marketers spend billions of dollars per year. The TiVo recorder and other similar devices enable consumers to download programming information and allow users to record many hours of TV programming onto a hard drive without the hassle of videocassettes. Users can program the recorder by topic or keyword, easily play back selected segments, and, to the delight of many viewers, hit a single button for preprogrammed quick skips of strings of TV commercials. It is clear that TiVo and other similar devices have and continue to shift the power over viewing behavior from the broadcaster to the viewer-consumer. What is not established yet is whether (or how) broadcasters are going to respond to this particular challenge.

Related to this issue, as consumers spend more time online and have more technological tools that enable them to avoid exposure to TV ads, marketers have been reducing their advertising expenditures on the major networks and investing their advertising dollars instead in the newer media, especially in Web and e-mail advertising, and increasingly exploring cell phone advertising. Advertisers have also begun to insist that broadcasters develop new measurement systems to more accurately estimate the number and demographics of their viewers.

CONSUMERS HAVE MORE ACCESS TO INFORMATION THAN EVER BEFORE

They can easily find reviews for products they are considering buying that have been posted by previous buyers, click a button to compare the features of different product models at the sites of online retailers, and participate in *virtual communities* of persons who share the same interests they do. In turn, marketers must be aware of the limits of their promotional messages and assume that such consumers are highly likely to know all of their buying options.

MARKETERS CAN AND MUST OFFER MORE SERVICES AND PRODUCTS THAN EVER BEFORE

The digitization of information enables sellers to *customize* the products and services they are selling and still sell them at reasonable prices. It also allows marketers to customize the promotional messages directed at many customers. For example, Amazon.com regularly sends personalized e-mails to previous book purchasers announcing newly published books; these suggestions are based on a determination of the interests of the targeted consumers derived from their past purchases. Similarly, an online drugstore may vary the initial display returning buyers see when they revisit its Web site. Buyers whose past purchases indicate that they tend to buy national brands will see a display arranged by brand. Past purchasers who bought mostly products that were on sale or generic brands will see a display categorized by price and discounted products.

INCREASING INSTANTANEOUS EXCHANGES BETWEEN MARKETERS AND CUSTOMERS

Traditional advertising is a one-way street where the marketer pays a large sum of money to reach a large number of potential buyers via a mass medium, and then assesses (usually after the fact) whether or not the message was effective on the basis of future sales or market studies. On the other hand, digital or new media communication enables a two-way interactive exchange in which consumers can instantly react to the marketer's message by, say, clicking on links within a given Web site or even by leaving the site. Thus, marketers can quickly gauge the effectiveness of their promotional messages rather than rely on delayed feedback through sales information that is collected after the fact.

MARKETERS CAN GATHER MORE INFORMATION ABOUT CONSUMERS MORE QUICKLY AND EASILY

Marketers can track consumers' online behavior and also gather information by requiring visitors to the Web sites to register and provide some background information before they get access to the site's features. Thus, marketers can construct and update their consumer databases efficiently and inexpensively. As a result, many marketers now employ **narrowcasting**—a method that enables them to develop and deliver more customized messages to increasingly smaller market segments on an ongoing basis.

IMPACT REACHES BEYOND THE PC-BASED CONNECTION OF THE WEB

While computer access to the Internet is quite extensive and growing, in the future we are likely to see the mobile phone or PDA emerge as the preferred access tool, because it brings e-mail and text messaging to one particular device. These devices are easy to use (i.e., to "turn on and dial up"), small and compact in size, and quick to access when compared to even very small laptops. More than anything else, it is the existence of very large numbers of highly mobile consumers that are making a cell device a preferred communications tool.[20] Indeed, in some European countries, consumers can already purchase products via their mobile phones. Also, cell phones with built-in GPS systems are just starting to become a medium that will deliver customized promotional messages to consumers everywhere. In addition, many U.S. homes now have smart TV cable boxes that enable two-way communications with broadcasters (e.g., enabling the consumer to check morning traffic conditions on the route to work from the TV before leaving home). Still further, as we switch to high-definition TV, all cable subscribers will have such boxes. Therefore, as consumers will be able to receive more and more TV programming on their PCs, electronics companies will increasingly be merging the TV and the PC into a single device that provides households with hundreds of cable channels, interactive capabilities with broadcasters, and high-speed, wireless access to the Web. Supermarket scanners that keep track of households' purchases and instantly provide personalized coupons at the checkout counter, and telephone devices that enable us to identify callers without picking up the phone, are two of the many additional products made possible by recently developed technologies.

The Mobile Consumer

LEARNING OBJECTIVE

1.5 *To Understand How Marketers Are Increasingly Able to Reach Consumers Wherever Consumers Wish to Be Reached.*

Again, cellular service providers are increasingly seeing the cell phone's screen as an opportunity to secure advertising revenue, much the same as broadcast TV stations and movie theaters see their screens as an opportunity for advertisers to get their message to the viewing consumers. More specifically, cell phone companies are actively contracting for entertainment content providers to develop games, contests, and TV-like soap opera stories that engage consumers to act like an audience, and provide an opportunity to secure revenue from advertisers that are increasingly interested in reaching mobile consumers via their cell phones or PDAs.

We can expect expanded use of wireless media messages as: (1) the availability of flat-rate data traffic to consumers increases, (2) with creation of enhanced screen image quality, and (3) increased consumer-user experiences with improved Web-related applications.[21] Research gathered by Nielsen Mobile further reveals that 15.6 percent of U.S. mobile subscribers use the mobile Internet, followed by 12.9 percent of United Kingdom and 11.9 percent of Italian subscribers.[22] Figure 1.3 presents the findings for a total of 16 countries.

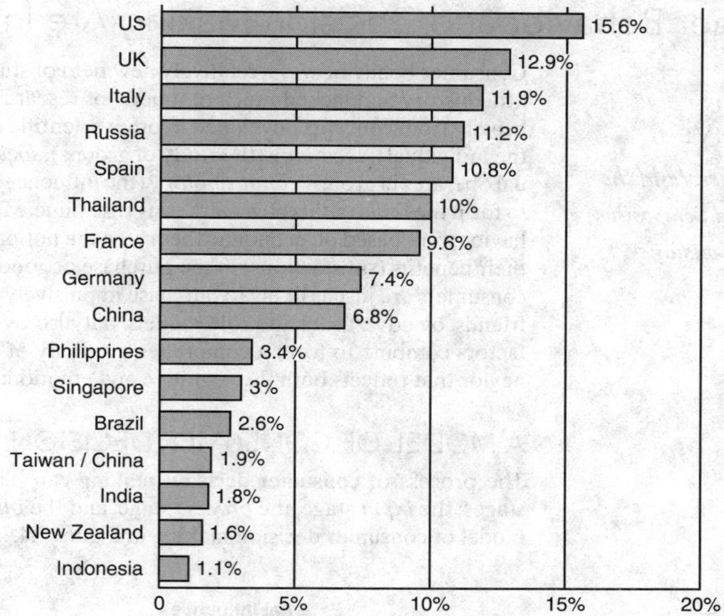

FIGURE 1.3
Penetration of Internet Usage Among Mobile Subscribers in 16 Economies

Source: *Critical Mass: The Worldwide State of the Mobile Web*, Nielsen Mobile, July 2008, 3. Copyright © 2008 The Nielsen Company. All rights reserved. Also, www.nielsenmobile.com/documents/CriticalMass.pdf.

Consumer Behavior in a World of Economic Instability

LEARNING OBJECTIVE

1.6 *To Understand How the World's Economic Condition Is Leading to Consumption Instability and Change.*

Near the end of preparing this edition of *Consumer Behavior*, we realized that we needed to address the recession and widespread economic downturn in consumer confidence that was at least, in part, initially caused by a dramatic drop in both home prices and sales of homes. This was followed by a striking decline in stock prices, and therefore the value of stocks, which in turn was followed by equally striking massive job layoffs and cut backs. This meant that many investors found that a significant portion of their financial holdings set aside for retirement, home purchases, children's education, and so on, were disappearing in front of their own eyes as banks were failing. All these negative occurrences happened in a relatively short period of time, creating an enormous downturn in the U.S. economy, which has resulted in a significant negative impact on consumers with respect to a wide range of purchasing.[23]

While the United States was initially the major victim, it did not take long for these economic instabilities to spread to European and Asian economic centers. All of a sudden we were in the midst of a worldwide economic recession, with unemployment, uncertainty, as well as falling stock prices occurring all over the globe. Great numbers of families were uncertain about their future, the future of their jobs, and the future prospects for their homes (i.e., could they continue to meet the mortgage payments).

We understand that such economic events will impact what and how much consumers are able to purchase, and that some consumers will really suffer. However, we also realize that much of the process of consumer decision making and the dynamics of consumer search and shopping will still go on, but it will be different. It will take time to secure an understanding as to what will remain the same, and what will change. Maybe the next edition of this book will be able to address the extent and nature of such a grand-scale recession—a recession that many economists, politicians, and consumers never expected could occur again. Indeed, recalling all previous editions of this book, we never remember so much concern and fear on the part of both consumers and businesses. In the past, we could easily ignore the generally mild "ups and downs" in the status of major world economic centers.

Wherever in the world you are reading and studying this edition of *Consumer Behavior*, please try to relate to what you are reading and consider what meaning it has to the economic crisis.

Consumer Behavior and Decision Making Are Interdisciplinary

LEARNING OBJECTIVE

1.7 *To Understand the Makeup and Composition of a Model of Consumer Behavior.*

Consumer behavior was a relatively new field of study in the mid- to late-1960s. Because it had little history and lacked much of a body of research of its own, marketing theorists borrowed heavily from concepts developed in other scientific disciplines, such as *psychology* (the study of the individual), *sociology* (the study of groups), *social psychology* (the study of how an individual operates in groups), *anthropology* (the influence of society on the individual), and *economics* to form the basis of this new marketing discipline. Many early theories concerning consumer behavior were based on economic theory, on the notion that individuals act rationally to maximize their benefits (satisfactions) in the purchase of goods and services. Later research revealed that consumers are just as likely to purchase impulsively and to be influenced not only by family and friends, by advertisers and role models, but also by mood, situation, and emotion. All of these factors combine to form a comprehensive body of thinking and research about consumer behavior that reflects both the cognitive and emotional aspects of consumer decision making.

A MODEL OF CONSUMER DECISION MAKING

The process of **consumer decision making** can be viewed as three distinct but interlocking stages: the *input* stage, the *process* stage, and the *output* stage. These stages are depicted in the model of consumer decision making in Figure 1.4.

FIGURE 1.4
A Model of Consumer Decision Making

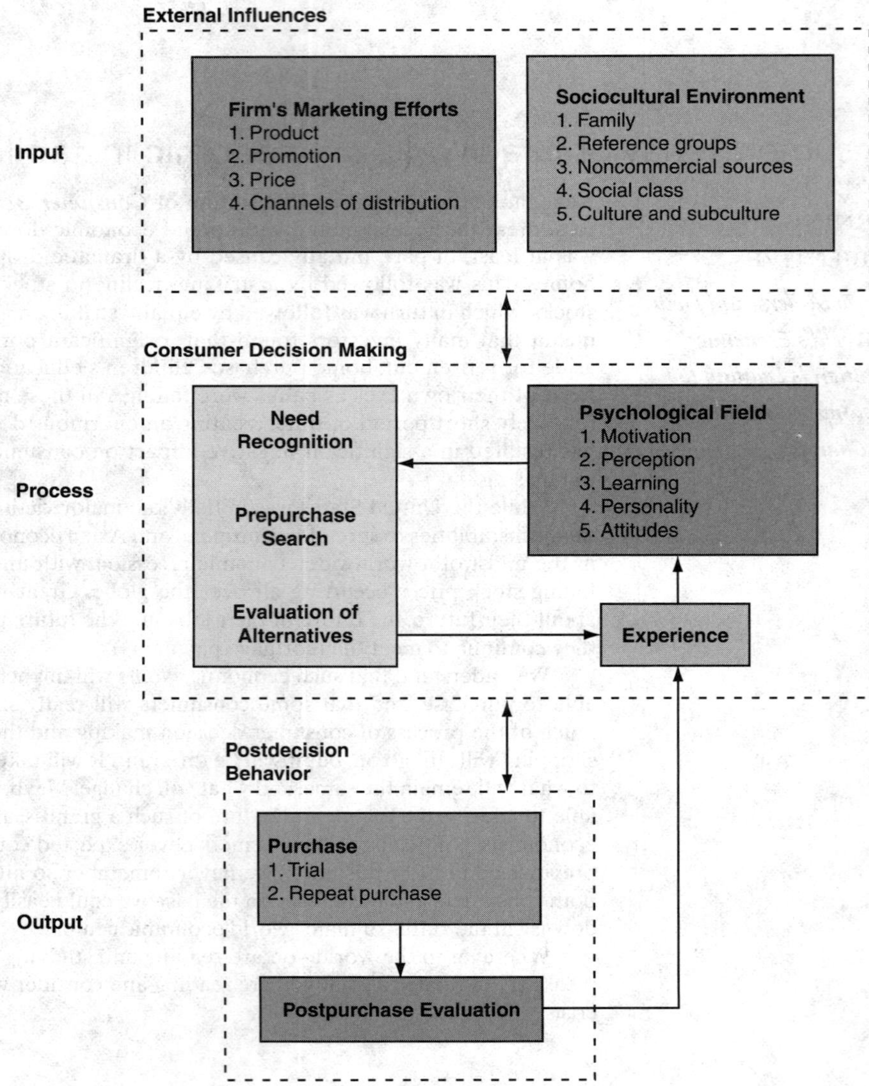

The *input* stage influences the consumer's recognition of a product need and consists of two major sources of information: the company's marketing efforts (the product itself, its price, its promotion, and where it is sold) and the external sociological influences on the consumer (family, friends, neighbors, other informal and noncommercial sources, social class, and cultural and subcultural memberships). The cumulative impact of the company's marketing efforts, the influence of family, friends, and neighbors, and society's existing code of behavior are all inputs that affect what consumers purchase and how they use what they buy.

The *process* stage of the model focuses on how consumers make decisions. The psychological factors inherent in each individual (motivation, perception, learning, personality, and attitudes) affect how the external inputs from the input stage influence the consumer's recognition of a need, prepurchase search for information, and evaluation of alternatives. The experience gained through evaluation of alternatives, in turn, affects the consumer's existing psychological attributes.

The *output* stage of the consumer decision-making model consists of two closely related postdecision activities: purchase behavior and postpurchase evaluation. Purchase behavior for a low-cost, nondurable product (e.g., a new shampoo) may be influenced by a manufacturer's coupon and may actually be a trial purchase; if the consumer is satisfied, he or she may repeat the purchase. The trial is the exploratory phase of purchase behavior in which the consumer evaluates the product through direct use. A repeat purchase usually signifies product adoption. For a relatively durable product such as a laptop ("relatively" durable because of the rapid rate of obsolescence), the purchase is more likely to signify adoption.

The consumer decision-making model is examined in greater depth in Chapter 15, where it ties together in great detail the psychological and sociocultural concepts explored throughout the book.

The Plan of This Book

LEARNING OBJECTIVE

1.8 *To Understand the Structure of This Book.*

In an effort to build a useful conceptual framework that both enhances understanding and permits practical application of consumer behavior principles to marketing strategy, this book is divided into four parts: Part 1 gives an introduction to the study of consumer behavior, Part 2 discusses the consumer as an individual, Part 3 examines consumers in their social and cultural settings, and Part 4 synthesizes all of the variables discussed earlier into the consumer decision-making process, and includes a discussion of the process of consuming or consumption of goods and services. The book ends with a new chapter that covers the important topics of *social responsibility* and *marketing ethics*.

Chapter 1 introduced the reader to the study of consumer behavior as an interdisciplinary science that investigates the consumption-related activities of individuals. It described the reasons for the development of consumer behavior as an academic discipline and as an applied science, and introduced a model of consumer decision making that links together all of the personal and group influences that affect consumption decisions. Chapter 2 examines the methodology of consumer research, including the assumptions underlying qualitative and quantitative research approaches. Chapter 3 discusses the process of market segmentation, bases for segmentation, strategic targeting, and sophisticated ways to reach customers more precisely.

Part 2 focuses on the psychological characteristics of the consumer. Chapter 4 discusses how individuals are motivated, Chapter 5 examines the impact of individual personality characteristics on consumer behavior, Chapter 6 explores consumer perception, Chapter 7 examines how consumers learn, Chapter 8 discusses consumer attitudes, and Chapter 9 concludes Part 2 with an examination of the communications process that links consumers to the world around them.

Part 3 focuses on consumers as members of society, subject to varying external influences on their buying behavior, such as their family setting and social class standing (see Chapter 10), and the broad cultural and specific subcultural groups to which they belong (Chapters 11 and 12). The importance of cross-cultural consumer research to international marketing is explored in Chapter 13.

Part 4 examines the consumer decision-making process. Chapter 14 discusses the consumers' reactions to innovation and change and describes the process by which new products are adopted and diffused throughout society, with Chapter 15 containing an in-depth discussion of consumer decision making that shows how all the psychological and sociocultural variables discussed in Parts 2 and 3 influence the consumer's decision-making process. The book concludes with Chapter 16 (a new chapter) that examines a range of important issues that deal with the interrelated topics of *social responsibility* and *marketing ethics*, as they impact consumer behavior.

SUMMARY

The study of consumer behavior enables marketers to understand and predict consumer behavior in the marketplace; it is concerned not only with what consumers buy but also with why, when, where, how, and how often they buy it. Consumer research is the methodology used to study consumer behavior and takes place at every phase of the consumption process: before, during, and after the purchase.

The field of consumer behavior is rooted in the marketing concept, a business orientation that evolved in the 1950s through several alternative approaches, referred to, respectively, as the *production concept*, the *product concept*, and the *selling concept*. The three major strategic tools of marketing are *market segmentation, targeting*, and *positioning*. The *marketing mix* consists of a company's service and/or product offerings to consumers and the pricing, promotion, and distribution methods needed to accomplish the exchange.

Skilled marketers make the customer the core of the company's organizational culture and ensure that all employees view any exchange with a customer as part of a *customer relationship*, not as a *transaction*. The three drivers of successful relationships between marketers and customers are *customer value*, high levels of *customer satisfaction*, and building a structure for *customer retention*.

Digital technologies allow much greater customization of products, services, and promotional messages than do older marketing tools. They enable marketers to adapt the elements of the marketing mix to consumers' needs more quickly and efficiently, and to build and maintain relationships with customers on a much greater scale. However, these technologies also represent significant challenges to marketers and to business models that have been used for decades.

Consumer behavior is interdisciplinary; that is, it is based on concepts and theories about people that have been developed by scientists in such diverse disciplines as *psychology*, *sociology*, *social psychology*, *cultural anthropology*, and *economics*.

Consumer behavior has become an integral part of strategic market planning. The belief that ethics and social responsibility should also be integral components of every marketing decision is embodied in a revised marketing concept—the *societal marketing concept*—that calls on marketers to fulfill the needs of their target markets in ways that improve society as a whole.

DISCUSSION QUESTIONS

1. Describe the interrelationship between consumer behavior and the marketing concept.
2. Describe the interrelationships between consumer research, market segmentation and targeting, and the development of the marketing mix for a manufacturer of HDTV sets.
3. Select any one of the company Web sites and product-specific site pairs listed in Table 1.1 that interests you. Then systematically examine each of the two sites in terms of how you as a consumer respond differently to the two sites.
4. Discuss the interrelationships among customer expectations and satisfaction, perceived value, and customer retention. Why is customer retention essential?
5. Discuss the role of the social and behavioral sciences in developing the consumer decision-making model.
6. Apply each of the two models depicted in Table 1.3 (i.e., traditional marketing and value and retention marketing) to the marketing of cell phone services. You may want to incorporate into your answer your own and your peers' experiences in selecting cellular communications providers.

EXERCISES

1. You are the marketing manager of Citibank's Online Banking Division. How would you apply the concepts of providing value, customer satisfaction, and customer retention to designing and marketing effective online banking?
2. Locate two examples (e.g., advertisements, articles, etc.) depicting practices that are consistent with the societal marketing concept and two examples of business practices that contradict this concept. Explain your choices.
3. Apply each of the business orientations featured in the section describing the development of the marketing concept to manufacturing and marketing iPods.

KEY TERMS

- consumer behavior *23*
- consumer decision making *36*
- consumer research *27*
- customer retention *30*
- customer satisfaction *29*
- customer value *29*
- market segmentation *28*
- market targeting *28*
- marketing concept *26*
- marketing mix *28*
- narrowcasting *34*
- organizational consumer *23*
- personal consumer *23*
- positioning *28*
- societal marketing concept *27*

Case One: The Pope, Jordan, and Religious Tourism

Pope Benedict XVI, the head of the Roman Catholic Church, visited the Middle East region, stopping in Jordan, Palestine, and Israel. Jordan's King Abdullah and Queen Rania met the pontiff at the spot southwest of the Jordanian capital and showed him around the archaeological site. The Pope's first stop was at the site on the Jordan River where Jesus is believed to have been baptized; in fact, nine years ago he officially recognized Bethany Beyond the Jordan as the baptism site of Jesus.

Tourism officials in Jordan are upbeat about the pontiff's visit; they expect the nation's religious tourism industry to get a significant boost and attract hundreds of thousands of religious tourists (pilgrims) from the Middle East region and other nations too. In an interview, Nayef Fayez, managing director of Jordan Tourism Board (JTB), stressed that JTB will concentrate on religious tourism and highlight sites such as Bethany Beyond the Jordan and Mount Nebo. He stated that JTB's strategy in the short term would be to extend tourists' stays from an average 4.4 days to a week.

Jordan is a country whose population is predominantly Muslim, with Christians making up less than 4 percent of its 5.8 million residents. However as a religion, Christianity has a 2,000-year history in the country, which is home to rich biblical sites. In the year 2000, the Catholic Church designated Jordanian sites, such as Bethany Beyond the Jordan, Mount Nebo, and Mukawir, as Great Jubilee 2000 pilgrimage sites.

QUESTIONS

1. Chapter 1 discusses such issues as segmentation and targeting. Based on the market segmentation categories and selected variables, discuss who would be the best target markets for Jordan Tourism Board (JTB)?
2. Can JTB use the benefit segmentation variable to market Jordan as a pilgrim tourism destination? Discuss.

Sources: Ma'ayeh Philip Suha, "Jordan Hopes Pilgrims Will Follow Papal Lead," *The National,* April 29, 2009, 10; and Philip Pullella, http://in.reuters.com/article/worldNews/idINIndia-39532120090510, May 12, 2009.

Case Two: Let's Buy Ways to Make Holes

Chapter 1 presented the comment that "consumers do not buy drill bits—they buy ways to make holes."

QUESTION

Assuming that this is true, what are consumers really purchasing when they buy the following five items?

1. A pair of sneakers
2. Lipstick
3. A life insurance policy
4. A Toyota Prius
5. Wrangler jeans

2 The Consumer Research Process

THE PREPARATION, use, and wide scale availability of large amounts of consumer research is a critical force in advancing the discipline of consumer behavior. This discipline is dedicated to building a body of knowledge and understanding as to what makes consumers tick, and how marketers can better satisfy consumers' needs and wants.

Indeed, consumer researchers regularly carry-out many different kinds of consumer research projects. For instance, they might conduct consumer depth interviews and focus groups to identify which benefits consumers seek from using their products or services. Also, they might conduct telephone surveys or mall intercept research to determine consumers' recall or recognition about their current advertising messages. To illustrate, Figure 2.1 presents a magazine ad for the Gillette Complete Skincare product. It is quite common in developing ad copy and supporting visual materials (be they for a magazine, newspaper, TV, radio, or Internet ad message) that marketers test the impact of the message before spending the often huge amount of money it takes to reach the targeted consumers with the right message. To this end, marketers might conduct a variety of different types of consumer research studies as they go through the process of developing their marketing messages, or to establish which product features are most important to consumers who make up the target market for a newly developed product. In this chapter, we will provide a foundation and understanding of the nature and scope of consumer research. In particular, the current chapter is dedicated to setting out the methodological research issues for planning and carrying out consumer research studies. It will introduce various forms of consumer research, and, where useful, illustrate what they are like and how they are used. If you wish to learn more about consumer and marketing research, we recommend that you go to a library and seek out textbooks on marketing research and/or behavioral science research methods. Alternatively, you might consider enrolling in a college-level marketing research course; or if you have completed your formal education, consider a course offered by a professional association (such as the American Marketing Association).

FIGURE 2.1

Source: © The Gillette Company. Used with permission. All rights reserved.

QUESTION: *Why Do Marketers Regularly Test Print Ads Like This One Before They Are Placed in the Media?*

Learning Objectives

2.1 *To Understand the Importance of Consumer Research for Firms and Their Brands, as Well as Consumers.*

2.2 *To Understand the Steps in the Consumer Research Process.*

2.3 *To Understand the Importance of Establishing Specific Research Objectives as the First Step in the Design of a Consumer Research Project.*

2.4 *To Understand the Purposes and Types of Secondary Consumer Research That Is Available for Making Decisions or Planning Future Consumer Research.*

2.5 *To Understand Specific Features and Applications of Different Research Methods to Be Carried Out in Consumer Research Studies.*

2.6 *To Understand Where Data Analysis and Reporting of Findings Fit in the Research Process.*

2.7 *To Understand How Each Element of the Consumer Research Process Adds to the Overall Outcome of the Research Study.*

Imperative to Conduct Consumer Research

Learning Objective

2.1 *To Understand the Importance of Consumer Research for Firms and Their Brands, as Well as Consumers.*

The field of consumer research, in part, has developed as an extension of the field of marketing research. It has also been strongly impacted by the academicians and research practitioners of psychology, sociology, and anthropology. As mentioned in Chapter 1, the methods and findings of these three behavioral disciplines have increasingly influenced the nature and approaches of consumer behavior research. The conceptual foundation and thinking of economics and other scholarly and applied disciplines have also influenced topics studied and the growth of consumer behavior research.

Very importantly, studying consumer behavior, in all its ramifications, enables marketers to predict or anticipate how marketers might better meet consumer needs by offering them more suitable products and marketing messages. Marketing practitioners also realize that the more they know about their target consumers' decision-making process, the more likely they are to design marketing strategies and promotional messages that will be attractive and favorably influence their target consumers. Still further, the task of knowing and satisfying the needs of consumers, and communicating with them, is becoming a greater challenge, as more companies seek to become global in scope, and to expand to more and more countries (with more and more insights needed to understand the uniqueness in needs and preferences of consumers in particular countries). To meet this important challenge, there has been a rapid increase in interest in executing more cross-cultural or regional consumer behavior studies, and even more interest in global-level consumer research and marketing. To meet the needs of expansion-oriented global marketers, there has been an increase in the number of global marketing strategic consulting companies, as well as an increase in the number of consumer and marketing research firms that are prepared to carry out worldwide consumer behavior studies.

An Overview of the Consumer Research Process

Learning Objective

2.2 *To Understand the Steps in the Consumer Research Process.*

The remainder of this chapter examines the major steps in the consumer research process. While we consider the importance of secondary information (i.e., information already collected for some other purpose, but able to provide in part or even in full answers about a current problem), most of our attention is concentrated on two categories of **primary research** (i.e., new research especially designed and collected for purposes of a current research problem). The two categories of primary consumer research that we focus on are: **qualitative research** (i.e., focus groups and depth interviews, and specific associated research approaches), and **quantitative research** (i.e., observational research, experimentation, and survey research, and their associated research approaches for collecting information from consumers).

FIGURE 2.2
The Consumer Research Process

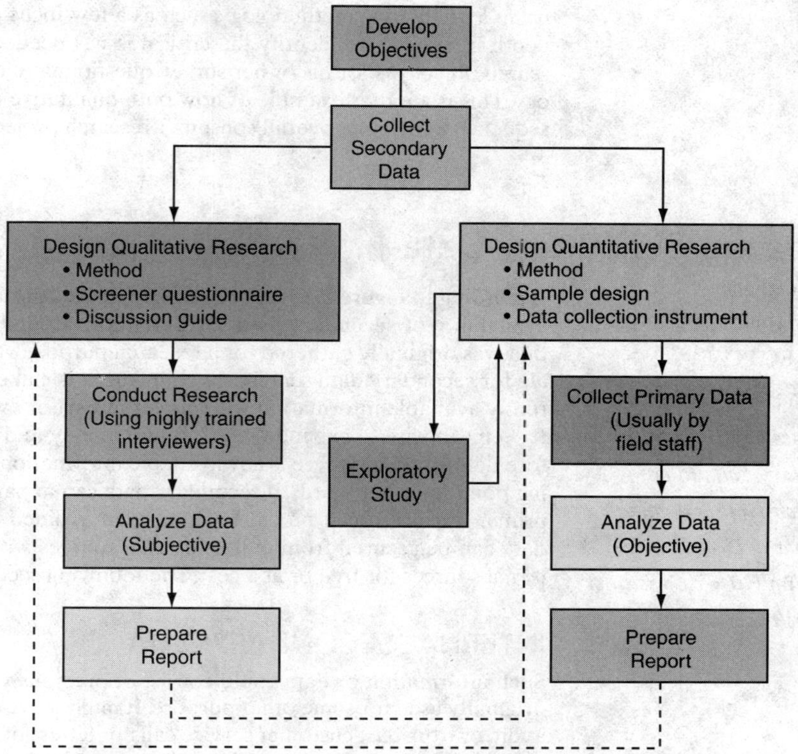

We have organized our discussion of the consumer research process into six steps: (1) defining the objectives of the research, (2) collecting and evaluating secondary data, (3) designing a primary research study, (4) collecting primary data, (5) analyzing the data, and (6) preparing a report of the findings. Figure 2.2 depicts a model of the consumer research process. The following major sections review each of the six steps of the consumer research process.

Developing Research Objectives

LEARNING OBJECTIVE

2.3 *To Understand the Importance of Establishing Specific Research Objectives as the First Step in the Design of a Consumer Research Project.*

The first and most difficult step in the consumer research process is to accurately define the objectives of the research. Is it to segment the market for HD television sets? Is it to examine consumer attitudes about the experience of online shopping? What percentage of households shop for food online? Whatever the key research question, it is important for the marketing manager and the research manager to agree at the outset as to the specific purposes and objectives of the proposed consumer study. Without such an understanding, it is questionable as to whether the core research questions are being communicated by those who need information and those who will carry out the research to secure strategic information. A carefully thought-out statement (in writing) of research objectives helps to insure that the information needed is secured, and that costly errors are avoided.

For example, if the purpose of a particular study is to come up with new ideas for product extensions or concepts for future promotional campaigns, then a qualitative study, consisting of focus group and/or one-on-one depth interviews are usually undertaken, in which consumer-participants spend a significant amount of time face-to-face with a highly trained professional interviewer-analyst who also does the analysis and writes the research report. Alternatively, if the purpose of the study is to find out *how many* target consumers there are in the population (i.e., what percentage of consumers) who use a particular product, and how frequently they use it, then a quantitative study is in order, because the research task is to provide quantitative information, upon which to derive strategic insights about how to better market a particular product to the appropriate consumer segment. Sometimes, in designing a quantitative study, the researcher may not know what questions to ask. In such cases, before undertaking a full-scale quantitative study, the researcher is likely to conduct a small-scale **exploratory study**, commonly using a qualitative methodology, such as a few focus group sessions or a series of one-on-one depth interviews, to identify the critical issues needed to develop focus and more precise research objectives for his or her survey questionnaire or other quantitative research methodology. This is another example of how both qualitative and quantitative research can be used in sequence to help the overall consumer research project.

Collecting Secondary Data

LEARNING OBJECTIVE

2.4 *To Understand the Purposes and Types of Secondary Consumer Research That Is Available for Making Decisions or Planning Future Consumer Research.*

According to Figure 2.2 , the second step in the consumer research process is to search for the availability of **secondary data**. By definition, secondary data is already existing information that was originally gathered for a research purpose *other than the present research*. The rationale for secondary data searches is simply that it makes good sense to investigate whether currently available information will answer in part or even in full the research question at hand. It seems unwise to expend the effort and money, and rush into collecting new information before determining if there is any available information that would provide at least a good starting point. In other words, if secondary data can in part or full answer the question, either new primary research can be cut back or even avoided altogether. Secondary consumer-related data can be secured from either internal sources within the company or organization, or external sources for free or at a cost. The following section explores secondary data.

INTERNAL SECONDARY DATA

Such information or data could consist of previously collected in-house information that was originally used for some other purpose. It might have originally been gathered as part of a sales audit, or from past customer service calls, or letters of inquiry from customers, or data collected via warranty cards. Increasingly, companies use internal secondary data to compute **customer lifetime value profiles** for various customer segments. These profiles include customer acquisition costs (the resources needed to establish a relationship with the customer), the profits generated from individual sales to each customer, the costs of handling customers and their orders (some customers may place more complex and variable orders that cost more to handle), and the expected duration of the relationship.

EXTERNAL SECONDARY DATA

This type of secondary data comes from sources outside of the firm or organization. They take many different forms. Some are free and can be found in a public library, other information is available for only a nominal fee, whereas still other data or information is quite expensive to secure. The following is a discussion of some of the specific types of consumer behavior secondary information available from outside of the firm.

Public and Government Secondary Data

Such data is collected by government bodies or their agencies, and is generally made available for a very nominal cost. For instance, within the United States, a major source of these data is the national government, which publishes information collected by scores of government agencies about the economy, business, and virtually all demographics of the U.S. population. An excellent way to access selected parts of these data is FedStats (**www.fedstats.gov**). The U.S. Census Bureau (**www.census.gov**) collects data on the age, education, occupation, and income of U.S. residents by state and region and also provides projections on the future growth or decline of various demographic segments. Any firm operating globally may find key statistics about any country in the world in the CIA's *World Factbook* (**www.cia.gov/cia/publications/factbook**). State and local governments, as well as studies prepared by the United Nations and various foreign governments, are also very useful for examining selective consumer behavior topics.

Periodicals and Articles Available from Online Search Services

Business-relevant secondary data from periodicals, newspapers, and books are readily accessible via a variety of online search engines. Two quite popular examples are: *ProQuest* and

LexisNexis. These two engines enable access to major newspapers such as the *Wall Street Journal* and the *New York Times*; business magazines such as *Business Week, Forbes, Fortune*, and *Harvard Business Review*; and marketing journals and applied publications focused specifically on marketing, such as *Advertising Age, Brandweek, Marketing News, Journal of Marketing, Journal of Marketing Research, Journal of Consumer Research,* and *European Journal of Marketing*. These materials are available in public and private libraries, especially business specialty libraries.

Syndicated Commercial Marketing and Media Research Services

Within the realm of commercially available information about consumers, there are syndicated and subscriber-based studies that are offered by marketing research companies that routinely sell data to subscribing marketers. For example, *Claritas* provides demographic and lifestyle profiles of the consumers residing in each U.S. postal area (**http://www.claritas.com/MyBestSegments**). *Ipsos Mendelsohn* (**www.ipsosmediact.com**) offers its Affluent Media Survey to advertisers and their ad agencies. Still further, *Yankelovich* monitors consumers' lifestyles and consumption patterns, as well as more targeted studies focused on the consumer behavior of specific ethnic groups (**www.yankelovich.com/ymonitor.asp**). *Mediamark Research Inc.* conducts segmentation studies of consumers' leisure activities, media habits, and buying styles, as well as studies focused specifically on consumer innovators (**www.mediamark.com**).

Secondary data is also provided by companies that routinely monitor a particular consumption-related behavior, and sell their data to marketing companies who use the insights to make more informed strategic decisions. For example, one of the primary challenges marketers face is placing their advertisements in media that are most likely to reach their target customers. For decades, *Nielsen Media Research* (**www.nielsenmedia.com**) has monitored the characteristics and audience size of TV programs. Nielsen did so through studying a presumably representative sample of U.S. households who agreed to install computerized boxes with modems connected to each set in their homes. Nielsen has been expanding into using people meters and mobile phones to track TV viewing behavior.[1]

Recognizing that new technologies provide opportunities for far more sophisticated monitoring techniques, media research rating companies, including Nielsen and Arbitron, are seeking out technology that might provide an advancement or possible breakthrough in terms of **portable people meters**, which are PDA-size devices, which individuals carry. Eventually, such devices will be able to monitor all media programming and advertising exposures of participating households. This would include individual exposures to all media programming and advertising, such as Web streaming, supermarket Muzak, and, when GPS systems are integrated into the new meter—exposure to outdoor advertising. At night, the meter devices are plugged into a cradle that transmits this data for analysis.

But perhaps the real future of researching consumers' exposure to media will not entail monitoring the behavior of several thousand consumers wearing portable meters, but monitoring the media exposure of almost all consumers via digital cable set-top boxes that are increasingly present in many homes and are likely to be placed in the majority of American homes, as digital TV replaces analog broadcasts. Presently, digital cable boxes are primarily used to send signals to consumers' TVs in order to enable them to watch movies on demand. However, the digital boxes can easily record all the programs that consumers are tuned into, including, of course, channel surfing, attempts at avoiding commercial breaks, and recordings for later viewing, using devices such as TiVo or digital video recorders that cable companies increasingly offer to subscribers. So far, cable companies have been reluctant to use this data due to privacy concerns. However, some companies are exploring methods that will transform data from digital cable boxes into information that can be used for precise targeting of consumers while still protecting privacy.[2] The portable people meters and the two-way digital cable boxes demonstrate the profound and dynamic changes that technology is bringing to consumer research. The influence of new technologies will increasingly enable marketers to study consumers' media exposure much more precisely and collect data that will allow them to better customize or *narrowcast* their promotional messages, and thus spend their advertising dollars more effectively.

Consumer Panels

For many decades, marketers have purchased data from secondary data providers who collected consumer behavior data from household or family **consumer panels**. The members of these consumer panels are paid for recording their purchases and/or media viewing habits in diaries that are then combined with thousands of households and analyzed by the data providers. On the other hand, marketers and advertising agencies pay the panel providers a subscription fee for the regular flow of reports of research findings. Often the information does not only tell subscribers about those individuals or families that buy and use their products, but the information also includes the same information about competitors' brands.

Today, online technology enables panel research companies to increasingly collect sophisticated data from respondents. For example, a manufacturer of customized snowboards had discovered that 10,000 snowboarding fans used its site's discussion forum to chat about their hobbies and buying habits, and also to rate different designs of snowboards. The snowboards marketer then started *selling* the data it collected from this online panel to other marketers interested in targeting the young, mostly male respondents who so enthusiastically revealed so much about themselves while discussing snowboards online. Similarly, automobile manufacturers purchase consumer behavior panel data about recent car purchases from independent panel companies. Again, information about a marketer's own brands and competitors' brands, as well as information about the demographic differences of households that buy their brand in contrast to competitors' brands are important insights for creating an effective competitive marketing campaign.

Obtaining secondary data before engaging in primary research offers several advantages. First, secondary data may provide a solution to the research problem and eliminate the need for primary research altogether. But even if this is not the case, secondary data, used in exploratory research, may help to clarify and redefine the objectives of the primary study and provide ideas for the methods to be used and the difficulties that are likely to occur during the full-scale study.

Although secondary information can be obtained more cheaply and quickly than primary data, it has some limitations. First, information may be categorized in units that are different from those that the researcher seeks (e.g., clustering consumers into the 15–20 and 21–25 age groups renders it useless to a researcher interested in consumers 17–24 years old). Some secondary data may not be accurate because of errors in gathering or analyzing the data for the original study or because the data had been collected in a biased fashion in order to support a particular point of view. Also, care must be taken not to use secondary data that may be outdated.

Designing Primary Research

LEARNING OBJECTIVE

2.5 *To Understand Specific Features and Applications of Different Research Methods to Be Carried Out in Consumer Research Studies.*

Figure 2.2 reveals that after considering the collection of secondary research, the diagram splits into two paths, with the left side route taking a path of qualitative research, and the right side route taking a path of quantitative research. The split reflects the purpose of the research and the orientation (i.e., preference for one or the other of the two routes of the research). If the purpose is to get new ideas (e.g., for positioning or repositioning a product), then a qualitative study is often undertaken; alternatively, if descriptive and quantitative information is sought, then some form of a quantitative study is likely to be undertaken. The merits of using the different measure instruments of qualitative and quantitative research are described in the two following sections.

DESIGNING AND CONDUCTING QUALITATIVE RESEARCH

Contemporary qualitative consumer research grew out of the *rejection* of the belief that consumer marketing was simply applied economics, and that consumers were rational decision makers who objectively evaluated the goods and services available to them and selected those that gave them the highest utility (satisfaction) at the lowest cost. Those rejecting this simplistic economic viewpoint included members of an early and important school of qualitative consumer researchers known as **motivational researchers**. The central tenet of their orientation was that consumers were not always consciously aware of why they made the decisions they did. Even when they were aware of their basic motivations, consumers were not always willing to reveal those reasons to others, or even to themselves.

The flamboyant early leader of the motivational research movement was the famous Viennese psychoanalyst Dr. Ernest Dichter, who after arriving in New York in the late 1930s began to apply qualitative Freudian psychoanalytic techniques to uncover the hidden or unconscious motivations of consumers.[3] By the late 1950s and early 1960s, this research orientation had become quite popular, and focus groups and depth interviews were being used by many advertising agencies and consumer products companies as a regular research tool to better understand consumer needs and motivations. Today, focus groups and depth interviews are very well-established research tools that are regularly used not only to secure insights about consumers' underlying needs and motivations but to have consumers provide their input into the new product development effort, including the creation of new products and even future advertising messages.[4] Because sample sizes are necessarily often small, findings cannot be generalized to larger popultions. Nevertheless, qualitative research contributes extensively to the initial identification and development of new promotional campaigns and new product development that can eventually be further refined through a variety of quantitative research methods.

In designing and implementing an appropriate research strategy for conducting a particular qualitative study, the researcher has to take into consideration the purpose of the study, the type of interviews that are likely to be best given the purpose of the research, and the types of data instruments most suitable for securing the information needed. Although the specific research methods used may differ in composition, most forms of qualitative research questioning have their roots in psychoanalytic and clinical aspects of psychology. Specifically, they tend to feature open-ended and free-response types of questioning and the related use of visual materials to stimulate respondents to reveal their innermost thoughts and beliefs.

The key types of interviews conducted in carrying out qualitative studies are depth interviews and/or focus group sessions. These two highly popular types of data collection methodologies, depth interviews and focus groups, as well as the processes of recruiting and questioning consumers in order to attempt to uncover their motivations, perceptions, attitudes, and beliefs are described next.

Depth Interviews

A **depth interview**, also frequently referred to as a "one-on-one" interview, is a somewhat lengthy nonstructured interview (often 20 to 60 minutes in duration) between a single respondent and a highly trained researcher (often the same person who moderates focus group sessions). Commonly, the strategy of the interviewer is to minimize his or her own talking time in order to provide as much time for the consumer to express his or her thoughts and behaviors, and respond to specific verbal and visual materials (e.g., mock-up of a potential print ad campaign). The researcher also must establish an atmosphere that encourages the consumer respondent to relax and open up in order to provide valuable insights. In many cases, the role of the researcher is to *probe* the respondent by encouraging the person to talk freely about the product category and/or brand under study. This is accomplished by gently and regularly asking "Why?" or "Can you try to explain that feeling a little more?" (see Figure 2.3 for some more examples of different probing phrases).

Generally, a series of the depth interviews takes place in a professionally set up interviewing room. These rooms are designed to provide audio and video recording equipment, and a one-way mirror for clients to view the interview without disrupting it ("yes," the researcher tells the participant that he or she is being observed). Audiotaping, videotaping, or "burning" of CDs are commonplace, and provide a means for the researcher and the clients to have a permanent recording of each interview.

Depth interview studies provide marketers with valuable ideas about product design or redesign, and provide insights for positioning or repositioning products. As already suggested, as part of a depth interview research project, a variety of stimulus materials are developed to enhance the discussion between the researcher and the respondent. They may take the form of written concept statements (describing a new product idea), drawings or photos of new products, actual product samples, or rough renditions or videotapes of print ads or TV commercials.

FIGURE 2.3
Examples of Different Probing Options for Focus Groups and Depth Interviews

Source: Naomi R. Henderson, "The Power of Probing," *Marketing Research* (Winter 2007): 39.

Request for elaboration: "Tell me more about that." "Give me an example of. . . ."

Request for definition: "What do you mean by . . . ?" "What does the term _____ mean to you?"

Request for word associations: "What other word(s) do you link with _____?" "Give me some synonyms that also describe _____."

Request for clarification: "How does that differ from . . ." "In what circumstances do you . . . ?"

Request for comparison: "How is _____ similar to _____?" "Which costs more, X or Y?"

Request for classification: "Where does _____ fit?" "What else is in the category of _____?"

"Silent" probe: This is a non-verbal probe and is characterized by such actions as raised eyebrows or hand gestures such as moving the right hand in a rolling motion that signifies "Tell me more."

In each application of such "stimulus materials," the purpose is to assist the respondent in expressing his or her inner thoughts and to encourage a more precise or accurate response to what is being investigated. Finally, over the course of a day of conducting depth interviews, a researcher is likely to be able to complete about five to eight hours of interviews, depending on the length of each interview.

Focus Groups

A "discussion group" or **focus group** often consists of 8 to 10 participants who meet with a moderator-researcher-analyst to "focus on" or "explore" a particular product or product category (or any other topic or subject of research interest). During a focus group session (often two hours in duration), participants are encouraged to discuss their reactions to product and service concepts, or new advertising or marketing communications campaigns.

Because a focus group generally takes about two hours to complete (sometimes they can last for three or more hours), a researcher can generally conduct two or three focus groups (with a total of about 30 respondents) in one day, while it might take that same researcher five or six days to conduct 30 individual depth interviews. Analysis of responses in both depth interviews and focus groups requires a great deal of skill on the part of the researcher. Like depth interviews, focus group sessions are invariably audiotaped and videotaped, to assist in the analysis, and to provide the client with a faithful record of the sessions. Like depth interviews, focus groups are usually held in specially designed conference rooms with one-way mirrors that enable marketers and advertising agency staff to observe the sessions without disrupting or inhibiting the responses.

For focus groups (and also depth interviews), respondents are recruited on the basis of a carefully drawn consumer profile that is detailed in the form of a questionnaire called a **screener questionnaire**. The purpose of the "screener" is to ensure that the appropriate individuals are invited to participate in the research study, and those who are not the target market are not invited. The specification of who is to attend and who is not to be invited is defined by the client. Also, keep in mind that today an appropriate respondent will often be paid $100 or more for his or her participation in the research process. In organizing focus group sessions, sometimes users of the company's brands are clustered in one or more groups, and their responses are compared to those of nonusers interviewed in separate sessions. Figure 2.4 presents a screener questionnaire that might be used to recruit participants for focus groups for a study that deals with introducing a premium line of canned vegetable soups. Carefully read the screener questionnaire; it is designed to identify target consumers to be invited to participate in either an all male or all female focus group session. Notice that individuals who are "screened out" (called "terminated" in research terminology) do not meet the desired specification for participation.

Some marketers prefer focus groups because they feel that the dynamic interaction between participants that takes place in focus groups tends to yield a greater number of new ideas and insights than depth interviews. Also, timing is sometimes very critical. In such cases, again, focus groups might be selected because it generally takes less time to complete a series of focus groups than a project of individual depth interviews. Other marketers (and in particular

FIGURE 2.4
Screener Questionnaire for Recruiting Respondents for a Consumer Study

FOOD PREFERENCE STUDY SCREENER

ASK TO SPEAK WITH A FEMALE OR MALE HOUSEHOLD MEMBER WHO IS BETWEEN 18 AND 35 YEARS OF AGE. WHEN THE CORRECT PERSON IS LOCATED INTRODUCE YOURSELF.

Hello, I'm ________, from ________. We are involved in a research project that is interested in knowing more about people's feeling and preferences with regard to food products. I want to assure you that this is research and not a "sales pitch." May I ask you a few questions.

1. CHECK ONE:
   Female .... [ ]-POTENTIAL FOR GROUP 1
   Male .... [ ]-POTENTIAL FOR GROUP 2

RECRUITER: Q1. RECRUIT 12 FEMALES AND 12 MALES.

2. In which of the following age groups are you? (READ CHOICES)
   Under 18 years of age .... [ ]-TERMINATE
   18-to-24 years of age .... [ ]
   25-to-29 years of age .... [ ]
   30-to-35 years of age .... [ ]
   Over 35 years of age .... [ ]-TERMINATE

RECRUITER: Q2. SECURE A GOOD MIX ACROSS THE AGE SPAN INDICATED.

3. Do you or anyone else in your household work for any of the following types of businesses? (READ CHOICES)

	No	Yes
A market research firm or agency	[ ]	[ ]-TERMINATE
An advertising or public relations firm or agency	[ ]	[ ]-TERMINATE
A company that sells, manufactures, or distributes any type of food products	[ ]	[ ]-TERMINATE

4. a. Have you ever participated in a depth interview, focus group, or discussion group?
   Yes .... [ ]-ASK Q4b.
   No .... [ ]-SKIP TO Q5.
   b. When was the last time you participated in a depth interview, focus group, or discussion group?
   Within the past 6 months .... [ ]-TERMINATE
   More than 6 months ago .... [ ]-CONTINUE

5. For classification purposes, please tell me how much formal education you have completed? (DO NOT READ CHOICES)
   Less than a college graduate .... [ ]-TERMINATE
   At least a college graduate .... [ ]

RECRUITER: Q5 ALL RESPONDENTS ARE TO BE COLLEGE GRADUATES.

6. Also, for classification purposes, please tell me into which of the following categories your total family's or personal income falls? (READ CHOICES)
   Under $25,000 .... [ ]-TERMINATE
   $25,000 to $49,999 .... [ ]
   $50,000 or more .... [ ]

RECRUITER: Q6 ALL PARTICIPANTS MUST HAVE INCOMES OF AT LEAST $25,000.

7. Which of the following food products have you eaten within the past 5 days? READ FULL LIST.

	Yes	No
Frozen pizzas	[ ]	[ ]
Prepackaged cold cuts	[ ]	[ ]
Pre-sliced packaged cheeses	[ ]	[ ]
Canned soup	[ ]	[ ]
Potato chips	[ ]	[ ]
Canned fruit	[ ]	[ ]
Peanut butter	[ ]	[ ]
Frozen vegetables	[ ]	[ ]

RECRUITER: Q7. RESPONDENT MUST SAY "YES" TO *CANNED SOUP*; OTHERWISE TERMINATE.

FIGURE 2.4
Continued

8. **FOR SOUP AND ANY ONE OTHER FOOD ITEMS ANSWERED "YES" ("EATEN") IN Q7, ASK:**
   a. During the course of one week how often do you eat ______?
      Number of time______
   b. During the course of one week how often do you have soup____?
      Number of time______

RECRUITER: Q8b. MUST SAY "AT LEAST TWO TIMES," OTHERWISE TERMINATE.

9. Now, I would like you to use your imagination. If you could serve dinner to a famous person from the past, who would it be? What would you serve for dinner?

RECRUITER: Q9 IS AN ARTICULATION QUESTION. THE RESPONDENTS SHOULD SHOW "CREATIVITY/GOOD IMAGINATION," AND BE ABLE TO ADD TO THE GROUP DISCUSSION.

10. As part of our current research we are conducting a discussion with 8 to 10 individuals. The discussion is called a "focus group." During the interview, you will have an opportunity to express your views and interact with the other participants on a variety of lifestyle and food consumption topics.

    The focus group will last for a full **2 hours.** You will receive $100.00 to help defray the cost of your time and travel.

    We would like to invite you to participate in the focus group session. It should prove to be an interesting and enjoyable session. The focus group will be held at (NAME OF FACILITY), which is located at (GIVE ADDRESS). It will take place on (DATE) at (GIVE CHOICE OF TIME). Can we count on having you attend?

    Yes .... [ ]-RECORD PARTICIPANT INFORMATION. REPEAT DAY, DATE, TIME, AND GIVE DIRECTIONS TO LOCATION.
    No .... [ ]-TERMINATE

THANK YOU FOR AGREEING TO PARTICIPATE, WE WILL CALL YOU THE DAY BEFORE THE RESEARCH TO REMIND YOU.

Record: A **female** participant, recruited for the 6:00 PM focus group ______
A **male** participant, recruited for the 8:00 PM focus group ______

advertising agency professionals) tend to prefer individual or depth interviews because they believe that individually interviewed respondents are free of group pressures and thus are less likely to give socially acceptable (and not necessarily truthful) responses. Moreover, the single participant is more likely to remain attentive during the entire interview, and—because of the greater personal attention received—is more likely to reveal private thoughts.

Discussion Guides

A discussion guide is a step-by-step outline that sets out the line of questioning that the researcher needs to cover with the respondent in a depth interview, or a group of respondents in the case of a focus group session. Some moderator-researchers prefer to closely follow (question by question) the order set out in a discussion guide; whereas other moderator-researchers prefer to "go with the flow" and allow the single respondent or focus group participants to go in the direction of what turns out to be particularly important to them. Surprisingly, a good researcher, following either the "question-by-question" or "go-with-the-flow" approach, will tend to finish with more information than was originally anticipated by the client. Indeed, it is not uncommon for qualitative research to produce strategically important insights that were not anticipated prior to conducting the actual qualitative research. Such "extra" insights are a special benefit of both depth interviews and focus groups—namely, that they can provide invaluable and unanticipated information. To provide you with an opportunity to examine a focus group discussion guide, Figure 2.5 presents one especially created to be used for an initial or first round of two focus groups, for the purpose of creating the new line of premium vegetable soups. While the screener questionnaire (in Figure 2.4) was designed to recruit a sample of the target consumer participants for the focus group sessions on the proposed premium line of vegetable soups, the discussion guide was created to help the moderator lead the discussion and manage the flow of the key themes or "lines of questioning."

It is extremely rare that a moderator-researcher would conduct depth interviews or focus group sessions without the aid of a discussion guide. In a sense, a discussion guide is a kind of

FIGURE 2.5
Focus Group Discussion Guide

ROUND #1 FOCUS GROUP:
CREATING A SUPERIOR LINE OF VEGETABLE SOUPS

Discussion Guide

I. INTRODUCTION

A. Introduce myself and my role
B. Tell participants about their roles
C. Identify session video-sound recording system and one-way mirror
D. Have each participant introduce him/herself—briefly talking about work, about household composition and interests/hobbies
E. Describe the "basic" purpose of the focus group discussion—TO CREATE A LINE OF SUPERIOR VEGETABLE SOUPS

II. SOUP BACKGROUND: *EARLIEST MEMORIES*

A. As you were growing up, what were your early memories of eating soup? Anything else?
B. In particular, what do you think of vegetable soup? In the "world of soup," where does "vegetable soup," fit in comparison to other soups? What do you think?
C. When you think of a "line of vegetable soups," what comes to mind? Are there six or more different vegetable soups?
D. Right now, what is your favorite vegetable soup?
E. Over the years, has your favorite vegetable soup been changing? In what ways?
F. How has your favorite vegetable changed from childhood to adulthood? Any other changes?
G. How would you characterize the difference between a really good restaurant vegetable soup, and a "home made" vegetable soup? Which do you prefer? Why?

III. SOUP CONSUMPTION CIRCUMSTANCES

A. For you, is vegetable soup "a meal" or is it "a part of a meal"? Why is it this way for you?
B. What is the difference between vegetable soup as a "meal" and as "part of meal"? Anything else?
C. Is there such a person as a "soup person?" Describe such a person? Give me a profile of a "soup person"? How do "soup people" tend to differ from non-soup people? Any other thoughts?

IV. SOUP SELECTION AND DECISION MAKING

A. In your household, how is the decision made as to which brand of soup is purchased and eaten? (Probe for various aspects of family choice and influence.)
B. Is there a single brand of soup that your family all agrees on? Which brand? Why?
C. How do you approach the selection of soup? Would you consider yourself to be: A specialist? An experimenter? A habitual purchaser?
D. What is your idea of a "soup connoisseur"? Describe such a person? Tell me more?
E. When it comes to food store soups, which is your favorite? Why?
F. In your mind's eye, what is a perfect vegetable soup?

V. SOUP TASTING EXERCISE
INTRODUCTION: "WE HAVE FIVE DIFFERENT VEGETABLE SOUPS FOR EACH OF YOU TO TRY, TONIGHT."

AFTER TRYING EACH ONE, I WANT YOU TO WRITE ON YOUR PADS YOUR THOUGHTS ABOUT THE PARTICULAR VEGETABLE SOUP.

A. What is your reaction to the ***first*** (repeat for each) vegetable soup that I gave you to try? Any other thoughts or feelings?
B. How would you describe it to a person who has not tasted it?
C. If this soup was available in a retail store, would you buy it? Why?/Why not?
D. Any ideas as to how to make the soup taste even better?
E. **REPEAT FOR THE NEXT VEGETABLE SOUP, UNTIL EACH OF THE FIVE ARE SAMPLED**
F. [**WRITE ON YOUR PAD**] Which of the five soups did you like the best? Which soup did you like the least? Again, write your answers down on your pad.
G. [**AROUND THE ROOM**] So, which one was the best?
H. Let's reflect on your reactions to the five soups?
I. [WRITE ON YOUR PAD] Considering the five vegetable soups, are there any other distinctive vegetables that need to be featured to make the overall selection better?

VI. ANY FINAL FEELINGS/THOUGHTS

A. Any final ideals or thoughts about the line of premium vegetable soups?
B. What would make it better? Anything else?
C. Where would you expect to purchase such a line of vegetable soups?

"agenda" of topics and issues that need to be covered over the course of each depth interview or each focus group session. However, also keep in mind that qualitative research is much like "jazz," the expertise is in the ability to improvise depending on the circumstance of the interview, or the makeup of the group session.

We will now consider several well-established and emerging qualitative research tools or instruments that are used by moderator-researchers to assist them in their efforts to engage participants in the tasks that enable them to better express their underlying or true feelings, or to faithfully report their actions or behavior.

Projective Techniques

When it comes to tapping into the underlying motives of individuals, **projective techniques** are a useful tool borrowed from psychoanalytic theory and practice, and adapted for studying the unconscious associations of consumers who may be concealing or suppressing some of their thoughts or reactions. Thus, projective exercises consist of a variety of disguised "tests" that contain ambiguous stimuli, such as incomplete sentences, untitled pictures or cartoons, word-association tests, and other-person characterizations. They are all designed to make it easier for consumers to express themselves and reveal their inner motivations. Projective techniques are sometimes administered as part of focus group research, but more often are used during depth interviews. Some of the well established exercises that are used by qualitative researchers to "tease-out" true consumer-related feelings and reflection are: (1) word associations (2) sentence completions (3) photo/visuals for storytelling, and (4) role playing. Table 2.1 describes each of these four exercises and their applications in consumer research.

Metaphor Analysis

Starting in the 1990s, there has been a stream of consumer research that suggests that since most communication is nonverbal and that people do not think in words but in images, it is important to use a set of engaging tasks and exercises to get consumer participants to get in touch with their own inner feelings. Moreover, if consumers' thought processes consist of a series of images or pictures in their minds, then it is likely that many respondents cannot adequately convey their feelings and attitudes about the research subject (such as a product or brand) through the use of words alone. Therefore, it is important to provide consumers with the opportunity to

TABLE 2.1 Some Commonly Used Qualitative Projective Exercises

	DESCRIPTION	APPLICATIONS
Word Associations	The researcher has a list of words, some of them to be studied and some just as "filler." The researcher asks the respondent(s) to react, one-at-a-time, to each word by stating or (in a focus group setting) writing on a pad the first word that comes to mind, and to explain the link.	The word association exercise tends to be used when marketers seek to know what certain words (or a phrase) mean to consumers. The exercise is used to determine if a word or words have a sufficiently positive meaning or relevance to a product, or even a proposed product's name or description.
Sentence Completions	The researcher has a series of incomplete sentences that the respondent(s) needs to complete with a word or phrase.	The sentence completion exercise is an alternative to the word association exercise (it is used for the same purpose). In reality, it is easier to use and generally provides for more useable consumer insights than the word association exercise.
Photo/Visual for Storytelling	The researcher creates/selects a series of photos of consumers, different brands or products, range of print ads, etc., to serve as stimuli. The respondents are asked to discuss or tell a story based on their response to a photo or some other visual stimulus.	The product or consumer ideas secured from responding to the photos/visuals, in the form of "free-association" or "storytelling" reveals how the participants feel about a topic, brands, or consumer within the context of the photos or other visual forms (e.g., cartoons). Ideas for new products or communication themes are possible outcomes.
Role Playing	Is quite similar to storytelling; however, instead of telling a story, the participant(s) will be given a situation and asked to "act out" the role(s), often with regard to a product or brand, or particular selling situation.	Role playing is appropriate in a focus group environment where different participants can be asked to role play and to act out different interacting roles.

represent their images in an alternate, nonverbal form—through the use, say, of sounds, music, drawings, or pictures. The use of one form of expression to describe or represent feelings about another is called a *metaphor*. A number of consumer theorists have come to believe that people use metaphors as the most basic method of thought and communication.

The **Zaltman Metaphor Elicitation Technique (ZMET)**—the first patented marketing research tool in the United States—relies on visual images to assess consumers' deep and subconscious thoughts about products, services, and marketing strategies. In one study about consumer perceptions of advertising, prescreened respondents were asked to bring into a depth interview pictures that illustrated their perceptions of the value of advertising. They were asked to bring pictures from magazines, newspapers, artwork, photos they took especially for the study or from existing collections, but not actual print advertisements. Each respondent participated in a two-hour videotaped interview (on average, each respondent brought in 13 images representing his or her impressions of the value of advertising). The interview used several methods that are part of the ZMET technique to elicit key metaphors and the interrelationships among them from the respondents. The interviews were then analyzed by qualified researchers according to the ZMET criteria. The findings revealed that the *ambivalent* respondents had both favorable (e.g., information and entertainment values) and unfavorable (e.g., misrepresentation of reality) impressions of advertising; *skeptics* had mostly negative, but some positive impressions of advertising; and *hostile* respondents viewed advertising as an all-negative force.[5]

The Growing Presence of Online Focus Groups

Over the past 5 to 10 years, there has been a substantial amount of interest in, trial of, and acceptance of online focus groups and depth interviews. However, what is being called an "online focus groups," can vary greatly. On the one hand, they can be very similar in nature and quality to a traditional focus group (i.e., sessions held in a local focus group facility, with moderator and participants interacting together. In such cases, they are often real focus group sessions that are "broadcasted" to individual client's laptops, or to a "sister" research facility in the client's hometown, and viewed by a gathering of clients. Alternatively, there is the option to select an online specialty research company, such as Harris Interactive (**www.harrisinteractive.com/services**) that provides focus group recruiting services from their very large panel of online consumers ready to participate. In addition, Harris Interactive also has the capability of offering clients access to a "virtual version" of traditional focus groups. Specifically, they can provide a "virtual focus group room" environment—one where consumer participants and a moderator can log on to participate in an online focus group session. In certain ways, it can be similar to a regular off-line focus group session.

In contrast, there is the online "quasi-focus group" that does not provide the dynamic environment that makes a focus group something special. Instead, such sessions are generally no more than a simplistic "back and forth" of a series of e-mailed questions from the moderator and replies from the respondents. There is little or no opportunity for participants to bond, or to establish a give-and-take, that are important ingredients of focus group research.

Looking-In (Online) Research

There is an established stream of consumer research that considers ways in which consumer-oriented Web sites, online consumer communities, as well as consumer blogs can be systematically studied to add to our understanding of the importance of contemporary consumers' online activities.[6] Moreover, for formulating marketing strategies, consumers' online social and product-related postings can provide a rich and powerful source of strategic insights that can be easily accessed by marketers who are willing to systematically listen in to involved consumers' give-and-take on discussion forums, blogs, and a wide range of online social media. To add to this stream of consumer research, a recently proposed approach to qualitative research, called looking-in, describes and illustrates the uses of a methodology designed to capture consumers' experiences, opinions, forecasts, and most important, these involved consumers' "wish list" of sought-out features that they are hoping will be included, say, in the next model of a particular digital camera.[7]

To conduct **looking-in research**, researchers perform a key phrase search of the stored threads and related postings. In the relevant preview "Canon Talk"—one of the consumer discussion forums maintained by the leading digital camera Web site, **www.dpreview.com**, a key phrase search revealed more than 200 pages of consumer postings and responses that clearly revealed significant consumer insight as to the features that the next generation of Canon G-series cameras should contain. This type of research is an inexpensive and powerful research approach to include consumers in the product development process.

Now that we have examined the design and conduct of qualitative research, and in particular data collection methods and a variety of tools used by practitioners of this branch of consumer research, we turn our attention to considering the different but parallel design and research tools associated with quantitative consumer research.

DESIGNING AND CONDUCTING QUANTITATIVE RESEARCH

A substantial portion of quantitative research is used by consumer researchers to better understand the acceptance of various products or specific brands, as well as the impact of promotional messages on consumers. In other cases, the objectives are to assist marketers in pinpointing consumers' level of satisfaction with a product, service, distributor, or retailer, or to possibly attempt to identify areas in which the consumer has unmet needs, or even to attempt to better "predict" future consumer needs or behavior. The broad category of quantitative research includes experimentation, survey techniques, and observation. The findings are descriptive, empirical, and, if collected randomly (i.e., using a probability sample), can be generalized to larger populations. Because the data collected are quantitative, they lend themselves to sophisticated statistical analysis.

When it comes to quantitative research studies, there are research and sample designs as well as data collection methods and instruments that are important for investigating a wide range of consumer behavior topics and issues. Next, we consider three basic research designs: observational research, experimentation (in a laboratory or in the field, such as in a retail store), and surveys (i.e., questioning people).

Observational Research

Watching or carefully observing consumers' actions of purchasing and consuming, especially in realistic surroundings (i.e., in stores, in malls, watching TV, and even in their home environments), is an extremely insightful way to learn what is valuable or meaningful to consumers. Indeed, **observational research** is an important research tool because marketers recognize that often the best way to gain an in-depth understanding of the relationship between people and products is by watching them in the process of buying and/or using the products.[8] Observing consumers in action enables researchers to comprehend what the product symbolizes to a consumer and provides greater insight into the bond between people and products that is the essence of brand loyalty. It is also important in uncovering issues or problems with a product. Many large corporations and advertising agencies use trained researchers/observers to watch, note, and sometimes videotape consumers in stores, malls, or even with permission in their own homes. For example, in studying responses to a new mint-flavored Listerine, the marketers hired a research firm that paid 37 New York City families to let it install cameras in their bathrooms to videotape mouthwash usage. The study found that consumers who used Scope gave the product a swish and spit it out. On the other hand, users of the new Listerine kept the mouthwash in their mouths for much longer (one subject even held the mouthwash in his mouth as he left home and got into the car, and only spit it out after driving a couple of blocks).[9] Procter & Gamble (P&G) sent video crews to scores of households around the world, which enabled P&G executives in Cincinnati to watch a mother in Thailand feed her baby. They discovered that the mother was multitasking while feeding her baby and even glanced at her TV from time to time. Understanding such behavior can lead to the development of products and packages that will give P&G a strong competitive advantage in the marketplace.[10]

As an alternative to having trained observers view consumers, some firms prefer to use mechanical or electronic devices, such as counting or video recording devices to capture customers' behaviors or responses to a particular marketing stimulus. For example, when Duane Reade—a large chain of drugstores in and around New York City—considers a location for a new store, the company uses electronic beams or hand counters to count the numbers of passersby at different times and under different weather conditions.[11] Government planners use data collected from electronic E-ZPass devices in passenger cars to decide which roads should be expanded, and banks use security cameras to observe problems customers may have in using ATMs.

Increasingly, consumers use automated systems in their purchases because these instruments make purchases easier and often provide rewards for using them. For example, consumers who use supermarket frequent shopper cards often receive special offers for promotional discounts tailored for them at checkout counters. Moviegoers who order tickets online can pick them up at ATM-like devices at movie theaters and avoid waiting in line at the box office. As consumers use more and more highly convenient technologies, such as credit and ATM cards, E-ZPasses, frequent shopper cards, cellular phones, and most of all online shopping, there are more and more electronic records of their consumption patterns. As a consequence, observation of consumer behavior via electronic means has grown significantly and, as illustrated in the earlier discussion of portable people meters and two-way digital cable boxes, electronic observation of consumption behavior will become increasingly sophisticated.

Gambling casinos have been in the forefront of developing systems that track individual customer data collected during the various stages of a customer's visit, and cross-matching them with data collected on previous visits by that customer (including spending usage). They use this data to classify visitors into categories based on their "loyalty levels," and implement corresponding rewards that are delivered almost immediately. For example, normally about 50,000 people a day visit the Foxwoods Resort Casino in Connecticut. Most of them use magnetic cards called "frequent player cards." Sophisticated electronic network systems monitor the gaming patterns, eating habits, and room preferences of all visitors. When a player sits at a table, within seconds, the casino's manager can read the guest's history on the screen, including alcoholic beverages preferred and gaming habits. Because there are electronic tags in the chips issued to each player, when a player leaves the table, his or her record is updated instantly and made available at any contact point for that customer throughout the entire casino complex. Thus, the casino can instantly reward customers who are good for business by giving free meals and room upgrades and inviting them to gamble in designated VIP lounges. The customers love the frequent player cards because they enable them to keep track of their spending, and the casinos benefit from each swipe of the card because it provides more information about each customer. The casino has two identical computer systems and, if needed, can switch to a backup immediately and thus avoid the many thousands of dollars that may be lost during an even brief period of operating without computers.[12] More casinos are employing increasingly sophisticated software to create real-time and personal rewards to day-trippers who bet relatively small amounts of money—$50 to $100 per visit—but who visit the casinos frequently. Casinos have recognized that although these consumers wage little money per trip, they view gaming as their primary entertainment, and observing their behavior and immediately using the data to encourage them to spend more money is likely to increase profits greatly over time.[13]

An audit is another type of mechanical observation that entails monitoring the sales of products. A key component of Wal-Mart's competitive advantage is the retailing giant's use of technology in its product audits. At any given moment, the company knows what is selling, how fast, and how much of the product remains in its inventory. Maintaining small inventories and moving products quickly enables the company to lower its prices and attract more customers. Wal-Mart's record profits are derived from low per-item profits multiplied by selling billions of products quickly, and also moving products rapidly to where consumers are likely to buy them. For example, after observing that the sales of strawberry Pop-Tarts increased dramatically before a hurricane and that the top preseller before a hurricane was beer, the company quickly transports large quantities of these items to areas expected to be hit by an approaching storm.[14]

Marketers also use **physiological observation** devices that monitor respondents' patterns of information processing. For example, an electronic eye camera may be used to monitor the eye movements of subjects looking at a series of advertisements for various products, and electronic sensors placed on the subjects' heads can monitor the brain activity and attentiveness levels involved in viewing each advertisement. Neuroscientists monitoring cognitive functions in 12 different regions of the brain while consumers watched commercials for different products claimed that the data collected shows the respondents' levels of attention and the decoding and recall of the promotional messages.[15]

Experimentation

There are a variety of experimental designs that a researcher needs to select from in formulating a particular consumer-related experiment. For our purposes here, we will keep it simple and general. For instance, it is possible to test the relative sales appeal of many types of variables, such as package designs, alternative price points, or different promotional offers by experiments designed to identify cause and effect. In the simplest form of such experiments (called *causal research*), only one variable is manipulated (called the *independent variable*), while all other elements are kept constant. A **controlled experiment** of this type ensures that any difference in the outcome (the *dependent variable*, which is most often sales) is due to different treatments of the variable under study and not to extraneous factors. For example, one study tested the effectiveness of using an attractive versus unattractive endorser in promoting two types of products: products that are used to enhance one's attractiveness (e.g., a men's cologne) and products that are not (e.g., a pen). The endorser used was a fictitious character named Phil Johnson who was described as a member of the U.S. Olympic water polo team. The photograph depicting the attractive endorser was a scanned image of an attractive athletic man, whereas the picture depicting the unattractive endorser was the same image graphically modified to reduce attractiveness. The subjects viewed each endorser-product combination for 15 seconds (simulating the viewing of an actual print ad) and then filled out a questionnaire that measured their attitudes and purchase intentions toward the products advertised. In this study, the combinations of the product (i.e., used/not used to enhance one's attractiveness) and the endorser's attractiveness (i.e., attractive/nonattractive endorser) were the *manipulated treatments* (i.e., the independent variables) and the combination of the attitudes and purchase intentions toward the product was the *dependent variable*. The study discovered that the attractive endorser was more effective in promoting both types of products.[16]

A major application of causal research is **test marketing**. Sometimes after conducting depth interviews, focus groups, and surveys research, there is realization by the marketing firm that it still needs to secure additional real-world feedback for a new product, service, or marketing communications program that it is considering, before it commits itself to full-scale marketing rollout. It is in such situations that test marketing is a logical next step. Test marketing typically includes the selection of a representative single market area and then conducting a market introduction (only in that market) in order to test the actual response of consumers to the marketing effort under actual marketing conditions. From the test marketing effort, the marketing firm hopes to be able to project how the entire market may respond to its marketing effort, without the full risks associated with skipping a test marketing stage. Still further, some research firms carry out for clients small-scale experiments that test consumer responses to alternative marketing strategies. This can be done prior to selecting a new product, redesigning a package, changing the price of a product, or trying out a new marketing campaign—all of these are marketing actions that can benefit from small-scale experimentation that manipulates variables in a controlled setting in order to predict sales or gauge the possible responses to the product. Unlike a test market that is usually in the real world, many experiments are conducted in a lab environment. Today some researchers employ *virtual reality methods*. For example, in a market test, respondents can view, on a computer screen, supermarket shelves that are stocked with many products, including different versions of the same product; they can "pick up" an item by touching the image, examine it by rotating the image with a track ball, and place it in a shopping cart if they decide to buy it. The researchers observe how long the respondents spend in looking at the product, the time spent in examining each side of the package, the products purchased, and the order of the purchases. In general terms, it is quite important for marketers to continuously experiment and test market their products and services.[17]

Survey Research

If researchers wish to ask consumers about their purchase preferences and consumption experiences, they can do so in person, by mail, by telephone, or online. Each of these survey methods has certain advantages and certain disadvantages that the researcher must weigh when selecting the method of contact (see Table 2.2).

Personal interview surveys (that are face-to-face) most often take place in a public space or a retail shopping area, such as within the public area of a mall, or a rented space within an office that is located in a mall. The latter, referred to as *mall intercepts*, are used more frequently, as a replacement for in-home interviews that used to be commonplace, because of the high incidence of not-at-home working women and the reluctance of many people today to allow a stranger into their homes.

Telephone interview surveys are also used to collect consumer data; however, evenings and weekends are often the only times to reach telephone respondents, who tend to be less responsive—even hostile—to calls that interrupt dinner, television viewing, or general relaxation. The difficulties of reaching people with unlisted telephone numbers have been solved through random-digit dialing, and the costs of a widespread telephone survey are often minimized by using toll-free telephone lines. Other problems arise, however, from the increased use of answering machines, telephone company voice mail systems, and caller ID to

TABLE 2.2 Comparative Advantages and Disadvantages of Mail, Telephone, Personal Interview, and Online Surveys

	MAIL	TELEPHONE	PERSONAL INTERVIEW	ONLINE
Cost	Low	Moderate	High	Low
Speed	Slow	Immediate	Slow	Fast
Response Rate	Low	Moderate	High	Self-selected
Geographic Flexibility	Excellent	Good	Difficult	Excellent
Interviewer Bias	N/A	Moderate	Problematic	N/A
Interviewer Supervision	N/A	Easy	Difficult	N/A

screen calls. Some market research companies have tried to automate telephone surveys, but many respondents are even less willing to interact with an electronic voice than with a live interviewer.

Mail surveys are conducted by sending questionnaires directly to individuals at their homes. One of the major problems of mail questionnaires is a low response rate, but researchers have developed a number of techniques to increase returns, such as enclosing a stamped, self-addressed envelope, using a provocative questionnaire, and sending prenotification letters as well as follow-up letters. Also, to deal with the ongoing problems of low response rates to unsolicited mail surveys, some consumer marketing companies are establishing their own ongoing consumer panels and periodically mail or e-mail a questionnaire to consumer panel participants to fill out. As a motivation to complete the task, and insure a satisfactory response rate, it is commonplace that for each round of completed surveys, respondents are paid a prearranged participation fee. Sometimes panel members are also asked to keep diaries of their purchases.[18]

E-mail surveys are an increasingly popular alternative to using the postal service as a means of distributing questionnaires to target consumers. One of the key attractions of using e-mail is that it is as easy and quick to distribute a survey around the world as it is to distribute it down the block. Moreover, with an accurate list of e-mail addresses, it is very inexpensive to distribute even a large number of questionnaires. We can expect that as the world increasingly turns to the Web for many types of social communications, we will see continued growth of e-mailing as a way to distribute surveys.[19]

Furthermore, there has been a rapid increase in the number of consumers who are interested in participating in **online** or **Internet-based surveys**. Potential respondents are directed to the marketer's (or researcher company's) Web site by online ads or targeted e-mail invitations. Often, responses to online surveys are from consumer respondents who are self-selected, and therefore the results cannot be projected to the larger population. Most computer polls ask respondents to complete a profile consisting of demographic questions that enable the researchers to classify the responses to the substantive product or service questions.

Another online option are established online research companies that maintain a database of potential consumers who are willing (for a fee) to participate in online consumer research projects. The advantage of established online survey research firms is their substantial databases and comprehensive profiles of each potential participant. This acts as a significant safeguard that only invites individuals who qualify to participate in the particular online survey. Since members of the database desire to continue earning money for their participation, there is a very good chance that they will be reliable and actually complete those surveys that they have been qualified to complete; otherwise they will eventually be dropped for not participating.

Research firms that conduct computer surveys believe that the anonymity of the Internet encourages respondents to be more forthright and honest than they would be if asked the same questions in person or by mail. Still further, online survey research organizations cite the inherent advantages of their geographically wide reach and the affordability of online consumer surveys. However, in contrast, there are other marketers who are largely skeptical about online research because they fear that the data collected may be suspect because some respondents may create false online personalities that do not reflect their own beliefs or behaviors.

QUANTITATIVE RESEARCH DATA COLLECTION INSTRUMENTS

Data collection instruments are developed as part of a study's total research design to systematize the collection of data and to ensure that all respondents are asked the same questions in the same order. Data collection instruments include questionnaires, personal inventories, and attitude scales. These instruments are usually pretested and "debugged" to assure the validity and reliability of the research study. A study is said to have **validity** if it does, in fact, collect the appropriate data needed to answer the questions or objectives stated in the first (objectives) stage of the research process. A study is said to have **reliability** if the same questions, asked of a similar sample, produce the same findings. Often a sample is systematically divided in two, and each half is given the same questionnaire to complete. If the results from each half are similar, the questionnaire is said to have *split-half reliability*.

Questionnaires

For quantitative research, the primary data collection instrument is the questionnaire, which can be sent through the mail or online to selected respondents for self-administration or can be administered by field interviewers in person or by telephone. In order to motivate respondents to take the time to respond to surveys, researchers have found that questionnaires must be interesting, objective, unambiguous, easy to complete, and generally not burdensome. To enhance the analysis and facilitate the classification of responses into meaningful categories, questionnaires include both substantive questions that are relevant to the purposes of the study and pertinent demographic questions.

The questionnaire itself can be *disguised* or *undisguised* as to its true purpose; a disguised questionnaire sometimes yields more truthful answers and avoids responses that respondents may think are expected or sought. Questions can be *open-ended* (requiring answers in the respondent's own words) or *closed-ended* (the respondent merely checks the appropriate answer from a list of options). Open-ended questions yield more insightful information but are more difficult to code and to analyze; closed-ended questions are relatively simple to tabulate and analyze, but the answers are limited to the alternative responses provided (i.e., to the existing insights of the questionnaire designer).

Wording the questions represents the biggest challenge in constructing questionnaires; Table 2.3 includes guidelines for writing clear and effective questions. The sequence of questions is also important: The opening questions must be interesting enough to "draw" the respondent into participating, they must proceed in a logical order, and demographic (classification) questions should be placed at the end, where they are more likely to be answered. The format of the questionnaire and the wording and sequence of the questions affect the validity of the responses and, in the case of mail questionnaires, the number (rate) of responses received.

TABLE 2.3 Guidelines for Wording Questions

1. *Avoid leading questions.* For example, questions such as "Do you often shop at such cost-saving stores as Staples?" or "Weren't you satisfied with the service you received at Staples today?" introduce bias into the survey
2. *Avoid two questions in one.* For example, "In your view, did you save money and receive good service when you last visited Staples?" is really two questions combined, and they should be stated separately.
3. *Questions must be clear.* For example, "Where do you usually shop for your home office supplies?" is unclear because the term *usually* is vague.
4. *Use words that consumers routinely use.* For example, do not use the verb *to rectify*; use the verb *to correct*.
5. *Respondents must be able to answer the question.* For example, it is unlikely that any respondent can accurately answer a question such as, "How many newspaper or TV ads for Staples did you read or see during the past month?"
6. *Respondents must be willing to answer the question.* Questions about money, health issues, personal hygiene, or sexual preferences can embarrass respondents and cause them not to answer. Sometimes, asking the question in a less personal fashion might help generate more responses. For example, rather than asking older consumers whether they experience incontinence, the researcher should ask, "Millions of Americans experience some level of incontinence. Do you or anyone you know experience this difficulty?"

There are many types of questionnaires that are commonly used in carrying out consumer research studies. In the real world of consumer research, one form of consumer survey is a **magazine readership survey**, like the one for *EARTH* (a fictitious magazine) that is presented in Figure 2.6. Such surveys are conducted to provide the publisher, editors, and circulation directors with reader feedback, as well as to provide the marketing and sales

FIGURE 2.6

Magazine Readership Survey

Source: *EARTH Magazine* Readership Survey (New York, Ipsos Mendelsohn, 2008).

EARTH Magazine: IPSOS MENDELSOHN READERSHIP SURVEY

ABOUT YOU AND *EARTH MAGAZINE*

1. Where did you purchase this issue of *EARTH Magazine?*
   - Local newsstand ☐1
   - Airport terminal newsstand ☐2
   - Bookstore (e.g., Borders, Barnes & Noble) ☐3
   - Other ☐4

2. Why did you buy this issue of *EARTH Magazine? (Please 'X' all that apply.)*
   - Intrigued by headlines on cover wrap ☐1
   - Attracted by the cover art ☐2
   - Curious about a specific article ☐3

   Heard about issue through:
   - Word-of-mouth ☐4
   - Print medium ☐5
   - Broadcast medium ☐6
   - Internet ☐7

   For a regular feature:
   - Index ☐1
   - Notebook ☐2
   - Readings ☐3
   - Puzzle ☐4
   - Findings ☐5
   - Annotation ☐6
   - Reviews ☐7
   - Forum ☐8

   For a regular feature (Cont't):
   - Photo essay ☐1
   - Fiction ☐2
   - Political reporting ☐3
   - Overseas reporting ☐4
   - Narrative non-fiction ☐5
   - Personal essays ☐6

3. How many issues of *EARTH Magazine* did you buy on the newsstand/bookstore in the last 12 months?
   - 1 issue ☐1
   - 2–3 issues ☐2
   - 4–5 issues ☐3
   - 6–7 issues ☐4
   - 8–9 issues ☐5
   - 10–11 issues ☐6
   - 12 issues ☐7
   - **None** ☐8

4. How long have you been a reader of *EARTH Magazine?*
   - Less than 6 months ☐1
   - 7–12 months ☐2
   - 1 to under 2 years ☐3
   - 2 years or more ☐4

5. How many of the last 4 issues of *EARTH Magazine* have you read or looked into?
   - 4 out of the last 4 ☐1
   - 3 out of the last 4 ☐2
   - 2 out of the last 4 ☐3
   - 1 out of the last 4 ☐4
   - **None** out of the last 4 ☐5

6. On average, how much time do you spend reading or looking into a typical issue of *EARTH Magazine?*
   - Less than 1 hour ☐1
   - 1 hour to less than 2 hours ☐2
   - 2 hours to less than 3 hours ☐3
   - 3 hours to less than 4 hours ☐4
   - 4 hours or more ☐5

7. Have you ever made a purchase as a result of advertising you saw in *EARTH Magazine?*
   - Yes ☐1
   - No ☐2

8. How do you rate *EARTH Magazine* overall compared to other publications you read?
   - One of my favorites ☐1
   - Very good ☐2
   - Good ☐3
   - Average ☐4
   - Poor ☐5

EARTH MAGAZINE WEBSITE

1. Have you visited *EARTH Magazine* website in the past 12 months?
   - Yes ☐1
   - No ☐2 → *Please go to Question 4*

2. How often do you visit the *EARTH Magazine* website?
   - Once a month ☐1
   - Less than once a week ☐2
   - Once a week ☐3
   - 2–3 times a week ☐4
   - 4–5 times a week ☐5
   - More than 5 times a week ☐6

3. On average, how much time do you spend on *EARTH Magazine* website per visit?
   - Less than 5 minutes ☐1
   - 5–9 minutes ☐2
   - 10–19 minutes ☐3
   - 20–29 minutes ☐4
   - 30–59 minutes ☐5
   - One hour or more ☐6

Continued

FIGURE 2.6
Continued

4. Would you be willing to pay for archived issues of *EARTH Magazine* going back to 1950 if they were available on the EARTH Magazine website?
   Yes. . . . .☐1 No . . . .☐2→*Please go to "About You" section below*

5. *(If yes)* How much would you be willing to pay per year for archived issues of *EARTH Magazine?*

$1–$9 . . . . ☐1	$20–$29 . . . . ☐3	$40–$49 . . . . ☐5
$10–$19 . . . . ☐2	$30–$39 . . . . ☐4	$50 or more. . . . . ☐6

ABOUT YOU

1. Are you: a man . . . .☐1 a woman . . . . ☐2
2. Please 'X' your age group.

Under 21 . . . . ☐1	35 to 44 . . . . ☐3	55 to 64. . . . . ☐5
21 to 34 . . . . ☐2	45 to 54 . . . . ☐4	65 or older. . . . . ☐6

3. Are you . . .

Married . . . . ☐1	Single . . . . ☐3	Separated. . . . . ☐5
Partnered . . . . ☐2	Widowed . . . . ☐4	Divorced . . . . ☐6

4. Please 'X' the highest level of education you have attained.

Some high school or less . . . . ☐1	Some college . . . . ☐3	Postgraduate study . . . . ☐5
High school graduate . . . . ☐2	College degree . . . . ☐4	Postgraduate degree . . . . ☐6

5. Please indicate your employment status.

Employed full time (35 hrs or more per week) . . . . ☐1	Not currently employed . . . . ☐3	Please skip
Employed part time (less than 35 hrs per week) . . . . ☐2	Retired . . . . ☐4	to Question 6

   What is your job title, position or rank?
   (Please be specific: e.g., partner, CEO, president, vice president, etc.) ________________

   What do you do for a living? (Please be specific: e.g., accountant, bookkeeper, lawyer, architect, etc.) ________________

6. What was your total estimated household income, before taxes, for last year? (Please include income for all household members and from all sources, including salaries or wages, profits, capital gains, rentals, social security, etc.)

Less than $50,000 . . . . ☐1	$500,000 to $749,999 . . . . . . ☐1	$2,500,000 to $2,999,999. . . . . ☐1
$50,000 to $99,999 . . . . ☐2	$750,000 to $999,999 . . . . . . ☐2	$3,000,000 to $3,999,999. . . . . ☐2
$100,000 to $199,999 . . . . ☐3	$1,000,000 to $1,499,999 . . . . ☐3	$4,000,000 to $4,999,999. . . . . ☐3
$200,000 to $299,999 . . . . ☐4	$1,500,000 to $1,999,999 . . . . ☐4	$5,000,000 or more. . . . . ☐4
$300,000 to $499,999 . . . . ☐5	$2,000,000 to $2,499,999 . . . . ☐5	

Please join us! The *EARTH Magazine* **Reader Advisory Panel** is an exclusive panel made up of *EARTH Magazine* readers. Through future surveys, your perspective on consumer trends – from tech innovations, culture, and travel – will have a direct impact on what you see and read in the pages of *EARTH Magazine.* If you would like to join our Reader Advisory Panel, please print your e-mail address below:

Your e-mail address:________________@________________

THANK YOU VERY MUCH

Please mail the completed survey in the reply envelope *(no postage necessary).*

Source: EARTH Magazine Readership Survey (New York, Ipsos Mendelsohn, 2008)

staff with information that would enable them to create a more convincing marketing package for selling adverting pages to potential advertisers and their advertising agencies. In particular, a standard use of the data secured from magazine readership surveys is preparation of a profile of a publication's readers so that potential advertisers can determine whether the publication delivers the audience that is most likely to positively respond to their advertising.

While any publication can conduct a readership survey, they are generally conducted by smaller circulation publications whose audience is not large enough to be measured in major syndicated media surveys, such as those conducted by Mediamark Research and Ipsos Mendelsohn (The Mendelsohn Affluent Survey).

Attitude Scales

Researchers often present respondents with a list of products or product attributes for which they are asked to indicate their relative feelings or evaluations. The instruments most frequently used to capture this evaluative data are called **attitude scales**. The most frequently used attitude scales are Likert scales, semantic differential scales, behavior intention scales, and rank-order scales.

The **Likert scale** is the most popular form of attitude scale because it is easy for researchers to prepare and to interpret, and simple for consumers to answer. They check or write the number corresponding to their level of "agreement" or "disagreement" with a series of statements, each referring to the object under investigation. The scale consists of an equal number of agreement/disagreement choices on either side of a neutral choice. A principal benefit of the Likert scale is that it gives the researcher the option of considering the responses to each statement separately or of combining the responses to produce an overall score.

The **semantic differential scale**, like the Likert scale, is relatively easy to construct and administer. The scale typically consists of a series of bipolar adjectives (such as *good/bad*, *hot/cold*, *like/dislike*, or *expensive/inexpensive*) anchored at the ends of an odd-numbered (e.g., five- or seven-point) continuum. Respondents are asked to evaluate a concept (or a product or company) on the basis of each attribute by checking the point on the continuum that best reflects their feelings or beliefs. Care must be taken to vary the location of positive and negative terms from the left side of the continuum to the right side to avoid consumer response bias. Sometimes an even-numbered scale is used to eliminate the option of a neutral answer. An important feature of the semantic differential scale is that it can be used to develop graphic consumer profiles of the concept under study. Semantic differential profiles are also used to compare consumer perceptions of competitive products and to indicate areas for product improvement when perceptions of the existing product are measured against perceptions of the "ideal" product.

The **behavior intention scale** measures the likelihood that consumers will act in a certain way in the future, such as buying the product again or recommending it to a friend. These scales are easy to construct, and consumers are asked to make subjective judgments regarding their future behavior.

With **rank-order scales**, subjects are asked to rank items such as products (or retail stores or Web sites) in order of preference in terms of some criterion, such as overall quality or value for the money. Rank-order scaling procedures provide important competitive information and enable marketers to identify needed areas of improvement in product design and product positioning. Figure 2.7 provides examples of the attitude scales, described here, that are frequently utilized in consumer research.

Customer Satisfaction Measurement

Gauging the level of customer satisfaction and its determinants is critical for every company. Marketers can use such data to retain customers, sell more products and services, improve the quality and value of their offerings, and operate more effectively and efficiently. **Customer satisfaction measurement** includes quantitative and qualitative measures, as well as a variety of contact methods with customers.

Customer satisfaction surveys measure how satisfied the customers are with relevant attributes of the product or service, and the relative importance of these attributes (using an importance scale). Generally, these surveys use 5-point semantic differential scales, ranging from "very dissatisfied" to "very satisfied" (see Figure 2.7). Research shows that customers who indicate they are "very satisfied" (typically a score of 5 on the satisfaction scale) are much more profitable and loyal than customers who indicate that they are "satisfied" (a score of 4). Therefore, companies that merely strive to have "satisfied" customers are making a crucial error.[20] Some marketers maintain that customers' satisfaction or dissatisfaction is a function of the difference between what they had *expected* to get from the product or service purchased and their perceptions of what they *received*. A group of researchers developed a scale that measures the performance of the service received against two expectation levels: *adequate* service and *desired* service, and also measures the customers' future intentions regarding purchasing the service.[21] This approach is more sophisticated than standard customer satisfaction surveys and more likely to yield results that can be used to develop corrective measures for products and services that fall short of customers' expectations.

Mystery shoppers are professional observers who pose as customers and interact with and provide unbiased evaluations of the company's service personnel in order to identify opportunities for improving productivity and efficiency. For example, one bank used mystery shoppers who, while dealing with a bank employee on another matter, dropped hints about

FIGURE 2.7
Attitude Scales

LIKERT SCALE

Next to each of the following statements, please record the number that best describes the extent to which you agree or disagree with each statement.

1. Strongly Agree	2. Somewhat Agree	3. Neither Agree nor Disagree	4. Somewhat Disagree	5. Strongly Disagree

_______ It's fun to shop online.
_______ I am afraid to give my credit card number online.

CUSTOMER SATISFACTION GUIDE

Overall, how satisfied are you with Bank X's online banking? _______

1. Very Satisfied	2. Somewhat Satisfied	3. Neither Satisfied nor Dissatisfied	4. Somewhat Dissatisfied	5. Very Dissatisfied

IMPORTANCE SCALE

The following list of features are associated with shopping on the Internet. Next to each feature, please record the number that best expresses how important or unimportant that feature is to you.

1. Extremely Important	2. Somewhat Important	3. Neither Important nor Unimportant	4. Somewhat Unimportant	5. Not at all Important

_______ Speed of downloading the order form
_______ Being able to register with the site

SEMANTIC DIFFERENTIAL SCALE

For each of the following features, please check one alternative that best expresses your impression of how that feature applies to **online banking:**

Competitive rates |—|—|—|—|—|—|—| Noncompetitive rates
Reliable |—|—|—|—|—|—|—| Unreliable

Note: The same semantic differential scale can be applied to two competitive offerings, such as online banking and regular banking, and a graphic representation of the profiles of the two alternatives, along with the bipolar adjectives included in the scale, can be easily constructed.

BEHAVIOR INTENTION SCALES

How likely are you to continue using Bank X's online banking for the next six months? _______

1. Definitely Will Continue	2. Probably Will Continue	3. Might or Might Not Continue	4. Probably Will Not Continue	5. Definitely Will Not Continue

How likely are you to recommend Bank X's online banking to a friend? _______

1. Definitely Will Recommend	2. Probably Will Recommend	3. Might or Might Not Recommend	4. Probably Will Not Recommend	5. Definitely Will Not Recommend

RANK ORDER SCALE

We would like to find out about your preferences regarding banking methods. Please rank the following banking methods by placing a "1" in front of the method that you prefer most, a "2" next to your second preference, and continuing until you have ranked all of the methods.

_______ Inside the bank _______ Online banking _______ Banking by telephone
_______ ATM _______ Banking by mail

buying a house or seeking to borrow college funds. Employees were scored on how quickly and effectively they provided information about the bank's pertinent products or services. A company that requires sales clerks to check youthful customers' IDs when they seek to buy video games with violent content may employ mystery shoppers to see whether their employees are actually doing so.

Analyzing customer complaints is crucial for improving products and customer service. Research indicates that only a few unsatisfied customers actually complain. Most unsatisfied customers say nothing but switch to competitors. A good **complaint analysis** system should encourage customers to (1) complain about an unsatisfactory product or service and (2) provide suggestions for improvements by completing forms asking specific questions beyond the routine "how was everything?" and (3) establish "listening posts" such as hotlines where specially designated employees either listen to customers' comments or actively solicit input from them (e.g., in a hotel lobby or on checkout lines). Since each complaint, by itself, provides little information, the company must have a system in which complaints are categorized and analyzed so that the results may be used to improve its operations.

Analyzing customer defections consists of finding out *why* customers leave the company. Customer loyalty rates are important because it is generally much cheaper to retain customers than to get new ones. Therefore, finding out why customers defect, and also *intervening* when customers' behaviors show that they may be considering leaving, is crucial. For example, one bank that was losing about 20 percent of its customers every year compared 500 transaction records of loyal customers with 500 transaction records of defectors, using such dimensions as number of transactions, frequency of transactions, and fluctuations in average balances. The bank then identified transaction patterns that may indicate future defection and started targeting potential defectors and encouraging them to stay.[22]

Sampling and Data Collection

Since it is almost always impossible to obtain information from *every* member of the *population* or *universe* being studied, researchers use samples. A **sample** is a subset of the population that is used to estimate the characteristics of the entire population. Therefore, the sample must be *representative* of the universe under study. As the well-established Nielsen Media Research company recently found out, suspicions that a sample may not be representative of its universe endanger the credibility of all the data collected, and therefore must be addressed promptly. Although Nielsen's TV ratings have been used to estimate TV audiences and calculate advertising rates for many decades, its clients recently charged that the Nielsen sample was no longer representative of the U.S. population because it did not reflect accurately America's changing demographics and the large numbers of consumers who use devices such as TiVo to "time shift" and to avoid commercials during both live and recorded programs. In response to these criticisms, Nielsen has redesigned its sample to include significantly more ethnic groupings and to reflect the changes in TV viewing habits.[23]

An integral component of a research design is the sampling plan. Specifically, the sampling plan addresses three questions: whom to survey (the sampling unit), how many to survey (the sample size), and how to select them (the sampling procedure). Deciding whom to survey requires explicit definition of the *universe* or boundaries of the market from which data are sought so that an appropriate sample can be selected (such as working mothers). The size of the sample is dependent both on the size of the budget and on the degree of confidence that the marketer wants to place in the findings. The larger the sample, the more likely the responses will reflect the total universe under study. It is interesting to note, however, that a small sample can often provide highly reliable findings, depending on the sampling procedure adopted.

There are two types of samples: in a **probability sample**, respondents are selected in such a way that every member of the population studied has a known, nonzero chance of being selected. In a **nonprobability sample**, the population under study has been predetermined in a nonrandom fashion on the basis of the researcher's judgment or decision to select a given number of respondents from a particular group. Table 2.4 summarizes the features of various types of probability and nonprobability designs.

TABLE 2.4 Types of Sampling

PROBABILITY SAMPLE	
Simple Random Sample	Every member of the population has a known and equal chance of being selected.
Systematic Random Sample	A member of the population is selected at random and then every *n*th person is selected.
Stratified Random Sample	The population is divided into mutually exclusive groups (such as age groups), and random samples are drawn from each group.
Cluster (area) Sample	The population is divided into mutually exclusive groups (such as blocks), and the researcher draws a sample of the groups to interview.
NONPROBABILITY SAMPLE	
Convenience Sample	The researcher selects the most accessible population members from whom to obtain information (e.g., students in a classroom).
Judgment Sample	The researcher uses his or her judgment to select population members who are good sources for accurate information (e.g., experts in the relevant field of study).
Quota Sample	The researcher interviews a prescribed number of people in each of several categories (e.g., 50 men and 50 women).

The step following the sample selection is the data collection. As indicated earlier, qualitative studies usually require highly trained social scientists to collect data. A quantitative study generally uses a field staff that is either recruited and trained directly by the researcher or contracted from a company that specializes in conducting field interviews. In either case, it is often necessary to verify whether the interviews have, in fact, taken place. This is sometimes done by a postcard mailing to respondents asking them to verify that they participated in an interview on the date recorded on the questionnaire form. Completed questionnaires are reviewed on a regular basis as the research study progresses to ensure that the recorded responses are clear, complete, and legible.

COMBINING QUALITATIVE AND QUANTITATIVE RESEARCH FINDINGS

Today, it is quite common for marketers, especially those associated with major consumer brands, to frequently conduct research projects that combine both a qualitative component (often composed of focus groups and/or depth interviews) and a quantitative component (often consisting of a survey research). For example, they use qualitative research findings to discover new ideas and to develop promotional strategy, and quantitative research findings to estimate the extent or amount of consumers who react in a particular way (i.e., positive or negative) to various promotional inputs. Frequently, ideas stemming from qualitative research are tested empirically through quantitative studies. The predictions made possible by quantitative research and the understanding provided by qualitative research together produce a richer and more robust profile of consumer behavior than either research approach used alone.

In reality, many consumer research studies carry out concurrently or in sequence a series of interrelated qualitative and quantitative studies, or move back and forth between one or more rounds of qualitative research and one or more rounds of quantitative research. In the many studies that the lead author of this book conducted for AT&T, it was quite common for him to undertake a number of focus groups or depth interview research studies to be followed by a quantitative stage using a very large internal consumer database, or the services of survey research companies that specialized in mail or telephone questionnaire surveys. The main point to keep in mind is that among marketing-oriented firms, consumer research is not commonly composed of a single study, but rather consists of a series of studies, often composed of a mix

TABLE 2.5 A Comparison of the Elements of Quantitative and Qualitative Research Designs

	QUALITATIVE RESEARCH (QUAL)	QUANTITATIVE RESEARCH (QUAN)
Study Purpose	QUAL studies are designed to provide insights about new product ideas and identify positioning strategies aimed at a target market. Ideas uncovered should be tested via QUAN studies. QUAL studies are also often used to refine the objectives and wording of QUAN studies.	QUAN studies are aimed at describing a target market—its characteristics and possible reactions of various segments to the elements of the marketing mix. Results are used for making strategic marketing decisions.
Types of Questions and Data Collection Methods	Open-ended, unstructured questions, stressing probing by the moderator or highly skilled interviewer. QUAL research also uses projective techniques including disguised questions and response to pictures or prototypes.	QUAN research often consists of closed-ended questions with predefined response choices and limited numbers of open-ended questions that need to be coded.
Main Methods	Focus groups and depth interviews.	Survey questionnaires including attitude scales and questions that are not disguised. QUAN questioning often consists of surveys that are self-administered, or conducted in person, by phone or mail, or online. Observation of consumers, experimentation, and consumer panels are other QUAN data collection methods.
Sampling Methods	Small, nonprobability samples; where findings are generally not representative of the universe under study.	Large, probability samples. If the data collection instruments are valid and reliable, the results can be viewed as representative of the universe.
Data Analysis	Data consists of transcripts or tapes of the verbal responses. The analysis is performed by skilled behavioral science researchers. Researchers seek to identify reoccurring "themes" of responses coming from participants.	After data is collected, it is coded and entered in the database. The researcher analyzes the data, using a variety of statistical methods of analysis, and estimates the extent to which the results represent the universe.

of qualitative research (most commonly focus groups and/or depth interviews) and quantitative research (most commonly some form of survey research, consumer panel data, or possibly an experiment). Commonly, the insights secured from a particular round of research are evaluated to determine whether more research is required, and if "yes," what should be the purpose and type of additional research conducted. The combined findings enable marketers to design more meaningful and effective marketing strategies. Table 2.5 compares the quantitative and qualitative research designs.

Data Analysis and Reporting Research Findings

LEARNING OBJECTIVE

2.6 *To Understand Where Data Analysis and Reporting of Findings Fit in the Research Process.*

In qualitative research, the moderator-researcher usually analyzes the responses received. In quantitative research, the researcher supervises the analysis: Open-ended responses are first coded and quantified (i.e., converted into numerical scores); then all the responses are tabulated and analyzed using sophisticated analytical programs that correlate the data by selected variables and cluster the data by selected demographic characteristics.

In both qualitative and quantitative research, the research report includes a brief executive summary of the findings. Depending on the assignment from marketing management, the research report may or may not include recommendations for marketing action. The body of the report includes a full description of the methodology used and, for quantitative research, also includes tables and graphics to support the findings. A sample of the questionnaire is usually included in the appendix to enable management to evaluate the objectivity of the findings.

Conducting a Research Study

Learning Objective

2.7 *To Understand How Each Element of the Consumer Research Process Adds to the Overall Outcome of the Research Study.*

In designing a research study, researchers adapt the research processes described in the previous sections to the special needs of the study. For example, if a researcher is told that the purpose of the study is to develop a segmentation strategy for a new online dating service, he or she would first collect secondary data, such as population statistics (e.g., the number of men and women online in selected metropolitan areas within a certain age range, their marital status, and occupations). Then, together with the marketing manager, the researcher would specify the parameters (i.e., define the sampling unit) of the population to be studied (e.g., single, college-educated men and women between the ages of 18 and 45 who live or work within the Boston metropolitan area). A qualitative study (e.g., focus groups) might be undertaken first to gather information about the target population's attitudes and concerns about meeting people online, their special interests, and the specific services and precautions they would like an online dating service to provide. This phase of the research should result in tentative generalizations about the specific age group(s) to target and the services to offer.

The marketing manager then might instruct the researcher to conduct a quantitative study to confirm and attach "hard" numbers (percentages) to the findings that emerged from the focus groups. The first-phase study should have provided sufficient insights to develop a research design and to launch directly into a large-scale survey. If, however, there is still doubt about any element of the research design, such as question wording or format, the marketing manager and the researcher might decide first to do a small-scale exploratory study. Then, after refining the questionnaire and any other needed elements of the research design, they would launch a full-scale quantitative survey, using a probability sample that would allow them to project the findings to the total population of singles (as originally defined). The analysis should cluster prospective consumers of the online dating service into segments based on relevant sociocultural or lifestyle characteristics and on media habits, attitudes, perceptions, and geodemographic characteristics.

SUMMARY

The field of consumer research developed in part as an extension of the applied field of marketing research and as part of the scholarly interests of academicians pursuing a more comprehensive understanding of consumers. In both cases, the goals have been to enlarge the understanding of consumers. However, there are differences in motivation carrying out consumer research. Specifically, marketing practitioners have concentrated on the practical application of predicting how consumers will react in the marketplace, and on understanding the reasons that drive consumers to make the purchase decisions they do. In contrast, academic consumer researchers tend to be more concerned with advancing the knowledge and principles that are associated with consumers' behaviors.

Consumer research can also be divided in terms of a qualitative or quantitative perspective. In this chapter we have considered both, because in reality there is a great amount of both qualitative and quantitative consumer research being conducted by both practitioners and academic consumer researchers.

This chapter was guided by the consumer research process (set out in Figure 2.2). Whether qualitative or quantitative, the consumer research process includes six steps: defining objectives, collecting secondary data, developing a research design, collecting primary data, analyzing the data, and preparing a report of the findings. The research objectives should be formulated jointly by the marketer and the person or company that will conduct the actual research. Findings from secondary data and exploratory research are used to refine the research objectives. The collection of secondary data includes both internal and external sources. Qualitative research design stressed the use of focus groups and depth interviews. A variety of different tools in preparing for qualitative research, including screener questionnaires and discussion guides, were described and illustrated. So were various specialized qualitative methodologies—most notably, metaphor analysis, in particular the Zaltman Metaphor Elicitation Techniques (ZMET), and the looking-in method, as well as several methods for collecting data online. Alternatively, quantitative research designs consist of observation, experimentation, or surveys, and, for the most part, questionnaires (that often include attitude scales) are used to collect the data. Again, we illustrated the application of quantitative consumer studies. In particular, we considered the selection and design of the sample, and why it is crucial (since the type of sample used determines the degree to which the results of the study are representative of the population). Following the data collection, the results are analyzed and specific analytic techniques applied respectively to qualitative or quantitative data. Consumer researchers must also observe specific ethical guidelines to ensure the integrity of their studies and the privacy of respondents (see Chapter 16).

DISCUSSION QUESTIONS

1. Have you ever been selected as a respondent in a marketing research survey? If yes, how were you contacted and where were you interviewed? Why do you think you, in particular, were selected? Did you know or could you guess the purpose of the survey? Do you know the name of the company or brand involved in the survey?
2. What is the difference between primary and secondary research? Under what circumstances might the availability of secondary data make primary research unnecessary? What are some major sources of secondary data?
3. What are the advantages and limitations of secondary data?
4. A manufacturer of a new product for whitening teeth would like to investigate the effects of package design and label information on consumers' perceptions of the product and their intentions to buy it. Would you advise the manufacturer to use observational research, experimentation, or a survey? Explain your choice.
5. Why might a researcher prefer to use focus groups rather than depth interviews? When might depth interviews be preferable?
6. How would the interpretation of survey results change if the researcher used a probability sample rather than a nonprobability sample? Explain your answer.
7. Why is observation becoming a more important component of consumer research? Describe two new technologies that can be used to observe consumption behavior and explain why they are better to use than questioning consumers about the same behavior.

EXERCISES

1. Neutrogena is a manufacturer of personal care products for young adults. The company would like to extend its facial cleansers product line. Design (1) a qualitative and (2) a quantitative research design for the company focused on this objective.
2. Based on the discussion of focus groups and depth interviews, as well the discussion guide presented in Figure 2.5, develop a discussion guide to studying college students' reaction to their brand and model of cell phone.
3. Using one of the attitude scales in Figure 2.7, construct an instrument to assess your fellow students' opinions regarding the technological support services provided by your university.
4. Using the scales in Figure 2.7, develop a questionnaire to measure students' attitudes toward the instructor in this course according to the following guidelines:
   a. Prepare five statements measuring students' attitudes via a Likert scale.
   b. Prepare five semantic differential scales measuring students' attitudes.
   c. Can the same dimensions be measured by using either scaling technique? Explain your answer.

KEY TERMS

- attitude scales *61*
- behavior intention scale *61*
- complaint analysis *63*
- consumer panel *46*
- controlled experiment *55*
- customer lifetime value profiles *44*
- customer satisfaction measurement *61*
- customer satisfaction survey *61*
- depth interview *47*
- e-mail surveys *57*
- experimentation *55*
- exploratory study *43*
- focus group *48*
- Likert scale *61*
- looking-in research *53*
- magazine readership survey *59*
- mail surveys *57*
- motivational researcher *46*
- mystery shoppers *61*
- nonprobability sample *63*
- observational research *54*
- online or Internet-based surveys *57*
- personal interview surveys *56*
- physiological observation *55*
- portable people meters *45*
- primary research *42*
- probability sample *63*
- projective techniques *52*
- qualitative research *42*
- quantitative research *42*
- questionnaire *58*
- rank-order scale *61*
- reliability *58*
- sample *63*
- screener questionnaire *48*
- secondary data *44*
- semantic differential scale *61*
- telephone interview surveys *56*
- test marketing *56*
- validity *58*
- Zaltman Metaphor Elicitation Technique (ZMET) *53*

Case One: Using Secondary Data in Targeting Consumers

Many big and successful companies are capturing information every time a consumer comes into contact with the company. These touch points include any inquiries (personal, telephone, or online), customer purchases, and requested services. The data from these transactions are collected by the company's contact center and organized into a data warehouse.

The environment faced by motor manufacturers is very volatile. The profits made on new vehicle sales are decreasing because of the introduction of many new car manufacturers like Suzuki, Daihatsu, Daewoo, etc. As a result, the motor manufacturers and dealers are trying to focus on advertising their products to the right people. This is where the data warehouse becomes important.

The database of a Toyota dealer, for example, will have information such as the customer's contact, the date when the car was purchased, the date the car was serviced, additional services that the customer always needs, demographic data (e.g., age), and the psychographic data (e.g., lifestyle). If Toyota SA introduces a new car, or new service, the Toyota dealers will use the information they have in their database to decide to whom and how they should advertise the car, or service. The database can be made available to the other companies that need to advertise their products and services.

It is believed that to sell more and increase profits, companies should focus attention on the existing (20 percent) customers. The 80-20 Rule predicts that 20 percent of the customers generate 80 percent of the profits. After phasing out the Tazz, Toyota had to come up with a smaller car to replace it. Toyota Yaris was introduced. To increase the sales, the dealers had to identify the existing Toyota customers who will be interested in the Yaris. The Yaris being a smaller car, the dealers had to target young and single men and women, and young couples with 1 or 2 children. The dealers had to use the existing database to draw out their target group. The dealers could, for example, send the target group personalized mails with the Toyota Yaris catalogue, or the dealer could use a lady or a gentleman or a small family in their TV or newspaper adverts.

QUESTIONS

1. In your own view, what other important information can Toyota dealers capture in their database? Explain your choice.
2. Rather than relying on Toyota's database, should the other car manufacturers collect their own data about the customers? Why or why not? In your answer be sure to describe the advantages and limitations of relying on secondary research data in making strategic marketing decisions.

Source: www.toyota.co.za.

Case Two: Please Talk to Me

A few years ago, a blogger named Jeff Javis repeatedly complained about his Dell brand laptop computer. His repeated slamming of Dell "became a case study in how one man's website could shred a corporate reputation."

So what did Dell do? It launched a Web site called IdeaStorm **(www.ideastorm.com)**, which allows Dell customers to offer suggestions about how to improve Dell products and services. The result has been thousands of suggestions and tens of thousands of comments. And Dell has been responsive. For example, after receiving a number of suggestions that Linux (an operating system) be available pre-installed on Dell machines, the computer maker conducted a detailed survey that over 100,000 consumers responded to. The result was that Dell began offering Linux pre-installed on a number of its desktop and notebook systems.

QUESTION

Since Chapter 2 discusses consumer research, what other techniques might Dell employ in order to find out what types of laptops and desktop computer systems consumers (including business users) want?

Source: Based on: Matthew Creamer, "Dell Quells Critics with Web 2.0 Tack," *Advertising Age,* (June 11, 2007): 1, 45.

3

Market Segmentation and Strategic Targeting

MARKET SEGMENTATION is the *opposite* of **mass marketing**. As stated in Chapter 1, before the emergence of the *marketing concept*, the prevailing way of doing business was mass marketing—that is, offering the same product and marketing mix to all consumers. This approach is summed up by the saying that consumers "can have a car in any color they want, as long as it is black." This saying is attributed to Henry Ford who, in 1908, introduced the Model T—the first affordable car, which also brought about America's car culture and, to a large extent, U.S. dependence on foreign oil. In 1924, Alfred Sloan, the chairman of General Motors (which at that time was a weak competitor of Ford), declared that GM will offer "a car for every purse and purpose," and introduced different models that appealed to consumers' changing needs and preferences as they matured and their buying power increased. Sloan realized that identifying distinct consumer segments and offering specific, clearly differentiated products that fit their particular needs is far superior to mass marketing. While Henry Ford focused on his *company's needs* (i.e., offering a uniformed product is easier and more economical than producing numerous different models), Sloan focused on *consumers' needs.* Sloan's strategy was a great success; GM overtook Ford's seemingly unbeatable domination and, for many decades, was the leader of the American car market.

The market segmentation and targeting process is the identification of distinct segments within a given market or population, evaluation of each segment's marketing potential, selection of the segments to be targeted, and the creation of a marketing mix (i.e., product, price, place, and promotion) for each target segment selected. Consumers can be segmented along several factors, such as their demographics, lifestyles (including hobbies), usage behavior associated with a given product and other factors. For example, the ad featured in Figure 3.1 targets runners who are physically active people and also relish the outdoors.

After segmenting a consumer market and selecting one or several target markets, the product or service must be positioned. Positioning is the unifying element of each marketing mix because it expresses the offering's value proposition which details the product's or service's capability to deliver specific benefits corresponding to consumers' unfulfilled needs. This chapter details the factors and processes of segmentation and targeting, and a discussion of positioning is part of Chapter 6.

FIGURE 3.1
Source: © asics.

QUESTION: *What Kind of Consumer Does This Ad Target?*

Learning Objectives

3.1 *To Understand Why Market Segmentation Is Essential.*

3.2 *To Understand the Criteria for Targeting Selected Segments Effectively.*

3.3 *To Understand the Bases for Segmenting Consumers.*

3.4 *To Understand How Segmentation and Strategic Targeting Are Carried Out.*

Why Is Market Segmentation Necessary?

Learning Objective

3.1 *To Understand Why Market Segmentation Is Essential.*

If all consumers were alike—if they all had the same needs, wants, and desires, and the same background, education, and experience—mass (undifferentiated) marketing would be a logical strategy. Its primary advantage is that it costs less: Usually, a single standardized product is offered, backed by a uniformed marketing strategy. Companies producing agricultural products or very basic manufactured goods successfully follow a mass-marketing strategy. However, the majority of marketers cannot follow an undifferentiated marketing approach. When trying to sell the same product to every prospective customer with a single advertising campaign, the marketer must portray its product as a means for satisfying a common or generic need and, therefore, often ends up appealing to nearly no one. A refrigerator provides the home with a place to store perishable food, but a standard-size refrigerator may be too big for a grandmother who lives alone and too small for a family of six. If a marketer offered the same model to the grandmother and the family of six, a competitor would come up with two different models designed to fulfill the specific needs of the two types of consumers. Therefore, any company of consumer goods that offers a single product is unlikely to survive, unless the product offered is extremely specialized and designed for a very specific consumer niche.

Segmentation, targeting, and positioning enable producers to avoid head-on competition in the marketplace by differentiating their offerings on the basis of such features as price, styling, packaging, promotional appeal, method of distribution, and level of service. Marketers discovered that effectively catering to the distinct needs of consumers by offering them clearly differentiated products is significantly more profitable than mass marketing, in spite of the much higher research, production, advertising, and distribution costs that accompany segmentation and strategic targeting.

Market segmentation, strategic **targeting,** and product (or service) **positioning** are the key elements of marketing most consumer goods. For example, in the chewing gum market, each of the brands available offers versions based on flavor and the existence or absence of sugar. Going beyond the flavor and sugar or no-sugar attributes, more sophisticated approaches to marketing chewing gum are illustrated in Figure 3.2, where each of the two ads proclaims a distinct benefit that the brand advertised delivers. One brand provides a social benefit (i.e., being in the same physical space with friends rather than chatting online) and the other provides both a health related benefit (i.e., quitting smoking) and a physically desirable one (i.e., whiter teeth). In yet another example of creative positioning, one company is introducing gum made with "green tea extract that kills the bacteria that causes bad breath" (in part, this claim is based on the premise that green tea provides health benefits).[1] Assumingly, through consumer research, the marketers of these brands uncovered specific market segments with distinct needs. After evaluating each of these segments along predefined criteria (discussed in the following section), the marketers developed the products and devised strategies to price, promote, and distribute them. As a result of repetitive and effective advertising stemming from a positioning strategy, in the consumers' minds, each brand of chewing gum will become differentiated from other brands and strongly associated with the unique benefit that it promises to provide.

Services also segment their markets and target different offerings to different market segments. For example, under the slogan "Be hospitable" (i.e., an "umbrella" positioning), Hilton's offerings include its flagship Hilton Hotels and Conrad Hotels and Resorts for both business and leisure travelers who want full-service, luxury, and a global and widely recognized brand for their accommodations. Hilton's Doubletree and Embassy Suites provide comfort and distinctive rooms, the Hampton Inn offers quality and value, and the Hilton Garden Inn caters to smart and practical travelers by offering them a casual and relaxing hotel stay.[2]

Marketers use segmentation research to identify the most appropriate media in which to place advertisements. Almost all media vehicles—from TV and radio stations to newspapers and magazines—use segmentation research to determine the characteristics of their audiences so that they can attract advertisers seeking to reach a given audience. For example, *People* created a separate magazine for teenagers titled *Teen People*, and *TIME* offers *Time for Kids* and separate issues for readers in Europe, Asia, and the South Pacific. With most magazines now appearing online in addition to selling paper copies, the number of magazines' versions targeting very specific audiences increased dramatically.

Criteria for Effective Targeting

LEARNING OBJECTIVE

3.2 *To Understand the Criteria for Targeting Selected Segments Effectively.*

Before describing how market segments are identified, we must point out that not *every* segment that can be identified is viable or profitable. The challenge marketers face is to select one or more segments to target with an appropriate marketing mix. To be an effective target, a market segment should be: (1) identifiable, (2) sizeable, (3) stable or growing, (4) accessible (reachable), and (5) congruent with the marketer's objectives and resources.

IDENTIFIABLE

To divide the market into separate segments on the basis of *common* or *shared needs* or characteristics that are relevant to the product or service, a marketer must be able to identify these characteristics. The types of these characteristics and the advantages and shortcomings of each one are discussed in the section titled "Bases for Segmentation." Some segmentation variables, such as *demographics* (e.g., age, gender, ethnicity), are easy to identify, and others can be determined through questioning (e.g., education, income, occupation, marital status). Other features, such as *benefits sought* (in a product or service) or *lifestyle*, are more difficult to identify and measure.

SIZEABLE

In order to be a viable market, a segment must consist of enough consumers to make targeting it profitable. A segment can be identifiable and stable (the stability criterion is discussed next) but not be large enough to be profitable. For example, consumers who are unusually tall or have uncommonly wide feet are often unable to find clothes and shoes that fit them in regular stores and have to shop at specialized outlets. To measure a segment's size and profitability, marketers use secondary data (e.g., census figures) and consumer surveys; such data estimate a given group of buyers' size, spending power, and buying propensity.

STABLE

Most marketers prefer to target consumer segments that are relatively stable in terms of lifestyles and consumption patterns (and are also likely to grow larger and more viable in the future) and avoid "fickle" segments that are unpredictable. For example, teenagers are a sizeable and easily identifiable market segment, eager to buy, able to spend, and easily reached. Yet, they are also likely to embrace fads and by the time marketers produce merchandise for a popular teenage trend, interest in it may have waned.

ACCESSIBLE

To be targeted, a segment must be accessible, which means that marketers must be able to reach that market segment in an economical way. With the diversification of magazines (and their online versions), the emergence of TV channels that target narrowly defined interests, and the growth of new media (e.g., sending ads to cell phones), marketers have significantly more avenues to reach unique segments and do so with customized products and promotional messages. (Customized targeting is discussed later in this chapter and also in Chapter 9.)

FIGURE 3.2A

Source: Dentyne: Courtesy of Cadbury.

QUESTION: *Which Distinct Benefit Does Each of the Two Brands Shown in This Figure Deliver?*

CONGRUENT WITH THE COMPANY'S OBJECTIVES AND RESOURCES

Not every company is interested or has the means to reach every market segment, even if that segment meets the four preceding criteria. For example, several international airlines now offer such classes as "Ultra First" and "Economy Premium" in addition to the conventional offerings of "Economy," "Business," and "First" classes. However, Southwest Airlines offers only one class of service because the focus and business objective of this company is to provide uniformed, inexpensive, and no-frills air transportation. At Hermès stores worldwide, customers entering the stores and asking for a Birkin bag (costing between $4,000 and $40,000) are routinely told that none are available and advised to put their names on a waiting list for an unspecified period of time.[3] Hermès's objective is to sell these prestigious bags only to people who

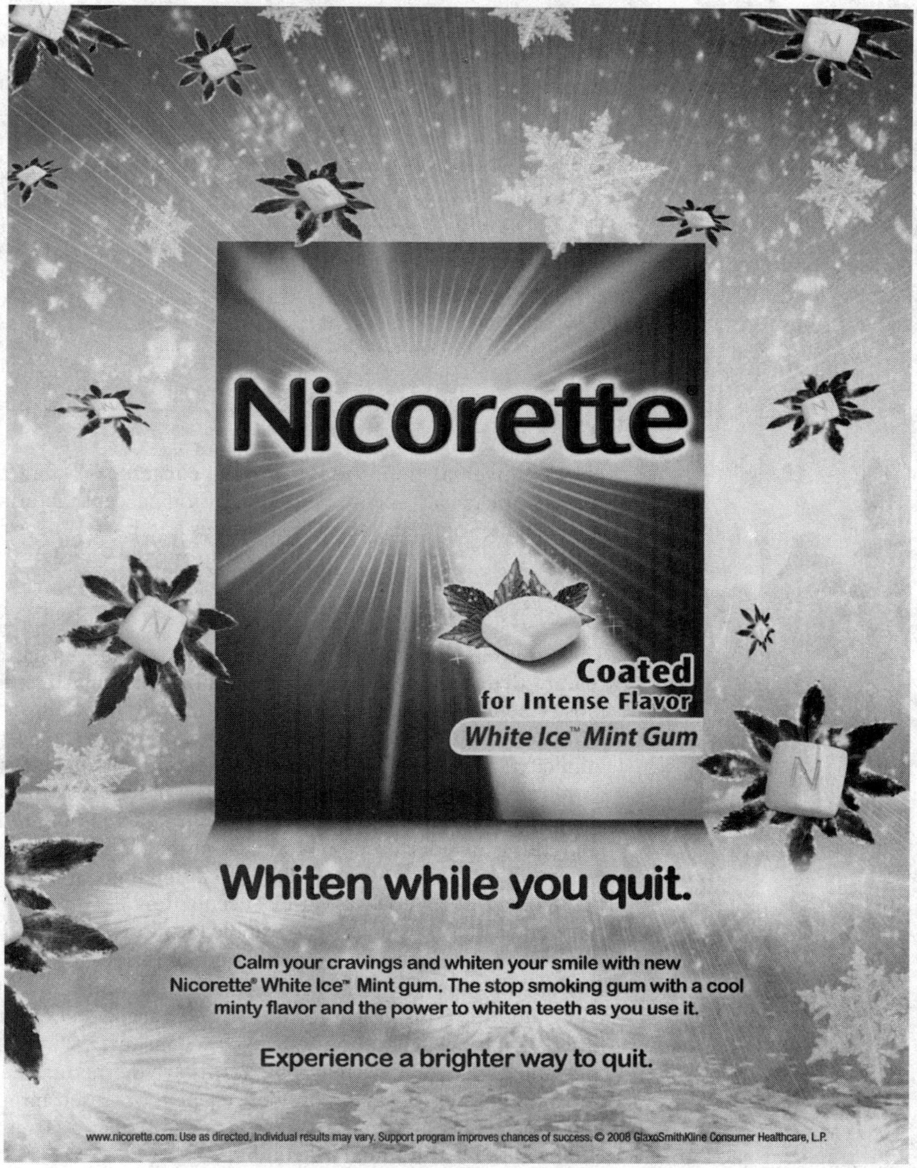

FIGURE 3.2B
Source: Nicorette: Courtesy of GlaxoSmithKline.

buy other Hermès products *first*, and also limit purchases by *resellers* who make money by reselling Birkins online.

Bases for Segmentation

LEARNING OBJECTIVE

3·3 *To Understand the Bases for Segmenting Consumers.*

A segmentation strategy begins by selecting the base(s) representing the core attribute(s) of a group of existing or potential customers. Figure 3.3 depicts a four-way classification of the characteristics used to segment the buyers of consumer goods.[4] It must be noted that a single characteristic is never used alone and that virtually all segmentation plans are in the forms of **hybrid segmentation** that includes attributes from two or more of the four quadrants of Figure 3.3.

The four groupings in Figure 3.3 stem from dividing consumers' characteristics along two criteria: (1) *facts*, which can be determined from direct questioning and categorized by a single objective measure, versus *cognitions*, which are abstract, can be determined only through more complex questioning, and where most of the constructs measured have no

FIGURE 3.3
Bases for Market Segmentation

Source: Joseph Wisenblit, "Segmentation: From Traditional Bases to Behavioral and Micro-Targeting," Working Paper (June 2008), Stillman School of Business, Seton Hall University, South Orange, New Jersey.

	Consumer-Rooted	Consumption-Specific
Facts	*Empirical Personal Features* * Demographics: age, age cohorts, gender, marital status, family life cycle, income, education, occupation, social class * Geographic location, address, and geodemographics	*Usage and Purchase Behaviors* * Usage rate * Usage situation/occasion * Brand loyalty (the behavior component) * Psychographics—factual behaviors (e.g., leisure activities, hobbies)
Cognitions	*Personality, Lifestyles, and Sociocultural Values* * Personality traits * Lifestyles, psychographics, and VALS * Sociocultural values and beliefs	*Attitudes and Preferences Regarding the Product* * Benefits wanted * Level of involvement * Awareness of product alternatives * Brand loyalty—perceived commitment and level of relationship

single, universal definitions; and (2) **consumer-rooted** features stemming from the consumer's physical, social, and psychological characteristics versus consumption-specific usage-behaviors (i.e., facts) or attitudes and preferences toward specific products or buying situations (i.e., cognitions). The four groups of characteristics are discussed next.

CONSUMER-ROOTED SEGMENTATION BASES

This group includes two types of personal attributes: *facts* that are evidence-based and can be readily determined and categorized along an objective criterion and *cognitions,* which can mostly be determined through indirect, psychological tests and classified into subjective categories, depending on the researcher. For example, **demographics** such as a person's age, gender, ethnicity, and income are objective and empirical, can be easily determined through questioning (some can even be observed) and enable a precise classification of each respondent into a given category (e.g., an "age group" or "income bracket"). Similarly, one's **social class** is defined by computing an index based on three quantifiable variables—*income* (number of dollars earned), *education* (number of years it takes to attain a given degree), and *occupation* (numerical prestige scores associated with various occupations). (Chapter 10 describes social class and its measurement.) The consumer's geographic location and zip code are also measurable and objective factors. On the other hand, **psychographics** (also known as *lifestyles*) consist of **activities**, **interests**, and **opinions** (i.e., **AIOS**), which are mostly attitudes (or cognitions) toward various issues, and cannot be classified according to standardized definitions. For instance, there are no fact-based, empirical denotations of a "green consumer," "impulse buyer," and the like; these attributes and almost all psychographic terms are defined in the scope of specific studies. Similarly, **personality traits** (e.g., self-confidence, open- or closed-mindedness, or being a high achiever) or one's sociocultural values are abstract cognitions that can be measured via one of several psychological or a attitudinal instruments.

Demographic Segmentation

The core of almost all segmentations is demographics, due to the following reasons: (1) demographics are the easiest and most logical way to classify people and can be measured more precisely than the other segmentation bases; (2) demographics offer the most cost-effective way to locate and reach specific segments because most of the secondary data compiled about any population is based on demographics (e.g., census bureau, audience profiles of various media); (3) demographics enable marketers to identify business opportunities enabled by shifts in populations' age, income or geographic location; and (4) many consumption behaviors, attitudes, and media exposure patterns are directly related to demographics. For example, many products are gender-specific, and music preferences are very closely related to one's age; for this reason, local radio stations specializing in various types of music are an efficient and economical way to target different age groups. Leisure activities and interests are a function of a person's age, education, and income, as are the media that consumers are exposed to. As an illustration, Table 3.1 lists the age, gender composition, and income of readers of popular magazines and newspapers (note the large differences in the median household income figures among the publications).[5]

TABLE 3.1 Key Demographics of the Audiences of Popular Magazines and Newspapers

MAGAZINE	CIRCULATION	AUDIENCE (000)			MEDIAN AGE			HOUSEHOLD INCOME		
		ADULTS	MEN	WOMEN	ADULTS	MEN	WOMEN	ADULTS	MEN	WOMEN
Total Adult Population		*220,896*	*106,548*	*114,348*	*44.8*	*44.0*	*45.6*	*55,462.00*	*58,936.0*	*51,964.0*
Architectural Digest	814	4,482	1,995	2,487	49.0	46.6	50.8	95,054.0	89,966.0	100,416.0
Bicycling	419	1,586	1,126	459	42.4	42.7	41.3	82,579.0	85,739.0	74,235.0
Business Week	919	4,729	3,085	1,644	45.9	45.1	47.1	91,599.0	95,501.0	82,496.0
Family Circle	3,943	21,274	2,038	19,236	51.3	52.4	51.2	51,859.0	52,835.0	51,721.0
Fortune	865	3,939	2,637	1,302	44.1	43.7	45.0	96,904.0	100,807.0	89,264.0
Guns & Ammo	454	6,410	5,736	674	37.5	36.9	41.6	56,113.0	57,497.0	44,693.0
Martha Stewart Living	1,914	11,662	1,267	10,395	46.7	46.5	46.7	68,987.0	74,468.0	68,202.0
Maxim	2,468	12,888	9,907	2,981	28.7	29.0	27.6	63,561.0	63,796.0	62,590.0
Men's Health	1,788	11,292	9,496	1,796	37.9	37.5	39.8	75,527.0	74,619.0	81,672.0
National Enquirer	1,008	8,797	2,979	5,818	44.6	41.3	46.0	45,832.0	54,576.0	42,691.0
New York Times (Daily)	1,142	3,174	1,816	1,358	47.6	47.7	47.6	103,177.0	101,746.0	105,174.0
New York Times (Sunday)	1,661	4,334	2,297	2,037	49.4	47.9	50.8	99,917.0	102,752.0	97,900.0
Newsweek	3,170	18,729	10,455	8,274	46.8	46.0	47.7	73,204.0	74,622.0	71,009.0
Outdoor Life	956	5,783	4,664	1,120	44.4	44.2	45.3	59,535.0	63,561.0	43,031.0
People	3,699	42,427	13,444	28,983	40.7	41.2	40.3	65,292.0	69,408.0	63,176.0
Reader's Digest	9,955	37,249	14,643	22,607	51.9	51.9	51.9	56,158.0	62,383.0	51,978.0
Soap Opera Digest	515	5,315	417	4,898	40.6	40.6	40.6	39,365.0	48,072.0	38,095.0
Star	1,404	10,482	2,517	7,965	35.7	34.1	36.4	51,296.0	55,585.0	49,361.0
Town & Country	468	3,927	1,127	2,800	48.8	48.1	49.2	58,883.0	64,396.0	56,800.0
USA Today	2,290	3,995	2,652	1,342	46.1	45.5	47.3	76,279.0	83,645.0	61,850.0
Vibe	910	7,734	3,769	3,965	27.9	27.7	28.0	41,853.0	44,043.0	38,865.0
Vogue	1,211	10,627	1,299	9,327	35.8	34.4	36.1	64,984.0	64,195.0	65,100.0

Source: MRI 2008, accessed at www.mriplus.com.

AGE Product needs often vary with consumers' age, and age is a key factor in marketing many products and services. For instance, younger investors—in their mid-20s to mid-40s—are often advised to invest aggressively and in "growth" stocks, whereas people who are older and closer to retirement should be much more cautious, keep a significant portion of their assets in bonds (which provide stable and safe income), and avoid risky, long-term investments. Age also influences our buying priorities. For example, as a young student, would you say that your opinions regarding what is a "luxury" product and whether or not you will continue buying that item even if it increased significantly in price are the same as those of your parents or grandparents? The most probable answer is illustrated in Table 3.2 which describes age-related perceptions toward buying luxury items.[6] As yet another example of age's impact on buying behavior, a study discovered that **marketplace decision difficulty (MPDD)**—an attribute depicting one's hardship in making buying decisions—was more typical of older, less-educated female consumers.[7]

The largest age segment in the U.S. population is *baby boomers*, the 76 million consumers born between 1946 and 1964 (about 72 million are left). They spend over $1 trillion annually,

TABLE 3.2 Cohort Perception of Luxury Goods

For each product or service on the list below, the numerical figures represent the percentage of buyers, within each age group, who said that they would continue to buy the product even if their income and the prices of other goods stayed stable while the price of the focal product doubled.

	<25 YEARS MEAN	25–50 YEARS MEAN	>50 YEARS MEAN
Designer handbag	32.2	40.8	29.1
Gold jewelry	34.5	35.2	42.2
MP3 player	35.0	33.3	42.7
HBO	35.4	28.7	34.5
Facial	37.2	28.6	31.9
Massage	37.8	28.3	35.3
Taxi	40.3	47.0	53.9
Laptop computer	41.7	49.7	70.7
Movies	44.0	39.0	37.3
Salon shampoo	44.0	47.5	44.3
Coffeehouse coffee	44.2	43.1	35.7
Live concert	45.5	30.0	36.6
Live game	45.8	29.1	42.9
Department store cosmetics	46.6	36.5	39.8
First-class airline ticket	46.6	52.7	51.9
Wine	48.1	46.9	46.3
Perfume	49.8	42.3	40.8
Dinner out	49.9	49.1	50.5
Down coat	53.5	45.8	50.3
Wool blanket	55.8	50.0	54.2
Lunch out	56.7	58.8	57.0
Chocolate	61.7	56.3	62.7
High speed Internet	66.1	57.5	62.8
Cell phone	69.6	62.6	60.9

Note: Products classified as necessities that were included in the source article are not listed.

Source: William E. Hauck and Nancy Stanforth, "Cohort Perception of Luxury Goods and Services," *Journal of Fashion Marketing and Management,* 11 no. 2 (2007): 185. Copyright © 2007, Emerald Group Publishing Limited.

control a large amount of the nation's wealth and disposable income, and, as more of them reach retirement age, will also account for most of the governmental expenditures on social security and medical benefits. As the baby boomers age, for the first time in history, the U.S. population will include a very large older population that has been born during economic growth, lived mostly during affluent times, and has had the opportunity to plan its long-term finances and accumulate significant wealth. Due to modern medicine, these consumers are also likely to live longer, be more active, and consume more products and services than previous cohorts of older people. Table 3.3 depicts a recent segmentation of this age group.[8]

The age cohorts following the baby boomers are Generations X and Y (Generation Y is also termed "echo boomers"), representing distinct and important target markets that are discussed in detail when age is examined as a subculture in Chapter 12.

GENDER Like age, gender is a factual distinguishing segmentation variable, and many products and services are inherently designed for either males or females. For instance, women have traditionally been the main users of such products as hair coloring and cosmetics, and men have been the main users of tools and shaving preparations. However, sex roles have blurred, and gender is no longer an accurate way to distinguish consumers in these and other product categories. Today, women are buying household repair tools, many men use skin and hair care cosmetics, and there are more and more magazine ads and TV commercials that depict men and women in roles traditionally occupied by the opposite sex. For example, many ads reflect the expanded child-nurturing roles of young fathers in today's society.

MARITAL STATUS Traditionally, the family has been the focus of most marketing efforts, and the household continues to be the focal consuming unit of many products and services. Marketers study the number and kinds of households that buy and own certain products and the media profiles of household decision makers (the persons involved in the actual selection of the product) in order to develop appropriate marketing appeals. Marketers have also discovered the benefits of targeting specific marital status groupings, such as singles, divorced individuals, single parents, and dual-income married couples. For instance, urban, one-person households with incomes greater than $75,000 tend to buy premium alcoholic drinks and beer, books, organic products, fresh produce, and shop in green markets and specialized food stores rather than in conventional supermarkets.

TABLE 3.3 Segmenting Baby Boomers

SEGMENT NAME	LOOKING FOR BALANCE	CONFIDENT AND LIVING WELL	AT EASE	OVERWHELMED
Percent of Boomers	27%	23%	31%	19%
Characteristics	Very active and busy lifestyle. Money is important, but so is saving time.	Have highest incomes, are first to buy a new product or service. Technologically oriented, stylish, and trendy.	At peace with themselves and do not worry about the future. Lowest interest in luxury goods, and do not travel much. Most home-centric and family-oriented group.	Lowest income segment, worried about the future and financial security. Least active group—health is a big concern. Least social group. Do not use high-tech products.
Marketing Implications	Want great experiences—a market for travel-related businesses and food service businesses.	Travel is a favorite interest. Want luxury goods and services.	A good market for traditional household products and services. Like trusted brand names. Low interest in new products.	Opportunity for marketers of certain financial service and health care products/services.

Source: Dick Chay, "New Segments of Boomers Reveal New Marketing Implications," *Marketing News* (March 15, 2005): 24.

FAMILY LIFE CYCLE This segmentation is based on the premise that many families pass through similar phases in their formation, growth, and final dissolution. At each phase, the family unit needs different products and services. Young single people, for example, need basic furniture for their first apartment, whereas their parents, finally free of child rearing, often refurnish their homes with more elaborate pieces. **Family life cycle** is a classification stemming from factual variables including *marital status*, *employment status*, and the *presence or absence of children* in the household. In most cases, these factors also reflect the relative age and income of the family members. Each stage in the traditional family life cycle (*bachelorhood, honeymooners, parenthood, postparenthood*, and *dissolution*) represents an important target segment to many marketers, and examples of such prospects are described in Chapter 10. Many major *life events* are part of the family life cycle. A recent study discovered that occasions such as moving, marriage, the birth or adoption of a child, birth or death of a close family member, significant changes in one's employment, and caring for older relatives represent viable segmentation variables when used together with age cohorts.[9]

INCOME, EDUCATION, AND OCCUPATION Income has long been an important variable for distinguishing between market segments because it is an indicator of the ability (or inability) to pay for a product or a specific version of a given offering. Income is often combined with other demographic variables to define target markets more accurately. To illustrate, high income has been combined with age to identify the important *affluent elderly* segment. It also has been combined with both age and occupational status to produce the so-called *yuppie* segment, a sought-after subgroup of the baby boomer market.

Education, occupation, and income tend to be closely correlated; high-level occupations that produce high incomes usually require advanced education and are more prestigious than occupations requiring less education. *Social class* is a base for market segmentation and is commonly computed as a weighted index of education, occupation, and income. The concept of social class also implies a hierarchy in which individuals in the same class generally have the same degree of status, whereas members of other classes have either higher or lower status. Studies have shown that consumers in different social classes vary in terms of values, product preferences, and buying habits. Chapter 10 discusses the lifestyles and buying patterns of different social classes.

Geodemographic Segmentation

Where a person lives determines some aspects of consumption behavior. For example, climates determine the types of clothing most people own, and fashions and styles in large cities are often very different from those in nonurban areas. Local customers, as opposed to visiting tourists, are also a distinct segment. For instance, one study investigated the *local resident gambler segment* in Las Vegas and found that the gaming habits of this group were distinctly different from those of tourists—a segment on which most marketing studies have focused.[10] Sometimes, geographic destinations lead to the emergence of market segments. While such exotic destinations as glaciers, coral reefs, ice fields, and tropical rain forests erode due to climate change and other factors, there are many customers willing to pay unusually high prices for traveling to these places in order to see them *before* they become much less majestic or disappear altogether; in the travel industry, this segment is known as "Tourism of Doom."[11] Another creative example of using geography is Absolut Vodka's introduction of limited editions of flavored vodkas in major cities with the cities' names integrated into the brand (e.g., "Absolut New York" and "Absolut Chicago") and with well-recognized features of the city embedded in the ads (e.g., in an ad for Absolut Chicago, wind is blowing the letters off the bottle).[12]

The most popular use of geography in strategic targeting is **geodemographics**—a hybrid segmentation scheme based on the premise that people who live close to one another are likely to have similar financial means, tastes, preferences, lifestyles, and consumption habits (as an old adage states, "Birds of a feather flock together"). The primary commercial application of this technique is the Claritas PRIZM NE classification (a product of the Nielsen Company). This system uses the ZIP + 4 postal system to classify households into 66 segments. As illustrated in Table 3.4, each cluster is described in demographic and behavioral terms; the list of behaviors consists of about 10,000 items (e.g., "owns a mutual fund," "plays football"). PRIZM's classification database includes 890,000 household records from diverse sources, including the census bureau and commercial surveys of factors such as lifestyles, media habits, financial decisions, new car buying, and health care choices.[13]

TABLE 3.4 Four PRIZM NE Geodemographic Segments

MOVERS & SHAKERS

- 1.59 percent of U.S. households
- Median household income: $95,372
- Predominant employment: Professional
- Social group: Elite suburbs
- Lifestage group: Midlife success
- Key education level: College grad+
- Adult age range: 35–64

CHARACTERISTICS: Movers & Shakers is home to America's up-and-coming business class: a wealthy suburban world of dual-income couples who are highly educated, typically between the ages of 35 and 54 and often with children. Given its high percentage of executives and white-collar professionals, there's a decided business bent to this segment: Movers & Shakers rank number-one for owning a small business and having a home office.

LIFESTYLE TRAITS:

- Go scuba diving/snorkeling
- Plan travel on the Internet
- Read *PC Magazine*
- Listen to adult contemporary radio
- Drive a Porsche

NEW EMPTY NESTS

- 1.05 percent of U.S. households
- Median household income: $65,832
- Predominant employment: Professional, white-collar
- Social group: The Affluentials
- Lifestage group: Conservative classics
- Key education level: College Grad+
- Adult age range: 65+

CHARACTERISTICS: With their grown-up children recently out of the house, New Empty Nests is composed of upscale older Americans who pursue active—and activist—lifestyles. Nearly three-quarters of residents are over 65 years old, but they show no interest in a rest-home retirement. This is the top-ranked segment for all-inclusive travel packages; the favorite destination is Italy.

LIFESTYLE TRAITS:

- Choose all-inclusive travel pkg.
- Belong to a fraternal order
- Read *Smithsonian*
- Watch *Meet the Press*
- Drive a Buick Park Avenue

BOOMTOWN SINGLES

- 1.22 percent of U.S. households
- Median household income: $37,407
- Predominant employment: White-collar, service
- Social group: City Centers
- Lifestage group: Young Achievers
- Key education level: H.S./College
- Adult age range: Under 35

CHARACTERISTICS: Affordable housing, abundant entry-level jobs and a thriving singles scene—all have given rise to the Boomtown Singles segment in fast-growing satellite cities. Young, single, and working-class, these residents pursue active lifestyles amid sprawling apartment complexes, bars, convenience stores, and Laundromats.

Continued

TABLE 3.4 Four PRIZM NE Geodemographic Segments *Continued*

LIFESTYLE TRAITS:
- Buy alternative music
- Play football
- Read *Muscle & Fitness*
- Watch MTV
- Drive a Daewoo

BEDROCK AMERICA
- 1.79 percent of U.S. households
- Median household income: $26,037
- Predominant employment: Service, BC, Farm
- Social group: Rustic living
- Lifestage group: Sustaining families
- Key education level: Elementary/H.S.
- Adult age range: Under 35

CHARACTERISTICS: Bedrock America consists of young, economically challenged families in small, isolated towns located throughout the nation's heartland. With modest educations, sprawling families, and blue-collar jobs, many of these residents struggle to make ends meet. One quarter live in mobile homes. One in three haven't finished high school. Rich in scenery, Bedrock America is a haven for fishing, hunting, hiking, and camping.

LIFESTYLE TRAITS:
- Go freshwater fishing
- Buy kids' bicycles
- Read baby magazines
- Watch *Days of Our Lives*
- Drive a Chevy S10 pickup

Source: Courtesy of Claritas Inc.

In recent years, Claritas also categorized the segments into *Lifestage Groups* (stages similar to those of the *family life cycle*). The PRIZM segments have been used in a wide array of targeting applications such as cost-effective direct marketing, selecting media for advertising campaigns, tailoring offers and promotional content to specific segments, identifying a product's or service's customers' composition and targeting by geographic area.[14] "Geodemographic clustering" is further discussed within the context of social class in Chapter 10.

Personality Traits

If asked directly, people are unlikely to disclose their personality traits either because they are guarded or because they do not consciously recognize them. (*Projective techniques* designed to overcome this barrier are discussed in Chapters 2 and 4). However, through personality tests—which are generally in the form of questions or statements presented to the respondent—researchers can determine one's personality and use it in segmentation. For example, consumers who are *open-minded* and generally *perceive less risk* than others in trying new things are likely to be *consumer innovators*—that is, more likely to buy a new product when it is first introduced and before many other consumers buy it. Therefore, marketers of new products must identify these individuals (and also find out their demographics, lifestyles, and values) and target them during the new product's introduction. Furthermore, if personality tests also discover that innovators tend to score high on *exhibition*—a trait where a person wants to be the center of a group—the promotion directed at this group should encourage the innovators to initiate positive *word of mouth* and tell others about the new product.

Table 3.5 depicts three distinct groups of online shoppers segmented mostly on the basis of personality traits. Note that the sample statements for measuring some personality dimensions (i.e., trust and perceived risk) were adapted specifically for online shopping, which is the focal consumption behavior of this study.[15]

TABLE 3.5 Segments of Online Shoppers

CONSTRUCT	SAMPLE STATEMENTS	SEGMENT 1: *RISK-AVERSE DOUBTERS*	SEGMENT 2: *OPEN-MINDED ONLINE SHOPPERS*	SEGMENT 3: *RESERVED INFORMATION SEEKERS*
Extraversion	• I like to have a lot of people around me. • I really enjoy talking to people • I am a very active person • My life is fast-paced	Reserved and not extraverted	High on extraversion	Reserved
Neuroticism	• I often feel inferior to others • Sometimes I feel completely worthless • I often get angry at the way people treat me • I often feel helpless and want someone else to solve my problems		Low on neuroticism and show little fear	Careful
Trust	• This online shop is genuinely committed to my satisfaction • When I see an advertisement of this store, I believe the information in it is accurate • This online shop is very reliable • I know what to expect from this online shop	Skeptical about new experiences	High trust of online vendors	Reasonable degree of trust
Attitude toward online shopping	Online shopping is: . . . good . . . enjoyable . . . convincing . . . positive . . . entertaining . . . diversified	Not favorable	High on the pleasure derived from shopping	Favorable attitude toward online shopping higher than shopping pleasure
Perceived risk	• I believe buying a product on the Internet is a significant risk • I believe buying a product on the Internet has a high potential for loss • The decision to purchase on the Internet involved a high level of risk • When I shop on the Internet, the transmission of my personal data involves a high degree of risk	High perceived risk	Low perceived risk	High perceived risk
Willingness to buy	• I could imagine buying products in an online shop • I would be willing to buy gifts in this online shop • I would be willing to recommend this online shop to my friends • How likely is it that you would consider purchasing from an online shop?	Low willingness to buy	Affinity for online shopping	Positive attitude toward online shopping

Source: Stuart J. Barnes, "Segmenting Cyberspace: A Customer Typology for the Internet," *European Journal of Marketing*, 41, no. 1/2 (2007): 71–93.

Lifestyles

Lifestyles, also known as psychographics, consist of *activities, interests,* and *opinions (AIOS)*. The interests and opinions portions are cognitive constructs, which can be measured via surveys but are not evidence-based. A psychographic study includes a battery of statements selected from a *psychographic inventory* and usually accompanied by *Likert scales* on which respondents are asked to indicate their level of agreement or disagreement with each statement. Some of the factors examined are similar to personality traits, and others include measures of buying motives, interests, attitudes, beliefs, and values. Because of their versatility, psychographics are widely used in segmentation and are part of almost any hybrid segmentation framework.

It is often stated that while *demographics determine consumers' needs* for products (e.g., males and females need and buy different products) and the *ability* to buy them (e.g., income), *psychographics explain buyers' purchase decisions and the choices they make* within the buying options available to them. For example, age is a factual demographic factor, and when people retire, their consumption, outlook on life and priorities change. However, not all people reaching retirement experience the same mind-set. Table 3.6 describes four distinct perceptions of retirement. In fact, these views represent different anticipated lifestyles following retirement and reflect varied types of future consumption behavior. As such, they are very valuable to any marketer targeting the rapidly growing and mostly financially secure segment of mature consumers.[16]

VALS (an acronym for "values and lifestyles") is the most popular segmentation system combining lifestyles and values. Drawing on Maslow's need hierarchy (see Chapter 4) and the concept of *social character* (see Chapter 5), researchers at SRI International developed a segmentation scheme of the American population known as VALS™. The original system was revised and the current VALS focus more explicitly on explaining consumer purchasing behavior. This typology classifies the American adult population into eight distinctive subgroups (segments) based on consumer responses to both attitudinal and demographic questions. Figure 3.4

TABLE 3.6 Four Views of Post-Retirement Lifestyle

AS AN OPPORTUNITY TO MAKE A NEW START

This group regards retirement as an exciting time. Work will have been largely unrewarding, so the transition is seen as a freedom from the constraints of their former role. Retirement will invigorate such people and inspire them towards undertaking activities that work largely prevented them from pursuing.

AS A CONTINUATION OF THEIR PRE-RETIREMENT LIFESTYLE

To such people, retirement is not perceived as signaling a drastic change. Work life has not been as unsatisfying as for others, hence its ending is not greeted with euphoria. There is, however, some satisfaction that retirement permits more opportunity to devote time to existing activities outside of their working role. The future is likely to see an increase in such activities but no real desire to engage in new ones.

AS AN UNWELCOME DISRUPTION

Work was an integral part of life for this group, who feel that part of their identity is removed when the stage ends. A sense of frustration materializes at the belief that a key opportunity for self-fulfillment has been taken away. Such retirees attempt to regain their focus by undertaking activities that act as a substitute for their working role. This behavior corroborates claims made in other studies that some individuals feel the need to prove their worth by undertaking and conquering new challenges.

AS A TRANSITION INTO OLD AGE

Here, retirement prompts a sense of resignation that old age beckons. It signals a time to slow down, rather than try anything new and energetic. That work might have become increasingly unwelcome and wearying substantiates this belief. As activity levels subside, the move towards introspection gathers pace.

Source: Christopher D. Hopkins, Catherine A. Roster, and Charles M. Wood, "Making the Transition to Retirement: Appraisals, Post-Transition Lifestyle, and Changes in Consumption Patterns," *Journal of Consumer Marketing*, 23 no. 2 (2006): 100.

FIGURE 3.4
A Diagram of the VALS Segments

Source: Reprinted with permission of SRI Consulting Business Intelligence.

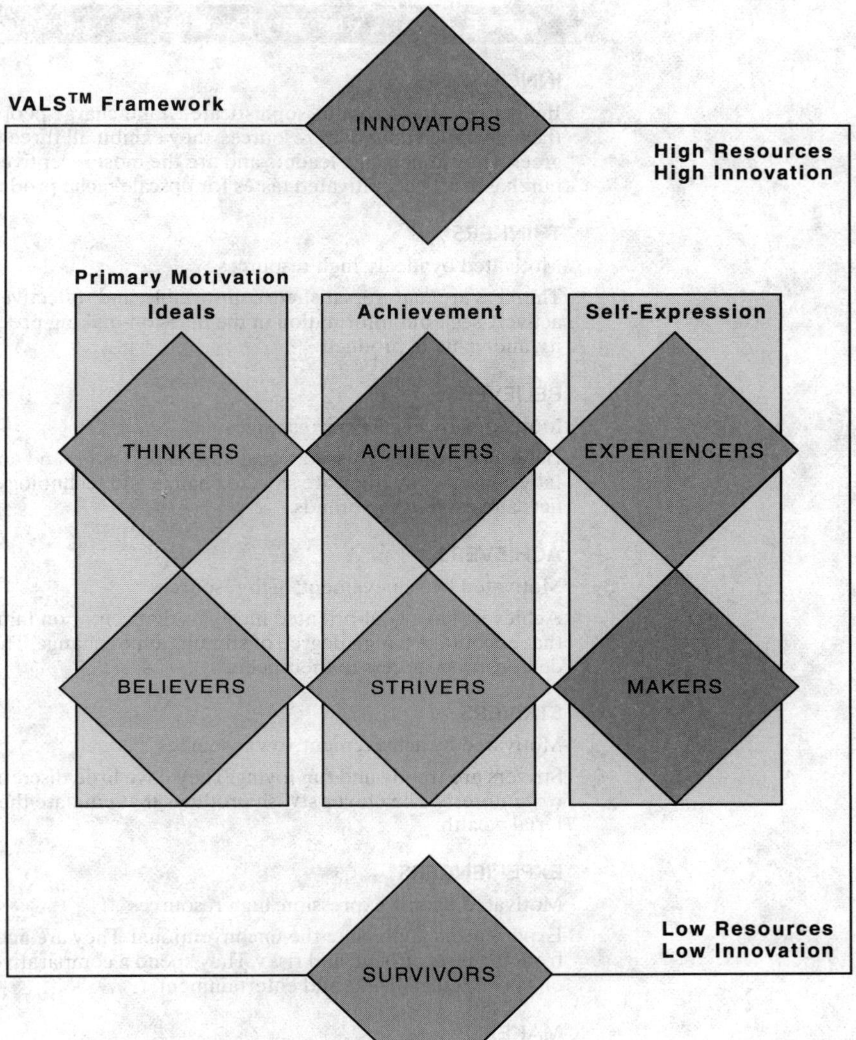

depicts the current VALS classification scheme, and Table 3.7 includes descriptions of the eight VALS segments. Examining the diagram (Figure 3.4) from left to right, there are three *primary motivations*: the *ideals motivated* (these consumer segments are guided by knowledge and principles), the *achievement motivated* (these consumer segments are looking for products and services that demonstrate success to their peers), and the *self-expression motivated* (these consumer segments desire social or physical activity, variety, and risk). Furthermore, each of these three major self-motivations represents distinct attitudes, lifestyles, and decision-making styles. Examining Figure 3.4, from top to bottom, the diagram reveals a kind of continuum in terms of resources and innovation—that is, *high resources-high innovation* (on the top) to *low resources-low innovation* (on the bottom). This range of resources/innovation (again, from most to least) includes the range of psychological, physical, demographic, and material means and capacities consumers have to draw upon, including education, income, self-confidence, health, eagerness to buy, and energy level, as well as the consumer's propensity to try new products.

Each of the eight VALS segments contains between 10 and 17 percent of the U.S. adult population, with Believers, at 17 percent, being the largest VALS group. In terms of consumer characteristics, the eight VALS segments differ in some important ways. For instance, *Believers* tend to buy American-made products and are slow to alter their consumption-related habits, whereas *Innovators* are drawn to top-of-the-line and new products, especially innovative technologies.

TABLE 3.7 Summary Descriptions of the Eight VALS Segments

INNOVATORS

Innovators are successful, sophisticated, take-charge people with high self-esteem. Because they have such abundant resources, they exhibit all three primary motivations in varying degrees. They are change leaders and are the most receptive to new ideas and technologies. Their purchases reflect cultivated tastes for upscale niche products and services.

THINKERS*

Motivated by ideals; high resources

Thinkers are mature, satisfied, comfortable, and reflective. They tend to be well educated and actively seek out information in the decision-making process. They favor durability, functionality, and value in products.

BELIEVERS

Motivated by ideals; low resources

Believers are strongly traditional and respect rules and authority. Because they are fundamentally conservative, they are slow to change and technology averse. They choose familiar products and established brands.

ACHIEVERS

Motivated by achievement; high resources

Achievers have goal-oriented lifestyles that center on family and career. They avoid situations that encourage a high degree of stimulation or change. They prefer premium products that demonstrate success to their peers.

STRIVERS

Motivated by achievement; low resources

Strivers are trendy and fun loving. They have little discretionary income and tend to have narrow interests. They favor stylish products that emulate the purchases of people with greater material wealth.

EXPERIENCERS

Motivated by self-expression; high resources

Experiencers appreciate the unconventional. They are active and impulsive, seeking stimulation from the new, offbeat, and risky. They spend a comparatively high proportion of their income on fashion, socializing, and entertainment.

MAKERS

Motivated by self-expression; low resources

Movers value practicality and self-sufficiency. They choose hands-on constructive activities and spend leisure time with family and close friends. Because they prefer value to luxury, they buy basic products.

SURVIVORS

Survivors lead narrowly focused lives. Because they have the fewest resources, they do not exhibit a primary motivation and often feel powerless. They are primarily concerned about safety and security, so they tend to be brand loyal and buy discounted merchandise.

*VALS™ segments the U.S. English-speaking population age 18 or older into eight consumer groups. Their primary motion and ability to express themselves in the marketplace distinguish the groups.

Source: Reprinted with permission of SRI Consulting Business Intelligence.

Therefore, for example, it is not surprising that marketers of intelligent in-vehicle technologies (e.g., global positioning devices) must first target *Innovators*, because they are early adopters of new products. VALS have been used in many business plans, and Table 3.8 includes examples of their strategic applications.

The VALS framework was developed as a result of administering a large psychographic inventory to sizeable samples of consumers. As discussed earlier, psychographics are highly versatile and can be adapted to survey many facets of one's attitudes, values, and opinions. For

TABLE 3.8 Examples of the Strategic Applications of VALS

COMMERCIALIZATION

- A European luxury automobile manufacturer used VALS to identify online, mobile applications that would appeal to affluent, early-adopter consumers within the next five years. VALS research identified early-adopter groups and explored their reactions to a variety of mobile services for use in automobiles. The VALS analysis enabled the company to prioritize applications for development and determine the best strategic alliances to pursue.
- A major telecommunications-product company used VALS to select an early-adopter target for a new telecommunications concept. VALS enabled the company to develop the product prototype and prioritize features and benefits, with a focus on the early-adopter target. The company used VALS to select the best name and logo, choose an overall positioning strategy, and set an initial price point.

POSITIONING

- A major stock brokerage firm focused on providing excellent service to a select group of affluent consumers used VALS to redefine its image and develop a new corporate slogan. Within 18 months, advertising recall scores increased dramatically from 8 to 55.
- A Minnesota medical center planned to offer a new line of service: cosmetic surgery. It used VALS to identify target consumers (those most interested and able to afford the service). By understanding the underlying motivations of the target, the center and its ad agency were able to develop a compelling selling proposition. The resulting advertising was so successful that just a few weeks into the campaign, the center exceeded its scheduling capabilities.

COMMUNICATIONS

- U.S. long-distance carrier used VALS to select its spokesperson in a major television campaign to increase its customer base. By understanding consumers who are heavy users of long-distance service, the company was able to select a spokesperson to whom the target could relate.
- An electric utility used VALS to increase participation in its energy-conservation program by developing a targeted direct mail campaign. Two distinctly different VALS segments were key targets. By developing unique strategies for each audience and identifying ZIP codes with high percentages of each target, the utility reported a 25% increase in participation.

Source: Reprinted with permission of SRI Consulting Business Intelligence.

example, a recent study developed a questionnaire designed to measure the extent of the consumer's difficulty in making choices among the many alternatives available when purchasing consumer goods. This psychological attribute was named the *marketplace decision difficulty* (or MPDD), and some of the statements used to measure it are listed in Table 3.9.[17]

Sociocultural Values and Beliefs

Sociological (group) and *anthropological* (cultural) variables—that is, *sociocultural variables*—provide further bases for market segmentation. For example, consumer markets have been successfully subdivided into segments on the basis of core cultural values, subcultural memberships, and cross-cultural affiliations.

CULTURE AND SUBCULTURE Marketers can segment some populations on the basis of cultural heritage because members of the same culture tend to share the same values, beliefs, and customs. Companies using cultural segmentation focus on widely held cultural values with which most consumers identify (e.g., *youthfulness* and *fitness and health*). Within the larger culture, distinct subgroups (subcultures) often are united by certain characteristics associated with specific values and beliefs. These groupings can be based on a demographic characteristic, ethnicity, or some other factor. In the United States, for example, African Americans, Hispanic Americans, Asian Americans, and the elderly are important subcultural market segments. (Subcultural differences are discussed in Chapter 12.) Culturally distinct segments can be prospects for the same product but often are targeted more efficiently with different promotional appeals. For example, a bicycle might be promoted as an efficient means of transportation in parts of Asia and as a health-and-fitness product in the United Kingdom.

TABLE 3.9 The Marketplace Decision Difficulty (MPDD) Scale

1. Products such as CD players or VCRs often have so many features that a comparison of different brands is barely possible.
2. The information I get from advertising often is so vague that it is hard to know what a product can actually perform.
3. When buying a product, I rarely feel sufficiently informed.
4. When purchasing certain products, such as a computer or hi-fi, I feel uncertain as to product features that are particularly important to me.
5. I do not always know exactly which products meet my needs best.
6. There are so many brands to choose from that I sometimes feel confused.
7. Owing to the host of stores it is sometimes difficult to decide where to shop.
8. Owing to the great similarity of many products it is often difficult to detect new products.
9. Some brands look so similar that it is uncertain whether they are made by the same manufacturer or not.
10. In the store, I tend to recognize my favorite brands immediately.

Source: Gianfranco Walsh and Vincent-Wayne Mitchell, "Demographic Characteristics of Consumers Who Find It Difficult to Decide," *Marketing Intelligence & Planning,* 23 nos. 2/3 (2005): 285.

CROSS-CULTURAL OR GLOBAL MARKETING SEGMENTATION As the world became more integrated—largely because of shared communication media—a global marketplace has emerged. For example, as you read this you may be sitting on an IKEA chair or sofa (made in Sweden), drinking Earl Grey tea (England), or wearing a Swatch watch (Switzerland), Nike sneakers (China), a Polo golf shirt (Mexico), or Dockers pants (Dominican Republic). Some global market segments, such as teenagers, appear to want the same types of products, regardless of which nation they call home—products that are trendy, entertaining, and image oriented. This global "sameness" allows, for example, a sneaker marketer to launch styles appealing to segments in different countries using the same global advertising campaign. On the other hand, cross-cultural differences also force marketers to adapt products to overseas markets. As an illustration, the core benefit that McDonald's provides is consistency and value by having a standardized, almost identical menu in each of its U.S. outlets. But, McDonald's had to adapt its uniform offerings to the needs and cultures of global consumers. Thus, in India, McDonald's does not serve beef products, and in Saudi Arabia, McDonald's outlets include separate dining sections for men and women (global marketing strategies and cross-cultural differences are discussed in Chapter 13).

CONSUMPTION-SPECIFIC SEGMENTATION BASES

This group includes two types of *consumption-specific* bases for segmentation: *facts* about actual consumption *behavior* and *cognitions* consumers have about products and services in the form of *attitudes*, *preferences*, and the like. Usage behaviors examined include **usage rate** and **usage situation**. Segmentation bases in the form of consumption-specific cognitions include **benefit segmentation** and **brand loyalty and relationship**.

Usage Rate Segmentation

This segmentation stems from differences among *heavy*, *medium,* and *light users*, and *nonusers* of a specific product, service, or brand. Marketers of many products such as soup, laundry detergent, beer, and dog food have found that a relatively small group of heavy users accounts for a disproportionately large percentage of the total product usage. For example, about 25 percent of all beer drinkers account for about 75 percent of all beer consumed. Therefore, most beer companies direct their advertising campaigns to heavy users rather than spend money trying to attract medium or light users. This also explains the successful targeting of light beer to heavy drinkers under the positioning that it is less filling (and, thus, can be consumed in greater quantities) than regular beer.

Targeting heavy users is a common marketing strategy, and it can certainly be more profitable than targeting other user categories. However, since all competitors within a given market are likely to target the same heavy users, trying to attract these buyers requires a lot of expensive advertising. Some marketers prefer to target light and medium users with products that are distinct from those preferred by heavy users. For example, every Super Bowl broadcast includes many very expensive commercials for mainstream brands of American beer directed at the product's heavy users. On the other hand, the beer section at a Whole Foods Supermarket consists of numerous brands from different countries and microbreweries, and with more exotic flavors; these products also cost more than top-selling beer brands and are backed by minimal advertising. Whole Foods targets consumers who drink less beer than those targeted by the Super Bowl ads but who have more discerning tastes and also greater disposable incomes.

A sophisticated approach to usage rate involves identifying the factors that directly impact the usage behavior. For instance, a recent study of supermarket customers found differences between two segments of buyers in terms of usage frequency, defined as the number of times per week buyers visited the supermarket. Then, usage frequency was examined in relation to buyers' reasons for purchasing at that chain, levels of expenditure at the store, travel times to the store and modes of transportation, and whether buyers came in from home, a job, or were simply passing by.[18] Understanding *nonusers* is also essential. For instance, a recent study found two distinct segments among nonadopters of Internet banking: *prospective adopters* and *persistent nonadopters*. Clearly, lumping all nonadopters into a single category would have resulted in overlooking targeting opportunities.[19]

In addition to segmenting customers in terms of rate of usage or other usage patterns, consumers can also be segmented in terms of their *awareness status* and also *level of involvement* (these factors represent cognitive factors strongly related to usage behaviors). The consumer's degree of awareness of the product, interest level in the product, readiness to buy the product, and whether the consumer is unaware and needs to be informed about the product represent distinct targeting opportunities. *Product involvement* (fully discussed in Chapter 7) is also a segmentation factor. For example, a recent study identified three clusters of consumers based on their varied involvement with a wine's "background or history" (i.e., its "appellation of origin") and found significant differences among the clusters in terms of knowledge of wine brands and wine purchases.[20]

Usage-Situation Segmentation

Because the occasion or situation often determines what consumers will purchase or consume, marketers sometimes use the *usage situation* as a segmentation variable. The following three statements reveal the potential of situation segmentation: "Whenever our son celebrates a birthday, we take him out to dinner at the Gramercy Tavern" "When I'm away on business for a week or more, I try to stay at a Suites hotel" "I always buy my wife candy on Valentine's Day." Under other circumstances, in other situations, and on other occasions, the same consumer might make other choices. Some situational factors that might influence a purchase or consumption choice includes whether it is a weekday or weekend (e.g., going to a movie); whether there is sufficient time (e.g., use of regular mail or express mail); whether it is a gift for a girlfriend, a parent, or a self-gift.

Many products are promoted for special usage occasions. The greeting card industry, for example, promotes special cards for a variety of occasions that seem to be increasing annually in the form of such additions as Grandparents' Day, Secretaries' Day, etc. The florist and candy industries promote their products for Valentine's Day and Mother's Day, the diamond industry promotes diamond rings as an engagement symbol, and expensive wristwatches and fountain pens are often promoted as graduation gifts with heavier advertising during the May–June graduation season. The Russell Stover® ad in Figure 3.5 is an example of situational, special usage segmentation. It appeared in magazines several weeks prior to holidays such as Christmas and Valentine's Day. The particular ad is making the point that they have been around for the holiday—since 1923.

A recent study found that individuals who purchase their magazines at newsstands are more active consumers and are more receptive to advertising than consumers who subscribe to the very same magazines. Clearly, this finding has important implications for advertisers.[21] Table 3.10 presents a comparison of newsstand magazine buyers versus magazine subscribers.

FIGURE 3.5

Source: © Russell Stover Candies Inc. Used with permission. All rights reserved.

QUESTION: *Which Consumption-Related Segmentation Is Featured in This AD?*

Benefit Segmentation

The benefits that consumers seek from products and services are the essence of *benefit segmentation* and many believe also the core of *all* segmentation strategies. Sought benefits represent unfilled consumer needs whereas buyers' perceptions that a given brand delivers a unique and prominent benefit result in loyalty to that brand. Therefore, benefit segmentation is often used to develop a positioning approach (as stated earlier, positioning guides all four elements of the marketing mix). The chewing gum ads at the start of this chapter (Figure 3.2) depict unique benefits offered by different brands. In the case of beer, another nondurable consumer good, a study examining what drives consumer preferences for micro or craft beer, identified the following five brand benefits: (1) functional (i.e., quality), (2) value for the money, (3) social benefit, (4) positive emotional benefits, and (5) negative emotional benefits.[22]

A recent study investigated the benefits that consumers seek when visiting each of three service providers: a dentist, hairdresser, and travel agent. The statistical analysis revealed three distinct groups of benefits (see Table 3.11, Part A). Then, subjects were classified into four age groups and asked how important each benefit-group was to them in determining their continued loyalty to each service provider (see Table 3.11, Part B).[23] Applying the results of the study

TABLE 3.10 Newsstand Magazine Buyers Versus Magazine Subscribers

CONSUMERS WHO BUY MAGAZINES ON THE NEWSSTAND ARE

- Two times as likely to enjoy reading ads in magazines
- 63 percent more likely to remember products advertised in magazines when they are shopping
- 48 percent more likely to shop frequently
- 50 percent more likely to buy things on the spur of the moment
- Twice as likely to spend more money on cosmetics than subscribers
- 58 percent more likely to buy leading cosmetic brands
- Nearly twice as likely to enjoy shopping for clothes
- 50 percent more likely to try new alcoholic drinks than subscribers
- 58 percent more likely to drink super-premium vodka
- Four times more likely to download music than subscribers
- More than twice as likely to purchase video games in the last 12 months
- Twice as likely to purchase designer jeans

Source: "New Study Reveals Newsstand Magazine Buyers to Be More Active Consumers and More Receptive to Advertising," *Business Wire*, September 8, 2004, 1.

TABLE 3.11 Benefits Sought from Service Providers

PART A—THREE TYPES OF BENEFITS SOUGHT

SCALE ITEM MY (SERVICE PROVIDER) WILL	SOCIAL BENEFITS (FACTOR LOADINGS)	SPECIAL TREATMENT BENEFITS (FACTOR LOADINGS)	CONFIDENCE BENEFITS (FACTOR LOADINGS)
Always recognize me the moment I contact them	0.80		
Would have a genuine relationship with me	0.89		
Are more likely to treat me as a personal friend	0.76		
Are more likely to make me feel important	0.67		
Will give me special deals and discounts that others don't get		0.80	
Will go out of their way to search for the best treatment for me		0.65	
Will pay more attention to my specific needs		0.75	
Will always search for the most reasonably priced solution		0.67	
Will more likely help me when something goes wrong		0.68	
Will more likely do what I want		0.79	
I will have more confidence the service will be performed correctly			0.69
I know what to expect when I go in			0.66
I will have less anxiety when I use the service			0.83
I believe there is less risk that something will go wrong			0.69
I feel I can trust my (*service provider*)			0.75
Total variance explained = 72.5%	7.5%	53.7%	11.3%
Coefficient Alpha (α):	0.87	0.81	0.91

Continued

TABLE 3.11 Benefits Sought from Service Providers *Continued*

PART B—MAINTAINING LOYALTY TO EACH OF THREE SERVICE PROVIDERS AS REPORTED BY RESPONDENTS CLASSIFIED INTO FOUR AGE GROUPS

HIGHER BEHAVIOR LOYALTY SCORES INDICATE *LESS* LOYALTY. HIGHER REPURCHASE INTENTION SCORES INDICATE *GREATER* LOYALTY.

	DENTAL		HAIRDRESSER		TRAVEL AGENT	
AGE GROUPS (YEARS)	BEHAVIOR LOYALTY	REPURCHASE INTENTION	BEHAVIOR LOYALTY	REPURCHASE INTENTION	BEHAVIOR LOYALTY	REPURCHASE INTENTION
18–24	1.94^{a} (0.9)	7.8^{a} (3.1)	2.41^{a} (1.6)	7.07^{a} (2.7)	1.26^{a} (1.2)	5.53^{a} (2.7)
25–34	1.45^{b} (1.2)	8.50^{b} (2.0)	2.89^{a} (1.8)	7.27^{ab} (3.0)	1.38^{a} (1.3)	6.57^{ab} (2.9)
35–54	1.03^{b} (1.1)	8.84^{b} (2.2)	1.21^{b} (1.2)	9.02^{c} (1.8)	1.04 (1.0)	7.72^{c} (2.4)
>55 years	0.91^{bc} (1.0)	9.42^{c} (1.3)	0.90^{b} (0.9)	8.57^{bc} (1.6)	0.91 (0.9)	7.69^{c} (2.0)
n		231		279		265
F	4.21	1.449	20.01	8.48	1.504	6.35
ANOVA sig.	0.007	0.230	0.000	0.000	0.214	0.000

Note: Means with different letters are significantly different from each other at $p \leq 0.05$. Standard deviations appear in parentheses.

Source: Paul G. Patterson, "Demographic Correlates of Loyalty in a Service Context," *Journal of Services Marketing*, 21 no. 2 (2007): 116, 118. Copyright © 2007, Emerald Group Publishing Limited.

to business practice, since *confidence benefits* emerged as a distinct factor, a dentist can enhance patients' confidence in her skills by, for example, post-visit contacts inquiring if patients experienced any problems following a dental procedure, and also sending them press clippings of her appearances at conferences or other media.

Another study investigated the motivations of people who donate money to intercollegiate athletic programs and identified four groups of benefits that these donors receive as a result of their monetary pledges (see Table 3.12).[24] Universities can use these findings in trying to persuade people to bestow money on their sports programs and create more persuasive messages targeting potential donors. A researcher specializing in tourism identified several groups of tourists—that is, benefit segments—who differed on what they look for when traveling to a national park. Sample survey statements used to identify each group and the characteristics of each segment are shown in Table 3.13.[25]

MEDIA BENEFITS As more and more forms of media emerge, marketers must study the benefits that consumers seek from adopting these communication tools in order to advertise in these media effectively. In one study, consumers singled out *immediacy*, *accessibility* and *free cost* as the most relevant features of digital newspapers, while identifying *writing style* and more *depth* and *details* as the key features of traditional newspapers. These findings indicate that publishers of traditional newspapers should position online and paper newspapers as complementing one another and that the two versions represent opportunities for somewhat different types of ads.[26] Another study found that, among car buyers, online information searches were perceived as substitutes for reading print ads and a way to reduce the amount of time spent on negotiating prices with car dealers.[27] Clearly, this means that car buyers who have consulted the Internet should be targeted differently than those who have not. Yet another study identified six types of benefits that users of mobile digital devices seek from these technologies (see Table 3.14 Part A) and five segments among these users (see Table 3.14 Part B).[28] The descriptions of the segments indicate which types of users are likely to be receptive to ads appearing on their mobile devices and the kind of users that will probably resent such messages.

Brand Loyalty and Relationship

Brand loyalty consists of two components: (1) *behavior*—the frequency and consistency of buying a given brand and (2) *attitude*—the consumer's feeling of commitment to the brand (see Chapter 7). The most common applications of brand loyalty are **frequency award programs**

TABLE 3.12 Benefits Received from Donating Money to Athletic Programs

	FACTOR 1	FACTOR 2	FACTOR 3	FACTOR 4
Factor 1: Belongingness				
Being associated with the school	0.930			
Identify with the university	0.774			
Being affiliated with the university	0.754			
Being loyal to the school	0.541			
Being part of a successful athletic program	0.430			
Keep up with the tradition	0.422			
Factor 2: Trusting				
Believing in the vision of the institution		−0.836		
Believing in the leadership of the university		−0.728		
Factor 3: Social-practical motivation				
Social contacts			0.838	
Professional contacts			0.746	
Meeting friends			0.558	
Priority seating in football games			0.416	
Tax deductions			0.380	
Factor 4: Prestige				
Increasing the prestige of the university through a quality athletic program				0.880
Supporting a high prestige institution				0.539
Eigenvalue	5.740	2.174	1.178	0.945
Variance (%)	33.108	9.711	9.765	3.660
Cumulative variance (%)	33.108	42.819	52.584	56.244
Cronbach's alpha	0.858	0.899	0.722	0.787
Number of items (total = 15)	6	2	5	2

Source: Rodoula Tsiotsou, "An Empirically Based Typology of Intercollegiate Athletic Donors: High and Low Motivation Scenarios," *Journal of Targeting, Measurement and Analysis for Marketing,* 15 no. 2 (2007): 84.

where marketers offer rewards and special benefits to buyers who purchase their offerings consistently (e.g., frequent flyer awards issued by airlines and points given by credit card companies). Many marketers apply their knowledge of the characteristics of their brand-loyal consumers in targeting other buyers with similar attributes. Other marketers target consumers who show no brand loyalty ("brand switchers") in the belief that they represent greater market potential than consumers who are brand loyal. A recent study demonstrated that when shopping and evaluating prices and discounts, *switchers* seek to obtain bargains and are also concerned about paying higher prices than usual for products. Thus, they are likely to respond to coupons and price cuts more readily than other segments.[29] Also, another key consumer segment—*consumer innovators*—often a prime target for new products—tend *not* to be brand loyal. (Chapter 14 discusses the characteristics of consumer innovators.)

Increasingly, marketers realize that their relationships with customers are complex and multidimensional. A recent study examined seven aspects of customers' relationships with a

TABLE 3.13 Benefits Visiting Tourists Seek in a National Park

SEGMENT	SAMPLE SURVEY STATEMENTS[a]	DESCRIPTION
Environmentalists	• Noise in hotels and camping sites should be reduced. • Humans must live in harmony with nature in order to survive. • There's a need for more aggressive enforcements of the park's rules. • Tourists to the park are severely abusing the environment.	Interested in an unpolluted, unspoiled natural environment and in conservation. Not interested in socializing, entertainment, or sports. Desire authenticity and less man-made structures and vehicles in the park.
Want-it-all Tourists	• The park should have more special areas for bird watching. • The park should initiate more tourism projects, which benefit the local people. • There's a need for better-equipped tourists centers at the park. • Humans have the right to modify the natural environment to suit their needs.	Value socializing and entertainment more than conservation. Interested in more activities and opportunities for meeting other tourists. Do not mind the "urbanization" of some park sections.
Independent Tourists	• The park should have more short walking trails. • Safaris should encompass interacting with the local people. • There is a need for more and better sign posting. • Need better access roads.	Looking for calm and unpolluted environment, exploring the park by themselves and staying at a comfortable place to relax. Influenced by word of mouth in choosing travel destinations.

[a]Travelers in this segment had higher levels of agreement with these statements than members of the other two segments.

Source: Wanjohi Kibicho, "Tourists to Amboseli National Park: A Factor-Cluster Segmentation Analysis," *Journal of Vacation Management,* 12 no. 3 (2006): 218–231. Copyright © 2006, SAGE Publications.

marketer; Part A of Table 3.15 depicts the survey statements used to measure each dimension. Then, the study distinguished between *active* customers who were *more relational* and with greater trust and commitment to the marketers, and *passive* customers who are *less relational*; Part B of Table 3.15 shows the differences between the two segments.[30] Another study investigated the factors that consumers of two national retail chains sought from their relationships with the retailers. The research discovered that customers seek both *personal connections* (e.g., emotion, sense of loyalty) and *functional features* (e.g., a wide variety of products, carrying the product the customer seeks). Customers who had solid personal *and* functional ties to the store were more likely to remain loyal and recommend the store to others.[31] Yet another study explored the relational benefits that banking customers seek from financial firms. The result indicated that there are three types of sought benefits: (1) *special treatment* (e.g., priority treatment in queues and faster service, better interest rates), (2) *confidence benefits* (e.g., clear and reasonable services, work done well and correctly), and (3) *social benefits* (e.g., the staff and employees knowing the customer by name).[32]

Implementing Segmentation Strategies

LEARNING OBJECTIVE

3·4 *To Understand How Segmentation and Strategic Targeting Are Carried Out.*

This section describes the implementation of segmentation frameworks and the strategic targeting of selected segment. Due to the rapidly increasing sophistication of data-collection and analysis technologies, including data mined from Web surfing, *behavioral targeting,* and *microtargeting* have become popular terms for describing narrower and more precise applications of market segmentation. Also, firms using market segmentation can pursue a *concentrated* marketing strategy or a *differentiated* marketing strategy. In certain instances, they might use a *countersegmentation* strategy.

TABLE 3.14 Benefit Segments of Users of Mobile Digital Devices

PART A—SIX TYPES OF BENEFITS SOUGHT FROM MOBILE DIGITAL DEVICES

M-SERVICES FACTOR*	1	2	3	4	5	6
Locator services						
Use location/map/directions services	0.686					
Use personal locator service (in case missing or injured)	0.529					
Receive weather reports	0.528					
Receive and read news	0.477					
Communication services						
Send/receive pictures		–0.670				
Send/receive SMS		–0.581				
Receive calendar/reminder services		–0.483				
Send/receive MMS		–0.374				
Sports/entertainment services						
Receive sports information			0.535			
Access adult entertainment			0.525			
Place bets online			0.449			
Play online games			0.422			
Mobile online "chat" services						
Chat online with strangers				0.656		
Send/receive e-mail				0.437		
Search for and compare prices of products while shopping				0.404		
Listen to/download music				0.312		
Value-added shopping services						
Receive shopping coupons					–0.750	
Receive personalized shopping alerts (of bargains etc.)					–0.715	
Search for/receive product information while shopping					–0.536	
Book cinema/theatre tickets					–0.462	
Use routine banking (pay bills etc.)					–0.370	
Financial services						
Use advanced banking services (e.g., apply for loans)						0.769
Send insurance damage reports						0.699
Take part in online auctions						0.628
Trade stock						0.626
Buy products online						0.519
Book travel tickets						0.427
Make micro-payments in shops or elsewhere						0.398
Remote activation of appliances						0.390
Access and use transaction services						0.389
Use online currency conversion service						0.360

*Negative item loadings result from oblique rotation method.
SMS, short message services; MMS, multimedia messaging service

PART B—FIVE SEGMENTS OF MOBILE DIGITAL DEVICES USERS

INNOVATORS	TECHNO-CONFIDENTS	SHOPPING LOVERS	BELONGING SEEKERS	CONSULTERS
Likely to use all six benefits. Strong need for information for financial services, communication services, and "chat" features.	Confident in ability to use the devices. Likely to use the locator/information features more than the shopping and financial features.	Have an emotional bond with shopping and are likely to use all of the benefits the devices provide except the sports/entertainment features.	Buy products and brands used by others. Seek approval from others and likely to use all six benefits of the devices as others adopt them.	Likely to use communication features such as pictures and text messages to consult with others. Unlikely to use shopping services.

Source: Gillian Sullivan Mort and Judy Drennan, "Marketing M-services: Establishing a Usage Benefit Typology Related to Mobile User Characteristics," *Database Marketing & Customer Strategy Management,* 12 no. 4 (2005): 327–341. Part A is directly from page 334.

TABLE 3.15 Customer Relationships as a Segmentation Base

PART A—SURVEY STATEMENTS USED TO STUDY THE DIMENSIONS OF THE RELATIONSHIP:

CONSTRUCT		MEASUREMENT ITEM	TYPE OF SCALE[a]
Endogenous constructs			
Overall satisfaction	A1	How satisfied are you with the company?	SD
	A2	How would you rate the company compared to X?	Cm
	A3	How would you rate the company compared to Y?	Cm
Trust	B1	The photo processing always meets my expectations	Lkt
	B2	The company always provides good products/services	Lkt
	B3	I can always rely on the company to deliver what it promises	Lkt
	B4	I have great confidence in the company	Lkt
	B5	The company rewards its loyal customers	Lkt
Commitment	C1	I am proud to be a customer of the company	Lkt
	C2	The staff are committed to me as customer	Lkt
	C3	I feel I want to be a customer of the company	Lkt
	C4	I have been a customer for many years	Lkt
	C5	I talk positively about company and recommend it	Lkt
Future intentions	D1	I plan to use the processing service in the future	Lkt
	D2	It should be negative if the relationship couldn't last	Lkt
	D3	I will continue to be a loyal customer	Lkt
	D4	I will continue if I get good products and services	Lkt
Exogenous constructs			
Brand satisfaction	E1	How would you rate your overall satisfaction with the film processing of the company?	SD
	E2	The quality of processing is high	Lkt
	E3	Photo deliveries are reliable	Lkt
Brand familiarity	F1	I enjoy my personal contact with the company	Lkt
	F2	Special price offers are essential in my choosing the company	Lkt
Brand attitudes	G1	In general, how satisfied are you with the offerings?	SD
	G2	The company does high quality photo processing	Lkt
	G3	I like the design of the photo bags	Lkt
	G4	The company has a useful picture guarantee	Lkt
	G5	The company provides fast and reliable deliveries	Lkt

[a]SD = Semantic Differential Scale; Cm = Comparative scale; Lkt = Likert Scale.

PART B—THE DIFFERENCES BETWEEN TWO RELATIONAL SEGMENTS

CONSTRUCTS WITH INDICATORS (MEASUREMENT ITEMS)	ACTIVE CONSUMERS MORE RELATIONAL	PASSIVE CONSUMERS LESS RELATIONAL
Overall satisfaction Overall satisfaction	Significantly more sastisfied with the company.	Significantly less sastisfied with the company.
Trust Always meet expectations Provide good offerings Reliable and safe High confidence Rewarding loyal customers	Believe the company is reliable and safe and always meets expectations. No different than passive regarding company rewarding loyal customers.	Significantly lower trust than active patrons in terms of reliability and the company meeting expectations.
Commitment Proud of being customer Engage in me as customer Feel I want to be a customer Been a customer many years Speak for the company	More proud of being the company's customer, wanting to be such, being a long-term patron and more likely to speak for the company.	Significantly lower than active customers on being proud of and wanting to be the company's customer. Unlikely to speak for the company.

TABLE 3.15 Customer Relationships as a Segmentation Base *Continued*

CONSTRUCTS WITH INDICATORS (MEASUREMENT ITEMS)	ACTIVE CONSUMERS MORE RELATIONAL	PASSIVE CONSUMERS LESS RELATIONAL
Future intentions Processing in the future Negative couldn't go on Continue as loyal customer	Highly likely to continue being the company's loyal customer.	View possible termination of relationship with the company as significantly less negative than active patrons.
Brand satisfaction Satisfaction with the film processing High quality of processing The photo deliveries are safe	Very satisfied with all aspects of the service they receive from the company.	Significantly less satisfied than active customers on all aspects of the service received.
Brand familiarity Like personal contacts Special price offers are essential	No significant differences between active and passive patrons on these dimensions.	
Brand attitudes Satisfaction with offerings A high valued photo processing Like design of photo bags Valuable picture guarantee Fast and reliable deliveries Continue if good offerings	Significantly more satisfied and believe the company guarantees fast and reliable delivery of the service.	Less satisfied than active patrons and do not view the company as highly as active patrons regarding all the items that comprise this factor.

Source: Based on Bertil Hulten, "Customer Segmentation: The Concepts of Trust, Commitment and Relationship," *Journal of Targeting, Measurement and Analysis for Marketing*, 15 no. 4 (2007): 262, 267.

BEHAVIORAL TARGETING

The methods termed **microtargeting** and **behavioral targeting** are capable of providing the kind of specificity that enables marketers to deliver *personalized advertising messages* to buyers. Generally, marketers use the term *behavioral targeting* to describe segmentation based on usage behavior. The more innovative use of behavioral targeting is sending ads to people depending on which Web sites they have visited. Major Web entities, such as Google and AOL, monitor the sites Web surfers visit and the patterns of these visits (e.g., length of visit, the sections a surfer reaches within a site, and click-through searches of other destinations) and then charge advertisers for placing personalized messages, based on individuals' interests as inferred from their Web surfing, on their sites and other Web destinations; these destinations are part of networks established by Google, AOL, or other large Web entities. In addition, advertisers are beginning to combine Web surfing data with geographic and demographic information.[33] Another form of behavioral targeting is Web portals issuing customers who use certain Web services coupons for various discounts.[34] Coupons based on people's online surfing habits are more linked to consumers' specific needs and more likely to be redeemed than mass issues of paper coupons distributed via newspapers or mailings. Recently, regulators have become concerned about marketers' increased use of behavioral targeting.[35]

MICROTARGETING

Long ago, marketers recognized that, even with elaborate segmentation plans, they were still reaching a lot of consumers who were neither interested in nor ever likely to purchase the products advertised. For instance, an expensive car commercial on TV may reach a large and diverse audience where up to 95 percent of the viewers are not looking to purchase a car. Early on, marketers have attempted to reach more defined *niches* within the consumer population targeted, and they supplemented demographics with psychographics. Then, they combined the two factors into elaborate hybrid models, such as *VALS*. Later on, marketers developed *geodemographic* designs aimed at reaching increasingly smaller and more precise groups of potential customers. Now, with the advancement in data collection technologies and the expansion of analytical tools capable of effectively cross-analyzing large sets of data originating from different sources, *microtargeting* is becoming viable and effective.

Microtargeting is aggregating individual consumers into relatively small groups, based on data available about them from many different databases, and targeting them with tailor-made messages. The individualized messages are transmitted via **narrowcasting**—the opposite of *broadcasting*—consisting of using e-mail, mobile devices, and even door-to-door presentations on small screens to deliver *personalized messages* to individuals. Microtargeting stands out in several ways: (1) the very large number and diverse origins of the sources used to classify people; (2) the cross-tabulation of large amounts of very detailed behavioral data consisting of very specific information on purchases, down to a narrow product category or even a particular brand purchased; (3) many providers of microtargeting claim to have developed "formulas" (or *propriety algorithms*) that assign consumers into groups in a way that enables predicting the impact of the messages sent; and (4) some models include peoples' online surfing patterns and purchases.

The data sources of microtargeting include virtually any piece of information available about people: voting records, residence and address change information, neighborhoods' demographics, tax records, political contributions, telephone records, media exposure, motor vehicle registrations, real estate records, credit card records, catalogs received, surveys and warrantee cards filled out by consumers, and online purchases and site visits (the means of collecting some of these data and the ethics involved are discussed in Chapter 16).

The major company providing customized profiles derived from cross-tabulating data from scores of sources is called Acxiom. Upon request, this firm can provide, for example, a list of Hispanic consumers who own two pets, have caller ID, drive a sedan, buy certain personal care products, subscribe to certain TV cable channels, read specified magazines, and whose income and education are within a given range. More detailed reports can even include the types of shoes the targeted buyers wear and whether or not they have bought sun tan lotions within the past six months. Acxiom's Personicx® *Life Stage Segmentation System* consists of 70 segments that are classified into 21 life stage groups (see Table 3.16). These segments can be integrated with a company's own data (mostly behavioral and transactional information about individual buyers) to classify current and potential consumers into subsets whose purchase behavior can be predicted and measured.[36] Acxiom also sells marketers descriptive clusters of specific target markets, such as Hispanics (see Figure 3.6).[37]

The practice now termed *microtargeting* originated in the 2004 presidential elections. After a very narrow and contested victory in 2000, the Republicans realized that Democrats watched more TV than Republicans, and that by running political ads on TV they were reaching many people who were unlikely to vote Republican. This discovery led to more focused and detailed research on the media habits, buying behavior, and opinions and values of voters, especially those residing in "swing states," which resulted in categorizing these audiences into smaller and smaller groups. Then, campaign workers armed with small digital screens would knock on doors of, for example, low-income, minority voters concerned with losing their jobs and show each voter a short video explaining how a given candidate was going to approach the problem. Using the same communication technique, voters with other concerns, such as gun control, were shown different messages corresponding to their particular concerns. This approach also enabled transmitting messages about issues that were too polarizing, controversial, and sometimes too explicit to be shown on commercial TV (e.g., abortion, the death penalty, stem cell research). The Democrats also quickly adopted tailoring messages to specific audiences; for example, a campaign commercial in one city showed workers talking about their jobs, while a political ad shown in a different city depicted a celebrity who suffers from Parkinson's disease and advocated embryonic stem cell research.[38] The popularity of microtargeting increased during the 2008 presidential campaign when foods and brands were studied as possible predictors of voting behavior. For example, studies showed that Republicans drank more

TABLE 3.16 Sample Acxiom Personicx Clusters

SHOOTING STARS

Still relatively young at a mean age of 36, and with top rankings for income, college education, home value and net worth, these consumers have the world by the tail. Feeling financially secure with large Investment portfolios, Shooting Stars spend their disposable Income making life a comfortable one, focusing on health, exercise, gourmet food, golf and travel.

TOTS & TOYS

Two things—work and family—consume these professional working couples. They're putting their college degrees into action, climbing the corporate ladder for lucrative careers, while saving for their children's education through do-it-yourself home improvements and trips to the zoo for entertainment. With time at a premium, it's not surprising that the radio is the most relied-upon source for news and entertainment.

MID AMERICANA

Still trying to win the lottery (and ready to quit their jobs once they do) this suburban, middle-income cluster would really rather make time for their favorite television shows than do housework. Often supporting extended families, they are wise investors who remain active in local government and religious clubs.

CORPORATE CLOUT

Firmly tied to American corporate culture, this exceedingly well-educated group defines themselves as "workaholics," perhaps because they were growing up when Jimi Hendrix died and women started wearing business suits. Savvy investors who like to read *Forbes* and travel magazines; they are also heavy users of air travel cards right along with their corporate credit cards.

SUMMIT ESTATES

In every sense, these families are enjoying the good life—luxury travel, entertainment and consumption of every kind are within close and easy reach. Serious and savvy about investing their wealth, they are not shy about leveraging their large disposable incomes for luxury cars, gourmet food and wine, expensive sports outings, and international travel.

Source: Acxiom, *Life Stage Segmentation System, Personicx*, 2007, 7. Used with permission of Acxiom Corporation and The Gadberry Group.

bourbon, subscribers to gourmet cooking magazines tended to vote Democratic, and even that specific cereal brands reflected political views: supporters of Barack Obama preferred *Bear Naked* cereal, Hillary Clinton's voters liked *GoLean* and John McCain's fans preferred *Fiber One*.[39] With the ongoing emergence of new media and marketers' increasing ability to deliver customized messages, behavioral and microtargeting will become mainstream strategies.

FIGURE 3.6
Sample Hispanic Clusters and Households

Source: Used with permission of Acxiom Corporation and The Gadberry Group.

CORPORATE LADDER	TOTS & TRADITION	INVESTING IN FUTURES
Average Age–38	Average Age–40	Average Age–37
Single	Single	Single
No Kids	Toddlers/School–Age Kids	School–Age Kids
Homeowner	Renter	Homeowner
Length of Residence–4 Years	Length of Residence–3 Years	Length of Residence–5 Years
Upper Income of $75,000–$99,999	Middle Income of $40,000–$49,999	Low–Middle Income of $20,000–$29,999
Medium Net Worth	Low Net Worth	Medium–High Net Worth
Live in Outer Suburbs and Towns	Live in Cities & Surrounds	Live in Outer Suburbs & Towns
Very Assimilated	Low Assimilation	Medium Assimilation
Speak mostly English at home	Speak mostly Spanish at home	Speak English & Spanish at home

CONCENTRATED VERSUS DIFFERENTIATED MARKETING

Once an organization has identified its most promising market segments, it must decide which ones to target and how to do so. Sometimes, each targeted segment receives a specially designed marketing mix (i.e., a specially tailored product, price, distribution network, and/or promotional campaign). Targeting several segments using individual marketing mixes is called **differentiated marketing**. At other times, a company may choose to target just one segment with a unique marketing mix, and this strategy is called **concentrated marketing**.

Differentiated marketing is a highly appropriate segmentation strategy for financially strong companies that are well established in a product category and competitive with other firms that also are strong in that category (e.g., soft drinks, automobiles, or detergents). However, if a company is small or new to the field, concentrated marketing is probably a better bet. Concentrated marketing is also appropriate for the final stage of the *product life cycle* when the product is being purchased by increasingly smaller numbers of consumers and is being phased out.

COUNTERSEGMENTATION

Periodically, companies must reconsider the extent to which they segment their markets because, over time, some segments may have contracted and no longer warrant individually designed marketing programs. In such cases, research aimed at discovering a more generic need or consumer characteristic applicable to the members of two or more segments should be undertaken. If a more generic need or characteristic is identified, two or more segments can be combined and targeted with a redesigned marketing mix. This is called a **countersegmentation** strategy. For example, some business schools with wide course offerings in each department were forced to adopt a countersegmentation strategy when they discovered that students simply did not have enough available credits to take all or even most of the electives offered in their majors. As a result, courses had to be canceled each semester because of inadequate registration. A countersegmentation strategy effectively solved the problem by, for example, combining *advertising, publicity, sales promotion*, and *personal selling* courses into a single course called promotion.

SUMMARY

Market segmentation is the opposite of mass marketing and is part of the segmentation, targeting, and positioning framework. Segmentation is defined as the process of dividing a potential market into distinct subsets of consumers with a common need or characteristic and selecting one or more segments to target with a specially designed marketing mix. Besides aiding in the development of new products, segmentation studies assist in the redesign and repositioning of existing products, in the creation of promotional appeals, and the selection of advertising media.

In order to be a viable target market, a segment must be identifiable (by some criteria such as demographics, lifestyles, or others), sizeable (i.e., large enough to be profitable), stable or growing, accessible (i.e., can be reached economically), and congruent with the marketer's objectives and resources.

Consumer-rooted behaviors and cognitions as well as consumption-specific facts and attitudes can be used to segment consumers. The most common categories used in segmentation are demographics and psychographics (or lifestyles). However, in most cases, hybrid segmentations are used. The primary examples of hybrid frameworks are VALS™ and the PRIZM™ geodemographic clusters. Other consumer-rooted variables used to segment markets are personality traits and sociocultural values and beliefs. The key consumption-specific segmentation factors are usage behavior (including usage rate and situation), benefit segmentation, and brand loyalty and relationship.

Behavioral targeting and microtargeting are emerging techniques rooted in marketers' abilities to identify and target increasingly smaller segments and even individual buyers with tailor-made messages (i.e., narrowcasting). In conventional segmentation, a company can choose to target several segments (differentiated marketing) or just one segment (concentrated marketing). In certain instances, a company must use countersegmentation and combine two or more segments into a single large segment.

DISCUSSION QUESTIONS

1. What is market segmentation? How is the practice of market segmentation related to the marketing concept?
2. How are market segmentation, targeting, and positioning interrelated? Illustrate how these three concepts can be used to develop a marketing strategy for a product of your choice.
3. Apply the five criteria for effective targeting to marketing a product of your choice to college students.
4. Discuss the advantages and disadvantages of using demographics as a basis for segmentation. Can demographics and psychographics be used together to segment markets? Illustrate your answer with a specific example.
5. Many marketers have found that a relatively small group of heavy users accounts for a disproportionately large amount of the total products consumed. What are the advantages and disadvantages of targeting these heavy users?
6. Under which circumstances and for what types of products should a marketer segment the market on the basis of (a) awareness status, (b) brand loyalty, and (c) usage situation?
7. Some marketers consider benefit segmentation as the segmentation approach most consistent with the marketing concept. Do you agree or disagree with this view? Why?
8. Regent Seven Seas Cruises and Royal Caribbean International are two companies in the vacation and travel industry. After looking at their Web sites, describe the kind of consumers that each company is seeking to attract. Also, describe how either company can use demographics and psychographics to identify TV shows and magazines in which to place its advertisements.
9. How can a marketer for a chain of health clubs use the VALS™ segmentation profiles to develop an advertising campaign? Which segments should be targeted? How should the health club be positioned to each of these segments?
10. For each of the following products, identify the segmentation base that you consider best for targeting consumers: (a) coffee, (b) soups, (c) cell phones, and (d) designer sunglasses. Explain your choices.

EXERCISES

1. Select a product and brand that you use frequently and list the benefits you receive from using it. Without disclosing your list, ask a fellow student who uses a different brand in this product category (preferably a friend of the opposite sex) to make a similar list for his or her brand. Compare the two lists and identify the implications for using benefit segmentation to market the two brands.
2. Does your lifestyle differ significantly from your parents' lifestyle? If so, how are the two lifestyles different? What factors cause these differences?
3. Visit two Web sites that you are familiar with and write down every click that you make and the patterns and time periods corresponding to your surfing. Then, describe how a marketer—of a product of your choice—who had tracked your Web visits to the sites—can used the observation of your surfing in designing a customized advertising message directed at you.
4. The owners of a local health-food restaurant have asked you to prepare a psychographic profile of families living in the community surrounding the restaurant's location. Construct a 10-question psychographic inventory appropriate for segmenting families on the basis of their dining-out preferences.
5. Find two print advertisements. One ad should be directed at one of the PRIZM clusters (Table 3.4) and the other at one of the Acxiom groups (Table 3.16). How effective do you think each ad is in terms of achieving its objective? Why?

KEY TERMS

- activities, interests, and opinions (AIOS) *76*
- behavioral targeting *97*
- benefit segmentation *88*
- brand loyalty and relationship *88*
- concentrated marketing *100*
- consumer-rooted segmentation bases *76*
- consumption-specific segmentation bases *88*
- countersegmentation *100*
- demographics *76*
- differentiated marketing *100*
- family life cycle *80*
- frequency award programs *92*
- geodemographics *80*
- hybrid segmentation *75*
- market segmentation *72*
- marketplace decision difficulty (MPDD) *78*
- mass marketing *70*
- microtargeting *97*
- narrowcasting *98*
- personality traits *76*
- positioning *72*
- psychographics *76*
- social class *76*
- sociocultural values and beliefs *87*
- targeting *72*
- usage rate *88*
- usage situation *88*
- VALS *84*

Case One: Matching Geodemographic Segments and Magazines' Audiences

The key demographics of the audiences of several popular magazines are listed in Table 3.1. The descriptions of several PRIZM NE geodemographic segments are listed in Table 3.4, and more descriptions can be looked up by zip code at **www.claritas.com/MyBestSegments/Default.jsp**.

Look up the zip code where you live and two other zip codes where some of your friends or family members live. Within each zip code, look up two segments that differ in terms of household incomes and lifestyles. By now, you should have selected a total of six segments.

QUESTIONS

1. For each of the segments selected, from Table 3.1, choose two or three magazines that, in your view, members of the segment are likely to read (many of PRIZM's segments' descriptions include titles of publications read by members of those segments). Explain the rationale supporting all the matches you have made.

2. The information in Table 3.1 was generated by a company named MRI+ located at: **www.mriplus.com/site/index.aspx**. You can easily register at that site and look up the audience profiles of many magazines. Select up to five magazines that you did not discuss in question 1, generate audience profiles for these magazines from MRI+ and also look at the magazines', Web sites. Now, go back to the geodemographic site and, for each magazine selected, find one geodemographic segment whose members are likely to read that publication. Explain your choices.

Case Two: Benefit Segmentation in the Oral Care Market

As discussed in the chapter, the benefits that consumers seek from products and services are the essence of *benefit segmentation* and many believe also the core of *all* segmentation strategies. Also, benefit segmentation is often used to develop a *positioning* approach for a given product. For many consumer products, such as tootpaste, finding unfulfilled benefits or creating products that satisfy several benefits is the key to gaining market share.

The two major competitors in the oral care market are Crest and Colgate, and both offer complete lines of oral care products. This assignment focuses on the many versions of toothpaste each brand offers. Visit the Web sites for Crest and Colgate. For each brand, select five product versions that offer mostly dissimilar benefits (there will be some overlaps in the benefits offered by the diverse product versions).

QUESTIONS

1. For each version of each brand that you had selected, make a list of the benefits that the product delivers. Compare the two lists and rank, as you see it, the benefits in your list from "most important" to "least important." Now, select the brand and version that most closely matches your rankings and explain your choice. If you are not presently using the product you chose, would you replace the toothpaste you are using now with this product? Why or why not?
2. Select another oral care (e.g., toothbrush) product where there are at least two major brands and each one is offering multiple versions of the same product. Repeat the analysis you performed in question 1 for the two brands.

4

Consumer Motivation

HUMAN NEEDS—consumer needs—are the basis of all modern marketing. Needs are the essence of the marketing concept. The key to a company's survival, profitability, and growth in a highly competitive marketplace is its ability to identify and satisfy unfulfilled consumer needs better and sooner than the competition.

The philosophy and marketing strategy of Charles Revson, the builder of the Revlon cosmetics empire, depict an insightful understanding of consumer needs. Charles Revson started by manufacturing nail polish, but he defined nail polish as a fashion accessory and not merely a nail covering. His strategy was designed to induce women to use different shades of nail polish to match different outfits, moods, and occasions. This approach vastly broadened the market for the product, because it persuaded women to buy and use many different colors of nail polish in the same season rather than wait to finish one bottle before buying another one. And Revson ensured that women would buy more and more bottles of nail polish by introducing new nail color fashions every season. Emulating GM's strategy of planned obsolescence (i.e., introducing new automobile models every year), Revlon would introduce new nail colors every fall and spring and, through heavy and effective advertising, would persuade women that buying the new colors would satisfy their needs to appear fashionable and attractive.[1]

Most importantly, Revson understood that he was not selling women the physical product (e.g., nail lacquer to cover their nails) but the fantasy that the nail polish would attract attention and bestow class and glamour on the user. Thus, Revson did not sell deep red polish; he sold *Fire and Ice.* He did not sell dark red polish; he sold *Berry Bon Bon.* Charles Revson summed up his philosophy by saying "In the factory, we make cosmetics; in the store, we sell hope." And selling hope, rather than the physical product known as cosmetics, allowed Revson to charge much more for his products. Rather than compete with other manufacturers on the basis of price, Revson competed on the basis of perceived quality and greater satisfaction of women's needs for fantasy and attention.[2] Similarly, although the ad featured in Figure 4.1 is for a home, it does not appeal to one's need for a home or a place where one lives and seeks physical shelter. Instead, it presents the

FIGURE 4.1

QUESTION: *To Which Consumer Needs Does This Ad Appeal?*

luxury condominium advertised as a possession that satisfies a buyer's psychological needs for self-esteem, success, and personal satisfaction.

Marketers do not create needs, although in many instances they strive to make consumers more keenly aware of unfelt or dormant needs. Savvy companies define their business in terms of the consumer needs they satisfy rather than the products they produce and sell. Because consumers' basic needs do not change but the products that satisfy them do, a corporate focus on developing products that will satisfy consumers' needs ensures that the company stays in the forefront of the search for new and effective solutions. By doing so, such companies are likely to survive and grow despite strong competition or adverse economic conditions. On the other hand, companies that define themselves in terms of the products they make may suffer or even go out of business when their products are replaced by competitive offerings that better satisfy the same need.

For example, Procter and Gamble defines its business as "providing branded products and services of quality and value that improve the lives of the world's consumers"—a need-focused definition—rather than stating that the company sells products such as detergents, shampoos, diapers, household cleaners, and dozens of other items (i.e., a product-oriented approach). Similarly, Logitech states that it is focused on innovation and quality and designs "personal peripherals to help people enjoy a better experience with the digital world" rather than stating that the company makes and sells mice, pointers, keyboards, and webcams. Likewise, rather than emphasizing the company's spacious and luxurious hotel rooms and facilities (i.e., a product-oriented definition), the credo of The Ritz Carlton defines the firm's business from the customer's perspective as "the genuine care and comfort of guests," and providing customers an experience that "enlivens the senses, instills well-being, and fulfills even the unexpressed needs and wishes" of guests.[3]

This chapter discusses human needs that motivate behavior and explores the influence that such needs have on consumption behavior.

Learning Objectives

4.1 *To Understand the Types of Human Needs and Motives and the Meaning of Goals.*

4.2 *To Understand the Dynamics of Motivation, Arousal of Needs, Setting of Goals, and Interrelationship Between Needs and Goals.*

4.3 *To Learn About Several Systems of Needs Developed by Researchers.*

4.4 *To Understand How Human Motives Are Studied and Measured.*

Motivation as a Psychological Force

Learning Objective

4.1 *To Understand the Types of Human Needs and Motives and the Meaning of Goals.*

Motivation is the *driving force within individuals that impels them to action.* This driving force is produced by a state of tension, which exists as the result of an unfulfilled need. Individuals strive both consciously and subconsciously to reduce this tension through selecting goals and subsequent behavior that they anticipate will fulfill their needs and thus relieve them of the tension they feel. Whether gratification is actually achieved depends on the course of action pursued. The specific goals that consumers wish to achieve and the courses of action they take to attain these goals are selected on the basis of their personality characteristics (discussed in Chapter 5), perceptions (discussed in Chapter 6), previous learning and experiences (discussed in Chapter 7) and attitudes (discussed in Chapter 8). Figure 4.2 presents a model of the motivational process.

NEEDS

Every individual has needs: Some are innate, others are acquired. **Innate needs** are physiological (i.e., *biogenic*); they include the needs for food, water, air, clothing, shelter, and sex. Because they are needed to sustain biological life, the biogenic needs are considered **primary needs** or motives.

Acquired needs are needs that we learn in response to our culture or environment. These may include needs for self-esteem, prestige, affection, power, and learning. Because acquired needs are generally psychological (i.e., *psychogenic*), they are considered **secondary needs** or

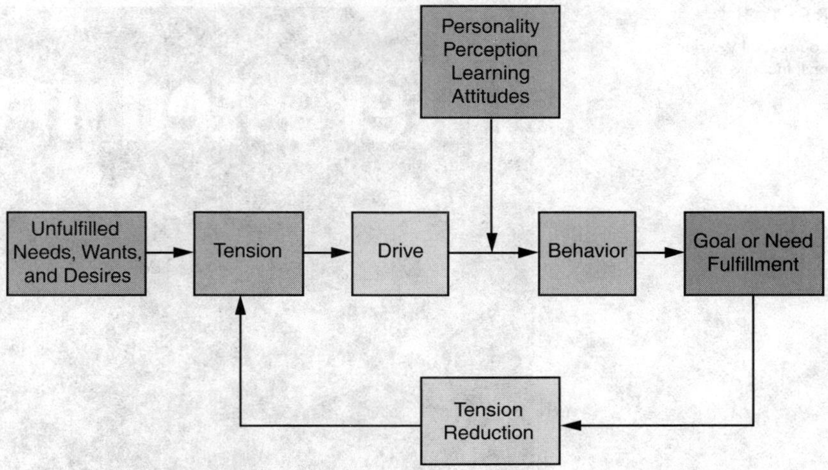

FIGURE 4.2
Model of the Motivation Process

Source: From "Observations: Translating Values into Product Wants," by Jeffrey F. Durgee et al. in *Journal of Advertising Research, 36,* 6 (November 1996). Reprinted by permission from the *Journal of Advertising Research,* © copyright 1996 by the Advertising Research Foundation.

motives. They result from the individual's subjective psychological state and from relationships with others. For example, all individuals need shelter from the elements; thus, finding a place to live fulfills an important primary need for a young, upwardly mobile couple. However, the kind of home they rent or buy may be the result of secondary needs. The couple may seek a place in which they can entertain large groups of people (and fulfill social needs); they may want to live in an exclusive community to impress their friends and family (and fulfill ego needs). Thus, the place where individuals ultimately choose to live fulfills both primary and secondary needs.

Motives or needs can have a *positive* or *negative* direction. We may feel a driving force *toward* some object or condition or a driving force *away* from some object or condition. For example, a person may be impelled to start exercising in order to avoid health problems (i.e., a negative outcome) or in order to look more attractive and dynamic (i.e., a positive outcome).

Some psychologists refer to positive drives as needs, wants, or desires and to negative drives as fears or aversions. However, although positive and negative motivational forces seem to differ dramatically in terms of physical (and sometimes emotional) activity, they are basically similar in that both serve to initiate and sustain human behavior. For this reason, researchers often refer to both kinds of drives or motives as *needs, wants*, and *desires.* Some theorists distinguish *wants* from *needs* by defining wants as product-specific needs. Others differentiate between desires, on the one hand, and needs and wants on the other. Thus, there is no uniformly accepted distinction among the terms *needs*, *wants*, and *desires*.

GOALS

Goals are the sought-after results of motivated behavior. As Figure 4.2 indicated, all behavior is goal oriented. Our discussion of motivation in this chapter is in part concerned with **generic goals**, that is, the general classes or categories of goals that consumers see as a means to fulfill their needs. If a student tells his parents that he wants to become an entrepreneur, he has stated a generic goal. If he says he wants to get an MBA degree from the Harvard Business School, he has expressed a **product-specific goal**. Marketers are particularly concerned with product-specific goals, that is, the specifically branded products and services that consumers select for goal fulfillment. Figure 4.3 depicts an ad that portrays subscribing to a health magazine as a means to achieve several physical appearance-related goals.

Individuals set goals on the basis of their personal values, and they select means (or behaviors) that they believe will help them achieve their desired goals. For example, blogs are personal journals posted online that generally encourage comments from others. Many people start their own blogs or regularly post comments on the blogs of others. Part A of Table 4.1 depicts the motivations behind blogging. Part B depicts how marketers can use their acquired understanding of the needs and goals of bloggers in targeting them. Bloggers are an important market segment because they are likely to post their consumption experiences online and create positive exposure for the brands they like.

FIGURE 4.3

Source: Courtesy of Weider Publications, Inc.

QUESTION: *How Does This Ad Appeal to One's Goals?*

The Selection of Goals

For any given need, there are many different and appropriate goals. The goals selected by individuals depend on their personal experiences, physical capacity, prevailing cultural norms and values, and the goal's accessibility in the physical and social environment. For example, a young woman may wish to get a deep, even tan and may envision spending time in the sun as a way to achieve her goal. However, if her dermatologist advises her to avoid direct exposure to the sun, she may settle for a self-tanning cosmetic product instead. The goal object has to be both socially acceptable and physically accessible. If cosmetic companies did not offer effective alternatives to tanning in the sun, our young woman would have to either ignore the advice of her dermatologist or select a substitute goal, such as untanned (but undamaged) youthful-looking skin.

Like needs, goals can be positive or negative. A positive goal is one toward which behavior is directed; thus, it is often referred to as an **approach object**. A negative goal is one from which behavior is directed away and is referred to as an **avoidance object**. Because both approach and avoidance goals are the results of motivated behavior, most researchers refer to

TABLE 4.1 Bloggers' Motivations and Corresponding Marketing Opportunities

PART A: A SCALE USED TO STUDY THE MOTIVATIONS BEHIND BLOGGING SUBJECTS RESPONDED ON A 7-POINT LIKERT SCALE RANGING FROM "STRONGLY AGREE" TO "STRONGLY DISAGREE."

CONSTRUCT	ITEMS
Blogging for self-expressing	I use my blog to free my mind when I am moody. I express myself by writing in my blog. My blog is the place where I express what I feel.
Blogging for life documenting	I use my blog as my diary to document my life. By writing text and posting video/audio files, I keep a record of my life.
Blogging for commenting	I'm willing to comment on what other bloggers say. I'd like to respond to other blogs that I read (no matter if I know of the blogger or not). I'd like to receive people's comments on what I post on my blog.
Blogging for forum participating	Blogging helps me to make more like-minded friends. In my blogroll I have friends with whom I can share things. By blogging I interact with a set of blogs that have contents similar to what I put in my blog.
Blogging for information seeking	Blogging helps me extract information behind events that interest me. Blogging helps me explore more information about products and/or services. To me it is convenient to search for information by blogging.
Interaction by blogging	I'm used to setting up my blog for easy response to visitors' comments. I'm used to sharing what I think and feel on my blog. I'm used to discussing things that interest me by blogging.
Information search by blogging	I'm used to looking for information by exploring blogs in my blogroll. I'm used to looking for information by blog search engines such as Technorati and Google Blog Search. I'm used to looking for information by looking at classified articles in blogs that I visit. I'm used to looking for information by looking at blog articles that are frequently quoted.

PART B: MARKETING PRODUCTS BY APPEALING TO VARIOUS BLOGGING MOTIVATIONS

BLOGGING MOTIVATIONS	COMMUNICATION OPPORTUNITIES FOR BRANDS
Self-expression	• Provide platforms (e.g., events, competitions) to encourage brand-related self-expressions. • Explore opportunities to link such self-expressions with the brand's communication messages for conventional media.
Life documenting	• Create brand-related experiences for bloggers to document. • Make bloggers' brand experiences a part of the brand's experiences (e.g., have a meta-blog run by the brand that empathetically documents brand-related personal anecdotes recorded by bloggers).
Commenting	• Locate the influential commentator blogs; subscribe to their RSS feeds so as to sense the pulses of the blogsphere. • Make quick and proactive responses to unfriendly comments. • Invite bloggers to join the brand's public relations activities.
Forum participation	• Encourage staff to participate in brand-related online communities. • Sponsor forums to discuss the brand. • Provide stimulating information for discussion to keep the dialogue ongoing.
Information seeking	• Pay attention to SEO (search engine optimization) on blog-specific search engines. • Provide rich information and easy-to-find paths for eyeballs to converge. • Synthesize internal and external pro-brand blogging activities on the brand's main Web site.

Source: Chung-Yao Huang, Yong-Zheng Shen, Hong-Xiang Lin, and Shin-Shin Chang, "Bloggers' Motivations and Behaviors: A Model," *Journal of Advertising Research,* 47, no. 4 (December 2007): 472–484.

both simply as *goals.* Consider this example: A young person who genuinely wants to attain higher education views going to college as a *positive* goal and college represents an *approach object*. Another person may view the lack of getting higher education and the likely resulting criticism by family and friends as a *negative* goal and go to college to avoid such a negative outcome; for this person, avoiding criticism is an *avoidance object*.

Many studies applied goal selection into consumption situations. One study found that approach-oriented and avoidance-oriented consumers are likely to respond differently to promotional appeals.[4] Another study identified two types of people: (1) persons with *promotion focus* are interested in their growth and development, have more hopes and aspirations, and favor the presence of positive outcomes; (2) persons with a *prevention focus* are interested in safety and security, are more concerned with duties and obligations and favor the absence of negative outcomes, and also favor status quo and inaction over action in their consumption decisions.[5] Yet another study discovered that *utilitarian* product features (e.g., a car's antilock brakes) fulfill consumers' prevention goals and enhance their satisfaction while *hedonic* features (e.g., a six-speaker audio system) fulfill promotion goals and evoke feelings of delight, rather than mere satisfaction.[6]

Goals are also related to negative forms of consumption behavior. One study found that personal goals that focus on *extrinsic* benefits (such as financial success, social status, and being attractive to others) are associated with higher degrees of compulsive buying than goals that stress *intrinsic* benefits (such as self-acceptance, affiliation, and connection with community).[7] These studies illustrate the complexity of the ways consumers conceptualize goals and the impact of set or achieved goals on consumption behavior.

Interdependence of Needs and Goals

Needs and goals are interdependent; neither exists without the other. However, people are often not as aware of their needs as they are of their goals. For example, a teenager may not consciously be aware of his social needs but may join a number of chat groups online to meet new friends. A person may not consciously be aware of a power need but may choose to run for public office when an elective position becomes available. A college student may not consciously recognize her need for achievement but may strive to attain a straight A grade point average.

Individuals are usually somewhat more aware of their *physiological* needs than they are of their *psychological* needs. Most people know when they are hungry, thirsty, or cold, and they take appropriate steps to satisfy these needs. The same people may not consciously be aware of their needs for acceptance, self-esteem, or status. They may, however, subconsciously engage in behavior that satisfies their psychological (acquired) needs.

RATIONAL VERSUS EMOTIONAL MOTIVES

Some consumer behaviorists distinguish between so-called **rational motives** and **emotional motives**. They use the term *rationality* in the traditional economic sense, which assumes that consumers behave rationally by carefully considering all alternatives and choosing those that give them the greatest utility. In a marketing context, the term *rationality* implies that consumers select goals based on totally objective criteria, such as size, weight, price, or miles per gallon. Emotional motives imply the selection of goals according to personal or subjective criteria (e.g., pride, fear, affection, or status). A recent study found that emotions arising from buying or not buying, when facing an unintended purchase, impact the impressions of advertising viewed subsequently. People who gave in when tempted and made an unintended purchase preferred subsequent happiness appeals while those who refrained from buying preferred pride appeals.[8] Another study illustrated that providing unique emotional experiences to customers is crucial in keeping customers of services coming back and recommending the service to others.[9]

Recent studies illustrate the complexity of rational versus emotional motivation during consumption. One study demonstrated that when the prices of two chocolate products—a Swiss product known for its superior taste and an American everyday chocolate item—were reduced by the same amount, most consumers bought the high-quality chocolate. However, when the prices were further reduced by the same amount but one that resulted in the lower-quality product being free, most consumers took the free, lower-quality product and gave up the chance to buy the superior chocolate for a ridiculously low price. Apparently, the word *free* triggered an emotional and irrational buying behavior.[10] Another study illustrated that consumers who had more ambiguous information about a product expected to be happier with their purchases than those who used more specific and detailed information in their purchases. The researchers named this finding "The Blissful Ignorance Effect."[11]

Obviously, what may appear irrational to an outside observer may be perfectly rational in the context of the consumer's own psychological field. For example, people who pursue extensive facial cosmetic surgery in order to appear younger use significant economic resources (e.g., hefty surgical fees, time lost in recovery, inconvenience, and the risk that something may go wrong) to achieve their goals. For such people, undergoing the surgery, and expending the considerable financial and physical costs required, are perfectly rational decisions to achieve their goals. However, to many other persons within the same culture who are less concerned with aging, and to persons from other cultures that are not so preoccupied with personal appearance, these decisions appear completely irrational.

The Dynamics of Motivation

LEARNING OBJECTIVE

4.2 *To Understand the Dynamics of Motivation, Arousal of Needs, Setting of Goals, and Interrelationship Between Needs and Goals.*

Motivation is a highly dynamic construct that is constantly changing in reaction to life experiences. Needs and goals change and grow in response to an individual's physical condition, environment, interactions with others, and experiences. As individuals attain their goals, they develop new ones. If they do not attain their goals, they continue to strive for old goals or they develop substitute goals. Some of the reasons why need-driven human activity never ceases include the following: (1) Many needs are never fully satisfied; they continually impel actions designed to attain or maintain satisfaction. (2) As needs become satisfied, new and higher-order needs emerge that cause tension and induce activity. (3) People who achieve their goals set new and higher goals for themselves.

NEEDS ARE NEVER FULLY SATISFIED

Most human needs are never fully or permanently satisfied. For example, at fairly regular intervals throughout each day, individuals experience hunger needs that must be satisfied. Most people regularly seek companionship and approval from others to satisfy their social needs. Even more complex psychological needs are rarely fully satisfied. For example, a person may partially satisfy a need for power by working as an administrative assistant to a local politician, but this vicarious taste of power may not sufficiently satisfy her need; thus, she may strive to work for a legislator or even to run for political office herself. In this instance, temporary goal achievement does not adequately satisfy the need for power, and the individual strives ever harder to more fully satisfy that need.

NEW NEEDS EMERGE AS OLD NEEDS ARE SATISFIED

Some motivational theorists believe that a hierarchy of needs exists and that new, higher-order needs emerge as lower-order needs are fulfilled.[12] For example, a man whose basic physiological needs (e.g., food, housing, etc.) are fairly well satisfied may turn his efforts to achieving acceptance among his neighbors by joining their political clubs and supporting their candidates. Once he is confident that he has achieved acceptance, he then may seek recognition by giving lavish parties or building a larger house.

SUCCESS AND FAILURE INFLUENCE GOALS

A number of researchers have explored the nature of the goals that individuals set for themselves. Broadly speaking, they have concluded that individuals who successfully achieve their goals usually set new and higher goals for themselves; that is, they raise their **levels of aspiration**. This may be due to the fact that their success in reaching lower goals makes them more confident of their ability to reach higher goals. Conversely, those who do not reach their goals sometimes lower their levels of aspiration.[13] Thus, goal selection is often a function of success and failure. For example, a college senior who is not accepted into medical school may try instead to become a dentist or a podiatrist.

The nature and persistence of an individual's behavior are often influenced by expectations of success or failure in reaching certain goals. Those expectations, in turn, are often based on past experience. A person who takes good snapshots with an inexpensive camera may be motivated to buy a more sophisticated camera in the belief that it will enable him to take even better photographs, and eventually he may upgrade his camera by several hundred dollars. On the other hand, a person who has not been able to take good photographs is just as likely to keep the same camera or even lose all interest in photography.

These effects of success and failure on goal selection have strategy implications for marketers. Goals should be reasonably attainable. Advertisements should not promise more than the product will deliver. Products and services are often evaluated by the size and direction of the gap between consumer expectations and objective performance. Thus, even a good product will not be repurchased if it fails to live up to unrealistic expectations created by ads that "overpromise." Similarly, a consumer is likely to regard a mediocre product with greater satisfaction than it warrants if its performance exceeds the person's expectations.

Substitute Goals

When an individual cannot attain a specific goal or type of goal that he or she anticipates will satisfy certain needs, behavior may be directed to a **substitute goal**. Although the substitute goal may not be as satisfactory as the primary goal, it may be sufficient to dispel uncomfortable tension. Continued deprivation of a primary goal may result in the substitute goal assuming primary-goal status. For example, a woman who has stopped drinking whole milk because she is dieting may actually begin to prefer skim milk. A man who cannot afford a BMW may convince himself that a new sporty and less expensive Japanese car has an image he clearly prefers.

Frustration

Failure to achieve a goal often results in feelings of frustration. At one time or another, everyone has experienced the frustration that comes from the inability to attain a goal. The barrier that prevents attainment of a goal may be personal to the individual (e.g., limited physical or financial resources) or an obstacle in the physical or social environment (e.g., a storm that causes the postponement of a long-awaited vacation). Regardless of the cause, individuals react differently to frustrating situations. Some people manage to cope by finding their way around the obstacle or, if that fails, by selecting a substitute goal. Others are less adaptive and may regard their inability to achieve a goal as a personal failure. Such people are likely to adopt a defense mechanism to protect their egos from feelings of inadequacy.

Products may represent creative responses to the concept of frustration. For example, consumers may feel frustrated by having to throw away fresh, unconsumed produce and fish only days after buying it. The FoodSaver product includes a vacuum sealing machine and corresponding bags and containers that enable consumers to store perishable foods that either cannot be frozen at all or lose a lot of their flavor while frozen. Also, readily accessible online help agents who chat with computer users alleviate many of the frustrations of having to go through endless "frequently asked questions" or call help lines with annoying directions and long waits.

Defense Mechanisms

People who cannot cope with frustration often mentally redefine their frustrating situations in order to protect their self-images and self-esteem. For example, a young woman may yearn for a European vacation she cannot afford. The coping individual may select a less expensive vacation trip to Disneyland or to a national park. The person who cannot cope may react with anger toward her boss for not paying her enough money to afford the vacation she prefers, or she may persuade herself that Europe is unseasonably warm this year. These last two possibilities are examples, respectively, of *aggression* and *rationalization*, **defense mechanisms** that people sometimes adopt to protect their egos from feelings of failure when they do not attain their goals. Other defense mechanisms include *regression*, *withdrawal*, *projection*, *daydreaming*, *identification*, and *repression*. These defense mechanisms are described in Table 4.2. This listing of defense mechanisms is far from exhaustive, because individuals tend to develop their own ways of redefining frustrating situations to protect their self-esteem from the anxieties that result

TABLE 4.2 Defense Mechanisms

DEFENSE MECHANISM	DESCRIPTION AND ILLUSTRATIONS
Aggression	In response to frustration, individuals may resort to aggressive behavior in attempting to protect their self-esteem. The tennis pro who slams his tennis racket to the ground when disappointed with his game or the baseball player who physically intimidates an umpire for his call are examples of such conduct. So are consumer boycotts of companies or stores.
Rationalization	People sometimes resolve frustration by inventing plausible reasons for being unable to attain their goals (e.g., not having enough time to practice) or deciding that the goal is not really worth pursuing (e.g., how important is it to achieve a high bowling score?).
Regression	An individual may react to a frustrating situation with childish or immature behavior. A shopper attending a bargain sale, for example, may fight over merchandise and even rip a garment that another shopper will not relinquish rather than allow the other person to have it.
Withdrawal	Frustration may be resolved by simply withdrawing from the situation. For instance, a person who has difficulty achieving officer status in an organization may decide he can use his time more constructively in other activities and simply quit that organization.
Projection	An individual may redefine a frustrating situation by projecting blame for his or her own failures and inabilities on other objects or persons. Thus, the golfer who misses a stroke may blame his golf clubs or his caddy.
Daydreaming	Daydreaming, or fantasizing, enables the individual to attain imaginary gratification of unfulfilled needs. A person who is shy and lonely, for example, may daydream about a romantic love affair.
Identification	People resolve feelings of frustration by subconsciously identifying with other persons or situations that they consider relevant. For example, slice-of-life commercials often portray a stereotypical situation in which an individual experiences a frustration and then overcomes the problem by using the advertised product. If the viewer can identify with the frustrating situation, he or she may very likely adopt the proposed solution and buy the product advertised.
Repression	Another way that individuals avoid the tension arising from frustration is by repressing the unsatisfied need. Thus, individuals may "force" the need out of their conscious awareness. Sometimes repressed needs manifest themselves indirectly. The wife who is unable to bear children may teach school or work in a library; her husband may do volunteer work in a boys' club. The manifestation of repressed needs in a socially acceptable form is called *sublimation*, another type of defense mechanism.

from experiencing failure. Marketers often consider this fact in their selection of advertising appeals and construct advertisements that portray a person resolving a particular frustration through the use of the advertised product.

MULTIPLICITY OF NEEDS AND VARIATION OF GOALS

A consumer's behavior often fulfills more than one need. In fact, it is likely that specific goals are selected because they fulfill several needs. We buy clothing for protection and for a certain degree of modesty; in addition, our clothing fulfills a wide range of personal and social needs, such as acceptance or ego needs.

One cannot accurately infer motives from behavior. People with different needs may seek fulfillment through selection of the same goal; people with the same needs may seek fulfillment through different goals. Consider the following examples. Five people who are active in a neighborhood association may each belong for a different reason. The first may be genuinely concerned with protecting the interests of the neighborhood's residents; the second may be concerned about the possibility of increased crime in the area; the third may seek social contacts from organizational meetings; the fourth may enjoy the power of directing a large group; and the fifth may enjoy the status and attention provided by membership in a public organization.

Similarly, five people may be driven by the same need (e.g., an ego need) to seek fulfillment in different ways. The first may seek advancement and recognition through a professional career; the second may become active in a political organization; the third may run in regional marathons; the fourth may take professional dance lessons; and the fifth may seek attention by monopolizing classroom discussions.

AROUSAL OF MOTIVES

Most of an individual's specific needs are dormant much of the time. The arousal of any particular set of needs at a specific moment in time may be caused by internal stimuli found in the individual's physiological condition, by emotional or cognitive processes, or by stimuli in the outside environment.

Physiological Arousal

Bodily needs at any one specific moment in time are based on the individual's physiological condition at that moment. A drop in blood sugar level or stomach contractions will trigger awareness of a hunger need. Secretion of sex hormones will awaken the sex need. A decrease in body temperature will induce shivering, which makes the individual aware of the need for warmth. Most of these physiological cues are involuntary; however, they arouse related needs that cause uncomfortable tensions until they are satisfied. For example, a person who is cold may turn up the heat in his bedroom and also make a mental note to buy a warm cardigan sweater to wear around the house.

Emotional Arousal

Sometimes daydreaming results in the arousal or stimulation of latent needs. People who are bored or who are frustrated in trying to achieve their goals often engage in daydreaming (autistic thinking), in which they imagine themselves in all sorts of desirable situations. These thoughts tend to arouse dormant needs, which may produce uncomfortable tensions that drive them into goal-oriented behavior. A young woman who daydreams of a torrid romance may spend her free time in Internet single chat rooms; a young man who dreams of being a famous novelist may enroll in a writing workshop.

Cognitive Arousal

Sometimes random thoughts can lead to a cognitive awareness of needs. An advertisement that provides reminders of home might trigger instant yearning to speak with one's parents. This is the basis for many long-distance telephone company campaigns that stress the low cost of international long-distance rates.

Advertisements are cues designed to arouse needs. Without these cues, the needs might remain dormant. Creative advertisements arouse needs and create a psychological imbalance in the consumer's mind. For example, the ad featured in Figure 4.4 is designed to arouse one's yearning for an adventurous vacation by appealing to the sense of touch, attempting to make the advertised vacation seem more *real* to the ad's reader.

When people live in a complex and highly varied environment, they experience many opportunities for need arousal. Conversely, when their environment is poor or deprived, fewer needs are activated. This explains why television has had such a mixed effect on the lives of people in underdeveloped countries. It exposes them to various lifestyles and expensive products that they would not otherwise see, and it awakens wants and desires that they have little

FIGURE 4.4
Source: Courtesy of Innovation Norway.

QUESTION: *How Does This Ad Arouse One's Needs?*

opportunity or even hope of satisfying. Thus, while television enriches many lives, it also serves to frustrate people with little money, education, or hope, and may result in the adoption of such aggressive defense mechanisms as robbery, boycotts, or even revolts.

There are two opposing philosophies concerned with the arousal of human motives. The **behaviorist school** considers motivation to be a mechanical process; behavior is seen as the response to a stimulus, and elements of conscious thought are ignored. An extreme example of the *stimulus–response* theory of motivation is the impulse buyer who reacts largely to external stimuli in the buying situation. According to this theory, the consumer's cognitive control is limited; he or she does not act but reacts to stimuli in the marketplace (e.g., an ice cream truck on the corner). The **cognitive school** believes that all behavior is directed at goal achievement. Needs and past experiences are reasoned, categorized, and transformed into attitudes and beliefs that act as predispositions focused on helping the individual satisfy needs; together, these factors determine the actions that a person takes to satisfy a particular need.

Types and Systems of Needs

LEARNING OBJECTIVE

4.3 *To Learn About Several Systems of Needs Developed by Researchers.*

For many years, psychologists and others interested in human behavior have attempted to develop exhaustive lists of human needs. Most lists of human needs tend to be diverse in content as well as in length. Although there is little disagreement about specific physiological needs, there is considerable disagreement about needs with nonphysical origins, that is psychological (or psychogenic) needs.

In 1938, the psychologist Henry Murray prepared a detailed list of 28 psychogenic needs. This research was the first systematic approach to the understanding of nonbiological human needs. Murray believed that everyone has the same basic set of needs but that individuals differ in their priority ranking of these needs. Murray's basic needs include many motives that are assumed to play an important role in consumer behavior, such as acquisition, achievement, recognition, and exhibition (see Table 4.3).

MASLOW'S HIERARCHY OF NEEDS

Dr. Abraham Maslow, a clinical psychologist, formulated a widely accepted theory of human motivation based on the notion of a universal hierarchy of human needs.[14] Maslow's theory identifies five basic levels of human needs, which rank in order of importance from lower-level (biogenic) needs to higher-level (psychogenic) needs. The theory postulates that individuals seek to satisfy lower-level needs before higher-level needs emerge. The lowest level of chronically unsatisfied need that an individual experiences serves to motivate his or her behavior. When that need is "fairly well" satisfied, a new (and higher) need emerges that the individual is motivated to fulfill. When this need is satisfied, a new (and still higher) need emerges, and so on. Of course, if a lower-level need experiences some renewed deprivation (e.g., thirst or hunger), it may temporarily become dominant again.

Figure 4.5 presents a diagram of **Maslow's hierarchy of needs**. For clarity, each level is depicted as mutually exclusive. According to the theory, however, there is some overlap among the levels, as no need is ever completely satisfied. For this reason, although all levels of need below the level that is currently dominant continue to motivate behavior to some extent, the prime motivator—the major driving force within the individual—is the lowest level of need that remains largely unsatisfied.

Physiological Needs

In the hierarchy-of-needs theory, physiological needs are the first and most basic level of human needs. These needs, which are required to sustain biological life, include food, water, air, shelter, clothing, sex—all the biogenic needs, in fact, that were listed as primary needs earlier.

According to Maslow, physiological needs are dominant when they are chronically unsatisfied: "For the man who is extremely and dangerously hungry, no other interest exists but food. He dreams food, he remembers food, he thinks about food, he emotes only about food, he perceives only food, and he wants only food."[15] For many people in this country, the biogenic needs

FIGURE 4.5
Maslow's Hierarchy of Needs

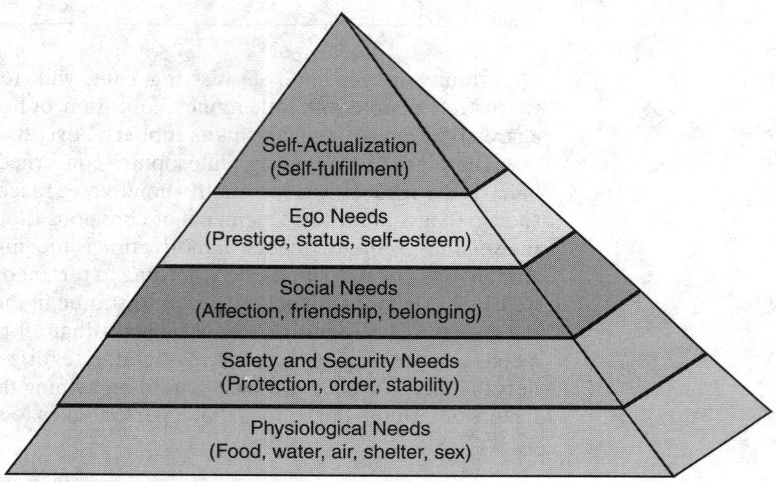

TABLE 4.3 Murray's List of Psychogenic Needs

NEEDS ASSOCIATED WITH INANIMATE OBJECTS
Acquisition
Conservancy
Order
Retention
Construction

NEEDS THAT REFLECT AMBITION, POWER, ACCOMPLISHMENT, AND PRESTIGE
Superiority
Achievement
Recognition
Exhibition
Inviolacy (inviolate attitude)
Infavoidance (to avoid shame, failure, humiliation, ridicule)
Defendance (defensive attitude)
Counteraction (counteractive attitude)

NEEDS CONCERNED WITH HUMAN POWER
Dominance
Deferrence
Similance (suggestible attitude)
Autonomy
Contrariance (to act differently from others)

SADOMASOCHISTIC NEEDS
Aggression
Abasement

NEEDS CONCERNED WITH AFFECTION BETWEEN PEOPLE
Affiliation
Rejection
Nurturance (to nourish, aid, or protect the helpless)
Succorance (to seek aid, protection, or sympathy)
Play

NEEDS CONCERNED WITH SOCIAL INTERCOURSE (THE NEEDS TO ASK AND TELL)
Cognizance (inquiring attitude)
Exposition (expositive attitude)

Source: Adapted from Henry A. Murray, "Types of Human Needs," in David C. McClelland, *Studies in Motivation* (New York: Appleton-Century-Crofts, 1955), 63–66. Reprinted by permission of Irvington Publishers, Inc.

tend to be satisfied, and higher-level needs are dominant. Unfortunately, however, the lives of the many homeless people in major cities and in physically devastated areas are focused almost entirely on satisfying their biogenic needs, such as the needs for food, clothing, and shelter.

Safety Needs

After the first level of needs is satisfied, safety and security needs become the driving force behind an individual's behavior. These needs are concerned not only with physical safety but also include order, stability, routine, familiarity, and control over one's life and environment. For example, health and the availability of health care are important safety concerns. Savings accounts, insurance policies, education, and vocational training are all means by which individuals satisfy the need for security.

FIGURE 4.6

Source: Courtesy of New York Magazine.

QUESTION: *To Which of Maslow's Needs Does This Ad Appeal?*

Social Needs

The third level of Maslow's hierarchy includes such needs as love, affection, belonging, and acceptance. People seek warm and satisfying human relationships with other people and are motivated by love for their families. Because of the importance of social motives in our society, advertisers of many product categories emphasize this appeal in their advertisements. Figure 4.6 portrays an ad appealing to both physiological and social needs.

Egoistic Needs

When social needs are more or less satisfied, the fourth level of Maslow's hierarchy becomes operative. This level is concerned with egoistic needs. These needs can take either an inward or an outward orientation, or both. Inwardly directed ego needs reflect an individual's need for self-acceptance, self-esteem, success, independence, and personal satisfaction with a job well done. Outwardly directed ego needs include the needs for prestige, reputation, status, and recognition from others. Figure 4.7 shows an ad for luxury apartment building based on a person's egoistic needs.

FIGURE 4.7

Source: Platinumnyc.com.
Photograhy: Bill Taylor Photo.
Rendering: Neoscape.
Ad Design: Sherman Advertising.

QUESTION: *To Which of Maslow's Needs Does This Ad Appeal?*

Need for Self-Actualization

According to Maslow, most people do not satisfy their ego needs sufficiently to ever move to the fifth level—the need for self-actualization (self-fulfillment). This need refers to an individual's desire to fulfill his or her potential—to become everything he or she is capable of becoming. In Maslow's words, "What a man can be, he must be."[16] This need is expressed in different ways by different people. A young man may desire to be an Olympic star and work single-mindedly for years to become the best in his sport. An artist may need to express herself on canvas; a research scientist may strive to find a new drug that eradicates cancer. Maslow noted that the self-actualization need is not necessarily a creative urge but that it is likely to take that form in people with some capacity for creativity. Some of our largest corporations encourage their highly paid employees to look beyond their paychecks to find gratification and self-fulfillment in the workplace—to view their jobs as the way to become "all they can be." Figure 4.8 shows an ad for athletic shoes based on a self-actualization appeal (note that the shoes themselves are not featured in the ad).

FIGURE 4.8
Source: Courtesy of Converse.

QUESTION: *To Which of Maslow's Needs Does This Ad Appeal?*

AN EVALUATION OF THE NEED HIERARCHY AND ITS MARKETING APPLICATIONS

Maslow's hierarchy-of-needs theory postulates a five-level hierarchy of prepotent human needs. Higher-order needs become the driving force behind human behavior as lower-level needs are satisfied. The theory says, in effect, that dissatisfaction, not satisfaction, motivates behavior.

The need hierarchy has received wide acceptance in many social disciplines because it appears to reflect the assumed or inferred motivations of many people in our society. The five levels of need are sufficiently generic to encompass most individual needs. The major problem with the theory is that it cannot be tested empirically; there is no way to measure precisely how satisfied one level of need must be before the next higher need becomes operative. The need hierarchy also appears to be very closely bound to contemporary American culture (i.e., it appears to be both culture- and time-bound).

Despite these limitations, the hierarchy offers a highly useful framework for marketers trying to develop appropriate advertising appeals for their products. It is adaptable in two ways: First, it enables marketers to focus their advertising appeals on a need level that is likely to be shared by a large segment of the target audience; second, it facilitates product positioning or repositioning.

Segmentation and Promotional Applications

Maslow's need hierarchy is readily adaptable to market segmentation and the development of advertising appeals because there are consumer goods designed to satisfy each of the need levels and because most needs are shared by large segments of consumers. For example, individuals buy health foods, medicines, and low-fat products to satisfy physiological needs. They buy insurance, preventive medical services, and home security systems to satisfy safety and security needs. Almost all personal care and grooming products (e.g., cosmetics, mouthwash, shaving cream), as well as most clothes, are bought to satisfy social needs. A recent study illustrates the importance of the sociability dimension when designing Web sites for both hedonic and utilitarian products (Table 4.4). High-tech products such as elaborate sound systems and luxury products (e.g., furs, big cars, or expensive furniture) are often bought to fulfill ego and esteem needs. Postgraduate college education, hobby-related products, and exotic and physically challenging adventure trips are sold as ways of achieving self-fulfillment.

Advertisers can also use the need hierarchy for *positioning* products—that is, deciding how the product should be perceived by prospective consumers. The key to positioning is to find a niche—an unsatisfied need—that is not occupied by a competing product or brand. The need hierarchy is a versatile tool for developing positioning strategies because different appeals for the same product can be based on different needs included in this framework. For example, a recent study tested different military recruitment slogans in the context of the needs of young recruits. The slogans and the needs the most popular slogans appealed to are shown in Table 4.5.

A TRIO OF NEEDS

Some psychologists believe in the existence of a **trio of** (basic) **needs:** the needs for power, for affiliation, and for achievement. These needs can each be subsumed within Maslow's need hierarchy; considered individually, however, each has a unique relevance to consumer motivation.

Power

The power need relates to an individual's desire to control his or her environment. It includes the need to control other persons and various objects. This need appears to be closely related to the ego need, in that many individuals experience increased self-esteem when they exercise power over objects or people.

Affiliation

Affiliation is a well-known and well-researched social motive that has far-reaching influence on consumer behavior. The affiliation need is very similar to Maslow's social need and suggests that behavior is strongly influenced by the desire for friendship, for acceptance, and for belonging. People with high affiliation needs tend to be socially dependent on others. They often select goods they feel will meet with the approval of friends. Teenagers who hang out at malls or techies who congregate at computer shows often do so more for the satisfaction of being with others than for making a purchase. An appeal to the affiliation needs of young, environmentally concerned adults is shown in Figure 4.9A. Another ad based on the affiliation need is featured in Figure 4.9B.

Achievement

Individuals with a strong need for achievement often regard personal accomplishment as an end in itself. The achievement need is closely related to both the egoistic need and the self-actualization need. People with a high need for achievement tend to be more self-confident, enjoy taking calculated risks, actively research their environments, and value feedback. Monetary

TABLE 4.4 A Low- Versus High-Social Web Site

SAMPLE WEB SITES FOR TRAVEL (HEDONIC PURCHASE)

SOCIAL CUES	HIGH-SOCIAL WEB SITE	LOW-SOCIAL WEB SITE
Language	Written text and spoken language	Written text
Social role	Using voice, a female interactive character identified herself as a tour guide. She greeted participants in a pop-up window on the home page. She also said "good-bye" when participants logged off.	No tour guide
Voice	In addition to the use of voice to create social role, the female voice gave a brief summary of each Web page.	No voice incorporated
Interactivity	Interactive Web pages: Before linking to the next page that participants selected from the home page, two interactive Web pages intervened. • First page: The tour guide asked, "Have you ever been to the Caribbean?" • Second page: The tour guide replied, "Thanks! That will help me provide you with the most appropriate travel information."	Not included

SAMPLE WEB SITES FOR CUSTOM-MADE HOME WINDOW BLINDS (UTILITARIAN PURCHASE)

SOCIAL CUES	HIGH-SOCIAL WEB SITE	LOW-SOCIAL WEB SITE
Language	Written text and spoken language	Written text
Social role	A female interactive character acting as a shopping guide appears on-screen, speaking to the visitor.	No shopping guide
Voice	In addition to the use of voice to create social role, the female voice gave a brief summary of each Web page: • *Homepage:* What's your style? Honey-combed shades or verticals? Roller shades or sheer? Well, click on me to see the most popular blinds in wood, fabric, wovens, and even, yes, woven woods, which just so happens to be my personal favorite. So, go ahead, select the product category that best fits your style. • *Product overview:* To view individual products, click on "view colors" in the gallery under the product description. To decorate your windows, simply click on the titled link. To compare all products in this category, select the "compare products" link at the bottom of the screen.	No voice incorporated
Interactivity	The character asks visitors to "click on her" to find out more about various products. The character provides oral directions on how to use the various Web page links and shopping aids.	Not included

Source: Liz C. Want, Julie Baker, Judy A. Wagner, and Kirk Wakefield, "Can a Retail Web Site Be Social?" *Journal of Marketing,* 71 (July 2007): 143–157. Copyright 2007 by American Marketing Association. Reproduced with permission of American Marketing Association in the format print & electronic usage via Copyright Clearance Center.

rewards provide an important type of feedback as to how they are doing. People with high achievement needs prefer situations in which they can take personal responsibility for finding solutions. High achievement is a useful promotional strategy for many products and services targeted to educated and affluent consumers. Figure 4.10 features an ad appealing to both power and achievement needs.

In summary, individuals with specific, heightened psychological needs tend to be receptive to advertising appeals directed at those needs. They also tend to be receptive to certain kinds of products. Thus, a knowledge of motivational theory provides marketers with key bases for segmenting markets and developing promotional strategies.

TABLE 4.5 Needs and Military Recruitment Slogans

PART A: THE FOLLOWING SLOGANS WERE TESTED AND COMPARED WITH THE RESPONDENTS' NEEDS

1. This is the Army
2. Today's Army Wants to Join You
3. Accelerate Your Life
4. I Want You
5. Join the People Who've Joined the Army
6. An Army of One
7. The Few, the Proud, the Marines
8. Let the Journey Begin
9. Be All You Can Be

PART B: THE MOST PREFERRED SLOGANS

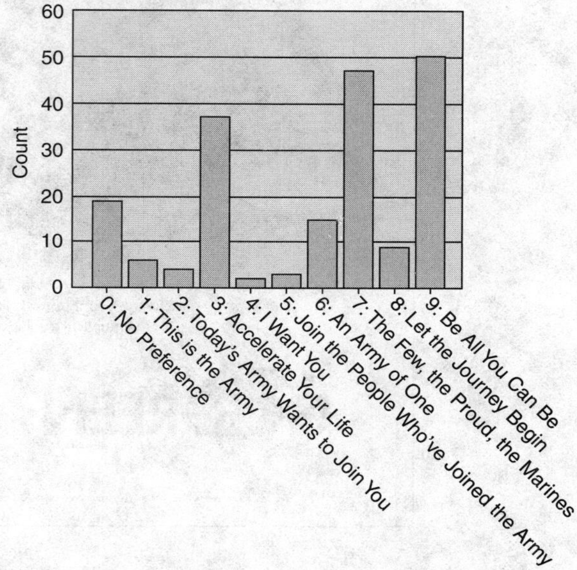

PART C: SLOGANS' APPEALS AND CORRESPONDING NEEDS

Subjects who preferred "Be All You Can Be," "The Few, the Proud, the Marines," and "Accelerate Your Life"—the most preferred slogans—were found to have higher motivators of esteem, autonomy, and self-actualization. It can logically be inferred that "Be All You Can Be" incorporates a self-actualization theme, "The Few, the Proud, the Marines" incorporates an esteem theme, and "Accelerate Your Life" appeals to motivators of self-actualization.

In terms of needs, subjects who preferred "This Is the Army," "Today's Army Wants to Join You," "I Want You," "Join the People Who've Joined the Army," "An Army of One," and "Let the Journey Begin"—the six less preferred slogans—scored significantly lower on their needs for achievement and dominance and significantly higher on their need for affiliation.

Source: From Sylvia A. Miller, M. Suzanne Clinton, and John P. Camey, "The Relationship of Motivators, Needs, and Involvment Factors to Preferences for Military Recruitment Slogans," *Journal of Advertising Research,* 47, no. 1 (March 2007): 66–78. The material in Part C is a direct quote from page 75 of this source.

FIGURE 4.9A
Source: Courtesy of Perf Go Green. www.perfgogreen.com.

QUESTION: *To Which of the Trio of Needs Does This Ad Appeal?*

The Measurement of Motives

LEARNING OBJECTIVE

4.4 *To Understand How Human Motives Are Studied and Measured.*

How are motives identified? How are they measured? How do researchers know which motives are responsible for certain kinds of behavior? These are difficult questions to answer because motives are hypothetical constructs—that is, they cannot be seen or touched, handled, smelled, or otherwise tangibly observed. For this reason, no single measurement method can be considered a reliable index. Instead, researchers usually rely on a combination of research techniques to try to establish the presence and/or the strength of various motives. By combining a variety of research methods—including responses to questionnaires or surveys' data (i.e., self-reports of opinions and behaviors), and insights from focus group sessions and depth interviews (i.e., to discover underlying motives)—consumer researchers achieve more valid insights into consumer motivations than they would by using any one technique alone.

Table 4.6 includes two scales used to obtain self-reports from potential recruits regarding their motives (the study featured in Table 4.5). The scale in Part A assesses needs based on respondents' self-reported priorities, and the one in Part B does the same based on reported frequency of engaging in certain behaviors.

Oftentimes respondents may be unaware of their motives or are unwilling to reveal them when asked directly. In such situations, researchers use *qualitative research* to delve into the consumer's unconscious or hidden motivations. Many qualitative methods also are termed **projective techniques** because they require respondents to interpret stimuli that do not have clear meanings, with the assumption that the subjects will reveal or "project" their subconscious, hidden motives into (or onto) the ambiguous stimuli. Table 4.7 includes a summary of

FIGURE 4.9B

Source: Photograph by James Mollison. Courtesy of United Colors of Benetton.

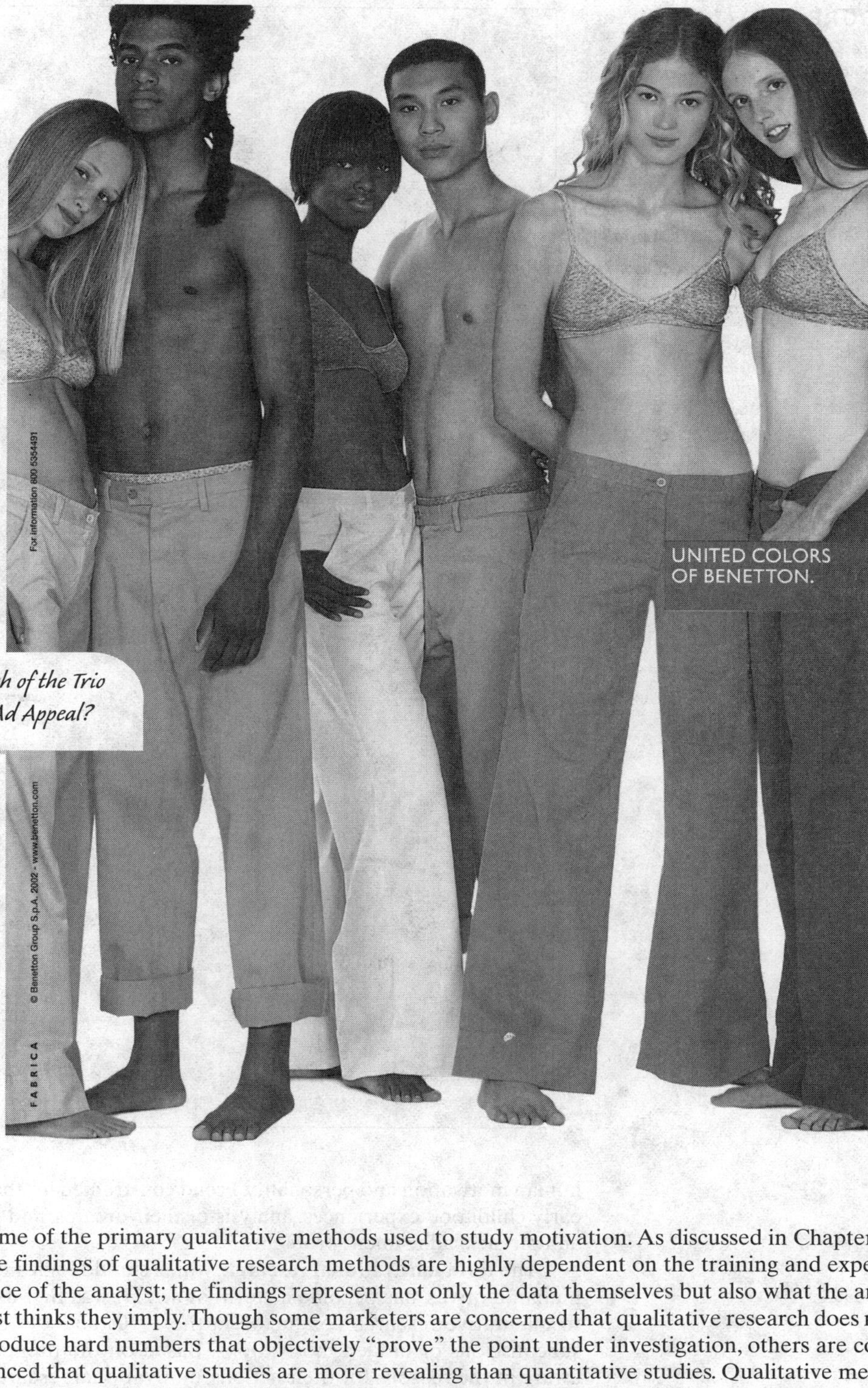

QUESTION: *To Which of the Trio of Needs Does This Ad Appeal?*

some of the primary qualitative methods used to study motivation. As discussed in Chapter 2, the findings of qualitative research methods are highly dependent on the training and experience of the analyst; the findings represent not only the data themselves but also what the analyst thinks they imply. Though some marketers are concerned that qualitative research does not produce hard numbers that objectively "prove" the point under investigation, others are convinced that qualitative studies are more revealing than quantitative studies. Qualitative methods were used in the studies described in the following section.

MOTIVATIONAL RESEARCH

Sigmund Freud's psychoanalytic theory of personality (discussed in Chapter 5) provided the foundation for the development of motivational research. This theory was built on the premise that unconscious needs or drives—especially biological and sexual drives—are at the heart of

FIGURE 4.10

Source: Courtesy of General Motors Corporation.

QUESTION: *To Which of the Trio of Needs Does This Ad Appeal?*

human motivation and personality. Freud constructed his theory from patients' recollections of early childhood experiences, analysis of their dreams, and the specific nature of their mental and physical adjustment problems.

The term **motivational research**, which should logically include all types of research into human motives, has become a "term of art." It was first used by Dr. Ernest Dichter to refer to qualitative research conducted in the 1950s and 1960s designed to uncover consumers' subconscious or hidden motivations. Based on the premise that consumers are not always aware of the reasons for their actions, motivational research attempts to discover underlying feelings, attitudes, and emotions concerning product, service, or brand use. When Dr. Ernest Dichter, trained as a clinical psychoanalyst in Vienna, arrived in the United States in the late 1930s, he sought a position with a major New York advertising agency, rather than establishing a clincal practice of psychotherapy. Up to this time, the little marketing research that was being conducted focused on what consumers did (i.e., quantitative, descriptive studies). Dr. Dichter adapted Freud's psychoanalytical techniques to the study of consumer buying habits. He used qualitative research methods to find out *why* consumers did what they did.

TABLE 4.6 Self-Reported Measures of Motives

PART A: A SCALE MEASURING SECURITY, SOCIAL, ESTEEM, AUTONOMY, AND SELF-ACTUALIZATION NEEDS

The scale includes 13 job-related statements. Subjects responded on a 7-point semantic differential scale ranging from "Least Important" to "Most Important."

1. The feeling of self-esteem a person gets from being in that job.
2. The opportunity for personal growth and development in that job.
3. The prestige of the job inside the company (that is, regard received from others in the company).
4. The opportunity for independent thought and action in that job.
5. The feeling of security in that job.
6. The feeling of self-fulfillment a person gets from being in that position (that is, the feeling of being able to use one's own unique capabilities, realizing one's potential).
7. The prestige of the job outside the company (that is, regard received from others not in the company).
8. The feeling of worthwhile accomplishment in that job.
9. The opportunity in that job to give help to other people.
10. The opportunity in that job for participation in the setting of goals.
11. The opportunity in that job for participation in the determination of methods and procedures.
12. The authority connected with the job.
13. The opportunity to develop close friendships in the job.

PART B: A SCALE MEASURING ACHIEVEMENT, AFFILIATION, AUTONOMY, AND DOMINANCE NEEDS

The scale includes 20 behavioral statements. Subjects responded on a 7-point semantic differential scale ranging from "Never" to "Always."

1. I do my best work when my job assignment is fairly difficult.
2. When I have a choice, I try to work in a group instead of by myself.
3. In my work assignments, I try to be my own boss.
4. I seek an active role in the leadership of a group.
5. I try very hard to improve on my past performance at work.
6. I pay a good deal of attention to the feelings of others at work.
7. I go my own way at work, regardless of the opinions of others.
8. I avoid trying to influence those around me to see things my way.
9. I take moderate risks and stick my neck out to get ahead at work.
10. I prefer to do my own work and let others do theirs.
11. I disregard rules and regulations that hamper my personal freedom.
12. I find myself organizing and directing the activities of others.
13. I try to avoid any added responsibilities on my job.
14. I express my disagreements with others openly.
15. I consider myself a "team player" at work.
16. I strive to gain more control over the events around me at work.
17. I try to perform better than my coworkers.
18. I find myself talking to those around me about nonbusiness-related matters.
19. I try my best to work alone on a job.
20. I strive to be "in command" when I am working in a group.

Source: From Sylvia A. Miller, M. Suzanne Clinton, and John P. Camey, "The Relationship of Motivators, Needs, and Involvment Factors to Preferences for Military Recruitment Slogans," *Journal of Advertising Research,* 47, no. 1 (March 2007): 66–78. As noted in this source, the scale in Part A was developed by Porter (1964), and the one in Part B was developed by Steers and Braunstein (1976).

TABLE 4.7 Qualitative Measures of Motives

METAPHOR ANALYSIS: This method, including the tool termed ZMET, was discussed in detail in Chapter 2. When DuPont used metaphor analysis to study women's emotions regarding pantyhose, women revealed that they evoked feelings of sensuality and being sexy and attractive to men. These findings indicated that pantyhose ads must appeal less to women's sensual feelings, even when the women targeted happen to be business executives.

STORYTELLING: This method consists of having customers tell real-life stories regarding their use of the product under study. By using this method to study parents' perceptions of diapers, Kimberly-Clark discovered that parents viewed diapers as clothing related to a particular stage in the child's development. Thus, if their children wore diapers too long, parents became distressed and embarrassed because it was an overt sign of their failure to toilet train their children. The company introduced its highly successful Huggies Pull-Ups training pants—a product that established a new category in the U.S. diaper industry.

WORD ASSOCIATION AND SENTENCE COMPLETION: In the word association method, respondents are presented with words, one at a time, and asked to say the first word that comes to mind. This method is highly useful in determining consumers' associations with existing brand names and those under development. In sentence completion, respondents are asked to complete a sentence upon hearing the opening phrase (e.g., "People who drive convertibles . . .").

THEMATIC APPERCEPTION TEST: Developed by Henry A. Murray, this test consists of showing pictures to individual respondents and asking them to tell a story about each picture. For example, Clearasil employed an image of a female looking into a mirror under the caption "Here is a teenager looking into the mirror and seeing pimples." The researchers discovered that teenagers view their lives as fast-paced and socially active and that the discovery of a pimple abruptly disturbs the swiftness of their lives. The resulting advertising depicted a teenage male walking briskly down the street and spotting a pimple on his face in a store window. All motion around him stops. He applies Clearasil, the pimple disappears, and life resumes its pace.

DRAWING PICTURES AND PHOTO SORTS: Visual images are often used to study consumers' perceptions of various brands and to develop new advertising strategies. For example, when respondents were asked to draw pictures of the typical Pillsbury cake-mix user, their drawings depicted old-fashioned, chubby females wearing frilly aprons. When asked to draw pictures of the Duncan Hines cake-mix user, their drawings showed slim, "with it" women wearing heels and miniskirts. These findings provided important input to Pillsbury concerning the need to reposition its product.

In a study using photo sorts conducted by the advertising agency for Playtex (a manufacturer of bras), respondents received stacks of photos depicting different types of women and asked to select pictures portraying their own self-images. Although many of the respondents were overweight, full-breasted, and old-fashioned in appearance, they selected photos showing physically fit, well-dressed, and independent women. The advertising agency advised Playtex to stop stressing the comfort of its bras in its ads and designed a new campaign showing sexy, thin, and big-bosomed women under the slogan "The fit that makes the fashion."

Sources: Emily Eakin, "Penetrating the Mind by Metaphor," *New York Times*, February 23, 2002, B9, Bl 1; Ronald B. Leiber, "Storytelling: A New Way to Get Close to Your Customer," *Fortune*, February 3, 1997; and Bernice Kramer, "Mind Games," *New York*, May 8, 1989, 33–40.

Marketers were quickly fascinated by the glib, entertaining, and usually surprising explanations offered for consumer behavior, especially since many of these explanations were grounded in sex. For example, marketers were told that cigarettes and Life Saver candies were bought because of their sexual symbolism, that men regarded convertible cars as surrogate mistresses, and that women baked cakes to fulfill their reproductive yearnings. Before long, almost every major advertising agency had a psychologist on staff to conduct motivational research studies. Four product profiles developed by Dichter and his colleagues are presented in Table 4.8.

Building on the contributions of Dr. Dichter and other motivational researchers, qualitative consumer research expanded from its focus on Freudian and neo-Freudian concepts to a broader perspective that embraced not only other schools of psychology, but included methodologies and concepts borrowed from sociology and anthropology. The Qualitative Research Consultants Association (QRCA) was established with the objective of applying

TABLE 4.8 Subconscious Meanings of Products

SELECT PRODUCT PERSONALITY PROFILES CONSTRUCTED BY ERNEST DICHTER

BAKING

Dichter described baking as an expression of femininity and motherhood, evoking nostalgic memories of delicious odors pervading the house when the mother was baking. He said that when baking a cake, a woman is subconsciously and symbolically going through the act of giving birth, and the most fertile moment occurs when the baked product is pulled from the oven. Dichter also maintained that when a woman bakes a cake for a man, she is offering him a symbol of fertility."[a] The Betty Crocker image was based on this profile.

AUTOMOBILES

According to Dichter, the car allows consumers to convert their subconscious urges to destroy and their fear of death—two key forces in the human psyche—into reality. For example, the expression "step on it" stems from the desire to feel power, and the phrase "I just missed that car by inches" reflects the desire to play with danger. Based on this view, Dichter advised Esso (now Exxon) to tap into consumers' aggressive motives for driving cars in promoting the superiority of its gasoline product. The slogan "Put a tiger in your tank" was developed as a result of his advice.[b] Dichter also maintained that cars have personalities, and that people become attached to their cars and view them as companions rather than objects. This notion stands behind his views that a man views a convertible as a mistress and a sedan as his wife.

DOLLS

Dolls play an important part in the socialization of children and are universally accepted as an essential toy for girls. Parents choose dolls that have the kind of characteristics they want their children to have, and the doll is an object for both the parents and the children to enjoy. When Mattel introduced Barbie in 1959, the company hired Dichter as a consultant. His research indicated that while girls liked the doll, their mothers detested the doll's perfect bodily proportions and Teutonic appearance. Dichter advised Mattel to market the doll as a teenage fashion model, reflecting the mother's desire for a daughter's proper and fashionable appearance. The advertising themes used subtly told mothers that it is better for their daughters to appear attractive to men rather than nondescript.[c]

ICE CREAM

Dichter described ice cream as an effortless food that does not have to be chewed and that melts in your mouth, a sign of abundance, an almost orgiastic kind of food that people eat as if they want it to run down their chins. Accordingly, he recommended that ice cream packaging should be round, with illustrations that run around the box panel, suggesting unlimited quantity.

Sources: [a]Ernest Dichter, *Handbook of Consumer Motivations* (New York: McGraw-Hill, 1964); Jack Hitt, "Does the Smell of Coffee Brewing Remind You of Your Mother?" *New York Times Magazine*, May 7, 2000, 6, 71. [b]Phil Patton, "Car Shrinks," *Fortune*, March 18, 2002, 6. [c]Barbara Lippert, "B-Ball Barbie," *Adweek*, November 9, 1998, 39.

an interdisciplinary orientation to research on consumer motivation. The membership of QRCA consists of qualitative researchers who regularly conduct focus groups and one-to-one or depth interviews for client marketing companies who seek to identify the underlying needs and motives of their customers. Through its publications and conferences, QRCA has done much to expand the methodologies aimed at the understanding of consumers' motives and other aspects of their consumer behavior. To learn more about contemporary qualitative research, visit QRCA's Web site, **www.qrca.org**.

EVALUATION OF MOTIVATIONAL RESEARCH

Today, the evolution of early motivational research, with its broadened qualitative orientation, not only embraces aspects of its Freudian origin, but also incorporates a largely expanded range of qualitative methods and procedures that made it a well-established part of "everyday" consumer research (see Chapter 2). Qualitative consumer research methods, consisting of focus group sessions and depth interviews, and a wide range of "lines of questioning and probing," are routinely used by large and small businesses seeking to gain deeper insights into the *whys* of consumer behavior. Since motivational research often reveals unsuspected consumer motivations concerning product or brand usage, one of its srtrategic uses today is the development of new ideas for promotional campaigns aimed at penetrating consumers' conscious awareness by appealing to unrecognized needs.

Qualitative research also enables marketers to explore consumer reactions to ideas and advertising copy at an early stage and avoid the costly errors resulting from placing ineffective and untested ads. Furthermore, as with all qualitative research techniques, motivational research findings provide consumer researchers with insights that serve as the foundations of structured, quantitative marketing research studies conducted on larger, more representative samples of consumers.

SUMMARY

Motivation is the driving force within individuals that impels them to action. This driving force is produced by a state of uncomfortable tension, which exists as the result of an unsatisfied need. All individuals have needs, wants, and desires. The individual's subconscious drive to reduce need-induced tensions results in behavior that he or she anticipates will satisfy needs and thus bring about a more comfortable internal state. Motivation can be either positive or negative.

Innate needs—those an individual is born with—are physiological (biogenic) in nature; they include all the factors required to sustain physical life (e.g., food, water, clothing, shelter, sex, and physical safety). Acquired needs—those an individual develops after birth—are primarily psychological (psychogenic); they include love, acceptance, esteem, and self-fulfillment.

All behavior is goal oriented. Goals are the sought-after results of motivated behavior. The form or direction that behavior takes—the goal that is selected—is a result of thinking processes (cognition) and previous learning (i.e., experience). There are two types of goals: generic goals and product-specific goals. A generic goal is one that may fulfill a certain need; a product-specific goal is a specifically branded or labeled product that the individual sees as a way to fulfill a need. Product-specific needs are sometimes referred to as wants. For any innate or acquired need, there are many different and appropriate goals. The specific goal selected depends on the individual's experiences, physical capacity, prevailing cultural norms and values, and the goal's accessibility in the physical and social environment. Needs and goals are interdependent and change in response to the individual's physical condition, environment, interaction with other people, and experiences. As needs become satisfied, new, higher-order needs emerge that must be fulfilled.

Failure to achieve a goal often results in feelings of frustration. Individuals react to frustration in two ways: "fight" or "flight." They may cope by finding a way around the obstacle that prohibits goal attainment or by adopting a substitute goal (fight); or they may adopt a defense mechanism that enables them to protect their self-esteem (flight). Defense mechanisms include aggression, regression, rationalization, withdrawal, projection, daydreaming, identification, and repression.

Motives cannot easily be inferred from consumer behavior. People with different needs may seek fulfillment through selection of the same goals; people with the same needs may seek fulfillment through different goals. Although some psychologists have suggested that individuals have different need priorities, others believe that most human beings experience the same basic needs, to which they assign similar priority rankings. Maslow's hierarchy-of-needs theory proposes five levels of human needs: physiological needs, safety needs, social needs, egoistic needs, and self-actualization needs. Other needs widely integrated into consumer advertising include the needs for power, affiliation, and achievement.

There are self-reported and qualitative methods for identifying and "measuring" human motives, and researchers use these techniques in tandem to assess the presence or strength of consumer motives. Motivational research and its current extended form (commonly referred to as "qualitative research"), seeks to delve below the consumer's level of conscious awareness, and to identify underlying needs and motives. Moreover, quantitative research has proved to be of value to marketers in developing new ideas and advertising copy appeals.

DISCUSSION QUESTIONS

1. Discuss the statement "marketers don't create needs; needs preexist marketers." Can marketing efforts *change* consumers' needs? Why or why not? Can they *arouse* consumer needs? If yes, how?

2. Consumers have both innate and acquired needs. Give examples of each kind of need and show how the same purchase can serve to fulfill either or both kinds of needs.

3. Specify both innate and acquired needs that would be useful bases for developing promotional strategies for:

a. global positioning systems

b. sunglasses that can be customized online

c. a new version of the iPhone

4. Why are consumers' needs and goals constantly changing? What factors influence the formation of new goals?

5. How can marketers use consumers' failures at achieving goals in developing promotional appeals for specific products and services? Give examples.

6. For each of the situations listed in question 3, select one level from Maslow's hierarchy of human needs that can be used to promote and position the product to a given market segment. Describe how you would use the need you selected in promoting the product and the market segment you selected. What are the advantages and disadvantages of using Maslow's need hierarchy in segmentation and positioning?

7. a. How do researchers identify and measure human motives? Give examples.

b. Does motivational research differ from quantitative research? Discuss.

c. What are the strengths and weaknesses of motivational research?

EXERCISES

1. Find two advertisements that depict two different defense mechanisms (Table 4.2) and discuss their effectiveness.

2. Examine Murray's List of Psychogenic Needs (Table 4.3). Can you identify any human needs not listed there? If not, why? If yes, explain your findings.

3. Find three advertisements that appeal to the needs for power, affiliation, and achievement and discuss their effectiveness.

4. Find two examples of ads that are designed to arouse consumer needs and discuss their effectiveness.

KEY TERMS

- acquired needs *106*
- approach object *108*
- avoidance object *108*
- behaviorist school *115*
- cognitive school *115*
- defense mechanisms *112*
- emotional motives *110*
- generic goals *107*
- innate needs *106*
- levels of aspiration *111*
- Maslow's hierarchy of needs *116*
- motivation *106*
- motivational research *126*
- primary needs *106*
- product-specific goals *107*
- projective techniques *124*
- rational motives *110*
- secondary needs *106*
- substitute goals *112*
- trio of needs *121*

Case One: Nintendo Wii's Success

The Japan giant video game producer Nintendo launched its new product Wii in late 2006. The Wii home video game console that primarily competes with Microsoft's Xbox 360 and Sony's PlayStation 3. The unique selling point for this new video game console is its wireless controller, which can be used as a handheld pointing device and detect movement in three dimensions. The Wii not only provides a new way of playing video games but also widens its target customers to almost everybody simply because of its user-friendliness.

Since its successful launch in 2006, Nintendo continues to innovate the Wii's peripheral products, like Wii sports and Wii fit. On March 25, 2009, at the Game Developers Conference, the president of Nintendo Japan, Satoru Iwata, reported that the worldwide shipments of Wii had reached 50 million.

What makes Nintendo Wii an outright success in the market? The president of Nintendo America, Reggie Fils-Aime, suggested that it is simply because of Nintendo's customer-driven marketing strategy—to drive the company's business through the eyes of their customers. Wii's country of origin—Japan—is well known as a health-conscious nation in which people live longer. This collective nature of its culture makes its members highly value family and social bonds. However, nowadays people have very busy work lives and have less time for exercise and family gatherings. The Nintendo Wii enables users to solve these dilemmas through exercise by playing the Wii games with their family members or friends at home after work or on the weekends.

QUESTIONS

1. What consumer needs are driving the success of the market adoption of Nintendo Wii? Consider the innate and acquired needs.
2. On the basis of the market success of the Nintendo Wii, explain the importance of understanding customer needs and motivation in new product adoption?

Sources: Tor Thorsen, "Nintendo's GDC Conference," *GameSpot*, March 25, 2009; Dave Parrack, "Nintendo President Explains Wii Success—We Focus on Consumers," *Gamer.Blorge*, October 30, 2007, accessed at www.gamer.blorge.com; and Nintendo, www.nintendo.com.

Case Two: Need-Focused Definition of Business

Savvy companies define their missións and business domains in terms of the needs that they satisfy rather than the products that they create. Doing so enables such companies to be in the forefront of searching for new products and solutions that satisfy consumers' needs more effectively than competing products.

Here are several companies whose business philosophies illustrate need-focused definitions of business:

1. Merck—at **www.merck.com** go to "About Merck" and then "Mission Statement."
2. Whole Foods Market—at **www.wholefoodsmarket.com** go to "Company Information" and then "Core Values."
3. Johnson & Johnson—at **www.jnj.com** go to "Our Company," and then "Our Credo Values."

QUESTIONS

1. Go to the sites listed above and prepare a short summary of each company's vision and definition of its business.
2. How does each of the three business definitions reflect the material covered in this chapter?
3. Based on their Web sites, list the major product lines of each of the three companies. Then describe how each company's products stem from its definition of the business in which it operates.

5

Personality and Consumer Behavior

MARKETERS have long tried to appeal to consumers in terms of their personality characteristics. They have intuitively felt that what consumers purchase, and when and how they consume, are likely to be influenced by their personality factors. For this reason, marketing and advertising people have frequently depicted (or incorporated) specific personality traits or characteristics in their marketing and advertising messages. Some recent examples are an appeal to *other-directedness* for the Toyota United Pro Cycling Team (headline: "Join the Team Now!"), an appeal to *low dogmatism* (or open mindedness) for the Travel Channel's show *Bizarre Foods with Andrew Zimmern* (headline: "One Man's Weird Is Another Man's Wonderful"), an appeal to drivers' sense of *nonconformity* or *sensation seeking* with the Hummer H3 (headline: "The Greatest Explorers Had No Maps"), and an appeal by BEDAT & Co wristwatches to consumers' *need for uniqueness* (headline: "Very Famous Amongst Very Few People"—**www.bedat.com**). Figure 5.1 presents an ad that would be particularly appealing to enthusiastic or extremely involved collectors (e.g., some stamp, coin, and Barbie collectors). This personality trait is known as "fixated consumption." It is discussed in greater detail later in this chapter.

This chapter provides the reader with an understanding of how *personality* and *self-concept* are related to various aspects of consumer behavior. It examines what personality is, reviews several major personality theories, and describes how these theories have stimulated marketing interest in the study of consumer personality. The chapter considers the important topics of *brand personality,* how the related concepts of *self* and *self-image* influence consumer attitudes and behavior. The chapter concludes with an exploration of *virtual personality* or *virtual self.*

FIGURE 5.1

Source: Courtesy of the U.S. Mint.

QUESTION: *What Is the Personality Trait Characterizing the Consumers to Whom This Ad Appeals?*

LEARNING OBJECTIVES

5.1 *To Understand How Personality Reflects Consumers' Inner Differences.*

5.2 *To Understand How Freudian, Neo-Freudian, and Trait Theories Each Explain the Influence of Personality on Consumers' Attitudes and Behavior.*

5.3 *To Understand How Personality Reflects Consumers' Responses to Product and Marketing Messages.*

5.4 *To Understand How Marketers Seek to Create Brand Personalities-Like Traits.*

5.5 *To Understand How the Products and Services That Consumers Use Enhance Their Self-Images.*

5.6 *To Understand How Consumers Can Create Online Identities Reflecting a Particular Set of Personality Traits.*

What Is Personality?

LEARNING OBJECTIVE

5.1 *To Understand How Personality Reflects Consumers' Inner Differences.*

The study of **personality** has been approached by theorists in a variety of ways. Some have emphasized the dual influence of heredity and early childhood experiences on personality development; others have stressed broader social and environmental influences and the fact that personalities develop continuously over time. Some theorists prefer to view personality as a unified whole; others focus on specific traits. The wide variation in viewpoints makes it difficult to arrive at a single definition. However, we propose that personality can be defined as *those inner psychological characteristics that both determine and reflect how a person responds to his or her environment.*

The emphasis in this definition is on *inner characteristics*—those specific qualities, attributes, traits, factors, and mannerisms that distinguish one individual from other individuals. As discussed later in the chapter, the deeply ingrained characteristics that we call personality are likely to influence the individual's product choices: They affect the way consumers respond to marketers' promotional efforts, and when, where, and how they consume particular products or services. Therefore, the identification of specific personality characteristics associated with consumer behavior has proven to be highly useful in the development of a firm's market segmentation strategies.

THE NATURE OF PERSONALITY

In the study of personality, three distinct properties are of central importance: (1) *personality reflects individual differences*; (2) *personality is consistent and enduring*; and (3) *personality can change.*

Personality Reflects Individual Differences

Because the inner characteristics that constitute an individual's personality are a unique combination of factors, no two individuals are exactly alike. Nevertheless, many individuals may be similar in terms of a single personality characteristic but not in terms of others. For instance, some people can be described as "high" in consumer *ethnocentrism* (e.g., willingness to accept a foreign-made product), whereas others can be described as "low" in *ethnocentrism* (e.g., afraid or reluctant to buy a foreign-made product). Personality is a useful concept because it enables us to categorize consumers into different groups on the basis of one or even several traits. If each person were different in terms of all personality traits, it would be impossible to group consumers into segments, and there would be little reason for marketers to develop products and promotional campaigns targeted to particular segments.

Personality Is Consistent and Enduring

An individual's personality tends to be both consistent and enduring. Indeed, the sibling who comments that her sister "has always cared a great deal about her clothes from the time she was a toddler" is supporting the contention that personality has both consistency and endurance.

Both qualities are essential if marketers are to explain or predict consumer behavior in terms of personality.

Although marketers cannot change consumers' personalities to conform to their products, if they know which personality characteristics influence specific consumer responses, they can attempt to appeal to the relevant traits inherent in their target group of consumers.

Even though consumers' personalities may be consistent, their consumption behavior often varies considerably because of the various psychological, sociocultural, environmental, and situational factors that affect behavior. For instance, although an individual's personality may be relatively stable, specific needs or motives, attitudes, reactions to group pressures, and even responses to newly available brands may cause a change in the person's behavior. Personality is only one of a combination of factors that influence how a consumer behaves.

Personality Can Change

Under certain circumstances personalities change. For instance, an individual's personality may be altered by major life events, such as marriage, the birth of a child, the death of a parent, or a change of job and/or profession. An individual's personality changes not only in response to abrupt events but also as part of a gradual maturing process—"She's more mature, and now she's willing to listen to points of view other than those she agrees with," says an aunt after not seeing her niece for several years.

There is also evidence that personality stereotypes may change over time. More specifically, although it is felt that men's personality has generally remained relatively constant over the past 50 years, women's personality has seemed to become increasingly more masculine and should continue to do so over the next 50 years. This prediction indicates a *convergence* in the personality characteristics of men and women.[1] The reason for this shift is that women have been moving more and more into occupations that have traditionally been dominated by men and, therefore, have increasingly been associated with masculine personality attributes.

Theories of Personality

LEARNING OBJECTIVE

5.2 *To Understand How Freudian, Neo-Freudian, and Trait Theories Each Explain the Influence of Personality on Consumers' Attitudes and Behavior.*

This section reviews three major theories of personality: (1) **Freudian theory**, (2) **neo-Freudian theory**, and (3) **trait theory**. These theories have been chosen for discussion from among many theories of personality because each has played a prominent role in the study of the relationship between consumer behavior and personality.

FREUDIAN THEORY

Sigmund Freud's **psychoanalytic theory of personality** is one of the cornerstones of modern psychology. This theory was built on the premise that *unconscious needs* or *drives*, especially sexual and other biological drives, are at the heart of human motivation and personality. Freud constructed his theory on the basis of patients' recollections of early childhood experiences, analysis of their dreams, and the specific nature of their mental and physical adjustment problems.

Id, Superego, and Ego

Based on his analyses, Freud proposed that the human personality consists of three interacting systems: the *id*, the *superego*, and the *ego*. The id was conceptualized as a "warehouse" of primitive and impulsive drives—basic physiological needs such as thirst, hunger, and sex—for which the individual seeks immediate satisfaction without concern for the specific means of satisfaction. The ad for Godiva Chocolatier (see Figure 5.2) captures some of the mystery and the excitement associated with the "forces" of primitive drives.

In contrast to the id, the *superego* is conceptualized as the individual's internal expression of society's moral and ethical codes of conduct. The superego's role is to see that the individual satisfies needs in a socially acceptable fashion. Thus, the superego is a kind of "brake" that restrains or inhibits the impulsive forces of the id.

Finally, the *ego* is the individual's conscious control. It functions as an internal monitor that attempts to balance the impulsive demands of the id and the sociocultural constraints of the

FIGURE 5.2

Source: © Godiva Chocolatier, Inc. Photography by CLANG.

QUESTION: *How Does This Marketing Message Apply the Notion of the Id?*

superego. Figure 5.3 represents the interrelationships among the three interacting systems. In addition to specifying a structure for personality, Freud emphasized that an individual's personality is formed as he or she passes through a number of distinct stages of infant and childhood development. These are the *oral, anal, phallic, latent*, and *genital* stages. Freud labeled four of these stages of development to conform to the area of the body on which he believed the child's sexual instincts are focused at the time.

According to Freudian theory, an adult's personality is determined by how well he or she deals with the crises that are experienced while passing through each of these stages (particularly the first three). For instance, if a child's oral needs are not adequately satisfied at the first stage of development, the person may become fixated at this stage and as an adult display a personality that includes such traits as dependence and excessive oral activity (e.g., gum chewing and smoking). When an individual is fixated at the anal stage, the adult personality may display other traits, such as an excessive need for neatness.

FIGURE 5.3
A Representation of the Interrelationships Among the Id, Ego, and Superego

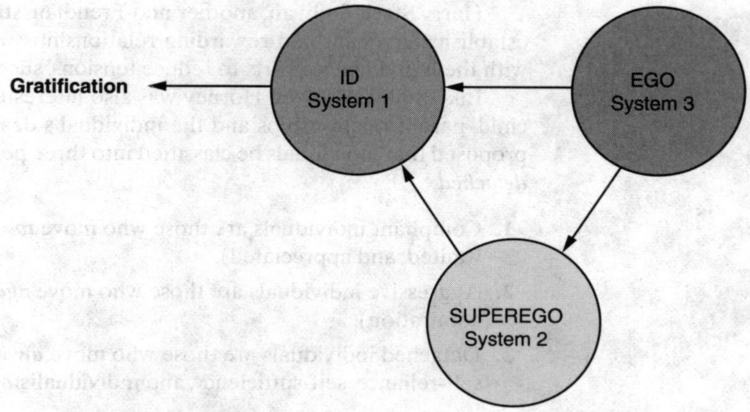

Freudian Theory and "Product Personality"

Researchers who apply Freud's psychoanalytic theory to the study of consumer personality believe that human drives are largely *unconscious* and that consumers are primarily unaware of their true reasons for buying what they buy. These researchers tend to see consumer purchases and/or consumption situations as a reflection and an extension of the consumer's own personality. In other words, they consider the consumer's appearance and possessions—grooming, clothing, jewelry, and so forth—as reflections of the individual's personality. Table 5.1 presents the results of a study of 19,000 consumers that examines the link between snack food perceptions and selected personality traits.[2] The findings of the research, for example, reveal that potato chips are associated with being ambitious, successful, and a high achiever and impatient with less than the best, whereas popcorn seems to be related to a personality that takes charge, pitches in often, and is modest and self-confident but not a show-off. (The related topics of *brand personality*, and the self and *self-images* are considered later in the chapter.)

NEO-FREUDIAN PERSONALITY THEORY

Several of Freud's colleagues disagreed with his contention that personality is primarily instinctual and sexual in nature. Instead, these neo-Freudians believed that *social relationships* are fundamental to the formation and development of personality. For instance, Alfred Adler viewed human beings as seeking to attain various rational goals, which he called *style of life.* He also placed much emphasis on the individual's efforts to overcome *feelings of inferiority* (i.e., by striving for superiority).

TABLE 5.1 Snack Foods and Personality Traits

SNACK FOODS	PERSONALITY TRAITS
Potato chips	Ambitious, successful, high achiever, impatient with less than the best.
Tortilla chips	Perfectionist, high expectations, punctual, conservative, responsible.
Pretzels	Lively, easily bored with same old routine, flirtatious, intuitive, may overcommit to projects.
Snack crackers	Rational, logical, contemplative, shy, prefers time alone.
Cheese curls	Conscientious, principled, proper, fair, may appear rigid but has great integrity, plans ahead, loves order.
Nuts	Easygoing, empathetic, understanding, calm, even tempered.
Popcorn	Takes charge, pitches in often, modest, self-confident but not a show-off.
Meat snacks	Gregarious, generous, trustworthy, tends to be overly trusting.

Source: From *What Flavor Is Your Personality? Discover Who You Are by Looking at What You Eat*, by Alan Hirsch, MD (Naperville, IL: Sourcebooks, 2001).

Harry Stack Sullivan, another neo-Freudian, stressed that people continuously attempt to establish significant and rewarding relationships with others. He was particularly concerned with the individual's efforts to reduce tensions, such as anxiety.

Like Sullivan, Karen Horney was also interested in *anxiety.* She focused on the impact of child–parent relationships and the individual's desire to conquer feelings of anxiety. Horney proposed that individuals be classified into three personality groups: *compliant, aggressive*, and *detached.*[3]

1. Compliant individuals are those who move *toward* others (they desire to be loved, wanted, and appreciated).
2. Aggressive individuals are those who move *against* others (they desire to excel and win admiration).
3. Detached individuals are those who move *away* from others (they desire independence, self-reliance, self-sufficiency, and individualism or freedom from obligations).

A personality test based on Horney's theory (the CAD) has been developed and tested within the context of consumer behavior.[4] The initial CAD research uncovered a number of tentative relationships between college students' scores and their product and brand usage patterns. For example, highly *compliant* students were found to prefer name-brand products such as Bayer aspirin; students classified as *aggressive* showed a preference for Old Spice deodorant over other brands (seemingly because of its masculine appeal); and highly *detached* students proved to be heavy tea drinkers (possibly reflecting their desire not to conform). More recent research has found that children who scored high in self-reliance—who preferred to do things independently of others (i.e., *detached* personalities)—were *less* likely to be brand loyal and were *more* likely to try different brands.[5]

Many marketers use some of these neo-Freudian theories intuitively. For example, marketers who position their products or services as providing an opportunity to belong or to be appreciated by others in a group or social setting would seem to be guided by Horney's characterization of the *compliant* individual. To illustrate, imagine an ad for sleepwear that is created to appeal to a compliant individual when it suggests that wearing the sleepwear will lead to "counting compliments," since compliant individuals particularly wish to be complimented and appreciated. In a similar fashion, Figure 5.4 shows an ad for Carmichael Training Systems® that in its headline is "speaking" to the aggressive individual who seeks to excel and achieve recognition. Specifically, the ad's headline makes a point of this when it states "Create Your Own Comeback."

TRAIT THEORY

Trait theory constitutes a major departure from the *qualitative* measures that typify the Freudian and neo-Freudian movements (e.g., personal observation, self-reported experiences, dream analysis, projective techniques).

The orientation of trait theory is primarily quantitative or empirical; it focuses on the measurement of personality in terms of specific psychological characteristics, called traits. A *trait* is defined as "any distinguishing, relatively enduring way in which one individual differs from another."[6] Trait theorists are concerned with the construction of personality tests (or inventories) that enable them to pinpoint individual differences in terms of specific traits.

Selected *single-trait personality* tests (which measure just one trait, such as self-confidence) are often developed specifically for use in consumer behavior studies. These tailor-made personality tests measure such traits as **consumer innovativeness** (how receptive a person is to new consumer-related experiences), **consumer materialism** (the degree of the consumer's attachment to "worldly possessions"), and **consumer ethnocentrism** (the consumer's likelihood to accept or reject foreign-made products).

Trait researchers have found that it is generally more realistic to expect personality to be linked to how consumers *make their choices* and to the purchase or consumption of *a broad product category* rather than a specific brand. For example, there is more likely to be a relationship between a personality trait and whether or not an individual regularly eats peanut butter and jelly sandwiches than between a personality trait and the brand of peanut better purchased. It is of interest to note that a study of over 1,000 U.S. adults found very different traits among soup lovers having preferences for different types of soups (e.g., chicken noodle versus New England clam chowder).[7] Table 5.2 presents the traits associated with six different types of soups.

FIGURE 5.4
Source: Courtesy of Carmichael Training Systems.

QUESTION: *Why Is Appealing to an Aggressive Consumer a Logical Position for This Product?*

The next section shows how measures of personality traits are used to expand our understanding of consumer behavior.

Personality and Understanding Consumer Behavior

LEARNING OBJECTIVE

5.3 *To Understand How Personality Reflects Consumers' Responses to Product and Marketing Messages.*

Marketers are interested in understanding how personality influences consumption behavior because such knowledge enables them to better understand consumers and to segment and target those consumers who are likely to respond positively to their product or service communications. Several specific personality traits that provide insights about consumer behavior are examined next.

CONSUMER INNOVATIVENESS AND RELATED PERSONALITY TRAITS

Marketing practitioners try to learn all they can about **consumer innovators**—those who are *open* to new ideas and to be among the first to try new products, services, or practices—for the

TABLE 5.2 Soup and Soup-Lovers' Traits

CHICKEN NOODLE SOUP LOVERS
- Watch a lot of TV
- Are family oriented
- Have a great sense of humor
- Are outgoing and loyal
- Like daytime talk shows
- Most likely to go to church

TOMATO SOUP LOVERS
- Passionate about reading
- Love pets
- Like meeting people for coffee
- Aren't usually the life of the party

VEGETABLE/MINESTRONE SOUP LOVERS
- Enjoy the outdoors
- Usually game for trying new things
- Spend more money than any other group dining in fancy restaurants
- Likely to be physically fit
- Gardening is often a favorite hobby

CHILI-BEEF SOUP LOVERS
- Generally preferred by males
- Are the most social of all soup lovers
- Are the life of the party
- Love telling jokes
- Watch sporting events
- Watch sitcoms on TV

NEW ENGLAND CLAM CHOWDER LOVERS
- Most conservative of all soup lovers
- Pride themselves on being realistic and down-to-earth
- Can occasionally be cynical

Source: Gwen Carden, "Your Favorite Soup Reveals Your Personality," *Sioux City Journal*, January 2, 2001, 5.

market response of such innovators is often a critical indication of the eventual success or failure of a new product or service.

Personality traits that have been useful in differentiating between consumer innovators and noninnovators include *consumer innovativeness, dogmatism, social character, need for uniqueness, optimum stimulation level, sensation seeking,* and *variety-novelty seeking.* (Chapter 14 examines nonpersonality characteristics that distinguish between consumer innovators and noninnovators.) However, according to a recent review of the literature of consumer innovativeness, innovators are frequently domain specific (i.e., innovators within a particular product or service category) with some overlapping likely between similar or closely related products and services.[8]

Consumer Innovativeness

Consumer researchers have endeavored to develop measurement instruments to gauge the level of consumer innovativeness, because such measures of personality traits provide important insights into the nature and boundaries of a consumer's "willingness to innovate." Over the years, the trait of consumer innovativeness has been linked to the need for stimulation, novelty

TABLE 5.3 Two Consumer Innovativeness Measurement Scales

A "GENERAL" CONSUMER INNOVATIVENESS SCALE

1. I would rather stick to a brand I usually buy than try something I am not very sure of.
2. When I go to a restaurant, I feel it is safer to order dishes I am familiar with.
3. If I like a brand, I rarely switch from it just to try something different.
4. I enjoy taking chances in buying unfamiliar brands just to get some variety in my purchase.
5. When I see a new brand on the shelf, I'm not afraid of giving it a try.

A DOMAIN-SPECIFIC CONSUMER INNOVATIVENESS SCALE

1. Compared to my friends, I own few rock albums.
2. In general, I am the last in my circle of friends to know the titles of the latest rock albums.
3. In general, I am among the first in my circle of friends to buy a new rock album when it appears.
4. If I heard that a new rock album was available in the store, I would be interested enough to buy it.
5. I will buy a new rock album, even if I haven't heard it yet.
6. I know the names of new rock acts before other people do.

Source: Reprinted from the *Journal of Business Research,* 57, Gilles Roehrich, Consumer Innovativeness: Concepts and Measurements, ©June 2004, p. 674, with permission from Elsevier.

seeking, and the need for uniqueness—three other traits that will be discussed later in this chapter.[9] Table 5.3 presents two alternative scales for measuring consumer innovativeness, the first scale measuring general innovativeness and the second measuring domain-specific (i.e., product-specific) innovativeness.

While previous studies of consumer innovativeness have treated this construct as a single personality trait, a recent research effort examining high-technology products, developed a hierarchical model consisting of three levels of personality, that is:[10]

1. *Global innovativeness*—a personal trait that exists independent of any context; one that represents the "very nature" of consumers' innovativeness
2. *Domain-specific innovativeness*—a more narrowly defined activity within a specific domain or product category
3. *Innovative behavior*—a pattern of actions or responses that indicate early acceptance of change and adoption of innovations (e.g., being among the first to purchase new and different products or services).

Available consumer research indicates a positive relationship between innovative use of the Internet and buying online.[11] Other research exploring the association between personality traits and innovative Internet behavior has reported that Internet shoppers tend to see themselves as being able to control their own future, using the Internet to seek out information, enjoying change, and ***not*** being afraid of uncertainty.[12] One study has found that while online banking is positively associated with Internet-related innovativeness (i.e., domain specific innovativeness), more general consumer innovativeness was negatively related to embracing online banking, thus highlighting the importance of domain-specific innovativeness.[13]

Additionally, consumer innovativeness can be an important consideration when firms contemplate brand extensions (e.g., a toothpaste brand begins marketing a line of toothbrushes under the same brand name). For instance, one research study found that consumer innovativeness is a key factor influencing brand extensions, and therefore firms bringing out a brand extension should consider developing a strategy that targets the more innovative consumer.[14] Another study, examining private or store brand purchasing in Korea, found consumer innovativeness to be more important than other factors (such as price consciousness, value consciousness, and perceived price variation) when it came to accounting for the attitudes of Korean shoppers toward private brands.[15]

Consumer Dogmatism

Many marketers are keenly interested in managing consumers' responses to distinctively unfamiliar products or product features, especially marketers of technologically rich products. Within this context **consumer dogmatism** is a personality trait that measures the degree of rigidity (versus openness) that individuals display toward the unfamiliar and toward information that is contrary to their own established beliefs.[16] A person who is *highly dogmatic* approaches the unfamiliar defensively and with considerable discomfort and uncertainty. At the other end of the spectrum, a person who is *low dogmatic* will readily consider the unfamiliar or opposing beliefs. In a recent print ad, McDonald's asks potential consumers to "Be open to new possibilities," a concept that should be appealing to low-dogmatic consumers.

Consumers who are low in dogmatism (*open-minded*) are more likely to prefer innovative products to established or traditional alternatives. In contrast, highly dogmatic (*closed-minded*) consumers are more likely to choose established, rather than innovative, product alternatives.

Highly dogmatic consumers tend to be more receptive to ads for new products or services that contain an appeal from an authoritative figure. To this end, marketers have used celebrities and experts in their new-product advertising to make it easier for potentially reluctant consumers (noninnovators) to accept the innovation. In contrast, low-dogmatic consumers (who are frequently high in innovativeness) seem to be more receptive to messages that stress factual differences, product benefits, and other forms of product-usage information.

Related to the concept of dogmatism, researchers found that Austrian consumers scoring high on the traits of openness to experience (similar to low dogmatism) and extraversion (which is associated with energy, ambition, venturesomeness, and being outgoing) respond stronger to emotional messages. Specifically, the stronger the responses to emotional messages, the stronger attitudinal and purchase loyalty is likely to be. To put it another way, "brands that make customers feel happiness, joy or affection are most likely to get a positive response."[17]

Social Character

The personality trait known as *social character* has its origins in sociological research, which focuses on the classification of individuals into distinct sociocultural types. As used in consumer psychology, social character is a personality trait that ranges on a continuum from **inner-directedness** to **other-directedness**. Inner-directed consumers tend to rely on their own inner values or standards in evaluating new products and are likely to be consumer innovators. Conversely, other-directed consumers tend to look to others for guidance as to what is appropriate or inappropriate; thus, they are *less* likely to be consumer innovators. Figure 5.5 presents an ad for Outward Bound Wildness that is likely to be appealing to the inner-directed person. In this ad, a sole person is experiencing the joys and adventure of the wildness. The ad ends with the inner-directed thought: "This challenge belongs to you."

To sum up, inner- and other-directed consumers are attracted to different types of promotional messages. Inner-directed people seem to prefer ads that stress product features and personal benefits (enabling them to use their own values and standards in evaluating products), whereas other-directed people prefer ads that feature an approving social environment or social acceptance (this is in keeping with their tendency to look to others or to act as part of a group). Thus, other-directed individuals may be more responsive to appeals that are based on social or group affiliations, rather than the informational content of an ad.

Need for Uniqueness

We all know people who seek to be unique. For these people, conformity to others' expectations or standards, either in appearance or in their possessions, is something to be avoided. Moreover, we would expect that it is easier to express or act uniquely if one does not have to pay a price in the form of others' criticism. Supporting this perspective, research indicates that when consumers with a high need for uniqueness (high NFU) are asked to explain their choices, and are not concerned about being criticized by others, they are more receptive to making unique choices (demonstrating their high NFU).[18] Seeing the importance of NFU, other consumer researchers have developed an inventory to measure the trait within the context of consumer behavior. Table 5.4 presents a sample of items drawn from the inventory.

FIGURE 5.5
Source: Courtesy of Outward Bound.

QUESTION: *In Picture and Words, How Does This Ad Target the Inner-Directed Outdoors Person?*

Optimum Stimulation Level

Some people seem to prefer a simple, uncluttered, and calm existence, whereas others prefer an environment crammed with novel, complex, and unusual experiences. Consumer research has examined how such variations in individual needs for stimulation may be related to consumer behavior. Research has found that high **optimum stimulation levels (OSLs)** are linked with greater willingness to take risks, to try new products, to be innovative, to seek purchase-related information, and to accept new retail facilities than low OSLs. Indeed, "individuals who seek high levels of stimulation are more likely to engage in "exploratory behaviors" during shopping in order to maintain an optimum level of arousal."[19] An example of exploratory shopping behavior is the "mixing and matching" of items of clothing on a virtual mannequin or model. Another fairly recent study investigating college students' willingness to select *mass customization* of fashion items (e.g., a pair of jeans that are especially measured, cut, and sewn so they offer a better fit or appearance), found that OSL predicted two factors—students'

TABLE 5.4 Sample Items from a Consumers' Need for Uniqueness Scale[a]

I collect unusual products as a way of telling people I'm different.
When dressing, I have sometimes dared to be different in ways that others are likely to disapprove.
When products or brands I like become extremely popular, I lose interest in them.
As far as I'm concerned, when it comes to the products I buy and the situations in which I use them, customs and rules are made to be broken.
I have sometimes purchased unusual products or brands as a way to create a more distinctive personal image.
I sometimes look for one-of-a-kind products or brands so that I create a style that is all my own.
I avoid products or brands that have already been accepted and purchased by the average consumer.

[a]This inventory is measured on a 5-point Likert scale ranging from "strongly agree" to "strongly disagree."

Source: Kelly Tepper Tian, William O. Bearden, and Gary L. Hunter, "Consumers' Need for Uniqueness: Scale Development and Validation," *Journal of Consumer Research*, 28, June 2001, pp. 50–66. Copyright © 2001, JCR, Inc.

openness to *experimentation with appearance* (e.g., "I try on some of the newest clothes each season to see how I look in the styles") and *enhancement of individuality* (e.g., "I try to buy clothes that are very unusual").[20]

OSL scores also seem to reflect a person's desired level of lifestyle stimulation.[21] For instance, consumers whose actual lifestyles are equivalent to their OSL scores appear to be *quite satisfied,* whereas those whose lifestyles are understimulated (i.e., their OSL scores are greater than the lifestyle they are currently living) are likely to be *bored.* Those whose lifestyles are overstimulated (i.e., their OSLs are lower than current reality) are likely to seek *rest* or *relief.* This suggests that the relationship between consumers' lifestyles and their OSLs is likely to influence their choices of products or services and how they manage and spend their time. For instance, a person who feels bored (an understimulated consumer) is likely to be attracted to a vacation that offers a great deal of activity and excitement. In contrast, a person who feels overwhelmed (an overstimulated consumer) is likely to seek a quiet, isolated, relaxing, and rejuvenating vacation.

Sensation Seeking

Closely related to the OSL concept is **sensation seeking (SS)**, which has been defined as "a trait characterized by the need for varied, novel, and complex sensations and experience, and the willingness to take physical and social risks for the sake of such experience." Research evidence indicates that teenage males with higher SS scores are more likely than other teenagers to prefer listening to heavy metal music and to engage in reckless or even dangerous behavior.[22]

Variety or Novelty Seeking

Still another personality-driven trait quite similar to and related to OSL is **variety** or **novelty seeking.** There appear to be many different types of consumer-variety seeking: *exploratory purchase behavior* (e.g., switching brands to experience new, different, and possibly better alternatives), *vicarious exploration* (e.g., securing information about a new or different alternative and then contemplating or even daydreaming about the option), and *use innovativeness* (using an already adopted product in a new or novel way).[23] The use innovativeness trait is particularly relevant to technological products (such as home electronics products), in which some models offer an abundance of features and functions, whereas others contain just a few essential features or functions. For example, a consumer with a high variety-seeking score might purchase a high-definition television with more features than a consumer with a lower variety-seeking score. Consumers with high variety-seeking scores are also more likely to be attracted to brands that claim to have novel features or multiple uses or applications. Still further, there appears to be a relationship between variety seeking and time of day, with greater variety-seeking behavior occurring when the consumer is experiencing arousal lows (as opposed to arousal peaks). And during the time of day when arousal seeking is relatively minimal, leader brands fare better, while follower brands do better during periods of the day when variety seeking is heightened.[24] Interestingly, there is also research evidence to indicate that variety seeking is greater when individuals are making choices for others, rather than for themselves.[25]

Recent research has also found evidence that variety seeking can be domain specific, such as fitness group participants choosing a larger variety of fruit juice drinks or members of a travel group selecting a wider variety of alternative holiday activities (e.g., beach, sports, nature). And, in general, hungry consumers opt for more variety in their food choices—hunger and visual food cues increase variety seeking with respect to food items.[26]

The stream of research examined here indicates that the consumer innovator differs from the noninnovator in terms of personality orientation. A knowledge of such personality differences should help marketers select target segments for new products and then to design distinctive promotional strategies for specific segments.

COGNITIVE PERSONALITY FACTORS

Consumer researchers have been increasingly interested in how **cognitive personality factors** influence various aspects of consumer behavior. In particular, two cognitive personality traits—**need for cognition** and **visualizers versus verbalizers**—have been useful in understanding selected aspects of consumer behavior.

Need for Cognition

A promising cognitive personality characteristic is need for cognition (NFC). It measures a person's craving for or enjoyment of *thinking.* Available research indicates that consumers who are *high* in NFC are more likely to be responsive to the part of an ad that is rich in product-related information or description; whereas consumers who are relatively *low* in NFC are more likely to be attracted to the background or peripheral aspects of an ad, such as an attractive model or well-known celebrity.[27] In this realm, research among adolescents compared the effectiveness of a cartoon message and a written message. As expected, for those low in NFC, the cartoon message was more effective in changing attitudes and subjective norms, whereas the written message was more effective for those high in NFC.[28] In still another study, research suggests that consumers who are high in NFC are likely to spend more time processing print advertisements, which results in superior brand and ad claim recall.[29] Another recent study using a Chinese sample shows that the inclusion of diagnostic product information in advertising (e.g., information that allows consumers to evaluate product quality and distinguish between brands) increases ad persuasion for high NFC consumers, but not for low NFC consumers.[30] Along the same lines, another Chinese research effort found that individuals low in NFC will more readily accept a marketer's recommended alternatives, allowing the consumer to more easily make a purchase decision.[31]

Need for cognition also seems to play a role in an individual's use of the Internet. More precisely, NFC has been positively related to using the Internet to seek product information, current events and news, and learning and education—all activities that incorporate a cognitive element.[32] Other studies have found that people high in NFC are able to better filter out distractions in order to concentrate on their online activities and are more motivated to learn online, and that the addition of interactive properties to a company's Web site will increase information processing for low NFC individuals.[33] Such research insights provide advertisers with valuable guidelines for creating online advertising messages (including supporting visuals) that appeal to a particular target audience grouping's *need for cognition.*

Visualizers Versus Verbalizers

It is fairly well established that some people seem to be more open to and prefer the written word as a way of securing information, whereas others are more likely to respond to and prefer visual images or messages as sources of information. Consistent with such individual differences, cognitive personality research classifies consumers into two groups: *visualizers* (consumers who prefer visual information and products that stress the visual, such as membership in a videotape club) or *verbalizers* (consumers who prefer written or verbal information and products, such as membership in book clubs or audiotape clubs). Some marketers stress strong visual dimensions in order to attract visualizers (see Figure 5.6); others feature a detailed description or point-by-point explanation to attract verbalizers (see Figure 5.7).

FIGURE 5.6
Source: Courtesy of Bontrager.

QUESTION: *Why Is This Ad Particularly Appealing to Visualizers?*

A recent research effort consisting of four separate studies found that there are two distinctly different types of visualizers. *Object visualizers* encode and process images as a single perceptual unit, while *spatial visualizers* process images piece by piece. Individuals scoring high on object visualization tend to score low in spatial visualization, and vice versa. Furthermore, while visual artists generally excel in object imagery, scientists and engineers do best with spacial imagery.[34]

FROM CONSUMER MATERIALISM TO COMPULSIVE CONSUMPTION

Consumer researchers have become increasingly interested in exploring various consumption and possession traits. These traits range from *consumer materialism* to *fixated consumption behavior* to *consumer compulsive behavior.*

Consumer Materialism

Materialism (the extent to which a person is considered materialistic) is a topic frequently discussed in newspapers, in magazines, and on TV (e.g., "Americans are very materialistic") and in everyday conversations between friends ("He's so materialistic!"). Materialism, as a

FIGURE 5.7
Source: Tempurpedic.com.

QUESTION: *Why Is This Ad Particularly Appealing to Verbalizers?*

personality-like trait, distinguishes between individuals who regard possessions as essential to their identities and their lives and those for whom possessions are secondary.[35] Researchers have found some general support for the following characteristics of materialistic people: (1) They especially value acquiring and showing off possessions; (2) they are particularly self-centered and selfish; (3) they seek lifestyles full of possessions (e.g., they desire to have lots of "things," rather than a simple, uncluttered lifestyle); and (4) their many possessions do not give them greater personal satisfaction (i.e., their possessions do not lead to greater happiness).[36]

Table 5.5 presents sample items from a materialism scale. The scale covers what are considered to be the three dimensions of "materialism–centrality" (does the consumer place possessions at the center of his or her life), "happiness" (are possessions necessary for well-being and satisfaction in life), and "success" (does the individual measure his or her success and the success of others based on possessions).[37] A recent study found that the most important predictor of the amount of time a consumer shopped and the amount he or she spent was that individual's total score on the materialism scale.[38]

TABLE 5.5 Sample Items from a Materialism Scale

SUCCESS

- I admire people who own expensive homes, cars, and clothes.
- I like to own things that impress people.
- I don't place much emphasis on the amount of material objects people own as a sign of success. (R)

CENTRALITY

- I usually buy only the things I need. (R)
- I try to keep my life simple, as far as possessions are concerned. (R)
- I like a lot of luxury in my life.

HAPPINESS

- I have all the things I really need to enjoy life. (R)
- My life would be better if I owned certain things I don't have.
- It sometimes bothers me quite a bit that I can't afford to buy all the things I'd like.

Note: Measured on a 5-point "agreement" scale. Items with an (R) are scored inversely.

Source: Marsha L. Richins, "The Material Values Scale: Measurement Properties and Development of a Short Form," *Journal of Consumer Research*, 31 (June 2004): 217–218. Copyright © 2004, JCR, Inc.

With regard to consumers' willingness to spend, individuals often react differently than they would ideally like to. "Tightwads" generally spend less than they would ideally like to because of the anticipated pain they associate with paying for their purchases, while "spendthrifts" find little pain in paying and therefore they typically spend more. Table 5.6 presents a spendthrift-tightwad scale validated in research with over 13,000 respondents.[39]

Materialism has often been linked to advertising, and researchers have suggested that in the United States there has been an increasing emphasis on materialism in the print media. It is important to remember, though, that the extent of consumer materialism can vary from country to country (e.g., consumer materialism is less developed in Mexico than in the United States), and, therefore, marketers must be careful when trying to export a successful U.S. marketing mix to another country.[40]

Related to the topic of materialism is *consumption dreaming,* during which time the consumer dreams about material objects and experiences. A research study involving 195 Canadian consumers found that most did indulge in consumption dreaming, with about 25 percent of these dreams involving a house and 20 percent dealing with travel. Such dreams are often related to consumer behavior, under one of the following five categories: (1) consumption (purchasing a product related to the dream), (2) information (searching for information related to the dream), (3) planning (making plans to realize the dream), (4) communication (talking about the dream with others), and (5) visualization (envisioning the dream in the conscious mind).[41]

Fixated Consumption Behavior

Somewhere between materialism and compulsion, with respect to buying or possessing objects, is the notion of being *fixated* with regard to consuming or possessing. Like materialism, *fixated consumption behavior* is in the realm of normal and socially acceptable behavior. Fixated consumers do not keep their objects or purchases of interest a secret; rather, they frequently display them, and their involvement is openly shared with others who have a similar interest. In the world of serious collectors (Barbie dolls, late 1940s art deco neckties, Carnival glass, rare antique teddy bears, or almost anything else that has drawn collectors), there are countless millions of *fixated consumers* pursuing their interests and trying to add to their collections.

Fixated consumers typically possess the following characteristics: (1) a deep (possibly passionate) interest in a particular object or product category, (2) a willingness to go to considerable lengths to secure additional examples of the object or product category of interest, and (3) the dedication of a considerable amount of discretionary time and money to search out the

TABLE 5.6 Spendthrift-Tightwad Scale

1. Which of the following descriptions fits you better?

1	2	3	4	5	6	7	8	9	10	11
Tightwad (difficulty spending money)					About the same or neither					Spendthrift (difficulty controlling spending)

2. Some people have trouble limiting their spending: They often spend money—for example on clothes, meals, vacations, phone calls—when they would do better not to.

   Other people have trouble spending money. Perhaps because spending money makes them anxious, they often don't spend money on things they should spend it on.

   a. How well does the first description fit you? That is, do you have trouble limiting your spending?

1	2	3	4	5
Never	Rarely	Sometimes	Often	Always

   b. (–) How well does the second description fit you? That is, do you have trouble spending money?

1	2	3	4	5
Never	Rarely	Sometimes	Often	Always

3. (–) Following is a scenario describing the behavior of two shoppers. After reading about each shopper, please answer the question that follows.

   Mr. A is accompanying a good friend who is on a shopping spree at a local mall. When they enter a large department store, Mr. A sees that the store has a "one-day-only sale" where everything is priced 10–60% off. He realizes he doesn't need anything, yet can't resist and ends up spending almost $100 on stuff.

   Mr. B is accompanying a good friend who is on a shopping spree at a local mall. When they enter a large department store, Mr. B sees that the store has a "one-day-only sale" where everything is priced 10–60% off. He figures he can get great deals on many items that he needs, yet the thought of spending the money keeps him from buying the stuff.

   In terms of your own behavior, who are you more similar to, Mr. A or Mr. B?

1	2	3	4	5
Mr. A		About the same or neither		Mr. B

Note: Items 2b and 3 are reverse scored=(–).

Source: Scott I. Rick, Cynthia E. Cryder, and George Loewenstein, "Tightwads and Spendthrifts," *Journal of Consumer Research*, 34 (April 2008): 780. Copyright © 2008, JCR, Inc.

object or product.[42] This profile of the fixated consumer describes many collectors, hobbyists, or enthusiasts. Thus, the traits that portray the fixated consumer reveal a person who is not only enduringly involved in the object category itself but is also deeply involved in the process of acquiring the object (sometimes referred to as the "hunt").

Compulsive Consumption Behavior

Unlike materialism and fixated consumption, **compulsive consumption** is in the realm of abnormal behavior—an example of the dark side of consumption. Consumers who are compulsive have an *addiction;* in some respects they are out of control, and their actions may have damaging consequences to them and to those around them. Examples of compulsive consumption problems are uncontrollable shopping, gambling, drug addiction, alcoholism, and various food and eating disorders. For instance, there are many women and a small number of men who are *chocoholics*—they have an intense craving (also termed an addiction) for chocolate.[43] Indeed, past research efforts have found that anywhere from 74 to 93 percent of those categorized as compulsive buyers are female.[44] There is even a new term used to describe the 17 million U.S. consumers who suffer from a shopping addiction—*oniomania*. The term is defined as a "shop 'til you drop" behavior based on the belief that buying will make the individual feel better.[45] As a consequence, the shopper purchases items that he or she doesn't need, will most likely never use, and often does not remember purchasing. From a marketing and consumer behavior perspective, *compulsive buying* can also be included in any list of compulsive activities. To control or possibly eliminate such compulsive problems generally requires some type of intervention therapy or clinical treatment.

Figure 5.8 presents the results of a study conducted with women in the UK, some of whom were classified as "compulsive buyers." The research found that compulsive buyers were less

FIGURE 5.8
Compulsive and Ordinary Consumers' Buying Motivations

Source: JOURNAL OF SOCIAL AND CLINICAL PSYCHOLOGY. ONLINE by Dittmar, Helga. Copyright 2005 by Guilford Publications, Inc. Reproduced with permission of Guilford Publications, Inc. in the format Textbook & Electronic via Copyright Clearance Center.

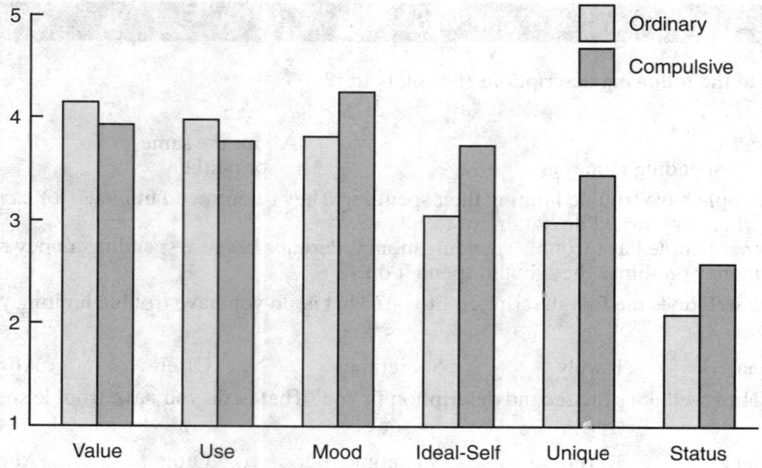

concerned than ordinary consumers with buying motivations that were economic/rational (i.e., good value for the money and useful), but psychological buying motives were instead the focus of attention for them (i.e., mood improvement, self-expression, social status improvement, and ideal self).[46]

There have been some research efforts to develop a screener inventory to pinpoint compulsive buying behavior. Table 5.7 presents sample questions from several of these scales. Evidence suggests that some consumers use self-gifting, impulse buying, and compulsive buying as a way to influence or manage their moods; that is, the act of purchasing may convert a negative mood to a more positive one ("I'm depressed, I'll go out shopping and I'll feel better").[47]

It is necessary to mention that quite a number of consumers (more women than men, and more younger rather than older individuals) exhibit impulse buying tendencies. However, while mild impulse purchasing might be viewed as "harmless fun," chronic levels of impulse purchasing are a serious matter and can have negative consequences. This is why, for example, a number of liquor manufacturers tell consumers to "drink responsibly." Research has also

TABLE 5.7 Sample Items from Scales to Measure Compulsive Buying

VALENCE, D'ASTOUS, AND FORTIER COMPULSIVE BUYING SCALE

1. When I have money, I cannot help but spend part or the whole of it.
2. I am often impulsive in my buying behavior.
3. As soon as I enter a shopping center, I have an irresistible urge to go into a shop to buy something.
4. I am one of those people who often responds to direct-mail offers (e.g., books or compact discs).
5. I have often bought a product that I did not need, while knowing I had very little money left.

FABER AND O'GUINN COMPULSIVE BUYING SCALE

1. If I have any money left at the end of the pay period, I just have to spend it.
2. I felt others would be horrified if they knew my spending habits.
3. I have bought things even though I couldn't afford them.
4. I wrote a check when I knew I didn't have enough money in the bank to cover it.
5. I bought something in order to make myself feel better.

Source: Gilles Valence, Alain d'Astous, and Louis Fortier, "Compulsive Buying: Concept and Measurement," *Journal of Consumer Policy,* 11 (1988): 419–433; Ronald J. Faber and Thomas C. O'Guinn, "A Clinical Screener for Compulsive Buying," *Journal of Consumer Research,* 19 (December 1992): 459–469; and Leslie Cole and Dan Sherrell, "Comparing Scales to Measure Compulsive Buying: An Exploration of Their Dimensionality," in *Advances in Consumer Research*, 22, ed. Frank R. Kardes and Mita Sujan (Provo, UT: Association for Consumer Research, 1995), 419–427.

found associations between impulse buying and negative emotions, and between impulse buying and excessive snacking.[48] A recent study conducted with China's Hong Kong consumers revealed that a compulsive buying tendency tends to be a predictor of being "premium prone"—that is the propensity to purchase products that include a premium or free gift.[49]

CONSUMER ETHNOCENTRISM: RESPONSES TO FOREIGN-MADE PRODUCTS

In an effort to distinguish between consumer segments that are likely to be receptive to foreign-made products and those that are not, researchers have developed and tested the *consumer ethnocentrism* scale, called CETSCALE (see Table 5.8).[50] The CETSCALE has been successful in identifying consumers with a predisposition to accept (or reject) foreign-made products, and has been shown to be a reliable measure in many nations.[51] Consumers who are highly ethnocentric are likely to feel that it is inappropriate or wrong to purchase foreign-made products because of the resulting economic impact on the domestic economy, whereas nonethnocentric consumers tend to evaluate foreign-made products—ostensibly more objectively—for their extrinsic characteristics (e.g., "how good are they?"). Research has also found that the concept of consumer ethnocentrism even applies in transitional economies where foreign goods tend to be preferred.[52] Moreover, in a post-9/11 study in the United States intended to assess Generation Y's (those consumers born between the years 1977 and 1994) attitudes toward foreign and domestic brands found few signs of ethnocentrism among this cohort, while other research found that for consumers in general, ethnocentrism increased in the United States as a result of 9/11, terrorist attacks, and natural disasters.[53]

TABLE 5.8 The Consumer Ethnocentrism Scale—CETSCALE

1. American people should always buy American-made products instead of imports.
2. Only those products that are unavailable in the United States should be imported.
3. Buy American-made products. Keep America working.
4. American products, first, last, and foremost.
5. Purchasing foreign-made products is un-American.
6. It is not right to purchase foreign products, because it puts Americans out of jobs.
7. A real American should always buy American-made products.
8. We should purchase products manufactured in America instead of letting other countries get rich off us.
9. It is always best to purchase American products.
10. There should be very little trading or purchasing of goods from other countries unless out of necessity.
11. Americans should not buy foreign products, because this hurts American business and causes unemployment.
12. Curbs should be put on all imports.
13. It may cost me in the long run but I prefer to support American products.
14. Foreigners should not be allowed to put their products on our markets.
15. Foreign products should be taxed heavily to reduce their entry into the United States.
16. We should buy from foreign countries only those products that we cannot obtain within our own country.
17. American consumers who purchase products made in other countries are responsible for putting their fellow Americans out of work.

Notes: Response format is a 7-point Likert-type scale (strongly agree = 7, strongly disagree = 1). Range of scores is from 17 to 119. Calculated from confirmatory factor analysis of data from four-area study.

Country-by-Country Ethnocentrism

Available evidence suggests that ethnocentrism has been found to vary by country and product. Mexican consumers, for example, are more ethnocentric than their French and American counterparts; and Malaysian consumers, while preferring to purchase slacks, shirts, undergarments, and belts that are locally manufactured, want to buy imported sunglasses and watches.[54] Other evidence suggests that some older American consumers, in remembrance of World War II, still refuse to purchase German- and/or Japanese-made products, whereas some German and Japanese consumers may feel similarly about American-made products.[55] Still further, for some consumers, country of assembly (COA) and/or country of design (COD) also play a role in their decision to purchase or refrain from purchasing a particular product.[56]

Targeting the Ethnocentric Consumer

Marketers successfully target ethnocentric consumers in any national market by stressing a nationalistic theme in their promotional appeals (e.g., "Made in America" or "Made in France") because this segment is predisposed to buy products made in their native land. To illustrate the ethnocentric appeal, Honda, the Japanese automaker, in an indirect appeal to ethnocentric Americans, had advertised that its Accord wagon is "Exported from America" to other markets (reinforcing that some of its automobiles are made in the United States). However, a study examining the preferences of UK consumers across eight product categories found that domestic country bias (i.e., a preference for products manufactured in a consumer's country of residence) varied among product categories. This means that a domestic manufacturer cannot expect that local consumers will automatically prefer their offerings over imported ones.[57] Still further, one research study found that low-knowledge consumers' product attitude (i.e., the consumer has little knowledge about the product) is more strongly influenced by country-of-origin perceptions than high-knowledge consumers' product attitude.[58] Table 5.10 presents a marketing mix strategy that can be used to manage country-of-origin effects. Specifically, if marketers determine that the potential customers in a particular country possess a *positive* image of products made in the country in which their products originate, the marketers may be able to create a marketing mix strategy that follows options in the *Positive* column. In contrast, if marketers assess that the potential customers in a particular country possess a *negative* image of products made in the country in which their products originate, the marketers might be wise to elect a marketing mix strategy that follows options in the *Negative* column of Table 5.9. As an additional consideration in the marketing of products, a recent study of Chinese consumers found that individuals exhibiting high consumer ethnocentrism had less favorable attitudes and buying intentions toward signs and messages that were bilingual.[59]

In this era of multinational marketing, it may be unclear to many consumers as to whether a particular product is domestic or imported. Consider Toyota, for example. Some of the models it sells in the United States are manufactured in Japan, some are manufactured in the United States, and some are manufactured in both nations (and end up being sold in the United

TABLE 5.9 Strategies for Managing Country-of-Origin Effects

	COUNTRY IMAGE	
MARKETING MIX	**POSITIVE**	**NEGATIVE**
Product	Emphasize "made in"	Emphasize brand name
Price	Premium price	Low price to attract value conscious
Place (Channel of distribution)	Exclusive locations	Establish supply chain partners
Promotion	Country image	Brand image
	Nation sponsored	Manufacturer sponsored

Source: Osman Mohamad, Zafar U. Ahmed, Earl D. Honeycutt, Jr., and Taizoon Hyder Tyebkhan, "Does 'Made In . . .' Matter to Consumers? A Malaysian Study of Country of Origin Effect," *Multinational Business Review* (Fall 2000): 73. Reprinted with permission.

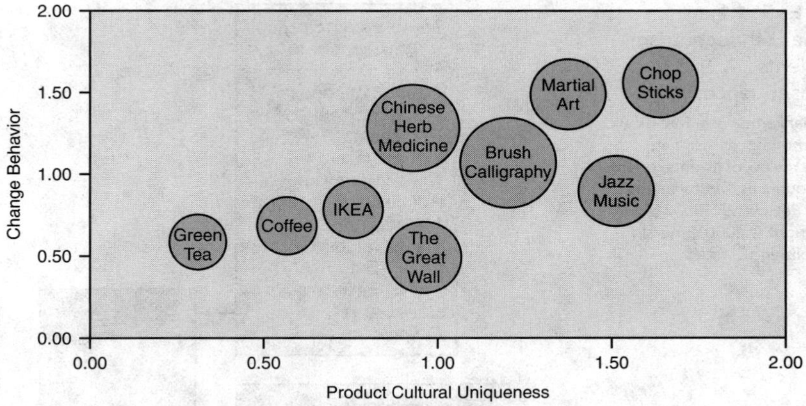

FIGURE 5.9
Object Degree of Globalization

Source: ADVANCES IN CONSUMER RESEARCH by Kao, Jufei. Copyright 2004 by Association for Consumer Research. Reproduced with permission of Association for Consumer Research in the format Textbook & Electronic via Copyright Clearance Center.

States). One study conducted among business school students in New York City has examined eight different products, from green tea to jazz music, to determine if they differ in terms of "degree of globalization." As presented in Figure 5.9, products in the lower-left corner have a higher degree of globalization, meaning that consumers view them to be low in product cultural uniqueness (i.e., they are viewed as nonforeign), while those in the upper right-hand corner are thought of as being "foreign."[60] Still further, Figure 5.10 illustrates the factors, including product cultural uniqueness, that lead to cross-cultural product adoption intention.

Figure 5.11 presents an integrated graphic framework of what is currently known about consumer ethnocentrism, its antecedents and its consequences, based on previous research studies. For example, there are a wide range of factors that impact consumer ethnocentrism (e.g., demographic, economic, political, sociopsychological factors).[61] Research efforts continue to relate consumer ethnocentrism to other personality traits. For example, a recent study among visitors to an automobile show in Australia found that higher NFC consumers (NFC was discussed earlier in this chapter) tended to rely on influences other than nationalism for their evaluations of component systems within products (e.g., a German engine in an Australian brand automobile), and that such component system evaluations can change an individual's product evaluation and purchase intention.[62]

COSMOPOLITANISM

The consumer trait of cosmopolitanism is in a sense quite the opposite of an ethnocentric view; that is, a consumer with a cosmopolitan orientation would consider the world to be his or her marketplace, and would consciously be attracted to products, experiences, and places from other cultures. Recent qualitative research conducted in Australia suggests that the increase in multiculturalism found in many countries can allow an individual to develop a cosmopolitan outlook within his or her home country and culture.[63]

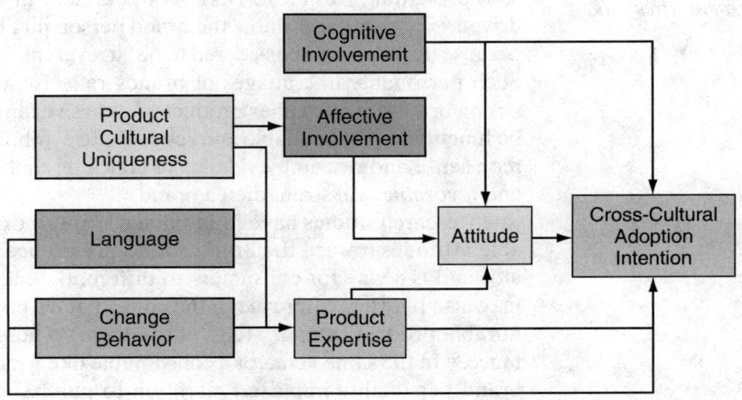

FIGURE 5.10
Casual Relationship Among Foreign Product Competence, Product Expertise, Involvement, Attitude, and Cross-Cultural Adoption Intention

Source: ADVANCES IN CONSUMER RESEARCH by Kao, Jufei. Copyright 2004 by Association for Consumer Research. Reproduced with permission of Association for Consumer Research in the format Textbook & Electronic via Copyright Clearance Center.

FIGURE 5.11
Consumer Ethnocentrism: Antecedents and Consequences

Source: Shankarmahesh, Mahesh N., "Consumer ethnocentrism: an integrative review of its antecedents and consequences," *International Marketing Review*, 23, No. 2 (2006): 161. Copyright © 2006, Emerald Group Publishing Limited.

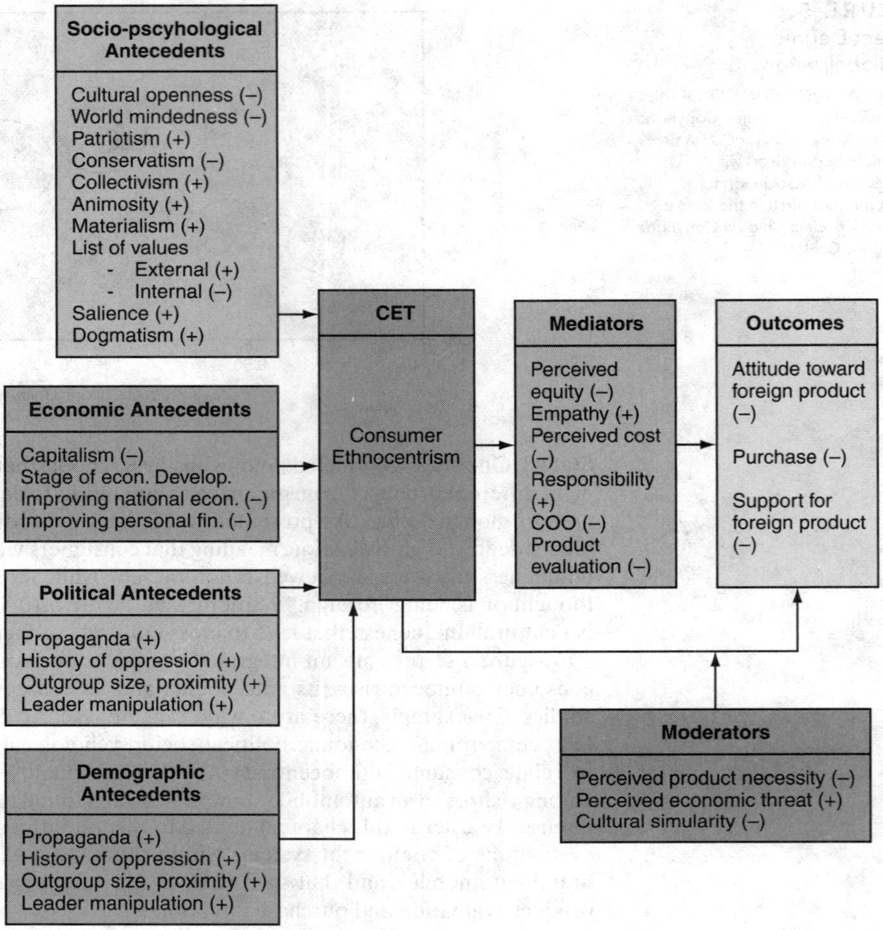

Brand Personality

Learning Objective

5.4 *To Understand How Marketers Seek to Create Brand Personalities-Like Traits.*

Earlier in this chapter, as part of our discussion of Freudian theory, we introduced the notion of *product personality.* Consumers also subscribe to the notion of *brand personality*; that is, they attribute various descriptive personality-like traits or characteristics to different brands in a wide variety of product categories. Moreover, a brand personality provides an emotional identity for a brand, and encourages consumers to respond with feelings and emotions toward the brand.[64] For instance, with some help from frequent advertising, consumers tend to see Perdue (chickens) as representing freshness, Nike as the athlete in all of us, and BMW as being performance driven.[65] In a similar fashion, the brand personality for Snapple has been referred to as "quirky," because the product is considered to be "irreverent," "fun," "approachable," and "down to earth."[66] Such personality-like images of brands reflect consumers' visions of the inner core of many strong brands of consumer products. As these examples reveal, a brand's personality can either be functional ("dependable and rugged") or symbolic ("the athlete in all of us").[67] There is common sense and research evidence to conclude that any brand personality, as long as it is *strong* and *favorable*, will strengthen a brand.[68]

Research studies have found that a strong, positive brand personality leads to more favorable attitudes toward the brand, brand preference, higher purchase intentions, and brand loyalty, and is a way for consumers to differentiate among competing brands. Brand personality may also play a greater role in the consumables product category (e.g., toothpaste) than in the durable product category (e.g., automobile), where the value proposition is of greater importance.[69] In the same vein, for a consumable like wine, a study of wine label designs revealed that brand personality impacted intention to purchase the wine.[70] Also, consider that Coca-Cola Zero is marketed without any particular reference to it being a diet beverage. It appears that

Coca-Cola is marketing Zero to young people, especially young men, who may see a stigma attached to the word *diet*.[71] A stream of research on product/brand personality has found that of all the marketing mix elements, marketing communication most often has the greatest influence in creating a brand personality. A recent research effort examined the dimensions of brand personality for products marketed by 64 American multinational corporations. The study looked at 270 Web sites created by these corporations in the UK, France, Germany, the United States, and Spain, and concluded that the five underlying "intended" dimensions of brand personality stimuli are excitement, sophistication, affection, popularity, and competence. Furthermore, these dimensions of brand personality were found to be traceable from the creative advertising appeals that these multinational corporations represent on their Web sites.[72]

It is also important to note that like product brands, service brands also have personalities. Service brand personality traits are presented, with examples, in Table 5.10. These traits are divided into two categories: (1) traits derived from the Brand Personality Scale, which are typically used to measure brand personality, and (2) traits derived from the Five Factor Model of Personality to further refine the dimensions of service personality.[73]

PRODUCT ANTHROPOMORPHISM

Anthropomorphism can be loosely defined as attributing human characteristics to something that is not human. For example, a recent study focusing on anthropomorphized products found that the ease with which consumers could anthropomorphize an offering was a function of how the product was presented to the public and the inclusion or absence of human-like product features. Products presented as human but which lack human features tend to be evaluated less favorably by consumers than products that are presented as human and have human-like attributes.[74]

TABLE 5.10 Service Personality Traits

TRAIT	DESCRIPTION	SERVICES EXAMPLE
BPS TRAITS		
Sincerity	Service is perceived as honest, genuine, cheerful, and domestic	Employees exhibit genuine interest in meeting customers' needs and striving to meet customer goals
Excitement	Customers perceive service as daring and spirited	Employees exhibit a liveliness that they attempt to instill into service
Competence	Service is perceived as responsible, reliable, efficient, and dependable	Employees demonstrate applicable knowledge about the service
Sophistication	Customers perceive service as charming, romantic, and glamorous	Employees carry themselves in a manner that dignifies themselves, and the service
Ruggedness	Service is perceived as tough, strong, and outdoorsy	Employees exhibit strong, bold confident behaviors
FFM TRAITS		
Agreeableness	A disposition to express kindness, sympathy, and compassion to others	Employees treat customers with both kindness and politeness
Extroversion	Operationalized as introversion, this trait represents a tendency to reveal feelings of bashfulness and preferences to be alone	Employees tend to approach customers with natural ease and confidence
Creativity	A tendency to use original ideas and find novel solutions to problems, to use the imagination	Employees find creative solutions to customers' problems
Stability	A disposition to be moody and temperamental; a tendency toward emotionality	Employees maintain a consistent level of emotionality during interactions with customers
Conscientiousness	The extent to which one is careful, diligent, and organized	Employees appear well prepared and organized during customer interactions

Source: Eric G. Harris and David E. Fleming, "Assessing the Human Element in Service Personality Formation: Personality Congruency and the Five Factor Model," *Journal of Services Marketing,* 19, no. 4 (2005): 191.

Some marketers encourage anthropomorphism by giving their product a personality. Two examples are Tony the Tiger or Mr. Peanut. Still further, you may know people who name their cars or argue with their PCs when they are experiencing computer problems. Additional aspects of product anthropomorphism will be discussed in the following two sections—brand personification and brand personality and gender.

BRAND PERSONIFICATION

Some marketers find it useful to create a **brand personification**, which tries to recast consumers' perception of the attributes of a product or service into a human-like character. For instance, in focus group research, well-known brands of dishwashing liquid have been likened to "demanding task masters" or "high-energy people." Many consumers express their inner feelings about products or brands in terms of their association with known personalities. Identifying consumers' current brand–personality links and creating personality links for new products are important marketing tasks.

The M&M "people" are an ongoing "fun" example of brand personification. It is based on the line of questioning that could ask the following: "If an M&M (or a chocolate-coated peanut variety) was a person, what kind of person would it be?" Additional questioning would be likely to explore how the color of the coating impacts consumers' perceived personality for the "M&M people" (see the discussion of personality and color).

To personify and humanize its model consumer, Celestial Seasonings, Inc., **(www.celestialseasonings.com)** a specialty tea maker, refers in its advertising to "Tracy Jones." And just who is Tracy Jones? According to Celestial Seasonings, she is "female, upscale, well educated, and highly involved in life in every way."[75] In a similar fashion, Mr. Coffee, a popular brand of automatic-drip coffeemakers, unexpectedly found in its focus group research that consumers were referring to Mr. Coffee as if the product were a person (e.g., "he makes good coffee" and "he's got a lot of different models and prices").[76] After careful consideration, the marketers decided to explore the possibility of creating a *brand personification.* Initial consumer research indicated that Mr. Coffee was seen as being "dependable," "friendly," "efficient," "intelligent," and "smart."

Figure 5.12 presents a *brand personality framework* that reflects extensive consumer research designed to pinpoint the structure and nature of a brand's personality. The framework suggests that there are five defining *dimensions* of a brand's personality ("sincerity," "excitement," "competence," "sophistication," and "ruggedness"), and 15 *facets* of personality that flow from the five dimensions (i.e., "down-to-earth," "daring," "reliable," "upper class," and "outdoors").[77] If we carefully review these brand personality dimensions and facets, it appears that this framework tends to accommodate the brand personalities pursued by many consumer products.

It is important to point out that the consumer sometimes develops a relationship with a brand that is similar in certain respects to the relationships they have with other humans (e.g., friends, family, neighbors). Some consumers, for example, become "brand zealots," and develop a relationship that goes beyond a functional need. An example of this would be VW Beetle

FIGURE 5.12
A Brand Personality Framework

Source: JOURNAL OF MARKETING RESEARCH by Aaker, Jennifer L. Copyright 1997 by American Marketing Association. Reproduced with permission of American Marketing Association in the format Textbook via Copyright Clearance Center.

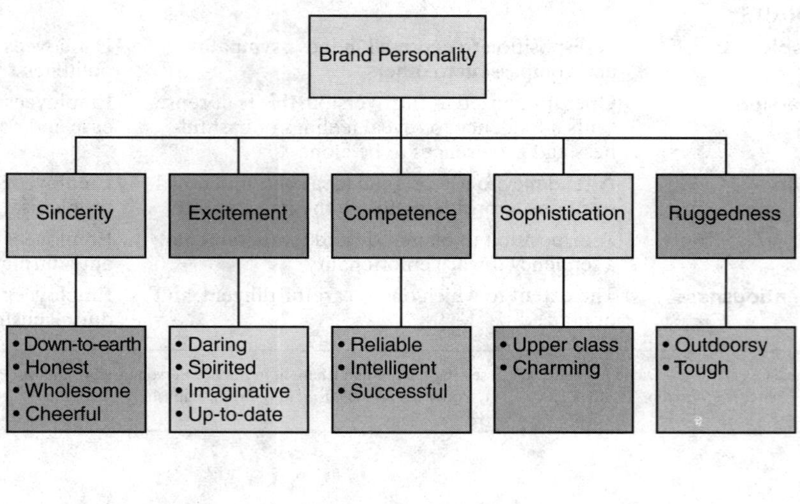

FIGURE 5.13

Source: Used with permission from Volkswagen Group of America, Inc.

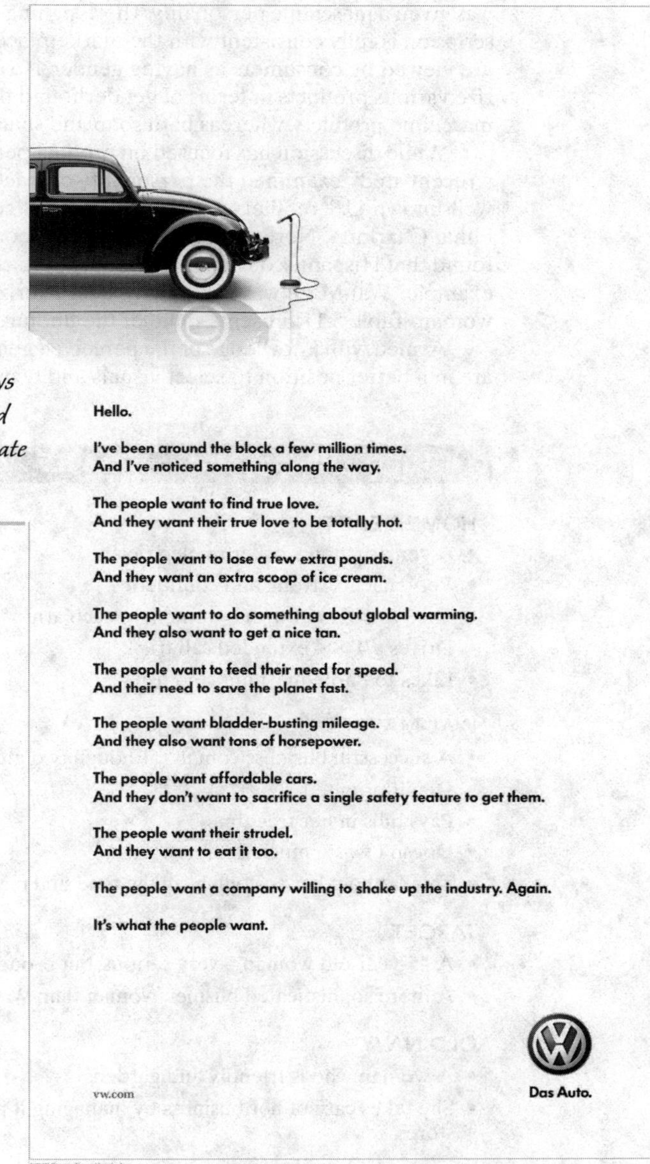

QUESTION: *In What Ways Do Max and Other Brand Personifications Help Create VW's Brand Image?*

owners who give their cars names and who can be seen talking to their vehicles and affectionately stroking them (i.e., anthropomorphism, which was discussed previously). Going a step further, Volkswagen recently introduced into some of its advertising messages an original 1950s Beetle, Max, who in the United States, speaks English with a German accent and is often "interviewed" about VW products. Further, Max serves as a personification for the Volkswagen brand, and more specifically as a reference point for the new Beetle (see Figure 5.13). He also reinforces the continuation of the notion of treating one's "beloved" VW Beetle as a "friend." Another example would be the Harley-Davidson motorcycle owners who go so far as getting a Harley tattoo. While in an "exchange relationship" the consumer gets something back in return, brand zealots develop a "communal relationship" with the product and demonstrate a passion that is typically associated only with close friends and family.[78]

PRODUCT PERSONALITY AND GENDER

A product personality, or persona, frequently endows the product or brand with a gender. For instance, Celestial Seasonings' Tracy Jones was given a feminine persona, whereas Mr. Coffee was given a masculine personality. The assigning of gender as part of a product's personality description is fully consistent with the marketplace reality that products and services, in general, are viewed by consumers as having gender. A study that asked Chinese consumers to categorize various products in terms of gender found that they perceived coffee and toothpaste to be masculine products, whereas bath soap and shampoo were seen as feminine products.[79]

While discussion has focused on product personality with respect to products and services, a recent study examined the personality characteristics that Hispanic shoppers associate with well-known U.S. retailers. Using focus groups conducted in Spanish in Columbia, South Carolina; Charlotte, North Carolina; Atlanta, Georgia; and Siloam Springs, Arkansas, the study found that Hispanic consumers definitely do ascribe personality characteristics to retailers. For example, Wal-Mart was frequently characterized as a detail-oriented, successful businesswoman. Table 5.11 presents some of the findings of the research.[80]

Armed with knowledge of the perceived gender of a product or a specific brand, marketers are in a better position to select visuals and text copy for various marketing messages.

TABLE 5.11 Personification of U.S. Retailers by Hispanic Consumers

HOME DEPOT
- A construction worker or electrician
- Very macho, strong and confident
- The type of man with a woman on each arm
- Drives a 4 × 4 extended cab truck
- Likes to barbeque, hunt, and fish

WAL-MART
- A successful businesswoman (although two groups described Wal-Mart as male)
- Detail-oriented
- Pays bills in her free time
- Doesn't waste much time
- Thinks about her customers all the time, and makes sure she has what they need in emergencies

TARGET
- A 45-year-old woman—very serious, but proud
- A more sophisticated businesswoman than Wal-Mart

OLD NAVY
- A woman who is friendly and gardens
- She takes care of her business by managing it herself, and tries to get more people into her stores

SEARS
- An elegant man driving an expensive car
- Attends cocktail parties and dabbles in politics

MARSHALLS
- A sophisticated man

TJMAXX
- A woman who is fashionable, young, and scatterbrained

ROSS
- A thin, blond, tall, elegant businesswoman who wears long skirts

Source: Scarlett C. Wesley, Deborah C. Fowler, and Maria Elena Vazquez, "Retail Personality and the Hispanic Consumer: An Exploration of American Retailers," *Managing Service Quality,* 16, no. 2 (2006): 177–180.

PRODUCT PERSONALITY AND GEOGRAPHY

Marketers learned long ago that certain products, in the minds of consumers, possess a strong geographical association (e.g., New England clam chowder). Consequently, by employing geography in the product's name, the product's manufacturer creates a geographic personality for the product. Such a geographic personality can lead to geographic equity for the brand, meaning that in the consumer's memory, the knowledge of the brand reflects a strong geographic association.

Interestingly, geographic brand names can be either familiar or unfamiliar (or fictitious). For example, take Philadelphia Cream Cheese. In fact, it is manufactured in the U.S. state of Illinois, even though it uses the name of one of the largest cities in the United States. Still further, although we all know that Arizona is a state, AriZona Iced Tea is brewed and bottled in the state of New York. Fictitious geographic product names include Hidden Valley salad dressings and Bear Creek soups.[81]

But more important than whether the name is real or fictitious is whether the location and its image add to the product's brand equity.[82] Although Texas Best Barbecue Sauce may be made in the U.S. state of New Jersey, many Americans associate barbecue with the state of Texas. Similarly, the Old El Paso brand of salsa capitalizes on the Mexican influence in the Southwest. The product may be made in Minneapolis, but a brand of salsa named Twin Cities Salsa (e.g., Minneapolis/St. Paul) just does not have the same cachet. Table 5.12 provides a list of familiar and not-so-familiar geographic brand names.

PERSONALITY AND COLOR

Consumers not only ascribe personality traits to products and services, but they also tend to associate personality factors with specific colors. For instance, Coca-Cola (www.coca-cola.com) is associated with red, which connotes excitement. Blue bottles are often used to sell wine because the color blue appeals particularly to female consumers, and they buy the majority of wine.[83] Yellow is associated with novelty, and black frequently connotes sophistication.[84] For this reason, brands wishing to create a sophisticated persona (such as Pasta LaBella) or an upscale or premium image (e.g., Miller Beer's Miller Reserve) use labeling or packaging that is primarily black. A combination of black and white communicates that a product is carefully engineered, high tech, and sophisticated in design. The Thinkpad (now the Lenovo Thinkpad, formerly the IBM Thinkpad) has consistently been an all-black case with a red button to house a very successful line of laptops. Nike has used black, white, and a touch of red for selected models of its sports shoes. This color combination seems to imply advanced-performance sports

TABLE 5.12 Examples of Geographic Brand Names

GEOGRAPHIC ORIENTATION	BRAND NAME	PRODUCT	LOCALE
Familiar/Actual	*KC Masterpiece*	BBQ sauce	Oakland, CA
	London Pub	Vinegar	Bloomfield, NJ
	Old El Paso	Salsa	Minneapolis, MN
	Old Milwaukee	Beer	Detroit, MI
	Philadelphia	Cream cheese	Glenview, IL
	San Francisco Intl.	Buns and rolls	Totowa, NJ
	AriZona Iced Tea	Iced tea	Lake Success, NY
Unfamiliar/Fictitious	*Bear Creek*	Soup	Harbor City, UT
	Green Forest	Paper towels	Mexico
	Hidden Valley	Salad dressing	Oakland, CA
	Italian Village	Ravioli	Secaucus, NJ
	Pepperwood Grove	Wine	Oakville, CA
	Sorrel Ridge	Jam	Port Reading, NJ

Source: Reprinted with permission from Proceedings of the American Marketing Association's Winter Educators' Conference, published by the American Marketing Association, K. Damon Aiken, Eric C. Koch, and Robert Mandrigal, Winter 2000, Vol. 11, 301–308.

TABLE 5.13 The Personality-Like Associations of Selected Colors

COLOR	PERSONALITY LINK	MARKETING INSIGHTS
Blue	Commands respect, authority	• America's favored color • IBM holds the title to blue • Associated with club soda • Men seek products packaged in blue • Houses painted blue are avoided • Low-calorie, skim milk • Coffee in a blue can perceived as "mild"
Yellow	Caution, novelty, temporary, warmth	• Eyes register it fastest • Coffee in yellow can taste "weak" • Stops traffic • Sells a house
Green	Secure, natural, relaxed or easygoing, living things	• Good work environment • Associated with vegetables and chewing gum • Canada Dry ginger ale sales increased when it changed its sugar-free package from red to green and white
Red	Human, exciting, hot, passionate, strong	• Makes food "smell" better • Coffee in a red can perceived as "rich" • Women have a preference for bluish red • Men have a preference for yellowish red • Coca-Cola "owns" red
Orange	Powerful, affordable, informal	• Draws attention quickly
Brown	Informal and relaxed, masculine, nature	• Coffee in a dark-brown can was "too strong" • Men seek products packaged in brown
White	Goodness, purity, chastity, cleanliness, delicacy, refinement, formality	• Suggests reduced calories • Pure and wholesome food • Clean, bath products, feminine
Black	Sophistication, power, authority, mystery	• Powerful clothing • High-tech electronics
Silver, Gold, Platinum	Regal, wealthy, stately	• Suggests premium price

Source: From "Color Schemes," by Bernice Kannaer in *New York Magazine,* April 3, 1989. Reprinted by permission of Primedia.

shoes. A recent print and outdoor advertising campaign for Life Savers, based on consumer flavor and color research, characterizes *cherry* as "Ms. Popularity," *lime* as "The Outsider," and *sour apple* and *cherry* (targeted to teens) as "The Troublemakers."[85] Many fast-food restaurants use combinations of bright colors, like red, yellow, and blue, for their roadside signs and interior designs. These colors have come to be associated with fast service and inexpensive food. In contrast, fine dining restaurants tend to use sophisticated colors like gray, white, shades of tan, or other soft, pale, or muted colors to reflect the feeling of fine, leisurely service. Table 5.13 presents a list of various colors, their personality-like meanings, and associated marketing insights.

As part of its *2005 Color Survey*, BuzzBack Market Research asked consumers to look over a palette of 44 color shades and to indicate which one best reflects their nature. The six color shades cited with the greatest frequency were Palace Blue (11 percent), Fiery Red (9 percent), Sunshine (7 percent), Little Boy Blue (6 percent), Sailor Blue (5 percent), and Black Limo (4 percent). Interestingly, while the top selection for males was Palace Blue (17 percent), two top selections among women were Fiery Red and Sunshine (9 percent each).[86] Table 5.14 presents the associations made by consumers with a "personal shade."

TABLE 5.14 Consumers' Associations with a Personal Shade

PALACE BLUE IS . . .	
"calming/peaceful"	27%
FIERY RED IS . . .	
"fiery/hot" and "energetic"	24%
SUNSHINE IS . . .	
"happy/cheerful"	58%
"bright"	30%
"optimistic"	25%
"sunny"	19%
LITTLE BOY BLUE IS . . .	
"calming/peaceful"	28%
a "favorite color"	21%
"easygoing/laid back"	16%
"happy/cheerful"	16%
SAILOR BLUE IS . . .	
a "favorite color"	19%
"strong/powerful"	18%
"calming/peaceful"	17%
BLACK LIMO IS . . .	
"dark"	19%
"matches everything/basic"	19%
"mysterious"	14%
"fits my mood"	14%
a "favorite color"	13%
"strong/powerful"	12%

Source: *Brandweek*, April 4, 2005, 24.

Self and Self-Image

LEARNING OBJECTIVE

5.5 *To Understand How the Products and Services That Consumers Use Enhance Their Self-Images.*

Consumers have a variety of enduring images of themselves. These self-images, or perceptions of self, are very closely associated with personality in that individuals tend to buy products and services and patronize retailers whose images or personalities relate in some meaningful way to their own self-images. In essence, consumers seek to depict themselves in their brand choices—they tend to approach products with images that could enhance their self-concept and avoid those products that do not.[87] In this section, we examine the issue of *one* or *multiple* selves, explore the makeup of the self-image, the notion of **extended self**, and the possibilities or options of *altering the self-image.*

ONE OR MULTIPLE SELVES

Historically, individuals have been thought to have a single self-image and to be interested, as consumers, in products and services that satisfy that single self. However, it is more accurate to think of consumers as having **multiple selves.**[88] This thinking reflects the understanding that a single consumer is likely to act quite differently with different people and in different situations. For instance, a person is likely to behave in different ways with parents, at school, at work, at a museum opening, or with friends at a nightclub. The healthy or normal person is likely to display a somewhat different personality in each of these different situations or social **roles**. In fact, acting exactly the same in all situations or roles and not adapting to the situation at hand may be considered a sign of an abnormal or unhealthy person.

In terms of consumer behavior, the idea that an individual embodies a number of different "selves" (i.e., has multiple self-images) suggests that marketers should target their products and services to consumers *within the context of a particular "self,"* and in certain cases, a choice of different products for different *selves.* (The notion of a consumer having multiple selves or playing multiple roles supports the application of usage situation as a segmentation base discussed in Chapter 3.)

The Makeup of the Self-Image

Consistent with the idea of multiple self-images, each individual has an image of himself or herself as a certain kind of person, with certain traits, skills, habits, possessions, relationships, and ways of behaving. As with other types of images and personality, the individual's self-image is unique, the outgrowth of that person's background and experience. Individuals develop their self-images through interactions with other people—initially their parents, and then other individuals or groups with whom they relate over the years.

In examining the growth of self-image and brand connections (i.e., using brands to communicate self-concept), there is evidence that these brand connections increase with age, and first develop between middle childhood and early adolescence. A limited number of such connections are formed in middle childhood, and these connections stem from concept associations with the brand (i.e., buying/owning branded items). Moving into adolescence, not only do the number of self-brand connections increase, but brands are now viewed as being connected to the person's self-concept, because the brand "has the same personality, user characteristics, or reference group affiliation."[89]

Products and brands have symbolic value for individuals, who evaluate them on the basis of their consistency (congruence) with their personal pictures or images of themselves. Some products seem to match one or more of an individual's self-images; others seem totally alien. It is generally believed that consumers attempt to preserve or enhance their self-images by selecting products and brands with "images" or "personalities" that they believe are congruent with their own self-images and avoiding products that are not.[90] Indeed, a research study on product personality and consumer preference found "that people prefer products with a product personality that matches their self-image.[91] This seems to be especially true for women; research reveals that more women than men (77 percent versus 64 percent) feel that the brands they select reflect their personalities.[92]

Given this relationship between brand preference and consumers' self-images, it is natural that consumers use brands to help them in their task of defining themselves. Research indicates that consumers who have strong links to particular brands—a positive self-brand connection—see such brands *as representing an aspect of themselves.* For marketers, such *connections* are certainly an important step in the formation of consumer loyalty and a positive relationship with consumers.[93] Consider the two charts presented in Figure 5.14, which show purchase intent to be strongest when there is a good fit between brand image and self-image.[94]

A variety of different self-images have been recognized in the consumer behavior literature for a long time. In particular, many researchers have depicted some or all of the following kinds of self-image: (1) **actual self-image** (how consumers in fact see themselves), (2) **ideal self-image** (how consumers would like to see themselves), (3) **social self-image** (how consumers feel others see them), and (4) **ideal social self-image** (how consumers would like others to see them). The headline in Figure 5.15 "Try telling her it's too late for full locks" appeals to actual self-image because it is communicating with "middle-aged" women who like their hair long to continue doing so.

It also seems useful to think in terms of two other types of self-images—**expected self** and the **"ought-to" self**. The *expected self-image* (how consumers expect to see themselves at some specified future time) is somewhere between the *actual* and *ideal* self-images. It is a future-oriented combination of what is (the actual self-image) and what consumers would like to be (the ideal self-image). As another interesting type of self-image—the *"ought-to" self*—consists of traits or characteristics that an individual believes it is his or her duty or obligation to possess.[95] Examples of this form of self-image might be the striving to achieve a deeper religious understanding or the seeking of a fair and just solution to a challenging ethical problem. Because the expected self and the ought-to self provide consumers with a realistic opportunity to change the self, they are both likely to be more valuable to marketers than the actual or ideal self-image as a guide for designing and promoting products.

FIGURE 5.14
Self-Image, Brand Image, and Purchase Intent.
(a) Fragrance Commercial: Self-Image and Brand-Image Convergence Among Respondents with Strong Purchase Intent.
(b) Fragrance Commercial: Self-Image and Brand-Image Convergence Among Respondents with Weak Purchase Intent

Source: Abhilasha Mehta, "Using Self-Concept to Assess Advertising Effectiveness," *Journal of Advertising Research* (February 1999): 87.

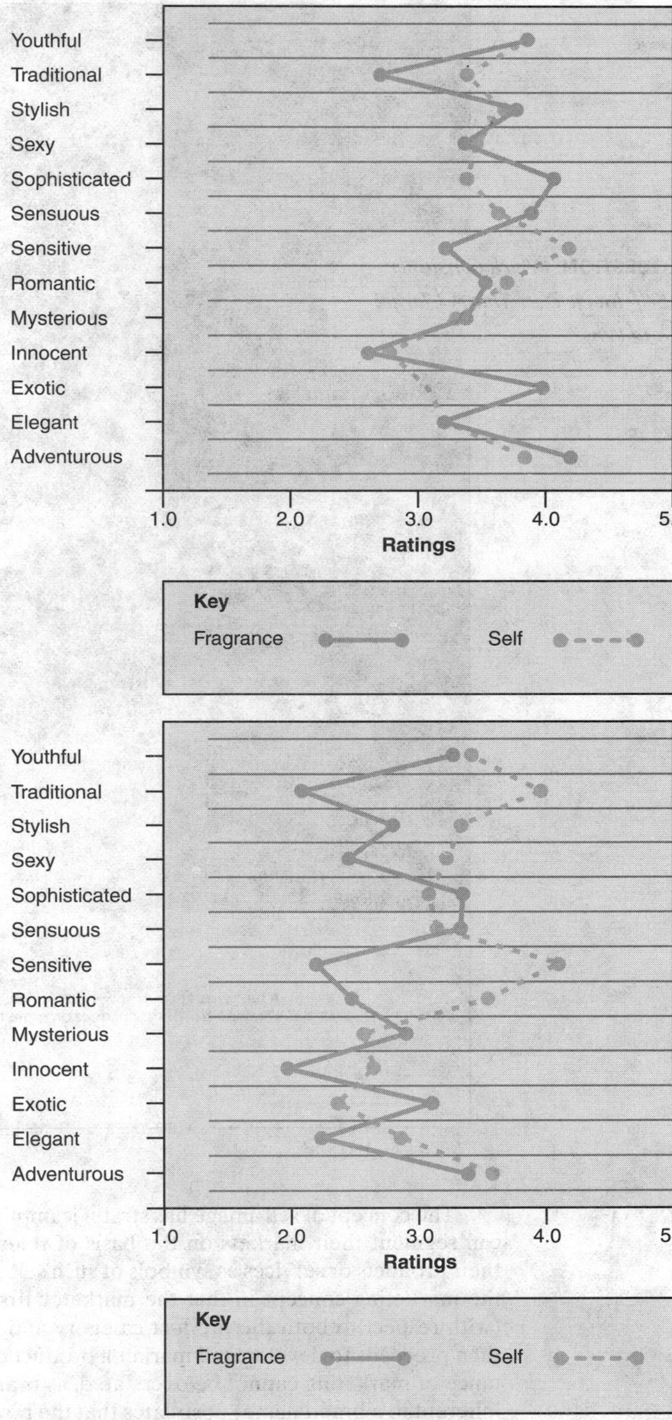

In different contexts (i.e., in different situations and/or with respect to different products), consumers might select a different self-image to guide their attitudes or behavior. For instance, with some everyday household products, consumers might be guided by their actual self-image, whereas for some socially enhancing or socially conspicuous products, they might be guided by their social self-image. When it comes to an important and a strong personal goal or wish, like losing weight and feeling better about oneself and one's appearance, individuals might be guided by either their ideal self-images or ideal social self-images.

FIGURE 5.15
Source: Courtesy of Dove.

QUESTION: *Which Consumer Self-Image Does This Ad Target and Why?*

The concept of self-image has strategic implications for marketers. For example, marketers can segment their markets on the basis of relevant consumer self-images and then position their products or services as symbols of such self-images. Such a strategy is fully consistent with the marketing concept in that the marketer first assesses the needs of a consumer segment (with respect to both the product category and to an appropriate symbol of self-image) and then proceeds to develop and market a product or service that meets both criteria. The importance of marketing cannot be overstated, as brand equity theory (which focuses on the value inherent in a brand name) postulates that the power of a brand resides in the consumer's mind from both lived (purchase and usage) and mediated (advertising and promotion) experiences.[96]

THE EXTENDED SELF

The interrelationship between consumers' self-images and their possessions (i.e., objects they call their own) is an exciting topic. Specifically, consumers' possessions can be seen to confirm or extend their self-images. For instance, acquiring a desired or sought-after pair of "vintage" Levi jeans might serve to expand or enrich a Brazilian teenager's image of self. The teenager

TABLE 5.15 Sample Items from an Extended Self-Survey[a]

My ________ holds a special place in my life.
My ________ is central to my identity.
I feel emotionally attached to my ________.
My ________ helps me narrow the gap between what I am and try to be.
If my ________ was stolen from me, I would feel as if part of me is missing.
I would be a different person without my ________.
I take good care of my ________.
I trust my ________.

[a]A 6-point agree–disagree scale was used.

Source: From "Peak Experiences and Mountain Biking: Incorporating the Bike in the Extended Self," by Kimberly J. Dodson in *Advances in Consumer Research,* 1996. Reprinted by permission of Association for Consumer Research.

might now see herself as being more desirable, more fashionable, and more successful because she has a pair of the sought-after "vintage jeans." In a similar manner, if the watch that a college student (let's call him Fred) received as a gift from his aunt was stolen, Fred is likely to feel diminished in some way. Indeed, the loss of a prized possession may lead Fred to "grieve" and to experience a variety of emotions, such as frustration, loss of control, the feeling of being violated, even the loss of magical protection. Table 5.15 presents sample items from a measurement instrument designed to reflect how particular possessions (e.g., a watch) might become part of one's extended self.

The previous examples suggest that much human emotion can be connected to valued possessions. In such cases, possessions are considered extensions of the self. It has been proposed that possessions can extend the self in a number of ways: (1) *actually*, by allowing the person to do things that otherwise would be very difficult or impossible to accomplish (e.g., problem solving by using a computer); (2) *symbolically*, by making the person feel better or "bigger" (receiving an employee award for excellence); (3) by *conferring status or rank* (e.g., among collectors of rare works of art because of the ownership of a particular masterpiece); (4) by *bestowing feelings of immortality* by leaving valued possessions to young family members (this also has the potential of extending the recipients' selves); and (5) by *endowing with magical powers* (e.g., a pair of cuff links inherited from one's grandfather might be perceived as magic amulets bestowing good luck when they are worn).[97]

ALTERING THE SELF

Sometimes consumers wish to change themselves to become a different or improved self. Clothing, grooming aids or cosmetics, and all kinds of accessories (such as sunglasses, jewelry, tattoos, or even colored contact lenses) offer consumers the opportunity to modify their appearances (to create a "makeover") and thereby to alter their "selves." In using *self-altering products*, consumers are frequently attempting to express their individualism or uniqueness by creating a new self, maintaining the existing self (or preventing the loss of self), and extending the self (modifying or changing the self). Still further, sometimes consumers use self-altering products or services to conform to or take on the appearance of a particular type of person (such as a military person, a physician, a business executive, or a college professor).

Closely related to both self-image and altering the self is the idea of *personal vanity.* As a descriptor of people, vanity is often associated with acting self-important, self-interested, or admiring one's own appearance or achievements. Using a "vanity scale" (Table 5.16), researchers have investigated both *physical vanity* (an excessive concern for and/or a positive—or inflated—view of one's physical appearance) and *achievement vanity* (an excessive concern for and/or a positive or inflated view of one's personal achievements). They have found both these ideas are related to materialism, use of cosmetics, concern with clothing, and country club membership.[98]

There is also research evidence to suggest that self-monitoring may serve as a moderating variable when it comes to how well a person is guided by situational cues regarding social appropriateness. Low self-monitors are individuals who are typically guided by their inner feelings, whereas high self-monitors claim that they act differently in different situations and

TABLE 5.16 Sample Items from a Vanity Scale

PHYSICAL-CONCERN ITEMS

1. The way I look is extremely important to me.
2. I am very concerned with my appearance.
3. It is important that I always look good.

PHYSICAL-VIEW ITEMS

1. People notice how attractive I am.
2. People are envious of my good looks.
3. My body is sexually appealing.

ACHIEVEMENT-CONCERN ITEMS

1. Professional achievements are an obsession with me.
2. Achieving greater success than my peers is important to me.
3. I want my achievements to be recognized by others.

ACHIEVEMENT-VIEW ITEMS

1. My achievements are highly regarded by others.
2. I am a good example of professional success.
3. Others wish they were as successful as me.

Source: From "Trait Aspects of Vanity: Measurement and Relevance to Consumer Behavior," by Netemeyer, Burton, and Lichtenstein in *Journal of Consumer Research,* Vol. 21, March 1995. Reprinted by permission of the publisher.

with different people.[99] Consequently, high self-monitors might be more prone to employ a self-altering product in order to enhance their ideal social self-image.

Altering one's self, particularly one's appearance or body parts, can be accomplished by cosmetics, hair restyling or coloring, getting a tattoo, switching from eyeglasses to contact lenses (or the reverse), undergoing cosmetic surgery, or a "makeover."

Virtual Personality or Self

LEARNING OBJECTIVE

5.6 *To Understand How Consumers Can Create Online Identities Reflecting a Particular Set of Personality Traits.*

With the widespread interest in using the Internet as a form of entertainment and as a social vehicle to meet new people with similar interests, there has been a tremendous growth in the use of online chat rooms. People who visit chat rooms are able to carry on real-time conversations about themselves and topics of mutual interest with people from all over the globe. Because at the present time most chats are actually text conversations rather than live video broadcasts, the participants usually never get to see each other. This creates an opportunity for chat room participants to try out new identities or to change their identities while online. For instance, one can change from male to female (known as "gender swapping"), from old to young, from married to single, from white-collar professional to blue-collar worker, or from grossly overweight to svelte. In terms of personality, one can change from mild-mannered to aggressive, or from introvert to extrovert.

The notion of a **virtual personality** or **virtual self** provides an individual with the opportunity to try on different personalities or different identities, much like going to the mall and trying on different outfits in a department or specialty store. If the identity fits, or the personality can be enhanced, the individual may decide to keep the new personality in favor of his or her old personality. From a consumer behavior point of view, it is likely that such opportunities to try out a new personality or alter the self may result in changes in selected forms of purchase behavior. This may in turn offer marketers new opportunities to target various "online selves."

Want to find out about your personality online? One Web site, **www.outofservice.com/bigfive**, offers Internet users an online test called "The Big Five Personality Test," which takes a few minutes to finish and measures five fundamental dimensions of personality. Give it a try.

SUMMARY

Personality can be described as the psychological characteristics that both determine and reflect how a person responds to his or her environment. Although personality tends to be consistent and enduring, it may change abruptly in response to major life events, as well as gradually over time.

Three theories of personality are prominent in the study of consumer behavior: psychoanalytic theory, neo-Freudian theory, and trait theory. Freud's psychoanalytic theory provides the foundation for the study of motivational research, which operates on the premise that human drives are largely unconscious in nature and serve to motivate many consumer actions. Neo-Freudian theory tends to emphasize the fundamental role of social relationships in the formation and development of personality. Alfred Adler viewed human beings as seeking to overcome feelings of inferiority. Harry Stack Sullivan believed that people attempt to establish significant and rewarding relationships with others. Karen Horney saw individuals as trying to overcome feelings of anxiety and categorized them as compliant, aggressive, or detached.

Trait theory is a major departure from the qualitative (or subjective) approach to personality measurement. It postulates that individuals possess innate psychological traits (e.g., innovativeness, novelty seeking, need for cognition, materialism) to a greater or lesser degree, and that these traits can be measured by specially designed scales or inventories. Because they are simple to use and to score and can be self-administered, personality inventories are the preferred method for many researchers in the assessment of consumer personality. Product and brand personalities represent real opportunities for marketers to take advantage of consumers' connections to various brands they offer. Brands often have personalities—some include "human-like" traits and even gender. These brand personalities help shape consumer responses, preferences, and loyalties.

Each individual has a perceived self-image (or multiple self-images) as a certain kind of person with certain traits, habits, possessions, relationships, and ways of behaving. Consumers frequently attempt to preserve, enhance, alter, or extend their self-images by purchasing products or services and shopping at stores they perceive as consistent with their relevant self-image(s) and by avoiding products and stores they perceive are not. With the growth of the Internet, there appear to be emerging virtual selves or virtual personalities. Consumer experiences with chat rooms sometimes provide an opportunity to explore new or alternative identities.

DISCUSSION QUESTIONS

1. How would you explain the fact that, although no two individuals have identical personalities, personality is sometimes used in consumer research to identify distinct and sizable market segments?
2. Contrast the major characteristics of the following personality theories: (a) Freudian theory, (b) neo-Freudian theory, and (c) trait theory. In your answer, illustrate how each theory is applied to the understanding of consumer behavior.
3. Describe personality trait theory. Give five examples of how personality traits can be used in consumer research.
4. How can a marketer of cameras use research findings that indicate a target market consists primarily of inner-directed or other-directed consumers? Of consumers who are high (or low) on innovativeness?
5. Describe the type of promotional message that would be most suitable for each of the following personality market segments and give an example of each: (a) highly dogmatic consumers, (b) inner-directed consumers, (c) consumers with high optimum stimulation levels, (d) consumers with a high need for cognition, and (e) consumers who are visualizers versus consumers who are verbalizers.
6. Is there likely to be a difference in personality traits between individuals who readily purchase foreign-made products and those who prefer American-made products? How can marketers use the consumer ethnocentrism scale to segment consumers?
7. A marketer of health foods is attempting to segment a certain market on the basis of consumer self-image. Describe the four types of consumer self-image and discuss which one(s) would be most effective for the stated purpose.

EXERCISES

1. How do your clothing preferences differ from those of your friends? What personality traits might explain why your preferences are different from those of other people?
2. Find three print advertisements based on Freudian personality theory. Discuss how Freudian concepts are used in these ads. Do any of the ads personify a brand? If so, how?
3. Administer the nine items from the materialism scale (listed in Table 5.5) to two of your friends. In your view, are their consumption behaviors consistent with their scores on the scale? Why or why not?

KEY TERMS

- actual self-image *164*
- brand personification *158*
- cognitive personality factors *147*
- compulsive consumption *151*
- consumer dogmatism *144*
- consumer ethnocentrism *140*
- consumer innovativeness *140*
- consumer innovators *141*
- consumer materialism *140*
- expected self *164*
- extended self *163*
- Freudian theory *137*
- ideal self-image *164*
- ideal social self-image *164*
- inner-directedness *144*
- multiple selves *163*
- need for cognition *147*
- neo-Freudian theory *137*
- optimum stimulation levels (OSLs) *145*
- other-directedness *144*
- "ought-to" self *164*
- personality *136*
- psychoanalytic theory of personality *137*
- roles *163*
- sensation seeking (SS) *146*
- social self-image *164*
- trait theory *137*
- variety or novelty seeking *146*
- virtual personality or self *168*
- visualizers versus verbalizers *147*

Case One: Hello Hong Kong Starbucks!

Strolling along the streets in any major districts in China's Hong Kong, you'll easily find at least one Starbucks, if not more. And there is a tendency for the Maxim Caterers Ltd., the sole distributor of Starbucks in Hong Kong, to increase the number of stores in the high-traffic areas of Hong Kong, for example, Central and the airport. Starbucks has already expanded to more than 100 stores in Hong Kong and about 400 stores in mainland China.

For many a coffee lover in Hong Kong, Starbucks has conquered their minds. Traditionally, people would socialize in Chinese restaurants, however today, many people have become accustomed to spending their time at the nearby Starbucks. Not only can people buy coffee from Starbucks, but also specialty beverages, merchandise and gifts, Starbucks cards, and fresh food (e.g., puff and pie, bakery, dessert, salad, etc.). Due to the availability of Wi-Fi technology, people work on their laptops, have a chat with their friends, or have a meeting with suppliers in Starbucks. Is there any working adult in Hong Kong who doesn't know what Starbucks is?

QUESTIONS

Since everybody knows Starbucks, answer the following questions (if you need any help with your answers, you might want to access **www.starbucks.com**):

1. If Starbucks was an animal, which animal would it be, and why?
2. If Starbucks was a color, which color would it be, and why?
3. If Starbucks was a celebrity (e.g., a sports figure, a movie or TV star), which celebrity would it be, and why? And why was your choice male or female?

Source: Data on store numbers obtained from www.starbucks.com and www.starbucks.com.hk/.

Case Two: Where Was Your Food Grown?

Malaysia, as a developing market, has attracted a wide range of overseas investors and marketers. The creation of the ASEAN Free Trade Area (AFTA) in 2003 opened up the country to foreign products, making them far more affordable to Malaysian consumers.

A study by Universiti Utara Malaysia in 2004 sought to identify the level of consumer ethnocentrism and measure consumers' buying preferences in terms of imported or domestic products and services. The key findings from the study showed that 80 percent of the respondents could be considered highly consumer ethnocentric. More broadly, the respondents had a higher regard for domestic products compared to foreign ones, but actual preferences to buy differed from one type of product or service to another.

Most respondents preferred to buy domestic food products, but were less ethnocentric as far as consumer goods were concerned, such as automobiles and personal computers. The study also revealed that demographic variables such as age, gender, income, and education had little impact on the degree of consumer ethnocentrism.

However, the study was only a small one, with just 350 questionnaires circulated and just 54 percent of these returned or deemed usable for the research.

QUESTIONS

1. Considering Chapter 5's discussion of consumer ethnocentrism, do you believe that it is a positive or a negative for multinational companies that many consumers might perceive their products to be foreign in certain markets?

2. Over 60 percent of the population of Malaysia are Muslim consumers. Most domestic food products have the JAKIM logo printed on the packaging, which certifies that it is safe to be consumed by Muslims. This may be a key reason for the preference for domestic certified food products in Malaysia, but why might it not be the full explanation?

Source: www.eprints.uum.edu.my.

6 Consumer Perception

CONSUMERS ACT and react on the basis of their perceptions, not on the basis of objective reality. For each individual, *reality* is a totally personal phenomenon, based on that person's needs, wants, values, and personal experiences. Thus, to the marketer, consumers' perceptions are much more important than their knowledge of objective reality. For if one thinks about it, it's not what actually is so, but what consumers *think* is so, that affects their actions and their buying habits. And, because individuals make decisions and take actions based on what they perceive to be reality, it is important that marketers understand the notion of perception and its related concepts to determine more readily what factors influence consumers to buy.

Through advertising, marketers create and shape consumers' perceptions of their products by *positioning* their offerings as fulfilling consumers' needs and delivering important benefits more effectively than competing alternatives. As discussed in Chapters 1 and 2, positioning is shaping the consumer's view or perception of the product rather than changing the product itself. The most effective positioning is getting consumers to believe that a given brand delivers a *product* or *service benefit* that is important to consumers. Such a benefit becomes the core identity of the brand, is also termed *unique value proposition*, and is the essence of the brand's *competitive advantage*.

The most difficult products to *position* or *differentiate* clearly from competition are commodities, which are largely the same and with little real physical differences among competing alternatives. For example, in form and appearance, water is an entirely uniformed product. And yet, consumers now have a choice of two types of bottled water and, within each type, a choice among many brands that range in price and are promoted as distinct and different from one another. The first type of bottled water is generically termed mineral or spring water. All the products in this category are the same in color and appearance, but different brands are positioned as delivering distinct and sophisticated attributes. For example, Figure 6.1 depicts two advertisements for bottled water with distinct promised benefits, which differentiate each

FIGURE 6.1

Source: Courtesy of Jana North America; Courtesy of Fiji.

QUESTION: *How Is Each Brand Positioned, and What Is the Benefit Each Delivers?*

TABLE 6.1 Positioning and Advertised Benefits of Bottled Water Brands

BRAND	POSITIONING	ADVERTISED BENEFIT
Tŷ Nant	From Wales. Award winning. Highly innovative packaging. Served at top hotels and restaurants.	Style. Status. Attention from others when one consumes it.
Voss	From Norway. From an aquifer that was shielded by ice and rock for centuries. The company is committed to environmental sustainability.	Purity.
Mist	From the Tennessee mountains. Naturally filtered by earth. Award-winning visionary package.	Nitrate and sodium free. Good pH balance.
Fiji	From the rain forest. The company is committed to conservation.	Soft, smooth taste. Environmental appeal—"drink with a clear conscience."
Jana	From Croatia. Artesian water from deep beneath the surface. Pure and balanced.	The perfect pH.
ESKA	From Canadian glaciers. Comes from a self-replenishing source. Water as nature intended it.	Purified by nature, not man.
Function Drinks	Eleven drinks with different colors and flavors.	Each drink claims to address a distinct health issue, such as fatigue, stress, or a hangover.
Vitaminwater	Fifteen drinks with different colors and flavors.	Each drink claims to deliver a distinct combination of vitamins and provide energy.
SoBe Life Water	Eight drinks with different colors and flavors.	Each flavor claims to deliver a distinct benefit, for example, "immunity," "strength," "calm," "enlighten."
Skinny Water	Five versions of flavored water.	No calories, controlling cravings, energy, getting skinny, staying fit.

brand from other offerings. Jana proclaims to deliver a healthy product (pH is a measure of a liquid's acidity) and Fiji proclaims that by buying the brand one helps the environment.

The second category of bottled water is flavored water products. Table 6.1 describes several brands of mineral and flavored water and their advertised benefits. For example, SoBe Life Water promise's to improve one's health and energy; each of the eleven products under the Function Drinks brand promises to deliver relief from a particular adverse physical condition such as fatigue, stress or a hangover.

Some of the brands listed in Table 6.1 are much more expensive than most bottled water products and come in distinct and innovative packaging (www.tynant.com, www.voss.com). The intricate package and high price are perceptual cues aimed at convincing consumers that the product is of much higher quality than competing brands; the impact of price and packaging on consumers' perception are discussed in this chapter.

This chapter examines the psychological and physiological bases of human perception and discusses the principles that influence our perception and interpretation of the world we see. Knowledge of these principles enables astute marketers to develop advertisements that have a better chance of being seen, noticed, and remembered by their target consumers.

Learning Objectives

6.1 *To Understand the Sensory Dynamics of Perception.*

6.2 *To Learn About the Three Elements of Perception.*

6.3 *To Understand the Components of Consumer Imagery and Their Strategic Applications.*

Sensory Dynamics of Perception

LEARNING OBJECTIVE

6.1 *To Understand the Sensory Dynamics of Perception.*

Perception is defined as *the process by which an individual selects, organizes, and interprets stimuli into a meaningful and coherent picture of the world.* It can be described as "how we see the world around us." Two individuals may be exposed to the same stimuli under the same apparent conditions, but how each person recognizes, selects, organizes, and interprets these stimuli is a highly individual process based on each person's own needs, values, and expectations.

SENSATION

Sensation is the immediate and direct response of the sensory organs to stimuli. A **stimulus** is any unit of input to any of the senses. Examples of stimuli (i.e., sensory input) include products, packages, brand names, advertisements, and commercials. **Sensory receptors** are the human organs (the eyes, ears, nose, mouth, and skin) that receive sensory inputs. Their sensory functions are to see, hear, smell, taste, and touch. All of these functions are called into play, either singly or in combination, in the purchase, use, and evaluation of consumer products. Human sensitivity refers to the experience of sensation. Sensitivity to stimuli varies with the quality of an individual's sensory receptors (e.g., eyesight or hearing) and the amount (or *intensity*) of the stimuli to which he or she is exposed. For example, a blind person may have a more highly developed sense of hearing than the average sighted person and may be able to hear sounds that the average person cannot, and a loud sound is more noticeable than a lesser one.

Sensation itself depends on energy change within the environment where the perception occurs (i.e., on differentiation of input). A perfectly bland or unchanging environment, regardless of the strength of the sensory input, provides little or no sensation at all. Thus, a person who lives on a busy street in midtown Manhattan would probably receive little or no sensation from the inputs of such noisy stimuli as horns honking, tires screeching, and fire engines clanging, because such sounds are so commonplace in New York City. In situations in which there is a great deal of sensory input, the senses do not detect small changes or differences in input. Thus, one honking horn more or less would never be noticed on a street with heavy traffic.

As sensory input *decreases*, however, our ability to detect changes in input or intensity *increases*, to the point that we attain maximum sensitivity under conditions of minimal stimulation. This accounts for the statement, "It was so quiet I could hear a pin drop." The ability of the human organism to accommodate itself to varying levels of sensitivity as external conditions vary not only provides more sensitivity when it is needed but also serves to protect us from damaging, disruptive, or irrelevant bombardment when the input level is high.

Most of the marketing communications today appeal to sight and sound. However, smell and touch also represent considerable opportunities for targeting consumers. The importance of smell in communication was strongly supported by two Americans who developed a scientific explanation as to how people associate memories with smells (and won the 2004 Nobel Prize in Physiology for this work) and other studies demonstrating the impact of fragrance on product and store choices.[1] Recognizing that the use of an ambient scent in a retail environment enhances the shopping experience for many consumers and makes the time they spend examining merchandise, waiting in line, and waiting for help seem shorter than it actually is, stores like Abercrombie & Fitch use strong fragrances throughout their facilities. A recent study indicated that *touching* a product influences persuasion and that touching could be used as a persuasive tool.

THE ABSOLUTE THRESHOLD

The lowest level at which an individual can experience a sensation is called the **absolute threshold**. The point at which a person can detect a difference between "something" and "nothing" is that person's absolute threshold for that stimulus. To illustrate, the distance at which a driver can note a specific billboard on a highway is that individual's absolute threshold. Two people riding together may first spot the billboard at different times (i.e., at different distances); thus, they appear to have different absolute thresholds. Under conditions of constant stimulation, such as driving through a "corridor" of billboards, the absolute threshold increases (i.e., the senses tend to become increasingly dulled). After an hour of driving through billboards, it is doubtful that any one billboard will make an impression. Hence, we often speak of "getting used to" a hot bath, a cold shower, or the bright sun. As our exposure to the stimulus increases,

TABLE 6.2 Promotional Methods Aimed at Increasing Sensory Input

METHOD	DESCRIPTION AND EXAMPLES
Experiential Marketing	Providing consumers with a chance to try the product, be photographed with it and, hopefully, post the photos online. Examples: Consumers closely examining NASCAR's race cars in Times Square, NY; Ford asked owners of its cars to hold house parties where guests can see, sit in, and even drive the cars. In an innovative promotion of its Stove Top stuffing brand, Kraft Foods heated several bus stops featuring ads for the brand, located in Chicago during one winter month. The objective was to convey the product's "warmth" to waiting passengers.
Sophisticated Scented Ads	Scented strips have been part of perfume ads for years. Now, this method is being extended to other products. Examples: scented stickers with coffee aromas on the front page of a daily newspaper; the scent of chocolate cookies being omitted from an ad for milk placed in a bus stop.
Sophisticated Inserts and Pop-Ups	Technology now enables marketers to place more elaborate inserts in magazines at relatively low costs. Examples: pop-ups with blinking lights and some that include samples of shampoo, perfume, and mint bars.
Ambush Advertising	Placing ads in places where consumers cannot avoid them. Examples: Brand names stamped on eggs in a supermarket, placed on video screens in taxis, on subway turnstiles, and on examination tables in doctors' offices; placing giant, fake pieces of advertised sushi on an airport's baggage carousel; placing ads on the bottom of the trays where consumers place small personal items during security checks at airports; placing ads on drycleaners' shirt boxes; projecting ads on the sides of large buildings at night in large cities; ads across from and inside urinals in men's restrooms; ads placed on muffin displays in small shops; ads placed on the security pedestals in retail stores; placing an ad display on the hood of a car as the attendant is filling it up with gas.
Product Placements	Also known as "branded entertainment," this method entails integrating products into TV shows, films, and even webisodes.

Sources: Louise Story, "Times Sq. Ads Spread via Tourists' Cameras," www.nytimes.com, December 11, 2006; Stuart Elliott, "Show and Tell Moves into Living Room," www.nytimes.com, April 4, 2008; Stuart Elliott, "Joint Promotion Adds Stickers to Sweet Smell of Marketing," www.nytimes.com, April 2, 2007; Louise Story, "Anywhere the Eye Can See, It's Likely to See an Ad," www.nytimes.com, January 15, 2007; Stuart Elliott, "Brainy Brand Names Where They're Least Expected," www.nytimes.com, October 3, 2008; Stuart Elliott, "You Are Here (and Probably Seeing an Ad)," www.nytimes.com, August 14, 2008; Elizabeth Olson, "Practicing the Subtle Sell of Placing Products on Webisodes," www.nytimes.com, January 3, 2008; and Stephanie Clifford, "More Bells, Whistles and Packets of All Sorts," www.nytimes.com, April 22, 2008.

we notice it less. In the field of perception, the term *adaptation* refers specifically to "getting used to" certain sensations; that is, becoming accommodated to a certain level of stimulation.

Sensory adaptation is a problem that concerns many national advertisers, which is why they try to change their advertising campaigns regularly. They are concerned that consumers will get so used to their current print ads and TV commercials that they will no longer "see" them; that is, the ads will no longer provide sufficient sensory input to be noted.

In an effort to cut through the advertising clutter and ensure that consumers note their ads, some marketers try to *increase* sensory input. Table 6.2 lists promotional methods aimed at increasing sensory input.

THE DIFFERENTIAL THRESHOLD

The minimal difference that can be detected between two similar stimuli is called the **differential threshold**, or the **just noticeable difference (j.n.d.)**. A nineteenth-century German scientist named Ernst Weber discovered that the j.n.d. between two stimuli was not an absolute amount, but an amount relative to the intensity of the first stimulus. **Weber's law**, as it has come to be known, states that the stronger the initial stimulus, the greater the additional intensity needed for the second stimulus to be perceived as different. For example, if the price of a half-gallon container of premium, freshly squeezed orange juice is $5.50, most consumers will probably not notice an increase of 25 cents (i.e., the increment would fall below the j.n.d.), and it may take an increase of 50 cents or more before a differential in price would be noticed. However, a 50-cent increase in the price of gasoline would be noticed very quickly by consumers because it is a significant percentage of the initial (base) cost of the product.

Marketing Applications of the J.N.D.

Weber's law has important applications in marketing. Manufacturers and marketers endeavor to determine the relevant j.n.d. for their products for two very different reasons: (1) so that negative changes (e.g., reductions in product size or quality, or increases in product price) are not readily discernible to the public (i.e., remain below the j.n.d.), and (2) so that product improvements (e.g., improved or updated packaging, larger size, or lower price) are very apparent to consumers without being wastefully extravagant (i.e., they are at or just above the j.n.d.).

When it comes to product improvements, marketers very much want to meet or exceed the consumer's differential threshold; that is, they want consumers to readily perceive any improvements made in the original product. Marketers use the j.n.d. to determine the amount of improvement they should make in their products. Less than the j.n.d. is wasted effort because the improvement will not be perceived; more than the j.n.d. is wasteful because it reduces the level of repeat sales. For example, let us say that Goddard's, a well-known manufacturer of fine polishes, wants to improve its Silver Care polish sufficiently to claim that it retards tarnish longer than the leading competing brand. In a series of experiments, the company determines that the j.n.d. for its present polish (which now gives a shine that lasts about 20 days) is 5 days, or one-fourth longer. That means that the shine given by the improved silver polish must last at least 25 days (or one-fourth) longer if the new polish is to be perceived by the majority of users as, in fact, improved. By finding this j.n.d. of 5 days, the company has isolated the minimum amount of time necessary to make its claim of "lasts longer" believable to the majority of consumers. If it had decided to make the polish effective for 23 days (just 3 extra days of product life), its claim of "lasts longer" would not be perceived as true by most consumers and, from the marketer's point of view, would be "wasted." On the other hand, if the company had decided to make the silver polish effective for 40 days, it would have sacrificed a good deal of repeat purchase frequency. Making the product improvement just equal to the j.n.d. is therefore the most efficient decision that management can make.

On the other hand, when it comes to price increases, less than the j.n.d. is desirable because consumers are unlikely to notice it. Since many routinely purchased consumer goods are relatively inexpensive, companies are reluctant to raise prices when their profit margins on these items are declining. Instead, many marketers decrease the product *quantity* included in the packages, while leaving the prices unchanged—thus, in effect, increasing the per unit price. When the costs of basic ingredients such as sugar, milk, eggs, corn syrup and coffee rise, manufacturers of such foods as chewing gum, canned coffee, cereals and ice cream do not decrease the size of the package but put less quantity of the product inside. For example, they reduce the amount of coffee in a can from 1 pound to 11 or 10 ounces, and the amount of ice cream placed in a typical half-gallon package from 64 ounces to 56 ounces.[3] Presumably, the decreases in the weight of these products reflect j.n.d.-focused research; any of the reductions in quantity should be below most consumers' j.n.d. for these products.

Marketers often want to update their existing package designs without losing the ready recognition of consumers who have been exposed to years of cumulative advertising impact. In such cases, they usually make a number of small changes, each carefully designed to fall below the j.n.d., so that consumers will perceive only minimal difference between succeeding versions. For example, Betty Crocker, the General Mills symbol, has been updated seven times from 1936 to 1996 (see Figure 6.2), but the basic elements of the symbol changed only minimally from one update to the next in order to maintain continous consumer recognition.

FIGURE 6.2
Sequential Changes in the Betty Crocker Symbol Fall Below the J.N.D.
Source: Courtesy of General Mills Company.

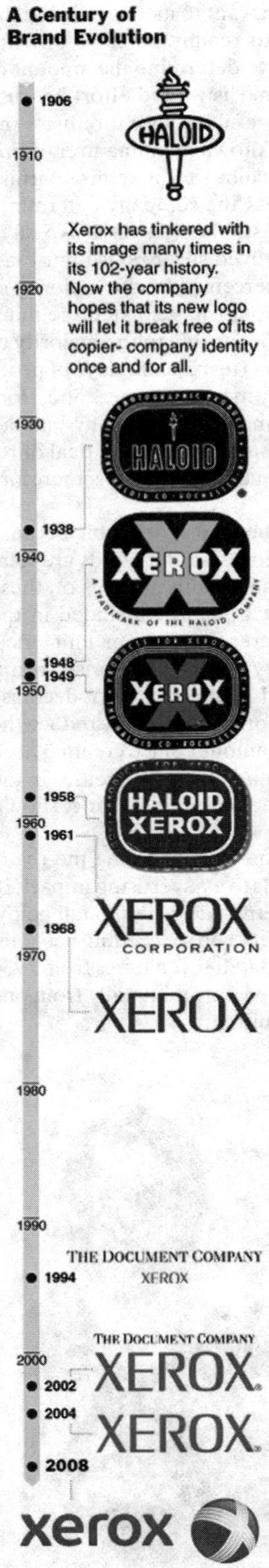

FIGURE 6.3
The Evolution of the Xerox Logo with J.N.D. Considerations in Mind
Source: Claudia H. Deutsch, "Xerox Hopes Its New Logo Doesn't Say 'Copy,'" www.nytimes.com, January 8, 2008. Courtesy of Xerox.

During its over 100 years history, the Xerox Company updated its logo many times. However, the logo was almost always updated carefully, with the j.n.d. in mind and without moving too drastically away from the logo that consumers readily recognized (see Figure 6.3).

SUBLIMINAL PERCEPTION

In Chapter 4 we spoke of people being *motivated* below their level of conscious awareness. People are also *stimulated* below their level of conscious awareness; that is, they can perceive stimuli without being consciously aware that they are doing so. Stimuli that are too weak or too brief to be consciously seen or heard may nevertheless be strong enough to be perceived by one or more receptor cells. This process is called **subliminal perception** because the stimulus is beneath the threshold, or "limen," of conscious awareness, though obviously not beneath the absolute threshold of the receptors involved. (Perception of stimuli that are above the level of conscious awareness technically is called *supraliminal perception*, though it is usually referred to simply as *perception*.)

The effectiveness of so-called subliminal advertising was reportedly first tested at a drive-in movie theatre in New Jersey in 1957, where the words *Eat popcorn* and *Drink Coca-Cola* were flashed on the screen during the movie. Exposure times were so short that viewers were unaware of seeing a message. It was reported that during the six-week test period, popcorn sales increased 58 percent and Coca-Cola sales increased 18 percent, but these findings were later reported to be false. Years later, it was discovered that although the simple subliminal stimulus *COKE* served to arouse thirst in subjects, the subliminal command *DRINK COKE* did not have a greater effect, nor did it have any behavioral consequences.

Over the years, there have been sporadic reports of marketers using subliminal messages in their efforts to influence consumption behavior. For example, in 1995, Disney was accused of using subliminal messages in the movies *Aladdin* (where the hero allegedly whispers "good teenagers, take off your clothes" in a subaudible voice) and *The Lion King* (where the letters "S-E-X" are allegedly formed in a cloud of dust). At times, it has been difficult to separate truth from fiction regarding such alleged manipulations. When some of the subliminal methods were tested methodically using scientific research procedures, the research results did not support the notion that subliminal messages can persuade consumers to act in a given manner.

Evaluating the Effectiveness of Subliminal Persuasion

Despite the many studies undertaken by academicians and researchers since the 1950s, there is no evidence that subliminal advertising persuades people to buy goods or services. A comprehensive review of the literature indicates that subliminal perception has no effect on attitudes toward products and consumption behavior, and that most of its effects were discovered in highly artificial situations.[4] A recent study in a laboratory setting supports this conclusion. Subjects were asked to keep a running total of numbers flashed on a screen where they were also exposed to images of either IBM or Apple logos, shown at a speed faster than could be consciously seen. Then, the subjects performed a creativity exercise. The subjects subliminally exposed to the Apple logo scored higher on the creativity test than those exposed to the IBM logo or to no logo at all.[5] Some interpret these results to mean that a brand can make you perform better. For example, if you wear a swimsuit worn and endorsed by a champion swimmer, you will swim faster. Others argue that the results of the experiment simply mean that a subliminal stimulus may trigger certain associations and motivations but not necessarily lead to different behavior. However, there is tangential indication that subliminal advertising may reduce antisocial behavior (e.g., subliminal, antishoplifting messages broadcasted in malls may lower shoplifting), but there is no credible evidence that such advertising can get consumers to engage in shopping—a voluntary and generally pleasant and social behavior.

As to sexual embeds, most researchers are of the opinion that "what you see is what you get"; that is, a vivid imagination can see whatever it wants to see in just about any situation. And that pretty much sums up the whole notion of perception: Individuals see what they want to see (e.g., what they are motivated to see) and what they expect to see.

Elements of Perception

Learning Objective

6.2 *To Learn About the Three Elements of Perception.*

The preceding section explained how the individual receives sensations from stimuli in the outside environment and how the human organism adapts to the level and intensity of sensory input. We now come to one of the major principles of perception: Raw sensory input by itself does not produce or explain the coherent picture of the world that most adults possess. Indeed, the study of perception is largely the study of what we subconsciously add to or subtract from raw sensory inputs to produce our own private picture of the world.

Human beings are constantly bombarded with stimuli during every minute and every hour of every day. The sensory world is made up of an almost infinite number of discrete sensations that are constantly and subtly changing. According to the principles of sensation, intensive stimulation "bounces off" most individuals, who subconsciously block (i.e., adapt to) a heavy bombardment of stimuli. Otherwise, the billions of different stimuli to which we are constantly exposed might serve to confuse us and keep us perpetually disoriented in a constantly changing environment. However, neither of these consequences tends to occur, because perception is not a function of sensory input alone. Rather, perception is the result of two different kinds of inputs that interact to form the personal pictures—the perceptions—that each individual experiences.

One type of input is *physical stimuli* from the outside environment; the other type of input is provided by individuals in the form of certain predispositions (expectations, motives, and learning) based on *previous experience.* The combination of these two very different kinds of inputs produces for each of us a very private, very personal picture of the world. Because each person is a unique individual, with unique experiences, needs, wants, desires, and expectations, it follows that each individual's perceptions are also unique. This explains why no two people see the world in precisely the same way.

Individuals are very selective as to which stimuli they "recognize"; they subconsciously organize the stimuli they do recognize according to widely held psychological principles, and they interpret such stimuli (they give meaning to them) subjectively in accordance with their personal needs, expectations, and experiences. The following sections examine each of these three aspects of perception: the *selection, organization,* and *interpretation* of stimuli.

PERCEPTUAL SELECTION

Consumers subconsciously exercise a great deal of selectivity as to which aspects of the environment (which stimuli) they perceive. An individual may look at some things, ignore others, and turn away from still others. In actuality, people receive (i.e., perceive) only a small fraction of the stimuli to which they are exposed. Consider, for example, a woman at a Whole Foods Market. She may be exposed to over 30,000 products of different colors, sizes, and shapes; to perhaps 300 people (looking, walking, searching, talking); to smells and tastes (from fruit, meat, and sample displays); to sounds within the store (audio announcements, music, cooking demonstrations) and many other stimuli. Yet she manages on a regular basis to visit the store, select the items she needs, pay for them, and leave, all within a relatively brief period of time, without losing her sanity or her personal orientation to the world around her. This is because she exercises *selectivity* in perception.

Which stimuli get selected depends on two major factors in addition to the nature of the stimulus itself: (1) consumers' *previous experience* as it affects their *expectations* (what they are prepared, or "set," to see) and (2) their *motives* at the time (their needs, desires, interests, and so on). Each of these factors can serve to increase or decrease the probability that a stimulus will be perceived.

Nature of the Stimulus

Marketing stimuli include an enormous number of variables that affect the consumer's perception, such as the *nature* of the product, its *physical attributes*, the *package* design, the *brand* name, the *advertisements* and commercials (including copy claims, choice and sex of model, positioning of model, size of ad, typography), the *position* of a print ad or a commercial, and the *editorial* environment.

In general, *contrast* is one of the most attention-compelling attributes of a stimulus. Advertisers often use extreme attention-getting devices to achieve maximum contrast and, thus, penetrate the consumer's perceptual "screen." For example, a number of magazines and newspapers carry ads that readers can unfold to reveal oversized, poster-like advertisements for products ranging from cosmetics to automobiles, because of the "stopping power" of giant ads

FIGURE 6.4

Source: Courtesy of Mogul Foot Care, www.footnewyork.com.

QUESTION: *Why Are Consumers Likely to Notice This Ad?*

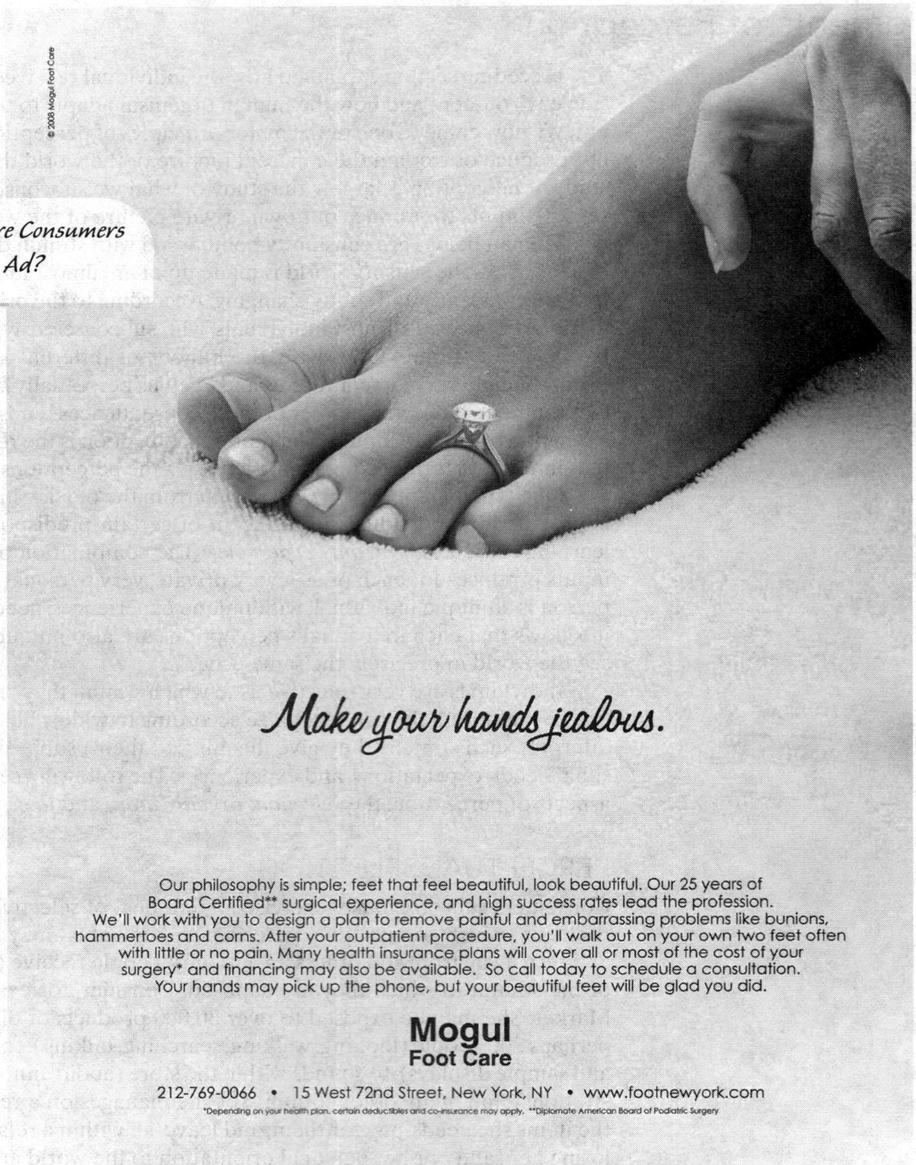

among more traditional sizes. Advertising that stands in contrast to its environment achieves a high degree of differentiation. The use of a dramatic image of the product against a white background with little copy in a print advertisement, the absence of sound in a commercial's opening scene, an ad appearing where consumers do not expect it—all offer sufficient contrast from their environments to achieve differentiation and merit the consumer's attention. Figure 6.4 illustrates the attention-getting nature of a dramatic image of a product in an advertisement.

With respect to packaging, astute marketers usually try to differentiate their packages to ensure rapid consumer perception. Since the average package on the supermarket shelf has about 1/10th of a second to make an impression on the consumer, it is important that every aspect of the package—the name, shape, color, label, and copy—provide sufficient sensory stimulation to be noted and remembered.

Expectations

People usually see what they expect to see, and what they expect to see is usually based on familiarity, previous experience, or preconditioned set of expectations. In a marketing context, people tend to perceive products and product attributes according to their own expectations. A student who has been told by his friends that a particular professor is interesting and dynamic will probably perceive the professor in that manner when the class begins; a teenager who attends a horror movie that has been billed as terrifying will probably find it so. On the other hand, stimuli that conflict sharply with expectations often receive more attention than those that conform to expectations.

For years, some marketers have used blatant sexuality in advertisements for products to which sex is not relevant, in the belief that such advertisements would attract a high degree of attention. However, ads with irrelevant sexuality often defeat the marketer's objectives because readers tend to remember the sexual aspects of the ad (e.g., the innuendo or the model), not the product or brand advertised. Nevertheless, some advertisers continue to use erotic appeals in promoting a wide variety of products, from office furniture to jeans. (The use of sex in advertising is discussed in Chapter 9.)

Motives

People tend to perceive the things they need or want; the stronger the need, the greater the tendency to ignore unrelated stimuli in the environment. A student who is looking for a new cell phone provider is more likely to notice and read carefully ads for deals and special offers regarding such services than his roommate, who may be satisfied with his present cellular service. In general, there is a heightened awareness of stimuli that are relevant to one's needs and interests and a decreased awareness of stimuli that are irrelevant to those needs. An individual's perceptual process simply attunes itself more closely to those elements in the environment that are important to him or her. Someone who is overweight is more likely to notice ads for diet foods; a sexually repressed person may perceive sexual symbolism where none exists.

Marketing managers recognize the efficiency of targeting their products to the perceived needs of consumers. For example, a marketer can determine through marketing research what different segments of consumers view as the ideal attributes of the product category or what they perceive their needs to be in relation to the product category. The marketer can then segment the market on the basis of those needs and vary the product advertising so that consumers in each segment will perceive the product as meeting their own special needs, wants, or interests.

Selective Perception

As the preceding discussion illustrates, the consumer's "selection" of stimuli from the environment is based on the interaction of expectations and motives with the stimulus itself. These factors give rise to four important concepts concerning perception.

SELECTIVE EXPOSURE Consumers actively seek out messages that they find pleasant or with which they are sympathetic, and they actively avoid painful or threatening ones. They also selectively expose themselves to advertisements that reassure them of the wisdom of their purchase decisions.

SELECTIVE ATTENTION Consumers exercise a great deal of selectivity in terms of the attention they give to commercial stimuli. They have a heightened awareness of stimuli that meet their needs or interests and minimal awareness of stimuli irrelevant to their needs. Thus, consumers are likely to note ads for products that would satisfy their needs and disregard those in which they have no interest. People also vary in terms of the kinds of information in which they are interested and the form of message and type of medium they prefer. Some people are more interested in price, some in appearance, and some in social acceptability. Some people like complex, sophisticated messages; others like simple graphics.

PERCEPTUAL DEFENSE Consumers subconsciously screen out stimuli that they find psychologically threatening, even though exposure has already taken place. Thus, threatening or otherwise damaging stimuli are less likely to be consciously perceived than are neutral stimuli at the same level of exposure. Furthermore, individuals sometimes unconsciously distort information that is not consistent with their needs, values, and beliefs. One way to combat *perceptual defense* is to vary and increase the amount of sensory input. For example, since surveys showed that most smokers no longer pay attention to the written warning labels on cigarette packs, some laws now require tobacco firms to feature graphic health warnings on cigarette packs (e.g., in Canada) and vary the text of these messages.

PERCEPTUAL BLOCKING Consumers protect themselves from being bombarded with stimuli by simply "tuning out"—blocking such stimuli from conscious awareness. They do so out of self-protection because of the visually overwhelming nature of the world in which we live. The popularity of such devices as TiVo and DVRs, which enable viewers to skip over TV commercials with great ease, is, in part, an outcome of individuals' quest for *perceptual blocking*.

PERCEPTUAL ORGANIZATION

People do not experience the numerous stimuli they select from the environment as separate and discrete sensations; rather, they tend to organize them into groups and perceive them as unified wholes. Thus, the perceived characteristics of even the simplest stimulus are viewed as a function of the whole to which the stimulus appears to belong. This method of perceptual organization simplifies life considerably for the individual.

The principles underlying perceptual organization are often referred to by the name **Gestalt psychology**. (*Gestalt*, in German, means "pattern or configuration.") Three of the most basic principles of perceptual organization are *figure and ground, grouping*, and *closure*.

Figure and Ground

As was noted earlier, stimuli that contrast with their environment are more likely to be noticed. A sound must be louder or softer, a color brighter or paler. The simplest visual illustration consists of a figure on a ground (i.e., background). The figure is perceived more clearly because, in contrast to its ground, it appears to be well defined, solid, and in the forefront. The ground is usually perceived as indefinite, hazy, and continuous. The common line that separates the figure and the ground is generally attributed to the figure rather than to the ground, which helps give the figure greater definition. Consider the stimulus of music. People can either "bathe" in music or listen to music. In the first case, music is simply background to other activities; in the second, it is the figure. Figure is more clearly perceived because it appears to be dominant; in contrast, ground appears to be subordinate and, therefore, less important.

Advertisers have to plan their advertisements carefully to make sure that the stimulus they want noted is seen as figure and not as ground. The musical background must not overwhelm the jingle; the background of an advertisement must not detract from the product. Print advertisers often silhouette their products against a nondistinct background to make sure that the features they want noted are clearly perceived.

A marketing technique dating back to the time when TV first became a mass medium, which is experiencing tremendous growth and stems from the figure-and-ground concept, is **product placement** (or "**branded entertainment**"). When this method is employed, the advertised product (i.e., the figure) is integrated into the TV show or film (i.e., the ground) in one or more of the following ways: (1) the product is used by the cast (e.g., in such shows as Survivor and American Idol); (2) the product is integrated into the plot (e.g., a Sex and the City episode centered around a new vodka entitled "Absolut Hunk"); or (3) the product is associated with a character (e.g., the character is also the product's advertising spokesperson).[6] A recent study found that a brand integrated and prominently featured in a TV program may produce negative feelings toward the brand among viewers who liked the program a lot, but those who liked the program less were more likely to develop positive attitudes toward the brand.[7] Thus, advertisers must be extremely careful in using product placement. Product placement is also discussed in Chapters 9 (Communications) and 16 (Ethics).

Grouping

Individuals tend to group stimuli so that they form a unified picture or impression. The perception of stimuli as groups or chunks of information, rather than as discrete bits of information, facilitates their memory and recall. Marketers use **grouping** to imply certain desired meanings in connection with their products. For example, an advertisement for tea may show a young man and woman sipping tea in a beautifully appointed room before a blazing hearth. The overall mood implied by the grouping of stimuli leads the consumer to associate the drinking of tea with romance, fine living, and winter warmth.

Most of us can remember and repeat our social security numbers because we automatically group them into three *chunks*, rather than try to remember nine separate numbers. Similarly, we recall and repeat our phone number in three segments—the area code, first three digits, and the last four digits. Also, for decades, Americans had five-digit postal codes grouped as a single chunk; as four additional digits were added to postal codes, the U.S. Postal Service faced a challenge in getting Americans to recall the extra digits and add a chunk to their recollection of postal codes.

Closure

Individuals have a need for **closure**. They express this need by organizing their perceptions so that they form a complete picture. If the pattern of stimuli to which they are exposed is incomplete, they tend to perceive it, nevertheless, as complete; that is, they consciously or subconsciously fill in the missing pieces. Thus, a circle with a section of its periphery missing is invariably perceived as a circle, not an arc.

Incomplete messages or tasks are better remembered than completed ones. One explanation for this phenomenon is that a person who hears the beginning of a message or who begins a task develops a need to complete it. If he or she is prevented from doing so, a state of tension is created that manifests itself in improved memory for the incomplete task. For example, hearing the beginning of a message leads to the need to hear the rest of it—like waiting for the second shoe to drop.

The need for closure has interesting implications for marketers. Promotional messages in which viewers are required to "fill in" information beg for completion by consumers, and the very act of completion serves to involve them more deeply in the message (see Figure 6.5 where the reader has to turn the ad upside down to find the answers to the questions posed). In a related vein, advertisers have discovered that they can achieve excellent results by using the soundtrack of a frequently viewed television commercial on radio. Consumers who are familiar with the TV commercial perceive the audio track alone as incomplete; in their need for completion, they mentally play back the visual content from memory.

PERCEPTUAL INTERPRETATION

The preceding discussion has emphasized that perception is a personal phenomenon. People exercise selectivity as to which stimuli they perceive, and they organize these stimuli on the basis of certain psychological principles. The interpretation of stimuli is also uniquely individual, because it is based on what individuals expect to see in light of their previous experiences, the number of plausible explanations they can envision, and their motives and interests at the time of perception.

Stimuli are often highly ambiguous. Some stimuli are weak because of such factors as poor visibility, brief exposure, high noise level, or constant fluctuation. Even stimuli that are strong tend to fluctuate dramatically because of such factors as different angles of viewing, varying distances, and changing levels of illumination. When stimuli are highly ambiguous, an individual will usually interpret them in such a way that they serve to fulfill personal needs, wishes, interests, and so on. It is this principle that provides the rationale for the *projective tests* discussed in Chapter 4. Such tests provide ambiguous stimuli (such as incomplete sentences, unclear pictures, or untitled cartoons) to respondents who are asked to interpret them. How a person describes a vague illustration is a reflection not of the stimulus itself, but of the subject's own needs, wants, and desires. Through the interpretation of ambiguous stimuli, respondents reveal a great deal about themselves.

Stereotypes

Individuals tend to carry biased pictures in their minds of the meanings of various stimuli, which are termed **stereotypes**. Sometimes, when presented with sensory stimuli, people "add" these biases to what they see or hear and form distorted impressions. Several years ago, an ad for Benetton featuring two men—one black and one white—handcuffed together, which was part of the "United Colors of Benetton" campaign promoting racial harmony, produced a public outcry because people perceived it as depicting a white man arresting a black man. Clearly, this perception was the result of *stereotypes,* since there was nothing in the ad to indicate that the white person was arresting the black person rather than the other way around. Marketers must be aware of possible stereotypes because these images reflect people's expectations and influence how stimuli are

FIGURE 6.5

Source: Courtesy of Levi Strauss & Co.

QUESTION: *What Element of Perceptual Organization Is Featured in This Ad?*

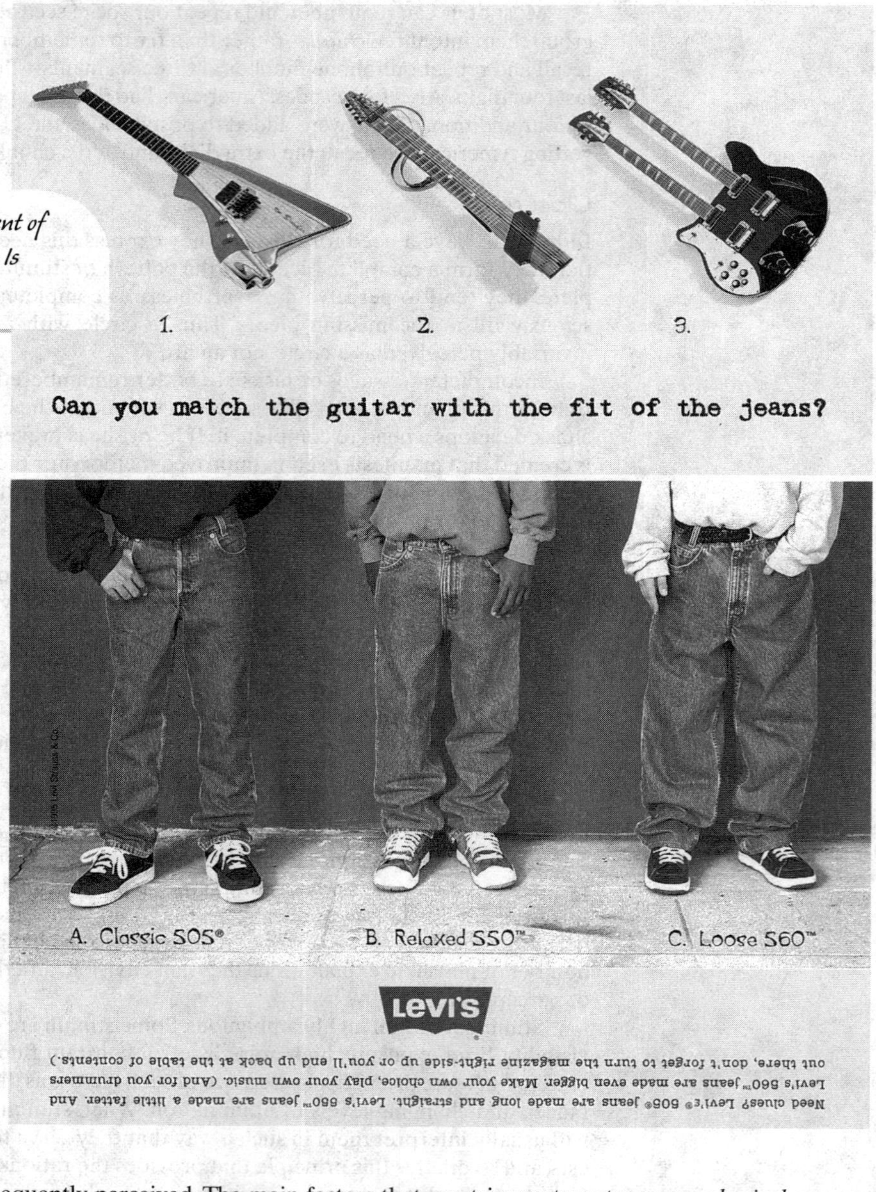

subsequently perceived. The main factors that can trigger stereotypes are *physical appearances*, *descriptive terms*, *first impressions*, and the *halo effect*.

PHYSICAL APPEARANCES People tend to attribute the qualities they associate with certain types of people to others who resemble them, whether or not they consciously recognize the similarity. For this reason, the selection of models for print advertisements and for television commercials can be a key element in their ultimate persuasiveness. Culturally, attractive models are likely to be more persuasive and have a more positive influence on consumer attitudes and behavior than average-looking models; attractive men are perceived as more successful businessmen than average-looking men. However, using attractive models without any other considerations does not increase ads' effectiveness. Thus, advertisers must ensure that there is a rational match between the product advertised and the physical attributes of the model used to promote it. For example, highly attractive models are likely to be perceived as having more expertise regarding enhancement products (e.g., jewelry, lipstick, perfume) but not problem-solving products (e.g., products that correct beauty flaws such as acne or dandruff).

The physical appearance of products often influences consumers' judgments. A recent study indicated that perceived taste of orange juice and distinguishing between three levels of sweetness were influenced by subtle color variations of the juice and also, somewhat unexpectedly, that such variations influenced perceived taste more than brand and price.[8] The shape of packages has great influence on consumers' impressions (as discussed later in the chapter) and impacts consumers' expectations. For this reason, ice cream packages are round because this shape was found to communicate abundance. An experimental study investigated how consumers construed the attributes of facial tissue products from print ads, each including one of the following three objects (in varied forms): cats, sunsets, and abstract paintings. The study found that a *fluffy* cat communicated a *soft* and expensive tissue while a *colorful* cat conveyed a soft and colorful tissue. Among the sunset images, the soft sunset expressed a soft, expensive, and colorful tissue while a *roadside* sunset conveyed a neither soft nor colorful and an inexpensive product.[9]

DESCRIPTIVE TERMS Stereotypes are often reflected in verbal messages. For example, consumers who eat foods with elaborate names such as "succulent Italian seafood filet" are very likely to rate those foods as more tasty and appealing than those who eat the same foods with such regular names as "seafood filet." The ad featured in Figure 6.6 contrasts the powerful and rugged Dodge Durango, termed "a big fat juicy cheeseburger" with other, less rugged and "weaker" cars referred to in the ad as the "land of tofu." One Asian student interpreted the ad as contrasting typically American cars with foreign cars manufactured in Southeast Asia, where tofu originated. Clearly, the student was interpreting the ad in terms of stereotypes associated with a product's country of origin.

Although distinct brand names are important to all products or services, associations that consumers make with certain names are particularly crucial in marketing services due to the abstract and intangible nature of many services. For example, names such as *Federal Express* (later abbreviated to *FedEx*) and *Humana* (a provider of health services) are excellent names because they are distinctive, memorable, and relevant to the services they feature. On the other hand, *Allegis*—a short-lived brand name aimed at creating a business travel concept by combining United Airlines, Hertz, and Hilton and Westin Hotels under one umbrella—failed because it conveyed consumers nothing about the type of services it offered.[10]

Advertisers must be careful about using canned stereotypes and "common wisdom" in their persuasive messages. For example, gender-role stereotypes view young boys as having "instrumental" orientation focused on problem solving and young girls as having "communal" orientation focused on relationships and group harmony. A recent study examined young children's attitudes toward ads that included *instrumental* scripts (e.g., eating a cracker will make you strong) and *communal* scripts (e.g., a cracker is a great snack to have with your

FIGURE 6.6

Source: © DaimlerChrysler Corporation. Used with permission. All rights reserved.

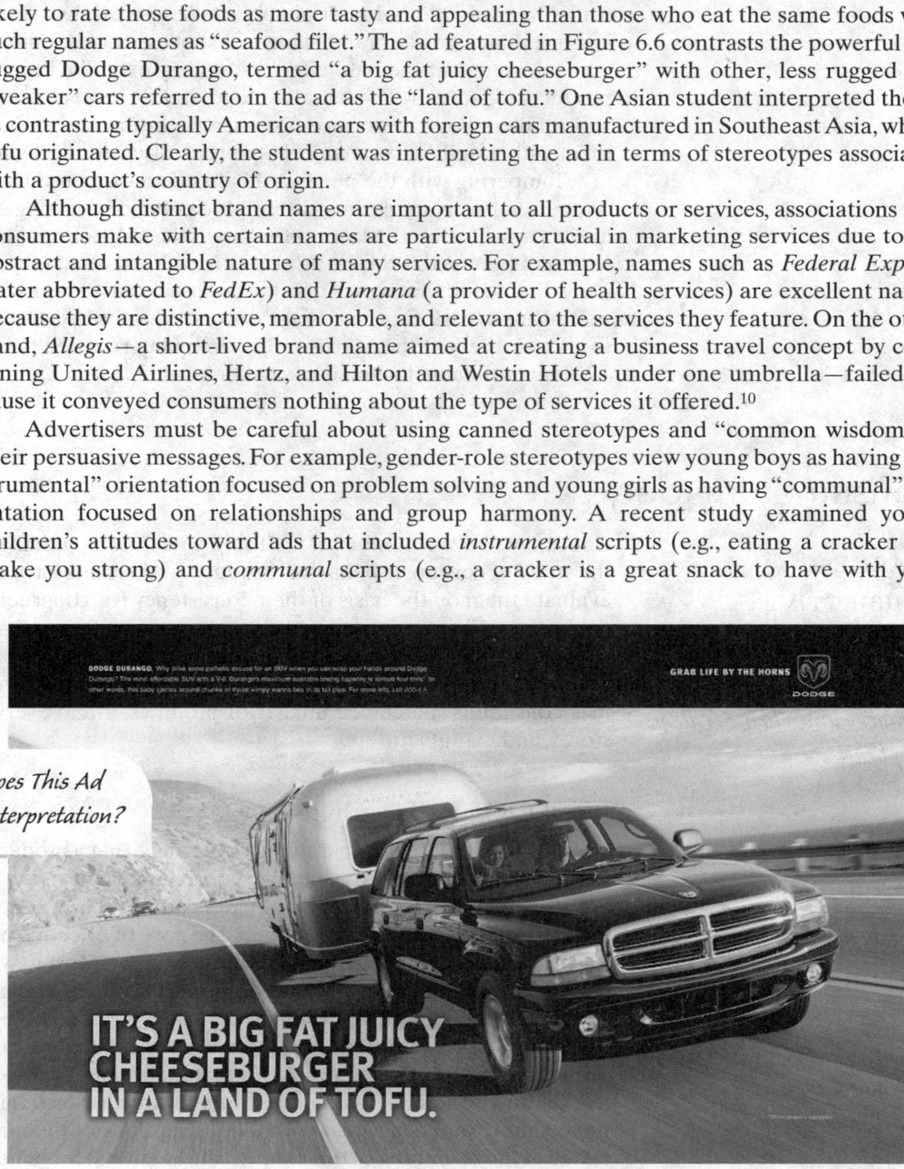

QUESTION: *How Does This Ad Depict Perceptual Interpretation?*

friends). The study found that preadolescent children did not necessarily respond more favorably to messages that included stereotypical gender-role attributes.[11]

FIRST IMPRESSIONS First impressions tend to be lasting, as illustrated by a shampoo commercial using the line "You'll never have a second chance to make a first impression." Since first impressions are often lasting, introducing a new product before it has been perfected may prove fatal to its ultimate success; subsequent information about its advantages, even if true, will often be negated by the memory of its early performance. When one retailer put a picture of an aloe vera leaf and the wording *aloe vera* on the surface of the mattress, at first impression, consumers assumed that aloe vera was a component of the ticking (the mattress cover) and the retailer had great difficulty dispelling this initial impression.[12]

HALO EFFECT Historically, the **halo effect** has been used to describe situations in which the evaluation of a single object or person on a multitude of dimensions is based on the evaluation of just one or a few dimensions (e.g., a man is trustworthy, fine, and noble because he looks you in the eye when he speaks). Consumer behaviorists broaden the notion of the halo effect to include the evaluation of multiple objects (e.g., a product line) on the basis of the evaluation of just one dimension (a brand name or a spokesperson). Using this broader definition, marketers take advantage of the halo effect when they extend a brand name associated with one line of products to another. The lucrative field of *licensing* is based on the halo effect. Manufacturers and retailers hope to acquire instant recognition and status for their products by associating them with a well-known name. (Chapter 7 discusses licensing in greater detail.)

Tampering with the perceived halo effect of a product or brand can have disastrous consequences. For example, in an attempt to enhance the image of JW Marriott, the Marriott hotel chain's upscale brand, Marriott took over the Rihga Royal Hotel, an upscale hotel in New York City, and renamed it the JW Marriott New York. When the new name signs went up, the company discovered that scores of regular, upscale customers who always stayed at the Rihga when visiting New York City canceled their reservations because they did not want to tell colleagues to contact them at the Marriott. The company restored the *Rihga Royal Hotel* name, with the JW Marriott name included in smaller print.[13]

Consumer Imagery

LEARNING OBJECTIVE

6.3 *To Understand the Components of Consumer Imagery and Their Strategic Applications.*

Consumers have a number of enduring perceptions, or images, that are particularly relevant to the study of consumer behavior. Products and brands have symbolic value for individuals, who evaluate them on the basis of their consistency (or congruence) with their personal pictures of themselves. Chapter 5 discussed consumer self-images and how consumers attempt to preserve or enhance their self-images by buying products and using services that they believe are congruent with their self-images and by avoiding those that are not. The following section examines consumers' perceived images of products, brands, services, prices, product quality, retail stores, and manufacturers.

PRODUCT POSITIONING

The essence of successful marketing is the image that a product has in the mind of the consumer—that is, its **positioning**. Positioning is more important to the ultimate success of a product than are its actual characteristics, although products that are poorly made will not succeed in the long run on the basis of image alone. The core of effective positioning is a unique position that the product occupies in the mind of the consumer. Most new products fail because they are perceived as "me too" offerings that do not offer potential consumers any advantages or unique benefits over competitive products.

Marketers of different brands in the same category can effectively differentiate their offerings only if they stress the *benefits* that their brands provide rather than their products' physical features. The benefits featured in a product's positioning must reflect attributes that are important to and congruent with the perceptions of the targeted consumer segment. As illustrated at the beginning of this chapter, although water is a homogeneous commodity, marketers have created numerous successful brands of bottled water, each positioned as having a unique attribute.

Take, for example, the activity of washing clothes, where the benefit provided to the consumer is clean clothes—a straightforward and obvious benefit. However, the *manner* in which the promised cleanliness is achieved, and the product's *specific strength* were used very creatively to differentiate detergent brands from one another. To illustrate, here are the positioning claims of several brands of detergents:

- **Ecos:** made by *Earth Friendly Products* in three scents (i.e., Magnolia & Lilies, Lavender, and Lemongrass) claims to provide better price performance than the competition and has soy fabric softener and cellulose-based optical brightener.
- **Caldrea:** this *Sweet Pea Detergent* is mild but highly effective in removing stains and especially formulated for babies and children. It is tested by dermatologists and includes oils and surfactants derived from plants.
- **Cheer:** one of the nine brands of the *Laundry and Fabric Care* product division of P&G protects against fading, color transfer, and fabric wear. It comes in powder or liquid and with or without bleach.
- **Ivory:** *Ivory Snow Gentle Care Detergent*, also made by P&G, promises mild cleansing and purity for a simple clean.
- **Tide:** often the best-selling detergent in the United States and also made by P&G, is "fabric cleaning and care at its best." This positioning is an "umbrella" approach within which P&G developed over 30 versions of this product, each with a unique promised benefit. For example: Ultra Tide with Bleach (an alternative to chlorine bleach), Tide Downy (with a touch of softness and freshness), and Tide Free ("No dyes. No perfumes. No worries").[14]

Another example of "umbrella positioning" is featured in the two ads shown in Figures 6.7 a and b. Suzuki, the maker of many car models, is using the same slogan to describe the consumer benefits that its products provide. The appeal featured here is also based on the principal of *contrast* (discussed earlier). Suzuki's ads convey to buyers the notion that the company's cars are compact (i.e., "drive small") and fuel efficient, and yet powerful and suited for many types of travel (i.e., "live large"). Note that the same slogan differs in its appearance in the two ads. For the smaller car, the slogan is featured using a "softer" tone and for the larger vehicle a bolder typeface is used. These differences reflect the principle that the visual components of an ad should reflect its product's positioning.

The result of successful positioning strategy is a distinctive brand image on which consumers rely in making product choices. A positive brand image also leads to consumer loyalty, positive beliefs about brand value, and a willingness to search for the brand. A positive brand image also promotes consumer interest in future brand promotions and *inoculates* consumers against competitors' marketing activities. An advertiser's positioning strategy forms consumer beliefs about its brand's attributes and also determines the prices consumers are willing to pay.

As products become more complex and the marketplace more crowded, consumers rely more on the product's image and claimed benefits than on its actual attributes in making purchase decisions. At the same time, in today's highly competitive marketplace, a distinctive product image is very difficult to create and maintain. A model of strategic positioning and a typology of positioning strategies derived from interviews of executives in highly profitable companies are depicted in Table 6.3.[15]

PACKAGING AS A POSITIONING ELEMENT

Packaging must convey the image that the brand communicates to buyers. For example, the Tide detergent version that promises predominantly stain removal comes in an orange plastic container with a large handle on its side and conveys the "heaviness" of the product because consumers tend to associate heaviness with the power needed to remove stains. On the other hand, the New Tide Total Care products, which promise scents of fresh morning, rain and spring days, come in slimmer, slicker packages in brighter shades of orange than the regular Tide and the handle is angled and congruent with the more sophisticated benefit claim of this brand. The packaging of Ivory Snow is white, round, and without a handle, almost implying

FIGURE 6.7A

Source: Courtesy of Suzuki.

QUESTION: *Which Concepts of Perception Are Applied in These Ads and How So?*

that the detergent should be squeezed into the washer, in support of the "gentle cleanliness" positioning of this brand.

The perception of scent and the associations made with different aromas vary greatly among individuals. For this reason, it is extremely difficult to convey an "image" of a fragrance. To buyers of perfumes, the only tangible evidence of the product's nature and quality is the packaging, whose costs often accounts for up to 40 percent of the fragrance's cost. A recent study identified several holistic (or Gestalt) designs of packages, each conveying a distinct, prominent brand impression. For each package type, the study also identified the brand personality features that consumers associate with it. The package types, associated personality features, and samples of brands depicting each package appear in Figure 6.8.[16]

PRODUCT REPOSITIONING

Regardless of how well positioned a product appears to be, the marketer may be forced to reposition it in response to market events, such as a competitor cutting into the brand's market

FIGURE 6.7B
Source: Courtesy of Suzuki.

share or too many competitors stressing the same attribute. Another reason to reposition a product or service is to satisfy changing consumer preferences. For example, for years, GM tried to convince consumers that Oldsmobile was not an "old folks'" car by trying to reposition the car as "not your father's Oldsmobile." However, this effort failed because the "old folks'" image of the brand was very strongly set in the minds of car buyers, and GM discontinued this brand.

The roots of the financial crisis that occurred in fall 2008 were excessive use of credit by consumers enabled by their ability to borrow large amounts of money easily against their real estate. Traditionally, Americans looked forward to paying off their mortgages (the ritual of burning the mortgage note was part of several sitcoms in the 1960s and 1970s) and the term *second mortgage* was associated with desperate borrowing as a last resort. However, over the years, bank marketers *repositioned* this negatively-perceived loan and lured more and more consumers to get the so called *equity loans* and use the funds for discretionary spending. The

TABLE 6.3 Positioning Products and Services

MODEL OF STRATEGIC POSITIONING

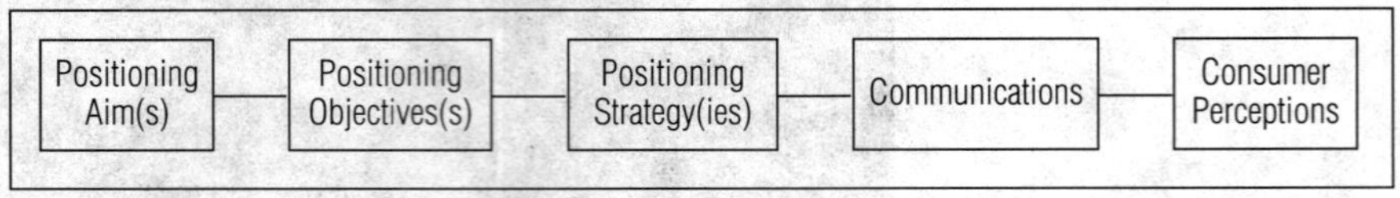

TYPOLOGY OF POSITIONING STRATEGIES

Strategy 1	**Top of the range:** *Upper class, top of the range, status, prestigious, posh*
Strategy 2	**Service:** *Impressive service, personal attention, consider people as important, friendly service*
Strategy 3	**Value for money:** *Reasonable price, value for money, affordability*
Strategy 4	**Reliability:** *Durability, warranty, safety, reliability*
Strategy 5	**Attractive:** *Good aesthetics, attractive, cool, elegant*
Strategy 6	**Country of origin:** *Patriotism, country of origin, youth market*
Strategy 7	**The Brand Name:** *The brand name, leaders in the market, extra features, choice, wide range, expensive*
Strategy 8	**Selectivity:** *Discriminatory, selective in the choice of customers, high principles*

Sources: Charles Blankson and Stavros P. Kalafatis, "Congruence Between Positioning and Brand Advertising," *Journal of Advertising Research* (March 2007): 79–94; and Charles Blankson, Stavros P. Kalafatis, Julian Ming-Sung Cheng, and Costas Hadjicharalambous, "Impact of Positioning Strategies on Corporate Image," *Journal of Advertising Research* (March 2008): 106–122.

first successful repositioning effort appeared in the form of the slogan "Live Richly" and was supported by such claims as "There's got to be at least $25,000 hidden in your house. We can help you find it." Over the years, marketers replaced the term *equity loans* with *equity access* (a term less associated with borrowing) and encouraged consumers to use it through such persuasive advertisements as "Is your mortgage squeezing your wallet? Squeeze back," "The smartest place to borrow? Your place," "The easiest way to haul money out of your house," and "You've put a lot of work into your home. Isn't it time for your home to return the favor?" The repositioning of the second mortgage was a spectacular success and since the 1980s equity loans ballooned from $1 billion to $1 trillion.[17] Apparently, consumers needs were fulfilled, but the same strategies that filled these needs also significantly contributed to destabilizing the world's financial structure.

PERCEPTUAL MAPPING

The analytical technique termed **perceptual mapping** enables marketers to determine just how they want their products or services to appear to consumers in relation to competitive brands on one or more relevant characteristics. It allows them to see gaps in the positioning of all brands in the product or service class and identify areas in which new offerings can be developed. Figure 6.9 portrays a perceptual map based on the slogans used to position new condominium residences recently offered for sale in New York City (the names of the buildings appear in the diagram and their positioning themes/slogans appear underneath). These residences vary greatly in price, form, and location, but the prices buyers were willing to pay were to a large extent a function of the images of these offerings, as determined by their respective positioning. Potential builders can use the map for uncovering marketing opportunities. For example, if they discover that in a particular neighborhood many condos are positioned as "modern trophies" (i.e., the upper right quadrant of the map) they should consider building more "traditional homes" (i.e., the lower left quadrant) in that area. Of course, before doing so, the developers must conduct marketing research in order to determine whether there is indeed a need for such residencies in that area and whether the prospective positioning of these buildings is congruent with consumers' perceptions of that neighborhood.[18]

Because unfilled gaps or "unowned" perceptual positions present opportunities for competitors, sophisticated marketers create several distinct offerings, often in the form of different

FIGURE 6.8
Holistic Package Design, Corresponding Brand Impressions, and Illustrations

[a]The features listed here are for fragrances. For each package design, the brand personality features associated with that design are described in relation to the entire sample that included 120 fragrances.

Source: Ulrich R. Orth and Keven Malkewitz, "Holistic Package Designs and Consumer Brand Impressions," *Journal of Marketing,* 72 (May 2008): 64–81. Copyright 2008 by American Marketing Association. Reproduced with permission of American Marketing Association in the format print & electronic usage via Copyright Clearance Center.

Package	Massive	Contrasting	Natural	Delicate	Nondescript
Perceived distinguishing factors	Robust and massive in the size of the package and typography. Low on resemblance to natural schemes and elaborateness.	Non-harmonious shape, color scheme, and typography. Low on resemblance to natural schemes. Include irregular designs.	Harmonious, symmetrical, resembling natural schemes. Viewed as archetypical, but may include designs from different periods.	Muted, sleek, and delicate. Elaborate structure and typography. Attracting attention. Low resemblance to natural schemes. Small in size and weight.	Simple, clean, discreet, and transparent but no factors that clearly differentiate these packages from others.
Brand personality features[i]	Lower excitement and sophistication and higher ruggedness.	Higher excitement and ruggedness and lower competence.	Appear sincere and sophisticated	Higher competence and sophistication and lower ruggedness.	Associated with low sincerity, excitement, and ruggedness.

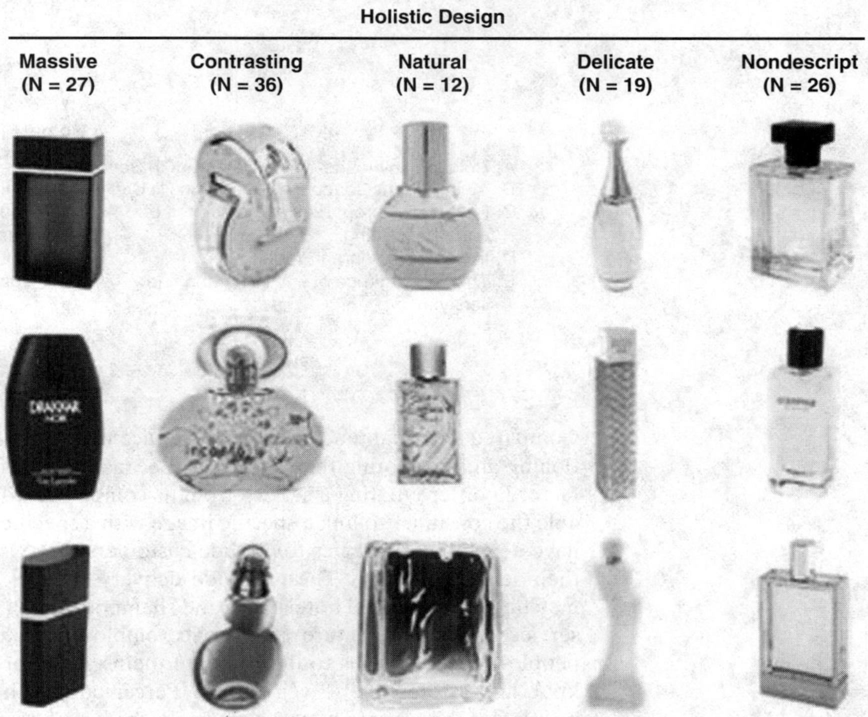

brands, to fill several identified niches. For example, Visine originally consisted of eye drops to relieve redness. Now, Visine's line of eye care offerings includes 10 versions for relieving eye redness and irritation due to allergies, dust, and pollen; drops for lubricating eyes; and several versions of an advanced formula named Visine Tears.[19] Crest Toothpaste's line includes 12 categories of toothpaste offering distinct benefits such as tartar, cavity, and sensitive teeth protection; toothpastes with baking soda and stripes; and Crest Kids. In response to the highly successful Colgate Total, Crest introduced a new line named Crest Pro-Health. Crest's Expressions line claims to "amaze the mouth," "awaken the senses," and "keep the taste buds tingling."[20] Within each Crest category, the product is offered in a variety of pastes, gels, liquid gels, and flavors. It would be virtually impossible for a manufacturer to penetrate either the eye care or the toothpaste market with a product that offers a benefit that is not already provided by Visine or Crest, in their respective markets.

FIGURE 6.9
Perceptual Map of New Condominiums in New York City

Source: Joseph Wisenblit, "Positioning New Condominiums in New York City," Working Paper (October 2008), Stillman School of Business, Seton Hall University, South Orange, New Jersey.

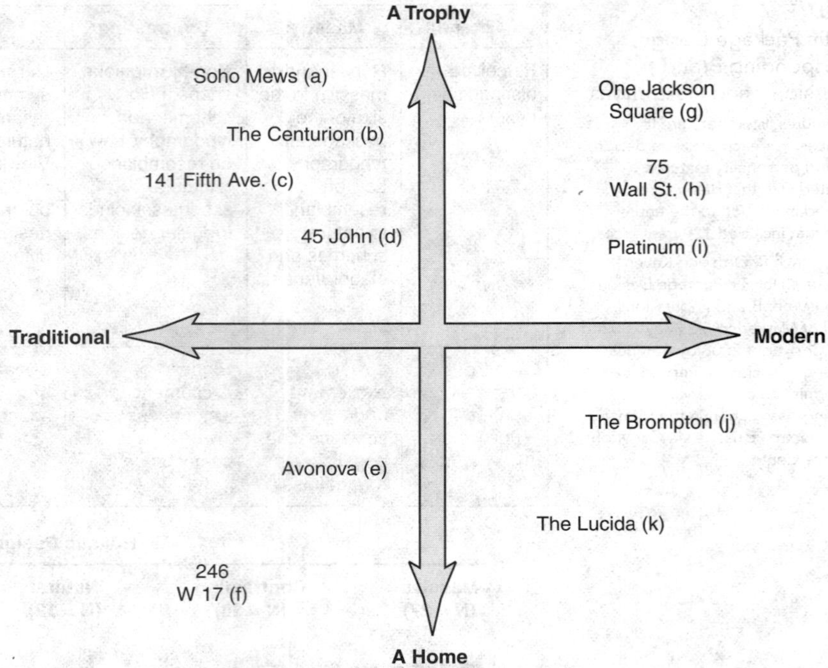

A: Hold the key to the only private park in Soho
B: 48 Important Condo Residences in NYC
C: Four trophy properties at the summit of a trophy building.
D: Impeccable. Vibrant. Yours.
E: The convergence of fine living and fine lifestyle.
F: Great apartments. Great lofts. A great place to live.
G: Your private island in the sky
H: A million stars above, five stars bellow
I: Cutting edge condo residences.
J: Your stylishly proper New York home.
K: A smarter kind of living on the Upper East Side

POSITIONING OF SERVICES

Compared with manufacturing firms, service marketers face several unique problems in positioning and promoting their offerings. Because services are *intangible*, image becomes a key factor in differentiating a service from its competition. Thus, the marketing objective is to enable the consumer to link a specific image with a specific brand name. Many service marketers have developed strategies to provide customers with visual images and tangible reminders of their service offerings. These include delivery vehicles painted in distinct colors, restaurant matchbooks, packaged hotel soaps and shampoos, and a variety of other specialty items. Many service companies feature real service employees in their ads (as tangible cues) and use people-focused themes to differentiate themselves. For example, Figure 6.10 depicts a steak knife and a reference to vegetarians. Perceived together, these tangible objects convey the position of the restaurant as a well-established steakhouse.

Many service companies market several versions of their service to different market segments by using a differentiated positioning strategy. However, they must be careful to avoid perceptual confusion among their customers. For example, as many flyers upgraded their tickets to business and first class, the "superior" image of these alternatives (relative to economy class) and the perceived distinction between business and first class became less pronounced. In response, several airlines upgraded their first class to offer such features as personal suites with beds, and also made their business classes more spacious and luxurious. After learning that many flyers are willing to pay more for larger seats and more legroom only, but not for extras such as fancy meals, wine, and toiletries, some airlines introduced the *premium economy* class. As another example, in theaters, traditionally, all orchestra seats were part of the same service class and equal in price. Now, most theaters offer *premium* orchestra seats, typically located in the very front or next to the center aisles, and many also offer premium balcony seats.

FIGURE 6.10
Source: Courtesy of Post House.

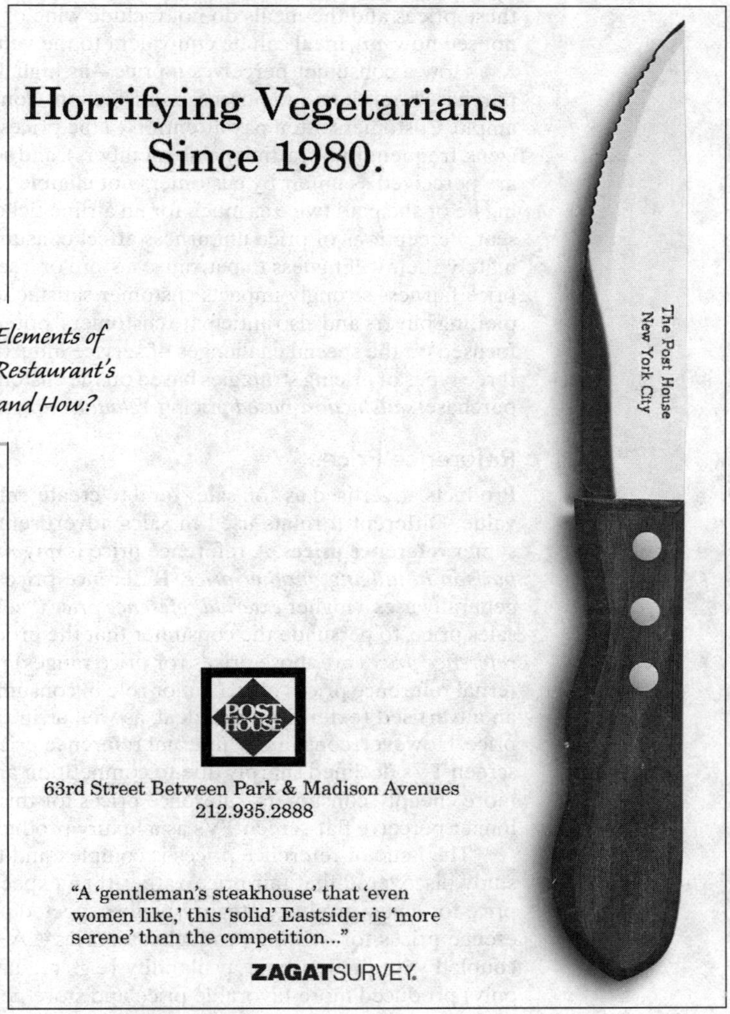

QUESTION: *Which Elements of This Ad Convey the Restaurant's Perceptual Position and How?*

The design of the service environment is an important aspect of service positioning strategy and sharply influences consumer impressions. For example, targeting the dynamic and technologically oriented Generation Y, many stores significantly increased the sensory stimuli provided within the store, including live DJs, dim lighting, scented environments, loud ultramodern music, flat-screen TVs, and live models. Some Apple stores are open 24 hours and are designed to keep Apple users there even if they are not buying products. Thus, the stores include long tables and chairs with electrical outlets and wireless online access so that Apple users can work on projects and interact with other users. A recent study indicated that the arousal level within the store environment must match the expectations of the shoppers in order to avoid perceived over- or understimulation.[21]

PERCEIVED PRICE

Perceived price should reflect the value that the customer receives from the purchase. For example, consumers generally perceive a low price for a meal at a fast-food outlet as well as a high price for a meal at a gourmet restaurant as consistent with the value that they received in both instances and therefore as fair. However, most reasonable consumers may argue that paying about $500 per person for a meal (there are several restaurants in New York City that charge these prices and the meals do not include wine or alcohol) is unreasonable because they cannot see how *any* meal can be equivalent to the value of $500.

How a consumer perceives a price—as high, low, or fair—has a strong influence on both purchase intentions and purchase satisfaction. Consider the perception of price fairness, for example. Customers often pay attention to the prices paid by other customers (such as senior citizens, frequent flyers, affinity club members), and sometimes such differential pricing strategies are perceived as unfair by customers not eligible for the special prices. No one is happy knowing he or she paid twice as much for an airline ticket or a movie ticket as the person in the next seat. Perceptions of price unfairness affect consumers' perceptions of product value and, ultimately, their willingness to patronize a store or a service. A recent study showed that perceived price fairness strongly impacts customer satisfaction and that sellers should steer clear of exploiting buyers and also anticipate customers' potential feelings of being exploited.[22] One study, focused on the special challenges of service industries in pricing intangible products, proposed three types of pricing strategies based on the customer's perception of the value provided by the purchase: *satisfaction-based* pricing, *relationship* pricing, and *efficiency* pricing (see Table 6.4).[23]

Reference Prices

Products advertised as "on sale" tend to create enhanced customer perceptions of savings and value. Different formats used in sales advertisements have differing impacts, based on consumer **reference prices**. A reference price is *any price that a consumer uses as a basis for comparison in judging another price.* Reference prices can be external or internal. An advertiser generally uses a higher *external reference price* ("sold elsewhere at . . .") in an ad offering a lower sales price, to persuade the consumer that the product advertised is a really good buy. *Internal reference prices* are those prices (or price ranges) retrieved by the consumer from memory. Internal reference prices play a major role in consumers' evaluations and perceptions of value of an advertised (external) price deal, as well as in the believability of any advertised reference price. However, consumers' internal reference prices change. For example, as the prices of flat-screen TVs declined sharply due to competition and manufacturers' abilities to produce them more cheaply, consumers' reference prices for this product have declined as well, and they no longer perceive flat-screen TVs as a luxury product that only few can afford.

The issue of reference prices is complex and the focus of many studies. For example, one study discovered that fair price, rather than expected price, determined consumers' reference price for a *new* product category, while expected price had more impact than fair price on reference prices for *existing* product categories.[24] A recent study showed that reference pricing coupled with limited-time availability (e.g., regularly $599, now $359 and on sale, three days only) produced more favorable price and store perceptions than each technique used alone.[25]

TABLE 6.4 Three Pricing Strategies Based on Perceived Value

PRICING STRATEGY	PROVIDES VALUE BY . . .	IMPLEMENTED AS . . .
Satisfaction-based pricing	Recognizing and reducing customers' perceptions of uncertainty, which the intangible nature of services magnifies.	Service guarantees. Benefit-driven pricing. Flat-rate pricing.
Relationship pricing	Encouraging long-term relationships with the company that customers view as beneficial.	Long-term contracts. Price bundling.
Efficiency pricing	Sharing with customers the cost savings that the company has achieved by understanding, managing, and reducing the costs of providing the service.	Cost-leader pricing.

Source: Leonard L. Berry and Yadav S. Manjit, "Capture and Communicate Value in the Pricing of Services," *Sloan Management Review* (Summer 1996): 41–51.

Another study illustrated the "right side effect" in relation to consumers' perceptions of discounts. When consumers saw regular and sale prices with the same left digits (e.g., 23 and 22), they perceived larger discounts when the *right digits* were smaller than 5 than when the right digits were higher than 5. Thus, consumers may perceive a discount from $23 to $22 as providing more value than a discount from $19 to $18.[26] Yet another study demonstrated that price discounts immediately increased buying intentions, and also lowered consumers' future reference prices.[27]

Naturally, consumers tend to believe that the selling prices of market offerings are considerably higher than their perceived fair prices. When an advertised reference price is within a given consumer's acceptable price range, it is considered plausible and credible. If the advertised reference point is outside the range of acceptable prices (i.e., implausible), it contrasts with existing attitudes and will not be perceived as a valid reference point, adversely affecting both consumer evaluations and the advertiser's credibility. When consumers encounter prices that are significantly different from their expectations, they engage in *dissonance reduction.* That is, they seek additional information to justify the high price or they trivialize their own expectations by, for example, saying that their expectations were unrealistic because it has been a while since they last were in the market to buy the product in question.[28] Table 6.5 depicts the possible changes in the perceptions of consumers who encounter unexpected prices. (The theory of *cognitive dissonance* is fully explored in Chapter 8.)

PERCEIVED QUALITY

Consumers' perceived quality of a product (or service) is based on a variety of informational cues that they associate with the product. Some of these cues are **intrinsic** to the product or service; others are **extrinsic**. Either singly or together, such cues provide the basis for perceptions of product and service quality.

Perceived Quality of Products

Cues that are *intrinsic* concern physical characteristics of the product itself, such as size, color, flavor, or aroma. In some cases, consumers use physical characteristics (e.g., the flavor of ice cream or cake) to judge product quality. Consumers like to believe that they base their

TABLE 6.5 Consumer Reactions to Unexpected Prices

CONSUMER ENCOUNTERS WITH UNEXPECTED PRICES

↓

CONSUMERS REDUCE DISSONANCE USING ONE OF THE FOLLOWING MODES

SEEKING CONSONANT INFORMATION	CHANGING ATTITUDE	TRIVIALIZING
Evaluate alternative suppliers Evaluate substitute products	Update Price Expectations	Reduce the importance of: (1) money (2) shop around savings (3) saving money (4) a good deal (5) fair pricing (6) value
Plan to search for additional information	Attribute higher prices to: (1) product quality (2) updated product information (3) product attributes (4) general rising prices	
Seek consonant information from another retailer or a substitute product (or) remain dissonant		
Change attitude, trivialize or remain dissonant	Dissonance is reduced	Dissonance is reduced

Source: Joan Lindsey-Mullikin, "Beyond Reference Price: Understanding Consumers' Encounters with Unexpected Prices," *Journal of Product and Brand Management,* 12, nos. 2/3 (2003): 141. Copyright © 2003, MCB UP Ltd.

evaluations of product quality on intrinsic cues, because that enables them to justify their product decisions (either positive or negative) as being "rational" or "objective" product choices. More often than not, however, they use *extrinsic* characteristics to judge quality. For example, though many consumers claim they buy a brand because of its superior taste, they are often unable to identify that brand in blind taste tests. The colors of such products as powdered fruit drinks and orange juice are a more important determinant than their labels and actual taste in determining the consumer's ability to identify the flavor correctly. For example, subjects are likely to view purple or grape-colored drinks as "tart" in flavor, and the orange-colored version as "flavorful, sweet, and refreshing." Many studies showed that the packaging influences consumers' perceptions of products. For example, a study reported that both consumers who rated a popcorn's taste as unfavorable and those who rated the same taste as favorable consumed more of the product when the container size was increased.[29] A recent study compared the differences in quality perceptions of store brands and national brands; the study discovered that the factors contributing to such perceived differences are customers' perceptions of the stores and their beliefs in the extrinsic attributes of the product as indicators of quality.[30] An experimental study of how people judge the quality of two foods—shrimp and cheese—at two price levels and two consumption situations (i.e., elegant and less elegant surroundings) found out that perceived price had a positive impact on *perceived quality* among highly involved consumers, and that the elegant physical surroundings positively impacted the subjects' perceived quality of the foods and the pleasure felt when eating them.[31]

In the absence of actual experience with a product, consumers often evaluate quality on the basis of cues that are external to the product itself, such as price, brand image, manufacturer's image, retail store image, or even the perceived country of origin. For example, Häagen-Dazs, an American-made ice cream, has been incredibly successful with its made-up (and meaningless) Scandinavian-sounding name. The success of Smirnoff vodka, made in Connecticut, can be related to its so-called Russian derivation. A recent study found that the wine region was the most important determinant of consumers' perceived quality of wines and that Napa Valley and Sonoma had the strongest regional images among American vineyards.[32]

There are numerous ways to measure perceptions of quality. A scale that measures perceptions of brand luxury—a construct that is often related to perceived quality—is shown in Figure 6.11.[33]

Perceived Quality of Services

It is more difficult for consumers to evaluate the quality of services than the quality of products. This is true because of certain distinctive characteristics of services: They are *intangible*, they are *variable*, they are *perishable*, and they are *simultaneously produced and consumed*. To overcome the fact that consumers are unable to compare competing services side-by-side as they do with competing products, consumers rely on surrogate cues (i.e., extrinsic cues) to evaluate service quality. In evaluating a doctor's services, for example, they note the quality of the office and examining room furnishings, the number (and source) of framed degrees on the wall, the pleasantness of the receptionist, and the professionalism of the nurse; all contribute to the consumer's overall evaluation of the quality of a doctor's services. A recent study found that online dating services generally fail to meet users' expectations because potential daters want to screen prospective partners by *experiential* attributes (e.g., rapport) while online dating providers only enable users to screen by *searchable* attributes (e.g., income). The study also found that using "virtual dates" (thus providing a tangible cue about the service) increased users' satisfaction with the online dating service.[34]

Because the actual quality of services can vary from day to day, from service employee to service employee, and from customer to customer (e.g., in food, in waitperson service, in haircuts, even in classes taught by the same professor), marketers try to standardize their services in order to provide consistency of quality. The downside of service standardization is the loss of customized services, which many consumers value.

Unlike products, which are first produced, then sold, and then consumed, most services are first sold and then produced and consumed simultaneously. Whereas a defective product is likely to be detected by factory quality control inspectors before it ever reaches the consumer, an inferior service is consumed as it is being produced; thus, there is little opportunity to correct

FIGURE 6.11
Measuring Perceptions of Brand Luxury

Source: Frank Vigneron and Lester W. Johnson, "Measuring Perceptions of Brand Luxury," *Journal of Brand Management*, 11, no. 6 (July 2004): 484.

Non-personally-oriented perceptions			
Conspicuousness	Conspicuous	___:___:___:___:___:___:___	Noticeable
	Popular	___:___:___:___:___:___:___	Elitist*
	Affordable	___:___:___:___:___:___:___	Extremely expensive*
	For wealthy	___:___:___:___:___:___:___	For well-off
Uniqueness	Fairly exclusive	___:___:___:___:___:___:___	Very exclusive*
	Precious	___:___:___:___:___:___:___	Valuable
	Rare	___:___:___:___:___:___:___	Uncommon
	Unique	___:___:___:___:___:___:___	Unusual
Quality	Crafted	___:___:___:___:___:___:___	Manufactured
	Upmarket	___:___:___:___:___:___:___	Luxurious*
	Best quality	___:___:___:___:___:___:___	Good quality
	Sophisticated	___:___:___:___:___:___:___	Original
	Superior	___:___:___:___:___:___:___	Better
Personally-oriented perceptions			
Hedonism	Exquisite	___:___:___:___:___:___:___	Tasteful
	Attractive	___:___:___:___:___:___:___	Glamorous*
	Stunning	___:___:___:___:___:___:___	Memorable
Extended self	Leading	___:___:___:___:___:___:___	Influential
	Very powerful	___:___:___:___:___:___:___	Fairly powerful
	Rewarding	___:___:___:___:___:___:___	Pleasing
	Successful	___:___:___:___:___:___:___	Well regarded

* Indicates item is reverse-scored

it. For example, a defective haircut is difficult to correct, just as the negative impression caused by an abrupt or careless waiter is difficult to correct.

During peak demand hours, the interactive quality of services often declines, because both the customer and the service provider are hurried and under stress. Without special effort by the service provider to ensure consistency of services during peak hours, service image is likely to decline. Many marketers try to change demand patterns in order to distribute the service more equally over time. Cell phone service providers offer unlimited minutes during weekends, and restaurants offer significantly less expensive "early bird" dinners for consumers who come in before 7:00 P.M.

The most widely accepted framework for researching service quality stems from the premise that a consumer's evaluation of service quality is a function of the magnitude and direction of the gap between the customer's *expectations of service* and the customer's *assessment (perception) of the service actually delivered.*[35] For example, a brand-new graduate student enrolled in an introductory marketing course at a highly reputable university has certain expectations about the intellectual abilities of her classmates, the richness of classroom discussions, and the professor's knowledge and communication skills. At the end of the term, her assessment of the course's quality is based on the differences between her expectations at the start of the term and her perceptions of the course at the end of the semester. If the course falls below her expectations, she will view it as a service of poor quality. If her expectations are exceeded, she will view the course as a high-quality educational experience.

The expectations of a given service vary widely among different consumers of the same service. These expectations stem from word-of-mouth consumers have heard about the service, their past experiences, the promises made about the service in its ads and by its salespersons, the purchase alternatives available, and other situational factors. If the level of service received significantly exceeds these expectations, the service is perceived as of high quality and generates more customer satisfaction, increased probability of repeat patronage, and favorable word of mouth.[36] Also, marketers should never make promises that they cannot realistically deliver because such claims raise customers' expectations and significantly increase the likelihood of lower perceived service quality when the service delivered is good, but not outstanding.

The SERVQUAL scale was designed to measure the gap between customers' expectations of services and their perceptions of the actual service delivered, based on the following five dimensions: *reliability*, *responsiveness*, *assurance*, *empathy*, and *tangibility*. These dimensions are divided into two groups: the **outcome dimension**, which focuses on the *reliable* delivery of the core service, and the **process dimension**, which focuses on *how* the core service is delivered (i.e., the employees' responsiveness, assurance, and empathy in handling customers) and the service's tangible aspects. The process dimension offers the service provider a significant opportunity to exceed customer expectations.[37] For example, although Amazon.com provides the same core service as other online booksellers (the *outcome* dimension), it provides a superior *process* dimension through its advanced database that generates recommendations for customers, shipment tracking system, the ability to preorder books yet to be published months in advance, subscriptions that include unlimited deliveries without shipping fees, and many other options. Thus, Amazon.com uses the *process* dimension as a method to exceed customers' expectations and has acquired the image of a company that has an important, customer-focused competitive advantage among the companies providing the same core service. Figure 6.12 illustrates using a process dimension in advertising a newly-formed business class on an airline.

PRICE/QUALITY RELATIONSHIP

Perceived product value has been described as a trade-off between the product's perceived benefits (or quality) and the perceived sacrifice—both monetary and nonmonetary—necessary to acquire it. Studies have repeatedly found that consumers rely on price as an indicator of product quality and, in the absence of other knowledge, view more expensive products as higher quality and value. Some suggest that consumers using a **price/quality relationship** are actually relying on a well-known (and, hence, more expensive) brand name as an indicator of quality without actually relying directly on price per se. Because price is so often considered an indicator of quality, some product advertisements deliberately emphasize a high price to underscore the marketers' claims of quality. The ad in Figure 6.13 illustrates using price/quality relationship (the slogan on the ad's bottom left reads "Perfection Has Its Price"). Marketers understand that, at times, products with lower prices may be interpreted as reduced quality. At the same time, consumers rely on the price and brand name when evaluating the product's prestige and symbolic value and use more concrete attributes of a product, such as performance and durability, to judge its overall performance. For these reasons, marketers must understand all the attributes that customers use to evaluate a given product and include all applicable information in order to counter any perceptions of negative quality associated with a lower price. A recent study validated the concept of price/quality perception. Subjects rated the pain in their wrist, artificially caused by an electric shock, after taking a pain reliever, which was actually a dummy, placebo pill. Half the subjects were told that the medication they took costs $2.50 per dose and the others learned that it costs 10 cents; in reality, all subjects received identical pills. Eighty-five percent of those who received the more expensive pill reported significant pain reduction while only 61% of those who took the cheaper pill reported such relief. Clearly, consumers tend to believe that more expensive medications are more effective; this finding is consistent with previous research showing that consumers perceive generic drugs as less effective than brand name medications, although, chemically, the two medications are identical.[38]

In most consumption situations, in addition to price, consumers also use such cues as the brand and the store in which the product is bought to evaluate its quality. Consumers use price as a surrogate indicator of quality if they have little information to go on, or if they have little confidence in their own ability to make the product or service choice on other grounds. When the consumer is familiar with a brand name or has experience with a product (or service) or the store where it is purchased, price declines as a determining factor in product evaluation and purchase.

The form in which products are sold may alter the product's perceived value. Many products and services are sold as *bundles* (e.g., sets of different pens, tickets to a series of ballet performances), and price discounts lead to more sales of bundled products. A recent study showed that bundle discounts may have unforeseen results in the form of perceptions of lower quality of all the items in the bundle, which will negatively impact future sales when these items are sold individually.[39]

FIGURE 6.12

Source: Courtesy of Singapore Airlines, Ltd.

QUESTION: *How Can This Ad Affect the Service's Perceived Quality?*

RETAIL STORE IMAGE

Retail stores have images of their own that serve to influence the perceived quality of products they carry and the decisions of consumers as to where to shop. These images stem from the merchandise they carry, the brands sold and their prices, the level of service, the store's physical environment and ambiance, and its typical clientele (this can often be determined from the cars parked in the store's parking lot). A recent study demonstrated that consumers who have a strong positive image of a store will not find negative word of mouth about that store credible.[40]

The *width and type of product assortment* affects retail store image. Grocery retailers, for example, are often reluctant to reduce the number of products they carry out of concern that perceptions of a smaller assortment will reduce the likelihood that consumers will shop in their stores; they carry primarily widely advertised, best-selling brands. On the other hand, Whole Foods Markets—a relatively small supermarket chain—has carved itself a profitable niche by

FIGURE 6.13
Source: Courtesy of Anheuser-Busch.

QUESTION: *Which of the Ad's Elements Conveys the Product's Quality?*

carrying a smaller but highly selective range of products in comparison to conventional supermarkets. Whole Foods stores carry organic (perceived as healthier) products, many of which are bought from mom-and-pop producers; all food products carried are screened for artificial ingredients; and the chain no longer sells products with hydrogenated fats. The chain has been much more profitable than conventional supermarkets in spite of its limited product assortment. Clearly, the unique benefit that a store provides is more important than the number of items it carries in forming a favorable store image in consumers' minds.

Customers often use brand, store image, and price together as a product's quality indicators. When brand and retailer images become associated, the less favorable image becomes enhanced at the expense of the more favorable image. Thus, when a low-priced store carries a brand with a high-priced image, the image of the store will improve, whereas the image of the brand will be adversely affected. For that reason, marketers of prestigious designer goods often attempt to control the outlets where their products are sold. Also, when upscale stores sell leftover expensive items to discount stores, they remove the designer labels from these goods as part of the agreements they have with the manufacturers of these products.

Pricing discounts also impact retail store image. Stores that offer frequent, small discounts on large numbers of items are more likely to be perceived as "discount stores" and less prestigious than stores offering larger discounts on a smaller number of products. This has important implications for retailers' *positioning strategies.* In times of heavy competition, when it is tempting to hold frequent large sales covering many items, such strategies may result in an unwanted change in store image. For example, Lord & Taylor in New York City, formerly positioned as an upscale, high-class department store, advertises sales so frequently and fills its aisles with sales racks proclaiming bargain prices, so that its upscale image has been tarnished, and its customer mix has changed. Marketers must also consider how price reductions of *specific* products impact consumers' perceptions. Poorly chosen price promotions cause confusion and may negatively impact consumers' perceptions of the store.

MANUFACTURERS' IMAGE

Consumer imagery extends beyond perceived price and store image to the producers themselves. Manufacturers who enjoy a favorable image generally find that their new products are accepted more readily than those of manufacturers who have a less favorable or even a "neutral" image. Consumers also associate certain attributes with manufacturers. For example, Apple is perceived as "different" from other computers for personal use. A Swiss-made Tissot watch is perceived as much more commonplace and inexpensive, while watches made by Rolex and Patek Philippe are perceived as expensive, status symbols

Some major marketers introduce new products under the guise of supposedly smaller, pioneering (and presumably more forward-thinking) companies. The goal of this so-called *stealth* (or faux) *parentage* is to persuade consumers that the new brands are produced by independent, nonconformist free spirits, rather than by giant corporate entities. Companies sometimes use stealth parentage when they enter a product category totally unrelated to the one with which their corporate name has become synonymous. For example, when Disney Studios—a company with a wholesome, family-focused image—produces films that include violence and sex, it does so under the name Touchstone Pictures.

Many companies use advertising, exhibits, and sponsorship of community events to enhance their images. Although some marketers argue that product and service advertising do more to boost the corporate image than *institutional* (image) advertising does, others see both types of advertising—product and institutional—as integral and complementary components of a total corporate communications program. When the reputation of Wal-Mart was tarnished by allegations of unfair labor practices, sexual discrimination, and the publication of data indicating that the company caused most of America's trade imbalance with China, the company published ads stating that "Wal-Mart Is Working for Everyone." In addition, the company's executives appeared on TV talk shows and met with community groups and government officials to dispel the negative associations.[41] Wal-Mart's troubles continued when a consumer advocacy group initiated an ad campaign that posed the question "Where would Jesus shop?" and stated that people of faith should *not* shop at the store during the holiday season because of the store's bad wages, benefits, and overseas child labor policies. This advertising also illustrates using Jesus's "halo effect"—a term discussed earlier.[42]

PERCEIVED RISK

Consumers must constantly make decisions regarding what products or services to buy and where to buy them. Because the outcomes (or consequences) of such decisions are often uncertain, the consumer perceives some degree of "risk" in making a purchase decision. **Perceived risk** is defined as *the uncertainty that consumers face when they cannot foresee the consequences of their purchase decisions.* This definition highlights two relevant dimensions of perceived risk: uncertainty and consequences.

The degree of risk that consumers perceive and their own tolerance for risk taking are factors that influence their purchase strategies. It should be stressed that consumers are influenced by risks that they perceive, whether or not such risks actually exist. Risk that is not perceived—no matter how real or how dangerous—will not influence consumer behavior. The major types of risks that consumers perceive when making product decisions include *functional risk, physical risk, financial risk, social risk, psychological risk*, and *time risk* (see Table 6.6, Part A).

Perception of Risk Varies

Consumer perception of risk varies, depending on the person, the product, the situation, and the culture. The amount of risk perceived depends on the specific consumer. Some consumers tend to perceive high degrees of risk in various consumption situations; others tend to perceive little risk. For example, adolescents who engage in high-risk activities, such as fast, complicated, and daring rollerblading or bicycling maneuvers, obviously have lower perceived risk than those who do not engage in high-risk activities. *High-risk perceivers* are often described as **narrow categorizers** because they limit their choices (e.g., product choices) to a few safe alternatives. They would rather exclude some perfectly good alternatives than chance a poor selection. *Low-risk perceivers* have been described as **broad categorizers** because they tend to make

TABLE 6.6 Perceived Risk

PART A: TYPES OF PERCEIVED RISK

Functional risk is the risk that the product will not perform as expected. ("Can the new FDA operate a full week without needing to be recharged?")

Physical risk is the risk to self and others that the product may pose. ("Is a cellular phone really safe, or does it emit harmful radiation?")

Financial risk is the risk that the product will not be worth its cost. ("Will a new and cheaper model of a Plasma TV monitor become available six months from now?")

Social risk is the risk that a poor product choice may result in social embarrassment. ("Will my classmates laugh at my purple mohawk haircut?")

Psychological risk is the risk that a poor product choice will bruise the consumer's ego. ("Will I be embarrassed when I invite friends to listen to music on my five-year old stereo?")

Time risk is the risk that the time spent in product search may be wanted if the product does not perform as expected. ("Will I have to go through the shopping effort all over again?")

PART B: HOW CONSUMERS HANDLE RISK

Consumers seek information: Consumers seek information about the product and product category through word-of-mouth communication (from friends and family and from other people whose opinions they value), from salespeople, and from the general media. They spend more time thinking about their choice and search for more information about the product alternatives when they associate a high degree of risk with the purchase.

Consumers are brand loyal: Consumers avoid risk by remaining loyal to a brand with which they have been satisfied instead of purchasing new or untried brands. High-risk perceivers are more likely to be loyal to their old brands and less likely to purchase newly introduced products.

Consumers select by brand image: When consumers have had no experience with a product, they tend to "trust" a favored or well-known brand name. They often think well-known brands are better and are worth buying for the implied assurance of quality, dependability, performance, and service.

Consumers rely on store image: If consumers have no other information about a product, they often trust the judgment of the merchandise buyers of a reputable store and depend on them to have made careful decisions in selecting products for sale. Store image also provides assurance of return privileges and adjustment in case of dissatisfaction.

Consumers buy the most expensive model: As indicated in the discussion of price/quality relationship, consumers often feel that the most expensive model is probably the best in terms of quality.

Consumers seek reassurance: Consumers seek reassurance through money-back guarantees, government and private laboratory test results, warranties, and prepurchase trial (e.g., a test drive). Products that do not easily lend themselves to free or limited trial, such as a refrigerator, present a selling challenge to marketers.

their choices from a much wider range of alternatives. They would rather risk a poor selection than limit the number of alternatives from which they can choose.

An individual's perception of risk varies with product categories. For example, consumers are likely to perceive a higher degree of risk (e.g., functional risk, financial risk, time risk) in the purchase of a high-definition recorder (a very new product category) than in the purchase of an automobile; this type of risk is termed *product-category* perceived risk. There are also *product-specific* perceived risks. For example, consumers generally perceive service decisions to be riskier than product decisions.

The degree of risk perceived by a consumer is also affected by the shopping situation (e.g., a traditional brick-and-mortar retail store, online, catalog, or direct-mail solicitations). The sharp increase in online sales in recent years indicates that, on the basis of positive experiences and word of mouth, consumers now perceive much less risk in online shopping than they once did. In part, this perceived risk reduction may be due to better technologies that enable buyers to examine the product online in greater detail and from different viewing angles. A recent study of online banking demonstrated that most consumers want to use online payments (mostly to meet deadlines and avoid past-due late penalties), but their willingness to do so is a function of their perceived risk of the security of online payment systems.[43] Studies also found that perceptions of trust and risk were the major determinants of consumers' attitudes toward shopping online and that trust reduced consumers' perceived risk in the electronic marketplace.[44]

How Consumers Handle Risk

Consumers characteristically develop their own strategies for reducing perceived risk. These risk-reduction strategies enable them to act with increased confidence when making product decisions, even though the consequences of such decisions remain somewhat uncertain. The means that consumers generally use to handle risk are summarized in Table 6.6 (Part B).

The concept of perceived risk has major implications for the introduction of new products. Because high-risk perceivers are less likely than low-risk perceivers to purchase new or innovative products, it is important for marketers to provide such consumers with persuasive risk-reduction strategies, such as a well-known brand name (sometimes achieved through licensing), distribution through reputable retail outlets, informative advertising, publicity, impartial test results, free samples, and money-back guarantees. Also, consumers can reduce perceived risk by using online resources enabling them to generate side-by-side comparisons depicting detailed charts of the features, prices, and ratings of all the available models within a given product category.

SUMMARY

Perception is the process by which individuals select, organize, and interpret stimuli into a meaningful and coherent picture of the world. Perception has strategy implications for marketers because consumers make decisions based on what they perceive rather than on the basis of objective reality.

The lowest level at which an individual can perceive a specific stimulus is that person's absolute threshold. The minimal difference that can be perceived between two stimuli is called the differential threshold or just noticeable difference (j.n.d.). Consumers perceive most sensory stimuli above the level of their conscious awareness; however, weak stimuli can be perceived below the level of conscious awareness (i.e., subliminally). Research refutes the notion that subliminal stimuli influence consumers' buying decisions.

Consumers' selections of stimuli from the environment are based on the interaction of their expectations and motives with the stimulus itself. People usually perceive things they need or want, and block the perception of unnecessary, unfavorable, or painful stimuli. The principles of selective perception include the following concepts: selective exposure, selective attention, perceptual defense, and perceptual blocking.

Consumers organize their perceptions into unified wholes according to the principles of Gestalt psychology: figure and ground, grouping, and closure. The interpretation of stimuli is highly subjective and is based on what the consumer expects to see in light of previous experience, on motives and interests at the time of perception, and on the clarity of the stimulus itself. Stereotypes that distort objective interpretation stem from physical appearances, descriptive terms, first impressions, and the halo effect.

Just as individuals have perceived images of themselves, they also have perceived images of products and brands. The perceived image of a product or service (how it is positioned) is more important to its ultimate success than are its actual physical characteristics. Products and services that are perceived distinctly and favorably have a much better chance of being purchased than products or services with unclear or unfavorable images.

Compared with manufacturing firms, service marketers face several unique problems in positioning and promoting their offerings because services are intangible, inherently variable, perishable, and are simultaneously produced and consumed. Regardless of how well positioned a product or service appears to be, the marketer may be forced to reposition it in response to market events, such as new competitor strategies or changing consumer preferences.

Consumers often judge the quality of a product or service on the basis of a variety of informational cues; some are intrinsic to the product (such as color, size, flavor, and aroma), while others are extrinsic (e.g., price, store image, brand image, and service environment). In the absence of direct experience or other information, consumers often rely on price as an indicator of quality. How a consumer perceives a price—as high, low, or fair—has a strong influence on purchase intentions and satisfaction. Consumers rely on both internal and external reference prices when assessing the fairness of a price.

Consumer imagery also includes perceived images of retail stores that influence the perceived quality of products they carry, as well as decisions as to where to shop. Manufacturers who enjoy a favorable image generally find that their new products are accepted more readily than those of manufacturers with less favorable or even neutral images.

Consumers often perceive risk in making product selections because of uncertainty as to the consequences of their product decisions. The most frequent types of risk that consumers perceive are functional risk, physical risk, financial risk, social risk, psychological risk, and time risk. Consumer strategies for reducing perceived risk include increased information search, brand loyalty, buying a well-known brand, buying from a reputable retailer, buying the most expensive brand, and seeking reassurance in the form of money-back guarantees, warranties, and prepurchase trials. The concept of perceived risk has important implications for marketers, who can facilitate the acceptance of new products by incorporating risk-reduction strategies in their new-product promotional campaigns.

DISCUSSION QUESTIONS

1. How does sensory adaptation affect advertising effectiveness? How can marketers overcome sensory adaptation?
2. Discuss the differences between the absolute threshold and the differential threshold. Which one is more important to marketers? Explain your answer.
3. For each of these products—chocolate bars and cereals—describe how marketers can apply their knowledge of the differential threshold to packaging, pricing, and promotional claims during periods of (a) rising ingredient and materials costs and (b) increasing competition.
4. Does subliminal advertising work? Support your view.
5. How do advertisers use contrast to make sure that their ads are noticed? Would the lack of contrast between the ad and the medium in which it appears help or hinder the effectiveness of the ad?
6. What are the implications of figure-and-ground relationships for print ads and for online ads? How can the figure-and-ground construct help or interfere with the communication of advertising messages?
7. Why are marketers sometimes "forced" to reposition their products or services? Illustrate your answers with examples.
8. Why is it more difficult for consumers to evaluate the effective quality of services than the quality of products?
9. Discuss the roles of extrinsic and intrinsic cues in the perceived quality of:

   a. wines.

   b. restaurants.

   c. cell phones.

   d. graduate education.

EXERCISES

1. Find three print examples of the kind of promotional methods described in Table 6.2. For each example, evaluate the effectiveness of the sensory input provided.
2. Define *selective perception*, and relate one or two elements of this concept to your own attention patterns in viewing print advertisements and online commercials.
3. Find two print advertisements depicting two of the positioning strategies listed in Table 6.3 and evaluate the effectiveness of each ad.
4. Select a company that produces several versions of the same product under the same brand name (do not use one of the examples discussed in this chapter). Visit the firm's Web site and prepare a list of the product items and the benefits that each item offers to consumers. Are all these benefits believable and will they persuade consumers to buy the different versions of the product? Explain your answers.
5. Relate two of the chapter's applicable concepts explaining consumers' evaluations of service quality to your evaluation of this course up to this point in the semester.

KEY TERMS

- absolute threshold *175*
- branded entertainment *182*
- broad categorizers *202*
- closure *183*
- consumer imagery *186*
- differential threshold *176*
- extrinsic cues *195*
- figure and ground *182*
- Gestalt psychology *182*
- grouping *182*
- halo effect *186*
- intrinsic cues *195*
- just noticeable difference (j.n.d.) *176*
- manufacturer's image *201*
- narrow categorizers *202*
- outcome dimension *198*
- perceived price *193*
- perceived quality *195*
- perceived risk *201*
- perception *175*
- perceptual blocking *182*
- perceptual defense *181*
- perceptual mapping *190*
- positioning *186*
- price/quality relationship *198*
- process dimension *198*
- product placement *182*
- reference prices *194*
- retail store image *199*
- selective attention *181*
- selective exposure *181*
- sensation *175*
- sensory adaptation *176*
- sensory receptors *175*
- stereotypes *183*
- stimulus *175*
- subliminal perception *178*
- Weber's law *176*

Case One: Packaging and the J.N.D.

One of the key elements of perception is the *j.n.d.*, which is defined as the minimal difference that consumers can detect between two similar stimuli. Recognizing this concept, marketers should update their existing package designs without losing the existing, easy and instant consumer recognition of these packages. Such recognition is the result of years of cumulative advertising and careful planning. Three recent examples of updating packages illustrate both effective and ineffective uses of the j.n.d.:

1. After 24 years, the Coca-Cola Company decided to drop the *Classic* designation from the red packaging of its Coca-Cola cans. It should also be noted that, over the last decade, the font size of the *Classic* designation has been steadily made smaller. (Stephanie Clifford, "Coca Cola Deleting 'Classic' from Coke Label," www.nytimes.com, January 31, 2009.)
2. In the first major change of its ketchup label, the Heinz Company replaced the pickle symbol, which had appeared on the label, under the words *tomato ketchup*, since the 1940s, with the tomato still on the vine. In addition, the word *tomato* was made larger than the word *ketchup*, and the words *Grown, not made* now appear above the picture of the tomato. (Stuart Elliott, "Heinz Ketchup Waves Goodbye to the Gherkin," www.nytimes.com, February 17, 2009).
3. After decades of being sold under the same label and packaging, the package of Tropicana Pure Premium orange juice was redesigned. Within one month after introduction and in response to public pressure, the old packaging of the product was being reinstated and the new one discontinued. (Stuart Elliott, "Tropicana Discovers Some Buyers Are Passionate About Packaging," www.nytimes.com, February 23, 2009).

QUESTION

1. Read the three articles quoted above describing the three package changes and look at the accompanying photos of the actual packages. Evaluate each of the changes in the context of what you had learned about the j.n.d.

Case Two: Perception and Product Placements

The *distinction* between *figure and ground* is an element of perception. A marketing technique dating back to the time when TV first became a mass medium that is experiencing tremendous growth and stems from the figure-and-ground concept is *product placement* (or "branded entertainment"). When this method is employed, the advertised product (i.e., the figure) is integrated into a TV show, film, or even news broadcast (i.e., the ground). As consumers increasingly and more efficiently avoid viewing TV commercials through "time shifting" and automatic "skip" features on their remote controls, marketers are turning to product placements where consumers are "forced" to view the products because they are integrated into the shows' contents. Furthermore, the recent move of comedian Jay Leno from his late night program to a daily prime-time show was viewed, in part, as an attempt to create a better platform for "elevating brands into the show" by NBC—the new show's sponsor. Several articles about product placements are listed below and you can easily find more readings about this topic online. Read five or more articles about product placements, as well as the applicable part discussing the ethical considerations of this practice in Chapter 16 (under the heading "Forced Exposure to Advertising"). Then, answer the following questions.

QUESTIONS

1. What are the ethical implications of product placements in the context of consumer perception?
2. Have you noticed an increase in product placements in movies and TV programs? Explain your answer.
3. Good product placements are "seamlessly" integrated into a movie's or TV program's story line. List and describe one movie or TV program that you recall seeing where there was a good fit between the product placed and the story line, and one example where the opposite was the case.
4. How does the increase in the number of product placements over the last few years reflect the changing business model of TV broadcasting?

SUGGESTED READINGS

1. Stuart Elliott, "More Products Get Roles in Shows, and Marketers Wonder If They're Getting Their Money's Worth," www.nytimes.com, March 29, 2005.
2. Lorne Manly, "On Television, Brands Go from Props to Stars," www.nytimes.com, October 2, 2005.
3. Louise Story, "So That's Why They Drink Coke on TV," www.nytimes.com, December 9, 2007.
4. Bill Carter, "Where Is Leno Going? To Prime Time, on NBC," www.nytimes.com, December 9, 2008.
5. Stuart Elliott, "A Show Meant to Cure the Ills of Network TV," www.nytimes.com, December 10, 2008.

7 Consumer Learning

WHAT COMES to one's mind upon seeing the V8 symbol? Thinking of foods, the most likely answer is a small can of vegetable juice sold via vending machines and convenience stores and larger bottles of the brand sold in supermarkets. Most consumers associate drinking vegetable juice and eating vegetables with the health benefits provided by these products, such as vitamins, antioxidants, and agents boosting one's immune system.

While most consumers associate V8 with vegetables, they probably do not connect the brand with fruit or with soup, especially since vegetable juice is consumed cold and most soups are served hot. If so, why is Campbell's, the owner of V8, going against consumers' awareness by introducing the Fusion fruit juices and soups featured in Figure 7.1 under the V8 brand? The answer stems from understanding *consumer learning*.

The new products represent *extensions* of a highly successful brand and follow the principles of consumer learning. For years, V8 effectively fulfilled consumers' needs for a quick and efficient way to consume multiple vegetables together. Each time consumers bought V8 products, they were *rewarded* because the juice tasted good and they knew they were consuming a healthy product. Therefore, when new products carrying the V8 brand name are advertised, consumers are likely to *associate* them with the rewarding experiences they have had for decades of consuming V8 vegetable juice, including the perceived health benefits that are the core of this brand. In order to succeed, the Fusion Juices and V8 Soups must fulfill consumers' needs (e.g., taste good), and also be promoted (or positioned) effectively. If so, consumers will apply what they already know about V8 to the new products introduced under the V8 name and buy them. Relating one's past knowledge to present circumstances and the applying past and present experiences to future behaviors represent **learning**.

Any company driven by the marketing concept must always look for growth opportunities in the form of new markets. By extending its offerings from vegetable juice into selling fruit juices and soups, Campbell's is taking advantage of the credibility, huge name recognition, and consumers'

FIGURE 7.1

Source: Courtesy of Campbells, Inc.

QUESTION: *In Terms of Consumer Learning, Are These New Products Likely to Succeed? Why or Why Not?*

emotional bonds with the V8 and Campbell's brand names. Apparently, the company is confident that prior consumer learning will drive people's enthusiastic acceptance of the new products tied with the V8 name.

Repeating advertising messages about brands and their benefits, rewarding people for purchase behavior by selling products that provide superior benefits, getting consumers to make associations among different offerings under the same brand name, and developing brand loyalty are all elements of consumer learning. The reason that marketers are concerned with how individuals learn is that they are vitally interested in teaching them, in their roles as consumers, about products, product attributes, and their potential benefits; where to buy them, how to use them, how to maintain them, and even how to dispose of them. They are also interested in how effectively they have taught consumers to prefer their brands and to differentiate their products from competitive offerings. Marketing strategies are based on communicating with the consumer—directly, through advertisements, and indirectly, through product appearance, packaging, price, and distribution channels. Marketers want their communications to be noted, believed, remembered, and recalled. For these reasons, they are interested in every aspect of the learning process.

Learning Objectives

7.1 *To Understand the Process and Four Elements of Consumer Learning.*

7.2 *To Study Behavioral Learning and Understand Its Applications to Consumption Behavior.*

7.3 *To Study Information Processing and Cognitive Learning and Understand Their Strategic Applications to Consumer Behavior.*

7.4 *To Study Consumer Involvement and Passive Learning and Understand Their Strategic Affects on Consumer Behavior.*

7.5 *To Understand How Consumer Learning and Its Results Are Measured.*

The Elements of Consumer Learning

Learning Objective

7.1 *To Understand the Process and Four Elements of Consumer Learning.*

Because not all psychologists agree on how learning takes place, it is difficult to come up with a generally accepted definition of learning. From a marketing perspective, learning is defined as *the process by which individuals acquire the purchase and consumption knowledge and experience that they apply to future related behavior.* Several points in this definition are worth noting.

First, consumer learning is a *process;* that is, it continually evolves and changes as a result of newly acquired *knowledge* (which may be gained from reading, from discussions, from observation, from thinking) or from actual *experience.* Both newly acquired knowledge and personal experience serve as *feedback* to the individual and provide the basis for *future behavior* in similar situations.

The role of *experience* in learning does not mean that all learning is deliberately sought. Though much learning is *intentional* (i.e., it is acquired as the result of a careful search for information), a great deal of learning is also *incidental,* acquired by accident or without much effort. For example, some ads may induce learning (e.g., of new products under familiar brand names such as the ones shown in Figure 7.1), even though the consumer's attention is elsewhere (on a magazine article rather than the advertisement on the facing page). Other ads are sought out and carefully read by consumers contemplating a major purchase decision.

The term *consumer earning* encompasses the total range of learning, from simple, almost reflexive responses, to the learning of abstract concepts and complex problem solving. Most learning theorists recognize the existence of different types of learning and explain the differences through the use of distinctive models of learning.

Despite their different viewpoints, learning theorists agree that in order for learning to occur, certain basic elements must be present. These elements are *motivation, cues, response,* and *reinforcement.* These concepts are discussed first because they recur in the theories discussed in this chapter.

MOTIVATION

Uncovering consumer motives is the prime tasks of marketers, who then try to teach motivated consumer segments why and how their products will fulfill the consumers' needs. Unfilled needs lead to *motivation,* which spurs learning. For example, men and women who want to take up bicycle riding for fitness and recreation are motivated to learn all they can about bike riding and also to practice often. They may seek information concerning the prices, quality, and characteristics of bicycles and "learn" which bicycles are the best for the kind of riding that they do. They will also read any articles in their local newspapers about bicycle trails and may seek online information about "active vacations" that involve biking or hiking. Conversely, individuals who are not interested in bike riding are likely to ignore all information related to the activity. The goal object (bicycle riding in order to relax and stay fit) simply has no relevance for them. The degree of relevance, or *involvement,* determines the consumer's level of motivation to search for knowledge or information about a product or service. (*Involvement theory,* as it has come to be known, is discussed later in the chapter.)

CUES

If motives serve to stimulate learning, *cues* are the stimuli that direct these motives. An advertisement for an exotic trip that includes bike riding may serve as a cue for bike riders, who may suddenly "recognize" that they "need" a vacation. The ad is the cue, or *stimulus,* that suggests a specific way to satisfy a salient motive. In the marketplace, price, styling, packaging, advertising, and store displays all serve as cues to help consumers fulfill their needs in product-specific ways.

Cues serve to direct consumer drives when they are consistent with consumer expectations. Marketers must be careful to provide cues that do not upset those expectations. For example, consumers expect designer clothes to be expensive and to be sold in upscale retail stores. Thus, a high-fashion designer should sell his or her clothes only through exclusive stores and advertise only in upscale fashion magazines. Each aspect of the marketing mix must reinforce the others if cues are to serve as the stimuli that guide consumer actions in the direction the marketer desires.

RESPONSE

How individuals react to a drive or cue—how they behave—constitute their *response.* Learning can occur even when responses are not overt. The automobile manufacturer that provides consistent cues to a consumer may not always succeed in stimulating a purchase. However, if the manufacturer succeeds in forming a favorable image of a particular automobile model in the consumer's mind, it is likely that the consumer will consider that make or model when he or she is ready to buy.

A response is not tied to a need in a one-to-one fashion. Indeed, as was discussed in Chapter 4, a need or motive may evoke a whole variety of responses. For example, there are many ways to respond to the need for physical exercise besides riding bicycles. Cues provide some direction, but there are many cues competing for the consumer's attention. Which response the consumer makes depends heavily on previous learning; that, in turn, depends on how previous, related responses have been reinforced.

REINFORCEMENT

Reinforcement increases the likelihood that a specific response will occur in the future as the result of particular cues or stimuli. If a consumer is rewarded, by enjoying a product or service purchased, that consumer has learned to associate the purchase with a pleasant feeling and, therefore, is likely to repeat the learned behavior and become a loyal customer. For example, if a person visits a restaurant for the first time, likes the food, service, and ambience and also feels he or she received value for the money paid, that customer was reinforced and is likely to dine at the restaurant again. If that person becomes a regular customer, the restaurant's owner should further reinforce the customer's continued patronage by, for example, giving the customer a free drink and recognizing the person by name upon arrival. Of course, the quality of the food and service must be maintained since they are the key elements of reinforcing the customer's continued visits. On the other hand, if a patron leaves a restaurant disappointed with the quality of the food or the service or feels "ripped off," reinforcement has not occurred. Because of the absence of reinforcement, it is unlikely that the customer would visit the restaurant again. With these basic principles established, we can now discuss some well-known theories or models of how learning occurs.

There is no single, universal theory of how people learn. In this chapter, we examine the two general categories of learning theory: **behavioral learning** and **cognitive learning**. Although these theories differ markedly in a number of essentials, each theory offers insights to marketers on how to shape their messages to consumers to bring about desired purchase behavior. We also discuss how consumers store, retain, and retrieve information, and how learning is measured.

Behavioral Learning

LEARNING OBJECTIVE

7.2 *To Study Behavioral Learning and Understand Its Applications to Consumption Behavior.*

Behavioral learning is sometimes referred to as **stimulus-response learning** because it is based on the premise that observable responses to specific external stimuli signal that learning has taken place. When a person acts (responds) in a predictable way to a known stimulus, he or she is said to have "learned." Behavioral learning is not so much concerned with the *process* of learning as it is with the *inputs* and *outcomes* of learning; that is, in the stimuli that consumers select from the environment and the observable behaviors that result. Two forms of behavioral learning with great relevance to marketing are **classical conditioning** and **instrumental** (or **operant) conditioning**.

CLASSICAL CONDITIONING

Early classical conditioning theorists regarded all organisms (both animal and human) as relatively passive entities that could be taught certain behaviors through repetition (i.e., *conditioning*). In everyday speech, the word *conditioning* has come to mean a kind of "knee-jerk" (or automatic) response to a situation built up through repeated exposure. If you get a headache every time you think of visiting your Aunt Gertrude, your reaction may be conditioned from years of boring visits with her.

Ivan Pavlov, a Russian physiologist, was the first to describe conditioning and to propose it as a general model of how learning occurs. According to Pavlovian theory, conditioned learning results when a stimulus that is paired with another stimulus that elicits a known response serves to produce the same response when used alone. Pavlov demonstrated what he meant by conditioned learning in his studies with dogs. Genetically, dogs are always hungry and highly motivated to eat. In his experiments, Pavlov sounded a bell and then immediately applied a meat paste to the dogs' tongues, which caused them to salivate. Learning (conditioning) occurred when, after a sufficient number of repetitions of the bell sound followed almost immediately by the food, the bell sound alone caused the dogs to salivate. The dogs associated the bell sound (the *conditioned* stimulus) with the meat paste (the *unconditioned* stimulus) and, after a number of pairings, gave the same unconditioned response (salivation) to the bell alone as they did to the meat paste. The unconditioned response to the meat paste became the conditioned response to the bell. Figure 7.2A models this relationship. An analogous situation would be one in which the smells of dinner cooking would cause your mouth to water. If you usually listen to the six o'clock news while waiting for dinner to be served, you would tend to associate the six o'clock news with dinner, so that eventually the sounds of the six o'clock news alone might cause your mouth to water, even if dinner was not being prepared and even if you were not hungry. Figure 7.2B diagrams this basic relationship.

In a consumer behavior context, an *unconditioned stimulus* might consist of a well-known brand symbol. For example, after more than 50 years of advertising (that is, a long period of learning by consumers), the name Crest implies that the product is the best alternative for preventing teeth decay (Crest was the first toothpaste with fluoride and endorsed by the American Dental Association). This previously acquired consumer perception of Crest is the *unconditioned response. Conditioned stimuli* are the scores of versions of toothpaste, toothbrushes, teeth whitening, flossing, and mouth-rinsing products, all presently marketed under the Crest brand name. The *conditioned response* would be consumers trying

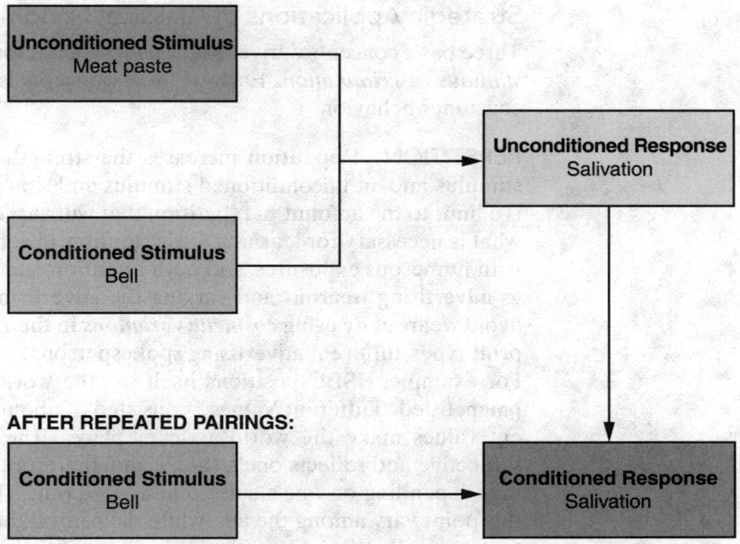

FIGURE 7.2A
Pavlovian Model of Classical Conditioning

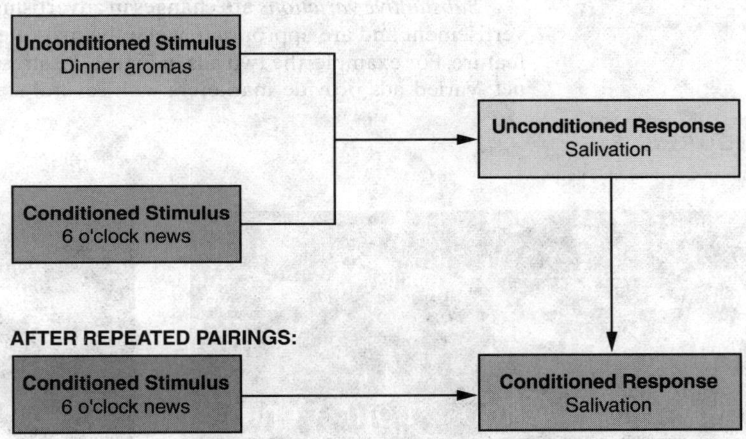

FIGURE 7.2B
Analogous Model of Classical Conditioning

these products because of the belief that they embody the same attributes with which the Crest name is associated.

Cognitive Associative Learning

Contemporary behavioral scientists view classical conditioning as the learning of associations among events that allows the organism to anticipate and "represent" its environment. According to this view, the relationship (or contiguity) between the conditioned stimulus and the unconditioned stimulus (the bell and the meat paste) influenced the dogs' expectations, which in turn influenced their behavior (salivation). Classical conditioning, then, rather than being a reflexive action, is seen as **cognitive associative learning**—not the acquisition of new reflexes, but the acquisition of new knowledge about the world. Optimal conditioning—that is, the creation of a strong association between the conditioned stimulus (CS) and the unconditioned stimulus (US)—requires (1) forward conditioning (i.e., the CS should precede the US); (2) repeated pairings of the CS and the US; (3) a CS and US that logically belong together; (4) a CS that is novel and unfamiliar; and (5) a US that is biologically or symbolically salient. This model is known as **neo-Pavlovian conditioning**.

Under neo-Pavlovian theory, the consumer can be viewed as an information seeker who uses logical and perceptual relations among events, along with his or her own preconceptions, to form a sophisticated representation of the world. Conditioning is the learning that results from exposure to relationships among events in the environment; such exposure creates expectations as to the structure of the environment.

Strategic Applications of Classical Conditioning

Three basic concepts derive from classical conditioning: *repetition, stimulus generalization,* and *stimulus discrimination.* Each of these concepts is important to the strategic applications of consumer behavior.

REPETITION Repetition increases the strength of the association between a conditioned stimulus and an unconditioned stimulus and slows the process of forgetting. However, there is a limit to the amount of repetition that will aid retention. Although some repetition beyond what is necessary for learning aids retention, at some point an individual can become satiated with numerous exposures, and both attention and retention will decline. This effect is known as **advertising wearout** and varying the advertising message can reduce it. Some marketers avoid wearout by using *cosmetic variations* in their ads (using different backgrounds, different print types, different advertising spokespersons) while repeating the same advertising theme. For example, HSBC positions itself as "the world's local bank." A recent advertising campaign, titled "Different Values," consisted of about 20 ads centered on the theme that "different values make the world a richer place." The ads illustrate that one's point of view is subjective and reflects one's values and, therefore, the same object can have different meanings depending on one's culture and viewpoint. The objects that are being used to illustrate this point vary among the ads, while the central theme remains the same. For example, a container of pills (the object pictured in one of the ads) may represent "prevention" (e.g., vitamins), "cure" (e.g., antibiotics) or "escape" (e.g., illegal substances).

Substantive variations are changes in advertising content across different versions of an advertisement and are appropriate when the marketer wishes to convey more than one product feature. For example, the two ads in Figure 7.3 stress two different attributes of the same product. Varied ads provide marketers with several strategic advantages. Consumers exposed to

FIGURE 7.3

Source: Courtesy of Gillette.

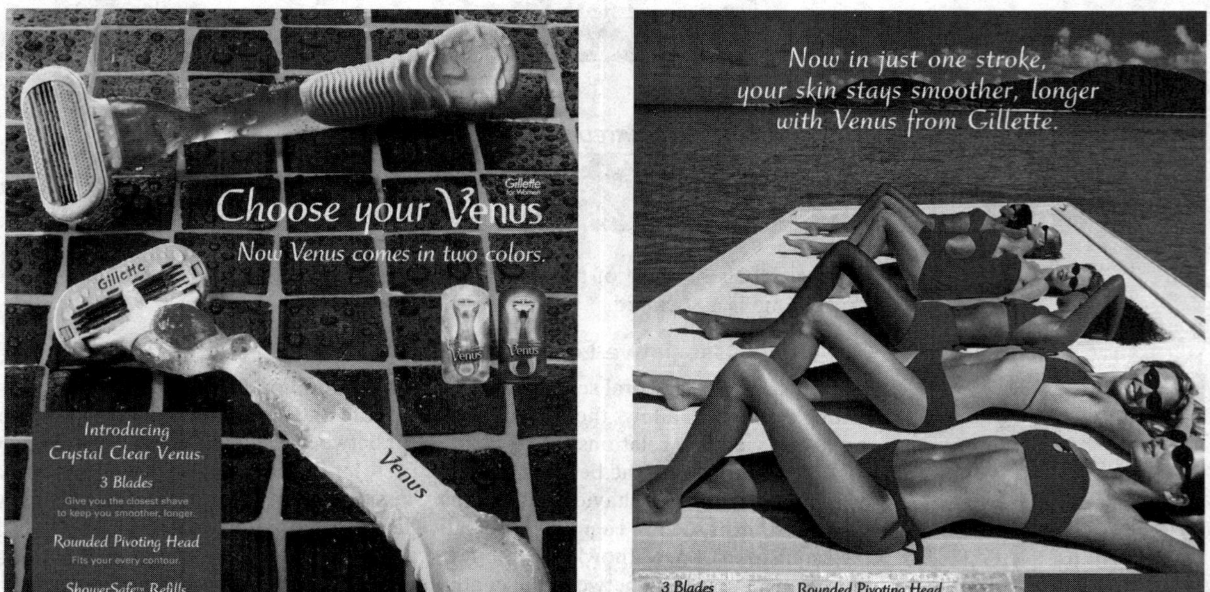

QUESTION: *Why Did Gillette Use Two Different Ads to Advertise the Same Product?*

substantively varied ads process more information about product attributes, and attitudes formed as a result of exposure to such messages are often more resistant to change in the face of competitive attacks.

Although the principle of repetition is well established among advertisers, not everyone agrees on how much repetition is enough. Some marketing scholars believe that just three exposures to an advertisement are needed: one to make consumers aware of the product, a second to show consumers the relevance of the product, and a third to remind them of its benefits. This is known as the *three-hit theory.* Others think it may take 11 to 12 repetitions to achieve the three objectives of the so-called three-hit theory.

The effectiveness of repetition is somewhat dependent on the amount of competitive advertising to which the consumer is exposed. The higher the level of competitive ads, the greater the likelihood that *interference* will occur causing consumers to forget previous learning that resulted from repetition.

STIMULUS GENERALIZATION According to classical conditioning theorists, learning depends not only on repetition but also on the ability of individuals to generalize. Pavlov found, for example, that a dog could learn to salivate not only to the sound of a bell but also to the somewhat similar sound of jangling keys. Making the same response to slightly different stimuli is called **stimulus generalization**.

Stimulus generalization explains why some imitative me-too products succeed in the marketplace: Consumers confuse them with the original product they have seen advertised. It also explains why manufacturers of private-label brands try to make their packaging closely resemble the national brand leaders. They are hoping that consumers will confuse their packages with the leading brand and buy their product rather than the leading brand. Similarly packaged competitive products result in millions of lost sales for well-positioned and extensively advertised brands.

Product Line, Form, and Category Extensions The principle of stimulus generalization is applied by marketers to *product line, form,* and *category extensions.* In **product line extensions**, the marketer adds related products to an already established brand, knowing that the new products are more likely to be adopted when they are associated with a known and trusted brand name. Figure 7.4 depicts two ads illustrating product line extension. The initial product introduced under the brand shown in Figure 7.4A was plain yogurt and, after the brand gained some market share, the strawberry-flavored yogurt featured here was introduced. The product featured in Figure 7.4B is an extension of a highly popular, decades-old brand.

Marketers also offer **product form extensions**, such as Listerine mouthwash to Listerine Paks and Chloraseptic to Allergen Block Gel (see Figure 7.5). Marketers also offer **product category extensions** that generally target new market segments. The product category extension shown in Figure 7.6 is part of a growing trend among chocolate marketers of introducing higher-end products with exotic flavors.[1]

The success of product extensions depends on a number of factors. If the image of the parent brand is one of quality and the new item is logically linked to the brand, consumers are more likely to bring positive associations to the new offerings introduced as product line, form, or category extensions. For example, Tylenol, a highly trusted brand, initially introduced line extensions by making its products available in a number of different forms (tablets, capsules, gel caps), strengths (regular, extra strength, and children's), and package sizes. It then extended its brand name to a wide range of related remedies for colds, flu, sinus congestion, and allergies, further segmenting the line for adults, children, and infants. The number of different products affiliated with a brand strengthens the brand name, as long as the company maintains a quality image across all brand extensions. Failure to do so, in the long run, is likely to negatively affect consumer confidence and evaluations of all the brand's offerings. One study showed that brands that include diverse products are likely to offer more successful brand extensions than brands that include similar products. The study also confirmed that the likely associations between the benefits offered by the brand and its new extension are the key to consumers' reactions to the brand extension.[2]

Family Branding **Family branding**—the practice of marketing a whole line of company products under the same brand name—is another strategy that capitalizes on the consumer's ability to generalize favorable brand associations from one product to others. Campbell's, originally a marketer of soups, continues to add new food products to its product line under the Campbell's brand name (e.g., chunky, condensed, kids, and lower sodium soups; frozen meals

FIGURE 7.4A

Source: Courtesy of Fage USA Dairy Industry Inc. and Ogilvy & Mather Worldwide. Image © Martin Wonnacott.

QUESTION: *Which Concept of Behavioral Learning Applies to the Introduction of the Two Products Shown in Figures 7.4A and B and Why?*

named Campbell's Super Bakes; and tomato juice), thus achieving ready acceptance for the new products from satisfied consumers of other Campbell's food products.

While many marketers use family branding effectively, Procter & Gamble (P&G) was built on the strength of its many individual brands in the same product category. For example, the company offers multiple brands of laundry products, antiperspirants, and hair care products, including shampoo. Although offering many brands of the same product is expensive, the combined weight of its brands has always provided P&G with great power in negotiating with advertising media and securing desirable shelf space for its products around the world. It also enables the company to effectively combat any competitors who may try to introduce products in markets dominated by P&G.

Retail private branding often achieves the same effect as family branding. For example, Wal-Mart used to advertise that its stores carried only "brands you trust." Now, the name Wal-Mart itself has become a "brand" that consumers have confidence in, and the name confers brand value on Wal-Mart's store brands.

FIGURE 7.4B

Source: The Procter & Gamble Company. Used by permission. All rights reserved.

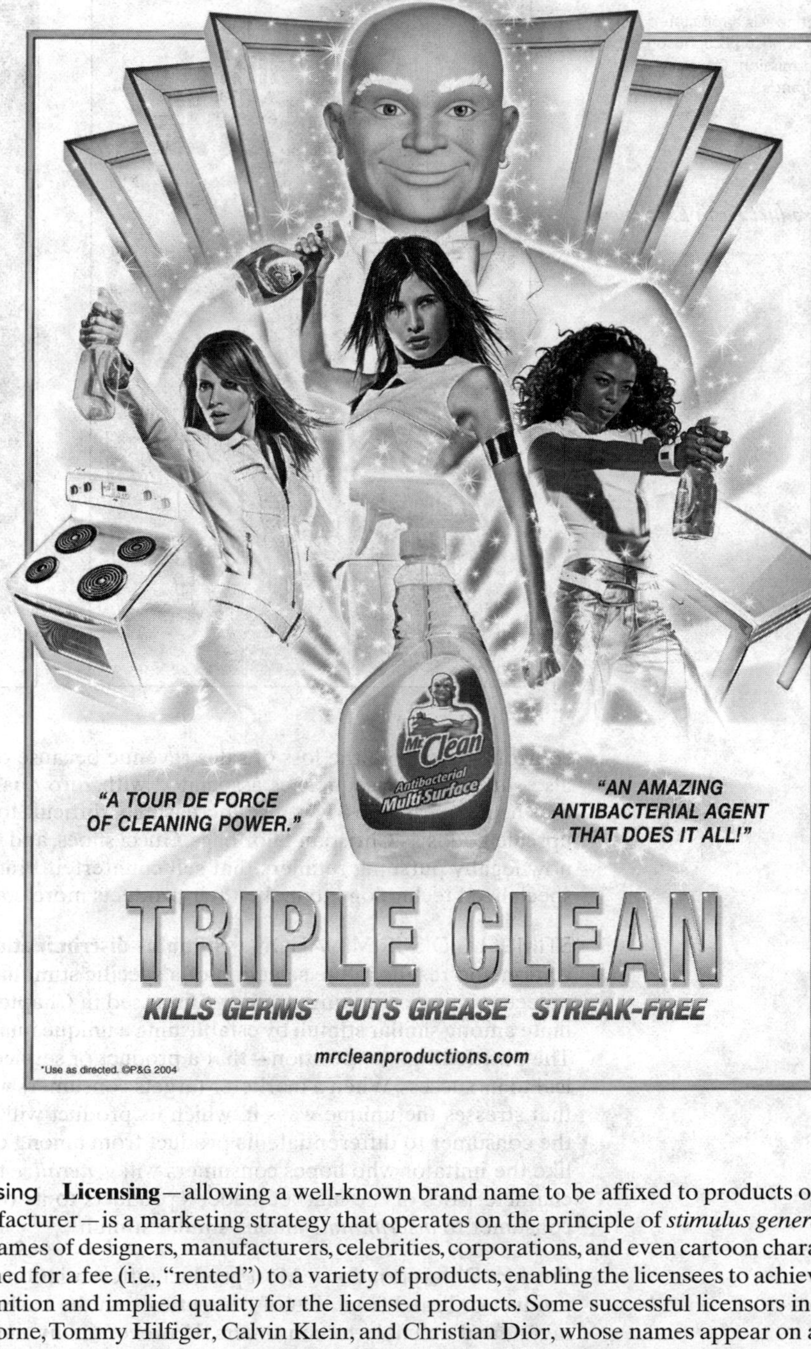

Licensing **Licensing**—allowing a well-known brand name to be affixed to products of another manufacturer—is a marketing strategy that operates on the principle of *stimulus generalization.* The names of designers, manufacturers, celebrities, corporations, and even cartoon characters are attached for a fee (i.e., "rented") to a variety of products, enabling the licensees to achieve instant recognition and implied quality for the licensed products. Some successful licensors include Liz Claiborne, Tommy Hilfiger, Calvin Klein, and Christian Dior, whose names appear on an exceptionally wide variety of products, from sheets to shoes and luggage to perfume. Figure 7.7 shows an ad for eyeglasses bearing the name of the well-known shoe manufacturer Kenneth Cole.

Corporations also license their names and trademarks, usually for some form of brand extension, where the name of the corporation is licensed to the maker of a related product and thereby enters a new product category (e.g., Godiva chocolates licensed its name for Godiva liqueur). Corporations also license their names for purely promotional licensing, in which popular company logos (such as "Always Coca-Cola") are stamped on clothing, toys, coffee mugs, and the like.

The increase in licensing has made *counterfeiting* a booming business, as counterfeiters add well-known licensor names to a variety of products without benefit of contract or quality

FIGURE 7.5

Source: Listerine® is a registered trademark of Johnson & Johnson. Used with permission. Courtesy of Prestige Brands.

Product Form Extensions

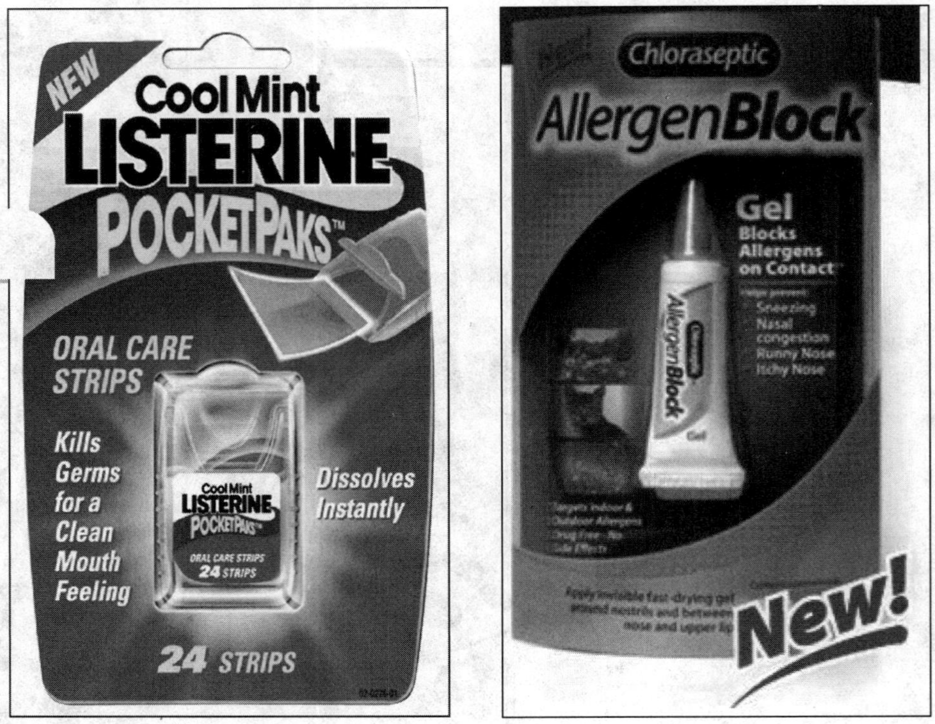

control. Aside from the loss of sales revenue because of counterfeiting, the authentic brands also suffer the consequences associated with zero quality control over counterfeit products that bear their names. It is also increasingly difficult to identify fakes of such expensive and upscale goods as Christian Dior bags, Gucci shoes, and Chanel No. 5 perfume. Many firms are now legally pursuing retailers that sell counterfeit branded goods; many also are employing specialized technology to make their products more counterfeit-proof.

STIMULUS DISCRIMINATION **Stimulus discrimination** is the opposite of stimulus generalization and results in the selection of a specific stimulus from among similar stimuli. The key objective of a positioning strategy (discussed in Chapter 6) is to get the consumer to discriminate among similar stimuli by establishing a unique image for a brand in the consumer's mind. The positioning—or position—that a product or service holds in the consumer's mind is critical to its success. When a marketer targets consumers with a strong communications program that stresses the unique ways in which its product will satisfy the consumer's needs, it wants the consumer to differentiate its product from among competitive products on the shelf. Unlike the imitator who hopes consumers will *generalize* their perceptions and attribute special characteristics of the market leader's products to its own products, market leaders want the consumer to *discriminate* among similar stimuli.

Product Differentiation Most product differentiation strategies are designed to distinguish a product or brand from that of competitors on the basis of an attribute that is relevant, meaningful, and valuable to consumers. However, many marketers also successfully differentiate their brands on an attribute that may actually be irrelevant to creating the implied benefit, such as a noncontributing ingredient, color, or a distinctive package. It often is quite difficult to unseat a brand leader once stimulus discrimination has occurred. One explanation is that the leader is usually first in the market and has had a longer period to "teach" consumers (through advertising and selling) to associate the brand name with the product. In general, the longer the period of learning—of associating a brand name with a specific product—the more likely the consumer is to discriminate and the less likely to generalize the stimulus. Figure 7.8 depicts an example of stimulus discrimination where the advertiser of a Greek-style yogurt brand demonstrates that its product is substantially different from other yogurts because it is "ridiculously thick."

FIGURE 7.6

Source: M&M'S® is a registered trademark owned by Mars, Incorporated and its affiliates. This trademark is used with permission. Mars, Incorporated is not associated with Pearson Prentice Hall. M&M'S® images printed with permission of Mars, Incorporated. © Mars, Inc. 2008.

QUESTION: *What Is the Name of the Marketing Application Featured Here and Which Concept of Behavioral Learning Is It Based On?*

The principles of classical conditioning provide the theoretical underpinnings for many marketing applications. Repetition, stimulus generalization, and stimulus discrimination are all major applied concepts that help to explain consumer behavior in the marketplace. However, they do not explain all forms of behavioral learning. Although a great deal of consumer behavior (e.g., the purchase of branded convenience goods) is shaped to some extent by repeated advertising messages stressing a unique competitive advantage, a significant amount of purchase behavior results from careful evaluation of product alternatives. Our assessments of products are often based on the degree of satisfaction—the rewards—we experience as a result of making specific purchases; in other words, from instrumental conditioning.

INSTRUMENTAL CONDITIONING

Like classical conditioning, instrumental conditioning requires a link between a stimulus and a response. However, in instrumental conditioning, the stimulus that results in the most satisfactory response is the one that is learned.

Instrumental learning theorists believe that learning occurs through a trial-and-error process, with habits formed as a result of rewards received for certain responses or behaviors.

FIGURE 7.7
Source: Courtesy of Kenneth Cole Productions, Inc.

QUESTION: *What Is the Name of the Marketing Application Featured Here and Which Concept of Behavioral Learning Is It Based On?*

This model of learning applies to many situations in which consumers learn about products, services, and retail stores. For example, consumers learn which stores carry the type of clothing they prefer at prices they can afford to pay by shopping in a number of stores. Once they find a store that carries clothing that meets their needs, they are likely to patronize that store to the exclusion of others. Every time they purchase a shirt or a sweater there that they really like, their store loyalty is rewarded (*reinforced*), and their patronage of that store is more likely to be repeated.

The name most closely associated with instrumental (*operant*) conditioning is that of the American psychologist B. F. Skinner. According to Skinner, most individual learning occurs in a controlled environment in which individuals are "rewarded" for choosing an appropriate behavior. In consumer behavior terms, instrumental conditioning suggests that consumers learn by means of a trial-and-error process in which some purchase behaviors result in more favorable outcomes (i.e., rewards) than other purchase behaviors. A favorable experience is "instrumental" in teaching the individual to repeat a specific behavior.

Like Pavlov, Skinner developed his model of learning by working with animals. Small animals, such as rats and pigeons, were placed in his "Skinner box"; if they made appropriate

FIGURE 7.8
Source: Courtesy of Fage USA Dairy Industry Inc. and Ogilvy & Mather Worldwide. Image © Martin Wonnacott.

QUESTION: *What Are the Names of the Marketing Application Featured Here and the Behavioral Learning Concept It Is Based On? What Is the Ad's Strategic Objective?*

movements (e.g., if they depressed levers or pecked keys), they received food (a positive reinforcement). Skinner and his many adherents have done amazing things with this simple learning model, including teaching pigeons to play Ping-Pong and even to dance. In a marketing context, the consumer who tries several brands and styles of jeans before finding a style that fits her figure (positive reinforcement) has engaged in instrumental learning. Presumably, the brand that fits best is the one she will continue to buy. This model of instrumental conditioning is presented in Figure 7.9.

Reinforcement of Behavior

Skinner distinguished two types of reinforcement (or reward) that influence the likelihood that a response will be repeated. The first type, **positive reinforcement**, consists of events that strengthen the likelihood of a specific response. Using a shampoo that leaves your hair feeling silky and clean is likely to result in a repeat purchase of the shampoo. **Negative reinforcement** is an unpleasant or negative outcome that also serves to encourage a specific behavior. Recent advertising campaigns, by the so-called "thought leader magazines" (e.g., *The Atlantic*, *The New Yorker,* and *The Economist*), are designed to "jolt" young viewers and inspire them to subscribe

FIGURE 7.9
A Model of Instrumental Conditioning

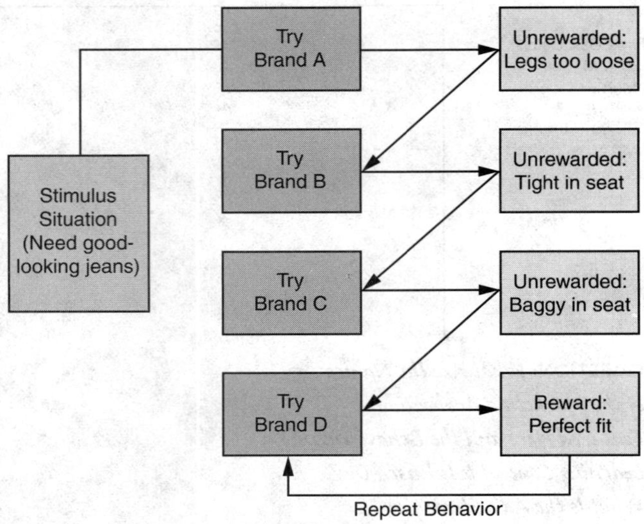

to these publications in order to avoid being uninformed. The slogan for *The Atlantic* is "Think. Again" and the one for *The Economist* is "Get a world view."[3]

Fear appeals in ad messages are examples of negative reinforcement. Many life insurance advertisements rely on negative reinforcement to encourage the purchase of life insurance. The ads warn husbands of the dire consequences to their wives and children in the event of their sudden death. Marketers of headache remedies use negative reinforcement when they illustrate the unpleasant symptoms of an unrelieved headache, as do marketers of mouthwash when they show the loneliness suffered by someone with bad breath. In each of these cases, the consumer is encouraged to avoid the negative consequences by buying the advertised product.

Either positive or negative reinforcement can be used to elicit a desired response. However, negative reinforcement should not be confused with punishment, which is designed to *discourage* behavior. For example, extra fees for rented DVDs returned late are not negative reinforcement; they are a form of "punishment" designed to discourage consumers from keeping the DVDs too long. In consumption situations, using "punishment" is tricky. In a frequently cited study, researchers discovered that when a day care center started "punishing" parents who picked up their kids late by charging them about $3, late pickups actually *increased* because parents viewed the fine as the price for being tardy.[4] The "punishment" legitimized being late to pick up a child and encouraged the behavior it was designed to lessen.

EXTINCTION AND FORGETTING When a learned response is no longer reinforced, it diminishes to the point of *extinction,* that is, to the point at which the link between the stimulus and the expected reward is eliminated. If a consumer is no longer satisfied with the service a retail store provides, the link between the stimulus (the store) and the response (expected satisfaction) is no longer reinforced, and there is little likelihood that the consumer will return. When behavior is no longer reinforced, it is "unlearned." There is a difference, however, between extinction and *forgetting.* A couple who have not visited a once-favorite restaurant for a very long time may simply forget how much they used to enjoy eating there and not think to return. Thus, their behavior is unlearned because of lack of use rather than lack of reinforcement. Forgetting is often related to the passage of time; this is known as the process of *decay.* Marketers can overcome forgetting through repetition, and can combat extinction through the deliberate enhancement of consumer satisfaction. Sometimes, marketers may cause extinction deliberately and "undo" a previously learned association. For example, a large car service in New York City known for many years as Tel Aviv Car Service is now called the "Dial 7s" car service in reference to its phone number (consisting of seven consecutive sevens) and, quite possibly, to undo its association in the consumer's mind with Israeli ownership.

Strategic Applications of Instrumental Conditioning

Marketers effectively utilize the concepts of consumer instrumental learning when they provide positive reinforcement by assuring customer satisfaction with the product, the service, and the total buying experience.

CUSTOMER SATISFACTION (REINFORCEMENT) The objective of all marketing efforts should be to maximize customer satisfaction. Marketers must provide the best possible product for the money and avoid raising consumer expectations for product (or service) performance beyond what the product can deliver. Aside from the experience of using the product itself, consumers can receive reinforcement from other elements in the purchase situation, such as the environment in which the transaction or service takes place, the attention and service provided by employees, and the amenities provided. For example, an upscale beauty salon, in addition to a beautiful environment, may offer coffee and soft drinks to waiting clients and provide free local telephone service at each hairdressing station. Even if the styling outcome is not so great, the client may feel so pampered with the atmosphere and service that she looks forward to her next visit and is confident that she will be able to get better styling next time. On the other hand, even with the other positive reinforcements in place, if the salon's employees are so busy talking with each other while the service is being rendered that the client feels ignored, she is not likely to return.

Also, companies should not assume that lower prices and more diverse product lines make customers more satisfied. Instead, it appears that companies that create personal connections with customers, and also offer diverse product lines and competitive prices, are the ones providing the best reinforcement, resulting in satisfaction and repeat patronage. Most frequent shopper programs are based on enhancing positive reinforcement and encouraging continued patronage. The more a consumer uses the service, the greater the rewards. Another form of reinforcement is rewarding customers for referring other customers to the vendor. The result of a recent study about referrals and awards are somewhat surprising: Although rewards increased referrals, there was no difference in referral likelihood between smaller and larger rewards. In addition, for existing customers with strong ties to the marketer providing the reward, these incentives did not increase referral likelihood.[5] Also, in situations where there is a lot of competition and where each competitor is trying to lure consumers with extra offers, or where the consumers themselves tend to be fickle, satisfaction may not guarantee loyalty. A study of cell phone usage discovered that consumers eight to twelve years old tend to be less loyal than adults even when satisfied with the service received.[6]

Relationship marketing—developing a close personalized relationship with customers—is another form of nonproduct reinforcement. Knowing that she will be advised of a forthcoming sale or that selected merchandise will be set aside for her next visit cements the loyalty that a consumer may have for a retail store. The ability to telephone his "personal" banker to transfer funds between accounts or to make other banking transactions, without coming into the bank, reinforces the satisfaction a consumer has with his bank. Service companies are particularly vulnerable to interruptions in customer reinforcement because of service failures that cannot be controlled in advance. As a result, astute service providers have implemented *service recovery* measures that provide extra rewards to customers who have experienced service failures. Such rewards are essential for loyal customers who emotionally bonded with the service provider (as a result of substantial reinforcement received over a period of time) and are unlikely to simply forgive the company because they feel truly "betrayed."

REINFORCEMENT SCHEDULES Product quality must be consistently high and provide satisfaction to the customer with each use for desired consumer behavior to continue. However, some rewards do not have to be offered each time the transaction takes place because even an occasional reward provides reinforcement and encourages consumer patronage. For example, airlines may occasionally upgrade a passenger at the gate, or a clothing discounter may from time to time announce a one-hour sale over the store sound system. The promise of possibly receiving a reward provides positive reinforcement and encourages consumer patronage.

Psychologists identified three types of reinforcement schedules: *total* (or continuous) reinforcement, *systematic* (fixed ratio) reinforcement, and *random* (variable ratio) reinforcement. An example of a total (or continuous) reinforcement schedule is the free after-dinner drink or fruit plate always served to patrons at certain restaurants. Needless to say, the basic product or service rendered is expected to provide total satisfaction (reinforcement) each time it is used. A *fixed ratio* reinforcement schedule provides reinforcement every *n*th time the product or service is purchased (say, every third time). For example, a retailer may send a credit voucher to account holders every three months based on a percentage of the previous quarter's purchases. A *variable ratio* reinforcement schedule rewards consumers on a random basis or on an average frequency basis (such as every third or tenth transaction). Gambling casinos operate on the basis of variable ratios. People pour money into slot machines (which are programmed to pay off on a variable ratio), hoping for the big win. Variable ratios tend to engender high rates of desired behavior and are somewhat resistant to extinction—perhaps because, for many consumers, hope springs eternal. Other examples of variable ratio schedules include lotteries, sweepstakes, door prizes, and contests that require certain consumer behaviors for eligibility.

SHAPING Reinforcement performed *before* the desired consumer behavior actually takes place is called **shaping**. Shaping increases the probabilities that certain desired consumer behavior will occur. For example, retailers recognize that they must first attract customers to their stores before they can expect them to do the bulk of their shopping there. Many retailers provide some form of preliminary reinforcement (shaping) to encourage consumers to visit only their store. For example, some retailers offer loss leaders—popular products at severely discounted prices—to the first hundred or so customers to arrive, since those customers are likely to buy more products at the store rather than only buy the discounted item. By reinforcing the behavior that's needed to enable the desired consumer behavior to take place, marketers increase the probability that the desired behavior will occur. Car dealers recognize that in order to sell new model cars, they must first encourage people to visit their showrooms and to test-drive their cars. Hopefully, the test drive will result in a sale. Using shaping principles, many car dealers encourage showroom visits by providing small monetary or other gifts to test-drive the car, and a rebate check upon placement of an order. They use a multistep shaping process to achieve desired consumer learning.

Massed Versus Distributed Learning

As illustrated previously, *timing* has an important influence on consumer learning. Should a learning schedule be spread out over a period of time (*distributed learning*), or should it be "bunched up" all at once (*massed learning*)? The question is an important one for advertisers planning a media schedule, because massed advertising produces more initial learning, whereas a distributed schedule usually results in learning that persists longer. When advertisers want an immediate impact (e.g., to introduce a new product or to counter a competitor's blitz campaign), they generally use a massed schedule to hasten consumer learning. However, when the goal is long-term repeat buying on a regular basis, a distributed schedule is preferable. A distributed schedule, with ads repeated on a regular basis, usually results in more long-term learning and is relatively immune to extinction.

MODELING OR OBSERVATIONAL LEARNING

Learning theorists have noted that a considerable amount of learning takes place in the absence of direct reinforcement, either positive or negative, through a process psychologists call **modeling** or **observational learning** (also called *vicarious learning*). Consumers often observe how others behave in response to certain situations (stimuli) and the ensuing results (reinforcement) that occur, and they imitate (model) the positively reinforced behavior when faced with similar situations. Modeling is *the process through which individuals learn behavior by observing the behavior of others and the consequences of such behavior.* Their role models are usually people they admire because they are related to them or due to such traits as appearance, accomplishment, skill, and even social class.

Advertisers recognize the importance of observational learning in their selection of models—whether celebrities or unknowns. If a teenager sees an ad that depicts social success as the outcome of using a certain brand of shampoo, she will want to buy it. If her brother sees a commercial that shows a muscular young athlete eating Wheaties—"the breakfast of champions"—he will want to eat it, too. Indeed, vicarious (or observational) learning is the basis of much of today's advertising. Consumer models with whom the target audience can identify are shown achieving positive outcomes to common problem situations through the use of the advertised product. Children learn much of their social behavior and consumer behavior by observing their older siblings or their parents. They imitate the behavior of those they see rewarded, expecting to be rewarded similarly if they adopt the same behavior.

Sometimes ads depict negative consequences for certain types of behavior. This is particularly true of public policy ads, which may show the negative consequences of smoking, driving too fast, or taking drugs. By observing the actions of others and the resulting consequences, consumers learn vicariously to recognize and distinguish between appropriate and inappropriate behavior.

Information Processing and Cognitive Learning

LEARNING OBJECTIVE

7.3 *To Study Information Processing and Cognitive Learning and Understand Their Strategic Applications to Consumer Behavior.*

Not all learning takes place as the result of repeated trials. A considerable amount of learning takes place as the result of consumer thinking and problem solving. When confronted with a problem, we sometimes see the solution instantly. More often, however, we are likely to search for information on which to base a decision, and we carefully evaluate what we learn in order to make the best decision possible for our purposes.

Learning based on mental activity is called cognitive learning. Cognitive learning theory holds that the kind of learning most characteristic of human beings is *problem solving,* which enables individuals to gain some control over their environment. Unlike behavioral learning theory, cognitive theory holds that learning involves complex *mental processing of information.* Instead of focusing on the importance of repetition or the association of a reward with a specific response, cognitive theorists emphasize the role of motivation and mental processes in producing a desired response. The coverage of cognitive learning begins with a discussion of the human memory—the key tool for information processing. Then, we present theoretical models of cognitive learning followed by a discussion of several forms of cognitive learning.

INFORMATION PROCESSING

Just as a computer processes information received as input, so too does the human mind process the information it receives as input. Consumers process product information by attributes, brands, comparisons between brands, or a combination of these factors. The attributes included in the brand's message, and the number of available alternatives, influence the intensity or degree of **information processing**. Also, consumers with higher cognitive ability generally acquire more product information and consider more product attributes and alternatives than consumers with lesser ability.

The more experience a consumer has with a product category, the greater his or her ability to make use of product information. Greater familiarity with the product category also increases learning during a new purchase decision, particularly with regard to technical information. Some consumers learn by analogy; that is, they transfer knowledge about products they are familiar with to new or unfamiliar products in order to enhance their understanding.

How Consumers Store, Retain, and Retrieve Information

The human memory is the center of information processing. We now examine how information gets stored in memory, how it is retained, and how it is retrieved. Because information processing occurs in stages, it is generally believed that there are separate and sequential "storehouses" in memory where information is kept temporarily before further processing: a **sensory store,** a **short-term store,** and a **long-term store.**

SENSORY STORE All data come to us through our senses; however, the senses do not transmit whole images as a camera does. Instead, each sense receives a piece of information (such as the smell, color, shape, and feel of a flower) and transmits it to the brain in parallel, where the perceptions of a single instant are synchronized and perceived as a single image, in a single moment of time. The image of a sensory input lasts for just a second or two in the mind's sensory store. If it is not processed, it is lost immediately. As noted in Chapter 6, we are constantly bombarded with stimuli from the environment and subconsciously block out a great deal of information that we do not "need" or cannot use. For marketers, this means that although it is relatively easy to get information into the consumer's sensory store, it is difficult to make a lasting impression. Furthermore, the brain automatically and subconsciously "tags" all perceptions with a value, either positive or negative; this evaluation, added to the initial perception in the first microsecond of cognition, tends to remain unless further information is processed. This explains why first impressions tend to last and why it is hazardous for a marketer to introduce a product prematurely into the marketplace.

SHORT-TERM STORE The short-term store (known as "working memory") is the stage of real memory in which information is processed and held for just a brief period. Anyone who has ever looked up a number in a telephone book, only to forget it just before dialing, knows how briefly information lasts in short-term storage. If information in the short-term store undergoes the process known as *rehearsal* (i.e., the silent, mental repetition of information), it is then transferred to the long-term store. The transfer process takes from 2 to 10 seconds. If information is not rehearsed and transferred, it is lost in about 30 seconds or less. The amount of information that can be held in short-term storage is limited to about four or five items. A recent experiment illustrates the operation of the short-term store. A researcher walked over to a pedestrian and asked for directions. As the person was responding, workmen carrying a large door walked between the researcher and respondent and, while hidden by the door being moved, the researcher switched places with someone else. Only about half the pedestrians noticed that they were talking to someone else afterward.[7]

LONG-TERM STORE In contrast to the short-term store, where information lasts only a few seconds, the long-term store retains information for relatively extended periods of time. Although it is possible to forget something within a few minutes after the information has reached long-term storage, it is more common for data in long-term storage to last for days, weeks, or even years. A recent study of three generations of automobile consumers discovered that people's earliest memories and experiences regarding cars defined what car brands meant to them and impacted their brand preferences later in life.[8] Figure 7.10 depicts the transfer of information received by the sensory store, through the short-term store, to long-term storage.

REHEARSAL AND ENCODING The amount of information available for delivery from short-term storage to long-term storage depends on the amount of **rehearsal** it receives. Failure to rehearse an input, either by repeating it or by relating it to other data, can result in fading and eventual loss of the information. Information can also be lost because of competition for attention. For example, if the short-term store receives a great number of inputs simultaneously from the sensory store, its capacity may be reduced to only two or three pieces of information.

"Learning" a picture takes less time than learning verbal information, but both types of information are important in forming an overall mental image. A print ad with both an illustration and body copy is more likely to be encoded and stored than an illustration without verbal information. High-imagery copy produces greater recall than low-imagery copy, and marketers realize that almost every ad should include some form of an illustration. In a recent study, consumers were given goals and then asked to memorize ads. The study found that an ad-memorization goal enhanced attention to the body text, pictures, and brand design. A brand-learning goal produced attention to the body text but also inhibited attention to the pictorial design. One may conclude that text-dominant ads activate brand learning and pictorial-dominant ads activate ad appreciation.[9]

The purpose of rehearsal is to hold information in short-term storage long enough for encoding to take place. **Encoding** is the process by which we select a word or visual image to represent a perceived object. Marketers, for example, help consumers encode brands by using brand symbols. Kellogg's uses Tony the Tiger on its Frosted Flakes; the Green Giant Company has its Jolly Green Giant. Dell Computer turns the *e* in its logo on its side for quick name recognition, and Apple uses its stylish and distinctive insignia.

Encoding commercials is related to the context in which they are featured. For example, while watching TV, some parts of a program may require viewers to commit a larger portion of their cognitive resources to processing (e.g., when a dramatic event takes place versus a casual conversation). When viewers commit more cognitive resources to the program itself, they encode and store less of the information conveyed by a commercial. This suggests that commercials requiring relatively little cognitive processing may be more effective within or adjacent to a dramatic program setting than commercials requiring more elaborate processing. Viewers who are very involved with a television show respond more positively to commercials adjacent

FIGURE 7.10
Information Processing and Memory Stores

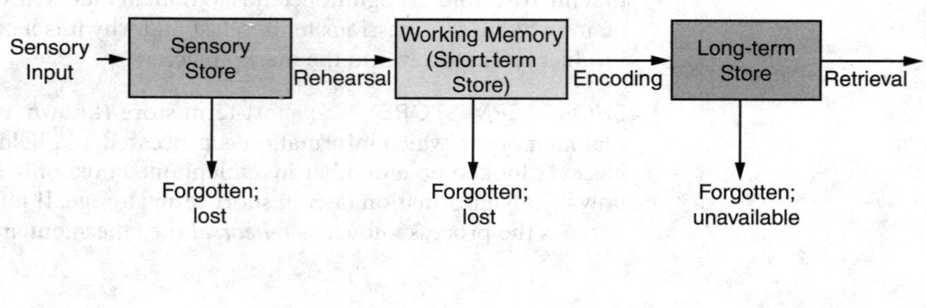

to that show and have more positive purchase intentions. Recent exposure to related information also facilitates encoding. A study found that publicity about advertising campaigns before they started facilitated better recall of subsequently advertised brands.[10]

When consumers are presented with too much information (called **information overload**), they encounter difficulty in encoding and storing it all. Therefore, consumers often find it difficult to remember product information from ads for new brands in heavily advertised categories. Consumers can become cognitively overloaded when they are given a lot of information in a limited time. Such overload may lead to consumer frustration, confusion, and even poor purchase decisions.

RETENTION Information does not just sit in long-term storage waiting to be retrieved. Instead, information is constantly organized and reorganized as new links between chunks of information are forged. In fact, many information-processing theorists view the long-term store as a network consisting of nodes (i.e., concepts), with links between and among them. As individuals gain more knowledge about a subject, they expand their network of relationships and sometimes their search for additional information. This process is known as *activation,* which involves relating new data to old to make the material more meaningful. Consumer memory for the name of a product may also be activated by relating it to the spokesperson used in its advertising. The total package of associations brought to mind when a cue is activated is called a *schema.*

Product information stored in memory tends to be brand based, and consumers interpret new information in a manner consistent with the way in which it is already organized. Consumers are confronted with thousands of new products each year, and their information search is often dependent on how similar or dissimilar (discrepant) these products are to product categories already stored in memory. Therefore, consumers are more likely to recall the information they receive on new products bearing a familiar brand name, and take more time to retain information about previously unfamiliar brands.

One study demonstrated that *brand imprinting*—messages that merely establish the brand's identity—conducted before the presentation of the brand's benefits facilitates consumer learning and retention of information about the brand.[11] Studies also showed that a brand's *sound symbolism* (a theory suggesting that the *sounds* of words convey meanings) and the brand's *linguistic characteristics* (e.g., unusual spelling) impacted the encoding and retention of the brand name.[12]

Consumers recode what they have already encoded to include larger amounts of information (called **chunking**). Marketers should research the kinds and numbers of groupings (chunks) of information that consumers can handle. When the chunks offered in an advertisement do not match those in the consumer's frame of reference, information recall may be hampered. The extent of prior knowledge is also an important consideration. Knowledgeable consumers can take in more complex chunks of information than those who are less knowledgeable about the product category. Thus, the amount and type of technological information contained in a computer ad can be much more detailed in a magazine such as *PC Magazine* or *Wired* than in a general-interest magazine such as *TIME.*

Information is stored in long-term memory in two ways: *episodically* (by the order in which it is acquired) and *semantically* (according to significant concepts). We may remember having gone to a movie last Saturday because of our ability to store data episodically, and we may remember the plot, the stars, and the director because of our ability to store data semantically. Learning theorists believe that memories stored semantically are organized into frameworks by which we integrate new data with previous experience. For information about a new brand or model of printer to enter our memory, for example, we would have to relate it to our previous experience with printers in terms of such qualities as speed, print quality, and resolution.

RETRIEVAL **Retrieval** is the *process by which we recover information from long-term storage.* Retrieval is most often triggered by situational cues. For example, when we see a product in the store or on TV we automatically retrieve the applicable information our brain has stored. If the brand is distinctive and heavily advertised, or if we had a memorable experience using it, the retrieval will be quicker than that for less sought-after brands. Some scientists used brain-imaging technologies, normally used in medicine, to examine information retrieval. For example, when men looked at racy sports cars, their reward centers were activated. The brain scans of consumers who were split as to whether they prefer Coke or Pepsi and were given blind taste tests indicated that two different brain regions were at play. When the subjects tasted either of the soft drinks, their brain's reward system was activated. But when these persons were told which brand they were drinking, their brain's memory region (where information regarding brand loyalty is stored) was activated and overrode the preferences the participants indicated after tasting the soft drink, but before knowing which brand they had tasted.[13]

Incongruent (or unexpected) message elements pierce consumers' perceptual screens and improve the retention of an ad when these elements are relevant to the advertising message. For example, an ad for a brand of stain-resistant, easy-to-clean carpet shows an elegantly dressed couple in a beautiful dining room setting where the man inadvertently knocks the food, the flowers, and the china to the floor. The elegance of the actors and the upscale setting make the accident totally incongruous and unexpected, whereas the message remains highly relevant: The mess can be cleaned up easily without leaving a stain on the carpet. Since this ad is very dramatic, it is likely to be remembered (or retrieved) when the consumer is exposed to any of the elements of the ad subsequently. Incongruent elements that are not relevant to an ad also pierce the consumer's perceptual screen but do not help in retaining the ad or product in one's memory. An ad showing a nude woman sitting on a piece of office furniture would very likely attract readers' attention, but would probably not increase the likelihood that the ad will be remembered or subsequently retrieved. A recent experiment, where subjects were manipulated into making choices among four desserts based on memory or on the actual stimuli (the desserts themselves), discovered that memory-based product choices were guided more by feelings (e.g., an urge for tasty food) where stimulus-based choices are guided more by deliberative considerations (e.g., the need to follow a sensible diet).[14]

The greater the number of competitive ads in a product category, the lower the recall of brand claims in a specific ad. These **interference effects** are caused by confusion with competing ads, and make information retrieval difficult. Ads can also act as retrieval cues for a competitive brand. An example of such consumer confusion occurred when consumers attributed the long-running and attention-getting television campaign featuring the Eveready Energizer Bunny to the leader in the field, Duracell. The level of interference experienced can depend on the consumer's previous experiences, prior knowledge of brand attribute information, and the amount of brand information available at the time of choice. There are actually two kinds of interference: *New learning* can interfere with the retrieval of previously stored material, and *old learning* can interfere with the recall of recently learned material.

THEORETICAL MODELS OF COGNITIVE LEARNING

Cognitive learning occurs when a person has a goal and must search for and process data in order to make a decision or solve a problem. For a long time, consumer researchers believed that all consumers passed through a complex series of mental and behavioral stages in arriving at a purchase decision. These stages ranged from awareness of the purchase options (exposure to information), to evaluation and preferences regarding the alternatives available, to possibly trying one or more versions of the product and then buying it or not buying it (behavior expressed as adoption or rejection). This same series of stages is often presented as the *consumer adoption process* (discussed in Chapter 14). For example, a consumer looking to purchase a super-slim, point-and-shoot digital camera (the goal) must choose among many brands and models (problem solving). The consumer will first get to know the features of different models (exposure to information resulting in knowledge), then develop preferences and evaluations toward the different alternatives, and then decide which model to buy (adoption) and which ones not to purchase (rejection).

Over the years, several models expressing sequential information processing and cognitive learning have been developed (see Table 7.1). Although the models use different terms to designate the sequences they depict, in essence, they follow the same phases as the consumer adoption process. For example, the *tricomponent attitude model* (fully discussed in Chapter 8), as applied to purchase behavior, consists of three stages: (1) the *cognitive stage*—the person's knowledge and beliefs about a product; (2) the *affective stage*—the person's feeling toward and evaluations of a product as "favorable" or "unfavorable"; and (3) the *conative stage*—the person's level of intention to buy the product.

The models listed in Table 7.1 are theoretical because they cannot be tested empirically. They are based mostly on surveys of consumers and reflect the views of several researchers as to how goal-oriented, problem-solving learning occurs. Initially, marketing scholars believed

TABLE 7.1 Models of Cognitive Learning Based on Sequential Information Processing

GENERIC FRAMEWORK	PROMOTIONAL MODEL (AIDA)	TRICOMPONENT MODEL	DECISION MAKING MODEL	INNOVATION ADOPTION MODEL	INNOVATION DECISION MODEL
Knowledge	Attention	Cognitive	Awareness Knowledge	Awareness	Knowledge
Evaluation	Interest Desire	Affective	Evaluation	Interest Evaluation	Persuasion
Behavior	Action	Conative	Purchase Postpurchase Evaluation	Trial Adoption	Decision Confirmation

that the complex processing of information by consumers depicted in the cognitive learning models was applicable to all purchase decisions. However, on the basis of their own subjective experiences as consumers, some theorists began to realize that many, especially routine purchases do not call for extensive information processing and evaluation. Such purchases are of minimal personal relevance, as opposed to highly relevant, search-oriented purchases. Purchases of minimal personal importance are called *low-involvement purchases,* and complex, search-oriented purchases are considered *high-involvement purchases.* Another learning concept that somewhat contradicts the cognitive learning paradigm is *passive learning* where consumers go from awareness of a need to a purchase, without a great deal of information search and mental evaluation. The following sections describe the concepts of *involvement* and *passive learning* and discuss their applications to marketing strategy.

Consumer Involvement and Passive Learning

Learning Objective

7.4 *To Study Consumer Involvement and Passive Learning and Understand Their Strategic Affects on Consumer Behavior.*

Consumer involvement is focused on the *degree of personal relevance* that the product or purchase holds for that consumer. High-involvement purchases are those that are very important to the consumer (e.g., in terms of perceived risk) and thus provoke extensive problem solving and information processing. An automobile and a dandruff shampoo both may represent high-involvement purchases under this scenario—the automobile because of its high perceived financial risk and the shampoo because of high perceived social risk. Low-involvement purchases are purchases that are not very important to the consumer, hold little relevance, and have little perceived risk, and, thus, provoke very limited information processing. Highly involved consumers find fewer brands acceptable (they are called *narrow categorizers*); uninvolved consumers are likely to be receptive to a greater number of advertising messages regarding the purchase and will consider more brands (they are *broad categorizers*).

DEFINITIONS AND MEASURES OF INVOLVEMENT

There is great variation in the conceptualization and measurement of consumer involvement. Throughout the marketing research literature, involvement has been defined in numerous ways, including product involvement, brand involvement, and advertising involvement. Because there is no single, clear definition of involvement, there are varied measures of this dimension. Some measures address cognitive factors such as the importance of a purchase to a buyer and the risk perceived with the purchase, while other measures focus on the behavioral aspects of involvement and appraise such factors as the search for and evaluation of product information. The most sensible approach to measuring involvement is using self-administered surveys that assess the consumer's cognitions or behaviors regarding a particular product or product category, and where involvement is measured on a continuum rather than as a dichotomy. Table 7.2 presents a semantic differential scale designed to measure involvement.[15] Table 7.3 shows a scale measuring a person's involvement with an ad for military recruiting.[16]

TABLE 7.2 Measuring Involvement on a Semantic Differential Scale

TO ME, [INSERT PRODUCT OR PRODUCT CATEGORY] IS

	1	2	3	4	5	6	7	
1. Important	—	—	—	—	—	—	—	Unimportant
2. Interesting	—	—	—	—	—	—	—	Boring
3. Relevant	—	—	—	—	—	—	—	Irrelevant
4. Exciting	—	—	—	—	—	—	—	Unexciting
5. Meaningful	—	—	—	—	—	—	—	Meaningless
6. Appealing	—	—	—	—	—	—	—	Unappealing
7. Fascinating	—	—	—	—	—	—	—	Ordinary
8. Priceless	—	—	—	—	—	—	—	Worthless
9. Involving	—	—	—	—	—	—	—	Uninvolving
10. Necessary	—	—	—	—	—	—	—	Unnecessary

Source: Based on Judith Lynne Zaichowsky, "The Personal Involvement Inventory: Reduction, Revision, and Application to Advertising," *Journal of Advertising*, 23, no. 4 (December 1994): 59–70. Reprinted by permission.

TABLE 7.3 Measuring Involvement with an Advertisement

Subjects respond to the following statements on a 7-point Likert scale ranging from "Strongly Agree" to "Strongly Disagree."

1. The message in the slogan was important to me.
2. The slogan didn't have anything to do with my needs. (rev)
3. The slogan made me think about joining the military.
4. The slogan made me want to join the military.
5. While reading the slogan, I thought about how the military might be useful for me.
6. The slogan did not show me anything that would make me join the military. (rev)
7. I have a more favorable view of the military after seeing the slogan.
8. The slogan showed me the military has certain advantages.
9. The slogan was meaningful to me.
10. The slogan was worth remembering.

Source: From Sylvia A. Miller, M. Suzanne Clinton, and John P. Camey, "The Relationship of Motivators, Needs, and Involvement Factors to Preferences for Military Recruitment Slogans," *Journal of Advertising Research*, 47, no. 1 (March 2007): 66–78.
rev = reverse coding.

MARKETING APPLICATIONS OF INVOLVEMENT

Marketers aspire to have consumers who are involved with the purchase and also view its brand as unique. Many studies showed that high purchase involvement coupled with perceived brand differences lead to a high favorable attitude toward the brand, which in turn leads to less variety seeking and brand switching and to strong brand loyalty.[17] Therefore, many studies have focused on the factors that increase involvement. For example, one study discovered that consumers who were highly involved in the sports program they watched recalled commercials significantly better than those who were less involved with the program watched.[18] Many advertisers now place ads and products in online video games, and a study found that game involvement was one of the factors impacting brand memory. Players who were highly involved with the game, because this was their first time playing it and they did not know what to anticipate, were more likely to recall the brands embedded in the game. When they became more experienced, the players also became less involved with the game and less likely to recall the brands embedded.[19] Online, many advertisers use **avatars**—animated, virtual reality graphical figures representing people—in their Web sites. One study found that an attractive avatar sales agent was effective at moderate levels of consumers' product involvement, but an expert avatar was a more effective sales agent for high levels of product involvement.[20] While there is no generalized profile of a highly involved consumer, many studies investigated the personal characteristics related to one's involvement level. For example, researchers found a relationship between ethnicity and involvement. Their study showed that appealing to strong Hispanic identities is desirable when advertising low-involvement products but is not an important cue for high-involvement products.[21] Finally, many researchers have examined the effects of promotional appeals on involvement. To illustrate, one study tested the impact of two copy appeals on consumers' involvement with ads for a cell phone and ascertained that a *narrative* appeal elicited more ad involvement and produced more favorable product evaluations than the *factual* appeal.[22]

Marketers can take steps to increase customer involvement with their ads. For example, advertisers can use sensory appeals, unusual stimuli, and celebrity endorsers to generate more attention for their messages. Since highly involved consumers are more likely to engage in long-term relationships with products and brands, marketers should simultaneously increase customer involvement levels and create bonds with their customers. The best strategy for increasing the personal relevance of products to consumers is the same as the core of modern marketing itself: Provide benefits that are important and relevant to customers, improve the product and add benefits as competition intensifies, and focus on forging *bonds* and *relationships* with customers rather than just engaging in *transactions*.

CENTRAL AND PERIPHERAL ROUTES TO PERSUASION

The framework of **central** and **peripheral routes to persuasion** illustrates the concepts of extensive and limited problem solving for high- and low-involvement purchase situations. The major premise of this model is that consumers are more likely to carefully evaluate the merits and weaknesses of a product when the purchase is of high relevance to them. Conversely, it is very likely that consumers will engage in very limited information search and evaluation when the purchase holds little relevance or importance for them. Thus, for high-involvement purchases, the *central route to persuasion*—which requires considered thought and cognitive processing—is likely to be the most effective marketing strategy. For low-involvement purchases, the *peripheral route to persuasion* is likely to be more effective. In this instance, because the consumer is less motivated to exert cognitive effort, learning is more likely to occur through repetition, the passive processing of visual cues, and holistic perception. Highly involved consumers use more attributes to evaluate brands, whereas less involved consumers apply simpler decision rules. In marketing to highly involved consumers, the quality of the argument presented in the persuasive message, rather than merely the imagery of the promotional message, has the greater impact on the consumption decision.

The level of information processing has important implications for promotion. For example, comparative ads (see Chapter 9) are more likely to be processed centrally (purposeful processing of message arguments), whereas noncomparative ads are commonly processed peripherally (with little message elaboration and a response derived from other elements in the ad). A study demonstrated that the correlation between a consumer's product involvement and objective product knowledge is higher for *utilitarian* products than in products designed to bring about pleasure (termed *hedonic* products); for hedonic products, the correlation between subjective knowledge and product involvement was higher than for utilitarian products.[23] Assuming that *subjective* knowledge is the result of interpreting the imagery presented in the ad while *objective* knowledge is the outcome of the factual information that the ad provides, marketers should consider the degree of the product's utilitarianism in selecting either the central or peripheral route in promoting that product.

HEMISPHERIC LATERALIZATION AND PASSIVE LEARNING

Hemispheric lateralization, or split-brain theory, originated in the 1960s (as part of medical research focused on epileptic seizures) and became popular in the 1980s.[24] The premise of *split-brain theory* is that the human brain is divided into two distinct cerebral hemispheres that operate together but "specialize" in the kinds of cognitions they process. The *left* hemisphere is the center of human language; it is the linear side of the brain and primarily responsible for reading, speaking, and attributional information processing. The *right* hemisphere of the brain is the home of spatial perception and nonverbal concepts; it is nonlinear and the source of imagination and pleasure. Put another way, the left side of the brain is rational, active, and realistic; the right side is emotional, metaphoric, impulsive, and intuitive. Some argue that computers emulate many of the sequential functions of the left side of the brain and that we should employ the imaginative, right brain to a greater degree in making business decisions.[25] Figure 7.11 shows an ad literally depicting split-brain theory.

Passive Learning and Media Strategy

Building on the notion of hemispheric lateralization, a pioneer consumer researcher theorized that when consumers watch advertising on TV they *passively* process and store right-brain (nonverbal, pictorial) information—that is, without active involvement.[26] Because TV is primarily a pictorial medium, TV viewing is often considered a right-brain activity (passive and holistic processing of images viewed on the screen), and TV itself is therefore considered a low-involvement medium. This research concluded that **passive learning** occurs through repeated exposures to a TV commercial (i.e., low-involvement information processing) and produces changes in consumer behavior (e.g., product purchases) *prior* to changes in the consumer's attitude toward the product. This view contradicts the models presented in Table 7.1, all of which maintain that cognitive evaluation and the formation of a favorable attitude toward a product take place before the actual purchase behavior.

Extending this reasoning to other media, print media (e.g., newspapers and magazines) and static copy on digital media consist largely of verbal information that is processed by the brain's left side; thus, these media are considered high-involvement media. According to the

FIGURE 7.11
Source: Courtesy of American Airlines. Image © Abrams Lacagnina/GettyImages/The Image Bank.

QUESTION: *What Is the Name of the Learning Theory Concept Featured in This Ad and How Is It Applied to Air Travel?*

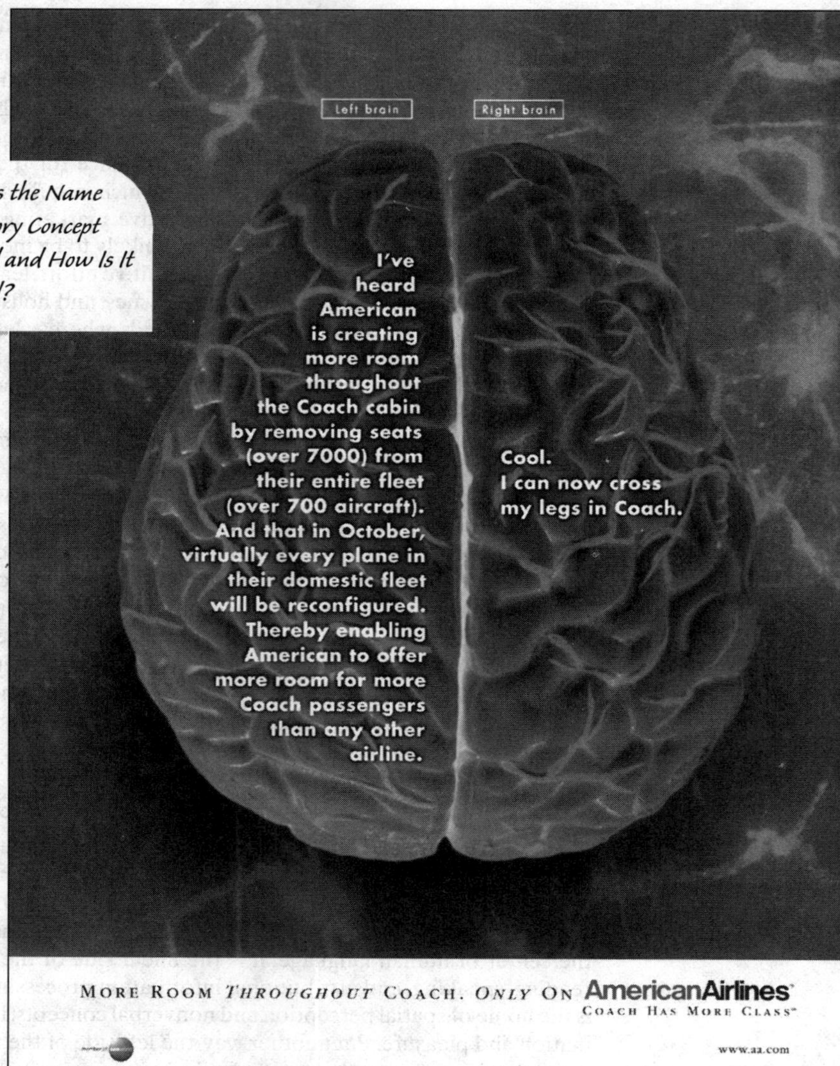

split-brain concept, print advertising is processed in the complex sequence of cognitive stages depicted in the cognitive models of information processing. On the other hand, advertising that consists mostly of moving images and pictorial information is processed holistically by the right side of the viewer's brain, with minimum involvement.

The right-brain theory of passive processing of information is consistent with classical conditioning. Through repetition, the product is paired with a visual image (e.g., a distinctive package) to produce the desired response: purchase of the advertised brand. According to this theory, in situations of passive learning (generated by low-involvement media), repetition is the key factor in producing purchase behavior. In marketing terms, the theory suggests that television commercials are most effective when they are of short duration and repeated frequently, thus ensuring brand familiarity without provoking detailed evaluation of the message content.

The right-brain processing theory stresses the importance of the *visual component* of advertising, including the creative use of symbols. Under this theory, highly visual TV commercials, packaging, and in-store displays generate familiarity with the brand and induce purchase behavior. Pictorial cues are more effective at generating recall and familiarity with the product, whereas verbal cues (which trigger left-brain processing) generate cognitive activity that encourages consumers to evaluate the advantages and disadvantages of the product. The ad in Figure 7.12 illustrates a promotional appeal targeting the left-brain (in comparison, the yogurt ads shown in Figures 7.4 and 7.8 are aimed at the right brain).

FIGURE 7.12

Source: © The Procter & Gamble Company. Used by permission. All rights reserved.

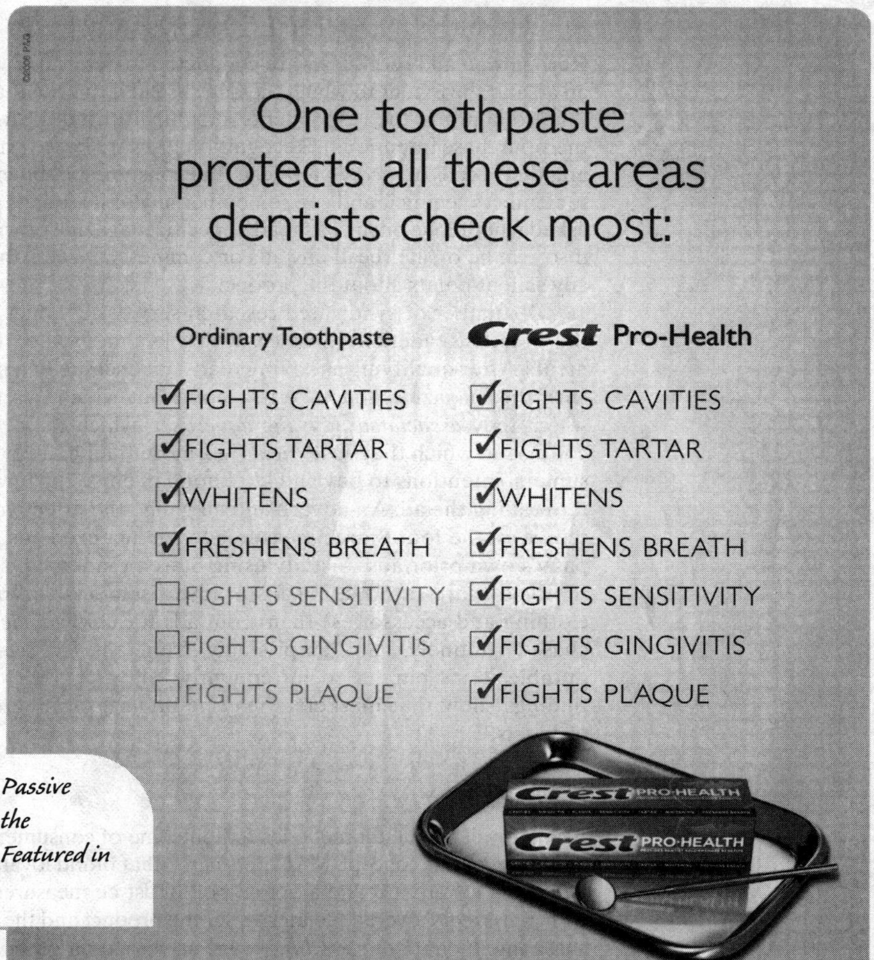

QUESTION: *How Is Passive Learning Applied to the Promotional Appeal Featured in This Ad?*

Although the right and left hemispheres of the brain process different types of cues, they do not operate independently of each other but work together to process information. Some individuals are *integrated processors* (they readily engage both hemispheres during information processing). Integrated processors have better overall recall of both the verbal and the visual portions of print ads than individuals who primarily exhibit either right or left hemispheric processing.

Outcomes and Measures of Consumer Learning

LEARNING OBJECTIVE

7.5 *To Understand How Consumer Learning and Its Results Are Measured.*

For marketers, the dual goals of consumer learning are increased market share and brand-loyal consumers. These goals are interdependent: Brand-loyal customers provide the basis for a stable and growing market share, and brands with larger market shares have proportionately larger groups of loyal buyers. Marketers focus their promotional budgets on trying to teach consumers that their brands are best and that their products will best solve the consumers' problems and satisfy their needs. Thus, it is important for the marketer to measure how effectively consumers have "learned" its message. The following sections will examine various measures of consumer learning: *recognition* and *recall measures,* and the *attitudinal and behavioral dimensions of brand loyalty.*

RECOGNITION AND RECALL MEASURES

Recognition and **recall tests** are conducted to determine whether consumers remember seeing an ad and the extent to which they have read it or seen it and can recall its content (some studies also appraise the respondents' resulting attitudes toward the product and the brand, and their purchase intentions). Recognition tests are based on **aided recall**, whereas recall tests use **unaided recall**. In *recognition* tests, the consumer is shown an ad and asked whether he or she remembers seeing it and can remember any of its salient points. In *recall* tests, the consumer is asked whether he or she has read a specific magazine or watched a specific television show, and, if so, can he or she recall any ads or commercials seen, the product advertised, the brand, and any salient points about the product.

A number of syndicated research services conduct recognition and recall tests, such as the Starch Readership Service, which evaluates the effectiveness of magazine advertisements. After qualifying as having read a given issue of a magazine, respondents are presented with the magazine and asked to point out which ads they *noted* (i.e., remember seeing), which they *associated with the advertiser,* which they *read some* (i.e., any part of the ad's copy), and which they *read most* (i.e., more than half of the copy). Starch also appraises consumers' intentions to buy and likelihood in engaging in word of mouth about the product after reading the ad. An advertiser can gauge the effectiveness of a given ad by comparing its scores on the four Starch measures to similar-sized ads, to competitive ads, and to the company's own prior ads. A study using Starch readership scores demonstrated that consumers received more information from advertisements for *shopping products* (e.g., high-priced clothing and accessories) than from ads for *convenience goods* (e.g., low-priced items purchased routinely) and, surprisingly, from ads for *search products* (e.g., very expensive, durable items purchased infrequently following an extensive information search). These findings show that marketers may be underinforming consumers when advertising search products.[27]

BRAND LOYALTY

Brand loyalty is the ultimate desired outcome of consumer learning. However, there is no single definition of this concept. Marketers agree that brand loyalty consists of both attitudes and actual behaviors toward a brand and that both must be measured. *Attitudinal measures* are concerned with consumers' overall feelings about the product and the brand (i.e., evaluation), and their purchase intentions. *Behavioral measures* are based on observable, factual behaviors regarding the brand, such as quantity purchased, purchase frequency and repeated buying. A measure on one's propensity to be brand loyal (i.e., an attitudinal measure) is shown in Table 7.4.[28]

Behavioral scientists who favor the theory of instrumental conditioning believe that brand loyalty results from an initial product trial that is reinforced through satisfaction, leading to re-

TABLE 7.4 A Measure of Propensity to Be Brand Loyal

x_1	I would rather stick with a brand I usually buy than try something I am not very sure of.
x_2	If I like a brand, I rarely switch from it just to try something different.
x_3	I rarely introduce new brands and products to my colleagues.
x_4	I rarely take chances by buying unfamiliar brands even if it means sacrificing variety.
x_5	I buy the same brands even if they are only average.
x_6	I would rather wait for others to try a new brand than try it myself.
x_7	I would rather stick to well-known brands when purchasing directory advertising.

Source: Rebekah Bennett and Sharyn Rundle-Thiele, "A Comparison of Attitudinal Loyalty Measurement Approaches," *Journal of Brand Management* (January 2002): 193–209.

peat purchase. *Cognitive* researchers, on the other hand, emphasize the role of mental processes in building brand loyalty. They believe that consumers engage in extensive problem-solving behavior involving brand and attribute comparisons, leading to a strong brand preference and repeat purchase behavior. Therefore, brand loyalty is the synergy among such attitudinal components as perceived product superiority, customer satisfaction, and the purchase behavior itself.

Behavioral definitions (such as frequency of purchase or proportion of total purchases) lack precision, because they do not distinguish between the "real" brand-loyal buyer who is intentionally faithful and the *spurious* brand-loyal buyer who repeats a brand purchase out of mere habit or because it is the only one available at the store. Often consumers buy from a mix of brands within their acceptable range (i.e., their **evoked set**). The greater the number of acceptable brands in a specific product category, the less likely the consumer is to be brand loyal to one specific brand. Conversely, products having few competitors in the marketplace, as well as those purchased with great frequency, are likely to have greater brand loyalty. Thus, a more favorable attitude toward a brand, service, or store, compared to potential alternatives, together with repeat patronage, are seen as the requisite components of customer loyalty. Behavioral brand loyalty leads to a higher market share, and attitudinal loyalty often enables the marketer to charge a higher price for the brand relative to the competition.

An integrated conceptual framework views consumer loyalty as the function of three groups of factors: (1) personal degree of risk aversion or variety seeking; (2) the brand's reputation and availability of substitute brands; and (3) social group influences and peers' recommendations. These influences produce four types of loyalty: (1) *no loyalty*—no purchase at all and no cognitive attachment to the brand; (2) *covetous loyalty*—no purchase but strong attachment and predisposition toward the brand that was developed from the person's social environment; (3) *inertia loyalty*—purchasing the brand because of habit and convenience but without any emotional attachment to the brand; and (4) *premium loyalty*—high attachment to the brand and high repeat purchase.[29] This framework also reflects a correlation among consumer involvement and the cognitive and behavioral dimensions of brand loyalty. Due to social perceptions regarding the importance of a car, and the symbolism of a particular car brand (e.g., Mercedes) as representing prestige and achievement, consumers may become involved with and attached to the brand without purchasing it (covetous loyalty), but may purchase the brand when they have the money to do so. Low involvement leads to exposure and brand awareness and then to brand habit (inertia loyalty). Consumers operating in this condition perceive little differentiation among brands and buy the brand repeatedly due to familiarity and convenience. On the other hand, premium loyalty represents truly brand-loyal consumers who have a strong commitment to the brand, are less likely to switch to other brands in spite of the persuasive promotional efforts of competitors, and may even go out of their way to obtain the strongly preferred brand.

Loyalty programs are generally designed with the intention of forming and maintaining brand loyalty. One study showed that brand managers believe that all reward programs impact incremental purchases and that low and moderate reward programs are the most cost-effective. The study proposed three types of brand-loyalty reward programs (see Table 7.5).[30] This research illustrates the options of tailoring loyalty programs to the purchase patterns of different market segments and the importance of doing so.

TABLE 7.5 Three Brand-Loyalty Reward Programs

REWARD PROGRAM	MEMBERSHIP NEWSLETTER	DISCOUNT COUPONS	PRODUCT LINE MERCHANDISE
Low	A quarterly one-page newsletter with information concerning new and existing products in the product line.	Coupons included in the newsletter for a $0.25 discount off any product in the product line.	Receive product line merchandise (e.g., coffee mugs or T-shirts) with 20 proofs of purchase and a $5.00 postage and handling fee.
Moderate	A quarterly full-color booklet with recipes and information concerning new and existing products in the product line.	Coupons included in the booklet for a $0.50 discount off any product in the product line.	Receive product line merchandise (e.g., coffee mugs or T-shirts) with 20 proofs of purchase.
High	A monthly full-color booklet with recipes, games and puzzles, and information concerning new and existing products in the product line.	Coupons included in the booklet for a $1.00 discount off any product in the product line.	Receive product line merchandise (e.g., coffee mugs or T-shirts) with 10 proofs of purchase.

Source: Brian Wansink, "Developing a Cost-Effective Brand Loyalty Program," *Journal of Advertising Research,* 43, no. 3 (September 2003): 305.

In marketing services, the potential for losing customers is greater than in selling products because the "production" of most services is less controllable and more susceptible to errors than the manufacturing of physical products. Therefore, understanding why customers stay is of utmost importance to service providers. A recent study of bank customers identified two groups of factors as the keys to maintaining customer loyalty: *switching barriers* and reasons that *affirm* the customer's relationship with the service vendor. The factors and survey items designed to measure them are shown in Table 7.6.[31]

Brand Equity

The term **brand equity** refers to the value inherent in a well-known brand name. This value stems from the consumer's perception of the brand's superiority, the social esteem that using it provides, and the customer's trust and identification with the brand. For many companies, their most valuable assets are their brand names. Well-known brand names are referred to as **megabrands**. Among the best-known brands are Coca-Cola, Campbell's Soup, Disney, Google, Hallmark Cards, and Sony. Their names have become global, "cultural icons" and enjoy powerful advantages over the competition.

Because of the escalation of new-product costs and the high rate of new-product failures, many companies prefer to leverage their brand equity through brand extensions rather than risk launching a new brand. Brand equity facilitates the acceptance of new products and the allocation of preferred shelf space, and enhances perceived value, perceived quality, and premium pricing options. Brand equity is most important for low-involvement purchases, such as inexpensive consumer goods that are bought routinely and with little processing of cognitive information. Thus, competitors of a strong brand will find it difficult to "teach" brand-loyal customers about the benefits of their brands.

While measuring brand loyalty is straightforward, gauging the factors leading to brand equity is more complex and requires more sophisticated analysis. A recent study identified perceived quality, brand loyalty, brand image, and brand awareness as the key drivers of a hotel's brand equity and also developed a scale measuring these factors (see Table 7.7).[32] A study of durable products, home appliances, discovered that the image of the product's country of origin significantly impacted brand equity and also identified other factors that strengthen brand equity (see Table 7.8).[33]

Because a brand that has been promoted heavily in the past retains a cumulative level of name recognition, companies buy, sell, and rent (i.e., license) their brand names, knowing that it is easier for a new company to buy, rather than to create, a brand name that has enduring strength. Brand equity enables companies to charge a price premium—an additional amount over and above the price of an identical store brand. A relatively new strategy among some marketers is **co-branding** (also called double branding). The basis of co-branding, in which two

TABLE 7.6 The Reasons Customers Remain Loyal to a Service Provider

CATEGORY	REASONS TO STAY
Switching Barriers	
Time and effort	Time and effort involved in looking for a new service provider
	Time and effort involved in switching
	Time and effort in learning about the new service provider
	Effort in establishing a new relationship
Alternatives	I do not know of any alternatives to move to
	I do not think that the alternatives are any better (5)
	I am concerned that the alternatives may be worse (4)
Emotional bonds	I'd be too embarrassed to tell my current service provider that I was leaving
	I am afraid I would hurt my current service provider's feelings
	I feel a sense of loyalty toward my current service provider
Switching costs	Financial cost of switching
	Possible problems caused by moving to new service provider
	Current service provider is convenient
	Current service provider has specialized knowledge
	Friends and family use service provider
Affirmatory Factors	
Confidence	There has not been a bad enough incident to make me switch (1)
	I am familiar with my current service provider (2)
	I have a history with my current service provider (3)
	I trust my current service provider
	I am comfortable with my current service provider
	I am satisfied with my current service provider
Social bonds	I get on well with staff at my current service provider
	I am recognized by staff at my current service provider
	I know staff at my current service provider
	Staff at my current service provider understand me
	Staff are friendly at my current service provider
Service recovery	A complaint was handled well
	A problem was handled well

Source: Mark Colgate, Vicky Thuy-Uyen Tong, Christina Kwal-Choi Lee, and John U. Farley, "Back from the Brink: Why Customers Stay," *Journal of Service Research,* 9, no. 3 (February 2007): 224.

brand names are featured on a single product, is to use another product's brand equity to enhance the primary brand's equity. Strong brands can cooperate in other creative ways. For example, Procter & Gamble partnered with the retailer Ann Taylor and used its stores to launch Tide Total Care and Downy Total Care—two products claiming to help clothes look new for a longer time, thus lowering one's expenditures on dry cleaning. The two detergents were featured in Ann Taylor's stores (and also in some ads), where consumers who bought machine-washable clothes got product samples and coupons.[34]

Brand equity reflects brand loyalty, which, as presented here, is a *learned* construct and one of the most important applications of learning theory to consumption behavior. Brand loyalty and brand equity lead to increased market share and greater profits. To marketers, the major function of learning theory is to teach consumers that their product is best, to encourage repeat purchase, and, ultimately, to develop loyalty to the brand name and brand equity for the company.

TABLE 7.7 Factors and Measures of a Hotel's Brand Equity

SCALE ITEMS
Brand Loyalty
I usually use this hotel as my first choice compared to other hotel brands
I am satisfied with the visit to this hotel
I would recommend this hotel to others
I would not switch to another hotel the next time
Perceived Quality
The hotel has modern looking equipment
The physical facilities at the hotel are visually appealing
Staff at the hotel appear neat
Materials associated with the service are visually appealing
When the hotel promised to do something by a certain time, it did it
When patrons have problems, the hotel shows a genuine interest in solving them
The hotel performs the service right the first time
The hotel provides its services at the time it promises to do so
The hotel insists on error free service
Staff at the hotel were able to tell patrons exactly when services would be performed
Staff at the hotel give prompt service to the patrons
Staff at the hotel are always willing to help patrons
Staff at the hotel are never too busy to respond to patrons
The behavior of staff instills confidence in patrons
Patrons of the hotel feel safe in their transactions
Staff of the hotel are consistently courteous with patrons
Staff of the hotel have the knowledge to answer patrons
The hotel gives patrons individualized attention
The hotel has opening hours convenient to all of its patrons
The hotel has staff who give its patrons personalized attention
The hotel has the patrons' best interest at heart
The staff of the hotel understand the specific needs of their patrons
Brand Image
It is comfortable
It has a very clean image
It is luxurious
It is a suitable place for high class
I become special by visiting this hotel
The staff is very kind
It has a long history
It has a differentiated image from other hotel brands

Source: Ruchan Kayaman and Huseyin Arasli, "Customer Based Brand Equity: Evidence from the Hotel Industry," *Managing Service Quality*, 17, no. 1 (2007): 100.

TABLE 7.8 Factors Driving the Brand Equity of Household Electrical Appliances

ITEMS
Country-of-Origin Image
The country from which brand *X* originates is a country that is innovative in manufacturing
The country from which brand *X* originates is a country that has a high level of technological advance
The country from which brand *X* originates is a country that is good in designing
The country from which brand *X* originates is a country that is creative in its workmanship
The country from which brand *X* originates is a country that has high quality in its workmanship
The country from which brand *X* originates is a country that is prestigious
X originates from a country that has an image of advanced country
Brand Distinctiveness
I associate *X* with dynamism
I associate *X* with high technology
I associate *X* with innovativeness
I associate *X* with sophistication
I associate *X* with distinctiveness
I associate *X* with excellence
I associate *X* with prestige
Brand Loyalty
If I am going to buy other electrical goods other than air-conditioner/refrigerator/television (either one), I will choose brand *X*
Compared to other brands that have similar features, I am willing to pay a premium (higher) price for *X*
I will not buy other brands if *X* is available at the store
I will think twice to buy another brand if it is almost the same with *X*
I make my purchase selection of air-conditioner (or refrigerator or television) according to my favorite brand name, regardless of price
Brand Awareness/Associations
I know what the symbol of brand *X* looks like
I have no difficulties in imagining *X* in my mind
I can quickly recall the symbol or logo of *X*
I have an opinion about this brand
Brand Equity
Even if another brand has the same features as *X*, I would prefer to buy *X*
If I have to choose among brands of air-conditioner/refrigerator/television, *X* is definitely my choice
If I have to buy an air-conditioner/refrigerator/television, I plan to buy *X* even though there are other brands as good as *X*
Even if another brand has the same price as *X*, I would still buy *X*
If there is another brand as good as *X*, I prefer to buy *X*
If another brand is not different from *X* in any way, it seems smarter to purchase *X*
It makes sense to buy *X* instead of any other brands, even if they are the same

Source: Norjaya Mohd Yasin, Mohd Nasser Noor, and Osman Mohamad, "Does Image of Country-of-Origin Matter to Brand Equity?" *Journal of Product & Brand Management,* 16, no. 1 (2007): 43. Copyright © 2007, Emerald Group Publishing Limited.

SUMMARY

Consumer learning is the process by which individuals acquire the purchase and consumption knowledge and experience they apply to future related behavior. Although some learning is intentional, much learning is incidental. Basic elements that contribute to an understanding of learning are motivation (drives), cues, response, and reinforcement.

There are two schools of thought as to how individuals learn—behavioral theories and cognitive theories. Both contribute to an understanding of consumer behavior. Behavioral theorists view learning as observable responses to stimuli, whereas cognitive theorists believe that learning is a function of mental processing.

Three major behavioral learning constructs are classical conditioning, instrumental conditioning, and observational (vicarious) learning. The principles of classical conditioning that provide theoretical underpinnings for many marketing applications include repetition, stimulus generalization, and stimulus discrimination. Neo-Pavlovian theories view traditional classical conditioning as cognitive associative learning rather than as reflexive action.

Instrumental learning theorists believe that learning occurs through a trial-and-error process in which positive outcomes (i.e., rewards) result in repeat behavior. Both positive and negative reinforcement can be used to encourage the desired behavior. Reinforcement schedules can be total (consistent) or partial (fixed ratio or random). The timing of repetitions influences how long the learned material is retained. Massed repetitions produce more initial learning than distributed repetitions; however, learning usually persists longer with distributed (i.e., spread out) reinforcement schedules.

Cognitive learning models maintain that the kind of learning most characteristic of humans is problem solving. Cognitive theorists are concerned with how information is processed by the human mind: how it is stored, retained, and retrieved. A basic model of the structure and operation of memory suggests the existence of three separate storage units: the sensory store, short-term store (or working memory), and long-term store. The processes of memory include rehearsal, encoding, storage, and retrieval.

The consumer involvement model proposes that people engage in limited information processing in situations of low importance or relevance to them and in extensive information processing in situations of high relevance. Hemispheric lateralization (i.e., split-brain) theory gave rise to the theory that television is a low-involvement medium that results in passive learning and that print and interactive media encourage more cognitive information processing.

Measures of consumer learning include recall and recognition tests, and attitudinal and behavioral measures of brand loyalty. Brand loyalty consists of both attitudes and actual behaviors toward a brand, and both must be measured. For marketers, the major reasons for understanding how consumers learn are to teach them that their brand is best and to develop brand loyalty. Brand equity refers to the inherent value a brand name has in the marketplace.

DISCUSSION QUESTIONS

1. How can the principles of (a) classical conditioning and (b) instrumental conditioning be applied to the development of marketing strategies?
2. Describe in learning terms the conditions under which family branding is a good policy and those under which it is not.
3. Neutrogena, a company known for its "dermatologist recommended" skin care products, introduced a line of shaving products for men. How can the company use stimulus generalization to market these products? Is instrumental conditioning applicable to this marketing situation? If so, how?
4. Which form of learning (classical conditioning, instrumental conditioning, observational learning, or cognitive learning) best explains the following consumption behaviors: (a) buying a six-pack of Gatorade, (b) preferring to purchase jeans at a Diesel Store, (c) buying a digital camera for the first time, (d) buying a new car, and (e) switching from one cell phone service to another? Explain your choices.
5. a. Define the following memory structures: sensory store, short-term store (working memory), and long-term store. Discuss how each of these concepts can be used in the development of an advertising strategy.
   b. How does information overload affect the consumer's ability to comprehend an ad and store it in his or her memory?
6. Discuss the differences between low- and high-involvement media. How would you apply the knowledge of hemispheric lateralization to the design of TV commercials and print advertisements?
7. Why are both attitudinal and behavioral measures important in measuring brand loyalty?
8. What is the relationship between brand loyalty and brand equity? What role do concepts play in the development of marketing strategies?
9. How can marketers use measures of recognition and recall to study the extent of consumer learning?

EXERCISES

1. Imagine you are the instructor in this course and that you are trying to increase student participation in class discussions. How would you use reinforcement to achieve your objective?
2. Visit a supermarket. Can you identify any packages where you think the marketer's knowledge of stimulus generalization or stimulus discrimination was incorporated into the package design? Note these examples and present them in class.

KEY TERMS

- advertising wearout *214*
- aided and unaided recall tests *234*
- avatars *230*
- behavioral learning *212*
- brand equity *236*
- brand loyalty *234*
- central route to persuasion *231*
- chunking *227*
- classical conditioning *212*
- co-branding *236*
- cognitive associative learning *213*
- cognitive learning *212*
- consumer involvement *229*
- encoding *226*
- evoked set *235*
- family branding *215*
- hemispheric lateralization *231*
- information overload *227*
- information processing *225*
- instrumental conditioning *212*
- interference effects *228*
- learning *208*
- licensing *217*
- long-term store *225*
- megabrands *236*
- modeling *224*
- negative reinforcement *221*
- neo-Pavlovian conditioning *213*
- observational learning *224*
- operant conditioning *212*
- passive learning *232*
- peripheral route to persuasion *231*
- positive reinforcement *221*
- product category extensions *215*
- product form extensions *215*
- product line extensions *215*
- recall tests *234*
- recognition tests *234*
- rehearsal *226*
- relationship marketing *223*
- retrieval *227*
- sensory store *225*
- shaping *224*
- short-term store *225*
- stimulus discrimination *218*
- stimulus generalization *215*
- stimulus-response learning *212*

Case One: The Dental Care Aisle of Confusion

Stimulus generalization is one of the outcomes of consumer learning. It enables marketers to extend the number of product versions and also introduce new forms of products under existing brand names that are strongly recognized and favored by consumers. However, such extensions, designed to provide more choice to consumers, sometimes result in consumer confusion and frustration. For example, in stores' toothpaste aisles, consumers must choose among scores of toothpastes providing different benefits (e.g., tartar control, special benefits for sensitive teeth, control of gum disease), that are offered in different forms (e.g., paste, gel, in combination with mouthwash) and in almost any conceivable flavor and packaging. In addition to toothpastes that claim to provide consumers with bright smiles and perfectly white teeth, there are many teeth-whitening products in the forms of strips, gels, and liquids. There are also many versions of manual toothbrushes in different sizes, designs, and degrees of softness or gentleness. And, there are electric toothbrushes and teeth-cleaning "systems." Furthermore, there are now many versions of dental floss, varied in flavor, thickness, and proclaimed strength to penetrate tight spaces between teeth.

Almost all the toothpastes and other oral-care products are offered by either Crest or Colgate—two highly successful brands that have been competitng with one another for decades. Facing saturated markets and competition, the two brands recognized the strategic value of stimulus generalization. Using the consumers' strong and favorable associations with the terms Crest and Colgate, the two brands have been trying to get consumers to use more toothpaste and related products, and households to buy more than a single version of toothpaste. The two marketers do so by offering consumers a seemingly endless array of ways to care for their teeth. However, some experts point out that the result is consumer confusion and frustration. First, consumers must decide which toothpaste is right for them. Then, they must find it in shelves crowded with many versions, and doing so takes time. Since stores cannot carry all of the versions all the time, they often alternate the toothpaste items carried and, at times, consumers may be unable to purchase their preferred versions of toothpaste in the stores where they regularly shop. There is also the anxiety that one is missing out on something by being brand loyal to a particular brand or flavor while all the new and "exciting" toothpastes are coming out. While it is apparent that stimulus generalization benefits marketers, it can also produce consumer confusion.

QUESTIONS

1. Do the potential negative outcomes of using stimulus generalization outweigh the benefits of using this concept to offer consumers more choice and ways to care for their teeth and oral hygeine? Explain your answer.
2. How can the marketers of Crest and Colgate reduce consumer confusion regarding toothpastes and related oral-care products?
3. Discuss the problem of consumer confusion regarding oral-care products with a few of your peers and find out how many had experienced it or were unable to find easily their preferred products at some point. Based on these conversations, would you say that Colgate and Crest should consider consumer confusion regarding oral-care products a significant issue? Why or why not?

Case Two: HSBC's "Different Values" Campaign

Learning includes making associations between stimuli and applying these cognitions into future behavior. Marketers repeat advertising messages so that consumers associate their products with the benefits and value that they promise to deliver, and remember these connections over time.

However, there is a limit to the amount of repetition that will aid retention and, at some point, an individual can become satiated with numerous exposures, and both attention and retention will decline. This effect is known as advertising wearout and varying the advertising messages for a given product or service can reduce it. Therefore, marketers try to lessen potential advertising wearout by employing different backgrounds or other cues in their ads, while repeating the same advertising theme. For example, HSBC positions itself as "the world's local bank." A recent advertising campaign, termed "Different Values," consisted of about 20 ads centered on the theme that "different values make the world a richer place." The ads illustrated that one's point of view is subjective and reflects one's values and, therefore, the same object can have different meanings stemming from one's culture and viewpoint. The *objects* depicted in the different ads varied, while the *central theme* remained the same.

In each "Different Values" ad, a single image (or object) was repeated three times, with a different one-word interpretation imposed over each photo. For example, in one ad, the words *style*, *soldier*, and *survivor* appeared over three identical photos of the back of a gender-neutral shaved head, illustrating that various people view the same object differently. You should have no trouble locating online other ads used in this campaign.

QUESTIONS

1. How does this campaign illustrate the concepts of consumer learning (Chapter 7) and also of perception (Chapter 6)?
2. Do you believe that the technique used by HSBC is likely to enhance the initial learning and subsequent recall of HSBC's message? Explain your answer.

8

Consumer Attitude Formation and Change

AS CONSUMERS, each of us has a vast number of attitudes toward products, services, advertisements, direct mail, the Internet, and retail stores. Whenever we are asked whether we like or dislike a product (e.g., a Casio watch), a service (e.g., American Airlines), a particular retailer (e.g., Macy's), a specific direct marketer (e.g., **www.Amazon.com**), or an advertising theme (e.g., "Saab—Born from Jets"), we are being asked to express our *attitudes.* Still further, when it comes to a particular product and an advertisement for that product (or for that matter any other marketing-related messages for the product), it is quite possible for a consumer to have a different attitude toward the product (e.g., "disliking it") than the attitude toward the ad for the product (e.g., "liking it"). Figure 8.1 presents an ad for Lysol's® sanitizing wipes. Examine the ad. Then answer for yourself what is your attitude toward the brand/product and the ad for the brand/product? Are they similar or different? Later in this chapter you will examine in detail the issues of attitudes toward products and attitudes toward advertisements.

Within the context of consumer behavior, an appreciation of prevailing consumer attitudes has considerable strategic merit. For instance, there has been very rapid growth in the sales of natural ingredient bath, body, and cosmetic products throughout the world. This trend seems linked to the currently popular attitude that things "natural" are good and things "synthetic" are bad. Yet, in reality, the positive attitude favoring things natural is not based on any systematic evidence that natural cosmetic products are any safer or better for consumers.

To get at the heart of what is driving consumers' behavior, *attitude research* has been used to answer a wide range of strategic marketing questions. For example, attitude research is frequently undertaken to determine whether consumers will accept a proposed new-product idea, to gauge why a firm's target audience has not reacted more favorably to its new promotional theme, or to learn how target customers are likely to react to a proposed change in the firm's packaging design. To illustrate, major athletic shoe marketers such as Nike or Reebok frequently conduct research among target consumers of the different functional types of athletic footwear products that they market. They seek attitudes of target consumers with respect to size, fit, comfort, and fashion elements of

FIGURE 8.1

Source: © Reckitt Benckiser Inc. Used with permission.

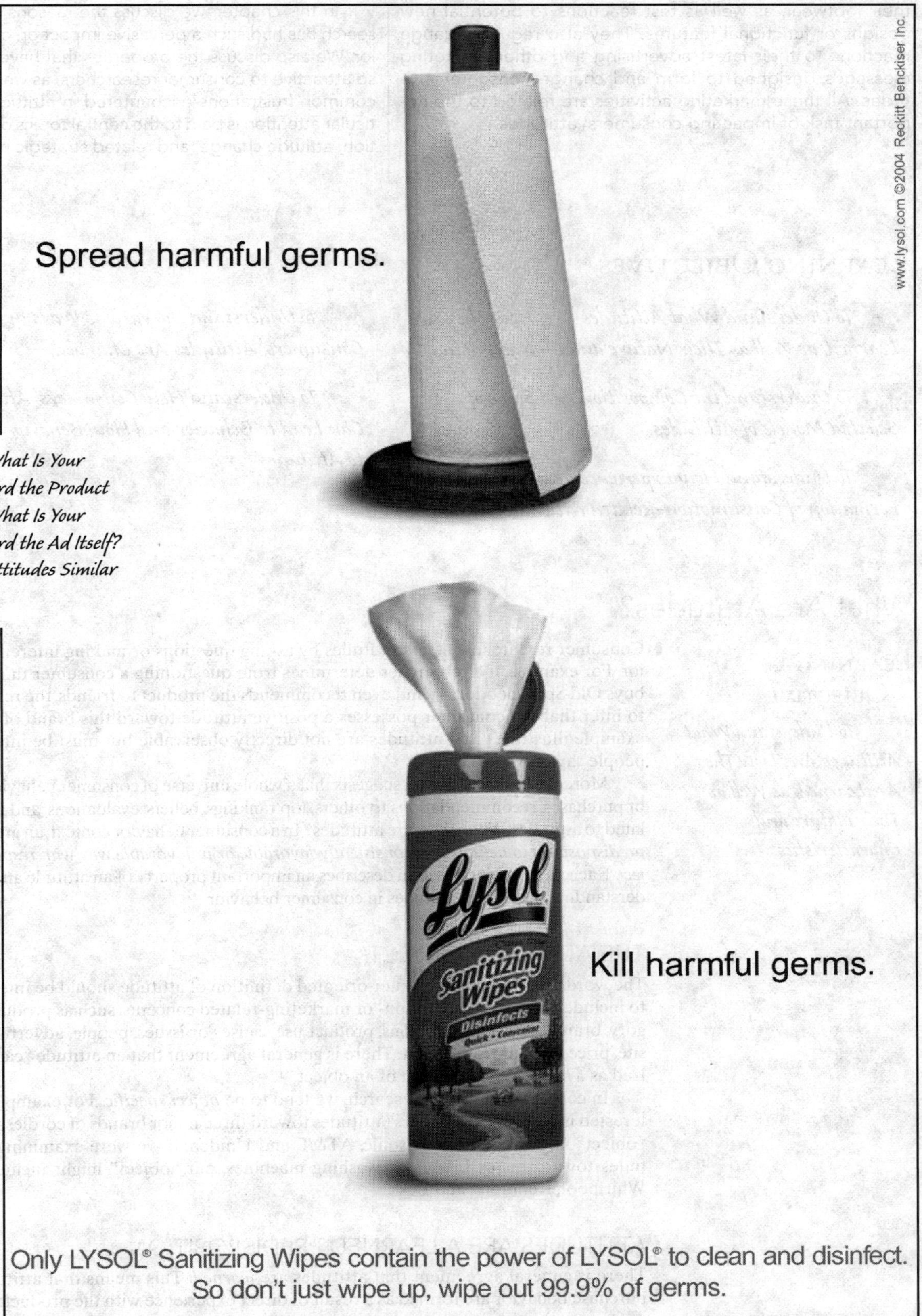

QUESTION: *What Is Your Attitude Toward the Product Advertised? What Is Your Attitude Toward the Ad Itself? Are the Two Attitudes Similar or Different?*

their footwear, as well as test reactions to potential new designs or functional features. They also regularly gauge reactions to their latest advertising and other marketing messages designed to form and change consumer attitudes. All these marketing activities are related to the important task of impacting consumers' attitudes.

In this chapter, we discuss the reasons why attitude research has had such a pervasive impact on consumer behavior. We also discuss the properties that have made attitudes so attractive to consumer researchers, as well as some of the common frustrations encountered in attitude research. Particular attention is paid to the central topics of attitude formation, attitude change, and related strategic marketing issues.

LEARNING OBJECTIVES

8.1 *To Understand What Attitudes Are, How They Are Learned, as Well as Their Nature and Characteristics.*

8.2 *To Understand the Composition and Scope of Selected Models of Attitudes.*

8.3 *To Understand How Experience Leads to the Initial Formation of Consumption-Related Attitudes.*

8.4 *To Understand the Various Ways in Which Consumers' Attitudes Are Changed.*

8.5 *To Understand How Consumers' Attitudes Can Lead to Behavior and How Behavior Can Lead to Attitudes.*

What Are Attitudes?

LEARNING OBJECTIVE

8.1 *To Understand What Attitudes Are, How They Are Learned, as Well as Their Nature and Characteristics.*

Consumer researchers assess attitudes by asking questions or making inferences from behavior. For example, if a researcher determines from questioning a consumer that he consistently buys Old Spice deodorant and even recommends the product to friends, the researcher is likely to infer that the consumer possesses a positive attitude toward this brand of deodorant. This example illustrates that attitudes are not directly observable but must be inferred from what people say or what they do.

Moreover, the illustration suggests that a whole universe of consumer behaviors—consistency of purchases, recommendations to others, top rankings, beliefs, evaluations, and intentions are related to attitudes. What, then, are attitudes? In a consumer behavior context, an **attitude** *is a learned predisposition to behave in a consistently favorable or unfavorable way with respect to a given object.* Each part of this definition describes an important property of an attitude and is critical to understanding the role of attitudes in consumer behavior.

THE ATTITUDE "OBJECT"

The word *object* in our consumer-oriented definition of attitude should be interpreted broadly to include specific consumption- or marketing-related concepts, such as product, product category, brand, service, possessions, product use, causes or issues, people, advertisement, Internet site, price, medium, or retailer. There is general agreement that an attitude "can be conceptualized as a summary evaluation of an object."[1]

In conducting attitude research, we tend to be *object specific.* For example, if we were interested in learning consumers' attitudes toward three major brands of cordless telephones, our "object" might include Panasonic, AT&T, and Uniden; if we were examining consumer attitudes toward major brands of washing machines, our "object" might include GE, Maytag, Whirlpool, Kenmore, and LG.

ATTITUDES ARE A LEARNED PREDISPOSITION

There is general agreement that attitudes are *learned.* This means that attitudes relevant to purchase behavior are formed as a result of direct experience with the product, word-of-mouth information acquired from others, or exposure to mass-media advertising, the Internet, and various forms of direct marketing (e.g., a retailer's catalog). It is important to remember that although attitudes may result from behavior, they are not synonymous with behavior. Instead, they reflect either a favorable or an unfavorable evaluation of the attitude object. As *learned predispositions,* attitudes have a motivational quality; that is, they might propel a consumer *toward* a particular behavior or repel the consumer *away* from a particular behavior.

ATTITUDES HAVE CONSISTENCY

Another characteristic of attitudes is that they are relatively consistent with the behavior they reflect. However, despite their *consistency,* attitudes are not necessarily permanent; they do change. (Attitude change is explored later in this chapter.)

It is important to illustrate what we mean by consistency. Normally, we expect consumers' behavior to correspond with their attitudes. For example, if a Mexican consumer reported preferring Japanese over Korean automobiles, we would expect that the individual would be more likely to buy a Japanese brand when his current vehicle needed to be replaced. In other words, when consumers are free to act as they wish, we anticipate that their actions will be consistent with their attitudes. However, circumstances often preclude consistency between attitudes and behavior. For example, in the case of our Mexican consumer, the matter of affordability may intervene, and the consumer would find a particular Korean car to be a more cost-effective choice than a Japanese car. Therefore, we must consider possible *situational* influences on consumer attitudes and behavior.

ATTITUDES OCCUR WITHIN A SITUATION

It is not immediately evident from our definition that attitudes occur within and are affected by the *situation.*[2] By "situation," we mean events or circumstances that, at a particular point in time, influence the relationship between an attitude and behavior. A specific situation can cause consumers to behave in ways seemingly inconsistent with their attitudes. For instance, let us assume that Margaret purchases a different brand of suntan lotion cream each time she runs low. Although her brand-switching behavior may seem to reflect a negative attitude or dissatisfaction with the brands she tries, it actually may be influenced by a specific situation, for example, her wish to economize. Thus, she will buy whatever is the least expensive brand, and it is not a matter of a negative attitude.[3]

The opposite can also be true. If Edward stays at a Hampton Inn each time he goes out of town for business, we may erroneously infer that he has a particularly favorable attitude toward Hampton Inn. On the contrary, Edward may find Hampton Inn to be "just okay." However, because he owns his own business and travels at his own expense, he may feel that Hampton Inn is "good enough," given that he may be paying less than he would be paying if he stayed at a Marriott, Sheraton, or Hilton hotel.

Indeed, consumers can have a variety of attitudes toward a particular object, each corresponding to a particular situation or application. For instance, Scott needs to replace his family's old station wagon, which is ready for the junkyard. On the one hand, he is thinking of a new SUV so he can drive his young children and their friends to after-school and weekend activities (i.e., he needs the room of an SUV in order to tote his children, their friends, and all their sports equipment). However, on the other hand, when he realizes that he would need to drive that SUV about 30 miles each way to work, he becomes concerned as to whether he really should purchase an SUV. This is especially true, given the rising cost of gasoline and that he is a high school earth science teacher who is personally committed to protecting the environment and conserving energy. He is genuinely concerned about making the right decision. One evening, while going through a magazine, he spots a magazine ad for a new Saturn Vue hybrid, (see Figure 8.2) and wonders whether this might be the solution to his dilemma. After doing a little "homework" (comparing it to other SUV hybrids), he concludes that the Saturn Vue would be a particularly good choice for him. After discussing the matter with his wife, he visited the local Saturn dealer, and after some further consideration, he purchases the new Vue hybrid.

It is important to understand how consumer attitudes vary from situation to situation. For instance, it is useful to know whether consumer preferences for various brands of hybrid SUVs

FIGURE 8.2

Source: Courtesy Saturn Car Company.

QUESTION: *What Information Does This Ad Provide to Assist Consumers in Forming Attitudes Toward the Saturn Vue Hybrid?*

(e.g., Honda CRV, Jeep Liberty, Ford Escape, and Saturn Vue) might be dependent on gas prices, miles received per amount of fuel, or a sense of "doing the right thing" (e.g., being "ecology minded"). In Scott's case, his attitudes and information-gathering process led him to select the Saturn Vue. He feels good about his decision, it provides a vehicle that enables him to take his children and their friends to their after-school and weekend activities, to get good gas mileage (important for his rather long commute to and from work), to align his purchase with his environmental concerns (important given his personal values), and to buy an American auto brand (which is an additional plus for him).

Clearly, when measuring attitudes, it is important to consider the situation in which the behavior takes place, or we can misinterpret the relationship between attitudes and behavior. Table 8.1 presents additional examples of specific situations that might influence consumer attitudes toward specific brands of products or services.

TABLE 8.1 Examples of How Situations Might Influence Attitudes

PRODUCT/SERVICE	SITUATION	ATTITUDE
Energizer Batteries	Hurricane is coming	"I know that the hurricane is going to knock out my electricity, so I'd better be prepared."
Mini Cooper	Buying a new car	"With gas prices so high, I've got to trade in my SUV and buy a car that gets 30 mpg!"
Cheerios	High cholesterol	"They've been advertising how Cheerios can lower cholesterol for so long that it must be true."
Wall Street Journal	Extra cash on hand	"I have to decide whether to invest in stocks or just put my money in a money market fund."
Delta Airlines	Friend's bachelor party	"My friend's bachelor party is in Las Vegas, and I want to be there."
Dunkin' Donuts	Need to stay awake	"I had a late date last night, but I've got a lot of work to do this morning at the office."
Stouffer's Easy Express Meals	Want dinner at home	"I'm tired of eating out night after night."

Structural Models of Attitudes

LEARNING OBJECTIVE

8.2 *To Understand the Composition and Scope of Selected Models of Attitudes.*

Motivated by a desire to understand the relationship between attitudes and behavior, psychologists have sought to construct models that capture the underlying dimensions of an attitude. To this end, the focus has been on specifying the composition of an attitude to better explain or predict behavior. The following section examines several important attitude models: the *tricomponent attitude model,* the *multiattribute attitude model,* the *trying-to-consume model,* and the *attitude-toward-the-ad model.* Each of these models provides a somewhat different perspective on the number of component parts of an attitude and how those parts are arranged or interrelated.

TRICOMPONENT ATTITUDE MODEL

According to the **tricomponent attitude model**, attitudes consist of three major components: a *cognitive* component, an *affective* component, and a *conative* component (see Figure 8.3).[4]

The Cognitive Component

The first part of the tricomponent attitude model consists of a person's *cognitions,* that is, the knowledge and perceptions that are acquired by a combination of direct experience with the *attitude object* and related information from various sources. This knowledge and resulting perceptions commonly take the form of *beliefs;* that is, the consumer believes that the attitude object possesses various attributes and that specific behavior will lead to specific outcomes.

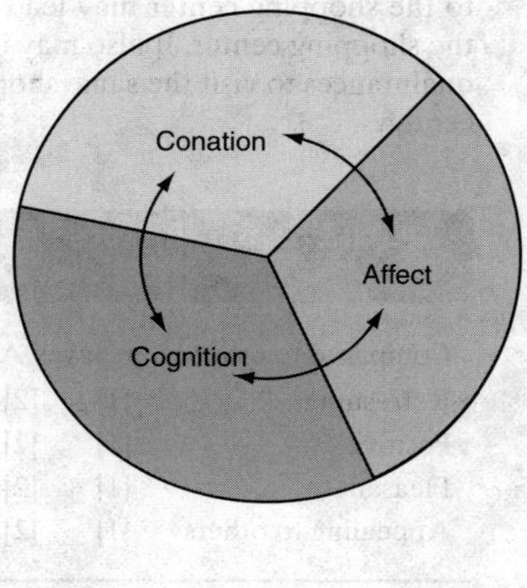

FIGURE 8.3 A Simple Representation of the Tricomponent Attitude Model

TABLE 8.2 A Consumer's Belief System for Two Types of HDTV Sets

	HDTV							
PRODUCT	**LCD**				**PLASMA**			
Brand Attributes	**Off-Angle Viewing**	**Reflectivity of Screen**	**Motion Blur**	**Color Saturation**	**Off-Angle Viewing**	**Reflectivity of Screen**	**Motion Blur**	**Color Saturation**
Beliefs	Image fades slightly from the side	Reflects less light	More than plasma	A bit worse than plasma	Excellent from all angles	Glass Screens can reflect light, so may be an issue	Negligible	Generally a bit better than LCD
Evaluations	(++)	(++++)	(−)	(++)	(++++)	(−)	(+++)	(++)

Although it captures only a part of Roy's belief system about two types of HDTV sets (e.g., LCD and plasma), Table 8.2 illustrates the composition of a consumer's belief system about these two alternatives. Roy's belief system for both types of connections consists of the same basic four attributes: off-angle viewing, screen reflectivity, motion blur, and color saturation. However, Roy has somewhat different beliefs about the two HDTV alternatives with respect to these attributes. For instance, he knows from friends that LCD HDTV set screens reflect less light (a positive), but he does not like the fact that LCD sets are subject to more blurring than plasma sets. Roy is thinking of asking a few of his friends about the differences between LCD and plasma HDTV sets and is also planning to go online to a number of Web sites that discuss this topic (e.g., **www.cnet.com**).

The Affective Component

A consumer's *emotions* or *feelings* about a particular product or brand constitute the *affective component* of an attitude.[5] These emotions and feelings are frequently treated by consumer researchers as primarily *evaluative* in nature; that is, they capture an individual's direct or global assessment of the attitude object (i.e., the extent to which the individual rates the attitude object as "favorable" or "unfavorable," "good" or "bad"). To illustrate, Table 8.3 shows a series of evaluative (affective) scale items that might be used to assess consumers' attitudes toward Aramis Aftershave (an Estée Lauder product).

Affect-laden experiences also manifest themselves as *emotionally charged states* (e.g., happiness, sadness, shame, disgust, anger, distress, guilt, or surprise). Research indicates that such emotional states may enhance or amplify positive or negative experiences and that later recollections of such experiences may impact what comes to mind and how the individual acts.[6] For instance, a person visiting a shopping center is likely to be influenced by his or her emotional state at the time. If the shopper is feeling particularly joyous at the moment, a positive response to the shopping center may be amplified. The emotionally enhanced response to the shopping center may lead the shopper to recall with great pleasure the time spent at the shopping center. It also may influence the individual shopper to persuade friends and acquaintances to visit the same shopping center and to make the personal decision to revisit the center.

TABLE 8.3 Selected Evaluative Scale Used to Gauge Consumers' Attitudes Toward Aramis Aftershave

Compared to other aftershaves, Aramis aftershave is:

Refreshing	[1]	[2]	[3]	[4]	[5]	[6]	[7]	Not refreshing
Positive	[1]	[2]	[3]	[4]	[5]	[6]	[7]	Negative
Pleasant	[1]	[2]	[3]	[4]	[5]	[6]	[7]	Unpleasant
Appealing to others	[1]	[2]	[3]	[4]	[5]	[6]	[7]	Unappealing to others

TABLE 8.4 Measuring Consumers' Feelings and Emotions with Regard to Using Aramis Aftershave

For the past 30 days you have had a chance to try Aramis Aftershave. We would appreciate it if you would identify how your face felt after using the product during this 30-day trial period. For each of the words below, we would appreciate it if you would mark an "X" in the box corresponding to how your face felt after using Aramis Aftershave during the past 30 days.

	VERY				NOT AT ALL
Relaxed	[]	[]	[]	[]	[]
Attractive looking	[]	[]	[]	[]	[]
Tight	[]	[]	[]	[]	[]
Smooth	[]	[]	[]	[]	[]
Supple	[]	[]	[]	[]	[]
Clean	[]	[]	[]	[]	[]
Refreshed	[]	[]	[]	[]	[]
Younger	[]	[]	[]	[]	[]
Revived	[]	[]	[]	[]	[]
Renewed	[]	[]	[]	[]	[]

Recent research suggests that "positive and negative forms of affect operate differently, and that their direct and indirect effects on attitudes are influenced by brand familiarity." For familiar brands, cognition mediates the impact of positive affect, while negative affect appears to have a direct impact on brand attitudes. For unfamiliar brands, "the direct effects between positive and negative affect and brand attitudes are all significant (i.e., cognition plays less of a role in attitude formation for unfamiliar brands).[7]

In addition to using direct or global evaluative measures of an attitude object, consumer researchers can also use a battery of affective response scales (e.g., that measure feelings and emotions) to construct a picture of consumers' overall feelings about a product, service, or ad. Table 8.4 gives an example of a 5-point scale that measures affective responses.

The Conative Component

Conation, the final component of the tricomponent attitude model, is concerned with the *likelihood* or *tendency* that an individual will undertake a specific action or behave in a particular way with regard to the attitude object. According to some interpretations, the conative component may include the actual behavior itself.

In marketing and consumer research, the conative component is frequently treated as an expression of the consumer's *intention to buy.* Buyer intention scales are used to assess the likelihood of a consumer purchasing a product or behaving in a certain way. Table 8.5 provides several examples of common **intention-to-buy scales**. Interestingly, consumers who are asked to respond to an intention-to-buy question appear to be more likely to actually make a brand purchase for positively evaluated brands (e.g. "I will buy it"), as contrasted to consumers who are not asked to respond to an intention question.[8] This suggests that a positive brand commitment in the form of a positive answer to an attitude intention question impacts in a positive way on the actual brand purchase.

MULTIATTRIBUTE ATTITUDE MODELS

Multiattribute attitude models portray consumers' attitudes with regard to an attitude object (e.g., a product, service, direct-mail catalog, or cause or an issue) as a function of consumers' perception and assessment of the key attributes or beliefs held with regard to the particular attitude object. Although there are many variations of this type of attitude model, we have selected the following three models to briefly consider here: the *attitude-toward-object model,* the *attitude-toward-behavior model,* and the *theory-of-reasoned-action model.*

The **attitude-toward-object model** is especially suitable for measuring attitudes toward a *product* (or *service*) category or specific *brands.*[9] According to this model, the consumer's attitude toward a product or specific brands of a product is a function of the presence (or absence)

TABLE 8.5 Two Examples of Intention-to-Buy Scales

Which of the following statements best describes the chance that you will buy Aramis Aftershave the next time you purchase an aftershave product?

_______I definitely will buy it.
_______I probably will buy it.
_______I am uncertain whether I will buy it.
_______I probably will not buy it.
_______I definitely will not buy it.

How likely are you to buy Aramis Aftershave during the next three months?

_______Very likely
_______Likely
_______Unlikely
_______Very unlikely

and evaluation of certain product-specific beliefs and/or attributes. In other words, consumers generally have favorable attitudes toward those brands that they believe have an adequate level of attributes that they evaluate as positive, and they have unfavorable attitudes toward those brands they feel do not have an adequate level of desired attributes or have too many negative or undesired attributes. As an illustration, we return to the HDTV example (see Table 8.2). Each alternative has a different "mix" of features (a "feature set"). The defining features might include available screen sizes, depth, weight, off-angle viewing, screen reflectivity, PC connectivity, motion blur, black-level performance, color saturation, resolution, and so on. For instance, one of the two types of HDTV sets might be found to excel on core features, whereas the other may be really good on a few of the core features, but offer some additional features. It is also possible that neither the current LCD nor plasma HDTV manufacturers may be more than "second rate." However, what consumers will purchase is likely to be a function of "how much they know," "what they feel are important features for them," and in the current example, their "awareness as to which type of HDTV set possesses (or lacks) the valued attributes." Supporting the "trade-off" nature of this evaluative process, a recent study of Chinese consumers' responses to the content of advertisements found that consumers tended to judge product messages both subjectively and objectively.[10]

Conducting consumer attitude research with children, especially gauging their attitudes toward products and brands, is an ongoing challenge. What is needed are new and effective measurement approaches that allow children to express their attitudes toward brands. To this end, researchers have labored to develop an especially simple and short attitude measurement instrument for questioning children between 8 and 12 years of age. In the case of the example presented in Table 8.6, the questionnaire is set up to assess children's attitudes toward the Kellogg's brand.

TABLE 8.6 A Scale Used to Measure Attitude Toward Brands for 8- to 12-Year-Olds

	DEFINITELY DISAGREE	DISAGREE	AGREE	DEFINITELY AGREE
Kellogg's—I like it.	❒	❒	❒	❒
Kellogg's—It is fun.	❒	❒	❒	❒
Kellogg's—It is great.	❒	❒	❒	❒
Kellogg's—It is useful.	❒	❒	❒	❒
Kellogg's—I like it very much.	❒	❒	❒	❒
Kellogg's—It is practical/handy.	❒	❒	❒	❒
Kellogg's—It is useless.	❒	❒	❒	❒

Source: Based on: Claude Pecheux and Christian Derbaix, "Children and Attitude Toward the Brand. A New Measurement Scale," *Journal of Advertising Research* (July/August 1999): 19–27.

The Attitude-Toward-Behavior Model

The **attitude-toward-behavior model** is designed to capture the individual's *attitude toward behaving* or *acting* with respect to an object rather than the attitude toward the object itself.[11] The appeal of the attitude-toward-behavior model is that it seems to correspond somewhat more closely to actual behavior than does the attitude-toward-object model. For instance, knowing Ralph's attitude about the act of purchasing a BMW (i.e., his attitude toward the *behavior*) reveals more about the potential act of purchasing than does simply knowing his attitude toward expensive automobiles or specifically BMW vehicles (i.e., the attitude toward the *object*). This seems logical, for a consumer might have a positive attitude toward an expensive BMW automobile but a negative attitude as to his prospects for purchasing such an expensive car.

A study conducted in China's Taiwan examined the relationship between consumer characteristics and attitude toward the behavior of online shopping. The researcher found that attitudes toward online shopping are significantly different based on various consumer behavior factors. For example, the research identified the following nine benefits of online shopping: (1) effectiveness and modern, (2) purchase convenience, (3) information abundance, (4) multiform and safety, (5) service quality, (6) delivery speed, (7) homepage design, (8) selection freedom, and (9) company name familiarity. These nine attributes were selected because they tend to reflect consumers' attitudes toward online shopping.[12] The researcher goes on to explore a model (see Figure 8.4) that suggests that *consumer characteristics* (on the left side of the model) impact *attitudes toward online shopping* (in the middle of the model—the nine attitudinal attributes listed previously) and the *rating of the online shopping experience* (on the right side of the model).

Theory-of-Reasoned-Action Model

The **theory-of-reasoned-action (TRA) model** represents a comprehensive integration of attitude components into a structure that is designed to lead to both better explanation and better predictions of behavior. Like the basic tricomponent attitude model, the theory-of-reasoned-action model incorporates a *cognitive* component, an *affective* component, and a *conative* component; however, these are arranged in a pattern different from that of the tricomponent model (see Figure 8.5).

In accordance with this expanded model, to understand *intention* we also need to measure the *subjective norms* that influence an individual's intention to act. A subjective norm can be measured directly by assessing a consumer's feelings as to what relevant others (family, friends, roommates, coworkers) would think of the action being contemplated; that is, would they look favorably or unfavorably on the anticipated action? For example, if an undergraduate student was considering getting a tattoo and stopped to ask herself what her parents or boyfriend would

FIGURE 8.4
Consumer Characteristics, Attitude, and Online Shopping

Source: Shwu-Ing Wu, "The Relationship Between Consumer Characteristics and Attitude Toward Online Shopping," *Marketing Intelligence and Planning*, 21, no. 7 (2003): 40.

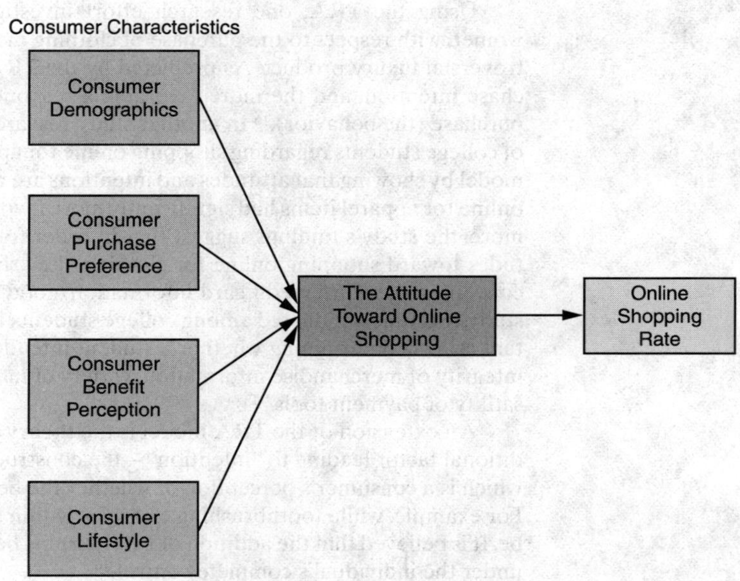

FIGURE 8.5
A Simplified Version of the Theory of Reasoned Action
Source: Adapted from Icek Ajzen and Martin Fishbein, *Understanding Attitudes and Predicting Social Behavior* (Upper Saddle River, NJ: Prentice Hall, 1980), 84. © 1980. Adapted by permission of Prentice Hall, Inc.

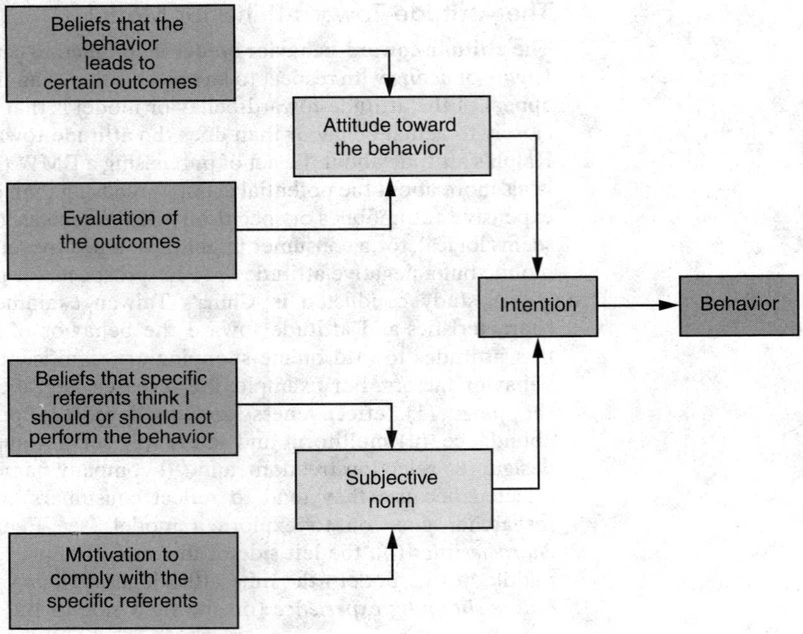

think of such behavior (i.e., approve or disapprove), such a reflection would constitute her subjective norm. In line with this model, a recent study of organic food consumption in Finland found that "the path from buying intentions of organic food to buying behavior of organic food was positive and significant."[13]

Consumer researchers can get behind the *subjective norm* to the underlying factors that are likely to produce it. They accomplish this by assessing the *normative beliefs* that the individual attributes to relevant others, as well as the individual's *motivation to comply* with each of the relevant others.[14] For instance, consider the undergraduate student contemplating a tattoo. To understand her subjective norm about the desired purchase, we would have to identify her relevant others (parents and boyfriend); her beliefs about how each would respond to her tattoo (e.g., "Mom would consider the tattoo as too gangsterish, but my boyfriend would love it"); and, finally, her motivation to comply with her parents and/or her boyfriend. A recent study also indicates that incorporating the consumer's emotional experience into the multiattribute model has the potential of enhancing the predictability of motives and preferences.[15]

Using the TRA, one research effort investigated the purchase intentions of affluent women with respect to the purchase of clothing made from American alligator leather, a controversial luxury product. As predicted by the TRA, attitude had the most influence on purchase intention, and the more favorable a respondent's attitude, the more likely she was to purchase (the behavior).[16] In another study, researchers used TRA to investigate the attitudes of college students regarding shopping online for apparel products. Results supported the TRA model by showing that attitudes and intentions are related—students with the intention to shop online for apparel items had significantly more favorable attitudes toward this activity. Furthermore, the study's findings suggest that in order for online retailers to improve students' attitudes toward shopping online for clothing, they should focus on "fit of products, good price, convenience, secure credit card information, good quality and easy return policy."[17] A similar study, this time conducted among college students in Taiwan, determined that the most important criteria determining whether a student intended to shop online were "shopping facilities, integrity of merchandise information, variety of merchandise, merchandise discounts, and versatility of payment tools."[18]

An extension of the TRA model is the **theory of planned behavior**, which includes an additional factor leading to "intention"—the construct of perceived behavioral control (PBC)—which is a consumer's perception of whether the behavior is or is not within his or her control. For example, while toothbrushing clearly is within an individual's control, weight loss may not be. It is believed that the addition of PBC permits better prediction of behaviors not completely under the individual's complete control.[19]

THEORY OF TRYING-TO-CONSUME MODEL

There has been an effort underway to extend attitude models so that they might better accommodate consumers' goals as expressed by their "trying" to consume.[20] The **theory of trying to consume** is designed to account for the many cases in which the action or outcome is not certain but instead reflects the consumer's attempts to consume (i.e., purchase). In trying to consume, there are often *personal impediments* (a consumer is trying to find just the tie to go with a newly purchased suit for under $50 or trying to lose weight but loves cookies) and/or *environmental impediments* (only the first 50 in line will be able to purchase this $200 color inkjet printer for the special Saturday 9:00 A.M. to 10:00 A.M. price of $69) that might prevent the desired action or outcome from occurring. Again, the key point is that in these cases of trying, the outcome (e.g., purchase, possession, use, or action) is not and cannot be assumed to be certain. Table 8.7 lists a few examples of possible personal and environmental impediments that might negatively impact the outcome for a consumer trying to consume. Researchers have recently extended this inquiry by examining those situations in which consumers do *not* try to consume—that is, *fail to try to consume.* In this case, consumers appear to (1) fail to see or are ignorant of their options and (2) make a conscious effort not to consume; that is, they might seek to self-sacrifice or defer gratification to some future time.[21]

ATTITUDE-TOWARD-THE-AD MODELS

In an effort to understand the impact of advertising or some other promotional vehicle (e.g., a catalog) on consumer attitudes toward particular products or brands, considerable attention has been paid to developing what has been referred to as **attitude-toward-the-ad models**.

Figure 8.6 presents a schematic of some of the basic relationships described by an attitude-toward-the ad model. As the model depicts, the consumer forms various feelings (affects) and judgments (cognitions) as the result of exposure to an ad. These feelings and judgments in turn affect the consumer's *attitude toward the ad* and *beliefs about the brand* secured from exposure to the ad. Finally, the consumer's attitude toward the ad and beliefs about the brand influence his or her *attitude toward the brand*.[22]

Research among Asian Indian U.S. immigrants have explored attitudes toward 12 advertisements and purchase intention of six different products that the ads feature. The study found a positive relationship between attitude toward the advertisement and purchase intention for each of the advertised products; that is, if consumers "like" the ad, they are more likely to purchase the product.[23] It should also be stated, though, that the utilitarian aspect of attitude-toward-the-ad can also be an important influence on purchase intention, and therefore it is important that an ad contain both subjective and objective information.[24] Another study

TABLE 8.7 Selected Examples of Potential Impediments That Might Impact on Trying

POTENTIAL PERSONAL IMPEDIMENTS

"I wonder whether my nails will be long enough by the time of my wedding so that I can have the manicure I want."

"I want to try to lose 2 inches off my waist by my birthday."

"I'm going to try to get us tickets for the Jimmy Buffet concert for our anniversary."

"I'm going to attempt to be able to run 5 miles by my birthday."

"I am going to increase how often I exercise from three to five times a week."

"Tonight I'm not going to have dessert at the restaurant."

POTENTIAL ENVIRONMENTAL IMPEDIMENTS

"The first 500 people at the football game will receive a team cap."

"Sorry, the Jaguar you ordered didn't come in from England on the ship that docked yesterday."

"There are only two cases of Merlot in our stockroom. You better come in sometime today."

"I am sorry. We cannot help you. We are closing the gas station because of an electrical outage."

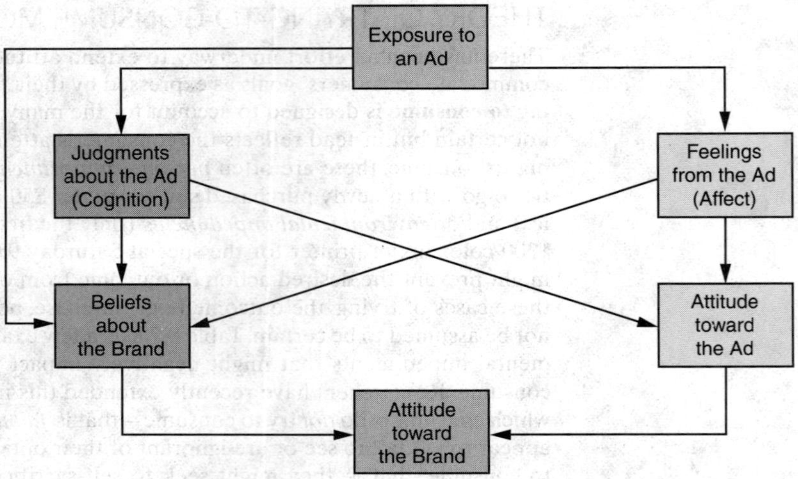

FIGURE 8.6
A Conception of the Relationship Among Elements in an Attitude-Toward-the-Ad Model
Source: Inspired by and based on Julie A. Edell and Marian Chapman Burke, "The Power of Feelings in Understanding Advertising Effects," *Journal of Consumer Research*, 14 (December 1987): 431. Reprinted by permission of University of Chicago Press as publisher.

explored general attitudes toward advertising in Bulgaria and Romania, the European Union's two recent member states. The research found that consumers in these two nations were more positive about the institution of advertising than they were to the instruments (i.e., techniques) used to promote advertising. Furthermore, while the main personal use of advertising in Bulgaria was information acquisition, the entertainment value of advertising was the strongest personal use in Romania.[25]

A study conducted in New Zealand examined when and why consumers were offended by advertisements. The research examined over 300 complaint reports that referred to ads, and concluded that: (1) consumers were more likely to be offended by an ad's offensive theme, than by the actual good, service, or idea being advertised; (2) some advertising themes were inherently more offensive than others; and (3) the more intrusive the media delivering the ad, the greater the odds were that the ad was considered offensive (e.g., direct mail was considered a more offensive media than magazine).[26]

Finally, consumer socialization has also shown itself to be an important determinant of a consumer's attitudes toward advertising. One study, for example, found that parental communication, peer communication, social utility of advertising, amount of television watched, gender, and race were all associated with attitude toward advertising. African Americans and women were found to have more positive attitudes toward advertising.[27]

Attitude Formation

LEARNING OBJECTIVE

8.3 *To Understand How Experience Leads to the Initial Formation of Consumption-Related Attitudes.*

How do people, especially young people, form their initial *general* attitudes toward "things"? Consider their attitudes toward clothing they wear, for example, underwear, casual wear, and business attire. On a more specific level, how do they form attitudes toward Hanes or Calvin Klein underwear, or Eddie Bauer or Gap casual wear, or Anne Klein or Brooks Brothers business clothing? Also, what about where such clothing is purchased? Would they buy their underwear, casual wear, and business clothing at Wal-Mart, Sears, Saks Fifth Avenue, or Nordstrom? How do family members and friends, admired celebrities, mass-media advertisements, even cultural memberships, influence the formation of their attitudes concerning consuming or not consuming each of these types of apparel items? Why do some attitudes seem to persist indefinitely while others change fairly often? The answers to such questions are of vital importance to marketers, for without knowing how attitudes are formed, they are unable to understand or to influence consumer attitudes or behavior.

Our examination of attitude formation is divided into three areas: *how attitudes are learned,* the *sources of influence* on attitude formation, and the impact of *personality* on attitude formation.

HOW ATTITUDES ARE LEARNED

When we speak of the formation of an attitude, we refer to the shift from having no attitude toward a given object (e.g., noise-canceling headphones) to having *some* attitude toward it (e.g.,

FIGURE 8.7

Source: Advertisement reprinted with the permission of Nestlé. LEAN CUISINE® is a registered trademark of Société des Produits Nestlé S.A., Vevey, Switzerland.

QUESTION: *How Does a Favorably Known Brand Name Impact the Formation of Consumer Attitudes Toward a New Product Introduced Under the Same Brand?*

noise-canceling headphones are great when listening to music or watching a movie on an airplane). The shift from no attitude to an attitude (i.e., the *attitude formation*) is a result of learning (see Chapter 7 for detailed exploration of consumer behavior and learning theories).

Consumers often purchase new products that are associated with a favorably viewed brand name. Their favorable attitude toward the brand name is frequently the result of repeated satisfaction with other products produced by the same company. In terms of *classical conditioning,* an established brand name is an *unconditioned* stimulus that through past positive reinforcement resulted in a favorable brand attitude. A new product, yet to be linked to the established brand, would be the *conditioned* stimulus. To illustrate, Société des Produits Nestlé S.A., by giving its new Chicken Tuscan Panini the benefit of its well-known and respected family name Lean Cuisine, is expecting a transfer of the favorable attitude already associated by the Lean Cuisine brand name to the new product (see Figure 8.7). They are counting on stimulus generalization from the Lean Cuisine brand names to the new product. Research suggests that the "fit" between a brand name (e.g., in this case Lean Cuisine) and a brand extension (e.g., in this case the Chicken Tuscan Panini) is likely to be quite a good fit.[28]

Sometimes attitudes *follow* the purchase and consumption of a product. For example, a consumer may purchase a brand-name product *without* having a prior attitude toward it because it is the only product of its kind available (e.g., the last disposable razor in a gas station mini-mart). Consumers also make trial purchases of new brands from product categories in which they have little personal involvement (see Chapter 7). If they find the purchased brand to meet or exceed their expectations, then they are likely to develop a favorable attitude toward it.

In situations in which consumers seek to solve a problem or satisfy a need, they are likely to form attitudes (either positive or negative) about products on the basis of information exposure and their own cognition (knowledge and beliefs). In general, the more information consumers have about a product or service, the more likely they are to form attitudes about it, either positive or negative. However, regardless of available information, consumers are not always ready or willing to process product-related information. Furthermore, consumers often use only a limited amount of the information available to them. Specifically, only two or three important beliefs about a product are likely to dominate in the formation of attitudes, and less important beliefs provide little additional input.[29] This suggests that marketers should fight off the impulse to include *all* the features of their products and services in their ads; rather, they should focus on the few key points that are at the heart of what distinguishes their product from the competition.

SOURCES OF INFLUENCE ON ATTITUDE FORMATION

The formation of consumer attitudes is strongly influenced by *personal experience,* the *influence* of family and friends, *direct marketing, mass media,* and the *Internet.*

A primary means by which attitudes toward goods and services are formed is through the consumer's direct experience in trying and evaluating them.[30] Recognizing the importance of direct experience, marketers frequently attempt to stimulate trial for products by offering cents-off coupons or even free samples. Figure 8.8 illustrates this strategy; the ad for Sweet'N Low, which includes a cents-off coupon for any box of the zero calorie sweeter. In such cases, the marketer's objective is to get new consumers to try and evaluate the product, and reward existing customers. For new customers, if a product proves to be to their liking, then it is likely that they will form a positive attitude and be more likely to repurchase the product.

As we come in contact with others, especially family, close friends, and admired individuals (e.g., a respected teacher), we form attitudes that influence our lives. The family is an extremely important source of influence on the formation of attitudes, for it is the family that provides us with many of our basic values and a wide range of less central beliefs. For instance, young children who are rewarded for good behavior with sweet foods and candy often retain a taste for (and positive attitude toward) sweets as adults.

Marketers are increasingly using highly focused direct-marketing programs to target small consumer niches with products and services that fit their interests and lifestyles. (Niche marketing is sometimes called *micromarketing.*) Marketers very carefully target customers on the basis of their demographic, psychographic, or geodemographic profiles with highly personalized product offerings (e.g., watches for left-handed people) and messages that show they understand their special needs and desires. Direct-marketing efforts have an excellent chance of favorably influencing target consumers' attitudes, because the products and services offered and the promotional messages conveyed are very carefully designed to address the individual segment's needs and concerns and, thus, are able to achieve a higher "hit rate" than mass marketing.

In countries where people have easy access to newspapers and a variety of general and special-interest magazines and television channels, consumers are constantly exposed to new ideas, products, opinions, and advertisements. These mass-media communications provide an important source of information that influences the formation of consumer attitudes. Other research indicates that for consumers who lack direct experience with a product, exposure to an emotionally appealing advertising message is more likely to create an attitude toward the product than for consumers who have beforehand secured direct experience with the product category.[31] The net implications of these findings appear to be that emotional appeals are most effective with consumers who lack product experience.

Still another issue with regard to evaluating the impact of advertising messages on attitude formation is the level of realism that is provided. Research has shown that attitudes that develop through *direct experience* (e.g., product usage) tend to be more confidently held, more enduring, and more resistant to attack than those developed via *indirect experience* (e.g., reading a print ad). And just as television provided the advertiser with more realism than is possible in

FIGURE 8.8
Source: forms@cpack.com.

QUESTION: *How Does a Cents-Off Coupon Impact Consumers' Attitudes?*

a radio or print ad, the Internet has an even greater ability to provide "telepresence," which is the simulated perception of direct experience. The Internet also has the ability to provide the "flow experience," which is a cognitive state occurring when the individual is so involved in an activity that nothing else matters. Research on telepresence suggests that "perceptions of telepresence grew stronger as levels of interactivity and levels of vividness (i.e., the way an environment presents information to the senses) of web sites increased."[32]

PERSONALITY FACTORS

Personality also plays a critical role in attitude formation. For example, individuals with a *high need for cognition* (i.e., those who crave information and enjoy thinking) are likely to form positive attitudes in response to ads or direct mail that are rich in product-related information. On the other hand, consumers who are relatively *low in need for cognition* are more likely to form positive attitudes in response to ads that feature an attractive model or well-known celebrity. In a similar fashion, attitudes toward new products and new consumption situations are strongly influenced by specific personality characteristics of consumers.

Strategies of Attitude Change

LEARNING OBJECTIVE

8.4 *To Understand the Various Ways in Which Consumers' Attitudes Are Changed.*

It is important to recognize that much of what has been said about *attitude formation* is also basically true of attitude change. That is, attitude changes are *learned;* they are influenced by *personal experience* and other *sources of information,* and *personality* affects both the receptivity and the speed with which attitudes are likely to be altered.

Altering consumer attitudes is a key strategy consideration for most marketers. For marketers who are fortunate enough to be market leaders and to enjoy a significant amount of customer goodwill and loyalty, the overriding goal is to fortify the existing positive attitudes of customers so that they will not succumb to competitors' special offers and other inducements designed to win them over. For instance, in many product categories (e.g., laundry detergent, in which Tide has been the leader, or sneakers, in which Nike has dominated), most competitors take aim at the market leaders when developing their marketing strategies. Their objective is to change the attitudes of the market leaders' customers and win them over. Among the *attitude-change strategies* that are available to them are (1) changing the consumer's basic motivational function, (2) associating the product with an admired group or event, (3) resolving two conflicting attitudes, (4) altering components of the multiattribute model, and (5) changing consumer beliefs about competitors' brands.

CHANGING THE BASIC MOTIVATIONAL FUNCTION

An effective strategy for changing consumer attitudes toward a product or brand is to make particular needs prominent. One method for changing motivation is known as the **functional approach**.[33] According to this approach, attitudes can be classified in terms of four functions: the **utilitarian function**, the **ego-defensive function**, the **value-expressive function**, and the **knowledge function**.

The Utilitarian Function

We hold certain brand attitudes partly because of a brand's utility. When a product has been useful or helped us in the past, our attitude toward it tends to be favorable. One way of changing attitudes in favor of a product is by showing people that it can serve a utilitarian purpose that they may not have considered. For example, the ad for new Green Works™ (Figure 8.9) points out that the 99 percent natural cleaner either works as well or better than conventional cleaners; and it is good for the environment.

The Ego-Defensive Function

Most people want to protect their self-images from inner feelings of doubt—they want to replace their uncertainty with a sense of security and personal confidence.[34] Ads for cosmetics and fashion clothing, by acknowledging this need, increase both their relevance to the consumer and the likelihood of a favorable attitude change by offering reassurance to the consumer's self-concept.

The Value-Expressive Function

Attitudes are an expression or reflection of the consumer's general values, lifestyle, and outlook. If a consumer segment generally holds a positive attitude toward owning the latest designer jeans, then their attitudes toward new brands of designer jeans are likely to reflect that orientation. Similarly, if a segment of consumers has a positive attitude toward being "high tech," then their attitudes toward thin wall-mountable HDTV sets are likely to reflect this viewpoint. Thus, by knowing target consumers' attitudes, marketers can better anticipate their values, lifestyle, or outlook and can reflect these characteristics in their advertising and direct-marketing efforts. The print ad for Mott's Healthy Harvest line of all-natural fruit flavored apple sauces in Figure 8.10, states: "Treat yourself healthy." The headline and the woman enjoying a spoonful of the product are consistent with a lifestyle that includes healthy eating and snacking.

The Knowledge Function

Individuals generally have a strong need to know and understand the people and things they encounter. The consumer's "need to know," a cognitive need, is important to marketers concerned with product positioning. Indeed, many product and brand positionings are attempts to satisfy the *need to know* and to improve the consumer's attitudes toward the brand by emphasizing its advantages over competitive brands. For instance, a message for a new OTC allergy

FIGURE 8.9

Source: Courtesy of the Clorox Company.

QUESTION: *Why and How Does This Ad Appeal to the Utilitarian Function?*

medication might point out how it is superior to other OTC allergy medications in alleviating the symptoms of allergies. The message might even use a bar graph to contrast its allergy symptom relief abilities to other leading allergy medications. Figure 8.11 is an ad for Neutrogena® that raised the question, "SPF measures UVB rays, but what about UVA rays?" The remainder of the magazine print ad goes on to answer the question, and thereby provides product and sun protection information to guide consumers in their seeking of more knowledge about the subject. Finally, note that this advertisement uses a bar graph to help present the case for being concerned about the two types of sun protection.

Combining Several Functions

Because different consumers may like or dislike the same product or service for different reasons, a functional framework for examining attitudes can be very useful. For instance, three consumers may all have positive attitudes toward Suave hair care products. However, one may be responding solely to the fact that the products work well (the utilitarian function); the second may have the inner confidence to agree with the point "When you know beautiful hair

FIGURE 8.10

Source: Mott's® is a registered trademark of Mott's LLP.

QUESTION: *Which Lifestyle-Related Attitudes Are Expressed or Reflected in This Ad?*

doesn't have to cost a fortune" (an ego-defensive function). The third consumer's favorable attitudes might reflect the realization that Suave has for many years stressed value (equal or better products for less)—the *knowledge function*.

ASSOCIATING THE PRODUCT WITH A SPECIAL GROUP, EVENT, OR CAUSE

Attitudes are related, at least in part, to certain groups, social events, or causes. It is possible to alter attitudes toward companies and their products, services, and brands by pointing out their relationships to particular social groups, events, or causes. For instance, Payless ShoeSource® has a partnering relationship with the American Ballet Theatre™, whereby it carries quality dance products at particularly reasonable prices, at its Payless stores. Similarly, Figure 8.12 presents an ad that shows thatYoplait yogurt supports the fight against breast cancer by making a 10-cent contribution for every unit of its yogurt sold that has a pink ribbon printed on its lid.

FIGURE 8.11
Source: Courtesy of Neutrogena, Inc.

QUESTION: *How Does This Ad Provide Information to Establish or Reinforce Consumer Attitudes?*

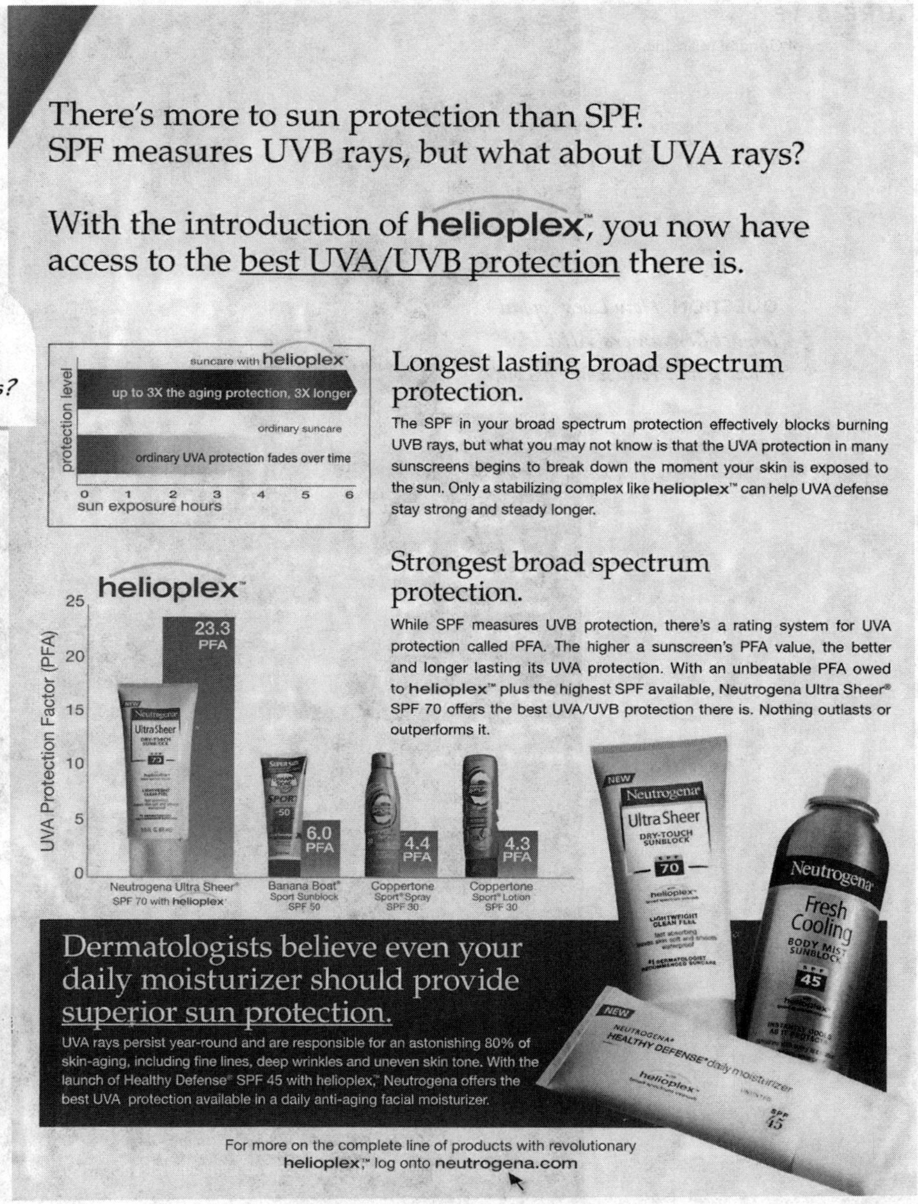

Recent research into brand-cause alliances has investigated the relationship between the "cause" and the "sponsor." The findings of one study found that while both the brand and the cause benefit from such alliances, a *low familiar cause* benefited more from its association with a positive brand than did a *highly familiar cause*.[35] The results of another study further suggests that if corporate sponsors fail to explicitly indicate their motives for a company-cause or a product-cause association, it is likely that consumers will form their own motives for the association between the company, product or service, and the cause.[36] This finding seems to indicate that it is likely to be a good idea for a sponsor to reveal to target consumers the reasoning behind their sponsorship, so that consumers know the sponsor's motives rather than form their own potentially inaccurate or negative motives. To this end, the ad in Figure 8.13 specifically states that Fiji Water is committed to working with Conservation International to help protect Fiji's (the island) largest lowland rainforest, because it is a way to give back to the environment, and there is a win-win outcome.

FIGURE 8.12
Source: Courtesy of General Mills, Inc.

QUESTION: *How Does Yoplait Impact Consumers' Attitudes Toward Its Product in This Ad?*

RESOLVING TWO CONFLICTING ATTITUDES

Attitude-change strategies can sometimes resolve actual or potential conflict between two attitudes. Specifically, if consumers can be made to see that their negative attitude toward a product, a specific brand, or its attributes is really not in conflict with another attitude, they may be induced to change their evaluation of the brand (i.e., moving from negative to positive). For example, Richard is an amateur photographer who has been thinking of moving from his point-and-shoot digital camera to a digital single lens reflex (DSLR) camera in order to take better pictures and to be able to change lenses. However, with the recent improvements in point-and-shoot cameras, Richard is unsure of whether his move to a DSLR camera will be worthwhile. Richard loves the idea of having the ability to change lenses (attitude 1), but he may feel that purchasing a DSLR camera is an unwise investment because these cameras may be supplanted in the near future by newer types of cameras (attitude 2). However, if Richard learns that Olympus and Panasonic are developing a "micro four-thirds format" small point-and-shoot-size cameras that will offer interchangeable lenses, he might change his mind and thereby resolve his conflicting attitudes.

FIGURE 8.13
Source: Courtesy Fiji Water.

QUESTION: *How Is Fiji Water's Link to an Environmental Cause Likely to Impact Consumers' Attitudes Toward Its Product?*

ALTERING COMPONENTS OF THE MULTIATTRIBUTE MODEL

Earlier in this chapter we discussed a number of multiattribute attitude models. These models have implications for attitude-change strategies; specifically, they provide us with additional insights as to how to bring about attitude change: (1) changing the relative evaluation of attributes, (2) changing brand beliefs, (3) adding an attribute, and (4) changing the overall brand rating.

Changing the Relative Evaluation of Attributes

The overall market for many product categories is often set out so that different consumer segments are offered different brands with different features or benefits. For instance, within a product category such as deodorants, there are brands such as Mitchum that stress potency and brands such as Secret that stress gentleness. These two brands of deodorant have historically appealed to different segments of the overall deodorant market. Similarly, when it comes to coffee, the market can be divided into regular coffee, flavored coffee (e.g., hazelnut), and decaffeinated coffee, or when it comes to headache remedies, there is the division between aspirin (e.g., Bayer), acetaminophen (e.g., Tylenol), and naproxen sodium (e.g., Aleve).

In general, when a product category is naturally divided according to distinct product features or benefits that appeal to a particular segment of consumers, marketers usually have an opportunity to persuade consumers to "cross over," that is, to persuade consumers who prefer one version of the product (e.g., standard bifocal eyeglass lenses) to shift their favorable attitudes toward another version of the product (e.g., progressive bifocal lenses).

Changing Brand Beliefs

A second cognitive-oriented strategy for changing attitudes concentrates on changing beliefs or perceptions about the brand itself. This is by far the most common form of advertising appeal. Advertisers constantly are reminding us that their product has "more" or is "better" or "best" in terms of some important product attribute. As a variation on this theme of "more," ads for Palmolive dishwashing liquid are designed to *extend* consumers' brand attitudes with regard to the product's gentleness by suggesting that it be used for hand washing of fine clothing items. Yet, another example would be an ad for Kraft's Miracle Whip that indicates that it makes for a better turkey sandwich than does mayonnaise. To support such a claim, it might points out that Miracle Whip has "more flavor and half the fat" of mayonnaise.

Within the context of brand beliefs, there are forces working to stop or slow down attitude change. For instance, consumers frequently resist evidence that challenges a strongly held attitude or belief and tend to interpret any ambiguous information in ways that reinforce their preexisting attitudes.[37] Therefore, information suggesting a change in attitude needs to be compelling and repeated enough to overcome the natural resistance to letting go of established attitudes.

Adding an Attribute

Another cognitive strategy consists of *adding an attribute.* This can be accomplished either by adding an attribute that previously has been ignored or one that represents an improvement or technological innovation.

The first route, adding a previously ignored or unknown attribute or benefit, is illustrated by the point that yogurt has more potassium than a banana (a fruit associated with a high quantity of potassium). For consumers interested in increasing their intake of potassium, the comparison of yogurt and bananas has the power of enhancing their attitudes toward yogurt. Figure 8.14 contains an ad for Listerine® Antiseptic that presents a newly identified potential benefit for its product. Specifically, it notes that "science suggests that there may be a link between the health of your mouth and the health of your whole body." This ad also illustrates the first route to adding an attribute to influence brand or product attitudes.

The second route of adding an attribute reflects an actual product change or technological innovation is easier to accomplish than stressing a previously ignored attribute. To illustrate, imagine Wish-Bone® Salad Spritzer™, which provides a pump device that allows a consumer to spray a mist of dressing on a salad, thus allowing consumers to more precisely control how much dressing they put on their salads.

Sometimes eliminating a characteristic or feature has the same enhancing outcome as adding a characteristic or attribute. For instance, a number of skin care or deodorant manufacturers offer versions of their products that are unscented (i.e., *deleting an ingredient*). For example, NIVEA for Men markets an unscented and alcohol-free version of its aftershave balm. Another example of removing a product attribute is depicted in Figure 8.15, where Gummy Bear Vitamins stresses that it has no artificial colors, flavors, or preservatives.

Changing the Overall Brand Rating

Still another cognitive-oriented strategy consists of attempting to alter consumers' *overall assessment of the brand* directly, without attempting to improve or change their evaluation of any single brand attribute. Such a strategy frequently relies on some form of global statement that "this is the largest-selling brand" or "the one all others try to imitate," or a similar claim that sets the brand apart from all its competitors. For instance, when Verizon Wireless mentions in many of its marketing communications that it is "America's Most Reliable Wireless Network," it is applying the strategy of changing the overall brand rating in the minds of its target consumers and it current customers (see Figure 8.16).

FIGURE 8.14

Source: Listerine® is a registered trademark of Johnson & Johnson. Used with permission.

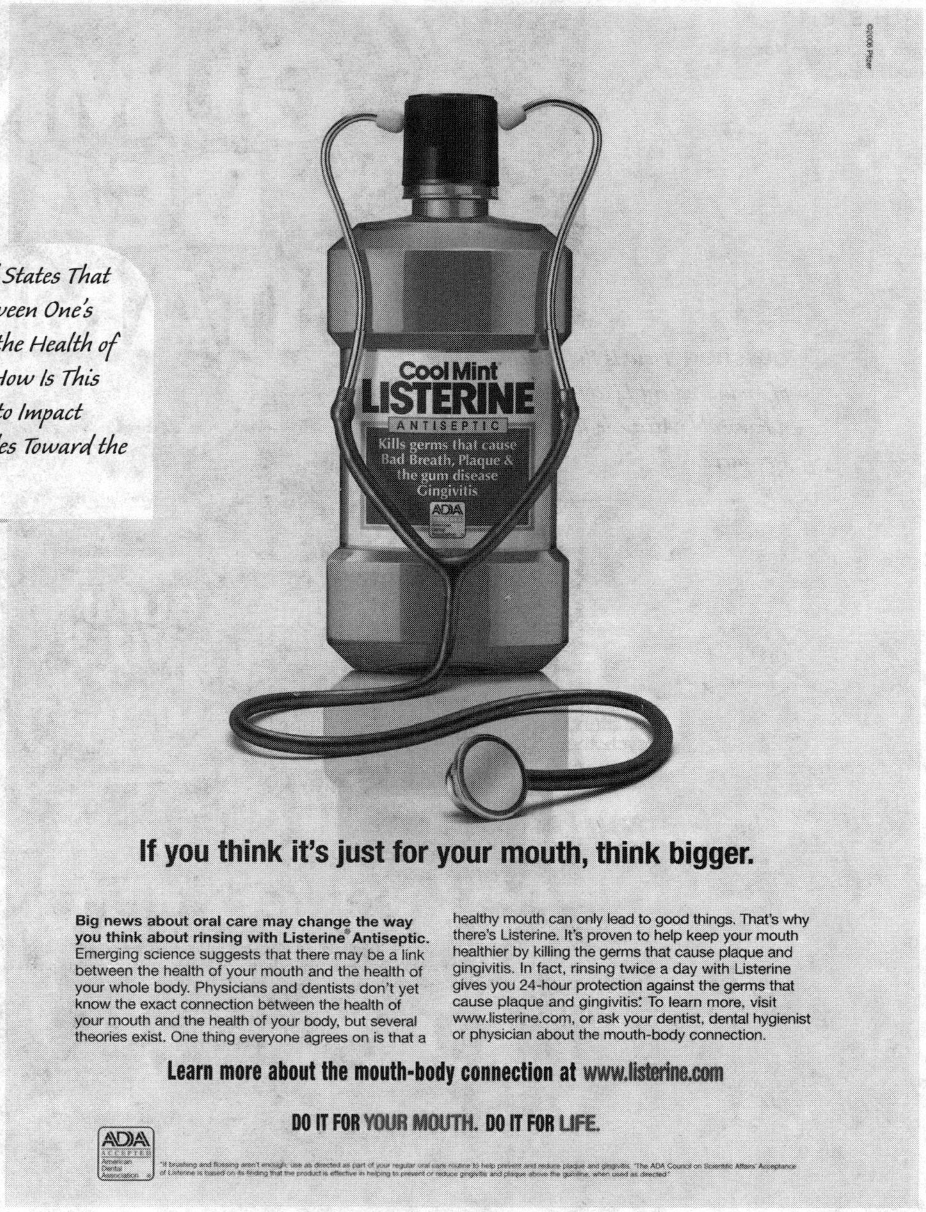

QUESTION: *The Ad States That There Is a Link Between One's Mouth Health and the Health of One's Whole Body. How Is This New Benefit Likely to Impact Consumers' Attitudes Toward the Product?*

CHANGING BELIEFS ABOUT COMPETITORS' BRANDS

Another approach to the attitude-change strategy involves changing consumer beliefs about the *attributes of competitive* brands or product categories. For instance, an advertisement for Eclipse chewing gum makes a dramatic assertion of product superiority over other gums by claiming that "Most other gums just mask bad breath. We kill the germs that cause it." Similarly, Caltrate calcium supplement claims that one of its tablets contains nearly twice the calcium of Citracel (a principal competitor). Still further, Valvoline® SynPower full synthetic 5W-30 motor oil claims superiority in terms of "better wear protection than its major competitor" Mobil 1 (see Figure 8.17). While potentially very effective, such comparative advertising can boomerang by giving visibility to a competing brand and their claims.

FIGURE 8.15

Source: Courtesy of Northwest Natural Products.

QUESTION: *How Is the Absence of an Ingredient Likely to Lead to a Favorable Attitude Toward a Product?*

THE ELABORATION LIKELIHOOD MODEL (ELM)

Compared to the various specific strategies of attitude change that we have reviewed, the **elaboration likelihood model (ELM)** proposes the more global view that consumer attitudes are changed by two distinctly different "routes to persuasion": a central route or a peripheral route (see also Chapter 7).[38] The *central route* is particularly relevant to attitude change when a consumer's motivation or ability to assess the attitude object is *high;* that is, attitude change occurs because the consumer actively seeks out information relevant to the attitude object itself. When consumers are willing to exert the effort to comprehend, learn, or evaluate the available information about the attitude object, learning and attitude change occur via the central route. Additionally, recent research has found that even such largely cognitive processing can have an emotional core.[39]

In contrast, when a consumer's motivation or assessment skills are low (e.g., low involvement), learning and attitude change tend to occur via the *peripheral route* without the consumer focusing on information relevant to the attitude object itself. In such cases, attitude change often is an outcome of secondary inducements (e.g., cents-off coupons, free samples, beautiful

FIGURE 8.16

Source: Courtesy of Verizon Wireless.

QUESTION: *Which Attitude Change Strategy Is Depicted in This Ad?*

background scenery, great packaging, or the encouragement of a celebrity endorsement). Research indicates that even in low-involvement conditions (e.g., such as exposure to most advertising), in which both central and secondary inducements are initially equal in their ability to evoke similar attitudes, it is the central inducement that has the greatest "staying power"—that is, over time it is more persistent. Additionally, for subjects low in product knowledge, advertisements with terminology result in the consumer having a better attitude toward the brand and the ad.[40] Figure 8.18 presents the elaboration likelihood model of persuasion, and shows that both central variables and peripheral variables impact a consumer's depth of information processing.

An offshoot of the ELM is the *dual mediation model (DMM)*. The DMM adds a link between attitude toward the ad and brand cognitions.[41] It acknowledges the possibility that the central route to persuasion could be influenced by a peripheral cue (i.e., attitude toward the ad). Thus, this model demonstrates the interrelationship between the central and peripheral processes. This model has recently been used in a research study that concluded that an advertisement's effect is important in the formation of an attitude, and therefore the DMM can be employed to explain how advertising impacts consumer behavior.[42]

FIGURE 8.17
Source: Courtesy of Valvoline, a division of Ashland Inc.

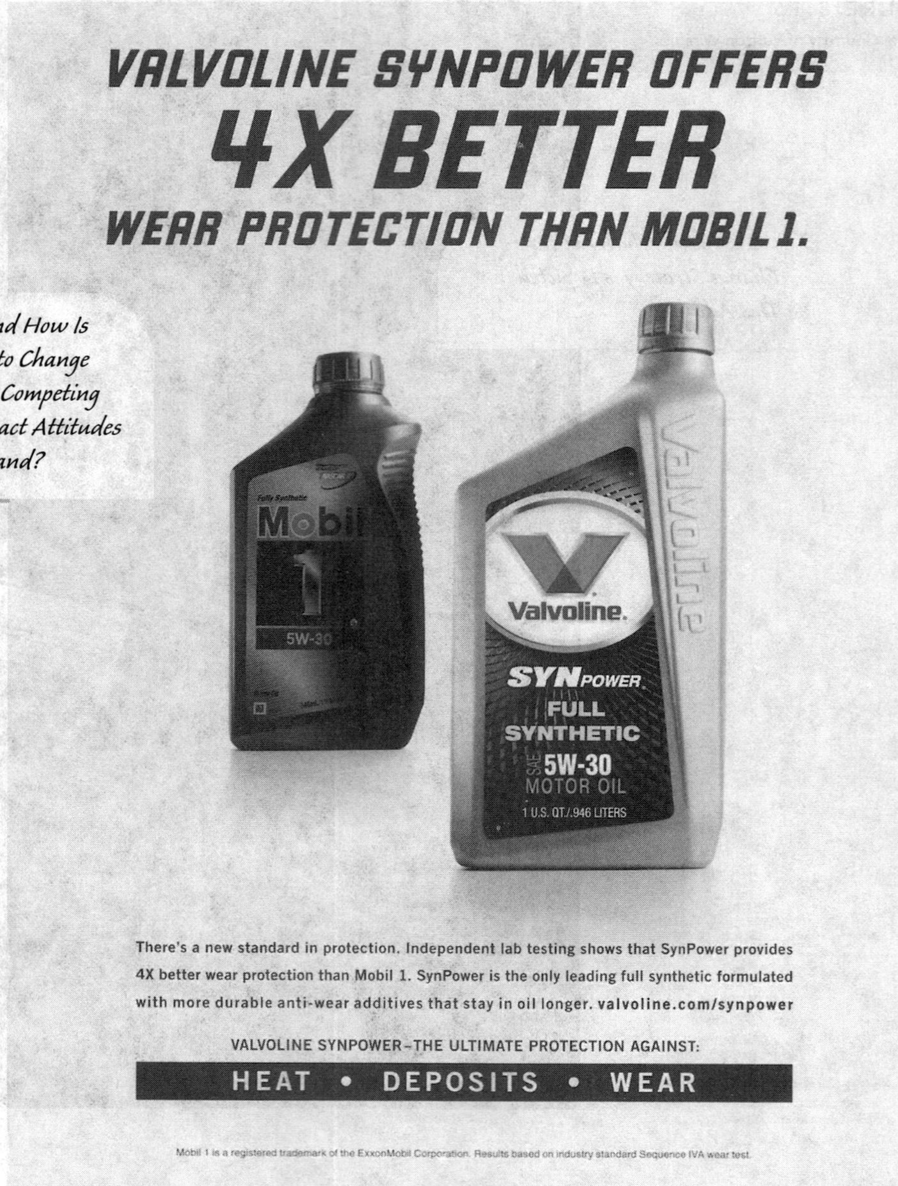

QUESTION: *Why and How Is Valvoline's Attempt to Change Attitudes Toward a Competing Brand Likely to Impact Attitudes Toward Its Own Brand?*

Behavior Can Precede or Follow Attitude Formation

LEARNING OBJECTIVE

8.5 *To Understand How Consumers' Attitudes Can Lead to Behavior and How Behavior Can Lead to Attitudes.*

Our discussion of attitude formation and attitude change has stressed the traditional "rational" view that consumers develop their attitudes before taking action (e.g., "Know what you are doing before you do it"). There are alternatives to this "attitude precedes behavior" perspective, alternatives that, on careful analysis, are likely to be just as logical and rational. For example, *cognitive dissonance theory* and *attribution theory* each provide a different explanation as to why behavior might precede attitude formation.

COGNITIVE DISSONANCE THEORY

According to **cognitive dissonance theory**, discomfort or dissonance occurs when a consumer holds conflicting thoughts about a belief or an attitude object. For instance, when consumers have made a commitment—made a down payment or placed an order for a product, particu-

FIGURE 8.18
Elaboration Likelihood Model (ELM) of Persuasion

Source: Kar Yan Tam and Shuk Ting Ho, "Web Personalization as a Persuasion Strategy: An Elaboration Likelihood Model Perspective," *Information Systems Research*, 16, no. 3 (September 2005): 274.

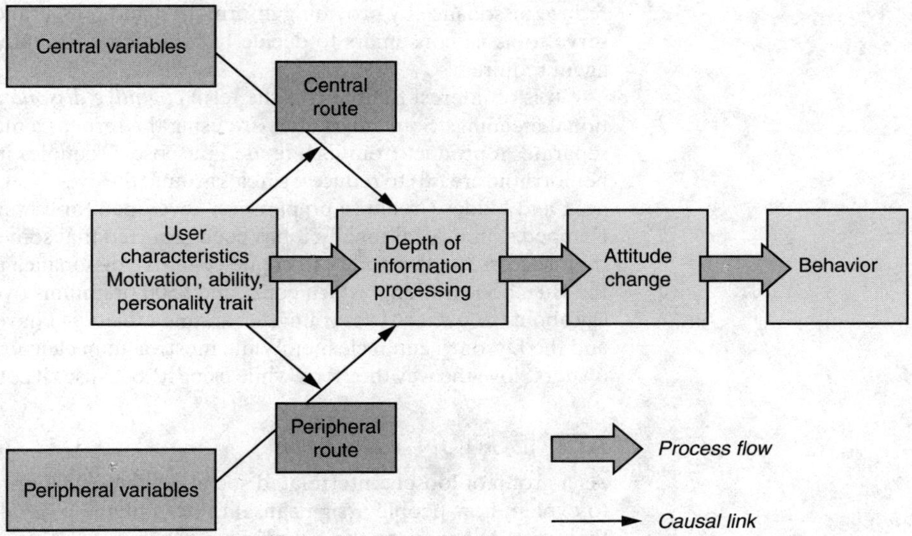

larly an expensive one such as an automobile or a personal computer—they often begin to feel cognitive dissonance *when they think of the unique, positive qualities of the brands not selected ("left behind")*. When cognitive dissonance occurs after a purchase, it is called *postpurchase dissonance.* Because purchase decisions often require some amount of compromise, postpurchase dissonance is quite normal. Nevertheless, it is likely to leave consumers with an uneasy feeling about their prior beliefs or actions—a feeling that they would seek to resolve by changing their attitudes to conform to their behavior.[43]

Thus, in the case of postpurchase dissonance, attitude change is frequently an *outcome* of an action or behavior. The conflicting thoughts and dissonant information following a purchase are prime factors that induce consumers to change their attitudes so that they will be consonant with their actual purchase behavior.

What makes postpurchase dissonance relevant to marketing strategists is the premise that *dissonance* propels consumers to reduce the unpleasant feelings created by the rival thoughts. A variety of tactics are open to consumers to reduce postpurchase dissonance. The consumer can rationalize the decision as being wise, seek out advertisements that support the choice (while avoiding dissonance-creating competitive ads), try to "sell" friends on the positive features of the brand (i.e., *"the consumer as a sales agent"*), or look to known satisfied owners for reassurance. For example, consider the response of a young man who just purchased an engagement ring for his girlfriend to the following ad headline he spots in a magazine: "How can you make two months' salary last forever?" This thought is likely to catch his attention. It says to him that although an engagement ring costs a great deal of money, it lasts forever because the future bride will cherish it for the rest of her life. Such ad exposure is bound to help him reduce any lingering dissonance that he might have about how much he just spent on the ring.

While it has traditionally been viewed, with respect to a particular purchase, that cognitive dissonance was something that a consumer either had or did not have, a recent study found that there can exist different types and levels of dissonance. The research studied consumer durable purchases, and found three distinct segments of consumers: a high dissonance segment, a low dissonance segment, and a "concerned about needing the purchase" segment.[44] In addition to such consumer-initiated tactics for reducing postpurchase uncertainty, marketers can help consumers relieve their dissonance by including messages in their advertising specifically aimed at reinforcing consumers' decisions by complimenting their wisdom, offering stronger guarantees or warranties, increasing the number and effectiveness of its services, or providing detailed brochures on how to use its products correctly. However, with respect to product and service advertisements, there is evidence that as many as 75 percent of Americans feel that advertisers, on purpose, stretch the truth about their products in their advertising.[45] A recent study also suggests that dissonance can be created by a retailer's sales staff, because the consumer may feel that he or she was "persuaded" into the purchase. Conversely, a store's sales staff can reduce dissonance by providing information and reassurance.[46] Such positive support can also serve to assist consumers to decide to repurchase the same product, when such a product is again required.

It is of interest to note that the term *cognitive dissonance* has recently taken on two additional meanings. Some marketers are using the term as a manipulative marketing strategy that separates a product from its intended purpose. Examples include the use of Preparation H (a hemorrhoid cream) to reduce wrinkles around the eyes, New Generation Shampoo to fight baldness, and Udder Cream (a preparation developed for cows) to restore moisture to dry, human chapped skin.[47] Additionally, it has been reported that some innovative high-end products owe their success to their ability to create cognitive dissonance in observers. Such products include the Bugaboo strollers, "which command $500 premiums over non-urban-assault strollers" and say about the owner "I am young, urban, and athletic—I have a life beyond tending to my child," and the Dyson vacuum cleaner. While most vacuum cleaners are relegated to the closet, Dyson owners "love the way they look while using it" because "it corners more fluidly than a Porsche."[48]

ATTRIBUTION THEORY

As a group of loosely interrelated social psychological principles, **attribution theory** attempts to explain how people assign causality (e.g., blame or credit) to events on the basis of either their own behavior or the behavior of others.[49] In other words, a person might say, "I contributed to the American Red Cross because it really helps people in need," or "He tried to persuade me to buy that unknown brand of MP3 player because he'd make a bigger commission." In attribution theory, the underlying question is why: "Why did I do this?" "Why did he try to get me to switch brands?" This process of making inferences about one's own or another's behavior is a major component of attitude formation and change.

Attribution theory is certainly part of our everyday lives, as companies continue to have their names on football stadiums and sponsor all types of charitable events. Research results indicate that the better the "match" between a sponsor and an event, the more positive the outcome is likely to be. Still further, there is evidence to suggest that consumers are willing to reward high-effort firms (i.e., they will pay more and/or evaluate the product higher) if they feel that the company has made an extra effort to make a better product or provide better consumer services.[50]

Self-Perception Theory

Of the various perspectives on attribution theory that have been proposed, **self-perception theory**—individuals' inferences or judgments as to the causes of their own behavior—is a good beginning point for a discussion of attribution.

In terms of consumer behavior, self-perception theory suggests that attitudes develop as consumers *look at and make judgments about their own behavior.* Simply stated, if a young advertising agency management supervision observes that she routinely purchases the *New York Times* on her way to the office, she is apt to conclude that she likes the *New York Times* (i.e., she has a positive attitude toward this newspaper).[51] Drawing inferences from one's own behavior is not always as simple or as clear-cut as the newspaper example might suggest. To appreciate the complexity of self-perception theory, it is useful to distinguish between **internal and external attributions**. Let us assume that Bradley has just finished using a popular computer video-editing software (e.g., Adobe's Premier Elements) for the first time and that his digital video of his South American vacation was well received when it was shown to the members of the photography club that he belongs to. After receiving the compliments, he says to himself, "I'm really a natural at editing my digital videos," this statement would be an example of an *internal attribution.* It is an internal attribution because he is giving himself credit for the outcome (e.g., his ability, his skill, or his effort). That is, he is saying, "These photos are good because of me." On the other hand, if Bradley concluded that the successful digital video editing was due to factors beyond his control (e.g., a user-friendly video-editing program, the assistance of another club member, or just "luck"), this would be an example of an *external attribution.* In such a case, he might be saying, "My great video is beginner's luck."

This distinction between internal and external attributions can be of strategic marketing importance. For instance, it would generally be in the best interest of the firm that produces the video-editing software if users, especially inexperienced users, *internalized* their successful use of the software package. If they internalized such a positive experience, it is more likely that they will repeat the behavior and become a satisfied regular user. Alternatively, however, if they were to *externalize* their success, it would be preferable that they attribute it to the particular software rather than to an incidental environmental factor such as "beginner's luck" or another's "foolproof" instructions. Additionally, recent studies suggest that when advertisers accurately target their message to consumers, with the proper cognitive generalizations about the self ("self-schema"), the consumer perceives the argument quality of the ad as being higher, and therefore has a more favorable attitude toward the message.[52]

According to the principle of **defensive attribution**, consumers are likely to accept credit personally for success (internal attribution) and to credit failure to others or to outside events (external attribution). For this reason, it is crucial that marketers offer uniformly high-quality products that allow consumers to perceive themselves as the reason for the success; that is, "I'm competent." Moreover, a company's advertising should serve to reassure consumers, particularly inexperienced ones, that its products will not let them down but will make them heroes instead.

FOOT-IN-THE-DOOR TECHNIQUE Self-perception researchers have explored situations in which consumer compliance with a minor request affects subsequent compliance with a more substantial request. This strategy, which is commonly referred to as the **foot-in-the-door technique**, is based on the premise that individuals look at their prior behavior (e.g., compliance with a minor request) and conclude that they are the kind of person who says "yes" to such requests (i.e., an internal attribution). Such self-attribution serves to increase the likelihood that they will agree to a similar more substantial request. Someone who donates $15 to the Michael J. Fox Foundation for Parkinson's Research might be persuaded to donate a much larger amount when properly approached. The initial donation is, in effect, the *foot in the door.*

Research into the foot-in-the-door technique has concentrated on understanding how specific incentives (e.g., cents-off coupons of varying amounts) ultimately influence consumer attitudes and subsequent purchase behavior. It appears that different-size incentives create different degrees of internal attribution, which, in turn, lead to different amounts of attitude change. For instance, individuals who try a brand without any inducements or individuals who buy a brand repeatedly are more likely to infer increasingly positive attitudes toward the brand from their respective behaviors (e.g., "I buy this brand because I like it"). In contrast, individuals who try a free sample are less committed to changing their attitudes toward the brand ("I tried this brand because it was free").

Thus, contrary to what might be expected, it is not the biggest incentive that is most likely to lead to positive attitude change. If an incentive is too big, marketers run the risk that consumers might externalize the cause of their behavior to the incentive and be *less* likely to change their attitudes and *less* likely to make future purchases of the brand. Instead, what seems most effective is a *moderate* incentive, one that is just big enough to stimulate initial purchase of the brand but still small enough to encourage consumers to internalize their positive usage experience and allow a positive attitude change to occur.[53]

In contrast with the foot-in-the-door technique is the **door-in-the-face technique**, in which a large, costly or high first request that is probably refused is followed by a second, more realistic, less costly request. Under certain situations, this technique may prove more effective than the foot-in-the-door technique.[54]

Attributions Toward Others

In addition to understanding self-perception theory, it is important to understand **attributions toward others** because of the variety of potential applications to consumer behavior and marketing. As already suggested, every time a person asks "why?" about a statement or action of another or "others"—a family member, a friend, a salesperson, a direct marketer, a shipping company—attribution theory is relevant. To illustrate, in evaluating the words or deeds of others, say, a salesperson, a consumer tries to determine if the salesperson's motives are in the consumer's best interests. If the salesperson's motives are viewed as favorable to the consumer, the consumer is likely to respond favorably. Otherwise, the consumer is likely to reject the salesperson's words and go elsewhere to make a purchase. In another case, a consumer orders a new MP3 player from a major direct marketer such as **Amazon.com** or **TigerDirect.com**. Because the consumer wants it immediately, she agrees to pay an extra $8 to $15 for next-day delivery by FedEx or UPS. If on the next day the package with the MP3 player fails to show up as expected, the consumer has two possible "others" to which she might attribute the failure—that is, the direct marketer (failing to get the product out on time) or the delivery service (failing to get the package to the consumer on time). In addition, she might blame them both (a dual failure); or if the weather was really bad, she might conclude that it was the bad weather (an attribution that neither of them was at fault).[55]

Attributions Toward Things

Consumer researchers also are interested in consumers' **attributions toward things** because products (or services) can readily be thought of as "things." It is in the area of judging product performance that consumers are most likely to form product attributions. Specifically, they want to find out why a product meets or fails to meet their expectations. In this regard, they could attribute the product's successful performance (or failure) to the product itself, to themselves, to other people or situations, or to some combination of these factors.[56] To recap an earlier example, when Bradley edited a challenging vacation digital video, he could attribute his success to the Adobe software (product attribution), to his own skill (self or internal attribution), or to a fellow photo club member who helped him (external attribution).

How We Test Our Attributions

After making initial attributions about a product's performance or a person's words or actions, we often attempt to determine whether the inference we made is correct. According to a leading attribution theorist, individuals acquire conviction about particular observations by acting like "naive scientists," that is, by collecting additional information in an attempt to confirm (or disconfirm) prior inferences. In collecting such information, consumers often use the following criteria:[57]

1. **Distinctiveness**—The consumer attributes an action to a particular product or person if the action occurs when the product (or person) is present and does not occur in its absence.
2. **Consistency over time**—Whenever the person or product is present, the consumer's inference or reaction must be the same, or nearly so.
3. **Consistency over modality**—The inference or reaction must be the same, even when the situation in which it occurs varies.
4. **Consensus**—The action is perceived in the same way by other consumers.

To illustrate how the process of testing our attributions work, Table 8.8 provides three scenarios that depict (for three of the four "attributions testing criteria"), how people might use information to determine why a corporation has given a grant for an after-school program to benefit public school children, and whether the giving is either internally or externally driven or caused.

The following example illustrates how each of these criteria might be used to make inferences about product performance and people's actions.

If Paul, a high school art teacher who loves taking pictures, observes that the photographs he prints at home seem to be sharper and more colorful when using his new Canon photo inkjet printer (**www.canonusa.com**), he is likely to credit the new Canon printer with the improved appearance of his photos (i.e., distinctiveness). Furthermore, if Paul finds that his new Canon printer produces the same high-quality results each time he uses it, he will tend to be more confident about his initial observation (i.e., the inference has consistency over time). Similarly, he will also

TABLE 8.8 Testing Attributions of a Corporate Grant to Support an After-School Program

CONSENSUS	DISTINCTIVENESS	CONSISTENCY	RESULTING ATTRIBUTION
High Many groups support the after-school program.	**High** The corporation supports only the school.	**High** The corporation supports the school regularly.	**External Influence** Support of the school is related to the quality of the school.
Low Only the corporation supports the after-school program.	**Low** The corporation supports several schools and other programs.	**High** The corporation supports the school regularly.	**Internal disposition** Support of the school is related to the benevolence of the corporation.
Either High or Low	**Either High or Low**	**Low** The corporation gave a grant to the school only once.	**External influence** Support of the school is related to an undefined aspect of the particular situation that occurred at the time of the grant.

Source: Andrea M. Sjovall and Andrew C. Talk, "From Actions to Impressions: Cognitive Attribution Theory and the Formation of Corporate Reputation," *Corporate Reputation Review*, 7 (Fall 2004): 277. Reproduced with permission of Palgrave Macmillan.

be more confident if he finds that his satisfaction with the Canon printer extends across a wide range of other related tasks, from printing out text and spreadsheets to printing graphs and charts (i.e., consistency over modality). Finally, Paul will have still more confidence in his inferences to the extent that his friends who own Canon printers also have similar experiences (i.e., consensus).

Much like Paul, we go about gathering additional information from our experiences with people and things, and we use this information to test our initial inferences.

SUMMARY

An attitude is a learned predisposition to behave in a consistently favorable or unfavorable way with respect to a given object (e.g., a product category, a brand, a service, an advertisement, a Web site, or a retail establishment). Each property of this definition is critical to understanding why and how attitudes are relevant in consumer behavior and marketing.

Of considerable importance in understanding the role of attitudes in consumer behavior is an appreciation of the structure and composition of an attitude. Four broad categories of attitude models have received attention: tricomponent attitude model, multiattribute attitude model, trying-to-consume attitude model, and attitude-toward-the-ad model.

The tricomponent model of attitudes consists of three parts: a cognitive component, an affective component, and a conative component. The cognitive component captures a consumer's knowledge and perceptions (i.e., beliefs) about products and services. The affective component focuses on a consumer's emotions or feelings with respect to a particular product or service. Evaluative in nature, the affective component determines an individual's overall assessment of the attitude object in terms of some kind of favorableness rating. The conative component is concerned with the likelihood that a consumer will act in a specific fashion with respect to the attitude object. In marketing and consumer behavior, the conative component is frequently treated as an expression of the consumer's intention to buy.

Multiattribute attitude models (i.e., attitude-toward-object, attitude-toward-behavior, and the theory-of-reasoned-action models) have received much attention from consumer researchers. As a group, these models examine consumer beliefs about specific product attributes (e.g., product or brand features or benefits). Recently, there has been an effort to better accommodate consumers' goals as expressed by their "trying to consume" (i.e., a goal the consumer is trying or planning to accomplish). The theory of trying is designed to account for the many cases in which the action or outcome is not certain. The attitude-toward-the-ad model examines the influence of advertisements on the consumer's attitudes toward the brand.

How consumer attitudes are formed and how they are changed are two closely related issues of considerable concern to marketing practitioners. When it comes to attitude formation, it is useful to remember that attitudes are learned and that different learning theories provide unique insights as to how attitudes initially may be formed. Attitude formation is facilitated by direct personal experience and influenced by the ideas and experiences of friends and family members and exposure to mass media. In addition, it is likely that an individual's personality plays a role in attitude formation.

These same factors also have an impact on attitude change; that is, attitude changes are learned, and they are influenced by personal experiences and the information gained from various personal and impersonal sources. The consumer's own personality affects both the acceptance and the speed with which attitudes are likely to be altered.

Strategies of attitude change can be classified into six distinct categories: (1) changing the basic motivational function, (2) associating the attitude object with a specific group or event, (3) relating the attitude object to conflicting attitudes, (4) altering components of the multiattribute model, (5) changing beliefs about competitors' brands, and (6) the elaboration likelihood model. Each of these strategies provides the marketer with alternative ways of changing consumers' existing attitudes.

Most discussions of attitude formation and attitude change stress the traditional view that consumers develop attitudes before they act. However, this may not always, or even usually, be true. Both cognitive dissonance theory and attribution theory provide alternative explanations of attitude formation and change that suggest that behavior might precede attitudes. Cognitive dissonance theory suggests that the conflicting thoughts, or dissonant information, following a purchase decision might propel consumers to change their attitudes to make them consonant with their actions. Attribution theory focuses on how people assign causality to events and how they form or alter attitudes as an outcome of assessing their own behavior or the behavior of other people or things.

DISCUSSION QUESTIONS

1. Explain how situational factors are likely to influence the degree of consistency between attitudes and behavior.

2. Because attitudes are learned predispositions to respond, why don't marketers and consumer researchers just measure purchase behavior and forget attitudes?

3. Explain a person's attitude toward visiting Disney World in terms of the tricomponent attitude model.

4. How can the marketer of a "nicotine patch" (a device that assists individuals to quit smoking) use the *theory of trying* to segment its market? Using this theory, identify two segments that the marketer should target and propose product positioning approaches to be directed at each of the two segments.

5. Explain how the product manager of a breakfast cereal might change consumer attitudes toward the company's brand by (a) changing beliefs about the brand, (b) changing beliefs about competing brands, (c) changing the relative evaluation of attributes, and (d) adding an attribute.
6. The Department of Transportation of a large city is planning an advertising campaign that encourages people to switch from private cars to mass transit. Give examples of how the department can use the following strategies to change commuters' attitudes: (a) changing the basic motivational function, (b) changing beliefs about public transportation, (c) using self-perception theory, and (d) using cognitive dissonance.
7. Should the marketer of a popular computer graphics program prefer consumers to make internal or external attributions? Explain your answer.
8. A college student has just purchased a new personal computer. What factors might cause the student to experience postpurchase dissonance? How might the student try to overcome it? How can the retailer who sold the computer help reduce the student's dissonance? How can the computer's manufacturer help?

EXERCISES

1. Find two print ads, one illustrating the use of the affective component and the other illustrating the cognitive component. Discuss each ad in the context of the tricomponent model. In your view, why has each marketer taken the approach it did in each of these ads?
2. What sources influenced your attitude about this course before classes started? Has your initial attitude changed since the course started? If so, how?
3. Describe a situation in which you acquired an attitude toward a new product through exposure to an advertisement for that product. Describe a situation in which you formed an attitude toward a product or brand on the basis of personal influence.
4. Find advertisements that illustrate each of the four motivational functions of attitudes. Distinguish between ads that are designed to reinforce an existing attitude and those aimed at changing an attitude.
5. Think back to the time when you were selecting a college. Did you experience dissonance immediately after you made a decision? Why or why not? If you did experience dissonance, how did you resolve it?

KEY TERMS

- attitudes *246*
- attitude-toward-behavior model *253*
- attitude-toward-object model *251*
- attitude-toward-the-ad models *255*
- attribution theory *272*
- attributions toward others *273*
- attributions toward things *274*
- cognitive dissonance theory *270*
- defensive attribution *273*
- door-in-the-face technique *273*
- ego-defensive function *260*
- elaboration likelihood model (ELM) *268*
- foot-in-the-door technique *273*
- functional approach *260*
- intention-to-buy scales *251*
- internal and external attributions *272*
- knowledge function *260*
- multiattribute attitude models *251*
- self-perception theory *272*
- theory of planned behavior *254*
- theory-of-reasoned-action (TRA) model *253*
- theory of trying to consume *255*
- tricomponent attitude model *249*
- utilitarian function *260*
- value-expressive function *260*

Case One: Skin Care Products for Men

The beauty industry used to be monopolized by the female market. However, over the last decade, this perception has changed. Men have become more conscious about their appearance and are more willing to spend on various kinds of skin care products or treatments. To meet this increasing demand, more and more skin care products or services for men have appeared in the Hong Kong market in the last few years.

Men's skin care has become a fast-growing business in Hong Kong. Margaret Leung, the president of Clarins, predicted that the men's skin care market will grow by double digits each year for the next five to eight years. In fact, in the past few years many cosmetic brands have released comprehensive men's lines, for example, L'Oréal's Men Expert, Biotherm Homme, and Clinque's Skin Supplies for Men. Local retailers are confident about the growing popularity of the industry. Watsons has recently opened its first "Pure Beauty"–a 3,000 square feet beauty outlet located in Times Square in Causeway Bay that sells more than 400 men's beauty products.

Apart from product development, cosmetic companies are also putting a lot of emphasis on promoting their men's lines. For example, Biotherm Homme invited Asian film star Takeshi Kaneshiro to be its spokesperson while L'Oréal's Men Expert employed the famous actor Daniel Wu as their celebrity spokesperson. Different integrated marketing communications efforts were used to increase the popularity and boost the sales of men's skin care products and services in Hong Kong.

QUESTIONS

1. On the basis of the theory of reasoned action presented in Chapter 8, how would you explain the positive attitude formation toward men's skin care products or services in the Hong Kong market?
2. Use the attitude-toward-the-ad model to discuss if the advertisements for men's skin care products or services help to accelerate their positive attitude formation.

Source: Carol Chan, "Well-Groomed Men Give Beauty Industry a New Face—Growing Competition Has Forced Local Retailers to Expand Their Services as Modern Males Embrace Skin Care," *South China Morning Post*, Hong Kong, September 9, 2006.

Case Two: The Redesign of McDonald's

McDonald's is a leading American fast-food chain in Hong Kong. Most people believe that McDonald's is a restaurant that sells primarily unhealthy junk food like hamburgers, french fries, and soft drinks.

In recent years, McDonald's has undergone some major changes in its marketing strategies to change customers' attitudes about its image and positioning. It started to offer healthy foods like sweet corn, salad, and yogurt in order to capitalize on the growing consumer interest in health and wellness. Many branches are now open late or even 24 hours; and they provide Wi-Fi access to customers.

Many McDonald's used to include a play area for children, but recently it has redesigned some of its restaurants in a more natural and flexible style of decoration that emphasizes warm feelings and customer comforts. For example, it introduced some lounge areas and replaced the fixed plastic chairs and tables with wooden ones that provide flexible seating. McDonald's also brought in some modern hanging lights and contemporary art prints to hang on the walls. Also, the Uncle McDonald's figures are gradually being eliminated from the brand. Advertisements also changed from a child focus to being teenage-centered. McDonald's is now relying more on celebrity endorsements, like pop singer Joey Yung, in its advertising to capture the attention of the teenage market.

All these marketing strategies are being implemented to change McDonald's target market from the family or child market to the teenage market. And it also aims to change the customers' beliefs about unhealthy fast food so that they believe that eating in McDonald's could be a healthy decision.

QUESTIONS

1. Use the attitude-toward-object model presented in Chapter 8 to explain how the customer attitudes toward McDonald's could be changed by its recent marketing efforts.
2. Referring to the redesign of McDonald's marketing strategies in Hong Kong, explain how important the marketer's role is in influencing customer attitude formation or change.

9

Communication and Consumer Behavior

Through the process of communication, companies convey to consumers information and ideas designed to persuade them to take action. Creating a unique, persuasive message that induces a specific response on the part of consumers is very difficult because consumers are bombarded with thousands of competing messages, and they ignore most of them (as discussed in previous chapters). Furthermore, many competing messages are creative and innovative, and coming up with a message that is more persuasive than other ads is a very challenging task. For example, although most persuasive messages are in the form of *verbal* statements, there are also *nonverbal* forms of communication, such as hand gestures, body language, and facial expressions. The ad featured in Figure 9.1 stands out because it demonstrates how nonverbal means are used in communication and also relates this concept to the positioning of HSBC—the *message's sender*—as a bank possessing a unique understanding of global cultures.

And yet, even at a time when most communicators are preoccupied with the technically innovative means of communication, highly effective messages sometimes stem from traditional concepts. For example, most travelers encounter signs at hotel bathrooms asking them to reuse their towels in order to "help save the environment." In one study, such a "standard" message was replaced by one implying that many *other* travelers had reused towels, and guests were asked to "join fellow guests in helping save the environment." This "social norm" message persuaded about 25 percent more people to reuse towels. When messages telling people that guests who had stayed in the *very same room* had reused the towels were posted, the number of people reusing towels increased further.[1] From a communication perspective, the "social norm" message was more persuasive than the "standard" message because it was more *credible* and *believable*. Apparently, many travelers perceived the standard messages, at least partially, as efforts by hotels to cut down their expenses. However, since most people adhere to social norms, stating that others have taken an ecologically friendly action made the message substantially more convincing.

Speaking further on the issue of credibility, think back to the time you graduated high school and you and your family

FIGURE 9.1

Source: © HSBC North America Holdings, Inc. Used with permission. All rights reserved. (www.hsbc.com).

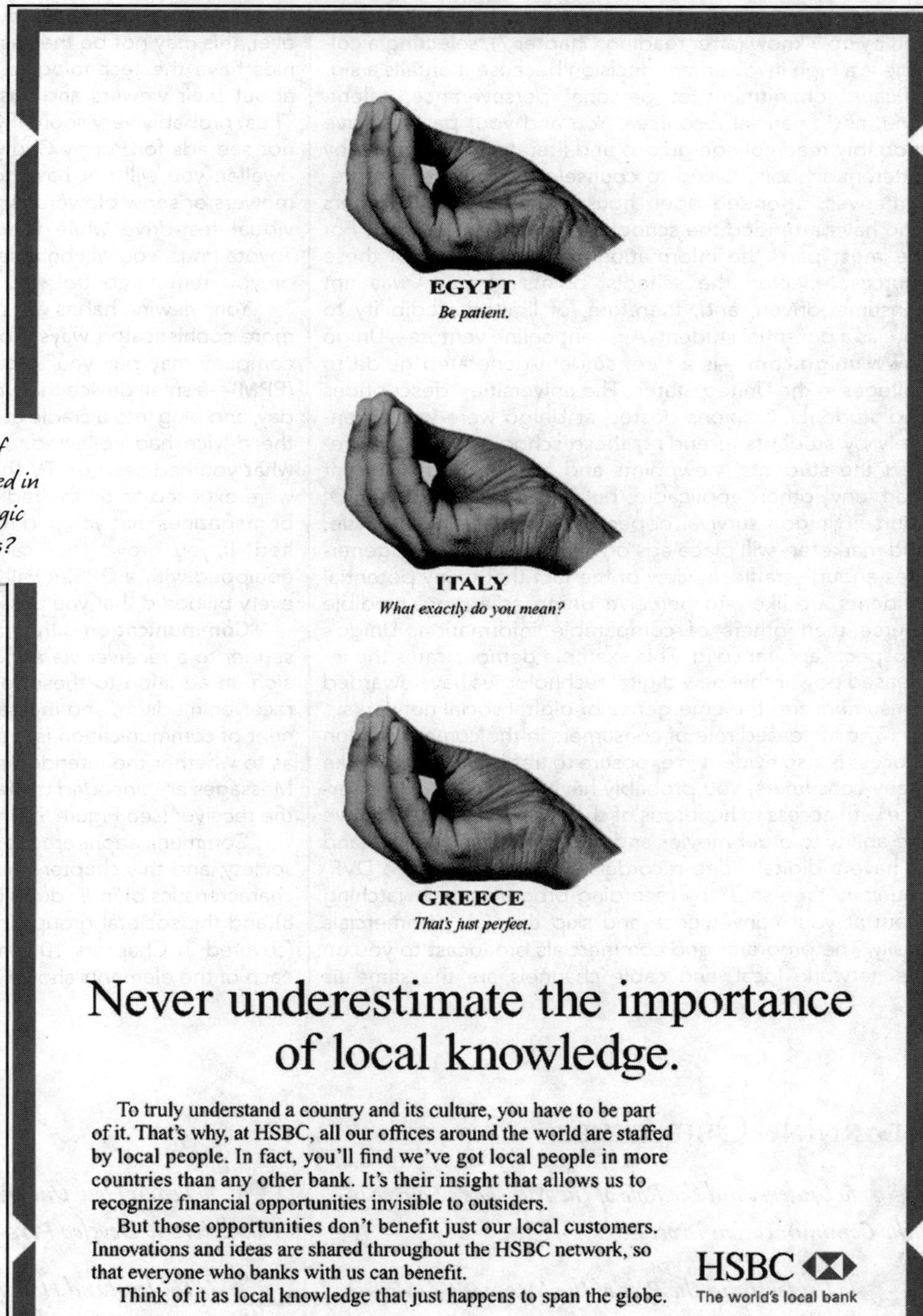

QUESTION: *Which Type of Communication Is Featured in This Ad, and What Strategic Concept Does It Get Across?*

were trying to decide which college you should attend. As you by now know (after reading Chapter 7), selecting a college is a high involvement decision because it entails a significant commitment of personal perseverance, talent, time, and financial resources. You and your parents have probably read college guides and literature distributed by different schools, talked to counselors and college representatives, attended open houses, and spoke to others who have attended the schools you were considering. For the most part, the information you received from these sources reflected the schools' points of view, was not consumer-driven, and, therefore, of limited credibility to you, as a potential student. A recent online venture—Unigo (**www.unigo.com**)—is a free, student-generated guide to colleges in the United States. The universities' descriptions and students' opinions posted at Unigo were written entirely by students attending these schools. Thus, they reflect the students' viewpoints and are also more current than any other applicable published information.[2] Of course, Unigo's survival depends on advertising revenue, and marketers will place ads on the site only after it generates enough traffic. In view of the fact that many potential students are likely to perceive Unigo as a more credible source than others of comparable information, Unigo's prospects appear solid. This example demonstrates the increased power that new digital technologies have awarded consumers and the emergence of digital social networks.

The increased role of consumers in the communication process is also evident in exposure to traditional media. Like many consumers, you probably have cable or satellite service with access to hundreds of channels. You may also have the ability to order movies and other programs on-demand or have a digital video recorder (DVR). If you have a DVR, you can "time shift" by recording programs and watching them at your convenience and skip through commercials easily. The programs and commercials broadcast to you on the network, local, and cable channels are the same as those transmitted to other viewers of these channels. However, this may not be the case for long. Most cable companies have the technological means to gather information about their viewers and customize the ads sent to them. Thus, probably very soon, if you do not own a dog, you will not see ads for Puppy Chow, and if you are an apartment dweller, you will not have to watch commercials for lawn mowers or snow blowers. And if you would like to go on a virtual test-drive while watching a TV commercial for a Toyota Prius, you will be able to do so by pressing a button on your remote control.

Your viewing habits will still be closely monitored, but in more sophisticated ways. For example, Nielsen or another company may pay you to carry a **portable people meter (PPM)**—a small device that you will clip to your belt, wear all day, and plug into a cradle at night that will transmit the data the device had collected. That data will include not only what you had seen on TV that day but also all the ads you were exposed to on the radio, in stores, in the newspapers or magazines that you had read, and the Web sites you visited. If you drove your car that day and your PPM was equipped with a GPS, it will also record the ads posted on every billboard that you passed.

Communication is *the transmission of a message from a sender to a receiver via a medium (or channel) of transmission.* In addition to these four basic components—sender, receiver, medium, and message—the fifth essential component of communication is *feedback,* which alerts the sender as to whether the intended message was, in fact, received. Messages are *encoded* by the sender and then *decoded* by the receiver (see Figure 9.2).

Communications are the link between the individual and society, and this chapter bridges the material covering the characteristics of individuals (covered in Chapters 3 through 8) and the societal groups in which they live and consume (covered in Chapters 10 through 15). This chapter covers each of the elements shown in Figure 9.2.

Learning Objectives

9.1 *To Understand the Role of the Message's Source in the Communication Process.*

9.2 *To Understand the Role of the Message's Audience (Receivers) in the Communication Process.*

9.3 *To Learn About Advertising Media and How to Select the Right Media When Sending Promotional Messages Targeting Selected Consumer Groups.*

9.4 *To Learn How Understanding Consumers Enables Marketers to Develop Persuasive Messages.*

9.5 *To Understand How Marketers Measure the Effectiveness of Their Promotional Messages.*

FIGURE 9.2
Communication Model

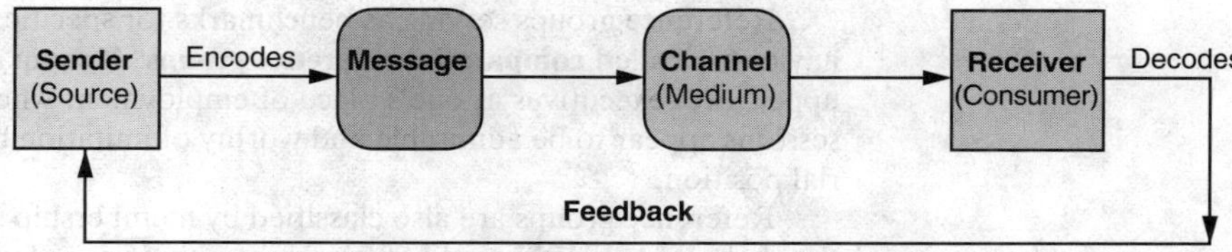

The Source as the Message Initiator

LEARNING OBJECTIVE

9.1 *To Understand the Role of the Message's Source in the Communication Process.*

A company's marketing communications are designed to make the consumer aware of the product or service, induce purchase or commitment, create a positive attitude toward the product, or show how it can solve the consumer's problem better than a competitive product (or service). The sender, as the initiator of the communication, can be a formal or an informal source. In marketing communications, a **formal source** represents either a for-profit (commercial) or a not-for-profit organization; an **informal source** was originally defined as a person whom the message receiver knows personally, such as a parent or friend who gives product information or advice. However, today, informal sources also include people who influence one's consumption via online **social networks** and other Web forums. Consumers often rely on informal communications sources in making purchase decisions because, unlike formal sources, these sources are perceived as having nothing to gain from the receiver's subsequent actions. Therefore, marketers must always encourage and even initiate positive **word-of-mouth (WOM)** communications about their products and services.

IMPERSONAL AND INTERPERSONAL COMMUNICATIONS

Communications can be either impersonal or interpersonal. In marketing, the sources of **impersonal communications** are organizations (either for-profit or not-for-profit) that develop and transmit appropriate messages through their marketing departments, advertising or public relations agencies, and spokespersons. The targets, or receivers, of such messages usually are a specific audience or several audiences that the organization is trying to inform, influence, or persuade. The senders of **interpersonal communications** can be either formal sources (e.g., a salesperson in a physical or virtual retail location) or informal sources (e.g., peers with whom the consumer communicates face to face or via electronic means). The key factor underlying the persuasive impact of a personal or interpersonal message received from either a formal or informal source is the source's credibility; that is, the extent to which the receiver trusts and believes the source sending the message.

Source Credibility

The perceived honesty and objectivity of the sponsor of the communication have enormous influence on how the communication is accepted by the receiver(s). When the source is well respected and highly thought of by the intended audience, the message is much more likely to be believed. Conversely, a message from a source considered unreliable or untrustworthy is likely to be received with skepticism and probably rejected.

Reference Groups

From a marketing perspective, **reference groups** are groups that serve as frames of reference for individuals in their consumption decisions because they are perceived as credible sources. Reference groups influencing broadly defined values or behavior are called **normative reference groups**. An example of a child's normative reference group is the immediate family, which plays an important role in molding the child's general consumer values and behavior (such as which foods to select for good nutrition, appropriate ways to dress for specific occasions, how and where to shop, or what constitutes "good" value). During the holiday shopping season that followed the financial crisis of fall 2008, many affluent consumers were embarrassed to be seen coming out of luxury stores carrying expensive shopping bags because many other people were financially strapped. These consumers resorted to buying luxury products at special, by-invitation-only sales events organized by dealers and retailers that were held in hotel suites and private living rooms.[3] This consumption behavior illustrates normative reference group influence.

Reference groups serving as benchmarks for specific or narrowly defined attitudes or behavior are called **comparative reference groups**. A comparative reference group might be the upper-level executives at one's place of employment whose lifestyle, clothing, and other possessions appear to be admirable and worthy of imitation by a person holding a lower managerial position.

Reference groups are also classified by membership status. A group to which a person either belongs or would qualify for membership in is called a **membership group**. For example, the group of men with whom a young executive plays poker weekly would be considered, for him, a membership group. There are also groups in which an individual is not likely to receive membership, despite acting like a member by adopting the group's values, attitudes, and behavior. Each such group is considered a **symbolic group**. For instance, professional tennis players may constitute a symbolic group for an amateur tennis player who identifies with certain players by imitating their behavior whenever possible (e.g., by purchasing a specific brand of tennis racket or tennis sneaker). However, the amateur tennis player does not (and probably never will) qualify for membership as a professional tennis player because she has neither the skills nor the opportunity to compete professionally.

THE CREDIBILITY AND DYNAMICS OF INFORMAL SOURCES AND WORD-OF-MOUTH

Informal sources such as friends, neighbors, relatives, and other consumers a person "meets" online in social networks, chat-rooms, and digital comment boards have a strong influence on that person's consumption behavior because they are perceived as having nothing to gain from their purchase recommendations. Such informal groups also serve as comparative and normative frames of reference for a person's overall values and behaviors. Originally, sociologists who studied the informal communications process named it **opinion leadership** and defined it as *the process by which one person (the opinion leader) informally influences the actions or attitudes of others, who may be opinion seekers or opinion recipients.* The key characteristic of the influence is that it is interpersonal and informal and takes place between two or more people, none of whom represents a commercial selling source that would gain directly from the sale of something. Later on, marketers realized that informal communications are a *two-way process* and named such interactions *word-of-mouth (WOM)*.

A word-of-mouth encounter may indeed start by one party offering advice or information about a product to another party. However, this **opinion leader** may become an **opinion receiver** later on. For example, a new father contemplating the purchase of a baby car seat sought information and advice from other people in deciding which brand to select. Once the car seat was purchased, he experienced postpurchase dissonance (see Chapter 8) and was compelled to talk favorably about the purchase to other people, thus confirming the wisdom of his own choice. In the first instance, he was an opinion receiver (seeker); in the second, he assumed the role of opinion leader.

In word-of-mouth communications, the parties involved perceive each other as highly credible sources of information because they view one another as objective concerning the product or service information or advice they dispense. Opinion receivers view the intentions of opinion leaders as being in their best interests because the opinion leaders receive no material gain for the advice; therefore, their opinion receivers are likely to consider such recommendations seriously. Because opinion leaders often base their product comments on firsthand experience, their advice reduces the opinion receivers' perceived risk or anxiety inherent in buying new products. Extending this logic further, the opinion leader is likely to view any feedback he or she receives from the opinion receiver about a suggestion made previously as credible and also be receptive to additional advice and information provided by the receiver.

Opinion leadership tends to be *category specific;* that is, opinion leaders often "specialize" in certain product categories about which they offer information and advice. When other product categories are discussed, however, they are just as likely to reverse their roles and become opinion receivers. A person who is considered particularly knowledgeable about home electronics may be an opinion leader in terms of this subject, yet when it comes to purchasing a new washing machine, the same person may seek advice from someone else—perhaps even from someone who has sought his advice on home electronics.

Although the term **word-of-mouth** implies personal, or face-to-face, communication, it may also take place in a telephone conversation or online. Consumers rely on word-of-mouth in selecting restaurants, travel destinations and hotels, physicians, personal care providers (e.g., hairdressers and nail salons), movies, books, financial services providers, and many other products and services.

THE WORD-OF-MOUTH ENVIRONMENT AND e-WOM

Until about 15 years ago, any consumption-related information transmitted by a consumer could reach relatively few people (e.g., the person's friends, family, work groups, and members of other organizations to which people belong). Today, one's review of a movie, book, product, university, professor, and even employer can be easily and quickly posted online and reach thousands of people. Furthermore, constantly emerging new technologies allow people to compile and post increasingly sophisticated, appealing, and attention-getting materials online and vividly share their consumption experience with others both visually and verbally. Word-of-mouth taking place online is called **e-WOM**. Consumption-related, e-WOM occurs online in *social networks, brand communities, blogs,* and *consumer message boards*.

Social Networks

Online social networks are *virtual communities* where people share information about themselves with others, generally with similar interests, with whom they establish relationships that, for the most part, exist only in cyberspace. Since consumption and the products people buy are integral parts of their lives, their online profiles and discussions with others include a tremendous amount of explicit and implicit purchase information and advice. The major social networks are **www.facebook.com**, **www.myspace.com**, and **www.youtube.com**.

A recent study identified three dimensions underlying consumers' engagement in e-WOM in online social networks: (1) *Tie strength*—the degree of intimacy and frequency of contacts between the information seeker and the source; (2) *Similarity* among the group's members in terms of demographics and lifestyles; and (3) *Source credibility*—the information seeker's perceptions of the source's expertise in the area of sought advice.[4] Another study investigated how consumers react to negative e-WOM and found that readers of negative reviews of *hedonic* products attributed the comments to the reviewers' internal and nonproduct-related reasons and did not consider the reviews useful. However, readers of negative reviews for *utilitarian* products (i.e., pleasure-focused products) attribute the reviews to product-related reasons and found them more useful than positive reviews.[5] Another study investigated the extent to which consumers—with varied levels of social *connectedness*—were likely to engage in word-of-mouth. The results showed that word-of-mouth did not come only from the highly connected people, and that moderately connected people (the majority of the sample) were as willing as highly connected persons to engage in word-of-mouth. The researchers attributed these findings to people's need to give advice and enjoy sharing information.[6] The results of the study and the survey questions used to gauge respondents' likelihood in engaging in word-of-mouth appear in Table 9.1.

Brand Communities

These online forums focus on particular products or brands. Generally, admirers of a particular item, often with nostalgic emotions and in possession of versions of the brand that are no longer made, find others with similar interests and form a community fostering a feeling of belonging across geographic, linguistic, and cultural barriers. Brands around which such networks emerged include Harley-Davidson motorcycles, Barbie dolls, and PEZ candy. While marketers may attempt to join communities centered on their brands, such efforts may be unwise because the brand community's members have joined the forum to interact with other consumers and may view the marketer as an unwelcome outsider.

Consumer Message Boards and Weblogs

Scores of Web portals enable anyone wishing to do so to post information on anything and everything quickly, cost free, and from any location and at any time. Many sites also offer continued access to chat rooms where discussions among many take place in real time. On these sites, consumers are free to express opinions, describe experiences with products and services, solicit purchase advice, and read others' testimonials about products and brands. Another medium for disseminating e-WOM is the **blog** (short for Weblog). A blog is a personal online journal initiated and managed by a *blogger*, which also includes comments entered by the

TABLE 9.1 The Effectiveness of Word-of-Mouth Among Three Groups of Consumers with Varied Levels of Connectedness to Social Networks

Respondents indicated how likely they are to take the action described in each statement. A seven-point scale was used ranging from "very likely" to "very unlikely."

SURVEY ITEM	LESS CONNECTED	MODERATELY CONNECTED	HIGHLY CONNECTED
If an advertisement offers a discount or coupon for a particular drug, how likely would you be to share the advertisement with others?	4.90	5.25	5.38
If you see an advertisement about a health product that you think would be useful to someone you know, how likely would you be to share information from the advertisement with others?	5.55	5.97	6.05
If you see an advertisement that focuses on how easy a medicine is to use, how likely would you be to share information from the advertisement with others?	4.96	5.27	5.45
If you see an advertisement that focuses on the symptoms of a disease disorder that may be experienced by someone you know, how likely would you be to share information from the advertisement with others?	5.60	5.92	5.95
If you see an advertisement that focuses on the positive outcomes of a medicine or treatment, how likely would you be to share information from the advertisement with others?	5.37	5.70	5.79
If you see an advertisement that focuses on how to better control a disease or disorder, how likely would you be to share information from the advertisement with others?	5.43	5.77	5.85
If you see an advertisement that mentions how patients are getting good results from a medication or treatment, how likely would you be to share information from the advertisement with others?	5.38	5.68	5.77

Source: Ted Smith, James R. Coyle, Elizabeth Lightfoot, and Amy Scott, "Reconsidering Models of Influence: The Relationship Between Consumer Social Networks and Word-of-Mouth Effectiveness," *Journal of Advertising Research,* 47, no. 4 (December 2007): 394.

readers, as well as responses to previous entries. With millions of these online journals appearing online and multiplying daily, they are now probably the most powerful platform for the exchange of consumption-related information. As an illustration of the enormous impact of this forum, consider the following example. After a person posted information on a group discussion site that U-shaped Kryptonite bicycle locks could be picked with a Bic ballpoint pen, within a few days, a number of blogs had videos demonstrating how this could be done. Four days after the original posting, Kryptonite issued a statement promising that their new line of bicycle locks would be tougher. But bloggers kept up the pressure, and shortly thereafter the *New York Times* and the Associated Press published articles about the problem. Over the following 10 days, about 1.8 million people read postings about Kryptonite, and the company announced that it would offer free exchange for any affected lock.[7]

There is an interesting paradox in the dynamics of e-WOM occurring in digital social networks, brand communities, online message boards, chat rooms, and blogs: While marketers have virtually no control over the information exchanged in these forums, these platforms are probably the most important sources of consumer information. First, online sources can be accessed instantly from almost any location and at any time. The fact that the phrase "I googled" a particular topic, person, or product is now part of America's language demonstrates the nearly universal use of the Web as one's primary source of information. Second, about any given product, digital platforms provide more comprehensive product data than the advertising messages for these offerings, and a lot of this information is likely to be perceived as more credible than data the ads provide. Third, all the major Web portals now enable consumers to *compare* prices, outlets, and versions of products instantly and upon the entry of the product or brand in the "search" window. Lastly, consumers can find scores of suggestions online regarding using a product in a variety of ways. For example, a person bored with his or her routine in tying a necktie or scarf can easily discover online more exciting ways of performing this mundane daily chore. Although marketers have little control of e-WOM, its existence and scope provide marketers with significant strategic promotional tools, which are discussed next.

STRATEGIC MARKETING APPLICATIONS OF WORD-OF-MOUTH

Marketers have long ago realized the power of word-of-mouth communications between consumers. They understand that it is often more effective than paid promotional messages initiated by manufacturers. Long before the emergence of the Web and e-WOM, marketers have portrayed word-of-mouth in advertisements, stimulated word-of-mouth among consumers through advertising slogans such as "tell your friends how much you like our product," and instituted *referral programs* where customers were rewarded for bringing in new clients. For example, a campaign for Vaseline Clinical Therapy asked the female consumer who received a free sample of the product to "freely prescribe it to anyone she thought might need it." The venue selected for the campaign was Kodiak Island—a remote location in Alaska known for its harsh weather.[8] In support of the value of interpersonal communications, a recent study discovered that the amount of word-of-mouth was directly related to the box office revenue of a movie in the early weeks after the movie opened.[9]

While stimulating WOM is not a new strategy, the emergence of e-WOM brought upon a huge surge in the amount of money and creativity devoted to campaigns and strategic initiatives centered on WOM, including using *buzz agents, viral marketing, e-referrals and recommendations,* and responding effectively to *negative rumors*.

Buzz Agents

Many firms enlist typical consumers to serve as their **buzz agents**; these agents agree to promote products by bringing them to family gatherings, read books promoted by publishers on mass transit with the titles clearly visible, suggest to store owners who do not carry a given product that they should do so, and talk other consumers into trying certain products during shopping trips. Generally, these "agents" do not receive direct payment from the companies they represent, although they often receive free samples. They are motivated by being called upon to serve as opinion leaders and get an ego boost by appearing so knowledgeable to their peers and having access to new products before others do.[10]

There are several companies offering marketers buzz-related services. For example, bzzagent.com recruits buzz agents and assists its clients in creating buzz marketing campaigns. Similarly, P&G has created a company known as Tremor (**www.tremor.com**) specializing in targeting teens and their families. Tremor screens applicants for buzz agent positions and only selects those who meet specific standards in terms of being likely to be an effective word-of-mouth communicator.

Some marketers hire actors or fashion models to go out and simulate demand for a product. For instance, a campaign for a new brand of flavored Vodka can use paid actors or models to visit bars and nightclubs and order martinis made with the new brand. The actors or models would appear as if they were ordering a well-established fad drink, while the real objective of this effort was to *create* a new drink. Similarly, in a recent campaign for an online gambling site in London, cab drivers were asked to steer passengers to a discussion about poker, direct them to the gambling site, and even provide "free hand" coupons to passengers who expressed considerable interest.[11]

Viral Marketing

Viral marketing consists of encouraging individuals to pass on an e-mail message to others, thus creating the potential for exponential growth in the message's exposure and influence. For example, Hotmail.com—the first free Web e-mail service—gave away free e-mail addresses and attached a tag to the bottom of every message encouraging receivers of e-mail to sign up with the company. Recently, a company marketing a hair gel product posted humorous audio-visual clips on the Web as part of a continued spoof and satire of a hair product and encouraged viewers to pass along the clips' Web location to others.[12] In another example, Facebook asked users if they would like to tell their friends about their brand preferences. Then, Facebook sent a message to the friends of a cooperating member; for example, the friends of a *Facebook* user who rented a movie received an invitation to rent the same movie from Blockbuster.[13]

E-mail is the key tool of viral marketing because so many people routinely forward e-mails to others, and many have different preset email groups for sharing different types of information. Table 9.2 presents the motives for sending pass-along e-mail. Note how four of the six top-rated reasons deal with enjoyment and/or entertainment, and the other two concern social motivations.[14] However, viral campaigns must be carefully planned. A recent study showed that

TABLE 9.2 Motives for Pass Along E-mail

Respondents were asked to indicate the importance of 28 reasons for communicating with others via pass-along e-mail. The reasons are listed in descending order of importance.

Because it's fun
Because I enjoy it
Because it's entertaining
To help others
To have a good time
To let others know I care about their feelings
To thank them
To get away from what I'm doing
Because it peps me up
To show others encouragement
Because it allows me to unwind
Because it's exciting
Because it relaxes me
Because it's stimulating
To get something I don't have
To get away from pressures
Because it's a pleasant rest
Because I'm concerned about them
Because it makes me feel less tense
To put off something I should be doing
Because I have nothing better to do
Because it's reassuring to know someone's there
Because I want someone to do something for me
Because it's thrilling
To tell others what to do
Because I just need to talk
Because I need someone to talk to
Because it makes me feel less lonely

Source: Joseph E. Phelps, Regina Lewis, Lynne Mobilio, David Perry, and Niranjan Raman, "Viral Marketing or Electronic Word-of-Mouth Advertising: Examining Consumer Responses and Motivations to Pass Along Email," *Journal of Advertising Research*, (December 2004): 343.

some viral marketing campaigns were viewed as too aggressive and generated negative postings in blogs and chat forums, including accusations of invasion of privacy and generating spam.[15] Another effective form of viral marketing is online **e-referrals and recommendations**. Highly successful e-merchants such as eBay and Amazon.com routinely attach links encouraging users to send notices of their selections to their friends.

Tackling Negative Rumors

Long ago, marketers realized that it is impossible to control word-of-mouth communications. Negative comments, frequently in the form of rumors that are untrue, can sweep through the marketplace and undermine a product. Some rumor themes that have plagued marketers in recent years and unfavorably influenced sales include the following: (1) the product was produced under unsanitary conditions; (2) the product contained an unwholesome or culturally unacceptable ingredient; (3) the product functioned as an undesirable depressant or stimulant; (4) the product included a cancer-causing element or agent; and (5) the firm was owned or influenced by an unfriendly or misguided foreign country, governmental agency, or religious cult.

The Web is a prolific ground for spreading negative rumors. Consider a disgruntled airline passenger, an unhappy retail customer, or even a student unhappy with a professor—all of whom can post their stories and opinions online for all to see and respond. Digital technologies now enable disgruntled consumers to reach millions of people easily and describe their often-exaggerated negative experiences with products and services. Persistent critics of marketers who initiate bad publicity online are called **determined detractors**. Many companies have been subject to such online attacks; perhaps the best-known example is the individual who ate nothing but McDonald's food for 30 days and produced an extremely critical documentary about this company entitled *Super Size Me.*[16] Furthermore, with the emergence of YouTube as a highly popular forum, disgruntled buyers can reach very large audiences with their *audio-visual* depictions of negative consumption encounters. A recent study identified the following factors as the primary motives behind e-WOM: venting negative feelings, concern for others, extraversion and positive self-enhancement, social benefits, economic incentives, helping the company, and advice seeking.[17]

THE CREDIBILITY OF FORMAL SOURCES, SPOKESPERSONS, AND ENDORSERS

Because consumers recognize that the intentions of commercial sources (e.g., manufacturers, service companies, financial institutions, retailers) are clearly profit oriented, they judge commercial **source credibility** on such factors as past performance, reputation, the kind and quality of products and service they are known to render, the image and attractiveness of the spokesperson used, the type of retail outlets through which they sell, and the media carrying their promotions.

Firms with well-established reputations have an easier time selling their products than do firms with lesser reputations. The ability of a quality image to invoke credibility is one of the reasons for the growth of *family brands* (discussed in Chapter 7). Manufacturers with favorable and well-established brand images prefer to give their new products the existing brand name in order to obtain ready acceptance from consumers. Marketers also use **institutional advertising**, which is designed to promote a favorable company image rather than to promote specific products.

Not-for-profit sources generally have more credibility than for-profit (commercial) sources. Formal sources that are perceived to be "neutral"—such as *Consumer Reports* or newspaper articles—have greater credibility than commercial sources because of the perception that they are more objective in their product assessments. That is why **publicity** is so valuable to a manufacturer: Citations of a product in an editorial context, rather than in a paid advertisement, give the reader much more confidence in the message. A recent study found that the publicity surrounding the Super Bowl increased viewers' attention to and recall of the advertisements shown during the game.[18]

Consumers sometimes regard the *spokesperson* delivering the product message as the source (or initiator) of the message. Thus, the "pitchman" (whether male or female) who appears in person or in a commercial or advertisement has a major influence on message credibility. Marketers often use celebrities as *endorsers* of their offerings, and a given celebrity's persuasive power is a function of consumers' awareness and likeability of the person (see Figure 9.3).[19] When a celebrity endorser has damaged his or her credentials through engaging in scandalous behavior, the marketer immediately disassociates itself from the endorser in question.

Many studies have investigated the relationship between the effectiveness of the message and the spokesperson or endorser employed. Here are some of the key findings of this body of research:

- The effectiveness of the spokesperson is related to the message itself. For example, when message comprehension is low, receivers rely on the spokesperson's credibility in forming attitudes toward the product, but when comprehension (and, thus, systematic information processing) is high, the expertise of the spokesperson has far less impact on a receiver's attitudes.
- The synergy between the endorser and the type of product or service advertised is very important, because, according to *associative learning theory* (Chapter 7), celebrities are conditioned with the products they promote. A recent study demonstrated that when there is an appropriate fit (or belongingness) between the celebrity and the product endorsed the conditioning will be more effective, robust, and enduring (this synergy is also termed *the match-up hypothesis*).[20] Therefore, for example, for attractiveness-related products (such as cosmetics), a physically attractive celebrity spokesperson is likely to enhance message credibility and generate a favorable and enduring attitude toward the brand. For attractiveness-unrelated products (e.g., a camera), an attractive endorser is

FIGURE 9.3
Source Credibility: Consumer Awareness and Likeability of Celebrities
Source: Julie Creswell, "Nothing Sells Like Celebrity," www.nytimes.com, June 22, 2008.

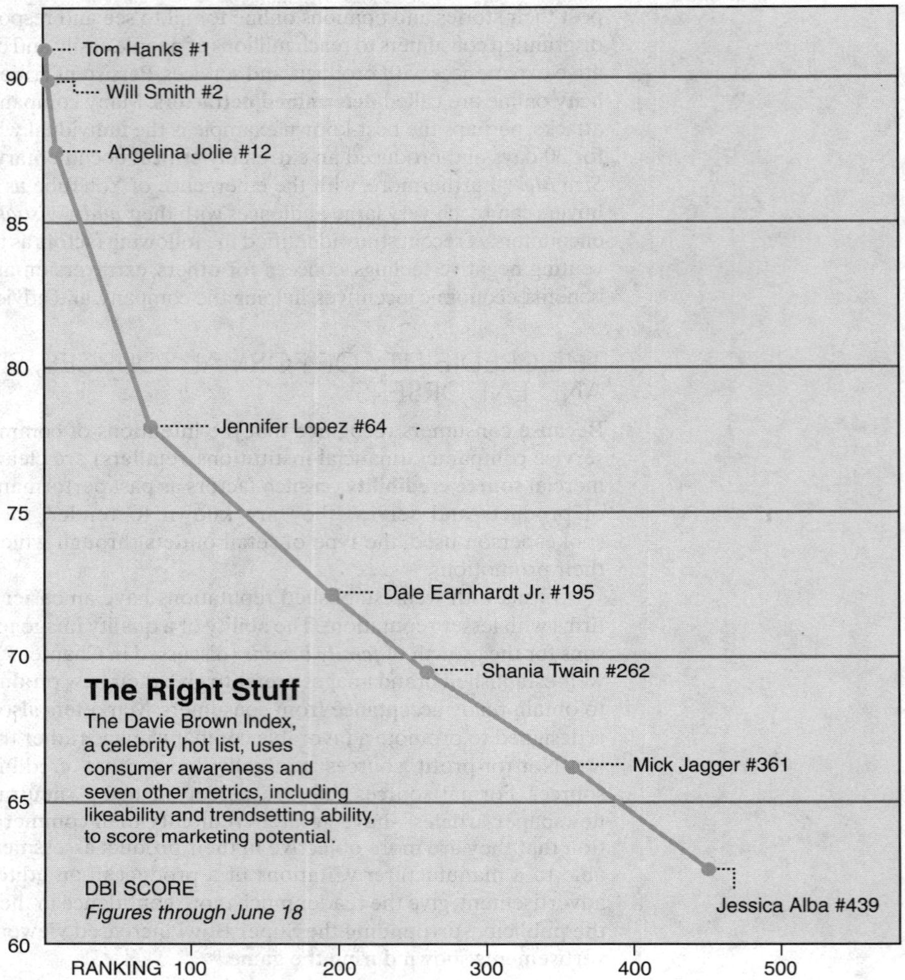

unlikely to have an effect. A glamorous celebrity endorser is more likely to be perceived as a credible source and positively impact attitudes toward the brand if featured in an ad for a hedonistic product (e.g., a very expensive watch) than for a utilitarian one (e.g., an inexpensive watch). The ad shown in Figure 9.4 illustrates such a synergy.

- Endorsers who have demographic characteristics (e.g., age, social class, and ethnicity) that are similar to those of the target audience are viewed as more credible and persuasive than those that do not. Also, consumers with strong ethnic identification are more likely to be persuaded by endorsers with similar ethnicity than individuals with weaker ethnic identification.
- The endorser's credibility is not a substitute for corporate credibility. Although an endorser's credibility may impact the audience's attitudes toward the *ad*, the perceived corporate credibility strongly impacts attitudes toward the advertised *brand.* Thus, marketers must develop multiple measures to evaluate the credibility and persuasiveness of advertising messages, such as attitudes toward the ad, attitudes toward the brand, and consumer purchase intentions.
- Marketers who use celebrities to give testimonials or endorse products must be sure that the specific wording of the endorsement lies within the recognized competence of the spokesperson. A tennis star can believably endorse a brand of analgesic with comments about how it relieves sore muscle pain; however, a recitation of medical evidence supporting the brand's superiority over other brands is beyond his or her expected knowledge and expertise, and thus may reduce (rather than enhance) message credibility.

FIGURE 9.4
Source: Courtesy of Omega.

QUESTION: *Why Are Consumers Likely to Perceive This Ad as Credible?*

Somewhat surprisingly, one study of advertising agencies found that none of the agencies surveyed had a written strategy regarding the selection of celebrity endorsers. The study's authors developed a list of factors to be considered in selecting celebrity endorsers, such as a careful match with the target audience, product, and brand; the celebrity's overall image; prior endorsements; trustworthiness; familiarity; expertise; profession; physical attractiveness; and whether the celebrity is a brand user.[21]

In formal interpersonal communications, consumers are more likely to be persuaded by salespersons who engender confidence and who give the impression of honesty and integrity. Consumer confidence in a salesperson is created in diverse ways, whether warranted or not. A salesperson who "looks you in the eye" often is perceived as more honest than one who evades direct eye contact. For many products, a sales representative who dresses well and drives an expensive, late-model car may have more credibility than one without such outward signs of success (and inferred representation of a best-selling product). For some products, however, a salesperson may achieve more credibility by dressing in the role of an expert. For example, a man selling home improvements may achieve more credibility by looking like someone who just climbed off a roof or out of a basement than by looking like a banker.

Vendor Credibility

The reputation of the retailer who sells the product has a major influence on message credibility. Products sold by well-known quality stores seem to carry the added endorsement (and implicit guarantee) of the store itself (e.g., "If Amazon.com recommends it, it must be a good book"). The aura of credibility generated by reputable vendor advertising reinforces the manufacturer's message as well. That is why so many ads for national brands often list the stores carrying the product.

The consumer's previous experience with the product or the vendor has a major impact on the credibility of the message. Fulfilled product expectations increase the credibility accorded future messages by the same advertiser; unfulfilled product claims or disappointing product experiences reduce the credibility of future messages. Thus, the key basis for message credibility is the ability of the product, service, or brand to deliver consistent quality, value, and satisfaction to consumers.

Medium Credibility

The reputation of the medium that carries the advertisement also enhances the credibility of the message. For example, the image of *Vogue* confers added status on the products advertised within. The reputation of the medium for honesty and objectivity also affects the believability of the advertising. Consumers often think that a medium they respect would not accept advertising for products it did not "know" were good. Because specialization in an area implies knowledge and expertise, consumers tend to regard advertising they see in special-interest magazines with more credibility than those they note in general-interest magazines.

Consumers today have more media options than ever before in new forms of media (such as the Web) and traditional media in new forms (such as online editions of well-established newspapers), but there is no single answer as to which medium has the most credibility. One study discovered that individuals interested in politics are shifting from television to the Web for political information.[22] Another study reported that the public generally considers opinion polls reported in traditional news media as more credible than online polls;[23] still another study reported that cable television newscasts are viewed as the most credible, and that differences in the perceived credibility of various media were related to the consumer's age.[24] Other sources report drastic increases in the number of people who do not believe what is reported by mass media channels.[25]

Effects of Time on Source Credibility: The Sleeper Effect

When information is transferred from the short-term memory to the cerebral cortex (where long-term memory is located), over time, it is separated from the context in which it was learned. For example, although you know what your nation's capital is, you probably do not remember how you learned this piece of information. This phenomenon is called **source amnesia** or the **sleeper effect**.[26] Thus, though a high-credibility source is initially more influential than a low-credibility source, research suggests that both positive and negative credibility effects tend to disappear after six weeks or so. Consumers forget the source of the message but remember the message itself. The sleeper effect is caused by *disassociation* of the message from the source over time, leaving just the message content in one's memory. This proposition supports using negative attack advertising in political campaigns. Over time, the initial negative perception of the "assailant" (i.e., the sender initiating the negative ad) is likely to fade while the negative information itself will probably be remembered.

The theory of **differential decay** suggests that the memory of a negative cue (e.g., a low-credibility source) simply decays faster than the message itself, leaving behind the primary message content. However, reintroduction of the same or similar message by the source serves to jog the audience's memory, and the original effect re-manifests itself; that is, the high-credibility source remains more persuasive than the low-credibility source. The implication for marketers who use high-credibility spokespersons is that they must repeat the same series of ads or commercials regularly in order to maintain a high level of persuasiveness.

The Receivers as the Target Audience

LEARNING OBJECTIVE

9.2 *To Understand the Role of the Message's Audience (Receivers) in the Communication Process.*

The sponsor (initiator) of the message first must decide to whom the message should be sent and what meaning it should convey. The *receiver* of formal marketing communications is generally a targeted prospect or customer (e.g., a member of the marketer's target audience). *Intermediary* and *unintended* audiences are also likely to receive marketers' communications. Examples of intermediary audiences are wholesalers, distributors, and retailers, who receive trade advertising from marketers designed to persuade them to order and stock merchandise, and relevant professionals (such as architects or physicians), who are sent *professional advertising* in the hopes that they will specify or prescribe the marketer's products. Unintended audiences include everyone who is exposed to the message who is not specifically targeted by the sender but often include publics that are important to the marketer, such as shareholders, creditors, suppliers, employees, bankers, and the local community. It is important to remember that all audiences are composed of *individual receivers,* each of whom interprets the message according to his or her own personal perceptions and experiences.

The message's source (or sender) must **encode** the message in such a way that its meaning is interpreted by the targeted audience in precisely the intended way. Marketers encode messages by using words, pictures, symbols, spokespersons, and special channels. The messages' receivers **decode** the messages they receive on the basis of their personal experiences, characteristics, and motives. The factors affecting the *decoding* and *comprehension* of persuasive messages include the receiver's personal characteristics and motives, involvement with the product or product category, the congruency of the message with the medium, and the receiver's mood. There are also barriers to communication that impact the receivers' reception and interpretations of promotional messages.

PERSONAL CHARACTERISTICS AND MOTIVES

The meaning derived from the message is a function of the message itself, the receiver's opportunity and ability to process the message, and the receiver's motivation. In fact, all of an individual's personal characteristics (described in earlier chapters) influence the accuracy with which the individual decodes a message. A person's demographics (such as age, gender, marital status), sociocultural memberships (social class, race, religion), and lifestyle determine how a message is interpreted. A bachelor may interpret a friendly comment from his unmarried neighbor as a "come-on"; a student may interpret a professor's easygoing manner as an indication of "relaxed" grading rigor. Personality, attitudes, and prior learning all affect how a message is decoded. Perception, based as it is on expectations, motivation, and past experience, also influences message interpretation. Therefore, not everyone reads and understands the marketing communications they receive in the same way that the sender intended.

One study, focused on gender-based differences in responding to charity ads, reported that women found altruistic appeals that stressed helping others more persuasive, whereas men tended to choose self-oriented themes that stressed helping oneself.[27] Another study discovered that persons who view themselves as more individualistic and unique and who tend to enjoy effortful thinking (i.e., they are high in the personality trait termed *need for cognition*) were more likely to be persuaded by comparative advertising than persons who possess lower levels of these personality traits.[28] Other researchers discovered that persons with a high need for cognition were more persuaded by messages that consisted of high-quality arguments followed by implicit, rather than explicit, conclusions.[29]

As discussed earlier, some promotional messages are focused at stimulating WOM. What motivates a person to talk about a product or service? Some people provide information or advice to others to satisfy some basic need of their own (e.g., an affiliation or ego need). However, opinion leaders may be unaware of their own underlying motives. As suggested earlier, opinion leaders may simply be trying to reduce their own postpurchase dissonance by confirming their own buying decisions. For instance, if Bradley subscribes to a satellite radio service and then is uncertain that he made the right choice, he may try to reassure himself by "talking up" the service's advantages to others. In this way, he relieves any doubts he may have about the recent purchase. Opinion receivers and seekers also have motivations that go beyond simply seeking information. Table 9.3 compares the motivations of opinion receivers with those of opinion leaders.

TABLE 9.3 A Comparison of the Motivations of Opinion Leaders and Opinion Receivers

OPINION LEADERS	OPINION RECEIVERS
Self-Improvement Motivations	
• Reduce postpurchase uncertainty or dissonance • Gain attention or status • Assert superiority and expertise • Feel like an adventurer • Experience the power of "converting" others	• Reduce the risk of making a purchase commitment • Reduce search time (e.g., avoid the necessity of shopping around)
Product-Involvement Motivations	
• Express satisfaction or dissatisfaction with a product or service	• Learn how to use or consume a product • Learn what products are new in the marketplace
Social-Involvement Motivations	
• Express neighborliness and friendship by discussing products or services that may be useful to others	• Buy products that have the approval of others, thereby ensuring acceptance
Message-Involvement Motivations	
• Express one's reaction to a stimulating advertisement by telling others about it	

Just who are opinion leaders? Can those consumers who are more likely to initiate WOM and become "buzz agents" be recognized by any distinctive characteristics? Can they be reached through specific media? Marketers have long sought answers to these questions, for if they are able to identify the relevant opinion leaders for their products, they can design marketing messages that encourage them to communicate with and influence the consumption behavior of others. Therefore, consumer researchers have attempted to develop a profile of the opinion leader. As was pointed out earlier, opinion leadership tends to be category specific; that is, an individual who is an opinion *leader* in one product category may be an opinion *receiver* in another product category, and it is therefore difficult to construct a generalized profile of the opinion leader without considering a particular product or service category of interest. However, the evidence indicates that opinion leaders across all product categories generally have several defining characteristics. First, they reveal a *keen sense of knowledge and interest* in the particular product or service area, and they are *likely to be consumer innovators*. They also demonstrate a greater *willingness to talk* about the product, service, or topic; they are *more self-confident*; and they are *more outgoing and gregarious* ("more sociable") than nonleaders. Furthermore, within the context of a specific subject area, opinion leaders *receive more information via nonpersonal sources* than nonleaders and are considered to have *expertise in their area of influence*. They also usually belong to the *same socioeconomic and age groups as their opinion receivers*.

People who generate WOM read special-interest publications and visit Web sites devoted to the specific topic or product category in which they "specialize." Thus, the opinion leader tends to have greater exposure to media specifically relevant to his or her area of interest than the other consumers. Several studies identified a special type of consumer influencer, the **market maven**. Market mavens possess a wide range of information about many different types of products, retail outlets, and other dimensions of markets. They initiate discussions with other consumers, respond to requests for market information, and like to shop and share their shopping expertise with others. While most opinion leaders are experts in categories of high-involvement products (e.g., cars, electronics), the influence of market mavens extends into such low-involvement products as razor blades and laundry detergents. Market mavens appear to be motivated by a sense of obligation to share information, a desire to help others, and the feeling of pleasure that comes with telling others about products.[30] Table 9.4 depicts a self-administered scale used to identify market mavens (similar scales are used to identify opinion leaders).[31] A recent study focused on the impact on one's *susceptibility to normative influence (SNI)*—a trait somewhat related to one's likelihood to be a leader or follower. The study discovered that people who scored high on SNI were more influenced by ads that included testimonials while those low on SNI were influenced mostly by information on product attributes.[32]

INVOLVEMENT AND CONGRUENCY

A person's level of involvement (see Chapter 7) plays a key role in how much attention is paid to the message and how carefully it is decoded; thus, involvement is an important consideration in the design and content of persuasive communications. One study discovered a relationship

TABLE 9.4 Market Maven Scale (Six-Point Agree/Disagree Response Format)

1. I like introducing new brands and products to my friends.
2. I like helping people by providing them with information about many kinds of products.
3. People ask me for information about products, places to shop, or sales.
4. If someone asked where to get the best buy on several products, I could tell him or her where to shop.
5. My friends think of me as a good source of information when it comes to new products or sales.

Source: Copyright © 2003 by M. E. Sharpe, Inc. From Ronald E. Goldsmith, Leisa R. Flynn, and Elizabeth B. Goldsmith, "Innovation Consumers and Market Mavens," *Journal of Marketing Theory and Practice*, vol. 11, no. 4 (Fall 2003): 58. Used with permission of M. E. Sharpe, Inc. All Rights Reserved. Not for reproduction.

between level of involvement and the style and context of an ad. Subjects with low involvement with the product preferred messages placed within a *congruent* context (e.g., a humorous ad within a humorous TV series) while persons highly involved with the product preferred messages that *contrasted* the style of ad and the context within which it was placed (e.g., a humorous ad within a rational context such as a TV documentary).[33] Another study showed that cognitively involving commercials shown in a cognitively involving program context produced higher recall among viewers than low-involvement commercials placed within an affective program context.[34]

MOOD

Mood, or affect (e.g., cheerfulness or unhappiness) plays a significant role in how a message is decoded, perceived, recalled, and acted upon. Marketers of many image-centered products such as perfume, fashion, and liquor have found that appeals focused on emotions and feelings associated with these products are more effective than rational appeals depicting the product's benefits. Generally, positive mood is likely to enhance the consumer's reaction to any ad. The consumer's mood is influenced by the *content* of the ad and by the *context* in which the advertising message appears (such as the accompanying TV program or adjacent newspaper story); these in turn affect the consumer's evaluation and recall of the message. One study showed that consumers with low familiarity with a service category prefer ads based on story appeals rather than lists of attributes and that such appeals work better when the receivers are in a happy mood while decoding the message.[35]

BARRIERS TO COMMUNICATION

Various "barriers" to communication may affect the accuracy with which consumers interpret messages. These include selective perception and psychological noise.

Selective Exposure to Messages

Consumers selectively perceive advertising messages. They read ads carefully for products they are interested in and tend to ignore advertisements that have no interest or relevance to them. Furthermore, technology provides consumers with increasingly sophisticated means to control their exposure to media. Consumers can now control their exposure to mass media and avoid commercials while watching TV by using the pause function when a string of commercials starts and then quickly returning to the broadcast once the ads are over. Viewers can also "time shift" by recording TV shows and viewing them at their leisure while skipping over commercials. Readers of newspapers and magazines online can create personalized editions of these publications and avoid many ads, and satellite radio allows consumers to avoid hearing radio ads. Caller ID, phone answering machines, the government's "do not call" list, and other devices allow consumers to screen out telemarketing and other unsolicited contacts from marketers. In response, marketers have increased their advertising via nontraditional media (discussed later in this chapter).

Psychological Noise

Just as telephone static can impair a phone conversation, **psychological noise** in the form of competing advertising messages or distracting thoughts, can impact the reception of a promotional message. A viewer faced with the clutter of nine successive commercial messages during a program break may actually receive and retain almost nothing of what he has seen. Similarly, an executive planning a department meeting while driving to work may be too engrossed in her thoughts to "hear" a radio commercial. There are various strategies that marketers use to overcome psychological noise:

- Repeated exposure to an advertising message (through *repetition* or *redundancy* of the advertising appeal) helps surmount psychological noise and facilitates message reception. Thus, repeating an ad several times is a must. (The effects of repetition on learning were discussed in Chapter 7.) The principle of redundancy also is seen in advertisements that use both illustrations and copy to emphasize the same points. To achieve more advertising redundancy, many marketers now place their messages in such places as video games, movie theaters, elevators, floors in supermarkets, and even public restrooms.

- Copywriters often use *contrast* to break through the psychological noise and advertising clutter. Contrast (discussed in Chapter 6) entails using features within the message itself to attract additional attention. Such strategies include featuring an unexpected outcome, increasing the amount of sensory input (such as color, scent, or sound), and identifying, through testing, message appeals that attract more attention.
- Digital technologies allow marketers to monitor the consumer's visits to Web sites, infer the person's interests from this data, and design and send customized promotional messages to that person. Indeed, personalization of promotional messages is a key feature of nontraditional (or "new") media discussed in the following section.

Of course, effective *positioning* and a *unique value (and selling) proposition* are the most effective ways to ensure that a promotional message stands out and is received and decoded appropriately by the target audience. Advertisements for products that are perceived to be unique and provide better value than competitive products are more likely to be received in their intended ways than other promotional messages within the advertising clutter.

The Media as the Channels for Transmitting Messages

Learning Objective

9.3 *To Learn About Advertising Media and How to Select the Right Media When Sending Promotional Messages Targeting Selected Consumer Groups.*

Media and communications models that have been used for decades are presently undergoing fundamental changes. Advertisers are unhappy with the current broadcast media because they are reaching increasingly smaller and more fragmented audiences and getting less "eyeballs" for the money they spend for TV ads. Consumers can avoid commercials with increasing ease, and a large number of broadcasted advertising messages reach many people who are not interested in (and unlikely to purchase) the products advertised. Advertisers complain that the Nielsen ratings do not accurately reflect the ethnic composition of the U.S. population and poorly monitor TV viewing via DVRs and other means. Cable operators realize that they have the means to monitor media viewing more accurately but are deeply aware of the privacy concerns of their subscribers. The TV networks, who have lost vast audiences to cable channels, realize that continuing to provide free programming underwritten by advertising revenues generated from reaching massive audiences of prime-time shows—a model in place since the early 1950s—may no longer be feasible. The networks, cable companies, and advertisers agree that the new communications model calls for targeting smaller groups of consumers who are already interested in the products advertised, and to whom they must provide more interactive and enticing ways of viewing promotional messages. In short, driven by technology, mass communication is going through the greatest changes since the development of spoken and written language.

The **medium**, or communications channel, can be *impersonal* (e.g., a mass medium) or *interpersonal* (a formal conversation between a salesperson and a customer, or an informal conversation between two or more people that takes place face-to-face, by telephone, by mail, or online). Today, there are two types of media that marketers use: mass media and new communication technologies grouped under the term **new media** (also termed *alternative* or *nontraditional media*). **Mass media** are the traditional avenues advertisers have used and are generally classified as *print* (newspapers, magazines, billboards) and *broadcast* (radio, television). Generally, mass media are *impersonal* because all receivers get the same message transmitted by a given source. The two types of media are discussed next.

TARGETING CONSUMERS THROUGH MASS MEDIA

Selecting the appropriate audience is the key component of a communications strategy. It is important to remember that an audience is made up of individuals—in many cases, great numbers of individuals. Because each individual has his or her own traits, characteristics, interests, needs, experience, and knowledge, the sender must segment the audience into groups that are homogeneous in terms of some relevant characteristic. Segmentation enables the sender to create specific messages for each target group and to run them in specific media that are seen, heard, or read by the relevant target group. It is unlikely that a marketer could develop a single message that would appeal simultaneously to its total audience. Efforts to use "universal" appeals phrased in simple language that everyone can understand invariably result in unsuccessful advertisements to which few people relate.

Companies that have many diverse audiences sometimes develop a communications strategy that consists of an overall (or umbrella) communications message to all their audiences, from which they spin off a series of related messages targeted directly to the specific interests of individual segments. In addition, to maintain positive communications with all of their publics, most large organizations use *public relations* to broadcast favorable information about the company and to suppress unfavorable information.

Media strategy is an essential component of a communications plan. It calls for the placement of ads in the specific media read, viewed, or heard by each targeted audience. To accomplish this, advertisers develop, through research, a **consumer profile** of their target customers that includes the specific media they read or watch. Media organizations research their own audiences and develop descriptive **audience profiles**. A cost-effective media choice is one that closely matches the advertiser's consumer profile to a medium's audience profile. Before selecting specific media vehicles, advertisers must select general media categories that will enhance the message they want to convey. Rather than select one media category to the exclusion of others, many advertisers use a multimedia campaign strategy, with one primary media category carrying the major burden of the campaign and other categories providing supplemental support. Table 9.5 compares the advantages and limitations of traditional advertising media along the dimensions of targeting precision (i.e., the ability to reach exclusively the intended audience), the ability to construct and send a persuasive message, degree of psychological noise, feedback, and relative cost.

TARGETING CONSUMERS THROUGH NEW (NONTRADITIONAL) MEDIA

New media are more *dynamic* than traditional mass media. While mass media transmit the same message to all the members of a given audience and the receivers are passive, messages transmitted via new media are: (1) **addressable**—they can be customized and addressed to a particular receiver and different receivers can get varied renderings of the same basic message; (2) **interactive**—the receivers can interact with the sender during its transmission; and (3) **response-measurable**—a receiver's response to a promotional message can be measured more precisely and directly than his or her response to a message transmitted via mass media.[36] New media consist of *digital technologies* that meet the three criteria stated above such as certain TV platforms and personal digital devices, cell phones, and computers. Over the past few years, marketers have steadily shifted advertising expenditures from traditional media to nontraditional media. New or nontraditional media is sometimes called "**unmeasured media**" because the organizations monitoring companies' advertising expenditures have not developed distinct means for computing the amount of money spent on each "unmeasured" medium separately. Such measurements have existed for decades for print and TV advertising, which is considered "measured media." This drastic shift in advertising expenditures is depicted in Figure 9.5.

There is no standard definition of what is considered "new," "nontraditional," or "alternative," media. The new media described here were classified, in part, according to a system developed by PQ Media—a research company focused on the study of unmeasured media.[37] Each form of new media is discussed next.

Out-of-Home and On-the-Go Media

This category consists of new promotional tools as well as some older means that were significantly updated with new technology. These media target mobile customers in more innovative, captivating, and interactive ways than mass media. The media group includes: (1) *Captive advertising screens* placed in buildings (e.g., hotels or office buildings), stores, theaters, and transit vehicles (e.g., taxis); (2) *Digital billboards and displays* placed within roads, transit locations, events, and stores; and (3) *Ambient advertising* (also know as *experiential advertising*) which includes messages delivered through platforms and means that have not been used before. For example, during the cold holiday season, Kraft Foods built and maintained heated bus shelters (in Chicago and other northern cities) designed to convey to consumers the warm feeling they would get if they eat stuffing.[38]

Some of the out-of-home media described above are actually more technologically sophisticated forms of such traditional advertising tools as transit advertising and billboards. While these technologically advanced media can somewhat successfully penetrate the clutter and "psychological noise" (discussed earlier) and some are interactive, they are generally neither addressable nor more response measurable than traditional mass media.

TABLE 9.5 Persuasive Capabilities and Limitations of Traditional Advertising Media

	TARGETING PRECISION	MESSAGE DEVELOPMENT AND EXECUTION	DEGREE OF PSYCHOLOGICAL NOISE	OBTAINING FEEDBACK	RELATIVE COST
Newspapers	Access to large audiences. Not very selective in reaching consumers with specific demographics. Effective for reaching local consumers.	Flexible. Messages can be designed and published quickly. Limited production quality and short message life.	High clutter. Many messages competing for attention.	Sales volume. Redemptions of special promotions and level of store traffic provide immediate feedback.	Determined by size of ad and the medium's circulation. Affordable for local businesses. Permits joint advertising by national manufacturers and local sellers.
Magazines	High geographic and demographic selectivity. *Selective binding* [a] allows more precise targeting of subscribers with the desired demographics.	High quality of production. High credibility of ads in special-interest magazines. Long message life and pass-along readership. Long lead time required.	High clutter. Some magazines may not guarantee ad placement in a particular position within the magazine.	Delayed and indirect feedback, such as the Starch scores that measure recall and attention.	Determined by cost of page and circulation. Top magazines charge very high rates.
Television	Reaches very large audiences. Many programs lack audience selectivity.	Appeals to several senses. Enables messages that draw attention and generate emotion. Short-duration messages must be repeated. Long lead time.	High clutter. Viewers can avoid message exposures by channel surfing or using advanced technologies such as TiVo.	Day-after recall tests measure how many consumers were exposed to the message and, to a lesser degree, their characteristics.	Very high costs based on how many consumers watch a given program.
Radio	High geographic and demographic audience selectivity.	Audio messages only. Short exposure. Relatively short lead time.	High clutter. Listeners can easily switch among stations during commercials.	Delayed feedback, such as day-after recall tests.	Based on size of the audience reached. Local radio may be relatively inexpensive.
Direct Mail [b]	High audience selectivity. Enables personalization. Perceived by many as "junk mail" and discarded.	Enables novel, visually appealing, and dramatic messages (including the addition of sensory inputs).	No competing messages within the mailing.	Easy to measure feedback through limited pretests and cost per inquiry and cost per order. Delayed feedback.	Relatively high cost per person per mailing due to "junk mail" image.
Direct Marketing[c]	Enables building and refining electronic databases of qualified buyers based on inquiries and purchases. Permits the development of selective customer segments. Privacy concerns make this practice difficult.	A function of the medium used to solicit the direct response from the customer.	Can be relatively free of clutter, even in media where there is generally a lot of noise. For example, infomercials provide advertisers with a "clutter-free" environment.	Generates measurable responses and enables marketers to measure the profitability of their efforts directly.	Determined through such variables as cost per inquiry, cost per sale, and revenue per advertisement.

Notes: [a]Selective binding is a technique that enables publishers to narrowly segment their subscription bases. When readers subscribe, they are asked to provide demographic information, which the publisher enters into a database. Through a sophisticated computerized system, the publisher is able to select specific subscribers, based on reader demographic profiles, to receive special sections that are bound into a limited number of magazines. [b]Direct mail includes catalogs, letters, brochures, promotional offers, and any materials mailed directly to customers at their homes or offices. [c]Direct marketing is not a medium but an interactive marketing technique that uses various media (such as mail, print, broadcast, telephone, and cyberspace) for the purpose of soliciting a direct response from a consumer. Electronic shopping (through home-shopping TV channels or interactive cable) is also considered direct marketing.

FIGURE 9.5
The Drastic Shift of Advertising Expenditures from Traditional to New Media
Sources: *Advertising Age* and *The New York Times*.

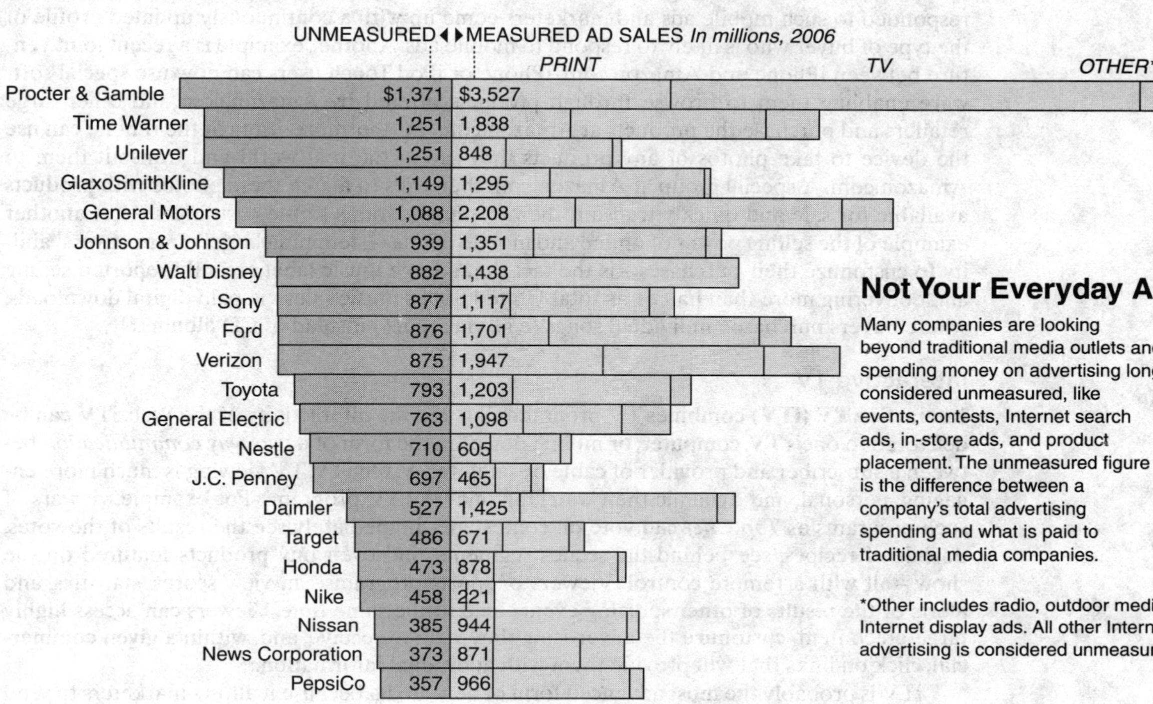

Not Your Everyday Ad

Many companies are looking beyond traditional media outlets and spending money on advertising long considered unmeasured, like events, contests, Internet search ads, in-store ads, and product placement. The unmeasured figure is the difference between a company's total advertising spending and what is paid to traditional media companies.

*Other includes radio, outdoor media, and Internet display ads. All other Internet advertising is considered unmeasured.

Online and Mobile Media

This category is also called **consumer-generated media** and **mobile advertising** and it includes all ads reaching the consumer online and on any mobile communication devices such as personal digital assistants (e.g., Palm), cell phones, and smartphones (e.g., BlackBerry and iPhone). The message-transmission tools used within this media include search engines (also called search and lead generation), online classifieds and yellow pages, online video and rich media, consumer-generated ads, and e-direct marketing.

Online and mobile media permit marketers to send *addressable*, customized messages, based on data gathered from tracing consumers' surfing and clicks online, in combination with other information. Such additional data includes the receiver's location (which can be determined from an IP address or a GPS integrated into a mobile device) and information from "cookies" installed on the hard drive of a digital device. These messages are often *interactive* because an action by the consumer—in the form of a click on a link or banner—triggers the transmission of a message. In addition, addressable communications—often termed **narrowcast messages**—are significantly more *response measurable* than traditional broadcasted ads.

Advertising on cell phones is gaining popularity because mobile phones are an ideal forum for personalized advertising. A TV network has teamed up with an online social network in recruiting participants in an experiment in addressable and location-based advertising.[39] A publishing company started delivering educational content via cell phones.[40] Several providers of wireless services teamed up with companies by rewarding subscribers who agree to receive ads on their cell phones with reduced rates and other incentives.[41] As the number of cell phones and other wireless communications devices continues to grow, mobile advertising is likely to become a component of most advertisers' media plans.

The following examples illustrate the tremendous marketing potential of online and mobile media. Consider a consumer driving with a GPS navigation device (or a GPS-enabled smartphone) who receives an ad for a sale in a store located near a highway exit several miles away. The consumer reacts to the message, stops by the store, purchases the item, and pays by credit card. The data about the purchase is immediately entered into a database that includes demographic information about the consumer, as well as the person's usage of mobile digital devices. Later on, the consumer receives an e-mail thanking her for the purchase and asking her to subscribe to "alerts" about future sales. Probably immediately, the data about the entire shopping encounter is integrated with the consumer data of thousands of persons who responded to such mobile ads and marketers come up with a continuously updated profile of the type of buyer who is likely to respond to mobile ads. Another example is a recent joint venture between iPhone and Amazon.com. iPhone or iPod Touch users can now use special software enabling them to browse through products offered by Amazon.com and other large retailers and purchase the products at Amazon.com. Furthermore, users of the iPhone can use the device to take photos of any products they see in the real world and transmit them to Amazon.com. A special group at Amazon.com then tries to match these photos with products available for sale and quickly transmit the recommendations to the customers.[42] Yet another example of the selling power of online and mobile media—stemming largely from buyers' ability to customize their purchases—is the fact that a large music label recently reported selling and delivering more than half of its total United States music sales via paid digital downloads, where buyers purchased individual songs (e.g., via iTunes) instead of CD albums.[43]

Interactive TV

Interactive TV (iTV) combines TV programming and the interactivity of the Web. iTV can be delivered to one's TV, computer, or mobile device in the form of a *two-way communication* between a subscriber and provider of cable or satellite TV. On iTV, TV viewing is much more engaging, personal, and dynamic than watching one-way TV programs. For example, viewers of such programs as *Top Chef* can vote on contestants, immediately see the results of the votes, download recipes, see behind-the-scenes segments, and even buy products featured on the show—all with a remote control. Viewers of sports programs can view scores, statistics, and alerts of the results of other sporting events held at the same time. Viewers can access highly targeted content, customize the advertising they wish to receive, and, within a given commercial, click on links that will provide them with additional information.[44]

iTV is probably the most advanced form of new media because it allows marketers to send *addressable ads*, allows *interactivity between the sender and the receiver* (which increases the receiver's level of engagement with the content), and permits marketers to *measure the results* and the persuasive impact of their messages very effectively.

MEDIA AND MESSAGE CONGRUENCE

The fusion of digital technologies and personal communication devices and the integration of TV—the most powerful persuasive medium—into computers and mobile devices fundamentally changed the format of the advertising content. For decades, the **broadcast model** meant that all the viewers of a given TV program (or all the readers of a particular newspaper or magazine) received the *same* advertising message. Presently, marketers can customize advertisements and send addressable promotional messages directed at individuals, or *narrowcast messages* to relatively small audiences defined by special interests or geographical locations. Also, in order to bypass the clutter in the advertising sphere and consumers' reluctance to view ads, marketers increasingly use sophisticated forms of **branded entertainment**. However, advertisers in new media must ensure that the message, product, and medium are a good match. For example, one study discovered that advertising old and unexciting brands on mobile phones was ineffective.[45]

Addressable Advertising

Many of the readers of this text probably purchased products at Amazon.com, rented a movie or program at Netflix.com, or traded an item on eBay.com. These premier online merchants analyze the purchase behaviors of their users (including consumers' ratings of the products rented or bought) and utilize this data to make customized recommendations to individual users about future offerings. Digitas (and other similar companies) uses data from major Web portals such as Google and Yahoo! to build proprietary models utilized to design the different ads a customer sees when he views an ad for the first time, the second time, after buying the product, and so on; the various ads are also a function of the viewer's demographics and past advertising exposure.[46] The ethics of collecting the data used to develop addressable ads are discussed in Chapter 16. A recent study demonstrated that consumers favor interactive Web sites where they feel that they receive personalized messages when they seek feedback (and especially when they complain) and where they can easily and quickly engage in two-way communications.[47] Figure 9.6 depicts an example of customized ads.

FIGURE 9.6
Hypothetical Customized Ads Based on Consumers' Online Behavior

Source: Fictitious advertisement created for educational purposes by Joe Wisenblitt. Photo credit: Courtesy of PlasticLogic.com.

INITIAL APPEAL
The ad's objective is to create interest in the product – a super-thin light and robust electronic reader positioned as a replacement for one's bulky and heavy briefcase.

LATER APPEAL
The product's picture is enlarged since already-interested viewers are likely to want to take a closer look. The tagline establishes brand identity and product features are detailed.

ANOTHER LATER APPEAL
The product's picture is lighter and less dramatic. The tag line is a personal appeal and product features are stated in more technical terms.

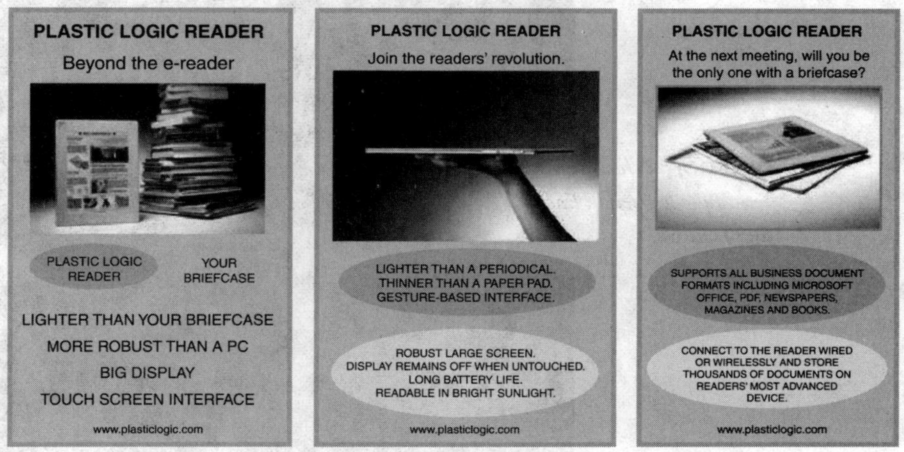

Branded Entertainment

Branded entertainment—often called *product placement*—dates back to the 1950s, an era when most popular TV shows were sponsored by companies and prominently displayed products throughout their broadcast. Over the years, thousands of paid-for embeds of products and brands appeared in many films and TV shows. Due to the consumers' ability to avoid viewing commercials (discussed earlier), in recent years, advertisers' expenditures on branded entertainment have increased significantly, and this method has spread beyond movies and TV and into other vehicles of communications. Apparently, marketers believe that they can build significant product awareness by integrating brands into the content of entertainment programs, where consumers cannot avoid them (the forms of such integration were discussed in Chapter 6).

In addition to embedding brands in films and TV programs, marketers now develop **webisodes** (i.e., short videos shown online featuring entertainment centered around a brand) and use **advergaming** (i.e., brands embedded in video games played at homes, arcades, or online). In addition, many recent programs billed as "entertainment" are actually showcases for prominently featuring products in ways designed to form emotional connections between brands and consumers (e.g., *The Apprentice*, *Top Chef*, *Survivor*, and various "makeover" programs). Products have also appeared on the sets on news broadcasts and within the dialogues of programs, and some advertisers and legislators have increasingly criticized such product placements (the ethical issues related to branded entertainment are discussed in Chapter 16).[48] By some estimates, the expenditures on branded entertainment have grown at an annual rate of 15 percent over the past five years and will shortly reach $7 billion.[49]

Designing Persuasive Messages

LEARNING OBJECTIVE

9.4 *To Learn How Understanding Consumers Enables Marketers to Develop Persuasive Messages.*

A **message** can be **verbal** (spoken or written), **nonverbal** (a photograph, an illustration, or a symbol), or a combination of the two. For example, Figure 9.1 (featured at the start of this chapter) depicts an ad portraying nonverbal, symbolic communications (in the form of hand gestures) in three different cultures. The message is the thought, idea, attitude, image, or other information that the sender wishes to convey to the intended audience. The sponsor, who may be an individual or an organization, must first establish the objectives of the message, select an appropriate medium for sending it, and design (encode) the message in a manner that is appropriate to each medium and to each audience. The objectives of a persuasive message include creating awareness of a service, promoting sales of a product, encouraging (or discouraging) certain practices, attracting retail patronage, reducing postpurchase dissonance, creating goodwill

FIGURE 9.7A

Source: Bertolli/Unilever.
© Gentl & Hyers, photographers and Shari Warren, illustrator. Used courtesy of Unilever, Inc.

QUESTION: *Which Advertising Technique Is Used in Each Ad, and How So?*

or a favorable image, or any combination of these and other communications objectives. In order to encode the message in a form that the audience will understand its intended meaning (i.e., decode it successfully), the sender must know exactly what he or she is trying to say and why (i.e., message objectives) and understand the target audience's personal characteristics. The impact of psychological and sociocultural factors on consumers' responses to communications is discussed throughout this book. For example, the *cognitive learning models* (discussed in Chapter 7) depict a process in which exposure to a message leads to interest and desire for the product and, ultimately, to buying behavior, and an explanation of how one's personality traits impact a person's reactions to various promotional appeals was discussed in Chapter 5.

MESSAGE STRUCTURE AND PRESENTATION

Some of the decisions that marketers must make in designing a message include the use of *resonance, positive* or *negative message framing, one-sided* or *two-sided messages*, and the *order* of presentation.

FIGURE 9.7B
Source: Courtesy of Nokia, Inc.

Resonance

Advertising resonance is wordplay, often consisting of a humorous double meaning, and usually accompanied by a relevant picture (see Figure 9.7). By using resonance in ads, marketers hope to increase the chances that consumers will notice their ads, remember them, and view them favorably. As an example, research has examined the effectiveness of metaphors and puns, such as a car seat with a package of motion sickness remedy serving as the seat belt's buckle. The study concluded that using rhetorical figures and symbols in ads increased the recall and memory of these messages; these findings are consistent with data from Starch Readership Surveys (see Chapter 7) showing that consumers are more likely to read ads that employ resonance than those that do not.[50]

Message Framing

Should a marketer stress the benefits to be gained by using a specific product (*positive* message framing) or the benefits to be lost by not using the product (*negative* message framing)?

Research suggests that the appropriate message framing decision depends on the consumer's attitudes and characteristics as well as the product itself. For example, one study found that persons with a low need for cognition were more likely to be persuaded by negatively framed messages.[51] Another study found that individuals with an independent self-image (i.e., who view themselves as defined by unique characteristics) were more persuaded by messages stressing an *approach* goal (positive framing); and those with an interdependent self-view (i.e., who view themselves as defined by others) found messages that stress *avoidance* goals more convincing (negative framing).[52] A study of advertised products that enabled the early detection of disease indicated that positively framed anecdotal messages were less persuasive than negatively framed anecdotal messages.[53] A recent study discovered that negative message framing was more effective than positive framing when respondents had less opportunity to process the information in the ad, but less effective when respondents had more opportunity to process the ad's content.[54]

One-Sided Versus Two-Sided Messages

Should marketers pretend that their products are the only ones of their kind, or should they acknowledge competing products? Some marketers stress only positive factors about their products and pretend that competition does not exist. However, when competition does exist and when it is likely to be vocal, such advertisers tend to lose credibility with the consumer. The credibility of an advertised claim can often be enhanced by actually disclaiming superiority of some product features in relation to a competing brand or by not claiming that the product is a universal cure. For example, an ad for a men's hair regrowth product may state that, after clinical testing, while almost half the men using the product experienced modest to dense hair regrowth, about a third experienced minimal hair regrowth, and about one-sixth had no regrowth whatsoever. The admission that the product did not always work enhanced the credibility of the ad.

The decision whether to use a one- or two-sided message also depends on the nature of the audience and the nature of the competition. If the audience is friendly (e.g., if it uses the advertiser's products), if it initially favors the communicator's position, or if it is not likely to hear an opposing argument, then a *one-sided (supportive) message* that stresses only favorable information is most effective. However, if the audience is critical or unfriendly (e.g., if it uses competitive products), if it is well educated, or if it is likely to hear opposing claims, then a *two-sided (refutational) message* is likely to be more effective. Two-sided messages can also be very effective when consumers are likely to see competitors' negative counterclaims or when consumer attitudes toward the brand are already negative.

Order Effects

Is it best to present your commercial first or last? Communications researchers have found that the *order* in which a message is presented affects audience receptivity. For example, on TV, the commercials shown first are recalled the best, whereas those in the middle are recalled the least. When just two competing messages are presented, one after the other, the evidence as to which position is more effective is somewhat conflicting. Some researchers have found that the material presented first produces a greater effect (*primacy effect*), whereas others have found that the material presented last is more effective (*recency effect*). Magazine publishers recognize the impact of **order effects** by charging more for ads on the front, back, and inside covers of magazines than for the inside magazine pages because of their greater visibility and recall.

Order is also important in listing product benefits within an ad. If audience interest is low, the most important point should be made first to attract attention. However, if interest is high, it is not necessary to pique curiosity, so product benefits can be arranged in ascending order, with the most important point mentioned last. When both favorable information and unfavorable information are to be presented (as in an annual stockholders' report), placing the favorable material first often produces greater tolerance for the unfavorable news. A recent study found that revealing the brand name at the onset of a message enhances brand recall and message persuasiveness.[55]

ADVERTISING APPEALS

Marketers have many options in selecting the appeal to be conveyed by a promotional message. The advertising appeals most commonly used are discussed next.

Comparative Advertising

Comparative advertising is a widely used marketing strategy in which a marketer claims product superiority for its brand over one or more explicitly named or implicitly identified competitors, either on an overall basis or on selected product attributes. Some critics of the technique maintain that comparative ads often assist recall of the competitor's brand at the expense of the advertised brand. However, the wide use of comparative advertising indicates that marketers are confident that comparative ads exert positive effects on brand attitudes, purchase intentions, and actual purchases. Among more sophisticated consumers, comparative ads elicit higher levels of cognitive processing and better recall, and are likely to be perceived as more relevant than noncomparative ads. A study that tested the degree of negativity in comparative messages (by using positive, negative, and mildly negative comparative messages) for several products reported that negative elements in an ad contributed to its effectiveness as long as they were believable or were offset by some elements that made the ad appear neutral.[56] Another study uncovered gender differences in response to comparative ads; comparative ads generated greater levels of brand-evaluation involvement among men but not among women. Among women, attention-getting comparative appeals produced inferences regarding the ads' manipulative intentions and reduced purchase likelihood.[57] Yet another study found that *promotion-focused* consumers (i.e., those who focus on the aspirational aspects and the likely positive consequences of a purchase) react to messages differently than *prevention-focused* consumers (i.e., those who focus on the presence or absence of negative outcomes such as safety). In comparative ads, negative framing led prevention-focused consumers to evaluate the advertised brand positively and the other brand negatively. Among promotion-focused consumers, positive framing led to positive evaluation of the advertised brand but did not impact evaluations of the comparison brand.[58]

Overall, comparative advertising has been used more in the United States than in other countries. However, one study of American and Thai consumers discovered that the persuasive ability of comparative ads was related to the two personality traits—*self-construal* (the degree to which people view themselves as autonomous and independent) and *need for cognition*—in the same way in both countries.[59] Another study compared American and Korean consumers and demonstrated that cultural values were more important in influencing reactions to comparative ads than reactions to noncomparative ads, and also that *need for cognition* impacted the persuasiveness of comparative ads for both groups.[60] These studies and many others support the view that, if used properly and in the right context, comparative marketing is a highly effective positioning strategy.

There has been considerable concern expressed as to the ability of comparative advertising to mislead consumers, including several legal actions against companies by the U.S. Federal Trade Commission. Many consumer advocates have pursued the development of specific measures designed to gauge a comparative ad's ability to mislead consumers. Figure 9.8 depicts two examples of comparative advertising.

Fear

Fear is an effective appeal often used in marketing communications. Some researchers have found a negative relationship between the intensity of fear appeals and their ability to persuade, so that strong fear appeals tend to be less effective than mild fear appeals. A number of explanations have been offered for this phenomenon. Strong fear appeals concerning a highly relevant topic (such as cigarette smoking) cause the individual to experience cognitive dissonance, which is resolved either by rejecting the practice or by rejecting the unwelcome information. Because giving up a comfortable habit is difficult, consumers more readily reject the threat. This they do by a variety of techniques, including denial of its validity ("There still is no real proof that smoking causes cancer"), the belief that they are immune to personal disaster ("It can't happen to me"), and a diffusing process that robs the claim of its true significance ("I play it safe by smoking only filter cigarettes"). Therefore, marketers should use reasonable but not extreme fear appeals and also recognize that fear appeals are not always appropriate. For example, information labels affixed to full-fat, reduced-fat, and nonfat products are likely to be more effective than warning labels.

Fear appeals are commonly used in antidrug campaigns. Such ads are more likely to be effective if they portray both the negative social consequences of drug use and the physical damages that drugs inflict on one's body. Fear appeals are unlikely to be effective among persons who score high on the personality variable termed *sensation seeking*. A high sensation seeker is more likely to use drugs and react negatively to fear-focused antidrug messages, feeling that

FIGURE 9.8A

Source: Courtesy of Campbells.

QUESTION: *Which Advertising Appeal Is Shown in Each Ad, and Why Is It Used?*

he or she is immortal. Male and females appear to react differently to fear appeals. A five-month study of high school students discovered that short-term cosmetic fear appeals (such as yellow teeth or bad breath) used in ads to stop or reduce smoking were more persuasive for males, while long-term health fear appeals (such as getting cancer later in life) were more persuasive for females.[61]

There is no single explanation of the relationship between fear appeals and persuasiveness. One theory proposes that individuals cognitively appraise the available information regarding the severity of the threat, then they appraise the likelihood that the threat will occur; they evaluate whether coping behavior can eliminate the threat's danger, and if so, whether they have the ability to perform the coping behavior. This theory is called the *ordered protection motivation model* (OPM).

In some cases, marketers are required to mention some possibly detrimental side effects of using a product; they must recognize that these mentions may have a negative impact on the product's proclaimed benefits and may result in negative attitudes toward the product itself. For that reason, when the benefits of a new pharmaceutical are discussed by actors in a TV ad,

FIGURE 9.8B

Source: Advertisement reprinted with the permission of Nestlé. CARNATION® is a registered trademark of Société des Produits Nestlé S.A., Vevey, Switzerland."

the negative side effects—which the company is required to mention although they may provoke fear—are usually rapidly intoned by a voice-over while the actors cheerfully repeat the drug's benefits. Figure 9.9 illustrates a humorous fear appeal (using humor in advertising is discussed next).

Humor

Many marketers use humorous appeals in the belief that humor will increase the acceptance and persuasiveness of their advertising communications. Therefore, humor is the most common advertising appeal used and also the most studied one. The findings of scores of studies on using humor in advertising indicated that: (1) Humor attracts attention and enhances one's liking of the product advertised; (2) Humor does not harm the comprehension of ads, and, in some cases, it aids comprehension; (3) Humor does not increase an ad's persuasive impact or a source's credibility; (4) Humor that is relevant to the product is more effective than humor unrelated to the product; (5) Humor is more effective in ads of existing products than in ads of new products, and more effective in targeting consumers that already have a positive attitude for the product;

FIGURE 9.9

Source: Courtesy of ConsumerSearch.com. All rights reserved.

QUESTION: *Which Two Advertising Appeals Are Shown in This Ad, and What Are the Advantages and Limitations of Each?*

(6) Using humor is more appropriate for advertising low-involvement than high-involvement products; and (7) The effects of humorous ads vary by the audience's demographics.

A recent study developed a measure of a personality trait named *need for humor* (NFH) that is focused on a person's tendency to enjoy, engage, or seek out amusement and suggested that these cognitive factors can better explain how consumers respond to humorous advertisements.[62] Another study discovered that ad recall was damaged when the humor was expected and this adverse effect was more pronounced for individuals with low need for humor.[63] Humorous ads were found to be more memorable when humor was strong and related to the message.[64] Placing product in humorous movie scenes evoked positive emotions, but other variables played a part in the resulting decision process regarding purchase.[65] Figure 9.10 is the photo board of a TV spot using humor. In this commercial, Sanjaya – a former contestant on *American Idol* – is trying to enter the fortress residence of a famous spiritual guru. Sanjaya is

FIGURE 9.10

Source: © 2008, Nationwide Mutual Insurance Company.

QUESTION: *Which Advertising Appeal Is Featured Here, and What Are Its Persuasive Capabilities and Limitations?*

Continued

FIGURE 9.10
Continued

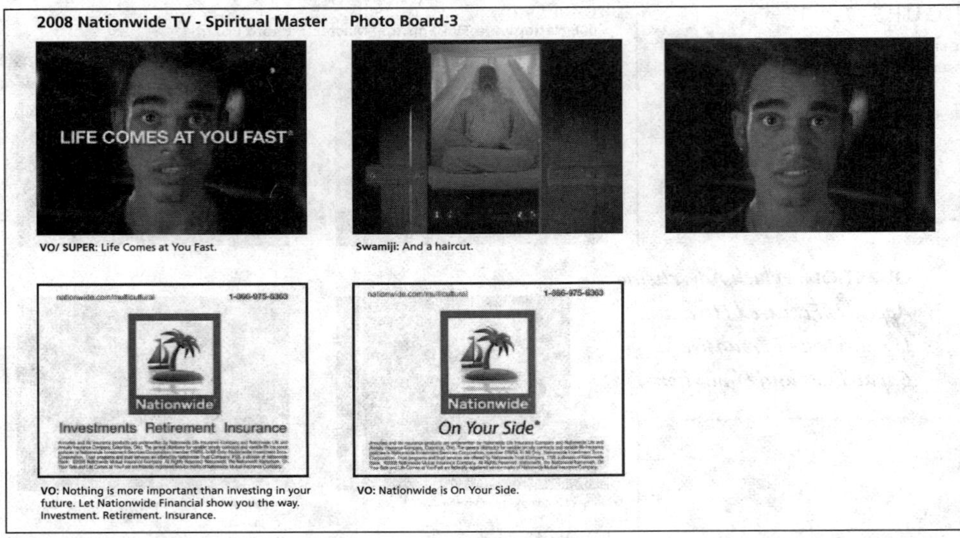

singing and the varying weather, his clothing, and hairstyles indicate that he has been standing and singing in an attempt to gain entry for a long time. Finally, in an apparent attempt to stop Sanjaya's singing, the guru's assistant allows Sanjaya to enter and he meets the "Spiritual Master." The commercial ends with a funny exchange between Sanjaya and the guru setting the humorous background for the punch line that is a promotional message from Nationwide Insurance.

Abrasive Advertising

How effective can unpleasant or annoying ads be? All of us have at one time or another been repelled by so-called *agony commercials*, which depict in diagrammatic detail the internal and intestinal effects of heartburn, indigestion, clogged sinus cavities, hammer-induced headaches, and the like. Nevertheless, pharmaceutical companies often run such commercials with great success because they appeal to a certain segment of the population that suffers from ailments that are not visible and thus elicit little sympathy from family and friends. Their complaints are legitimized by commercials with which they immediately identify. With the sponsor's credibility established ("They really understand the misery I'm going through"), the message itself tends to be highly persuasive in getting consumers to buy the advertised product.

Sex in Advertising

In our highly permissive society, sensual advertising seems to permeate the print media and the airwaves. Advertisers are increasingly trying to provoke attention with suggestive illustrations, crude language, and nudity in their efforts to appear "hip" and contemporary. In today's advertising, there is a lot of explicit and daring sexual imagery, extending far beyond the traditional product categories of fashion and fragrance into such categories as shampoo, beer, cars, and home construction.

There is little doubt that sexual themes have attention-getting value, but studies show that they rarely encourage actual consumption behavior. However, sexual advertising appeals often detract consumers from the message content. Sexual appeals tend to interfere with message comprehension, particularly when there is substantial information to be processed. Because the visual sexual elements in an ad are more likely to be processed than the ad's verbal content, the cognitive processing of the product information may be incomplete. In addition, nudity may negatively impact the product message.

The type of interest that sexual advertising evokes often stops exactly where it starts—with sex. If a sexually suggestive or explicit illustration is not relevant to the product advertised, it has little effect on consumers' buying intentions. This highlights the potential risk of sexually oriented advertising: The advertiser may be giving up persuasiveness to achieve "stopping power." When using sex to promote a product, the advertiser must be sure that the product, the ad, the

TABLE 9.6 Types of Celebrity Appeals

TYPES	DEFINITION
Testimonial	Based on personal usage, a celebrity attests to the quality of the product or service.
Endorsement	Celebrity lends his or her name and appears on behalf of a product or service with which he or she may or may not be an expert.
Actor	Celebrity presents a product or service as part of character endorsement.
Spokesperson	Celebrity represents the brand or company over an extended period of time.

target audience, and the use of sexual themes and elements all work together. When sex is relevant to the product, it can be an extremely potent copy theme. For example, the advertisers of fragrances for either men or women often use highly romantic or suggestive visuals in their ads, implying that the use of the fragrance will result in a meaningful or sultry romance.

Audience Participation

Earlier we spoke about the importance of feedback in the communications process. The provision of feedback changes the communications process from one-way to two-way communication. This is important to senders because it enables them to determine whether and how well communication has taken place. But feedback also is important to receivers because it enables them to participate, to be involved, to experience in some way the message itself. Participation by the receiver reinforces the message. An experienced communicator asks questions and opinions of an audience to draw them into the discussion. Many professors use the participative approach in classrooms rather than the more sterile lecture format because they recognize that student participation tends to facilitate internalization of the information covered.

Timely Advertising

The financial crisis of September 2008 had a significant impact on advertising. For example, an ad for a health club urged consumers to make "a renewed commitment to lead a healthy life during these changing times." An ad for a chain restaurant promoting an inexpensive meal used humor by stating: "It's one thing to bail out Wall Street. But who's gonna bail you out?"[66] Ads for several Broadway shows emphasized hope for better times ahead.[67] Other marketers came up with appeals promoting products as affordable and sensible rather than indulgent and fabulous.[68] An ad campaign for a shopping district consisted of ads that did not suggest products to buy but instead listed fun and upbeat things one can do, such as catching snowflakes on one's tongue.[69] Finally, some Halloween ads reflected the tough economic times with such appeals as "Incredible savings that are almost scary."[70]

Celebrities

Using spokespersons in advertising was discussed earlier in this chapter. A firm employing a celebrity to promote its product or service can use the celebrity in a **testimonial**, an **endorsement**, as an **actor** in a commercial, or as a company **spokesperson** (see Table 9.6).

Feedback Determines the Message's Effectiveness

LEARNING OBJECTIVE

9.5 *To Understand How Marketers Measure the Effectiveness of Their Promotional Messages.*

Since marketing communications are usually designed to persuade a target audience to act in a desired way (e.g., to purchase a specific brand or product, to vote for a presidential candidate), their ultimate test is the receiver's response. Therefore, the sender must obtain feedback as promptly and as accurately as possible. Only through feedback can the sender determine whether and how well the message has been received. **Communication feedback** is an essential component of both interpersonal and impersonal communications because it enables the sender to reinforce or change the message to ensure that it is understood in the intended way.

An important advantage of interpersonal communications is the ability to obtain *immediate feedback* through verbal as well as nonverbal cues. Experienced speakers are very attentive to feedback and constantly modify their messages based on what they see and hear from the audience. Immediate feedback is the factor that makes personal selling so effective because it enables the salesperson to tailor the sales pitch to the expressed needs and observed reactions of each prospect. Similarly, immediate feedback in the form of inattention serves to alert the college professor to jolt a dozing class awake; thus, the professor may make a deliberately provocative statement such as: "This material will probably appear in your final exam."

Because of the high cost of space and time in mass media, it has always been very important for sponsors of impersonal communications to obtain feedback as promptly as possible, so that they could revise a message if its meaning is not being received as intended or if the messages did not reach, at least mostly, the intended audience. Unlike interpersonal communications feedback, mass communications feedback *is rarely direct*; instead, it is *usually inferred*. Senders infer how persuasive their messages are from the resulting action (or inaction) of the targeted audience. Receivers buy (or do not buy) the advertised product; they renew (or do not renew) their magazine subscriptions; they vote (or do not vote) for the political candidate. Another type of feedback that companies seek from mass audiences is the degree of *customer satisfaction* (or dissatisfaction) with a product purchase. They try to discover and correct as swiftly as possible any problems with the product in order to retain their brand's image of reliability (e.g., through hotlines, online contacts, and other ways).

Since advertising in mass media started (initially in newspapers and magazines) approximately in the middle of the nineteenth century, advertisers had recognized that many messages were reaching consumers that had no interest in the products advertised and that accurately gauging the persuasive effectiveness of ads placed in mass media was impossible. In evaluating the impact of their advertising messages, marketers must measure their **exposure effects** (i.e., how many consumers were exposed to the message?), **persuasion effects** (i.e., was the message received, understood, and interpreted correctly?), and their **sales effects** (i.e., did the ad increase sales?) of their advertising messages. Advertisers gauge the *exposure* and *persuasion effects* of their messages by buying data from firms monitoring media audiences (e.g., from Nielsen) and conducting audience research to find out which media are read, which television programs are viewed, and which advertisements were remembered by their target audience(s).

The *sales effects* of mass communications are difficult to assess (although retailers usually can assess the effectiveness of their morning newspaper ads by midday on the basis of sales activity for the advertised product). A widely used method of measuring the sales effects of food and other packaged goods advertising is based on the Universal Product Code (UPC), which is tied to computerized cash registers. Supermarket scanner data can be combined with data from other sources (e.g., media and promotional information) to measure the correlation between advertisements, special promotions, and sales. Selected measures of advertising feedback are described next.

MEDIA AND MESSAGE EXPOSURE MEASURES

These measures assess *how many* consumers received the message and construct a profile of those *who* received it. The largest syndicated company that collects such data and sells it to advertisers and other organizations is Nielsen. Originally, Nielsen monitored TV viewing but it now maintains many panels consisting of groups of consumers who have consented to the monitoring of certain aspects of their media exposure and consumption[71] Nielsen is pursuing a strategy called "Anytime Anywhere Media Measurement" (also called A2/M2). The company intends to monitor a person's total exposure to media, including online page views, video streams, and visits to Web sites, viewing of TV screens and billboards outside of the home (e.g., in stores or shopping malls), and, of course, watching TV and listening to radio. The tools used to monitor the total media exposure are *portable people meters*—small, GPS-enabled personal devices that were described in the introduction to this chapter.

There are many other companies monitoring consumers' media and advertising exposure. For example, comScore monitors online traffic and Web visits; M:Metrics tracks mobile advertising on cell phones; Mediamark Research Inc. (MRI) provides, for a given magazine, data on its *circulation* as well as a descriptive *audience profile* (a breakdown of its readers by gender, median age, and household income); and Arbitron measures the audiences of radio broadcasts.

Broadcasters, publishers, and owners of Web sites use media exposure measures to determine the size of their audiences and set the rates they charge advertisers for placing promotional messages in their media. However, disputes regarding the results of audience measurements are not uncommon. For example, for years advertisers argued that Nielsen's panels did not adequately represent minorities, and media companies claimed that the company failed to properly measure viewers who use "time shifting" devices. More recently, one Web site's estimate of its monthly number of visitors was 1.8 million while comScore's estimate of the same audience was only 421,000. The major sources of such discrepancies are how to measure Internet use in the work place and consumers who delete "cookies," which are small identifying files placed on a computer's hard drive that are essential in counting Web sites' visits. Many believe that a better tracking system is crucial for the growth of online advertising.[72]

MESSAGE ATTENTION, INTERPRETATION, AND RECALL MEASURES

Physiological measures track bodily responses to stimuli. For example, *eye tracking* is a method where a camera tracks the movement of the eye across store shelves and gauges to which labels or brands respondents paid more attention. Another method, *brain wave analysis*, tracks the degree of attention paid to the components of viewed advertisements through monitoring electrical impulses produced by the viewer's brain. *Facial Electromyography* (Facial EMG) is a technique that tracks the electrical activity and subtle movements of facial muscles in order to gauge the emotions generated by different types of TV commercials.

Attitudinal measures gauge consumers' cognitive responses to messages, including their levels of engagement and involvement with the messages tested. For example, in *theater tests*, TV programs or commercials are shown in a theater setting and viewers use dials (located in their armrests) to indicate their levels of interest or disinterest during the showing of the program or advertisement. Semantic-differential and Likert scales (see Chapter 2) are used in *copy pretests* or *posttests* to assess whether respondents like the message, understand it correctly, and regard it as effective and persuasive.

In addition to the *recall and recognition measures* discussed in Chapter 7, researchers use *day-after recall tests* in which viewers of TV shows or listeners to radio broadcasts are interviewed a day after watching or listening to a given program. Participants are asked to describe which commercials they recall. The recall of a commercial and its central theme is evidence of its attention-getting and persuasive power. The *Starch Readership Survey* (discussed in Chapter 7) measures both attention and recall.

MEASURES OF THE IMPACT OF ADDRESSABLE ADVERTISEMENTS

The measures discussed previously assess the extent to which consumers noticed, paid attention to, liked, and remembered promotional messages, but none gauges the actual buying behavior induced by a given ad. As discussed earlier, for the most part, marketers *infer* the purchase behaviors triggered by ads from broad sets of sales data, where it is rarely possible to identify a cause-and-effect relationship between a given message and the resulting purchase behavior.

Addressable advertising is significantly more response measurable than standard "broadcast" advertising because addressable messages are sent to individual consumers and often include a digital tracking device that enables the sender to monitor the receiver's responses. The most common such tool is the electronic "cookie;" an ad used by AOL to explain the intricacies of this device is featured in Figure 9.11.[73] Some innovative companies like ADISN and Tumri are now developing addressable ads and also measuring their effectiveness based on criteria set by the advertiser, viewers' clicks, and the number of people who actually bought products after clicking on ads. These companies also buy space on Web sites and use their databases to find ads that are likely to appeal to the sites' visitors. A new service—Google's Ad Planner—helps media buyers to identify sites where their ads are likely to have the most impact.[74] As addressable advertising becomes more commonplace, more sophisticated measures of promotional messages' persuasive impact—in terms of actual consumer behavior—will certainly emerge.

FIGURE 9.11
Source: Courtesy of AOL.

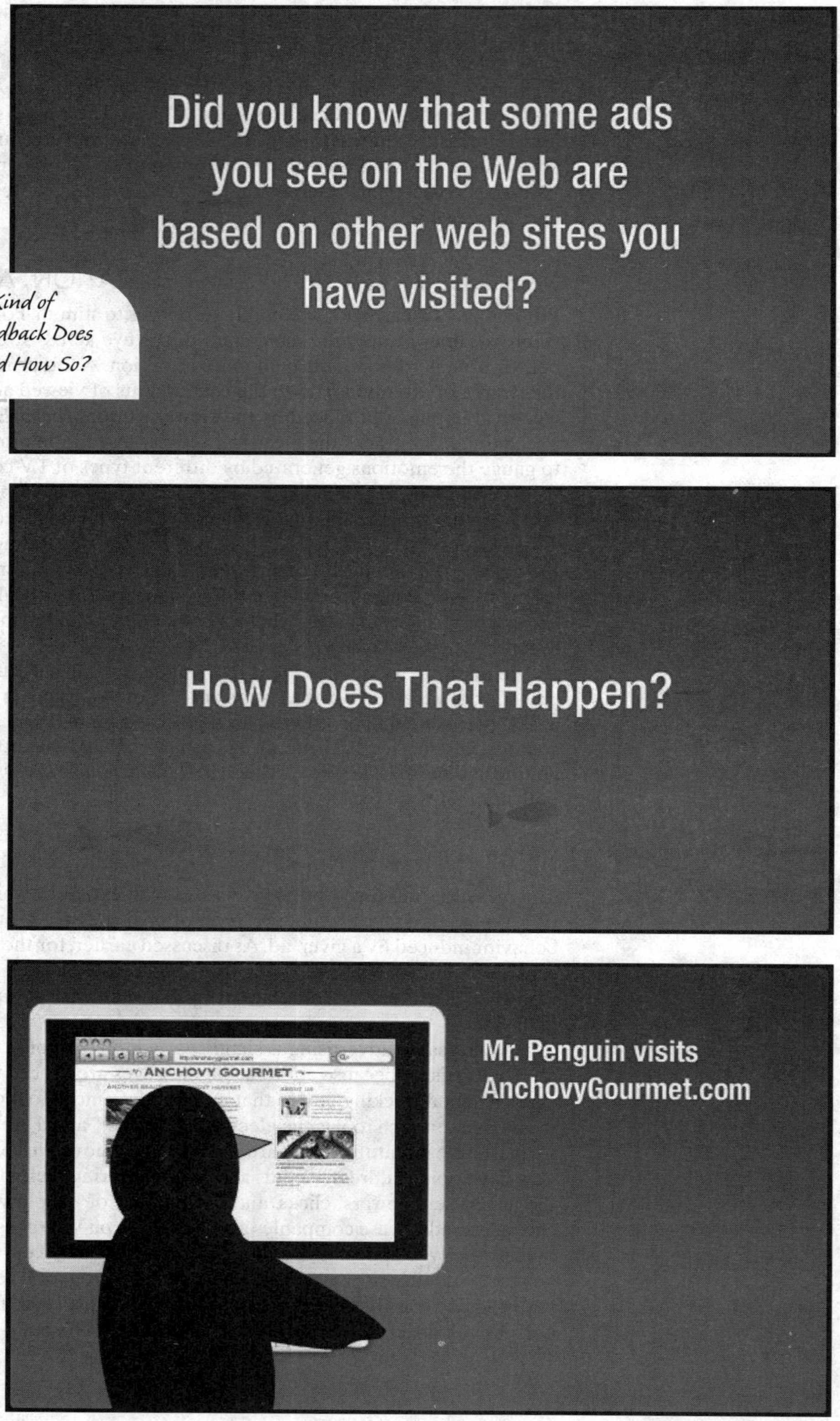

QUESTION: *What Kind of Communication Feedback Does This Ad Explain, and How So?*

FIGURE 9.11
Continued

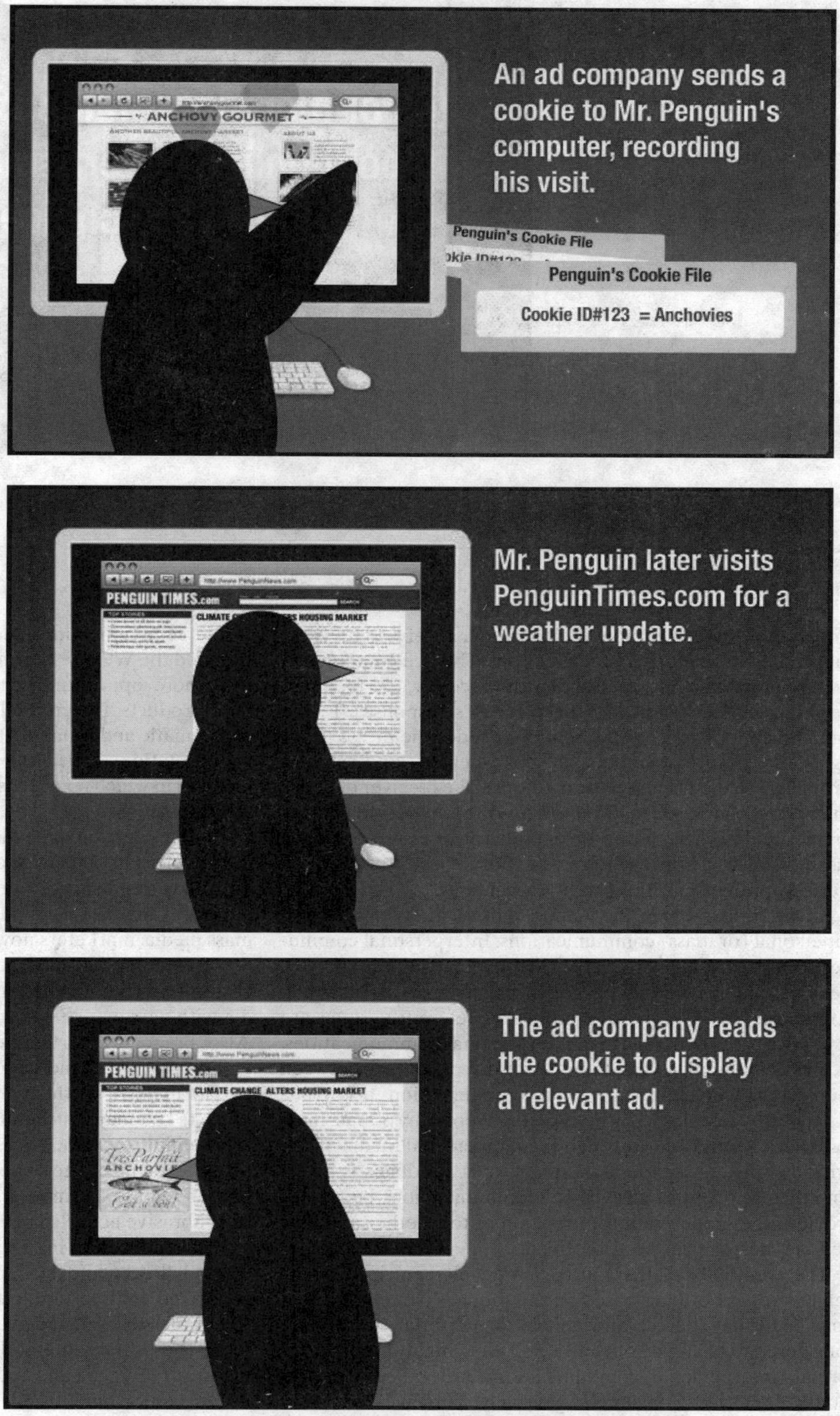

Continued

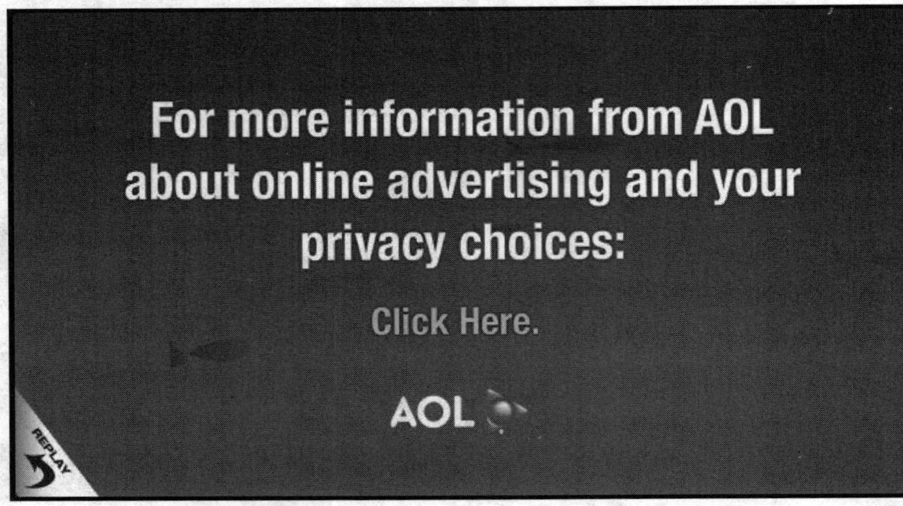

FIGURE 9.11
Continued

SUMMARY

This chapter described how the consumer receives and is influenced by marketing communications. The five components of communication are: the sender, the receiver, the medium, the message, and feedback (the receiver's response). In the communications process, the sender encodes the message using words, pictures, symbols, or spokespersons and sends it through a selected channel (or medium). The receiver decodes (interprets) the message based on his or her personal characteristics and experience, and responds (or does not respond) based on such factors as selective exposure, selective perception, comprehension, and psychological noise.

There are two types of communications: interpersonal and impersonal (or mass) communications. Interpersonal communications occur on a personal level between two or more people and may be verbal or nonverbal, formal or informal. Consumers' comparative and normative reference groups are key sources of their informal, interpersonal communications. In mass communications, there is no direct contact between source and receiver. Interpersonal communications take place in person, by telephone, by mail, on the Web, or by e-mail; mass communications occur through such impersonal media as television, radio, newspapers, and magazines. Feedback is an essential component of all types of communications because it provides the sender with some notion as to whether and how well the message has been received.

The credibility of the source, a vital element in message persuasiveness, often is based on the source's perceived intentions. Informal sources and neutral or editorial sources are considered to be highly objective and, thus, highly credible. Informal, interpersonal communications are called word-of-mouth (WOM). Consumers generally perceive WOM as highly credible, and marketers must devise strategies that stimulate positive WOM about their offerings. The growth of online communications and social networks has significantly widened the WOM environment and also provided marketers with more opportunities to use such networks to promote their products. The credibility of a commercial source is more problematic and usually is based on a composite evaluation of its reputation, expertise, and knowledge and that of the medium in which it advertises, the retail channel, and company spokespersons.

Media selection depends on the product, the audience, and the advertising objectives of the campaign. Each medium has advantages and shortcomings that must be weighed in the selection of media for an advertising campaign. In addition to mass media, marketers now have access to new media that are more dynamic and interactive and enable developing more customized communications that can reach consumers via media with narrowcasting, rather than broadcasting, capabilities. Also, branded entertainment has been growing significantly and is now part of most promotional communications.

The manner in which a message is presented influences its impact. The major structural aspects of advertising messages are framing, one-sided versus two-sided messages, and advertising resonance. The major advertising appeals used include humor, fear, sex, comparative advertising, audience participation, abrasive advertising, and using celebrities.

The feedback of interpersonal communications is immediate and direct while the impact of impersonal communications is delayed, indirect, and often inferred. The impact of promotional messages includes exposure, persuasion, and sales effects. The primary methods of communications feedback are measures of media and audience exposure, message attention, interpretation and recall, and recently developed methods gauging the impact of addressable advertising.

DISCUSSION QUESTIONS

1. Explain the differences between feedback from interpersonal communications and feedback from impersonal communications. How can the marketer obtain and use each kind of feedback?
2. How do some new media enable obtaining better advertising feedback than traditional media?
3. Why is an opinion leader a more credible source of product information than an advertisement for the same product? Are there any circumstances in which information from advertisements is likely to be more influential than word-of-mouth?
4. Why would a consumer who has just purchased an expensive digital camera attempt to influence the purchase behavior of others?
5. List and discuss the effects of psychological noise on the communications process. What strategies can a marketer use to overcome psychological noise?
6. List and discuss factors that affect the credibility of formal communications sources of product information. What factors influence the perceived credibility of informal communications sources?
7. You are the marketing vice president of a large soft-drink company. Your company's advertising agency is in the process of negotiating a contract to employ a superstar female singer to promote your product. Discuss the reference group factors that you would consider before the celebrity is hired.
8. What are the implications of the sleeper effect for the selection of spokespersons and the scheduling of advertising messages?
9. Compared with mass media, what are the advantages and unique features of new media?
10. For what kinds of audiences would you consider using comparative advertising? Why?

EXERCISES

1. Bring two print advertisements to class: one illustrating a one-sided message and the other a two-sided message. Which of the measures discussed in the chapter would you use to evaluate the effectiveness of each ad? Explain your answers.
2. Describe two situations in which you served as an opinion leader and two situations in which you sought consumption-related advice or information from an opinion leader. Indicate your relationship to the persons with whom you interacted. Are the circumstances during which you engaged in word-of-mouth communications consistent with those described in the text? Explain.
3. a. Find ads that encourage consumers to engage in word-of-mouth communications and present them in class.
   b. Can you think of negative rumors that you have heard recently about a company or a product? If so, present them in class.
4. With a paper and pencil, spend one hour watching a network television channel during prime time. Record the total number of commercials that aired. For each commercial using a celebrity endorser, record the celebrity's name, the product or service advertised, and whether the celebrity was used in a testimonial, as an endorser, as an actor, or as a spokesperson. For each listing, in the context of the text's discussion on using celebrities in advertising, discuss whether the celebrity chosen was a good choice or not.
5. Find one example of each of the following two advertising appeals: fear and sex. One example must be a print ad and the other a TV commercial. Analyze the placement of each ad in the medium where it appeared according to the media selection criteria presented in Table 9.5.
6. Watch one hour of TV on a single channel during prime time and also tape the broadcast. Immediately after watching the broadcast, list all the commercials you can recall seeing. For each commercial, identify (a) the message framing approach used, and (b) whether the message was one-sided or two-sided. Compare your list with the actual taped broadcast. Explain any discrepancies between your recollections and the actual broadcast on the basis of concepts discussed in this chapter.

KEY TERMS

- addressable advertising *298*
- addressable messages *295*
- advergaming *299*
- advertising resonance *301*
- attitudinal measures *311*
- audience profiles *295*
- blog *283*
- brand communities *283*
- branded entertainment *298*
- broadcast model *298*
- buzz agents *285*
- celebrity actor *309*
- celebrity endorsement *309*
- celebrity spokesperson *309*
- celebrity testimonial *309*
- communication *280*
- communication feedback *309*
- comparative advertising *303*
- comparative reference groups *282*
- consumer profile *295*
- consumer-generated media *297*
- decoding *290*
- determined detractors *287*
- differential decay *290*
- encoding *290*
- e-referrals and recommendations *286*

Case One: The Viewer's Voice Influences TV Programming

American TV producers broadcasted entertainment programs supported by advertising fees for over 60 years. Much like a book or a movie, the contents of these programs were without significant input from the audience—the receivers of these communications. Generally, Nielsen ratings have been used to gauge the "success" of TV programs and determine the advertising rates on various broadcasts. After watching them, many viewers frequently discussed TV programs at their offices' water coolers, and some may have even talked back to their televisions while watching. But, the writers and producers of these programs had no reliable and continuous way to listen to what viewers were saying.

Today, online Web sites such as **www.televisionwitoutpity.com** (TWOP) give consumers a forum to discuss, rate, complain about, and occasionally compliment scores of TV shows and even some movies. TWOP is an online site where vast numbers of viewers can virtually "gather" after or even during a broadcast and discuss their views about a particular show. Because the viewers who post their comments are very involved with the programs they watch, the producers of TV shows can read their postings, get a sense of their publics' reactions to plotlines, dialogues, and other show features, and incorporate such feedback into the content of future show episodes. Since TV shows are filmed several weeks prior to a broadcast, writers can now change yet-to-be-broadcast programming to address concerns expressed by viewers' TWOP posts. For example, if a given story line on the highly popular show *Mad Men* appears to bore or irritate viewers, the story line can be shortened and concluded sooner than planned.

QUESTIONS

1. How does the communications' feedback that TV shows' writers and producers (the communications' sources) receive through Web sites like TWOP differ from input derived from conventional fan mail and standard TV shows' ratings?
2. Should television programmers and producers consider the comments viewers post on TWOP in designing future broadcasts? Why or why not?
3. For a TV show of your choice, apply the concept of source credibility (as discussed in Chapter 9) to current viewer comments posted on TWOP.
4. Compare and contrast the Nielsen rating or a given episode on a TV series with the comments posted about the same show on TWOP. Are the two measures of viewer feedback consistent with one another or not? Explain your answer.

Case Two: Advertising Appeals

A. Go to **www.nytimes.com/interactive/2009/02/02/business/media/20090202-business-superbowlads.html**.

This Web site depicts a summary of Super Bowl ads starting in 1984, including the percentages of ads, by yearly broadcast, that featured appeals and elements commonly used in advertising. Examine these posted figures for all the annual broadcasts, starting with the 1984 data.

B. Now, go to **www.livingroomcandidate.org**.

This Web site features presidential campaign TV commercials starting in 1952. Under "Type of Commercial," the political ads are classified according to the communication appeal used. View the ads categorized by appeals and also the ones under "Curator's Choice."

QUESTIONS

1. Which of the advertising appeals discussed in the chapter has been used most often in Super Bowl ads? What are the advantages and shortcomings of using this appeal?
2. Which of the advertising appeals discussed in the chapter has been used most often in presidential campaigns' TV commercials? What are the advantages and shortcomings of using this appeal?
3. Is it realistic to use the appeal that you had identified in question 1 in political marketing? Explain your answer.
4. Is it realistic to use the appeal that you had identified in question 2 to promote the kind of consumer goods typically featured in Super Bowl ads? Explain your answer.

10

The Family and Its Social Class Standing

ALTHOUGH THE TERM **family** is a basic concept, it is not easy to define because family composition and structure, as well as the roles played by family members, are almost always in transition. Traditionally, however, *family* is defined as *two or more persons related by blood, marriage, or adoption who reside together.* In a more dynamic sense, the individuals who constitute a family might be described as members of the most basic social group who live together and interact to satisfy their personal and mutual needs. Currently, in the United States, for example, about 68 percent of the 114.4 million **households** are families.[1] According to many sources, the *family* remains the central or dominant institution in providing for the welfare of its members and is the major household consumer and consuming unit. In this spirit, the ad for Bayliner family boating in Figure 10.1 reminds parents of the importance of creating "quality time" for the whole family; that is, "good times" that will provide everlasting family memories.

This chapter describes the influence of the family on its members' development as consumers, as well as how the family functions as a basic consuming unit. It also examines how different demographic stages (i.e., family life cycle stages) influence both traditional and nontraditional families by impacting the dynamics of family decision-making. In addition, we explore a number of non-family households that have been growing in number in western societies, as well as Dual Spousal Work Involvement—a contemporary system for understanding and targeting of families and households.

We will also explore in this chapter how a child's family is initially his or her primary reference group (reference groups were discussed in Chapter 9). As children grow older, they begin to compare themselves with others who are both similar and different in demographic features, such as income, education, and occupation. These demographics are frequently used variables to determine a person's and/or a family's social class standing. In terms of an individual consumer, social class represents a person's prestige and status relative to others within the same or different social class groupings. The second part of this chapter also examines a social class framework, the measurement of social class and its value in segmenting and targeting consumers. The chapter concludes with a discussion of several markets corresponding to select social classes, including their consumption habits, tastes and values.

FIGURE 10.1

Source: © Brunswick Boat Group. Used with permission. All rights reserved.

QUESTION: *As You See It, What Is the Main "Family Message" of This Ad?*

Learning Objectives

10.1 *To Understand the Changing Nature of U.S. Families, Including Their Composition and Spending Patterns.*

10.2 *To Understand the Socialization Process and Other Roles of the Family.*

10.3 *To Understand the Dynamics of Husband-Wife Decision Making, as Well as the Influence of Children in Family Consumption Decision-Making.*

10.4 *To Understand How Traditional and Non-traditional Family Life Cycles Impact Consumer Behavior.*

10.5 *To Understand What Social Class Is and How It Relates to Consumer Behavior.*

10.6 *To Understand the Various Measures of Social Class and Their Role in Consumer Behavior.*

10.7 *To Appreciate the Distinctive Profiles of Specific Social Class Groupings.*

10.8 *To Understand the "Ups and Downs" of Social Class Mobility.*

10.9 *To Understand the Relationship Between Social Class and Geodemographic Clusters.*

10.10 *To Understand the Affluent Consumer.*

10.11 *To Understand the Middle-Class Consumer.*

10.12 *To Understand the Working Class and Other Nonaffulent Consumers.*

10.13 *To Understand the Nature and Influence of the "Techno-Class."*

10.14 *To Understand How Social Class Is Used in Consumer Research Studies.*

The Changing U.S. Family

Learning Objective

10.1 *To Understand the Changing Nature of U.S. Families, Including Their Composition and Spending Patterns.*

Although families sometimes are referred to as households, not all households are families. For example, a household might include individuals who are not related by blood, marriage, or adoption, such as unmarried couples, family friends, roommates, or boarders. However, within the context of consumer behavior, households and families usually are treated as synonymous, and we will continue this convention.

In most Western societies, three types of families dominate: the married couple, the nuclear family, and the extended family. The simplest type of family, in number of members, is the *married couple*—a husband and a wife. As a household unit, the married couple generally is representative of either new marrieds who have not yet started a family or older couples who have already raised their children.

A husband and wife and one or more children constitute a **nuclear family**. This type of family is still commonplace but has been on the decline. The nuclear family, together with at least one grandparent living within the household, is called an **extended family**. Within the past 30 years the incidence of the extended family has also declined because of the geographic mobility that splits up families. Moreover, because of divorce, separation, and out-of-wedlock births, there has been a rapid increase in the number of **single-parent family** households consisting of one parent and at least one child.

Not surprisingly, the type of family that is most typical can vary considerably from culture to culture. For instance, in an individualistic society such as that in Canada, the nuclear family is most common. In a kinship culture (with extended families), such as that in Thailand, a family would commonly include a head of household, married adult children, and grandchildren.[2]

There are the many factors associated with how family lifestyles are changing that impact on family consumer behavior. For example, about 55 percent of career women who are

35 years old are childless, between a third and half of 40-year-old career women have no children, and the number of childless women between the ages of 40 and 44 has doubled during the past 20 years. Moreover, 49 percent of female corporate executives earning $100,000 or more annually are childless (but only 10 percent of high-income male executives have no children).[3]

With the huge number of wives and mothers employed outside the home, studies have examined the question of whether an employed wife behaves at home the same as a nonworking wife. Research results indicated that there was little to no difference between working and nonworking wives with respect to their purchases of time-saving goods; indeed, nonworking married women were even more likely to buy time-saving durables (i.e., if they were doing the domestic work themselves, they wanted to save time). The research also showed that a married man's behavior with respect to household chores remained the same whether the wife was or was not employed, and the ultimate responsibility for household management still belonged to the wife. Still further, the evidence also indicated that the more traditional the division of household labor in a household, the higher the marital satisfaction was of the man (husband) and the lower the satisfaction of the woman (wife). Interestingly, though, husbands of working wives made fewer decisions by themselves.[4]

There is no doubt that the "typical" or "traditional" family or household has changed. Although families represented 81 percent of households in 1970, by 2006 this percentage has shrunk to 68 percent, and households consisting of married couples with children under 18 have decreased from 40.3 percent in 1970 to just 22.7 percent in 2006, and "not married, no children" households (i.e., nonfamily households) rose from almost 19 percent in 1970 to 32 percent in 2006, making nonfamily households more numerous than married couples with children households (see Figure 10.2). During this same time frame, the percentage of family households without a spouse present rose significantly from 11 to almost 17 percent, and people living alone grew from 17 percent in 1970 to almost 27 percent in 2006. Also, while in 1970, 65 percent of

FIGURE 10.2
Evidence of the Dynamic Nature of U.S. Households

Source: U.S. Census Bureau, Statistical Abstract of the United States, 2008, Tables 58 & 61, accessed at http://www.censu.gov/compendia/; U.S. Census Bureau, "American's Families and Living Arrangements: 2003," November 2004, 4, accessed at www.census.gov/prod/2004pubs/p20-553.pdf.

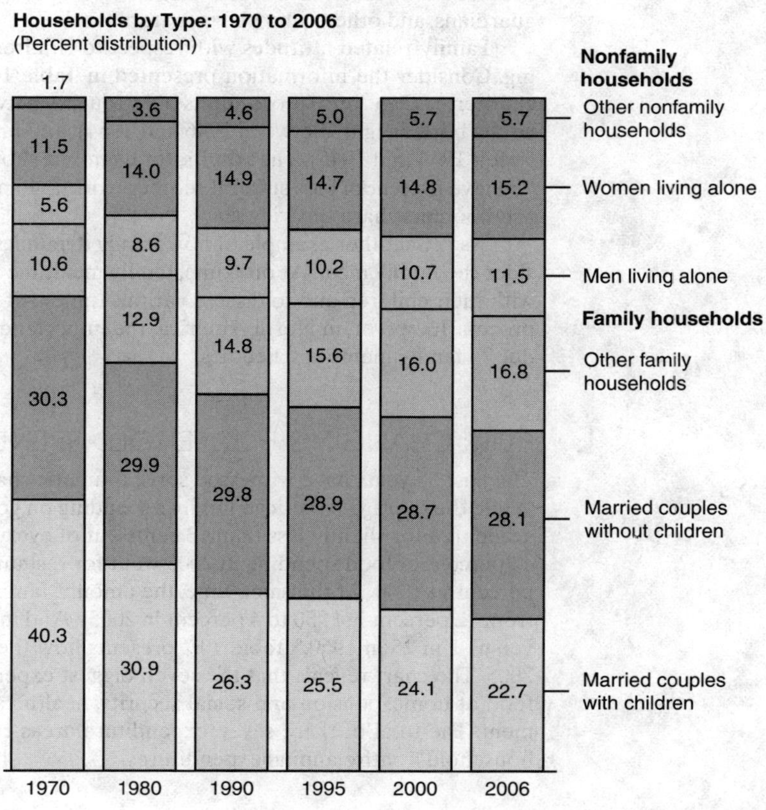

TABLE 10.1 How Different Generations Feel About Children and Family

	GEN XERS	BABY BOOMERS	PRE-BOOMERS
Ideal number of children is two.	52%	55%	50%
Ideal number of children is three.	27%	21%	30%
Favor spanking to discipline a child.	74%	76%	76%
Favor sex ed in public schools.	91%	87%	80%
Believe preschool kids suffer if mother works.	37%	46%	57%
Believe it's better for the man to work and the woman to tend home.	29%	37%	64%
Believe a working mother doesn't hurt children.	67%	63%	52%
Believe a wife should help husband put career first.	12%	15%	32%
I spend too little time with my kids.	45%	46%	25%
Divorce laws should be tougher.	50%	52%	59%

Source: Pamela Paul, "Meet the Parents," *American Demographics* (January 2002): 46. Reprinted by permission of Primedia.

men and 60 percent of women age 18 and older were married, by 2006 these figures were reduced to 53 percent of men and 50 percent of women; during this same time period, the percentage of men and women either separated or divorced almost tripled. Still further, households have decreased in size. The percent of households with five or more people dropped from 21 percent in 1970 to just under 10 percent in 2006, while households with only one or two members grew from 46 percent to almost 60 percent over the same period of time.[5] Because of these changes in family dynamics, companies such as American Greetings sell Mother's Day cards for single moms, divorced moms, stepmothers, foster mothers, caregivers, guardians, and others who play a maternal role.

Family-related attitudes with respect to children and child rearing have also been changing. Consider the information presented in Table 10.1, which compares the attitudes toward children of Gen Xers (those adults born roughly between 1965 and 1978), baby boomers (those adults born roughly between 1946 and 1964), and pre-boomers (those adults born roughly between 1934 and 1945). The results, for example, show that while only 37 percent of Gen Xers "believe preschool kids suffer if mother works," 46 percent of baby boomers and 57 percent of pre-boomers share this view.[6]

As yet another example of how family dynamics and childrearing has been changing, consider the family meal. At one time, family mealtime was an opportunity for parents to interact with their children and to discuss various topics—it was an important part of the socialization process. However, in North America, the importance of family mealtime has decreased, often due to family member schedules.

EVER-CHANGING HOUSEHOLD SPENDING PATTERNS

The past 50 years have witnessed some dramatic changes in how families spend their incomes. While the average American family's spending on goods and services in 2005 was $46,409, food accounted for slightly less than 13 cents out of every dollar, down from 32 cents in 1950, while 44 percent of food spending in 2005 went for restaurant dining and takeout food—up from 21 percent in 1960. At the same time, the amount families spent on apparel and shoes decreased from 12 percent in 1950 to 4 percent in 2005.[7] And in 2004, 1 in 17 Americans bought a new car, versus 1 in 25 in 1960.[8] Table 10.2 presents how the "average" U.S. family spent its money in 2005. The chart reveals that the seven biggest expenditure areas are: housing, transportation, food at home, pension and social security, health care, food away from home, and entertainment. The total of these seven expenditure areas constitute a major portion of a family's or household's entire annual expenditures.

TABLE 10.2 How the "Average" Family Spends Its Money

EXPENDITURE CATEGORY	DOLLARS	PERCENT
Food at home	5,931	12.8
Food away from home	2,634	5.7
Alcoholic beverages	426	1
Housing	15,167	32.7
Apparel and services	1,886	4.1
Transportation	8,344	18
Health care	2,664	5.7
Entertainment	2,388	5.1
Reading	126	0.3
Tobacco products	319	0.7
Life and other personal insurance	381	0.8
Pensions and social security	4,823	10.4
Misc.	1,320	2.8
	46,409	

Source: U.S. Census Bureau, "Average Annual Expenditures of All Consumer Units by Selected Major Types of Expenditures: 1990 to 2005," *Statistical Abstract of the United States: 2008,* Table 662, accessed at www.census.gov/compendia.

Socialization and Related Roles of Family Members

LEARNING OBJECTIVE

10.2 *To Understand the Socialization Process and Other Roles of the Family.*

The **socialization of family members**, ranging from young children to adults, is a central family function. In the case of young children, this process includes imparting to children the basic values and modes of behavior consistent with the culture. These generally include moral and religious principles, interpersonal skills, dress and grooming standards, appropriate manners and speech, and the selection of suitable educational and occupational or career goals (see Figure 10.3).

Parental socialization responsibility seems to be constantly expanding. For instance, parents are often anxious to see their young children possess adequate computer skills, almost before they are able to talk or walk—as early as 12 months after their birth. Another sign of parents' constant pressure to help their young children secure an "advantage" or "keep ahead" are the demanding daily schedules that rule the lives of many children (e.g., daily preschool classes, after-school classes, play dates, weekend enrichment, and/or sports programs). Such hectic schedules foster a concentration on competition and results and not on having fun or on being creative. In contrast, as kids, their parents may have been frequently engaged in creative play tasks such as building forts out of blankets or pillows. However, with the structured activities of today and with the child constantly surrounded by media, there is little opportunity for the child to explore his or her world in such an imaginative fashion.[9]

Marketers frequently target parents looking for assistance in the task of socializing their children. To this end, marketers are sensitive to the fact that the socialization of young children provides an opportunity to establish a foundation on which later experiences continue to build throughout life. These experiences are reinforced and modified as the child grows into adolescence, the teenage years, and eventually into adulthood.

CONSUMER SOCIALIZATION OF CHILDREN

The aspect of childhood socialization that is particularly relevant to the study of consumer behavior is **consumer socialization**, which is defined as the *process by which children acquire the skills, knowledge, attitudes, and experiences necessary to function as consumers.* A variety of studies have focused on how children develop consumption skills. Many preadolescent children

FIGURE 10.3
Source: Courtesy of the U.S. Army.

QUESTION: *What Is the Name and Definition of the Process Depicted in This Ad?*

acquire their *consumer behavior norms* through observation of their parents and older siblings, who function as role models and sources of cues for basic consumption learning. Indeed, "children perceive their families as a close and reliable source of information, in contrast with other sources of information, such as advertising.[10] In contrast, adolescents and teenagers are likely to look to their friends for models of acceptable consumption behavior.[11] Other research has shown that younger children generally also react positively to advertisements employing a spokesperson who seems to fulfill a parental role, whereas teens often like products for the simple reason that their parents disapprove of them.[12]

Shared shopping experiences (i.e., coshopping—when mother and child shop together) also give children the opportunity to acquire in-store shopping skills. Coshopping is a way of spending time with one's children while at the same time accomplishing a necessary task. Consumer socialization also serves as a tool by which parents influence other aspects of the socialization process. For instance, parents frequently use the promise or reward of material goods

TABLE 10.3 U.S. Mom Segments

MARKETING RECEPTIVE

- The Balancer (25.4% of U.S. population)
  - She has figured out how to have it all—career, marriage, and family. She can multitask and believes in teaching her children to be good consumers. She lets her kids sometime make mistakes, which is not too much of a problem because of her higher income level.
- The Nurturer (9.6% of U.S. population)
  - She is completely focused on her family, and often sacrifices her own desires to meet the wants of her children. She is very trusting of people and of "traditional family" companies and brands. This mother is very happy and content.
- The Diva (7.2% of U.S. population)
  - She is self-focused and seeks acceptance and attention from others—she is a conspicuous consumer. This mother is concerned about her image and sees her children as a part of her image. Often gives in to children's requests to make her life easier.

MARKETING RESISTANT

- The Protector (21% of U.S. population)
  - Highest income and level of education of all mom segments. A very rational and deliberate decision maker, she teaches her children to shop and spend responsibly. Protective of her children and resents the influence of the media, marketing, etc., on her children.
- The Struggler (21.6% of U.S. population)
  - Her financial situation does not permit her to be as indulgent with her children as she would like. May have to deny some of her children's requests in order to live within her means. Very price and value conscious as a shopper. Has a negative impression of herself and life in general.
- The Stoic (15.1% of U.S. population)
  - Often culturally or socially isolated, she values her privacy. She views her role as a caretaker and homemaker. Loves her children but feels she is emotionally distanced from them. Makes every decision with great deliberation.

Source: Copyright © 2007 by M.E. Sharpe, Inc. From Sabrina M. Neeley and Tim Coffey, "Understanding the 'Four-eyed, Four-legged' Consumer: A Segmentation Analysis of U.S. Moms," *Journal of Marketing Theory and Practice*, Vol. 15, No. 3 (Summer 2007): 254-255. Used with permission of M.E. Sharpe, Inc. All Rights Reserved. Not for reproduction.

as a device to modify or control a child's behavior. A mother may reward her child with a gift when the child does something to please her, or she may withhold or remove it when the child disobeys. Research conducted by one of the authors supports this behavior-controlling function. Specifically, adolescents reported that their parents frequently used the promise of chocolate candy as a means of controlling their behavior (e.g., getting them to complete homework or to clean their rooms).

A **socialization agent** is a person or organization involved in the socialization process "because of frequency of contact with the individual and control over the rewards and punishments given to the individual."[13] Mothers are generally considered to be stronger consumer socialization agents than their husbands, because they tend to be more involved with their children, and are more likely to mediate their children's exposure to commercial messages. Additionally, they provide instruction in the skills needed by consumers, and serve as gatekeepers to information and influence by regulating the money that their offspring can spend. When investigating how mothers interact and relate to marketplace influences, a recent study found six distinct segments of mothers—three with a positive attitude toward marketing (marketing receptive) and three with a negative attitude (marketing resistant). For example, while "Diva" mothers see the influence of promotional media and marketing activities as normal, "Protector" mothers tend to mistrust marketing and promotional messages aimed at their children because they see these influences as threats to their own protective instincts.[14] Table 10.3 presents information on these six segments of U.S. moms.

It is important to point out that consumer socialization of children does not function identically in all cultures. For example, research indicates that American mothers emphasize autonomy more than Japanese mothers and want their children to develop independent consumption skills at an early age. In contrast, Japanese mothers maintain greater control over their children's consumption, and, therefore, their offspring's understanding of how advertising works and other consumer-related skills develop at a somewhat later age.[15]

Growing Up in a Materialistic World

Children learn to attach importance to worldly possession at an early age, such as seeing a commercial for a doll or action figure on television, pointing to the screen, and shouting "I want that!" A recent study conducted with school-aged children in Minnesota found that materialism increases from middle childhood (ages 8–9) to early adolescence (ages 12–13), and then declines from early to late adolescence (ages 16–18). The research also found an inverse relationship between self-esteem and materialism in children and adolescents (i.e., children with high self-esteem are more likely to express lower levels of materialism, and vice versa).[16] Furthermore, the study notes that rather than blaming the media for the materialism exhibited by children and adolescents, finding ways to increase this group's self-esteem might serve as a more positive approach. Interestingly, another research effort found that expert "informants identified middle school as the period that marked the onset and peak of ridicule about possessions, the start of their fashion awareness and brand consciousness, and the beginning of their interest in shopping." Indeed, the study found that ridicule is a mechanism used by adolescents to exchange information about what should and should not be consumed and valued, and that ridicule is used "to ostracize, haze, or admonish peers who violate consumption norms."[17] Still further, a recent Canadian study of college students (with the majority being full-time students, and 85 percent living at home with parents) suggests "that older college students are more likely to be influenced by their parents and school, and less influenced by their peers and media" (such as television, Internet, and magazines).[18] In the same study, the older college students were also found to be more competent consumers than their younger counterparts.

Yet another aspect of the consumer socialization process, particularly for adolescents, is the development of skepticism toward product and service claims and advertising. One study found that older and higher socially ranked adolescents tended to be less skeptical, while adolescents with after-school jobs who talk about shopping-related issues with parents and have some knowledge of the marketplace tend to develop more healthy levels of skepticism. Lower socioeconomic status adolescents, having less money than their wealthier peers, were more critical when evaluating advertising claims. Additionally, the study found that Internet usage was negatively related to skepticism, possibly because Internet surfers can skip ads and only visit Web sites that interest them.[19]

ADULT CONSUMER SOCIALIZATION

The socialization process is not confined to childhood, but is an ongoing process. It is now accepted that socialization begins in early childhood and extends throughout a person's entire life. For example, when a newly married couple establishes their own household, their adjustment to living and consuming together is part of this continuing process. Similarly, the adjustment of a soon-to-be-retired couple who decide to move from Minneapolis to Phoenix is also part of the ongoing socialization process. Even a family that is welcoming a pet into their home as a new family member must face the challenge of socializing the pet so that it fits into the family environment. Survey research reveals that pet owners commonly treat their pets as full-fledged family members. For instance, 58 percent of those surveyed indicated that they have sent or received a holiday card from their dog or cat, and 78 percent regularly talk in a different voice ("I wov you") to their pets.[20]

INTERGENERATIONAL SOCIALIZATION

It appears that it is quite common for certain product loyalties or brand preferences to be transferred from one generation to another—*intergenerational brand transfer*—maybe for even three or four generations within the same family.[21] For instance, specific brand preferences for products such as peanut butter, mayonnaise, ketchup, coffee, and canned soup are all product categories that are frequently passed on from one generation to another generation. The

FIGURE 10.4
A Simple Model of the Socialization Process

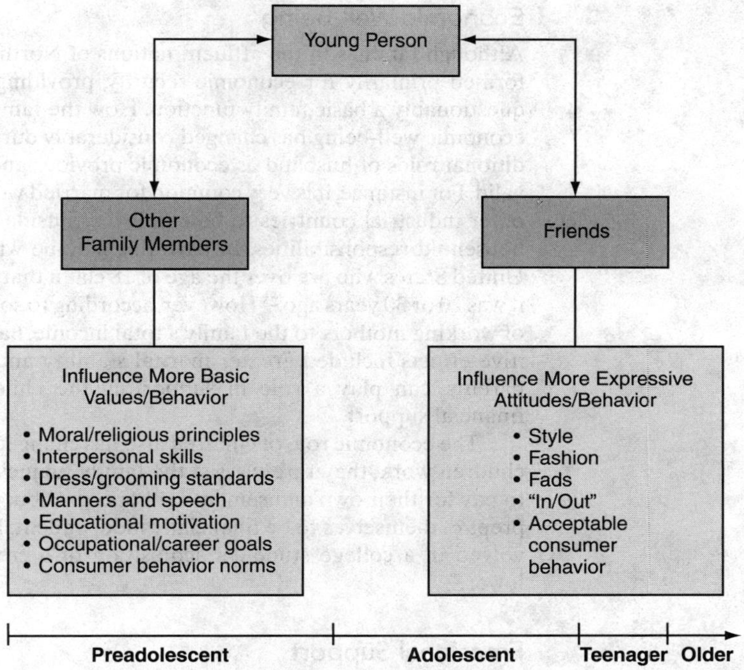

following is a verbatim from research with college-aged consumers as to how they feel about product usage extending over several generations:[22]

> I find it hard to break away from the things I've been using since I was little, like Vaseline products, Ivory soap, Lipton tea, and cornflakes. I live on campus so I have to do my own shopping, and when I do I see a lot of my mother in myself. I buy things I'm accustomed to using . . . products my mother buys for the house. (Respondent is West Indian American female.)

Not only is there a strong intergenerational transfer of brand preferences between generations, but grandparents frequently play an instrumental role in the socialization of their grandchildren, as they did earlier in the socialization of their own children.

Figure 10.4 presents a model of the socialization process that focuses on the socialization of young children that can also be extended to family members of all ages. Note that the arrows run both ways between the young person and other family members and between the young person and his or her friends. This two-directional arrow signifies that socialization is really a "two-way street," one in which the young person is both socialized and influences those who are doing the socializing. Supporting this view is the reality that children of all ages often influence the opinions and behavior of their parents. As an example, research with elementary school–aged children has found that parental warmth relates positively to (1) the extent to which a child's interest in the Internet serves as a catalyst for increased parental Internet interest, (2) how much the child teaches a parent about the Internet, and (3) whether the child acts as the parent's Internet agent (e.g., the child shops for the parent on the Internet).[23] Because children are often more comfortable than their parents with digital and electronic media, they are often the ones in the family who do the teaching. Another research study examined the influence of family on consumer innovativeness, and found that the perceptions of adult children regarding their parent's innovativeness influenced their own innovativeness.[24]

OTHER FUNCTIONS OF THE FAMILY

Three other basic functions provided by the family are particularly relevant to a discussion of consumer behavior. These include economic well-being, emotional support, and suitable family lifestyles.

Economic Well-Being

Although families in the affluent nations of North America, Europe, and Asia are no longer formed primarily for economic security, providing financial means to its dependents is unquestionably a basic family function. How the family divides its responsibilities for providing economic well-being has changed considerably during the past 30 years. No longer are the traditional roles of husband as economic provider and wife as homemaker and child rearer still valid. For instance, it is very common for married women with children in the United States and other industrial countries to be employed outside the home and for their husbands to share household responsibilities. In part, this may be why more than 70 percent of women in the United States who are over the age of 18 claim that it is more difficult to be a mother now than it was 20 or 30 years ago.[25] However, according to some sociologists, the increased contributions of working mothers to the family's total income, has had mostly a positive net effect. The positive effects included greater marital stability and greater marital equality.[26] Again, grandparents, can play a role in supporting the children and grandchildren in supplemental financial support.

The economic role of children also has changed. Today, despite the fact that many teenage children work, they rarely assist the family financially. Instead, many teenagers are expected to pay for their own amusements; others contribute to the costs of their formal education and prepare themselves to be financially independent. It is of interest to note when parents are involved in a college student's acquisition of a credit card, credit card balances tend to be lower.[27]

Emotional Support

The provision of emotional nourishment (including love, affection, and intimacy) to its members is an important core function of the contemporary family. In fulfilling this function, the family provides support and encouragement and assists its members in coping with decision making and with personal or social problems.

The *San Francisco Chronicle* asked its younger readers: "What is the key to happiness?" Many responses dealt specifically with the child's family:[28]

> The key to happiness is when my dad is making me laugh.
>
> The key to my happiness is my family, because they love and trust me.
>
> My family is a very good family. My mom and dad are very nice and listen to me.

If the family cannot provide adequate assistance when it is needed, it may turn to a counselor, psychologist, or other helping professional as an alternative. For instance, in most communities, educational and psychological centers are available that are designed to assist parents who want to help their children improve their learning and communication skills or to generally better adjust to their environments.

Suitable Family Lifestyles

Another important family function in terms of consumer behavior is the establishment of a suitable *lifestyle* for the family. Upbringing, experience, and the personal and jointly held goals of the spouses determine the importance placed on education or career, on reading, on television viewing, on the learning of computer skills, on the frequency and quality of dining out, and on the selection of other entertainment and recreational activities. Researchers have identified a shift in the nature of family "togetherness." Whereas a family being together once meant doing things together, today it often means being in the same household and each person doing his or her own thing.[29]

Family lifestyle commitments, including the allocation of time, are greatly influencing consumption patterns. For example, a series of diverse pressures on moms has reduced the time that they have available for household chores and has created a market for convenience products and fast-food restaurants. Also, with both parents working, an increased emphasis is being placed on the notion of "quality time" rather than on the "quantity of time" spent with children and other family members.

Family Decision Making and Consumption-Related Roles

Learning Objective

10.3 *To Understand the Dynamics of Husband-Wife Decision Making, as Well as the Influence of Children in Family Consumption Decision-Making.*

Although many marketers recognize the family as the basic consumer decision-making unit, they most frequently examine the attitudes and behavior of the one family member whom they believe to be the major *decision maker*. In some cases, they also examine the attitudes and behavior of the person most likely to be the primary *user* of the product or service. For instance, in the case of men's underwear, which is frequently purchased by women for their husbands and unmarried sons, it is commonplace to seek the views of both the men who wear the underwear and the women who buy it. By considering both the likely user and the likely purchaser, the marketer obtains a richer picture of the consumption process.

DYNAMICS OF HUSBAND–WIFE DECISION MAKING

Marketers are interested in the relative amount of influence that a husband and a wife have when it comes to family consumption choices. The relative influence of husbands and wives can be classified as: **husband dominated**, **wife dominated**, **joint** (either equal or syncratic), and **autonomic** (where either the husband or the wife is the primary or only decision maker).[30]

The relative influence of a husband and wife on a particular consumer decision depends in part on the product and service category. For instance, during the 1950s, the purchase of a new automobile was strongly husband dominated, whereas food and financial banking decisions more often were wife dominated. Fifty years later, the purchase of the family's principal automobile is still often husband dominated in many households. However, in other contexts or situations (e.g., a car to transport the children around or a car for a working mother), female car buyers are a segment on which many car manufacturers are currently showering a great deal of marketing attention. Also, in the case of financial decision making, there has been a general trend over the past decade to have the female head of household make financial decisions.[31]

Husband–wife decision making also appears to be related to cultural influence. Research comparing husband–wife decision-making patterns in the People's Republic of China and in the United States reveals that among Chinese there were substantially fewer "joint" decisions and more "husband-dominated" decisions for many household purchases.[32] However, when limiting the comparison to urban and rural Chinese households (i.e., a "within-China" comparison), the research showed that in a larger city such as Beijing, married couples were more likely than rural couples to share equally in purchase decisions. Still further, because of China's "one child" policy and the ensuing custom of treating a single child as a "little emperor," many of the parents' purchase decisions are influenced by the input of their child.[33]

In another cross-cultural study that examined American and Singaporean family decision making, the researchers found that American families engage in more joint decision making than the Singaporean family, whereas Singaporean family decision making was more husband dominant.[34]

THE EXPANDING ROLE OF CHILDREN IN FAMILY DECISION MAKING

Over the past several decades, there has been a trend toward children playing a more active role in what the family buys, as well as in the family decision-making process. This shift in influence has occurred as a result of families having fewer children (which increases the influence of each child), more dual-income couples who can afford to permit their children to make a greater number of the choices, and the encouragement by the media to allow children to "express themselves." Still further, single-parent households often push their children toward household participation and self-reliance. As one example of children's influence, kids in supermarkets with a parent make an average of 15 requests, of which about half are typically granted.[35] Table 10.4 enumerates some of the tactics employed by children to influence their parents, and Table 10.5 presents the amount of influence children perceive they have with respect to their family's purchasing of a variety of items. Table 10.5 also indicates that children's influence tends to be greatest when the purchase was for themselves, although many claimed to be influential in the purchase of "family products," such as meals, vacations, and automobiles.

TABLE 10.4 Tactics Used by Children to Influence Their Parents

Pressure Tactics	The child makes demands, uses threats, or intimidation to persuade you to comply with his/her request
Upward Appeal	The child seeks to persuade you, saying that the request was approved or supported by an older member of the family, a teacher, or even a family friend
Exchange Tactics	The child makes an explicit or implicit promise to give you some sort of service such as washing the car, cleaning the house, or taking care of the baby, in return for a favor
Coalition Tactics	The child seeks the aid of others to persuade you to comply with his/her request or uses the support of others as an argument for you to agree with him/her
Ingratiating Tactics	The child seeks to get you in a good mood or think favorably of him or her before asking you to comply with a request
Rational Persuasion	The child uses logical arguments and factual evidence to persuade you to agree with his/her request
Inspirational Appeals	The child makes an emotional appeal or proposal that arouses enthusiasm by appealing to your values and ideals
Consultation Tactics	The child seeks your involvement in making a decision

Source: "Tactics Used by Children to Influence Their Parents," Joyantha S. Wimalasiri–*Journal of Consumer Marketing* (2004, Vol. 21, No. 4) © MCB UP Limited www.emeraldinsight.com/msq.htm. Copyright © 2004, Emerald Group Publishing Limited.

In a recent study of family holidays conducted in France and Germany, it was found that while parents think that their children have a moderate impact on holiday decision making, their children consider their level of impact to be high.[36]

There is also research evidence supporting the notion that the extent to which children influence a family's purchases is related to family communication patterns. As might be expected, children's influence has been found to be highest in families where the parents are *pluralistic*

TABLE 10.5 Items Children Perceive Themselves to Have Influenced the Purchase Of

	%
Casual clothes for me	91
Trainers for me	88
CDs for me	84
Sweets for me	83
Computers for me	83
Soft drinks for me	80
School shoes for me	80
A family trip to the cinema	73
Food for me for lunch at the weekend	73
A holiday I would go on with the family	63
Going out for a family meal	52
A family car	37

Source: "The Influence of Children on Purchases: The Development of Measures of Gender Role Orientation and Shopping Savvy." Reproduced from the *International Journal of Market Research* with permission (www.ijmr.com). Copyright The Market Research Society.

parents (i.e., parents who encourage children to speak up and express their individual preferences on purchases) and *consensual parents* (i.e., parents who encourage children to seek harmony, but are nevertheless open to the children's viewpoint on purchases), because such parents allow their children a significantly greater amount of influence than do *protective parents* (i.e., parents who stress that children should not stress their own preferences, but rather go along with the parents' judgment on what is to be purchased).[37]

Still further, there is other research that has explored the notion of the *teen Internet maven*—teenagers who spend considerable time on the Internet and know how to search for and find information, and respond to requests from others to provide information. It has been shown that teen Internet mavens contribute significantly to the family's decision making.[38] Specifically, they perceive themselves to be more influential in researching and evaluating family purchases; indeed, their parents tend to concur that they are more influential with regard to family decision making.

Finally, advertisers have long recognized the importance of children's "pester power," and therefore encourage children to "pester" their parents to purchase what they see in ads. A recent study of the strategies children use to influence their parents' food-purchasing decisions began with the proposed framework that there are four types of influence: individual differences, interpersonal influences, environmental influences, and societal influences that children employ to influence their parents so that food-purchase decisions reflect their choices or preferences. This framework is depicted in Figure 10.5. This research goes on to reveal that 10-year-old French Canadian children (living in Montreal) considered it important to eat foods similar to those eaten by others, to eat in front of the television, to suggest that the family eat foods advertised on TV, and to develop strategies to influence parental food-purchasing decisions. Still further, it was more important for boys than for girls to select foods eaten by others, and boys were more likely to eat in front of the TV and to eat in their bedrooms. The strategies used by children to influence their parents' food-purchasing decisions, included such *persuasive* strategies as: stating their preferences or begging, and *emotional* strategies, such as asking repetitively for a product (in a way that irritates the parents).[39]

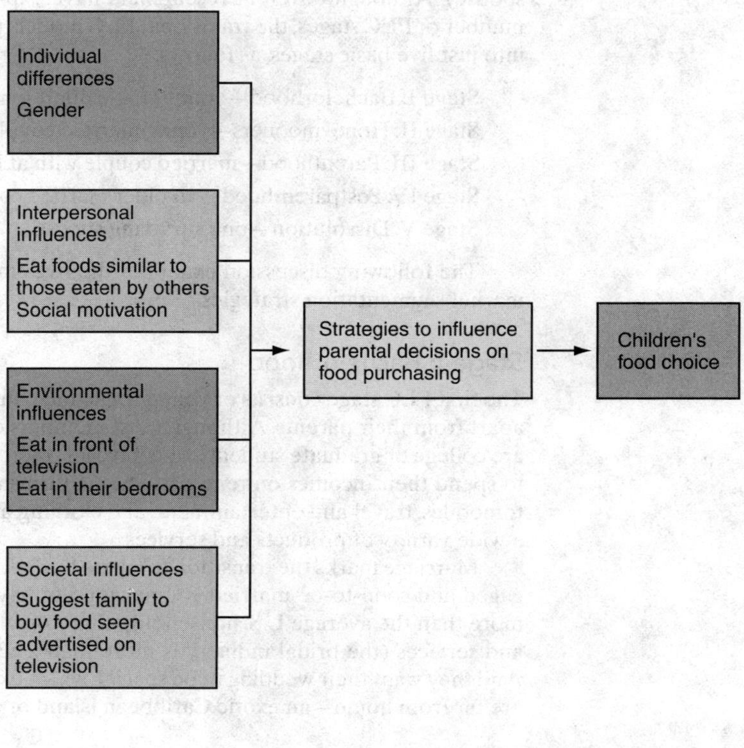

FIGURE 10.5
Conceptual Framework Related to Factors Explaining the Development of Strategies by 10-Year-Old Children to Influence Parental Decisions on Food Purchasing

Source: Marie Marquis, "Strategies for Influencing Parental Decisions on Food Purchasing," *Journal of Consumer Marketing*, 21, no. 2 (2004): 135.

The Family Life Cycle

LEARNING OBJECTIVE

10.4 *To Understand How Traditional and Non-traditional Family Life Cycles Impact Consumer Behavior.*

Sociologists and consumer researchers have long been attracted to the concept of the **family life cycle (FLC)** as a means of depicting what was once a rather steady and predictable series of stages through which most families progressed. However, with the advent of many diverse family and lifestyle arrangements, what was the rule has been on the decline. This decline in the percentage of families that progress through a traditional FLC (to be explored shortly) seems to be caused by a host of societal factors, including an increasing divorce rate, the explosive number of out-of-wedlock births, and the 40-plus year decline in the number of extended families that transpired as many young families moved away from where they grew up in order to advance their job and career opportunities.

The notion of the FLC remains a useful marketing tool when one keeps in mind that there are family and lifestyle arrangements that are not fully accounted for by the traditional representation. FLC analysis enables marketers to segment families in terms of a series of stages spanning the life course of a family unit. The FLC is a composite variable created by systematically combining such commonly used demographic variables as *marital status, size of family, age of family members* (focusing on the age of the oldest or youngest child), and *employment status* of the head of household. The ages of the parents and the relative amount of disposable income usually are inferred from the stage in the family life cycle.

To reflect the current realities of a wide range of family and lifestyle arrangements, our treatment of the FLC concept is divided into two sections. The first section considers the traditional FLC schema. This model is increasingly being challenged because it fails to account for modern, nontraditional family living arrangements. To rectify these limitations, the second section focuses on alternative FLC stages, including increasingly important nontraditional family structures.

TRADITIONAL FAMILY LIFE CYCLE

The **traditional family life cycle** is a progression of stages through which many families pass, starting with bachelorhood, moving on to marriage (and the creation of the basic family unit), then to family growth (with the birth of children), to family contraction (as grown children leave the household), and ending with the dissolution of the basic unit (due to the death of one spouse). Although different researchers have expressed various preferences in terms of the number of FLC stages, the traditional FLC models proposed over the years can be synthesized into just five basic stages, as follows:

Stage I: Bachelorhood—young single adult living apart from parents
Stage II: Honeymooners—young married couple
Stage III: Parenthood—married couple with at least one child living at home
Stage IV: Postparenthood—an older married couple with no children living at home
Stage V: Dissolution—one surviving spouse

The following discussion examines the five stages in detail and shows how they apply to market segmentation strategies.

Stage I: Bachelorhood

The first FLC stage consists of young single men and women who have established households apart from their parents. Although most members of this FLC stage are fully employed, many are college or graduate students who have left their parents' homes. Young single adults are apt to spend their incomes on rent, basic home furnishings, the purchase and maintenance of automobiles, travel and entertainment, and clothing and accessories. Marketers target singles for a wide variety of products and services.

Marriage marks the transition from the bachelorhood stage to the honeymooner stage. Engaged and soon-to-be-married couples tend to have a combined discretionary income that is more than the average U.S. household); therefore, they are often the target for many products and services (the bridal industry is more than a $30-billion-a-year market—see Figure 10.6). And they want their wedding to be special, which explains the recent trend in wedding sites that are far from home—an exotic Caribbean island or a major European capital city.

FIGURE 10.6

Source: © Bed Bath & Beyond Inc. and its subsidiaries. Used with permission.

QUESTION: *To Which Stage of the Family Life Cycle Does This Ad Apply, and Why?*

Stage II: Honeymooners

The *honeymoon* stage starts immediately after the marriage vows are taken and generally continues until the arrival of the couple's first child. This FLC stage serves as a period of adjustment to married life. Because many young husbands and wives both work, these couples have an available combined income that often permits a lifestyle that provides them with the opportunities of more indulgent purchasing of possessions or allows them to save or invest their extra income.

Honeymooners have considerable start-up expenses when establishing a new home (major and minor appliances, bedroom and living room furniture, carpeting, drapes, dishes, and a host of utensils and accessory items). During this stage, the advice and experience of other married couples are likely to be important to newlyweds. Also important as sources of new product information are the so-called shelter magazines, such as *Better Homes and Gardens* and *Metropolitan Home.*

Stage III: Parenthood

When a couple has its first child, the honeymoon is considered over. The *parenthood* stage (sometimes called the full-nest stage) usually extends over more than a 20-year period. Because of its long duration, this stage can be divided into shorter phases: the preschool phase, the elementary school phase, the high school phase, and the college phase. Throughout these parenthood phases, the interrelationships of family members and the structure of the family gradually change. Furthermore, the financial resources of the family change significantly, as one (or both) parents progress in a career and as child rearing and educational responsibilities gradually increase and finally decrease as children become self-supporting.

Many magazines cater to the information and entertainment needs of parents and children. For example, there are many other special-interest publications, such as *Humpty Dumpty,* designed for the young child just learning to read; *Scholastic Magazine,* for the elementary school pupil; *Boy's Life,* for young boys; and *American Girl*, *Seventeen,* and *Glamour* for teen and young adult girls interested in fashion. In addition, a relatively new magazine, *Cookie,* is targeting the parents in the more than 22 million U.S. homes with annual incomes in excess of $75,000 who also have children under 10 years of age.[40]

Stage IV: Postparenthood

Because parenthood extends over many years, it is only natural to find that *postparenthood,* when all the children have left home, is traumatic for some parents and liberating for others. This so-called *empty-nest stage* signifies for many parents almost a "rebirth," a time for doing all the things they could not do while the children were at home and they had to worry about soaring educational expenses.

It is during this stage that married couples tend to be most comfortable financially. Today's empty nesters have more leisure time. They travel more frequently, take extended vacations, and are likely to purchase a second home in a warmer climate. They have higher disposable incomes because of savings and investments, and they have fewer expenses (no mortgage or college tuition bills). They look forward to being involved grandparents. For this reason, families in the postparenthood stage are an important market for luxury goods, new automobiles, expensive furniture, and vacations to faraway places.

For some empty nesters, the decision to retire provides the opportunity to pursue new interests, to travel, and to fulfill unsatisfied needs. Of course, for retired couples it is really important to have sufficient savings and investments to maintain a successful retirement (see Figure 10.7). Finally, there are subsegments of older individuals who do *not* wish to retire—they simply love what they do at work too much to think of retiring. Older consumers tend to use television as an important source of information and entertainment (within Chapter 12 we will have more to say about older consumers).

Stage V: Dissolution

Dissolution of the basic family unit occurs with the death of one spouse. When the surviving spouse is in good health, is working or has adequate savings, and has supportive family and friends, the adjustment is easier. The surviving spouse (usually, the wife) often tends to follow a more economical lifestyle. Many surviving spouses seek each other out for companionship; others enter into second (or third and even fourth) marriages.

Marketing and the Traditional FLC

Whereas the foregoing discussion of the traditional family life cycle concept indicated the types of products and services that a household or family might be most interested in at each stage, it is also possible to trace how the FLC concept impacts a single product or service over time. An example, a recent qualitative study conducted in Denmark indicates that family life cycle stage influences the experiences that consumers are seeking during their vacations (e.g., less "traditional" vacations when single, such as backpacking through Europe; more "traditional" vacations when married with a young child, such as a week at a Caribbean island hotel). Consequently, FLC stage is an important consideration for vacation marketing.[41]

MODIFICATIONS—THE NONTRADITIONAL FLC

As we already noted, the traditional FLC model has lost some of its ability to fully represent the progression of stages through which current family and lifestyle arrangements move. To

FIGURE 10.7

Source: © Rarity Communities, Inc. Used with permission. All rights reserved.

QUESTION: *Which Subgroup of "Empty Nesters" Does This Ad Most Likely Target?*

compensate for these limitations, consumer researchers have been attempting to search out expanded FLC models that better reflect the diversity of family and lifestyle arrangements.[42] The underlying sociodemographic forces that have typically driven the need for an expanded FLC model include divorce and later marriages, with and without the presence of children. However, since such modified FLC models only recognize families that started in marriage, ignoring such single-parent households as unwed mothers and families formed because a single person or single persons adopt a child, they are limited in their scope and in their ability to account for contemporary realities of family composition.

Nontraditional FLC Stages

Table 10.6 presents an extensive categorization of nontraditional FLC stages that are derived from the dynamic sociodemographic forces operating during the past 30 years or so. These nontraditional stages include not only family households but also **nonfamily households**: those consisting of a single individual and those consisting of two or more unrelated individuals. At one time, nonfamily households were so uncommon that it was not really important whether they were considered or not. However, as Table 10.7 reveals, over 30 percent of all households are currently nonfamily households (i.e., men or women living alone or with another person as an unmarried couple). The table points out how FLC stages have shifted so that today nonfamily households actually outnumber married couples with children, the

TABLE 10.6 Noteworthy Nontraditional FLC Stage

ALTERNATIVE FLC STAGES	DEFINITION/COMMENTARY
Family Households	
Childless couples	It is increasingly acceptable for married couples to elect not to have children. Contributing forces are more career-oriented married women and delayed marriages.
Couples who marry later in life (in their late 30s or later)	More career-oriented men and women and greater occurrence of couples living together. Likely to have fewer or even no children.
Couples who have first child later in life (in their late 30s or later)	Likely to have fewer children. Stress quality lifestyle: "Only the best is good enough."
Single parents I	High divorce rates (about 50 percent) contribute to a portion of single-parent households.
Single parents II	Young man or woman who has one or more children out of wedlock.
Single parents III	A single person who adopts one or more children.
Extended family	Young single-adult children who return home to avoid the expenses of living alone while establishing their careers. Divorced daughter or son and grandchild(ren) return home to parents. Frail elderly parents who move in with children. Newlyweds living with in-laws.
Nonfamily Households	
Unmarried couples	Increased acceptance of heterosexual and homosexual couples.
Divorced persons (no children)	High divorce rate contributes to dissolution of households before children are born.
Single persons (most are young)	Primarily a result of delaying first marriage; also, men and women who never marry.
Widowed persons (most are elderly)	Longer life expectancy, especially for women, means more over-75 single-person households.

once stereotypical family. Additionally, there is some research evidence to show that cohabitating couples make decisions differently than married couples. For example, married couples make more purchase decisions separately, while cohabitating couples make their decisions together.[43]

Consumption in Nontraditional Families

When households undergo status changes (divorce, temporary retirement, a new person moving into the household, or the death of a spouse), they often undergo spontaneous changes in

TABLE 10.7 Family and Nonfamily Households

	NUMBER OF HOUSEHOLDS BY TYPE IN 2006 (IN 000S)	DISTRIBUTION OF HOUSEHOLDS BY TYPE
All Households	**114,384**	**100.0%**
Family Households	**77,402**	**67.7%**
Married couples	58,179	50.9%
With own children under 18	25,982	22.7%
Female householder (no husband present)	14,093	12.3%
Nonfamily Households	**36,982**	**32.3%**
Householder living alone	30,453	26.6%

Average household size = 2.57

Average family size = 3.20

Source: U.S. Census Bureau, "Households, Families, Subfamilies, and Married Couples," and "Households and Persons Per Household by Type of Household," *Statistical Abstract of the United States: 2008,* Tables 58, and 61, accessed at www.census.gov/compendia/statab.

consumption-related preferences and, thus, become attractive targets for many marketers. For example, divorce often requires that one (or both) former spouses find a new residence, get new telephones (with new telephone numbers), buy new furniture, and perhaps find a job. These requirements mean that a divorced person might need to contact real estate agents, call the local and long-distance telephone companies, visit furniture stores, and possibly contact a personnel agency or career consultant. There are also the special needs of the children who are experiencing the divorce. Still further, "children in single-parent households have greater influence in the choice of the large item, the holiday, than do children from intact families."[44]

Dual Spousal Work Involvement (DSWI): An Alternative Family/Household Classification System

DSWI is a new composite index that uses occupational status and the career commitment of both spouses as a basis for segmentation. The result is an eight-category schema: (1) retired couples, (2) nonworking wife, low husband-occupation status couples, (3) nonworking wife, high husband-occupation status couples, (4) dual low occupation status, blue-collar husband couples, (5) dual low occupation status, low white-collar husband couples, (6) high husband, low wife-occupation status couples, (7) medium–high wife-occupation status couples, and (8) dual–very high occupation status career couples. Empirical research has shown that this model (see Figure 10.8) can explain both attitudes/motivations and consumer spending. For example, dual low occupation and nonworking wife, low husband-occupation households exhibited the highest consumption of junk and convenience foods, and the lowest consumption of healthy foods. In contrast, dual, very high occupation career couples were heavy users of healthy staples and restaurant meals, and low users of convenience foods.[45]

FIGURE 10.8
A Conceptual Model of DSWI

Source: Charles M. Schaninger and Sanjay Putrevu, "Dual Spousal Work Involvement: An Alternative Method to Classify Households/Families," *Academy of Marketing Science Review, Vol. 10* no. 8 (2006): 3.

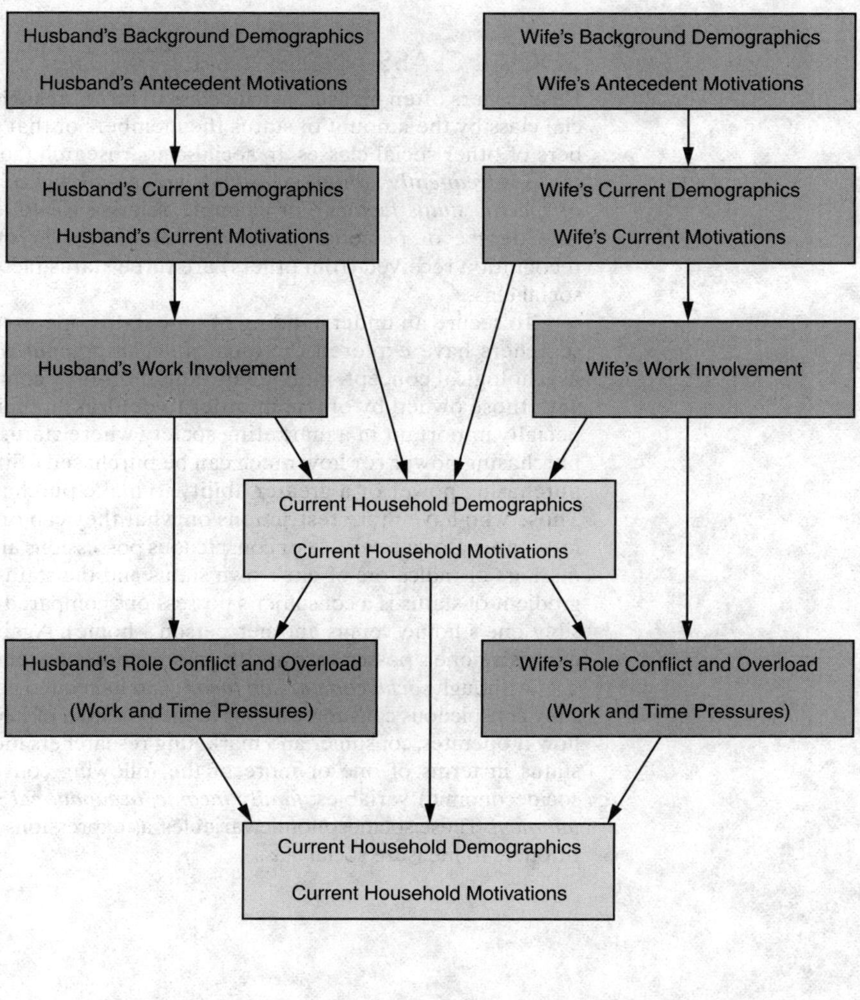

What Is Social Class?

LEARNING OBJECTIVE

10.5 *To Understand What Social Class Is and How It Relates to Consumer Behavior.*

We have just examined the concept of the family, which is one of the most important social groupings for all of us, especially during our formative years when many qualities associated with our consumer- and consumption-related values, preferences, and behavior are established. As we get older and interact more and more outside of the family, we begin to compare ourselves with those around us, often developing some type of "pecking order" so that we know where we stand within our social system. Consequently, the notion of social class is important as a consumer behavior variable.

Some form of class structure or social stratification has existed in all societies throughout the history of human existence. In contemporary societies, an indication that social classes exist is the common reality that people who are better educated or have more prestigious occupations such as physicians and lawyers often are more highly valued than those who are truck drivers and farmhands. This is so, even though all four occupations are necessary for a society's well-being. Moreover, as will be discussed later, a wide range of differences in values, attitudes, and behavior exists among members of different social classes.

Social class can be thought of as a continuum which includes a range of social positions on which each member of society can be placed, divided into a small number of specific social classes, or *strata*. Within this framework, the concept of social class is used to assign individuals or families to a social-class category. Consistent with this practice, social class is defined as *the division of members of a society into a hierarchy of distinct status classes, so that members of each class have relatively the same status and members of all other classes have either more or less status.*

To appreciate more fully the nature and complexity of social class, now consider several underlying concepts pertinent to this definition.

SOCIAL CLASS AND SOCIAL STATUS

Researchers often measure social class in terms of **social status**; that is, they define each social class by the amount of status the members of that class have in comparison with members of other social classes. In social-class research (sometimes called *social stratification*), *status is frequently thought of as the relative rankings of members of each social class in terms of specific status factors.* For example, relative *wealth* (amount of economic assets), *power* (the degree of personal choice or influence over others), and *prestige* (the degree of recognition received from others) are three status factors frequently used when estimating social class.

To secure an understanding of how status operates within the minds of consumers, researchers have explored the idea of *social comparison theory.* According to this social-psychological concept, individuals quite normally compare their own material possessions with those owned by others in order to determine their relative social standing. This is especially important in a marketing society where status is often associated with consumers' purchasing power (or how much can be purchased). Simply stated, an individual with more purchasing power or a greater ability to make purchases often tends to have more status. Those who have more restrictions on what they can or cannot buy frequently tend to have less status. Because visible or conspicuous possessions are easy to spot, they especially serve as markers or indicators of one's own status and the status of others. Not surprisingly, a key ingredient of status is a consumer's possessions compared with others' similar possessions (possibly one's home versus another person's home). Again, the more possessions or the more expensive one's possessions are, the more status one tends to have.

Although *social comparison theory* and its related activity of *status consumption* (and possibly conspicuous consumption) have the potential of being very enlightening about status and how it operates, consumer and marketing researchers most often approach the actual study of status in terms of one or more of the following convenient demographic (more precisely socioeconomic) variables: *family income, occupational status or prestige,* and *educational attainment.* These socioeconomic variables, as expressions of status, are used by marketing practitioners to measure social class.

SOCIAL CLASS IS HIERARCHICAL AND A FORM OF SEGMENTATION

Social-class categories usually are ranked in a hierarchy, ranging from low to high status. Thus, members of a specific social class perceive members of other social classes as having either more or less status than they do. To many people, therefore, social-class categories suggest that others are either equal to them (about the same social class), superior to them (higher social class), or inferior to them (lower social class).

The hierarchical aspect of social class is important to marketers. Consumers may purchase certain products because these products are favored by members of either their own or a higher social class (e.g., a high-priced Swiss wristwatch), and consumers may avoid other products because they perceive the products to be "lower-class" products (e.g., a "no-name" brand of sneaker). Thus, the various social-class strata provide a natural basis for market segmentation for many products and services. In many instances, consumer researchers have been able to relate aspects of product usage to social-class membership. For example, when it comes to the consumption of instant coffee throughout Europe, it appears that for German consumers instant coffee tends to be a particularly upmarket or upscale product; and in contrast, for French consumers instant coffee is a particularly downmarket or downscale product.[46]

The classification of society's members into a small number of social classes has also enabled researchers to note the existence of shared values, attitudes, and behavioral patterns among members within each social class and differing values, attitudes, and behavior among social classes. Consumer researchers have been able to relate social-class standing to consumer attitudes concerning specific products and to examine social-class influences on the actual consumption of products.

SOCIAL-CLASS CATEGORIES

Little agreement exists among sociologists on how many distinct class divisions are necessary to adequately describe the class structure of the United States. Most early studies divided the members of specific communities into five or six social-class groups. However, other researchers have found nine-, four-, three-, and even two-class schemas suitable for their purposes. The choice of how many separate classes to use depends on the amount of detail that the researcher believes is necessary to explain adequately the attitudes or behavior under study. Marketers are interested in the social-class structures of communities that are potential markets for their products and in the specific social-class level of their potential customers. Table 10.8 provides a sense of the distribution of the U.S. population according to a five-category subdivision.

Table 10.8 also reveals the small size of the upper class, which is the reason why most mass marketers simply ignore it (or combine it with the upper-middle class). On the other hand, its small size and highly cultivated tastes make the upper class a particularly desirable target market for specialty firms with a specific expertise and the ability to cater to the small number of particularly affluent consumers.

TABLE 10.8 A Five-Category Social-Class Measure with Percent Distribution and Category Description

CLASS	TYPICAL CHARACTERISTICS
Upper class (1%)	Top-level executives, celebrities, heirs; income of $500,000+ common. Ivy league education common
Upper middle class (15%) (also referred to as the "professional class")	Highly educated (often with graduate degrees) professionals & managers with household incomes varying from the high 5-figure range to commonly above $100,000
Lower middle class (32%)	Semi-professionals and craftsman with some work autonomy; household incomes commonly range from $35,000 to $75,000. Typically, some college education.
Working class (32%)	Clerical, pink and blue collar workers with often low job security; common household incomes range from $16,000 to $30,000. High school education.
Lower class (14%–20%)	Those who occupy poorly-paid positions or rely on government transfers. Some high school education.

Source: William E. Thompson and Josephy V. Hickey, *Society in Focus* (Boston, MA: Pearson, Allyn & Bacon, 2005), http://en.wikipedia.org/wiki/Social_class_in_the_United_States.

The Measurement of Social Class

LEARNING OBJECTIVE

10.6 *To Understand the Various Measures of Social Class and Their Role in Consumer Behavior.*

There is no general agreement on how to measure social class. To a great extent, researchers are uncertain about the underlying dimensions of social-class structure. To attempt to resolve this dilemma, researchers have used a wide range of measurement techniques that they believe give a fair approximation of social class.

Systematic approaches for measuring social class fall into the following two broad categories: **subjective measures** and **objective measures** of social class.

SUBJECTIVE MEASURES

In the *subjective* approach to measuring social class, individuals are asked to estimate their own social-class positions. Typical of this approach is the following question:

Which one of the following four categories best describes your social class: the lower class, the lower-middle class, the upper-middle class, or the upper class?

Lower class	[ ]
Lower-middle-class	[ ]
Upper-middle class	[ ]
Upper class	[ ]
Do not know/refuse to answer	[ ]

The resulting classification of social-class membership is based on the participants' self-perceptions or self-images. Social class is treated as a personal phenomenon, one that reflects an individual's sense of belonging or identification with others. This feeling of social-group membership is often referred to as **class consciousness**.

Subjective measures of social-class membership tend to produce an overabundance of people who classify themselves as middle class (thus, understating the number of people—the "fringe people"—who would, perhaps, be more correctly classified as either lower or upper class).[47] Moreover, it is likely that the subjective perception of one's social-class membership, as a reflection of one's self-image, is related to product usage and consumption preferences. This is not only an American phenomenon. Every year in Japan, a "Life of the Nation" survey asks citizens to place themselves into one of five social-class categories: upper, upper-middle, middle-middle, lower-middle, and lower class. Whereas in the late 1950s over 70 percent of respondents placed themselves into one of the three middle-class categories, by the late 1960s, and continuing on through today, close to 90 percent categorize themselves as "middle class."[48] Again, this demonstrates the tendency for consumers to report seeing themselves as "middle class."

OBJECTIVE MEASURES

In contrast to the subjective methods, which require people to envision their own class standing or that of other community members, *objective* measures consist of selected demographic or socioeconomic variables concerning the individual(s) under study. These variables are measured through questionnaires that ask respondents several factual questions about themselves, their families, or their places of residence. When selecting objective measures of social class, most researchers use one or more of the following variables: *occupation, amount of income,* and *education*. To these socioeconomic factors they sometimes add geodemographic clustering data in the form of zip code and residence-neighborhood information. These socioeconomic indicators are especially important as a means of locating concentrations of consumers with specific social-class membership.

Socioeconomic measures of social class are of considerable value to marketers concerned with segmenting markets. Marketing managers who have developed socioeconomic profiles of their target markets can locate these markets (i.e., identify and measure them) by studying the socioeconomic data periodically issued by the U.S. Bureau of the Census and numerous commercial geodemographic data services. To reach a desired target market, marketers match the *socioeconomic profiles* of their target audiences to the *audience profiles* of selected advertising media. Socioeconomic audience profiles are regularly developed and routinely made available to potential advertisers by most of the mass media (see Table 10.9).

Objective measures of social class fall into two basic categories: **single-variable indexes** and **composite-variable indexes**.

TABLE 10.9 Socioeconomic Profile of *National Geographic Adventure* Readers

	AUDIENCE (OOO)	% COMPOSITION	INDEX
Total Adults	2,393	100.0%	100
Male	1,550	64.8%	134
Female	843	35.2%	68
Medians			
Age	43.1 years		
Household Income	$69,720		
Individual Employment Income	$41,642		
Age			
18–24	338	14.1%	111
25–34	489	20.4%	114
35–44	461	19.3%	98
45–54	428	17.9%	92
55+	677	28.3%	94
Household Income			
$100,000+	603	25.2%	117
$50,000+	1,506	62.9%	115
Education			
Attended/Graduated College+	1,647	68.8%	130
College Graduate Plus	932	39.0%	153
Post Graduate Degree	308	12.9%	154
Occupation			
Professional	486	20.3%	150
Professional/Managerial	763	31.9%	137
Household Composition			
Single	769	32.1%	128
Married	1,296	54.2%	97

Source: www.nationalgeographic.com/adverture/images/adverture-media-kit-2008.pdf.

Single-Variable Indexes

A single-variable index uses just one socioeconomic variable to evaluate social-class membership. Some of the variables that are used for this purpose are discussed next.

OCCUPATION Occupation is a widely accepted and probably the best-documented measure of social class because it reflects occupational status.[49] The importance of occupation as a social-class indicator is dramatized by the frequency with which people ask others they meet for the first time, "What do you do for a living?" The response to this question serves as a guide in sizing up (or evaluating and forming opinions of) others.

More important, marketers frequently think in terms of specific occupations when defining a target market for their products (such as "Accountants are our best customers for late Spring—after April 15—Caribbean Island vacations") or broader occupational categories ("We target our ultra-deluxe seven-day cruises to executives and professionals"). Still further, the likelihood that particular occupations would be receptive to certain products or services often provides the basis for an occupational screener requirement for participation in focus groups or survey research and for marketers to select occupational databases to target with direct-marketing campaigns (e.g., a list of female high school social studies teachers working in the San Diego area).

Figure 10.9 presents findings from a continuing survey undertaken by the Gallup organization that estimates the relative honesty and perceived ethical standards that people assign to a sample of basic occupational titles. Because this ranking is based more on respect or societal prestige (a form of status) than on wealth, it is not surprising that the rankings (i.e., from top to

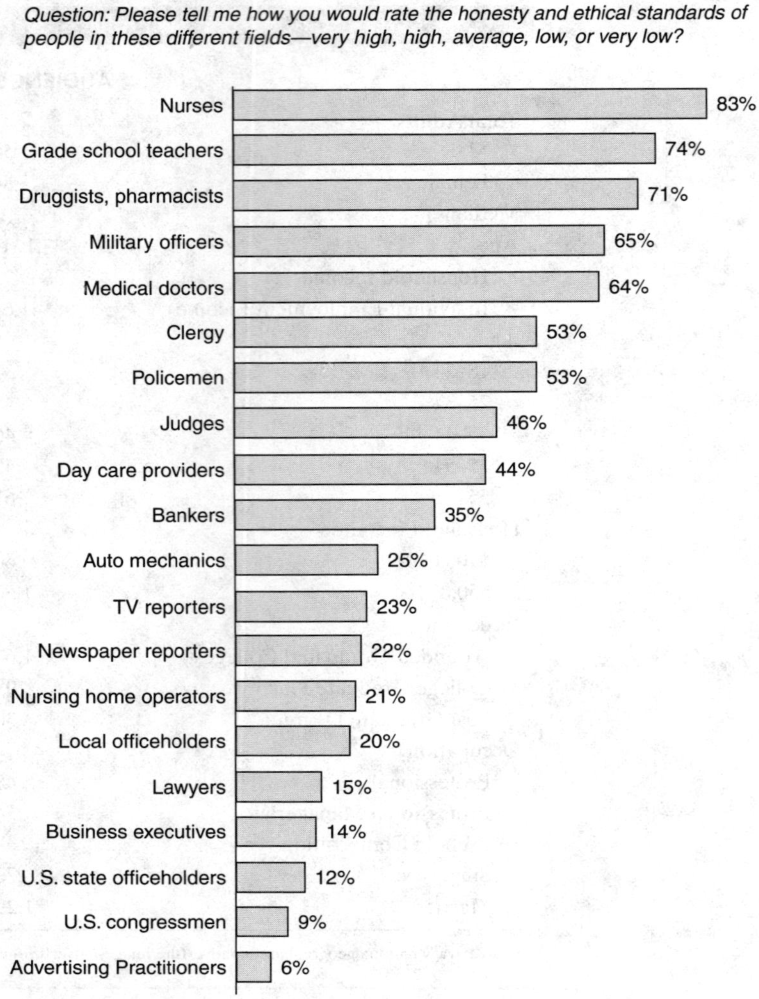

FIGURE 10.9 Occupational Rankings in Terms of Honesty and Ethical Standards

Source: *The Gallup Poll Monthly*, November 2007. Reprinted by permission. At www.gallup.com/poll/1654/Honesty-Ethics-Professions.aspx.

bottom) do *not* seem to suggest that occupations toward the top half of the figure earn higher incomes or require more formal education than those toward the bottom half.

Within the domain of occupational status, there has also been an increasing trend toward self-employment among business and professional people. Specifically, it appears that business executives and professionals who are self-employed or entrepreneurs are substantially more likely to be *very wealthy* than their counterparts who work for someone else.[50] This link between self-employment and higher incomes is consistent with the trend of increasing numbers of business school graduates seeking to work for themselves rather than going to work for a "big business."

EDUCATION The level of a person's formal education is another commonly accepted approximation of social-class standing. Generally speaking, the more education a person has, the more likely it is that the person is well paid (or has a higher income) and has an admired or respected position (high occupational status).[51] Using U.S. census data, Table 10.10 supports the close relationship between educational attainment and amount of household income.

Research has shown that different social classes often approach the notion of a college degree very differently. For example, students at the most selective universities in the United States are often the sons and daughters of upper-class Americans, while lower-class children are often encouraged to "get a good job." In a series of articles on social class, a 50-year-old man whose father was a factory worker, was quoted as saying: "The whole concept of life was that you should get a good job in the factory . . . if I'd said I wanted to go to college, it would have been like saying I wanted to grow gills and breathe underwater."[52] Almost one in three Americans in their

TABLE 10.10 The Relationship Between Formal Education and Family Income

	TOTAL	LESS THAN GRADE 9	SOME HIGH SCHOOL	HIGH SCHOOL GRADUATE	SOME COLLEGE (NO DEGREE)	ASSOCIATES DEGREE	BACHELOR'S DEGREE OR MORE
All Households[a]	100%	100%	100%	100%	100%	100%	100%
Under $15,000	8.1	21.1	20.6	9.6	7.0	5.1	2.3
$15,000 to $24,999	9.7	24.3	19.7	12.7	8.4	6.2	3.1
$25,000 to $34,999	10.5	18.8	17.6	13.0	11.2	9.1	4.5
$35,000 to $49,999	14.6	15.9	17.2	18.0	16.2	14.7	9.0
$50,000 to $74,999	20.6	12.4	14.9	22.7	22.4	25.1	19.1
$75,000 to $99,999	13.9	4.8	5.8	11.9	15.4	17.7	17.7
$100,000 and over	22.6	2.8	4.3	12.1	19.4	22.1	44.3
Number of families (000)	73,722	3,870	6,085	22,097	13,370	6,694	21,605
Median income	$56,194	$26,973	$30,275	$47,045	$56,841	$64,294	$91,010

[a]Persons 25 years old and over.

Source: U.S. Census Bureau, *Statistical Abstract of the United States*, 2008; from *Current Population Reports*, P60-231; and http://pubdb3.census.gov/macro/032006/faminc/new01_000.htm, released August 29, 2006.

mid-20s today is a college dropout (compared to one in five in the late 1960s), and most are members of poor and working-class families. In contrast, the children of the middle and upper classes more often stay in college until they graduate "because they can hardly imagine doing otherwise."[53]

INCOME Individual or family income is another socioeconomic variable frequently used to approximate social-class standing. Researchers who favor income as a measure of social class use either *amount* or *source* of income. Available research suggests that income works best in accounting for leisure consumption when measured in terms of "engaging in" or "doing or not doing" a particular leisure activity (such as snow skiing, bowling, or playing basketball or golf).[54]

A study to differentiate between "income" and "wealth" points out that: (1) Wealth, not income, is the primary driver to financial freedom—wealth, not income, is a function of savings, so to achieve wealth you have to increase your net worth, and not just your income; (2) Wealth and money are not the same—wealth deals with the creation of resources, and money deals more with consumption; (3) For wealth you need to network and build personal alliances, because a great deal of the information needed to create wealth is passed along via such relationships; and (4) You need to find ways to minimize your taxes, because taxes reduce your ability to create wealth.[55]

It is important to point out that the distribution of income and net worth in the United States has become more unbalanced over the past few decades. For example, in the year 2001, the richest 1 percent of households possessed almost 34 percent of all net worth, while the bottom 90 percent of all households had 28.5 percent. It is accurate to state that the trend has been that the rich get richer, and the poor get poorer. Table 10.11, which presents the distribution of income growth to income group for the historical period from 1979 to 2000, clearly shows that while the income of the richest 1 percent of all households grew 38.4 percent during this time period, the income growth for the poorest 20 percent of households was less than 1 percent.[56] Still further, between 1984 and 2005 on average, the net worth of the top two percentile of U.S. families rose from $1.07 million to over $2.1 million, while the poorest 5 percent of U.S. households had their negative net worth grow from $1,000 to almost $9,000.[57]

Although income is a commonly used estimate of social-class standing, not all consumer researchers agree that it is an appropriate index of social class. Some argue that a blue-collar electrician and a white-collar administrative assistant may both earn $77,000 a year, yet because of (or as a reflection of) social-class differences, each will spend that income in a different way. How they decide to spend their incomes reflects different values. Within this context, it is the difference in values that is an important discriminant of social class between people, not the amount of income they earn.

TABLE 10.11 Distribution of Income Growth to Income Group, 1979–2000

INCOME GROUP (HOUSEHOLDS)	SHARE OF INCOME GROWTH, 1979–2000
Poorest 20%	0.8%
Middle 20%	5.1
Richest 20%	74.0
80–85%	21.5
95–99%	14.1
Richest 1%	38.4

Source: Michael D. Yates, "A Statistical Portrait of the U.S. Working Class," *Monthly Review,* 56 (April 2005): 20.

Composite-Variable Indexes

Composite indexes systematically combine a number of socioeconomic factors to form one overall measure of social-class standing. Such indexes are of interest to consumer researchers because they may better reflect the complexity of social class than single-variable indexes. For instance, research exploring consumers' perceptions of mail and phone order shopping reveals that the *higher* the socioeconomic status (in terms of a composite of income, occupational status, and education), the more positive are the consumers' ratings of mail and phone order buying, relative to in-store shopping.[58] The same research also found that downscale consumers (a composite of lower scores on the three variables) were less positive toward magazine and catalog shopping and more positive toward in-store shopping than more upscale socioeconomic groupings. Armed with such information, retailers such as Kmart and Wal-Mart that especially target *working-class* consumers would have a real challenge using direct-marketing catalogs and telephone-selling approaches. In contrast, retailers concentrating on upscale consumers, such as Neiman Marcus and Saks, have been especially effective in developing catalog programs targeted to specific segments of affluent or upscale consumers.

Two popular composite indexes are the **Index of Status Characteristics** and the **Socioeconomic Status Score**:

1. **Index of status characteristics**—A classic composite measure of social class is Warner's Index of Status Characteristics (ISC). The ISC is a weighted measure of the following socioeconomic variables: occupation, source of income (not amount of income), house type, and dwelling area (quality of neighborhood).[59]
2. **Socioeconomic status scores**—The U.S. Bureau of the Census developed the Socioeconomic Status Score (SES), which combines three basic socioeconomic variables: occupation, family income, and educational attainment.[60]

Lifestyle Profiles of the Social Classes

LEARNING OBJECTIVE

10.7 *To Appreciate the Distinctive Profiles of Specific Social Class Groupings.*

Consumer research has found evidence that within each of the social classes, there is a constellation of specific lifestyle factors (shared beliefs, attitudes, activities, and behaviors) that tends to distinguish the members of each class from the members of all other social classes.

To capture the lifestyle composition of the various social-class groupings, Table 10.12 presents a consolidated portrait, pieced together from numerous sources, of the members of the following six social classes: upper-upper class, lower-upper class, upper-middle class, lower-middle class, upper-lower class, and lower-lower class. Each of these profiles is only a generalized picture of the class.

Clearly, most marketers target more than one social class. For example, Target stores can appeal to more than a single social class. Target, for example, is known as a marketer of "cheap chic," and while it offers general merchandise at discounted prices, it "also stocks inexpensive designer products to attract relatively affluent customers."[61]

TABLE 10.12 Social-Class Profiles

THE UPPER-UPPER CLASS—COUNTRY CLUB ESTABLISHMENT
- Small number of well-established families
- Belong to best country clubs and sponsor major charity events
- Serve as trustees for local colleges and hospitals
- Prominent physicians and lawyers
- May be heads of major financial institutions, owners of major long-established firms
- Accustomed to wealth, so do not spend money conspicuously

THE LOWER-UPPER CLASS—NEW WEALTH
- Not quite accepted by the upper crust of society
- Represent "new money"
- Successful business executives
- Conspicuous users of their new wealth

THE UPPER-MIDDLE CLASS—ACHIEVING PROFESSIONALS
- Have neither family status nor unusual wealth
- Career oriented
- Successful professionals, corporate managers, and business owners
- Most are college graduates, many with advanced degrees
- Active in professional, community, and social activities
- Have a keen interest in obtaining the "better things in life"
- Their homes serve as symbols of their achievements
- Consumption is often conspicuous
- Very child oriented

THE LOWER-MIDDLE CLASS—FAITHFUL FOLLOWERS
- Primarily nonmanagerial white-collar workers and highly paid blue-collar workers
- Want to achieve respectability and be accepted as good citizens
- Want their children to be well-behaved
- Tend to be churchgoers and are often involved in church-sponsored activities
- Prefer a neat and clean appearance and tend to avoid faddish or highly styled clothing
- Constitute a major market for do-it-yourself products

THE UPPER-LOWER CLASS—SECURITY-MINDED MAJORITY
- The largest social-class segment
- Solidly blue collar
- Strive for security (sometimes gained from union membership)
- View work as a means to "buy" enjoyment
- Want children to behave properly
- High wage earners in this group may spend impulsively
- Interested in items that enhance their leisure time (e.g., TV sets, hunting equipment)
- Husbands typically have a strong "macho" self-image
- Males are sports fans, heavy smokers, beer drinkers

THE LOWER-LOWER CLASS—ROCK BOTTOM
- Poorly educated, unskilled laborers
- Often out of work
- Children are often poorly treated
- Tend to live a day-to-day existence

Social-Class Mobility

Learning Objective

10.8 *To Understand the "Ups and Downs" of Social Class Mobility.*

Social-class membership in the United States is not as hard and fixed as it is in some other countries and cultures. Although individuals can move either up or down in social-class standing from the class position held by their parents, Americans have primarily thought in terms of **upward mobility** because of the availability of free education and opportunities for self-development and self-advancement. Indeed, the classic Horatio Alger tale of a penniless young orphan who managed to achieve great success in business and in life is depicted over and over again in American novels, movies, and television shows. Today many young men and women with ambition to get ahead dream of going to college and eventually starting their own successful businesses.

Because upward mobility has commonly been attainable in American society, the higher social classes often become reference groups for ambitious men and women of lower social status. Familiar examples of upward mobility are the new management trainee who strives to dress like the boss, the middle manager who aspires to belong to the status country club, or the graduate of a municipal college who wants to send her son to Yale.

Recognizing that individuals often aspire to the lifestyle and possessions enjoyed by members of a higher social class, marketers frequently incorporate the symbols of higher-class membership, both as products and symbols, in advertisements targeted to lower social-class audiences. For example, ads often present or display marketers' products within an upper-class setting.

Another characteristic of social-class mobility is that products and services traditionally within the realm of one social class may filter down to lower social classes. For instance, plastic surgery was once affordable only for movie stars and other wealthy consumers. Today, however, lower-middle class consumers and higher economic strata seek to undergo cosmetic procedures.

SOME SIGNS OF DOWNWARD MOBILITY

Although the United States is frequently associated with *upward mobility,* because it was the "rule" for much of its history that each generation within a family tended to "do better" than the last generation, there now are signs of some **downward mobility**. Social commentators have suggested that some young adults (such as members of Generation X in Chapter 12) are not only likely to find it difficult to "do better" than their successful parents (e.g., to get better jobs, own homes, have more disposable income, and have more savings) but also may *not* even do as well as their parents.

There is some evidence of such a slide in social-class mobility. Specifically, researchers have found that the odds that young men's income will reach middle-class levels by the time they reach their thirtieth birthday have been slowly declining.[62] This regressive pattern holds true regardless of race, parents' income, and young persons' educational level.

IS HORATIO ALGER DEAD?

While many Americans still believe in the Horatio Alger rags-to-riches story, there is a growing body of evidence that social mobility in America is not what it used to be. For example, while household income grew by $1,869 from 1969–1979, by $2,855 from 1979–1989, and by $3,888 from 1989–2000, from 2000–2007 the change in household income was a *minus* $324.[63] Additionally, income inequality is rising to levels not seen since the 1880s—the Gilded Age, and the gap between the rich and the poor has widened since 1970. Specifically, while the income of households in the top fifth grew 70 percent between 1979 and 2000, the real income of households in the bottom fifth rose only 6.4 percent. Although most Americans find little wrong with income inequality, as long as there still exists plenty of social mobility, there are signs that social mobility is falling.[64] One recent study examined 2,749 father-and-son pairs and found that few sons ever got to move up the class ladder.[65] Another research effort found that out of over 6,000 American families studied, 42 percent of the individuals born into the poorest fifth ended up there, at the bottom, with another 24 percent moving up only slightly, to the next-to-bottom group.[66] Only 10 percent of adult men born into the bottom quarter ever made it to the top quarter. It has been reported that currently, a child born into poverty in Europe or Canada has a better chance at prosperity than one born in the United States, and that "Americans are no more or less likely to rise above, or fall below, their parents' economic class than they were 35 years ago."[67]

Geodemographic Clustering

Learning Objective

10.9 *To Understand the Relationship Between Social Class and Geodemographic Clusters.*

In recent years, traditional social-class measures have been enhanced by linking consumer-related geographic and socioeconomic data to create comprehensive **geodemographic clusters**. The underlying rationale for geodemographic clustering is that "birds of a feather flock together." This is to say that families of similar socioeconomic backgrounds tend to reside in the same neighborhoods or communities—that is, "they cluster together." Furthermore, throughout a large and diversified country there are dispersed communities made up of similar people with similar geographic profiles. Employing a variety of consumer research methodologies, these communities can be defined and located in terms of their zip codes and/or postal routes. Still further, they can be combined to create a considerably larger "geodemographic cluster" (often given a distinctive name). These larger clusters can then be marketed to (often using direct marketing).

One of the most popular clustering services is **PRIZM NE** (i.e., "new edition") from Claritas (www.claritas.com/Default.jsp) which identifies a variety of socioeconomic and demographic factors (education, income, occupation, family life cycle, ethnicity, housing, and urbanization) drawn from U.S. census data. This material is combined with survey and panel data on actual consumer behavior (e.g., product purchase and usage, mail-order buying, and media-exposure habits) to locate concentrations of consumers with similar characteristics.

PRIZM NE assigns every one of the microneighborhoods in the United States (ZIP + 4 areas) to one of 66 PRIZM NE clusters, which are further collapsed into 14 *social groups* (that reflect the extent of wealth and a kind of geographic density or "urbanicity" continuum) and also some 11 *lifestage groups* (that reflect the extent of wealth and life-age stages). Figure 10.10 illustrates how these two groups arrange PRIZM NE clusters in terms of *level of wealth* (from the top "high," to the bottom "low"). Marketers can superimpose these geodemographic clusters onto a host of product and service usage data, media-exposure data, and lifestyle data (such as VALS, discussed in Chapter 3) to create a sharp, refined picture of their target markets. For example, the "Affluentials" (Social Group S2) is 12 percent more likely to visit real estate Web sites, while the "Micro-City Blues" (Social Group C3) is 12 percent less likely to do so.[68] To further illustrate the usefulness of such clustering of consumers, Table 10.13 presents brief descriptions of two higher-end, two mid-range, and two lower-end PRIZM NE clusters.

A recent study used geodemographic clustering to compare consumer attitudes toward commercial banks in Western Pennsylvania. The research found that local bank customers (as opposed to national bank customers) were mostly female, younger, college graduates, had higher incomes, and were holders of professional jobs. The researchers note that in order to be of use in commercial bank marketing, a segment must be as homogeneous as possible, the segment's size must be quantifiable, and it must be locatable.[69] Clearly, geodemographic clustering systems like PRIZM NE meet these requirements.

The Affluent Consumer

Learning Objective

10.10 *To Understand the Affluent Consumer.*

Affluent households constitute an especially attractive target segment because its members have incomes that provide them with a disproportionately larger share of all discretionary income—the "extras" that allow the purchase of luxury cruises, foreign sports cars, time-sharing ski-resort condos and fine jewelry. It has also been pointed out that there is a strong positive relationship between health and economic status—that is, "the healthiest people are those who are economically advantaged" and "poverty is bad for you."[70] Indeed, higher income and more highly educated people are less likely to die of heart disease, strokes, diabetes, and many types of cancer, and affluent Americans live longer and in better health than middle-class Americans, who live longer and in better health than individuals at the bottom.[71] Conversely, evidence suggests that children of the affluent may have problems with substance abuse, anxiety, and depression, which can be caused by excessive pressures to achieve and isolation from parents (both physically and emotionally).[72]

The wealth of Americans grew dramatically during the 1990s partially due to the longest bull market in U.S. history. By 2004, the total personal wealth of American households was a

FIGURE 10.10A
PRIZM NE Fourteen Social Groups That Reflect 66 Microneighborhoods
Source: Claritas, *PRIZM Segment Narratives*, August 2008.

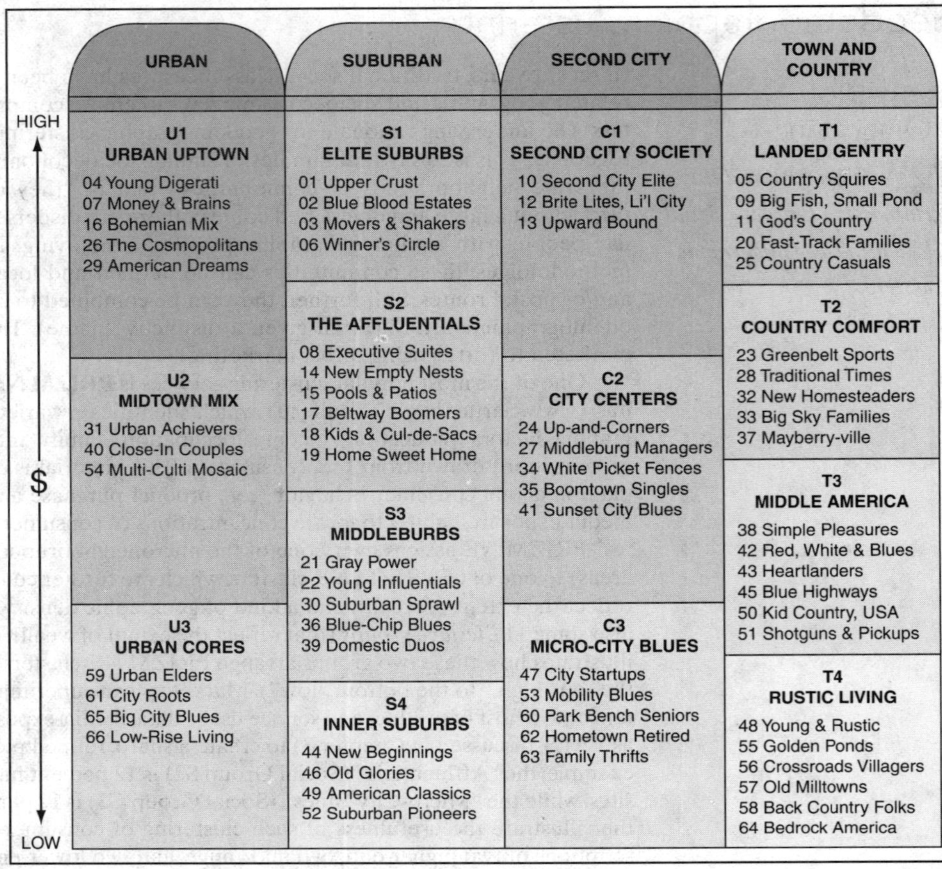

record $48.5 trillion, a gain of 8.8 percent over 2003.[73] From 2002 to 2004, the number of "high net worth individuals" (HNWIs) in North America, that is, individuals with a minimum net worth of $1 million, grew by 9.7 percent, for a total HNWI population of 2.7 million, and from 2006 to 2007 the number grew from 2.9 million to more than 3 million, a gain of 3.7 percent.[74] Indeed, although North America has only 6 percent of the world adult population, it accounts for 34 percent of the world's household wealth.[75] Figure 10.11 is a print ad especially targeting the affluent consumer market.

While the affluent market is most often defined by income or net worth, one research study explored this market to examine whether such a definition was sufficient. The study proposed that an operational definition of *affluent* should also include both lifestyle and psychographic factors because the heads of affluent households have a tendency to behave and think affluently.[76] Still further, a recent study found that almost 80 percent of individuals considered to be wealthy (defined as discretionary household incomes above $125,000) are themselves products of middle class households. Consequently, there are two types of affluent shoppers; passion shoppers (40 percent of luxury shoppers) who love the elegance of shopping in a luxury environment and are willing to pay full price, and logical shoppers (60 percent of luxury shoppers), who did not grow up with the brands and services that they can now afford, and may search online for discounts and/or require the brand to prove itself before they will purchase it.[77]

For over 30 years, Ipsos Mendelsohn (formally Mendelsohn Media Research) has conducted an annual study of the **affluent market** (defined in its 2008 survey as those with household incomes of $100,000 or more per year). The survey divides the affluent market into three segments: the *least affluent* segment has annual household incomes of $100,000 to $149,000 (12 percent of all households, $1.7 trillion estimated household income), the *middle affluent* segment with incomes from $150,000 to $249,000 (6 percent of all households, $1.3 trillion estimated household income), and the *most affluent* segment with household incomes of $250,000 or more

FIGURE 10.10B
PRIZM NE Eleven Lifestyle Groups
Source: Claritas, *PRIZM Segment Narratives*, August 2008.

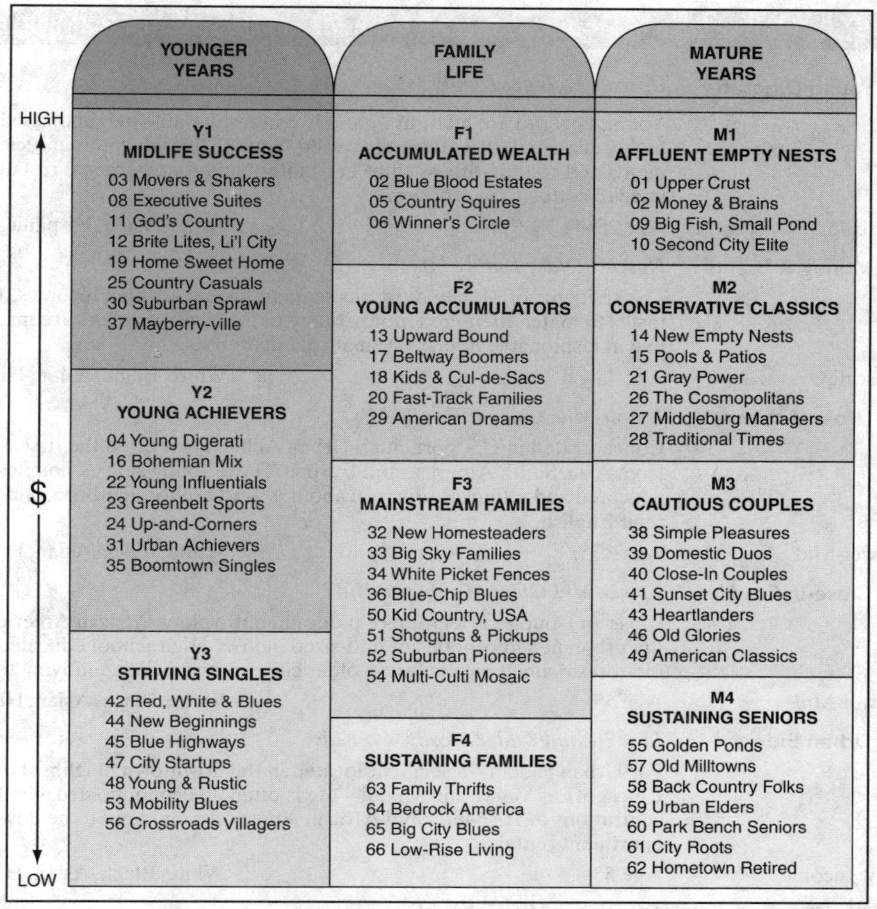

(2 percent of all households, \$1.6 trillion estimated household income). Although they consist of only 20 percent of total U.S. households (23.3 million households), these affluent market segments accounted for over half of all U.S. household income. The average household income for these consumers is \$195,600, with average household liquid assets of \$500,900.[78] Figure 10.12 presents additional information as to average household expenditures for selected purchases for the three affluent segments. The results reveal that although the first two segments of affluent consumers certainly spend ample amounts purchasing a wide variety of products, in many cases the "most affluent" purchasers spend significantly more. For instance, when it comes to computers and electronics, the "least affluent" spent \$2,970, and the "medium affluent" spent \$3,975, whereas the "most affluent" spent \$6,515. Figure 10.13 presents some further insights about this much sought after market segment in terms of a comparison of the sports participation of the three segments of affluent consumers. The results reveal that the "most affluent" are more likely than members of the two other affluent consumer segments to participate with many of the sports listed.[79] An examination of these two figures explains why marketers are so eager to target affluent consumers.

Still further, a growing subcategory of the overall affluent market are the *millionaires.* As already cited, there are currently over 3 million individuals or families in North America with a net worth that is at least \$1 million. Contrary to common stereotypes, these millionaires are quite similar to nonmillionaires. They are typically first-generation wealthy, often working for themselves in "ordinary" nonglamour businesses. They work hard and frequently live in nonpretentious homes, often next door to nonmillionaires. It is also important to note that The Mendelsohn Affluent Survey also makes a distinction between *affluence* and *wealth*, and defines a household having substantial wealth as one with liquid assets (i.e., cash or cash equivalents, such as CDs, mutual funds, stocks, bonds, etc.) of at least \$1 million. Out of the 23.3 million

TABLE 10.13 Examples of Upscale, Mid-Range, and Downscale PRIZM NE Clusters

04 Young Digerati	*Upscale Younger Family Mix*	
	Young Digerati are tech-savvy and live in fashionable neighborhoods on the urban fringe. Affluent, highly educated, and ethnically mixed, Young Digerati communities are typically filled with trendy apartments and condos, fitness clubs and clothing boutiques, casual restaurants and all types of bars—from juice to coffee to microbrew.	
Upscale	Age 25–44	White, Asian, Hispanic, Mix
07 Money & Brains	*Upscale Older Family Mix*	
	The residents of Money & Brains seem to have it all: high incomes, advanced degrees, and sophisticated tastes to match their credentials. Many of these city dwellers are married couples with few children who live in fashionable homes on small, manicured lots.	
Upscale	Age 45–64	White, Black, Asian, Hispanic, Mix
31 Urban Achievers	*Lower-Mid Younger Family Mix*	
	Concentrated in U.S. port cities, Urban Achievers is often the first stop for up-and-coming immigrants from Asia, South America, and Europe. These young singles, couples, and families are typically college-educated and ethnically diverse: about a third are foreign-born, and even more speak a language other than English.	
Lower-Mid	Age <35	White, Black, Asian, Hispanic, Mix
40 Close-In Couples	*Lower-Mid Older Mostly w/o Kids*	
	Close-In Couples is a group of predominantly older, African American couples living in older homes in the urban neighborhoods of mid-sized metros. High school educated and empty nesting, these mostly older residents typically live in older city neighborhoods, enjoying their retirements.	
Lower-Mid	Age 55+	White, Black, Asian, Hispanic, Mix
59 Urban Elders	*Low Income Older Mostly w/o Kids*	
	For Urban Elders—a segment located in the downtown neighborhoods of such metros as New York, Chicago, Las Vegas, and Miami—life is often an economic struggle. These communities have high concentrations of Hispanics and African Americans and tend to be downscale, with singles living in older apartment rentals.	
Low Income	Age 55+	White, Black, Asian, Hispanic, Mix
61 City Roots	*Downscale Mature Mostly w/o Kids*	
	Found in urban neighborhoods, City Roots is a segment of low income retirees, typically living in older homes and duplexes they've owned for years. In these ethnically diverse neighborhoods—more than a third are African American or Hispanic—residents are often widows or widowers living on fixed incomes and maintaining low-key lifestyles.	
Downscale	Age 65+	White, Black, Hispanic, Mix

Source: Claritas, *PRIZM Segment Narratives,* August 2008.

affluent households in the United States, the survey found that 2.672 million households have more than $1 million in liquid assets, and 1.029 million have both more than $1 million in wealth plus an annual household income of at least $250,000.[80]

In the United Kingdom, the affluent are often empty nesters with high disposable incomes and small or paid-off mortgages. These consumers have an abundance of money, but are time poor and are interested in improving the quality of their lives with overseas vacations and sports cars.[81] Moreover, researchers who have examined affluent consumers, in both the United Kingdom and United States, have found that they are likely to focus on saving or reducing time and effort and, not unsurprisingly, are willing to pay for many things that provide such convenience.[82]

THE MEDIA EXPOSURE OF THE AFFLUENT CONSUMER

As might be expected, the media habits of the affluent differ from those of the general population.[83] For example, those households earning more than $100,000 a year view *less* TV per day than less affluent households. A profile of the media habits of $100,000-plus affluent adult householders shows they read 8 different publications, listen to 11.3 hours of weekday radio and watch 19.5 hours of TV per week, and 95 percent of them view cable TV. Magazines that

FIGURE 10.11
Source: Courtesy of Marquis Jet Card.
marquisjet.com

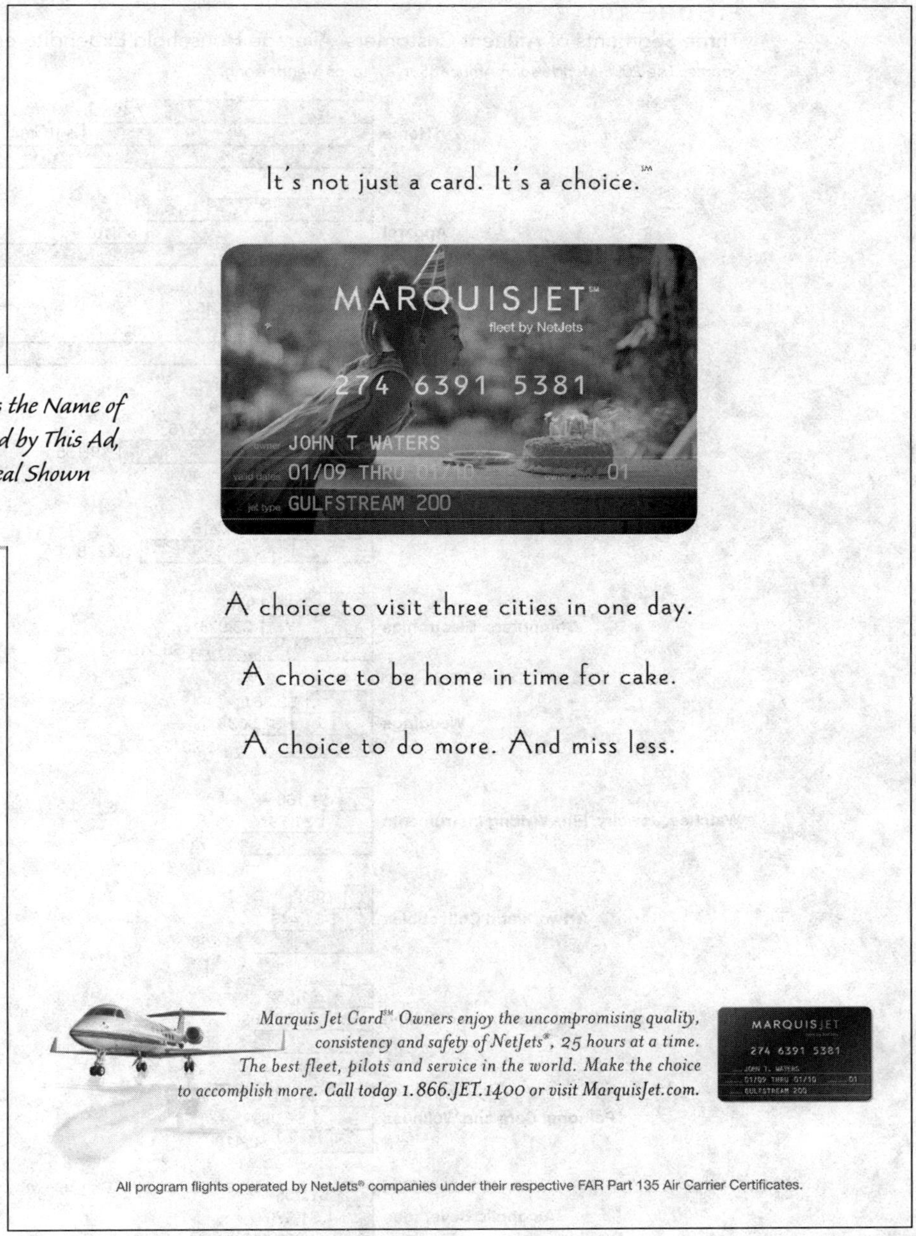

QUESTION: *What Is the Name of the Segment Targeted by This Ad, and Why Is the Appeal Shown Here Used?*

cater to the tastes and interests of the affluent include *Architectural Digest, Condé Nast Traveler, Gourmet, Southern Accents,* and *Town & Country.* Table 10.14 presents a selection of magazines and reveals the median household incomes of those among their readers with incomes of $100,000 or more.

Traditionally, when Nielsen Media Research provided information on TV viewership, the company's highest household income category had been $75,000-plus. Recently, Nielsen has begun providing demographic data for households earning $100,000-plus, which permits advertisers and television stations to gain new insights into the TV habits of more affluent Americans.[84]

The Luxury Institute recently surveyed over 1,500 consumers with annual household incomes of at least $150,000 about leading luxury fashion brands for men. Mentioned brands were ranked by quality, exclusivity, social status, and self-enhancement, and then the rankings for each brand were combined to form the Luxury Brand Status Index (LBSI). The number one brand was Brioni, with Armani and Ermenegildo Zegna tied for second place.[85]

FIGURE 10.12

Three Segments of Affluent Customers' Average Household Expenditures (Among Purchasing Households)

Source: *The 2008 Mendelsohn Affluent Survey*, Ipsos Mendelsohn.

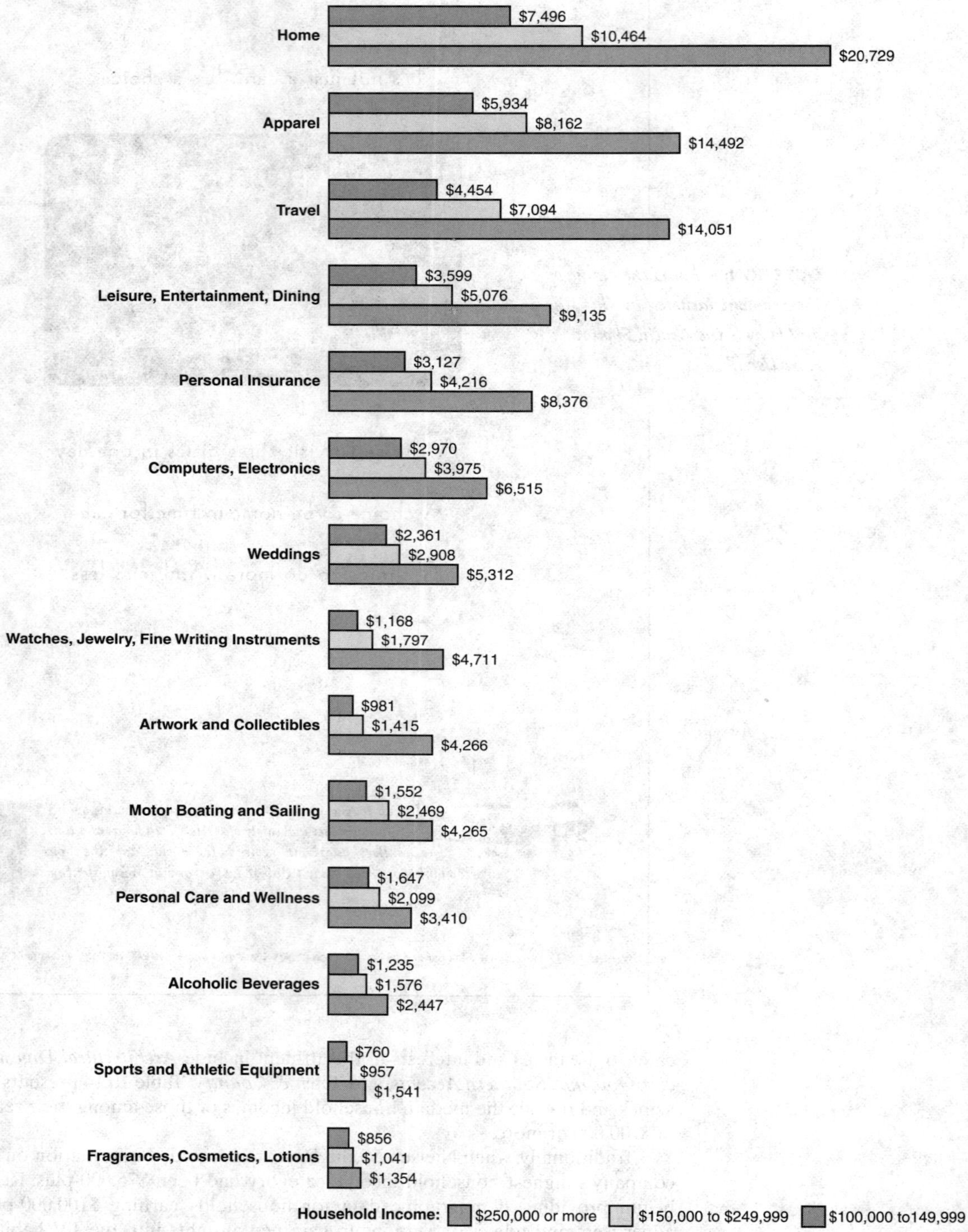

FIGURE 10.13
Affluent Consumers' Participation in Selected Sports (Number of Days in Past Year, Indexed to Each of the Three Income Segments)
Source: *The 2008 Mendelsohn Affluent Survey*, Ipsos Mendelsohn.

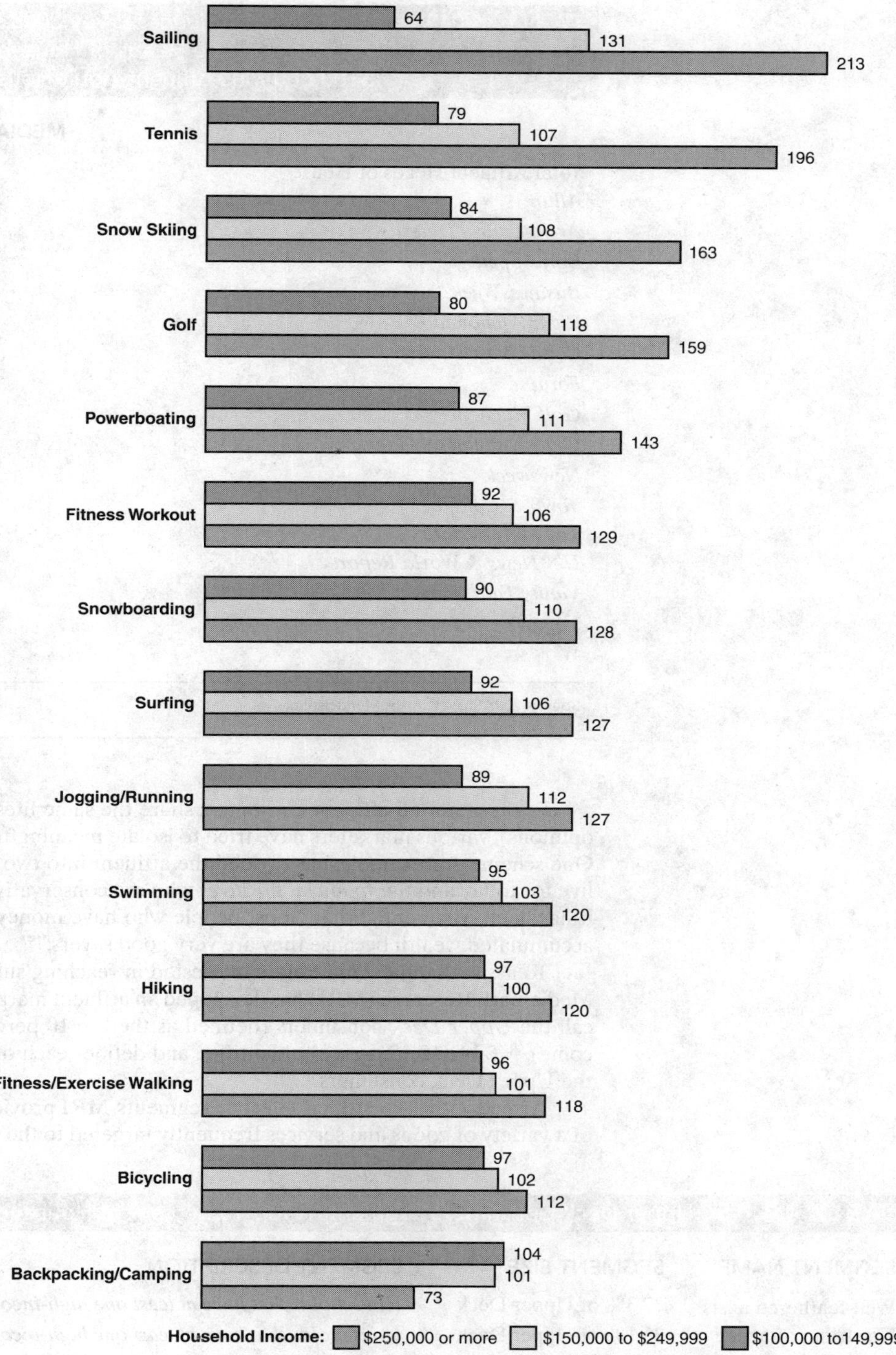

SEGMENTING THE AFFLUENT MARKET

In addition to Mendelsohn Media Research's division of the overall affluent consumer market into three subsegments, it is recognized that affluent consumers can be defined in terms of various other factors. For example, one study found that the wealth in America is not found only behind "the tall, cloistered walls of suburban country clubs, but is spread among niches, including Asian immigrants, single women, and young Cuban Americans, to name a few."[86]

TABLE 10.14 *Mendelsohn Affluent Survey 2008* Audiences: Male and Female Heads of Household ($100,000-Plus Affluent Adult Households)

	MEDIAN HOUSEHOLD INCOME
Total Affluent Heads of House	$138,800
Allure	$139,900
Architectural Digest	$163,200
Bon Appétit	$151,600
BusinessWeek	$163,300
Cigar Aficionado	$160,800
Condé Nast Traveler	$158,900
Fortune	$160,500
Golf Magazine	$154,500
GQ, Gentlemen's Quarterly	$157,900
Newsweek	$145,900
Town & Country	$156,200
Travel + Leisure	$155,000
U.S. News & World Report	$147,300
Vanity Fair	$153,900
Vogue	$144,900
W	$159,600

Source: 2008 Survey, Ipsos Mendelsohn.

Because not all affluent consumers share the same lifestyles (i.e., activities, interests, and opinions), various marketers have tried to isolate meaningful segments of the affluent market. One scheme, for example, has divided the affluent into two groups—the *upbeat enjoyers* who live for today and the *financial positives* who are conservative and look for value. Still further, it has been commented that "most people who have money are fairly conservative, and have accumulated wealth because they are very good savers."[87]

To assist the many marketers interested in reaching subsegments of the affluent market, Mediamark Research (MRI) has developed an affluent market-segmentation schema that they call the *Upper Deck* consumers (defined as the top 10 percent of households in terms of income).[88] Table 10.15 presents, identifies, and defines each of the five segments that constitute the Upper Deck consumers.

Armed with such affluent lifestyle segments, MRI provides its clients with profiles of users of a variety of goods and services frequently targeted to the affluent consumer and specifically

TABLE 10.15 Upper Deck Consumers Segments—Top 10 Percent of Household in Terms of Income

SEGMENT NAME	SEGMENT SIZE	SEGMENT DESCRIPTION
Well-feathered nests	37.3% of Upper Deck	*Households that have at least one high-income earner and children present*
No strings attached	35.1% of Upper Deck	*Households that have at least one high-income earner and no children*
Nanny's in charge	8.3% of Upper Deck	*Households that have two or more earners, none earning high incomes, and children present*
Two careers	9.4% of Upper Deck	*Households that have two or more earners, neither earning high incomes, and no children present*
The good life	10.0% of Upper Deck	*Households that have a high degree of affluence with no person employed or with the head of household not employed*

Source: *The Upper Deck* (Mediamark Research and Intelligence, 2007).

to the five segments of the Upper Deck. For instance, when it comes to leisure activities, members of the *Well-feathered nest segment* are more likely to be out flying a kite than members of the other four Upper Deck consumers, the *No strings attached segment* are more interested in going to live theater performances, the *Nanny's in charge segment* would rather attend a country music performance, the *Two career segment* are more likely to engage in model making, and members of the *Good life segment* are most interested in bird-watching.[89] What we have is different segments of the affluent consumer market interested in different leisure activities. This type of information is of considerable interest to marketers who always want to target their marketing messages to the most suitable segment of consumers.

Middle-Class Consumers

LEARNING OBJECTIVE

10.11 *To Understand the Middle-Class Consumer.*

It is not easy to define the boundaries of what is meant by *middle class*. Although the U.S. Bureau of the Census does not have a definition of middle class, there have nevertheless been many attempts to define it. For instance, "middle market" has been defined as the "middle" 50 percent of household incomes—that is, about 57 million households earning between $25,000 and $85,000.[90] It is interesting to note that some polls suggest that 90 percent or more of Americans consider themselves to be "middle class" or "upper-middle class" or "working class."[91]

For many marketers *middle class* can be thought of as including households that range from lower-middle to middle-middle class in terms of some acceptable variable or combination of variables (e.g., income, education, and/or occupation). This view of middle class does not include the *upper-middle class,* which over the years has increasingly been treated as a segment of affluent consumers.

The dynamic nature of social class in the United States has been working against the middle class. In particular, there is mounting evidence that the middle-class American is slowly disappearing. It appears that middle-class consumers are increasingly moving upstream to the ranks of the upper-middle class, and another smaller segment is losing ground and slipping backward to the ranks of the working class—creating a distribution that looks like an "hourglass."[92]

Although the middle class has been shrinking in the United States, there has been a fairly rapid increase in the number of middle-class consumers in select Asian and Eastern European countries. For example, within the past few years, Tropicana and other fruit juice companies have been successfully positioning their products to the expanding middle-class Indian consumers who are seeking more health-oriented products.[93]

THE EMERGING CHINESE MIDDLE CLASS

No discussion of the middle class would be complete without specific mention of what is currently going on in China. Today, lower-middle-class households in China earn 25,000 to 40,000 yuan ($3,200 to $5,100) a year, while upper-middle-class annual household earnings are 40,000 to 100,000 yuan ($5,100 to $14,000), and the percentage of households with 200,000 yuan or higher annual incomes (more than $28,571) is expected to grow 36 percent annually between now and 2012.[94] And while some observers predict that China will become the biggest consumer marketplace on the planet by 2020, others feel that this could occur by 2012. Many Chinese middle-class consumers feel that "the more products, the more stuff I have, the more happiness I feel," and it has been reported that "Chinese consumers are driven more and more by their desire for social status, which is reflected in their buying behaviors, particularly with respect to products positioned as status symbols."[95]

A number of American companies, like Procter & Gamble, have had great success in China (e.g., P&G introduced a green tea–flavored toothpaste), and many Chinese believe that the longer a brand has been around, "the better and more trustworthy" it is. It is also important to note that Chinese consumers are generally cautious with respect to consumer credit (hence the low incidence of credit card purchases), do not open their wallets easily (typically, over 25 percent of monthly income is saved, not spent), and are extremely price sensitive.[96]

MOVING UP TO MORE "NEAR" LUXURIES

Adding to the challenge of defining *middle class* is the reality that luxury and technological products have been becoming more affordable for more consumers (often because of the introduction of near-luxury models by major luxury-brand firms and/or the downward price trend for many technology products) and, therefore, more middle-class consumers have access to products and brands that were once considered beyond their reach.[97] Indeed, the $220 billion market for luxury goods has doubled in the past 10 years, as "people from Indiana to India . . . pay a premium for the thrill of owning something that makes them feel special."[98] Moreover, recently there has been an increasing interest in midlevel consumers seeking out more status upscale brands. As an outcome, when the first signs of an economic downturn appeared at the beginning of 2008, brands like Burberry, Tiffany, Coach, and Polo Ralph Lauren reported concerns about their profits, but brands like Cartier, which appeal to the recession-proof super-rich, were still reporting strong sales.[99]

The Working Class and Other Nonaffluent Consumers

LEARNING OBJECTIVE

10.12 *To Understand the Working Class and Other Nonaffulent Consumers.*

Although many advertisers would prefer to show their products as part of an affluent lifestyle, working-class or blue-collar people represent a vast group of consumers that marketers cannot ignore. In fact, households earning less than $40,000, control somewhere near 30 percent of the total income in the United States. Therefore, it is also important to consider the **downscale consumers** (frequently defined as having household incomes of $40,000 or less), because they may actually be more stable in terms of their brand loyalty than wealthier consumers, because they cannot afford to make mistakes by switching to unfamiliar brands.

Understanding the importance of speaking to (not *at*) the downscale consumers, companies such as RC Cola, MasterCard, and McDonald's target "average Joes" (and Janes) with ads reflecting the modest lifestyles of some of their customers.[100] For instance, marketers need to be sensitive to the reality that downscale consumers often spend a higher percentage of their available incomes on food than do their middle-class counterparts. Moreover, food is a particularly important purchase area for low-income consumers because it represents an area of "indulgence." For this reason, they periodically trade up the foods they purchase—especially favorite ethnic and natural foods—"where taste and authenticity matter."[101] Still further, a British writer, reflecting on a trend toward super-sized fast-food offerings in the United Kingdom noted that "It isn't the wealthy middle classes . . . that are generally obese—it's the underclass . . . with little budget, knowledge of diet . . . that is suffering."[102]

Recognizing the "Techno-Class"

LEARNING OBJECTIVE

10.13 *To Understand the Nature and Influence of the "Techno-Class."*

The degree of literacy, familiarity, and competency with technology, especially computers and the Internet, appears to be a new basis for a kind of "class standing," or status or prestige. Those who are unfamiliar with or lack computer skills are being referred to as "technologically underclassed."[103] Educators, business leaders, and government officials have warned that the inability to adequately use technology is negatively impacting lifestyles and the quality of life of those who are not computer literate.

Not wanting to see their children left out of the "sweep of computer technology," parents in all social-class groupings are seeking out early computer exposure for their children. Either based on their positive experiences using computers or possibly on fears produced as the result of a lack of personal computer experience, parents sense that an understanding of computers is a necessary tool of competitive achievement and success. At the other end of the life and age spectrum, even 55-year-old professionals, who were initially reluctant to "learn computers," are now seeking personal computer training—they no longer want to be left out, nor do they want to be further embarrassed by having to admit that they "don't know computers."

Consumers throughout the world have come to believe that it is critical to acquire a functional understanding of computers in order to ensure that they do not become obsolete or hinder themselves socially or professionally. In this sense, there is a technological class structure that centers on the amount of computer skills that one possesses. It appears that those without necessary computer skills will increasingly find themselves to be "underclassed" and "disadvantaged."

THE GEEK GETS STATUS

The importance of computers and other informational and communications technologies in everyday life has resulted in somewhat of a reversal of fortune, in that the "geek" is now often viewed by his or her peers as "friendly and fun." The increasingly positive image of geeks has made them and their lifestyles the target of marketers' messages designed to appeal to their great appetite for novel technological products (see Figure 10.14).

Indeed, according to a British National Opinion Poll (NOP) of 7- to 16-year-olds, "computer geeks are now the coolest kids in class."[104] The poll found that the archetypical geek is most typically a 14- to 16-year-old boy who is the family computer expert, and he is willing to teach his parents, siblings, and teachers about computers. Interestingly, in an environment where children naturally take to computers, it is often the parents who find themselves technologically disenfranchised. To remedy this situation, schools and libraries are offering classes to bring parents up to speed in the use of computers.

FIGURE 10.14

Source: © Yamaha Electronics Corporation, USA. Used with permission. All rights reserved.

QUESTION: *In What Ways Have the Prestige and Status of Geeks Been Changing?*

Selected Consumer Behavior Applications of Social Class

LEARNING OBJECTIVE

10.14 *To Understand How Social Class Is Used in Consumer Research Studies.*

Social-class profiles provide a broad picture of the values, attitudes, and behavior that distinguish the members of various social classes. This section focuses on specific consumer research findings about the consumption behaviors of various social classes.

CLOTHING, FASHION, AND SHOPPING

A Greek philosopher once said, "Know, first, who you are; and then adorn yourself accordingly."[105] This bit of wisdom is relevant to clothing marketers today, because most people dress to fit their self-image, which includes their perceptions of their own social-class membership. However, for many consumers, the notion of "keeping up with the Joneses" (i.e., trying to be like one's neighbors) has been replaced by looking to more upscale reference groups that they would like to emulate (most often, people earning substantially more than they do).

Members of specific social classes differ in terms of what they consider fashionable or in good taste. For instance, lower-middle-class consumers have a strong preference for T-shirts, caps, and other clothing that offer an *external point of identification,* such as the name of an admired person or group (e.g., Dale Earnhardt, Jr.), a respected company or brand name (Honda), or a valued trademark (FUBU). These consumers are prime targets for licensed goods (with well-known logos). In contrast, upper-class consumers are likely to buy clothing that is free from such supporting associations. Upper-class consumers also seek clothing with a more subtle look, such as the kind of sportswear found in an L.L.Bean, Lands' End, or Talbots catalog, rather than designer jeans.

Social class is also an important variable in determining where a consumer shops. People tend to avoid stores that have the image of appealing to a social class very different from their own. In the past, some mass merchandisers who tried to appeal to a higher class of consumers found themselves alienating their traditional customers. This implies that retailers should pay attention to the social class of their customer base to ensure that they send the appropriate message through advertising. For instance, Gap rolled out the Old Navy clothing stores in an effort to attract working-class families who usually purchased their casual and active wear clothing from general merchandise retailers such as Kmart, Wal-Mart, or Target. For Gap, trading down to the lower-income consumer with Old Navy has resulted in bigger sales, more leverage with suppliers, and increased traffic volume. However, in creating a lower-price alternative to itself, Gap has also tended to cannibalize itself—shifting loyal Gap customers to the Old Navy outlets.

THE PURSUIT OF LEISURE

Social-class membership is also closely related to the choice of recreational and leisure-time activities. For instance, upper-class consumers are likely to attend the theater and concerts, to play bridge, and to attend college football games. They may vacation by joining a travel club that allows them access to ultra-deluxe resorts for a specific number of days per year. For example, Exclusive Resort's 15-day package requires a $195,000 initial fee plus annual dues of up to $25,000.[106] Lower-class consumers tend to be avid television watchers and fishing enthusiasts, and they enjoy drive-in movies and baseball games. Furthermore, the lower-class consumer spends more time on commercial types of activities (bowling, playing pool or billiards, or visiting taverns) and craft activities (model building, painting, and woodworking projects) rather than cerebral activities (reading, visiting museums). In any case, among both middle-class and working-class consumers, there appears to be a trend toward more spending on "experiences" that bring the family together (family vacations or activities) and less spending on "things."[107]

SAVING, SPENDING, AND CREDIT

Saving, spending, and credit card usage all seem to be related to social-class standing. Upper-class consumers are more future oriented and confident of their financial acumen; they are more willing to invest in insurance, stocks, and real estate. In comparison, lower-class consumers are generally more concerned with immediate gratification; when they do save, they are

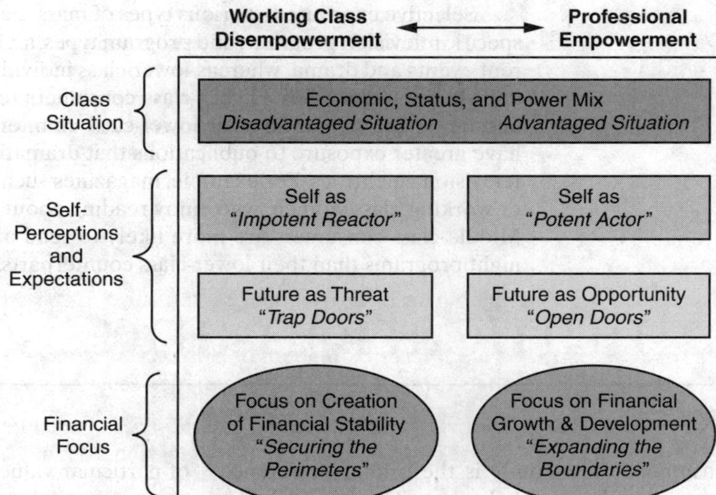

FIGURE 10.15
Class Situations, Self-Perceptions, and Financial Orientations
Source: Paul C. Henry, "Social Class, Market Situation, and Consumers' Metaphors of (Dis)Empowerment" *Journal of Consumer Research*, 31 (March 2005): 769.

primarily interested in safety and security. Therefore, it is not surprising that when it comes to bank credit card usage, members of the lower social classes tend to use their bank credit cards for installment purchases, whereas members of the upper social classes pay their credit card bills in full each month. In other words, lower-class purchasers tend to use their credit cards to "buy now and pay later" for things they might not otherwise be able to afford, whereas upper-class purchasers use their credit cards as a convenient substitute for cash.

A recent study examined the role of empowerment and disempowerment as a central phenomenon of social class among working-class and young professionals (25–30 years of age) in Sydney, Australia. The study focused on money management, and financial planning practices and priorities. As shown in Figure 10.15, young professionals perceived themselves to be empowered in the sense that they could achieve whatever they set their minds to, and they were disciplined and results oriented. Working-class participants, in contrast, perceived themselves as being average, were more likely to describe a range of personal weaknesses (e.g., "I can never finish things") and, unlike the young professionals, had a strong uncertainty about the future.[108]

SOCIAL CLASS AND COMMUNICATION

Social-class groupings differ in terms of their media habits and in how they transmit and receive communications. Knowledge of these differences is invaluable to marketers who segment their markets on the basis of social class.

When it comes to describing their world, lower-class consumers tend to portray it in rather personal and concrete terms, whereas middle-class consumers are able to describe their experiences from a number of different perspectives. A simple example illustrates that members of different social classes tend to see the world differently. The following responses to a question asking where the respondent usually purchases gasoline were received:

Upper-middle-class answer: At Exxon or Sunoco.

Lower-middle-class answer: At the station on Seventh Street and Post Avenue.

Lower-class answer: At Charlie's.

Such variations in response indicate that middle-class consumers have a broader or more general view of the world, while lower-class consumers tend to have a narrow or personal view—seeing the world through their own immediate experiences.

Regional differences in terminology, choice of words and phrases, and patterns of usage also tend to increase as we move down the social-class ladder. Therefore, in creating messages targeted to the lower classes, marketers try to word advertisements to reflect particular regional preferences that exist (e.g., the children's game hopscotch is called *potsy* in Manhattan and *blue sky* in Chicago).

Selective exposure to various types of mass media differs by social class. In the selection of specific television programs and program types, higher-social-class members tend to prefer current events and drama, whereas lower-class individuals tend to prefer soap operas, quiz shows, and situation comedies. Higher-class consumers tend to have greater exposure to magazines and newspapers than do their lower-class counterparts. Lower-class consumers are likely to have greater exposure to publications that dramatize romance and the lifestyles of movie and television celebrities. For example, magazines such as *True Story* appeal heavily to blue-collar or working-class women, who enjoy reading about the problems, fame, and fortunes of others. Middle-class consumers are more likely to read a newspaper and to prefer movies and late-night programs than their lower-class counterparts.[109]

SUMMARY

For many consumers, their family is the primary reference group for many attitudes and behaviors. The family is the prime target market for most products and product categories. As the most basic membership group, families are defined as two or more persons related by blood, marriage, or adoption who reside together. There are three types of families: married couples, nuclear families, and extended families. Socialization is a core function of the family. Other functions of the family are the provision of economic and emotional support and the pursuit of a suitable lifestyle for its members.

The majority of consumer studies classify family consumption decisions as husband-dominated, wife-dominated, joint, or autonomic decisions. The extent and nature of husband–wife influence in family decisions depend, in part, on the specific product or service and selected cultural influences.

Classification of families by stage in the family life cycle (FLC) provides valuable insights into family consumption-related behavior. The traditional FLC begins with bachelorhood, moves on to marriage, then to an expanding family, to a contracting family, and to an end with the death of a spouse. Dynamic sociodemographic changes in society have resulted in many nontraditional stages that a family or nonfamily household might pass through (such as childless couples, couples marrying later in life, single parents, unmarried couples, or single-person households). These nontraditional stages are becoming increasingly important to marketers in terms of specific market niches.

Social stratification, the division of members of a society into a hierarchy of distinct social classes, exists in all societies and cultures. Social class usually is defined by the amount of status that members of a specific class possess in relation to members of other classes. Social-class membership often serves as a frame of reference (a reference group) for the development of consumer attitudes and behavior.

The measurement of social class is concerned with classifying individuals into social-class groupings. These groupings are of particular value to marketers, who use social classification as an effective means of identifying and segmenting target markets. There are two basic methods for measuring social class: subjective measurement and objective measurement. Subjective measures rely on an individual's self-perception, and objective measures use specific socioeconomic measures, either alone (as a single-variable index) or in combination with others (as a composite-variable index). Composite-variable indexes, such as the Index of Status Characteristics and the Socioeconomic Status Score, combine a number of socioeconomic factors to form one overall measure of social-class standing.

Class structures range from two-class to nine-class systems. A frequently used classification system consists of six classes: upper-upper, lower-upper, upper-middle, lower-middle, upper-lower, and lower-lower classes. Profiles of these classes indicate that the socioeconomic differences among classes are reflected in differences in attitudes, in leisure activities, and in consumption habits. This is why segmentation by social class is of special interest to marketers.

In recent years, some marketers have turned to geodemographic clustering as an alternative to a strict social-class typology. Geodemographic clustering is a technique that combines geographic and socioeconomic factors to locate concentrations of consumers with particular characteristics. Particular attention currently is being directed to affluent consumers, who represent the fastest-growing segment in our population; however, some marketers are finding it extremely profitable to cater to the needs of nonaffluent consumers.

Research has revealed social-class differences in clothing habits, home decoration, and leisure activities, as well as saving, spending, and credit habits. Thus, astute marketers tailor specific product and promotional strategies to each social-class target segment.

DISCUSSION QUESTIONS

1. How does the family influence the consumer socialization of children? What role does television advertising play in consumer socialization?
2. As a marketing consultant, you were retained by the Walt Disney Company to design a study investigating how families make vacation decisions. Whom, within the family, would you interview? What kind of questions would you ask? How would you assess the relative power of each family member in making vacation-related decisions?
3. Which of the five stages of the traditional family life cycle constitute the most lucrative segment(s) for the following products and services: (a) TV cable subscriptions, (b) a Club Med vacation, (c) Domino's pizza, (d) iPods, (e) mutual funds, and (f) motor homes? Explain your answers.
4. Marketing researchers generally use the objective method to measure social class rather than the subjective method. Why is the objective method preferred by researchers?
5. Under what circumstances would you expect income to be a better predictor of consumer behavior than a composite measure of social class (e.g., based on income, education, and occupation)? When would you expect the composite social-class measure to be superior?
6. Which status-related variable—occupation, education, or income—is the most appropriate segmentation base for: (a) expensive vacations, (b) opera subscriptions, (c) *People* magazine subscriptions, (d) fat-free foods, (e) personal computers, (f) cellular telephones, and (g) health clubs?
7. Consider the Rolex watch, which has a retail price range starting at about $4,500 for a stainless-steel model to thousands of dollars for a solid-gold model. How might the Rolex company use geodemographic clustering in its marketing efforts?
8. You are the owner of two furniture stores, one catering to upper-middle-class consumers and the other to lower-class consumers. How do social-class differences influence each store's (a) product lines and styles, (b) advertising media selection, (c) the copy and communications style used in the ads, and (d) payment policies?

EXERCISES

1. In this chapter, we have considered how parents and siblings play a role in the consumer socialization of their children and young brothers and sisters, and how adults continue to be socialized throughout their lives. However, we have not considered how children (especially teens and young adults) influence the socialization of their parents. Make a list of ten ways by which you have contributed or influenced the ongoing socialization of your parents.
2. Identify one traditional family and one nontraditional family (or household) featured in a TV sitcom or series. (The two family households can be featured in the same or in different TV shows.) Classify the traditional group into one stage of the traditional FLC. Classify the nontraditional group into one of the categories described in Table 10.6. Select two characters of the same gender and approximate age, one from each group, and compare their consumption behavior (such as clothes, furniture, or stated or implied attitudes toward spending money).
3. Copy the list of occupations in Figure 10.9 and ask students majoring in areas other than marketing (both business and nonbusiness) to rank the relative prestige of these occupations. Are any differences in the rankings related to the students' majors? Explain.
4. Select two households featured in two different TV series or sitcoms. Classify each household into one of the social classes discussed in the text and analyze its lifestyle and consumption behavior.

KEY TERMS

- affluent market *348*
- autonomic decisions *329*
- class consciousness *340*
- composite-variable indexes *340*
- consumer socialization *323*
- downscale consumers *356*
- downward mobility *346*
- extended family *320*
- family *318*
- family life cycle (FLC) *332*
- geodemographic clusters *347*
- household *318*
- husband-dominated decisions *329*
- Index of Status Characteristics *344*
- joint (equal or syncratic) decisions *329*
- nonfamily households *335*
- nontraditional families *336*
- nuclear family *320*
- objective measures *340*
- PRIZM NE *347*
- single-parent family *320*
- single-variable index *340*
- social class *338*
- social status *338*
- socialization agent *325*
- socialization of family members *323*
- Socioeconomic Status Score *344*
- subjective measures *340*
- traditional family life cycle *332*
- upward mobility *346*
- wife-dominated decisions *329*

Case: Keeping Up with the Joneses

Finland, like the United States, is a wealthy country. Its economy is open—providing consumers a wide variety of choices when it comes to consumer products. What sets Finland apart, though, is that the country keeps very detailed records about its citizens—including everything from the ages, sex, and incomes of people living in the same household, the amount they spend annually on commuting, and vehicle purchases.

Consider this: Researchers have determined that when a Finnish household buys a new car, the odds that one of that household's nearest 10 neighbors will purchase the same brand of vehicle during the next week and a half increases by 86 percent!

QUESTION

1. What factors contained in Chapter 10 might be used to explain this phenomenon?

Source: David Leonhardt, "See the New Car in the Jones's Driveway? You May Soon Be Driving One Just Like It," *New York Times,* June 13, 2005, C5.

11

Influence of Culture on Consumer Behavior

THE STUDY of culture is a challenging undertaking because its primary focus is on the broadest component of social behavior—*an entire society*, or in comparing and contrasting the cultural differences and similarities of more than one culture. Also, in contrast to the psychologist, who is principally concerned with the study of individual behavior, or the sociologist, who is concerned with the study of groups, the anthropologist is primarily interested in identifying the very fabric of society itself. In marketing and consumer behavior, culture is frequently reflected in products' features and designs, as well as the layout, visuals and contents of promotional messages (i.e., in print, TV, and Internet advertising). Figure 11.1 presents a magazine ad for Bush's Baked Beans that suggests that they could not make their beans any better, so they made it easier to prepare (by placing them in a microwavable cup). In terms of cultural values, such an ad is likely to appeal to U.S. consumers who particularly value convenience in food preparation. On the other hand, certain other cultures might require some appeal (e.g., "slow old fashion cooking").

This chapter explores the basic concepts of culture, with particular emphasis on the role that culture plays in influencing consumer behavior. We will first consider the specific dimensions of culture that make it a powerful force in regulating human behavior. After reviewing several measurement approaches that researchers use to understand the impact of culture on consumption behavior, we will show how a variety of core American cultural values influence consumer behavior.

Still further, the chapter is concerned with the general aspects of culture; the following two chapters focus on subculture and on global and/or cross-culture and show how marketers can use such knowledge to shape and modify their marketing strategies in order to effectively reach and communicate with target consumers.

FIGURE 11.1

Source: © Bush Brothers & Company.

QUESTION: *To Which Cultural Value or Values Is This Product's Advertising Appealing?*

Learning Objectives

11.1 *To Understand What Culture Is and How It Impacts Consumer Behaviors.*

11.2 *To Understand How Culture Acts as an "Invisible Hand" That Guides Consumption-Related Attitudes, Values, and Behavior.*

11.3 *To Understand How Culture Sets Standards for What Satisfies Consumers' Needs.*

11.4 *To Understand How Culture Is Learned and Expressed in Language, Symbols, and Rituals.*

11.5 *To Understand How Consumers Are Always Adapting to Culture-Related Experiences.*

11.6 *To Understand How the Impact of Culture on Consumer Behavior Is Measured.*

11.7 *To Understand How Core Cultural Values Impact American Consumers.*

11.8 *To Understand How the American Culture Became a "Shopping Culture."*

What Is Culture?

Learning Objective

11.1 *To Understand What Culture Is and How It Impacts Consumer Behavior.*

Given the broad and pervasive nature of culture, its study generally requires a detailed examination of the character of the total society, including such factors as language, knowledge, laws, religions, food customs, music, art, technology, work patterns, products, and other artifacts that give a society its distinctive flavor. In a sense, culture is a society's personality. For this reason, it is not easy to define its boundaries.

Because our objective is to understand the influence of culture on consumer behavior, we define **culture** as the *sum total of learned beliefs, values, and customs that serve to direct the consumer behavior of members of a particular society.*

The *belief* and *value* components of our definition refer to the accumulated feelings and priorities that individuals have about "things" and possessions. More precisely, *beliefs* consist of the very large number of mental or verbal statements (i.e., "I believe . . .") that reflect a person's particular knowledge and assessment of something (another person, a store, a product, a brand). *Values* also are beliefs. Values differ from other beliefs, however, because they meet the following criteria: (1) They are relatively few in number; (2) they serve as a guide for culturally appropriate behavior; (3) they are enduring or difficult to change; (4) they are not tied to specific objects or situations; and (5) they are widely accepted by the members of a society.

Therefore, in a broad sense, both values and beliefs are mental images that affect a wide range of specific attitudes that, in turn, influence the way a person is likely to respond in a specific situation. For example, the criteria a person uses to evaluate alternative brands in a product category (such as a Volvo versus an Audi automobile), or his or her eventual preference for one of these brands over the other, are influenced by both a person's general values (perceptions as to what constitutes quality and the meaning of country of origin) and specific beliefs (particular perceptions about the quality of Swedish-made versus German-made automobiles).

In contrast to beliefs and values, customs are *overt modes of behavior that constitute culturally approved or acceptable ways of behaving in specific situations.* Customs consist of everyday or routine behavior. For example, a consumer's routine behavior, such as adding a diet sweetener to coffee, putting ketchup on scrambled eggs, putting mustard on frankfurters, and having a pasta dish *before* rather than *with* the main course of a meal, are customs. Thus, whereas beliefs and values are guides for behavior, customs are *usual and acceptable ways of behaving.*

By our definition, it is easy to see how an understanding of various cultures can help marketers predict consumer acceptance of their products.

The World Is Flat is the title of a particularly important nonfiction book that concentrates on the concept of the increasing globalization taking place at the beginning of the twenty-first century.[1] An important theme of the book is that at present, with satellite TV and the Internet, it is not difficult for one culture to embrace or adopt what it wishes from other cultures. With this premise as a backdrop, a recent research study commented:[2]

> Culture is becoming increasingly deterritorialized and penetrated by elements from other cultures. This is resulting in cultural contamination, cultural pluralism and hybridization. It has become more difficult to study culture as it is becoming diffused. At the same time, it is becoming more important to study it because of its pervasive influence on consumer behavior.

The Invisible Hand of Culture

Learning Objective

11.2 *To Understand How Culture Acts as an "Invisible Hand" That Guides Consumption-Related Attitudes, Values, and Behavior.*

The impact of culture is so natural and automatic that its influence on behavior is usually taken for granted. For instance, when consumer researchers ask people why they do certain things, they frequently answer, "Because it's the right thing to do." This seemingly superficial response partially reflects the ingrained influence of culture on our behavior. Often it is only when we are exposed to people with different cultural values or customs (as when visiting a different region or a different country) that we become better aware as to how culture has molded our own behavior. Thus, a true appreciation of the influence that culture has on our daily life requires some knowledge of at least one other society with different cultural characteristics. For example, to understand that brushing our teeth twice a day with flavored toothpaste is a cultural phenomenon requires some awareness that members of another society either do not brush their teeth at all or do so in a distinctly different manner than our own society.

Perhaps the following statement expresses it best:

> Consumers both view themselves in the context of their culture and react to their environment based upon the cultural framework that they bring to that experience. Each individual perceives the world through his own cultural lens.[3]

Culture can exist and sometimes reveal itself at different perceived or subjective levels.[4] For those of us interested in consumer behavior, we would be most concerned with three "levels" of subjective culture that are especially relevant to the exploration of consumer behavior and formation of marketing strategy. The first level can be thought of as the *supranational level;* it reflects the underlying dimensions of culture that impact multiple cultures or different societies (i.e., cross-national or cross-cultural boundaries). For instance, it might reflect regional character (e.g., people living in several nations in a particular region of South America), or racial and religious similarities or differences, or shared or different languages (mostly the concern of Chapter 13). The second level is concerned with *national level* factors, such as shared core values, customs, personalities, and predispositional factors that tend to capture the essence of the "national character" of the citizens of a particular country (mostly the content of this chapter). Finally, *group level* factors are concerned with various subdivisions of a country or society. They might include subcultures' difference, and membership and reference group differences (mostly the concern of Chapter 12). Table 11.1 summarizes this discussion, whereas Figure 11.2 presents a model depicting the role that subjective culture (on the left side of the model) plays in determining our beliefs, practices, and values, which in turn impact our social norms, attitudes, behavioral intentions, and, ultimately, our behavior (see the discussion of such attitude models in Chapter 8).

With regard to the supranational level of culture, which crosses national boundaries, researchers have recently developed a lifestyle matrix for global youth aged 14 to 24. The characteristics of each of the four segments of the matrix, as represented in Figure 11.3 are as follows:[5]

> The in-crowd: It's all about privilege and reinforcement. Generally seek approval when communicating, and prefer classic brands like Nike and Abercrombie & Fitch to uphold tradition.
>
> Pop mavericks: Word of mouth spreads rapidly, and passion, individuality, and instant gratification are important. They prefer brands that they can personalize—brands like Diesel and Adidas.

TABLE 11.1 Three Levels of Subjective Culture—Supranational, National, and Groups

LEVELS	DEFINITION/DIMENSIONS
Level 1: Supranational	Subjective cultural differences that cross national boundaries or can be seen to be present in more than one country Composed of the following consumer behavior relevant factors: regional makeup, ethnic-racial composition of population, language and symbolisms meaning
Level 2: National	Shared cultural characters (national character or identity) that uniquely or specifically define the citizens of particular countries
Level 3: Group	Cultural divisions or grouping (especially subcultures) that contain various collections of individuals (e.g., families, work groups, shopping groups, friendship groups)

Source: Inspired and adapted from: Elena Karahanna, J. Roberto Evaristo, and Mark Strite, "Levels of Culture and Individual Behavior: An Integrative Perspective," *Journal of Global Information Management*, 13 (April–June 2005): 5.

FIGURE 11.2
A Theoretical Model of Culture's Influence on Behavior

Source: Elena Karahanna, J. Roberto Evaristo, and Mark Strite, "Levels of Culture and Individual Behavior: An Integrative Perspective," *Journal of Global Information Management*, 13 (April–June 2005): 8.

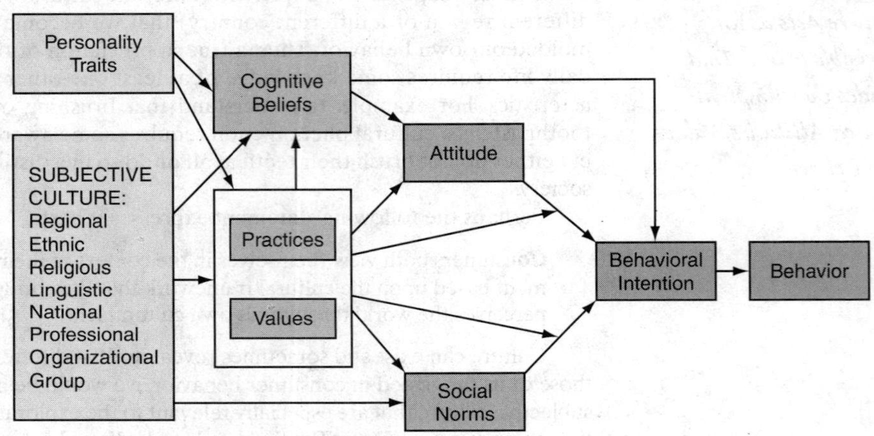

Networked intelligentsia: They are the hub of online social networks, and it's all about revolution, creativity, and deconstruction. They prefer cult brands, like Vespa (in America) and Vans, which add to their sense of obscurity.

Thrill renegades: It's all about infamy, adrenaline, and anarchy (law and order is nonexistent). They relate to the in-crowd by co-opting their brands, such as Tanqueray and Timberland, and then taking them to another level.

Culture Satisfies Needs

LEARNING OBJECTIVE

11.3 *To Understand How Culture Sets Standards for What Satisfies Consumers' Needs.*

Culture exists to satisfy the needs of the people within a society. It offers order, direction, and guidance in all phases of human problem solving by providing "tried-and-true" methods of satisfying physiological, personal, and social needs. For example, culture provides standards and "rules" about when to eat ("not between meals"); where to eat ("in a busy restaurant, because the food is likely to be good"); what is appropriate to eat for breakfast (pancakes), lunch (a sandwich), dinner ("something hot and good and healthy"), and snacks ("something with quick energy, but not too many calories"); and what to serve to guests at a dinner party ("a formal sit-down meal"), at a picnic (barbecued "franks and hamburgers"), or at a wedding (champagne). Culture is also associated with what a society's members consider to be a necessity and what they view as a luxury. For instance, 55 percent of American adults consider a microwave to be a necessity, and 36 percent consider a remote control for a TV, DVD, and other forms of consumer electronics to be a necessity.[6]

FIGURE 11.3
Lifestyle Matrix for Global Youth, Aged 14 to 24

Source: Tim Stock and Marie Lena Tupot, "Common Denominators: What Unites Global Youth?" *Young Consumers* (Quarter 1, 2006): 37.

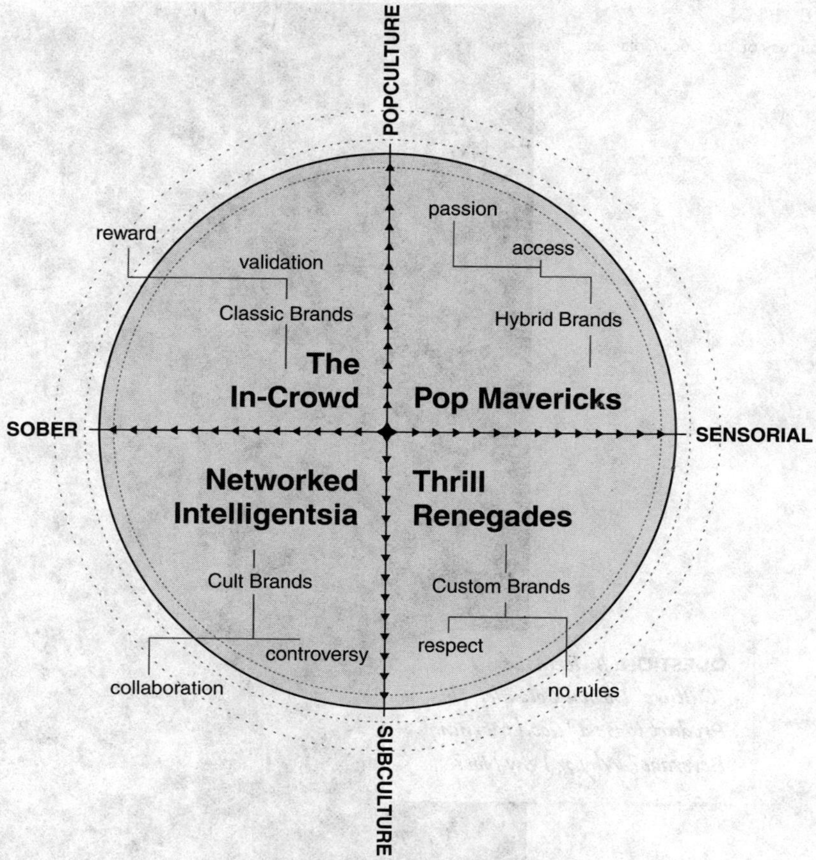

Similarly, culture also provides insights as to suitable dress for specific occasions (such as what to wear around the house, what to wear to school, to work, to church, at a fast-food restaurant, or to a movie theater). Dress codes have shifted dramatically; people are dressing more casually most of the time. Today, only a few big-city restaurants and clubs have business dress requirements. With the relaxed dress code in the corporate work environment, fewer men are wearing dress shirts, ties, and business suits, and fewer women are wearing dresses, suits, and panty hose. In their place, casual slacks, sports shirts and blouses, and jeans have been increasing in sales.

Soft-drink companies would prefer that consumers received their morning "jolt" of caffeine from one of their products rather than from coffee. Because most Americans do not consider soda a suitable breakfast beverage, the real challenge for soft-drink companies is to overcome culture, not only competition (see Figure 11.4). Indeed, coffee has been challenged on all fronts by juices, milk, teas (hot and iced), a host of different types of soft drinks, and now even caffeinated waters. Not resting on their "cultural advantage" as a breakfast drink and the namesake of the "coffee break," coffee marketers have been fighting back by targeting gourmet and specialty coffees (e.g., espresso, cappuccino, and café mocha) to young adults (those 18 to 24 years of age). These efforts have been paying off as young adults (an important segment of the soft-drink market) have been responding positively to gourmet coffees.

Cultural beliefs, values, and customs continue to be followed as long as they yield satisfaction. When a specific standard no longer satisfies the members of a society, however, it is modified or replaced, so that the resulting standard is more in line with current needs and desires. For instance, it was once considered a sign of a fine hotel that it provided down or goose feather pillows in rooms. Today, with so many guests allergic to such materials, synthetic polyfill pillows are becoming more the rule. Thus, culture gradually but continually evolves to meet the needs of society.

FIGURE 11.4
Source: Courtesy of The Coca-Cola Company.

QUESTION: *In Terms of "Culture" Do You Consider This Product to Be a "Good Morning" Beverage? Why or Why Not?*

Culture Is Learned

LEARNING OBJECTIVE

11.4 *To Understand How Culture Is Learned and Expressed in Language, Symbols, and Rituals.*

Unlike innate biological characteristics (e.g., sex, skin, hair color, or intelligence), culture is learned. At an early age, we begin to acquire from our social environment a set of beliefs, values, and customs that make up our culture. For children, the learning of these acceptable cultural values and customs is reinforced by the process of playing with their toys. As children play, they act out and rehearse important cultural lessons and situations. This cultural learning prepares them for later real-life circumstances.

HOW CULTURE IS LEARNED

Anthropologists have identified three distinct forms of cultural learning: *formal learning,* in which adults and older siblings teach a young family member "how to behave"; *informal learning,* in which a child learns primarily by imitating the behavior of selected others, such as family, friends, or TV heroes; and *technical learning*, in which teachers instruct the child in an educational environment about what should be done, how it should be done, and why it should be done. Our ethical values tend to be formed in childhood from the examples provided by parents, teachers, and other significant adults, and we learn the importance of kindness, honesty, and responsibility from family.[7]

MARKETING INFLUENCES CULTURAL LEARNING

Although a firm's advertising and marketing communications can influence all three types of cultural learning, it is likely that many product marketing messages enhance informal cultural learning by providing the audience with a model of behavior to imitate. This is especially true for visible or conspicuous products that are evaluated in public settings (such as designer clothing, cell phones, or status golf clubs), where peer influence is likely to play an important role. Additionally, "not only are cultural values cited in advertising copy, they also are often coded in the visual imagery, colors, movements, music, and other nonverbal elements of an advertisement."[8]

The repetition of marketing messages creates and reinforces cultural beliefs and values. For example, many advertisers continually stress the same selected benefits of their products or services. Ads for wireless phone service often stress the clarity of their connection, or the nationwide coverage of their service, or the free long-distance calling, as well as the flexibility of their pricing plans. It is difficult to say whether wireless phone subscribers *inherently* desire these benefits from their wireless service providers or whether, after several years of cumulative exposure to advertising appeals stressing these benefits, they have been taught by marketers to desire them. In a sense, although specific product advertising may reinforce the benefits that consumers want from the product (as determined by consumer behavior research); such advertising also "teaches" future generations of consumers to expect the same benefits from the product category.

We can think of cultural meaning flowing from social-cultural values and practices to consumer goods and from there to the individual consumer by means of various forms of social communications or media (e.g,, TV advertising or online social networks). Imagine the ever-popular baseball cap and how it can furnish cultural meaning and identity for wearers. Baseball caps can function as *trophies* (as proof of participation in sports or travel) or as self-proclaimed labels of belonging to a cultural category ("Harley-Davidson Owner"). Baseball caps can also be used as a means of *self-expression,* which may provide wearers with the additional benefit of serving as a "topic" initiating social dialogue with others. Still further, although we might expect that a San Diego Padres baseball cap would be worn by a person who has been to San Diego (or has received it as a gift from someone else who has visited San Diego), this is not necessarily so. In such a world of "virtual identities," consumers can now just buy a San Diego Padres baseball cap at a local retailer and create the impression that they have been there.

Many marketers and advertisers share the view that advertising mirrors the values and needs of society, and therefore the claims and/or appeals contained in ads reflect the behavior or aspirations of potential customers. However, a study conducted in New Zealand, using fashion-related advertisements from major United Kingdom magazines and examining the period from 1950 to 2000, came to a somewhat different conclusion. After analyzing more than 7,500 half-page and larger ads, the research concluded that many of the changes in advertising styles or appeals that occur over time may primarily be the result of "an internally (industry) driven 'fashion' and/or 'investment' cycle," rather than the commonly held notion that "advertising is society driven."[9]

ENCULTURATION AND ACCULTURATION

When discussing the acquisition of culture, anthropologists often distinguish between the learning of one's own, or native, culture and the learning of some "new" (other) culture. The learning of one's own culture is known as **enculturation**. The learning of a new or foreign culture is known as **acculturation**. In Chapter 13, we will see that acculturation is an important concept for marketers who plan to sell their products in foreign or multinational markets. In such cases, marketers must study the specific culture(s) of their potential target markets to determine whether their products will be acceptable to its members and, if so, how they can best communicate the characteristics of their products to persuade the target market to buy.

It is also important to point out that a consumer can be a "foreigner" in his or her own country. For example, using ethnographic fieldwork, a recent study traced a group of provincial women in Thailand as they enrolled in a university in Bangkok, that nation's capital city. As their first semester began, they quickly formed a provincial group and generally kept to themselves, rather than mixing with Bangkokian students and the Bangkok social scene. As the study reports, "Ironically, the longer they live in Bangkok, the more they seem to resist becoming Bangkokians and want to reclaim their provincial selves."[10]

LANGUAGE AND SYMBOLS

To acquire a common culture, the members of a society must be able to communicate with each other through a common language. Without a common language, shared meaning could not exist and true communication would not take place.

To communicate effectively with their audiences, marketers must use appropriate **symbols** to convey desired product images or characteristics. These symbols can be verbal or nonverbal. Verbal symbols may include a television announcement or an advertisement in a magazine. Nonverbal communication includes the use of such symbols as figures, colors, shapes, and even textures to provide additional meaning to print or broadcast advertisements, to trademarks, and to packaging or product designs (see Figure 11.5).

Basically, the symbolic nature of human language sets it apart from all other animal communication. A symbol is anything that stands for something else. Any word is a symbol. The word *house* calls forth a specific image related to an individual's own knowledge and experience. The word *hurricane* calls forth the notion of waves and water and also has the power to

FIGURE 11.5
Source: Courtesy of General Electric.

QUESTION: *How Does a Symbol Convey the Product's Advertised Benefits?*

stir us emotionally, arousing feelings of danger and the need for protection and safety. Similarly, the word *Cadillac* has symbolic meaning: To some it suggests a fine luxury automobile; to others it implies wealth and status (e.g., the following phrase may be used to indicate that a refrigerator is the best in its product category. "This is the Cadillac of refrigerators!").

Because the human mind can process symbols, it is possible, for example, for a person to "experience" cognitively a visualization for a product, like the advertisement for a skin moisturizing gel, which contrasts two scenes—one of a parched desert without the gel and one of a rich green landscape with the gel. Such a comparison presents the idea that a skin-moisturizing gel will transform a person's dry skin to a comfortable moist state. The capacity to learn symbolically is primarily a human phenomenon; most other animals learn by direct experience. Clearly, the ability of humans to understand symbolically how a product, service, or idea can satisfy their needs makes it easier for marketers to sell the features and benefits of their offerings. Through a shared language and culture, individuals already know what the image means; thus, an association can be made without actively thinking about it.

A symbol may have several, even contradictory, meanings, so the advertiser must ascertain exactly what the symbol is communicating to its intended audience. For example, the advertiser who uses a trademark depicting an old craftsman to symbolize careful workmanship may instead be communicating an image of outmoded methods and lack of style. The marketer who uses slang in an advertisement to attract a teenage audience must do so with great care; slang that is misused or outdated will symbolically date the marketer's firm and product.

Price and channels of distribution also are significant symbols of the marketer and the marketer's product. For example, price often implies quality to potential buyers. For certain products (such as clothing), the type of store in which the product is sold also is an important symbol of quality. In fact, all the elements of the marketing mix—the product, its promotion, price, and the stores at which it is available—are symbols that communicate ranges of quality to potential buyers.

Brands are symbols of the popular culture as well as expressions of management or ad agency strategy. For example, advertisements of the 1950s suggested a fantasy involving time-saving appliances, stylish automobiles, and fewer cavities. In contrast, ads of the 1960s were more rebellious counterculture messages. Additionally, consumers may not always agree with the meaning originally conceived by the product managers or ad agencies. For example, while some people might consider Spam as something good to take on a camping trip, others might view it as "the antithesis of *nouvelle cuisine*."

RITUALS

In addition to language and symbols, culture includes various ritualized experiences and behaviors that are increasingly receiving the attention of consumer researchers. A **ritual** is a type of symbolic activity consisting of a series of steps (multiple behaviors) occurring in a fixed sequence and repeated over time.[11]

In practice, rituals extend over the human life cycle from birth to death, including a host of intermediate events (such as confirmation, graduations, and marriage). These rituals can be very public, elaborate, religious, or civil ceremonies, or they can be as mundane as an individual's grooming behavior or flossing. Typically, ritualized behavior is formal and often is scripted behavior (as a religious service requiring a prayer book or the code of proper conduct in a court of law). It is also likely to occur repeatedly over time (such as singing the national anthem before a hockey game).

Most important from the standpoint of marketers is the fact that rituals tend to be replete with ritual artifacts (products) that are associated with or somehow enhance the performance of the ritual. For instance, turkey, stuffing, and other various food items are linked to the ritual of Thanksgiving Day, New Year's Day, or other holiday celebrations; other rituals (such as a graduation, a wedding or wedding anniversary, a Tuesday night card game, or a Saturday morning visit to the hair salon) have their own specific artifacts associated with them. For special occasions, such as wedding anniversaries, some types of artifacts are perceived as more appropriate gifts than others. Table 11.2 lists the artifacts that are culturally appropriate for various special occasions.

In addition to a ritual, which is the way that something is traditionally done, there is also *ritualistic behavior,* which can be defined as any behavior that is made into a ritual. For

TABLE 11.2 Selected Rituals and Associated Artifacts

SELECTED RITUALS	TYPICAL ARTIFACTS
Wedding	White gown (something old, something new, something borrowed, something blue)
Birth of child	U.S. savings bond, silver baby spoon
Birthday	Card, present, cake with candles
50th wedding anniversary	Catered party, card and gift, display of photos of the couple's life together
Graduation	Pen, U.S. savings bond, card, wristwatch
Valentine's Day	Candy, card, flowers
New Year's Eve	Champagne, party, fancy dress
Thanksgiving	Prepare a turkey meal for family and friends
Going to the gym	Towel, exercise clothes, water, iPod
Sunday football	Beer, potato chips, pretzels
Super Bowl party	Same as Sunday football (just more)
Starting a new job	Get a haircut, buy some new clothing
Getting a job promotion	Taken out to lunch by coworkers, receive token gift
Retirement	Company party, watch, plaque
Death	Send a card, give to charity in the name of the deceased

example, a golfer may take a few practice swings before moving up to the golf ball, setting his feet and then swinging to actually hit the ball. Table 11.3 describes the ongoing ritualistic behavior of a woman performing her daily facial beauty care.

CULTURAL CUSTOMS AND BELIEFS ARE SHARED

To be considered a cultural characteristic, a particular belief, value, or practice must be shared by a significant portion of the society. Thus, culture frequently is viewed as group *customs* that link together the members of a society. Of course, common language is the critical cultural component that makes it possible for people to share values, experiences, and customs.

Various social institutions within a society transmit the elements of culture and make the sharing of culture a reality. Chief among such institutions is the *family,* which serves as the primary agent for enculturation—the passing along of basic cultural beliefs, values, and customs to society's newest members. A vital part of the enculturation role of the family is the *consumer socialization* of the young (see Chapter 10). This includes teaching such basic consumer-related values and skills as the meaning of money; the relationship between price and quality; the

TABLE 11.3 Facial Beauty Ritual of a Young TV Advertising Sales Representative

1. I pull my hair back with a headband.
2. I take all my makeup off with L'Oréal eye makeup remover.
3. Next, I use a Q-tip with some moisturizer around my eyes to make sure all eye makeup is removed.
4. I wash my face with Noxzema facial wash.
5. I apply Clinique Dramatically Different Lotion to my face, neck, and throat.
6. If I have a blemish, I apply Clearasil Treatment to the area to dry it out.
7. Twice weekly (or as necessary) I use Aapri Facial Scrub to remove dry and dead skin.
8. Once a week I apply Clinique Clarifying Lotion 2 with a cotton ball to my face and throat to remove deep-down dirt and oils.
9. Once every three months I get a professional salon facial to deep-clean my pores.

establishment of product tastes, preferences, and habits; and appropriate methods of response to various promotional messages.[12]

In addition to the family, two other institutions traditionally share much of the responsibility for the transfer of selected aspects of culture: *educational institutions* and *houses of worship.* Educational institutions specifically are charged with imparting basic learning skills, history, patriotism, citizenship, and the technical training needed to prepare people for significant roles within society. Religious institutions provide and spread religious consciousness, spiritual guidance, and moral training. Although the young receive much of their consumer training within the family setting, the educational and religious systems reinforce this training by teaching economic and ethical concepts.

A fourth frequently overlooked, social institution that plays a major role in the transfer of culture throughout society is the mass media and other forms of marketing communications. Given the extensive exposure of the American population to print, broadcast, and more and more online media, as well as the easily ingested, entertaining format in which the contents of such media usually are presented, it is not surprising that such media are powerful vehicles for imparting a wide range of cultural values.

We are exposed daily to advertising, an important component of the media. Advertising not only underwrites, or makes economically feasible, the editorial or programming contents of the media, but it also transmits much about our culture. Without advertising, it would be almost impossible to disseminate information about products, ideas, and causes.

Consumers receive important cultural information from advertising. For example, it has been hypothesized that one of the roles of advertising in sophisticated magazines such as *Vogue* (**www.vogue.com**), *Bon Appetit* (**www.bonappetit.com**), and *Architectural Digest* (**www.architecturaldigest.com**) is to instruct readers how to dress, how to decorate their homes, and what foods and wines to serve guests, or in other words, what types of behavior are most appropriate to their particular social class. Thus, although the scope of advertising is often considered to be limited to influencing the demand for specific products or services, in a cultural context, advertising has the expanded mission of reinforcing established cultural values and aiding in the dissemination of new tastes, habits, and customs. In planning their advertising, marketers should recognize that advertising is an important agent for social change in our society.

A fifth and somewhat more recent social institution for the sharing of cultural values are *virtual communities,* such as chat rooms. It has been estimated that over 40 million consumers, worldwide, participate in such communities. A recent study systematically examined over 2,500 apparel retailers' Web sites, and found that 13 of these retailers hosted virtual communities. Such virtual communities are typically facilitated through the use of message or bulletin boards, and may or may not require that the consumer register.[13] Consider the welcome message from one of these retailers:

> This is a place we created for you, so you can talk with others about fashion, beauty, travel, or whatever's on your mind—as a company, we stay completely out of it (if you wish to contact us, click here). Our only request is that you respect other members and only post messages that are appropriate for all. Thanks and enjoy![14]

Culture Is Dynamic

LEARNING OBJECTIVE

11.5 *To Understand How Consumers Are Always Adapting to Culture-Related Experiences.*

To fulfill its need-gratifying role, culture continually must evolve if it is to function in the best interests of a society. For this reason, the marketer must carefully monitor the sociocultural environment in order to market an existing product more effectively or to develop promising new products that are congruent with changing cultural trends.

Understanding cultural changes is not an easy task because many factors are likely to produce cultural changes within a given society (new technology, population shifts, resource shortages, wars, changing values, and customs borrowed from other cultures). For example, major ongoing cultural changes in American society reflect the expanded career options open to women. Today, most women work outside the home, frequently in careers that once were considered exclusively male oriented. These career women are increasingly not waiting for marriage or a man to buy them luxury items—such as fur coats, expensive wristwatches, and diamond rings. More and more such women are saying, "I earn a good living, why wait? I will buy it for myself."

The changing nature of culture means that marketers have to consistently reconsider *why* consumers are now doing what they do, *who* the purchasers and the users of their products are (males only, females only, or both), *when* they do their shopping, *how* and *where* they can be reached by the media, and *what* new product and service needs are emerging. Marketers who monitor cultural changes also often find new opportunities to increase corporate profitability. For example, marketers of such products and services as life insurance, financial and investment advice, casual clothing, toy electric trains, and cigars are among those who have attempted to take advantage of shifts in what is feminine and how to communicate with female consumers. As yet another example, "design has (re)emerged as a major force in American consumers' lives." Since today even basic consumer goods deliver on their promises of performance, design has become a way for a company to differentiate its products.[15] If all MP3 players, for example, sound great, then why not purchase the one that looks the "coolest," which is probably the iPod. One writer has recently described the period we are now living in "as the age of aesthetics," wherein the way things look, feel, and smell have come to matter—not just among the upper-middle classes but among all consumers.[16] Consider the typical shopping center—an enclosed mall with perhaps two large department stores as the "anchor" tenants. Today this format has evolved into an "open-air revolution," with the old-fashioned shopping mall morphing into an open-air lifestyle center where "creating a sense of place and space can be as important to good design as are the retail amenities."[17]

A recent longitudinal study of how women have been depicted in *Fortune* magazine serves as yet another example of how culture is dynamic. The study employed *content analysis* (discussed briefly later in this chapter) and concluded that the changes in advertising tended to reflect the changing role of women during the decade starting in 1990.[18] In particular, the research reveals a fourfold increase in the number of women as the "figure" (i.e., presented in the foreground of the print advertisement) compared to men. Women were also substantially more likely to be portrayed as being "professionals".

The Measurement of Culture

LEARNING OBJECTIVE

11.6 *To Understand How the Impact of Culture on Consumer Behavior Is Measured.*

A wide range of measurement techniques are used in the study of culture. Some of these techniques were already described in Chapter 2. For example, the projective tests used by psychologists to study motivation and personality and the attitude measurement techniques used by social psychologists and sociologists are relatively popular tools in the study of culture.

In addition, *content analysis, consumer fieldwork,* and *value measurement instruments* are three research approaches that are frequently used to examine culture and to spot cultural trends. There are also several commercial services that track emerging values and social trends for businesses and governmental agencies.

CONTENT ANALYSIS

The portrayal of a society, or specific aspects of a society, or a comparison of two or more societies sometimes can be drawn from examining the content of particular messages. **Content analysis**, as the name implies, focuses on the content of verbal, written, and pictorial communications (such as the text and art composition of an ad).

Content analysis can be used as a relatively objective means of determining what social and cultural changes have occurred in a specific society or as a way of contrasting aspects of two different societies. A content analysis of more than 250 ads appearing in eight issues of *Seventeen* magazine, four Japanese issues, and four American issues, found that teenage girls are portrayed differently. The research concluded that these "differences correspond to each country's central concepts of self and society." Whereas American teen girls are often associated with images of "independence and determination," Japanese teen girls are most often portrayed with a "happy, playful, childlike girlish image."[19] In another content analysis study—this one comparing American and Chinese television commercials targeted to children—the research revealed that 82 percent of the Chinese ads aimed at children were for food products, whereas 56 percent of the ads directed at American children were for toys.[20]

Content analysis is useful to both marketers and public policymakers interested in comparing the advertising claims of competitors within a specific industry, as well as for evaluating the nature of advertising claims targeted to specific audiences (e.g., women, the elderly, or children).

CONSUMER FIELDWORK

When examining a specific society, anthropologists frequently immerse themselves in the environment under study through **consumer fieldwork**. As trained researchers, they are likely to select a small sample of people from a particular society and carefully observe their behavior. Based on their observations, researchers draw conclusions about the values, beliefs, and customs of the society under investigation. For example, if researchers were interested in how women select jeans, they might position trained observers in department and clothing stores and note how jeans are selected (straight leg versus tapered leg, with or without back pocket designs, and so on). The researchers also may be interested in the degree of search that accompanies the choice—that is, how often consumers tend to take a pair of jeans off the shelf, examine it, compare it to other jeans in the store, and place it back again before selecting the pair of jeans that they finally purchase.

The distinct characteristics of **field observation** are that (1) it takes place within a natural environment; (2) it is performed sometimes without the subject's awareness; and (3) it focuses on observation of behavior. Because the emphasis is on a natural environment and observable behavior, field observation concerned with consumer behavior often focuses on in-store shopping behavior and, less frequently, on in-home preparation and consumption.

In some cases, instead of just observing behavior, researchers become **participant-observers** (i.e., they become active members of the environment that they are studying). For example, if researchers were interested in examining how consumers select a washing machine, they might take a sales position in an appliance store to observe directly and even to interact with customers in the transaction process.

Today, there are consumer research firms that specialize in studying consumer rituals and values. These firms often videotape subjects at work, at home, in their cars, and in public places. For instance, researchers might ask a teenager why he's buying a certain T-shirt, and you might not get a useful response. Rather, watching a teenager as he shops for that T-shirt, and you might "learn a few things." This type of research, used by Nissan in the 1990s when it was designing its line of Infiniti automobiles, discovered that the Japanese notion of luxury was very different than the American version—whereas the Japanese crave simplicity, Americans crave visible opulence.[21]

Both field observation and participant-observer research require highly skilled researchers who can separate their own preferences and emotions from what they actually observe in their professional roles. Both techniques provide valuable insight that might not easily be obtained through survey research that simply asks consumers questions about their behavior.

In addition to fieldwork methods, depth interviews and focus-group sessions (see Chapter 2) are also often used by marketers to get a "first look" at an emerging social or cultural change. In the relatively informal atmosphere of focus group discussions, consumers are apt to reveal attitudes or behavior that may signal a shift in values that, in turn, may affect the long-run market acceptance of a product or service. For instance, focus group studies can be used to identify marketing programs that reinforce established customer loyalty and goodwill (i.e., relationship marketing). A common thread running throughout these studies showed that established customers, especially for services (such as investment and banking services), want to have their loyalty acknowledged in the form of personalized services. These observations have led various service and product companies to refine or establish loyalty programs that are more personalized in the way that they treat their established customers (e.g., by recognizing the individuality of such core customers). This is just one of numerous examples showing how focus groups and depth interviews are used to spot social trends.

Consider the following recent research study dealing with the symbolic meanings of contemporary food consumption. A total of 30 in-depth interviews, each lasting 1.5 to 2.5 hours, were conducted with subjects (15 male, 15 female) 22 to 71 years of age. The research revealed that the social and cultural categories of food consumption can be broken down into seven distinctly different categories: *symbolic* foods (e.g., home made food and comfort food), *individual* foods (e.g., healthy food and guilty food), *social* foods (e.g., sharing food and connecting food with family), *cultural* foods (e,g., sexual attraction food and taboo food), *ritualistic* foods (e.g., event food and nostalgia food), *context* foods (e.g., date food and coffee break food , and *experience* foods (global food and unfamiliar food).[22]

VALUE MEASUREMENT SURVEY INSTRUMENTS

Anthropologists have traditionally observed the behavior of members of a specific society and inferred from such behavior the dominant or underlying values of the society. In recent years, however, there has been a gradual increase in measuring values by means of survey (questionnaire) research. Researchers use data collection instruments to ask people how they feel about such basic personal and social concepts as freedom, comfort, national security, and peace.

A variety of value measurement instruments have been used in consumer behavior studies, including the **Rokeach Value Survey**, the *List of Values (LOV),* and the *Values and Lifestyles—VALS*. The Rokeach Value Survey is a self-administered value inventory that is divided into two parts, each part measuring different but complementary types of personal values. The first part consists of 18 *terminal value* items, which are designed to measure the relative importance of end states of existence (or personal goals). The second part consists of 18 *instrumental value* items, which measure basic approaches an individual might take to reach end-state values. Thus, the first half of the measurement instrument deals with *ends* (e.g., aspects of "happiness"), and the second half considers *means* (e.g., being "cheerful").

Using the Rokeach Value Survey, adult Brazilians were categorized into six distinctive value segments.[23] For example, Segment A (representing 13 percent of the sample) was most concerned with "world peace," followed by "inner harmony" and "true friendship." Members of this segment were found to be especially involved in domestic-oriented activities (such as gardening, reading, and going out with the family to visit relatives). Because of their less materialistic and nonhedonistic orientation, this segment also may be the least prone to experimenting with new products. In contrast, Segment B (representing 9 percent of the sample) was most concerned with self-centered values such as self-respect, a comfortable life, pleasure, an exciting life, a sense of accomplishment, and social recognition. They were least concerned with values related to the family, such as friendship, love, and equality. These self-centered, achievement-oriented pleasure seekers were expected to prefer provocative clothes in the latest fashion, to enjoy an active lifestyle, and be more likely to try new products.

The LOV scale is another measurement instrument that is also designed to be used in surveying consumers' personal values. The LOV scale asks consumers to identify their two most important values from a nine-value list (such as "warm relationships with others," "a sense of belonging," or "a sense of accomplishment") that is based on the terminal values of the Rokeach Value Survey.[24]

American Core Values

LEARNING OBJECTIVE

11.7 *To Understand How Core Cultural Values Impact American Consumers.*

What is the American culture? In this section, we identify a number of **core values** that both affect and reflect the character of American society. This is a difficult undertaking for several reasons. First, the United States is a diverse country, consisting of a good number of *subcultures* (religious, ethnic, regional, racial, and economic groups), each of which interprets and responds to society's basic beliefs and values in its own specific way. Second, America is a dynamic society that has undergone an almost constant change in response to the development of new technology. This element of rapid change makes it especially difficult to monitor changes in cultural values. Finally, the existence of contradictory values in American society is somewhat confusing. For instance, Americans traditionally embrace freedom of choice and individualism, yet simultaneously they show great tendencies to conform (in dress, in furnishings, and in fads) to the rest of society. In the context of consumer behavior, Americans like to have a wide choice of products and prefer those that uniquely express what they envison to be their personal lifestyles. Yet, there is often a considerable amount of implicit pressure to conform to the values of family members, friends, and other socially important groups. It is difficult to reconcile these seemingly inconsistent values; their existence, however, demonstrates that America is a complex society with numerous paradoxes.

When selecting the specific core values to be examined, we were guided by three criteria:

1. The value must be pervasive. *A significant portion of the American people must accept the value and use it as a guide for their attitudes and actions.*

2. The value must be enduring. *The specific value must have influenced the actions of the American people over an extended period of time (as distinguished from a short-run trend).*
3. The value must be consumer related. *The specific value must provide insights that help us to understand the consumption actions of the American people.*

Meeting these criteria are a number of basic values that expert observers of the American scene consider the "building blocks" of that rather elusive concept called the "American character."

ACHIEVEMENT AND SUCCESS

In a broad cultural context, achievement is a major American value, with historical roots that can be traced to the traditional religious belief in the Protestant work ethic, which considers hard work to be wholesome, spiritually rewarding, and an appropriate end in itself. Indeed, substantial research evidence shows that the achievement orientation has historically been closely associated with the technical development and general economic growth of American society.[25]

Individuals who consider a "sense of accomplishment" an important personal value tend to be achievers who strive hard for success. Although traditionally associated with men, especially male business executives, *achievement* is very important for women, who are increasingly enrolled in undergraduate and graduate business programs and are more commonly seeking top-level business careers.

A recent study that examined the interplay between the Internet and personal values found that those individuals scoring high in "sense of accomplishment" were more likely to use the Internet for learning or gathering information, making reservations or researching travel, for work/business tasks, buying goods or services, looking up stock quotes, and participating in online auctions by buying or selling products. Conversely, Internet activities not associated with a high "sense of accomplishment" included surfing the Web, communication with others in chat rooms, and gathering product or retail store information.[26]

Success is a closely related American cultural theme. However, achievement and success do differ. Specifically, achievement is its own direct reward (it is implicitly satisfying to the individual achiever), whereas success implies an extrinsic reward (such as luxury possessions, financial compensation, or status improvement). Moreover, it is the widespread embracing of achievement and success that has led to the great success and progress of the United States.[27] A recent study examining what influences college students' choice of major found that the most important influence for incoming freshmen was interest in the subject. However, while for female students the next most influential factor was aptitude in the subject, for male students it was "the major's potential for career advancement, and job opportunities and the level of compensation in the field."[28]

Both achievement and success influence consumption. They often serve as social and moral justification for the acquisition of goods and services. For example, "You owe it to yourself," "You worked for it," and "You deserve it" are popular achievement themes used by advertisers to coax consumers into purchasing their products. Regardless of gender, achievement-oriented people often enjoy conspicuous consumption because it allows them to display symbols of their personal achievement (e.g., a Rolex wristwatch). When it comes to personal development and preparation for future careers, the themes of achievement and success are also especially appropriate. In this vein, a study had undergraduate business majors read stories about successful fellow business majors. As a result, these research participants forecasted high annual salaries for themselves and an increased desire for luxury brands like Lexus and Rolex. Reading stories of unsuccessful business students had the opposite effect with respect to salaries and luxury goods.[29]

ACTIVITY

Americans attach an extraordinary amount of importance to being *active* or *involved.* Keeping busy is widely accepted as a healthy and even necessary part of the American lifestyle. The hectic nature of American life is attested to by foreign visitors, who frequently comment that they cannot understand why Americans are always "on the run" and seemingly unable to relax. It is easy to identify ads in the mass media for products and services that are designed to assist consumers in dealing with their hectic or "overfull" lives. The premium placed on activity has had both positive and negative effects on the popularity of various products. For example, a principal reason for the enormous growth of fast-food chains, such as McDonald's and Kentucky Fried Chicken, is that so many people want quick, prepared meals when they are away from the house. Americans rarely eat a full breakfast because they usually are too rushed in the morning to prepare and consume a traditional morning meal. According to a recent Yankelovich poll, half of all consumers, across all income brackets, now claim that a lack of time is a bigger problem for them than a lack of money.[30]

Research suggests that "being busy," in and of itself, is not enough and not necessarily healthy. For example, some researchers have reported that although it is important for elderly people to "keep busy," it is important that the activities they engage in be fulfilling. Similarly, it is being questioned whether keeping young children busy all the time is healthy for them—it's been suggested that kids need time to relax![31]

EFFICIENCY AND PRACTICALITY

With a basic philosophy of down-to-earth pragmatism, Americans pride themselves on being efficient and practical. When it comes to *efficiency,* they admire anything that saves time and effort. In terms of *practicality,* they generally are receptive to any new product that makes tasks easier and can help solve problems. For example, today it is possible for manufacturers of many product categories to offer the public a wide range of interchangeable components. Thus, a consumer can design his or her own customized wall unit from such standard components as compatible metals and woods, legs, door facings, and style panels at a cost not much higher than a completely standardized unit. The capacity of manufacturers to create mass-produced components offers consumers the practical option of a customized product at a reasonable price. If you are unfamiliar with such furniture, just browse through an IKEA catalog or the "virtual catalog" on the IKEA Web site (**www.ikea.com**). As another example, if you go to the Dell Computer Web site (**www.dell.com**) you can observe the myriad of ways in which almost any model of a Dell computer can be customized by the purchaser (e.g., memory upgrades, video card upgrades, hard drive size upgrades, software upgrades, etc.).

Another illustration of Americans' attentiveness to efficiency and practicality is the extreme importance attached to *time.* Americans seem to be convinced that "time waits for no one," which is reflected in their habitual attention to being prompt. Another sign of America's preoccupation with time is the belief that time is in increasingly short supply; for instance, consumers want good food, but we want it "fast." Americans place a great deal of importance on getting there first, on the value of time itself, on the notion that time is money, on the importance of not wasting time, and on identifying "more" time. In an attempt to get more and more out of each day, one author has concluded that Americans may become trapped in a vicious circle in which they feel as if they are getting less and less out of each day.[32]

While today many teens and young adults have given up wearing a watch and instead rely on their cell phones to provide the time, the frequency with which Americans look at their watches (or cell phones) and the importance attached to carrying an accurate timepiece (whether in watch or cell phone form) tend to support the American value of *punctuality.*

PROGRESS

Progress is another watchword of American society. Americans respond favorably to the promise of progress. Receptivity to progress appears to be closely linked to the other core values already examined (*achievement, success, efficiency,* and *practicality*) and to the central belief that people can always improve themselves and that tomorrow should be better than today. In a consumption-oriented society, such as that of the United States, progress often means the acceptance of change, new products, or services designed to fulfill previously undersatisfied or unsatisfied needs. A new type of counselor, the "life coach" or "personal coach," works with individuals in order to help them improve themselves and seek "fulfillment and balance in careers, family, health, and hobbies." The coach tracks the client's progress and tries to keep the client heading in the direction of his or her fulfillment. Ideally, the coach makes the client excited about prospects for the future.

In the name of progress, Americans appear to be receptive to product claims that stress "new," "improved," "longer-lasting," "speedier," "quicker," "smoother and closer," "increased strength," and "smarter" (see Figure 11.6).

FIGURE 11.6
Source: Courtesy of Samsung.
Photo Credit © Vincent Dixon.

QUESTION: *Which Cultural Value Is Portrayed, and How So?*

MATERIAL COMFORT

For most Americans (even young children), *material comfort* signifies the attainment of "the good life," a life that may include a new car, a dishwasher, an air conditioner, a hot tub, and an almost infinite variety of other convenience-oriented and pleasure-providing goods and services. It appears that consumers' idea of material comfort is largely a *relative* view; that is, consumers tend to define their own satisfaction with the amount of material goods they have in terms of a comparison of what they have to what others have. If a comparison suggests that they have more than others do, then they are more likely to be satisfied.[33] On the other hand, as many popular songs point out, the ownership of material goods does not always lead to happiness. For instance, many people, especially affluent people, might be willing to trade money for more free time to spend with family and friends.

The desire of Americans for material comfort is nothing new. In an *Atlantic Monthly* essay in 1924 entitled "Things Are in the Saddle," Samuel Strauss coined the term *consumptionism*, which he defined as "the science of compelling men to use more and more things." Strauss felt that this was changing the nature of America by "bringing it about that the American citizen's first importance to his country is no longer that of citizen, but that of consumer."[34]

Vivre (**www.vivre.com**) offers a mail-order and online catalog aimed at "connecting luxury brands with affluent shoppers and providing material comfort for its customers." Consider a portion of how the company responds to the question "What is Vivre?" (taken from its Web site):

> One might consider Vivre to be a revival of the classic "first floor" of a department store, which traditionally displayed only the best of the best to a discriminating clientele. Likewise, Vivre presents only that which is deemed to be relevant, inspiring and exquisitely crafted. With a modern sensibility, the resulting treasure trove is delivered to doorsteps in the form of a glossy catalog . . . and to desktops via a full-service e-commerce website. Therein shoppers will find the best of the world at their fingertips.
>
> By presenting each season's collection in a lifestyle context, we create an emotional connection with our customers, who rely upon us to offer an edited collection of the very best of each season. By interspersing our selections with editorial and advice, we create an inspirational shopping experience—one where Vivre is considered to be a trusted advisor to "A Beautiful Life."[35]

Material comfort has often been associated with "bigger quantities of things" or "more of something." Recently, however, there has been a noticeable shift away from such a "more is better" viewpoint to a "better is better" vision—one that stresses better quality and better design. Americans today increasingly want *better,* and *better looking,* products. Such a state of affairs has been referred to as "the design economy"—that is, an economy that is based on the interaction of four elements: sustained prosperity, ongoing technology, a culture open to change, and marketing expertise.[36] Consider, for example, how the famous designer, Michael Graves, has helped Target (the mass-merchandise retailer) accomplish its goal of being a standout provider of finely designed products at mass-market prices.

INDIVIDUALISM

Americans value "being themselves." Self-reliance, self-interest, self-confidence, self-esteem, and self-fulfillment are all exceedingly popular expressions of *individualism.* Striving for individualism seems to be linked to the rejection of dependency; that is, it is better to rely on oneself than on others. Indeed, the opposite of *individualism* is *collectivism*, which implies that "being in a group is a basic human endeavor, so that self-concept involves group membership."[37]

American "rugged individualism" is a form of individualism. It is based on the notion of self-reliance with competition (i.e., we try to meet our needs through personal effort, and in a way that outperforms our peers). Still further, solo performance, to the rugged individualist, is more important than teamwork—tasks should be accomplished alone, and victory should be earned alone.[38] Table 11.4 presents an interesting elaboration of the concept of "rugged individualism."

In terms of consumer behavior, an appeal to individualism frequently takes the form of reinforcing the consumer's sense of identity with products or services that both reflect and emphasize that identity. For example, advertisements for high-style clothing and cosmetics usually promise that their products will enhance the consumer's exclusive or distinctive character and set him or her apart from others. Additionally, while the purchase of a well-known brand may reduce the perceived risk of the product not performing as expected (i.e., perceived performance risk), many consumers today exhibit enough self-confidence, optimism, and trust in their own ability to prefer modified or customized products, and are willing to pay a higher price for such goods.[39]

FREEDOM

Freedom is another very strong American value, with historical roots in such democratic ideals as freedom of speech, freedom of the press, and freedom of worship. As an outgrowth of these beliefs in freedom, Americans have a strong preference for *freedom of choice,* the opportunity to choose from a wide range of alternatives. This preference is reflected in the large number of competitive brands and product variations that can be found on the shelves of the modern supermarket or department store. For many products, consumers can select from a wide variety

TABLE 11.4 An Elaboration of the Cultural Dynamics of the "Rugged Individual"

LABEL	DEFINITION	IMAGERY
Competition against self/ Competition against others	Sees both self-weakness and others' strengths as foes to overcome.	Transforming self from a weakling to a warrior.
Manual labor/Purchased labor	The choice to make or buy competitive equipment.	Becoming completely self-sufficient.
Solo performance/Team work		The solo performer as the ideal.
Technology and machines/ Aesthetics and fashion	Exaltation to utility, denigration of beauty.	Aesthetics as a seductive siren.
Instrumentalism/Anthropomorphism	The extended self as alive, nonself as target or tool.	Dog as partner, deer as prey.
Nature/Culture	Culture as inadequate for testing manhood; nature as both refuge and providing ground.	The wilderness as heaven and hell.
Individual freedom/Rule of law	Any form of government is restrictive of personal freedom and therefore undesirable.	The warrior as the quintessence of selfhood, the embodiment of freedom, and the exemplar of natural law.

Source: Copyright © 2003 by American Academy of Advertising, from Elizabeth C. Hirschman, "Men, Dogs, Guns, and Cars: The Semiotics of Rugged Individualism," *Journal of Advertising,* vol. 32, no. 1 (Spring 2003): 11. Used with permission of M.E. Sharpe, Inc.

of sizes, colors, flavors, features, styles, and even special ingredients. It also explains why many companies offer consumers many choices.

However, there are decision-making situations when consumers are faced with too many choices. In such cases, they may feel overwhelmed by the shear number of choices and respond by running away from the stressful situation (see Chapter 15). Research with English consumers found that many of the respondents reported feeling bewildered and irritated by the fact that they were being offered "too much choice."[40]

EXTERNAL CONFORMITY

Although Americans deeply embrace freedom of choice and individualism, they nevertheless accept the reality of conformity. *External conformity* is a necessary process by which the individual adapts to society.

In the realm of consumer behavior, conformity (or uniformity) takes the form of standardized goods and services. Standardized products have been made possible by mass production. The availability of a wide choice of standardized products places the consumer in the unique position of being *individualistic* (by selecting specific products that close friends do not have) or of *conforming* (by purchasing a similar or identical product). In this context, individualism and conformity exist side by side as choices for the consumer.

An interesting example of the "Ping-Pong" relationship between seeking individualism and accepting conformity is the widespread acceptance of casual dressing in the workplace. For instance, male and female executives are conforming less to workplace dress codes (i.e., there are more "total" dress options open to business executives). As a result, some male executives are wearing casual slacks and sport shirts to work; others are wearing blazers and slacks rather than business suits. Greater personal confidence and an emphasis on comfort appear to be the reasons that many executives are wearing less traditional business attire. Nevertheless, in some companies, the appearance of male executives in blue blazers and gray slacks does seem like a "business uniform" (which is a kind of conformity).

HUMANITARIANISM

Americans are often generous when it comes to giving to those in need. They support with a passion many humane and charitable causes, and they sympathize with the underdog who must overcome adversity to get ahead. They also tend to be charitable and willing to come to the aid of people who are less fortunate than they are. To make the study of charitable giving more fruitful, consumer researchers have validated two scales that deal with *attitudes toward helping*

TABLE 11.5 A Scale to Measure Attitude Toward Helping Others (AHO) and Attitude Toward Charitable Organizations (ACO)

SCALE ITEM
ATTITUDE TOWARD HELPING OTHERS (AHO)
People should be willing to help others who are less fortunate.
Helping troubled people with their problems is very important to me.
People should be more charitable toward others in society.
People in need should receive support from others.
ATTITUDE TOWARD CHARITABLE ORGANIZATIONS (ACO)
The money given to charities goes to good causes.
Much of the money donated to charity is wasted. (R)
My image of charitable organizations is positive.
Charitable organizations have been quite successful in helping the needy.
Charity organizations perform a useful function for society.

Note: (R)= reverse scored.

Source: Deborah J. Webb, Corliss L. Green, and Thomas G. Brashear, "Development and Validation of Scales to Measure Attitudes Influencing Monetary Donations to Charitable Organizations," *Journal of the Academy of Marketing Science,* 28, no. 12 (Spring 2000): 299–309. Reprinted by permission of the publisher. Copyright © 2000, Springer Netherlands.

others (AHO) and *attitudes toward charitable organizations* (ACO).[41] Table 11.5 presents the nine-item scale used to measure AHO and ACO.

Within the context of making charitable decisions, the Web site of the Planned Giving Design Center (**www.pgdc.net**) assists charities in their efforts to establish and cultivate relationships with professionals who advise clients in a position to make charitable contributions (e.g., lawyers, financial planners, trust officers).[42] Other Web sites are designed to provide individual givers with assistance in donating to specific charities (e.g., **www.charityguide.org**, **www.guidestar.org**, and **www.charitynavigator.org**).

Beyond charitable giving, other social issues have an impact on both what consumers buy and where they invest. For example, some investors prefer mutual funds that screen companies for such social concerns as military contracts, pollution problems, and equal opportunity employment. Investments in socially conscious mutual funds are now quite commonplace. Many companies try to appeal to consumers by emphasizing their concern for environmental or social issues.

An annual survey, Cone's Trend Tracker, has found that Americans claimed that when it comes to Christmas shopping, companies' charitable choices influenced their purchase decisions. The number of consumers indicating that they intend to purchase from retailers "that support a cause" has been steadily increasing.[43]

YOUTHFULNESS

Americans tend to place an almost sacred value on *youthfulness*. This emphasis is a reflection of America's preoccupation with technological development, and "new" and "improved." Specifically, in an atmosphere where "young" and "youthfulness" are constantly stressed, "old" is often equated with being outdated. This is in contrast to more traditional European, African, and Asian societies, in which older people are respected and looked-up to for their wisdom and experience that comes with age.

Nevertheless, *youthfulness* should not be confused with youth, which describes an age grouping. Americans are preoccupied with *looking* and *acting* young, regardless of their chronological age. For Americans, youthfulness is a state of mind and a state of being, sometimes expressed as being "young at heart," "young in spirit," or "young in appearance."

A great deal of advertising and other marketing messages are directed to creating a sense of urgency about retaining one's youth and fearing aging.[44] Hand-cream ads talk about "young hands"; skin-treatment ads state "I dreaded turning 30"; fragrance and makeup ads stress looking "sexy and young" or "denying your age"; detergent ads ask the reader, "Can you match their hands with their ages?" These advertising themes, which promise the consumer the benefits of youthfulness, reflect the high premium Americans place on appearing and acting young.

FITNESS AND HEALTH

Americans' preoccupation with *fitness* and *health* has emerged as a core value. This value has manifested itself in a number of ways, including tennis, racquetball, biking and jogging, and the continued increases in sales of vitamins. Added to these trends is an enhanced consciousness on the part of Americans that "You are what you eat." It has been suggested that the American fitness boom was a result of a perceived lack of social control in America—people just felt anxious, insecure, and had self-doubts. A person feeling a lack of external self-control turns inward—if you can't control the world, you can control and change your own body through exercise.[45]

Fitness and health have become lifestyle choices for an increasing number of consumers. Indeed, survey research reveals that 95 percent of shoppers are "health active," which means that "they select food for healthful reasons at least some of the time."[46] Therefore, it is not surprising to find an almost constant stream of new products and services designed to assist health-focused consumers to achieve a healthier lifestyle (see Figure 11.7).

This trend has stimulated Reebok to open a series of exercise–retail complexes that seek to build a cultural connection with consumers that goes beyond the normal marketing approach. Traditional food manufacturers have begun modifying their ingredients to cater to the health-conscious consumer. Frozen dinners have become more nutritious in recent years, and manufacturers of traditional "junk food" are trying to make it more healthful. "Light" or "fat-free" versions of snack chips or pretzels, along with "low-sodium," "no-cholesterol," "no-preservative," "no trans fat" snack products, are attempts to provide consumers with tasty and healthy options. And it has been reported that two of the most important trends in the beverage industry are: (1) weight management and obesity, and (2) digestive health and immunity.[47] There are also Web sites for the fitness-minded consumer (see **www.fitnessonline .com**) offering workout tips, nutritional information, and fitness-related products and services.

According to PEW/INTERNET, "eight in ten Internet users have looked online for information on at least one of 16 health topics, with increased interest in diet, fitness, drugs, health insurance, experimental treatments, and particular doctors and hospitals."[48] A recent article in *Progressive Grocer,* a leading food retailing publication, suggests that "the most lucrative consumer trend in the next five to 10 years" is going to be "health and wellness," and consumers who now make their grocery shopping decisions based on price, taste, and convenience, will upgrade "health benefits to a No. 1 or No. 2 priority."[49] There has also been an increasing emphasis on the healthy home, evidenced by the introduction of new antimicrobial home-cleaning products.[50]

Although there is no denying the "fitness and healthy living" trend in American society, there is evidence that consumers find it difficult "to be good" in terms of their personal health. The World Health Organization has released a report stating that obesity is an increasing problem in both developed and developing countries.[51] Despite these negative indications, when Franklin Covey polled over 15,000 consumers about their top three New Year's resolutions for 2008, two of the top three were lose weight, and develop a healthy habit like exercise or healthy eating (the third was to get out of debt or save money).[52]

CORE VALUES ARE NOT ONLY AN AMERICAN PHENOMENON

The cultural values just examined are not all uniquely or originally American. Some may have originally been borrowed, particularly from European society, as people immigrated to the United States. Some values that originated in America are now part of the fabric of other societies. For example, there is evidence that the good life may be nearly a universal notion and that global brands are used as an external sign of attaining the good life.[53]

In addition, not all Americans necessarily accept each of these values. However, as a whole, these values do account for much of the American character. Table 11.6 summarizes a number of American core values and indicates their relevance to consumer behavior.

FIGURE 11.7
Source: Thomas® English Muffins are a registered trademark of Entenmann's Products, Inc.

QUESTION: *Which Cultural Value Is This Ad Stressing, and How So?*

Toward a Shopping Culture

LEARNING OBJECTIVE

11.8 *To Understand How the American Culture Became a "Shopping Culture."*

It appears that the role that shopping plays in the American life has been elevated to the point that the American culture has become a *shopping culture* (which is a parallel perspective to the commonly held view that America's culture is a *consumer culture*). One authority has even noted that shopping has remade our culture and now defines the way we understand the world around us—"shopping is what we do to create value in our lives."[54] Making this possible is the reality that great shopping experiences are no longer just for the rich, as consumers from all walks of life can enjoy the low prices found in discount stores. Still further, shopping "has become an increasingly acceptable and popular pastime even for younger, single guys." Specifically, men between 25 and 49 years of age now account for over half of all male buying power, and this market is expected to grow to more than $6.7 trillion over the next several years, an

TABLE 11.6 Summary of American Core Values

VALUE	DEFINITION	RELEVANCE TO CONSUMER BEHAVIOR
Achievement and success	Hard work is good; success flows from hard work.	Acts as a justification for acquisition of goods ("You deserve it").
Activity	Keeping busy is healthy and natural.	Stimulates interest in products that are time savers and enhance leisure time.
Efficiency and practicality	Admiration of things that solve problems (e.g., saves time and effort).	Stimulates purchase of products that function well and save time.
Progress	People can improve themselves; tomorrow should be better than today.	Stimulates desire for new products that fulfill unsatisfied needs better than existing products and are positioned as "new" or "improved."
Material comfort	"The good life."	Fosters acceptance of convenience and luxury products that make life more comfortable and enjoyable.
Individualism	Being oneself (e.g., self-reliance, self-interest, self-esteem).	Stimulates acceptance of customized or unique products that enable a person to "express his or her own personality."
Freedom	Freedom of choice.	Fosters interest in wide product lines and differentiated products.
External conformity	Uniformity of observable behavior; desire for acceptance.	Stimulates interest in products that are used or owned by others in the same social group.
Humanitarianism	Caring for others, particularly the underdog.	Stimulates patronage of firms that compete with market leaders.
Youthfulness	A state of mind that stresses being "young at heart" and having a youthful appearance.	Stimulates acceptance of products that provide the illusion of maintaining or fostering youthfulness.
Fitness and health	Caring about one's body, including the desire to be physically fit and healthy.	Stimulates acceptance of food products, activities, and equipment perceived to maintain or increase physical fitness.

increase of almost 25 percent. A recent study found that one in four men under age 40 claim to shop frequently, compared to less than 20 percent of men in their 40s and 50s.[55]

Much of this "shop 'til you drop" mentality has propelled shopping to the "all American" pastime, an obsession that is driving an increasing number of Americans to be in credit card debt. It appears that consumers' credit card usage is more and more defining the meaning of a *consumption lifestyle,* one that unfortunately fosters consumers' attainment through their consumption of unfulfilling possessions and burdensome debt.[56]

SUMMARY

The study of culture is the study of all aspects of a society. It is the language, knowledge, laws, and customs that give that society its distinctive character and personality. In the context of consumer behavior, culture is defined as the sum total of learned beliefs, values, and customs that serve to regulate the consumer behavior of members of a particular society. Beliefs and values are guides for consumer behavior; customs are usual and accepted ways of behaving.

The impact of culture on society is so natural and so ingrained that its influence on behavior is rarely noted. Yet, culture offers order, direction, and guidance to members of society in all phases of human problem solving. Culture is dynamic and gradually and continually evolves to meet the needs of society.

Culture is learned as part of social experience. Children acquire from their environment a set of beliefs, values, and customs that constitutes culture (i.e., they are encultured). These are acquired through formal learning, informal learning, and technical learning. Advertising enhances formal learning by reinforcing desired modes of behavior and expectations; it enhances informal learning by providing models for behavior.

Culture is communicated to members of society through a common language and through commonly shared symbols. Because the human mind has the ability to absorb and to process symbolic communication, marketers are able to promote to consumers both tangible and intangible products, services and concepts.

All the elements in the marketing mix serve to communicate symbolically with the audience. Products project an image of their own; so does promotion. Price and retail outlets symbolically convey images concerning the quality of products.

The elements of culture are transmitted by three pervasive social institutions: the family, the church, and the school. A fourth social institution that plays a major role in the transmission of culture is the mass media, both through editorial content and through advertising.

A wide range of measurement techniques is used to study culture. The range includes projective techniques, attitude measurement methods, field observation, participant observation, content analysis, and value measurement survey techniques.

A number of core values of the American people are relevant to the study of consumer behavior. These include achievement and success, activity, efficiency and practicality, progress, material comfort, individualism, freedom, conformity, humanitarianism, youthfulness, and fitness and health.

Because each of these values varies in importance to the members of our society, each provides an effective basis for segmenting consumer markets.

DISCUSSION QUESTIONS

1. Distinguish among beliefs, values, and customs. Illustrate how the clothing a person wears at different times or for different occasions is influenced by customs.
2. A manufacturer of fat-free granola bars is considering targeting school-age children by positioning its product as a healthy, nutritious snack food. How can an understanding of the three forms of cultural learning be used in developing an effective strategy to target the intended market?
3. The Citrus Growers of America is planning a promotional campaign to encourage the drinking of orange and grapefruit juice in situations in which many consumers normally consume soft drinks. Using the Rokeach Value Survey researchers identified "family security" (providing for loved ones) a promising "terminal value" and "honest" (trustworthy or believable) as a likely "instrumental value" for marketers to use in future advertising campaign for citrus juices as an alternative to soft drinks. How can these two values be portrayed in an advertising campaign designed to increase the consumption of citrus juices?
4. For each of the following products and activities:
   a. Identify the core values most relevant to their purchase and use.
   b. Determine whether these values encourage or discourage use or ownership.
   c. Determine whether these core values are shifting and, if so, in what direction. The products and activities are:
      1. Donating money to charities
      2. Donating blood
      3. Digital video recorders
      4. Personal GPS devices
      5. Toothpaste
      6. Diet soft drinks
      7. Foreign travel
      8. Suntan lotion
      9. Cellular smartphones
      10. Interactive TV home-shopping services
      11. Fat-free foods
      12. Products in recyclable packaging

EXERCISES

1. Identify a singer or singing group whose music you like and discuss the symbolic function of the clothes that person (or group) wears.
2. Think of various routines in your everyday life (such as grooming or food preparation). Identify one ritual and describe it. In your view, is this ritual shared by others? If so, to what extent? What are the implications of your ritualistic behavior to the marketer(s) of the product(s) you use during your routine?
3. a. Summarize an episode of a weekly television series that you watched recently. Describe how the program transmitted cultural beliefs, values, and customs.
   b. Select and describe three commercials that were broadcast during the program mentioned in 3a. Do these commercials create or reflect cultural values? Explain your answer.
4. a. Find two different advertisements for deodorants in two magazines that are targeted to different audiences. Content-analyze the written and pictorial aspects of each ad, using any core values discussed in this chapter. How are these values portrayed to the target audiences?
   b. Identify symbols used in these ads and discuss their effectiveness in conveying the desired product image or characteristics

KEY TERMS

- acculturation *371*
- consumer fieldwork *377*
- content analysis *376*
- core values *378*
- culture *366*
- enculturation *371*
- field observation *377*
- participant-observers *377*
- ritual *373*
- Rokeach Value Survey *378*
- symbols *372*

Case One: Tweeting and Facebooking in the United Arab Emirates

Various social institutions within a society transmit the elements of culture and make the sharing of culture a reality. The most recent social institution for the sharing of cultural values is the virtual community, such as chat rooms. It has been estimated that over 40 million consumers, worldwide, participate in such communities. Two such virtual communities making waves in the United Arab Emirates are Twitter and Facebook. Twitter has been given an enormous boost by celebrities like Ashton Kutcher and Oprah Winfrey, who have helped to fuel Twitter mania.

Facebook is a phenomena in itself in social networking, as it uses the power of virtual communities. Recently a Facebook page created by Dusty Sorg and Michael Jedrzejewski, two Coca-Cola enthusiasts, attracted more than 3 million members to the site. The growing popularity of Twitter and Facebook in the UAE is making new enterprises like the Wild Peeta, a Dubai-based, Quick-Service Restaurant (QSR) choose this social networking site as part of the business promotional strategy.

QUESTION

1. Discuss the role of Twitter and Facebook as agents of change for culture. Which group/s are most likely to change their traditional ways of doing things because of these social networking sites?

Sources: Basma Al Jadaly, "Parents Outraged over Facebook Parties," *Gulf News Business*, April 9, 2009, 3; Tim Bradshaw and David Gelles, "Facebook Puts a Fizz into COKE," *Gulf News*, April 9, 2009, 40; Scott Shuey Scott, "Dubai Firms Tweet to Log On to Customers' Minds," *Gulf News Business*, May 7, 2009, 40; Anonymous, "Celebrity Following," *7 Days*, March 25, 2009, 9; and Anonymous, "All That Twitters Isn't Gold," *Khaleej Times*, April 24, 2009, 36.

Case Two: Privacy: A New Facet of American Culture?

For many of us, the Internet is a wonderful tool. It makes it possible to e-mail our friends and family, helps us bank and pay our bills, compare different brands that we might consider purchasing, and find the best price for a desired item. But how much of this "wonderfulness" are we willing to exchange for our personal data?

Marketers want to know who we are, and where we go on the Internet. So, for example, they've been installing cookies on our computers for years. That's why once we've visited a Web site, the next time we want to click on it its listing is a different color. And if you increase the security level of your computer so that your PC does not accept cookies, then it will take you longer to enter most Web Sites.

Google has been particularly criticized by those with security concerns because of how it operates its Gmail system. Gmail automatically delivers ads to the user, based on e-mail content. Many users are not happy that Google is monitoring their e-mail in order to send them ads, even if, based on e-mail content, the ads are relevant.

In today's world of identify theft and computer viruses, consumers are resisting swapping personal information for increased value, whether it is taking place online or offline. Jupiter Research has recently found that 58 percent of Internet users say that they have deleted cookies, with as many as 39 percent claiming to do so monthly. And 28 percent of Internet users are selectively rejecting third-party cookies, like those placed by online ad networks.

QUESTION

1. Is personal privacy a new U.S. cultural value?

Source: Based on: Jack Neff, "Are We Too Targeted?," *Advertising Age's Point Magazine*, June 2005: 8–11.

12

Subcultures and Consumer Behavior

CULTURE HAS a potent influence on all consumer behavior. Individuals are brought up to follow the beliefs, values, and customs of their society and to avoid behavior that is judged unacceptable or considered taboo. In addition to segmenting in terms of cultural factors, marketers also segment overall societies into smaller subgroups (subcultures) that consist of people who are similar in terms of their ethnic origin, their customs, and the ways they behave. These subcultures provide important marketing opportunities for astute marketing strategists.

Our discussion of subcultures, therefore, has a narrower focus than the discussion of culture. Instead of examining the dominant beliefs, values, and customs that exist within an entire society, this chapter explores the marketing opportunities created by the existence of certain beliefs, values, and customs shared by members of specific subcultural groups within a society.

These subcultural divisions are based on a variety of sociocultural and demographic variables, such as nationality, religion, geographic locality, race, age, and sex. As you will read later in this chapter, when marketers decide to single-out members of a particular subculture that they wish to provide extra or special attention to, they sometimes need to adapt the product to better meet the needs of the targeted consumers. However, they very often need to change the marketing message to better suit the needs, interests, or tastes of the members of the particular subculture. For instance, Figure 12.1 shows an ad that is presenting an insurance message to Hispanic American consumers who either need to be communicated to in Spanish, or alternatively prefer to be communicated to in Spanish.

Later in this chapter, as part of the discussion of the Hispanic subculture, you will learn that companies often supplement their English language advertising with ads in Spanish, which are more effective than the English ads when targeting the rapidly growing Hispanic–American market.

FIGURE 12.1

Source: Copyright © State Farm Mutual Automobile Insurance Company, 2005. Used by permission.

QUESTION: *Why Is State Farm Sometimes Running Magazine Ads in Spanish? At Whom Are These Ads Directed?*

Learning Objectives

12.1 *To Understand What Subculture Is, and Its Relationship to Culture.*

12.2 *To Understand Nationality as a Subcultural Influence on Consumer Behavior.*

12.3 *To Understand Religious Affiliation as a Subcultural Influence on Consumer Behavior.*

12.4 *To Understand Geographic and Regional Residences as Subcultural Influences on Consumer Behavior.*

12.5 *To Understand Racial Identity as a Subcultural Influence on Consumer Behavior.*

12.6 *To Understand Age as a Subcultural Influence on Consumer Behavior.*

12.7 *To Understand Gender as a Subcultural Influence on Consumer Behavior.*

12.8 *To Understand How Multiple Subcultural Memberships Jointly Influence Consumer Behavior.*

What Is Subculture?

Learning Objective

12.1 *To Understand What Subculture Is, and Its Relationship to Culture.*

The members of a specific **subculture** possess beliefs, values, and customs that set them apart from other members of the same society. In addition, they adhere to most of the dominant cultural beliefs, values, and behavioral patterns of the larger society. We define subculture, then, as *a distinct cultural group that exists as an identifiable segment within a larger, more complex society*.

Thus, the cultural profile of a society or nation is a composite of two distinct elements: (1) the unique beliefs, values, and customs subscribed to by members of specific subcultures; and (2) the central or core cultural themes that are shared by most of the population, regardless of specific subcultural memberships. Figure 12.2 presents a model of the relationship between two subcultural groups (Hispanic Americans and Asian Americans) and the larger or "more general" culture. As the figure depicts, each subculture has its own unique traits, yet both groups share the dominant traits of the overall American culture.

Let us look at it in another way: Each American is, in large part, a product of the "American way of life." Each American, however, is at the same time a member of various subcultures. For example, a 10-year-old girl may simultaneously be African American, Baptist, a preteen, and a Texan. We would expect that membership in each different subculture would provide its own set of specific beliefs, values, attitudes, and customs. Table 12.1 lists typical subcultural categories and corresponding examples of specific subcultural groups. This list is by no means exhaustive: Plumbers, Republicans, Girl Scouts, and billionaires—in fact, any group that shares common beliefs and customs—may be classified as a subculture.

Subcultural analysis enables the marketing manager to focus on sizable and natural market segments. When carrying out such analyses, the marketer must determine whether the

FIGURE 12.2
Relationship Between Culture and Subculture

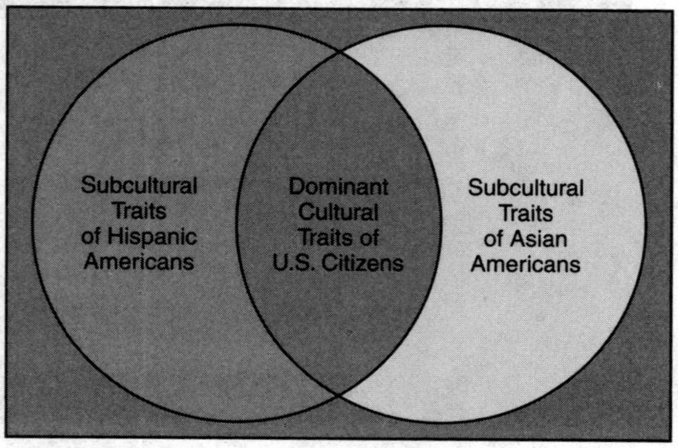

TABLE 12.1 Examples of Major Subcultural Categories

CATEGORIES	EXAMPLES
Nationality (i.e., birthplace of ancestors)	Greek, Italian, Russian
Religion	Catholic, Hindu, Mormon
Geographic region	Eastern, Southern, U.S. Southwestern
Race	African American, Asian, Caucasian
Age	Teenager, Xers, elderly
Gender	Female, male
Occupation	Bus driver, cook, scientist
Social class	Lower, middle, upper

beliefs, values, and customs shared by members of a specific subgroup make them desirable candidates for special marketing attention. Subcultures, therefore, are relevant units of analysis for market research. And these subcultures are dynamic—for example, the different ethnic groups that comprise the U.S. population have been changing and will continue to change in size and economic power in the coming years. More specifically, the white (non-Hispanic) population of the United States, which made up 71 percent of Americans in the year 2000 (date of the last U.S. Census), is projected to represent about 46 percent of the U.S. population by the year 2050.[1] Indeed, the U.S. Census Bureau has estimated that by 2042, "Americans who identify themselves as Hispanic, black, Asian, American Indian, Native Hawaiian and Pacific Islander will together outnumber non-Hispanic whites. Four years ago, officials had projected the shift would come in 2050."[2] Frequently a "window on the future," the State of California has estimated that the state's multicultural or combined minority population is now the state's majority population.

A study of ethnic media usage in California also found that over 80 percent of Asian American, African American, and Hispanic American respondents claimed to get information from ethnic television, radio, and publications. Furthermore, 68 percent preferred ethnic-language TV stations over English channels for news, and 40 percent reported paying greater attention to ethnic language ads than English-language ads.[3]

The following sections examine a number of important subcultural categories: nationality, religion, geographic location, race, age, and sex. (Occupational and social-class subgroups were discussed in detail in Chapter 11.)

Nationality Subcultures

LEARNING OBJECTIVE

12.2 *To Understand Nationality as a Subcultural Influence on Consumer Behavior.*

For many people, **nationality subcultures** guide what they value and what they buy. This is especially true for the population of a country like the United States that has a history of attracting people from all over the globe. Supporting this pattern are the results of the 2005 U.S. Census American Community Survey, which found that more than one in ten Americans (12.4 percent) is foreign born, and that 22.2 percent of this foreign-born population entered the United States in 2000 or later.[4] It has also been reported that Queens County (one of the five boroughs that make up the City of New York) is the most multicultural county in America, and that 46 percent of its residents were born outside of the United States.[5] For these Americans, as well as Americans born in the United States, there is frequently a strong sense of identification and pride in the language and customs of their ancestors.

When it comes to consumer behavior, this ancestral pride is manifested most strongly in the consumption of ethnic foods, in travel to the "homeland," and in the purchase of numerous cultural artifacts (ethnic clothing, art, music, foreign-language newspapers). Interest in these goods and services has expanded rapidly as younger Americans attempt to better understand and more closely associate with their ethnic roots. To illustrate the importance of ethnic origin as a subcultural market segment, the next section examines the **Hispanic American subculture**.

THE HISPANIC SUBCULTURE

The most recent U.S. Census (year 2000) found that the number of Hispanic Americans (of all races) had grown by 58 percent during the decade of the 1990s (compared to an overall U.S. population growth of 13.2 percent). And, according to the U.S. Census Bureau, in July 2002 Hispanics replaced African Americans as the largest minority group in the United States. Hispanics are currently 15 percent of the U.S. population, and their number is estimated to reach 30 percent of the population by the year 2050, giving the United States a Hispanic population of almost 133 million.[6] These Hispanic Americans had an estimated purchasing power in 2004 of $687 billion, which is expected to climb to $1.2 trillion by 2011.[7] In contrast to other American population segments, Hispanic Americans are younger—in 2006 almost 34 percent of Hispanics were under 18 years of age, whereas only 25 percent of the U.S. population is under 18. The median age for Hispanics is 27 years of age, whereas the median age for all of America is 36 years of age.[8] Hispanic Americans also tend to be members of larger families (an average Hispanic household size is 3.34 people compared to an average U.S. household size of 2.57 people).[9] They are also more likely to live in an extended family household consisting of several generations of family members. Not only are Hispanic households more likely than black or non-Hispanic American white families to contain children, but also Hispanics spend more time caring for their children.[10] In general, Hispanics, more so than non-Hispanics, tend to more highly value social relationships and networks among family members and friends.[11]

Approximately 88 percent of all Hispanics under the age of 18 living in the United States were born here. And by 2020, only 34 percent of Hispanics living here will be foreign-born first generation, 36 percent will be U.S.-born second-generation children of immigrants, and 30 percent will be third-generation children of U.S.-born Hispanics.[12] In terms of acculturation, only 20 percent of the Hispanic/Latino market has recently migrated to the United States and speak only Spanish. Of the remaining 80 percent, 20 percent speak only English and 60 percent speak both Spanish and English.

Of the more than 44 million Hispanics and Latinos currently living in the United States, 77 percent live in the seven U.S. states that have a Hispanic population of 1 million or more (California, Texas, New York, Florida, Illinois, Arizona, and New Jersey). Still further, while Hispanics represented 42 percent of New Mexico's total population, the highest percentage of any state, some counties in North Carolina, Georgia, Iowa, Arkansas, Minnesota, and Nebraska are between 6 and 25 percent Hispanic.[13] Table 12.2 presents the 25 largest U.S. Hispanic markets, the Hispanic population of each, and the Hispanic percentage of the total residents of that market.

This subcultural group can be considered as a single market, based on a common language and culture, or as separate subcultural markets that correspond to different Hispanic countries of origin. There are 12 Hispanic subgroups identified in the United States. The three largest Hispanic subcultural groups consist of Mexican Americans (about 67 percent of total Hispanic Americans), Puerto Ricans (approximately 8 percent of the total), and Cubans (about 4 percent of the total). These subcultures are heavily concentrated geographically, with more than 70 percent of their members residing in California, Texas, New York, and Florida; Los Angeles alone is home to one-fifth of the Hispanic population of the United States. Also, whereas more than 60 percent of all Mexican Americans (the largest Hispanic group) were born in the United States, 72 percent of Cuban Americans were born in Cuba. Figure 12.3 presents the U.S. Hispanic population by place of origin.[14]

Understanding Hispanic Consumer Behavior

Available evidence indicates that Hispanic and Anglo consumers differ in terms of a variety of important buyer behavior variables. For instance, Hispanic consumers have a strong preference for well-established brands and traditionally prefer to shop at smaller stores. Recently, though, "as Hispanics become more acculturated, there is less evidence of brand loyalty."[15] And in the New York metropolitan area, for example, Hispanic consumers spend a substantial portion of their food budgets in *bodegas* (relatively small food specialty stores), despite the fact that supermarket prices generally are lower. Table 12.3 presents these and other distinctive characteristics of the overall Hispanic market.

Although mindful of their tradition, Hispanic Americans, like other major subcultural groups, are a dynamic and evolving portion of the overall society. For this reason, a growing number of Hispanic consumers are shifting their food shopping to nonethnic, large, American-style supermarkets. They appear to be engaged in a process of acculturation; that is, they are gradually adopting the consumption patterns of the majority of U.S. consumers. Similarly, when it

TABLE 12.2 Top 25 U.S. Hispanic Markets

RANK	MARKET	AREA POPULATION	% OF TOTAL
1	Los Angeles	8,507,000	48.1
2	New York	4,434,700	21.1
3	Miami	2,152,300	49.2
4	Houston	2,064,300	34.5
5	Chicago	1,972,700	20.3
6	Dallas-Fort Worth	1,757,500	25.9
7	San Francisco	1,712,300	23.7
8	Phoenix	1,378,200	27.4
9	San Antonio, Texas	1,259,400	54.6
10	McAllen, Texas	1,153,200	96.5
11	San Diego	998,200	33.1
12	Fresno-Visalia, Calif.	982,300	51.3
13	Sacramento	886,100	23.4
14	El Paso, Texas	817,200	85.9
15	Denver	791,000	20.8
16	Albuquerque, N.M.	767,600	45.0
17	Washington	688,600	11.1
18	Philadelphia	626,500	7.9
19	Atlanta	623,500	10.1
20	Las Vegas	532,500	28.5
21	Orlando, Fla.	529,600	14.8
22	Tampa, Fla.	521,200	12.0
23	Austin, Texas	496,600	29.6
24	Boston	465,100	7.3
25	Tucson, Ariz. (Nogales)	442,500	38.3

Source: "2008 Hispanic Fact Pack," A Supplement to *Advertising Age*, (July 28, 2008): 48.

comes to clothes shopping, Hispanic youths are more fashion conscious and are more likely to seek out and be loyal to well-known brands and to generally like the act of shopping more than their non-Hispanic counterparts.[16] Interestingly, a recent study found that female Hispanic high school students show a significantly higher need for uniqueness than female non-Hispanic students. As a consequence, marketers might try to reach this group with advertising appeals based on the notions of nonconformity, independence, and/or a departure from both family and non-Hispanic peers.[17] While more than 60 percent of Hispanic Americans have a desktop computer at home (as compared to more than 80 percent of U.S. households), the number of Hispanic households with computers with Internet access has been increasing annually.[18] In fact, 78 percent of English-dominant Hispanics and 76 percent of bilingual Hispanics are Internet users,

FIGURE 12.3
U.S. Hispanic Population by Place of Origin
Source: "2008 Hispanic Fact Pack," A Supplement to *Advertising Age*, (July 28, 2008): 49.

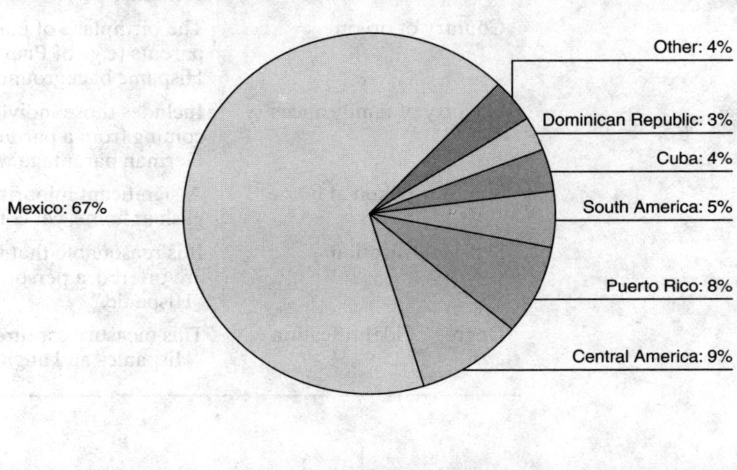

TABLE 12.3 Traditional Characteristics of the Hispanic American Market

Prefer well-known or familiar brands
Buy brands perceived to be more prestigious
Are fashion conscious
Historically prefer to shop at smaller personal stores
Buy brands advertised by their ethnic-group stores
Tend not to be impulse buyers (i.e., are deliberate)
Increasingly clipping and using cents-off coupons
Likely to buy what their parents bought
Prefer fresh to frozen or prepared items
Tend to be negative about marketing practices and government intervention in business

compared to only 32 percent of Spanish-dominant Hispanic adults.[19] Perhaps one of the reasons why Mattel has introduced a Spanish-language "Barbie" site targeted to young girls (**www.barbielatina.com**) is because of the increasing number of Hispanic households with personal computers and Internet connections.[20] At present, approximately "80 percent of online Hispanics have broadband access and 44 percent have wireless access to the Web," and a recent study reported that Hispanics prefer "web content that reflects the culture of their country of origin."[21] Still further, Hispanic American consumers are more likely than non-Hispanics to use their cell phones for purposes other than normal voice calls (e.g., 28.6 percent of Hispanics send photos or videos with their mobile phones, versus 15.3 percent of the general population).[22]

Defining and Segmenting the Hispanic Market

Marketers who are targeting the diversity within the Hispanic subculture are concerned with finding the best ways to define and segment this subculture. In terms of definition, Table 12.4 presents six variables marketers have used to determine who is a Hispanic. Of these measures, the combination of *self-identification* and *degree of identification* are particularly appealing, because they permit consumers to define or label themselves. Research shows that those who strongly identify with being Hispanic (*Strong Hispanic Identifiers*) are more frequent users of Spanish-language media, are more brand loyal, are more likely to buy prestige brands, are more likely to seek the advice of another and to more often be influenced by friends or family, and are more likely to buy brands advertised to Hispanics than *Weak Hispanic Identifiers.*[23] This pattern suggests that the degree of Hispanic identification is a useful segmentation variable.

TABLE 12.4 Ways in Which "Hispanic" Has Been Defined

NAME OF INDICATOR	NATURE/SCOPE AND COMMENTARY
Spanish surname	Not definitive; since a non-Hispanic person might have a Spanish surname, or a Hispanic person might have a non-Spanish surname.
Country of origin	The birthplace of persons born in the United States of Hispanic parents (e.g., of Puerto Rican parentage) would not reveal their Hispanic background.
Country of family ancestry	Includes those individuals who may not be Hispanic despite coming from a particular Spanish/Latin country (e.g., people of German parentage who may be brought up in a Latin country).
Spanish spoken at home	A significant minority of Hispanic households may speak English at home, yet consider themselves to be culturally Hispanic.
Self-identification	It is reasonable that if an adequate number of self-report choices are offered, a person might identify himself or herself as "Hispanic."
Degree of identification	This measure captures the "degree" of personal identification as "Hispanic" and augments the self-identification measure.

Some marketers feel that it is worthwhile to target each Hispanic American market separately. Other marketers, especially larger marketers, have been targeting the Hispanic market as a single market, using Spanish-language mass media. For instance, to cater to the Hispanic market, Toyota has a Spanish-language Web site (**www.toyota.com/español**), and in 2007 AT&T spent over $12 million advertising on Spanish-language Web sites.[24] And in 2008, Ford's Flex, a crossover vehicle, starred in Telemundo's 22-episode mini-novela *Amorres de Luna*. Ford's message was aimed at a new type of Hispanic consumer known as the *Nuevo Latino*, a 30- to 39-year-old bicultural consumer who lives up to traditional Hispanic norms but also embraces more contemporary attitudes.[25] Still further, many Hispanics are moving upscale; indeed, almost 4 million Hispanic Americans have annual incomes of $75,000 or more.[26]

While the Spanish language is often regarded as the bridge that links the various Hispanic subcultures, nevertheless, available research indicates that Hispanic Americans tend to spend the most time with mass media in the first language that they learn to speak. So those whose first language is Spanish tend to prefer TV, radio, magazines, and newspapers in Spanish (see Figure 12.4).[27]

FIGURE 12.4

Source: Courtesy Days Inn/Wyndham.

QUESTION: *Why Is Days Inn Running Ads in Spanish, and Who Are the Consumers Targeted by Such Ads?*

TABLE 12.5 Demographic Characteristics of U.S. Hispanic Ethnicity Types

	A-SYMBOLIC (%)	SYMBOLIC (%)	STRONG (%)	WEAK (%)
Gender				
Female	45	52	50	46
Male	55	48	50	54
Age				
18–20	11	12	6	16
21–24	10	7	12	9
25–34	28	35	29	28
35–49	30	23	31	28
50+	21	23	22	19
Refused	0	0	0	0
Marital status				
Single	31	45	29	35
Married	59	42	56	52
Divorced	8	13	12	10
Refused	2	0	3	3
Educational level				
Elementary	10	3	11	9
Jr. high	13	23	18	22
Some high school	15	29	16	18
Sr. high	19	23	17	20
Some college/junior college	15	10	13	13
College graduate	14	10	12	9
Postgraduate work	5	0	2	3
Technical/trade school	2	0	2	2
No formal schooling	1	2	1	1
Refused	6	0	8	3
Income level				
Less than 10K	6	13	11	10
10K–20K	15	16	11	15
21K–30K	15	19	10	18
31K–40K	10	10	12	9
41K–50K	6	10	8	6
51K–75K	10	7	8	4
76K–100K	5	0	6	2
Over 100K	2	2	2	2
Refused	31	23	32	34

Source: Richardo Villarreal and Robert A. Peterson, "Hispanic Ethnicity and Media Behavior," *Journal of Advertising Research* (June 2008): 183.

Over the years there have been a number of efforts to segment the Hispanic American market. In particular, a recent study segmented the Hispanic market based on the strength of their ethnic identify and family ties.[28] Specifically, while both of these variables are continuous in nature, the researchers were nevertheless able to develop a two-by-two matrix consisting of high versus low ethnic identity and high versus low familism (the strength of the family unit), and then to use this matrix as a basis to segment the Hispanic market, and to examine the media preferences of each of the four Hispanic consumer segments. Results of the study reveal that the four segments can be defined as follows: (1) *"A-Symbolic" Hispanic* (i.e., 24 percent of the sample who have relatively "weak" Hispanic identify but a high degree of familism; (2) *"Symbolic" Hispanic* (i.e., 4 percent of the sample who have the "strongest" ethnic identity and the "lowest" level of familism; (3) *"Strong" Hispanic*, (i.e., 36 percent of the sample who have the "highest" degree of familism and the "second-highest" ethnic identity; and (4) *"Weak" Hispanic*, also 36 percent of the sample, who have the "second-weakest" ethnic identity strength and the "second-lowest" degree of familism.[29] Table 12.5 presents a demographic profile of these U.S. Hispanic ethnicity types, and Figure 12.5 presents an illustrative media decision matrix for reaching these four consumer segments. For example, because Symbolic Hispanics are particularly influenced by the strength of their ethnic identity, it is appropriate to communicate with them by focusing on this identity; whereas those in the Weak Hispanics segement exhibit low ethnic identity and low familism, a message based on one or both of these factors should have little to do with determining a consumer's media behavior.

FIGURE 12.5
Decision Matrix for Reaching Hispanic Consumer Segments
Source: Richardo Villarreal and Robert A. Peterson, "Hispanic Ethnicity and Media Behavior," *Journal of Advertising Research* (June 2008): 183.

Decision Variables	Hispanicness Segments							
	Symbolic Hispanics				Strong Hispanics			
Advertising Context	Ethnic Identity (High)		Familism (Low)		Ethnic Identity (High)		Familism (Low)	
Advertisement Language	Spanish	English	Spanish	English	Spanish	English	Spanish	English
Broadcast Media	Yes	Yes	No	No	Yes	Yes	Yes	Yes
Print Media	Yes	Yes	No	No	Yes	Yes	Yes	Yes
	Weak Hispanics				A-Symbolic Hispanics			
Advertising Context	Ethnic Identity (Low)		Familism (High)		Ethnic Identity (Low)		Familism (High)	
Advertisement Language	Spanish	English	Spanish	English	Spanish	English	Spanish	English
Broadcast Media	?	?	?	?	No	No	Yes	Yes
Print Media	?	?	?	?	Yes	No	Yes	Yes

Religious Subcultures

LEARNING OBJECTIVE

12.3 *To Understand Religious Affiliation as a Subcultural Influence on Consumer Behavior.*

The United States alone reportedly has more than 200 different organized **religious subcultures**. Of this number, Protestant denominations, Roman Catholicism, Islam, and Judaism are the principal organized religious faiths. The members of all these religious groups at times are likely to make purchase decisions that are influenced by their religious identity. Commonly, consumer behavior is directly affected by religion in terms of products that are *symbolically* and *ritualistically* associated with the celebration of various religious holidays. For example, Christmas has become the major gift-purchasing season of the year.

While there is very little consumer research that focuses on religion, there are several recent studies that examine aspects of consumers' religion and their consumer behavior. First, consider born-again Christians—they are the fastest-growing religious affiliation in America (i.e., they make up about 72 million of the 235 million Christians in the United States). Moreover, born-again Christians are generally defined as individuals "who follow literal interpretations of the Bible and acknowledge being born again through religious conversion." From a marketer's perspective, born-again Christians tend to be fiercely loyal to a brand that supports their causes and viewpoint.[30]

A second recent study focusing on American Jews (there are about 6.7 million Jewish people living in the United States) found no significant differences with respect to brand loyalty and word of mouth between American Jews and non-Jews. However, the research did discover that the higher the degree of acculturation, the less likely a Jewish consumer would rely on word of mouth and the less likely he or she would be brand loyal.[31] Therefore, we would expect that more observant Jews would be more likely to engage in word of mouth and be more brand loyal. It would be interesting to see whether future research suggests that there is a general link between being observant or orthodox and a tendency to engage in more word of mouth and to also be more brand loyal.

Religious requirements or practices sometimes take on an expanded meaning beyond their original purpose. For instance, dietary laws for an observant Jewish family represent an obligation, so there are toothpastes and artificial sweeteners that are kosher for Passover. The *U* and *K* marks on food packaging are symbols that the food meets Jewish dietary laws. For nonobservant Jews and an increasing number of non-Jews, however, these marks often signify that the food is pure and wholesome—a kind of "Jewish *Good Housekeeping* Seal of Approval." In response to the broader meaning given to kosher-certified products, a number of national brands, such as Coors beer and Pepperidge Farm cookies, have secured kosher certification for their products. Indeed, most kosher food is consumed by non-Jews.[32] A kosher Manhattan steak house, the Prime Grill, claims that about half of its clientele are non-Jews, and that its success is based on the fact that it has a fine dining menu (without "Jewish types of food") that "just happens to be kosher."[33] Packaging and print ads for food items that are kosher often display a *K* or a *U* inside a circle and sometimes the word *parve.* This word tells the shopper that the product is kosher and that it can be eaten with either meat or dairy products (but not both). Targeting specific religious groups with specially designed marketing programs can be really profitable. For instance, the Shaklee Corporation, a multilevel marketer of the Shaklee Performance drink mix, recruits salespeople from a variety of different religious groups (e.g., Hasidic Jews, Amish, and Mennonites) to sell its products to members of their communities.[34] It is likely that such shared religious identity and membership aid a salesperson in his or her effort to communicate with and persuade potential customers.

Geographic and Regional Subcultures

LEARNING OBJECTIVE

12.4 *To Understand Geographic and Regional Residences as Subcultural Influences on Consumer Behavior.*

The United States, for example, is a large country, one that includes a wide range of climatic and geographic conditions. Given the country's size and physical diversity, it is only natural that many Americans have a sense of **regional** identification and use this identification as a way of describing themselves and others (such as "he is a true Southerner"). These labels often assist us in developing a mental picture and supporting a *stereotype* of the person in question.

Anyone who has traveled across the United States has probably noted many regional differences in consumption behavior, especially when it comes to food and drink. For example, a *mug* of black coffee typifies the West, while a *cup* of coffee with milk and sugar is preferred in the East. There also are **geographic** differences in the consumption of staple foods, such as bread. Specifically, in the South and Midwest, soft white bread is preferred, whereas on the East

TABLE 12.6 Product Purchase/Usage by Leading Metropolitan Market

PRODUCT PURCHASE/USAGE	HIGHEST PURCHASE/USAGE	LOWEST PURCHASE/USAGE
Mouth wash	Atlanta	Los Angeles
Hair growth product	Philadelphia	Detroit
Massage past 6 months	San Francisco	Boston
Artificial sweeteners	Dallas	Los Angeles
Energy drinks	Chicago	New York
Car rental for personal use	Washington, D.C.	Philadelphia
Frozen yogurt	New York	Dallas
Pretzels	Philadelphia	Los Angeles
Frozen pizza	Boston	Los Angeles
Infant cereal	Dallas	Detroit
Attend adult education course	Boston	Atlanta
Baking	Detroit	Los Angeles
Board games	Chicago	San Francisco
Go to museum	Washington, D.C.	Atlanta
Play bingo	Philadelphia	Dallas
Video games	Detroit	San Francisco
Make a speech	Chicago	Los Angeles
Recycle products	San Francisco	Atlanta
Attend movies once or more a week	Detroit	Boston
Baseball, watch TV	Boston	Los Angeles
Own a bowling ball	Detroit	Los Angeles

Source: Doublebase Mediamark Research, Inc. *2007 Doublebase Report*. All rights reserved by Mediamark. Reprinted by permission.

and West coasts, firmer breads (rye, whole wheat, and French and Italian breads) are favored. Regional differences also include brand preferences. Why do you suppose Skippy is the best-selling brand of peanut butter on both the East and West coasts, while Peter Pan sells best in the South and Jif sells best in the Midwest?[35]

Consumer research studies document regional differences in consumption patterns. For instance, Table 12.6 illustrates that differences in product purchase, ownership, or usage levels occur between major metropolitan areas. This distribution helps redefine local markets in terms of specific urban lifestyles. Still further, Table 12.7 reveals that New York leads the United States, 10 largest markets when it comes to ordering by catalog, mail order, telephone, and Internet from the Home Shopping Network. An examination of this table and the other evidence presented here supports marketers who argue that it is important to take geographic consumption patterns into account when planning marketing and promotional efforts.

In general, large metropolitan areas, with a substantial number of affluent middle-age households, dominate many, but not all, consumer-spending categories. Two examples are the San Jose, California, metro area, which leads in apparel purchasing, and Nassau-Suffolk counties in New York, which lead in purchasing of insurance and pension programs.[36]

Exactly what is a *national brand?* The simplest definition might be to consider a national brand as a brand that is available in all 50 U.S. states. But marketers can get themselves into trouble if they fail to realize that the sales and market shares of national brands can vary widely from one geographic region to another. As a recent research study noted, "Comments confirm that practitioners are well aware of the striking geographic differences in performance that many brands face across U.S. markets." Still further, a beer company Web site states that "The U.S. beer market operates as a series of smaller, very different markets, and that the company uses a marketing strategy tailored to the different conditions of each market."[37] These differences in market share across geographic markets may be the result of such factors as the common marketing practice of putting more merchandising dollars behind markets that sell more.[38] Still further, the availability of scanner data has allowed marketers to reallocate

TABLE 12.7 Leading Metropolitan Markets in Terms of Ordering Anything by Catalog, Mail Order, Telephone, and Internet from the Home Shopping Network During the Past 12 Months

MARKET	U.S. AVERAGE $$$ = 100
New York	197
Detroit	173
Philadelphia	149
Chicago	140
Washington, D.C.	129
Atlanta	96
Boston	69
San Francisco	68
Los Angeles	66
Dallas–Fort Worth	62

Source: Doublebase Mediamark Research, Inc. *2007 Doublebase Report*.

resources (e.g., moving inventory around the country and shifting ad expenditures) geographically in order to increase the profitability of their brands.[39]

While geographic differences in sales and market share are common for many brands of consumer packaged goods in large nations, brands in nations that are smaller in geographic area, such as France, often do not exhibit similar regional differences.[40] However, other nations do exhibit different types of geographic or regional differences, such as a study conducted in Mainland China that found that urban children were more skeptical toward advertising than rural children.[41] Table 12.8 presents the differences between the favorite products of rural Chinese consumers versus the favorite products of urban Chinese consumers. Note, for example, how rural consumers favor food as their favorite product by an 8 to 1 margin, while urban consumers consider their computers as their favorite product by a 15 to 0 score.[42] Still further, as a study of diversity in India noted:[43]

> Consumer behavior has been found to be affected by regional differences that come out of various geographic, topological and cultural factors including values, motives and life style. These give rise to distinct subcultures and can be an important determinant of both consumption and non-consumption behaviors.

Racial Subcultures

LEARNING OBJECTIVE

12.5 *To Understand Racial Identity as a Subcultural Influence on Consumer Behavior.*

The major **racial subcultures** in the United States are Caucasian, African American, Asian American, and American Indian. Although differences in lifestyles and consumer-spending patterns exist among these groups, the vast majority of racially oriented consumer research has focused on consumer differences between African Americans and Caucasians. More recently, particular research attention has been given to Asian American consumers.

THE AFRICAN AMERICAN CONSUMER

The U.S. Census Bureau estimates the African American population of the United States to be 38.9 million people in 2009, 40 million in 2010, and 70 million by 2050. This represents approximately 13 percent of the U.S. population.[44] While the overall U.S. population grew 20.9 percent between 1990 and 2007; the African American population in the United States grew by 26.8 percent, and is expected to grow an additional 6.7 percent between 2007 and 2012.[45] As such, **African American consumers** currently constitute the second largest minority in the United States. With a purchasing power estimated at $845 billion in 2007 and expected to break the $1 trillion mark by 2012, over 2 million African American households have annual incomes

TABLE 12.8 Mainland Chinese Consumers' Favorite Products

PRODUCT TYPES	RURAL CONSUMERS	URBAN CONSUMERS
Functional		
Food (rice, tea, etc.)	8	1
House/apartment	4	8
Bicycle	3	0
Bed	2	1
Cell phone	1	1
Clothes	0	1
Furniture/appliances	0	2
Total	18	14
Entertainment		
TV/DVD	10	11
Computer	0	15
Camera	0	1
Hobby (fishing gear, tea sets)	0	2
Total	10	29
Memento		
Personal		
Jewelry	2	1
Posters (NBA team)	1	0
Photographs	2	3
Toy	0	1
Political	1	0
Total	6	5
Hedonic		
Motorcycle	1	0
Pet	3	1
Artwork	0	2
Books and calligraphy	4	2
Total	7	5
Nothing	12	5
Total	53	58

Source: Francis Piron, "China's Changing Culture: Rural and Urban Consumers' Favorite Things," *Journal of Consumer Marketing*, 23, no. 6 (2006): 329.

over $75,000.[46] Still further, more than half of African American consumers are less than 35 years of age.[47] However, this important subcultural grouping is frequently portrayed as a single, undifferentiated African American market, consisting of consumers who have a uniform set of consumer needs. In reality they are a diverse group, consisting of numerous subgroups, each with distinctive backgrounds, needs, interests, and opinions. For example, in addition to the African Americans who have been in the United States for many generations, there are Caribbean Americans, from such islands as Jamaica and Haiti, who have recently immigrated to the United States.[48] Therefore, just as the white majority consist of a variety of market segments, each with its own distinctive needs and tastes, so, too, can the African American market be segmented. Still further, the five U.S. states with the highest population percentage of African Americans are Mississippi (37 percent), Louisiana (33 percent), Georgia (30 percent), Maryland (30 percent), and South Carolina (29 percent), and Washington, D.C.'s African American population is 55 percent.[49] Table 12.9 provides information on the top 10 African American/ Black markets in the United States.

TABLE 12.9 Top 10 African American/Black Markets

	GENERAL MARKET RANK	AA/B POPULATION (000)	PERCENT OF TOTAL U.S. AA/B POPULATION	PERCENT AA/B OF TOTAL MARKET POPULATION
New York	1	4,021	9.9%	19.0%
Chicago	3	1,906	4.7	19.4
Atlanta	9	1,614	4.0	28.7
Washington, D.C.	8	1,552	3.8	25.8
Philadelphia	4	1,542	3.8	19.7
Los Angeles	2	1,458	3.6	8.1
Detroit	11	1,200	3.0	23.4
Miami	15	1,011	2.5	22.9
Houston	10	983	2.4	17.3
Dallas	6	935	2.3	14.4
Total		**16,222**	**40.0**	**19.9**

AA/B = African-American/Black.

Source: "African-American/Black Market Profile 2008," *Magazine Publishers of America*, 8, accessed at www.magazine.org/marketprofiles.

Consumer Behavior Characteristics of African American Consumers

Although there are many similarities between African Americans and the rest of America in terms of consumer behavior, there are also some meaningful differences in terms of product preferences and brand purchase patterns. African American consumers tend to prefer popular or leading brands, are brand loyal, and are unlikely to purchase private-label and generic products. One study, for example, found that almost two-thirds of African Americans are willing to pay more to get "the best," even if the brand or product is not widely recognized (only 51 percent of whites were reported to feel this way), and African Americans have been reported to buy high fashions and name brands "as signals of their success."[50] Still further, African American consumers tend to make more trips during the course of a week to the grocery store (2.2 trips versus 1.8 trips for the average shopper), and they also spend more per week ($94 versus $85 for the average shopper) than other consumers.[51] With respect to the businesses that African Americans patronize, Radio One's study ("Black America Today") found that 64 percent favor businesses that give back to the Black Community, 49 percent prefer buying brands that are respectful of the Black culture, and 33 percent favor brands that are popular with their culture.[52]

African Americans account for over 30 percent of spending in the $4 billion hair care market, and they spend more on telephone services than any other consumer segment. Still further, they spend an average of $1,427 annually on clothing for themselves, which is $458 more than all U.S. consumers.[53] Similarly, African American teens spend more on clothing and video games than all U.S. teens. Table 12.10 compares total U.S. teens to African American/Black teens with respect to the median dollars spent in the past year on selected product categories. The table suggests that for every product category, African American teens spend more on average than the total U.S. teen market. Also, the research indicated for all product categories that African Americans were more brand loyal than the total U.S. teen market.[54]

Some meaningful differences exist among Anglo-White, African American, and Hispanic American consumers in the purchase, ownership, and use of a diverse group of products (see Table 12.11). For marketers, these findings confirm the wisdom of targeting racial market segments. In other research, focusing on segmenting the African American market, Radio One's 2008 research report "Black America Today" identifies some 11 segments for characterizing the African American market.[55] For example, there is the "Black Is Better" segment who shops in drugstores, convenience stores, and price clubs monthly, whereas the "New Middle Class" segment spends more than the other African American segments in terms of shopping on the Internet.[56]

TABLE 12.10 The African American/Black Teen Market Versus All U.S. Teens

MEDIAN DOLLARS SPENT IN THE PAST 12 MONTHS	TOTAL U.S. TEENS	AA/B TEENS
Clothing	$219	$258
Video Game Hardware	219	260
PC Software	114	123
Casual/Leisure Shoes	57	70
STRONG INFLUENCE ON HOUSEHOLD PURCHASE DECISION		
Male Teens	**Total U.S.**	**AA/B**
Athletic Shoes	39.8%	43.6%
Cereal	28.8	36.6
Fast Food (from restaurants)	29.3	34.4
Toothpaste	22.4	28.9
Female Teens		
Hand & Body Cream/Lotion/Oil	37.8%	43.0%
Cell Phones	34.8	41.4
Ice Cream	28.5	36.6
DVDs/Video Tapes	27.0	35.7
BRAND LOYAL—BOUGHT SAME BRAND LAST THREE TIMES		
Male Teens	**Total U.S.**	**AA/B**
Body Soap (liquid or bar)	35.5%	43.2%
Sneakers/Athletic Shoes	35.6	41.6
Potato Chips	35.3	41.0
Bottled Water	28.9	33.5
Female Teens		
Soda	55.6%	60.3%
Hair Styling Products	40.0	54.2
Cookies	28.6	43.6
Nail Polish	21.1	28.0

Source: "African-American/Black Market Profile 2008," *Magazine Publishers of America*, 11, accessed at www.magazine.org/marketprofiles (based on data from Mediamark Research and Intelligence, Teenmark, 2007).

Reaching the African American Audience

A question of central importance to marketers is how to best reach *African American consumers.* Traditionally, marketers have subscribed to one of two distinct marketing strategies. Some have followed the policy of running all their advertising in general mass media in the belief that African Americans have the same media habits as whites; others have followed the policy of running additional advertising in selected media directed exclusively to African Americans. A recent research study did conclude, though, that "African Americans are more than twice as likely to trust Black media as they are to trust Mainstream media."[57]

Both strategies may be appropriate in specific situations and for specific product categories. For products of very broad appeal (as aspirin or toothpaste), it is possible that the mass media (primarily television) may effectively reach all relevant consumers, including African American and white. For other products (such as personal grooming products or food products), marketers may find that mass media do not communicate effectively with the African American market.

Because the media habits of African American consumers differ from those of the general population, media specifically targeted to African Americans are likely to be more effective. Furthermore, other research reveals that African American adults tend to place a great deal of trust in African American–centric media (i.e., black magazines, black TV news, black-owned

TABLE 12.11 Comparison of Purchase Patterns of Anglo-White, African American, and Hispanic American Households

PRODUCT/ACTIVITY	ANGLO-WHITE	AFRICAN AMERICAN	HISPANIC AMERICAN
Breath fresheners	95*	128	105
Body powder	93	157	99
Massage/last 6 months	105	70	80
Chewing gum	96	117	113
Ready to drink ice tea	90	149	121
Car rental—business use	96	127	78
Own luggage	108	74	67
Frozen main course	108	87	72
Play bingo	102	111	91
Raising tropical fish	103	107	72
Religious club member	105	107	65
Attend a movies 2–3 times a month	93	118	132
Basketball, participate	89	165	102
Bicycling—mountain, participate	113	36	80
Fishing—freshwater, participate	115	50	52
Martial arts, participate	90	138	105
Bowling, attend	102	116	74
Own a hand gun	119	31	52
Foreign travel for personal reasons	90	74	137
Foreign travel for vacation or honeymoon	104	55	99

*These are index numbers. 100 = average for U.S. population.

Source: Mediamark Research and Intelligence. *Doublebase 2007 Report*.

local newspapers, and black radio news) as a source of information about companies and their products.[58] Approximately $400 million of the $1.7 billion spent annually on ads targeted to African Americans is spent on magazine advertising, which includes such publications as *Black Enterprise, Ebony, Essence, Jet,* and *Vibe.*[59] Also, from 2002 to 2006, more than 80 new magazines targeted to African Americans have been launched.[60] Because of the importance of "Black media" to African American consumers, many marketers supplement their general advertising expenditures with ads placed in magazines, newspapers, and other media directed specifically to African Americans (see Figure 12.6).

Still further, Internet usage among African Americans is essentially equal to that of all Americans (68 percent of African Americans are online versus 71 percent of all Americans), and two-thirds of African Americans shop online.[61]

ASIAN AMERICAN CONSUMERS

The **Asian American** population is approximately 14 million in size and is the fastest-growing American minority (on a percentage basis). This fast growing group increased 48 percent during the decade extending from 1990 to 2000, and has increased 9 percent since 2000 (currently constitutes about 5 percent of America's population). There are presently more than 11 million Asian Americans in the United States, and this number is expected to triple to 34 million over the next 50 years.[62] Presently, 64 percent of Asian Americans are immigrants, 23 percent are first generation, and only 13 percent are second generation or above.[63]

According to the 2000 Census, six different ethnicities make up almost 90 percent of the Asian American population: Chinese (2.4 million), Filipinos (1.9 million), Indian (1.7 million), Vietnamese (1.12 million), Korean (1.1 million), and Japanese (797,000).[64] Asian Americans are today the most diverse ethnic group in the United States, and includes the influences of 15 different cultures and a wide range of languages.[65] Consequently, many Asian Americans in the

FIGURE 12.6
Source: © Wisconsin Department of Tourism. Used with permission.

QUESTION: *What Are the Strategic Goals of This Ad?*

United States do not think of themselves as a separate single group, which could explain why relatively few Asian Americans consume ethnic media.[66]

Asian Americans are largely family oriented, highly industrious, and strongly driven to achieve a middle-class lifestyle. They are an attractive market for increasing numbers of marketers. Indeed, in 2005, Asian American families had a median income of $69,159, which is approximately 24 percent higher than the median family income for the entire U.S. population. With respect to occupations, a higher proportion of Asians and Pacific Islanders were concentrated in managerial and professional jobs. Still further, educational attainment is an important goal for this segment of the population. For the Asian American population age 25 and older, 49 percent have earned a bachelor's degree or more.[67] Still further, Asian Americans are younger than the average American—31.6 years of age versus 35.3 years of age.[68]

Where Are the Asian Americans?

Asian Americans are concentrated in neighborhoods situated in and around a small number of large American cities (95 percent live in metropolitan areas). Nearly half of all Asian Americans live in Los Angeles, San Francisco, New York, Honolulu, and Sacramento, and more than 10 percent of California's population is Asian American (which accounts for over one-third of the total U.S. Asian American population). Still further, specifically in the case

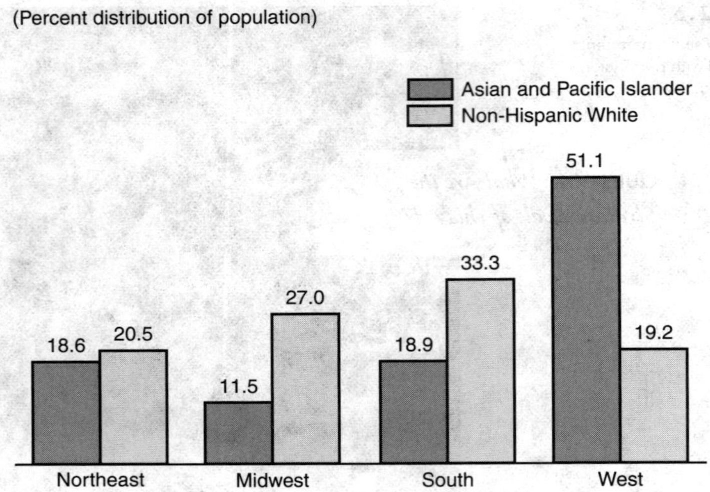

FIGURE 12.7
Region of Residence for Selected Subcultural Groups
Source: U.S. Census Bureau, Annual Demographic Supplement to the March 2002 Current Population Survey, as contained in "The Asian and Pacific Islander Population of the United States: March 2002," *U.S. Census Bureau*, accessed at www.census.gov/prod/2003pubs/p20–540.pdf, 2.

of Asian Indians, the largest Asian American communities are in the Northeast, South, and Midwest; with about 75 percent of this group born outside of the United States.[69]

Also, the stereotypical impression that most Chinese Americans live in a "Chinatown" is incorrect. In reality, most Chinese, as well as most other Asian Americans, do not live in downtown urban areas; they live in the suburb areas surrounding or near to urban areas.[70] Figure 12.7 presents a comparison of region of residence for Asian and Pacific Islanders versus non-Hispanic whites. It is of interest to note that while close to 20 percent of non-Hispanic whites live in the West, slightly more than half of Asians and Pacific Islanders do.

Understanding the Asian American Consumer

U.S. Census Bureau data reveal that more Asian Americans, on a per capita basis, own their own businesses than non–Asian American minorities. Those who do not own their own businesses are largely in professional, technical, or managerial occupations. Additionally, many Asian Americans are young and live a good part of their lives in multi-income households. Asian Americans also tend to be more computer literate than the general population. English-speaking Asian Americans are more likely than other Americans to get their news and information online. Asian Americans who go online also tend to be young. Still further, Asian American households are more likely than Hispanic and African American households to have Internet access.[71] Two general-interest Internet sites, **www.Click2Asia.com** and **www.Asianamericans.com**, are cyberspace communities for Asian Americans.[72] Still further, Asian Americans are much more likely to purchase online than other segments of the U.S. population.

Asian Americans as Consumers

During the decade of the 1990s, the buying power of Asian Americans increased about 125 percent, to over $250 billion, and it is anticipated to reach about $530 billion by 2009.[73] As consumers, Asian Americans value quality (associated quality with well-known upscale brands). This population segment tends to be loyal customers, frequently more male oriented when it comes to consumption decisions, and attracted to retailers that make it known that they welcome Asian American patronage. Table 12.12 lists the top 10 U.S. Asian American markets, including general market rank and percent of total U.S. Asian American population. Note, for example, that while San Francisco is the third largest Asian American market, it is only the 30th largest market in the United States.[74]

It is important to remember that Asian Americans are really drawn from diverse cultural backgrounds. Therefore, although Asian Americans have many similarities, marketers should avoid treating Asian Americans as a single market because they are far from being so homogeneous. For example, Vietnamese Americans are more likely to follow the traditional model, wherein the man makes the decision for large purchases; however, Chinese American husbands and wives are more likely to share in the decision-making process.[75] Vietnamese Americans also frown on credit, because in their culture owing money is viewed negatively. In contrast, Korean Americans and Chinese Americans, many of whom have been in the United States for years, accept credit as the American way.[76] A recent article, though, does mention several Asian

TABLE 12.12 Top U.S. Asian American Markets

DMA'S RANKED BY ASIAN AMERICAN POPULATION	GENERAL MARKET RANK	ASIAN AMERICAN POPULATION* (000)	% ASIAN AMERICAN POPULATION IN DMA	% OF TOTAL U.S. ASIAN AMERICAN POPULATION
Los Angeles	1	2,331	13	17
New York	2	1,578	8	11
San Francisco	30	1,511	22	11
Honolulu	68	860	65	6
Chicago	3	505	8.3	4
Sacramento	35	494	8	4
Washington, D.C.	5	434	8	3
Seattle	19	389	5	3
San Diego	15	360	6	3
Boston	10	339	6	2
Total Top 10 Markets		**5,301**		**64**

Source: "Asian-American Market Profile," *Magazine Publishers of America* (June 2006): 8, accessed at www.magazine.org/marketprofiles.

American youth trends, including the belief among females that the way to stay slim is through self-discipline, and not through fad diets, the desire to be the first to own high-tech gadgets, the addition of Canton Pop artists to MP3 playlists, and a more open-minded attitude toward interracial coupling.[77]

The use of Asian American models in advertising is effective in reaching this market segment. Research reveals that responses to an ad for stereo speakers featuring an Asian model were significantly more positive than responses to the same ad using a Caucasian model.[78] Additionally, the percentage of Asian Americans who prefer advertisements that are not in the English language varies among different Asian American groups. For instance, 93 percent of Vietnamese consumers prefer ad messages in the Vietnamese language, whereas only 42 percent of Japanese Americans prefer ad messages in Japanese.[79] Aware of the increased importance of the Asian American market, Procter & Gamble has named its first Asian American advertising agency, and Wal-Mart has just begun running TV commercials in Mandarin, Cantonese, and Vietnamese, as well as Filipino print ads.[80] In contrast, though, it is important to note that according to the most recent Census, almost 80 percent of Asian Americans speak English "very well," with 20 percent indicating that they speak only English. Figure 12.8 illustrates the percent of Asian Americans who say they speak English.

FIGURE 12.8
Percent of Asian Americans Who Say They Speak English

Source: "Asian-American Market Profile," *Magazine Publishers of America* (June 2006): 9, accessed at www.magazine.org/marketprofiles.

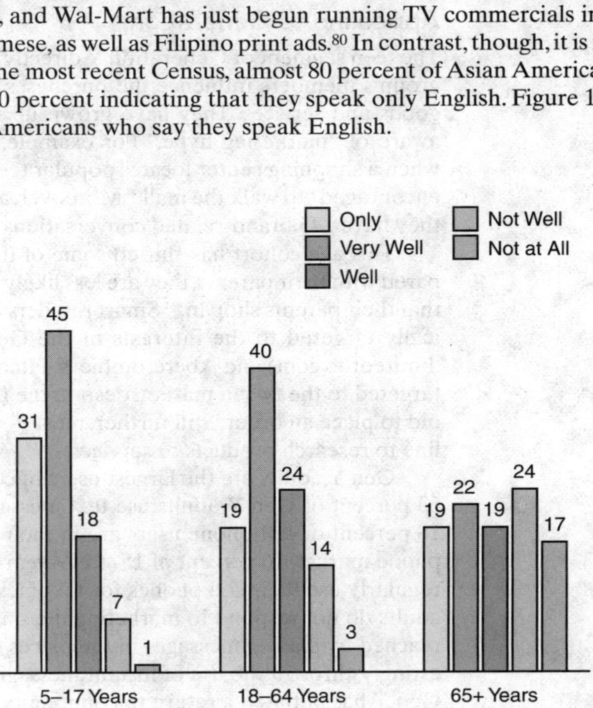

Age Subcultures

Learning Objective

12.6 *To Understand Age as a Subcultural Influence on Consumer Behavior.*

It's not difficult to understand why each major age subgrouping of the population might be thought of as a separate subculture. After all, don't you listen to different music than your parents and grandparents, dress differently, read different magazines, and enjoy different TV shows? Clearly, important shifts occur in an individual's demand for specific types of products and services as he or she goes from being a dependent child to a retired senior citizen. In this chapter, we will limit our examination of **age subcultures** to four age groups, moving from youngest to oldest: **Generation Y**, **Generation X**, **baby boomers**, and seniors. These four age segments have been singled out because their distinctive lifestyles qualify them for consideration as subcultural groups.

THE GENERATION Y MARKET

This age cohort (a cohort is a group of individuals born over a relatively short and continuous period of time) includes somewhere between 80 and 100 million Americans ages 30 and under in 2008. They are the children of baby boomers, and, depending on the source, were born between the years 1977 and 1994, or between 1982 and 2000. Members of Generation Y (also known as "echo boomers" and the "millennium generation") can be divided into three subsegments: Gen Y adults (ages 19–28), Gen Y teens (ages 13–18), and Gen Y kids, or "tweens" (ages 8–12).[81] Keep in mind that while tweens are too young to have been born between 1977 and 1994, they nevertheless are still considered to be part of the Gen Y market.

Clearly, undergraduate college students (18–22 years old) are members of Gen Y. In a recent survey of over 7,000 U.S. college students, researchers found that:[82]

- 97 percent own a computer
- 97 percent have downloaded music and other media using peer-to-peer file sharing
- 94 percent own a cell phone
- 76 percent use instant messaging and social networking sites
- 75 percent have a Facebook profile and most check it daily
- 60 percent own some type of portable music and/or video device, such as an iPod
- 34 percent use Web sites as their primary source of news
- 28 percent author a blog and 44 percent read blogs

Appealing to Generation Y

The teen segment of Generation Y directly spends over $150 billion annually; furthermore, this group's members influence the purchases of their parents for a substantial amount of other goods and services. They have grown up in a media-saturated environment and tend to be aware of "marketing hype." For example, they would tend to immediately understand that when a shopping center locates popular teen stores at opposite ends of the mall they are being encouraged "to walk the mall." Moreover, a recent survey of 13- to 17-year-old teens found that they have 145 brand-related conversations a week, about twice the number for adults.[83]

This age cohort has shifted some of its TV viewing time to the Internet and, when compared with their parents, they are less likely to read newspapers and often do not trust the stores that their parents shop in.[84] Smart retailers have found it profitable to develop Web sites specifically targeted to the interests of the Gen Y consumer. For example, Limited Too (www.limitedtoo.com) and Abercrombie & Fitch (www.abercrombiekids.com) have developed sites targeted to the tween market, despite the fact that a person is supposed to be at least 18 years old to place an order. Still further, most 9- to 17-year-olds are asked by their parents to go online to research products or services.

Gen Y adults are the largest users of cell phone text messaging. A recent study found that 63 percent of Gen Y adults use text messaging, compared with only 31 percent of Gen Xers; 18 percent of cell phone users are in their 40s, and 13 percent are in their 50s. In today's cell phone market, 76 percent of 15- to 19-year-olds and 90 percent of consumers in their early 20s regularly use their cell phones for text messaging, ringtones, and games.[85] Still further, Gen Y adults do not respond to marketing the same way their parents do. They are most likely to be reached by placing messages in the places they frequent, such as online and cable TV.[86] Interestingly, through the use of instant messaging, blogs, chat rooms, social networking, and so on, Gen Y has initiated a return to community, but this time it's "community" in virtual space.[87]

TABLE 12.13 Selected Profile of the Tween Market

- Consists of 8- to 14-year-olds
- Spend and influence $1.18 trillion in purchases worldwide
- They know brand images better than an advertising expert
- Tweens in the United Kingdom, United States, and Australia average seeing 20,000 to 40,000 commercials a year
- Tweens affect their parents' brand choices
  - They may influence up to 80 percent of family brand choices
  - They may have a substantial influence on the final decision in over 60 percent of choices
- They no longer expect to be informed by traditional media (e.g., TV, radio)
- The concept of individual brand loyalty may no longer exist—it is a group decision (i.e., the tween and his or her peers)
- Up to 25 percent of all tweens communicate every week with tweens in other countries
- Almost half of all tweens consider the use of grammatically correct language to be outdated, and prefer TweenSpeak, which combines words, icons, illustrations, and phrases
- Globally, 24 percent of tweens use the Internet as their primary communication tool
- 21 percent of tweens claim that the Internet is the easiest way to find new friends

Source: Adapted from Martin Lindstrom, "Branding Is No Longer Child's Play!" *Journal of Consumer Marketing*, 21, no. 3 (2004): 175–182.

Tweens

In the United States, the 29 million members of the "tween" market (generally considered to consist of 8- to 14-year-olds) spend an average of $1,294 each, for a total of $38 billion. And as an age group, their parents will spend almost $126 billion more on them. It has been estimated that worldwide, 8- to 12-year-olds spend $170 billion, and that "a lot of kids get cell phones in middle school."[88] Still further, in households that include a tween, food purchases account for almost 50 percent of total household spending.[89] Table 12.13 provides some additional information about the tween market. Tweens also visit shopping malls more frequently than any other age group, spending an average of $46.80 per mall visit.[90] At the mall, they are likely to find a branch of Five Below—a retailer that targets the tween customer, tends to sell products priced at $5 or less, and places a Media Center on the back wall of its stores.[91]

What about children too young to be considered tweens? A recent study noted that in the United States children are responsible for more than $30 billion in direct purchases, and indirectly influence over $600 billion in household spending. As a result of this influence, more than $15 billion is being spent annually on advertising to children.[92]

Twixters

Spanning the Gen Y and Gen X markets is a group of 21- to 29-year-olds who continue to live with their parents. Many of them are out of college and have decent jobs and incomes—but they are not moving out to get married, nor are they leaving their parents' home. Over half of these Twixters have graduated from college, and are more then $10,000 in debt. They tend to have trust in their parents and in established institutions, and often do not marry before they reach their 30th birthday. While these individuals cannot afford to purchase "anything that could be considered an asset," they do purchase gadgets and clothes.[93] In fact, twixters claim that they spend more than most people on eating out, clothes, entertainment, computers, and software.[94]

THE GENERATION X MARKET

This age grouping—often referred to as *Xers, busters,* or *slackers*—consists of the almost 50 million individuals born between about 1965 and 1979 (different experts quote different starting and ending years). As consumers, these 31- to 43-year-olds represented $1.4 trillion in spending power in 2004.[95] They do not like labels, are cynical, and do not want to be singled out and marketed to.

Also, unlike their parents, who are frequently baby boomers, they are in no rush to marry, start a family, or work excessive hours to earn high salaries. For Generation X consumers, job satisfaction is typically more important than salary. It has been said, for example, that "Baby Boomers live to work, Gen Xers work to live!" Xers reject the values of older coworkers who may neglect their families while striving to secure higher salaries and career advancement, and many have observed their parents getting laid off after many years of loyalty to an employer. They, therefore, are not particularly interested in long-term employment with a single company but instead prefer to work for a company that can offer some work–life flexibility and can bring some fun aspects into the environment. Gen Xers understand the necessity of money but do not view salary as a sufficient reason for staying with a company—the quality of the work itself and the relationships built on the job are much more important. For Generation X, it is more important to enjoy life and to have a lifestyle that provides freedom and flexibility.

Some additional facts about Generation X are:

- 62 percent are married
- 29.7 million are parents
- 51 percent of children under 18 living at home are in households headed by a Gen Xer
- 31 percent of Gen Xers have earned a college degree
- 81 percent of Gen Xers are employed full-time or part-time
- 37 percent of Gen Xers' mothers worked outside the home when they (as kids) were growing up[96]

Appealing to Generation X

Members of Generation X often pride themselves on their sophistication. Although they are not necessarily materialistic, they do purchase good brand names (such as Sony) but not necessarily designer labels. They want to be recognized by marketers as a group in their own right and not as mini–baby boomers. Therefore, advertisements targeted to this audience must focus on their style in music, fashions, and language. One key for marketers appears to be sincerity. Xers are not against advertising but only opposed to insincerity.

Baby boomer media does not work with Generation X members. For example, while 65 percent of 50- to 64-year-olds, and 55 percent of 30- to 49-year-olds read a newspaper regularly, only 39 percent of younger Xers regularly read a newspaper.[97] Xers are the MTV generation and use the Internet more than any other age cohort. For example, 60 percent of Xers have tried online banking, while only 38 percent of Generation Y has tried online banking.[98]

Hotel chains are also making changes in their offerings in order to better attract the Gen X traveler, the fastest-growing group of hotel patrons. Marriott, for example, is remodeling rooms to include flat-panel LCD TVs, high-speed Internet access, ergonomic desk chairs, and high thread-count sheets.[99] Additionally, Gen Xers are generally dissatisfied with most current shopping malls—they want to do more than just shop. Xers want to be able to eat a proper sit-down meal at the mall, rather than something quick at the food court. They also want to be able to get a cup of coffee while doing work on their laptop, and perhaps also see a movie.[100]

THE BABY BOOMER MARKET

Marketers have found baby boomers a particularly desirable target audience because (1) they are a large distinctive age category; (2) they frequently make important consumer purchase decisions; and (3) they contain small subsegments of trendsetting consumers (sometimes known as yuppies, or young upwardly mobile professionals) who have influence on the consumer tastes of other age segments of society.

Who Are the Baby Boomers?

The term *baby boomers,* refers to the age segment of the population that was born between 1946 and 1964. Thus, baby boomers are in the broad age category that extends from about 45 to 63. These 78 million or so baby boomers represent more than 40 percent of the adult population. The magnitude of this statistic alone would make them a much sought-after market segment. However, they also are valued because they comprise about 50 percent of all those in professional and managerial occupations and more than one-half of those with at least a college degree.

By 2010, fully one-third of all U.S. adults, 97.1 million of them, will be age 50 or older, and the American Association of Retired Persons (AARP) estimates that U.S. consumers in this age bracket own 80 percent of U.S. financial assets. Indeed, in a recent year, consumers 45 and older were responsible for almost 55 percent of total U.S. consumer spending.[101]

Although each year more baby boomers turn 50 years of age, they do not necessarily like the idea. Increases in health club memberships and a boom in the sales of vitamin and health supplements are evidence that these consumers are trying hard to look and feel "young"—they do not want to age gracefully but will fight and kick and pay whatever is necessary to look young. In advertisements they want to be portrayed as they see themselves—lively and attractive.[102] Most important to marketers, who understand them, they have money and they want to spend it on what they feel advances the quality of their lives. And while the AARP and other organizations may label anyone age 50 and over as a "senior," this is a brand that most baby boomers reject.[103]

Consumer Characteristics of Baby Boomers

Baby boomers tend to be motivated consumers. They enjoy buying for themselves, for their homes or apartments, and for others—they are consumption oriented. As baby boomers age, the nature of the products and services they most need or desire changes. For example, because of the aging of this market segment, sales of "relaxed fit" jeans and "lineless" bifocal glasses are up substantially, as is the sales of walking shoes. Men's and women's pants with elastic waistbands are also enjoying strong sales. Moreover, bank marketers and other financial institutions are also paying more attention to assisting boomers who are starting to think about retirement. Even St. Joseph's Aspirin has switched its target from babies to boomers, and Disney has ads to entice baby boomers to vacation at their theme parks without their kids. A recent study dealing with the purchase of luxury goods found that consumers 50 and older were more likely to buy such goods and services in order to beautify their homes, while consumers under the age of 25, in contrast, were more likely to purchase luxury goods and services to self-gift, buy for status reasons, and/or buy on impulse.[104] Still further, it is not true that boomers are set in their ways—they are open-minded and are as willing as younger consumers to try new products and services. Yuppies are by far the most sought-after subgroup of baby boomers. Although constituting only 5 percent of the population, they generally are well off financially, well educated, and in enviable professional or managerial careers. They often are associated with status brand names, such as BMWs or Volvo station wagons, Rolex watches, cable TV, and Cuisinart food processors.

Today, though, as many yuppies are maturing, they are shifting their attention away from expensive status-type possessions to travel, physical fitness, planning for second careers, or some other form of new life directions. Indeed, there has been a move away from wanting possessions, to wanting experiences—"boomers today are more interested in doing things than having things."[105] Still further, boomers are computer literate, with 70 percent of U.S. 55- to 64-year-olds using the Internet (compared, for example, to 11 percent for the same age cohort in Spain).[106]

No Rush into Retirement

Baby boomers are not anxious to retire. They plan to keep working, either full time or part time beyond age 65. While some continue working for the money, most just want to stay active, and/or are even planning, upon retirement, to start new careers.

Studies of baby boomers contemplating retirement have found that they adopt one of four lifestyle postures toward the retirement transition; that is, they see: (1) retirement as an opportunity to make a new start, (2) retirement as a continuation of preretirement lifestyle, (3) retirement as an unwelcome, imposed disruption, and (4) retirement as a transition to old age. While the first two viewpoints are positive toward retirement and are accompanied by an increase in available resources, the other two viewpoints are negative appraisals of retirement and are accompanied by a decrease in available resources. "New start" retirees feel that freedom from working offers them an opportunity to experience new things, while "continuation" retirees direct their energies toward inward-oriented or home-centric activities. "Disrupted" retirees, while having a negative view of retirement, seek outward and activity-oriented pursuits to replace their work role, while "old age" retirees give up their active lifestyle for what they believe to be the final phase of life.[107] Table 3.6 describes segmenting **older consumers** according to these four dimensions.

To sum up, Gen Yers, Gen Xers, and baby boomers differ in their purchasing behavior, attitudes toward brands, and behavior toward ads. Table 12.14 captures some of the differences among these three age cohorts.

TABLE 12.14 Comparison of Selected Age Cohorts Across Marketing-Related Issues

THEMES	GENERATION Y	GENERATION X	BOOMERS
Purchasing behavior	Savvy, pragmatic	Materialistic	Narcissistic
Coming of age technology	Computer in every home	Microwave in every home	TV in every home
Price–quality attitude	Value oriented: weighing price–quality relationships	Price oriented: concerned about the cost of individual items	Conspicuous consumption: buying for indulgence
Attitude toward brands	Brand embracing	Against branding	Brand loyal
Behavior toward ads	Rebel against hype	Rebel against hype	Respond to hype image-building type

Source: MARKETING THEORY: PROCEEDINGS AMA WINTER EDUCATORS' CONFERENCE, 1982 by Stephanie M. Noble. Copyright 2000 by American Marketing Association. Reproduced with permission of American Marketing Association in the format Textbook via Copyright Clearance Center.

OLDER CONSUMERS

America is aging. A portion of the baby boomers have already turned 60, with plenty more to come in the next decade. According to the U.S. Census Bureau (in 2006), there were more than 37 million people in this country who are 65 years of age or older (almost 12.5 percent of the population). Projecting ahead to the year 2050, it is anticipated that there will be more than 88 million Americans (20 percent of the total population) who will be 65 years of age or older.[108] Still further, from the start to the end of the twentieth century, life expectancy in the United States rose from about 47 years to 77 years, and whereas a 65-year-old in 1900 could expect, on average, to live about 12 more years, a 65-year-old in 2002 can expect about 18 more years of life.[109]

It should also be kept in mind that "later adulthood" (i.e., those who are 50 years of age or older) is the longest adult life stage for most consumers (i.e., often 29 or more years in duration). This is in contrast to "early adulthood" (i.e., those who are 18 to 34 years of age), a stage lasting 16 years, and "middle adulthood" (i.e., those who are 35 to 49 years of age), a stage lasting 14 years. Remember that people over age 50 comprise about one-third of the adult U.S. market.

Although some people think of older consumers as consisting of people without substantial financial resources, in generally poor health, and with plenty of free time on their hands, the fact is that more than 30 percent of men and more than 20 percent of women aged 65 to 69 are employed, as are 19 percent of men and 12 percent of women aged 70 to 74. Additionally, millions of seniors are involved in the daily care of a grandchild, and many do volunteer work. The annual discretionary income of this group amounts to 50 percent of the discretionary income of the United States, and these older consumers spend $200 billion a year on major purchases such as luxury cars, alcohol, vacations, and financial products. Americans over 65 now control about 70 percent of the net worth of American households.[110]

Defining "Older" in Older Consumer

Driving the growth of the elderly population are three factors: the declining birthrate, the aging of the huge baby boomer segment, and improved medical diagnoses and treatment. In the United States, "old age" is officially assumed to begin with a person's 65th birthday (or when the individual qualifies for full Social Security and Medicare). However, people over age 60 tend to view themselves as being 15 years younger than their chronological age.

It is generally accepted that people's perceptions of their ages are more important in determining behavior than their chronological ages (or the number of years lived). In fact, people may at the same time have a number of different perceived or **cognitive ages**. Specifically, elderly consumers perceive themselves to be younger than their chronological ages on four perceived age dimensions: *feel age* (how old they feel); *look age* (how old they look); *do age* (how involved they are in activities favored by members of a specific age group); and *interest age* (how similar their interests are to those of members of a specific age group).[111] The results support other research that indicates that elderly consumers are more likely to consider themselves younger (to have a younger cognitive age) than their chronological age.

For marketers, these findings underscore the importance of looking beyond chronological age to perceived or cognitive age when appealing to mature consumers and to the possibility that cognitive age might be used to segment the mature market.[112]

Segmenting the Elderly Market

The elderly are by no means a homogeneous subcultural group. There are those who, as a matter of choice, do not have color TVs or touch-tone telephone service, whereas others have the latest desktop computers and spend their time surfing the Internet (cyberseniors will be discussed later in this section).

One consumer gerontologist has suggested that the elderly are more diverse in interests, opinions, and actions than other segments of the adult population.[113] Although this view runs counter to the popular myth that the elderly are uniform in terms of attitudes and lifestyles, both gerontologists and market researchers have repeatedly demonstrated that age is not necessarily a major factor in determining how older consumers respond to marketing activities.

With an increased appreciation that the elderly constitute a diverse age segment, more attention is now being given to identifying ways to segment the elderly into meaningful groupings. One relatively simple segmentation scheme partitions the elderly into three chronological age categories: the *young-old* (65 to 74 years of age); the *old* (those 75 to 84); and the *old-old* (those 85 years of age and older). This market segmentation approach provides useful consumer-relevant insights.

The elderly can also be segmented in terms of motivations and *quality-of-life orientation.* Table 12.15 presents a side-by-side comparison of *new-age elderly* consumers and the more *traditional older* consumers. The increased presence of the new-age elderly suggests that marketers need to respond to the value orientations of older consumers whose lifestyles remain relatively ageless. Clearly, the new-age elderly are individuals who feel, think, and do according to a cognitive age that is younger than their chronological age. All this suggests the declining importance of chronological age, and increasing importance of perceived or cognitive age as an indicator of the "aging experience" and age-related quality of life.

TABLE 12.15 Comparison of New-Age and Traditional Elderly

NEW-AGE ELDERLY	TRADITIONAL/STEREOTYPICAL ELDERLY
• Perceive themselves to be different in outlook from other people their age	• Perceive all older people to be about the same in outlook
• Age is seen as a state of mind	• See age as more of a physical state
• See themselves as younger than their chronological age	• See themselves at or near their chronological age
• Feel younger, think younger, and "do" younger	• Tend to feel, think, and do things that they feel match their chronological age
• Have a genuinely youthful outlook	• Feel that one should act one's age
• Feel there is a considerable adventure to living	• Feel life should be dependable and routine
• Feel more in control of their own lives	• Normal sense of being in control of their own lives
• Have greater self-confidence when it comes to making consumer decisions	• Normal range of self-confidence when it comes to making consumer decisions
• Less concerned that they will make a mistake when buying something	• Some concern that they will make a mistake when buying something
• Especially knowledgeable and alert consumers	• Low-to-average consumer capabilities
• Selectively innovative	• Not innovative
• Seek new experiences and personal challenges	• Seek stability and a secure routine
• Less interested in accumulating possessions	• Normal range of interest in accumulating possessions
• Higher measured life satisfaction	• Lower measured life satisfaction
• Less likely to want to live their lives over differently	• Have some regrets as to how they lived their lives
• Perceive themselves to be healthier	• Perceive themselves to be of normal health for their age
• Feel financially more secure	• Somewhat concerned about financial security

Source: Reprinted from *Journal of Business Research,* Vol. 22, No.2, Leon G. Schiffman and Elaine Sherman, "The Value Orientation of New-Age Elderly: The Coming of an Ageless Market" 187–194, Copyright © 1991, with permission from Elsevier.

Cyberseniors

Although some people might think of older Americans as individuals who still use rotary phones and are generally resistant to change, this stereotype is far from the truth. Few older consumers are fearful of new technology, and there are more Internet users over the age of 50 than under the age of 20. Research studies have found that those over 55 are more likely than the average adult to use the Internet to purchase books, stocks, and computer equipment and that 92 percent of surfing seniors have shopped online.[114] In fact, older Internet users (aged 65 and older) are the fastest-growing demographic group with respect to the U.S. Internet market.[115]

What's the attraction for seniors to go online? Certainly, the Internet is a great way to communicate with friends and family members living in other states, including grandchildren in college. But the Web is also a place to find information (e.g., stock prices, health and medication-related information), entertainment, and a sense of community. There also appears to be a relationship between the amount of time an older adult spends on the Internet and his or her level of out-of-home mobility (using the Internet may serve as a substitute for going out of the house). Having a computer and modem "empowers" older consumers—it allows them to regain some of the control that was lost due to the physical and/or social deterioration in their lives. For example, a consumer can pay bills, shop, and e-mail friends. This may be part of the reason why the AARP claims that 2 million of its members are computer users.[116] Figure 12.9 presents the ways in which seniors have been using the Internet.

Marketing to the Older Consumer

Older consumers are open to be marketed to, but only for the "right" kinds of products and services and using the "right" advertising presentation. For example, older models tend to be underrepresented in advertisements or are often shown as being infirm or feeble. Part of the problem, according to some writers on the subject, is that the advertising professionals who create the ads are often in their 20s and 30s and have little understanding or empathy for older consumers. Seniors often want to be identified not for what they did in the past but by what they would like to accomplish in the future. Retirement or moving to a sunbelt community is viewed as the opening of a new chapter in life and not a quiet withdrawal from life. In the same vein, the increase in the number of older adults taking vacation cruises and joining health clubs signifies a strong commitment to remaining "functionally young." Research has also found that when considering how to advertise to seniors, older adults have a higher liking and better recall of emotional appeals (while younger consumers have a higher liking and recall of rational appeals).[117]

FIGURE 12.9
How Seniors Use the Internet

Source: Jacqueline K. Eastman and Rajesh Iyer, "The Elderly's Uses and Attitudes Towards the Internet," *Journal of Consumer Marketing*, 21, no. 3 (2004): 214.

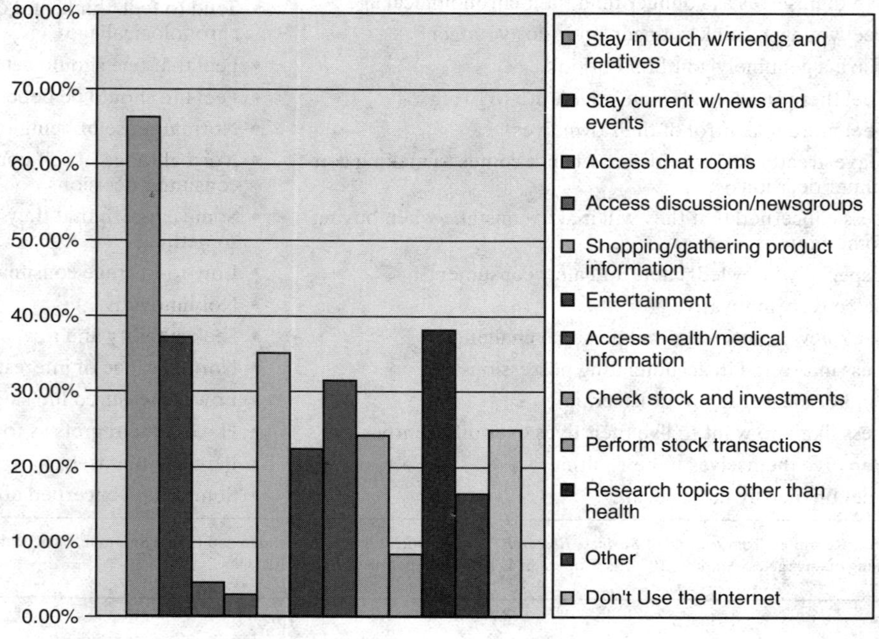

For some products and services, seniors do exhibit different shopping habits than younger consumers. For example, when shopping for a car, older consumers consider fewer brands, fewer models, and fewer dealers. They also are more likely to choose a long-established brand of automobile.[118] Older shoppers tend to be more store-loyal than younger age groups, especially with respect to supermarkets. Still further, the importance of factors like store location (e.g., distance from home) are often a function of the health status of the senior.[119]

The aging process can be difficult for consumers. Many elderly consumers do not hear as well as they did when they were younger, and many do not see as well. Jars and bottles that are easy to open for a 30-year-old often present problems when an 80-year-old tries to open them. While some marketers have redesigned their products to make them easier for the elderly to cope with, many more product redesigns are needed. To provide an example, consider the following:[120]

> When 80-year-old Martha Smith wants to boil a cup of water in her microwave, she turns the dial to the popcorn setting and hits "start." Unable to easily adjust the digital timer on the device, she repeats this three times before it is warm enough for a cup of tea. Martha has become a master of various microwave recipes, all measured in terms of how many "popcorns" it takes to cook the food.

Gender as a Subculture

Learning Objective

12.7 *To Understand Gender as a Subcultural Influence on Consumer Behavior.*

Because **sex roles** have an important cultural component, it is quite fitting to examine **gender** as a subcultural category.

SEX ROLES AND CONSUMER BEHAVIOR

All societies tend to assign certain traits and roles to males and others to females. In American society, for instance, aggressiveness and competitiveness often were considered traditional *masculine traits*; neatness, tactfulness, gentleness, and talkativeness were considered traditional *feminine traits.* In terms of role differences, women have historically been cast as homemakers with responsibility for child care and men as the providers or breadwinners. Because such traits and roles are no longer relevant for many individuals, marketers are appealing to consumers' broader vision of gender-related role options. However, many studies are still suggesting that even with the large number of middle-class women in the workplace, men are not doing more in terms of housework (e.g., cleaning, cooking, and laundry).[121]

One study also found that men and women exhibit different reactions to identical print advertisements. Women show superior affect and purchase intention toward ads that are verbal, harmonious, complex, and category-oriented. In contrast, men exhibit superior affect and purchase intention toward ads that are comparative, simple, and attribute-oriented. Consequently, it may be best, where feasible, to advertise differently to men and women.[122]

A recent study found that gender plays an important role with respect to shopping motives. Female shoppers tend to be more prone to such shopping motives as uniqueness and assortment seeking, social interaction, and browsing. In contrast, male shoppers tend to be motivated by information attainment and convenience seeking. Still further, women tend to be more loyal to local merchants than their male counterparts. The researchers suggest that local merchants could use this information to develop advertising campaigns that are gender specific.[123] It is also important to note that today women control 85 percent of family spending, which amounts to $500 billion a year. Because of this, "women have been called the household's CPO, or chief purchasing officer."[124]

CONSUMER PRODUCTS AND SEX ROLES

Within every society, it is quite common to find products that are either exclusively or strongly associated with the members of one sex. In the United States, for example, shaving equipment, cigars, pants, ties, and work clothing were historically male products; bracelets, hair spray, hair dryers, and sweet-smelling colognes generally were considered feminine products. For most of these products, the sex role link has either diminished or disappeared; for others, the prohibition still lingers. Specifically, although women have historically been the major market for vitamins, men are increasingly being targeted for vitamins exclusively formulated for men. Furthermore, in the past few years men have exhibited more of an interest in personal health and wellness, closing the gap with women with regard to these areas of personal concern.[125]

While initially women lagged behind men with respect to Internet usage, a recent study found that "women under 65 now outpace men in Internet usage, though only by a few percentage points." For example, in the 18- to 29-year-old age category, 86 percent of women are online, while only 80 percent of men are online.[126] The appeal of the Internet seems to differ somewhat for men and women. For instance, women go online to seek out reference materials, online books, medical information, cooking ideas, government information, and chat sites. In contrast, men tend to focus on exploring, discovery, identifying free software, and investments. This seems to provide further support for the notion that men are "hunters," whereas women are "nurturers."[127] Still further, although men and women are equally likely to browse commercial sites, women are less likely to purchase online (32 percent for men versus 19 percent for women). Evidence suggests that the lower incidence of women purchasing online is due to their heightened concerns about online security and privacy.[128]

In a recent study of coupon usage and bargain hunting, the authors note that while a 1995 study found that 10 percent of men were the primary grocery shopper for their household, by 2003, 36 percent of men performed this task. And a 2004 study reported that 84 percent of females and 68 percent males used coupons. This research explored the degree to which men of differing age groups considered various types of shopping as gender neutral. As presented in Table 12.16, men under the age of 60 were more likely than older men to consider grocery shopping as gender neutral, while men 40 and over were more likely to believe that the purchase of technical products (e.g., computers, cell phones, digital cameras) is appropriate for either gender.[129] Clearly, the role of men as shoppers is changing.

WOMEN AS DEPICTED IN MEDIA AND ADVERTISING

Many women feel that the media and advertising create an expectation of beauty that most women can never achieve. Consequently, they want the *definition* of beauty to change. Dove has an advertising campaign that is challenging the traditional sense of beauty and has been well received by women. "Real" women are portrayed in the company's ads—with gray hair, wrinkles, and flawed skin (i.e., real people!). Importantly, the campaign lets women know that beauty comes in many sizes, shapes, and ages.[130] Supporting Dove's realistic approach, a recent study found that 65 percent of women 35 to 40 years of age felt that most advertisements aimed at them were patronizing, and 50 percent also found the ads to be "old-fashioned."[131]

WORKING WOMEN

Marketers are keenly interested in **working women**, especially married working women. They recognize that married women who work outside of the home are a large and growing market segment, one whose needs differ from those of women who do not work outside the home (frequently self-labeled "stay-at-home moms"). It is the size of the working woman market that makes it so attractive. Approximately 60 percent of American women 16 years of age and older are in the labor force, which represents a market of over 65 million individuals. Whereas more than half of all women with children under the age of 1 are working (55 percent), almost

TABLE 12.16 Age of Male and Egalitarian Gender Orientation

	MALE RESPONDENT BELIEVES PURCHASE IS GENDER NEUTRAL		
PRODUCT	**UNDER 40**	**40–59**	**60 AND OLDER**
Groceries	76%	73%	59%
Cars	50%	46%	46%
Clothes	58%	69%	57%
Technical	42%	61%	62%
Food delivery	74%	71%	71%
Oil change/tune up	50%	40%	40%

Source: C. Jeanne Hill and Susan K. Harmon, "Male Gender Role Beliefs, Coupon Use and Bargain Hunting," *Academy of Marketing Studies Journal*, 11, no. 2 (2007): 115.

78 percent of women with children ages 6 to 17 are employed.[132] When the time spent on everything that a working woman has to accomplish in a day is added together (e.g., work, childcare, shopping, cooking), it is no wonder that studies have concluded that this constitutes a "38-hour day."[133]

Because 40 percent of all business travelers today are women, hotels have begun to realize that it pays to provide the services women want, such as healthy foods, gyms, and spas and wellness centers. Female business travelers are also concerned about hotel security and frequently use room service because they do not want to go to the hotel bar or restaurant.

Segmenting the Working Women Market

To provide a richer framework for segmentation, marketers have developed categories that differentiate the motivations of working and nonworking women. For instance, a number of studies have divided the female population into four segments: *stay-at-home* housewives; *plan-to-work* housewives; *just-a-job* working women; and *career-oriented* working women.[134] The distinction between "just-a-job" and "career-oriented" working women is particularly meaningful. Just-a-job working women seem to be motivated to work primarily by a sense that the family requires the additional income, whereas career-oriented working women, who tend to be in a managerial or professional position, are driven more by a need to achieve and succeed in their chosen careers. Today, though, with more and more female college graduates in the workforce, the percentage of career-oriented working women is on the rise. As evidence of this fact, 25 percent of all working women bring home a paycheck that is larger than their husband's (10 years ago it was only 17 percent).[135]

Working women spend less time shopping than nonworking women. They accomplish this "time economy" by shopping less often and by being brand and store loyal. Not surprisingly, working women also are likely to shop during evening hours and on weekends, as well as to buy through direct-mail catalogs.

Businesses that advertise to women should also be aware that magazines are now delivering a larger women's audience than television shows. Whereas early 1980s' TV shows had higher ratings than popular magazines, today the top 25 women's magazines have larger audiences than the top 25 television shows targeted to females.[136]

Every year, more and more products and retailers target to women. Recent examples include Beringer's introduction of White Lie Early Season Chardonnay ("This wine speaks to us in our language") and Godiva Chocolate's notion that their product is something that a woman deserves to buy for herself (rather than as a gift for someone else). Best Buy and other similar electronics stores are trying harder than ever to make women feel comfortable shopping in their outlets, since women spend $55 billion annually on consumer electronics. A recent study by the Consumer Electronics Association found that 46 percent of women claim that they have the most influence in their households with respect to consumer electronics purchases.[137] Figure 12.10 shows the consumer electronics products that women are most interested in buying.

FIGURE 12.10
Consumer Electronics Products Women Are Most Interested in Buying

Source: Beth Snyder Bulik, "Electronics Retailers Woo Women," *Advertising Age*, (November 15, 2004): 16.

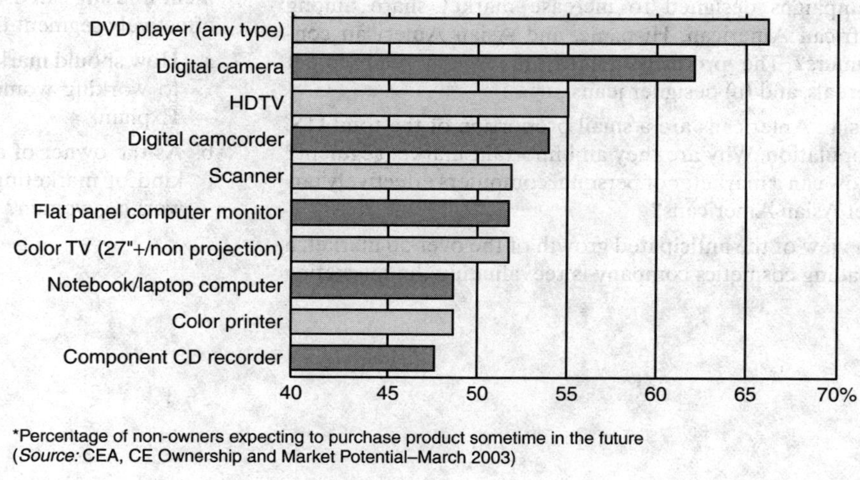

*Percentage of non-owners expecting to purchase product sometime in the future
(*Source:* CEA, CE Ownership and Market Potential–March 2003)

Subcultural Interaction

LEARNING OBJECTIVE

12.8 *To Understand How Multiple Subcultural Memberships Jointly Influence Consumer Behavior.*

All consumers are simultaneously members of more than one subcultural segment (e.g., a consumer may be a young, Hispanic, Catholic homemaker living in the Midwest). The reality of **subcultural interaction** suggests that marketers should strive to understand how multiple subcultural memberships *interact* to influence target consumers' relevant consumption behavior.

SUMMARY

Subcultural analysis enables marketers to segment their markets to meet the specific needs, motivations, perceptions, and attitudes shared by members of a specific subcultural group. A subculture is a distinct cultural group that exists as an identifiable segment within a larger, more complex society. Its members possess beliefs, values, and customs that set them apart from other members of the same society; at the same time, they hold to the dominant beliefs of the overall society. Major subcultural categories in this country include nationality, religion, geographic location, race, age, and sex. Each of these can be broken down into smaller segments that can be reached through special copy appeals and selective media choices. In some cases (such as the elderly consumer), product characteristics should be tailored to the specialized needs of the market segment. Because all consumers simultaneously are members of several subcultural groups, the marketer must determine how specific subcultural memberships interact to influence the consumer's purchases of specific products and services.

DISCUSSION QUESTIONS

1. Why is subcultural analysis especially significant in a country such as the United States?
2. Discuss the importance of subcultural segmentation to marketers of food products. Identify a food product for which the marketing mix should be regionalized. Explain why and how the marketing mix should be varied across geographic areas.
3. How can marketers of the following products use the material presented in this chapter to develop promotional campaigns designed to increase market share among African American, Hispanic, and Asian American consumers? The products are (a) iPods, (b) ready-to-eat cereals, and (c) designer jeans.
4. Asian Americans are a small proportion of the total U.S. population. Why are they an important market segment? How can a marketer of personal computers effectively target Asian Americans?
5. In view of the anticipated growth of the over-50 market, a leading cosmetics company is reevaluating the marketing strategy for its best-selling moisturizing face cream for women. Should the company market the product to younger (under 50) as well as older women? Would it be wiser to develop a new brand and formula for consumers over 50 rather than target both age groups with one product? Explain your answer.
6. Marketers realize that people of the same age often exhibit very different lifestyles. Using the evidence presented in this chapter, discuss how developers of retirement housing can use older Americans' lifestyles to more effectively segment their markets.
7. a. How should marketers promote products and services to working women? What appeals should they use? Explain.
   b. As the owner of a BMW automobile dealership, what kind of marketing strategies would you use to target working women?

EXERCISES

1. Using one of the subculture categories listed in Table 12.1, identify a group that can be regarded as a subculture within your university or college.
   a. Describe the norms, values, and behaviors of the subculture's members.
   b. Interview five members of that subculture regarding attitudes toward the use of credit cards.
   c. What are the implications of your findings for marketing credit cards to the group you selected?
2. Interview one baby boomer and one adult Generation Y consumer regarding the purchase of a car. Prepare a report on the differences in attitudes between the two individuals. Do your findings support the text's discussion of the differences between boomers and echoboomers? Explain.
3. Many of your perceptions regarding price versus value are likely to be different from those of your parents or grandparents. Researchers attribute such differences to *cohort effects,* which are based on the premise that consumption patterns are determined early in life. Therefore, individuals who experienced different economic, political, and cultural environments during their youth are likely to be different types of consumers as adults. Describe instances in which your parents or grandparents disagreed with or criticized purchases you had made. Describe the cohort effects that explain each party's position during these disagreements.
4. Find two good and two bad examples of advertising directed toward elderly consumers. To what degree are these ads stereotypical? Do they depict the concept of perceived age? How could these ads be improved by applying some of this chapter's guidelines for advertising to elderly consumers?

KEY TERMS

- African American Consumer *402*
- age subcultures *410*
- Asian Americans *406*
- baby boomers *410*
- cognitive ages *414*
- gender subcultures *417*
- Generation X *410*
- Generation Y *410*
- geographic and regional subcultures *400*
- Hispanic American subculture *393*
- nationality subcultures *393*
- older consumers *413*
- racial subcultures *402*
- religious subcultures *400*
- sex roles *417*
- subcultural interaction *420*
- subculture *392*
- working women *418*

Case One: The Growth of the Halal Industry

The global halal food industry has grown to a whopping $2.1 trillion worldwide industry, catering to some 1.8 billion consumers. According to industry observers, like consulting firm A.T. Kearney, this growth is only going to increase given that Islam is the world's fastest-growing religion. Very few people are aware that halal does not only cover the food sector, but also covers ecotourism, logistics, pharmaceuticals, software development, and personal care products—these latter ones are only now being investigated by marketers and associations that certify halal.

Halal literally means "what is permissible" under Islam. The world's largest fast-food brands, such as McDonalds, KFC, and Burger King, have been selling halal burgers and chicken nuggets for some years now. In addition, the conglomerate Nestlé, which entered the halal market a decade ago, is now a major player with annual sales of $3 billion—480 of its factories worldwide adhere to halal food requirements. Recently, Colgate-Palmolive has launched a halal toothpaste, while an Australian company has begun marketing a halal makeup. The supermarket chains don't want to lag behind, and major players such as Carrefour, Tesco, and Wal-Mart are now developing in-house halal ranges.

One of the biggest players in the food industry in the Arab world is Al Islami foods. The company began operations in 1981, and has diversified its products to now include fresh and frozen chicken, meat, seafood, vegetables, and dairy products.

QUESTION

1. While there is very little consumer research that focuses on religion, there are several recent studies that examine aspects of consumers' religion and their consumer behavior. Since very little is done on research that focuses on religion, find out the background of the halal concept in Islamic religion.

Sources: Bontems Nathalie, "Totally Swamped," *Gulf Marketing Review* (May 2009): 43–49; and Husain Shakir, "Local Halal Food Companies Urged to Shape Up or Lose Out," *Gulf News*, September 16, 2006, 35.

Case Two: Kraft Woos Asian Americans

According to Vincent Tam, director of client services at Admerasia, a New York–based ad agency, "food companies have been slow to target Asian Americans . . . they find it daunting and complex that there are so many Asian groups. But as diverse as we are, we have shared values."

Tam's firm recently won Kraft's Asian business, and is in the process of developing in-language print ads aimed at immigrant Chinese-speaking moms that will appear in Chinese newspapers in Los Angeles and New York. These ads will feature such Kraft products as Oreos, Ritz, Kraft Barbecue Sauce, Capri Sun, and Philly Cream Cheese, and will do so in "culturally relevant settings." Interestingly, the focus of the campaign is not to get Chinese-speaking moms to use these products in their own Chinese cooking, but to teach them how to use Kraft products for Western-style meals.

The president of the Asian American Advertising Federation, Bill Imada, feels that "Kraft's entry will make a big difference to those food marketers who are on the fence." This could result in significantly more advertising money being channeled to the Asian American market.

QUESTION

1. Considering the text discussion of Asian American consumers (and a targeted search of this subcultural market on the Internet), why is this demographic segment particularly ripe for increased attention from marketers?

Source: Based on: Sonia Reyes, "Kraft Initiative Woos Asian American Moms," *Brandweek,* (July 25, 2005): 10.

13

Cross-Cultural Consumer Behavior: An International Perspective

IN OUR EXAMINATION OF psychological, social, and cultural factors, we have regularly pointed out how segments of consumers from a particular country or culture are in certain ways different in terms of their consumer attitudes and behavior. If such diversity exists among segments of a single society, then even more diversity is likely to exist among the members of two or more societies. To succeed, international marketers must understand the nature and extent of differences between the consumers of different societies—"cross-cultural" differences—so that they can determine whether they can use a similar marketing strategy across different countries, or develop somewhat different or even rather unique and differentiated marketing strategies for specific foreign markets.

Creating an effective strategy that works across different countries with different cultures is a real challenge. Moreover, while it is sometimes possible to create a single strategy (i.e., a global strategy), in other cases it is better to create different strategies for different countries (i.e., local strategies). To get you to think more about this challenge, Figure 13.1 presents an English language ad for the upscale Ritz-Carlton Golf Club & Spa®. While this ad was likely designed primarily for particularly affluent U.S. consumers, it is nevertheless likely to appear in selected upscale magazines that are also read by a segment of very-affluent consumers from all over the world who frequently visit the United States and regularly read American and other English language upscale magazines. As you read this chapter, you will continue to be challenged to think about when it is appropriate to market to consumers locally, and when a mixed or global strategy may be best.

FIGURE 13.1

Source: © 2005, DC Ranch L.L.C. The DC Ranch & Silverleaf names & related marks are registered trademarks. (www.silverleaf.com)

QUESTION: *Under What Circumstances Would This English Language Ad Attract Affluent Consumers from Largely Non-English Speaking Countries?*

Learning Objectives

13.1 *To Understand the Importance of Formulating an Appropriate Multinational or Global Marketing Strategy.*

13.2 *To Understand How to Study the Differences Among Cultures while Developing Marketing Strategies.*

13.3 *To Understand How Consumer-Related Factors Impact a Firm's Decision to Select a Global, Local, or Mixed Marketing Strategy.*

13.4 *To Understand How Lifestyle and Psychographic Segmentation Can Be Used in Developing Global or Local Marketing Strategies.*

Developing Multinational Marketing Strategies Is Imperative

Learning Objective

13.1 *To Understand the Importance of Formulating an Appropriate Multinational or Global Marketing Strategy.*

Today, almost all major corporations are actively marketing their products beyond their original homeland borders. In fact, the issue is generally not *whether* to market a brand in other countries but rather *how* to do it (the same product with the same "global" advertising campaign, or "tailored" products and localized ads for each country). Because of this emphasis on operating as a multinational entity, the vocabulary of marketing now includes terms such as *glocal*, which refers to companies that are both "global" and "local"; that is, they include in their marketing efforts a blend of standardized and local elements in order to secure the benefits of each strategy.

This challenge has been given special meaning by the efforts of the **European Union (EU)** to form a single market. Although the movement of goods and services among its 27 members (as of January 1, 2007) has been eased, it is unclear whether this diverse market will really be transformed into a single market of almost 495 million homogeneous "Euroconsumers" with the same or very similar wants and needs.[1] Many people hope that the introduction of the euro as a common EU currency will help shape Europe into a huge, powerful, unified market. Closer to home, the **North American Free Trade Agreement (NAFTA)**, which currently consists of the United States, Canada, and Mexico, provides free-market access to more than 440 million consumers. Since its inception (January 1, 1994), for example, the markets in Canada and Mexico for packaged software from U.S. firms have grown to three times their pre-NAFTA market size, and all trade between the United States, Canada, and Mexico has increased by 200 percent.[2] Other important trade associations include the Association of Southeast Asian Nations (ASEAN), consisting of Indonesia, Singapore, Thailand, the Philippines, Malaysia, Brunei; Mercosur (the largest Latin American trade agreement), which includes Argentina, Bolivia, Brazil, Chile, Columbia, Ecuador, Paraguay, Peru, and Uruguay; and the Central America Trade Agreement (CAFTA), which includes Costa Rica, the Dominican Republic, El Salvador, Guatemala, Honduras, and Nicaragua.

Many firms are developing strategies to take advantage of these and other emerging economic opportunities. A substantial number of firms are now jockeying for market share in foreign markets. For instance, Starbucks has been opening stores in China, and MTV Networks has formed a partnership with @Japan Media and running a 24-hour Japanese language music TV channel.[3]

Firms are selling their products worldwide for a variety of reasons. First, with an ongoing buildup of "multinational fever" and the general attractiveness of multinational markets, products or services originating in one country are increasingly being sought out by consumers in other parts of the world. Second, many firms have learned that overseas markets represent the single most important opportunity for their future growth when their home markets reach maturity. This realization is propelling them to expand their horizons and seek consumers scattered all over the world. Moreover, consumers all over the world are eager to try "foreign" products that are popular in different and far-off places. Consider the following story:

> There was this Englishman who worked in the London office of a multinational corporation based in the United States. He drove home one evening in his Japanese car. His wife, who worked in a firm which imported German kitchen equipment, was already home. Her small

TABLE 13.1 The Best Global Brands

RANK	BRAND	2008 BRAND VALUE ($BILLIONS)
1	Coca-Cola	66.7
2	IBM	59.0
3	Microsoft	59.0
4	GE	53.1
5	Nokia	35.9
6	Toyota	34.1
7	Intel	31.3
8	McDonald's	31.0
9	Disney	29.3
10	Google	25.6

Note: Only includes brands that obtain at least one-third of their earnings outside of their home country.

Source: Burt Helm, "Best Global Brands," *Business Week*, September 29, 2008, 56.

Italian car was often more maneuverable in London's heavy traffic than most other cars. After a meal which included New Zealand lamb, California carrots, Mexican honey, French cheese and Spanish wine, they settled down to watch a program on their television set, which has been made in Finland. The program was a retrospective celebration of the war to recapture the Falkland Islands. As they watched it they felt warmly patriotic, and very proud to be British.[4]

According to *BusinessWeek*, Coca-Cola is the most valuable brand in the world, with a brand value of almost $67 billion. Table 13.1 presents a list of the world's 10 best global brands.

WINNING EMERGING MARKETS

In 2006, for the first time, the GDP of emerging markets equaled the GDP of advanced nations. Much of this growth came from the "BRICET" nations—Brazil, Russia, India, China, Eastern Europe, and Turkey. Because emerging markets are home to about 85 percent of the world's population, multinational marketers who ignore these markets do so at their own peril.[5]

ACQUIRING EXPOSURE TO OTHER CULTURES

As more and more consumers come in contact with the material goods and lifestyles of people living in other parts of the world, they have the opportunity to adopt these different products and practices. How consumers in one culture secure exposure to the goods of other people living in other cultures is an important part of consumer behavior. It impacts the well-being of consumers worldwide and of marketers trying to gain acceptance for their products in countries that are often quite different from their home country. After all, by the time you read this, there may be a number of models of automobiles available for you to purchase that were made in China, thanks to a deal between Chery Automobiles of China and Malcolm Bricklin, chairman of Visionary Vehicles.[6]

Still further, a portion of consumers' exposure to different cultures tends to come about through consumers' own initiatives—their travel, their living and working in foreign countries, or even their immigration to a different country. For example, "Turkish migrant workers to Germany and the Netherlands have introduced the 'Doner Kebap,' a Turkish sandwich of roasted meat, and 'pide,' Turkish flat bread, into those countries."[7] Additionally, consumers obtain a "taste" of different cultures from contact with foreign movies, theater, art and artifacts, and most certainly, from exposure to unfamiliar and different products. This second major category of cultural exposure is often fostered by marketers seeking to expand their markets by bringing new products, services, practices, ideas, and experiences to potential consumers residing in a different country and possessing a different cultural view. Within this context, international marketing provides a form of "culture transfer."

COUNTRY-OF-ORIGIN EFFECTS

A number of recent research studies have examined **country-of-origin effects** both in the United States and in other countries. One study of the Samsung brand among U.S. consumers found no difference in brand image or purchase intention whether the subject thought that Samsung was a Japanese brand or a South Korean brand.[8] A study in Indonesia reported that with respect to relative quality and purchase intention, country-of-origin was more important than price for both intangible services and tangible goods, and this was true for consumers both high and low in consumer ethnocentrism (e.g., whether and how strongly consumers prefer products made in their own country, compared to other countries).[9] Using visitors to an automobile show as subjects, research conducted in Australia found that consumers exhibiting high levels of NFC (need for cognition—see Chapter 5) were "more engaged in more complex assessment of the country of origin (COO) cue in their product evaluation than those who have less NFC."[10] Still further, research studying COO in Turkey found that while products from Germany, France, Italy, and Israel were favored by Turkish consumers for their quality, design, and performance, products from the United States and England were chosen for their reliability and warranty. And although Chinese and South Korean products were rated highly with respect to price and innovativeness, Turkish consumers felt they were lacking in quality, performance, durability, and assortment.[11]

When consumers are making purchase decisions, they may take into consideration the COO of their choices. Researchers have shown that consumers use their knowledge of where products are made in the evaluation of their purchase options.[12] Such a country-of-origin effect seems to come about because consumers are often aware that a particular firm or brand name is associated with a particular country. For example, Volkswagen's current ad campaign features a vintage black VW Beetle that speaks English with a German accent in part to remind us of its German heritage. In contrast, Jaguar does not tend to play on its British heritage when marketing its cars in the United States. And then there's Chevrolet, the General Motors division responsible for over half of GM's vehicle sales. Over the years, Chevrolet has used slogans such as "See the U.S.A. in your Chevrolet," and most recently used the theme "An American Revolution."

Because of the sheer size of the Chinese consumer market and the recent growth in its spending power, a number of new studies have examined COO and the Chinese consumer. While the traditional view has been that Chinese consumers strongly prefer foreign brands, more recent evidence suggests that this may not be the case, as sales of local brands across many product categories have risen. However, one study found that while Chinese consumers say that they prefer buying local Chinese grocery brands, and that it is important to purchase local brands, actual purchase behavior often does not reflect this.[13] Still further, other research conducted in China found that the effect of COO can influence four different factors: (1) consumer ethnocentrism, (2) knowledge of the product and country of origin, (3) degree of a consumer's involvement in the product, and (4) individual differences in information processing. The researchers also found that the COO was more influential for consumers with low multicultural competence when making product quality evaluations than was true for consumers with greater multicultural competence.[14]

In general, many consumers associate France with wine, fashion clothing, perfume, and other beauty products; Italy with pasta, designer clothing, furniture, shoes, and sports cars; Japan with cameras and consumer electronics; and Germany with cars, tools, and machinery. Moreover, consumers tend to have an established *attitude* or even a preference when it comes to a particular product being made in a particular country. This attitude might be positive, negative, or neutral, depending on perceptions or experience. For instance, a consumer in one country might positively value a particular product made in another country (e.g., affluent American consumers may feel that an English Thomas Pink dress shirt or a Bosch dishwasher from Germany are worthwhile investments). In contrast, another consumer might be negatively influenced when he learns that a television set he is considering is made in a country that he does not associate with fine electronics (e.g., a TV made in Costa Rica). Such COO effects influence how consumers rate quality and which brands they will ultimately select.

Refining the COO concept, a study that contrasted U.S. and Mexican consumers decomposed COO into three separate entities: country of design (COD), country of assembly

FIGURE 13.2
Conceptual Model of COD and COM on the Branded Product

Source: Adapted from: Leila Hamzaoui Essoussi and Dwight Merunka, "Consumers' Product Evaluations in Emerging Markets," *International Marketing Review*, 24, no. 4 (2007): 413.

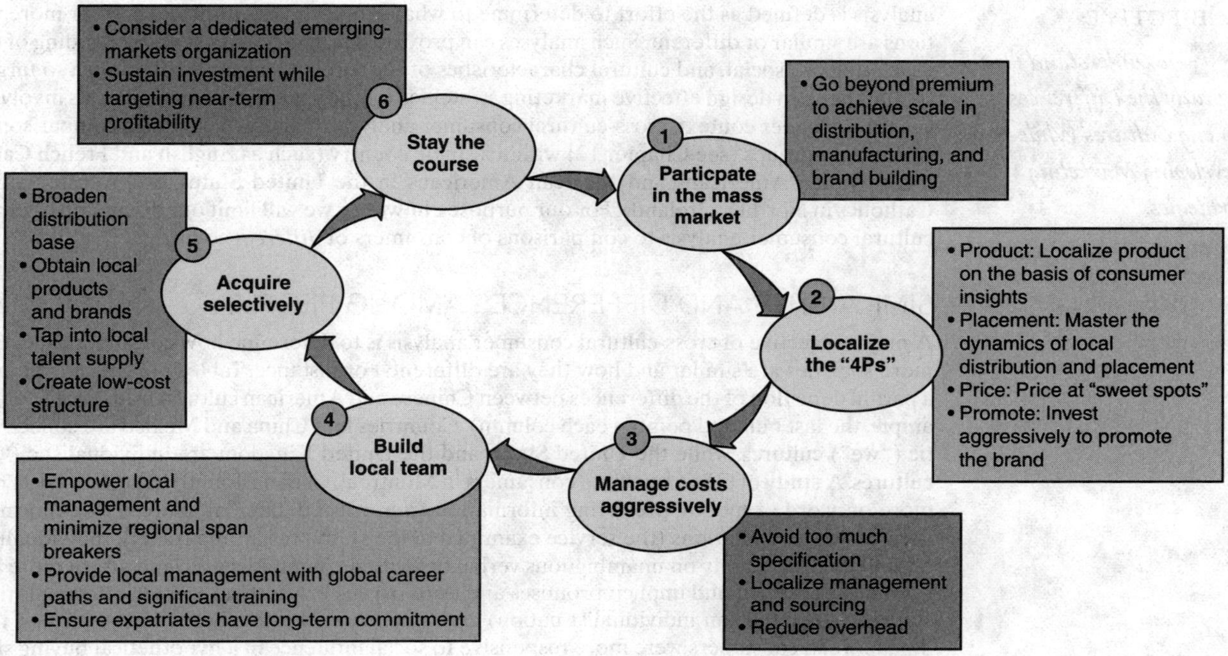

(COA), and country of parts (COP). Of the three, COP had the strongest influence on product evaluations.[15] The study also found that COD was a more important cue in the United States than in Mexico, and that younger Mexicans exhibited a stronger COO effect than older Mexicans. In a similar vein, a study in Tunisia, an emerging market, investigated the effects of COD, country of manufacture (COM), and brand image on consumers' perceptions of products that were designed and manufactured in different countries. The research found that in an emerging market, consumers place greater value in a product's COM than in its COD (i.e., COM is more influential in a consumer's perception of product quality). This is true, unless it is believed that the product is complex to design and manufacture.[16] Figure 13.2 presents a conceptual model of COD and COM impact on the perception of branded products. Note how the impact of COD and COM on perceived product quality includes the "fit," in the consumer's mind, of the perceived ability of the country to manufacture (or design) a product in that product category.[17]

ANIMOSITY AND COUNTRY OF MANUFACTURER

Beyond perceptions of a product's attributes based on its COM, research evidence suggests that some consumers may refrain from purchasing products from particular countries due to animosity. A study of this issue found that *high-animosity consumers* in the People's Republic of China owned fewer Japanese products than *low-animosity consumers* (during World War II, Japan occupied parts of China). Although some Chinese consumers might consider Sony to be a high-end, high-quality brand (or perceptions of the product itself might be very positive), they might nevertheless refuse to bring a product manufactured in Japan into their homes. Similarly, some Jewish consumers avoid purchasing German-made products due to the Holocaust, and some New Zealand and Australian consumers boycott French products due to France's nuclear tests in the South Pacific.[18]

Cross-Cultural Consumer Analysis

LEARNING OBJECTIVE

13.2 *To Understand How to Study the Differences Among Cultures While Developing Marketing Strategies.*

To determine whether and how to enter a foreign market, marketers need to conduct some form of **cross-cultural consumer analysis**. Within the scope of this discussion, cross-cultural consumer analysis is defined as the effort to determine to what extent the consumers of two or more nations are similar or different. Such analyses can provide marketers with an understanding of the psychological, social, and cultural characteristics of the foreign consumers they wish to target, so that they can design effective marketing strategies for the specific national markets involved.

In a broader context, cross-cultural consumer analysis might also include a comparison of subcultural groups (see Chapter 12) within a single country (such as English and French Canadians, Cuban Americans and Mexican Americans in the United States, or Protestants and Catholics in Northern Ireland). For our purposes, however, we will limit our discussion of cross-cultural consumer analysis to comparisons of consumers of *different* countries.

SIMILARITIES AND DIFFERENCES AMONG PEOPLE

A major objective of cross-cultural consumer analysis is to determine how consumers in two or more societies are similar and how they are different. For instance, Table 13.2 presents at least a partial depiction of the differences between Chinese and American cultural traits (note, for example, the last bulleted point in each column). Countries like China and Mexico are collectivistic ("we") cultures, while the United States and the United Kingdom are individualistic ("I") cultures. A study of "I" versus "we" consumers in Montreal, Canada, found that collectivists rely more on word of mouth, preferring information from trusted, familiar sources when forming their service expectations (the service examined in the study was airline travel). Individualists, on the other hand, rely on unambiguous verbal or written communication, and attach more importance to explicit and implicit promises and third parties.[19] Another research effort, this time studying Australia (an individualist nation) and Singapore (a collectivist country), found that Singaporean consumers were more responsive to social influence in a hypothetical buying situation than Australian consumers. Moreover, Australian subjects were more internally oriented, while Singaporean subjects were more externally oriented. This resulted in Australians attributing more responsibility to themselves for the good or bad outcome of a buying decision.[20]

Such an understanding of the similarities and differences that exist between nations is critical to the multinational marketer who must devise appropriate strategies to reach consumers in specific foreign markets. The greater the similarity between nations, the more feasible it is to use relatively *similar* marketing strategies in each nation. On the other hand, if the cultural be-

TABLE 13.2 A Comparison of Chinese and American Cultures

CHINESE CULTURAL TRAITS	AMERICAN CULTURAL TRAITS
• Centered on a set of relationships defined by Confucian doctrine	• Centered on the individual
• Submissive to authority	• Greater emphasis on self-reliance
• Ancestor worship	• Resents class-based distinctions
• Passive acceptance of fate by seeking harmony with nature	• Active mastery in the person–nature relationship
• Emphasizes inner experiences of meaning and feeling	• Concerned with external experiences and and the world of things
• A closed worldview, prizing stability and harmony	• An open view of the world, emphasizing change and movement
• Culture rests on kinship ties and tradition with a historical orientation	• Places primary faith in rationalism and is oriented toward the future
• Places weight on vertical interpersonal relationships	• Places weight on horizontal dimensions of interpersonal relationship
• Values a person's duties to family, clan, and state	• Values the individual personality

Source: Copyright © 2001 by American Academy of Advertising, from Carolyn A. Lin, "Cultural Values Reflected in Chinese and American Television Advertising," *Journal of Advertising*, vol. 30, no. 3 (Winter 2001): Used with permission of M.E. Sharpe, Inc. All Rights Reserved. Not for reproduction.

liefs, values, and customs of specific target countries are found to differ widely, then a highly *individualized* marketing strategy is indicated for each country. For example, a recent study of Internet banking among Swedish and Estonian customers found that while Swedish customers were demographically heterogeneous, Estonian customers could be segmented by age, gender, education, and income.[21]

As another illustration, in addition to IKEA furniture company's generic global Web site that uses English, the firm also offers 14 localized Web sites (in selected languages) and 30 mini-sites (in more languages) that only provide contact information. And whereas the IKEA Italian Web site shows a group of people frolicking on their IKEA furniture (nudity is acceptable and commonplace in Italian advertising), the Saudi Arabian Web site uses extremely conservative photographs (**www.ikea.com**).[22]

A recent study in four Central European nations (Croatia, The Czech Republic, Hungary, and Poland) found that although these nations are in the same geographic region, national differences would make it unwise to employ the same advertising content and imagery in all four countries.[23] As another example, while 88 percent of adults in both France and Germany drink mineral water, it appears that French consumption is strongly associated with concern for the quality of tap water, whereas German consumption is closely linked to vegetarians.[24] However, in contrast to the results presented previously, a recent study examined the notion of an Asian regional brand, and found that some marketers have been able to create a "multicultural mosaic" for their brand that can "appeal across national boundaries" (e.g., Singapore-based Tiger Beer and the 77th Street retail brand). They have done this by creating the image of an Asian consumer that is "urban, modern, and multicultural."[25]

A firm's success in marketing a product or service in a number of foreign countries is likely to be influenced by how similar the beliefs, values, and customs are that govern the use of the product in the various countries. For example, the worldwide TV commercials and magazine ads of major international airlines (American Airlines, British Airways, Continental Airlines, Air France, Lufthansa, Qantas, Swissair, United Airlines) tend to depict the luxury and pampering offered to their business-class and first-class international travelers. The reason for their general cross-cultural appeal is that these commercials speak to the same types of individual worldwide—upscale international business travelers—who share much in common (Figure 13.3). In contrast, knowing that "typical" American advertising would not work in China, Nike hired Chinese-speaking art directors and copywriters to develop specific commercials that would appeal to the Chinese consumer within the boundaries of the Chinese culture. The resulting advertising campaign appealed to national pride in China.[26] Yet another example of cultural differences necessitating a change in marketing would be the efforts of Western banks to attract Muslim customers. The Shari'ah (the sacred law of Islam based on what is written in the Koran) forbids Muslims from charging interest, and prohibits such Western-type financial transactions such as speculation, selling short, and conventional debt financing. Consequently, Western banks in the United Kingdom that want to appeal to that country's 2 million Muslim residents must develop a new range of products for this group of target consumers.[27]

A recent study in four countries (the United Kingdom, France, Germany, and the United States) examined whether there were differences in terms of "consumer style" (i.e., how a consumer approaches the purchase and consumption experience, including attitudes, beliefs, and consumers' decision rules about price, value, etc.).[28] Table 13.3 presents some of the consumer style differences among subject participants from the four countries. Also, based on consumer style, the researchers were able to segment these consumers into four clusters: (1) price-sensitive consumers, (2) variety-seeking consumers, (3) brand-loyal consumers, and (4) information-seeking consumers. Since German consumers, for example, tend to be less brand-loyal and more price-sensitive than their counterparts from the other three nations in the study, it is not surprising that German participants are underrepresented in the brand-loyal consumer cluster and overrepresented in the price-sensitive cluster. Table 13.4 contains a distribution of consumer clusters by country.

Further supporting the importance of cultural differences or orientation, consider that Southeast Asia is frequently the largest market for prestige and luxury brands from the West, and that luxury brand companies such as Louis Vuitton, Rolex, Gucci, and Prada are looking to markets such as Hanoi and Guangzhou when they are thinking of expanding their market reach. Indeed, in fine-tuning their marketing, these luxury-brand marketers need to be especially responsive to cultural differences that compel luxury purchases in the Asian and Western

FIGURE 13.3
Source: Courtesy of Qantas.

QUESTION: *Why Do Most Global Airlines Stress Pampering Business Travelers in Their Ads?*

markets. To this end, research suggests that while Western consumers tend to "use" a prestige item to enhance their sense of individualism or serve as a source of personal pleasure, for Southeast Asian consumers, the same prestige item might serve to further bond the individual with others and to provide visible evidence of the person's value to others.[29] Still further, within the scope of a visible luxury product, a woman in Hong Kong might carry a Fendi handbag (a visible and conspicuous item), but is not likely to be receptive to luxury lingerie because it is not an item that "shows" in public.[30] A recent study of international tourism in Hawaii found that Japanese tourists primarily travel to Hawaii for the shopping, especially for leather handbags and accessories.[31]

THE GROWING GLOBAL MIDDLE CLASS

Recent projections state that while the world's population will grow by about 1 billion people over the next 12 years, the middle class will increase by 1.8 billion people, of which 600 million will be in China. Moreover, by 2020, the middle class will grow from 30 percent to 52 percent of the world's population. And by 2025, China will have the world's largest middle class, and India's

TABLE 13.3 Differences in "Consumer Style" Among Consumers from Four Nations

- German Consumers:
  - Less brand loyal
  - More price-sensitive
  - Least likely to seek variety in products
  - Most likely to consider themselves impulsive shoppers
  - Least likely to say they dislike shopping
- U.S. Consumers
  - More likely to seek new and different products than French and German consumers
  - See advertising as more informative than French and German consumers
- United Kingdom Consumers
  - More likely to seek new and different products than French and German consumers
  - See advertising as more informative than French and German consumers
  - See advertising as insulting
- French Consumers
  - Believe shopping is no fun
  - Claim to engage in comparison shopping, but are not the most likely to purchase products on sale

Source: John A. McCarty, Martin I. Horn, Mary Kate Szenasy, and Jocelyn Feintuch, "An Exploratory Study of Consumer Style: Country Differences and International Segments," *Journal of Consumer Behaviour* (January–February 2007): 53–54. Copyright © 2007 John Wiley & Sons, Ltd.

middle class will be 10 times larger than it currently is.[32] The growing middle class in developing countries is a phenomenon that is very attractive to global marketers who are often eager to identify new customers for their products. The news media has given considerable coverage to the idea that the rapidly expanding middle class in countries of Asia, South America, and Eastern Europe is based on the reality that, although per capita income may be low, there is nevertheless considerable buying power in a country such as China, where most income is largely discretionary income. Today, top wage earners in Beijing earn about $12,000 annually, while the middle class averages about $7,000 a year. While this may not be a high income by Western standards, in a low-cost market it represents an impressive amount of buying power.[33] Indeed, this same general pattern of the growing middle class has also been observed in many parts of South America, Asia, and Eastern Europe.[34] In many parts of the world, an income equivalent to $5,000 is considered the point at which a person becomes "middle class," and it has been estimated that more than 1 billion people in the world's developing countries meet this income standard.[35] It is important to note though, that consumers in less-developed nations often cannot afford to pay as much for a product as consumers in the more advanced economies do. As an example, Nestlé has introduced low-price ice cream in China—the product sells for 12 cents.[36] Table 13.5 lists the size of the emerging middle class in 12 different countries. The

TABLE 13.4 Distribution of Consumer Clusters (Segments) by Country

CLUSTER	FRANCE	GERMANY	UNITED KINGDOM	UNITED STATES
Price-Sensitive Consumers	27.5	38.7	19.3	21.0
Variety-Seeking Consumers	22.0	19.4	22.4	23.3
Brand-Loyal Consumers	30.4	20.0	36.2	22.2
Information-Seeking Consumers	20.1	21.9	22.1	33.5

Source: John A. McCarty, Martin I. Horn, Mary Kate Szenasy, and Jocelyn Feintuch, "An Exploratory Study of Consumer Style: Country Differences and International Segments," *Journal of Consumer Behaviour* (January–February 2007): 56. Copyright © 2007 John Wiley & Sons, Ltd.

TABLE 13.5 Size of the Emerging Middle Class in Selected Countries

	PERCENT OF THE POPULATION	NUMBER OF PEOPLE (MILLIONS)
Brazil	35	57.9
China	23	290.4
India	9	91.4
Indonesia	10	21.0
Korea, Republic of	93	44.0
Malaysia	46	10.7
Mexico	46	45.1
Nigeria	<5	<6.3
Pakistan	<5	<6.9
Peru	27	6.9
Philippines	25	18.9
Russian Federation	45	65.5

Source: Benjamin Senauer and Linda Goetz, "The Growing Middle Class in Developing Countries and the Market for High-Value Food Products," *Prepared for the Workshop on Global Markets for High-Value Food, Economic Research Service, USDA*, Washington, D.C., February 14, 2003, 13, accessed at www.farmfoundation.org/documents/ben-sanauerpaper2—10—3-13-03_000.pdf.

results reveal that more than 90 percent of the population of South Korea can be considered middle class, whereas less than 5 percent of the populations of Nigeria and Pakistan can be similarly categorized.

The rather rapid expansion of middle-class consumers, over the past 50 years, have attracted the attention of many well-established marketing powerhouses, who were already finding their home markets to be rather mature and reaching what was felt to be a saturation point in terms of sales opportunities. While in 1960 two-thirds of the world's middle class lived in industrialized nations, by the year 2000, some 83 percent of middle-class citizens were living in developing countries. These changes strongly suggest that more people are now living longer, healthier, and better lives—literacy rates in developing countries have risen dramatically in the past 50 years, and today two-thirds, rather than only one-third, of the people living in these nations are literate.[37] Table 13.6 captures the global progress over the past 50 years and projects it to year 2050. Note how in 1950 the caloric intake in emerging markets was only 55 percent of industrial countries, while today it is more than 80 percent.

Although a growing middle class provides a market opportunity for products like Big Macs and fries, it should always be remembered that the same product may have different meanings in different countries. For example, whereas a U.S. consumer wants his or her "fast food" to be fast, a Korean consumer is more likely to view a meal as a social or family-related experience. Consequently, convenient store hours may be valued more by a Korean consumer than shorter service time.[38] In China, despite a traditional emphasis on "fresh" (just picked or killed) food, the emerging middle class consumers, with rising incomes and rising demands on their time, are often willing to spend money to save time, in the form of alternatives to home-cooked meals.[39]

The Global Teen Market

As part of growth of the world middle class, there has been a parallel growth in an affluent global teenage and young adult market, a segment which has attracted the attention of marketers. Overall, teenagers (and their somewhat older brothers and sisters—"the young adult segment") appear to have quite similar interests, desires, and consumption behavior no matter where they live. Therefore, in response to this perspective, consumer researchers have explored the makeup, composition, and behavior of this segment(s). One particular study considered the fashion consciousness of teenagers in Japan, the United States, and China.[40] The research revealed that American and Japanese teens were highly similar, differing only in that the Japanese teens were more likely than American teens to choose style over comfort (most likely

TABLE 13.6 Measured Global Progress 1950–2050

	1950	2000	2050
Global Output, Per Capita ($)	586	6,666	15,155
Global Financial Market Capitalization, Per Capita ($)	158	13,333	75,000
Percent of Global GDP			
Emerging Markets	5	50	55
Industrial Countries	95	75	45
Life Expectancy (years)			
Emerging Markets	41	64	76
Industrial Countries	65	77	82
Daily Caloric Intake			
Emerging Markets	1,200	2,600	3,000
Industrial Countries	2,200	3,100	3,200
Infant Mortality (per 1,000)			
Emerging Markets	140	65	10
Industrial Countries	30	8	4
Literacy Rate (per 100)			
Emerging Markets	33	64	90
Industrial Countries	95	98	99

Source: Bloomberg, World Bank, United Nations, and author's estimates. Output and financial market capitalization figures are inflation-adjusted. Peter Marber, "Globalization and Its Contents," *World Policy Journal* (Winter 2004–05): 30.

because of the importance, in the Japanese Confucian society, of meeting the expectations of group members). In contrast, Chinese teens were less fashion conscious than both the American and Japanese teens, which supports the idea that differences exist between highly developed and less high-developed nations with respect to teen fashion consciousness.[41]

Advertising agency BBDO's (Chicago) recent "GenWorld Global Teen Study" reported a significant change in the world's teenagers.[42] During the 1990s, according to the research, the "coolest" teens were found in the United States. Currently, though, the "coolest" teens, the *Creatives,* can be found in all of the 13 countries examined in the research. The *Creatives* represent about 30 percent of all teenagers, and are especially numerous in Western Europe (only 23 percent of U.S. teens are *Creatives*). Table 13.7 presents the top values and bottom values of both *Creatives* and all teenagers. Notice, for example, that while 13 percent of all teens value traditional gender roles, only 1 percent of *Creatives* do.[43] Still further, for the 13 nations examined in the GenWorld Global Teen Study, Figure 13.4 indicates the percentage of

TABLE 13.7 Teenage *Creatives* Versus All Teens: Top Values and Bottom Values

CREATIVES' TOP VALUES	ALL TEENS	CREATIVES	CREATIVES' BOTTOM VALUES	ALL TEENS	CREATIVES
Freedom	55%	66%	Public Image	30%	17%
Honesty	49%	61%	Status	22%	12%
Equality	39%	50%	Wealth	23%	11%
Learning	37%	47%	Looking Good	25%	9%
Preserving the Environment	31%	45%	Traditional Gender Roles	13%	1%
Curiosity	34%	40%	Faith	19%	2%
Creativity	29%	36%			

Source: Becky Ebenkamp, "Creative Consciousness," *Brandweek,* January 16, 2006, 14.

FIGURE 13.4
Percent of Teens Who Do Two or More of the Following Every Day

Source: Energy BBDO, "The GenWorld Teen Study," 17, accessed at www.businessfordiplomaticaction.com/learn/articles/genworld_leave_behind.pdf.

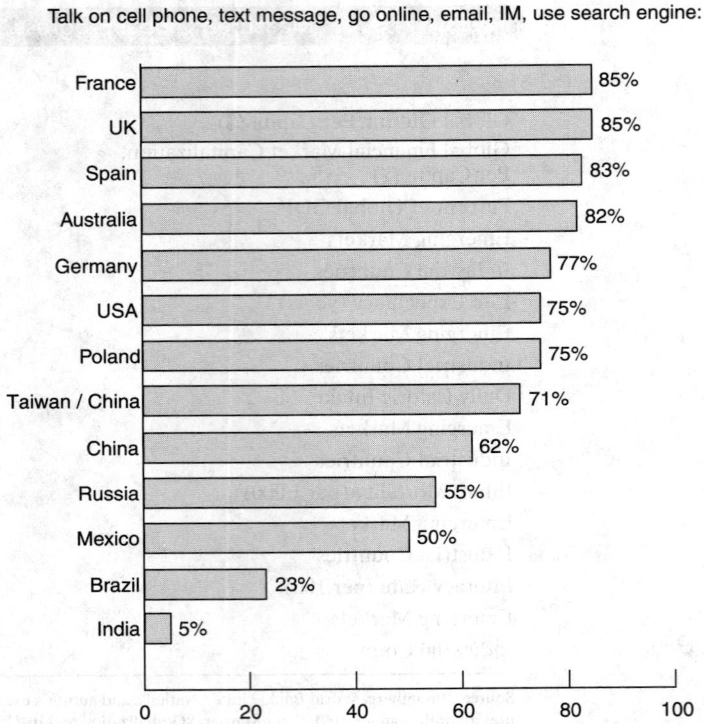

teenagers in each country who do two or more of the following every day—talk on a cell phone, text message, go online, e-mail, IM, and/or use a search engine. As shown, while 85 percent of French and UK teens meet the criteria, only 23 percent of Brazilian teens and 5 percent of teens in India do so.[44]

ACCULTURATION IS A NEEDED MARKETING VIEWPOINT

Too many marketers contemplating international expansion make the strategic error of believing that if its product is liked by local or domestic consumers, then everyone will like it. This biased viewpoint increases the likelihood of marketing failures abroad. It reflects a lack of appreciation of the unique psychological, social, cultural, and environmental characteristics of distinctly different cultures. To overcome such a narrow and culturally myopic view, marketers must also go through an *acculturation process*. They must learn everything that is relevant about the usage or potential usage of their products and product categories in the foreign countries in which they plan to operate. Take the Chinese culture, for example. For Western marketers to succeed in China, it is important for them to take into consideration *guo qing* (pronounced "gwor ching"), which means "to consider the special situation or character of China."[45] An example of *guo qing* for Western marketers is the Chinese policy of limiting families to one child. An appreciation of this policy means that foreign businesses will understand that Chinese families are open to particularly high-quality baby products for their single child (or "the little emperor").[46] One result of this one-child policy is that, in the large cities in China, children are given more than $3 billion a year by their parents to spend as they wish and influence approximately 68 percent of their parents' spending. These Chinese children are also less culture bound than their parents and are, therefore, more open to Western ideas and products.[47]

In a sense, cross-cultural **acculturation** is a dual process for marketers. First, marketers must thoroughly orient themselves to the values, beliefs, and customs of the new society to appropriately position and market their products (being sensitive to and consistent with traditional or prevailing attitudes and values). Second, to gain acceptance for a culturally new product in a foreign society, they must develop a strategy that encourages members of that society to modify or even break with their own traditions (to change their attitudes and possibly alter their behavior). To illustrate the point, a social marketing effort designed to encourage consumers in developing nations to secure polio vaccinations for their children would require a two-step acculturation process. First, the marketer must obtain an in-depth picture of a society's present attitudes and customs with regard to preventive medicine and related concepts. Then the marketer must devise promotional strategies that will convince the members of a target market to have their children vaccinated, even if doing so requires a change in current attitudes.

Distinctive Characteristics of Cross-Cultural Analysis

It is often difficult for a company planning to do business in foreign countries to undertake cross-cultural consumer research. For instance, it is difficult in the Islamic countries of the Middle East to conduct Western-style market research. In Saudi Arabia, for instance, it is illegal to stop people on the streets, and focus groups are impractical because most gatherings of four or more people (with the exception of family and religious gatherings) are outlawed.[48] American firms desiring to do business in Russia have found a limited amount of information regarding consumer and market statistics. Similarly, marketing research information on China is generally inadequate, and surveys that ask personal questions arouse suspicion. So marketers have tried other ways to elicit the data they need. For example, Grey Advertising has given cameras to Chinese children so they can take pictures of what they like and do not like, rather than ask them to explain it to a stranger. Moreover, ACNielsen conducts focus groups in pubs and children's playrooms rather than in conference rooms; and Leo Burnett has sent researchers to China to simply "hang out" with consumers.[49]

APPLYING RESEARCH TECHNIQUES

Although the same basic research techniques used to study domestic consumers are useful in studying consumers in foreign lands (see Chapter 2), in cross-cultural analysis an additional burden exists because language and word usage often differ from nation to nation. Another issue in international marketing research concerns scales of measurement. In the United States, a 5- or 7-point scale may be adequate, but in other countries a 10- or even 20-point scale may be needed. Still further, research facilities, such as telephone interviewing services, may or may not be available in particular countries or areas of the world.

To avoid such research measurement problems, consumer researchers must familiarize themselves with the availability of research services in the countries they are evaluating as potential markets and must learn how to design marketing research studies that will yield useful data. Researchers must also keep in mind that cultural differences may make "standard" research methodologies inappropriate. Table 13.8 identifies basic issues that multinational marketers must consider when planning cross-cultural consumer research.

TABLE 13.8 Research Issues in Cross-Cultural Analysis

FACTORS	EXAMPLES
Differences in language and meaning	Words or concepts (e.g., "personal checking account") may not mean the same in two different countries.
Differences in market segmentation opportunities	The income, social class, age, and sex of target customers may differ dramatically between two different countries.
Differences in consumption patterns	Two countries may differ substantially in the level of consumption or use of products or services (e.g., mail catalogs).
Differences in the perceived benefits of products and services	Two nations may use or consume the same product (e.g., yogurt) in very different ways.
Differences in the criteria for evaluating products and services	The benefits sought from a service (e.g., bank cards) may differ from country to country.
Differences in economic and social conditions and family structure	The "style" of family decision making may vary significantly from country to country.
Differences in marketing research and conditions	The types and quality of retail outlets and direct-mail lists may vary greatly among countries.
Differences in marketing research possibilities	The availability of professional consumer researchers may vary considerably from country to country.

Alternative Multinational Strategies: Global Versus Local

Learning Objective

13.3 *To Understand How Consumer-Related Factors Impact a Firm's Decision to Select a Global, Local, or Mixed Marketing Strategy.*

Some marketers have argued that world markets are becoming more and more similar and that standardized marketing strategies are, therefore, becoming more feasible. For example, Exxon Mobil had sponsored a $150 million marketing campaign to promote its brands (Exxon, Esso, Mobil, and General), and the firm wanted all the ads to carry the same look and feel, regardless of which one of the 100 countries in the world the ad will appear.[50] In contrast, other marketers feel that differences between consumers of various nations are far too great to permit a standardized marketing strategy. In a practical sense, a basic challenge for many executives contemplating multinational marketing is to decide whether to use *shared needs and values* as a segmentation strategy (i.e., to appeal to consumers in different countries in terms of their "common" needs, values, and goals) or to use *national borders* as a segmentation strategy (i.e., to use relatively different, "local," or specific marketing strategies for members of distinctive cultures or countries).

FAVORING A WORLD BRAND

An increasing number of firms have created **world brand** products that are manufactured, packaged, and positioned in exactly the same way regardless of the country in which they are sold. It is quite natural for a "world class" upscale brand of wristwatches such as Patek Philippe to create a global or uniform advertising campaign to reach its sophisticated worldwide target market (see Figure 13.5). Although the advertising copy is in specific target languages, one might speculate that many of Patek Philippe's affluent target customers do read and write English. Nevertheless, to maximize their "comfort zone," it is appropriate to speak to them in their native languages.

Marketers of products with a wide or almost mass-market appeal have also embraced a world branding strategy. For instance, multinational companies, such as General Motors, Gillette, Estée Lauder, Unilever, and Fiat, have each moved from a local strategy of nation-by-nation advertising to a global advertising strategy.

Still other marketers selectively use a world branding strategy. For example, you might think that P&G, which markets hundreds of brands worldwide, is a company with an abundance of world brands. Recently, though, it was revealed that of its 16 largest brands, only three are truly global brands—Always/Whisper, Pringles, and Pantene. Some of P&G's other brands, such as Pampers, Tide/Ariel, Safeguard, and Oil of Olay, are just starting to establish common positioning in the world market.[51]

A recent study explored two global-look strategies in Chinese advertising—the use of Western models and English brand names.[52] A content analysis of almost 2,500 ads found that Western models promoted products in slightly less than half of the ads, while English brand names were found in slightly more than half of the ads. These two strategies, it was reported, enhance the global perception of the brand and enhance the perception that the product comes from a developed Western nation. Interestingly, while the use of Western models tended to increase the consumer's perceived quality of the product, these same consumers rated products with Chinese brand names (as opposed to English brand names) higher on brand friendliness, brand trust, self-brand connections, and brand liking. Another recent study examined perceptions of "Western products" among Generation Y consumers in Kazakhstan, a transitional economy. The study found that because of increased contacts with the West, primarily through TV but also through the marketing campaigns of multinational companies, these consumers had a favorable attitude toward Western products and things, especially for global brands.[53]

As a possible further indication of the proliferation of world brands can be found in a recent study of global versus local online branding.[54] The research examined the online presence of 489 of the *Fortune* Global 500 companies, and found that more than 55 percent of non-U.S. companies employed a global ".com" domain rather than a local (e.g., ".com.jp" for a Japanese firm) domain. While all four Brazilian companies kept a local identity, as did most Japanese firms (86 percent), only 33 percent of Australian companies, 19 percent of French companies, and 18 percent of British companies used a local domain name.

It has been suggested that one reason why global brands often do not survive is due to tribal differences, similar to those occurring on the TV series *Survivor*. Certainly, while differences in language and cultural mores must be considered, the following five ideas may help in establishing a global brand: (1) begin by bringing together representatives from all key markets and disciplines—involve them early and often; (2) conduct marketing research in all key markets; (3) create a foundation for the brand based on what global communities share, not on their differences, and then permit local markets to adapt the strategy to meet local conditions;

FIGURE 13.5

Source: © Patek Philippe Geneva. Used with permission. All rights reserved.

QUESTION: *Why Does One of the World's Most Highly Regarded Wristwatch Brands Use a Single Global Advertising Strategy (Only Varying the Language)?*

(4) use inputs from all countries to develop creative concepts; and (5) talk over all country-specific issues to find commonalities.[55] Still further, an exploratory study considers how products, images, and activities associated with a popular culture, in this case the Japanese culture, support and sustain the brands associated with that culture (i.e., global Japanese brands). The study found that the main components of Japanese culture can be used to determine the level of

FIGURE 13.6
Cross-Border Diffusion of Popular Culture

Source: Roblyn Simeon, "A Conceptual Model Linking Brand Building Strategies and Japanese Popular Culture," *Marketing Intelligence & Planning*, 24, no. 5 (2006): 466.

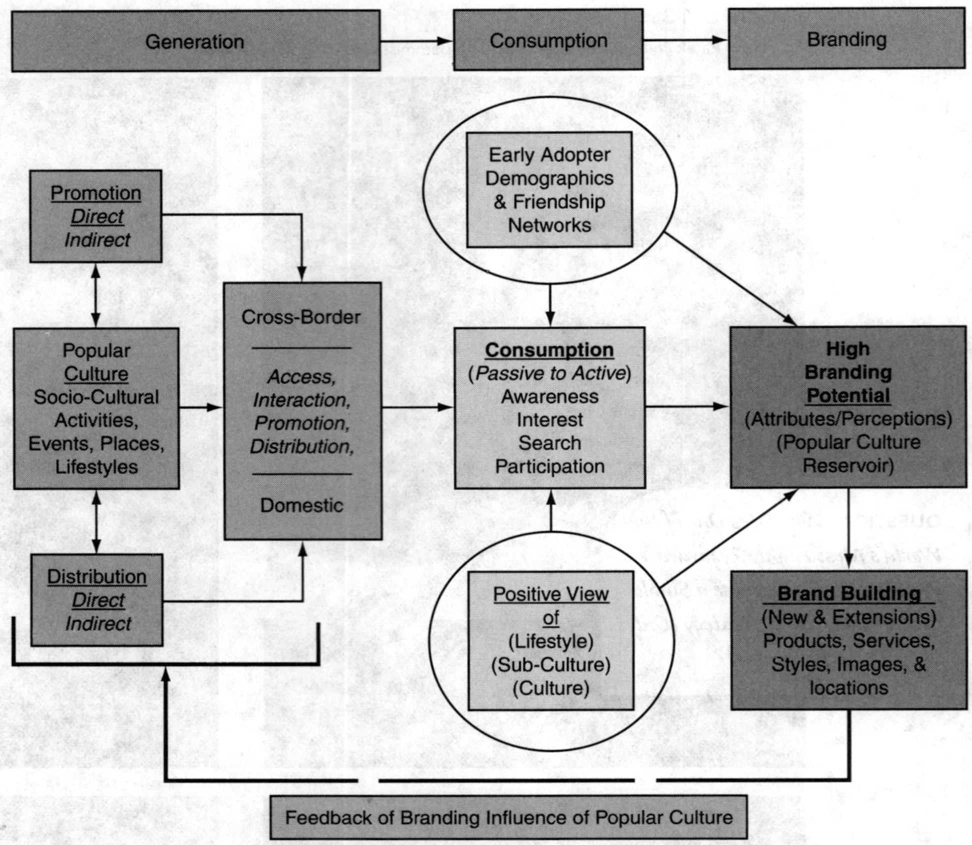

interest for these global brands in countries other than Japan. Figure 13.6 presents a model of cross-border diffusion of popular culture. Cross-border diffusion levels are strongly linked to the extent of promotion and distribution in other countries, as well as access and interaction of consumers of the countries involved.[56]

ARE GLOBAL BRANDS DIFFERENT?

According to a 12-nation consumer research project, global brands are viewed differently than local brands, and consumers, worldwide, associate global brands with three characteristics: *quality signal*, *global myth*, and *social responsibility*. First, consumers believe that the more people who purchase a brand, the higher the brand's quality (which often results in a global brand being able to command a premium price). Still further, consumers worldwide believe that global brands develop new products and breakthrough technologies at a faster pace than local brands. The second characteristic, global myth, refers to the fact that consumers view global brands as a kind of "cultural ideal," and their purchase and use makes the consumer feel like a citizen of the world, and gives them an identity (i.e., "*Local brands show what we are; global brands show what we want to be*"). Finally, global companies are held to a higher level of corporate social responsibility than local brands, and are expected to respond to social problems associated with what they sell. For the 12 nations studied in this research, the importance of these three dimensions was consistent, and accounted for 64 percent of the variation in the overall brand preferences (quality signal accounts for 44 percent of the explanation, global myth accounts for 12 percent of the explanation, and social responsibility accounts for 8 percent of the explanation).[57]

Additionally, while there was not much variation across the 12 nations studied, there were intracountry differences, which resulted in the conclusion that there were four major segments in each country with respect to how its citizens view global brands. *Global Citizens* (55 percent of the total respondents) use a company's global success as an indication of product quality and innovativeness, and are also concerned that the firm acts in a socially responsible manner.

Global Dreamers (23 percent of the total respondents) view global brands as quality products, and are not particularly concerned about the social responsibility issue. *Antiglobals* (13 percent of the total respondents) feel that global brands are higher quality than local brands, but they dislike brands that preach U.S. values and do not trust global companies to act responsibly. Generally, they try to avoid purchasing global brands. Lastly, *Global Agnostics* (8%) evaluate global brands in the same way they evaluate local brands.[58]

MULTINATIONAL REACTIONS TO BRAND EXTENSIONS

Just because a brand may be global in character does not mean that consumers around the world will necessarily respond similarly to a brand extension. A recent study examined reactions to brand extensions among Western culture (U.S.) and Eastern culture (India) consumers, hypothesizing that the Eastern holistic way of thinking (which focuses on the relationships between objects), rather than the Western analytic style of thinking (which focuses on the attributes or parts of objects) would affect the manner in which consumers judge the "fit" of a brand extension. Indeed, the research results confirmed this hypothesis—low-fit extensions (McDonald's chocolate bar and Coke popcorn) received more positive evaluations from the Eastern culture subjects, while moderate-fit extensions (Kodak greeting cards and Mercedes Benz watches) garnered equal responses from both cultural groups. For the Eastern culture participants, liking Coke products, and the fact that Coke and popcorn were complementary products, in that they can be consumed together, was enough to make the brand extension acceptable. The American subjects, in contrast, saw little product class similarity between Coke and popcorn.[59] More recently, these same researchers replicated their earlier study, went on to determine that American Indians were significantly more holistic in their thinking than Caucasian Americans, and reported that certain factors, such as corporate reputation, may be used more frequently by Easterners (than by Westerners) as a basis for judging the "fit" of a brand extension.[60]

ADAPTIVE GLOBAL MARKETING

In contrast to the marketing communication strategy that stresses a common message, some firms embrace a strategy that adapts their advertising messages to the specific values of particular cultures. McDonald's is an example of a firm that tries to localize its advertising and other marketing communications to consumers in each of the cultural markets in which it operates, making it a glocal company. For example, the Ronald McDonald that we all know has been renamed Donald McDonald in Japan, because the Japanese language does not contain the *R* sound. Additionally, the McDonald's menu in Japan has been localized to include corn soup and green tea milkshakes.[61] And in Sweden McDonald's developed a new package using woodcut illustrations and a softer design to appeal to the interest the consumers of that nation have in food value and the outdoors.[62]

Like McDonald's, Levi's and Reebok also tend to follow multilocal strategies that calculate cultural differences in creating brand images for their products. For instance, Levi's tends to position its jeans to American consumers, stressing a social-group image, whereas it uses a much more individualistic, sexual image when communicating with European consumers.[63] Still further, Yahoo!, one of the most successful Web sites on the Internet, modifies both its content and communications for each of its 23 country-specific Web sites. Moreover, in a number of Coke's 140-plus markets, what we know as Diet Coke is called Coca-Cola Light, because the word *diet* has an undesirable connotation or no relevance.[64] Similarly, Coke's best-selling beverage in Japan is not Coke Classic—it's Georgia Coffee—packaged in a can and available in more than 10 versions (e.g., black, black with sugar, with milk and sugar, and so on). Other marketers, too, feel that the world brand concept may be going too far. Specifically, when it comes to the marketing of Tiger Woods, one of the premier golfers of our time; in the United States, he is seen as an example of African American success, in Asia he is a sports star with Asian heritage, and in Europe he is seen as a great young athlete who regularly beats older golfers.[65]

Combining Global and Local Marketing Strategies

Some firms follow a mixed or combination strategy. For instance, Unilever, Playtex, and Black & Decker have augmented their global strategies with local executions. In taking such an adaptive approach, global advertisers with knowledge of cross-cultural differences can tailor their supplemental messages more effectively to suit individual local markets. For example, a study has indicated that while U.S. consumers focus more on the product-related claims made in advertisements, Chinese consumers focus more on the appropriateness of the ad, such as its aesthetic qualities.[66] There is also some evidence to suggest that Spanish ads may contain a larger proportion of affiliation appeals than U.S. ads do because of Spain's cultural inclination toward femininity in its societal norms (U.S. societal norms tend to reflect masculinity).[67] Because concepts and words often do not easily translate and many regions of the country have their own language, advertisements in China are likely to be more effective if they rely heavily on symbols rather than text.[68] A recent study dealing with visual standardization in print ads concluded that "the standardized approach to global advertising may be able to convey a degree of uniformity in meaning when relying on visually explicit messages. . . . This suggests that there is an ability to create a general consensus of meaning across various cultures by using strong visual images.[69] It is also important to note that consumers in different countries of the world have vastly different amounts of exposure to advertisements. For instance, the daily amount of advertising aimed at Japanese consumers, at almost $6 a day, is 14 times the amount aimed at the average Laotian consumer over the course of an entire year.[70] Even so, Cold Stone Creamery is attempting to convey a different image to Japanese consumers—that eating Cold Stone is ultracool—and therefore shuns traditional advertising and instead gives out free samples in upscale shopping areas and locates its outlets near ultra-high-end retailers like Versace and Louis Vuitton.[71]

A recent study of foreign advertisers in China found that 11 percent employed a standardized (or global) strategy, 12 percent used a localized strategy, and the remaining 77 percent favored a combination strategy. Of the seven advertising components that were studied, localizing language to blend with the local culture was considered to be the most important, followed by the need to localize product attributes, models, colors of ads, humor, scenic background, and music.[72] Additionally, it has been reported that many of the Western companies that have not been successful in China have acted as if what had worked well in other parts of the world would also prove successful in China.

FRAMEWORKS FOR ASSESSING MULTINATIONAL STRATEGIES

Global marketers face the challenge of creating multinational strategies in the form of marketing and advertising programs capable of communicating effectively with a diversity of target markets. To assist in this imposing task, various frameworks have been developed to determine the degree to which marketing and advertising efforts should be either globalized or localized, or mixed or combined.

To enable international marketers to assess the positions their products enjoy in specific foreign markets, Table 13.9 presents a five-stage continuum that ranges from mere awareness of a foreign brand in a local market area to complete global identification of the brand; that is, the brand is accepted "as is" in almost every market, and consumers do not think about its country of origin.

Table 13.10 presents a framework that focuses on four marketing strategies available to a firm contemplating doing business on a global basis. A firm might decide either to standardize or localize its product and either standardize or localize its communications program (thus forming a two-by-two matrix). The four possibilities that this decision framework considers range from a company incorporating a **global strategy** (or standardizing both product and communications program) to developing a completely **local strategy** (or customizing both the product and communications program) for each unique market. In the middle there are two **mixed strategies**. All four cells may represent growth opportunities for the firm. To determine which cell represents the firm's best strategy, the marketer must conduct cross-cultural consumer analysis to obtain consumer reactions to alternative product and promotional executions. To illustrate the strategic importance of product uniformity, Frito-Lay, the U.S. snack-food giant, has been standardizing quality and reducing the many local brand names of potato chip companies that it owns throughout the world. This effort is moving the company along a common global visual appearance that features the Lay's logo as a global brand. Its efforts are driven by research that reveals that potato chips are a snack food that has widespread appeal throughout much of the world.[73]

Another orientation for assessing whether to use a global versus local marketing strategy concentrates on a high-tech to high-touch continuum. **Product standardization** appears to be

TABLE 13.9 A Product Recognition Continuum for Multinational Marketing

FACTORS	EXAMPLES
Stage One	Local consumers have heard or read of a brand marketed elsewhere but cannot get it at home; a brand is "alien" and unavailable but may be desirable [e.g., Rover (English autos), Havana cigars (made in Cuba), or medicine not approved by the FDA but sold in Europe].
Stage Two	Local consumers view a brand made elsewhere as "foreign," made in a particular country but locally available (e.g., Saab autos, French wine). The fact that the brand is foreign makes a difference in the consumer's mind, sometimes favorable, sometimes not.
Stage Three	Local consumers accord imported brand "national status"—that is, its national origin is known but does not affect their choice (e.g., Molson beer in the United States, Ford autos in southern Europe).
Stage Four	Brand owned by a foreign company is made (wholly or partly) domestically and has come to be perceived by locals as a local brand; its foreign origins may be remembered, but the brand has been "adopted" ("naturalized"). Examples are Sony in Australia, Coca-Cola in Europe and Japan.
Stage Five	Brand has lost national identity and consumers everywhere see it as "borderless" or global; not only can people not identify where it comes from but they never ask this question. Examples include the Associated Press and CNN news services, Nescafé, Bayer aspirin.

Source: Based on: George V. Priovolos, "How to Turn National European Brands into Pan-European Brands." Working paper. Hagan School of Business, Iona College, New Rochelle, New York.

most successful for high-involvement products that approach either end of the high-tech/high-touch continuum. In other words, products that are at either extreme are more suitable for positioning as global brands. In contrast, low-involvement products in the midrange of the high-tech/high-touch continuum are more suitably marketed as local brands, using market-by-market executions.[74] To illustrate, on a worldwide basis, consumers interested in high-involvement, high-tech products share a common language (such as "bytes" and "microprocessors"), whereas advertisements for high-involvement, high-touch products tend to use more emotional appeals and to emphasize visual images. In either case, according to this perspective (high-involvement products that are either high-tech or high-touch), such products are candidates for global promotional communications.

Some researchers have written that globalization (or standardization) and localization should be viewed as two ends of a continuum and that often the key to success is to "be global but to act local." It is also generally an error to assume that demographic segments in other nations would want to be or act like Americans. When looking for success in a foreign market, it has been suggested that a company should remember the following **three Ps**—*place, people,* and *product.* Table 13.11 presents the specific elements of these three Ps and cites the appropriate marketing strategy when using a standardization approach and when using a localization approach.[75]

TABLE 13.10 A Framework for Alternative Global Marketing Strategies

PRODUCT STRATEGY	COMMUNICATION STRATEGY	
	STANDARDIZED COMMUNICATIONS	LOCALIZED COMMUNICATIONS
Standardized Product	**GLOBAL STRATEGY:** Uniform Product/Uniform Message	**MIXED STRATEGY:** Uniform Product/Customized Message
Localized Product	**MIXED STRATEGY:** Customized Product/Uniform Message	**LOCAL STRATEGY:** Customized Product/Customized Message

TABLE 13.11 Degree of Fit Between Marketing Strategies and the Three Ps

		MARKETING STRATEGIES	
THREE PS	**SPECIFIC ELEMENTS**	**STANDARDIZATION**	**LOCALIZATION**
Place	Economy	Prosperous	Struggling
	Partners	Few	Plentiful
	Competition	Low	Intense
People	Tastes	Little preference	High preference
	Sophistication	High	Low
	Segments	Few	Many
	Classification	Industrial/consumer durables	Consumer nondurables
Products	Technology	High	Low
	Culture bound	Low	High
	Reputation	Sterling	Poor or unknown
	Product perception	High	Low

Source: Copyright © 1999 by M.E. Sharpe, Inc. From *Journal of Marketing Theory and Practice,* vol. 7, no. 2 (Spring 1999): 101. Used with permission.

Global Web Sites

When it comes to the design of e-commerce Web sites, a five-nation research study suggests that consumers react best when content is adapted to their local needs. While in the past some companies felt that local adaptation involved no more than simply translating Web pages into the local language, it is now felt that special attention must also be paid to a number of other factors, including local time and date formats, units of measurement, addresses and telephone numbers, layout and orientation of Web pages, icons, symbols, color, and aesthetics.[76] Still further, one study of American and German Internet users revealed that German users were more likely to withhold or alter personal information on the Internet than American users. Analysis suggests that the German personality has a large private space and a small public space, which translates into a great sense of personal privacy; whereas the opposite is true of the American personality.[77] As a recent study suggests, "understanding the characteristics of local cultures and their impact on Internet use and access should facilitate more accurate projections of sales and customer acquisition growth rates.[78]

Perhaps because of the dominance of English-language pages on the Internet, non–English-speaking European nations appear to be out to distinguish themselves and their cultures by designing Web sites that in some way or other reflect their countries and specific cultures. So German Web sites might employ bright colors and a geometrical layout to give it a "German feel"; a French Web site might have a black background; a Dutch Web site might offer video downloads; and a Scandinavian Web site might provide a variety of images of nature.[79] Indeed, a recent study of global American brands examined how these brands standardize their Web sites in Europe (United Kingdom, France, Germany, and Spain). The study found that while manufacturers' Web sites did have a minimal level of uniformity with respect to color, logo, and layout, the textual information and visual images were dissimilar from one market to the next. Still further, as with traditional advertising media, standardization for durable goods was higher than for nondurables.[80] In yet another study, researchers examined the domestic and Chinese Web sites of U.S.-based multinational companies. Findings show that the Internet is not a culturally neutral medium, but is full of cultural markers that allow country-specific Web sites to possess a feel and a look that is unique to the local culture. For example, while Web sites intended for the U.S. consumer often contained patriotic phrases and references to September 11th, Chinese Web sites were loaded with Chinese cultural symbols (e.g., the Great Wall of China, Chinese festivals). The managerial implication of the research is that consumers relate best to Web sites that have a local feel because it reduces the anxiety associated with the Internet (it is a relatively new medium) and makes navigation easier.[81]

Cross-Cultural Psychographic Segmentation

LEARNING OBJECTIVE

13.4 *To Understand How Lifestyle and Psychographic Segmentation Can Be Used in Developing Global or Local Marketing Strategies.*

The paradox in cross-cultural consumer research is that although worldwide consumers may be similar in many ways (e.g., the increased number of women who work outside of the home), any differences in attitudes or behavior can be crucial and also provide opportunities for segmenting consumers in terms of cultural differences. For example, although more than 50 percent of Japanese and American women work outside the home (which enhances the need for many convenience and time-saving products), Japanese women have been slower to embrace the liberated attitudes of their counterpart working women in the United States.[82] Seen in this light, the determination of whether or not to market a time-saving cleaning device as a world brand is a critical strategic decision. Some firms might attempt to establish a global branding strategy, whereas others would design an individual or local marketing strategy—one that treats Japanese and American working women differently. One marketing authority aptly summed up the issues years ago by stating: "The only ultimate truth possible is that humans are both deeply the same and obviously different. . . ."[83]

This book endorses the same thesis. Earlier chapters have described the underlying similarities that exist between people and the external influences that serve to differentiate them into distinct market segments. If we believe in tailoring marketing strategies to specific segments of the American market, it follows then that we also believe in tailoring marketing strategies to the needs—psychological, social, cultural, and functional—of specific foreign segments.

Global psychographic research often reveals cultural differences of great importance to marketers. For example, Roper Starch Worldwide, a major multinational marketing research company, interviewed 35,000 consumers in 35 countries in order to identify shared values, irrespective of national borders. The research sought to uncover the bedrock values in peoples' lives in order to understand the motivations that drive both attitudes and behavior. After completing the interviews in North and South America, Asia, and Europe, six global value groups were uncovered: *Strivers* (e.g., ambitious and materialistic), *Devouts* (e.g., responsible, respectful, and conservative in outlook), *Altruists* (e.g., unselfish in their concern for others, society and the future), *Intimates* (e.g., focus on social relationships and family), *Fun Seekers* (e.g., young in age and outlook, they value adventure and good times), and *Creatives* (e.g., seek knowledge, insight and have a keen interest in books and new media).[84]

SUMMARY

When there is so much diversity present among the members of just one nation, it is easy to appreciate that numerous larger differences exist between citizens of different nations having different cultures, values, beliefs, and languages. If international marketers are to satisfy the needs of consumers in potentially very distinct markets effectively, they must understand the relevant similarities and differences that exist between the peoples of the countries they decide to target.

When consumers make purchase decisions, they seem to take into consideration the countries of origin of the brands that they are assessing. Consumers frequently have specific attitudes or even preferences for products made in particular countries. These country-of-origin effects influence how consumers rate quality and, sometimes, which brands they will ultimately select.

As increasing numbers of consumers from all over the world come in contact with the material goods and lifestyle of people living in other countries and as the number of middle-class consumers grows in developing countries, marketers are eager to locate these new customers and to offer them their products. The rapidly expanding middle classes in countries of Asia, South America, and Eastern Europe possess relatively substantial buying power because their incomes are largely discretionary (necessities like housing and medical care are often provided by the state for little or no cost).

For some international marketers, acculturation is a dual process: First, marketers must learn everything that is relevant to the product and product category in the society in which they plan to market, and then they must persuade the members of that society to break with their traditional ways of doing things to adopt the new product. The more similar a foreign target market is to a marketer's home market, the easier is the process of acculturation. Conversely, the more a foreign target market is different, the more difficult the process of acculturation.

Some of the problems involved in cross-cultural analysis include differences in language, consumption patterns, needs, product usage, economic and social conditions, marketing conditions, and market research opportunities. There is an urgent need for more systematic and conceptual cross-cultural analyses of the psychological, social, and cultural characteristics concerning the consumption habits of foreign consumers. Such analyses would identify increased marketing opportunities that would benefit both international marketers and their targeted consumers.

DISCUSSION QUESTIONS

1. With all the problems facing companies that go global, why are so many companies choosing to expand internationally? What are the advantages of expanding beyond the domestic market?
2. In terms of consumer behavior are the cultures of the world becoming more similar or more different? Discuss.
3. What is cross-cultural consumer analysis? How can a multinational company use cross-cultural research to design each factor in its marketing mix? Illustrate your answer with examples.
4. What are the advantages and disadvantages of global promotional strategies?
5. Should Head & Shoulders shampoo be sold worldwide with the same formulation? In the same packaging? With the same advertising message? Explain your answers.
6. a. If you wanted to name a new product that would be acceptable to consumers throughout the world, what cultural factors would you consider?
   b. What factors might inhibit an attempt by Apple to position a new laptop computer as a world brand?
7. An American company is introducing a line of canned soups in Poland.
   a. How should the company use cross-cultural research?
   b. Should the company use the same marketing mix it uses in the United States to target Polish consumers? Explain your answer.
   c. Which, if any, marketing mix components should be designed specifically for marketing canned soups in Poland? Explain your answer.
8. Mercedes-Benz, a German car manufacturer, is using cross-cultural psychographic segmentation to develop marketing campaigns for a new two-seater sports car directed at consumers in different countries. How should the company market the car in the United States? How should it market the car in Japan?
9. What advice would you give to an American retailer who wants to sell women's clothing in Japan?
10. Via online research, identify two mistakes that American companies have made in targeting consumers in other countries. Discuss how these mistakes could have been avoided if the companies involved had adequately researched some of the issues listed in Table 13.8.

EXERCISES

1. Have you ever traveled outside the United States? If so, please identify some of the differences in values, behavior, and consumption patterns you noted between people in a country you visited and Americans.
2. Interview a student from another culture about his or her use of (a) credit cards, (b) fast-food restaurants, (c) shampoo, and (d) sneakers. Compare your consumption behavior to that of the person you interviewed and discuss any similarities and differences you found.
3. Select one of the following countries: Mexico, Brazil, Germany, Italy, Israel, Kuwait, Japan, or Australia. Assume that a significant number of people in the country you chose would like to visit the United States and have the financial means to do so. Now, imagine you are a consultant for your state's tourism agency and that you have been charged with developing a promotional strategy to attract tourists from the country you chose. Conduct a computerized literature search of the databases in your school's library and select and read several articles about the lifestyles, customs, and consumption behavior of the people in the country you chose. Prepare an analysis of the articles and, on the basis of what you read, develop a promotional strategy designed to persuade tourists from that country to visit your state.

KEY TERMS

- acculturation *436*
- country-of-origin effects *428*
- cross-cultural consumer analysis *430*
- European Union *426*
- global strategy *442*
- local strategy *442*
- mixed strategies *442*
- multinational strategies *442*
- North American Free Trade Agreement (NAFTA) *426*
- product standardization *442*
- three Ps *443*
- world brand *438*

Case One: Japan to Apple's iPhone: "No Thanks!"

The new version of Apple's iPhone has generally been a strong seller worldwide, except in Japan. While some analysts had estimated that Apple would sell a million units of its latest iPhone in Japan, revised estimates put the number at more like 500,000 phones. So what's the problem? The phone uses the faster 3G network and offers a touch screen. And Apple iPods and computers are popular in Japan.

Well, it turns out that Apple iPhone's use of the 3G network is not a big deal in Japan, because 3G access has been a standard feature on Japanese cell phones for several years. And as far as the touch screen is concerned, some Japanese consumers feel that they would have problems getting used to it. Perhaps the biggest hurdle facing Apple, however, is what the iPhone doesn't have. Remember, Japanese consumers enjoy some of the world's most technologically advanced cell phone features, such as "a high-end color display, digital TV-viewing capability, satellite navigation service, music player and digital camera." Another "must have" feature in Japan, lacking in the iPhone, is "emoji," which is clip art that can be inserted into sentences to make e-mails more attractive. In addition, many mobile phones in Japan allow their users to use their phones as debit cards or train passes.

QUESTIONS

1. Did Apple err in trying to sell its latest iPhone in Japan?
2. Is the Japanese cell phone market similar to the cell phone markets in other countries?

Source: Yukari Iwatani Kane, "Apple's Latest iPhone Sees Slow Japan Sales," *Wall Street Journal,* September 15, 2008, B3.

Case Two: Would Mickey Mouse Eat Shark's Fin Soup?

Controversy started brewing at Hong Kong Disneyland even before the park opened in fall 2005. At Disney theme parks around the world, weddings and wedding receptions are a profitable business. Disney is planning to offer shark's fin soup as an option on wedding reception menus at Hong Kong Disneyland.

Clearly, Disney wants to show its appreciation for Chinese traditions, and claims that it is doing nothing more than following local standards—the dish is considered an essential part of a Chinese wedding banquet, and can be priced at up to $150 at the best restaurants. However, environmental groups from all over the world are up in arms over the prospect of Disney serving this soup, which points out a difference between Chinese and Western traditions.

Although shark's fin soup has been a Chinese favorite for 200 years, some environmental groups are concerned that China's increasing wealth has led to a greater appetite for rare species. For example, Hong Kong authorities recently stopped a shipment of 1,800 freeze-dried penguins that were being smuggled into mainland China. Some animal advocates are afraid that down the road entire species could be threatened.

QUESTION

1. As a member of the top management team at the Walt Disney Company, do you keep or delete shark's fin soup from the wedding banquet menu at Hong Kong Disneyland?

Source: Keith Bradsher, "Chinese Delicacy Has Disney in Turbulent Waters," *New York Times,* June 17, 2005, C1, C7.

14 Consumers and the Diffusion of Innovations

THIS CHAPTER deals with the dynamic processes that impact consumers' acceptance of new products and services. We will see that defining a new product or service is not an easy task. *New* can be revolutionary "new," like the first computer or building of a super network like the Internet. Alternatively, *new* can be a minor product variation, or a product that is new to consumers in a particular part of the world, but well established to consumers in another part of the world. Figure 14.1 presents an ad for a new flavor of sugarless gum (i..e, Cool Green Apple), that was introduced by Wrigley's. To simulate interest and trial, Wrigley's provided, as part of a special-offer, a coupon to encourage trial. Indeed, it is quite common for marketers to introduce new variations of a product, by stating that it is "new," and providing some form of incentives designed to stimulate trial.

In this chapter, we will explore factors that encourage and discourage acceptance (or rejection) of new products and services. For consumers, new products and services may represent increased opportunities to satisfy personal, social, and environmental needs and add to their quality of life. For the marketer, new products and services provide an important mechanism for keeping the firm competitive, profitable and growing.

FIGURE 14.1

Source: © Wm. Wrigley Jr. Company. Used with permission. All rights reserved.

QUESTION: *What Is Shown or Stated in This Ad That Is Designed to Attract Consumers to This New Product?*

Learning Objectives

14.1 *To Understand the Twofold Process of the Spread and Acceptance of Innovative Products and Services Within a Social System.*

14.2 *To Understand How Innovative Products and Services Spread (or Fail to Spread) Within a Social System.*

14.3 *To Understand How Individual Consumers Decide Whether or Not to Try and Adopt a Particularly Innovative Product or Service.*

14.4 *To Understand the Personal Characteristics of Innovators.*

Diffusion and Adoption of Innovations

Learning Objective

14.1 *To Understand the Twofold Process of the Spread and Acceptance of Innovative Products and Services Within a Social System.*

A major issue in marketing and consumer behavior is the acceptance of new products and services. The framework for exploring consumer acceptance of new products is drawn from the area of research known as the **diffusion of innovations**. Consumer researchers who specialize in the diffusion of innovations are primarily interested in understanding two closely related processes: the **diffusion process** and the **adoption process**. In the broadest sense, diffusion is a macro process concerned with the spread of a new product (an innovation) from its source to the consuming public. In contrast, adoption is a micro process that focuses on the stages through which an individual consumer passes when deciding to accept or reject a new product. In addition to an examination of these two interrelated processes, we present a profile of **consumer innovators**, those who are the first to purchase a new product. The ability of marketers to identify and reach this important group of consumers plays a major role in the success or failure of new-product introductions.

And why are new-product introductions so important? Consider GM's OnStar system, which is in widespread use today. When it was first introduced, it was a dealer-installed option that required consumers to obtain their own cellular accounts. When dealers informed GM that this procedure was overly cumbersome and was limiting sales, GM made a deal with a cellular telephone company, which allowed OnStar to be packaged as a factory-installed fully functioning communications device. GM was also told by consumers that they did not need the detailed diagnostic engine reports that the system was providing—they only needed to know the difference between a problem that required immediate emergency attention and one that could wait for a routine service appointment.[1] These changes to the original GM version of OnStar undoubtedly increased its popularity with GM vehicle purchasers.

The Diffusion Process

Learning Objective

14.2 *To Understand How Innovative Products and Services Spread (or Fail to Spread) Within a Social System.*

The diffusion process is concerned with how innovations spread, that is, how they are assimilated within a market. More precisely, diffusion is the process by which the acceptance of an innovation (a new product, new service, new idea, or new practice) is spread by communication (mass media, salespeople, or informal conversations) to members of a social system (a target market) over a period of time. This definition includes the four basic elements of the diffusion process: (1) the innovation, (2) the channels of communication, (3) the social system, and (4) time.

THE INNOVATION

No universally accepted definition of the terms **product or service innovation** or *new product* exists. Instead, there have been various approaches taken to define a new product or a new service; these can be classified as *firm-, product-, market-*, and *consumer-oriented definitions of innovations*.

Firm-Oriented Definitions

A *firm-oriented* approach treats the newness of a product from the perspective of the company producing or marketing it. When the product is "new" to the company, it is considered new. This definition ignores whether or not the product is actually new to the marketplace (i.e., to competitors or consumers). Consistent with this view, copies or modifications of a competitor's product would qualify as new. Although this definition has considerable merit when the objective is to examine the impact that a "new" product has on the firm, it is not very useful when the goal is to understand consumer acceptance of a new product.

Product-Oriented Definitions

In contrast to firm-oriented definitions, a *product-oriented* approach focuses on the features inherent in the product itself and on the effects these features are likely to have on consumers' established usage patterns. One product-oriented framework considers the extent to which a new product is likely to disrupt established behavior patterns. It defines the following three types of product innovations:[2]

1. A **continuous innovation** has the least disruptive influence on established patterns. It involves the introduction of a modified product rather than a totally new product. Examples include the newly redesigned Apple MacBook, the latest version of Microsoft Office, reduced-fat Oreo cookies, Hershey Cacao (i.e., a form of dark) chocolate bars, American Express gift cards, BAND-AID TOUGH-STRIPS, and the Oral-B® Advantage Glide (see Figure 14.2).
2. A **dynamically continuous innovation** is somewhat more disruptive than a continuous innovation but still does not alter established behavior patterns. It may involve the creation of a new product or the modification of an existing product. Examples include digital cameras, digital video recorders, MP3 players, DVRs, USB flash drives, and disposable diapers.
3. A **discontinuous innovation** requires consumers to adopt new behavior patterns. Examples include airplanes, radios, TVs, automobiles, fax machines, PCs, videocassette recorders, medical self-test kits, and the Internet.

Figure 14.3 shows how the telephone, a discontinuous innovation of major magnitude, has produced a variety of both dynamically continuous and continuous innovations and has even stimulated the development of other discontinuous innovations.

Market-Oriented Definitions

A *market-oriented* approach judges the newness of a product in terms of how much exposure consumers have to the new product. Two market-oriented definitions of product innovation have been used extensively in consumer studies:

1. A product is considered new if it has been purchased by a relatively small (fixed) percentage of the potential market.
2. A product is considered new if it has been on the market for a relatively short (specified) period of time.

Both of these market-oriented definitions are basically subjective because they leave the researcher with the task of establishing the degree of sales penetration within the market that qualifies the product as an "innovation" (such as the first 10 percent of the potential market to use the new product) or how long the product can be on the market and still be considered "new" (i.e., the first three months that the product is available).

Consumer-Oriented Definitions

Although each of the three approaches described have been useful to consumer researchers in their study of the diffusion of innovations, some researchers have favored a *consumer-oriented* approach in defining an innovation.[3] In this context, a "new" product is any product that a potential consumer judges to be new. In other words, newness is based on the consumer's perception of the product rather than on physical features or market realities. Although the consumer-oriented approach has been endorsed by some advertising and marketing practitioners, it has received little systematic research attention.

FIGURE 14.2
Source: Courtesy of the Procter & Gamble Company. All rights reserved.

QUESTION: *What Kind of Innovation Is Shown Here, and Why?*

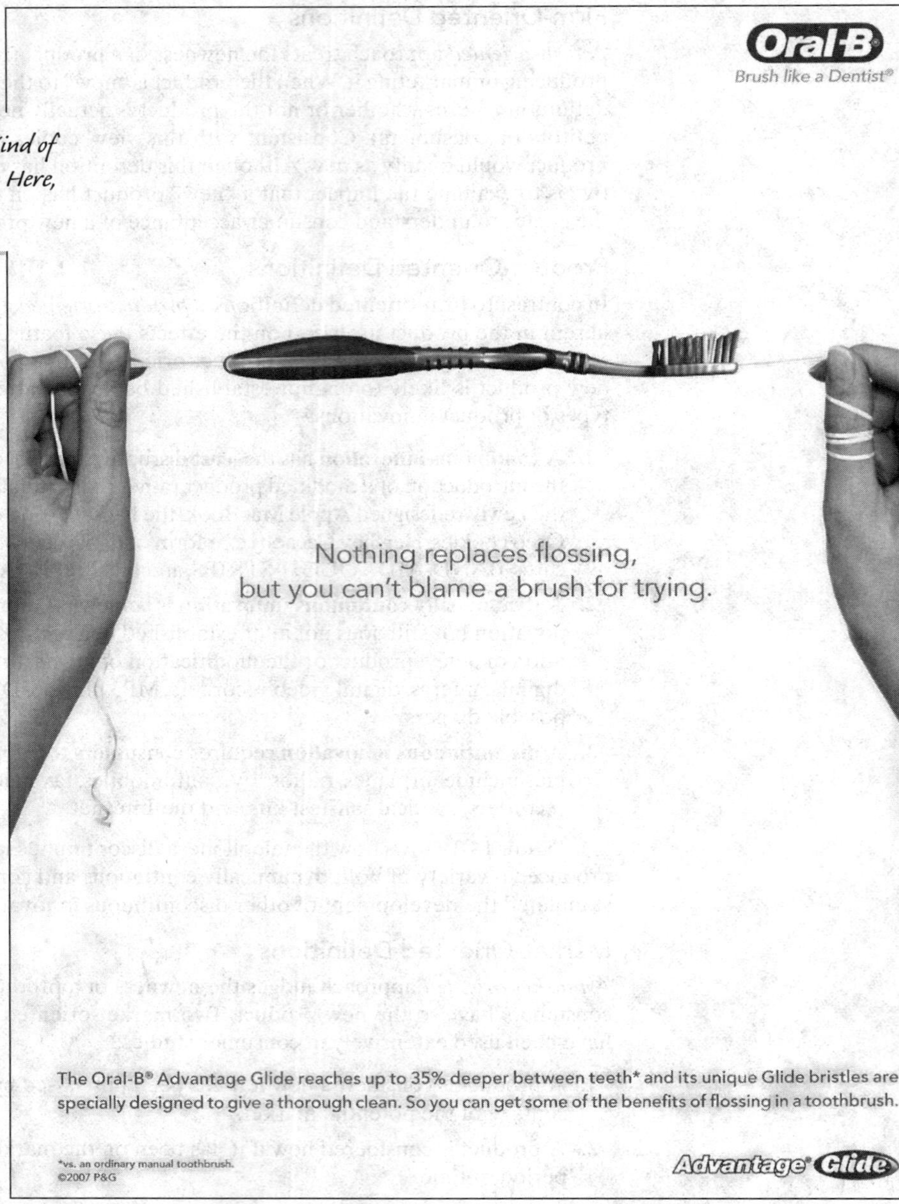

Additionally, it should be pointed out that although this portion of the chapter deals primarily with what might be described as "purchase" innovativeness (or time of adoption), a second type of innovativeness, "use innovativeness," has been the subject of some thought and research. A consumer is being *use innovative* when he or she uses a previously adopted product in a novel or unusual way, or very extensively. In one study that dealt with the adoption of VCRs and PCs, early adopters showed significantly higher use innovativeness than those who adopted somewhat later along the cycle of acceptance of the innovation.[4]

Product Characteristics That Influence Diffusion

All products that are new do not have equal potential for consumer acceptance. Some products seem to catch on almost overnight (e.g. cordless telephones), whereas others take a very long time to gain acceptance or never seem to achieve widespread consumer acceptance (e.g. trash compactors).

FIGURE 14.3
The Telephone Has Led to Related Innovations

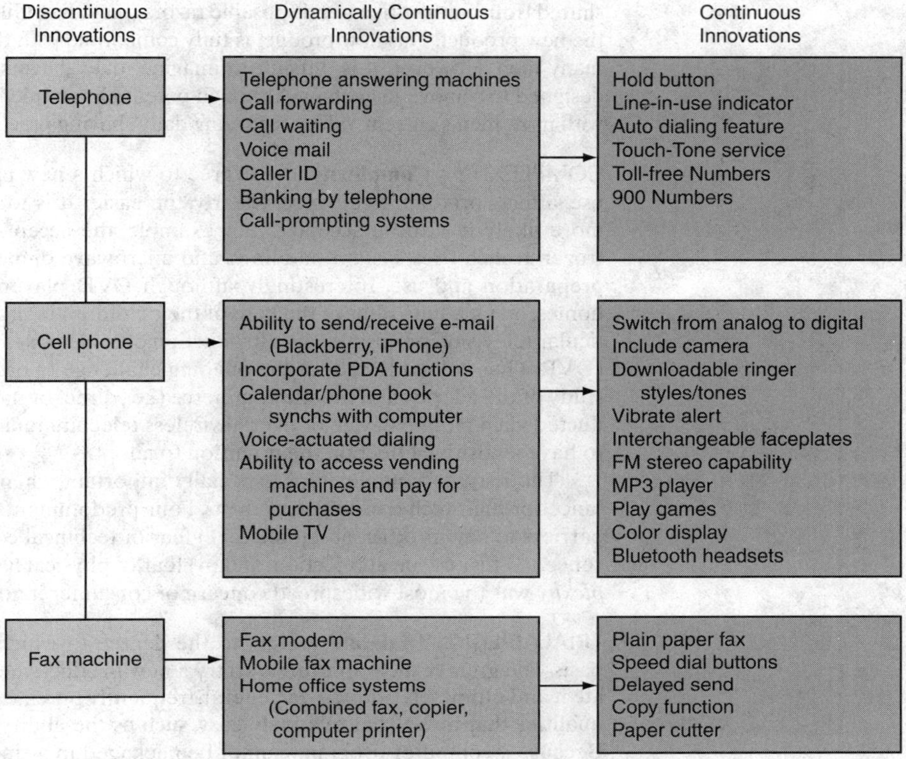

The uncertainties of product marketing would be reduced if marketers could anticipate how consumers will react to their products. For example, if a marketer knew that a product contained inherent features that were likely to inhibit its acceptance, the marketer could develop a promotional strategy that would compensate for these features or decide not to market the product at all. Pickup trucks are now being designed for the female driver, and manufacturers are careful to design door handles that do not break nails. Ford even offers adjustable gas and brake pedals in order to accomodate women's height.[5]

Although there are no precise formulas by which marketers can evaluate a new product's likely acceptance, diffusion researchers have identified five product characteristics that influence consumer acceptance of new products: (1) relative advantage, (2) compatibility, (3) complexity, (4) trialability, and (5) observability.[6] Based on available research, it has been estimated that these five product characteristics account for much of the rate or speed of adoption.[7]

RELATIVE ADVANTAGE The degree to which potential customers perceive a new product as superior to existing substitutes is its **relative advantage**. For example, although people can carry beepers so that their business offices or families can contact them, a cellular telephone enables users to be in nearly instant communication with the world and allows users to both receive and place calls. The fax machine is another example of an innovation that offers users a significant relative advantage in terms of their ability to communicate. A document can be transmitted in as little as 15 to 18 seconds at perhaps one-tenth the cost of an overnight express service, which will not deliver the document until the following day. Of course, sending the document as an attachment to an e-mail entails no cost and, like a fax, gets delivered in seconds.

COMPATIBILITY The degree to which potential consumers feel a new product is consistent with their present needs, values, and practices is a measure of its **compatibility**. For instance, an advantage of 3M's Scotch Pop-up Tape Strips is that they are easier to use than roll tape for certain tasks (such as wrapping gifts), yet they represent no new learning for the user. Similarly, in the realm of shaving products, it is not too difficult to imagine that a few years ago when Gillette introduced the Fusion razor, some men made the transition from inexpensive disposable razors and other men shifted from competitive nondisposable razors (including Gillette's own MACH3 razors) to using the new product. This new product is fully compatible with the established wet-shaving rituals of many men. However, it is difficult to imagine male shavers shifting to a new depilatory cream designed to remove facial hair. Although potentially simpler to use, such a cream is *incompatible* with most men's current values regarding daily shaving practices.

COMPLEXITY **Complexity**, the degree to which a new product is difficult to understand or use, affects product acceptance. Clearly, the easier it is to understand and use a product, the more likely it is to be accepted. For example, the acceptance of such convenience foods as frozen french fries, instant puddings, and microwave dinners is generally due to their ease of preparation and use. Interestingly, although DVD players can be found in most American homes, many adults require the help of their children in order to use the devices to record particular television programs. The introduction of cable boxes with built-in digital video recorders (DVRs) has helped to reduce the ongoing challenge to easily record a TV program. A recent study of the adoption of mobile commerce (i.e., direct or indirect commercial transactions conducted via a mobile device or over a wireless telecommunication) found perceived ease of use to have a positive effect on the intention to adopt.[8]

The issue of complexity is especially important when attempting to gain market acceptance for high-tech consumer products. Four predominant types of "technological fear" act as barriers to new-product acceptance: (1) fear of technical complexity, (2) fear of rapid obsolescence, (3) fear of social rejection, and (4) fear of physical harm. Of the four, *technological complexity* was the most widespread concern of consumer innovators.[9]

TRIALABILITY **Trialability** refers to the degree to which a new product tried on a limited basis. The greater the opportunity to try a new product, the easier it is for consumers to evaluate it and ultimately adopt it. In general, frequently purchased household products tend to have qualities that make trial relatively easy, such as the ability to purchase a small or "trial" size. Because a computer program cannot be packaged in a smaller size, many computer software companies offer free working models of their latest software to encourage computer users to try the program and subsequently buy the program.

Aware of the importance of trial, marketers of new supermarket products commonly use substantial cents-off coupons or free samples to provide consumers with direct product experience. On the other hand, durable items, such as refrigerators or ovens, are difficult to try without making a major commitment. This may explain why publications such as *Consumer Reports* are so widely consulted for their ratings of infrequently purchased durable goods.

OBSERVABILITY **Observability** (or communicability) is the ease with which a product's benefits or attributes can be observed, imagined, or described to potential consumers. Products that have a high degree of social visibility, such as fashion items, are more easily diffused than products that are used in private, such as a new type of deodorant. Similarly, a tangible product is promoted more easily than an intangible product (such as a service).

It is also important to recognize that a particular innovation may diffuse differently throughout different cultures. For example, although shelf-stable milk (milk that does not require refrigeration) has been successfully sold for years in Europe, Americans thus far have generally resisted the aseptic milk package. Table 14.1 summarizes the product characteristics that influence diffusion.

Resistance to Innovation

What makes some new products almost instant successes, while others must struggle to achieve consumer acceptance? After all, the dishwasher was first introduced in 1893, but it was more than 50 years later that it succeeded as a mainstream product.[10] To help answer such a question, marketers look at the product characteristics of an innovation. Such characteristics offer clues to help determine the extent of consumer resistance, which increases when perceived relative advantage, perceived compatibility, trialability, and communicability are low, and perceived complexity is high. The term *innovation overload* is used to describe the situation in which the increase in information and options available to the consumer is so great that it seriously impairs decision making. As a result, the consumer finds it difficult to make comparisons among the available choices. In a world in which consumers often find themselves with too little time

TABLE 14.1 Product Characteristics That Influence Diffusion

CHARACTERISTICS	DEFINITION	EXAMPLES
Relative Advantage	The degree to which potential customers perceive a new product as superior to existing substitutes	HDTV over standard TV, MP3 player over a traditional CD player
Compatibility	The degree to which potential consumers feel a new product is consistent with their present needs, values, and practices	Gillette MACH3 Turbo over disposable razors, digital alarm clocks over analog alarm clocks
Complexity	The degree to which a new product is difficult to understand or use	Products low in complexity include hot and cold cereals, disposable razors, and soap
Trialability	The degree to which a new product is capable of being tried on a limited basis	Trial-size jars and bottles of new products, free trials of software, free samples, cents-off coupons
Observability	The degree to which a product's benefits or attributes can be observed, imagined, or described to potential customers	Clothing, such as Ralph Lauren jeans, sneakers, laptops, messenger bags

and too much stress, increased complexity of products wastes time and may reduce or eliminate acceptance of the product.

Consider the screw cap wine bottle, which is preferred by less than 10 percent of U.S. wine consumers and used on no more than 5 percent of U.S. wines. In contrast, the screw cap wine bottle can be found on 40 percent of domestically sold wine bottles in Australia and 80 percent of domestically sold wine bottles in New Zealand. While many consumers, especially in the United States, associate a screw cap with "cheap" wine, the fact is that the screw cap eliminates a major wine industry quality problem known as "cork taint," which occurs when a bottle of wine takes on a musty flavor due to a poor quality cork. It appears that acceptance of the screw cap in Australia and New Zealand by wine consumers was accomplished by a cooperative effort of wineries in the two countries to promote the benefits of the screw cap. In contrast, in the United States, where distributors tend to be especially competitive, there has been a general lack of a uniform effort to promote the benefits of screw caps over the well established cork to consumers. Also, U.S. wineries have had only limited success in trying to establish niche markets of wine connoisseurs who know the benefits of the screw cap wine bottle. Moreover, in contrast, New Zealand wineries formed the New Zealand Wine Seal Initiative, with the purpose of promoting the screw cap.[11] Another study differentiated between receptive and resistant innovations. Figure 14.4 indicates how a marketer might develop a strategy for diffusing both receptive innovations and resistant innovations.

It is also important to note that the product characteristics that influence diffusion may vary from country to country. For example, a study that compared perceptions of electronic commerce among both U.S. and Indian consumers found that relative advantage, ease of use (complexity), compatibility, and image (degree to which the use of the innovation enhances the individual's image or social status) differed between the two countries. Some of these differences can be explained by India's limited access to PCs and the Internet, resulting in lower customer experience with these technologies.[12]

THE CHANNELS OF COMMUNICATION

How quickly an innovation spreads through a market depends to a great extent on communications between the marketer and consumers, as well as communication among consumers (word-of-mouth communication). Of central concern is the uncovering of the relative influence of impersonal sources (advertising and editorial matter) and interpersonal sources (salespeople and informal opinion leaders). Over the past decade or so, we have also seen the rapid increase of the Internet as a major consumer-related source of information. The Internet is particularly interesting since it can on the one hand be seen as an interpersonal source of information (e.g., with its Internet ads, Webpods, e-Commerce Web sites that function in a similar fashion to direct-mail catalogues). On the other hand, the Internet is an interpersonal source of information because it provides consumers with an incredible number of company- and noncompany-sponsored forums and discussion groups

FIGURE 14.4
Developing a Marketing Strategy for Diffusing Innovations

Source: Rosanna Garcia, Fleura Bardhi, and Colette Friedrich, "Overcoming Consumer Resistance to Innovation," *MIT Sloan Management Review*, 48, no. 4 (Summer 2007): 87.

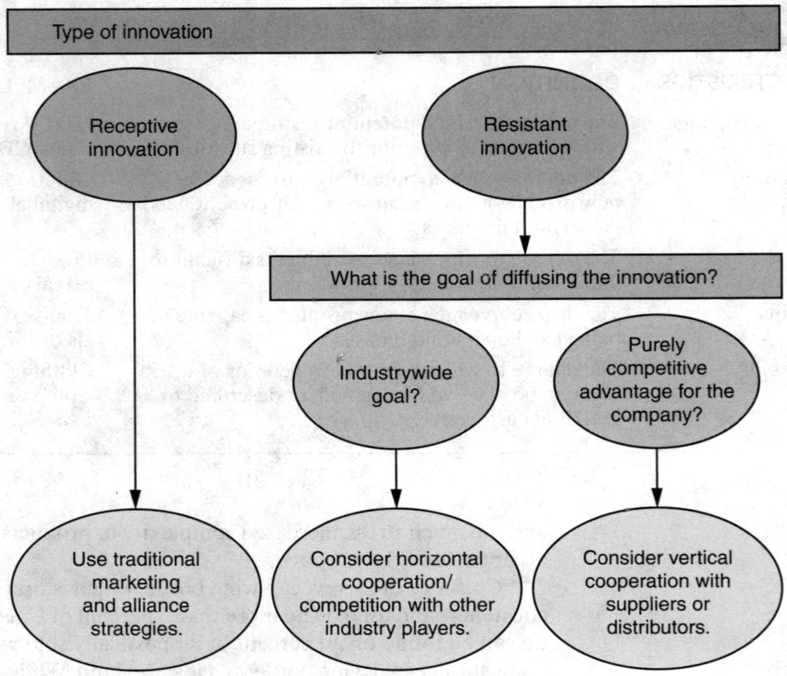

to chat away with people who have expertise and experience that is vital to making an informed decision.

Still further, in recent years, a variety of new channels of communication have been developed to inform consumers of innovative products and services. Consider the growth of interactive marketing messages, in which the consumer becomes an important part of the communication rather than just a "passive" message recipient. For example, for the past several years, an increasing number of companies, such as the Ford Motor Company, General Motors, and other major automobile manufactures, have used DVDs to promote their products.

Rapidly growing new media are creating or enhancing all types of additional word-of-mouth online. For instance, podcasts and social networking, which consumers are using to seek out information alternatives to TV, radio, and print information, is now commonplace. It has been estimated that there are now thousands of podcasts available on the Internet, which the consumer can download as audio files (e.g., computer, MP3 player). For example, the *Harvard Business Review* is available in audio format as a podcast.[13]

Sometimes, though, even old-fashioned ways of disseminating information about a new product can work effectively to reach innovators. Consider the Dyson vacuum cleaner, which seems to have dominated its product category almost overnight. In order to reach innovators and opinion leaders, Dyson issued no press releases, which meant that the only way for the media to get information was through interviews. As a result, between 1994 and 1998, interviews with Dyson appeared frequently in the media, and featured both the man and the product. The story of Dyson's success with overcoming the problems associated with "traditional" vacuum cleaners, and the fact that his product looked like no other vacuum cleaner, helped Dyson's product succeed in the marketplace.[14] In terms of *relative advantage,* the Dyson is superior to traditional vacuum cleaners because it does not lose suction power as it picks up dirt.

THE SOCIAL SYSTEM

The diffusion of a new product usually takes place in a social setting frequently referred to as a *social system.* In the context of consumer behavior, the terms *market segment* and *target market* may be more relevant than the term *social system* used in diffusion research. A social system is a physical, social, or cultural environment to which people belong and within which they function. For example, for a new hybrid-seed corn, the social system might consist of all farmers in a number of local communities. For a new drug, the social system might consist of all physicians within a specific medical specialty (e.g., all neurologists). For a new special diet product, the social system might include all residents of a geriatric community. As these examples indicate, the social system serves as the *boundary* within which the diffusion of a new product is examined. A recent study among 10- to 12-year-olds in England, for example, discovered that these children felt that the next logical step in mobile phone development was mobile TV—something that they are ready to adopt.[15] And a study of the diffusion of an innovative new computer program among 8- to 12-year-old school children in The Netherlands found that the children's social networks played a more important role in the diffusion process than information from the mass media.[16]

The orientation of a social system, with its own special values or norms, is likely to influence the acceptance or rejection of new products. When a social system is modern in orientation, the acceptance of innovations is likely to be high. In contrast, when a social system is traditional in orientation, innovations that are perceived as radical or as infringements on established customs are likely to be avoided. According to one authority, the following characteristics typify a *modern social system*:[17]

- A positive attitude toward change
- An advanced technology and skilled labor force
- A general respect for education and science
- An emphasis on rational and ordered social relationships rather than on emotional ones
- An outreach perspective, in which members of the system frequently interact with outsiders, thus facilitating the entrance of new ideas into the social system
- A system in which members can readily see themselves in quite different roles

Furthermore, a social system (either modern or traditional) may be national in scope and may influence members of an entire society or may exist at the local level and influence only those who live in a specific community. The key point to remember is that a social system's orientation is the climate in which marketers must operate to gain acceptance for their new products. For example, in recent years, the United States has experienced a decline in the demand for beef, from just under 80 pounds per person in 1970 to a little over 60 pounds per person in the first few years of this century.[18] The growing interest in health and fitness throughout the nation has created a climate in which beef is considered too high in fat and in caloric content. At the same time, the consumption of chicken and fish has increased because these foods satisfy the prevailing nutritional values of a great number of consumers.

Returning to the notion that the social system may be national in scope, a recent study explored cultural differences and consumers' propensity to adopt innovations among both French and German consumers. The research found consumers more likely to exhibit an inclination to innovate if their culture can be characterized by small power distance (i.e., they value equality, not hierarchical power), weak uncertainty avoidance (i.e., consumers accept uncertainty and take each day as it comes), and masculinity (i.e., the culture places value on masculine traits, such as high earnings, achievement, assertiveness).[19]

TIME

Time is the backbone of the diffusion process. It pervades the study of diffusion in three distinct but interrelated ways: (1) the *amount of purchase time,* (2) the identification of *adopter categories,* and (3) the *rate of adoption.*

Purchase Time

Purchase time refers to the amount of time that elapses between consumers' initial awareness of a new product or service and the point at which they purchase or reject it. Table 14.2 illustrates the scope of purchase time by tracking a hypothetical advertising agency director's purchase of a new HDTV for her home.

Table 14.2 illustrates not only the length and complexity of consumer decision making but also how different information sources become important at successive steps in the process. Purchase time is an important concept because the average time a consumer takes to adopt a new product is sometimes a useful predictor of the overall length of time it will take for the new

TABLE 14.2 Time Line for Selecting an HDTV

WEEK	PRECIPITATING SITUATIONS/FACTORS
0	Janet, a group account director for an advertising agency, has been living and working in Manhattan since graduating college 10 years ago. Last Spring she purchased a one-bedroom apartment in a very nice "doorman" building in Manhattan, in a location that allows her the luxury of being able to walk to work. This apartment replaced the studio she had been renting—one that was small and was not suitable for entertaining friends (at least not more than one or two at a time). Since moving into her new home she has been planning to replace her old inexpensive furniture with more fashionable furniture. But it takes her several months of living in her new home to have some idea of what style she wishes to decorate in and what pieces of furniture she wants to purchase. Also, because of the expense of moving, having the apartment painted, purchasing window blinds, etc., it takes about four months before she feels she is ready to being decorating.
	DECISION PROCESS BEGINS
16–20	Janet visits a number of furniture stores and talks to salespeople about the pros and cons of various types and styles of furniture. She also, when visiting friends, carefully evaluates how they have decorated their apartments.
21	Janet's parents live in a suburb of New York City and are presently redecorating a number of rooms in their home. At her mother's suggestion, Janet has her mother's decorator visit her in her new apartment to discuss decorating options and colors.
	A TV STORAGE UNIT IS PURCHASED
22	When shopping at a branch of a national furniture store chain, Janet sees a TV unit that she falls in love with. It is about 100 inches wide, and consists of a central storage piece—made for an HDTV set to sit on top—flanked by a tall thin bookcase on each side. She feels that this unit would be perfect for the long wall in her living room, and she purchases it.
23	The new furniture is delivered.
	CONSUMER ACQUIRES A MENTOR (OPINION LEADER)
24	Janet knows that her younger brother, who also lives and works in Manhattan, is pretty much of an expert on anything and everything electronic, including TVs. Her brother has been helping her for years with computer problems and whenever she moved he was the person who connected her TV to the cable box and DVD, got her broadband Internet service working properly with her wireless modem, and so on. So Janet asks her brother which HDTV sets she should consider buying.
	FEATURES AND BRAND OPTIONS ARE REVIEWED
25–27	While the wall unit can handle a 50-inch HDTV set, Janet decides that there is a limit to how much money she is willing to spend, because she still plans to purchase a dining room table and chairs in the very near future. She and her brother decide that a 40- to 42-inch HDTV set would look very good on top of her unit, and that the picture quality from a 720p set will be fine (rather than spending hundreds of dollars more for a 1080p picture). With the advice of her brother, and after visiting a number of electronics stores with him, Janet narrows down her choice to one Panasonic model, one Sony model, and one Samsung model. While the Panasonic is a plasma set, the other two are LCD HDTVs.
28–29	Janet revisits several electronics stores to again look at the Panasonic, Sony, and Samsung models of interest. She also spends time on the CNET Web site reading about these TVs. She concludes that all HDTVs look great to her. Her brother suggests that since the Panasonic is available in the 42-inch size, while the others are only available in a 40-inch size (she doesn't want to spend the extra money for the next size up, which is 46 inches), she might be better off purchasing the larger TV, since it got a very good review on CNET and its price is comparable.

TABLE 14.2 Time Line for Selecting an HDTV *Continued*

WEEK	PRECIPITATING SITUATIONS/FACTORS
	ORDERING THE HDTV
30	Janet prices the Panasonic HDTV model she is interested in. Big electronics stores in Manhattan (each is part of a national chain) are asking about $800 for the TV. She also prices the set online. While several e-tailers are asking $770–$780, with free delivery, the price on Buydig.com is $750 (again, with free delivery). Both her father and her uncle have purchased HDTVs from Buydig.com, and both were very pleased with this e-tailer. So Janet orders the set on a Sunday afternoon, using her laptop, and pays for the purchase with a credit card.
	Janet receives an e-mail Monday afternoon that her HDTV set has been shipped and that the trucking company will call her the day before delivery to give her a time. The e-mail also tells Janet that the truck driver will take off the top of the box for her so that she can inspect the screen for cracks. Janet receives a call on Wednesday telling her to expect delivery between 9:00 A.M. and 11:00 A.M. on Thursday. She lets her boss know that she will be coming to work a little late Thursday morning. At 9:15 A.M. Thursday morning the doorman in her building lets her know that a large package has arrived, and the deliveryman wants to bring it up to her apartment. Janet tells the doorman to please let him come into the building, and four minutes later the deliveryman and her new TV are in her apartment. The deliveryman takes off the top of the carton, Janet inspects the TV, which is in perfect condition, tips the deliveryman, and then heads off to her office. While walking to her office she calls her brother to let him know that her HDTV set has been delivered, and he promises to come over to her apartment after work that evening to hook it up. By 7:00 P.M. Janet's new HDTV set is sitting on top of her TV unit, connected, and Janet is marveling at how great the picture is. She thanks her brother and says to him "I'm buying, where would you like to eat dinner?"

product to achieve widespread adoption. For example, when the individual purchase time is short, a marketer can expect that the overall rate of diffusion will be faster than when the individual purchase time is long.

A recent research study, conducted in Mexico, investigated the importance of temporal distance (i.e., time) in the new-product adoption process. Findings indicate that while consumers considering adoption in the near future focus on uncertainties related to the negative aspects of adoption, such as switching-cost and affective uncertainties, those considering adoption in the distant future focus more on the uncertainties associated with the benefits of adoption (performance and symbolic uncertainties). Consequently, effective promotional strategy for a new product that is to be immediately adopted should focus on process simulation (how to deal with the constraints of adoption), while effective promotion targeted to those who will adopt in the distant future should focus on outcomes (the desirable reasons for adoption).[20]

Adopter Categories

The concept of **adopter categories** stems from a classification scheme that depicts where consumers stand in relation to other consumers in terms of their time of purchase of a new product or service (i.e., an innovation). Generally, *five* adopter categories are identified in the diffusion literature: *innovators* (first 2.5 percent to adopt), *early adopters* (next 13.5 percent to adopt), *early majority* (next 34 percent to adopt), *late majority* (next 34 percent to adopt), and *laggards* (last 16 percent to adopt). If drawn, these five adopter categories take on the shape of a normal or bell shape distribution, like the one appearing in statistics textbooks (see Figure 14.5 Part A).

The following is a concise description of the five adopter-categories in the context of the diffusion of a new product—a mini netbook PC (i.e., a small, light, thin, and wireless personal computer):

CONSUMER ADOPTER CATEGORY 1—*INNOVATORS* are the earliest consumers to buy the mini netbook. The innovative consumers of hi-tech products or services are often members of the "geek class" (see Chapter 10) who love technology, perceive little risk in adopting new products, and are even willing to pay higher prices for newly-introduced products because they enjoy being the first to own such gadgets. They are also very likely to provide information and advice to potential later adopters (i.e., to be opinion leaders in the realm of hi-tech products).

CONSUMER ADOPTER CATEGORY 2—*EARLY ADOPTERS* are consumers who are likely to buy the mini netbook within a short period of time following its introduction (but not as early as the innovators). Within their local neighborhoods or circles of friends, early adopters are also quite likely to provide information and assistance to others who are evaluating a new product like a mini netbook, and thus they are also likely to be opinion leaders.

CONSUMER ADOPTER CATEGORY 3—*EARLY MAJORITY* are members of the first half of the "mass market" of consumers who would purchase the now somewhat-established mini netbook. When the product was first introduced, they perceived purchasing it as risky because it was new. After a relatively small but not insignificant number of consumers purchased the product (and probably after the price of the product has gone down), these consumers concluded that purchasing the product is wise.

CONSUMER ADOPTER CATEGORY 4—*LATE MAJORITY* consumers are the second half of the "mass market" of consumers who purchase the now even older (possibly at or heading toward "maturity") mini netbook. The members of the "late majority" category of adopters have taken a relatively long time to evaluate whether or not they would benefit by owning a mini netbook and, most likely, perceive more risk in all consumption situations than members of the three preceding adopter groups. Together, the early and late majority adopter categories constitute the large and maturing market for any innovation.

CONSUMER ADOPTER CATEGORY 5—*LAGGARDS* are the very last group of consumers to purchase the mini netbook. When they get around to purchasing the product, the innovators and early adopters are already probably switching to more advanced innovations in this product category. Laggards are generally high risk-perceivers and the last ones to recognize the value of innovative products.

Clearly, in the case of most products, *not all* members of a given society are likely to adopt an innovation. In some cases a very large percentage of consumers purchase a product innovation within a social system and; in other cases a very small percentage of consumers will purchase. In either case, only those who adopted a product or service are included in one of the five categories. The remaining members of a particular society or consumer social system, that is, those who are not accounted for in the five categories, are called "non-adopters" or "non-purchasers."

As far as the exact percentage of consumers belonging to each of the five adopter-categories, marketing practitioners and researchers have *not* used the first 2.5 percent limit to classify consumers as "innovators." Instead, they have generally defined "innovators" as approximately the first 10 percent of the total purchasers or adopters of a particular products or services. This figure stems from considering real world historical data collected from various industries where product innovations are common. As an example, following the same practice, marketers might estimate the percentages of consumers belonging to the remaining four adopter categories as follows: *early adopters* as 15 percent, *early majority* as 30 percent, *late majority* as 30 percent, and *laggards* as 15 percent. Figure 14.5 Part B depicts the distribution of adopter categories that are formed from the above assumed percentages for each of the five adopter categories. In reality, while there are not fixed rules for defining the size of a product's or service's diffusion curve, there are patterns for various industries that serve as guidelines.

All Nonadopters May Not Be Equal

A recent research study that explored the diffusion of Internet banking services found that not only did differences exist between adopters and nonadopters, but there were also differences between "prospective adopters" (consumers likely to adopt Internet banking within the next 12 months) and "persistent nonadopters."[21] In this study, prospective adopters were most often heavier users of ATMs, phone banking, and used computers for work. In contrast, per-

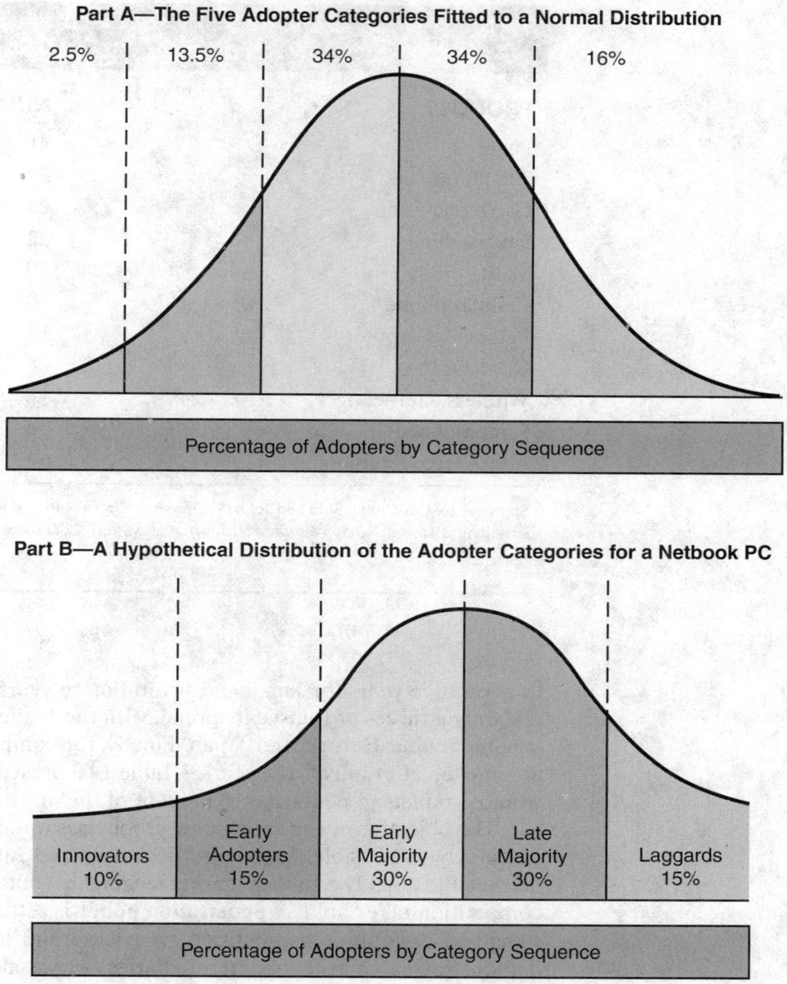

FIGURE 14.5
Two Different Diffusion Curves for the Five Adopter Categories

sistent nonadopters were generally less familiar with technology. There was also little difference between current adopters and prospective adopters with regard to such adoption factors as compatibility and experience with technology. Overall, the differences between adopters and prospective adopters were perceptual, while the differences between prospective adopters and persistent nonadopters reflected varying degrees of technological sophistication (of the lack if it). Perhaps the most important lesson to be learned from this research is that demographic characteristics alone are generally not an effective way to profile adopters versus nonadopters.

Rate of Adoption

The rate of adoption is concerned with how long it takes a new product or service to be adopted by members of a social system, that is, how quickly it takes a new product to be accepted by those who will ultimately adopt it. The general view is that the rate of adoption for new products is getting faster or shorter. Fashion adoption is a form of diffusion, one in which the rate of adoption is important. Cyclical fashion trends or "fads" are extremely "fast," whereas "fashion classics" may have extremely slow or "long" cycles.

In general, the diffusion of products worldwide is becoming a more rapid phenomenon. For example, it took black-and-white TVs about 12 years longer to reach the same level of penetration in Europe and Japan as in the United States. For color TVs, the lag time dropped

TABLE 14.3 Time Required for Electronic Products to Penetrate 10 Percent of the Mass Market in the United Kingdom

PRODUCT	NUMBER OF YEARS
Pager	41
Telephone	38
Cable television	25
Fax machine	22
VCR	9
Cellular phone	9
Personal computer	7
CD-ROM*	6
Wireless data service*	6
Screen-phone*	6
Interactive television*	3

Source: Eric Chi-Chung Shiu and John A. Dawson, "Cross-National Consumer Segmentation of Internet Shopping for Britain and Taiwan," *Service Industries Journal (London),* 22 (January 2002): 163. Reprinted by permission.

*Predicted.

to about five years for Japan and several more years for Europe. In contrast, for VCRs there was only a three- or four-year spread, with the United States (with its emphasis on cable TV) lagging behind Europe and Japan. Finally, for compact disk players, penetration levels were about even after only three years.[22] Table 14.3 presents the time required for a sample of electronic products to penetrate 10 percent of the mass market in the United Kingdom.

The objective in marketing new products is usually to gain wide acceptance of the product as quickly as possible. Marketers desire a rapid rate of product adoption to penetrate the market and quickly establish market leadership (obtain the largest share of the market) before competition takes hold. A **penetration policy** is setting a relatively low introductory price designed to discourage competition from entering the market. Rapid product adoption also demonstrates to marketing intermediaries (wholesalers and retailers) that the product is worthy of their full and continued support.

Under certain circumstances, marketers might prefer to avoid a rapid rate of adoption for a new product. For example, marketers who wish to use a pricing strategy that will enable them to recoup their development costs quickly might follow a **skimming policy**: They first make the product available at a very high price to consumers who are willing to pay top dollar and then gradually lower the price in a stepwise fashion to attract additional market segments at each price reduction plateau. For example, when Blu-ray disc players were first introduced, they sold for more than $700. Today they can be purchased for $200 or less.

In addition to how long it takes from introduction to the point of adoption (or when the purchase actually occurs), it is useful to track the extent of adoption (the diffusion rate). For instance, a particular corporation might not upgrade its employees' computer systems to the Windows Vista environment until after many other companies in the area have already begun to do so. However, once it decides to upgrade, it might install Windows Vista software in a relatively short period of time on all of its employees' PCs. Thus, although the company was relatively "late" with respect to *time* of adoption, its *extent* of adoption was very high.

Although sales graphs depicting the adoption categories (again, see Figure 14.5) are typically thought of as having a normal distribution in which sales continue to increase prior to reaching a peak (at the top of the curve), some research evidence indicates that a third to a half of such sales curves, at least in the consumer electronics industry, involve an initial peak, a trough, and then another sales increase. Such a "saddle" in the sales curve has been attributed to the *early* market adopters and the *main* market adopters being two separate markets.[23] Figure 14.6 presents two examples of sales curves with saddles—PCs and VCR decks with stereo.

FIGURE 14.6
"Sales Saddle" Differentiates Early Market Adopters from the Main Market Adopters

Source: Jacob Goldenberg, Barak Libai, and Eitan Muller, "Riding the Saddle: How Cross-Market Communications Can Create a Major Slump in Sales," *Journal of Marketing*, 66 (April 2002): 5.

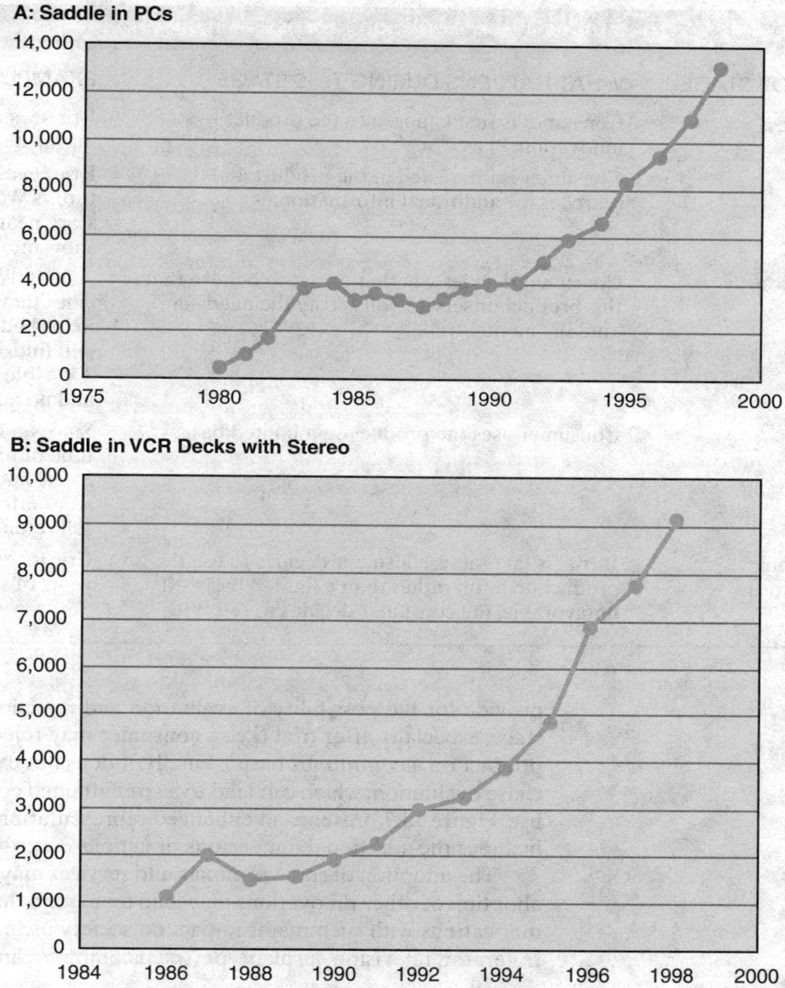

The Adoption Process

LEARNING OBJECTIVE

14.3 *To Understand How Individual Consumers Decide Whether or Not to Try and Adopt a Particularly Innovative Product or Service.*

The second major process in the diffusion of innovations is *adoption.* The focus of this process is the stages through which an individual consumer passes while arriving at a decision to try or not to try, or to continue using or to discontinue using a new product. (The *adoption process* should not be confused with *adopter categories.*)

STAGES IN THE ADOPTION PROCESS

It is often assumed that the consumer moves through five stages in arriving at a decision to purchase or reject a new product: (1) awareness, (2) interest, (3) evaluation, (4) trial, and (5) adoption (or rejection). The assumption underlying the adoption process is that consumers engage in extensive information search (see Chapter 7), whereas consumer involvement theory suggests that for some products, a limited information search is more likely (for low-involvement products). The five **stages in the adoption process** are described in Table 14.4.

Although the traditional adoption process model is insightful in its simplicity, it does not adequately reflect the full complexity of the consumer adoption process. For one, it does not adequately acknowledge that there is quite often a need or problem-recognition stage that consumers face before acquiring an awareness of potential options or solutions (a need recognition preceding the awareness stage). Moreover, the adoption process does not adequately

TABLE 14.4 The Stages in the Adoption Process

NAME OF STAGE	WHAT HAPPENS DURING THIS STAGE	EXAMPLE
Awareness	Consumer is first exposed to the product innovation.	Eric sees an ad for a 23-inch thin LCD HDTV in a magazine he is reading.
Interest	Consumer is interested in the product and searches for additional information.	Eric reads about the HDTV set on the manufacturer's Web site and then goes to an electronics store near his apartment and has a salesperson show him the unit.
Evaluation	Consumer decides whether or not to believe that this product or service will satisfy the need—a kind of "mental trial."	After talking to a knowledgeable friend, Eric decides that this TV will fit nicely on top of the chest in his bedroom. He also calls his cable company and finds out that he can exchange his "standard" TV cable box for an HDTV cable box at no cost and no additional monthly fee.
Trial	Consumer uses the product on a limited basis.	Since an HDTV set cannot be "tried" like a small tube of toothpaste, Eric buys the TV at his local electronics store on his way home from work. The store offers a 14-day (from the date of purchase) full refund policy.
Adoption (Rejection)	If trial is favorable, consumer decides to use the product on a full rather than a limited basis—if unfavorable, the consumer decides to reject it.	Eric loves his new HDTV set and expects many years of service from it.

provide for the possibility of evaluation and rejection of a new product or service after each stage, especially after trial (i.e., a consumer may reject the product after trial or never use the product on a continuous basis). Finally, it does not explicitly include postadoption or postpurchase evaluation, which can lead to a strengthened commitment or to a decision to discontinue use. Figure 14.7 presents an enhanced representation of the adoption process model, one that includes the additional dimensions or actions described here.

The adoption of some products and services may have minimal consequences, whereas the adoption of other innovations may lead to major behavioral and lifestyle changes. Examples of innovations with such major impact on society include the automobile, telephone, electric refrigerator, television, airplane, personal computer, and the Internet.

THE ADOPTION PROCESS AND INFORMATION SOURCES

The adoption process provides a framework for determining which types of information sources consumers find most important at specific decision stages. For example, early purchasers of USB storage devices or keys (often used to back up or store computer files) might first become aware of the products via mass-media sources (e.g., technology and computer magazines or Internet sites like **www.news.com**). Then these early or innovative consumers'

FIGURE 14.7
An Enhanced Adoption Process Model

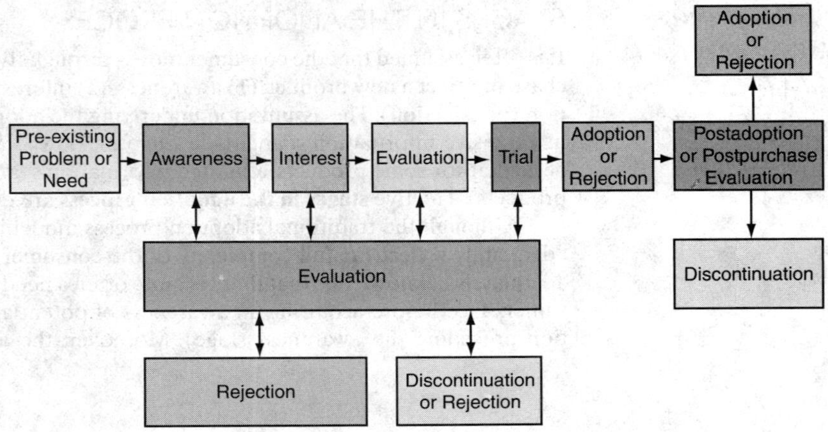

FIGURE 14.8
The Relative Importance of Different Types of Information Sources in the Adoption Process

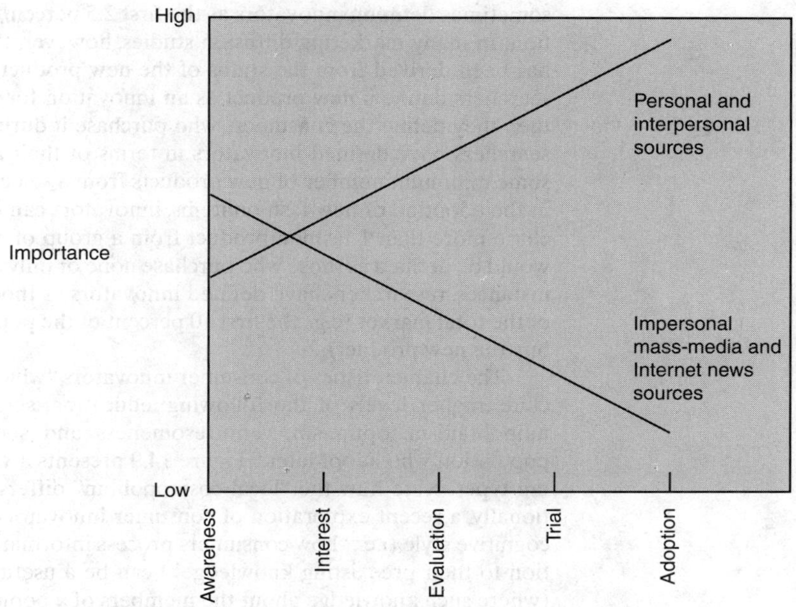

final pretrial information might be an outcome of informal discussions with personal sources (e.g., other innovators at a technology forum or chat room). The key point is that traditionally, impersonal mass-media sources were felt to be most valuable for creating initial product awareness; as the purchase decision progresses, however, the relative importance of these sources was believed to decline while the relative importance of interpersonal sources (friends, salespeople, and others) increased. Figure 14.8 depicts this relationship.

Changing the Relative Importance of Information Sources

There is reason to believe that the relationship depicted in Figure 14.8 may not fully reflect the reality of today's high-tech world. Indeed, while interpersonal sources are still important at the latter stages of the purchase decision process, it is believed that the nature of these interpersonal sources has changed. A person seeking information today no longer has to rely mostly on friends, relatives, and/or salespeople. For almost any product category, there are discussion forums, chat rooms, and blogs on the Web that can not only provide relevant information, but can also answer questions. Indeed, experts in the product or service category are often available via some online format. Often, when the questioner poses a question in the appropriate discussion group, he or she receives multiple responses. Such responses may prove to be extremely valuable to the consumer in the final stages of the purchase decision process, especially since they may be from individuals who have already purchased and used the product in question. Consequently, the consumer no longer has to personally know consumers who bought the product shortly after introduction because he or she can find such people electronically.

A Profile of the Consumer Innovator

LEARNING OBJECTIVE

14.4 *To Understand the Personal Characteristics of Innovators.*

Who is the consumer innovator? What characteristics set the innovator apart from later adopters and from those who never purchase? How can the marketer reach and influence the innovator? These are key questions for the marketing practitioner about to introduce a new product or service.

DEFINING THE CONSUMER INNOVATOR

Consumer innovators can be defined as the relatively small group of consumers who are the earliest purchasers of a new product. The problem with this definition, however, concerns the concept of *earliest,* which is, after all, a relative term. Sociologists have treated this issue by sometimes defining innovators as the first 2.5 percent of the social system to adopt an innovation. In many marketing diffusion studies, however, the definition of the consumer innovator has been derived from the status of the new product under investigation. For example, if researchers define a new product as an innovation for the first three months of its availability, then they define the consumers who purchase it during this period as "innovators." Other researchers have defined innovators in terms of their *innovativeness,* that is, their purchase of some minimum number of new products from a selected group of new products. For instance, in the adoption of new fashion items, innovators can be defined as those consumers who purchase more than 1 fashion product from a group of 10 new fashion products. Noninnovators would be defined as those who purchase none or only one of the new fashion products. In other instances, researchers have defined innovators as those falling within an arbitrary proportion of the total market (e.g., the first 10 percent of the population in a specified geographic area to buy the new product).

The characteristics of consumer innovators "which are well supported in the literature include higher levels of the following: education, social interaction, opinion leadership, cosmopolitanism, optimism, venturesomeness and social status; compared to those in the population who adopt later." Figure 14.9 presents a view of cosmopolitan and noncosmopolitan types. Note how the "local cosmopolitan" differs from the "global cosmopolitan." Additionally, a recent exploration of consumer innovators also reported that the characteristic of cognitive style (i.e., "how consumers process information and make purchase decisions in relation to their preexisting knowledge") can be a useful addition to the traditional list of traits (where such knowledge about the members of a population is known).[24]

FIGURE 14.9
Cosmopolitan and Noncosmopolitan Types

Source: Marylouise Caldwell, Kristen Blackwell, and Kirsty Tuulloch, "Cosmopolitanism as a Consumer Orientation," *Qualitative Market Research: An International Journal,* 9, no. 2 (2006): 128; and adapted from Hugh M. Cannon and Attila Yaprak, "Will the Real-World Citizen Please Stand Up!" *Journal of International Marketing,* 10, no. 4 (2002): 30–52.

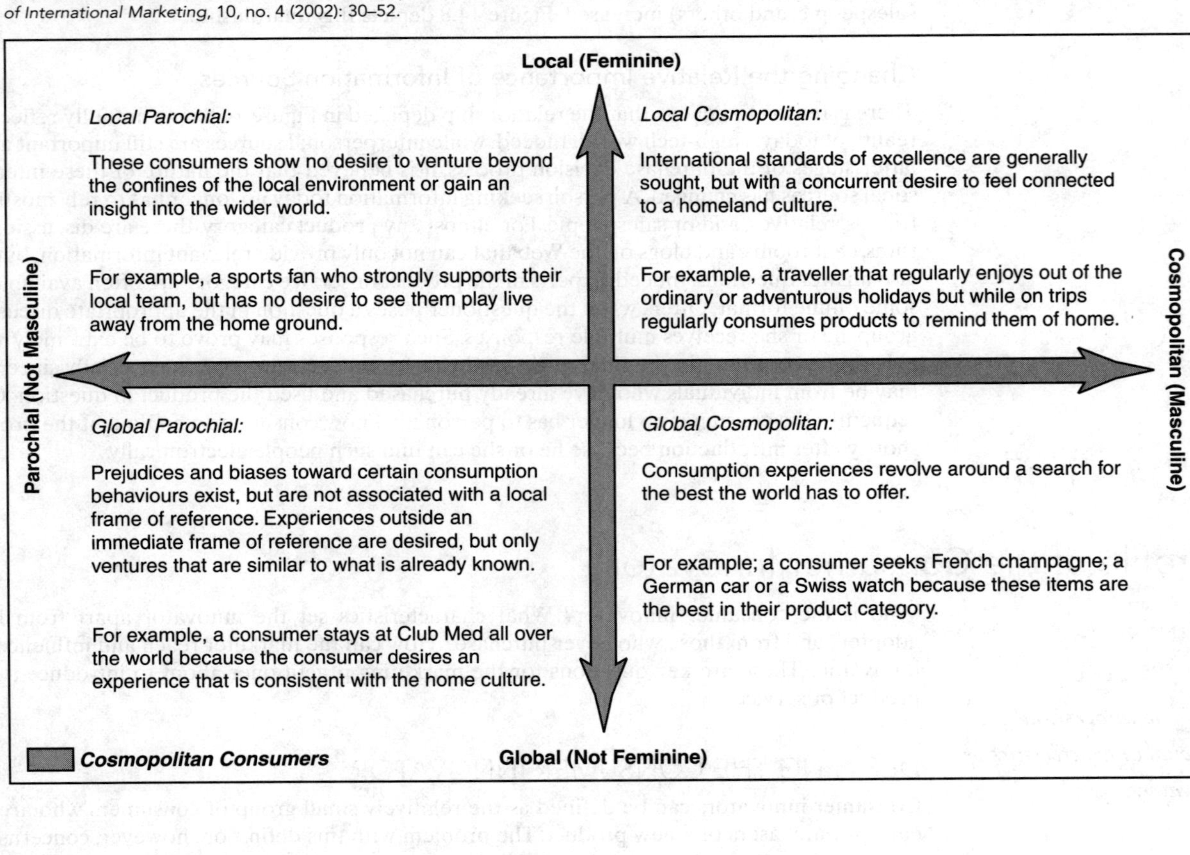

INTEREST IN THE PRODUCT CATEGORY

Not surprisingly, consumer innovators are much more interested than either later adopters or nonadopters in the product categories that they are among the first to purchase. If what is known from diffusion theory holds true in the future, the earliest purchasers of small electric automobiles are likely to have substantially greater interest in automobiles (they will enjoy looking at automotive magazines and will be interested in the performance and functioning of automobiles) than those who purchased conventional small cars during the same period or those who purchased small electric cars during a later period. Also, early adopters of products containing a nonfat synthetic cooking oil (i.e., olestra) were found to have a high interest in such a product because of health and diet concerns.

Consumer innovators are more likely than noninnovators to seek information concerning their specific interests from a variety of informal and mass-media sources. They are more likely to give greater deliberation to the purchase of new products or services in their areas of interest than noninnovators.

THE INNOVATOR IS AN OPINION LEADER

When discussing the characteristics of the opinion leader in Chapter 9, we indicated a tendency for consumer opinion leaders to be innovators. In the present context, an impressive amount of research on the diffusion of innovations has found that consumer innovators provide other consumers with information and advice about new products and that those who receive such advice frequently follow it. Thus, in the role of opinion leader, the consumer innovator often influences the acceptance or rejection of new products.

When innovators are enthusiastic about a new product and encourage others to try it, the product is likely to receive broader and quicker acceptance. When consumer innovators are dissatisfied with a new product and discourage others from trying it, its acceptance will be severely limited, and it may die a quick death. Also, for products that do not generate much excitement (either positive or negative), consumer innovators may not be sufficiently motivated to provide advice to others. In such cases, the marketer must rely almost entirely on mass media and personal selling to influence future purchasers; the absence of informal influence is also likely to result in a somewhat slower rate of acceptance (or rejection) of the new product. Because motivated consumer innovators can influence the rate of acceptance or rejection of a new product, they influence its eventual success or failure.

Is There a Noninnovator Opinion Leader?

Traditionally, diffusion of innovation literature has characterized the innovator as having more knowledge about the product or service in question than any other member of a consumer's social group. We believe that this is no longer an absolute. Consider computers, for example. Twenty years ago a PC user had to constantly purchase the latest and greatest computer in order to run the newest and most feature-laden software. And it was traditionally the innovator who was the first member of the group to purchase this "faster" computer. But today, a person with a three-year-old PC, for example, should have no trouble running the latest versions of Microsoft Excel, Word, or PowerPoint, and therefore this computer wiz might spend his money elsewhere. So this individual, whom other members of his or her social system recognize as a computer expert and whose advice they seek prior to purchasing a new PC for themselves, may actually purchase fewer computers than one or more other members of his or her social group.

PERSONALITY TRAITS

In Chapter 5, we examined the personality traits that distinguish the consumer innovator from the noninnovator. In this section, we will briefly highlight what researchers have learned about the personality of the consumer innovator.

First, consumer innovators generally are *less dogmatic* than noninnovators. They tend to approach new or unfamiliar products with considerable openness and little anxiety. In contrast, noninnovators seem to find new products threatening to the point where they prefer to delay purchase until the product's success has been clearly established.

Consistent with their open-mindedness, it appears that innovative behavior is an expression of an individual's *need for uniqueness*.[25] Some researchers have found that a tension exists in decision making between two opposing objectives—conformity and distinction. The need for uniqueness allows an individual to distinguish himself by purchasing a rare item, which is a socially acceptable behavior. Consequently, those new products, both branded and unbranded, that represent a greater change in a person's consumption habits were viewed as superior when it came to satisfying the need for uniqueness. Therefore, to gain more rapid acceptance of a new product, marketers might consider appealing to a consumer's need for uniqueness.

Still further, consumer innovators also differ from noninnovators in terms of *social character.* Consumer innovators are *inner-directed;* that is, they rely on their own values or standards when making a decision about a new product. In contrast, noninnovators are *other-directed,* relying on others for guidance on how to respond to a new product rather than trusting their own personal values or standards. Thus, the initial purchasers of a new line of automobiles might be inner-directed, whereas the later purchasers of the same automobile might be other-directed. This suggests that as acceptance of a product progresses from early to later adopters, a gradual shift occurs in the personality type of adopters from inner-directedness to other-directedness.

There also appears to be a link between *optimum stimulation level* and consumer innovativeness. Specifically, individuals who seek a lifestyle rich with novel, complex, and unusual experiences (high optimum stimulation levels) are more willing to risk trying new products, to be innovative, to seek purchase-related information, and to accept new retail facilities.

Researchers have isolated a link between *variety seeking* and purchase behavior that provides insights into consumer innovators. Variety-seeking consumers tend to be brand switchers and purchasers of innovative products and services. They also possess the following innovator-related personality traits: They are open-minded (or low in dogmatism), extroverts, liberal, low in authoritarianism, able to deal with complex or ambiguous stimuli, and creative.[26]

To sum up, consumer innovators seem to be more receptive to the unfamiliar and the unique; they are more willing to rely on their own values or standards than on the judgment of others. They also are willing to run the risk of a poor product choice to increase their exposure to new products that will be satisfying. The results of a recent study of webcasting adoption found support for measuring the innovativeness construct as a personality trait instead of a singular behavioral outcome (i.e., relative time of adoption)."[27] For the marketer, the personality traits that distinguish innovators from noninnovators suggest the need for separate promotional campaigns for innovators and for later adopters.

Perceived Risk and Venturesomeness

Perceived risk, which is discussed in detail in Chapter 6, is another measure of a consumer's likelihood to try new brands or products. Perceived risk is the degree of uncertainty or fear about the consequences of a purchase that a consumer feels when considering the purchase of a new product. For example, consumers experience uncertainty when they are concerned that a new product will not work properly or as well as other alternatives. Research on perceived risk and the trial of new products overwhelmingly indicates that consumer innovators are low-risk perceivers; that is, they experience little fear of trying new products or services. Consumers who perceive little or no risk in the purchase of a new product are much more likely to make innovative purchases than consumers who perceive a great deal of risk. In other words, high-risk perception limits innovativeness.

A study exploring consumer innovativeness and perceived risk related to the adoption of high-tech products enumerated seven different forms of risk that could be linked to the acquisition of novel information associated with such products, which is a precursor to adoption. These seven forms of risk are: (1) social risk, (2) time risk, (3) financial risk, (4) physical risk, (5) performance risk, (6) psychological risk, and (7) network externality risk (the consumer's evaluation of whether others in the social network also possess the new technology, so that if something goes wrong they can seek help).[28]

A study examined self-service technology (SST) adoption; in this research, the three technologies studied were ATMs, bank by phone, and online banking.[29] A conclusion of the research was that the more positive the consumer's attitude toward the SST, the more widely adopted it became. While almost 80 percent of subjects used ATMs, and 28 percent banked by phone, just under 13 percent used online banking. The research found that risk was an important determinant of a consumer's attitude toward online banking, but not for ATMs or bank by phone.[30] In a similar context, a recent study of wine retailing in Ireland concluded by stating that Irish wine consumers were adopting new wine products rapidly, especially "at the lower end of the market, where price discounting is high and risk is minimal.

An interesting focus group study was recently conducted in the United Kingdom and Germany regarding consumers' perceived risk in successive versions of the Nokia 9000 Communicator (a combined a mobile phone with a personal digital assistant).[31] The findings indicate that consumers perceived less risk regarding the original innovative product, because only through trials of the new products was it possible to become aware of the unique functionality and the associated risk of the new products. Regarding the improved versions, consumers knew what enhancement they would like to see, based on their use of the previous version, and could determine whether or not these enhancements had been incorporated into the latest or next version. For marketers, the lesson to be learned is that it is vital to obtain feedback from product users prior to designing and marketing a new version of a product.[32]

Venturesomeness is a broad-based measure of a consumer's willingness to accept the risk of purchasing new products. Measures of venturesomeness have been used to evaluate a person's general values or attitudes toward trying new products. A typical measurement scale might include such items as:

- I prefer to (try a shampoo when it first comes out) (wait and learn how good it is before trying it).
- When I am shopping and see a brand of coffee I know about but have never tried, I am (very anxious or willing to try it), (hesitant about trying it), (very unwilling to try it).
- I like to be among the first people to buy and use new products that are on the market (measured on a 5-point "agreement" scale).

Research that has examined venturesomeness has generally found that consumers who indicate a willingness to try new products tend to be consumer innovators (as measured by their actual purchase of new products). On the other hand, consumers who express a reluctance to try new products are, in fact, less likely to purchase new products. Therefore, venturesomeness seems to be an effective barometer of actual innovative behavior.

Purchase and Consumption Characteristics

Consumer innovators possess purchase and usage traits that set them apart from noninnovators. For example, consumer innovators are *less* brand loyal; that is, they are more apt to switch brands. This is not surprising, for brand loyalty would seriously impede a consumer's willingness to try new products.

Consumer innovators are more likely to be *deal prone* (to take advantage of special promotional offers such as free samples and cents-off coupons). They are also likely to be *heavy users* of the product category in which they innovate. Specifically, they purchase larger quantities and consume more of the product than noninnovators. Finally, for products like DVRs, PCs, microwave ovens, digital cameras, and food processors, usage variety is likely to be a relevant dimension of new-product diffusion. An understanding of how consumers might be "usage innovators"—that is, finding or "inventing" new uses for an innovation—might create entirely new market opportunities for marketers' products. Still further, a study of Indian consumers' attitudes toward the purchase of new food products found that "intention to buy" was an accurate predictor of behavior for highly innovative consumers, but failed to predict purchase behavior for less innovative Indian consumers.[33] This suggests that more innovative consumers are more likely to act on their reported intentions to purchase than less innovative consumers with the same intention of purchase.

To sum up, a positive relationship exists between innovative behavior and heavy usage. Consumer innovators are not only an important market segment from the standpoint of being the first to use a new product, but they also represent a substantial market in terms of product volume. However, their propensity to switch brands or to use products in different or unique ways and their positive response to promotional deals also suggest that innovators will continue to use a specific brand only as long as they do not perceive that a new and potentially better alternative is available.

Media Habits

Comparisons of the media habits of innovators and noninnovators across such widely diverse areas of consumption as fashion clothing and new automotive services suggest that innovators have somewhat greater total exposure to magazines than noninnovators, particularly to special-interest magazines devoted to the product category in which they innovate. For example, fashion innovators are more likely to read magazines such as *GQ* and *Vogue* than noninnovators; financial services innovators have greater exposure to such special-interest magazines as *Money* and *Forbes*.

Consumer innovators are also less likely to watch television than noninnovators. This view is consistently supported by research that over the past decade or so has compared the magazine and TV exposure levels of consumer innovators. The evidence indicates that consumer innovators have higher-than-average magazine exposure and lower-than-average TV exposure. It will be interesting, though, to observe over the next few years what the impact of the convergence of computers and television will be. Studies concerning the relationship between innovative behavior and exposure to other mass media, such as radio and newspapers, have been too few, and the results have been too varied to draw any useful conclusions.

SOCIAL CHARACTERISTICS

Consumer innovators are more socially accepted and socially involved than noninnovators. For example, innovators are more socially integrated into the community, better accepted by others, and more socially involved; that is, they belong to more social groups and organizations than noninnovators. This greater social acceptance and involvement of consumer innovators may help explain why they function as effective opinion leaders.

DEMOGRAPHIC CHARACTERISTICS

It is reasonable to assume that the age of the consumer innovator is related to the specific product category in which he or she innovates; however, research suggests that consumer innovators tend to be younger than either late adopters or noninnovators. This is no doubt because many of the products selected for research attention (such as fashion, convenience grocery products, or new automobiles) are particularly attractive to younger consumers.

Consumer innovators have more formal education, have higher personal or family incomes, and are more likely to have higher occupational status (to be professionals or hold managerial positions) than late adopters or noninnovators. In other words, innovators tend to be more upscale than other consumer segments and can, therefore, better afford to make a mistake should the innovative new product or service being purchased prove to be unacceptable.

Table 14.5 summarizes the major differences between consumer innovators and late adopters or noninnovators. The table includes the major distinctions examined in our current presentation of the *consumer innovator profile*.

ARE THERE GENERALIZED CONSUMER INNOVATORS?

Do consumer innovators in one product category tend to be consumer innovators in other product categories? The answer to this strategically important question has traditionally been a guarded "no." The overlap of innovativeness across product categories, like opinion leadership, seems to be limited to product categories that are closely related to the same basic interest area. Consumers who are innovators of one new food product or one new appliance are more likely to be innovators of other new products in the same general product category. In other words, although no single or generalized consumer-innovativeness trait seems to operate *across* broadly different product categories, evidence suggests that consumers who innovate *within* a specific product category will innovate again within the same product category. For example, up to the point of "innovator burnout" (i.e., "What I have is good enough"), a person who was an innovator in buying an early 2 megapixel digital camera in the 1990s was most likely again to be an innovator in buying a 5 megapixel digital camera, a 7 megapixel digital camera, and a 10 megapixel digital camera, and is likely again to be an innovator when it comes to the next generation of digital cameras. For the marketer, such a pattern suggests that it is generally a good marketing strategy to target a new product to consumers who were the first to try other products in the same basic product category.

Domain-Specific Versus Global Innovativeness

The literature dealing with diffusion of innovation traditionally treats innovativeness, as discussed in the previous paragraph, as being domain-specific (i.e., the individual is innovative

TABLE 14.5 Comparative Profiles of the Consumer Innovator and the Noninnovator or Late Adopter

CHARACTERISTIC	INNOVATOR	NONINNOVATOR (OR LATE ADOPTER)
Product interest	More	Less
Opinion leadership	More	Less
PERSONALITY		
Dogmatism	Open-minded	Closed-minded
Need for uniqueness	Higher	Lower
Social character	Inner-directed	Other-directed
Optimum stimulation level	Higher	Lower
Variety seeking	Higher	Lower
Perceived risk	Less	More
Venturesomeness	More	Less
PURCHASE AND CONSUMPTION TRAITS		
Brand loyalty	Less	More
Deal proneness	More	Less
Usage	More	Less
MEDIA HABITS		
Total magazine exposure	More	Less
Special-interest magazines	More	Less
Television	Less	More
SOCIAL CHARACTERISTICS		
Social integration	More	Less
Social striving (e.g., social, physical, and occupational mobility)	More	Less
Group memberships	More	Less
DEMOGRAPHIC CHARACTERISTICS		
Age	Younger	Older
Income	Higher	Lower
Education	More	Less
Occupational status	Higher	Lower

with respect to a specific product or service category). However, there has also been a stream of research dealing with innovativeness as a personality trait, independent of the need to be anchored to any particular domain. Research efforts have found the personality trait of innovativeness related to openness in information processing, willingness to change, inherent novelty seeking, variety seeking, and optimum stimulation level. There have also been some studies that suggest that innovativeness is bidimensional in perspective—it includes both cognitive and sensory traits. The cognitive trait gets the consumer to seek stimulation and to engage in new experiences, while the sensory trait leads the consumer to seek stimulation to arouse the senses. It would appear that the issue of exactly what innovativeness is and what it is not makes it far from a universally agreed upon concept.[34]

Technology and Innovators

In the realm of high-tech innovations, there is evidence suggesting that there is a generalized "high-tech" innovator—known as a "change leader."[35] Such individuals tend to embrace and popularize many of the innovations that are ultimately accepted by the mainstream population, such as computers, cellular telephones, and fax machines. They tend to have a wide range of personal and professional contacts representing different occupational and social groups; most often these contacts tend to be "weak ties" or acquaintances. Change leaders also appear to fall into one of two distinct groups: a *younger group* that can be characterized as being stimulation seeking, sociable, and having high levels of fashion awareness or a *middle-aged group* that is highly self-confident and has very high information-seeking needs.

Similar to change leaders, *technophiles* are individuals who purchase technologically advanced products soon after their market debut. Such individuals tend to be technically curious people. Also, another group responding to technology is adults who are categorized as *techthusiasts*—people who are most likely to purchase or subscribe to emerging products and services that are technologically oriented. These consumers are typically younger, better educated, and more affluent.[36]

Advancing our understanding of the relationship between technology and consumer innovation has been explored within the context of the technology acceptance model (TAM). Within the domain of work perceived usefulness or the utilitarian aspect of a technology has been revealed to be most important; however, within the consumer context of consumers' response to a new handheld Internet device, the most powerful determinant of attitudes toward usage was the "fun" of using the device—a hedonic aspect. The implication for marketers is clear—a consumer may purchase a new bit of technology more for the fun they can have with the device than for the ability it gives them to accomplish particular functions.[37]

Research conducted with over 500 adult Internet users found that purchasing online was positively related to technology-related innovativeness. Still further, the gathering of store or product information online was positively related to the number of years online and the weekly number of hours spent online.[38] Moreover, when exploring the adoption of mobile gaming (games delivered via cell phone), a market that is expected to have worldwide sales of $10 billion in 2009, researchers discovered important additions to the traditional list of product characteristics that influence the rate of adoption (e.g., relative advantage, complexity).[39] What they perceived as risk were navigation (maneuvering ergonomics associated with the mobile device), critical mass (the more people that have adopted the innovation, the more attractive it is to others), and payment options (because of the expense of the mobile device, trialability is not an option). Perceived risk was found to play the most important role in the adoption process, followed by complexity and compatibility.[40]

SUMMARY

The diffusion process and the adoption process are two closely related concepts concerned with the acceptance of new products by consumers. The diffusion process is a macro process that focuses on the spread of an innovation (a new product, service, or idea) from its source to the consuming public. The adoption process is a micro process that examines the stages through which an individual consumer passes when making a decision to accept or reject a new product.

The definition of the term *innovation* can be firm oriented (new to the firm), product oriented (a continuous innovation, a dynamically continuous innovation, or a discontinuous innovation), market oriented (how long the product has been on the market or an arbitrary percentage of the potential target market that has purchased it), or consumer oriented (new to the consumer). Market-oriented definitions of innovation are most useful to consumer researchers in the study of the diffusion and adoption of new products.

Five product characteristics influence the consumer's acceptance of a new product: relative advantage, compatibility, complexity, trialability, and observability (or communicability).

Diffusion researchers are concerned with two aspects of communication—the channels through which word of a new product is spread to the consuming public and the types of messages that influence the adoption or rejection of new products. Diffusion is always examined in the context of a specific social system, such as a target market, a community, a region, or even a nation.

Time is an integral consideration in the diffusion process. Researchers are concerned with the amount of purchase time required for an individual consumer to adopt or reject a new product, with the rate of adoption, and with the identification of sequential adopters. The five adopter categories are innovators, early adopters, early majority, late majority, and laggards.

Marketing strategists try to control the rate of adoption through their new-product pricing policies. Marketers who wish to penetrate the market to achieve market leadership try to acquire wide adoption as quickly as possible by using low prices. Those who wish to recoup their developmental costs quickly use a skimming pricing policy but lengthen the adoption process.

The traditional adoption process model describes five stages through which an individual consumer passes to arrive at the decision to adopt or reject a new product: awareness, interest, evaluation, trial, and adoption. To make it more realistic, an enhanced model is suggested as one that considers the possibility of a preexisting need or problem, the likelihood that some form of evaluation might occur through the entire process, and that even after adoption there will be postadoption or purchase evaluation that might either strengthen the commitment or alternatively lead to discontinuation.

New-product marketers are vitally concerned with identifying the consumer innovator so that they may direct their promotional campaigns to the people who are most likely to try new products, adopt them, and influence others. Consumer research has identified a number of consumer-related characteristics, including product interest, opinion leadership, personality factors, purchase and consumption traits, media habits, social characteristics, and demographic variables that distinguish consumer innovators from later adopters. These serve as useful variables in the segmentation of markets for new-product introductions.

DISCUSSION QUESTIONS

1. Describe how a manufacturer might use knowledge of the following product characteristics to speed up the acceptance of GPS-enabled car navigation systems:
   a. Relative advantage
   b. Compatibility
   c. Complexity
   d. Trialability
   e. Observability
2. Panasonic has introduced a digital camera that combines the size benefits of a digital point and shoot camera with the ability to use small interchangeable lenses. How can the company use the diffusion-of-innovations framework to develop promotional, pricing, and distribution strategies targeted to the following adopter categories?
   a. Innovators
   b. Early adopters
   c. Early majority
   d. Late majority
   e. Laggards
3. The adopter categories of the diffusion process consists of five stages: innovators, early adopters, early majority, late majority, and laggards. As Figure 14.5 reveals the normal distribution curve from college-level statistics describes the sequence and proportion of adopter categories among the population is similar in shape to the product life cycle curve? How would you use both of these curves to develop a marketing strategy?
4. Figure 14.8 presents a diagram of the relationship between different types of marketing-related information sources over the adoption process. What does it imply about an effective strategy of communicating with target consumers as they are going through the adoption process?
5. Panasonic is introducing a TV with a 60-inch wide screen that is only 1 inch deep and weighs about half the weight of any competitor's brand.
   a. What recommendations would you make to Panasonic regarding the initial target market for the new TV model?
   b. How would you identify the innovators for this product?
   c. Should Panasonic follow a penetration or a skimming policy in introducing the product? Why?
6. Create your own personal time line for an expensive product that you or your family have recently gone through. Use Table 14.2 as a guideline.
7. Table 14.5 contains a comparison of innovators and non-innovators. Concentrating on the innovators (i.e., the left side of the table), select the 10 characteristics that you think would be important for a consumer innovator to possess if he or she was to be among the very first to go out and purchase an advanced hybrid passenger automobile that gets 100 miles to a gallon of regular gas? Make sure to explain why you selected the 10 characteristics.

EXERCISES

1. Identify a product, service, or style that recently was adopted by you or some of your friends. Identify what type of innovation it is and describe its diffusion process up to this point in time. What are the characteristics of people who adopted it first? What types of people did not adopt it? What features of the product, service, or style are likely to determine its eventual success or failure?
2. With the advancement of digital technology, some TV cable companies are offering on-demand, pay-per-view systems that will allow viewers to select films from video libraries and view them on demand. Among people you know, identify two who are likely to be the innovators for such a new service and construct consumer profiles using the characteristics of consumer innovators discussed in the text.
3. Identify five friends that have recently purchased a new model of cell phone (with some features that they consider to be "new"). Arrange to interview each of the individuals, one at a time. Ask them the following questions, and any others you think are appropriate:
   a. Why did you select this cell phone over other cell phones that you were looking at or considering?
   b. Do you currently like the phone for the same reasons that you purchased, or have you found other reasons why you particularly like it?
   c. What would you recommend to make the next model of this cell phone even better?
   d. After you are finished with the assignment, get together with other students and discuss what you have found. Look for similarities and differences.

KEY TERMS

- adopter categories *459*
- adoption process *450*
- compatibility *453*
- complexity *454*
- consumer innovators *450*
- continuous innovation *451*
- diffusion of innovations *450*
- diffusion process *450*
- discontinuous innovation *451*
- dynamically continuous innovation *451*
- observability *454*
- penetration policy *462*
- product or service innovation *450*
- relative advantage *453*
- skimming policy *462*
- stages in the adoption process *463*
- trialability *454*

Case One: Now Talk Is Even Cheaper

MXit is a free instant messaging program for both mobile phones and personal computers, allowing members to talk to other MXit users anywhere in the world. This type of communication is not as personal and instant as a phone conversation, but it is faster than e-mail and considerably cheaper than an SMS. Users are allowed up to 1,000 characters at a fraction of the cost of an SMS—they send and receive free text messages via the Internet using GPRS or 3G, instead of standard SMS technology.

Normal instant messaging (IM), which forms the basis of MXit, was introduced in South Africa by MXit Lifestyle in May 2005. About 95 percent of MXit's users mainly use it for this purpose—they exchange messages with other users or other online chat communities at any time, which creates a virtual community.

Eighteen thousand mobile phone users register with MXit daily in South Africa. Figures vary, but MXit has about 12.5 million registered users, although it is not known how many of them are active. With more than 250 million text messages being sent per day, MXit offers companies excellent opportunities for brand exposure, building and owning communities, and advertising. This may explain why social networking providers, such as MXit, are regarded as the most powerful platform to reach South African youth.

MXit, however, has come under attack in the media for a number of issues such as adults who are sexually attracted to children targeting the youth and the circulation of defamatory lists and pornographic material. Some critics regard MXit as "extremely dangerous" and even suggest that MXit is involved in most crimes where the youth is involved. The CEO of MXit, Herman Heunis, believes these accusations are not true and often result from a misunderstanding of MXit technology and the responsibilities of the parties involved.

Heunis believes IM is very safe because every user can chat only to his or her circle of friends after they have been added as contacts on their mobile phones. Most of the cases where MXit is implicated stem from public chat rooms where users do not keep to basic Internet security practices such as not revealing personal information. Only about 5 percent of MXit users, however, use the chat rooms. They are not directly available to MXit users, and in order to be accessed, these chat rooms need to be purchased and added as a contact. Heunis further believes that in light of the fact that technology is growing constantly, the Internet will continue to be part of consumers' lives and that the development of children's Internet social skills should be an essential part of their education.

QUESTIONS

1. The chapter discussed a number of product characteristics that influence the diffusion process. How does MXit rate on each of these characteristics?
2. Based on the definitions of innovations discussed in the chapter, as which type of innovation could MXit be classified?
3. How would the social system for the diffusion of MXit be characterized?
4. Which characteristics would consumers who adopt MXit typically have?

Sources: www.mxit.co.za; "MXit—Can You 'Bare' It?" *Sunday Tribune*, Sports Edition, March 29, 2009 14; Z. Mokgata, "Chat Network Grows Rapidly in SA," *Daily Dispatch*, February 10, 2009 3; and E. Naidu, "Talk Is Cheap Among SA's Chatty Youth," *Sunday Independent*, March 1, 2009.

Case Two: We Have a Relationship—We Blog!

As a way to enhance relationships with customers, e-tailers are beginning to test Web logs (blogs). Online merchants feel that their blogs will give their e-stores more of a personality, and will get customers to return to their Web sites even when they are not in the mood to shop.

For example, eHobbies is a small company with 25 employees. On its new blog it posts photographs of employees and photos taken at trade shows. The firm believes that its blog helps "humanize" the company by showing that it is "a company of hobbyists," who in many ways are just like their customers.

But there can be problems with a company having a blog. One difficulty is how do you keep the customer from straying from the store Web site (where he or she can purchase merchandise) to the blog, and then not returning to the store's site? After all, most blogs contain links to other articles on the Web. Another issue is that some customers might not like the language used on the blog or might not appreciate a scorching review or comment.

Perhaps the most controversial company with a blog is GoDaddy.com, a firm offering Internet domains and hosting services. On its blog, the company's owner, Bob Parsons, offers his thoughts on a lot of different topics, and often his comments are highly opinionated. While this is enough for some individuals who visit this blog to never return, Parsons feels that his blog lets his company become more to consumers than just "some name with a URL on the Internet," and also lets people "understand why we do things the way we do them."

QUESTION

1. How do you think blogs fit into the diffusion process that you read about in Chapter 14?

Source: Bob Tedeschi, "Yes, You Sell Sweaters, but Should You Really Blog About It?" *New York Times,* July 4, 2005, C6.

15

Consumer Decision Making and Beyond

THIS CHAPTER combines many of the psychological, social, and cultural concepts developed throughout the book into an overview framework for understanding how consumers make decisions. Unlike Chapter 14, which examined the dynamics of *new-product* adoption, this chapter takes a broader perspective and examines **consumer decision making** in the context of all types of consumption choices, ranging from the consumption of new products to the use of old and established products. It also considers consumers' decisions not as the end point but rather as the beginning point of a **consumption process**.

We need to appreciate that sometimes consumers are unaware of or have never even thought of a particular product or service until they are actually exposed to the product or a marketing message about the product (i.e., often referred to as an "unsought good"). Figure 15.1 presents an ad for VPI Pet Insurance. For pet owners, pet insurance may be a product they have given little or no thought to, because they may be unaware of its availability. When learning of it existence, consumers' first impulse might be: "Is this something that I want or need for my pets?" Study and read the entire ad, and decide whether the words and illustration would motivate pet owners to go to the Web site or call the toll-free number to seek additional information about the insurance.

FIGURE 15.1

Source: © Veterinary Pet Insurance Company.

QUESTION: *What Would a Pet Owner Need to Know in Order to Make a Decision About Buying Pet Insurance?*

Learning Objectives

15.1 *To Understand What a Consumer Decision Is.*

15.2 *To Understand the Three Levels of Consumer Decision Making.*

15.3 *To Understand Four Different Views or Models of Consumer Decision Making.*

15.4 *To Understand in Detail the Model of Consumer Decision Making Originally Introduced in Chapter 1.*

15.5 *To Understand the Nature and Scope of Consumer Gift Giving.*

15.6 *To Understand the Significance of Consuming and Possessing.*

15.7 *To Understand the Need for Relationship Marketing.*

What Is a Consumer Decision?

Learning Objective

15.1 *To Understand What a Consumer Decision Is.*

Every day, each of us makes numerous decisions concerning every aspect of our daily lives. However, we generally make these decisions without stopping to think about how we make them and what is involved in the particular decision-making process itself. In the most general terms, a decision is the selection of an option from two or more alternative choices. In other words, for a person to make a decision, a choice of alternatives must be available. When a person has a choice between making a purchase and not making a purchase, a choice between brand X and brand Y, or a choice of spending time doing A or B, that person is in a position to make a decision. On the other hand, if the consumer has no alternatives from which to choose and is literally *forced* to make a particular purchase or take a particular action (e.g., use a prescribed medication), then this single "no-choice" instance does not constitute a decision; such a no-choice decision is commonly referred to as a "Hobson's choice."

In actuality, no-choice purchase or consumption situations are fairly rare. You may recall from our discussion of core American cultural values (Chapter 11) that for consumers, *freedom* is often expressed in terms of a wide range of product choices. Thus, if there is almost always a choice, then there is almost always an opportunity for consumers to make decisions. Moreover, experimental research reveals that providing consumers with a choice when there was originally none can be a very good business strategy, one that can substantially increase sales.[1] For instance, when a direct-mail electrical appliance catalog displayed two coffeemakers instead of just one (the original coffeemaker at $149 and a "new" only slightly larger one at $229), the addition of the second *comparison* coffeemaker seemed to stimulate consumer evaluation that significantly increased the sales of the original coffeemaker.

Table 15.1 summarizes various types of consumption and purchase-related decisions. Although not exhaustive, this list serves to demonstrate that the scope of consumer decision making is far broader than the mere selection of one brand from a number of brands.

Levels of Consumer Decision Making

Learning Objective

15.2 *To Understand the Three Levels of Consumer Decision Making.*

Not all consumer decision-making situations receive (or require) the same degree of information research. If all purchase decisions required extensive effort, then consumer decision making would be an exhausting process that left little time for anything else. On the other hand, if all purchases were routine, then they would tend to be monotonous and would provide little pleasure or novelty. On a continuum of effort ranging from very high to very low, we can distinguish three specific levels of consumer decision making: **extensive problem solving**, **limited problem solving**, and **routinized response behavior**.

TABLE 15.1 Types of Purchase or Consumption Decisions

DECISION CATEGORY	ALTERNATIVE A	ALTERNATIVE B
Basic Purchase or Consumption Decision Brand Purchase or Consumption Decision	To purchase or consume a product (or service)	Not to purchase or consume a product (or service)
	To purchase or consume a specific brand	To purchase or consume another brand
	To purchase or consume one's usual brand	To purchase or consume another established brand (possibly with special features)
	To purchase or consume a basic model	To purchase or consume a luxury or status model
	To purchase or consume a new brand	To purchase or consume one's usual brand or some other established brand
	To purchase or consume a standard quantity	To purchase or consume more or less than a standard quantity
	To purchase or consume an on-sale brand	To purchase or consume a nonsale brand
	To purchase or consume a national brand	To purchase or consume a store brand
Channel Purchase Decisions	To purchase from a specific type of store (e.g., a department store)	To purchase from some other type of store (e.g., a discount store)
	To purchase from one's usual store	To purchase from some other store
	To purchase in-home (by phone, catalog, or Internet)	To purchase in-store merchandise
	To purchase from a local store	To purchase from a store requiring some travel (outshopping)
Payment Purchase Decisions	To pay for the purchase with cash	To pay for the purchase with a credit card
	To pay the bill in full when it arrives	To pay for the purchase in installments

EXTENSIVE PROBLEM SOLVING

When consumers have no established criteria for evaluating a product category or specific brands in that category or have not narrowed the number of brands they will consider to a small, manageable subset, their decision-making efforts can be classified as *extensive problem solving.* At this level, the consumer needs a great deal of information to establish a set of criteria on which to judge specific brands and a correspondingly large amount of information concerning each of the brands to be considered. Extensive problem solving often occurs when a consumer is purchasing an expensive, important, or technically complicated product or service for the first time (e.g., replacing an old "tube" TV with a new HDTV).

LIMITED PROBLEM SOLVING

At this level of problem solving, consumers already have established the basic criteria for evaluating the product category and the various brands in the category. However, they have not fully established preferences concerning a select group of brands. Their search for additional information is more like "fine-tuning"; they must gather additional brand information to discriminate among the various brands. This type of problem solving frequently occurs when the consumer is purchasing a new, updated version of something that he or she has purchased before, such as replacing an old laptop with a new one—the new laptop having a faster processor, a larger hard drive, and so on.

ROUTINIZED RESPONSE BEHAVIOR

At this level, consumers have experience with the product category and a well-established set of criteria with which to evaluate the brands they are considering. In some situations, they may search for a small amount of additional information; in others, they simply review what they already know.

Just how extensive a consumer's problem-solving task is depends on how well established his or her criteria for selection are, how much information he or she has about each brand being considered, and how narrow the set of brands is from which the choice will be made. Clearly, extensive problem solving implies that the consumer must seek more information to make a choice, whereas routinized response behavior implies little need for additional information.

All decisions in our lives cannot be complex and require extensive research and consideration—we just cannot exert the level of effort required. Some decisions have to be "easy ones."

Models of Consumers: Four Views of Consumer Decision Making

LEARNING OBJECTIVE

15.3 *To Understand Four Different Views or Models of Consumer Decision Making.*

Before presenting an overview model of how consumers make decisions, we will consider several schools of thought that depict consumer decision making in distinctly different ways. The term *models of consumers* refers to a general view or perspective as to how (and why) individuals behave as they do. Specifically, we will examine models of consumers in terms of the following four views: (1) an *economic view*, (2) a *passive view*, (3) a *cognitive view*, and (4) an *emotional view*.

AN ECONOMIC VIEW

In the field of theoretical economics, which portrays a world of perfect competition, the consumer has often been characterized as making rational decisions. This model, called the *economic view*, has been criticized by consumer researchers for a number of reasons. To behave rationally in the economic sense, a consumer would have to (1) be aware of all available product alternatives, (2) be capable of correctly ranking each alternative in terms of its benefits and disadvantages, and (3) be able to identify the one best alternative. Realistically, however, consumers rarely have all of the information or sufficiently accurate information or even an adequate degree of involvement or motivation to make the so-called "perfect" decision.

It has been argued that the classical economic model of an all-rational consumer is unrealistic for the following reasons: (a) People are limited by their existing skills, habits, and reflexes; (b) people are limited by their existing values and goals; and (c) people are limited by the extent of their knowledge.[2] Consumers operate in an imperfect world in which they do not maximize their decisions in terms of economic considerations, such as price–quantity relationships, marginal utility, or indifference curves. Indeed, the consumer generally is unwilling to engage in extensive decision-making activities and will settle, instead, for a "satisfactory" decision, one that is "good enough."[3] For this reason, the economic model is often rejected as too idealistic and simplistic. As an example, recent research has found that consumers' primary motivation for price haggling, which was long thought to be the desire to obtain a better price (i.e., better dollar value for the purchase), may instead be related to the need for achievement, affiliation, and dominance.[4] Conversely, a study by an e-tailing group of the 2006 holiday shopping season found that the two most important reasons for purchasing gifts online were "saving time" and "saving money"—two very rational reasons.[5]

A PASSIVE VIEW

Quite opposite to the rational economic view of consumers is the *passive view* that depicts the consumer as basically submissive to the self-serving interests and promotional efforts of marketers. In the passive view, consumers are perceived as impulsive and irrational purchasers, ready to yield to the aims and into the arms of marketers. At least to some degree, the passive model of the consumer was subscribed to by the hard-driving super salespeople of old, who were trained to regard the consumer as an object to be manipulated.

The principal limitation of the passive model is that it fails to recognize that the consumer plays an equal, if not dominant, role in many buying situations—sometimes by seeking information about product alternatives and selecting the product that appears to offer the greatest satisfaction and at other times by impulsively selecting a product that satisfies the mood or emotion of the moment. All that we have studied about motivation (see Chapter 4), selective perception (Chapter 6), learning (Chapter 7), attitudes (Chapter 8), communication (Chapter 9), and opinion leadership (Chapter 9) supports the proposition that consumers are rarely objects of manipulation. Therefore, this simple and single-minded view should also be rejected as unrealistic.

A COGNITIVE VIEW

The third model portrays the consumer as a *thinking problem solver*. Within this framework, consumers frequently are pictured as either receptive to or actively searching for products and services that fulfill their needs and enrich their lives. The *cognitive view* focuses on the processes by which consumers seek and evaluate information about selected brands and retail outlets.

Within the context of the cognitive model, consumers are viewed as information processors. Moreover, information processing leads to the formation of preferences and, ultimately, to purchase intentions. The cognitive view also recognizes that the consumer is unlikely to even attempt to obtain all available information about every choice. Instead, consumers are likely to cease their information-seeking efforts when they perceive that they have sufficient information about some of the alternatives to make a "satisfactory" decision. As this information-processing viewpoint suggests, consumers often develop shortcut decision rules (called **heuristics**) to facilitate the decision-making process. A recent study found that consumer decision making is more heuristic in situations that involve spending time, rather than spending money.[6] They also use decision rules to cope with exposure to too much information (i.e., **information overload**).

The cognitive, or problem-solving, view describes a consumer who falls somewhere between the extremes of the economic and passive views, who does not (or cannot) have total knowledge about available product alternatives and, therefore, cannot make *perfect* decisions, but who nonetheless actively seeks information and attempts to make *satisfactory* decisions.

Consistent with the problem-solving view is the notion that a great deal of consumer behavior is goal directed. For example, a consumer might purchase a computer in order to manage finances or look for a laundry detergent that will be gentle on fabrics. Goal setting is especially important when it comes to the adoption of new products because the greater the degree of "newness," the more difficult it would be for the consumer to evaluate the product and relate it to his or her need (because of a lack of experience with the product). Figure 15.2 diagrams goal setting and goal pursuit in consumer behavior.

AN EMOTIONAL VIEW

Although long aware of the *emotional* or *impulsive view* of consumer decision making, marketers frequently prefer to think of consumers in terms of either economic or passive models. In reality, however, each of us is likely to associate deep feelings or emotions, such as joy, fear,

FIGURE 15.2
Goal Setting and Goal Pursuit in Consumer Behavior

Source: Richard P. Bagozzi and Utpal Dholakia, "Goal Setting and Goal Striving in Consumer Behavior," *Journal of Marketing*, 63 (1999): 21.

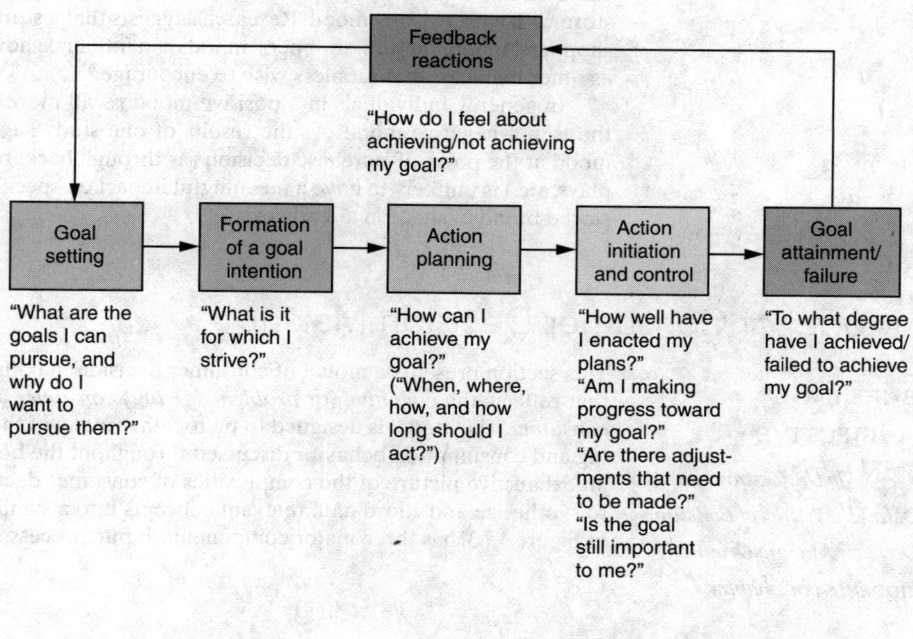

love, hope, sexuality, fantasy, and even a little "magic," with certain purchases or possessions. These feelings or emotions are likely to be highly involving. For instance, a person who misplaces a favorite fountain pen might go to great lengths to look for it, despite the fact that he or she has six others at hand. Still further, several interrelated studies found that consumers' *superstitious beliefs* can play a meaningful role in their purchasing-related decision making when such beliefs were nonconscious in nature.[7]

Possessions also may serve to preserve a sense of the past and act as familiar transitional objects when one is confronted with an uncertain future. For example, members of the armed forces invariably carry photographs of "the girl (or guy) back home," their families, and their lives in earlier times. These memorabilia frequently serve as hopeful reminders that normal activities will someday resume.

If we were to reflect on the nature of our recent purchases, we might be surprised to realize just how impulsive some of them were. Rather than carefully searching, deliberating, and evaluating alternatives before buying, we are just as likely to have made many of these purchases on impulse, on a whim, or because we were emotionally driven.

When a consumer makes what is basically an emotional purchase decision, less emphasis is placed on the search for prepurchase information. Instead, more emphasis is placed on current mood and feelings ("Go for it!"). This is not to say that emotional decisions are not rational. As Chapter 4 pointed out, buying products that afford emotional satisfaction is a perfectly rational consumer decision. Some emotional decisions are expressions that "you deserve it" or "treat yourself." For instance, many consumers buy designer-label clothing, not because they look any better in it, but because status labels make them feel better. This is a rational decision. Of course, if a man with a wife and three children purchases a two-seater Pontiac Solstice Roadster (**www.pontiac.com**) for himself, the neighbors might wonder about his level of rationality (although some might think it was deviously high). No such question would arise if the same man selected a box of Godiva chocolate (**www.godiva.com**), instead of a Whitman Sampler (**www.whitmans.com**), although in both instances, each might be an impulsive, emotional purchase decision.

Consumers' **moods** are also important to decision making. Mood can be defined as a "feeling state" or state of mind.[8] Unlike an emotion, which is a response to a particular environment, a mood is more typically an unfocused, preexisting state—already present at the time a consumer "experiences" an advertisement, a retail environment, a brand, or a product. Compared to emotions, moods are generally lower in intensity and longer lasting and are not as directly coupled with action tendencies and explicit actions as emotions.

Mood appears to be important to consumer decision making, because it impacts on *when* consumers shop, *where* they shop, and *whether* they shop alone or with others. It also is likely to influence *how* the consumer responds to actual shopping environments (i.e., at point of purchase). Some retailers attempt to create a mood for shoppers, even though shoppers enter the store with a preexisting mood. Research suggests that a store's image or atmosphere can affect shoppers' moods; in turn, shoppers' moods can influence how long they stay in the store, as well as other behavior that retailers wish to encourage.[9]

In general, individuals in a positive mood recall more information about a product than those in a negative mood. As the results of one study suggest, however, inducing a positive mood at the point-of-purchase decision (as through background music, point-of-purchase displays, etc.) is unlikely to have a meaningful impact on specific brand choice unless a previously stored brand evaluation already exists.[10]

A Model of Consumer Decision Making

Learning Objective

15.4 *To Understand in Detail the Model of Consumer Decision Making Originally Introduced in Chapter 1.*

This section presents a model of consumer decision making (briefly introduced in Chapter 1) that reflects the *cognitive* (or *problem-solving*) *consumer* and, to some degree, the *emotional consumer*. The model is designed to tie together many of the ideas on consumer decision making and consumption behavior discussed throughout the book. It does not presume to provide an exhaustive picture of the complexities of consumer decision making. Rather, it is designed to synthesize and coordinate relevant concepts into a significant whole. The model, presented in Figure 15.3, has three major components: input, process, and output.

FIGURE 15.3
A Model of Consumer Decision Making

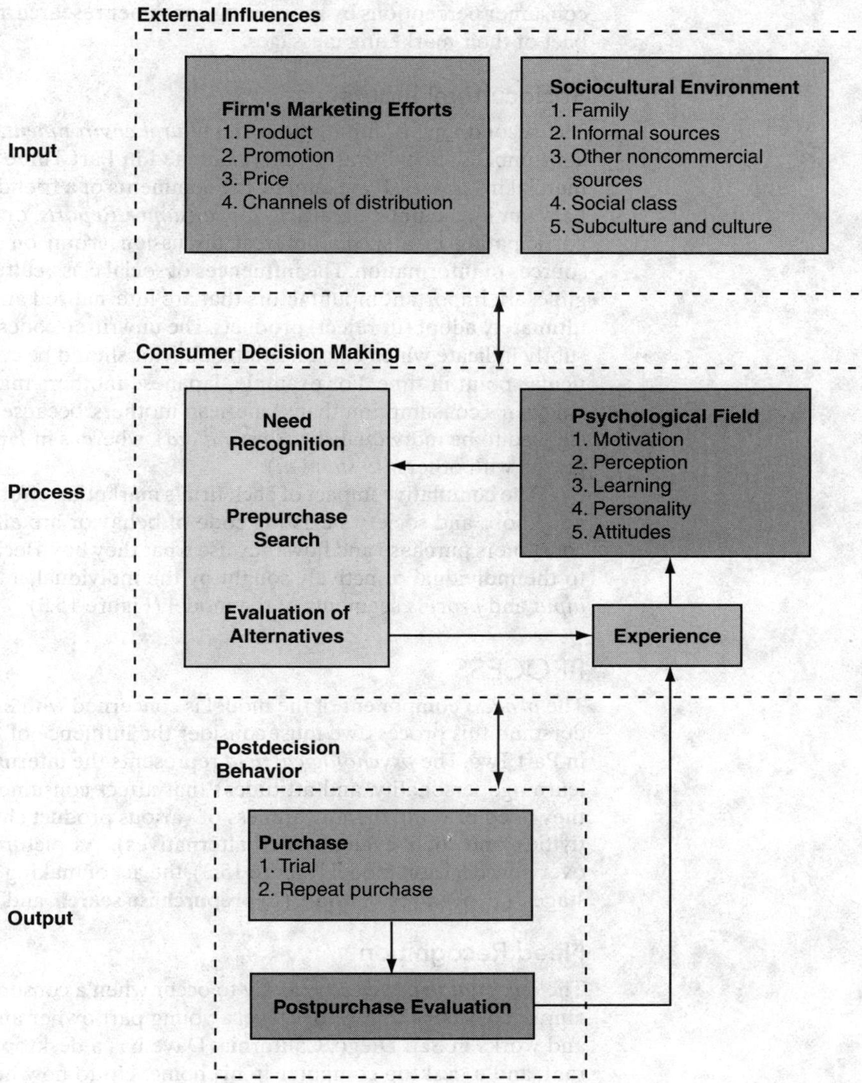

INPUT

The *input* component of our consumer decision-making model draws on external influences that serve as sources of information about a particular product and influence a consumer's product-related values, attitudes, and behavior. Chief among these input factors are the *marketing mix activities* of organizations that attempt to communicate the benefits of their products and services to potential consumers and the nonmarketing *sociocultural influences*, which, when internalized, affect the consumer's purchase decisions.

Marketing Inputs

The firm's marketing activities are a direct attempt to reach, inform, and persuade consumers to buy and use its products. These inputs to the consumer's decision-making process take the form of specific marketing mix strategies that consist of the product itself (including its package, size, and guarantees); mass-media advertising, direct marketing, personal selling, and other promotional efforts; pricing policy; and the selection of distribution channels to move the product from the manufacturer to the consumer.

Ultimately, the impact of a firm's marketing efforts in large measure is governed by the consumer's perception of these efforts. Thus, marketers do well to remain diligently alert to consumer perceptions by sponsoring consumer research, rather than to rely on the *intended* impact of their marketing messages.

Sociocultural Inputs

The second type of input, the *sociocultural environment*, also exerts a major influence on the consumer. Sociocultural inputs (examined in Part Three) consist of a wide range of noncommercial influences. For example, the comments of a friend, an editorial in the newspaper, usage by a family member, an article in *Consumer Reports*, or the views of experienced consumers participating in a special-interest discussion group on the Internet are all noncommercial sources of information. The influences of social class, culture, and subculture, although less tangible, are important input factors that are internalized and affect how consumers evaluate and ultimately adopt (or reject) products. The unwritten codes of conduct communicated by culture subtly indicate which consumption behavior should be considered "right" or "wrong" at a particular point in time. For example, Japanese mothers maintain much more control over their children's consumption than American mothers, because in the United States children are socialized to be individualistic (*to stand out*), whereas in Japan children are socialized to be integrated with others (*to stand in*).

The cumulative impact of each firm's marketing efforts, the influence of family, friends, and neighbors, and society's existing code of behavior are all inputs that are likely to affect what consumers purchase and how they use what they buy. Because these influences may be directed to the individual or actively sought by the individual, a two-headed arrow is used to link the *input* and *process* segments of the model (Figure 15.3).

PROCESS

The *process* component of the model is concerned with how consumers make decisions. To understand this process, we must consider the influence of the psychological concepts examined in Part Two. The *psychological field* represents the internal influences (motivation, perception, learning, personality, and attitudes) that affect consumers' decision-making processes (what they need or want, their awareness of various product choices, their information-gathering activities, and their evaluation of alternatives). As pictured in the *process* component of the overview decision model (Figure 15.3), the act of making a consumer decision consists of three stages: (1) **need recognition**, (2) **prepurchase search**, and (3) **evaluation of alternatives**.

Need Recognition

The *recognition of a need* is likely to occur when a consumer is faced with a "problem." For example, consider the case of Dave, a young part owner and manager of a restaurant, who lives and works in San Diego, California. Dave has a desktop computer in his office at the restaurant, and a desktop computer in his home. Up to now he has never had a desire for a laptop computer because he considers them to be too big, to break too often (from what he has observed from his friends with laptops), and to be somewhat uncomfortable to use (e.g., small keyboards without much "feel" to the keys, and a touchpad rather than a mouse).

Coincidentally, within the last two years, Dave has been investing in real estate. With some money he inherited from a "favorite" aunt, and money he had saved by having a comfortable but not extravagant lifestyle, he has purchased a condo in a new residential building in San Diego—as an investment, not to live there. He bought the condo at a very low "preconstruction" price, and the building, which is now completed, has tenants living there. Dave has found a renter for his condo, and at the rental price he was able to negotiate, will make a nice profit from this venture.

While it is true that in many areas real estate prices have plummeted, in the San Diego area real estate prices have dropped less than 5 percent. As a result, while Dave has the down payment to purchase two or three additional condominiums as investments, he feels that new construction in San Diego is just too expensive at present. Since Dave's job managing the restaurant gives him every Monday and Tuesday off, he begins driving to other nearby cities to investigate the real estate market. For example, over the past two weeks, he has taken overnight trips to Las Vegas and Phoenix, both just less than 350 miles from San Diego. Prior to both trips, Dave did research on the Internet to find out about new condominium construction in both locales, and was also in contact, via e-mail, with real estate agents who were serving as renting agents for these buildings. When in both cities, Dave also drove around to seek out new construction that he had not found on the Internet.

For the first time, Dave wishes that he had a laptop computer. He realized that when he was in Las Vegas and Phoenix, if he had a laptop he could have looked up any new construction he found in order to gain some knowledge about the building, such as layout, pricing, and amenities.

Among consumers, there seem to be two different need or problem recognition styles. Some consumers are *actual state* types, who perceive that they have a problem when a product fails to perform satisfactorily (as a cordless telephone that develops constant static). In contrast, other consumers are *desired state* types, for whom the desire for something new may trigger the decision process.[11] Since Dave currently does not own a laptop computer, he appears to be a desired state consumer.

Prepurchase Search

Prepurchase search begins when a consumer perceives a need that might be satisfied by the purchase and consumption of a product. The recollection of past experiences (drawn from storage in long-term memory) might provide the consumer with adequate information to make the present choice. On the other hand, when the consumer has had no prior experience, he or she may have to engage in an extensive search of the outside environment for useful information on which to base a choice.

The consumer usually searches his or her memory (the *psychological field* depicted in the model) before seeking external sources of information regarding a given consumption-related need. Past experience is considered an internal source of information. The greater the relevant past experience, the less external information the consumer is likely to need to reach a decision. Many consumer decisions are based on a combination of past experience (internal sources) and marketing and noncommercial information (external sources). The degree of perceived risk can also influence this stage of the decision process (see Chapter 6). In high-risk situations, consumers are likely to engage in complex and extensive information search and evaluation; in low-risk situations, they are likely to use very simple or limited search and evaluation tactics.

The act of shopping is an important form of external information. According to consumer research, there is a big difference between men and women in terms of their response to shopping. Whereas most men do not like to shop, most women claim to like the experience of shopping; and although the majority of women found shopping to be relaxing and enjoyable, the majority of men did not feel that way.[12]

An examination of the external search effort associated with the purchase of different product categories (TVs, DVD recorders, or personal computers) found that, as the amount of total search effort increased, consumer attitudes toward shopping became more positive, and more time was made available for shopping. Not surprisingly, the external search effort was greatest for consumers who had the least amount of product category knowledge.[13] It follows that the less consumers know about a product category and the more important the purchase is to them, the more time they will make available and the more extensive their prepurchase search activity is likely to be. Conversely, research studies have indicated that consumers high in subjective knowledge (a self-assessment of how much they know about the product category) rely more on their own evaluations than on dealer recommendations.

It is also important to point out that the Internet has had a great impact on prepurchase search. Rather than visiting a store to find out about a product or calling the manufacturer and asking for a brochure, manufacturers' Web sites can provide consumers with much of the information they need about the products and services they are considering. For example, many automobile Web sites provide product specifications, sticker prices and dealer cost information, reviews, and even comparisons with competing vehicles. Volvo's Web site (**www.volvocars.com/us**), for example, lets you "build" your own car, and see how it would look, for example, in different colors. Some auto company Web sites will even list a particular auto dealer's new and used car inventory. And then there are Web sites such as Joya Beauty (**www.joyabeauty.com/custom.html**) that allow women to customize any number of cosmetic products, and My Tailor (**www.mytailor.com**) that lets men design their own clothing, such as dress shirts.

With respect to surfing the Internet for information, consider one consumer's comments drawn from a recent research study: "I like to use the Web because it's so easy to find information, and it's really easy to use. The information is at my finger-tips and I don't have to search books in libraries."[14] However, a Roper Starch Survey found that an individual searching the

FIGURE 15.4
A Model of Search Regret

Source: Kristy E. Reynolds, Judith Anne Garretson Folse, and Michael A. Jones, "Search Regret: Antecedents and Consequences," *Journal of Retailing*, 82, no. 4 (2006): 342.

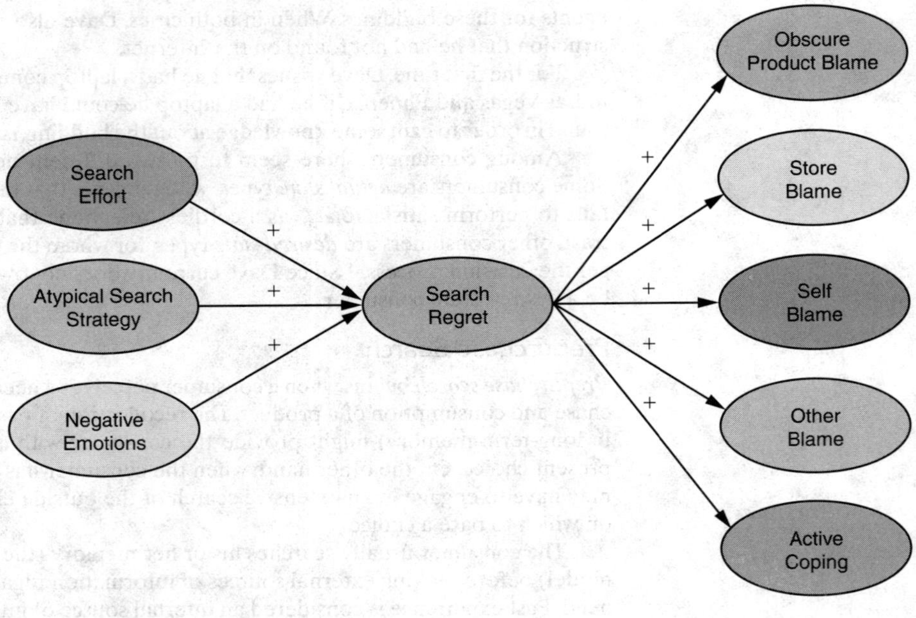

Internet gets frustrated in about 12 minutes, on average; and other research added to the thought by suggesting that although the Internet may reduce physical effort, there is nevertheless a "cognitive challenge" that limits consumers' online information search.[15]

What happens if the search is a failure? A recent article examined the issue of "search regret," which it defined as "a postsearch dissonance that results from an unsuccessful prepurchase search."[16] Search regret can have a damaging effect on retailers, because in this pilot study store blame and self-blame were not significantly correlated with each other. The study noted that retailers can help eliminate or reduce search regret by providing ample information, trying to reduce out-of-stock situations, and proper training of salespeople.[17] Figure 15.4 presents a model of search regret. Note how this negative outcome can lead to blaming the product, the store, oneself, others, or coping (where the consumer actively tries to resolve the issue).

How much information a consumer will gather also depends on various situational factors. Getting back to Dave, while he works long hours at the restaurant, he is willing to spend time researching his desired purchase. He starts by sitting at his computer table at home with his computer connected to the Internet via a broadband connection. He visits the Web sites of computer manufacturers such as Dell (**www.dell.com**), Hewlett-Packard (**www.hp.com**), and Toshiba (**www.toshiba.com**), the Web sites of stores in the San Diego area that sell computers, such as Best Buy (**www.bestbuy.com**) and Fry's Electronics (**www.frys.com**), as well as e-tailer Web sites like Amazon.com (**www.amazon.com**) and Buy.com (**www.buy.com**), to see which brands and models of laptop computers are small and lightweight. He knows that he is not looking for a "desktop replacement" type of laptop—he wants something that he can use when traveling in order to access his e-mail and surf the Web. Dave feels that something like a BlackBerry or an Apple iPhone or iTouch does not have a screen that is large enough for him to be comfortable with, especially since he often spends 30 minutes or more at a time on the Internet.

Dave also talks to some of his friends and coworkers who are considerably more knowledgeable about computers than he is (especially since he never really bothered to learn much about laptops). One of his friends tells him about a new class of laptop computer that has recently come onto the market. Called "Netbooks" or ultra-mobile personal computers (UMPCs), these PCs typically run a version of Microsoft OS or Linux, have an 8- to 10-inch screen, and typically weigh three pounds or less. His friend also suggests that he try to find product reviews of netbooks on such Web sites as CNET (**www.cnet.com**), *PC Magazine* (**www.pcmag.com**), and *Computer Shopper* (**www.computershopper.com**).

As Table 15.2 indicates, a number of factors are likely to increase consumers' prepurchase search. For some products and services, the consumer may have ongoing experience on which

TABLE 15.2 Factors That Are Likely to Increase Prepurchase Search

PRODUCT FACTORS

Long interpurchase time (a long-lasting or infrequently used product)
Frequent changes in product styling
Frequent price changes
Volume purchasing (large number of units)
High price
Many alternative brands
Much variation in features

SITUATIONAL FACTORS

Experience

First-time purchase
No past experience because the product is new
Unsatisfactory past experience within the product category

Social Acceptability

The purchase is for a gift
The product is socially visible

Value-Related Considerations

Purchase is discretionary rather than necessary
All alternatives have both desirable and undesirable consequences
Family members disagree on product requirements or evaluation of alternatives
Product usage deviates from important reference groups
The purchase involves ecological considerations
Many sources of conflicting information

CONSUMER FACTORS

Demographic Characteristics of Consumer

Well educated
High income
White-collar occupation
Under 35 years of age

Personality

Low dogmatic
Low-risk perceiver (broad categorizer)
Other personal factors such as high product involvement and enjoyment of shopping and search

to draw (such as a golfer purchasing a "better" set of golf clubs), or the purchase may essentially be discretionary in nature (rather than a necessity), so there is no rush to make a decision. In the case of Dave, our restaurant manager and real estate investor, while there is no particular need to rush into the purchase of the computer, he would like to have it in two weeks when he is planning to take another overnight trip to examine condos, this time to Tucson, Arizona.

Let's consider several of the prepurchase search alternatives open to a computer buyer. At the most fundamental level, search alternatives can be classified as either personal or impersonal. *Personal* search alternatives include more than a consumer's past experience with the product or service. They also include asking for information and advice from friends, relatives, coworkers, and sales representatives. For instance, Dave spoke with a few friends and coworkers and asked them what they know about laptops. Dave also investigated whether computer magazines, such

TABLE 15.3 Alternative Prepurchase Information Sources for an Ultralight Laptop

PERSONAL	IMPERSONAL
Friends	Newspaper articles
Neighbors	Magazine articles
Relatives	*Consumer Reports*
Coworkers	Direct-mail brochures
Computer salespeople	Information from product advertisements
Membership discussion forum	Online electronics retailer's Web site

as *PC Review* and *Computer Shopper* might have rated the various brands or models of laptops. Table 15.3 presents some of the sources of information that Dave might use as part of his prepurchase search. Any or all of these sources might be used as part of a consumer's search process.

Evaluation of Alternatives

When evaluating potential alternatives, consumers tend to use two types of information: (1) a "list" of brands (or models) from which they plan to make their selection (the evoked set) and (2) the criteria they will use to evaluate each brand (or model). Making a selection from a *sample* of all possible brands (or models) is a human characteristic that helps simplify the decision-making process.

EVOKED SET Within the context of consumer decision making, the **evoked set** refers to the specific brands (or models) a consumer considers in making a purchase within a particular product category. (The evoked set is also called the *consideration set*.) A consumer's evoked set is distinguished from his or her **inept set**, which consists of brands (or models) the consumer excludes from purchase consideration because they are felt to be unacceptable (or they are seen as "inferior"), and from the **inert set**, which consists of brands (or models) the consumer is indifferent toward because they are perceived as not having any particular advantages. Regardless of the total number of brands (or models) in a product category, a consumer's evoked set tends to be quite small on average, often consisting of only three to five brands (or models).

The evoked set consists of the small number of brands the consumer is familiar with, remembers, and finds acceptable. Figure 15.5 depicts the evoked set as a subset of all available brands in a product category. As the figure indicates, it is essential that a product be part of a

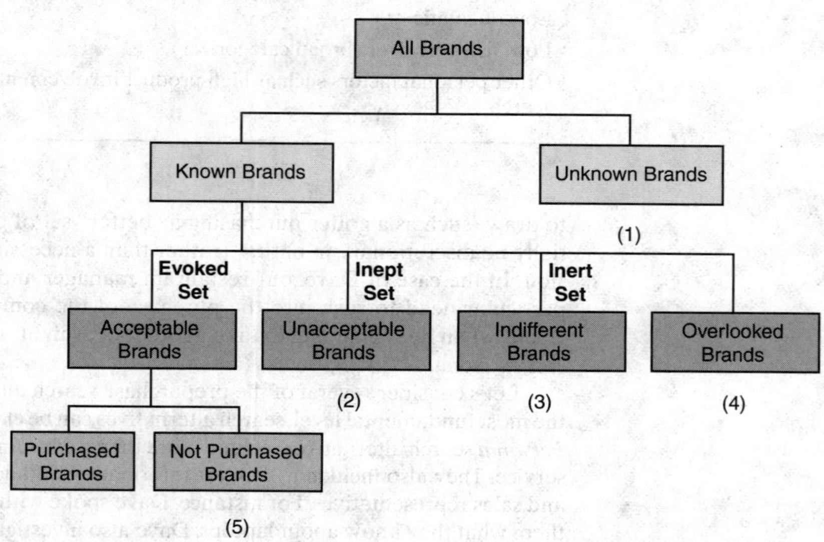

FIGURE 15.5 The Evoked Set as a Subset of All Brands in a Product Class

consumer's evoked set if it is to be considered at all. The five terminal positions in the model that do not end in purchase would appear to have perceptual problems. For example, (1) brands (or models) may be *unknown* because of the consumer's selective exposure to advertising media and selective perception of advertising stimuli; (2) brands (or models) may be *unacceptable* because of poor qualities or attributes or inappropriate positioning in either advertising or product characteristics; (3) brands (or models) may be perceived as not having any special benefits and are regarded *indifferently* by the consumer; (4) brands (or models) may be *overlooked* because they have not been clearly positioned or sharply targeted at the consumer market segment under study; and (5) brands (or models) may not be selected because they are perceived by consumers as *unable to satisfy* perceived needs as fully as the brand that is chosen.

In each of these instances, the implication for marketers is that promotional techniques should be designed to impart a more favorable, perhaps more relevant, product image to the target consumer. This may also require a change in product features or attributes (more or better features). An alternative strategy is to invite consumers in a particular target segment to consider a specific offering and possibly put it in their evoked set.

Research also suggests that the use of white space and choice of typeface in advertisements may influence the consumer's image of the product. For example, quality, prestige, trust, attitude toward the brand, and purchase intention have been shown to be positively conveyed by white space, and typefaces that were perceived as being attractive, warm, and liked when they were simple, more natural, and include a typeface with serifs.[18] It has also been suggested that consumers may not, all at once, reduce down the number of possible choices into their evoked set, but instead may make several decisions within a single decision process. These screening decisions, or decision waves, are used to eliminate unsuitable alternatives before gathering information or comparing options, and help reduce decision complexity to a more manageable level.[19]

CRITERIA USED FOR EVALUATING BRANDS The criteria consumers use to evaluate the alternative products that constitute their evoked sets usually are expressed in terms of important product attributes. Examples of product attributes that consumers have used as criteria in evaluating nine product categories are listed in Table 15.4.

TABLE 15.4 Possible Product Attributes Used as Purchase Criteria for Nine Product Categories

PERSONAL COMPUTERS	MP3 PLAYERS	WRISTWATCHES
Processing speed	Mega bass	Watchband
Price	Memory size	Alarm feature
Type of display	Length of play on batteries	Price
Hard-disk size	Random play feature	Water resistant
Amount of memory	Equalizer	Quartz movement
Laptop or desktop		Size of dial
DVD PLAYERS	**HDTVS**	**FROZEN DINNERS**
Ease of connecting to HDTV	Picture quality	Taste
Ability to record	Length of warranty	Type of main course
720p or 1080p	720p or 1080p	Type of side dishes
Slow-motion feature	Price	Price
Dolby	Size of screen	Preparation requirements
DIGITAL CAMERAS	**FOUNTAIN PENS**	**COLOR INKJET PRINTERS**
Auto focus	Balance	Output speed
Built-in flash	Price	Number of ink colors
Image stabilization	Gold nib	Resolution (DPI)
Lens type	Smoothness	Length of warranty
Size and weight	Ink reserve	USB capability

When a company knows that consumers will be evaluating alternatives, it sometimes advertises in a way that recommends the criteria that consumers should use in assessing product or service options.

We have probably all had the experience of comparing or evaluating different brands or models of a product and finding the one that just feels, looks, and/or performs "right." Interestingly, research shows that when consumers discuss such "right products," there is little or no mention of price; brand names are not often uppermost in consumers' minds; items often reflect personality characteristics or childhood experiences; and it is often "love at first sight." In one study, the products claimed to "just feel right" included Big Bertha golf clubs, old leather briefcases, Post-it notes, and the Honda Accord.[20] And, a product's country of origin can also play a role in how a consumer evaluates a brand (see Chapter 13).

Research has explored the role of brand credibility (which consists of trustworthiness and expertise) on brand choice, and has found that brand credibility improves the chances that a brand will be included in the consideration set. Three factors that impact a brand's credibility are: the perceived quality of the brand, the perceived risk associated with the brand, and the information costs saved with that brand (due to the time and effort saved by not having to shop around).[21] Still further, the study indicates that trustworthiness is more important than expertise when it comes to making a choice.

Let's return for a moment to Dave and his search for a small, lightweight portable computer. As part of his search process, he has acquired information about a number of relevant issues (or attributes) that could influence his final choice. For example, Dave has learned that the overall size of a computer is very much a function of the features that it contains, such as the speed of its processor, whether or not the computer has an optical drive (CD or DVD), the size of its hard drive and screen, and its battery life. Still further, Dave realizes that since he is planning to use this PC almost exclusively for e-mail and for surfing the Internet, he is more interested in small size (but not too small a screen or keyboard) than in hard drive size or whether the machine has a built-in optical drive. Consequently, Dave decides that a netbook is what he needs.

As part of his search process, Dave has also acquired information about other relevant issues (or attributes) that could influence his final choice (see Table 15.5). For example, he has learned that some models of netbooks have much larger hard drives than other models, and that some offer larger screens.

On the basis of his information search, Dave realizes that he is going to have to make a decision regarding what he really wants from this new UMPC. Does he want his mobile PC to have decent screen size, decent keyboard, and a large hard drive, or is he willing to sacrifice fea-

TABLE 15.5 Comparison of Selected Characteristics of Netbooks

FEATURE	DELL INSPIRON MINI 9	MSI WIND	HP 2133 MINI-NOTE PC	ACER ASPIRE ONE
Operating system	MS Windows XP Home	MS Windows XP Home	MS Windows Vista Business	Windows XP
Processor	Intel Atom	Intel Atom	VIA C7	Intel Atom
Processor speed	1.6 GHz	1.6 GHz	1.6 GHz	1.6 GHz
RAM	1 GB	1 GB	2 GB	1 GB
Weight	2.3 lbs.	2.6 lbs.	3.2 lbs.	2.3 lbs.
Screen Size	8.9 inches	10.1 inches	8.9 inches	8.9 inches
Graphics memory	64 MB	224 MB	256 MB	384 MB
Storage capacity	8 GB solid state	80 GB	120 GB	160 GB
Primary optical drive	External	External	External	External
Battery type	32 Watt hours	24 Watt hours	55 Watt hours	48 Watt hours
Price	$399	$400	$800	$399

Sources: Based on "PC Magazine—Compare Products," accessed at www.pcmag.com/compare; "Dell Joins the Netbook Fray," *PC Magazine,* December 2008, 23; and "Acer Aspire One," *Computer Shopper,* November 2008, 29.

Note: These netbooks are available in a variety of configurations.

tures in order to obtain a netbook that is smaller and lighter? He comes to realize that since he is not going to be replacing his current desktop computer, and he is not planning to put any of his "work" software on this new netbook (e.g., Microsoft Excel and Word), he is willing to give up some functionality (such as a large hard drive) in exchange for reduced size and weight.

CONSUMER DECISION RULES Consumer decision rules, often referred to as *heuristics, decision strategies*, and *information-processing strategies*, are procedures used by consumers to facilitate brand (or other consumption-related) choices. These rules reduce the burden of making complex decisions by providing guidelines or routines that make the process less taxing.

Consumer decision rules have been broadly classified into two major categories: **compensatory** and **noncompensatory decision rules**. In following a compensatory decision rule, a consumer evaluates brand or model options in terms of each relevant attribute and computes a weighted or summated score for each brand. The computed score reflects the brand's relative merit as a potential purchase choice. The assumption is that the consumer will select the brand that scores highest among the alternatives evaluated. Referring to Table 15.6, it is clear that when using a compensatory decision rule, the Acer Aspire One, configured with a 160 GB hard drive and the 6-cell battery, scores highest.

A unique feature of a compensatory decision rule is that it allows a positive evaluation of a brand on one attribute to balance out a negative evaluation on some other attribute.[22] For example, a positive assessment of the energy savings made possible by a particular brand or type of lightbulb may offset an unacceptable assessment in terms of the bulb's diminished light output.

In contrast, noncompensatory decision rules do not allow consumers to balance positive evaluations of a brand on one attribute against a negative evaluation on some other attribute. For instance, in the case of an energy-saving lightbulb, the product's negative (unacceptable) rating on its light output would not be offset by a positive evaluation of its energy savings. Instead, this particular lightbulb would be disqualified from further consideration. If Dave's choice of a netbook was based on the desire to have a standard hard drive, rather than a solid-state drive (refer again to Table 15.5), a noncompensatory decision rule would have eliminated the Dell Inspiron Mini 9.

Three noncompensatory rules are considered briefly here: the *conjunctive* rule, the *disjunctive* rule, and the *lexicographic* rule.

In following a **conjunctive decision rule**, the consumer establishes a separate, minimally acceptable level as a cutoff point for each attribute. If any particular brand or model falls below the cutoff point on any one attribute, the option is eliminated from further consideration. Because the conjunctive rule can result in several acceptable alternatives, it becomes necessary in such cases for the consumer to apply an additional decision rule to arrive at a final selection, for example, to accept the first satisfactory brand. The conjunctive rule is particularly useful in quickly reducing the number of alternatives to be considered. The consumer can then apply another more refined decision rule to arrive at a final choice.

TABLE 15.6 Hypothetical Ratings for Netbooks

FEATURE	DELL INSPIRON MINI 9	MSI WIND	HP 2133 MINI-NOTE PC	ACER ASPIRE ONE
Operating system	7	7	9	7
Processor	8	8	6	8
Processor speed	8	8	8	8
RAM	7	7	8	7
Weight	9	7	4	9
Screen size	7	8	7	7
Graphics memory	5	7	7	8
Storage capacity	4	6	7	8
Primary optical drive	5	5	5	5
Battery type	6	5	8	9
Price	8	8	4	8
Total	74	76	73	84

The **disjunctive rule** is the "mirror image" of the conjunctive rule. In applying this decision rule, the consumer establishes a separate, minimally acceptable cutoff level for each attribute (which may be higher than the one normally established for a conjunctive rule). In this case, if an option meets or exceeds the cutoff established for any one attribute, it is accepted. Here again, a number of brands (or models) might exceed the cutoff point, producing a situation in which another decision rule is required. When this occurs, the consumer may accept the first satisfactory alternative as the final choice, or apply another decision rule that is perhaps more suitable.

In following a **lexicographic decision rule**, the consumer first ranks the attributes in terms of perceived relevance or importance. The consumer then compares the various alternatives in terms of the single attribute that is considered most important. If one option scores sufficiently high on this top-ranked attribute (regardless of the score on any of the other attributes), it is selected and the process ends. When there are two or more surviving alternatives, the process is repeated with the second highest-ranked attribute (and so on), until reaching the point that one of the options is selected because it exceeds the others on a particular attribute.

With the lexicographic rule, the highest-ranked attribute (the one applied first) may reveal something about the individual's basic consumer (or shopping) orientation. For instance, a "buy the best" rule might indicate that the consumer is *quality oriented*; a "buy the most prestigious brand" rule might indicate that the consumer is *status oriented*; a "buy the least expensive" rule might reveal that the consumer is *economy minded*.

A variety of decision rules appear quite commonplace. According to a consumer survey, 9 out of 10 shoppers who go to the store for frequently purchased items possess a specific shopping strategy for saving money. The consumer segment and the specific shopping rules that these segments employ are:[23]

1. Practical loyalists—those who look for ways to save on the brands and products they would buy anyway.
2. Bottom-line price shoppers—those who buy the lowest-priced item with little or no regard for brand.
3. Opportunistic switchers—those who use coupons or sales to decide among brands and products that fall within their evoked set.
4. Deal hunters—those who look for the best bargain and are not brand loyal.

We have considered only the most basic of an almost infinite number of consumer decision rules. Most of the decision rules described here can be combined to form new variations, such as conjunctive-compensatory, conjunctive-disjunctive, and disjunctive-conjunctive rules. It is likely that for many purchase decisions, consumers maintain in long-term memory overall evaluations of the brands in their evoked sets. This would make assessment by individual attributes unnecessary. Instead, the consumer would simply select the brand with the highest perceived overall rating. This type of synthesized decision rule is known as the **affect referral decision rule** and may represent the simplest of all rules.

Table 15.7 summarizes the essence of many of the decision rules considered in this chapter in terms of the kind of mental statements that Dave might make in selecting a netbook.

TABLE 15.7 Hypothetical Use of Popular Decision Rules in Making a Decision to Purchase a Netbook

DECISION RULE	MENTAL STATEMENT
Compensatory rule	"I selected the netbook that came out best when I balanced the good ratings against the bad ratings."
Conjunctive rule	"I selected the netbook that had no bad features."
Disjunctive rule	"I picked the netbook that excelled in at least one attribute."
Lexicographic rule	"I looked at the feature that was most important to me and chose the netbook that ranked highest on that attribute."
Affect referral rule	"I bought the brand with the highest overall rating."

HOW DO FUNCTIONALLY ILLITERATE CONSUMERS DECIDE? The National Adult Literacy Survey found that a bit more than 20 percent of American consumers did not possess the rudimentary skills in language and arithmetic needed for the typical retail environment, and that perhaps as much as half of all U.S. consumers lack the skills needed to master specific aspects of shopping, such as sales agreements and credit applications. Furthermore, despite the fact that functionally illiterate consumers have only 40 percent as much purchasing power as their literate counterparts, they may spend as much as $380 billion annually.[24]

Research has found that functionally illiterate consumers do make decisions differently, in terms of cognitive predilections, decision rules and trade-offs, and coping behaviors (see Figure 15.6). For example, they use concrete reasoning and noncompensatory decision rules, meaning that they base the purchase decision on a single piece of information, without regard to other product attributes (e.g., "I just look at the tag and see what's cheapest. I don't look by their sizes"). Such consumers, if confronted with two boxes of a product at the same price, would tend to purchase the one in the physically larger box, even if the label on the smaller-sized package indicated a higher weight or greater volume. And through what might be referred to as "sight reading," they recognize brand logos the same way they might recognize people in a photograph. In fact, functionally illiterate consumers treat all words and numbers as pictorial elements. They also become anxious when shopping in a new store (they prefer to shop in the same store, especially if they have established a rapport with a friendly and helpful employee), and often give all their money to the cashier expecting him or her to return the proper change.[25] Table 15.8 presents the coping strategies used by functionally illiterate consumers. Note how such consumers avoid purchasing unknown brands and try to carry limited amounts of cash to the store.

GOING ONLINE TO SECURE ASSISTANCE IN DECISION MAKING For a while now, researchers have been examining how the Internet has impacted the way consumers make decisions. It is often hypothesized that because consumers have limited information-processing capacity, they must develop a choice strategy based on both individual factors (e.g., knowledge, personality traits, demographics) and contextual factors (characteristics of the decision tasks). The three major contextual factors that have been researched are *task complexity* (number of alternatives and amount of information available for each alternative), *information organization* (presentation, format, and content), and *time constraint* (more or less time to decide).[26] Table 15.9 compares these contextual factors for both the electronic and traditional environments.

A reason to go online is that a number of Web sites allow a consumer to build his or her "own anything." For example, you can order M&Ms imprinted with your own message at **www.mymms.com/customprint/?sc_cid=DR_LV1**, or order personalized shower gels at **www.myweddingaccents.com**. According to one source, about 75 percent of Mini Cooper purchasers went through 70 options to design their vehicles online (**www.miniusa.com**).[27]

FIGURE 15.6
The Decision Process for Functionally Illiterate Consumers

Source: Madhubalan Viswanathan, José Antonio Rosa, and James Edwin Harris, "Decision Making and Coping of Functionally Illiterate Consumers and Some Implications for Marketing Management," *Journal of Marketing*, 69 (January 2005): 19.

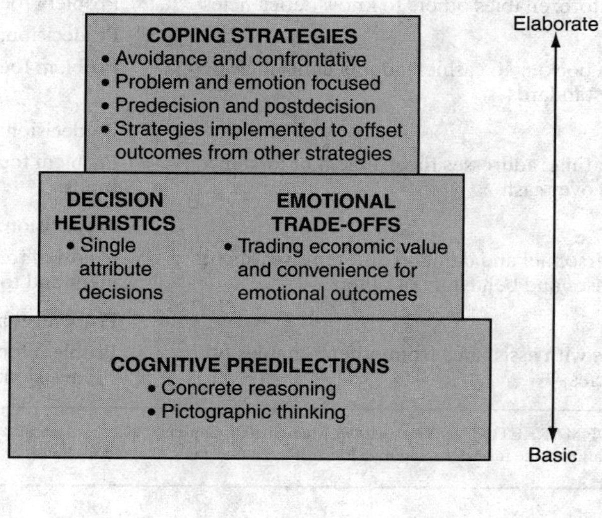

TABLE 15.8 Coping Strategies of Functionally Illiterate Consumers

COPING STRATEGIES	CLASSIFICATIONS
AVOIDANCE	
Shop at the same store: avoids stress of unfamiliar environment	Problem focused: shops effectively Predecision: habitual choice about store helps with choices about products
Shop at smaller stores: avoids cognitive demands from product variety	Emotion focused: reduces stress Predecision: requires advance planning
Single-attribute decisions: avoids stressful and complex product comparisons	Problem focused: makes decisions manageable Emotion focused: preserves image of competence Predecision: requires advance planning
Avoid percentage- and fraction-off discounted items: avoids difficult numerical tasks	Emotion focused: reduces stress Problem focused: less chance of mistakes Predecision: implements habitually
Buy only known brands (loyalty): avoids risks from unknown brands	Problem focused: facilitates shopping Predecision: implements habitually
Rationalize outcomes to shift responsibility: avoids responsibility for outcomes	Emotion focused: protects self-esteem Postdecision: implements after outcome is clear
Carry limited amounts of cash: avoids risks of overspending and being cheated	Problem focused: controls transactions Predecision: requires advance planning
Buy small amounts more often: avoids risk of large scale cheating	Problem focused: controls transactions Predecision: requires advance planning
Pretend disability: avoids revealing deficiencies and embarrassment	Problem focused: obtains assistance Emotion focused: preserves public image Predecision: requires advance planning
Pretend to evaluate products and prices: avoids revealing deficiencies indirectly	Emotion focused: preserves public image Predecision: requires advance planning
CONFRONTATION	
Shop with family members and friends: enables others to know deficiencies	Problem focused: helps shop on a budget Predecision: involves advance planning
Establish relationships with store personnel: enables others to know deficiencies	Emotion focused: avoids embarrassment and stress Predecision: Involves advance planning
Seek help in the store: enables others to know deficiencies	Problem focused: facilitates final decision Predecision: leads to a purchase decision
Give all money in pockets to cashier: admits deficiencies, plays on honesty standards	Problem focused: avoids not being able to count Predecision: implements habitually
Buy one item at a time: addresses the problem of loss of control when turning over cash	Problem focused: controls pace of transactions and flow of funds Predecision: requires advance planning
Confront store personnel and demand different treatment: focuses on responses and behaviors of others	Emotion focused: seeks to minimize or eliminate embarrassment and to preserve or restore public image Postdecision: implements in response to others
Plan expenditures with assistance from others: enables others to know deficiencies	Problem focused: facilitates a budget Predecision: involves advance planning

TABLE 15.9 Comparison of Electronic and Traditional Information Environment

ASSUMPTION		ELECTRONIC ENVIRONMENT CONSUMERS USE BOTH "HEADS" AND COMPUTERS TO MAKE DECISIONS. THE TOTAL CAPACITY IS EXTENDED.	TRADITIONAL ENVIRONMENT CONSUMERS USE "HEADS" TO MAKE DECISIONS. THEIR COGNITIVE CAPACITY IS FIXED.
Contextual factors	Task complexity	More alternatives and more information for each alternative are available.	Information is scattered and information search is costly.
	Information organization	Information is more accessible. Information presentation format is flexible. It can be reorganized and controlled by consumers. Product utilities can be calculated by computers without consumers' direct examination of the attributes.	Information presentation format and organization are fixed. They can only be "edited" by consumers manually (e.g., using pencil and paper).
	Time constraint	Time is saved by using computers to execute the decision rules; extra time is needed to learn how to use the application.	Complex choice strategies require more time to formulate and execute.

Source: AMERICAN MARKETING ASSOCIATION. SUMMER CONFERENCE PROCEEDINGS (1999) by Xia, Lan. Copyright 1999 by American Marketing Association. Reproduced with permission of American Marketing Association in the format print & electronic usage via Copyright Clearance Center.

LIFESTYLES AS A CONSUMER DECISION STRATEGY An individual's or family's decisions to be committed to a particular lifestyle (e.g., devoted followers of a particular religion) tends to impact a wide range of their specific everyday consumer behavior. For instance, the Trends Research Institute has identified "voluntary simplicity" as one of the top 10 lifestyle trends.[28] Researchers there estimate that 15 percent of all boomers seek a simpler lifestyle with reduced emphasis on ownership and possessions. Voluntary simplifiers are making do with less clothing and fewer credit cards (with no outstanding balances) and moving to smaller, yet still adequate, homes or apartments in less populated communities. Most importantly, it is not that these consumers can no longer afford their affluence or "lifestyle of abundance"; rather, they are seeking new, "reduced," less extravagant lifestyles. As part of this new lifestyle commitment, some individuals are seeking less stressful and lower-salary careers or jobs. In a telephone survey, for example, 33 percent of those contacted claimed that they would be willing to take a 20 percent pay cut in return for working fewer hours.[29] Time pressure may also play a role in the consumer's decision process, as research has positively associated this factor with both sale proneness (i.e., respond positively to cents-off coupons or special offers) and display proneness (e.g., respond positively to in-store displays offering a special price).[30]

A family also makes a lifestyle decision with regard to the foods it consumes. For some families, this may mean trying to eat healthy—lots of salads, plenty of fruit, few fried foods, and a minimum of sweets. For other families, dinner time may mean fried foods, extra gravy, and sugary desserts. Figure 15.7 presents a family food decision-making conceptual framework. Food events are situations in which food and eating goals are applied, and families must consider the available alternatives. Such goals may be negotiated among members of the family, or may have been provided by some adult decision maker. There also may be trade-offs, as different family members negotiate for his or her own food preferences. The result of a satisfactory decision may be the establishment of a routine; if unsuccessful, not doing it again may become part of the family's food policies.[31]

As another lifestyle issue, consider the humongous success of the Apple iPod. Especially among teenagers and young adults, the iPod is overwhelmingly the portable music player of choice. While some might argue that the inexpensive iPod Shuffle cheapens the product's image, it could also be a way for Apple to offer a product that allows more modest income parents to placate their teenagers. One industry analyst has commented that "The cachet is not in the price, it's in the brand. iPod is an affordable luxury item, and they're simply bringing it to another level of buyers. People who want an iPod will forgo buying an MP3 player at all saying 'If I buy, I will buy an iPod.'"[32]

FIGURE 15.7
A Family Food Decision-Making Conceptual Framework

Source: Ardyth H. Gillespie and Gilbert W. Gillespie, Jr., "Family Food Decision-Making: An Ecological Systems Framework," *Journal of Family and Consumer Sciences*, 99, no. 2 (April 2007): 25.

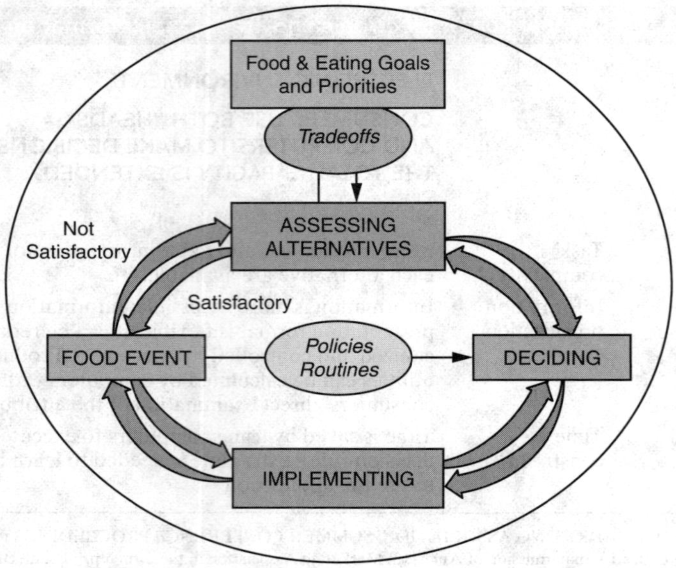

INCOMPLETE INFORMATION AND NONCOMPARABLE ALTERNATIVES In many choice situations, consumers face incomplete information on which to base decisions and must use alternative strategies to cope with the missing elements. Missing information may result from advertisements or packaging that mentions only certain attributes, the consumer's own imperfect memory of attributes for nonpresent alternatives, or because some attributes are experiential and can only be evaluated after product use. There are at least four alternative strategies that consumers can adopt for coping with missing information:[33]

1. Consumers may delay the decision until missing information is obtained.
2. Consumers may ignore missing information and decide to continue with the current decision rule (e.g., compensatory or noncompensatory), using the available attribute information.
3. Consumers may change the customarily used decision strategy to one that better accommodates missing information.
4. Consumers may infer ("construct") the missing information.

In discussing consumer decision rules, we have assumed that a choice is made from among the brands (or models) evaluated. Of course, a consumer also may conclude that none of the alternatives offers sufficient benefits to warrant purchase. If this were to occur with a necessity, such as a home water heater, the consumer would probably either lower his or her expectations and settle for the best of the available alternatives or seek information about additional brands, hoping to find one that more closely meets predetermined criteria. On the other hand, if the purchase is more discretionary (a second or third NFL team jersey), the consumer probably would postpone the purchase. In this case, information gained from the search up to that point would be transferred to long-term storage (in the psychological field) and retrieved and reintroduced as input if and when the consumer regains interest in making such a purchase.

APPLYING DECISION RULES It should be noted that, in applying decision rules, consumers may at times attempt to compare dissimilar (noncomparable) alternatives. For example, a consumer may be undecided about whether to buy a new computer system or a new set of golf clubs, because the individual can afford one or the other but not both. Another example: A consumer may try to decide between buying a new overcoat or a new raincoat. When there is great dissimilarity in the alternative ways of allocating available funds, consumers abstract the products to a level in which comparisons are possible. In the foregoing examples, a consumer might weigh the alternatives (golf clubs versus PC or overcoat versus raincoat) in terms of which alternative would offer more pleasure or which, if either, is more of a "necessity."

A SERIES OF DECISIONS Although we have discussed the purchase decision as if it were a single decision, in reality, a purchase can involve a number of decisions. For example, when purchasing an automobile, consumers are involved in multiple decisions such as choosing the make or country of origin of the car (foreign versus domestic), the dealer, the financing, and particular options. In the case of a replacement automobile, these decisions must be preceded by a decision as to whether or not to trade in one's current car.

DECISION RULES AND MARKETING STRATEGY An understanding of which decision rules consumers apply in selecting a particular product or service is useful to marketers concerned with formulating a promotional program. A marketer familiar with the prevailing decision rule can prepare a promotional message in a format that would facilitate consumer information processing. The promotional message might even suggest how potential consumers should make a decision. For instance, a direct-mail piece for a desktop computer might tell potential consumers "what to look for in a new PC." This mail piece might specifically ask consumers to consider the attributes of hard-disk size, amount of memory, processor speed, monitor size and maximum resolution, video card memory, and CD burner speed.

OUTPUT

The output portion of the consumer decision-making model concerns two closely associated kinds of postdecision activity: **purchase behavior** and **postpurchase evaluation**. The objective of both activities is to increase the consumer's satisfaction with his or her purchase.

Purchase Behavior

Consumers make three types of purchases: *trial purchases, repeat purchases*, and *long-term commitment purchases*. When a consumer purchases a product (or brand) for the first time and buys a smaller quantity than usual, this purchase would be considered a trial. Thus, a trial is the exploratory phase of purchase behavior in which consumers attempt to evaluate a product through direct use. For instance, when consumers purchase a new brand of laundry detergent about which they may be uncertain, they are likely to purchase smaller trial quantities than if it were a familiar brand. Consumers can also be encouraged to try a new product through such promotional tactics as free samples, coupons, and/or sale prices.

When a new brand in an established product category (cookies, cold cereal, or yogurt) is found by trial to be more satisfactory or better than other brands, consumers are likely to repeat the purchase. Repeat purchase behavior is closely related to the concept of *brand loyalty*, which most firms try to encourage because it contributes to greater stability in the marketplace (see Chapter 7). Unlike a trial, in which the consumer uses the product on a small scale and without any commitment, a repeat purchase usually signifies that the product meets with the consumer's approval and that he or she is willing to use it again and in larger quantities.

Trial, of course, is not always feasible. For example, with most durable goods (refrigerators, washing machines, or electric ranges), a consumer usually moves directly from evaluation to a long-term commitment (through purchase) without the opportunity for an actual trial. While purchasers of the new Volkswagen Beetle were awaiting delivery of their just-purchased cars, they were kept "warm" by being sent a mailing that included a psychographic tool called "Total Visual Imagery" that was personalized to the point that it showed them the precise model and color they had ordered.[34]

Consider Dave and his decision concerning the selection of a netbook. Since he lives and works in San Diego, it was easy for him to visit several of the large computer/electronics stores. His first stop was Best Buy, where three of the four netbooks he was considering were on display. He was able to hold each one, get the feel of the keyboard, and take note of the screen size and image quality, and, since the store keeps its computers plugged into their rechargers, Dave was able to surf the Web with each one (since the store was equipped with wireless). The salesperson was neutral in his opinion, feeling that all three of the netbooks that Best Buy carried were essentially equivalent, and that it was all just a matter of personal taste. A few days later, Dave stopped at Fry's Electronics on his way home from the restaurant. This store also sold three of the four netbooks Dave was considering, including the one that was not available at Best Buy. So Dave examined these three netbooks and surfed the Web with them. When he thought about his experiences with the four netbooks, it seemed to him that the Acer keyboard was easier for him to type on, based on key placement and key "feel" (i.e., he made fewer errors), the 8.9-inch screen was large enough and sharp enough to make e-mails and Web pages easy to read, and he liked the fact that this netbook had an SD card slot (the storage media his digital camera used) and several USB ports.

Next, Dave again went to the Internet. He had been told by a coworker that there were a number of computer discussion groups on the Internet, and that some of them probably contained consumer evaluations of specific netbook models. So he spent one morning in his apartment (before leaving for the restaurant) reading owner/user comments on the forums of **www.computerforums.com**, **www.hardwareforums.com**, and **http://forums.cnet.com**. He learned what some owners liked and disliked about each of the four netbooks that he was considering. He also learned approximately how long the battery in each netbook would last. On one of the forums he posted a message asking which netbook might make the best traveling companion, especially when its primary purpose was for retrieving e-mail and surfing the Internet. Within a day he had received several responses, each one offering an opinion that differed from the other replies.

Dave is now convinced that the Acer is the netbook he should purchase. He felt comfortable using its keyboard, he finds its screen to be bright and sharp, it has more hard disk storage space than he will ever need, and it weighs less than 2.5 pounds. So he checks the prices for this netbook both at several San Diego retailers and online. He finds that the lowest price for the netbook is at Buy.com, which includes free shipping, and he orders it.

Postpurchase Evaluation

As consumers use a product, particularly during a trial purchase, they evaluate its performance in light of their own expectations. There are three possible outcomes of these evaluations: (1) actual performance matches expectations, leading to a neutral feeling; (2) performance exceeds expectations, causing what is known as *positive disconfirmation of expectations* (which leads to satisfaction); and (3) performance is below expectations, causing *negative disconfirmation of expectations* and dissatisfaction. For each of these three outcomes, consumers' expectations and satisfaction are closely linked; that is, consumers tend to judge their experience against their expectations when performing a postpurchase evaluation.

An important component of postpurchase evaluation is the reduction of any uncertainty or doubt that the consumer might have had about the selection. As part of their postpurchase analyses, consumers try to reassure themselves that their choice was a wise one; that is, they attempt to reduce *postpurchase cognitive dissonance*. As Chapter 8 indicated, they do this by adopting one of the following strategies: They may rationalize the decision as being wise; they may seek advertisements that support their choice and avoid those of competitive brands; they may attempt to persuade friends or neighbors to buy the same brand (and, thus, confirm their own choice); or they may turn to other satisfied owners for reassurance.

The degree of postpurchase analysis that consumers undertake depends on the importance of the product decision and the experience acquired in using the product. When the product lives up to expectations, they probably will buy it again. When the product's performance is disappointing or does not meet expectations, however, they will search for more suitable alternatives. Thus, the consumer's postpurchase evaluation "feeds back" as *experience* to the consumer's psychological field and serves to influence future related decisions. Although it would be logical to assume that customer satisfaction is related to customer retention (i.e., if a consumer is satisfied with his Panasonic DVD player, he will buy other Panasonic products), one study found no direct relationship between satisfaction and retention. The findings show that customer retention may be more a matter of the brand's reputation—especially for products consumers find difficult to evaluate.[35] A recent study, though, found that since today's younger customers have more involvement and higher expectations of service, they are more likely to experience cognitive dissonance. This factor is something that store management should take into consideration, because of its implications for salesperson training.[36] Figure 15.8 presents postpurchase alternatives—from dissonance, to retention, to repeat purchases.

A satisfied customer is one who feels that he or she has received "value." As an outcome of an evaluative judgment (i.e., the consumer purchases one of the brands or models in his or her evoked set), value implies the notion of a trade-off of benefits—the features of the purchased item—versus the sacrifice necessary to purchase it (the product's price).[37] Still further, as early as 1911 it was suggested that one can view "consumption as voting." Just as a consumer

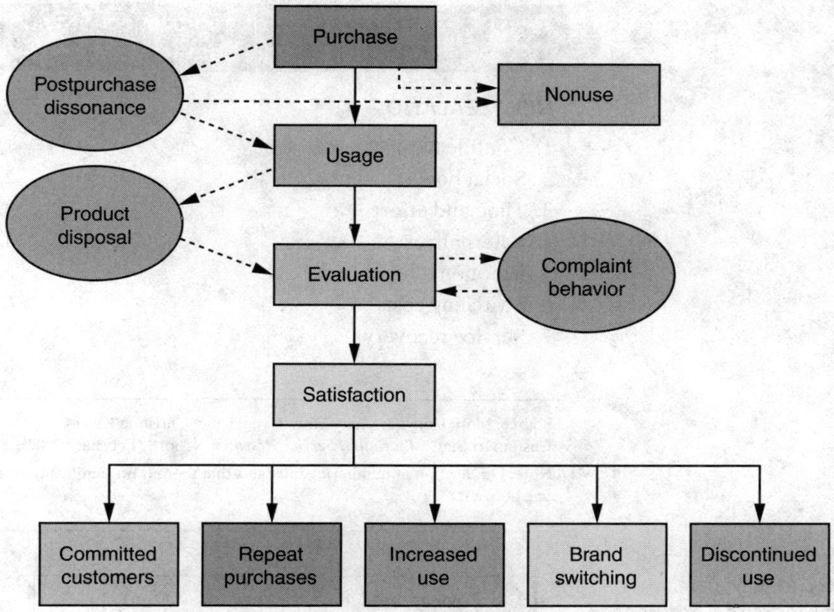

FIGURE 15.8
Postpurchase Dissonance: Satisfaction to Retention to Repeat Purchases

Source: Mohammed M. Nadeem, "Post-Purchase Dissonance: The Wisdom of the 'Repeat' Purchases," *Journal of Global Business Issues*, 1, no. 2 (Summer 2007): 184.

influences a political election by the act of voting, that same consumer influences the environment and society by his or her purchases.[38]

What was Dave's postpurchase evaluation of his new netbook? He is thrilled with his purchase. Shortly after the delivery of his netbook, Dave took it with him on his overnight trip to Tucson, Arizona. Over the two-day period he checked his e-mail often and spent at least two hours looking up potential information about new residential construction in Tucson. He had no problem in using the free wireless Internet service in the hotel he stayed at in Tucson, and also found connecting to the Internet in the two Starbucks he stopped at was, both times, a quick and painless process. And he accomplished all this without the need to recharge the netbook's battery. He's convinced that his Acer Aspire One will be with him on all of his trips out of the San Diego area—whether business or vacation.

The Decision to Do Nothing

It is important to mention that every so often a consumer may go through the entire purchase decision-making process and decide not to buy or not to switch from one brand or service provider to another. Indeed, a recent study examining "why customers stay" with their current service providers (e.g., bank, electric company, dentist) found that the reasons vary by type of service and by culture. Service providers were divided into three categories—high-contact, customized personal service (e.g., dentist, doctor, hairdresser); moderate-contact, semicustomized (e.g., auto mechanic, fitness center); and moderate-contact, standardized, nonpersonal (e.g., telephone, Internet service provider, mobile phone). The reasons for staying differed based on the type of service provider and also differed between consumers in New Zealand and consumers in China.[39] Table 15.10 presents a comparison of the reasons for the high-contact, customized service category, for both New Zealand and Chinese research participants. Interestingly, for all three categories of services, "confidence" was always the number one reason for staying among New Zealand consumers, while "time and effort" was the number one reason among Chinese consumers.

Information overload, a concept mentioned earlier in this chapter, can be another reason why a consumer elects to do nothing (i.e., to decide not to make a purchase). For a consumer, being overwhelmed with choice and information leads to confusion, which in turn can result in an abandonment of the purchase decision, postponement of the purchase, seeking additional information, and/or delegating the decision to someone else. Figure 15.9 presents a basic model of consumer confusion, which has been defined as "consumer failure to develop a correct interpretation of various facets of a product/service during the information processing procedure."[40] A recent research effort that explored Internet-based mass customization (in this

TABLE 15.10 Order of Importance: Staying Reasons by Service Type for High-Contact, Customized Services

NEW ZEALAND	CHINA
1. Confidence	1. Time and effort
2. Social bonds	2. Alternatives
3. Time and effort	3. Benefits of staying
4. Alternatives	4. Social bonds
5. Emotional bonds	5. Switching costs
6. Switching costs	6. Confidence
7. Service recovery	7. Emotional bonds
	8. Service recovery

Source: Mark Colgate, Vicky Thuy-Uyen Tong, Christina Kwai-Choi Lee, and John U. Farley, "Back from the Brink: Why Customers Stay," *Journal of Service Research,* 9, no. 3 (February 2007): 222. Copyright © 2007, SAGE Publications.

Note: Duplication in numbering indicates that there is no significant difference in score between that "reason" and the one above it.

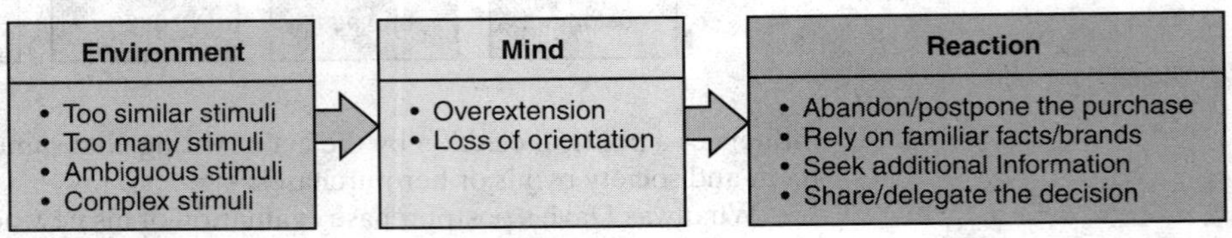

FIGURE 15.9
A Basic Model of Consumer Confusion

Source: Kurt Matzler, Martin Waiguny, and Johann Fuller, "Spoiled for Choice: Consumer Confusion in Internet-Based Mass Customization," *Innovative Marketing,* 3, no. 3 (2007): 9.

study, the ability of a computer manufacturer to make individually customized offers, such as the numerous possible configurations of a notebook computer on the computer manufacturer's Internet homepage) found that Internet retailers should provide a default setting for customers, which would help them cope with configuration overload. Other confusion reduction methods include having online providers offer trustable testimonials from previous purchasers and offering an online reviewing system like the one used by Amazon.com (**www.amazon.com**) and eBay (**www.ebay.com**).[41]

Consumer Gifting Behavior

LEARNING OBJECTIVE

15.5 *To Understand the Nature and Scope of Consumer Gift Giving.*

In terms of both dollars spent each year and how they make givers and receivers feel, gifts are a particularly interesting part of consumer behavior. Products and services chosen as gifts represent more than ordinary "everyday" purchases. Because of their symbolic meaning, they are associated with such important events as Mother's Day, births and birthdays, engagements, weddings, graduations, and many other accomplishments and milestones.

Gifting behavior can be thought of as the *gift exchange* that takes place between a giver and a recipient. The definition is broad in nature and embraces gifts given voluntarily ("Just to let you know I'm thinking of you"), as well as gifts that are an obligation ("I had to get him a gift").[42] It includes gifts given to (and received from) others and gifts to oneself, or **self-gifts**. Indeed, although 96 percent of Americans purchased at least one "gift" last year, the majority of products that we refer to as "gifts" are self-purchased (i.e., they are self-gifts).[43] Furthermore, gift purchases represent about 10 percent of all retail purchases in North America.[44]

Still further, gifting is an act of symbolic communication, with explicit and implicit meanings ranging from congratulations, love, and regret to obligation and dominance. The nature of the relationship between gift giver and gift receiver is an important consideration in choosing a gift. Indeed, gifting often impacts the relationship between the giver and the recipient.[45] There are different types of gifts. The following are five gifting subdivisions or different types of gift giving: (1) intergroup gifting, (2) intercategory gifting, (3) intragroup gifting, (4) interpersonal gifting, and (5) intrapersonal gifting.

Intergroup gifting behavior occurs whenever one group exchanges gifts with another group (such as one family with another). You will recall from Chapter 10 that the process and outcome of family decision making is different from individual decision making. Similarly, gifts given to families will be different than those given to individual family members. For example, a "common" wedding gift for a bride *and* a groom may include products for setting up a household rather than a gift that would personally be used by either the bride or the groom. When it comes to *intercategory gifting*, either an individual is giving a gift to a group (a single friend is giving a couple an anniversary gift) or a group is giving an individual a gift (friends chip in and give another friend a joint birthday gift). The gift selection strategies "buy for joint recipients" or "buy with someone" (creating intercategory gifting) are especially useful when it comes to a difficult recipient situation (when "nothing seems to satisfy her"). These strategies can also be applied to reduce some of the time pressure associated with shopping for the great number of gifts exchanged during the American Christmas season gift-giving ritual. For example, a consumer may choose to purchase five intercategory gifts for five aunt and uncle pairs (intercategory gifting), instead of buying 10 personal gifts for five aunts and five uncles (interpersonal gifting). In this way, less time, money, and effort may be expended.[46]

An *intragroup gift* can be characterized by the sentiment "we gave this to ourselves"; that is, a group gives a gift to itself or its members. For example, a dual-income couple may find that their demanding work schedules limit leisure time spent together as husband and wife. Therefore, an anniversary gift ("to us") of a long weekend in Las Vegas would be an example of an intragroup gift. It would also remedy the couple's problem of not spending enough time together. In contrast, *interpersonal gifting* occurs between just two individuals, a gift giver and gift receiver. By their very nature, interpersonal gifts are "intimate" because they provide an opportunity for a gift giver to reveal what he or she thinks of the gift receiver. Successful gifts are those that communicate that the giver knows and understands the receiver and their relationship. For example, a pair of cufflinks given to a friend in just the right shape and size can be viewed as "she really knows me." In contrast, an electric can opener given as a Valentine's Day gift, when the recipient is expecting a more "intimate" gift, can mean the deterioration of a relationship. Still further, researchers who have explored the gender of gift givers and their feelings about same-sex gifting (female to female or male to male) and opposite-sex gifting (male to female or female to male) have found that both male and female gift givers feel more comfortable in giving gifts to the same sex; however, they also reported that they felt more intense feeling with respect to gifts given to members of the opposite sex.[47] Additionally, although females get more pleasure than males from giving gifts and generally play the dominant role in gift exchanges, both sexes are strongly motivated by feelings of obligation. Still further, everyone knows that selecting and giving a gift can be the cause of "gifting anxiety" (which is related to social anxiety) on the part of the givers, the recipients, and the gifting situations themselves. Knowledge of such gender differences are useful for marketers to know because it implies that additional support might be appreciated at the point of purchase (while in a store) when a consumer is considering a gift for an opposite-sex recipient.

A recent study of gifts purchased online found that the variety-seeking trait (see Chapter 5) extends to gifting, as subjects with this trait considered a wider range of product categories when buying gifts for others.[48] Table 15.11 presents a picture of the dynamics of the gift continuum in Hong Kong. Note how a number of issues associated with the gift, such as risk, emotional expectations, and the "why," vary across the four categories of gifts. For example, a gift given to a "romantic other" involves a high emotional expectation, but one given to a friend has a low emotional expectation.[49] Still further, a recent study "found evidence of a consumer gift system in peer-to-peer music file sharing practices at Napster." This music sharing service was found to possess all three of the classic gift system indicators—its social distinctions, its norm of reciprocity, and its rituals and symbolisms.[50]

One study examined mothers giving gifts to their children (*interpersonal gifting*) across three different cultures: (1) Anglo-Celtic (mothers born in Australia), (2) Sino-Vietnamese (mothers born in Vietnam), and (3) Israeli (mothers born in Israel).[51] Whereas in all three of these cultures the mother plays a central role in family gift giving, Table 15.12 presents the major differences among these groups. For instance, when it comes to gift giving, Anglo-Celtic mothers were found to be motivated to select status or prestige gifts, whereas Sino-Vietnamese mothers were likely to pick practical gifts, and Israeli mothers tended to select gifts that they felt would be important to the recipient. Examine the table for other differences.

Intrapersonal gifting, or a self-gift (also called "monadic giving"), occurs when the giver and the receiver are the same individual. To some extent a self-gift is a "state of mind." If a consumer sees a purchase as the "buying of something I need," then it is simply a purchase. On the other hand, if the same consumer sees the same purchase as a "self-gift," then it is something special,

TABLE 15.11 The Dynamics of a Gift Continuum in Hong Kong

WHO	ROMANTIC OTHER	CLOSE FRIENDS	JUST FRIENDS	HI/BYE FRIENDS
Chinese Terminology	*Sui láih maht*	*Yihhei*	*Renqing*	*Guanxi*
When (examples)	(1) Birthday Gift (2) Special Occasions (e.g., Valentine's Day) (3) Spontaneous (e.g., small gifts) (4) Formal/Ceremonial (e.g., Mid-Autumn Festival)	(1) Birthday Gift (2) Special Occasions (e.g., leaving on a trip) (3) Spontaneous (e.g., special awards) (4) Formal/Ceremonial (e.g., New Year)	(1) Birthday Gift (2) Maintenance Gift (e.g., souvenir from a trip)	(1) Birthday Gift
Type of Gift	Expressive	Expressive	Expressive/Instrumental	Instrumental
Emotional Expectations	High	High	Medium	Low
Selection Criteria	Inexpensive (early) Expensive (later) No Gift (family)	Mostly Expensive	Somewhat Expensive	Inexpensive
Effort in Selection	Match Needs (e.g., jewelry)	Match Needs (e.g., desired clothing)	Typical Gift (e.g., having meal)	Typical Gift (e.g., birthday card)
Token Gift (Interim)	Often	Often	Occasionally	Occasionally
Why	Win Hearts	Care	Care/Build Network	Build Network
Face	Social (early) Moral (later)	Moral	Mostly Social	Social
Risks	Guilt/Shame	Guilt/Shame	Loss of Face	Loss of Face

Source: Annamma Joy, "Gift Giving in Hong Kong and the Continuum of Social Ties," *Journal of Consumer Research,* 28 (September 2001): 244. Reprinted by permission of the publisher.

with special meaning. Consumers may treat themselves to self-gifts that are products (clothing, compact disks, or jewelry), services (hairstyling, restaurant meals, spa membership), or experiences (socializing with friends). For example, while purchasing holiday gifts for others, some consumers find themselves in stores that they might not otherwise visit or find themselves looking at merchandise (such as a scarf) that they want but would not ordinarily buy. Such intrapersonal gifts have their own special range of meaning and context. Table 15.13 illustrates specific circumstances and motivations that might lead a consumer to engage in self-gift behavior.

Furthermore, consumers may make gift selections based on the decision process set out in Figure 15.10. The process starts with the question: "Should I give a gift to X?" The answer can be "yes" or "no" depending on a variety of factors (e.g., relationship, occasion). If the answer is "yes," the gift giver continues by asking: "What shall I give X as a gift?" This leads us to the next question: "Do I want to give X something that X desires (i.e., do I want to put in some "real" effort researching the gift)?" If the answer is "yes," then the gift giver is faced with the question, "How do I learn what X desires the gift given?" Here there are two choices; predicting the preferences of the recipient or asking the recipient what he/she desires. If answering "no," to the question: "Do I want to give X something that X desires?" then the gift giver has two choices (according to the model): (1) To give a gift that he or she would like (i.e., "To you for me"), or (2) To give a gift that attempts to "alter" or "improve" the gift receiver to the gift giver's liking: (i.e., "Identify imposition"). The symbolic messages associated with these gifts tend to be less valued by the recipient. If preference prediction rather than asking the recipient directly for a gift idea is chosen, then there will be an element of surprise. In addition, if the giver does not bother to learn recipient preferences, then the outcome can also be a surprise, but maybe not a good surprise.[52]

Finally, Table 15.14 summarizes the five gifting behavior subdivisions explored earlier.

TABLE 15.12 Major Differences Between Gift-Giving Behavior of Anglo-Celtic, Sino-Vietnamese, and Israeli Mothers

GIFT-GIVING ELEMENTS	ANGLO-CELTIC MOTHERS	SINO-VIETNAMESE MOTHERS	ISRAELI MOTHERS
1. Motivation			
Justification	Short-term goals	Long-term goals	Long-term/ short-term goals
Significance	Prestige gifts	Practical gifts	Importance to recipient
	Birthday gifts	Lucky money	
Timing	Special occasions (e.g., birthdays, Christmas)	Chinese New Year and academic reward	Birthdays and general needs
2. Selection			
Involvement	High priority	Low priority	Low priority
	Social and psychological risks	Financial risks	
Family Influences	Children	Mother	Mother dominant with younger children and influenced by older children
Promotional Influences	Status symbols	Sale items	Sale items
Gift Attributes	Quality	Price	Price
	Money unsuitable	Money suitable	Money suitable
3. Presentation			
Presentation Messages	Immediate self-gratification	Delayed self-gratification	Immediate self-gratification
Allocation Messages	Multiple gifts	Single gifts	Single gifts
	Mothers favored	Eldest child favored	
Understanding of Messages	Always	Not always	Never
4. Reaction			
Achievement	Often	Most of the time	Never
Feedback	More expressive	Less expressive	Least expressive
Usage	Often private	Often shared	Never shared

Source: ADVANCES IN CONSUMER RESEARCH by Hill, Constance. Copyright 1996 by Association for Consumer Research. Reproduced with permission of Association for Consumer Research in the format Textbook & Electronic via Copyright Clearance Center.

TABLE 15.13 Reported Circumstances and Motivations for Self-Gift Behavior

CIRCUMSTANCES	MOTIVATIONS
Personal accomplishment	To reward oneself
Feeling down	To be nice to oneself
Holiday	To cheer oneself up
Feeling stressed	To fulfill a need
Have some extra money	To celebrate
Need	To relieve stress
Had not bought for self in a while	To maintain a good feeling
Attainment of a desired goal	To provide an incentive toward a goal
Others	Others

Source: ADVANCES IN CONSUMER RESEARCH by Glen, David. Copyright 1990 by Association for Consumer Research. Reproduced with permission of Association for Consumer Research in the format Textbook & Electronic via Copyright Clearance Center.

FIGURE 15.10
A Gift Selection Decision-Making Process

Source: Based in part on: Leon G. Schiffman and Deborah Y. Cohn, "Are They Playing by the Same Rules? A Consumer Gifting Classification of Marital Dyads," *Journal of Business Research*, forthcoming.

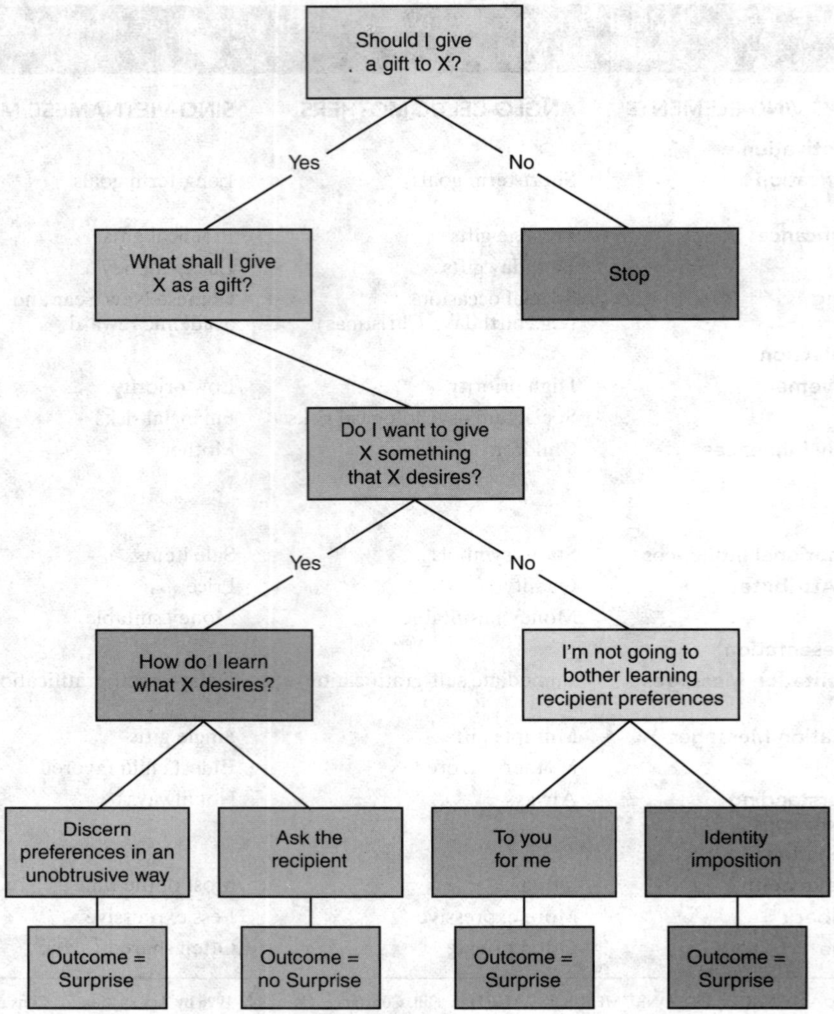

TABLE 15.14 Gifting Relationship Categories: Definitions and Examples

GIFTING RELATIONSHIP	DEFINITION	EXAMPLE
Intergroup	A group giving a gift to another group	A Christmas gift from one family to another family
Intercategory	An individual giving a gift to a group or a group giving a gift to an individual	A group of friends chips in to buy a new mother a baby gift
Intragroup	A group giving a gift to itself or its members	A family buys a DVD player for itself as a Christmas gift
Interpersonal	An individual giving a gift to another individual	Valentine's Day chocolates presented from a boyfriend to a girlfriend
Intrapersonal	Self-gift	A woman buys herself jewelry to cheer herself up

Source: Adapted from Deborah Y. Cohn and Leon G. Schiffman, "Gifting: A Taxonomy of Private Realm Giver and Recipient Relationships," Working Paper, City University of New York, Baruch College, 1996, 2.

Beyond the Decision: Consuming and Possessing

LEARNING OBJECTIVE

15.6 *To Understand the Significance of Consuming and Possessing.*

Historically, the emphasis in consumer behavior studies has been on product, service, and brand choice decisions. As shown throughout this book, however, there are many more facets to consumer behavior. The experience of using products and services, as well as the sense of pleasure derived from *possessing, collecting*, or *consuming* "things" and "experiences" (mechanical watches, old fountain pens, or a baseball card collection) contributes to consumer satisfaction and overall quality of life. These consumption outcomes or experiences, in turn, affect consumers' future decision processes.

Thus, given the importance of possessions and experiences, a broader perspective of consumer behavior might view consumer choices as the beginning of a *consumption process*, not merely the end of a consumer decision-making effort. In this context, the choice or purchase decision is an *input* into a process of consumption. The input stage includes the establishment of a *consumption set* (an assortment or portfolio of products and their attributes) and a *consuming style* (the "rules" by which the individual or household fulfills consumption requirements). The *process* stage of a simple model of consumption might include (from the consumer's perspective) the *using, possessing* (or having), *collecting*, and *disposing* of things and experiences. The output stage of this process would include changes in a wide range of feelings, moods, attitudes, and behavior, as well as reinforcement (positive or negative) of a particular lifestyle (e.g., a devotion to physical fitness), enhancement of a sense of self, and the level of consumer satisfaction and quality of life.[53] Figure 15.11 presents a *model of consumption* that reflects the ideas discussed here and throughout the book.

PRODUCTS HAVE SPECIAL MEANINGS AND MEMORIES

Consuming is a diverse and complex concept. It includes the simple utility derived from the continued use of a superior toothpaste, the stress reduction of an island holiday, the stored memories of a DVD reflecting one's childhood, the "sacred" meaning or "magic" of a grandparent's wristwatch, the symbol of membership gained from wearing a school tie, the pleasure and sense of accomplishment that comes from building a model airplane, and the fun and even financial rewards that come from collecting almost anything (even jokers from decks of cards). In fact, one man's hobby of collecting old earthenware drain tiles has become the Mike Weaver

FIGURE 15.11
A Model of Consumption

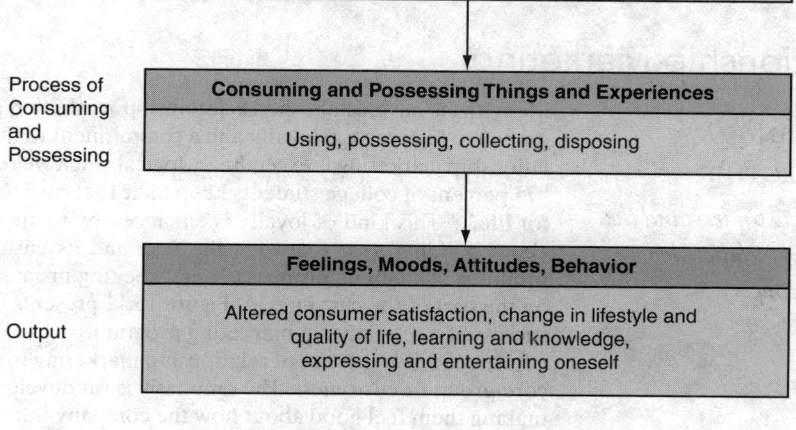

Drain Tile Museum.[54] There are special possessions that consumers resist replacing, even with an exact replica, because the replica cannot possibly hold the same meaning as the original. Such possessions are often tied, in the consumer's mind, to a specific physical time or person.

Consider the male love affair with cars, which can manifest itself in many ways. Clearly, some men identify themselves with the automobiles that they own—it becomes an extension of the self, and some men personalize their vehicles in order to bond more fully with them (e.g., special paint color, custom wheels). Some individuals even take on the characteristics of their vehicles, with a powerful engine giving the owner a sense of greater power, and high performance handling providing the man with the notion that he is similarly capable of high performance. Some even feel that the "right" car will make them irresistible to women. Cars can also sometimes serve as children, lovers, and friends (e.g., "It's kind of like my baby—I wouldn't sell the car to just anyone—they must take care of the car or it would be like child abuse"), and some men attribute certain personality characteristics to their vehicles, calling it a "she."[55] In a similar vein, a recent study of male motorcycle owners found that the type of "love" these bikers expressed toward their motorcycles was similar to interpersonal love—it is passionate, possessive, and selfless in nature.

Some possessions serve to assist consumers in their effort to create "personal meaning" and to maintain a sense of the past. To this end, it has been suggested that nostalgia permits people to maintain their identity after some major change in their life. This nostalgia can be based on family and friends; on objects such as toys, books, jewelry, and cars; or on special events, such as graduations, weddings, and holidays.[56] Providing the triple benefits of a sense of nostalgia, the fun of collecting, and the attraction of a potential return on investment, there is a strong interest in collecting Barbie dolls. It is estimated that there are currently more than 100,000 Barbie doll collectors, who are dedicated to hunting down rare and valuable Barbie dolls to add to their collections.

And it appears that you're never too young to start collecting, as evidenced by the following story about a child who started collecting at the age of 2:

> Cars have always interested Kevin LaLuzerne, a fifth-grader at Oakhurst Elementary in Largo. He has boxes and boxes of Hot Wheels, Micro Machines and other cars—more than 600! He started collecting them when he was just 2, and he still enjoys seeing all of the different cars and trucks he has collected over the years. He even has a "Weinermobile," the Oscar Meyer hot dog car. Kevin's newest addition to his collection is a limited-edition Chevron car that has a cartoon mouth, eyes and ears.[57]

There is even a Web site devoted to kids who collect, which includes "An A to Z Guide to What Kids Can Collect" (**www.countrycollector.com/kids.html**).

At the other end of the age continuum, older consumers are often faced with the issue of how they should dispose of such special possessions. Indeed, in the past several years, a number of researchers have examined this subject area. Sometimes it is some precipitating event, such as the death of a spouse, illness, or moving out of one's home (to a nursing home or retirement community), that gets the consumer thinking about the disposition of his or her possessions. Often the older person wants to pass a family legacy on to a child, ensure a good home for a cherished collection, and/or influence the lives of others.

Relationship Marketing

Learning Objective

15.7 *To Understand the Need for Relationship Marketing.*

Many firms have established **relationship marketing** programs (sometimes called *loyalty programs*) to foster usage loyalty and a commitment to their company's products and services. Relationship marketing is exceedingly logical when we realize credit card research has shown that "75 percent of college students keep their first card for 15 years, and 60 percent keep that card for life."[58] This kind of loyalty is enhanced by relationship marketing, which at its heart is all about building *trust* (between the firm and its customers) and keeping *promises* ("making promises," "enabling promises," and "keeping promises" on the part of the firm and, possibly, on the part of the customer).[59] Figure 15.12 presents the many factors that can account for the success of a relationship marketing program.

Indeed, it is the aim of relationship marketing to create strong, lasting relationships with a core group of customers. The emphasis is on developing long-term bonds with customers by making them feel good about how the company interacts (or does business) with them and by giving them some kind of personal connection to the business. For example, a good relationship

FIGURE 15.12
Factors Accounting for Relationship Marketing Success

Source: Shelby D. Hunt and Dennis B. Arnett, "The Explanatory Foundations of Relationship Marketing Theory," *Journal of Business and Industrial Marketing*, 21, no. 2 (2006): 78.

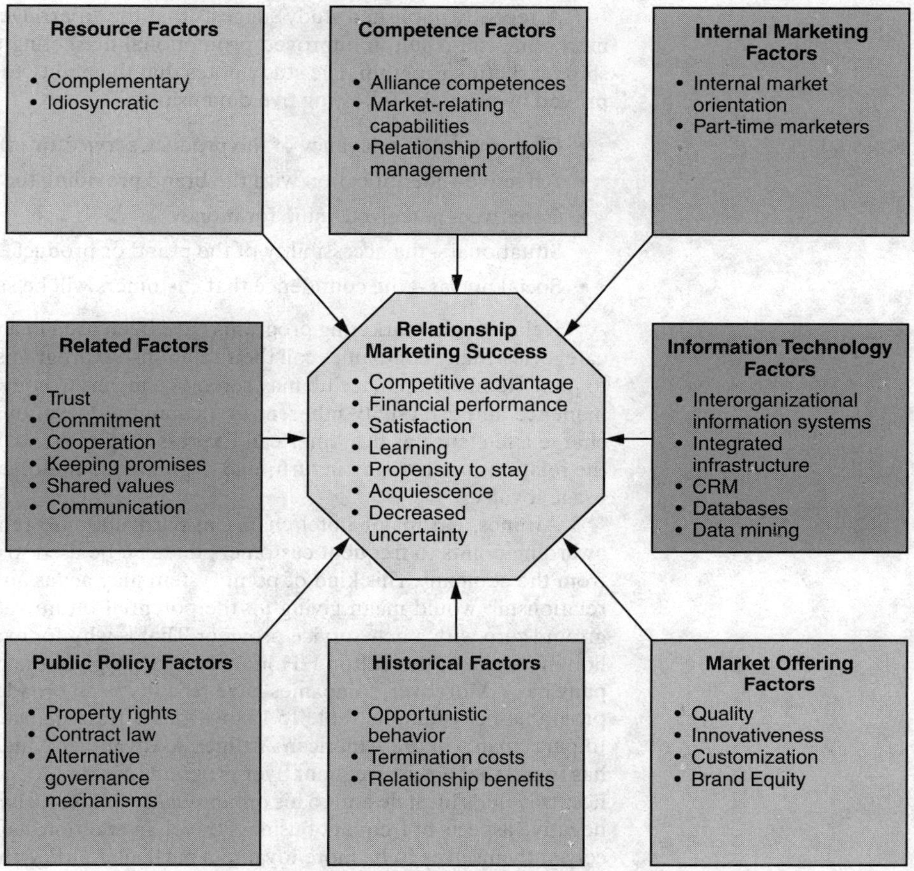

marketing program lengthens the relationship between retailers and their customers.[60] A review of the composition of 66 consumer relationship marketing programs revealed three elements shared by more than 50 percent of the programs. They are (1) fostering ongoing communication with customers (73 percent of the programs); (2) furnishing loyalty by building in extras like upgrades and other perks (68 percent of the programs); and (3) stimulating a sense of belonging by providing a "club membership" format (50 percent of the programs).[61] A real relationship marketing program is more than the use of database marketing tactics to better target customers—the consumer must feel that he or she has received something for being a participant in the relationship. In a positive vein, businesses have been finding that the Internet is an inexpensive, efficient, and more productive way to extend customer services. This has resulted in "permission marketing." It is the "art of asking consumers if they would like to receive a targeted e-mail ad, promotion, or message *before* it appears in their in-box." The opposite tact, sending a consumer spam and offering the option to "Click here to opt out," annoys consumers and is not permission marketing.[62] A recent article suggests that since 20 to 25 percent of online customers change their e-mail addresses each year, a company's Web site must include a good "preference center" where program participants can indicate a change of e-mail address and/or a change in preferences (e.g., how often they receive relationship marketing program–related e-mails).[63]

Although direct marketing, sales promotion, and general advertising may be used as part of a relationship marketing strategy, relationship marketing stresses long-term commitment to the individual customer. Advances in technology (such as UPC scanning equipment, and relational databases) have provided techniques that make tracking customers simpler, thus influencing the trend toward relationship marketing. Indeed, Wal-Mart's database is second in size only to the database of the U.S. government.[64] Still further, a recent study suggests that relationship marketing programs are more likely to succeed if the product or service is one that buyers consider to be high involvement due to its association with financial, social, or physical risk.[65]

A recently published study suggests that the "marriage" of market research and database marketing can result in improved promotional marketing to participants in a firm's relationship marketing program. The study notes that the ability to satisfy consumer needs can be improved by using the following five dimensions:

- Cognitive—the relevancy of the product, service, or offer
- Affective—identification with the brand providing the service or product
- Conative—perceived value for money
- Situational—the accessibility of the brand or product
- Social norms—the confidence that customers will be satisfied with what they buy[66]

Relationship marketing programs have been used in a wide variety of product and service categories. Many companies call their relationship programs a club, and some even charge a fee to join. Membership in a club may serve as a means to convey to customers the notions of permanence and exclusivity inherent in a committed relationship. Additionally, those firms that charge a fee (such as the American Express Platinum card) increase customers' investment in the relationship that may, in turn, lead to greater commitment to the relationship and increased usage loyalty.

Airlines and major hotel chains, in particular, use relationship marketing techniques by awarding points to frequent customers that can be used to obtain additional goods or services from the company. This kind of point system may act as an exit barrier because starting a new relationship would mean giving up the potential future value of the points and starting from ground zero with a new service provider. That is why, for example, Hilton considers the 6.5 million members of the Hilton HHonors loyalty program the most important customers the company has.[67] Moreover, companies have recently been broadening the scope of such relationship programs. For example, Table 15.15 provides a list of many of the products and services offered to participants in the American Airlines AAdvantage Mileage Program. Still further, research has found that airline frequent flyer programs contribute in a positive way to the frequent business traveler's lifestyle and to his or her quality of life, perhaps by compensating for some of the negative aspects of frequent business travel. In addition, happy frequent business travelers perceived themselves to be more loyal to a particular airline than their less happy counterparts.[68]

Ultimately, it is to a firm's advantage to develop long-term relationships with existing customers because it is easier and less expensive to make an additional sale to an existing customer than to make a new sale to a new consumer.[69] Figure 15.13 portrays some of the characteristics of the relationship between the firm and the customer within the spirit of relationship marketing.

TABLE 15.15 A Broad-Based Relationship Program

AIRLINES	**HOTELS**
Canadian Airlines International	Holiday Inns
Cathay Pacific Airlines	InterContinental Hotels
Hawaiian Airlines	ITT Sheraton Hotels, Inns, Resorts, and All-Suites
Qantas Airways	Marriott Hotels, Resorts, and Suites
Keno Air	Vista Hotels
Singapore Airlines	Wyndham Hotels and Resorts
TWA	**CAR RENTAL**
US Airways	Avis Rent A Car
HOTELS	Hertz
Conrad Hotels	**OTHER**
Forte Hotels	Citibank AAdvantage Visa or MasterCard application
Forum Hotels	MCI Long Distance
Hilton Hotels & Resorts	American AAdvantage Money Market Fund
Hilton International Hotels	The American Traveler Catalog

FIGURE 15.13
A Portrayal of the Characteristics of Relationship Marketing

Source: In part, this portrayal was inspired by: Mary Long, Leon Schiffman, and Elaine Sherman, "Understanding the Relationships in Consumer Marketing Relationship Programs: A Content Analysis," in *Proceedings of the World Marketing Congress VII-II*, eds. K. Grant and O. Walker (Melbourne, Australia: Academy of Marketing Science, 1995), 10/27–10/26.

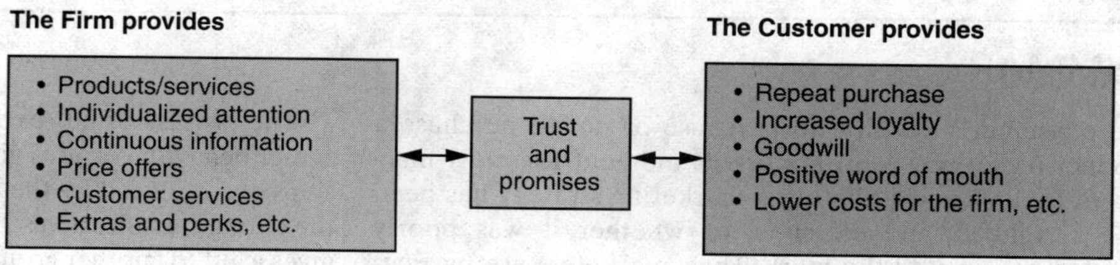

Why is relationship marketing so important? Research indicates that consumers today are less loyal than in the past, due to six major forces: (1) the abundance of choice, (2) availability of information, (3) entitlement (consumers repeatedly ask "What have you done for me lately?"), (4) commoditization (most products/services appear to be similar—nothing stands out), (5) insecurity (consumer financial problems reduce loyalty), and (6) time scarcity (not enough time to be loyal). These six forces result in consumer defections, complaints, cynicism, reduced affiliation, greater price sensitivity, and litigiousness.[70] Moreover, the bottom line for any relationship marketing or customer loyalty program, for the program's sponsor, has to be customer profitability. And it's not just how much the consumer who is a member of a firm's relationship marketing program spends—consumer commitment has been shown to also result in an increased share of customer.[71] A recent study lists six areas in which a loyalty building strategy can result in cost savings:

1. Reduced marketing costs—customer acquisition costs more.
2. Lower transaction costs, such as outbound efforts and order processing.
3. Reduced customer turnover expenses (fewer lost customers to replace).
4. Increased cross-selling success, leading to larger share of customer.
5. More positive word of mouth.
6. Reduced failure costs (reduction in returns, debt, claims, and complaints).[72]

Finally, Figure 15.14 presents a model of customer loyalty. Note that there are both behavioral and attitudinal dimensions to the notion of customer loyalty.

FIGURE 15.14
A Model of Customer Loyalty

Source: Jean Donio, Paola Massari, and Giuseppina Passiante, "Customer Satisfaction and Loyalty in a Digital Environment: An Empirical Test," *Journal of Consumer Marketing*, 23, no. 7 (2006): 447.

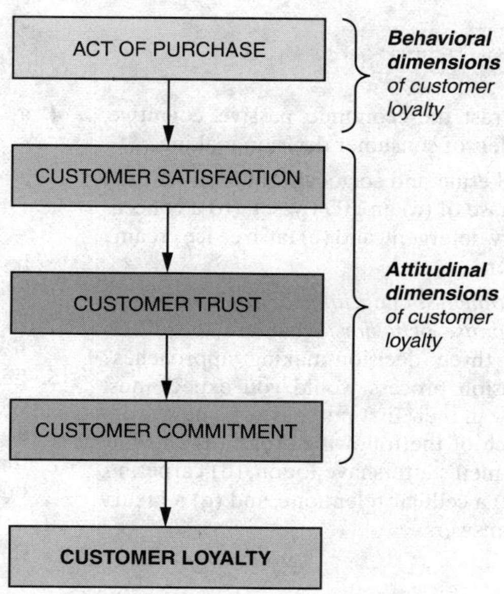

SUMMARY

The consumer's decision to purchase or not to purchase a product or service is an important moment for most marketers. It can signify whether a marketing strategy has been wise, insightful, and effective, or whether it was poorly planned and missed the mark. Thus, marketers are particularly interested in the consumer's decision-making process. For a consumer to make a decision, more than one alternative must be available. (The decision not to buy is also an alternative.)

Theories of consumer decision making vary depending on the researcher's assumptions about the nature of humankind. The various models of consumers (economic view, passive view, cognitive view, and emotional view) depict consumers and their decision-making processes in distinctly different ways.

An overview consumer decision-making model ties together the psychological, social, and cultural concepts examined in Parts Two and Three into an easily understood framework. This decision model has three sets of variables: input variables, process variables, and output variables.

Input variables that affect the decision-making process include commercial marketing efforts, as well as noncommercial influences from the consumer's sociocultural environment. The decision process variables are influenced by the consumer's psychological field, including the evoked set (or the brands in a particular product category considered in making a purchase choice). Taken as a whole, the psychological field influences the consumer's recognition of a need, prepurchase search for information, and evaluation of alternatives.

The output phase of the model includes the actual purchase (either trial or repeat purchase) and postpurchase evaluation. Both prepurchase and postpurchase evaluation feeds back in the form of experience into the consumer's psychological field and serves to influence future decision processing.

The process of gift exchange is an important part of consumer behavior. Various gift-giving and gift-receiving relationships are captured by the following five specific categories in the gifting classification scheme: (1) intergroup gifting (a group gives a gift to another group); (2) intercategory gifting (an individual gives a gift to a group or a group gives a gift to an individual); (3) intragroup gifting (a group gives a gift to itself or its members); (4) interpersonal gifting (an individual gives a gift to another individual); and (5) intrapersonal gifting (a self-gift).

Consumer behavior is not just making a purchase decision or the act of purchasing; it also includes the full range of experiences associated with using or consuming products and services. It also includes the sense of pleasure and satisfaction derived from possessing or collecting "things." The outputs of consumption are changes in feelings, moods, or attitudes; reinforcement of lifestyles; an enhanced sense of self; satisfaction of a consumer-related need; belonging to groups; and expressing and entertaining oneself.

Among other things, consuming includes the simple utility of using a superior product, the stress reduction of a vacation, the sense of having a "sacred" possession, and the pleasures of a hobby or a collection. Some possessions serve to assist consumers in their effort to create personal meaning and to maintain a sense of the past.

Relationship marketing impacts consumers' decisions and their consumption satisfaction. Firms establish relationship marketing programs (sometimes called loyalty programs) to foster usage loyalty and a commitment to their products and services. At its heart, relationship marketing is all about building trust (between the firm and its customers), and keeping promises made to consumers. Therefore, the emphasis in relationship marketing is almost always on developing long-term bonds with customers by making them feel special and by providing them with personalized services.

DISCUSSION QUESTIONS

1. Compare and contrast the economic, passive, cognitive, and emotional models of consumer decision making.
2. What kinds of marketing and sociocultural inputs would influence the purchase of (a) an HDTV set, (b) a concentrated liquid laundry detergent, and (c) fat-free ice cream? Explain your answers.
3. Define *extensive problem solving*, *limited problem solving*, and *routinized response behavior*. What are the differences among the three decision-making approaches? What type of decision process would you expect most consumers to follow in their first purchase of a new product or brand in each of the following areas: (a) chewing gum, (b) sugar, (c) men's aftershave lotion, (d) carpeting, (e) paper towels, (f) a cellular telephone, and (g) a luxury car? Explain your answers.
4. a. Identify three different products that you believe require a reasonably intensive prepurchase search by a consumer. Then, using Table 15.2 as a guide, identify the specific characteristics of these products that make an intensive prepurchase search likely.
   b. For each of the products that you listed, identify the perceived risks that a consumer is likely to experience before a purchase (see Table 6.6). Discuss how the marketers of these products can reduce these perceived risks.
5. Let's assume that this coming summer you are planning to spend a month touring Europe and are, therefore, in need of a good digital camera. (a) Develop a list of product attributes that you will use as the purchase criteria in evaluating various digital cameras. (b) Distinguish the differences that would occur in your decision process if you were to use compensatory versus noncompensatory decision rules.

6. How can a marketer of very light, very powerful laptop computers use its knowledge of customers' expectations in designing a marketing strategy?
7. How do consumers reduce postpurchase dissonance? How can marketers provide positive reinforcement to consumers after the purchase to reduce their dissonance?
8. Albert Einstein once wrote that "the whole of science is nothing more than a refinement of everyday thinking." Do you think that this quote applies to the development of the consumer decision-making model presented in Figure 15.3?

EXERCISES

1. Find two print advertisements, one that illustrates the cognitive model of consumer decision making and one that illustrates the emotional model. Explain your choices. In your view, why did the marketers choose the approaches depicted in the advertisements?
2. Describe the need recognition process that took place before you purchased your last can of soft drink. How did it differ from the process that preceded the purchase of a new pair of sneakers? What role, if any, did advertising play in your need recognition?
3. List the colleges that you considered when choosing which college or university to attend and the criteria that you used to evaluate them. Describe how you acquired information on the different colleges along the different attributes that were important to you and how you made your decision. Be sure to specify whether you used compensatory or noncompensatory decision rules.
4. Select one of the following product categories: (a) compact, portable DVD players, (b) fast-food restaurants, or (c) shampoo, and: (1) write down the brands that constitute your evoked set, (2) identify brands that are not part of your evoked set, and (3) discuss how the brands included in your evoked set differ from those that are not included in terms of important attributes.
5. Select a newspaper or magazine advertisement that attempts to provide the consumer with a decision strategy to follow in making a purchase decision. Evaluate the effectiveness of the ad you selected.

KEY TERMS

- affect referral decision rule *492*
- compensatory decision rules *491*
- conjunctive decision rule *491*
- consumer decision making *476*
- consumer decision rules *491*
- consumption process *476*
- disjunctive rule *492*
- evaluation of alternatives *484*
- evoked set *488*
- extensive problem solving *478*
- gifting behavior *500*
- heuristics *481*
- inept set *488*
- inert set *488*
- information overload *481*
- lexicographic decision rule *492*
- limited problem solving *478*
- moods *482*
- need recognition *484*
- noncompensatory decision rules *491*
- postpurchase evaluation *497*
- prepurchase search *484*
- purchase behavior *497*
- relationship marketing *506*
- routinized response behavior *478*
- self-gifts *500*

Case One: You Will Never Travel Alone

TomTom, manufacturers of various portable global positioning system (GPS) car navigation systems uses the slogan "The smart choice in personal navigation." It points out that its personal navigation devices enable users to arrive at their destinations on time, relaxed, and safely. Some of these devices may be relatively expensive in, for instance, emerging economies, but by using the TomTom savings calculator, users can calculate how much they could potentially save by using particular TomTom devices, based on the distance they travel each year.

The company offers various models, for instance, the TomTom Go 720. It offers various options for personalized use (such as a choice of voice, screen colors, and whether security warnings are required), a wider screen, and five hours of battery life, as well as a highly sensitive GPS receiver, which some believe sets it apart from similar devices.

TomTom's procedure for setting a destination ensures that users do not type in a word that is spelled incorrectly (as sometimes happens with phone GPS systems). Compared to most other GPS devices, the TomTom Go 720 has a thinner mounting bracket by which it is attached to the windshield, making it easier to operate and manipulate. Its screen width has been increased and its body made slimmer so that it easily fits into one's pocket and its carrier case.

The TomTom Go 720 has all the usual TomTom applications. At TomTom Home, users can check whether they have the latest maps and points of interest. TomTom's unique patented shared technology further ensures that users can report map errors and share them with one another. The "Help Me!" function directs users to the nearest emergency service or provides their exact location to enable an emergency service to find them.

The TomTom Go 720 can also be used a as a hands-free device for certain phones, but they need to be Bluetooth enabled. Users can consult the companies Web site to determine whether their phones are supported. On some mobile phones, the address book can be synchronized in order for users to phone directly from their TomTom.

Although some may regard these devices as off-road status symbols, they may be perceived as necessities in countries with poor road conditions, considering all the accessories they offer.

QUESTIONS

1. How could the model of consumer decision-making, discussed in this chapter, be applied to explain a consumer's decision on whether or not to purchase a TomTom Go 720?
2. What types of perceived risks would you decrease by buying the product?
3. Which factors would consumers probably take into account when considering the TomTom Go 720 as a gift?

Sources: www.tomtom.com; and www.smartcraft.biz.

Case Two: Chelsea Tractors

In London they are nicknamed Chelsea Tractors; in other countries people refer to them as Urban 4 × 4s. Whatever their name, they are large, gas-guzzling, environmentally unfriendly, dangerous to pedestrian sport utility vehicles that are not being used for the purpose that they were originally designed.

In London, there have been calls to ban these sport utility vehicles (SUVs) from the streets, and there are plans for at least 15,000 owners of larger cars living inside the congestion charging zone in London to lose their residents' discount, making their daily payment rise by 3,000 percent from $1.16 to $36.50.

In some cases, these SUVs are being used to take children to and from school, but increasingly they have been used in many urban locations by predominantly female drivers. In the Gulf region, the Ford Explorer has been the best-selling SUV for the past 15 years, yet it is rarely used by owners as an off-road vehicle.

High fuel prices in the United States in 2008 threaten to end the American love affair with the SUV. Dealers have seen a marked fall in the numbers of SUVs being sold. Market analysts believe that the shift from SUVs to smaller vehicles is a permanent one, and the most significant change in the market in 30 years.

Yet SUVs are still seen as a status symbol. Automobile makers have realized that women want vehicles that are stylish, safe, fun to drive, an expression of their personality, reliable, loaded with features, and reasonably priced.

QUESTIONS

1. How can the concept of self-gifting be used to explain the increased interest of women in purchasing nonfamily-type vehicles?
2. What level of market penetration has the SUV made in your own country and particularly how common is it in the urban environment?

16

Marketing Ethics and Social Responsibility

THE MARKETING CONCEPT as we know it—that is, fulfilling the needs of target consumer markets more effectively than competitors—is sometimes inconsistent or incongruous with society's well-being and best interests. For example, products such as tobacco and alcohol satisfy consumer "needs" but are harmful, and many products that are convenient to use significantly contribute to environmental deterioration and climate change (e.g., products packaged in convenient but not reusable packaging, single-usage protective coverings used by dry cleaners). Given the fact that all companies prosper when society prospers, companies must make social responsibility an integral component of every marketing decision. A more appropriate conceptualization of the traditional marketing concept, which balances the needs of society with the needs of the individuals and marketing organizations, is the societal marketing concept. The **societal marketing concept** requires that all marketers adhere to principles of social responsibility in the marketing of their goods and services; that is, they should endeavor to satisfy the needs and wants of their target markets in ways that preserve and enhance the well-being of consumers and society as a whole, while fulfilling the objectives of the organization. According to the societal marketing concept, fast-food restaurants should develop foods that contain less fat and starch but more nutrients, and marketers should not advertise foods to young people in ways that encourage overeating, or use professional athletes in liquor or tobacco advertisements, because celebrities often serve as role models for the young and using them in ads may result in underage or over consumption of these products. The ad shown in Figure 16.1—sponsored by a consumer advocacy group—criticized McDonald's for contributing to heart-disease deaths by using trans fats in preparing its products. Using trans fats is one example of ignoring consumers' interests (and the societal marketing concept) in a quest for profits, since other cooking agents, which are probably more expensive, are available.

A serious deterrent to widespread implementation of the societal marketing concept is the *short-term orientation* embraced by most business executives in pursuing increased market share and quick profits. This short-term orientation stems from the fact that managerial performance

FIGURE 16.1

Source: Center for Science in the Public Interest (CSSPI). www.cspinet.org.

QUESTION: *Why Is the Sponsor of This Ad Criticizing McDonald's, and What Business Concept Did McDonald's Ignore by Using Trans Fats?*

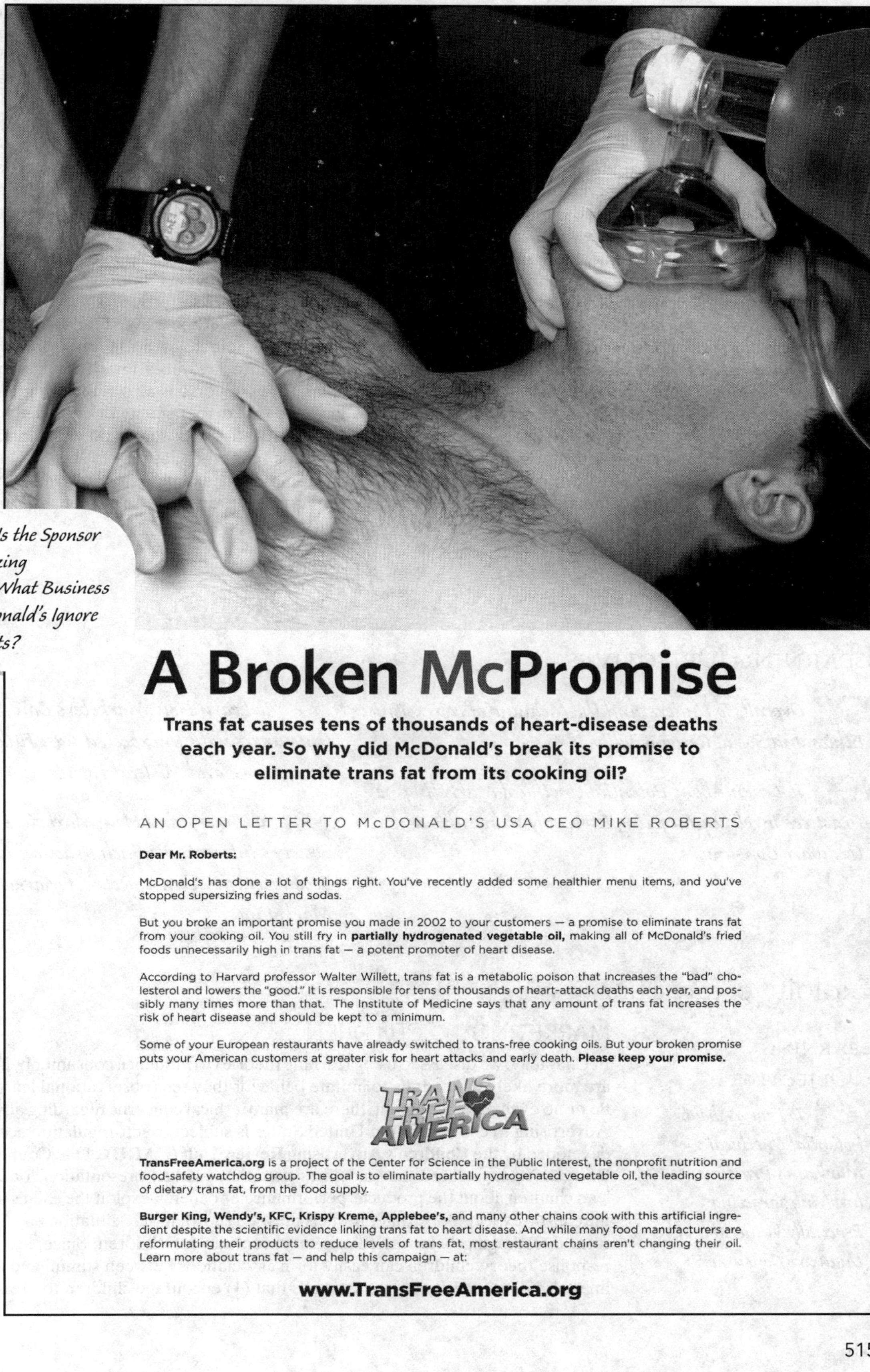

usually is evaluated on the basis of short-term results. Thus, a young and ambitious advertising executive may create a striking advertising campaign using unreasonably slim females with pale faces and withdrawn expressions in order to dramatically increase the sales of the advertised product, without considering the negative impact of the campaign, such as an increase in eating disorders among young women or the implicit approval of drug taking reflected in the models' appearances. The societal marketing concept advocates a *long-term perspective*. It proposes that all companies would be better off in a stronger, healthier society, and that companies that incorporate ethical behavior and social responsibility in all of their business dealings attract and maintain loyal consumer support over the long term.

The purpose of studying consumer behavior is to understand why and how consumers make their purchase decisions. These insights enable marketers to design more effective marketing strategies, especially today when advanced technologies allow them to collect more data about consumers and target customers more precisely. Some critics are concerned that an in-depth understanding of consumer behavior makes it possible for unethical marketers to exploit human vulnerabilities in the marketplace and engage in other unethical marketing practices in order to achieve corporate business objectives.

In response to public criticisms and concerns, many trade associations representing marketers of consumer goods developed industry-wide *codes of ethics*, because they recognize that industry-wide self-regulation is in marketers' best interests in that it deters government from imposing its own regulations on industries. A number of companies have incorporated specific social goals into their mission statements and include programs in support of these goals as integral components of their strategic planning. They believe that **marketing ethics** and social responsibility are important components of organizational effectiveness. Most companies also recognize that socially responsible activities improve their image among consumers, stockholders, the financial community, and other relevant publics. They have found that ethical and socially responsible practices are simply good business, resulting not only in a favorable image, but ultimately in increased sales. The converse is also true: Perceptions of a company's lack of social responsibility or unethical marketing strategies negatively affect consumer purchase decisions.

This chapter describes several unethical marketing strategies and examines socially responsible marketing in the forms of promoting social causes, green marketing, and consumer ethics.

Learning Objectives

16.1 *Overall: To Understand the Meaning of Marketing Ethics and Social Responsibility.*

16.2 *To Learn About Potential Unethical Marketing Practices Involving Targeting Especially Vulnerable or Unaware Consumers.*

16.3 *To Learn How Marketers Can Ambush Consumers with Unexpected Ads, Tinker with Their Perceptions, and Mislead Them.*

16.4 *To Understand How Marketers Can Advance Society's Interests via Such Practices as Advocating Social Benefits, Cause-Related Marketing, and Green Marketing.*

Exploitive Targeting

Learning Objective

16.2 *To Learn About Potential Unethical Marketing Practices Involving Targeting Especially Vulnerable or Unaware Consumers.*

MARKETING TO CHILDREN

In Chapter 7, we discussed using learning theories to influence consumer behavior. Since children are more likely than adults to imitate behavior they see (observational learning) on TV with little or no evaluative judgment, there are many ethical concerns regarding advertising to children. Advertising to children in the United States is subject to self-regulation according to guidelines developed by the **Children's Advertising Review Unit (CARU)** of the Council of Better Business Bureau. Among others, the guidelines state that product presentations or claims must not mislead children about the product's performance or benefits, exploit the child's imagination or create unrealistic expectations, that products must be shown in safe situations, and the ads must refrain from encouraging behavior that is inappropriate for children. Since, according to stimulus—response theory, children can easily form associations between stimuli and outcomes, the guidelines also direct marketers to *avoid* ads that (1) encourage children to pressure their parents to buy the products advertised, and (2) compel children to feel that ownership of a given product will make them more accepted by peers. Regarding loyalty-building measures such as kid's clubs, premiums, and sweepstakes, the CARU guidelines acknowledge that children not always understand the true purpose of such measures and direct marketers to ensure that loyalty programs do not exploit them.[1]

CARU's new releases illustrate many possible misuses in advertising to children and also the effectiveness of self-regulation. For example, in response to CARU's routine monitoring of children's advertising and CARU's subsequent request, a marketer of cotton candy machines agreed to modify a TV commercial that featured children operating an electrical candy machine without parental supervision and while dancing or talking on the phone. In another case, after viewing a commercial showing Oreo cookies going into a toaster and popping out as Kool-Stuf pastries, a four-year-old child inserted Oreos into a toaster and, when they did not pop out, tried to retrieve them with a pair of scissors. The child's mother complained to CARU, which brought it to the attention of Oreo's marketer, who subsequently agreed to modify the commercial. Procter & Gamble agreed to modify a TV spot for Pringles that CARU believed encouraged excessive consumption of the snack food.[2]

A major concern regarding the impact of marketing on children's behavior is whether food marketers "teach" children to eat more than they should and thus cause the surging obesity and health problems among young consumers. By some estimates, marketers spend $10 billion annually on marketing foods and beverages to America's children, significantly contributing to the number of obese or overweight children, a population that has doubled in the past 20 years (no pun intended). Figure 16.2 demonstrates the extensive targeting of children, across 12 product categories that include eight types of food, during both children's and nonchildren's TV programs.[3] Over the past few years, some lawmakers have called for legislation regulating food advertising to children and, presumably to avoid such regulation, several companies voluntarily modified their marketing practices. For example, Kraft Foods stopped TV advertising of certain products to children, and increased their advertising of sugar-free drinks and smaller packages of cookies. McDonald's, a company frequently accused of selling junk foods with too much fat and poor nutritional quality, has eliminated some of its "super-sized" offerings and begun selling more salads. They even offer apples as a dessert alternative to calorie-laden pies. More recently, McDonald's had a program that awarded food prizes to small kids who got good grades on their report cards; the program was advertised on book jackets and was discontinued after McDonald's was criticized by parents and consumer advocacy groups and even ridiculed by some media.[4]

Clearly, there are merits to the argument that, ultimately, any consumption behavior, including excessive eating, is the responsibility of the adults consuming overly rich foods or allowing their children to consume them and not the marketers who produced such foods. However, it must always be remembered that children are a vulnerable population. In addressing this issue and fearing that "McDonald's-made-me-fat" lawsuits will gain momentum, the food companies have pursued legislation that will not allow obese persons to sue them for personal damages.[5]

Regarding advertising to children, there is a consensus that even if children understand the purpose of promotional messages, marketers must take special care in advertising to them because of the amount of time kids spend viewing TV and online. Generally, advertising to children in the United States is less regulated than in European countries. Also, regulating marketing to children does not always fully work. Table 16.1 indicates that numerous practices generally forbidden in marketing to children online are widely employed by Web sites targeting children.[6]

OVERAGGRESSIVE PROMOTION

Children are not the only vulnerable population. Teenagers and college students are often provided with too much easy credit, which puts them into financial difficulties for years. For example, as a result of very aggressive marketing of credit cards to college students, college loan debt has been rising, and the average graduate leaves college with over $18,000 in credit card debt, often coupled with a low credit rating.[7] One study showed that, on average, students received their first credit card at age 18 (some did so when they were as young as 15), more than 10 percent owned more than five cards, and most of these young people did not keep credit card receipts, did not check their monthly statements against their purchases, were unaware of the

FIGURE 16.2
Percentage of Annual Exposure Within a Category by Program Type: 2004

Notes: Staff analysis of copyrighted Nielsen Media Research/Nielsen Monitor-Plus® data; four weeks projected annually.

Source: Debra M. Desrochers and Debra J. Holt, "Children's Exposure to Television Advertising: Implications for Childhood Obesity," *Journal of Public Policy and Marketing*, 26, no. 2 (Fall 2007): 191.

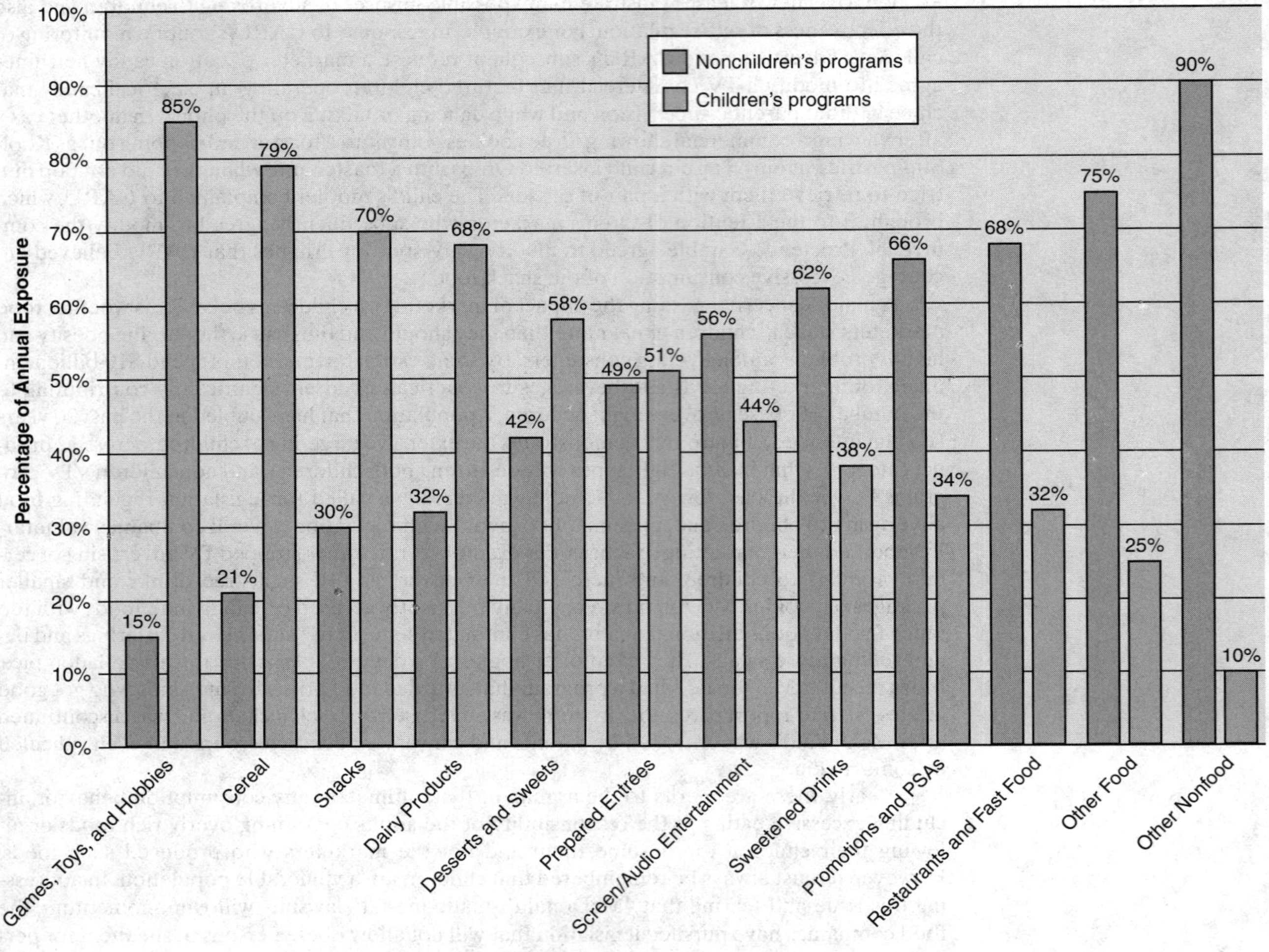

interest rates they were charged, and about 10 percent paid only the minimum required payment every month.[8] Recognizing that the marketing of credit cards to college students has become far too aggressive and against society's best interests, many U.S. states have passed, or are in the process of passing, strict rules limiting the marketing of banks and credit card companies on college campuses, and some banks developed codes of conduct limiting the promotion of credit cards directed at students.[9] A recent study identified several personality traits contributing to students' misuse of credit cards (e.g., impulsiveness and materialism) and outlined potential communication appeals stemming from this knowledge designed to promote more responsible credit card usage among students.[10]

Much of the financial credit crisis that struck the globe during fall 2008 has been attributed to Americans' ballooning credit debt, much of which has been in the form of home equity loans. The heavy usage of one's home value to finance discretionary and often excessive and impulsive spending on luxury items is the result of brilliant marketing by banks. In Chapter 6, we discussed how banks repositioned home equity loans and altered consumers perceptions toward widely (and maybe even wildly) using these financial instruments. This positioning was implemented via overaggressive ads, which now, in retrospect, most regulators and financial gurus believe were unwise and should have been scrutinized more closely.[11]

TABLE 16.1 Regulating Online Marketing to Children

PART A: COMMON PRACTICES IN MARKETING FOODS TO CHILDREN ONLINE THAT ARE GENERALLY FORBIDDEN UNDER U.S. OR SELF-REGULATION

1. Promoting foods of low nutritional quality; not providing enough nutritional labeling; misleading nutritional claims.
2. Embedding food ads in games and facilitating children's learning to consume the foods advertised.
3. Creating "buzz" about the products and encouraging children to send ads to their friends (i.e., viral marketing).
4. Offering children brand-related items that they can use after leaving the Web sites and tying the online advertising with other exposures to the brands.
5. Not including "ad breaks" and reminders that the content watched is advertising.
6. Offering children that may be too young opportunities and prizes if they register at the Web site.
7. Offering direct inducements to purchase (e.g., access to a secret site).

PART B: AN ILLUSTRATION OF THE LIMITED SUCCESS OF SELF AND U.S. REGULATION REGARDING WEB SITES TARGETING CHILDREN

Note: the ideas expressed in Part B are those of the authors of the second source, and not those of the authors of the first one.

CONTENT ANALYSIS FINDINGS	CURRENT GUIDE AND REGULATORY EFFORTS
64% of Web sites encouraged children to send e-mail greetings or invitations to visit the Web site to their friends.	Advertising should not urge children to ask parents or others to buy products. (CARU)
53% of Web sites offered unlimited viewing of television advertisements.	Advertisements are limited to 10.5–12 minutes per hour. (Children's Television Act of 1990 [47 U.S.C. § 303])
76% of Web sites offered at least one brand "extra," and 52% offered two or more: 43% offered sweepstakes: and 31% offered premiums to stimulate sales.	Advertisers should take special care in using these kinds of promotions to guard against exploiting children's immaturity. (CARU)
39% of Web sites offered specific purchase incentives, such as game rewards.	Advertisers should avoid using sales pressures in advertising to children. (CARU)
18% of the Web sites provided ad break reminders that the content was advertising.	The U.S. Federal Communications Commission requires ad breaks for children's television programming.
47% of the Web sites offered a tie-in to movie or television shows and characters.	Television advertising should not use program personalities (live or animated) adjacent to their shows. (CARU and U.S. Federal Communications Commission)

Sources: *Part A:* JOURNAL OF PUBLIC POLICY & MARKETING by Moore, Elizabeth S. Copyright 2007 by American Marketing Association. Reproduced with permission of American Marketing Association in the format print & electronic usage via Copyright Clearance Center.

Part B: JOURNAL OF PUBLIC POLICY & MARKETING by Seiders, Kathleen. Copyright 2007 by American Marketing Association. Reproduced with permission of American Marketing Association in the format print & electronic usage via Copyright Clearance Center.

SELLING PHARMACEUTICALS DIRECTLY TO CONSUMERS

Direct-to-consumer pharmaceutical advertising, permitted since 1997, has increased the consumption of numerous categories of medications. In studies, consumers confirm that they obtain most of the information about these medications from TV commercials rather than from their physicians.[12] Recognizing that direct-to-consumer advertising has become too aggressive, the pharmaceutical industry has developed voluntary restrictions regarding this marketing method. The Senate majority leader has called for a two-year moratorium on advertising new drugs to consumers; one major pharmaceutical company has volunteered not to advertise new drugs to consumers during their first year on the market.[13] Online search engines further complicate the direct selling of medications to consumers. Recently, the FDA strongly urged pharmaceutical companies to include risk information about drugs in the companies' search advertisements, that is, the short text that appears besides the results of one's Google search; since Google limits such ads to 95 characters, it is unclear how this can be done.[14]

THE PERILS OF PRECISION TARGETING

Consumers' loss of privacy is an increasingly problematic ethical issue as marketers identify and reach out to increasingly smaller audiences through innovative media and more sophisticated tracking. As explained in Chapter 9, it is apparent that the old *broadcasting* model—

FIGURE 16.3
Data Collection by Web Companies Tracking Their Users

Source: Louise Story, "How Do They Track You? Let Us Count the Ways," www.nytimes.com, March 9, 2008; and Louise Story, "Where Every Ad Knows Your Name," www.nytimes.com, March 10, 2008.

Part A:

They Know More Than You Think

Web companies are usually compared by how many people visit their sites each month. But looking at how many times a month each Web company collects data about a typical visitor may be a better comparison. These figures are based on the number of times consumers make search inquiries on these sites as well as the number of ads they see, pages they view and videos they watch.

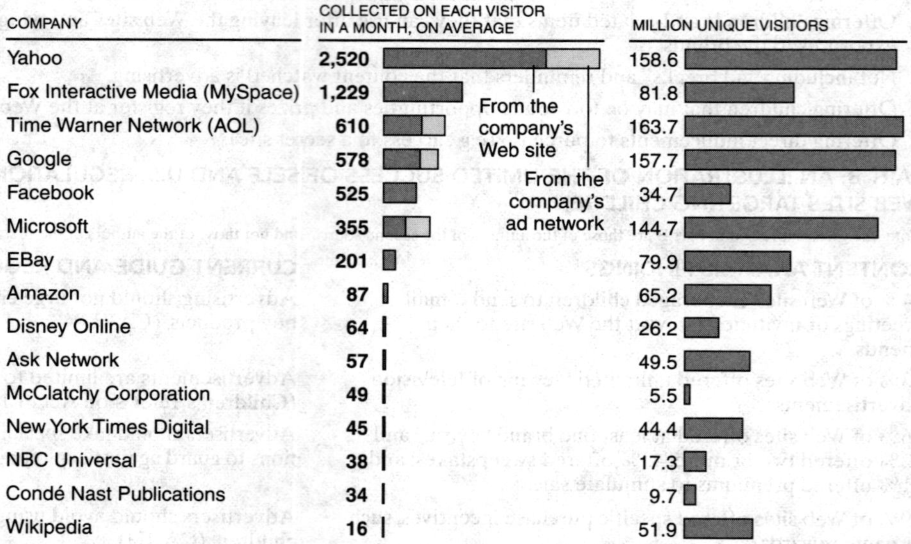

Notes: The ad networks are places these companies can collect data, but they do not in all of these instances. Also, the Time Warner figure is missing the ad network Tacoda, and the Microsoft number does not include its ad-serving company Atlas. Google's numbers do not include the ad-serving company DoubleClick.

where large audiences are reached with the same electronic or print messages—is rapidly becoming obsolete. Advertisers are increasingly adopting *narrowcasting*—a technique that allows them to send precisely directed messages to very small audiences on an ongoing basis. **Narrowcasting** is made possible through the efforts of sophisticated data providers who compile individual profiles from census data, tax records, credit card companies, banks, direct-mail responses, surveys and product warranty cards completed by consumers, and from internal sales records provided by companies. Sophisticated analysis of such data enables the compilation of extremely specialized lists of consumers. For example, a marketer can purchase a list of left-handed people with a specified income who own pets and are of Hispanic origin. Based on these characteristics, the marketer can develop and deliver a highly targeted and persuasive message designed specifically for this very narrowly defined consumer group.

On the Web, online marketers monitor and track consumers more closely and accurately than most people realize or would probably allow. For example, Facebook had a program called "beacon," which traced where users were going and sent their friends alerts about the goods that the users who were monitored bought or viewed online. After a public outcry, Facebook incorporated into the program a feature allowing users to opt out of it easily.[15] A recent analysis of online consumer data proved that Web companies are learning a lot about consumers from what people do and search for on the Internet, use this information to predict what ads and content consumers would like to see, and charge high fees for companies who buy this data and use it to place tailored ads online. Some companies even admit that they can identify some of the monitored consumers by name. Generally, consumers have not complained about these practices because the tracking is invisible to them.[16] However, some public advocates have expressed concerns that targeted ads based on data from Internet portal companies, collected without consumers' awareness, violate U.S. wiretap and privacy laws, and a Senate committee held hearings on this issue.[17]

FIGURE 16.3
Continued

Part B:

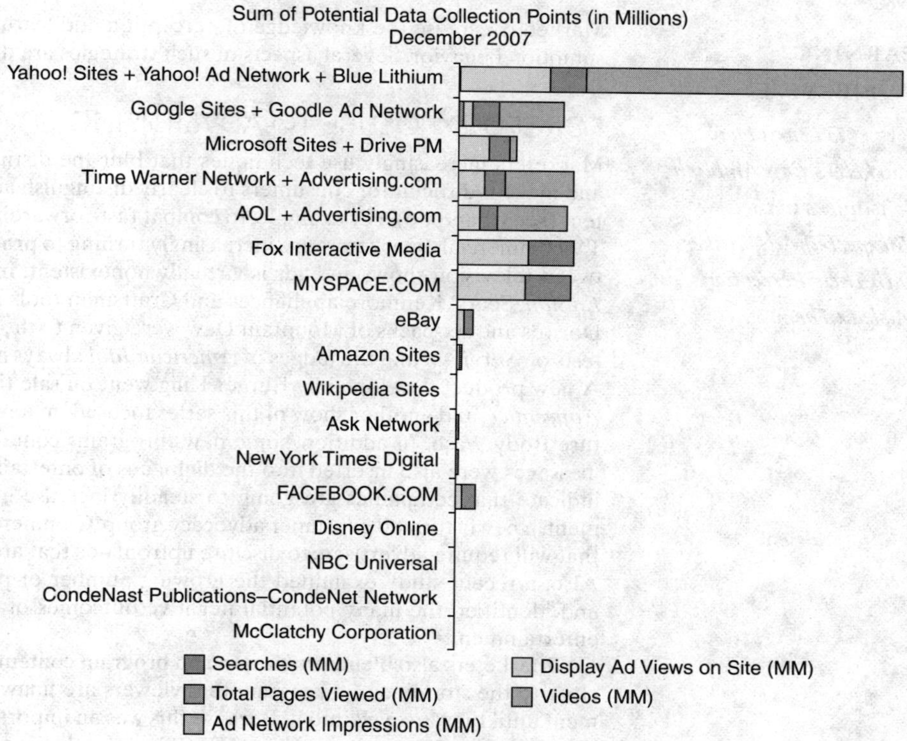

As discussed in Chapter 9, electronic, invisible "cookies" are the primary tool to identify consumers online. Studies found that both cookie use and disclosure by companies depositing the cookies have steadily increased. A study found that consumers' negative reactions toward cookies were decreased by a priori disclosure from the visited Web sites. Also, consumers' online experience and degree of privacy concern moderated their reactions to cookie use.[18] Figure 16.3 demonstrates the vast tracking and surveillance of consumers online.

Marketers can learn not only *who* you are (e.g., your personal characteristics) and *what* specific purchases you make, but now they can also learn *where* you are at any given moment because your cell phone, mobile e-mail device, or the GPS integrated into your car or sports watch serve as sort of "electronic bracelets" that monitor your movements. In one futuristic movie thriller set in 2054, the hero passes a billboard featuring the American Express card, which, upon scanning his eye retina, becomes a hologram (presumably only visible to him) portraying his picture and personal data and urging him to use the card. He then enters a Gap store where he is met by voices greeting him by name, asking how he liked his previous purchases, and suggesting items that he may like based on his past purchases. Although such scanning and recognition devices are not yet widespread, if you travel abroad and have a cell phone with a roaming service, upon landing at your destination your phone is likely to include a message welcoming you to that destination and offering you additional services designed for travelers. Clearly, in the not-too-distant future, when you drive a car equipped with a GPS with the radio on, the commercial that you will hear may alert you to, say, a McDonald's two exits down next to the highway; that ad will not be the same as the one heard by another driver in a different location and listening to the same radio station. In fact, in several large cities, advertisers experimented with using cabs equipped with GPS and advertising billboards on their roofs to create ever-changing advertising messages; the changing ad displays corresponded to the businesses the cabs passed as they traveled (in some cabs screens inside the cabs portrayed ads as well).

Manipulating Consumers

LEARNING OBJECTIVE

16.3 *To Learn How Marketers Can Ambush Consumers with Unexpected Ads, Tinker with Their Perceptions, and Mislead Them.*

Marketers can use the knowledge of perception and learning to manipulate consumers' consumption behavior. Several aspects of such strategies are discussed next.

FORCED EXPOSURE TO ADVERTISING

Marketers increasingly use techniques that blur the distinctions between *figure* and *ground* and make it difficult for consumers to clearly distinguish advertising from entertainment content (see Chapter 6). For example, to combat fast-forwarding by consumers who wish to avoid TV commercials, marketers are increasingly turning to **product placements**, where the line between television shows and ads is virtually nonexistent. In ABC's *Extreme Makeover: Home Edition*, Sears' Kenmore appliances and Craftsman tools are the "stars" of the show. Bags of Doritos and six-packs of Mountain Dew were given to the winners of personal challenge contests on *Survivor*, and the judges of *American Idol* always have a Coca-Cola within easy reach. A new product developed by Burger King went on sale the day after it was featured on *The Apprentice*, and another show of this series focused on developing an ad for Dove Cool Moisture Body Wash. In addition, some news programs contain embedded ads, and promotional messages were also inserted into the dialogues of entertainments programs.[19] While forecasts indicate that companies are going to steadily increase expenditures on branded entertainment, a newly formed consumer advocacy group, Commercial Alert, is lobbying for legislation that will require advertisers to disclose upfront ads that are designed as product placements.[20] Also, a recent study examined the growing number of pharmaceutical product placements and identified the many potential negative outcomes of medications' inclusions in fictional entertainment.[21]

Marketers also blend promotion and program content by positioning a TV commercial so close to the storyline of a program that viewers are unaware they are watching an advertisement until they are well into it. Because this was an important factor in advertising to children, the U.S. Federal Trade Commission (FTC) has strictly limited the use of this technique. TV stars or cartoon characters are now prohibited from promoting products during the children's shows in which they appear. Other potential misuse of figure-and-ground is print ads (called *advertorials*) that closely resemble editorial matter. For example, 30-minute commercials (called *infomercials*) appear to the average viewer as documentaries, and thus command more attentive viewing than obvious commercials would receive.

TINKERING WITH CONSUMERS' PERCEPTIONS

Researchers and public interest advocates have been increasingly concerned about Americans' steadily growing consumption of unhealthy foods. A recent study demonstrated that consumers believe that foods that are *less* healthy taste better, are enjoyed more, and preferred when a hedonic meal takes place.[22] Marketers can also use their knowledge of perception to increase the quantities of foods consumers eat by the way these items are packaged or presented. For example, studies showed that: (1) both children and adults consume more juice when the product is presented in short, wide glasses than in tall slender glasses; (2) candies placed in clear jars were eaten much quicker than those presented in opaque jars; (3) sandwiches in transparent wrap generated more consumption than those in opaque wraps; and (4) the visibility and aroma of tempting foods generated greater consumption.[23] Another study demonstrated that the organization of the merchandise, the size of the package, the symmetry of the display, and its perceived variety served to impact consumption quantities. The consumer implications of these findings are listed in Table 16.2.[24]

Marketers can also manipulate consumers' perception and behavior by using the physical setting where consumption occurs. It is widely known that supermarkets routinely move products around to encourage consumers to wander around the store, and keep the stores relatively cold because colder temperatures make people hungrier and so they increase their food purchases. (Some nutritionists advise consumers to go food shopping directly after a filling meal.)

Marketers can also manipulate consumers' interpretations of marketing stimuli through the context in which they are featured. For example, in QVC's *Extreme Shopping*, during which rare and expensive products are offered, consumers perceived $200 art prints as reasonably priced when the prints were shown immediately after much more expensive items.[25] Inadvertently,

TABLE 16.2 Implications for How Assortment Structure Influences Consumption Quantities

	ORGANIZATION INFLUENCES CONSUMPTION	SIZE INFLUENCES CONSUMPTION	SYMMETRY INFLUENCES CONSUMPTION	PERCEIVED VARIETY PARTIALLY MEDIATES CONSUMPTION	CONSUMPTION RULES INFLUENCE CONSUMPTION
Consumer Implications	Organization is relevant for mixed assortments in bowls (or "grab bags"), buffets, potlucks, or dinner table settings. It may also be relevant in retail contexts. Consumers may be able to control consumption by organizing less-structured offerings.	Assortment size or duplication is commonly found in the form of multiple product tastings, multiple offerings of party snacks, duplicate buffet lines, family dinners with multiple dishes, and perhaps even in retail displays. Duplicated offerings can stimulate consumption.	The symmetry of an assortment is an issue wherever multiple units (and perhaps sizes) of options are involved, such as at holiday dinners, toys in play areas, and collectibles and collecting. Minimal variation in the size of serving bowls may overstimulate consumption.	People are often surprised at how much they consume, showing that they may have been influenced at a basic or perceptual level.	Large inventory levels in one's home pantry could increase the quantity of food one believes is appropriate for a meal. Health care professionals and dieticians can stimulate consumption among nutritionally deficient individuals by offering smaller helpings of more items.

Source: Barbara E. Kahn and Brian Wansink, "The Influence of Assortment Structure on Perceived Variety and Consumption Quantities," *Journal of Consumer Research*, 30 (March 2004): 530. Reproduced with permission of the copyright owner. Further reproduction prohibited without permission. Copyright © 2004, JCR, Inc.

marketers can also impact the content and duration of news and other information-focused broadcasts. For example, many marketers carefully screen the context in which their messages are shown, because they recognize that advertisements are perceived more positively when placed within more positive programs. Thus, they may choose not to place ads in news broadcasts or programs that cover serious issues, such as wars and world hunger, where some of the content is bound to be unpleasant. Since broadcasts are driven by advertising revenue, media companies may choose to shorten the coverage of serious and disagreeable topics.

The principle of stimulus generalization can be used to confuse consumers and alter intended consumption behavior. In most drugstores, less expensive brands of personal care products such as shampoo, dental floss, skin care lotions, and soap come in packages that are extremely similar to instantly recognized and more expensive premium brands of these products, and are deliberately placed right next to them on the shelf. Consumers can easily be confused by such displays and also by brand names or logos similar to those of premium offerings. Therefore, the marketers of premium brands often secure legal protection (in the form of patents or trademarks) for their brand names, packages, and visual identities. One unscrupulous marketer used stimulus generalization especially to exploit children. Shortly after the inauguration of President Obama, a toy company introduced the Marvelous Malia and Sweet Sasha dolls, which clearly resembled the president's young daughters; this act violated the privacy rights of two young girls and also exploited the children who may have nagged their parents to purchase the dolls.

COVERT MARKETING

Covert marketing (also known as *masked* or *stealth marketing*) consists of marketing messages and promotional materials that appear to come from independent parties although, in fact, they are sent by marketers. Table 16.3 features a typology of such practices.[26] Some maintain that **masked marketing** strategies often violate the FTC's definition of deceptive advertising, endorsement guidelines, and other regulations of marketing, and believe that the FTC should establish clearer rules in order to reduce the use of masked advertising.[27] Others argue that the widespread use of **stealth marketing** abuses consumers' efforts to avoid advertising and will result in increased consumers' distrust of product information; of particular concern here is the

TABLE 16.3 A Typology of Masked Marketing Practices

PRACTICE	DESCRIPTION
Posers (disguised communicator)	Actors or salespeople who pretend to be ordinary people or researchers conducting a survey to explain product benefits and give potential consumers the chance to examine, sample, or use a product.
Buzz and viral marketing (disguised communicator)	Recruitment of people to talk about products through free samples or discounts before the product is available to the general public and suggestions on what to say and how to approach people about the product. Some refer to this as viral marketing when the contact with potential consumers is done electronically.
Advertorials (disguised format)	Advertisements that appear to be information from an independent source, such as prepared television news stories: infomercials that appear to be consumer television shows; and print advertisements that appear to be editorial content.
Disguised monitoring of queries via search engines	Employing invisible metatags to monitor queries submitted via search engines and using the data from these observations to target consumers with customized ads.
Urgent ad-formation (disguised format)	Advertisements that appear in the form of important account information from firms with an existing business relationship, government notices, sweepstakes prize notices, or checks that are simply discount coupons.
Advertainment (disguised format)	Product and advertising placement in television shows, at sporting events, and in video games.

increased involvement of companies in initiating and designing communications that are made to resemble genuine word-of-mouth.[28]

SOCIALLY UNDESIRABLE REPRESENTATIONS

Presumably unintentionally, marketers may convey socially undesirable stereotypes and images in products and advertisements. Some years ago, the makers of an American icon—G.I. Joe—introduced a substantially more muscular version of the doll and were subsequently accused of sanctioning the use of muscle-building drugs by teenagers. Similarly, the makers of Barbie—a doll that has gradually become thinner and bustier—were accused of conveying an unrealistic body image to young girls.[29] More recently, Tapout—a popular brand of clothing that is associated with the "sport" of Ultimate Fighting—was criticized by the media and some consumer advocates who believe that the brand promotes violence.[30]

In trying to illustrate that some ads may bring about undesirable, although unintended, behavior, a New Jersey professor showed his students a magazine ad featuring a fit, smiling young man on a sidewalk in New York City with yellow cabs, pedestrians, and buildings in the background. The bright red headline read, "Just once a day!" All other copy elements of the ad were concealed in order to disguise the actual product advertised. When the professor asked his students to guess what kind of product the ad was promoting, the consensus of the guesses was that the ad was for some kind of a pill, probably a vitamin. In fact, the ad was for a medication that is used as part of an HIV therapy by persons who are HIV positive. Since visual images are very persuasive, is it possible that the fit young man and the bright red caption "Just once a day!" conveys to young adults that being HIV positive is an easily "manageable" condition, and that one can engage in unsafe sex? And, if a study indicates that such a perception is indeed created by the ad, what should the marketer do? Clearly, featuring an individual who looks *unhealthy* in an ad for a pharmaceutical designed to control a serious medical condition will not be effective. The caption is an accurate representation of how often this drug should be taken (in combination, of course, with other drugs). Although the potential perception created here may not have been considered when this ad was designed, the problem addressed here is real. The Food and Drug Administration (FDA) has alerted marketers of HIV medications to the fact that some of their ads, which often show healthy-looking persons involved in rigorous physical activity, may be conveying the notion that since the drugs can restore one's health, they implicitly encourage unsafe sex.[31]

Some objectionable ads may be the result of good intentions. For example, a not-for-profit organization in New York City ran an ad campaign aimed at raising public awareness of such children's disorders as autism, depression, and eating-related illnesses. The ads featured "Ransom Notes" depicting how the diseases held the families of the sick children captive by taking over their lives. Although many agreed that this advertising approach was effective in the context of the campaign's objectives, some parents of children afflicted with the illnesses featured found the ads too emotional and personal, and the campaign was discontinued.[32]

Since advertising is part of our culture, the cumulative persuasive impact of promotional messages on societal values must be considered. By itself, one tasteless ad has little impact on our values. However, cumulatively, such ads may persuade consumers to act unwisely or develop undesirable attitudes. For example, repeated exposure to ads depicting perfectly tanned people is likely to result in excessive sun bathing or tanning via ultraviolet light, despite the fact that it has been documented that such practices significantly increase the chances of developing cancer. Interestingly, not all ads that promote a practice that may negatively impact one's health are treated the same way. For example, although it is known that tanning causes cancer, Americans have accepted ads portraying perfectly tanned models without criticism.

Following considerable research, it is now generally accepted that repeated exposure to very thin "ideal" figures in promotional messages leads to negative self-perceptions (particularly in women) and is partially responsible for the increase in eating-related disorders. Marketers now recognize that ads focused on beauty and attractiveness, especially if they stress the importance of these attributes over other personal characteristics, are likely to be scrutinized by the media, consumers, advocacy groups, or religious organizations. Subsequently, numerous advertisements now portray more realistic-looking models and some beauty-products ads integrate the notion that although the "outside" is important, the person's self-worth or "true beauty" comes from "within." A recent study of the sexual objectification of women in advertising showed that although the number of ads containing such portrayals has been increasing, compared with data collected in the past, females were less offended by these images, and that respondents' attitudes toward such ads had little impact on their purchase intentions.[33]

Although marketers continuously sponsor ads portraying values or behaviors that some (or many) consumers find distasteful or wrong, the importance of public scrutiny must not be underestimated. For example, the broadcast of the 2004 Super Bowl included many ads portraying crude humor and gags that were later criticized by many (and also amplified by the coincidental "wardrobe malfunction" of a female entertainer during the half-time show). As a result, advertisers during the 2005 Super Bowl broadcast took special care to develop ads that were more mainstream and traditional, not an easy task since Super Bowl ads—expected to be creative and unique—are the most analyzed group of ads in American broadcasting.[34]

Many studies focused on the use of objectionable themes in advertising. For example, one study of TV commercials directed at children discovered that diverse ethnicities were underrepresented compared to Caucasians and pointed out the need for more diverse ethnic representation in children's TV advertising. This is an important recommendation because children are generally deeply engaged in TV viewing and the advertising's ethnic portrayal influences their views of social ethnicity.[35] A study of promotional elements offending consumers found out that images and words unsuitable for children produced the most consumer complaints followed by bad language. The study also discovered that consumers felt more insulted by offensive themes than the products, services, or ideas featured in the ads, and that consumers viewed ads delivered via intrusive media as more offensive than those delivered via other media.[36]

FALSE OR MISLEADING ADVERTISING

The ethical issues related to advertising focus on the accuracy of the information provided and the potential misuse of promotional messages' persuasive abilities. Regarding accuracy, a toothpaste ad stating that "brand A is the best" is considered an acceptable form of advertising "puffery" because consumers generally understand that there is no credible way to determine what *best* means. A toothpaste ad stating that the brand was "endorsed by the American Dental Association" is an objective statement because it includes information that is easy to verify. However, is an ad stating that the brand "provides more cavity protection than any other toothpaste" permissible advertising puffery, or is it false or misleading? The answer depends on how most reasonable consumers are likely to interpret the ad. Do they believe that there is a scientific way to measure the degree of cavity protection and that the maker of the brand has conducted a scientific study of all brands of toothpaste on the market and whether the study proved the ad's claim? It is clear that determining how most reasonable consumers are likely to interpret the ad is a complex undertaking, and therefore there is no definitive answer to the question "At what point does puffery become deceptive?" As discussed in Chapter 9, humor is the most popular advertising appeal. A recent study discovered that deceptive claims were found in about three-quarters of humorous ads, and, in most cases, the humor was used to *mask* the deceptive claims.[37]

Truth-in-advertising laws protect consumers from false advertisements. Over time, the FTC has developed guidelines as to what constitutes **deceptive advertising** in the United States, and they hold marketers responsible for determining their ads' potential to mislead consumers. While the FTC is responsible for stopping false or misleading ads, it is apparent that such ads continue to exist. For example, the FTC's Web site has featured a "Red Flag" button alerting consumers that "misleading weight loss advertising is everywhere" and also warning them to beware of weight loss claims that are too good to be true, such as claims that the product causes "substantial weight loss no matter how much the consumer eats" or promising "a weight loss of two pounds or more a week for a month or more without dieting or exercise."[38] The FTC encourages and investigates complaints by consumers and companies regarding false or misleading ads, but its public advice for consumers regarding weight loss products illustrates that it cannot locate and stop all misleading ads. The FTC can also require companies that have misled consumers through their advertising to run **corrective advertising**. For example, years ago Listerine's maker was forced to correct the claim that the product prevents colds. A recent study indicated that corrective advertising sometimes resulted in consumers' distrust toward other products sold by the company and also toward similar products sold by unrelated marketers and suggested that corrective promotional messages may not achieve their desired objectives.[39]

In addition to the FTC, the National Advertising Review Council (NARC) is the self-regulatory group that monitors complaints from companies and consumers regarding truth in advertising and often determines what ads can or cannot state. For example, NARC determined that Colgate-Palmolive provided supportive evidence to the claim that its Oxy-Plus product "blasts away grease faster" than P&G's Ultra Dawn, but decided that there was no evidence supporting GlaxoSmithKline's claim that Super PoliGrip provides the "strongest hold ever," a claim that the company subsequently withdrew. NARC also supported a challenge of promotions for cancer treatment claiming that "Chemotherapy doesn't work for everyone."[40] In some cases, powerful companies can persuade media to stop running ads they deem deceptive. For example, Anheuser-Busch persuaded ABC, CBS, and NBC to stop running Miller Beer ads depicting consumers comparing beers and saying that the Miller beers have more flavor, on the grounds that these comparisons were flawed.[41]

Social Responsibility

LEARNING OBJECTIVE

16.4 *To Understand How Marketers Can Advance Society's Interests via Such Practices as Advocating Social Benefits, Cause-Related Marketing, and Green Marketing.*

Many not-for-profit organizations, including consumer advocacy groups, exist primarily to promote socially beneficial behaviors such as contributing to charity, using energy responsibly, and reducing such negative behaviors as using drugs, discrimination, and drunk driving. In addition, in accordance with the *societal marketing concept*, many companies try to increase their credibility by being "good corporate citizens" and integrating socially desirable practices into their operations. For example, earlier in this chapter we discussed how McDonald's and Facebook had altered their practices in ways that adhered to the public interest. As another example, recently, Disney agreed to not feature any smoking in Disney-branded films.[42] A recent study indicated that societal marketing program had a powerful impact on creating positive consumer attitudes toward companies.[43] Socially beneficial forms of doing business include promoting social cause, cause-related marketing, and producing and promoting ecologically sound products. These practices are described next and the chapter concludes with a discussion of consumer ethics.

ADVOCATING SOCIALLY BENEFICIAL CAUSES

The primary objective of many not-for-profit organizations is to promote socially desirable behaviors and discourage ones that produce negative outcomes. For example, The Advertising Council—a group founded during World War II and dedicated to the advancement of socially worthy causes through advertising—recently ran a campaign that discouraged the use of derogatory phrases regarding one's sexual orientation. The campaign's title was "Think Before You Speak," and its objective was to reduce the harassment and bullying of teenagers who are

FIGURE 16.4

Source: Courtesy The Jewish Guild for the Blind.

QUESTION: *What Is the Name and Meaning of the Marketing Approach Featured in this Ad?*

gay, lesbian, bisexual, or transgender.[44] With the increase of "digital harassment" among teenagers, The Advertising Council initiated a campaign entitled "That's Not Cool" alerting young adults that excessive and unwelcome sending of text messages can quickly become illegal stalking.[45] Still further, the Christopher Reeve Foundation is a not-for-profit group dedicated to raising money for treating people who live with spinal impairment and finding a cure for spinal injury; recently, the group ran an ad campaign under its new slogan "Today's Care. Tomorrow's Cure."[46] As a final example, a campaign by the Visiting Nurse Service of New York (a large not-for-profit organization) ran an ad campaign—under the slogan "Now What?"—featuring the difficulties that patients and their families faced when confronted with unexpected illnesses and limited mobility.[47] Figure 16.4 features an ad for a charitable organization that includes a subtle appeal for contributions.

FIGURE 16.5
Source: Center for Science in the Public Interest (CSPI). www.cspinet.org.

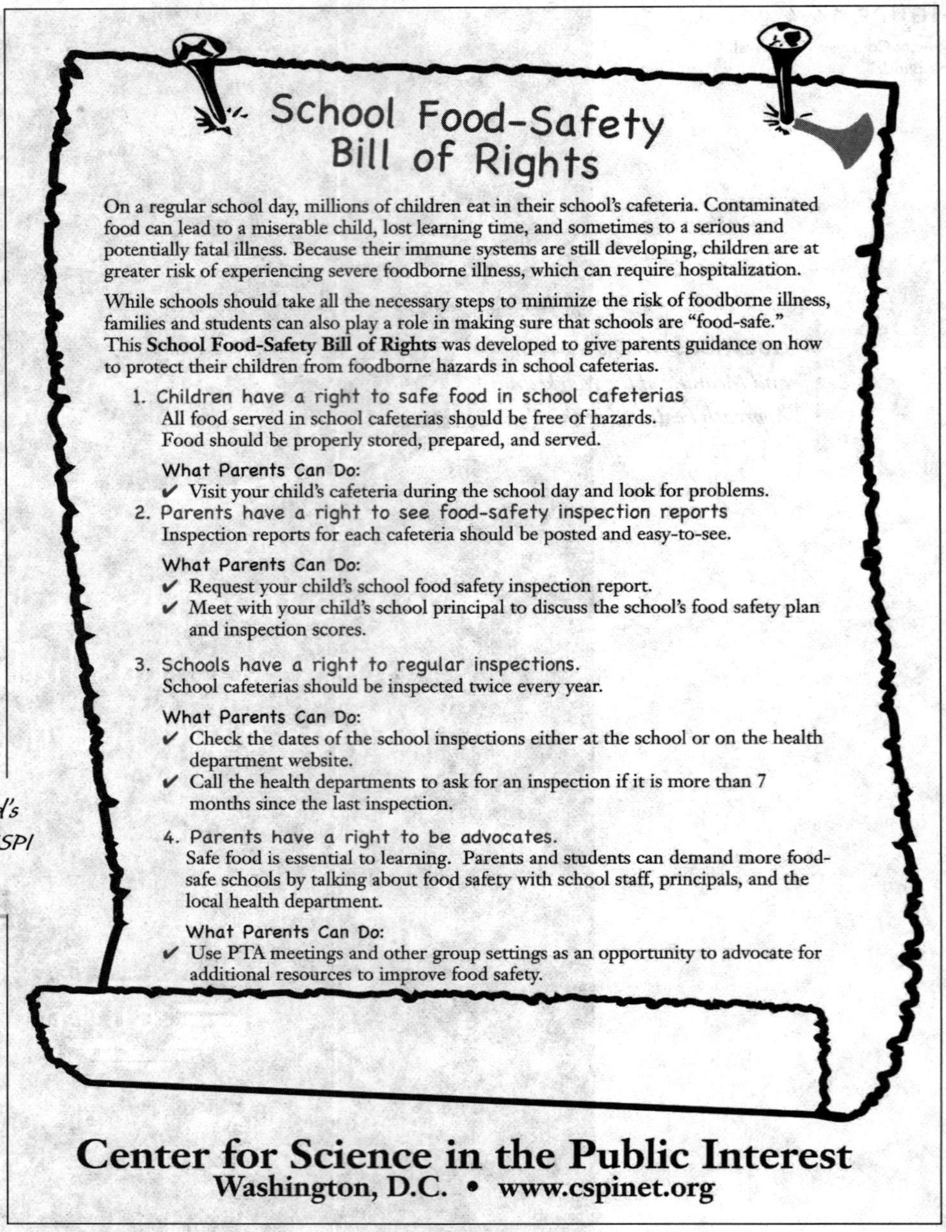

QUESTION: *What Is the Ad's Objective, and Why Is the CSPI Sponsoring It?*

Sometimes, even government organizations try to induce public behavior that they see fit. For example, since many TV series and films are shot on the streets of New York City, some hurried New Yorkers have grown increasingly annoyed at the delays and inconveniences caused by film crews who must often close and obstruct city blocks and sidewalks during filming. The city's Mayor's Office ran a campaign asking New Yorkers to play host to film crews even if they may be reluctant to do so; the ads featured New Yorkers who work in the film industry and stressed the economic benefits of the industry's strong presence in the city.[48]

Consumer advocacy groups sometimes resort to aggressive advertising when they believe the public is harmed by corporate practices. Figure 16.5 features an ad aimed at educating consumers about an unhealthy product; the ad is sponsored by the **Center for Science in the Public Interest** (CSPI)—a widely recognized consumer advocacy group.

CAUSE-RELATED MARKETING

Some firms engage in **cause-related marketing**, where they contribute a portion of the revenues they receive from selling certain products to such causes as helping people inflicted with incurable diseases or hurt by inclement weather. For example, fashion designers such as Armani and Ralph Lauren have donated selected portions of their sales to AIDS research and other charities. To acknowledge National Breast Cancer Awareness Month in October, many beauty and cosmetics companies earmark a portion of the selling price of their "pink-ribbon" products to breast cancer charities. Following the December 2004 tsunami in Southeast Asia, several designers sold tsunami-relief T-shirts; many others encouraged consumers to make donations to a fund that was set up to help the storm's victims and even included links to this fund on their Web sites. Other kinds of corporate-sponsored special events include marching bands, fireworks displays, parades, laser shows, and traveling art exhibits. The nature and quality of these sponsorships constitute a subtle message to the consumer: "We're a great (kind, good-natured, socially responsible) company; we deserve your business."

A recent study demonstrated the importance of the fit between the sponsored cause and the company's positioning strategy and that a low fit can harm the company's image.[49] In another study, an ad with a cause-related message elicited more favorable consumer attitudes than a similar ad without a cause-related message.[50] Yet another study showed that cause-related advertising is more effective among more involved consumers.[51]

GREEN MARKETING

With the increased global awareness of climate change and its potential dire consequences for our planet and its inhabitants, many companies have adopted forms of **green marketing** and now promote healthy, reusable, and ecofriendly products. Since emissions from cars are one of the most often blamed contributors to environmental deterioration, many automobile makers now produce environmentally sound cars (see Figure 16.6). In addition, many companies presently promote their use of renewable, clean, and sustainable energy and recycled and nonpolluting materials.

Several studies focused on consumers' likelihood to buy environmentally safe products. One study examined consumers' willingness to purchase such goods in the context of their desires to buy quality products at reasonable prices and also developed a scale measuring consumers' attitudes toward green products and the firms making them (see Table 16.4).[52] Another study found that consumers *said* that they like ecologically friendly products but only about a third actually bought such products, and most of the respondents did not know which lifestyle changes are the best means to reduce global warming.[53] Another study discovered that consumers find environmental labels difficult to understand and that this issue increases their price

TABLE 16.4 A Scale Measuring Consumers' Attitudes Toward Green Products

I believe there are a lot of exaggerations about companies taking environmental risks nowadays.
I believe the government is doing all that is possible to safeguard the environment.
I believe that we should not slow down industry progress because of concern for the environment.
I believe environmental safety is the responsibility of the government, not individual citizens.
I believe that government legislation adequately regulates environmental protection.
I believe a well-known brand is always a safe product to buy.
I believe that the quality of environmentally safe products is not as good as other products.
I believe that the price of environmentally safe products is usually more expensive than other products.
I believe Australian companies are generally doing a good job in helping to protect the environment.
I believe companies should place higher priority on reducing pollution than on increasing their own profitability.
I believe companies should place higher priority on reducing pollution than on increasing profitability even if jobs are at risk.

Source: Claire D'Souza, Mehdi Taghian, and Rajiv Khosla, "Examination of Environmental Beliefs and Its Impact on the Influence of Price, Quality and Demographic Characteristics with Respect to Green Purchase Intentions," *Journal of Targeting, Measurement and Analysis for Marketing,* 15, no. 2 (2007): 73.

FIGURE 16.6A

Source: Courtesy of Chevrolet/GM.

QUESTION: *What Is the Name and Purpose of the Marketing Practice Depicted in the Three Ads Shown in This Figure, and How Did Each of the Three Carmakers Featured Adopt This Practice?*

sensitivity regarding green ecologically sound products.[54] Yet another study indicated that even consumers with pro-environmental beliefs have difficulty correctly identifying green products (other than cleaning items) and do not find green marketing engaging.[55] Together, these studies indicate that marketers must improve the promotion of green products.

CONSUMER ETHICS

Marketers who implement ethical strategies do so in order "to do the right thing," to improve their image in the eyes of their constituencies, reduce scrutiny, and as an alternative to the likelihood of government legislation. A recent study focused on measuring consumers' views and perceptions of companies that tackle such issues as exploitation of the third world, animal testing, damage to the environment, and recycling. The study applied a model of personal acceptance of change to an increased awareness and action regarding an ethical issue (see Table 16.5A). Then, the researchers developed a scale measuring consumers' views regard-

FIGURE 16.6B
Source: Courtesy of Saab/GM.

ing ethical business issues and companies that adopt morally right strategies; the scale includes personal, social, and money aspects of adopting more ethical views, as well as possible positive and negative outcomes of doing so (see Table 16.5B).[56]

Another facet of **consumer ethics** is buyers' dishonest behavior in the marketplace. For example, many stores started charging restocking fees, limiting return policies, and tracking abnormal return patterns because of buyers who bought items, used them, and then returned them for a refund (some stores encountered shoplifters who tried to return stolen merchandise). Also, in the digital world, software piracy is a major problem. A recent study focused on ways to reduce consumers' software theft and discovered that increasing the risk of getting caught is unlikely to reduce this practice and may actually increase piracy levels. The study also found that consumers were less likely to pirate and more willing to pay for software if the Web sites involved offered them extra value, such as rare recordings or downloadable ringtones and videos.[57]

FIGURE 16.6C

Source: Courtesy of Lexus, a division of Toyota Motor Sales.

TABLE 16.5A An Application of the Stages of Change to Ethical Decision-Making

For illustration purposes, this exhibit applies each stage of change to a personal decision (i.e., quitting smoking) and then to ethical decision making.

STAGE	DESCRIPTION
Precontemplation	(a) During this stage, people are not giving any serious thought to quitting smoking and are likely to be defensive to the idea. They are unlikely to be aware of the consequences or are attached to the experience. (b) From an ethical perspective consumers are unlikely to have given much thought to the ethical issue and it is highly probable that they are not interested in taking any steps toward intervention. They may well be unaware or not bothered about the issue. They do not discuss the issue with others.

Continued

TABLE 16.5A An Application of the Stages of Change to Ethical Decision-Making *Continued*

Contemplation	(a) Smokers in this stage may well have given thought to the decision to quit smoking. Whilst aware of the harmful consequences, they are ambivalent to the next stage in the cessation process and perhaps doubt whether they will see any long-term benefits.
	(b) In the context of ethics research, during this stage the consumer becomes aware of the issue and moves from not being concerned at all to showing some signs of awareness and concern. However, they may feel that the negative aspects of taking action outweigh the positive and therefore remain in the comtemplation stage. From another perspective, they may well be more receptive to information regarding the issue and are more likely to reflect on their own thoughts and feelings regarding the issue.
Preparation	(a) The smoker has made the decision to quit and has built up the motivation to launch a serious attempt at cessation.
	(b) The ethical consumers is also preparing to take action. The pros begin to outweigh the cons. Motivations such as "I should do something about this" or "something has to change" drive the person's movements toward action.
Action	(a) The smoker is actively attempting to stop smoking through a number of techniques.
	(b) The consumer takes some level of action (minor or major) regarding an issue. They may also seek to influence others.
Maintenance	(a) Smokers in the maintenance phase are successfully avoiding the temptation to relapse back into their former habits. Their motivations suggest that what they are striving for is worthwhile.
	(b) Consumers in this stage continue to believe it is worthwhile to maintain action regarding an ethical issue.

TABLE 16.5B A Scale Measuring a Person's Ethical Awareness and Concerns

Respondents used a 7-point scale ranging from "strongly agree" to "strongly disagree."

PERSONAL POSITIVES

My friends are concerned with this issue
People who matter to me would respect me for being concerned about this issue
This is an issue that I like to be associated with
I feel better about myself if I take some form of action against firms that violate this issue

SOCIAL POSITIVES

It would be better for everyone in the long run if people favoured products that address this issue
It would help if people bought from firms that address this issue
Society would benefit from the removal of products that violate this issue
People could make fairer choices if they were aware of which companies had high ethical principles regarding this issue

PERSONAL NEGATIVES

It would be too much hassle to buy only from businesses that do not violate this issue
It is not my responsibility to punish firms that ignore this issue
It would take the pleasure out of shopping if I had to choose only from products that support this issue
It would make shopping less convenient if I had to choose only from products that support this issue

SOCIAL NEGATIVES

People would be annoyed if they were pressured into being concerned with this issue
People are too busy today to be concerned with this issue
People might think it was a waste of time to try to influence big business over this issue
Having to take account of this issue would make shopping less convenient for people

MONEY ISSUES

It does not cost me any more money to take this issue into account when shopping *(item reversed for these analyses)*
It costs more to take account of this issue when shopping

Source: Oliver M. Freestone and Peter J. McGoldrick, "Motivations of the Ethical Consumer," *Journal of Business Ethics,* 79 (2008): Part A— 463, Part B—455.

SUMMARY

The marketing concept is sometimes incongruous with society's best interests. Since all companies prosper when society prospers, companies must integrate social responsibility into all marketing decisions and many adopted the societal marketing concept. The societal marketing concept requires that all marketers adhere to principles of social responsibility in the marketing of their goods and services. A serious deterrent to widespread implementation of the societal marketing concept is the short-term orientation embraced by most business executives in their drive for quickly increasing market share and profits.

Since the study of consumer behavior allows marketers to understand why and how consumers make their purchase decisions, it also enables unethical marketers to exploit human vulnerabilities in the marketplace and engage in other unethical marketing practices. Such practices include targeting vulnerable consumers such as children, teenagers, the elderly, and less-educated consumers, who may not have the knowledge or experience to evaluate the products or services being promoted and the potential negative consequences of using these offerings. Marketers can also use their knowledge of learning and perception to forcefully expose consumers to advertising, tinker with people's perceptions, use covert marketing, depict socially undesirable themes in promotional messages and engage in misleading or false advertising.

Many not-for-profit organizations exist primarily to promote socially beneficial behaviors such as contributing to charity and reduce such negative behaviors as using drugs. Also, many companies try to increase their credibility by being "good corporate citizens" and integrating socially desirable practices into their operations in the form of cause-related marketing and green marketing. The study of consumer ethics allows marketers to understand consumers' reactions to societal marketing.

DISCUSSION QUESTIONS

1. Some say that targeting *any* group of consumers who are willing and able to purchase a product is simply good marketing. For example, advertising very sweet and fatty foods to young children is perfectly okay because children like sweets and, when parents buy these products at their children's requests, the needs of both the kids and their parents are met and satisfied. What is your reaction to this view?
2. A soft drink company distributed cell phones to preadolescents in low-income areas. The phones routinely received advertising messages for the drink. Following criticism, the company said that the benefits of the disadvantaged children's having the cell phones (e.g., safety) outweighed any "exploitive targeting" considerations. Do you agree with the company's position? Explain your answer.
3. At a time when many consumers can avoid advertising messages via sophisticated "time shifting" devices, marketers increasingly use product placements (also known as "branded entertainment"). In your view, is this a wise strategy or not? Explain your answer.
4. Is it right to advertise prescription medications *directly* to consumers? Why or why not?
5. Why are companies increasingly introducing green products and engaging in ecologically friendly practices?
6. Why is it important to study consumer ethics?
7. What are the privacy implications of the increasingly widespread monitoring of online consumers by companies?

EXERCISES

1. Find, bring to class, and discuss ads that depict each of the following:
   a. Exploitive targeting of children
   b. Overaggressive advertising
   c. Direct-to-consumer advertising of pharmaceuticals
   d. Green marketing
   e. Cause-related marketing
   f. Societal marketing by a not-for-profit group
   g. Societal marketing by a for-profit company
   h. Socially undesirable representation
2. Table 16.3 depicts examples of covert (or masked) marketing. Find an example of such marketing, bring it to class, and discuss.
3. Compile a list of consumption behaviors that *you* consider *unethical*. For each behavior listed, explain why you view it as wrong. Also, for each behavior listed, discuss the *possible reasons* a person engaging in that practice may use to *justify* doing so.
4. Visit the news section at www.caru.org. Select three of the press releases featured there (other than those discussed in the chapter) and illustrate how they depict the unethical applications of learning or perception concepts in targeting children.

KEY TERMS

- cause-related marketing *529*
- Center for Science in the Public Interest (CSPI) *528*
- Children's Advertising Review Unit (CARU) *516*
- consumer ethics *531*
- corrective advertising *526*
- covert, masked, or stealth marketing *523*
- deceptive advertising *526*
- exploitive targeting *516*
- false or misleading advertising *525*
- green marketing *529*
- marketing ethics *516*
- narrowcasting *520*
- product placements *522*
- societal marketing concept *514*
- truth-in-advertising laws *526*

Case One: Does Food Marketing to Children Cause Obesity?

For years, Americans believed that children learn and often imitate what they see on TV and expressed concern regarding the negative impact of TV on children's behavior. Increases in violent crime have been partially attributed to the once-widespread depiction of sex and violence on TV, and, as a result, TV programmers have curtailed showing such behaviors. In sitcoms and dramas, the "good guys" always win at the end and characters always end up doing "the right thing," even in story lines where opposite actions or outcomes appear to be more likely, in order to convey the "right values" to young viewers. Now, many attribute the growing rates of obesity and associated illnesses among children and teenagers to the overconsumption of high-calorie and high-fat foods that, these critiques claim, are the results of the heavy promotion of foods to children on which advertisers spend about $ 10 billion a year and in which most of the items advertised are high in fat and sugar but low in nutrition. In fact, several countries have already either banned advertising foods to children or restricted it. Several influential consumer advocacy groups have called for restricting the advertising of "junk foods" on TV, in movie placements and tie-ins, and in schools, and it appears likely that a bill giving the U.S. Federal Trade Commission more effective power to regulate advertising to children will be introduced in Congress. In addition, several individuals sued the food companies for causing them obesity or obesity-related health problems.

Recognizing these concerns and facing legal restrictions on their advertising to children, some fast-food companies eliminated the "super size" servings from their menus, started offering and advertising more vegetable and fruit products, and began stressing the importance of physical activity in their commercials. The marketers of major brands of soft drinks, voluntarily, stopped marketing full-calorie carbonated drinks in elementary schools and are developing healthier soft drinks. Food and restaurant companies are also pursuing legislation that will prevent consumers from suing them on the grounds that long-term consumption of their foods resulted in health problems. It is obvious that marketing foods to children has some negative results that concern society and that these concerns will result in changes, voluntary or mandated, in the ways food companies target the young.

QUESTIONS

1. Do you believe that the government, rather than parents only, should regulate the consumption behavior of children? Why or why not? Please list all the examples you can think of where laws and regulations already dictate to parents what their children can or cannot consume or how they must use certain products?

2. Some maintain that it is strictly up to parents to determine what their children eat and educate them about eating, and, therefore, food marketers should not be blamed for the increases in children's obesity and advertising of foods to children must not be regulated. Others say that parents who are trying to get their children to eat right cannot effectively compete with the heavy advertising of foods to the children and the widespread presence of "junk foods," and that children are likely to pick up bad eating habits regardless of what

their parents might try and teach them. Therefore, the advertising of foods to children must be regulated. Which position do you agree with and why?

3. Some schools now forbid parents to include such items as cookies or soft drinks in their children's lunch boxes. Thinking back to the time you were in school, do you wish that such school regulations would have been in place? Explain your answer.

Case Two: Should TV Advertisements for Personal Loans Be Banned?

The United Kingdom is cracking down on the loan industry and TV advertisements that casually invite viewers to borrow thousands of pounds. The country's Advertising Standards Authority (ASA) will use a new social responsibility code to stamp out reckless consumer credit promotions.

During the past decade, campaigners have criticized daytime TV ads that invite home owners to use their home as collateral for instant spending money. The ASA had only been able to ban loan ads if they have been misleading, but Lord Smith, the chairman of ASA, said he would use a social responsibility rule from the Broadcasting Committee in Advertising Practice (BCAP) to toughen its stance.

He singled out one example of a bad loan advertisement last year. In a TV commercial for a financial service company, there was a housewife surrounded by a busy household of kids getting ready for school and the husband coming down the stairs and grabbing a slice of toast. In the meantime, the housewife was talking on the phone saying that a loan of $45,000 would be alright. The advertisement implied that loan is the easiest way to solve any problem, even tedious housework, by making a telephone call and asking for big amount of money without any consideration. Lord Smith said that the ASA would brief firms about how they could advertise loans in future.

QUESTIONS

1. Is there any similar loan advertisement in your country? Do you think it is irresponsible advertising?

2. Do you believe that the government should have laws and regulations to dictate such loan advertising? Why or why not?

Source: Martin Hickman, "Advertising Regulator to Crackdown on 'Irresponsible' Lending Offers," *The Independent*, April 29, 2009.

Notes

Chapter 1

1. Karen Tumulty, "Obama's Viral Marketing Campaign," *Time*, July 5, 2007, accessed at www.time.com/time/magazine/article/0,9171,640402,00.html.
2. John Quelch, "How Better Marketing Elected Obama," *Harvard Business Publishing*, posted November 5, 2008, accessed at http://discussionleader.hbsp.com/quelch/2008/11/how_better_marketing_elected_b.html.
3. Adam Nagourney, "The '08 Campaign: See Change for Politics as We Know It," *New York Times*, November 4, 2008, accessed at www.nytimes.com/2008/11/04/us/politics/04memo.html.
4. "How He Did IT," *Newsweek*, November 5, 2008, accessed at www.newsweek.com/id/167582/output/print.
5. Leon Schiffman, Elaine Sherman, and Deborah Y. Cohn, "Looking In on Global Consumer Users: To Develop Better Product Feature Sets," *2008 Global Business and Technology Association (GBATA) International Conference*, Madrid, Spain, July 2008.
6. William M. Pride and O. C. Ferrell, *Foundations of Marketing* (Boston: Houghton Mifflin Company, 2004), 11.
7. *Colonel Sanders, America's Chicken King*, VHS Tape, A&E Television Networks, 1998.
8. *Ray Kroc, Fast Food McMillionaire*, VHS Tape, A&E Television Networks, 1998.
9. P. Kotler and S. Levy, "Broadening the Concept of Marketing," *Journal of Marketing*, 35 (1969): 10–15; Gi-Du Kang and J. James, "Revisiting the Concept of a Societal Orientation: Conceptualization and Delineation," *Journal of Business Ethics*, 73 (July 2007): 301–319; and A. Crane and, J. Desmond, "Societal Marketing and Morality," *European Journal of Marketing*, 36 (2002): 548–570.
10. C. Blankson, S. Kalafatis, J. Ming-Sung Cheng, and C. Hadjicharalambous, "Impact of Positioning Strategies on Corporate Performance," *Journal of Advertising Research*, 48 (March 2008): 106–122; and D. Florin, B. Callen, Sean Mullen, and J. Kropp, "Profiting from Mega-Trends," *Journal of Product and Brand Management*, 16 (2007): 220–225.
11. Thomas O. Jones and W. Earl Sasser, Jr., "Why Satisfied Customers Defect," *Harvard Business Review* (November–December 1995): 88–99.
12. Ibid.
13. L. Casalo, Carlos Flavian, and Miguel Guinaliu, "Fundaments of Trust Management in the Development of Virtual Communities," *Management Research News*, 31 (2008): 324–338.
14. *Trust in Advertising*: *A Global Nielsen Consumer Report*, October 2008, 1; and www2.acnielsen.com/reports/documents/TrustinAdvertisingOct07.pdf, accessed April 2009.
15. www.marketwire.com/press-release/Truste-930017.html, accessed April 2009.
16. Barry Berman, "How to Delight Your Customers," *California Management Review*, 48 (Fall 2005): 129–151.
17. Frederick F. Reichheld and W. Earl Sasser, Jr., "Zero Defections: Quality Comes to Services," *Harvard Business Review* (September–October 1990): 105–111; Michael Treacy and Fred Wiersema, "Customer Intimacy and Other Value Disciplines," *Harvard Business Review* (January–February 1993): 84–93.
18. Valerie A. Zeithaml, Roland T. Rust, and Katherine N. Lemon, "The Customer Pyramid: Creating and Serving Profitable Customers," *California Management Review* (Summer 2001): 118–142.
19. Glen L. Urban, "Customer Advocacy: A New Era in Marketing?" *Journal of Public Policy and Marketing*, 24 (Spring 2005): 155–159.
20. C. Peters, C. Amato, and C. Hollenbeck, "An Exploratory Investigation of Consumers' Perceptions of Wireless Advertising," *Journal of Advertising*, 26 (Winter 2007): 129–145.
21. Ibid.
22. *Critical Mass: The Worldwide State of Mobile Web*, Nielsen Mobile, July 2008, 3, Copyright © 2008 The Nielsen Company. All rights reserved, accessed at www.nielsenmobile.com/documents/criticalmas.pdf.
23. See for example, Dave Flessner, "Chattanooga: Sign of the Hard Times," *McClatchy-Tribune Business News*, Washington, D.C., October 26, 2008.

Chapter 2

1. "Nielson to Track TV Viewing on Mobile Phones," *FinancialWire*, June 14, 2006, 1.
2. Jon Gertner, "Our Rating, Ourselves," www.nytimes.com, April 10, 2005.
3. See Ernest Dichter, "Whose Lifestyle Is It Anyway? *Psychology and Marketing* (1986): 3; Ernest Dichter, *Handbook of Consumer Motivation* (New York: McGraw-Hill, 1964); and Emanuel H. Demby, "A Remembrance of Ernest Dichter," *Marketing News* 6 (January 6, 1992): 21. Also, see Michelle R. Nelson, "The Hidden Persuaders: Then and Now," *Journal of Advertising*, 37 (Spring 2008): 113–126.
4. Stan Maklan, Simon Knox, and Lynette Ryals, "New Trends in Innovation and Customer Relationship Management: A Challenge for Market Researchers," *International Journal of Market Research*, 50 (2008): 221–238.
5. Gerald Zaltman and Robin Higie Coulter, "See the Voice of the Consumer: Metaphor-Based Advertising Research," *Journal of Advertising Research* (July–August 1995): 35–51; Robin A. Coulter, Gerald Zaltman, and Keith S. Coulter, "Interpreting Consumer Perceptions of Advertising: An Application of the Zaltman Metaphor Elicitation Technique," *Journal of Advertising* (Winter 2001): 1–21; and Jim Edwards, "Victory Dance for the Vain: A Reporter Goes 'Under,'" *Brandweek*, October 3, 2005, 23.
6. Robert Kozinets, "'I Want To Believe': A Netnography of The X-Files' Subculture of Consumption," in *Advances in Consumer Research*, ed. M. Brucks and D. J. MacInnis (Provo, UT: Association for Consumer Research, 1997), 24, 470–475; Robert Kozinets, "The Field Behind the Screen: Using Netnography for Marketing Research in Online Communities," *Journal of Marketing Research,* 39 (February 2002): 61–72; D. Pitta and D. Fowler, "Online Consumer Communities and Their Value to New Product Development," *Journal of Product and Brand Management*, 14 (2007): 283–291; A. Puri, "The Web of Insights: The Art and Practice of Webnography," *International Journal of Marketing Research*, 49 (2007): 386–408; S. Pace "YouTube: An Opportunity for Consumer Narrative Analysis," *Qualitative*

Market Research: An International Journal, 11 (2008): 213–226; G. Urban and J. Hauser, "Listening In to Find and Explore New Combinations of Customer Needs," *Journal of Marketing*, 68 (April 2004): 72–87; B. Borrossey, "Blogs Growing into the Ultimate Focus Group," *Adweek*, June 20, 2005, 12.

7. Leon Schiffman, Elaine Sherman, and D. Y. Cohn, "Looking In on Global Consumer Users: To Develop Better Product Feature Sets," *2008 Global Business and Technology Association (GBATA) International Conference*, Taipei, Taiwan, 2008.
8. Nick Lee and Amanda J. Broderick, "The Past, Present and Future of Observational Research in Marketing," *Qualitative Market Research: An International Journal,* 10 (2007): 121–129.
9. Leslie Kaufman, "Enough Talk," *Newsweek*, August 19, 1997, 48–49.
10. Emily Nelson, "P&G Checks Out Real Life," *Wall Street Journal* (Eastern Edition), May 17, 2001, B1.
11. Ian Mount, "The Mystery of Duane Reade," *New York Magazine*, June 6, 2005, 28–31.
12. Kim S. Nash, "Casinos Hit Jackpot with Customer Data," *Computer World*, July 2, 2001, 16–17; and *Modern Marvels: Casino Technology*, VHS Tape, 1999, A&E Television Networks.
13. Alex Salkever, "The Technology of Personalized Pitches," *Business Week Online*, June 22, 2004.
14. Constance L. Hays, "What Wal-Mart Knows About Customers' Habits," www.nytimes.com, November 14, 2004.
15. Melanie Wells, "In Search of the Buy Button," *Forbes*, September 1, 2003, 62.
16. Brian D. Till and Michael Busler, "The Match-Up Hypothesis: Physical Attractiveness, Expertise, and the Role of Fit on Brand Attitude, Purchase Intent and Brand Beliefs," *Journal of Advertising* (Fall 2000): 1–13.
17. Yoram Wind, "Marketing by Experiment," *Marketing Research* (Spring 2007): 10–16.
18. See the following for additional viewpoints: Jenny Clark, Clive Nancarrow, and Lee Higgins, "Using Consumer Panel Participants to Generate Creative New Product Ideas," *Journal of American Academy of Business* 12 (September 2007): 139–144.
19. Nina Michaelidou and Sally Dibb, "Using Email Questionnaires for Research: Good Practice in Tackling Non-Response," *Journal of Targeting, Measurement and Analysis for Marketing*, 14 (July 2006): 289–296.
20. Thomas O. Jones and W. Earl Sasser, Jr., "Why Satisfied Customers Defect," *Harvard Business Review* (November–December 1995): 88–99.
21. A. Parasuraman, Valarie A. Zeithaml, and Leonard L. Berry, *Moving Forward in Service Quality Research: Measuring Different Customer-Expectation Levels, Comparing Alternative Scales, and Examining the Performance-Behavioral Intentions Link*, Report No. 94-114, (Cambridge, MA: Marketing Science Institute, 1994).
22. Michael M. Pearson and Guy H. Gessner, "Transactional Segmentation to Slow Customer Defections," *Marketing Management* (Summer 1999): 16–23.
23. Stuart Elliott, "Nielsen Presents a Research Plan to Quell Concerns About Accuracy," www.nytimes.com, February 22, 2005; and Stuart Elliott, "Nielsen Will Address Potential Undercounting of Minority TV Viewers," www.nytimes.com, March 24, 2005.

Chapter 3

1. Stuart Elliott, "It's in the Bag—the Tea Bag, That Is," www.nytimes.com, October 13, 2008.
2. http://hiltonworldwide1.hilton.com, accessed October 20, 2008.
3. Michael Tonello, *Bringing Home the Birkin*, (New York: William Morrow, 2008).
4. Joseph Wisenblit, "Segmentation: From Traditional Bases to Behavioral and Micro-Targeting," Working Paper (June 2008), Stillman School of Business, Seton Hall University, South Orange, New Jersey.
5. www.mriplus.com, accessed October 24, 2008.
6. William E. Hauck and Nancy Stanforth, "Cohort Perception of Luxury Goods and Services," *Journal of Fashion Marketing and Management,* 11 no. 2 (2007): 175–188.
7. Gianfranco Walsh and Vincent-Wayne Mitchell, "Demographic Characteristics of Consumers Who Find It Difficult to Decide," *Marketing Intelligence & Planning,* 23 nos. 2/3 (2005): 281–295.
8. Dick Chay, "New Segments of Boomers Reveal New Marketing Implications," *Marketing News*, March 15, 2005, 24.
9. Anil Mathur, Lee Euehun, and George P. Moschis, "Life-Changing Events and Marketing Opportunities," *Journal of Targeting, Measurement and Analysis for Marketing,* 14, no. 2 (January 2006): 115–128.
10. Stowe Shoemaker and Dina Marie V. Zemke, "The 'Locals' Market: An Emerging Gaming Segment," *Journal of Gambling Studies,* 21, no. 4 (Winter 2005): 379–407.
11. Allen Salkin, "Before It Disappears," www.nytimes.com, December 16, 2007.
12. Stuart Elliott, "Loved the Ads? Now Pour the Drink," www.nytimes.com, August 27, 2008.
13. www.claritas.com, accessed October 23, 2008.
14. Ibid.
15. Stuart J. Barnes, "Segmenting Cyberspace: A Customer Typology for the Internet," *European Journal of Marketing*, 41, nos. 1/2 (2007): 71–93.
16. Christopher D. Hopkins, Catherine A. Roster, and Charles M. Wood, "Making the Transition to Retirement: Appraisals, Post-Transition Lifestyle, and Changes in Consumption Patterns," *Journal of Consumer Marketing,* 23 no. 2 (2006): 89–101.
17. Walsh and Mitchell, "Demographic Characteristics of Consumers."
18. Jaime R. S. Fonseca and Margarida G. M. S. Cardoso, "Supermarket Customers Segments Stability," *Journal of Targeting, Measurement and Analysis for Marketing,* 15 no. 4 (2007): 210–221.
19. Eun-Ju Lee, Kyoung-Nan Kwon, and David W. Schumann, "Segmenting the Non-adopter Category in the Diffusion of Internet Banking," *International Journal of Bank Marketing,* 23 no. 5 (2005): 414–437.
20. Carmen Rodriguez Santos, Miguel Cervantes Blanco, and Ana Gonzalez Fernandez, "Segmenting Wine Consumers According to Their Involvement with Appellations of Origin," *Brand Management,* 13 nos. 4/5 (April–June 2006): 300–312.
21. "New Study Reveals Newsstand Magazine Buyers to Be More Active Consumers and More Receptive to Advertising," *Business Wire*, September 8, 2004, 1.
22. Ulrich R. Orth, Mina McDaniel, Tom Shellhammer, and Kannapon Lopetcharat, "Promoting Brand Benefits: The Role of Consumer Psychographics and Lifestyle," *Journal of Consumer Marketing*, 21 nos. 2/3 (2004): 97–108.
23. Paul G. Patterson, "Demographic Correlates of Loyalty in a Service Context," *Journal of Services Marketing,* 21 no. 2 (2007): 112–121.
24. Rodoula Tsiotsou, "An Empirically Based Typology of Intercollegiate Athletic Donors: High and Low Motivation Scenarios," *Journal of Targeting, Measurement and Analysis for Marketing,* 15 no. 2 (2007): 79–92.
25. Wanjohi Kibicho, "Tourists to Amboseli National Park: A Factor-Cluster Segmentation Analysis," *Journal of Vacation Management,* 12 no. 3 (2006): 218–231.
26. Carlos Flavian and Raquel Gurrea, "The Role of Readers' Motivations in the Choice of Digital Versus Traditional Newspapers," *Journal of Targeting, Measurement and Analysis for Marketing,* 14 no. 4 (2006): 325–335.
27. Brian T. Ratchford, Debabrata Talukdar, and Myung-Soo Lee, "The Impact of the Internet on Consumers' Use of Information Sources for Automobiles: A Re-Inquiry," *Journal of Consumer Research*, 34 (June 2007): 111–119.

28. Gillian Sullivan Mort and Judy Drennan, "Marketing M-services: Establishing a Usage Benefit Typology Related to Mobile User Characteristics," *Database Marketing & Customer Strategy Management,* 12 no. 4 (2005): 327–341.
29. Rodolfo Vazquez Casielles and Begona Alvarez Alvarez, "Consumers' Characteristics and Brand Choice Behavior: Loyalty and Consumption," *Journal of Targeting, Measurement and Analysis for Marketing,* 15, no. 2 (2007): 121–133.
30. Bertil Hulten, "Customer Segmentation: The Concepts of Trust, Commitment and Relationship," *Journal of Targeting, Measurement and Analysis for Marketing,* 15, no. 4 (2007): 256–269.
31. John Story and Jeff Hess, "Segmenting Customer-Brand Relationships: Beyond the Personal Relationship Metaphor," *Journal of Consumer Marketing,* 23, no. 7 (2006): 406–413.
32. David Martin-Consuegra, Arturo Molina, and Agueda Esteban, "The Customers' Perspective on Relational Benefits in Banking Activities," *Journal of Financial Services Marketing,* 10, no. 4 (2006): 98–108.
33. Pradnya Joshi, "Aiming Online Ads More Selectively," and Stuart Elliott, "1,200 Marketers Can't Be Wrong: The Future Is in Consumer Behavior," www.nytimes.com, October 15, 2007.
34. Steve Lohr, "Clip and Save Holds Its Own Against Point and Click," www.nytimes.com, August 30, 2006.
35. Louise Story, "F.T.C. Takes a Look at Web Marketing," www.nytimes.com, February 2, 2007.
36. Acxiom, "Building Blocks for Segmentation: Advancements in Market Segmentation," White Paper (2007); and Acxiom, *Life Stage Segmentation System, Personicx*, 2007.
37. Acxiom, *Personicx Hispanic, Household-Level Market Segmentation*, 2007; and Acxiom In-depth, *Breakthrough Merchandising for the Growing U.S. Hispanic Community*, 2007.
38. *The Persuaders* (a PBS broadcast), www.pbs.org/wgbh/pages/frontline/shows/persuaders, accessed October 30, 2008; and Katharine Q. Seelye, "How to Sell a Candidate to a Porsche-Driving Leno-Loving Nascar Fan," www.nytimes.com, December 6, 2004.
39. Kim Severson, "What's for Dinner? The Pollster Wants to Know," www.nytimes.com, April 16, 2008.

Chapter 4

1. Andrew Tobias, *Fire and Ice* (New York: William Morrow and Company, 1976), Chapter 8.
2. Ibid.
3. www.pg.com, www.logitech.com, http://corporate.ritzcarlton.com, accessed October 1, 2008.
4. Thomas Kramer and Song-On Yoon, "Approach-Avoidance Motivation and the Use of Affect as Information," *Journal of Consumer Psychology*, 17, no. 2 (2007): 128–138.
5. Alexander Chernev, "Goal Orientation and Consumer Preference for the Status Quo," *Journal of Consumer Research* (December 2004): 557–565.
6. Ravindra Chitturi, Rajagopal Raghunathan, and Vijay Mahajan, "Delight by Design: The Role of Hedonic Versus Utilitarian Benefits," *Journal of Marketing* (May 2008): 48–63.
7. James A. Roberts and Stephen F. Pirog, III, "Personal Goals and Their Role in Consumer Behavior: The Case of Compulsive Buying," *Journal of Marketing Theory and Practice* (Summer 2004): 61–73.
8. Anirban Mukhopadhyay and Gita Venkataramani Johar, "Tempted or Not? The Effect of Recent Purchase History on Responses to Affective Advertising," *Journal of Consumer Research* (March 2007): 445–453.
9. Sharon Morrison and Frederick G. Crane, "Building the Service Brand by Creating and Managing an Emotional Brand Experience," *Journal of Brand Management,* 14 (2007): 410–421.
10. Alina Tugend, "'Two for One' . . . 'Free Delivery' . . . Hooked Yet?" *New York Times*, July 5, 2008, C5.
11. Alina Tugend, "Some Blissful Ignorance Can Cure Chronic Buyer's Remorse," *New York Times*, March 15, 2008, C5.
12. See Abraham H. Maslow, "A Theory of Human Motivation," *Psychological Review,* 50 (1943): 370–396; Abraham H. Maslow, *Motivation and Personality* (New York: Harper & Row, 1954); and Abraham H. Maslow, *Toward a Psychology of Being* (New York: Van Nostrand Reinhold, 1968), 189–215.
13. A number of studies have focused on human levels of aspiration. See, for example, Kurt Lewin et al., "Level of Aspiration," in *Personality and Behavior Disorders*, ed. J. McV. Hunt (New York: Ronald Press, 1944); Howard Garland, "Goal Levels and Task Performance, a Compelling Replication of Some Compelling Results," *Journal of Applied Psychology,* 67 (1982): 245–248; Edwin A. Locke, Elizabeth Frederick, Cynthia Lee, and Philip Bobko, "Effect of Self Efficacy, Goals and Task Strategies on Task Performance," *Journal of Applied Psychology,* 69, no. 2 (1984): 241–251; Edwin A. Locke, Elizabeth Frederick, Elizabeth Buckner, and Philip Bobko, "Effect of Previously Assigned Goals on Self Set Goals and Performance," *Journal of Applied Psychology,* 72, no. 2 (1987): 204–211; and John R. Hollenbeck and Howard J. Klein, "Goal Commitment and the Goal Setting Process: Problems, Prospects and Proposals for Future Research," *Journal of Applied Psychology,* 2 (1987): 212–220.
14. Maslow 1954, 1968.
15. Ibid.
16. Ibid.

Chapter 5

1. Amanda B. Diekman and Alice H. Eagly, "Stereotypes as Dynamic Constructs: Women and Men of the Past, Present, and Future," *Personality and Social Psychology Bulletin* 26, no. 10 (October 2000): 1171–1188.
2. Ellen Creager, "Do Snack Foods Such as Nuts and Popcorn Affect Romance?" *The Patriot-News*, Harrisburg, PA, February 14, 2001, E11.
3. For example, see Karen Horney, *The Neurotic Personality of Our Time* (New York: Norton, 1937).
4. Joel B. Cohen, "An Interpersonal Orientation to the Study of Consumer Behavior," *Journal of Marketing Research* 6 (August 1967): 270–278; Arch G. Woodside and Ruth Andress, "CAD Eight Years Later," *Journal of the Academy of Marketing Science* 3 (Summer–Fall 1975): 309–313; see also Jon P. Noerager, "An Assessment of CAD: A Personality Instrument Developed Specifically for Marketing Research," *Journal of Marketing Research* 16 (February 1979): 53–59; and Pradeep K. Tyagi, "Validation of the CAD Instrument: A Replication," in *Advances in Consumer Research*, 10, ed. Richard P. Bogazzio and Alice M. Tybout (Ann Arbor, MI: Association for Consumer Research, 1983), 112–114.
5. Morton I. Jaffe, "Brand-Loyalty/Variety-Seeking and the Consumer's Personality: Comparing Children and Young Adults," in *Proceedings of the Society for Consumer Psychology*, ed. Scott B. MacKenzie and Douglas M. Stayman (La Jolla, CA: American Psychological Association, 1995), 144–151.
6. J. P. Guilford, *Personality* (New York: McGraw-Hill, 1959), 6.
7. Brian Wansink and Sea Bum Park, "Accounting for Tastes: Building Consumer Preference Prototypes," *Journal of Database Marketing* 7, no. 4 (2000): 308–320.
8. Jana Bowden and David Corkindale, "Identifying the Initial Target Consumer for Innovations: An Integrative Approach," *Marketing Intelligence & Planning,* 23, no. 6 (2005): 563, 570.
9. Gilles Roehrich, "Consumer Innovativeness: Concepts and Measurements," *Journal of Business Research* 57 (June 2004): 671–677.

10. Tanawat Hirunyawipada and Audhesh K. Paswan, "Consumer Innovativeness and Perceived Risk: Implications for High Technology Product Adoption," *Journal of Consumer Marketing* 23/4 (2006): 197.
11. Alka Varma Citrin, David E. Sprott, Steven N. Silverman, and Donald E. Stem, Jr., "From Internet Use to Internet Adoption: Is General Innovativeness Enough?" in *1999 AMA Winter Educators' Conference*, 10, ed. Anil Menon and Arun Sharma (Chicago: American Marketing Association, 1999), 232–233.
12. Gilles Roehrich, "Consumer Innovativeness," and Angela D'Auria Stanton and Wilbur W. Stanton, "To Click or Not to Click: Personality Characteristics of Internet Versus Non-Internet Purchasers," in *2001 AMA Winter Educators' Conference*, 12, ed. Ram Krishnan and Madhu Viswanathan (Chicago: American Marketing Association, 2001), 161–162.
13. Walfried M. Lassar, Chris Manolis, and Sharon S. Lassar, "The Relationship Between Consumer Innovativeness, Personal Characteristics, and Online Banking Adoption," *International Journal of Bank Marketing,* 23, no. 2 (2005): 190.
14. Isita Lahiri and Amitava Gupta, "Brand Extensions in Consumer Non-durables, Durables and Services: A Comparative Study," *South Asian Journal of Management,* 12, no. 4 (October–December 2005): 34.
15. Byoungho Jin and Yong Gu Suh, "Integrating Effect of Consumer Perception Factors in Predicting Private Brand Purchase in a Korean Discount Store Context," *Journal of Consumer Marketing,* 22, no. 2 (2005): 62.
16. Milton Rokeach, *The Open and Closed Mind* (New York: Basic Books, 1960).
17. Kurt Matzler, Sonja Bidmon, and Sonja Grabner-Kräuter, "Individual Determinants of Brand Affect: The Role of Personality Traits of Extraversion and Openness to Experience," *Journal of Product & Brand Management,* 15, no. 7 (2006): 434.
18. Itamar Simonson and Stephen M. Nowlis, "The Role of Explanations and Need for Uniqueness in Consumer Decision Making: Unconventional Choices Based on Reasons," *Journal of Consumer Research* 27 (June 2000): 49–68.
19. Ann Marie Fiore, Hyun-Jeong Jin, and Jihyun Kim, "For Fun and Profit: Hedonic Value from Image Interactivity and Responses Toward an Online Store," *Psychology & Marketing,* 22, no. 8 (2005): 675.
20. Ann Marie Fiore, Leung-Eun Lee, and Grace Kunz, "Individual Differences, Motivations, and Willingness to Use a Mass Customization Option for Fashion Products," *European Journal of Marketing* 38, no. 7 (2004): 835–849.
21. P. S. Raju, "Optimum Stimulation Level: Its Relationship to Personality, Demographics, and Exploratory Behavior," *Journal of Consumer Research* 7 (December 1980): 272–282; Leigh McAlister and Edgar Pessemier, "Variety Seeking Behavior: An Interdisciplinary Review," *Journal of Consumer Research* 9 (December 1982): 311–322; Jan-Benedict, E. M. Steenkamp, and Hans Baumgartner, "The Role of Optimum Stimulation Level in Exploratory Consumer Behavior," *Journal of Consumer Research* 19 (December 1992): 434; Russell G. Wahlers and Michael J. Etzel, "A Consumer Response to Incongruity Between Optimal Stimulation and Life Style Satisfaction," in *Advances in Consumer Research*, 12, ed. Elizabeth C. Hirschman and Morris B. Holbrook (Provo, UT: Association for Consumer Research, 1985), 97–101; and Jan-Benedict, E. M. Steenkamp, Frenkel ter Hofstede, and Michel Wedel, "A Cross-National Investigation into the Individual and National Cultural Antecedents of Consumer Innovativeness," *Journal of Marketing* 62 (April 1999): 55–69.
22. Linda McNamara and Mary E. Ballard, "Resting Arousal, Sensation Seeking, and Music Preference," *Genetic, Social, and General Psychology Monographs* 125, no. 3 (1999): 229–250.
23. Elizabeth C. Hirschman, "Innovativeness, Novelty Seeking and Consumer Creativity," *Journal of Consumer Research* 7 (1980): 283–295; Wayne Hoyer and Nancy M. Ridgway, "Variety Seeking as an Explanation for Exploratory Purchase Behavior: A Theoretical Model," in *Advances in Consumer Research*, 17, ed. Thomas C. Kinnear (Provo, UT: Association for Consumer Research, 1984), 114–119; and Minakshi Trivedi, "Using Variety-Seeking-Based Segmentation to Study Promotional Response," *Journal of the Academy of Marketing Science* 27 (Winter 1999): 37–49.
24. Harper A. Roehm, Jr. and Michelle L. Roehm, "Variety-Seeking and Time of Day: Why Leader Brands Hope Young Adults Shop in the Afternoon, but Follower Brands Hope for Morning," *Marketing Letters Boston* 15 (January 2005): 213–221.
25. Jinhee Choi, B. Kyu Kim, Incheol Choi, and Youjae Yi, "Variety-Seeking Tendency in Choice for Others: Interpersonal and Intrapersonal Causes," *Journal of Consumer Research,* 32 (March 2006): 590.
26. Caroline Goukens, Siegfried Dewitte, Mario Pandelaere, and Luk Warlop, "Wanting a Bit(e) of Everything: Extending the Valuation Effect to Variety Seeking," *Journal of Consumer Research,* 34 (October 2007): 386–595.
27. Richard Petty et al., "Personality and Ad Effectiveness: Exploring the Utility of Need for Cognition," in *Advances in Consumer Research*, 15, ed. Michael Houston (Ann Arbor, MI: Association for Consumer Research, 1988), 209–212; and Susan Powell Mantel and Frank R. Kardes, "The Role of Direction of Comparison, Attribute-Based Processing, and Attitude-Based Processing in Consumer Preference," *Journal of Consumer Research* 25 (March 1999): 335–352.
28. Arnold B. Bakker, "Persuasive Communication About AIDS Prevention: Need for Cognition Determines the Impact of Message Format," *AIDS Education and Prevention* 11, no. 2 (1999): 150–162.
29. Ayn E. Crowley and Wayne D. Hoyer, "The Relationship Between Need for Cognition and Other Individual Difference Variables: A Two-Dimensional Framework," in *Advances in Consumer Research*, 16, ed. Thomas K. Srull (Provo, UT: Association for Consumer Research, 1989), 37–43; and James W. Peltier and John A. Schibrowsky, "Need for Cognition, Advertisement Viewing Time and Memory for Advertising Stimuli," *Advances in Consumer Research* 21 (1994): 244–250.
30. Chingching Chang, "Diagnostic Advertising Content and Individual Differences," *Journal of Advertising,* 36, no. 3 (Fall 2007): 79.
31. Chien-Huang Lin and Pei-Hsun Wu, "The Effect of Variety on Consumer Preferences: The Role of Need for Cognition and Recommended Alternatives," *Social Behavior and Personality,* 34, no. 7 (2006): 874.
32. Tracy L. Tuten and Michael Bosnjak, "Understanding Differences in Web Usage: The Role of Need for Cognition and the Five Factor Model of Personality," *Social Behavior and Personality,* 29, no. 4 (2001): 391–398.
33. Dahui Li and Glenn J. Browne, "The Role of Need for Cognition and Mood in Online Flow Experience," *Journal of Computer Information Systems,* 46, no. 3 (Spring 2006): 15; and Maria Sicilia, Salvador Ruiz, and Jose L. Munuera, "Effects of Interactivity in a Web Site," *Journal of Advertising,* 34, no. 3 (Fall 2005): 40.
34. Maria Kozhevnikov, Stephen Kosslyn, and Jeffifer Shepard, "Spatial Versus Object Visualizers: A New Characterization of Visual Cognitive Style," *Memory and Cognition,* 33, no. 4 (2005): 710, 722.
35. Russell W. Belk, "Three Scales to Measure Constructs Related to Materialism" and "Materialism: Trait Aspects of Living in the Material World," *Journal of Consumer Research,* 12 (December 1985): 265–280.
36. Marsha L. Richins and Scott Dawson, "A Consumer Values Orientation for Materialism and Its Measurement: Scale Development and Validation," *Journal of Consumer Research,* 19 (December 1992): 303–316; and Jeff Tanner and Jim Roberts, "Materialism Cometh," *Baylor Business Review* (Fall 2000): 8–9.

37. James A. Roberts, Chris Manolis, and John F. Tanner, Jr., "Adolescent Autonomy and the Impact of Family Structure on Materialism and Compulsive Buying," *Journal of Marketing Theory and Practice,* 14, no. 4 (Fall 2006): 307.
38. Julie Fitzmaurice and Charles Comegys, "Materialism and Social Consumption," *Journal of Marketing Theory and Practice,* 14, no. 4 (Fall 2006): 295.
39. Scott I. Rick, Cynthia E. Cryder, and George Loewenstein, "Tightwads and Spendthrifts," *Journal of Consumer Research,* 34 (April 2008): 767–782.
40. Reto Felix, Roberto Hernandez, and Wolfgang Hinck, "An Empirical Investigation of Materialism in Mexico," in *2000 AMA Educators' Proceedings*, 11, ed. Gregory T. Gundlach and Patrick E. Murphy (Chicago: American Marketing Association, 2000), 279–286.
41. Alain d'Astous and Jonathan Deschenes, "Consuming in One's Mind: An Exploration," *Psychology and Marketing,* 22, no. 1 (January 2005): 1–30.
42. Ronald J. Faber and Thomas C. O'Guinn, "A Clinical Screener for Compulsive Buying," *Journal of Consumer Research,* 19 (December 1992): 459–469.
43. Kristen Bruinsma and Douglas L. Taren, "Chocolate: Food or Drug?" *Journal of the American Dietetic Association,* 99, no. 10 (October 1999): 1249–1256.
44. Helga Dittmar, "A New Look at 'Compulsive Buying': Self-Discrepancies and Materialistic Values as Predictors of Compulsive Buying Tendency," *Journal of Social and Clinical Psychology,* 24, no. 6 (September 2005): 832–859.
45. Christine Van Dusen, "Hooked on Shopping: Consumption Fuels the Economy—But for Some It Becomes a Debilitating Addition," *Atlanta Journal-Constitution,* February 27, 2005, F1.
46. Dittmar, "A New Look at 'Compulsive Buying'."
47. Ronald J. Faber and Gary A. Christenson, "Can You Buy Happiness?: A Comparison of the Antecedent and Concurrent Moods Associated with the Shopping of Compulsive and Non-Compulsive Buyers," in *1995 Winter Educator's Conference*, 6, ed. David W. Stewart and Naufel J. Vilcassin (Chicago: American Marketing Association, 1995), 378–379.
48. David H. Silvera, Anne M. Lavack, and Fredric Kropp, "Impulse Buying: The Role of Affect, Social Influence, and Subjective Wellbeing," *Journal of Consumer Marketing,* 25, no. 1 (2008): 23–33.
49. Gerard P. Prendergast, Derek T. Y. Poon, Alex S. L. Tsang, and Ting Yan Fan, "Predicting Premium Proneness," *Journal of Advertising Research* (June 2008): 287–296.
50. Terence A. Shimp and Subhash Sharma, "Consumer Ethnocentrism: Construction and Validation of the CETSCALE," *Journal of Marketing Research,* 24 (August 1987): 280–289; and Richard G. Netemeyer, Srinivas Durvaula, and Donald R. Lichtenstein, "A Cross-National Assessment of the Reliability and Validity of the CETSCALE," *Journal of Marketing Research,* 28 (August 1991): 320–327.
51. Kojo Saffu and John Hugh Walker, "An Assessment of the Consumer Ethnocentric Scale (CETSCALE) in an Advanced and Transitional Country: The Case of Canada and Russia," *International Journal of Management,* 22, 4 (December 2005): 556; and Hyokjin Kwak, Anupam Jaju, and Trina Larsen, "Consumer Ethnocentrism Offline and Online: The Mediating Role of Marketing Efforts and Personality Traits in the United States, South Korea, and India," *Academy of Marketing Science Journal,* 34, no. 3 (Summer 2006): 367–385.
52. Jill Gabrielle Klein, Richard Ettenson, and Balaji C. Krishnan, "Extending the Construct of Consumer Ethnocentrism: When Foreign Products Are Preferred," *International Marketing Review,* 23, 3 (2006): 316.
53. Olaf Werder and Marilyn S. Roberts, "Generation Y's Consumer Ethnocentrism: Implications for Advertisers in a Post September 11th World," *American Academy of Advertising Conference Proceedings* (2005): 185; and Gregory S. Black and Leon F. Dube, "Implications of Collective Trauma on Consumer Purchase Attitudes," *Atlantic Economic Journal,* published online December 20, 2006.
54. Osman Mohamad, Zafar U. Ahmed, Earl D. Honeycutt, Jr., and Taizoon Hyder Tyebkhan, "Does 'Made In . . .' Matter to Consumers? A Malaysian Study of Country of Origin Effect," *Multinational Business Review* (Fall 2000): 69–73; and Irvin Clarke, Mahesh N. Shankarmahesh, and John B. Ford, "Consumer Ethnocentrism, Materialism and Values: A Four Country Study," in *2000 AMA Winter Educators' Conference*, 11, ed. John P. Workman and William D. Perreault (Chicago: American Marketing Association, 2000), 102–103.
55. Subhash Sharma, Terence A. Shimp, and Jeongshin Shin, "Consumer Ethnocentrism: A Test of Antecedents and Moderators," *Journal of the Academy of Marketing Science*, 23 (1995): 27.
56. Hamin and Greg Elliott, "A Less-Developed Country Perspective of Consumer Ethnocentrism and 'Country of Origin' Effects: Indonesian Evidence," *Asia Pacific Journal of Marketing and Logistics,* 18, no. 2 (2006): 79–92.
57. George Balabanis and Adamantios Diamantopoulos, "Domestic Country Bias, Country-of-Origin Effects, and Consumer Ethnocentrism: A Multidimensional Unfolding Approach," *Journal of the Academy of Marketing Science,* 32 (Winter 2004): 80–95.
58. Byeong-Joon Moon, "Effects of Consumer Ethnocentrism and Product Knowledge on Consumers' Utilization of Country-of-Origin Information," *Advances in Consumer Research,* 31 (2004): 667–673.
59. Fang Liu, Jamie Murphy, Jianyao Li, and Xiangping Liu, "English and Chinese? The Role of Consumer Ethnocentrism and Country of Origin in Chinese Attitudes Towards Store Signs," *Australasian Marketing Journal,* 14, no. 2 (2006): 5–16.
60. Jufei Kao, "Is It a Foreign Product? A Scale to Classify Products in an Era of Globalization," *Advances in Consumer Research,* 31 (2004): 674–682.
61. Mahesh N. Shankarmahesh, "Consumer Ethnocentrism: An Integrative Review of Its Antecedents and Consequences," *International Marketing Review,* 23, no. 2 (2006): 146–172.
62. Amal R. Karunaratna and Pascale G. Quester, "Influence of Cognition on Product Component Country of Origin evaluation," *Asia Pacific Journal of Marketing,* 19, no. 4 (2007): 349–362.
63. Marylouise Caldwell, Kristen Blackwell, and Kirsty Tulloch, "Cosmopolitanism as a Consumer Orientation," *Qualitative Market Research: An International Journal,* 9, no. 2 (2006): 126–139.
64. Insa Matthiesen and Ian Phau, "The 'Hugo Boss' Connection: Achieving Global Brand Consistency Across Countries," *Journal of Brand Management,* 12, no. 5 (June 2005): 329–330.
65. David Martin, "Branding: Finding That 'One Thing,'" *Brandweek*, February 16, 1998, 18.
66. Lucy Raia, "New Tech for 'Non-Techies': Creating Excitement for a Valuable Tool," *Journal of Digital Asset Management,* 1, no. 2 (2005): 99.
67. Subodh Bhat and Srinivas K. Reddy, "Symbolic and Functional Positioning of Brands," *Journal of Consumer Marketing* 15 (1998): 32–43.
68. Traci L. Haigood, "The Brand Personality Effect: An Empirical Investigation," in *1999 AMA Winter Educators' Conference*, 10, ed. Anil Menon and Arun Sharma (Chicago: American Marketing Association, 1999), 149–150; and Traci L. Haigood, "Deconstructing Brand Personality," in *2001 AMA Educators' Proceedings*, 12, ed. Greg W. Marshall and Stephen J. Grove (Chicago: American Marketing Association, 2001), 327–328.
69. Traci H. Freling and Lukas P. Forbes, "An Empirical Analysis of the Brand Personality Effect," *Journal of Product & Brand*

Management, 14, no. 7 (2005): 409; Zhang Mengxia, "Impact of Brand Personality on PALI: A Comparative Research Between Two Different Brands," *International Management Review,* 3, no. 3 (2007): 44; and Ramesh Kumar, Amit Luthra, and Gaurav Datta, "Linkages Between Brand Personality and Brand Loyalty: A Qualitative Study in an Emerging Market in the Indian Context," *South Asian Journal of Management,* 13, no. 3 (April–June 2006): 20.

70. Clair A. Boudreaux and Stephen E. Palmer, "A Charming Little Cabernet: Effects of Wine Label Design on Purchase Intent and Brand Personality," *International Journal of Wine Business Research,* 19, no. 3 (2007): 170–186.
71. Andrea K. Walker, "Better Diet Soda," *Chicago Tribune,* August 1, 2005: 1.
72. Shintaro Okazaki, "Excitement or Sophistication? A Preliminary Exploration of Online Brand Personality," *International Marketing Review,* 23, no. 3 (2006): 279–303.
73. Eric G. Harris and David E. Fleming, "Assessing the Human Element in Service Personality Formation: Personality Congruency and the Five Factor Model," *Journal of Services Marketing,* 19, no. 4 (2005): 187–198.
74. Pankaj Aggarwal and Ann L. McGill, "Is That Car Smiling at Me? Schema Congruity as a Basis for Evaluating Anthropomorphized Products," *Journal of Consumer Research,* 34 (December 2007): 468–479.
75. Tim Triplett, "When Tracy Speaks, Celestial Listens," *Marketing News*, October 24, 1994, 14.
76. David M. Morawski and Lacey J. Zachary, "Making Mr. Coffee," *Quirk's Marketing Research Review* 6 (March 1992): 6–7, 29–33.
77. Jennifer L. Aaker, "Dimension of Brand Personality," *Journal of Marketing Research*, 35 (August 1997): 351–352.
78. Pankaj Aggarwal, "The Effects of Brand Relationship Norms on Consumer Attitudes and Behavior," *Journal of Consumer Research* 31 (June 2004): 87–101.
79. Laura M. Milner and Dale Fodness, "Product Gender Perception: The Case of China," in *1995 Winter Educators' Conference*, 6, ed. David W. Stewart and Naufel J. Vilcassin (Chicago: American Marketing Association, 1995), 331–336.
80. Scarlett C. Wesley, Deborah C. Fowler, and Maria Elena Vazquez, "Retail Personality and the Hispanic Consumer: An Exploration of American Retailers," *Managing Service Quality,*
81. K. Damon Aiken, Eric C. Koch, and Robert Mandrigal, "What's in a Name? Explorations in Geographic Equity and Geographic Personality," in *2000 AMA Winter Educators' Conference*, 11, ed. John P. Workman and William D. Perreault (Chicago: American Marketing Association, 2000), 301–308.
82. Max Blackston, "Observations: Building Brand Equity by Managing the Brand's Relationships," *Journal of Advertising Research* (November/December 2000): 101–105.
83. Elizabeth Jensen, "Blue Bottles, Gimmicky Labels Sell Wine," *Wall Street Journal*, July 7, 1997, B1.
84. Pamela S. Schindler, "Color and Contrast in Magazine Advertising," *Psychology & Marketing,* 3 (1986): 69–78.
85. Stephanie Thompson, "LifeSavers Effort Gets Personality," *Advertising Age*, January 21, 2002, 42. Also see Lawrence L. Garber, Jr., Eva M. Hyatt, and Richard G. Starr, Jr., "The Effects of Food Color on Perceived Flavor," *Journal of Marketing Theory and Practice* (Fall 2000): 59–72.
86. Becky Ebenkamp (ed.), "Living in Color," *Brandweek*, April 4, 2005, 22–24.
87. P. C. M. Govers and J. P. L. Schoormans, "Product Personality and Its Influence on Consumer Preference," *Journal of Consumer Marketing,* 22, no. 4 (2005): 189–197; and Kiran Karande, George M. Zinkhan, and Alyssa Baird Lum, "Brand Personality and Self Concept: A Replication and Extension," *AMA Summer 1997 Conference*, 165–171.
88. Hazel Markus and Paula Nurius, "Possible Selves," *American Psychologist* (1986): 954–969.
89. Lan Nguyen Chaplin and Deborah Roedder John, "The Development of Self-Brand Conncetions in Children and Adolescents," *Journal of Consumer Research,* 32 (June 2005): 127.
90. For a detailed discussion of self-images and congruence, see M. Joseph Sirgy, "Self-Concept in Consumer Behavior: A Critical Review," *Journal of Consumer Research,* 9 (December 1992): 287–300; C. B. Claiborne and M. Joseph Sirgy, "Self-Image Congruence as a Model of Consumer Attitude Formation and Behavior: A Conceptual Review and Guide for Future Research," in *Developments in Marketing Science*, 13, ed. B. J. Dunlap (Cullowhee, NC: Academy of Marketing Science, 1990), 1–7; and J. S. Johar and M. Joseph Sirgy, "Value-Expressive Versus Utilitarian Advertising Appeals: When and Why to Use Which Appeal," *Journal of Advertising,* 20 (September 1991): 23–33.
91. Govers and Schoormans, "Product Personality and Its Influence on Consumer Preference," 189.
92. "Sex Appeal," *Brandweek*, April 20, 1998, 26.
93. Susan Fournier, "Consumers and Their Brands: Developing Relationship Theory in Consumer Research," *Journal of Consumer Research,* 24 (March 1998); and Kimberly J. Dodson, "Peak Experiences and Mountain Biking: Incorporating the Bike in the Extended Self," in *Advances in Consumer Research*, 23, ed. Kim P. Cofman and John G. Lynch, Jr. (Provo, UT: Association for Consumer Research 1996), 317–322.
94. Abhilasha Mehta, "Using Self-Concept to Assess Advertising Effectiveness," *Journal of Advertising Research* (February 1999): 81–89.
95. Marlene M. Moretti and E. Tory Higgens, "Internal Representations of Others in Self-Regulation: A New Look at a Classic Issue," *Social Cognition,* 17, no. 2 (1999): 186–208.
96. Robert Underwood, Edward Bond, and Robert Baer, "Building Service Brands via Social Identity: Lessons from the Sports Marketplace," *Journal of Marketing Theory and Practice* (Winter 2001): 1–13.
97. Russell W. Belk, "Possessions and the Extended Self," *Journal of Consumer Research,* 15 (September 1988): 139–168; and Amy J. Morgan, "The Evolving Self in Consumer Behavior: Exploring Possible Selves," in *Advances in Consumer Research*, 20, ed. Leigh McAlister and Michael L. Rothschild (Provo, UT: Association for Consumer Research, 1992), 429–432.
98. Richard G. Netemeyer, Scot Burton, and Donald R. Lichtenstein, "Trait Aspects of Vanity: Measurement and Relevance to Consumer Behavior," *Journal of Consumer Research,* 21 (March 1995): 613.
99. Jennifer L. Aaker, "The Malleable Self: The Role of Self-Expression in Persuasion," *Journal of Marketing Research,* XXXVI (February 1999): 45–57.

Chapter 6

1. Daniel Milotic, "The Impact of Fragrance on Consumer Choice," *Journal of Consumer Behaviour* (December 2003): 179; Lawrence K. Altman, "Unraveling Enigma of Smell Wins Nobel for 2 Americans," *New York Times*, December 5, 2004, A18.
2. Joann Peck and Jennifer Wiggins, "It Just Feels Good: Customers' Affective Response to Touch and Its Influence on Persuasion," *Journal of Marketing*, 70 (October 2006): 59–69.
3. M.P. Dunleavey, "The Price Is the Same; It's the Size That Shrinks," www.nytimes.com August 9, 2008.
4. Sheri J. Broyles, "Subliminal Advertising and the Perpetual Popularity of Playing to People's Paranoia," *Journal of Consumer Affairs,* 40, no. 2 (Winter 2006): 392–406.
5. Rob Walker, "Subconscious Warm-Up: Can a Brand Make You Perform Better?" *New York Times Magazine*, October 5, 2008, 22; Grainne M. Fitzsimons, Tanya L. Chartrand, and Gavan J. Fitzsimons, "Automatic Effects of Brand Exposure on Motivated Behavior: How Apple Makes You 'Think Different,'" *Journal of Consumer Research,* 35, no. 1 (June 2008): 21–35.

6. Stephanie Clifford, "Product Placements Acquire a Life of Their Own on Shows," www.nytimes.com, July 14, 2008.
7. Elizabeth Cowley and Chris Barron, "When Product Placement Goes Wrong: The Effects of Program Liking and Placement Prominence," *Journal of Advertising,* 37, no. 1 (Spring 2008): 89–99.
8. Joandrea Hoegg and Joseph W. Alba, "Taste Perception: More Than Meets the Tongue," *Journal of Consumer Research,* 33 (March 2007): 490–498.
9. Linda M. Scott and Patrick Vargas, "Writing with Pictures: Toward a Unifying Theory of Consumer Response to Images," *Journal of Consumer Research,* 34 (October 2007): 341–356.
10. Leonard L. Berry, Edwin F. Lefkowith, and Terry Clark, "In Services, What's in a Name?" *Harvard Business Review* (September–October 1988): 28–30.
11. Aysen Bakir, Jeffrey G. Blodgett, and Gregory M. Rose, "Children's Response to Gender-Role Stereotyped Advertisements," *Journal of Advertising Research,* 48, no. 2 (June 2008): 255–266.
12. Karl Kunkel, "Making Mattresses Tick: Manufacturers Rely on Distinctive Colors and Textures to Create Products That Entice Consumers with a Great First Impression," *HFN: The Weekly Newspaper for the Home Furnishings Network,* December 12, 2005, 33.
13. Joe Sharkey, "Hotels Learn the Importance of Expectations Built into a Brand Name," *New York Times*, June 18, 2002, C12.
14. www.tide.com, accessed October 15, 2008.
15. Charles Blankson and Stavros P. Kalafatis, "Congruence Between Positioning and Brand Advertising," *Journal of Advertising Research* (March 2007): 79–94; Charles Blankson, Stavros P. Kalafatis, Julian Ming-Sung Cheng, and Costas Hadjicharalambous, "Impact of Positioning Strategies on Corporate Image," *Journal of Advertising Research* (March 2008): 106–122.
16. Ulrich R. Orth and Keven Malkewitz, "Holistic Package Designs and Consumer Brand Impressions," *Journal of Marketing* 72 (May 2008): 64–81.
17. Louise Story, "Home Equity Frenzy Was a Bank Ad Come True," www.nytimes.com, August 15, 2008.
18. Joseph Wisenblit, "Positioning New Condominiums in New York City," Working Paper (October 2008), Stillman School of Business, Seton Hall University, South Orange, New Jersey.
19. www.visine.com, accessed October 16, 2008.
20. www.crest.com, accessed October 16, 2008.
21. Jochen Wirtz, Anna S. Mattila, and Rachel L. P. Tan, "The Role of Arousal Congruency in Influencing Consumers' Satisfaction Evaluations and In-Store Behaviors," *International Journal of Service Industry Management,* 18, no. 1 (2007): 6–24.
22. Andreas Herrmann, Lan Xia, Kent B. Monroe, and Frank Huber, "The Influence of Price Fairness on Customer Satisfaction: An Empirical Test in the Context of Automobile Purchases," *Journal of Product and Brand Management,* 16, no. 1 (2007): 49–58.
23. Leonard L. Berry and Yadav S. Manjit, "Capture and Communicate Value in the Pricing of Services," *Sloan Management Review* (Summer 1996): 41–51.
24. Ben Lowe and Frank Alpert, "Measuring Reference Price Perceptions for New Product Categories: Which Measure Is Best?" *Journal of Product and Brand Management,* 16, no. 2 (2007): 132–141.
25. Daniel J. Howard and Roger A. Kerin, "Broadening the Scope of Reference Price Advertising Research: A Field Study of Consumer Shopping Involvement," *Journal of Marketing,* 70 (October 2006): 185–204.
26. Keith S. Coulter and Robin A. Coulter, "Distortion of Price Discount Perceptions: The Right Digit Effect," *Journal of Consumer Research,* 34, (August 2007): 162–173.
27. Sara Campo and Maria J. Yague, "Effects of Price Promotions on the Perceived Price," *International Journal of Service Industry Management,* 18, no. 3 (2007): 269–286.
28. Joan Lindsey-Mullikin, "Beyond Reference Price: Understanding Consumers' Encounters with Unexpected Prices," *Journal of Product and Brand Management,* 12, nos. 2/3 (2003): 140–154.
29. Brian Wansink and SeaBum Park, "At the Movies: How External Cues and Perceived Taste Impact Consumption Volume," *Food Quality and Preference,* 12 (2001): 69–74.
30. Celina Gonzalez Mieres, Ana Maria Diaz Martin, and J. A. T. Gutierrez, "Antecedents of the Difference in Perceived Risk Between Store Brands and National Brands," *European Journal of Marketing,* 40 nos. 1/2 (2006): 61–82.
31. Torben Hansen, "Understanding Consumer Perception of Food Quality: The Cases of Shrimp and Cheeses," *British Food Journal,* 107, no. 7 (2005): 500–525.
32. Ray Johnson and Johan Bruwer, "Regional Brand Image and Perceived Wine Quality: The Consumer Perspective," *International Journal of Wine Business Research,* 19, no. 4 (2007): 276–297.
33. Frank Vigneron and Lester W. Johnson, "Measuring Perceptions of Brand Luxury," *Journal of Brand Management,* 11, no. 6 (July 2004): 484.
34. Jeana H. Frost, Zoe Chance, Michael I. Norton, and Dan Ariely, "People Are Experience Goods: Improving Online Dating with Virtual Dates," *Journal of Interactive Marketing,* 22, no. 1 (Winter 2008): 51–61.
35. The research on expected versus perceived service quality and SERVQUAL appears in: Valarie A. Zeithaml, A. Parasuraman, and Leonard L. Berry, *Delivering Quality Service: Balancing Customer Perceptions and Expectations* (New York: The Free Press, 1990); Valarie A. Zeithaml, Leonard L. Berry, and A. Parasuraman, "The Nature and Determinants of Customer Expectation of Service," *Journal of the Academy of Marketing Science* (Winter 1993): 1–12; A. Parasuraman, Leonard L. Berry, and Valerie A. Zeithaml, "Refinement and Reassessment of the SERVQUAL Scale," *Journal of Retailing,* 67, no. 4 (Winter 1991): 420–450; and A. Parasuraman, Leonard L. Berry, and Valerie A. Zeithaml, "Understanding Customer Expectations of Service," *Sloan Management Review* (Spring 1991): 39–48.
36. Ibid.
37. Ibid.
38. Benedict Carey, "$2.50 Placebo Gives More Relief Than a 10 Cents One," www.nytimes.com, March 5, 2008.
39. Shibin Sheng, Andrew M. Parker, and Kent Nakamoto, "The Effects of Price Discounts and Product Complimentarity on Consumer Evaluations of Bundle Components," *Journal of Marketing Theory and Practice,* 15, no. 1 (Winter 2007): 53–64.
40. Thomas E. DeCarlo, Russell N. Laczniak, Carol M. Motley, and Sridhar Ramaswamy, "Influence of Image and Familiarity on Consumer Response to Negative Word-of-Mouth Communications About Retail Entities," *Journal of Marketing Theory and Practice,* 15, no. 1 (Winter 2007): 41–51.
41. Nat Ives, "Wal-Mart Turns to Ads to Address Its Critics," www .nytimes.com, January 14, 2005; and Stuart Elliott, "Wal-Mart's New Realm: Reality TV," www.nytimes.com, June 3, 2005.
42. Kevin Coupe, "The Halo Effect, Revisited," *Chain Store Age* (February 2006): 36–37.
43. Fang He and Peter P. Mykytyn, "Decision Factors for the Adoption of an Online Payment System by Customers," *International Journal of E-Business Research,* 3, no. 4 (October–December 2007): 1–32.
44. Tibert Verhagen, Sellmar Meents, and Yao-Hua Tan, "Perceived Risk and Trust Associated with Purchasing at Electronic Marketplaces," *European Journal of Information Systems* (2006): 542–555; and Sally Harridge-March, "Can Building of Trust Overcome Consumer Perceived Risk?" *Marketing Intelligence & Planning,* 24, no. 7 (2006): 747–761.

Chapter 7

1. Jeremy Caplan, "Chocolate, Meet Choco-Luxe," *TIME*, November 3, 2008, 69.
2. Tom Meyvis and Chris Janiszewski, "When Are Broader Brands Stronger Brands? An Accessibility Perspective on the Success of Brand Extensions," *Journal of Consumer Research* (September 2004): 346–358.
3. Stuart Elliott, Brainy Brand Names Where They're Least Expected," www.nytimes.com, October 3, 2008.
4. Uri Gneezy, and Aldo Rustichini, "A Fine Is a Price," *Journal of Legal Studies,* XXIX, no. 1, part 1 (2000): 1–18.
5. Gangseog Ryu and Lawrence Feick, "A Penny for Your Thoughts: Referral Reward Programs and Referral Likelihood," *Journal of Marketing,* 71 (January 2007): 84–94.
6. Anne Martensen, "Tweens' Satisfaction and Brand Loyalty in the Mobile Phone Market," *Young Consumers,* 8, no. 2 (2007): 108–116.
7. John Tierney, "How Many Memories Fit in Your Brain?" www.nytimes.com, June 22, 2007.
8. Kathryn A. Braun-LaTour, Michael S. LaTour, and George M. Zinkhan, "Using Childhood Memories to Gain Insight into Brand Meaning," *Journal of Marketing,* 71 (April 2007): 45–60.
9. Rik Pieters and Michel Wedel, "Goal Control of Attention to Advertising: The Yarbus Implication," *Journal of Consumer Research,* 34 (August 2007): 224–233.
10. Hyun Seung Jin, Jaebeom Suh, and Todd Donovan, "Salient Effects of Publicity in Advertised Brand Recall and Recognition: The List-Stretch Paradigm," *Journal of Advertising,* 37, no. 1 (Spring 2008): 45–58.
11. William E. Baker, "Does Brand Imprinting in Memory Increase Brand Information Retention?" *Psychology & Marketing* (December 2003): 1119+.
12. Tina M. Lowery, L. J. Shrum, and Tony M. Dubitsky, "The Relation Between Brand-Name Linguistic Characteristics and Brand-Name Memory," *Journal of Advertising* (Fall 2003): 7–18; and Eric Yorkston and Geeta Menon, "A Sound Idea: Phonetic Effects of Brand Names on Consumer Judgments," *Journal of Consumer Research* (June 2004): 43–52.
13. Sandra Blakeslee, "If Your Brain Has a 'Buy Button,' What Pushes It?" www.nytimes.com, October 19, 2004.
14. Yuval Rottenstreich, Sanjay Sood, and Lyle Brenner, "Feeling and Thinking in Memory Versus Stimulus-Based Choices," *Journal of Consumer Research*, 33 (March 2007): 461–469.
15. Judith Lynne Zaichowsky, "The Personal Involvement Inventory: Reduction, Revision, and Application to Advertising," *Journal of Advertising,* 23, no. 4 (December 1994): 59–70.
16. Sylvia A. Miller, M. Suzanne Clinton, and John P. Camey, "The Relationship of Motivators, Needs, and Involvement Factors to Preferences for Military Recruitment Slogans," *Journal of Advertising Research*, 47, no. 1 (March 2007): 66–78.
17. For example, Jan Meller Jensen and Torben Hansen, "An Empirical Examination of Brand Loyalty," *Journal of Product & Brand Management,* 15, no. 7 (2006): 442–449.
18. Marjolein Moorman, Peter C. Neijens, and Edith G. Smit, "The Effects of Program Involvement on Commercial Exposure and Recall in a Naturalistic Setting," *Journal of Advertising,* 36, no. 1 (Spring 2007): 121–138.
19. Mira Lee and Ronald J. Faber, "Effects of Product Placement in On-Line Games on Brand Memory," *Journal of Advertising,* 36, no. 4 (Winter 2007): 75–91.
20. Martin Holzwarth, Chris Janiszewski, and Marcus M. Neumann, "The Influence of Avatars on Online Consumer Shopping Behavior," *Journal of Marketing,* 70 (October 2006): 19–36.
21. Ivonne M. Torres and Elten Briggs, "Identification Effects on Advertising Response," *Journal of Advertising,* 36, no. 3 (Fall 2007): 97–109.
22. Kawpong Polyorat, Dana L. Alden, and Eugene S. Kim, "Impact of Narrative Versus Factual Print Ad Copy on Product Evaluation: The Mediating Effect of Message Involvement," *Psychology and Marketing,* 24, no. 6 (June 2007): 439–554.
23. Chan-Wook Park and Byeong-Joon Moon, "The Relationship Between Product Involvement and Product Knowledge: Moderating Roles of Product Type and Product Knowledge Type," *Psychology & Marketing* (November 2003): 977+.
24. Betty Edwards, *Drawing on the Right Side of the Brain* (New York: Tarcher/Putnam, 1989).
25. Janet Rae-Dupree, "Let Computers Compute. It's the Age of the Right Brain," www.nytimes.com, April 6, 2008.
26. Herbert E. Krugman, "The Impact of Television Advertising: Learning Without Involvement," *Public Opinion Quarterly,* 29 (Fall 1965): 349–356; "Brain Wave Measures of Media Involvement," *Journal of Advertising Research,* 11 (February 1971): 3–10; and "Memory Without Recall, Exposure Without Perception," *Journal of Advertising Research,* 1 (September 1982): 80–85.
27. George R. Franke, Bruce A. Huhmann, and David L. Mothersbaugh, "Information Content and Consumer Readership of Print Ads: A Comparison of Search and Experience Products," *Academy of Marketing Science Journal* (Winter 2004): 20+.
28. Rebekah Bennett and Sharyn Rundle-Thiele, "A Comparison of Attitudinal Loyalty Measurement Approaches," *Journal of Brand Management* (January 2002): 193–209.
29. Spiros Gounaris and Vlasis Stathakopoulos, "Antecedents and Consequences of Brand Loyalty: An Empirical Study," *Journal of Brand Management* (April 2004): 283–307.
30. Brian Wansink, "Developing a Cost-effective Brand Loyalty Program," *Journal of Advertising Research* (September 2003): 301–307.
31. Mark Colgate, Vicky Thuy-Uyen Tong, Christina Kwal-Choi Lee, and John U. Farley, "Back from the Brink: Why Customers Stay," *Journal of Service Research,* 9, no. 3 (February 2007): 211–228.
32. Ruchan Kayaman and Huseyin Arasli, "Customer Based Brand Equity: Evidence from the Hotel Industry," *Managing Service Quality*, 17, no. 1 (2007): 92–109.
33. Norjaya Mohd Yasin, Mohd Nasser Noor, and Osman Mohamad, "Does Image of Country-of-Origin Matter to Brand Equity?" *Journal of Product & Brand Management,* 16, no. 1 (2007): 38–48.
34. Douglas Quenqua, "A Way to Save and Still Have Crisp Clothes," www.nytimes.com, October 10, 2008.

Chapter 8

1. Naresh K. Malhotra, "Attitude and Affect: New Frontiers of Research in the 21st Century," *Journal of Business Research,* 58 (April 2005): 477–482.
2. See, for example, Gordon R. Foxall, M. Mirella, and Yani-de-Soriano, "Situational Influences on Consumers' Attitudes and Behavior," *Journal of Business Research,* 58 (April 2005): 518–525.
3. Jack Neff, "Suave Strokes," *Advertising Age,* August 20, 2001, 12.
4. Pamela E. Grimm, "A_b Components' Impact on Brand Preference," *Journal of Business Research,* 58 (April 2005): 508–517; and Steven A. Taylor, Gary L. Hunter, and Timothy A. Longfellow, "Testing an Expanded Attitude Model of Goal-Directed Behavior in a Loyalty Context," *Journal of Consumer Satisfaction, Dissatisfaction and Complaining Behavior,* 19 (2006), 18–39.
5. See, for example, Chris T. Allen, Karen A. Machleit, Susan Schultz Kleine, and Arti Sahni Notani, "A Place for Emotion in Attitude Models," *Journal of Business Research,* 58 (April 2005): 494–499.
6. Joel B. Cohen and Charles S. Areni, "Affect and Consumer Behavior," in *Perspectives in Consumer Behavior*, eds. Harold H. Kassarjian and Thomas S. Robertson(Dallas: Scott, Foresman and Company, 1968), 188–240; and Madeline Johnson and George M.

Zinkhan, "Emotional Responses to a Professional Service Encounter," *Journal of Service Marketing,* 5 (Spring 1991): 5–16. Also see John Kim, Jeen-Su Iim, and Mukesh Bhargava, "The Role of Affect in Attitude Formation: A Classical Condition Approach," *Journal of the Academy of Marketing Science,* 26 (1998): 143–152.

7. Pamela Miles Homer, "Relationships Among Ad-Induced Affect, Beliefs, and Attitudes: Another Look," *Journal of Advertising,* 35, no. 1 (Spring 2006): 35–51.
8. Jaideep Sengupta, "Perspectives on Attitude Strength" (a special session summary), in *Advances in Consumer Research,* 25, eds. Joseph W. Alba and J. Wesley Hutchinson (Provo, UT: Association for Consumer Research, 1998), 63–64.
9. Martin Fishbein, "An Investigation of the Relationships Between Beliefs About an Object and the Attitude Toward the Object," *Human Relations,* 16 (1963): 233–240; and Martin Fishbein, "A Behavioral Theory Approach to the Relations Between Beliefs About an Object and the Attitude Toward the Object," in *Readings in Attitude Theory and Measurement*, ed. Martin Fishbein (New York: Wiley, 1967), 389–400.
10. Shou-Shiung Chou, "Effects of Trope Advertisement on Chinese Consumers," *Journal of American Academy of Business,* Cambridge, 9, no. 1 (March 2006): 229–232.
11. Icek Ajzen and Martin Fishbein, *Understanding Attitudes and Predicting Social Behavior* (Upper Saddle River, NJ: Prentice Hall, 1980); and Martin Fishbein and Icek Ajzen, *Belief, Attitude, Intentions, and Behavior* (Reading, MA: Addison-Wesley, 1975), 62–63. Also see Robert E. Burnkrant, H. Rao Unnava, and Thomas J. Page, Jr., "Effects of Experience on Attitude Structure," in *Advances in Consumer Research,* 18, eds. Rebecca H. Holman and Michael R. Solomon (Provo, UT: Association for Consumer Research, 1991), 28–29.
12. Shwu-Ing Wu, "The Relationship Between Consumer Characteristics and Attitude Toward Online Shopping," *Marketing Intelligence and Planning,* 21, no. 1, (2003): 37–44.
13. Anssi Tarkiainen and Sanna Sundqvist, "Subjective Norms, Attitudes and Intentions of Finnish Consumers in Buying Organic Food," *British Food Journal,* 107, nos. 10/11 (2005), 808–822.
14. Terence A. Shimp and Alican Kavas, "The Theory of Reasoned Action Applied to Coupon Usage," *Journal of Consumer Research,* 11 (December 1984): 795–809; Blair H. Sheppard, Jon Hartwick, and Paul R. Warshaw, "The Theory of Reasoned Action: A Meta-Analysis of Past Research with Recommendations for Modifications and Future Research," *Journal of Consumer Research,* 15 (September 1986): 325–343; Sharon E. Beatty and Lynn R. Kahle, "Alternative Hierarchies of the Attitude-Behavior Relationship: The Impact of Brand Commitment and Habit," *Journal of the Academy of Marketing Science,* 16 (Summer 1988): 1–10; Richard P. Bagozzi, Hans Baumgartner, and Youjae Yi, "Coupon Usage and the Theory of Reasoned Action," in *Advances in Consumer Research,* 18, eds. Rebecca H. Holman and Michael R. Solomon (Provo, UT: Association for Consumer Research, 1991), 24–27; Hee Sun Park, "Relationships Among Attitudes and Subjective Norms: Testing the Theory of Reasoned Action Across Cultures," *Communication Studies,* 51, no. 2 (Summer 2000): 162–175; and Hung-Pin Shih, "An Empirical Study on Predicting User Acceptance of e-Shopping on the Web," *Information & Management (Amsterdam),* 41 (January 2004): 351.
15. Chris T. Allen, Karen A. Machleit, Susan Schultz Kleine, and Arti Sahni Notani, "A Place for Emotion in Attitude Models," *Journal of Business Research,* 58 (April 2005): 494–499.
16. Teresa A. Summers, Bonnie D. Belleau, and Yingjiao Xu, "Predicting Purchase Intention of a Controversial Luxury Apparel Product," *Journal of Fashion Marketing and Management,* 10, no. 4 (2006): 405–419.
17. Yingjiao Xu and V. Ann Paulins, "College Students' Attitudes Toward Shopping Online for Apparel Products," *Journal of Fashion Marketing and Management,* 9, no. 4 (2005): 430.
18. Tai-Kuei Yu and Guey-Sen Wu, "Determinants of Internet Shopping Behavior: An Application of Reasoned Behaviour Theory," *International Journal of Management,* 24, no. 4 (December 2007): 757.
19. Rob van Zanten, "Drink Choice: Factors Influencing the Intention to Drink Wine," *International Journal of Wine Marketing,* 17, no. 2 (2005): 49–61.
20. Richard P. Bagozzi and Paul R. Warshaw, "Trying to Consume," *Journal of Consumer Research,* 17 (September 1990): 127–140; Richard P. Bagozzi, Fred D. Davis, and Paul R. Warshaw, "Development and Test of a Theory of Technological Learning and Usage," *Human Relations,* 45, no. 7 (July 1992): 659–686; and Anil Mathur, "From Intentions to Behavior: The Role of Trying and Control," in *1995 AMA Educators' Proceedings*, eds. Barbara B. Stern and George M. Zinkan (Chicago: American Marketing Association, 1995), 374–375.
21. Stephen J. Gould, Franklin S. Houston, and Jonel Mundt, "Failing to Try to Consume: A Reversal of the Usual Consumer Research Perspective," in *Advances in Consumer Research*, eds. Merrie Brucks and Deborah J. MacInnis (Provo, UT: Association for Consumer Research, 1997), 211–216.
22. Rajeev Batra and Michael L. Ray, "Affective Responses Mediating Acceptance of Advertising," *Journal of Consumer Research,* 13 (September 1986): 236–239; Julie A. Edell and Marian Chapman Burke, "The Power of Feelings in Understanding Advertising Effects," *Journal of Consumer Research,* 14 (December 1987): 421–433; and Marian Chapman Burke and Julie A. Edell, "The Impact of Feelings on Ad-Based Affect and Cognition," *Journal of Marketing Research,* 26 (February 1989): 69–83.
23. Durriya Z. Khairullah and Zahid Y. Khairullah, "Relationships Between Acculturation, Attitude Toward the Advertisement, and Purchase Intention of Asian-Indian Immigrants," *International Journal of Commerce and Management,* 9, nos. 3/4 (1999): 46–65.
24. Eunsun Lee, Spencer Tinkham, and Steven M. Edwards, "The Multidimensional Structure of Attitude Toward the Ad: Utilitarian, Hedonic, and Interestingness Dimensions," *American Academy of Advertising, Conference Proceedings* (2005): 58–66.
25. Dan Petrovici and Marin Marinov, "Determinants and Antecedents of General Attitudes Towards Advertising: A Study of Two EU Accession Countries," *European Journal of Marketing,* 3, no. 4 (2007): 307–326.
26. Fred K. Beard, "How Products and Advertising Offend Consumers," *Journal of Advertising Research* (March 2008): 13–21.
27. Alan J. Bush, Rachel Smith, and Craig Martin, "The Influence of Consumer Socialization Variables on Attitude Toward Advertising: A Comparison of African-Americans and Caucasians," *Journal of Advertising,* 28, no. 3 (Fall 1999): 13–24.
28. Subodh Bhat and Srinivas K. Reddy, "Investigating the Dimensions of the Fit Between a Brand and Its Extensions," *1997 AMA Winter Educators' Conference Proceedings,* 8 (Chicago: American Marketing Association, 1997), 186–194.
29. Morris B. Holbrook, David A. Velez, and Gerard J. Tabouret, "Attitude Structure and Search: An Integrative Model of Importance-Directed Information Processing," in *Advances in Consumer Research,* 8, ed. Kent B. Monroe (Ann Arbor, MI: Association for Consumer Research, 1981), 35–41.
30. Richard P. Bagozzi, Hans Baumgartner, and Youjae Yi, "Coupon Usage and the Theory of Reasoned Action," in *Advances in Consumer Research,* 18, eds. Rebecca H. Holman and Michael R. Solomon (Provo, UT: Association for Consumer Research, 1991), 24–27.
31. Haksik Lee, Gilbert D. Harrell, and Cornelia L. Droge, "Product Experiences and Hierarchy of Advertising Effects," in *2000 AMA Winter Educators' Conference,* 11, eds. John P. Workman and William D. Perreault (Chicago: American Marketing Association, 2000), 41–42.

32. James R. Coyle and Esther Thorson, "The Effects of Progressive Levels of Interactivity and Vividness in Web Marketing Sites," *Journal of Advertising,* 30, no. 3 (Fall 2001): 65–77; and Lynn C. Dailey and C. Edward Heath, "Creating the Flow Experience Online: The Role of Web Atmospherics," in *2000 AMA Winter Educators' Conference,* 11, eds. John P. Workman and William D. Perreault (Chicago: American Marketing Association, 2000), 58.
33. Daniel Katz, "The Functional Approach to the Study of Attitudes," *Public Opinion Quarterly,* 24 (Summer 1960): 163–191; Sharon Shavitt, "Products, Personality and Situations in Attitude Functions: Implications for Consumer Behavior," in *Advances in Consumer Research,* 16, ed. Thomas K. Srull (Provo, UT: Association for Consumer Research, 1989), 300–305; and Richard Ennis and Mark P. Zanna, "Attitudes, Advertising, and Automobiles: A Functional Approach," in *Advances in Consumer Research,* 20, eds. Leigh McAlister and Michael L. Rothschild (Provo, UT: Association for Consumer Research, 1992), 662–666.
34. Maria Knight Lapinski and Franklin J. Boster, "Modeling the Ego-Defensive Function of Attitudes," *Communication Monographs,* 68, no. 3 (September 2001): 314–324.
35. Barbara A. Lafferty and Ronald E. Goldsmith, "Cause-Brand Alliances: Does the Cause Help the Brand or Does the Brand Help the Cause?" *Journal of Business Research,* 58 (April 2005): 423–429.
36. Nora J. Rifon, Sejung Marina Choi, Carrie S. Tripble, and Hairong Li, "Congruence Effects in Sponsorship," *Journal of Advertising,* 33 (Spring 2004): 29–42.
37. Geoffrey L. Cohen, Joshua Aronson, and Claude M. Steele, "When Beliefs Yield to Evidence: Reducing Biased Evaluation by Affirming the Self," *Personality and Social Psychology Bulletin,* 26, no. 9 (September 2000): 1151–1164.
38. Richard E. Petty, et al., "Theories of Attitude Change," in *Handbook of Consumer Theory and Research*, eds. Harold Kassarjian and Thomas Robertson (Upper Saddle River, NJ: Prentice Hall, 1991); and Richard E. Petty, John T. Cacioppo, and David Schumann, "Central and Peripheral Routes to Advertising Effectiveness: The Moderating Role of Involvement," *Journal of Consumer Research,* 10 (September 1983): 135–146. Also see Curtis P. Haugtvedt and Alan J. Strathman, "Situational Product Relevance and Attitude Persistence," in *Advances in Consumer Research,* 17, eds. Marvin E. Goldberg, Gerald Gorn, and Richard W. Pollay (Provo, UT: Association for Consumer Research, 1990), 766–769; and Scott B. Mackenzie and Richard A. Spreng, "How Does Motivation Moderate the Impact of Central and Peripheral Processing on Brand Attitudes and Intentions?" *Journal of Consumer Research,* 18 (March 1992): 519–529.
39. Jon D. Morris, ChongMoo Woo, and A. J. Singh, "Elaboration Likelihood Model: A Missing Intrinsic Emotional Implication," *Journal of Targeting, Measurement and Analysis for Marketing,* 14, no. 1 (December 2005): 79–98.
40. Shin-Chieh Chuang and Chia-Ching Tsai, "The Impact of Consumer Product Knowledge on the Effect of Terminology in Advertising," *Journal of the American Academy of Business,* 6 (March 2005): 154–158, and Jaideep Sgupta, Ronald C. Goldstein, and David S. Boninger, "All Cues Are Not Created Equal: Obtaining Attitude Persistence Under Low-Involvement Conditions," *Journal of Consumer Research,* 23 (March 1997): 351–361.
41. Keith S. Coulter and Girish N. Punj, "The Effects of Cognitive Resource Requirements, Availability, and Argument Quality on Brand Attitudes," *Journal of Advertising,* 33 (Winter 2004): 53–64; and Keith S. Coulter, "An Examination of Qualitative vs. Quantitative Elaboration Likelihood Effects," *Psychology & Marketing,* 22, no. 1 (January 2005): 31–49.
42. Lefa Teng, Michel Laroche, and Huihuang Zhu, "The Effects of Multiple-Ads and Multiple-Brands on Consumer Attitude and Purchase Behavior," *Journal of Consumer Marketing,* 24, no. 1 (2007): 27–35.
43. See, for example, David C. Matz and Wendy Wood, "Cognitive Dissonance in Groups," *Journal of Personality and Social Psychology,* 88 (January 2005): 22–37; Jillian C. Sweeney and Tanya Mukhopadhyay, "Cognitive Dissonance After Purchase: A Comparison of Bricks and Mortar and Online Retail Purchase Situations," *American Marketing Association Conference Proceedings: 2004 AMA Winter Educators' Conference, 15* (Chicago: American Marketing Association, 2004), 190–191; Martin O'Neill and Adrian Palmer, "Cognitive Dissonance and the Stability of Service Quality Perceptions," *Journal of Services Marketing,* 18, nos. 6/7 (2004): 433–449; Robert A Wicklund and Jack W. Brehm, "Internalization of Multiple Perspectives or Dissonance Reduction?" *Theory & Psychology (London),* 14 (June 2004): 355–371, and Alex R. Zablah, Danny N. Bellenger, and Westley J. Johnson, "Customer Relationship Management Implementation Gaps," *Journal of Personal Selling & Sales Management,* 24 (Fall 2004): 279–295.
44. Geoffrey N. Soutar and Jillian C. Sweeney, "Are There Cognitive Dissonance Segments?" *Australian Journal of Management,* 28 (December 2003): 227–239.
45. Phil Lampert, "Cognitive Dissonance," *Progressive Grocer,* 83 (May 15, 2004): 16.
46. Mohammed M. Nadeem, "Post-Purchase Dissonance: The Wisdom of the 'Repeat' Purchases," *Journal of Global Business Issues,* 1, no. 2 (Summer 2007): 183–193.
47. Steve Herman, "Chemical Reaction: Cognitive Dissonance," *Global Chemical Industry,* 174, no. 1 (January 2006): 58.
48. Stuart Hogue, "Making Designs Dissonant," *Design Management Review,* 16, no. 4 (Fall 2005): 34–36.
49. Edward E. Jones, et al., *Attribution: Perceiving the Causes of Behavior* (Morristown, NJ: General Learning Press, 1972); and Bernard Weiner, "Attributional Thoughts About Consumer Behavior," *Journal of Consumer Research,* 27, no. 3 (December 2000): 382–387.
50. Rifon et al., "Congruence Effects in Sponsorship," 29; and Andrea C. Morales, "Giving Firms an 'E' for Effort: Consumer Responses to High-Effort Firms," *Journal of Consumer Research,* 3 (March 2005): 806–812.
51. Chris T. Allen and William R. Dillon, "Self-Perception Development and Consumer Choice Criteria: Is There a Linkage?" in *Advances in Consumer Research,* 10, eds. Richard P. Bagozzi and Alice M. Tybout (Ann Arbor, MI: Association for Consumer Research, 1983), 45–50.
52. S. Christian Wheeler, Richard E. Petty, and George Y. Bizer, "Self-Schema Matching and Attitude Change: Situational and Dispositional Determinants of Message Elaboration," *Journal of Consumer Research,* 31 (March 2005): 787–797.
53. See, for example, Leslie Lazar Kanuk, *Mail Questionnaire Response Behavior as a Function of Motivational Treatment* (New York: CUNY, 1974).
54. Angelos Rodafinos, Arso Vucevic, and Georgios D. Sideridis, "The Effectiveness of Compliance Techniques: Foot in the Door Versus Door in the Face," *Journal of Social Psychology,* 145 (April 2005): 237–239.
55. John R. O'Malley, Jr., "Consumer Attributions of Product Failures to Channel Members," in *Advances in Consumer Research,* 23, eds. Kim P. Corfman and John F. Lynch, Jr. (Provo, UT: Association for Consumer Research, 1996), 342–345. Also see Charmine Hartel, Janet R. Mccoll-Kennedy, and Lyn McDonald, "Incorporating Attributional Theory and the Theory of Reasoned Action Within an Affective Events Theory Framework to Produce a Contingency Predictive Model of Consumer Reactions to Organizational Mishaps," in *Advances in Consumer Research,* 25, eds. Joseph W. Alba and J. Wesley Hutchinson (Provo, UT: Association for Consumer Research, 1998), 428–432.
56. Valerie S. Folkes, "Consumer Reactions to Product Failure: Attributional Approach," *Journal of Consumer Research,* 10 (March 1984): 398–409; and "Recent Attribution Research in

Consumer Behavior: A Review and New Dimensions," *Journal of Consumer Research,* 14 (March 1988): 548–565.

57. Harold H. Kelley, "Attribution Theory in Social Psychology," in *Nebraska Symposium on Motivation*, 15, ed. David Levine (Lincoln: University of Nebraska Press, 1967), 197.

Chapter 9

1. Marina Krakovsky, "Less Wash, More Dry," *Scientific American*, November 2008, 28–29.
2. Jonathan Dee, "The Tell-All Campus Tour," www.nytimes.com, September 21, 2008.
3. Ruth La Ferla, "Even in Recession, Spend They Must: Luxury Shoppers Anonymous," www.nytimes.com, December 11, 2008.
4. Jo Brown, Amanda J. Broderick, and Nick Lee, "Word of Mouth Communication Within Online Communities: Conceptualizing the Online Social Network," *Journal of Interactive Marketing,* 21, no. 3 (Summer 2007): 2–20.
5. Shahana Sen and Dawn Lerman, "Why Are You Telling Me This? An Examination into Negative Consumer Reviews on the Web," *Journal of Interactive Marketing,* 21, no. 4 (Autumn 2007): 76–94.
6. Ted Smith, James R. Coyle, Elizabeth Lightfoot, and Amy Scott, "Reconsidering Models of Influence: The Relationship Between Consumer Social Networks and Word-of-Mouth Effectiveness," *Journal of Advertising Research*, 47, no. 4 (December 2007): 387–397.
7. David Kirkpatrick and Daniel Roth, "Why There's No Escaping the BLOG," *Fortune,* January 10, 2005, 44–50.
8. Stephanie Clifford, "Spreading the Word (and the Lotion) in Small-Town Alaska," www.nytimes.com, October 9, 2008.
9. Yong Liu, "Word of Mouth for Movies: Its Dynamics and Impact on Box Office Revenue," *Journal of Marketing,* 70 (July 2006): 74–89.
10. Rob Walker, "The Hidden (in Plain Sight) Persuaders," www .nytimes.com, December 5, 2004.
11. Eric Pfanner, "Taxi Drivers in London Take a Turn as Pitchmen," www.nytimes.com, January 21, 2008.
12. Stuart Elliott, "Laugh at the Web Clips, Then Buy the Gel," www .nytimes.com, December 19, 2007.
13. Louise Story, "Facebook Is Marketing Your Brand Preferences (with Your Permission)," www.nytimes.com, November 7, 2007.
14. Joseph E. Phelps, Regina Lewis, Lynne Mobilio, David Perry, and Niranjan Raman, "Viral Marketing or Electronic Word-of-Mouth Advertising: Examining Consumer Responses and Motivations to Pass Along Email," *Journal of Advertising Research* (December 2004): 333–348.
15. Kirthi Kalyanam, Shelby McIntyre, and Todd Masonis, "Adaptive Experimentation in Interactive Marketing: The Case of Viral Marketing at Plaxo," *Journal of Interactive Marketing,* 21, no. 3 (Summer 2007): 72–85.
16. Nat Ives, "Marketing's Flip Side: The 'Determined Detractor'," *New York Times,* December 27, 2004, C1.
17. Thorsten Hennig-Thurau, Kevin P. Gwinner, Gianfranco Walsh, and Dwayne D. Gremler, "Electronic Word-of-Mouth Via Consumer-Opinion Platforms: What Motivates Consumers to Articulate Themselves on the Internet?" *Journal of Interactive Marketing* (Winter 2004): 38–52.
18. Hyun Seung Jin, "Compounding Consumer Interest: Effects of Advertising Campaign Publicity on the Ability to Recall Subsequent Advertisements," *Journal of Advertising* (Winter 2003/2004): 29–42.
19. Julie Creswell, "Nothing Sells Like Celebrity," www.nytimes.com, June 22, 2008.
20. Brian T. Till, Sarah M. Stanley, and Randi Priluck, "Classical Conditioning and Celebrity Endorsers: An Examination of Belongingness and Resistance to Extinction," *Psychology and Marketing* (February 2008): xx.
21. B. Zafer Erdogan, Michael J. Baker, and Stephen Tagg, "Selecting Celebrity Endorsers: The Practitioner's Perspective," *Journal of Advertising Research* (May/June 2001): 39–48.
22. Thomas J. Robinson and Barbara K. Kaye, "Using Is Believing: The Influence of Reliance on the Credibility of Online Political Information Among Politically Interested Internet Users," *Journalism and Mass Communication Quarterly* (Winter 2000): 865–879.
23. Sung Tae Kim, David Weaver, and Lars Willnat, "Media Reporting and Perceived Credibility of Online Polls," *Journalism and Mass Communication Quarterly* (Winter 2000): 846–864.
24. Mineabere Ibelema and Lary Powell, "Cable Television News Viewed as Most Credible," *Newspaper Research Journal* (Winter 2001): 41–51.
25. Patrick D. Healy, "Believe It: The Media's Credibility Headache Gets Worse," www.nytimes.com, May 22, 2005.
26. Carl I. Hovland, Arthur A. Lumsdaine, and Fred D. Sheffield, *Experiments on Mass Communication* (New York: Wiley, 1949): 182–200; and Sam Wang and Sandra Aamodt, "Your Brain Lies to You, www.nytimes.com, June 27, 2008.
27. Frédéric F. Brunel and Michelle R. Nelson, "Explaining Gender Responses to 'Help-Self' and 'Help-Others' Charity Ads Appeals: The Mediating Role of World-Views," *Journal of Advertising* (Fall 2000): 15–27.
28. Kawpong Polyorat and Dana L Alden, "Self-Construal and Need-for-Cognition Effects on Brand Attitudes and Purchase Intentions in Response to Comparative Advertising in Thailand and the United States," *Journal of Advertising* (Spring 2005): 37–49.
29. Bred A. S. Martin, Bodo Lang, and Stephanie Wong, "Conclusion Explicitness in Advertising: The Moderating Role of Need for Cognition (NFC) and Argument Quality (AQ) on Persuasion," *Journal of Advertising* (Winter 2003/2004): 57–66.
30. Gianfranco Walsh, Kevin P. Gwinner, and Scott R. Swanson, "What Makes Mavens Tick? Exploring the Motives of Market Mavens' Initiation of Information Diffusion," *Journal of Consumer Marketing,* 21, no. 2 (2004): 109–122.
31. Ronald E. Goldsmith, Leisa R. Flynn, and Elizabeth B. Goldsmith, "Innovation Consumers and Market Mavens," *Journal of Marketing Theory and Practice,* 11 (Fall 2003): 58.
32. Brett A. S. Martin, Daniel Wentzel, and Torsten Tomczak, "Effects of Susceptibility to Normative Influence and Type of Testimonial on Attitude Toward Print Advertising," *Journal of Advertising,* 37, no. 1 (Spring 2008): 29–43.
33. Patrick De Pelsmacker, Maggie Geuens, and Pascal Anckaert, "Media Context and Advertising Effectiveness: The Role of Context Appreciation and Context/Ad Similarity," *Journal of Advertising* (Summer 2002): 49–61.
34. Andrew Sharma, "Recall of Television Commercials as a Function of Viewing Context: The Impact of Program-Commercial Congruity on Commercial Messages," *Journal of General Psychology* (October 2000): 383–396.
35. Anna S. Mattila, "The Role of Narratives in the Advertising of Experiential Services," *Journal of Service Research* (August 2000): 35–45.
36. Joseph Wisenblit, "Segmentation: From Traditional Bases to Behavioral and Micro-Targeting," Working Paper (June 2008), Stillman School of Business, Seton Hall University, South Orange, New Jersey.
37. PQ Media "Alternative Out-of-Home Media Forecast 2007–2011," www.pqmedia.com, December 7, 2008.
38. Stuart Elliott, "Hot Food, and Air, at Bus Stops," www.nytimes .com, December 2, 2008.
39. Laura M. Holson, "In CBS Test, Mobile Ads Find Users," www .nytimes.com, February 6, 2008.
40. Edward Wyatt, "Publisher Aims at Cellphones," www.nytimes .com, February 18, 2008.
41. Louise Story, "Madison Avenue Calling," www.nytimes.com, January 20, 2007.

42. Brad Stone, "Amazon.com Invades the Apple App Store," www.nytimes.com, December 3, 2008.
43. Tim Arango, "Digital Sales Surpass CDs at Atlantic," www.nytimes.com, November 26, 2008.
44. www.ensequence.com, accessed December 12, 2008.
45. Shintaro Okazaki, Akihiro Katsukura, and Mamoru Nishiyama, "How Mobile Advertising Works: The Role of Trust in Improving Attitudes and Recall," *Journal of Advertising,* 47, no. 2, (June 2007): 165–178.
46. Louise Story, "It's an Ad, Ad, Ad, Ad World," www.nytimes.com, August 6, 2007.
47. Ji Hee Song and George M. Zinkhan, "Determinants of Perceived Web Site Interactivity," *Journal of Marketing,* 72 (March 2008): 99–113.
48. Doreen Carvajal, "Placing the Product in the Dialogue, Too," www.nytimes.com, January 17, 2006; Louise Story, "So That's Why They Drink Coke on TV," www.nytimes.com, December 9, 2007; Stuart Elliott, "Up Next, a Show From Our Sponsor," www.nytimes.com, June 12, 2008; and Stephanie Clifford, "A Product's Place Is on the Set," www.nytimes.com, July 22, 2008.
49. "Product Placement Spending in Media 2005: Executive Summary," A Special Report by PQMedia, March 2005.
50. Edward F. McQuarrie and David Glen Mick, "Visual and Verbal Rhetorical Figures Under Directed Processing Versus Incidental Exposure to Advertising," *Journal of Consumer Research* (March 2003): 579–588.
51. Richard Buda and Bruce H. Chamov, "Message Processing in Realistic Recruitment Practices," *Journal of Managerial Issues* (Fall 2003): 302+.
52. Jennifer L. Aaker and Angela Y. Lee, "'I' Seek Pleasure and 'We' Avoid Pains: The Role of Self-Regulatory Goals in Information Processing and Persuasion," *Journal of Consumer Research* (June 2001): 33–49.
53. Dena Cox and Anthony D. Cox, "Communicating the Consequences of Early Detection: The Role of Evidence and Framing," *Journal of Marketing* (July 2001): 91–103.
54. Baba Shiv, Julie A. Edell Britton, and John W. Payne, "Does Elaboration Increase or Decrease the Effectiveness of Negatively Versus Positively Framed Messages?" *Journal of Consumer Research* (June 2004): 199–209.
55. William E. Baker, Heather Honea, and Cristel Antonia Russell, "Do Not Wait to Reveal the Brand Name: The Effect of Brand-Name Placement on Television Advertising Effectiveness," *Journal of Advertising* (Fall 2004): 77–86.
56. Kenneth C. Manning, Paul W. Miniard, Michael J. Barone, and Randall L. Rose, "Understanding the Mental Representations Created by Comparative Advertising," *Journal of Advertising* (Summer 2001): 27–39.
57. Chingching Chang, The Relative Effectiveness of Comparative Advertising: Evidence for Gender Differences in Information-Processing Strategies," *Journal of Advertising,* 36, no. 1 (Spring 2007): 21–36.
58. Shailendra Pratap Jain, Charles Lindsey, Nidhi Agrawal, and Durairaj Maheswaran, "For Better or For Worse? Valenced Comparative Frames and Regulatory Focus," *Journal of Consumer Research,* 34 (June 2007): 57–65.
59. Kawpong Polyorat and Dana L Alden, "Self-Construal and Need-for-Cognition Effects on Brand Attitudes and Purchase Intentions in Response to Comparative Advertising in Thailand and the United States," *Journal of Advertising* (Spring 2005): 37–49.
60. Yung Kyun Choi and Gordon E. Miracle, "The Effectiveness of Comparative Advertising in Korea and the United States," *Journal of Advertising* (Winter 2004): 75–88.
61. Karen H. Smith and Mary Ann Stutts, "Effects of Short-Term Cosmetic Versus Long-Term Health Fear Appeals in Anti-Smoking Advertisements on the Smoking Behaviour of Adolescents," *Journal of Consumer Behaviour* (December 2003): 157+.
62. Thomas W. Cline, Moses B. Altsech, and James J. Kellaris, "When Does Humor Enhance or Inhibit Ad Responses? The Moderating Role of the Need for Humor," *Journal of Advertising* (Fall 2003): 31–46.
63. James J. Kellaris and Thomas W. Cline, "Humor and Ad Memorability: On the Contributions of Humor Expectancy, Relevancy, and Need for Humor," *Psychology and Marketing,* 24, no. 6 (June 2007): 497–509.
64. Thomas W. Cline and James J. Kellaris, "The Influence of Humor Strength and Humor-Message Relatedness on Ad Memorability: A Dual Process Model," *Journal of Advertising,* 36, no. 1 (Spring 2007): 55–68.
65. ChangHyun Jin and Jorge Villegas, "The Effect of the Placement of the Product in Film: Consumers' Emotional Responses to Humorous Stimuli and Prior Brand Evaluation," *Journal of Targeting, Measurement and Analysis for Marketing,* 15, no. 4 (2007): 244–255.
66. Stuart Elliott, "Striving for Balance Between Losses and Laughs," www.nytimes.com, October 15, 2008.
67. Patricia Cohen, "Marketing Broadway: Selling Hope for a Song," www.nytimes.com, December 10, 2008.
68. Stephanie Clifford and Stuart Elliott, "Goodbye Seduction, Hello Coupons," www.nytimes.com November 10, 2008.
69. Stuart Elliott, "Business District Tries Soft Selling for Holidays," www.nytimes.com, December 8, 2008.
70. Stuart Elliott, "Capitalizing on Consumer Anxiety, One Halloween Deal at a Time," www.nytimes.com, October 14, 2008.
71. Louise Story, "Nielsen Looks Beyond TV, and Hits Roadblocks," www.nytimes.com, February 26, 2008.
72. Louise Story, "How Many Site Hits? Depends Who's Counting," www.nytimes.com, October 22, 2007.
73. Louise Story, "AOL Brings Out the Penguins to Explain Ad Targeting," www.nytimes.com, March 9, 2008.
74. Stephanie Clifford, "Web Marketing That Hopes to Learn What Attracts a Click," www.nytimes.com December 3, 2008; and Stephanie Clifford, "Service from Google Gives Crucial Data to Ad Buyers," www.nytimes.com, June 25, 2008.

Chapter 10

1. U.S. Census Bureau, "USA Statistics in Brief—Households, Housing, and Construction," 2006, accessed at www.census.gov/compendia/statab/files/house.html.
2. Terry L. Childers and Akshay R. Rao, "The Influence of Familial and Peer-Based Reference Groups on Consumer Decisions," *Journal of Consumer Research,* 19 (September 1992): 198–211.
3. Maureen Dowd, "The Baby Bust," *New York Times,* April 10, 2001, A27; and Nancy Gibbs, "Making Time for a Baby," *TIME,* April 15, 2002, 48–54.
4. James W. Gentry and Lee Phillip McGinnis, "Doing Gender in the Family: Household Production Issues," *Advances in Consumer Research,* 30 (2003): 309–313.
5. U.S. Census Bureau, "Households, Families, Subfamilies, and Married Couples: 1980 to 2006," and "Households by Age of Householder and Size of Household: 1990 to 2006," *Statistical Abstract of the United States: 2008,* Tables 58 and 61, accessed at www.census.gov/compendia/statab; and U.S. Census Bureau, "Marital Status of People 15 Years and Over, by Age, Sex, Personal Earnings, Race, and Hispanic Origin, 2006," *Current Population Survey 2006, Annual Social and Economic Supplement*, March 27, 2007, Table A1.
6. Pamela Paul, "Meet the Parents," *American Demographics* (January 2002): 43–47.
7. *Statistical Abstract of the United States: 2008,* Table 662.
8. Bradley Johnson, "Families Spend Less on Food as They Pursue House, Car Dreams," *Advertising Age,* February 7, 2005, 34.
9. Pamela Kruger, "Why Johnny Can't Play," *Fast Company,* August 2000, 271–272. See also Daniel Thomas Cook, *The Co-modification*

of Childhood: The Children's Clothing Industry and the Rise of the Child Consumer (Durham: Duke University Press, 2004).

10. Rafael Bravo, Elena Fraj, and Eva Martinez, "Intergenerational Influences on the Dimensions of Young Customer-Based Brand Equity," *Young Consumers,* 8, no. 1 (2007): 63.
11. Deborah Roedder John, "Consumer Socialization of Children: A Retrospective Look at Twenty-Five Years of Research," *Journal of Consumer Research,* 26 (December 1999): 183–213.
12. Amy Rummel, John Howard, Jennifer M. Swinton, and D. Bradley Seymour, "You Can't Have That! A Study of Reactance Effects and Children's Consumer Behavior," *Journal of Marketing Theory and Practice* (Winter 2000): 38–45.
13. Jason E. Lueg and R. Zachary Finney, "Interpersonal Communication in the Consumer Socialization Process: Scale Development and Validation," *Journal of Marketing Theory and Practice,* 15 (Winter 2007), 25–39.
14. Sabrina M. Neeley and Tim Coffey, "Understanding the 'Four-Eyed, Four-Legged' Consumer: A Segmentation Analysis of U.S. Moms," *Journal of Marketing Theory and Practice,* 15, no. 3 (Summer 2007): 251–261.
15. Gregory M. Rose, "Consumer Socialization, Parental Style, and Developmental Timetables in the United States and Japan," *Journal of Marketing,* 63 (July 1999): 105–119.
16. Lan Nguyen Chaplin and Deborah Roedder John, "Growing Up in a Material World: Age Differences in Materialism in Children and Adolescents," *Journal of Consumer Research,* 34 (December 2007), 480–493.
17. David B. Wooten, "From Labeling Possessions to Possessing Labels: Ridicule and Socialization Among Adolescents," *Journal of Consumer Research,* 33 (September 2006): 188–198.
18. Marie J. Lachance and Frederic Legault, "College Students' Consumer Competence: Identifying the Socialization Sources," *Journal of Research for Consumers,* no. 13 (2007): 1–5.
19. Deborah Moscardelli and Catherine Liston-Heyes, "Consumer Socialization in a Wired World: The Effects of Internet Use and Parental Communication on the Development of Skepticism to Advertising," *Journal of Marketing,* 13, no. 3 (Summer 2005): 62–75.
20. John Fetto, "'Woof Woof' Means, 'I Love You,'" *American Demographics* (February 2002): 11.
21. See, for example, Carter A. Mandrik, Edward F. Fern, and Yeqing Bao, "Intergenerational Influence in Mothers and Young Adult Daughters," *Advances in Consumer Research,* 31 (2004): 697–699.
22. Barbara Olsen, "Brand Loyalty and Lineage: Exploring New Dimensions for Research," in *Advances in Consumer Research,* 20, eds. Leigh McAlister and Michael L. Rothschild (Provo, UT: Association for Consumer Research, 1993), 575–579; Marilyn Lavin, "Husband-Dominant, Wife-Dominant, Joint," *Journal of Consumer Marketing,* 10 (1993): 33–42; and Vern L. Bengtson, "Beyond the Nuclear Family: The Increasing Importance of Multigenerational Bond," *Journal of Marriage and Family* (February 2001): 1–16.
23. Sanford Grossbart, Stephanie McConnell Hughes, Cara Okleshen, Stephanie Nelson, Les Carlson, Russell N. Laczniak, and Darrel Muehling, "Parents, Children, and the Internet: Socialization Perspectives," in *2001 AMA Winter Educators' Conference,* 12, eds. Ram Krishnan and Madhu Viswanathan (Chicago: American Marketing Association, 2001), 379–385.
24. June Cotte and Stacy L. Wood, "Families and Innovative Consumer Behavior: A Triadic Analysis of Sibling and Parental Influence," *Journal of Consumer Research,* 31 (June 2004): 78–86.
25. Kevin Heubusch, "A Tough Job Gets Tougher," *American Demographics* (September 1997): 39.
26. Lynn White and Stacy J. Rogers, "Economic Circumstances and Family Outcomes: A Review of the 1990s," *Journal of Marriage and the Family,* 62 (November 2000): 1035–1051.
27. Todd Starr Palmer, Mary Beth Pinto, and Diane H. Parente, "College Students' Credit Card Debt and the Role of Parental Involvement: Implications for Public Policy," *Journal of Public Policy and Marketing,* 20, no. 1 (Spring 2001): 105–113.
28. Janice Greene, "Dogs, Dads and Laughter Bring Happiness to Kids," *San Francisco Chronicle,* November 2, 2001, 2.
29. Leah Haran, "Families Together Differently Today," *Advertising Age,* October 23, 1995, 1, 12.
30. Kim P. Corfman, "Perceptions of Relative Influence: Formation and Measurement," *Journal of Marketing Research,* 28 (May 1991): 125–136. Also, for additional articles on family decision-making roles and structures, see Christina Kwai-Choi and Roger Marshall, "Who Do We Ask and When: A Pilot Study About Research in Family Decision Making," in *Developments in Marketing Science,* 16, eds. Michael Levy and Dhruv Grewal (Coral Gables, FL: Academy of Marketing Science, 1993), 30–35.
31. Joan Raymond, "For Richer and for Poorer," *American Demographics* (July 2000): 58–64.
32. John B. Ford, Michael S. LaTour, and Tony L. Henthorne, "Perception of Marital Roles in Purchase Decision Processes: A Cross-Cultural Study," *Journal of the Academy of Marketing Science,* 23, no. 2 (1995): 120–131; and Tony L. Henthorne, Michael S. LaTour, and Robert Matthews, "Perception of Marital Roles in Purchase Decision Making: A Study of Japanese Couples," *Proceedings* (Chicago: American Marketing Association, 1995), 321–322.
33. James U. McNeal and Chyon-Hwa Yeh, "Development of Consumer Behavior Patterns Among Chinese Children," *Journal of Consumer Marketing,* 14 (1997): 45–59.
34. Yang Xia, Zafar U. Ahmed, Ng Kuan Hwa, Tan Wan Li, and Wendy Teo Chai Ying, "Spousal Influence in Singaporean Family Purchase Decision-Making Process: A Cross-Cultural Comparison," *Asia Pacific Journal of Marketing,* 18, no. 3 (2006): 201–222.
35. Joyantha S. Wimalasiri, "A Cross-National Study on Children's Purchasing Behavior and Parental Response," *Journal of Consumer Marketing,* 21, no. 4 (2004): 274–284; Michael J. Dotson and Eva M. Hyatt, "Major Influence Factors in Children's Consumer Socialization," *Journal of Consumer Marketing,* 22, no. 1 (2005): 35–42; Aviv Shoham, "He Said, She Said . . . They Said: Parents' and Children's Assessment of Children's Influence on Family Consumption Decisions," *Journal of Consumer Marketing,* 22, no. 3 (2005): 152–160, and L. A. Flurry and Alvin C. Burns, "Children's Influence in Purchase Decisions: A Social Power Theory Approach," *Journal of Business Research,* 58 (May 2005): 593–601.
36. Malene Gram, "Children as Co-decision Makers in the Family? The Case of Family Holidays," *Young Consumers,* 8, no. 1 (2007): 19–28.
37. Aviv Shoham, Gregory M. Rose, and Aysen Bakir, "The Effect of Family Communication Patterns on Mothers' and Fathers' Perceived Influence in Family Decision Making," *Advances in Consumer Behavior,* 31 (2004): 692.
38. Michael A. Belch, Kathleen A. Krentler, and Laura A. Willis-Flurry, "Teen Internet Mavens: Influence in Family Decision Making," *Journal of Business Research,* 58 (May 2005): 569–575.
39. N. Marie Marquis, "Strategies for Influencing Parental Decisions on Food Purchasing," *Journal of Consumer Marketing,* 21, no. 2 (2004): 134–143.
40. Stephanie Thompson, "Million-Dollar Baby," *Advertising Age,* May 30, 2005, 1, 50.
41. Bodil Stilling Blichfeldt, "A Nice Vacation: Variations in Experience Aspirations and Travel Careers," *Journal of Vacation Marketing,* 13, no. 2 (2007): 149–164.
42. Charles M. Schaninger and William D. Danko, "A Conceptual and Empirical Comparison of Alternative Household Life Cycle Models," *Journal of Consumer Research,* 19 (March 1993): 580–594.

43. Nabil Razzouk, Victoria Seitz, and Karen Prodigalidad Capo, "A Comparison of Consumer Decision-Making Behavior of Married and Cohabiting Couples," *Journal of Consumer Marketing,* 24, no. 5 (2007): 264–274.
44. Julie Tinson, Clive Nancarrow, and Ian Brace, "Purchase Decision Making and the Increasing Significance of Family Types," *Journal of Consumer Marketing,* 25, no. 1 (2008): 45–56.
45. Charles M. Schaninger and Sanjay Putrevu, "Dual Spousal Work Involvement: An Alternative Method to Classify Households/Families," *Academy of Marketing Science Review,*10 no. 8 (2006): 1–21.
46. "Brand Stats: Market Focus—Instant Coffee," *Brand Strategy (London),* May 10, 2005, 50.
47. Malcolm M. Knapp, "Believing 'Myth of the Middle Class' Can Be Costly Misreading of Consumer Spending," *Nation's Restaurant News,* January 1, 2001, 36.
48. Takashina Shuji, "The New Inequality," *Japan Echo,* August 2000, 38–39.
49. Rebecca Piirto Heath, "The New Working Class," *American Demographics* (January 1998): 52.
50. John P. Dickson and R. Bruce Lind, "The Stability of Occupational Prestige as a Key Variable in Determining Social Class Structure: A Longitudinal Study 1976–2000," in *2001 AMA Winter Educators' Conference,* 12, eds. Ram Krishnan and Madhu Viswanathan (Chicago: American Marketing Association, 2001), 38–44.
51. Diane Crispell, "The Real Middle Americans," *American Demographics* (October 1994): 28–35.
52. Tamar Lewin, "A Marriage of Unequals," *New York Times,* May 19, 2005, A1, 14–15.
53. David Leonhardt, "The College Dropout Boom," *New York Times,* May 24, 2005, A1, 18–19.
54. Eugene Sivadas, George Mathew, and David J. Curry, "A Preliminary Examination of the Continued Significance of Social Class to Marketing: A Geodemographic Replication," *Journal of Consumer Marketing,* 14, no. 6 (1997): 469.
55. David Hinson, "Closing the Wealth Gap; How African-Americans Can Sustain a Middle-Class Lifestyle," *Network Journal,* 11 (February 29, 2004): 8.
56. Michael D. Yates, "A Statistical Portrait of the U.S. Working Class," *Monthly Review,* 56 (April 2005): 12–31.
57. "Rich and Richer, Poor and Poorer," *The Futurist,* November–December 2007: 12.
58. Robert B. Settle, Pamela L. Alreck, and Denny E. McCorkle, "Consumer Perceptions of Mail Phone Order Shopping Media," *Journal of Direct Marketing,* 8 (Summer 1994): 30–45.
59. W. Lloyd Warner, Marchia Meeker, and Kenneth Eells, *Social Class in America: Manual of Procedure for the Measurement of Social Status* (New York: Harper & Brothers, 1960).
60. *Methodology and Scores of Socioeconomic Status,* Working Paper No. 15 (Washington, DC: U.S. Bureau of the Census, 1963).
61. Kevin Lamiman, "Target Corporation," *Better Investing,* 55, no. 12 (August 2006): 36.
62. Randy Kennedy, "For Middle Class, New York Shrinks as Home Prices Soar," *New York Times,* April 1, 1998, A1, B6; "Two Tier Marketing," *Business Week,* March 17, 1997, 82–90; and Keith Bradsher, "America's Opportunity Gap," *New York Times,* June 4, 1995, 4.
63. Jared Bernstein, "Income Picture: Median Income Rose as Did Poverty in 2007," *Economic Policy Institute* (August 26, 2008), accessed at www.epi.org/content.cfm/webfeatures_economindictors_iancome_20080826.
64. Ibid.
65. "Special Report: Ever Higher Society, Ever Harder to Ascend—Meritocracy in America," *The Economist,* January 1, 2005, 35–37. Arthur Cordell, "Rich Poor Gap in the US," *Wall Street Journal,* May 13, 2005, 19.
66. Cordell, "Rich Poor Gap in the US," 19.
67. Debra Branch McBrier and George Wilson, "Going Down?" *Work and Occupations,* 31 (August 2004): 283–322.
68. Housing Jitters Manifest: Internet Searches for 'Real Estate Bubble' Rise; Real Estate Traffic Levels up 19 Percent Versus Year-Ago," *Business Wire (New York),* June 16, 2005, 1.
69. Erdener Kaynak and Talha D. Harcar, "American Consumers' Attitudes Towards Commercial Banks: A Comparison of Local and National Bank Customers by Use of Geodemographic Segmentation," *International Journal of Bank Marketing,* 23, no. 1 (2005): 73–89.
70. Paul Bruder, "Economic Health: The Key Ingredient in the Personal Health of Global Communities," *Hospital Topics,* 79, no. 1 (Winter 2001): 32–35.
71. Janny Scott, "In America, Living Better and Living Longer Is a Major Factor in Health Care and the Gaps Are Widening," *International Herald Tribune,* May 17, 2005, 2.
72. Suniya S. Luthar and Shawn J. Latendresse, "Children of the Affluent; Challenges to Well-Being," *Current Directions in Psychological Science,* 14 (February 2005): 49.
73. "Kudlow's Money Politic$," March 11, 2005, http://lkmp.blogspot.com/2005/03/wealth-of-nations.html.
74. Merrill Lynch and Capgemini, *World Wealth Report, 2008*, accessed at www.capgemini.com/resources/thought_leadership/world_wealth_report_2008; and Merrill Lynch and Capgemini, *World Wealth Report, 2005*, accessed at www.capgemini.com/resources/thought_leadership/world_wealth_report_200.
75. James Davies, Susanna Sandstrom, Anthony Shorrocks, and Edward Wolff, "The World Distribution of Household Wealth," *World Institute for Development Economies Research of the United Nations University,* 2006, accessed at www.mindfully.org/WTO/2006/Household-Wealth-Gap5dec06.htm.
76. Michael R. Hyman, Gopala Ganesh, and Shaun McQuitty, "Augmenting the Household Affluence Construct," *Journal of Marketing Theory and Practice,* 10 (Summer 2002): 13–31.
77. Sandra O'Loughlin, "Affluent Consumers Don't Always 'Brand' Together," *Brandweek,* April 30, 2007, 10.
78. *The 2008 Mendelsohn Affluent Survey*, Ipsos Mendelsohn, 2008.
79. Ibid.
80. Ibid.
81. Geoffrey Holliman, "Once a Teenager, Now Affluent and Best Not Ignored," *Marketing,* December 2, 1999, 22.
82. Martha R. McEnally and Charles Bodkin, "A Comparison of Convenience Orientation Between U.S. and U.K. Households," in *2001 AMA Winter Educators' Conference,* 12, eds. Ram Krishnan and Madhu Viswanathan (Chicago: American Marketing Association, 2001), 332–338.
83. *The 2008 Mendelsohn Affluent Survey*, 2008.
84. Joe Mandese, "In Search of Affluent Viewers," *TelevisionWeek (Chicago),* January 12, 2004, 47.
85. "Men's Wear Grandeur," *DNR,* 37, no. 25 (June 18, 2007): 22.
86. "Marketing to Affluents: Hidden Pockets of Wealth," *Advertising Age,* July 9, 1990, S1.
87. Jeanie Casison, "Wealthy and Wise," *Incentive,* January 1999, 78–81.
88. *The Upper Deck* (Mediamark Research, Inc., 2004).
89. Ibid.
90. *Statistical Abstract of the United States 2008,* Table 671.
91. www.factcheck.org/askfactcheck/is_there_a_standard_accepted_definition_of.html, accessed October 2008.
92. Gregory L. White and Shirley Leung, "Stepping Up," *Wall Street Journal*, March 29, 2002, A1.
93. Rasul Bailay, "Juice Processors See Fruitful Future in India—Companies Hope to Lure Country's Middle Class—'The Taste of Good Health,'" *Wall Street Journal,* November 17, 2000, 28; and Clay Chandler, "GM to Make Small Cars in China; Buick Sail, Similar to Opel, Will Be Aimed at Middle Class," *Washington Post,* October 24, 2000, E1.

94. Noreen O'Leary, "Keeping Up with the Jiangs," *Brandweek*, January 2, 2007, 15.
95. "Consumer Revolution Underway in China as Dramatic Shift in Values Creates New Middle Case Mindset," *PR Newswire*, May 2008.
96. Claudia Suessmuth-Dyckerhoff, Jimmy Hexter, and Ian St-Maurice, "Marketing to China's New Traditionalists," *Far Eastern Economic Review* (April 2008): 28–33.
97. W. Michael Cox, "The Low Cost of Living," *The Voluntaryist*, October 1999, 3.
98. Peter Gumbel, "Mass vs. Class," *Fortune*, September 17, 2007, 82.
99. Eric Newman, "'Mass Affluents' Retreat En Masse," *Brandweek*, January 21, 2008, 4.
100. Karen Benezra, "Hardworking RC Cola," *Brandweek*, May 25, 1998, 18–19.
101. "Small Budgets Yield Big Clout for Food Companies—10.1 Million Low Income Consumers Can't (or Shouldn't) Be Ignored," *PR Newswire*, August 22, 2002, 1.
102. George Pitcher, "Being Super-Sized Boils Down to Personal Choice," *Marketing Week (London)*, October 7, 2004, 33.
103. Steve Rosenbush, "Techno Leaders Warn of a 'Great Divide,'" *USA Today*, June 17, 1998, B1.
104. "Computer Geeks Now the Cool Kids in Class," *The Press* (Christchurch, New Zealand), July 20, 2000, 31.
105. Epictetus, "Discourses" (second century) in *The Enchiridion*, 2, trans. Thomas Higginson (Indianapolis: Bobbs-Merrill, 1955).
106. Michael Applebaum, "Marketers of the Next Generation," *Brandweek*, April 17, 2006, 32–33.
107. Christina Duff, "Indulging in Inconspicuous Consumption," *Wall Street Journal*, April 14, 1997, B1, B2; and Christina Duff, "Two Family Budgets: Different Means, Similar Ends," *Wall Street Journal*, April 14, 1997, B1, B2.
108. Paul C. Henry, "Social Class, Market Situation, and Consumers' Metaphors of (Dis)Empowerment," *Journal of Consumer Research*, 31 (March 2005): 766–778.
109. Youn-Kyung Kim and Seunghae Han, "Perceived Images of Retail Stores and Brands: Comparison Among Three Ethnic Consumer Groups," *Journal of Family and Consumer Sciences*, 92, no. 3 (2000), 58–61.

Chapter 11

1. Thomas L. Friedman, *The World Is Flat* (New York: Farrar, Straus and Giroux, 2005).
2. C. Samuel Craig and Susan P. Douglas, "Beyond National Culture: Implications of Cultural Dynamics for Consumer Research," *International Marketing Review*, 23, no. 2 (2006): 322.
3. Linda C. Ueltschy and Robert F. Krampf, "Cultural Sensitivity to Satisfaction and Service Quality Measures," *Journal of Marketing Theory and Practice* (Summer 2001): 14–31.
4. Elena Karahanna, J. Roberto Evaristo, and Mark Strite, "Levels of Culture and Individual Behavior: An Integrative Perspective," *Journal of Global Information Management*, 13 (April–June 2005): 1–20.
5. Tim Stock and Marie Lena Tupot, "Common Denominators: What Unites Global Youth?" *Young Consumers* (Quarter 1, 2006): 36–43.
6. "Demo Memo," *American Demographics* (February 1998): 41.
7. Virginia Richards, "Perpetuating Core Consumer Sciences," *Journal of Family and Consumer Sciences*, 97, no. 3 (September 2005): 8–10.
8. Elizabeth C. Hirschman, "Men, Dogs, Guns, and Cars: The Seminotics of Rugged Individualism," *Journal of Advertising*, 32 (Spring 2003): 9–22.
9. Michael Fay, "Cyclical PATTERNS in the content of Advertisements: Replication, Confirmation, Extension and Revision," *European Journal of Marketing*, 40, nos. 1/2 (2006): 198–217.
10. Kritsadarat Wattanasuwan, "Balancing the Hybrid Self in the Competing Landscapes of Consumption," *Journal of the American Academy of Business, Cambridge*, 11, no. 1 (March 2007): 9–17.
11. Dennis W. Rook, "The Ritual Dimension of Consumer Behavior," *Journal of Consumer Research*, 12 (December 1985): 251–264.
12. For a discussion of socialization, see Jason E. Lueg and R. Zachary Finney, "Interpersonal Communication in the Consumer Socialization Process: Scale Development and Validation," *Journal of Marketing Theory and Practice*, 15, no. 1 (Winter 2007): 25–39.
13. Hye-Shin Kim and Byoungho Jin, "Exploratory Study of Virtual Communities of Apparel Retailers," *Journal of Fashion Marketing and Management*, 10, no. 1 (2006): 41–55.
14. Ibid., 51.
15. Andrew Zolli, "Why Design Matters More," *American Demographics* (October 2004): 52–53.
16. Virginia Postrel, *The Substance of Style: How the Rise of Aesthetic Value Is Remaking Commerce, Culture, and Consciousness* (New York: HarperCollins, 2003).
17. Debra Hazel, "Wide-Open Spaces," *Chain Store Age*, November 2005: 120–124.
18. Jeff Strieter and Jerald Weaver, "A Longitudinal Study of the Depiction of Women in a United States Business Publication," *Journal of the American Academy of Business*, 7 (September 2005): 229–235.
19. Michael L. Maynard and Charles R. Taylor, "Girlish Images Across Cultures: Analyzing Japanese Versus U.S. *Seventeen* Magazine Ads," *Journal of Advertising*, 28, no. 1 (Spring 1999): 39–45.
20. Mindy F. Ji and James U. McNeal, "How Chinese Children's Commercials Differ from Those of the United States: A Content Analysis," *Journal of Advertising*, 30, no. 3 (Fall 2001): 79–92.
21. Lawrence Osborne, "Consuming Rituals of the Suburban Tribe," *New York Times Magazine*, January 13, 2002, 28–31; Margaret Littman, "Science Shopping," *Crain's Chicago Business*, January 11, 1999, 3; and Marvin Matises, "Top of Mind: Send Ethnographers into New-SKU Jungle," *Brandweek*, September 25, 2000, 32–33.
22. Maria Kniazeva and Alladi Venkatesh, "Food for Thought: A Study of Food Consumption in Postmodern US Culture," *Journal of Consumer Behavior*, 6 (November–December 2007): 419–435.
23. Wagner A. Kamakura and Jose Afonso Mazzon, "Value Segmentation: A Model for the Measurement of Values and Value Systems," *Journal of Consumer Research*, 18 (September 1991): 208–218.
24. Lynn R. Kahle, ed., *Social Values and Social Change: Adaptation of Life in America* (New York: Praeger, 1983); Sharon E. Beatty et al., "Alternative Measurement Approaches to Consumer Values: The List of Values and the Rokeach Value Survey," *Psychology & Marketing*, 2 (1985): 181–200; and Lynn R. Kahle, Roger P. McIntyre, Reid P. Claxton, and David B. Jones, "Empirical Relationships Between Cognitive Style and LOV: Implications for Values and Value Systems," in *Advances in Consumer Research*, 22, ed. Frank R. Kardes and Mita Sujan (Provo, UT: Association for Consumer Research 1995), 141–146.
25. David C. McClelland, *The Achieving Society* (New York: Free Press, 1961), 150–151.
26. Leon G. Schiffman, Elaine Sherman, and Mary M. Long, "Toward a Better Understanding of the Interplay of Personal Values and the Internet," *Psychology and Marketing*, 20 (February 2003): 169–186.
27. Lawrence E. Harrison, "Culture Matters," *The National Interest*, 60 (Summer 2000): 55–65.
28. Charles A. Malgwi, Martha A. Howe, and Priscilla A. Burnaby, "Influences on Students' Choice of College Major," *Journal of Education for Business*, 80 (May/June 2005): 275–282.
29. Naomi Mandel, Petia K. Petrova, and Robert B. Cialdini, "Images of Success and the Preference for Luxury Brands," *Journal of Consumer Psychology*, 16, no. 1 (2006): 57–69.

30. Mark Dolliver, "The 24-Hour Limit," *Adweek*, 47, no. 46 (December 11–December 25, 2006): 26.
31. "Just Keeping Busy in Old Age Isn't the Key to Actively Enjoying Life; Seniors: The Quality and Purpose of Their Activities Determine Whether the Elderly Are Just Going Through the Motions or Truly Fulfilled, a Researcher Has Found," *Los Angeles Times*, November 26, 1999, 5C; and Evelyn Petersen, "Being Busy All The Time Isn't Healthy Series: Booked Solid," *Syracuse Herald American,* October 17, 1999, A13.
32. Peter Rojas, "Time-Out Guide," *Red Herring*, December 1999, 114.
33. Ramesh Venkat and Harold J. Ogden, "Material Satisfaction: The Effects of Social Comparison and Attribution," in *1995 AMA Educators' Proceedings,* eds. Barbara B. Stern and George M. Zinkan (Chicago: American Marketing Association, 1995), 314–349.
34. Joe Renouard, "The Predicaments of Plenty: Interwar Intellectuals and American Consumerism," *Journal of American Culture,* 30, no. 1 (March 2007): 59.
35. "What Is Vivre," accessed at www.vivre.com/control/about/whatis.
36. Frank Gibney, Jr. and Belinda Luscombe, "The Redesigning of America," *TIME,* June 26, 2000, unnumbered insert section.
37. Daphna Oyserman, "High Power, Low Power, and Equality: Culture Beyond Individualism and Collectivism," *Journal of Consumer Psychology,* 16 (2006): 354; and Norbert Schwarz, "Individualism and Collectivism," *Journal of Consumer Psychology,* 16, no. 4 (2006): 324.
38. Hirschman, "Men, Dogs, Guns, and Cars."
39. Mario J. Miranda and Laszlo Konya, "Customisation—Moving Customers away from the Dull Conformity of Brand Loyalty," *Managing Service Quality,* 17, no. 4 (2007): 449–466.
40. Virginia Matthews, "Simplicity Is the Consumer's Choice: Marketing Product Innovation: Shoppers Complain of Confusion as Companies Blitz Them with a Host of New Products, Writes Virginia Matthews," *Financial Times* (*London*), December 10, 1999, 16.
41. Deborah J. Webb, Corliss L. Green, and Thomas G. Brashear, "Development and Validation of Scales to Measure Attitudes Influencing Monetary Donations to Charitable Organizations," *Journal of the Academy of Marketing Science,* 28, no. 2 (Spring 2000): 299–309.
42. George R. Reis, "Building Bridges," *Fund Raising Management,* 30, no. 6 (August 1999): 19–23.
43. Becky Ebenkamp, "Out of the Box: Gifts That Keep on Giving," *Brandweek,* December 11–December 25, 2006, 12.
44. Richard A. Lee "The Youth Bias in Advertising," *American Demographics* (January 1997): 47–50.
45. Barbara J. Phillips, "Working Out: Consumers and the Culture of Exercise," *Journal of Popular Culture,* 38 (February 2005): 525–551.
46. D. Gail Fleenor, "Beyond Burgers," *Frozen Food Age,* 55, no. 6 (January 2007): 22.
47. Stacey Kappes, "Ask the Expert: R&D," *Beverage World,* 126, no. 1774 (May 15, 2007): 92.
48. www.pewinternet.org/PPF/r/156/report_display.asp, accessed November 2008.
49. Art Turock, "Health Consciousness Tipping Point," *Progressive Grocer,* 87, no. 6 (May 2008): 38.
50. Mike Duff, "Marketers Making Most of Healthy Home," *Retailing Today,* 45, no. 5 (April 9, 2007): 17.
51. Jeffrey A. Tannenbaum, "Fat-Free Store Pushes to Gain Weight in U.S.—Small New York Firm Targets Shrinking Market," *Asian Wall Street Journal,* February 14, 2001, N5; and Normita Thongtham, "You Are What You Eat," *Bangkok Post,* March 2, 2002, 1.
52. "Bike Retailers Can Tap into Consumers' Fitness Resolutions," *Bicycle Retailer and Industry News,* 17, no. 1 (January 1, 2008): 38.
53. George M. Zinkhan and Penelope J. Prenshaw, "Good Life Images and Brand Name Associations: Evidence from Asia, America, and Europe," in *Advances in Consumer Research,* vol. 21, eds. Chris T. Allen and Deborah Roedder John (Provo, UT: Association for Consumer Research, 1994), 496–500.
54. Juliet Schor, "Point of Purchase: How Shopping Changed American Culture," *Contemporary Sociology,* 34 (January 2005): 43–44.
55. Christine Van Dusen, "Shopping: It's More of a Man's World These Days," *Atlanta Journal-Constitution,* April 1, 2005, F1.
56. Matthew J. Bernthal, David Crockett, and Randall L. Rose, "Credit Cards as Lifestyle Facilitators," *Journal of Consumer Research,* 32 (June 2005): 130–145.

Chapter 12

1. U.S. Census Bureau, National Population Projections, Released 2008, "Table 4. Projections of the Population by Sex, Race, and Hispanic Origin for the United States: 2010 to 2050," accessed November 2008 at www.census.gov/population/www/projections/summarytables .html.
2. Sam Roberts, "In a Generation, Minorities May Be the U.S. Majority," *New York Times,* August 14, 2008, accessed November 2008 at www.nytimes.com/2008/08/14/washington/14census.html?_r=1&scp=6&sq=Sam%20Roberts&st=cse&oref=slogin.
3. Pui-Wing Tam, "Ethnic Media Muy Popular in California," *Wall Street Journal*, April 23, 2002, B1.
4. U.S. Census Bureau, 2005 American Community Survey, "Table 40: Native and Foreign-Born Population by State: 2005," *Statistical Abstract of the United States: 2008,* accessed November 2008 at www.census.gov/compendia/statab/tables/08s0040.pdf.
5. Matthew Monks, "Report Shows Nearly Half of Queens Is Foreign Born," *Jackson Heights Times*, January 27, 2005, accessed November 2008 at http://gothamgazette.com/community/21/news/1184.
6. U.S. Census Bureau, *Statistical Abstract of the United States 2008*, Table 8; "Largest Minority Group: Hispanics," *New York Times*, January 22, 2003, A17; and "Hispanic Fact Pack, 2004 Edition," A Supplement to *Advertising Age Magazine.*
7. Deborah L. Vence, "Pick Up the Pieces: Companies Target Lifestyle Segments of Hispanics," *Marketing News*, March 15, 2005, 13–15; and Richardo Villarreal and Robert A. Peterson, "Hispanic Ethnicity and Media Behavior," *Journal of Advertising Research* (June 2008): 179.
8. U.S. Census Bureau, *Statistical Abstract of the United States 2008*, Table 8.
9. U.S. Census Bureau, *America's Families and Living Arrangements*, 2006, accessed November 2008 at www.census.gov/population/www/socdemo/hh-fam/cps2006.html.
10. Jeanie Casison, "Snapshot of America," *Incentive*, October 2001, 33–36; Lynn Petrak, "Cultured Products," *Dairy Field*, April 2001, 34–38; and John Robinson, Bart Landry, and Ronica Rooks, "Time and the Melting Pot," *American Demographics* (June 1998): 18–24.
11. Christina Rafeedie, Lynn Godkin, Sean Valentine, and Robert A. Swerdlow, "The Development of a Model Specifying the Differences in Hispanic and White Adolescents' Consumer Behavior," *International Journal of Management,* 23, no. 3 (September 2006): 597–598.
12. Laurel Wentz, "Multicultural? No, Mainstream," *Advertising Age*, May 2, 2005, 3, 57.
13. U.S. Census Bureau, *Statistical Abstract of the United States 2008*, Table 18; and U.S. Department of Commerce, "The Hispanic Population: Census 2000 Brief," accessed November 2008 at www .census.gov; and "2003 American Community Survey Data Profile Highlights," *U.S. Census Bureau—American FactFinder*, accessed at: http://factfinder.census.gov.
14. Ibid.; Brad Edmondson, "Hispanic Americans in 2001," *American Demographics* (January 1997): 17; and "2008 Hispanic Fact Pack," A Supplement to *Advertising Age,* July 28, 2008, 49.
15. "Hispanic Power," *Chain Store Age,* 83, no. 11 (November 2007): 26.

16. Soyeon Shim and Kenneth C. Gehrt, "Native American and Hispanic Adolescent Consumers: Examination of Shopping Orientation, Socialization Factors and Social Structure Variables," in *1995 AMA Educators' Proceedings*, ed. Barbara B. Stern and George M. Zinkan (Chicago: American Marketing Association, 1995), 297–298.
17. Michael Chattalas and Holly Harper, "Navigating a Hybrid Cultural Identity: Hispanic Teenagers' Fashion Consumption Influences," *Journal of Consumer Marketing,* 24, no. 6 (2007): 351–357.
18. "2007 Hispanic Fact Pack," A Supplement to *Advertising Age,* July 23, 2007; and "Hispanic Fact Book, 2004 Edition," A Supplement to *Advertising Age,* 35.
19. "Multitaskers," *Brandweek,* April 23, 2007, 18.
20. Catharine P. Taylor, "Barbie Latina Says 'Hola' to Net," *Advertising Age*, October 1, 2001, 54.
21. Nitish Singh, Daniel W. Baack, Arun Pereira, and Donald Baack, "Culturally Customizing Websites for U.S. Hispanic Online Consumers," *Journal of Advertising Research* (June 2008): 224–234; and Hallie Mummert, "Culture: More Than a Language," *Target Marketing,* 30, no. 5 (May 2007): 54.
22. Della de Lafuente, "Text Market," *Adweek,* 49, no. 12 (April 7–April 14, 2008): A1.
23. Rohit Deshpandè, Wayne D. Hoyer, and Naveen Donthu, "The Intensity of Ethnic Affiliation: A Study of the Sociology of Hispanic Consumption," *Journal of Consumer Research,* 13 (September 1986): 214–220; and Cynthia Webster, "The Role of Hispanic Ethnic Identification on Reference Group Influence," in *Advances in Consumer Research* 21, eds. Chris T. Allen and Deborah Roedder John (Provo, UT: Association for Consumer Research, 1994), 458–463.
24. *2008 Hispanic Fact Pack*, 15; and "Toyota Corolla: Conill, Los Angeles," *Advertising Age*, April 18, 2005, 38.
25. Della de Lafuente, "Ford Flex Finds *Novela* Way to Reach Latino Consumers," *Brandweek,* June 30–July 7, 2008, 12.
26. Della de Lafuente, "Affluent in Spanish," *Adweek,* 49, no. 23 (July 14–July 21, 2008): 26.
27. Marcia Mogelonsky, "First Language Comes First," *American Demographics* (October 1995): 21.
28. Villarreal and Peterson, "Hispanic Ethnicity and Media Behavior," 182.
29. Ibid.
30. Michael Fielding, "The Halo: Christian Consumers Are a Bloc That Matters to All Marketers," *Marketing News*, February 1, 2005, 18, 20.
31. Jeffrey Steven Podoshen, "Word of Mouth, Brand Loyalty, Acculturation and the American Jewish Consumer," *Journal of Consumer Marketing,* 23, no. 5 (2006): 266–282.
32. Kevin Michael Grace, "Is This Kosher," *Report Newsmagazine*, 27, no. 1, May 8, 2000, 37; Laura Bird, "Major Brands Look for the Kosher Label," *Adweek's Marketing Week*, April 1, 1991, 18–19; and Judith Waldrop, "Everything's Kosher," *American Demographics* (March 1991): 4.
33. Victoria Rivkin, "Godly Gains," *Crain's New York Business*, October 13, 2003, 21, 27.
34. Heidi J. Shrager, "Closed-Circle Commerce," *Wall Street Journal*, November 19, 2001, B1, B11.
35. Florence Fabricant, "The Geography of Taste," *New York Times Magazine*, March 10, 1996, 40–41.
36. Marcia Mogelonsky, "America's Hottest Market," *American Demographics* (January 1996): 20–31, 55.
37. Bart J. Bronnenberg, Sanjay K. Dhar, and Jean-Pierre Dube, "Consumer Packaged Goods in the United States: National Brands, Local Branding" *Journal of Marketing Research,* 44 (February 2007): 4–14; and Bart J. Bronnenberg, Sanjay K. Dhar, and Jean-Pierre Dube, "National Brands, Local Branding: Conclusions and Future Research Opportunities," *Journal of Marketing Research,* 44 (February 2007): 26–28.
38. Michael W. Kruger, "How Geographic Variation Persists: Comments on 'Consumer Packaged Goods in the United States: National Brands, Local Branding,'" *Journal of Marketing Research,* 44 (February 2007): 21–22.
39. Leonard M. Lodish, "Another Reason Academics and Practitioners Should Communicate More," *Journal of Marketing Research,* 44 (February 2007): 23–25.
40. M. Berk Ataman, Carl F. Mela, and Harald J. Van Heerde, "Consumer Packaged Goods in France: National Brands, Regional Chains, and Local Branding," *Journal of Marketing Research,* 44 (February 2007): 14–20.
41. Kara Chan, "Chinese Children's Perceptions of Advertising and Brands: An Urban Rural Comparison," *Journal of Consumer Marketing,* 25, no. 2 (2008): 74–84; and John D. Nicholson and Philip J. Kitchen, "The Development of Regional Marketing—Have Marketers Been Myopic?" *International Journal of Business Studies,* 15, no. 1 (June 2007): 107–125.
42. Francis Piron, "China's Changing Culture: Rural and Urban Consumers' Favorite Things," *Journal of Consumer Marketing,* 23, no. 6 (2006): 327–334.
43. Himadri Roy Chaudhuri, Sr., and A. K. Haldar, "Understanding the Interrelationship Between Regional Differences and Material Aspiration in the Context of Indian Diversity: Results of an Exploratory Study," *Asia Pacific Journal of Marketing and Logistics,* 17, no. 4 (2005): 3.
44. Jeffrey Steven Podoshen, "The African American Consumer Revisited: Brand Loyalty, Word-of-Mouth and the Effects of the Black Experience," *Journal of Consumer Marketing,* 25, no. 4 (2008): 211–222.
45. "African-American/Black Market Profile 2008," *Magazine Publishers of America*, 3, accessed at www.magazine.org/marketprofiles.
46. Podoshen, "The African American Consumer Revisited," 211.
47. Mike Beirne, "Has This Group Been Left Behind?" *Brandweek*, March 14, 2005, 33–35.
48. "Understanding Nuances of Language and Culture Is Key in Marketing to Minority Women," *Marketing to Women,* 13, no. 2 (February 2000): S1.
49. "African American/Black Market Profile 2008," 7.
50. Youn-Kyung Kim and Seunghae Han, "Perceived Images of Retail Stores and Brands: Comparison Among Three Ethnic Consumer Groups," *Journal of Family and Consumer Sciences,* 92, no. 3 (2000): 58–61; and Christy Fisher, "Black, Hip, and Primed (to Shop)," *American Demographics* (September 1996): 52–58.
51. Gerda Gallop-Goodman, "Check This Out," *American Demographics*, 23, no. 5 (May 2001): 14–17.
52. "Black America Today," *Radio One,* June 2008, accessed at http://blackamericastudy.com/fact-sheets/black_consumer_final2.pdf.
53. "African American Market Profile 2008," 8.
54. Ibid., 11.
55. "Black America Today," 27.
56. Ibid.
57. Ibid.
58. "Understanding Nuances of Language and Culture Are Key in Marketing to Minority Women," S3.
59. Louise Witt, "Color Code Red: African American Magazines Have Loyal Readers, so Why Are They Still Having a Hard Time Attracting Advertisers?" *American Demographics* (February 2004): 23–25.
60. "African-American/Black Market Profile 2008," 15.
61. Pepper Miller, "The Truth About Black America," *Advertising Age,* July 15, 2008, accessed at www.adage.com.
62. "Asian-American Market Profile," *Magazine Publishers of America* (June 2006): 2, accessed November 2008 at www.magazine.org/marketprofiles.
63. Ibid., 5.

64. Ibid., and U.S. Census Bureau, Projections Table NP-T5-B; and see www.ewowfacts.com/pdfs/chapters/61.pdf.
65. "Asian-American Market Profile," 4.
66. Silvia Knobloch-Westerwick and Brendon Coates, "Minority Models in Advertisements in Magazines Popular with Minorities," *Journalism and Mass Communication Quarterly,* 83, no. 3 (Autumn 2006): 596–614.
67. U.S. Census Bureau, "2005 American Community Survey, Table 36: Selected Characteristics of Racial Groups and Hispanic/Latino Population: 2005," accessed November 2008 at www.census.gov.
68. "Asian-American Market Profile," 4.
69. Shashi Dewan and Shashi K. Dewan, "Cultural and Environmental Factors: Their Effect on the Home Buying Behavior of First Generation Asian Indian Immigrants," *Business Review,* 7, no. 2 (Summer 2007): 194–198.
70. www.ewowfacts.com/pdfs/chapters/61.pdf, accessed November 2008.
71. John Fetto, "Cyber Tigers," *American Demographics*, 24, 3 (March 2002): 9–10; and Sheila Thorne, "Reaching the Minority Majority," *Pharmaceutical Executive*, 21, 4 (April 2001): 156–158.
72. "Orienting the U.S. Food and Beverage Market: Strategies Targeting Asian Americans to 2010," Promar International, Alexandria, VA, June 2000.
73. "Asian-American Market Profile," 4.
74. Ibid., 8.
75. John Steere, "How Asian-Americans Make Purchase Decisions," *Marketing News*, March 13, 1995, 9.
76. Simpson, "The Future Cardholder," 36–42.
77. "Asian Youth Trends," *American Demographics* (October 2004): 14.
78. Judy Cohen, "White Consumer Response to Asian Models in Advertising," *Journal of Consumer Marketing* (Spring 1992): 17–27.
79. See www.ewowfacts.com/pdfs/chapter/61.pdf (page 609); and *Orienting the U.S. Food and Beverage Market: Strategies Targeting Asian American to 2010* (Alexandria, VA: Promar Internatonal: June 2000), 87.
80. Laurel Wentz, "AZN TV Makes It Easier to Reach Asians," *Advertising Age*, April 18, 2005, 38.
81. Stephanie M. Noble and Charles H. Noble, "Getting to Know Y: The Consumption Behaviors of a New Cohort," in *2000 AMA Winter Educators' Conference*, 11, ed. John P. Workman and William D. Perreault (Chicago: American Marketing Association, 2000), 293–303; and Pamela Paul, "Getting Inside Gen Y," *American Demographics* 23, 9 (September 2001): 42–49.
82. Reynol Junco and Jeanna Mastrodicase, "Connecting to the Net Generation: What Higher Education Professionals Need to Know About Today's Students," *NASPA*, 2007.
83. Kenneth Hein, "Teen Talk Is, Like, Totally Branded," *Brandweek,* August 6–August 13, 2007, 4.
84. Joyce M. Wolburg and James Pokrywczynski, "A Psychographic Analysis of Generation Y College Students," *Journal of Advertising Research,* 41, no. 5 (September/October 2001): 33–52.
85. Rob McGann, "Generation Y Embraces SMS," *ClickZ Stats*, accessed November 2008 at www.clickz.com/stats/sectors/wireless/article.php/3489776; and Jyoti Thottam, "How Kids Set the (Ring) Tone," *TIME*, April 4, 2005, 40–42, 45.
86. Marianne Wilson and Katherine Field, "Defining Gen Y," *Chain Store Age,* Vol. 83, No. 3 (Mar 2007): 36.
87. Mike Beirne, "Generation Gab," *Brandweek,* June 30–July 7, 2008, 16–20.
88. Natalie Hope McDonald, "Targeting Tweens," *Dealerscope,* 49, no. 11 (October 2007): 48.
89. David G. Kennedy, "Coming of Age in Consumerdom," *American Demographics* (April 2004): 14.
90. "Teen Market Profile," *Magazine Publishers of America*, accessed at www.magazine.org/marketprofiles.
91. Mike Duff, "The Tween Consumer: Price-Conscious Retailer Destination for Accessories," *Retailing Today,* 46, no. 1 (January 8, 2007): 24.
92. Aysen Bakir, Jeffrey G. Blodgett, and Gregory M. Rose, "Children's Responses to Gender-Role Stereotyped Advertisements," *Journal of Advertising Research* (June 2008): 255–266.
93. Clark Crowdus, "Pay Your Respects: Twixters More Like Parents Than You'd Think," *Marketing News*, March 15, 2005, 22, 25.
94. "How to Market to a New Demographic Segment: Twixters," *ABA Bank Marketing,* 37, no. 5 (June 2005): 5.
95. Scott Schroder and Warren Zeller, "Gent to Know Gen X—and Its Segments," *Multichannel News*, March 21, 2005, 55; and Tabitha Armstrong, "GenX Family Values," *The Lane Report*, January 1, 2005, 41.
96. "The Scoop on Gen X," *Work & Family Life,* 19 (January 2005): 1.
97. Paula M. Poindexter and Dominic L. Lasorsa, "Generation X: Is Its Meaning Understood?" *Newspaper Research Journal,* 20, no. 4 (Fall 1999): 28–36.
98. Rob McGann, "Only Banking Increased 47 Percent Since 2002," *ClickZ Stats*, accessed November 2008 at http://clickz.com/stats/sectors/finance/article.php.3481976.
99. "Marriott Revamp Targets Gen Xers," *Hotels*, 39 (May 2005): 14; and Ed Watkins, "Meet Your New Guest: Generation X," *Lodging Hospitality*, 61 (March 15, 2005): 2.
100. James Morrow, "X-It Plans," *American Demographics* (May 2004): 35–38.
101. Linda Jane Coleman, Marie Hladikova, and Maria Savelyeva, "The Baby Boomer Market," *Journal of Targeting, Measurement and Analysis for Marketing,* 14, no. 3 (April 2006): 191–209.
102. "Boomer Facts," *American Demographics* (January 1996): 14. Also see Diane Crispell, "U.S. Population Forecasts Decline for 2000, but Rise Slightly for 2050," *Wall Street Journal*, March 25, 1996, B3. "Advertising to 50s and Over," *Brand Strategy (London)*, April 5, 2005, 57.
103. Susan Dann, "Branded Generations: Baby Boomers Moving into the Seniors Market," *Journal of Product & Brand Management,* 16, no. 6 (2007): 429–431.
104. William E. Hauck and Nancy Stanforth, "Cohort Perception of Luxury Goods and Services," *Journal of Fashion Marketing and Management,* 11, no. 2 (2007): 175–188.
105. Paula Andruss, "The Golden Age," *Marketing News*, April 1, 2005, 21, 26.
106. Coleman, Hladikova, and Savelyeva, "The Baby Boomer Market," 200.
107. Christopher D. Hopkins, Catherine A. Roster, and Charles M. Wood, "Making the Transition to Retirement: Appraisals, Post-Transition Lifestyle, and Changes in Consumption Patterns," *Journal of Consumer Marketing,* 23, no. 2 (2006): 89–101.
108. "Table 2. Projections of the Population by Selected Age Groups and Sex for the United States: 2010 to 2050," accessed at www.census.gov/population/www/projections/summarytables.html; and "Table 8. Resident Population by Race, Hispanic Origin, and Age: 2000 and 2006," *Statistical Abstract of the United States 2008,* accessed November 2008 at www.census.gov/compendia/statab/cats/population .html.
109. Christine L. Himes, "Elderly Americans," *Population Bulletin,* 56, no. 4 (December 2001): 3–40; and "Table 98. Expectations of Life at Birth, 1970 to 2004, and Projections, 2010 and 2015" and "Table 99. Average Number of Years of Life Remaining by Sex and Age: 1979 to 2003," *Statistical Abstract of the United States 2008,* accessed November 2008 at www.census.gov/prod/2007pubs/08abstract/vitstat.pdf.
110. Tim Reisenwitz, Rajesh Iyer, David B. Kuhlmeier, and Jacqueline K. Eastman, "The Elderly's Internet Usage: An Updated Look," *Journal of Consumer Marketing,* 24, no. 7 (2007): 406–418.
111. Benny Barak and Leon G. Schiffman, "Cognitive Age: A Nonchronological Age Variable," in *Advances in Consumer Research*, 8, ed. Kent B. Monroe (Ann Arbor, MI: Association for Consumer Research, 1981), 602–606; Elaine Sherman, Leon G. Schiffman, and William R. Dillon, "Age/Gender Segments and Quality of Life Differences," in *1988 Winter Educators' Conference*, eds. Stanley Shapiro and A. H. Walle (Chicago:

American Marketing Association, 1988), 319–320; Stuart Van Auken and Thomas E. Barry, "An Assessment of the Trait Validity of Cognitive Age," *Journal of Consumer Psychology* (1995): 107–132; Robert E. Wilkes, "A Structural Modeling Approach to the Measurement and Meaning of Cognitive Age," *Journal of Consumer Research* (September 1992): 292–301; and Chad Rubel, "Mature Market Often Misunderstood," *Marketing News*, August 28, 1995, 28–29.

112. Elaine Sherman, Leon G. Schiffman, and Anil Mathur, "The Influence of Gender on the New-Age Elderly's Consumption Orientation," *Psychology & Marketing,* 18, no. 10 (October 2001): 1073–1089.
113. Elaine Sherman, quoted in David B. Wolfe, "The Ageless Market," *American Demographics* (July 1987): 26–28, 55–56.
114. Isabelle Szmigin and Marylyn Carrigan, "Leisure and Tourism Services and the Older Innovator," *The Service Industries Journal* (London), 21, no. 3 (July 2001): 113–129; and I. Polyak, "The Center of Attention," *American Demographic,* 22, (2000) 32.
115. Jacqueline K. Eastman and Rajesh Iyer, "The Elderly's Uses and Attitudes Towards the Internet," *Journal of Consumer Marketing,* 21, no. 3 (2004): 208–220.
116. Charles A. McMellon and Leon G. Schiffman, "Cybersenior Empowerment: How Some Older Individuals Are Taking Control of Their Lives," *Journal of Applied Gerontology,* 21, no. 2 (June 2002): 157–175; and Charles A. McMellon and Leon G. Schiffman, "Cybersenior Mobility: Why Some Older Consumers May Be Adopting the Internet," *Advances in Consumer Research,* 27 (2000): 138–144.
117. Patti Williams and Aimee Drolet, "Age-Related Differences in Responses to Emotional Advertisements," *Journal of Consumer Research,* 32 (December 2005): 343–354.
118. Raphaëlle Lambert-Pandraud, Gilles Laurent, and Eric Lapersoone, "Repeat Purchasing of New Automobiles by Older Consumers: Empirical Evidence and Interpretations," *Journal of Marketing,* 69 (April 2005): 97–113.
119. George Moschis, Carolyn Curasi, and Danny Bellenger, "Patronage Motives of Mature Consumers in the Selection of Food and Grocery Stores," *Journal of Consumer Marketing,* 21, no. 2 (2004): 112–133.
120. Cabrini Pak and Ajit Kambil, "Over 50 and Ready to Shop: Serving the Aging Consumer," *Journal of Business Strategy,* 27, no. 6 (2006): 18.
121. James W. Gentry, Suraj Commuri, and Sunkyu Jun, "Review of Literature on Gender in the Family," *Academy of Marketing Science Review* (Vancouver) (2003): 1.
122. Sanjay Putrevu, "Communicating with the Sexes," *Journal of Advertising,* 33 (Fall 204): 51–62.
123. Stephanie M. Noble, David A. Griffith, and Mavis T. Adjei, "Drivers of Local Merchant Loyalty: Understanding the Influence of Gender and Shopping Motives," *Journal of Retailing,* 82, no. 3 (2006): 177–188.
124. Debra Kaufman, "Look Who Controls the Pursestrings," *Television Week,* 27, no. 6 (February 18–February 25, 2008): 16–17.
125. "Dudes: Do I Look Fat in This Survey?" *Brandweek*, April 18, 2005, 20.
126. Yuki Noguchi, "Women Narrow the Internet Gender Gap, Survey Finds," *Washington Post,* December 29, 2005, D1.
127. Scott M. Smith and David B. Whitlark, "Men and Women Online: What Makes Them Click?" *Marketing Research,* 13, no. 2 (Summer 2001): 20–25.
128. Kara A. Arnold and Lyle R. Wetsch, "Sex Differences and Information Processing; Implications for Marketing on the Internet," in *2001 AMA Winter Educators' Conference* 12, eds. Ram Krishnan and Madhu Viswanathan (Chicago: American Marketing Association 2001), 357–365.
129. C. Jeanne Hill and Susan K. Harmon, "Male Gender Role Beliefs, Coupon Use and Bargain Hunting," *Academy of Marketing Studies Journal* 11, no. 2 (2007): 107–121.
130. Silvia Lagnado, "Getting Real About Beauty," *Advertising Age*, December 6, 2004, 20.
131. Kelley Skoloda, "Reaching Out to Today's 'Multiminding' Woman," *Brandweek*, April 25, 2005, 28–29.
132. Rifka Rosenwein, "The Baby Sabbatical," *American Demographics* (February 2002): 36–40.
133. Kelley Skoloda, "Reaching Out to Today's 'Multiminding' Woman," *Brandweek,* April 25, 2005, 28–29.
134. Thomas Barry, Mary Gilly, and Lindley Doran, "Advertising to Women with Different Career Orientations," *Journal of Advertising Research,* 25 (April–May 1985): 26–35.
135. Alice Z. Cuneo, "Advertisers Target Women, but Market Remains Elusive," *Advertising Age*, November 10, 1997, 1, 24–26.
136. Alison Stein Wellner, "The Female Persuasion," *American Demographics*, 24, 2 (February 2002): 24–29.
137. Kenneth Hein, "Beringer Fabricates New Ladies Wine," *Brandweek*, April 4, 2005, 15; Stephanie Thompson, "Lenart Turns Godiva Toward Stylish, Self-Indulgent Brand," *Advertising Age*, November 15, 2004, 46; and Beth Snyder Bulik, "Electronics Retailers Woo Women," *Advertising Age*, November 15, 2004, 16.

Chapter 13

1. "Panorama of the European Union," *Europa: The EU at a Glance,* accessed November 2008 at http://europa.eu/abc/panorama/index_en.htm.
2. Mauricio Hurtado and Edgar Ahrens, "International Tax Review, Regional Guides: North America," accessed November 2008 at www.internationaltaxreview.com; and "NAFTA 10 Years Later: Information and Communication Technologies," *U.S. Department of Commerce, International Trade Administration,* accessed November 2008 at www.ita.doc.gov/td/industry/otea/nafta/ict.pdf#search =nafta%20market%20size; and "North America Free Trade Agreement," accessed November 2008 at www.export.gov/fta/nafta/doc_fta_nafta.asp.
3. Larry Roellig, "Designing Global Brands: Critical Lessons," *Design Management Journal,* 12, no. 4 (Fall 2001): 40–45; and "MTV: Music Television and H&Q Asia Pacific's @ Japan Media Group to Launch New 24-Hour Channel in Japan," *PR Newswire,* August 29, 2000, 1.
4. Michael Silk and David L. Andrews, "Beyond a Boundary? Sport, Transnational Advertising, and the Reimagining of National Culture," *Journal of Sport and Social Issues,* 25, no. 2 (May 2001): 180–201.
5. Satish Shankar, Charles Ormiston, Nicolas Bloch, Robert Schaus, and Vijay Vishwanath, "How to Win in Emerging Markets," *MIT Sloan Management Review,* 49, no. 3 (Spring 2008): 19–23.
6. Jean Halliday, "Champion of the Yugo to Import Chinese Cars," *Advertising Age,* March 7, 2005, 12.
7. C. Samuel Craig and Susan P. Douglas, "Beyond National Culture: Implications of Cultural Dynamics for Consumer Research," *International Marketing Review,* 23, no. 3 (2006): 331.
8. Yungwook Kim, "Do South Korean Companies Need to Obscure Their Country-of-Origin Image? A Case of Samsung," *Corporate Communications: An International Journal,* 11, no. 2 (2006): 126–137.
9. Hamin and Greg Elliott, "A Less-Developed Country Perspective of Consumer Ethnocentrism and 'Country of Origin' Effects: Indonesian Evidence," *Asian Pacific Journal of Marketing,* 18, no. 2 (2006): 79–92.
10. Amal R. Karunaratna and Pascale G. Quester, "Influence of Cognition of Product Component Country of Origin Evaluation," *Asia Pacific Journal of Marketing,* 19, no. 4 (2007): 349–362.
11. Ekrem Cengiz and Fazil Kirkbir, "Turkish Consumers' Evaluation of Products Made in Foreign Countries: The Country of Origin Effect," *Innovative Marketing,* 3, no. 2 (2007): 72–92.
12. Sharyne Merritt and Vernon Staubb, "A Cross-Cultural Exploration of Country-of-Origin Preference," in *1995 AMA Winter Educators' Proceedings,* eds. David W. Stewart and Naufel J. Vilcassim (Chicago: American Marketing Association, 1995), 380; Jill Gabrielle Klein, Richard Ettenson, and Marlene D.

Morris, "The Animosity Model of Foreign Product Purchase: An Empirical Test in the People's Republic of China," *Journal of Marketing,* 62 (January 1998): 89–100; and Gillian Sullivan Mort, Hume Winzar, and C. Min Han, "Country Image Effects in International Services: A Conceptual Model and Cross-National Empirical Test," in *2001 AMA Educators' Proceedings* 12, eds. Greg W. Marshall and Stephen J. Grove (Chicago: American Marketing Association, 2001), 43–44.

13. Simon Kwok, Mark Uncles, and Yimin Huang, "Brand Preferences and Brand Choices Among Urban Chinese Consumers," *Asia Pacific Journal of Marketing and Logistics,* 18, no. 3 (2006): 163–172.
14. Siqing Peng and Yahui Zou, "The Moderating Effect of Multicultural Competence in Brand-of-Origin Effect," *International Management Review,* 3, no. 3 (2007): 57–65.
15. Gary S. Insch and J. Brad McBride, "The Impact of Country-of-Origin Cues on Consumer Perceptions of Product Quality: A Binational Test of the Decomposed Country-of-Origin Construct," *Journal of Business Research,* 57 (2004): 256–265.
16. Leila Hamzaoui Essoussi and Dwight Merunka, "Consumers' Product Evaluations in Emerging Markets," *International Marketing Review,* 24, no. 4 (2007): 409–426.
17. Ibid.
18. Klein, Ettenson, and Morris, "The Animosity Model," 89–100.
19. Michel Laroche, Maria Kalamas, and Mark Cleveland, "'I' Versus 'We': How Individualists and Collectivists Use Information Sources to Formulate Their Service Expectations," *International Marketing Review,* 22, no. 3 (2005): 279–308.
20. Kritika Kongsompong, "Cultural Diversities Between Singapore and Australia: An Analysis of Consumption Behavior," *Journal of the American Academy of Business,* 9, no. 2 (September 2006): 87–92.
21. Daniel Nilsson, "A Cross-Cultural Comparison of Self-Service Technology Use," *European Journal of Marketing,* 41, nos. 3/4 (2007): 367–381.
22. Olin Lagon, "Culturally Correct Site Design," *Web Techniques,* 5, no. 9 (September 2000): 49–51.
23. Ultrich R. Orth, Harold F. Koenig, and Zuzana Firbasova, "Cross-National Differences in Consumer Response to the Framing of Advertising Messages," *European Journal of Marketing,* 41, nos. 3/4 (2007): 327–348.
24. "Market Focus: Bottled Mineral Water," *Brand Strategy (London),* February 11, 2004, 42.
25. Julien Cayla and Giana M. Eckhardt, "Asian Brands and the Shaping of a Transnational Imagined Community," *Journal of Consumer Research,* 35 (August 2008): 216–230.
26. Robert G. Tian and Charles Emery, "Cross-Cultural Issues in Internet Marketing," *Journal of American Academy of Business,* 1, no. 2 (March 2002): 217–224; and Keith E. Thompson and Julia Engelken, "Mapping the Values Driving Organic Food Choice," *European Journal of Marketing,* 38, no. 8 (2004): 995–1012.
27. Michael Fielding, "Accrued Interest: Western-Style Banks Tailor Approach to Draw Muslims," *Marketing News,* May 15, 2005, 41–44.
28. John A. McCarty, Martin I. Horn, Mary Kate Szenasy, and Jocelyn Feintuch, "An Exploratory Study of Consumer Style: Country Differences and International Segments," *Journal of Consumer Behaviour* (January–February 2007): 53–63.
29. Nancy Y. Wong and Aaron C. Ahuvia, "Personal Taste and Family Face: Luxury Consumption in Confucian and Western Societies," *Psychology and Marketing,* 15, no. 5 (August 1998): 423–441. Also see Sarah Ellison, "Sex-Themed Ads Often Don't Travel Well," *Wall Street Journal,* March 31, 2000, 87.
30. Kitty Go, "Lessons in How to Love Lingerie: The Opening of Hong Kong's Largest Luxury Lingerie Store Heralds the Beginning of a Process to Educate Women on the Benefits of Wearing Their Wealth Close to the Skin," *Financial Times (London),* May 28, 2005, 9.
31. Mark S. Rosenbaum and Daniel L. Spears, "Who Buys That? Who Does What? Analysis of Cross-Cultural Consumption Behaviours Among Tourists in Hawaii," *Journal of Vacation Marketing* 11, no. 3 (2005): 235–247.
32. Moises Naim, "Can the World Afford a Middle Class?" *Foreign Policy,* 165 (March–April 2008): 95–96.
33. Dan Mintz, "Sagging Markets? Look to China," *Adweek,* 49, no. 21 (June 23, 2008): 16.
34. Chip Walker, "The Global Middle Class," *American Demographics* (September 1995): 40–46; Paula Kephart, "How Big Is the Mexican Market?" *American Demographics* (October 1995): 17–18; and Rahul Jacob, "The Big Rise," *Fortune,* May 30, 1994, 74–90.
35. Rainer Hengst, "Plotting Your Global Strategy," *Direct Marketing,* August 2000, 55.
36. Benjamin Senauer and Linda Goetz, "The Growing Middle Class in Developing Countries and the Market for High-Value Food Products," *Prepared for the Workshop on Global Markets for High-Value Food, Economic Research Service, USDA,* Washington, D.C., February 14, 2003, accessed at www.farmfoundation.org/documents/ben-sanauerpaper2—10—3-13-03_000.pdf.
37. Peter Marber, "Globalization and Its Contents," *World Policy Journal* (Winter 2004–2005): 29–37.
38. Mookyu Lee and Francis M. Ulgado, "Consumer Evaluations of Fast-Food Services: A Cross-National Comparison," *Journal of Services Marketing,* 11, no. 1 (1997): 39–52.
39. Ann Veeck and Alvin C. Burns, "Changing Tastes: The Adoption of New Food Choices in Post-Reform China," *Journal of Business Research,* 58 (2005): 644–652.
40. *R. Stephen Parker, Charles M. Hermans, and Allen D. Schaefer, "Fashion Consciousness of Chinese, Japanese and American Teenagers," *Journal of Fashion Marketing and Management,* 8, no. 2 (2004): 176–186.
41. R. Stephen Parker, Charles M. Hermans, and Allen D. Schaefer, "Fashion Consciousness of Chinese, Japanese and American Teenagers," *Journal of Fashion Marketing and Management,* 8 (2004): 182.
42. Energy BBDO, "The GenWorld Teen Study," accessed November 2008 at www.businessfordiplomaticaction.com/learn/articles/genworld_leave_behind.pdf.
43. Becky Ebenkamp, "Creative Consciousness," *Brandweek,* January 16, 2006, 14.
44. Energy BBDO, "The GenWorld Teen Study," 17.
45. Rick Yan, "To Reach China's Consumers, Adapt to Guo Qing," *Harvard Business Review* (September–October 1994): 66–67.
46. Kathy Chen, "Chinese Babies Are Coveted Consumers," *Wall Street Journal,* May 15, 1998, B1; and Fara Warner, "Western Markets Send Researchers to China to Plumb Consumers' Minds," *Wall Street Journal,* March 28, 1997, B5.
47. Mindy F. Ji and James U. McNeal, "How Chinese Children's Commercials Differ from Those of the United States: A Content Analysis," *Journal of Advertising,* 30, no. 3 (Fall 2001): 78–92.
48. Tara Parker-Pope, "Nonalcoholic Beer Hits the Spot in Mideast," *Wall Street Journal,* December 6, 1995, B1.
49. Warner, "Western Markets Send Researchers," B5.
50. Vanessa O'Connell, "Exxon 'Centralizes' New Global Campaign," *Wall Street Journal,* July 11, 2001, B6.
51. Robert L. Wehling, "Even at P&G, Only 3 Brands Make Truly Global Grade So Far," *Advertising Age International,* January 1998, 8.
52. Chingching Chang, "The Effectiveness of Using a Global Look in an Asian Market, *Journal of Advertising Research* (June 2008): 199–214.
53. Jung-Wan Lee and Simon Tai, "Young Consumers' Perceptions of Multinational Firms and Their Acculturation Channels Towards Western Products in Transition Economies," *International Journal of Emerging Markets,* 1, no. 3 (2006): 212–224.

54. Jamie Murphy and Arno Scharl, "An Investigation of Global Versus Local Online Branding," *International Marketing Review,* 24, no. 3 (2007): 297–312.
55. Maureen Mangiavas, "Global Brands, Tribal Pride," *Medical Marketing and Media,* 41, no. 3 (2006): 86.
56. Roblyn Simeon, "A Conceptual Model Linking Brand Building Strategies and Japanese Popular Culture," *Marketing Intelligence & Planning,* 24, no. 5 (2006): 463–476.
57. Douglas B. Holt, John A. Quelch, and Earl L. Taylor, "How Global Brands Compete," *Harvard Business Review* (September 2004): 68–75.
58. Ibid.
59. Alokparna Basu Monga and Debroah Roedder John, "Consumer Response to Brand Extensions: Does Culture Matter?" *Advances in Consumer Research,* 31 (2004): 216–222.
60. Alokparna Basu Monga and Debroah Roedder John, "Cultural Differences in Brand Extension Evaluation: The Influence of Analytic Versus Holistic Thinking," *Journal of Consumer Research,* 33 (March 2007): 529–536.
61. Friedman, "Big Mac II," A27; and Drew Martin and Paul Herbig, "Marketing Implications of Japan's Social-Cultural Underpinnings," *Journal of Brand Management,* 9, no. 3 (January 2002): 171–179.
62. Pamela Buxton, "Helping Brands Take on the World," *Marketing (London),* May 13, 1999, 32.
63. Martin S. Roth, "The Effects of Culture and Socioeconomics on the Performance of Global Brand Image Strategies," *Journal of Marketing Research,* 32 (1995): 163–175.
64. Roellig, "Designing Global Brands," 43.
65. Sicco Van Gelder, "Global Brand Strategy," *Journal of Brand Management,* 12 (September 2004): 39–48.
66. Sharon Shavitt, Michelle R. Nelson, and Rose Mei Len Yuan, "Exploring Cross-Cultural Differences in Cognitive Responding to Ads," in *Advances in Consumer Research,* 24, eds. Merrie Brucks and Deborah J. MacInnis (Provo, UT: Association for Consumer Research, 1997), 245–250.
67. Michael A. Callow, Dawn B. Lerman, and Mayo de Juan Vigaray, "Motivational Appeals in Advertising: A Comparative Content Analysis of United States and Spanish Advertising," in *Proceedings of the Sixth Symposium on Cross-Cultural Consumer and Business Studies,* ed. Scott M. Smith (Honolulu, HI: Association of Consumer Research and the Society for Consumer Psychology, 1997), 392–396.
68. Dean Foster, "Playing with China Dollars," *Brandweek,* November 10, 1997, 20–23.
69. Michael Callow and Leon G. Schiffman, "Sociocultural Meanings in Visually Standardized Print Ads," *European Journal of Marketing,* 38, nos. 9/10 (2004): 1113–1128.
70. Kip D. Cassino, "A World of Advertising," *American Demographics* (November 1997): 60.
71. Amy Chozick, "Cold Stone Aims to Be Hip in Japan; Ice-Cream Chain Uses Word of Mouth as Part of Bid for an Urban Image," *Wall Street Journal* (Eastern edition), December 14, 2006, B10.
72. Jiafei Yin, "International Advertising Strategies in China: A Worldwide Survey of Foreign Advertisers," *Journal of Advertising Research,* 39, no. 6 (November/December 1999): 25–35.
73. Robert Frank, "Potato Chips to Go Global—or So Pepsi Bets," *Wall Street Journal,* November 30, 1995, B1.
74. Teresa Domzal and Lynette Unger, "Emerging Positioning Strategies in Global Marketing," *Journal of Consumer Marketing,* 4 (Fall 1987): 27–29.
75. Sangeeta Ramarapu, John E. Timmerman, and Narender Ramarapu, "Choosing Between Globalization and Localization as a Strategic Thrust for Your International Marketing Effort," *Journal of Marketing Theory and Practice,* 7, no. 2 (Spring 1999): 97–105.
76. Nitish Singh, Olivier Furrer, and Massimiliano Ostinelli, "To Localize or to Standardize on the Web: Empirical Evidence from Italy, India, Netherlands, Spain, and Switzerland," *Multinational Business Review,* 12 (Spring 2004): 69–87.
77. Desmond Lam and Dick Mizerski, "Cross-Cultural Differences on the Internet: The Case of Internet Privacy," *American Marketing Association Conference Proceedings,* 14 (2003): 257–258.
78. Wen Gong, Zhan G. Li, and Rodney L. Stump, "Global Internet Use and Access: Cultural Considerations," *Asia Pacific Journal of Marketing,* 19, no. 1 (2007): 69.
79. Ben Vickers, "In Internet Age, Europe Looks to Define Its Many Cultures Against U.S. Online," *Wall Street Journal,* April 2, 2001, B9F.
80. Shintaro Okazaki, "Searching the Web for Global Brands: How American Brands Standardize Their Web Sites in Europe," *European Journal of Marketing,* 39, nos. 1/2 (2005): 87–109.
81. Nitish Singh, Hongxin Zhao, and Xiaorui Hu, "Cultural Adaptation on the Web: A Study of American Companies' Domestic and Chinese Websites," *Journal of Global Information Management,* 11 (July–September 2003): 63–80.
82. Jack Russell, "Working Women Give Japan Culture Shock," *Advertising Age,* January 16, 1995, 1–24.
83. Sidney J. Levy, "Myth and Meaning in Marketing," in *1974 Combined Proceedings,* ed. Ronald C. Curhan (Chicago: American Marketing Association, 1975), 555–556.
84. Stuart Elliott, "Research Finds Consumers Worldwide Belong to Six Basic Groups That Cross National Lines," *New York Times,* June 25, 1998, D8.

Chapter 14

1. Lauren Keller Johnson, "Harnessing the Power of the Customer," *Harvard Business Review* (March 2004): 3.
2. Thomas S. Robertson, "The Process of Innovation and the Diffusion of Innovation," *Journal of Marketing,* 31 (January 1967): 14–19.
3. Everett M. Rogers, *Diffusion of Innovations,* 4 (New York: Free Press, 1995); and Hubert Gatignon and Thomas S. Robertson, "Innovative Decision Processes," in *Handbook of Consumer Behavior,* eds. Thomas S. Robertson and Harold H. Kassarjian (Upper Saddle River, NJ: Prentice Hall, 1991), 316–348.
4. S. Ram and Hyung-Shik Jung, "Innovativeness in Product Usage: A Comparison of Early Adopters and Early Majority," *Psychology and Marketing,* 11 (January–February 1994): 57–67; A. R. Petrosky, "Gender and Use Innovation: An Inquiry into the Socialization of Innovative Behavior," in *1995 AMA Educators' Proceedings,* eds. Barbara B. Stern and George M. Zinkan (Chicago: American Marketing Association, 1995), 299–307; Kyungae Park and Carl L. Dyer, "Consumer Use Innovative Behavior: An Approach Toward Its Causes," in *Advances in Consumer Research* 22, ed. Frank R. Kardes and Mita Sujan (Provo, UT: Association for Consumer Research 1995), 566–572.
5. Earle Eldridge, "Pickups Get Women's Touch," *USA Today,* June 13, 2001, 1B, 2B.
6. Rogers, *Diffusion of Innovations,* 15–16.
7. Hsiang Chen and Kevin Crowston, "Comparative Diffusion of the Telephone and the World Wide Web: An Analysis of Rates of Adoption," in *Proceedings of WebNet '97—World Conference of the WWW, Internet and Intranet,* eds. Suave Lobodzinski and Ivan Tomek, (AACE: Toronto, Canada), 110–115.
8. Tariq Bhatti, "Exploring Factors Influencing the Adoption of Mobile Commerce," *Journal of Internet Banking and Commerce,* 12, no. 3 (2007): 1–13.
9. Susan H. Higgins and William L. Shanklin, "Seeding Mass Market Acceptance for High Technology Consumer Products," *Journal of Consumer Marketing,* 9 (Winter 1992): 5–14.
10. Rosanna Garcia, Fleura Bardhi, and Colette Friedrich, "Overcoming Consumer Resistance to Innovation," *MIT Sloan Management Review,* 48, no. 4 (Summer 2007): 82–88.
11. Ibid.

12. Craig Van Slyke, France Belanger, and Varadharajan Sridhar, "A Comparison of American and Indian Consumers Perceptions of Electronic Commerce," *Information Resources Management Journal,* 18, no. 2 (April–June 2005): 24–40.
13. Albert Maruggi, "Podcasting Offers a Sound Technique," *Brandweek,* May 2, 2005, 21.
14. "Dyson's Marketing Sensation," *Strategic Direction,* 21, no. 2 (February 2005): 17–19.
15. Shazia Ali, "Upwardly Mobile: A Study into Mobile TV Use Amongst Children," *Young Consumers,* 8, no. 1 (2007): 52–57.
16. Laurien Kunst and Jan Kratzer, "Diffusion of Innovations Through Social Networks of Children," *Young Consumers,* 8, no. 1 (2007): 36–51.
17. Everett M. Rogers and F. Floyd Shoemaker, *Communication of Innovations,* 2 (New York: Free Press, 1971), 32–33; see also Elizabeth C. Hirschman, "Consumer Modernity, Cognitive Complexity, Creativity and Innovativeness," in *Marketing in the 80's: Changes and Challenges,* eds. Richard P. Bagozzi et al. (Chicago: American Marketing Association, 1980), 135–139.
18. "BSE Economics: What's at Stake in Wisconsin?" Wisconsin Department of Agriculture, Trade & Consumer Protection, January 8, 2004, 1, accessed at www.datcp.state.wi.us/ah/agriculture/animals/disease/bse/pdf/economic_impacts_BSE.pdf.
19. Sangeeta Singh, "Cultural Differences in, and Influences on, Consumers' Propensity to Adopt Innovations," *International Marketing Review,* 23, no. 2 (2006): 173–191.
20. Raquel Castaño, Mita Sujan, Manish Kacher, and Harish Sujan, "Managing Consumer Uncertainty in the Adoption of New Products: Temporal Distance and Mental Simulation," *Journal of Marketing Research,* 45 (June 2008): 320–336.
21. Eun-Ju Lee, Kyoung-Nan Kwon, and David W. Schumann, "Segmenting the Non-adopter Category in the Diffusion of Internet Banking," *International Journal of Bank Marketing,* 23, no. 5 (2005): 414–437.
22. Kenichi Ohmae, "Managing in a Borderless World," *Harvard Business Review* (May–June 1989): 152–161.
23. Jacob Goldenberg, Barak Libai, and Eitan Muller, "Riding the Saddle: How Cross-Market Communications Can Create a Major Slump in Sales," *Journal of Marketing,* 66, no. 2 (April 2002): 1–16.
24. Jana Bowden and David Corkindale, "Identifying the Initial Target Consumer for Innovations: An Integrative Approach," *Marketing Intelligence & Planning,* 23, no. 6 (2005): 562–573.
25. David J. Burns and Robert F. Krampf, "A Semiotic Perspective on Innovative Behavior," in *Developments in Marketing Science,* ed. Robert L. King (Richmond, VA: Academy of Marketing Science, 1991), 32–35.
26. Wayne D. Hoyer and Nancy M. Ridgway, "Variety Seeking as an Explanation for Exploratory Purchase Behavior: A Theoretical Model," in *Advances in Consumer Research,* 11, ed. Thomas C. Kinnear (Provo, UT: Association for Consumer Research, 1984), 114–119.
27. Carolyn A. Lin, "Predicting Webcasting Adoption via Personal Innovativeness and Perceived Utilities," *Journal of Advertising Research* (June 2006): 234.
28. Tanawat Hirunyawipada and Audhesh K. Paswan, "Consumer Innovativeness and Perceived Risk: Implications for High Technology Product Adoption," *Journal of Consumer Marketing,* 23, no. 4 (2006): 182–198.
29. Agnes Murray and David Demick, "Wine Retailing in Ireland: The Diffusion of Innovation," *International Journal of Wine,* 18, no. 3 (2006): 215.
30. James M. Curran and Matthew L. Meuter, "Self-Service Technology Adoption: Comparing Three Technologies," *Journal of Services Marketing,* 19, no. 2 (2005): 103–113.
31. Maria Saakjarvi and Minttu Lampinen, "Consumer Perceived Risk in Successive Product Generations," *European Journal of Innovative Management,* 8, no. 2 (2005): 145–156.
32. Leon Schiffman, Elaine Sherman, and D.Y. Cohn, "Looking In on Global Consumer Users: To Develop Better Product Feature Sets," 2008 Global Business and Technology Association (GBATA) International Conference, Taipei, Taiwan.
33. HoJung Choo and Jae-Eun Chung, "Antecedents to New Food Product Purchasing Behavior among Innovator Groups in India," *European Journal of Marketing,* 38, nos. 5/6 (2004): 608–625.
34. Hirunyawipada and Paswan, "Consumer Innovativeness and Perceived Risk," 184.
35. Bruce MacEvoy, "Change Leaders and the New Media," *American Demographics* (January 1994): 42–48.
36. Susan Mitchell, "Technophiles and Technophobes," *American Demographics* (February 1994): 36–42.
37. Gordon C. Bruner II and Anand Kumar, "Explaining Consumer Acceptance of Handheld Internet Devices," *Journal of Business Research,* 58 (2005): 553–558.
38. Mary Long, Leon Schiffman, and Elaine Sherman, "Exploring the Dynamics of Online Retail-Related Activities," in *Retailing 2003: Strategic Planning in Uncertain Times,* Proceedings of the Seventh Triennial National Retailing Conference, Academy of Marketing Sciences, Columbus, Ohio, November 2003.
39. Windsor Holden, "Press Release: Juniper Research Predicts Mobile Games Market to Reach $10bn by 2009, Driven by Emerging Markets and Casual Gamers," *Juniper Research,* accessed December 2008 at http://juniperresearch.com/shop/viewpressrelease.php?pr=63.
40. Mirella Kleijnen, Ko de Ruyter, and Martin Wetzels, "Consumer Adoption of Wireless Services: Discovering the Rules While Playing the Game," *Journal of Interactive Marketing,* 18 (Spring 2004): 51–61.

Chapter 15

1. Itamar Simonson, "Shoppers' Easily Influenced Choices," *New York Times*, November 6, 1994, 11.
2. Herbert A. Simon, *Administrative Behavior*, 2 (New York: Free Press, 1965), 40.
3. James G. March and Herbert A. Simon, *Organizations* (New York: Wiley, 1958), 140–241.
4. Michael A. Jones, Philip J. Trocchia, and David L. Mothersbaugh, "Noneconomic Motivations for Price Haggling: An Exploratory Study," in *Advances in Consumer Research,* 24, eds. Merrie Brucks and Deborah J. MacInnis (Provo, UT: Association for Consumer Research, 1997), 388–391.
5. Samantha Murphy, "The Good, the Bad and the Ugly," *Chain Store Age,* 83, no. 11 (November 2007): 72.
6. Ritesh Saini and Ashwani Monga, "How I Decide Depends on What I Spend: Use of Heuristics Is Greater for Time Than for Money," *Journal of Consumer Research,* 34 (April 2008): 914–922.
7. Thomas Kramer and Lauren Block, "Conscious and Nonconscious Components of Superstitious Beliefs in Judgment and Decision Making," *Journal of Consumer Research,* 34 (April 2008): 783–793.
8. Meryl Paula Gardner, "Mood States and Consumer Behavior: A Critical Review," *Journal of Consumer Research,* 12 (December 1985): 281–300; and Robert A. Peterson and Matthew Sauber, "A Mood Scale for Survey Research," in *1983 AMA Educators' Proceedings,* eds. Patrick E. Murphy, et al. (Chicago: American Marketing Association, 1983), 409–414.
9. Ruth Belk Smith and Elaine Sherman, "Effects of Store Image and Mood on Consumer Behavior: A Theoretical and Empirical Analysis," in *Advances in Consumer Research,* 20, eds. Leigh McAlister and Michael L. Rothschild (Provo, UT: Association for Consumer Research, 1993), 631.
10. Knowles, Grove, and Burroughs, "An Experimental Examination."
11. Gordon C. Bruner, II, "The Effect of Problem-Recognition Style on Information Seeking," *Journal of the Academy of Marketing Science,* 15 (Winter 1987): 33–41.

12. Matthew Klein, "He Shops, She Shops," *American Demographics* (March 1998): 34–35.
13. Sharon E. Beatty and Scott M. Smith, "External Search Effort: An Investigation Across Several Product Categories," *Journal of Consumer Research,* 14 (June 1987): 83–95.
14. Niranjan V. Raman, "A Qualitative Investigation of Web-Browsing Behavior," in *Advances in Consumer Research*, eds. Brucks and MacInnis (Provo, UT: Association for Consumer Research, 1997), 511–516.
15. "Just the Facts," *Journal of Business Strategy*, 22, no. 2 (March/April, 2001): 3–4; and Kuan-Pin Chiang, Ruby Roy Dholakia, and Stu Westin, "Needle in the Cyberstack: Consumer Search for Information in the Web-Based Marketspace," *Advances in Consumer Research,* 31 (2004): 88–89.
16. Kristy E. Reynolds, Judith Anne Garretson Folse, and Michael A. Jones, "Search Regret: Antecedents and Consequences," *Journal of Retailing,* 82, no. 4 (2006): 339.
17. Ibid., 339–348.
18. John W. Pracejus, G. Douglas Olsen, and Thomas C. O'Guinn, "Nothing Is Something: The Production and Reception of Advertising Meaning Through the Use of White Space," *Advances in Consumer Research,* 30, eds. Punam Anand Keller and Dennis W. Rook (Valdosta, GA: Association for Consumer Research, 2003), 174; and Pamela Henderson, Joan Giese, and Joseph A. Cote, "Typeface Design and Meaning: The Three Faces of Typefaces," *Advances in Consumer Research,* 30 (2003), 175.
19. Ashley Lye, Wei Shao, and Sharyn Rundle-Thiele, "Decision Waves: Consumer Decisions in Today's Complex World," *European Journal of Marketing,* 39, nos. 1/2 (2005): 216–230.
20. Jeffrey F. Durgee, "Why Some Products 'Just Feel Right,' or, the Phenomenology of Product Rightness," in *Advances in Consumer Research,* 22, eds. Frank R. Kardes and Mita Sujan (Provo, UT: Association for Consumer Research, 1995), 650–652.
21. Tulin Erdem and Joffre Swait, "Brand Credibility, Brand Consideration, and Choice," *Journal of Consumer Research,* 31 (June 2004): 191–198
22. Alexander Chernev, "Jack of All Trades or Master of One? Product Differentiation and Compensatory Reasoning in Consumer Choice," *Journal of Consumer Research,* 33 (March 2007): 430–444.
23. Laurie Peterson, "The Strategic Shopper," *Adweek's Marketing Week*, March 30, 1992, 18–20.
24. Madhubalan Viswanathan, José Antonio Rosa, and James Edwin Harris, "Decision Making and Coping of Functionally Illiterate Consumers and Some Implications for Marketing Management," *Journal of Marketing,* 69 (January 2005): 15–31.
25. Ibid.
26. Lan Xia, "Consumer Choice Strategies and Choice Confidence in the Electronic Environment," in *1999 AMA Educators Proceedings,* 10, eds. Stephen P. Brown and D. Sudharshan (Chicago: American Marketing Association, 1999), 270–277.
27. Laura Daily, "If You Can Dream It, They Can Make It," *American Way*, April 1, 2005, 30.
28. Carey Goldberg, "Choosing the Joys of a Simplified Life," *New York Times*, September 21, 1995, C1, C9.
29. Ibid.
30. Nancy Spears, "The Time Pressured Consumer and Deal Proneness: Theoretical Framework and Empirical Evidence," in *2000 AMA Winter Educators' Conference*, 11, eds. John P. Workman and William D. Perreault (Chicago: American Marketing Association, 2000), 35–40.
31. Ardyth H. Gillespie and Gilbert W. Gillespie, Jr., "Family Food Decision-Making: An Ecological Systems Framework," *Journal of Family and Consumer Sciences,* 99, no. 2 (April 2007): 22–28.
32. Beth Snyder Bulik, "Apple Puts iPod Halo to Test with Shuffle and Mini," *Advertising Age*, January 17, 2005, 33, 28; and Walter S. Mossberg, "The Newest iPod Mini Rival: iRiver's $280 H10," *Wall Street Journal*, February 23, 2005, D4.
33. Sarah Fisher Gardial and David W. Schumann, "In Search of the Elusive Consumer Inference," in *Advances in Consumer Research*, eds. Goldberg, Gorn, and Pollay (Provo, UT: Association for Consumer Research, 1990), 283–287; see also Burke.
34. Emily Booth, "Getting Inside a Shopper's Mind," *Marketing (U.K.),* June 3, 1999, 33.
35. Kare Sandvik, Kjell Gronhaug, and Frank Lindberg, "Routes to Customer Retention: The Importance of Customer Satisfaction, Performance Quality, Brand Reputation and Customer Knowledge," in *AMA Winter Conference,* eds. Debbie Thorne LeClair and Michael Hartline (Chicago: American Marketing Association, 1997), 211–217.
36. Mohammed M. Nadeem, "Post-Purchase Dissonance: The Wisdom of the 'Repeat' Purchases," *Journal of Global Business Issues,* 1, no. 2 (Summer 2007): 183–193.
37. Raquel Sanchez-Fernandez and M. Angeles Iniesta-Bonillo, "Consumer Perception of Value: Literature Review and a New Conceptual Framework," *Journal of Consumer Satisfaction, Dissatisfaction and Complaining Behavior,* 19 (2006): 40–58.
38. Deirdre Shaw, Terry Newholm, and Roger Dickinson, "Consumption as Voting: An Exploration of Consumer Empowerment," *European Journal of Marketing,* 40, nos. 9/10 (2006): 1049–1067.
39. Mark Colgate, Vicky Thuy-Uyen Tong, Christina Kwai-Choi Lee, and John U. Farley, "Back from the Brink: Why Customers Stay," *Journal of Service Research,* 9, no. 3 (February 2007): 211–228.
40. Kurt Matzler, Martin Waiguny, and Johann Fuller, "Spoiled for Choice: Consumer Confusion in Internet-Based Mass Customization," *Innovative Marketing,* 3, no. 3 (2007): 9.
41. Ibid., 7–18.
42. Russell W. Belk and Gregory S. Coon, "Gift Giving as Agapic Love: An Alternative to the Exchange Paradigm Based on Dating Experiences," *Journal of Consumer Research,* 20 (December 1993): 393–417.
43. "More Consumers Buy Gifts for Themselves Than to Give as Gifts; 'Gift Market' Is a Misnomer, Since Most Consumers Buy Gift Products for Personal Consumption," *Business Wire*, April 17, 2000, 1.
44. Michel Laroche, Gad Saad, Elizabeth Browne, Mark Cleveland, and Chankon Kim, "Determinants of In-Store Information Search Strategies Pertaining to a Christmas Gift Purchase," *Revue Canadienne des Sciences de l'Administration,* 17, no. 1 (March 2000): 1–19.
45. Julie A. Ruth, Cele C. Otnes, and Frédéric F. Brunel, "Gift Receipt and the Reformulation of Interpersonal Relationships," *Journal of Consumer Research,* 25 (March 1999): 385–402.
46. Deborah Y. Cohn and Leon G. Schiffman, "A Taxonomy of Consumer Gifting Relationships," *Navigating Crisis and Opportunities in Global Markets: Leadership, Strategy and Governance, International Conference of the Global Business and Technology Association*, eds. Nejdet Delener and Chiang-nan Chaoin, June 8–12, 2004, 164–171.
47. Stephen J. Gould and Claudia E. Weil, "Gift-Giving and Gender Self-Concepts," *Gender Role,* 24 (1991): 617–637.
48. Tilottama G. Chowdhury, S. Ratneshwar, and Kalpesh K. Desai, "Do Unto Others As You Would Do Unto Yourself: Variety-Seeking Motives in Gift Giving," *Advances in Consumer Research,* 31, eds. Barbara E. Kahn and Mary Frances Luce (Valdosta, GA: Association for Consumer Research, 2004), 22–23.
49. Annamma Joy, "Gift Giving in Hong Kong and the Continuum of Social Ties," *Journal of Consumer Research,* 28, no. 2 (September 2001): 239–256.
50. Markus Giesler, "Consumer Gift Systems," *Journal of Consumer Research,* 33 (September 2006): 283–290.
51. Constance Hill and Celia T. Romm, "The Role of Mothers as Gift Givers: A Comparison Across Three Cultures," in *Advances in Consumer Research,* 23, eds. Kim P. Corfman and John G. Lynch, Jr. (Provo, UT: Association for Consumer Research, 1996), 21–27.

52. Leon G Schiffman and Deborah Y. Cohn, "Are They Playing by the Same Rules? A Consumer Gifting Classification of Marital Dyads," *Journal of Business Research*, forthcoming.
53. Kathleen M. Rassuli and Gilbert D. Harrell, "A New Perspective on Choice," in *Advances in Consumer Research*, eds. Goldberg, Gorn, and Pollay, 737–744.
54. James M. Perry, "Mike Weaver Proves That Everything Can Be a Collection," *Wall Street Journal*, August 16, 1995, 1.
55. Russell W. Belk, "Men and Their Machines," *Advances in Consumer Research,* 31, 2004, 273–278.
56. Stacey Menzel Baker and Patricia F. Kennedy, "Death by Nostalgia: A Diagnosis of Context-Specific Cases," in *Advances in Consumer Research,* 21, eds. Chris T. Allen and Deborah Roedder John (Provo, UT: Association for Consumer Research, 1994), 169–174.
57. Andy Wright, "Oh, the Stuff We Collect Series: XPRESS," *St. Petersburg Times*, August 30, 1999, 3D.
58. Robert Bryce, "Here's a Course in Personal Finance 101, the Hard Way," *New York Times*, April 30, 1995, F11.
59. Susan M. Lloyd, "Toward Understanding Relationship Marketing from the Consumer's Perspective: What Relationships Are and Why Consumers Choose to Enter Them," in *2000 AMA Educators' Proceedings,* 11, eds. Gregory T. Gundlach and Patrick E. Murphy (Chicago: American Marketing Association, 2000), 12–20; Leonard L. Berry, "Relationship Marketing of Services—Growing Interest, Emerging Perspectives," *Journal of the Academy of Marketing Science,* 23 (Fall 1995): 236–245; and Mary Jo Bitner, "Building Service Relationships: It's All About Promises," *Journal of the Academy of Marketing Science,* 23 (Fall 1995): 246–251.
60. Hussein Abdulla El-Omari, "Importance Attached to Relationship Marketing in the Emirate of Ajman (UAE): A Consumer's Point-of-View," *Journal of American Academy of Business,* 13, no. 1 (March 2008): 109–115.
61. Mary Long, Leon Schiffman, and Elaine Sherman, "Understanding the Relationships in Consumer Marketing Relationship Programs: A Content Analysis," in *Proceedings of the World Marketing Congress VII-II*, eds. K. Grant and Walker (Melbourne, Australia: Academy of Marketing Science, 1995), 10/27–10/32.
62. Lauren Barack, "Pretty, Pretty, Please," *Business 2.0,* April 2000, 176–180.
63. Regina Brady, "Preferential Treatment," *Target Marketing,* 31, no. 7 (July 2008): 23–24.
64. Emily Nelson, "Why Wal-Mart Sings, 'Yes, We Have Bananas,'" *Wall Street Journal*, October 6, 1998, B1, B4.
65. Mary Ellen Gordon and Kim McKeage, "Relationship Marketing Effectiveness: Differences between Women in New Zealand and the United States," in *1997 AMA Educators' Proceedings,* eds. William M. Pride and G. Tomas M. Hult (Chicago: American Marketing Association, 1997), 117–122.
66. Richard Cuthbertson and Steve Messenger, "Marrying Market Research and Customer Relationship Marketing: Are They Good Bedfellows?" *Journal of Direct, Data and Digital Marketing Practice,* 8, no. 2 (October–December 2006): 119.
67. Mike Beirne, "Burke Customizing Hilton Honors," *Brandweek*, October 11, 2004, 17.
68. Mary M. Long, Sylvia D. Clark, Leon G. Schiffman, and Charles McMellon, "In the Air Again: Frequent Flyer Relationship Programs and Business Travelers' Quality of Life," *International Journal of Tourism Research,* 5 (2003): 421–432.
69. Jagdish N. Sheth and Atul Parvatiyar, "Relationship Marketing in Consumer Marketing: Antecedents and Consequences," *Journal of the Academy of Marketing Science,* 23 (Fall 1995): 255–271.
70. Steve Schriver, "Customer Loyalty: Going, Going . . .," *American Demographics* (September 1997): 20–23.
71. Russell Lacey, "Relationship Drivers of Customer Commitment," *Journal of Marketing Theory and Practice,* 15, no. 4 (Fall 2007): 315–333.
72. Jean Donio, Paola Massari, and Giuseppina Passiante, "Customer Satisfaction and Loyalty in a Digital Environment: An Empirical Test," *Journal of Consumer Marketing,* 23, no. 7 (2006): 453.

Chapter 16

1. www.caru.com.
2. CARU New Releases: "Roseart Supports CARU and Children's Safety . . .," January 5, 2005; "Nabisco Puts Safety First in TV Ads," October 4, 2000; "Procter and Gamble Works with CARU on Pringles Commercial," April 15, 2004; and www.caru.org/news/index.asp.
3. Debra M. Desrochers and Debra J. Holt, "Children's Exposure to Television Advertising: Implications for Childhood Obesity," *Journal of Public Policy and Marketing,* 26, no. 2 (Fall 2007): 182–201.
4. Stuart Elliott, "McDonald's Ending Promotion on Jackets of Children's Report Cards," www.nytimes.com, January 18, 2008.
5. Melanie Warner, "The Food Industry Empire Strikes Back," www.nytimes.com, July 5, 2005.
6. Elizabeth S. Moore and Victoria J. Rideout, "The Online Marketing of Food to Children: Is It Just Fun and Games?" *Journal of Public Policy & Marketing*, 26, no. 2 (Fall 2007): 202–220. Kathleen Seiders and Ross D. Petty, "Taming the Obesity Beast: Children, Marketing, and Public Policy Considerations," *Journal of Public Policy & Marketing*, 26, no. 2 (Fall 2007): 236–242.
7. "Credit Scores Plummet as Student Debt Rises," *Business Wire*, New York, April 8, 2005.
8. So-hyun Joo, John E. Grable, and Dorothy C. Bagwell, "Credit Card Attitudes and Behaviors of College Students," *College Student Journal* (September 2003): 405–416.
9. "New York Law Targets Credit Card Ads at Universities," *Bank Marketing International* (December 2004): 1; and Jonathan D. Glater, "Marketing Code for Student Lenders," www.nytimes.com, September 10, 2008.
10. Stephen F. Pirog and James A. Roberts, "Personality and Credit Card Misuse Among College Students: The Mediating Role of Impulsiveness," *Journal of Marketing Theory and Practice*, 15, no. 1 (Winter 2007): 65–77.
11. Louise Story, "Home Equity Frenzy Was a Bank Ad Come True," www.nytimes.com, August 15, 2008.
12. R. Stephen Parker and Charles E. Pettijohn, "Ethical Considerations in the Use of Direct-to-Consumer Advertising and Pharmaceutical Promotions: The Impact on Pharmaceutical Sales and Physicians," *Journal of Business Ethics* (December 2003): 279–287; and Nat Ives, "Consumers Are Looking Past Commercials to Study Prescription Drugs," www.nytimes.com, March 25, 2005.
13. Stephanie Saul, "A Self-Imposed Ban on Drug Ads," www.nytimes.com, June 15, 2005.
14. Stephanie Clifford, "FDA Rules on Drug Ads Sow Confusion as Applied to Web," www.nytimes.com. April 16, 2009.
15. Louise Story and Brad Stone, "Facebook Retreats on Online Tracking," www.nytimes.com, November 30, 2007.
16. Louise Story, "How Do They Track You? Let Us Count the Ways," www.nytimes.com, March 9, 2008; Louise Story, "Where Every Ad Knows Your Name," www.nytimes.com, March 10, 2008.
17. Stephanie Clifford, "Ad-Targeting Companies and Critics Prepare for Senate Scrutiny," www.nytimes.com, July 8, 2008.
18. Anthony D. Miyazaki, "Online Privacy and the Disclosure of Cookie Use: Effects on Consumer Trust and Anticipated Patronage," *Journal of Public Policy and Marketing,* 27, no. 1 (Spring 2008): 19–33.

19. Nat Ives, "Ads Embedded in Online News Raise Questions," www.nytimes.com, February 24, 2005; and Doreen Carvajal, "Placing the Product in the Dialogue, Too," www.nytimes.com, January 17, 2006.
20. Johnnie L. Roberts, "TV's New Brand of Stars," *Newsweek*, November 22, 2004, 62–64; Stuart Elliott, "Burger King Takes a Product from TV to the Table," www.nytimes.com, January 21, 2005; Nat Ives, "Ads Embedded in Online News Raise Questions," www.nytimes.com, February 24, 2005; Stuart Elliott, "More Products Get Roles in Shows and Marketers Wonder If They're Getting Their Money's Worth," www.nytimes.com, March 29, 2005; and Rob Walker, "Soap Opera," www.nytimes.com, April 3, 2005.
21. Sony Ta and Dominick L. Frosch, "Pharmaceutical Product Placement: Simply Script or Prescription for Trouble?" *Journal of Public Policy and Marketing,* 27, no. 1 (Spring 2008): 98–106.
22. Rajagopal Raghunathan, Rebecca Walker Naylor, and Wayne D. Hoyer, "The Unhealthy = Tasty Intuition and Its Effects on Taste Inferences, Enjoyment, and Choice of Food Products," *Journal of Marketing,* 70, (October 2006): 170–184.
23. Brian Wansink and Koert van Ittersum, "Bottoms Up! The Influence of Elongation on Pouring and Consumption Value," *Journal of Consumer Research* (December 2003): 455–463; Brian Wansink, "Environmental Factors That Increase the Food Intake and Consumption Volume of Unknowing Consumers," *Annual Reviews* (Nutrition, 2004): 24, 455–479.
24. Barbara E. Kahn and Brian Wansink, "The Influence of Assortment Structure on Perceived Variety and Consumption Quantities," *Journal of Consumer Research* (March 2004): 519–534.
25. Thomas F. Stafford, "Alert or Oblivious? Factors Underlying Consumer Responses to Marketing Stimuli," *Psychology and Marketing* (September 2000): 745–760.
26. Ross D. Petty and J. Craig Andrews, "Covert Marketing Unmasked: A Legal and Regulatory Guide for Practices That Mask Marketing Messages," *Journal of Public Policy and Marketing,* 27, no. 1 (Spring 2008): 7–18.
27. Ibid.
28. Kelly D. Martin and Craig Smith, "Commercializing Social Interaction: The Ethics of Stealth Marketing," *Journal of Public Policy and Marketing,* 27, no. 1 (Spring 2008): 45–56.
29. Natalie Angier, "Drugs, Sports, Body Image and G.I. Joe," *New York Times*, December 22, 1998, F1.
30. Rob Walker, "Ultimate Branding," www.nytimes.com, August 31, 2008.
31. "FDA Faults 'Misleading' Drug-Ad Images," *Wall Street Journal,* May 4, 2001, B8.
32. Joanne Kaufman, "Ransom-Note Ads About Children's Health Are Cancelled," www.nytimes.com, December 20, 2007.
33. Amanda Zimmerman and John Dahlberg, "The Sexual Objectification of Women in Advertising: A Contemporary Cultural Perspective," *Journal of Advertising Research,* 48, no. 1 (March 2008): 21–38.
34. Stuart Elliott, "Emphasizing Taste, and Not Just in Beer, at Super Bowl," *New York Times,* January 26, 2005, C1; Stuart Elliott, "Ad Reaction Claims Super Bowl Casualty," www.nytimes.com, February 3, 2005; and Stuart Elliott, "Super Bowl Spot Provokes After Only One Broadcast," www.nytimes.com, February 8, 2005.
35. Jill K. Maher, Kenneth C. Herbst, Nancy M. Childs, and Seth Finn, "Racial Stereotypes in Children's Television Commercials," *Journal of Advertising,* 37, no. 1 (March 2008): 80–93.
36. Fred K. Beard, "How Product and Advertising Offend Consumers," *Journal of Advertising,* 37, no. 1 (March 2008): 13–21.
37. Haseeb Shabbir and Des Thwaites, "The Use of Humor to Mask Deceptive Advertising: It's No Laughing Matter," *Journal of Advertising,* 36, no. 2 (Summer 2007): 75–86.
38. www.ftc.gov/bcp/conline/edcams/redflag/falseclaims.
39. Peter R. Darke, Laurence Ashworth, and Robin J.B. Ritchie, "Damage from Corrective Advertising: Causes and Cures," *Journal of Marketing,* 72 (November 2008): 81–97.
40. Nat Ives, "Advertisers Have a Deep Concern for the Truth, Especially When It Comes to a Rival's Claim," *New York Times,* September 21, 2004, C4.
41. Ibid.
42. Brooks Barnes, "Bowing to Pressure, Disney Bans Smoking in Its Branded Movies," www.nytimes.com, July 26, 2007.
43. Apisit Chattananon, Meredith Lawley, Jirasek Trimetsoontorn, Numachi Supparekchaisakul, and Lackana Leelayouthayothin, "Building Corporate Image Through Societal Marketing Programs," *Society and Business Review,* 2, no. 3 (2007): 230–253.
44. Stuart Elliott, "A Push to Curb Casual Use of Ugly Phrases," www.nytimes.com, October 8, 2008.
45. Stephanie Clifford, "Teaching Teenagers About Harassment," www.nytimes.com, January 27, 2009.
46. Stuart Elliott, "Standing Up for Those Who Cannot," www.nytimes.com, September 29, 2008.
47. Stuart Elliott, "Campaign Seeks to Answer 'Now What?'" www.nytimes.com, December 15, 2008.
48. Stuart Elliott, "A New York Job Behind Every Light and Camera," www.nytimes.com, December 22, 2008.
49. Carolyn J. Simmons and Karen L. Becker-Olsen, "Achieving Marketing Objectives Through Social Sponsorships," *Journal of Marketing,* 70 (October 2006): 154–169.
50. Xiaoli Nan and Kwangjun Heo, "Consumer Responses to Corporate Social Responsibility (CSR) Initiatives: Examining the Role of Brand-Cause Fit in Cause-Related Marketing," *Journal of Advertising,* 36, no. 2 (Summer 2007): 63–75.
51. Stacy Landreth Grau and Judith Anne Garreston Folse, "The Influence of Donation Proximity and Message-Framing Cues on the Less-Involved Consumer," *Journal of Advertising,* 36, no. 4 (Winter 2007): 19–34.
52. Claire D'Souza, Mehdi Taghian, and Rajiv Khosla, "Examination of Environmental Beliefs and Its Impact on the Influence of Price, Quality and Demographic Characteristics with Respect to Green Purchase Intentions," *Journal of Targeting, Measurement and Analysis for Marketing,* 15, no. 2 (2007): 69–78.
53. Sheila Bonini and Jeremy Oppenheim, "Cultivating the Green Consumer," *Stanford Social Innovation Review* (Fall 2008): 56–61.
54. Claire D'Souza, Mehdi Taghian, and Peter Lamb, "An Empirical Study on the Influence of Environmental Labels on Consumers," *Corporate Communications: An International Journal,* 11, no. 2 (2006): 162–173.
55. Josephine Pickett-Baker and Ritsuko Ozaki, "Pro-environmental Products: Marketing Influence on Consumer Choice Decision," *Journal of Consumer Marketing,* 25, no. 5 (2008): 281–286.
56. Oliver M. Freestone and Peter J. McGoldrick, "Motivations of the Ethical Consumer," *Journal of Business Ethics,* 79 (2008): 445–467.
57. Rajiv K. Sinha and Naomi Mandel, "Preventing Digital Music Piracy: The Carrot or the Stick?" *Journal of Marketing,* 72 (January 2008): 1–15.

Glossary

Absolute Threshold. The lowest level at which an individual can experience a sensation. *p. 175*

Acculturation. The learning of a new or "foreign" culture. *p. 371*

Acquired Needs. Needs that are learned in response to one's culture or environment (such as the need for esteem, prestige, affection, or power). Also known as *psychogenic* or *secondary needs*. *p. 106*

Activities, Interests, and Opinions (AIOs). Psychographic variables that focus on activities, interests, and opinions. Also referred to as lifestyles. *p. 76*

Actual Self-Image. The image that an individual has of himself or herself as a certain kind of person, with certain characteristic traits, habits, possessions, relationships, and behavior. *p. 164*

Addressable Advertising. Mostly refers to advertising by premier online merchants who analyze the purchase behaviors of their users (including consumers' ratings of the products rented or bought) and utilize this data to make customized recommendations to individual users about future offerings. These marketers also use data from research companies who collect web surfing data from major Web portals and use it to build proprietary models utilized to design the different ads a customer sees when he views an ad for the first time, the second time, after buying the product, and so on; the various ads are also a function of the viewer's demographics and past advertising exposure. *p. 298*

Addressable Messages. Messages that can be customized and addressed to various receivers. Different receivers can get varied renderings of the same basic message. *p. 295*

Adopter Categories. A sequence of categories that describes how early (or late) a consumer adopts a new product in relation to other adopters. The five typical adopter categories are innovators, early adopters, early majority, late majority, and laggards. *p. 459*

Adoption Process. The stages through which an individual consumer passes in arriving at a decision to try (or not to try), to continue using (or discontinue using) a new product. The five stages of the traditional adoption process are awareness, interest, evaluation, trial, and adoption. *p. 450*

Advergaming. Embedding particular brands of products into video games played at homes, arcades, and online. *p. 299*

Advertising Resonance. Wordplay, often used to create a double meaning, used in combination with a relevant picture. *p. 301*

Advertising Wearout. Overexposure to repetitive advertising that causes individuals to become satiated and their attention and retention to decline. *p. 214*

Affect Referral Decision Rule. A simplified decision rule by which consumers make a product choice on the basis of their previously established overall ratings of the brands considered, rather than on specific attributes. *p. 492*

Affluent Market. Upscale market segment that consists of households with incomes that are higher than average (e.g., income over $75,000). *p. 348*

African American Consumers. Americans of African heritage constituting more than 39 million Americans or 13 percent of the U.S. population. *p. 402*

Age Subcultures. Age subgroupings of the population. *p. 410*

Aided and Unaided Recall Tests. In an aided recall test, the consumer is shown an ad and asked whether he or she remembers seeing it and recalls any of its salient points. In an unaided recall test, the consumer is asked whether he or she has read a particular magazine/seen a particular TV show and can recall any of the ads seen in them, as well as the ad's salient points. *p. 234*

Approach Object. A positive goal toward which behavior is directed. *p. 108*

Asian Americans. The fastest-growing American minority with a population of about 14 million in size made up of Chinese, Filipinos, Indian, Vietnamese, Korean, and Japanese. *p. 406*

Attitude. A learned predisposition to behave in a consistently favorable or unfavorable manner with respect to a given object. *p. 246*

Attitude Scales. Research measurement instrument used to capture evaluative data. *p. 61*

Attitude-Toward-Behavior Model. A model that proposes that a consumer's attitude toward a specific behavior is a function of how strongly he or she believes that the action will lead to a specific outcome (either favorable or unfavorable). *p. 253*

Attitude-Toward-Object Model. A model that proposes that a consumer's attitude toward a product or brand is a function of the presence of certain attributes and the consumer's evaluation of those attributes. *p. 251*

Attitude-Toward-the-Ad Model. A model that proposes that a consumer forms various feelings (affects) and judgments (cognitions) as the result of exposure to an advertisement, which, in turn, affect the consumer's *attitude toward the ad* and *beliefs and attitudes toward the brand*. *p. 255*

Attitudinal Measures. Measures concerned with consumers' overall feelings (i.e., evaluation) about the product and the brand and their purchase intentions. *p. 311*

Attribution Theory. A theory concerned with how people assign causality to events, and form or alter their attitudes after assessing their own or other people's behavior. *p. 272*

Attributions Toward Others. When consumers feel that another person is responsible for either positive or negative product performance. *p. 273*

Attributions Toward Things. Consumers judge a product's performance and attribute its success or failure to the product itself. *p. 274*

Audience Profiles. Psychographic/demographic descriptions of the audience of a specific medium. *p. 295*

Autonomic (Unilateral) Decision. A purchase decision in which either the husband or the wife makes the final decision. *p. 329*

Avatars. Animated, virtual reality graphical figures representing people. *p. 230*

Avoidance Object. A negative goal from which behavior is directed away. *p. 108*

Baby Boomers. Individuals born between 1946 and 1964 (approximately 40% of the adult population). *p. 410*

Behavior Intention Scale. An instrument that measures the likelihood that consumers will act a certain way in the future, such as if they will buy a product again or recommend it to friends. *p. 61*

Behavioral Learning. Theories based on the premise that learning takes place as the result of observable responses to external stimuli. (See also Stimulus-Response Learning.) *p. 212*

Behavioral Targeting. Segmentation based on usage behavior, such as sending targeted ads to people based on Web sites they have visited. *p. 97*

Behaviorist School. A philosophy of human motivation that views motivation as a mechanical process; behavior is viewed as a response to a stimulus. *p. 115*

Benefit Segmentation. Segmentation based on the kinds of benefits consumers seek in a product. *p. 88*

Blog. Short for Weblog, this is a personal online journal initiated and managed by an individual to express comments and receive feedback from readers. *p. 283*

Brand Communities. Online forums that focus on particular products or brands. *p. 283*

Brand Equity. The value inherent in a well-known brand name. *p. 236*

Brand Loyalty and Relationship. Consumers' consistent preference and/or purchase of the same brand in a specific product or service category. *p. 88*

Brand Personification. Specific "personality-type" traits or characteristics ascribed by consumers to different brands. *p. 158*

Branded Entertainment. (See Product Placement.) *p. 182*

Broad Versus Narrow Categorizers. Broad categorizers are uninvolved consumers who are likely to be receptive to a greater number of advertising messages regarding a product category and will consider more brands. Narrow categorizers are highly involved consumers that find fewer brands acceptable. *p. 202*

Broadcast Model. Advertising technique in which all the viewers of a given TV show or readers of a magazine receive the same advertising content. *p. 298*

Buzz Agents. Consumers who agree to promote products by bringing them to family gatherings, suggesting to store owners that they stock the items, reading certain books in public, and finding other ways to create "buzz" about a product. *p. 285*

Cause-Related Marketing. Process in which a firm contributes a portion of the revenues they receive from selling certain products to such causes as helping people with incurable diseases or those hurt by inclement weather. *p. 529*

Celebrity Actor. A celebrity who promotes a product or service as part of character endorsement. *p. 309*

Celebrity Endorsement. A celebrity who lends his or her name and appears on behalf of a product or service with which he or she may or may not be an expert. *p. 309*

Celebrity Spokesperson. A celebrity who represents a brand or company over an extended period of time. *p. 309*

Celebrity Testimonial. Based on personal usage, a celebrity attests to the quality of the product or service. *p. 309*

Center for Science in the Public Interest (CSPI). A widely recognized consumer advocacy group. *p. 528*

Central and Peripheral Routes to Persuasion. A promotional theory that proposes that highly involved consumers are best reached through ads that focus on the specific attributes of the product (the central route) while uninvolved consumers can be attracted through peripheral advertising cues such as the model or the setting (the peripheral route). *p. 231*

Children's Advertising Review Unit (CARU). Division of the Council of the Better Business Bureau that issues guidelines regulating advertising to children. *p. 516*

Chunking. The process by which consumers recode what they have already coded to include larger amounts of information. *p. 227*

Class Consciousness. A feeling of social-group membership that reflects an individual's sense of belonging or identification with others. *p. 340*

Classical Conditioning. According to Pavlovian theory, conditioned learning results when a stimulus paired with another stimulus that elicits a known response serves to produce the same response by itself. *p. 212*

Closure. A principle of Gestalt psychology that stresses the individual's need for completion. This need is reflected in the individual's subconscious reorganization and perception of incomplete stimuli as complete or whole pictures. *p. 183*

Co-Branding. When two brand names are featured on a single product. *p. 236*

Cognitive Age. An individual's perceived age (usually 10 to 15 years younger than his or her chronological age). *p. 414*

Cognitive Associative Learning. The learning of associations among events through classical conditioning that allows the organism to anticipate and represent its environment. *p. 213*

Cognitive Dissonance Theory. The discomfort or dissonance that consumers experience as a result of conflicting information. *p. 270*

Cognitive Learning. A theory of learning based on mental information processing, often in response to problem solving. *p. 212*

Cognitive Personality Factors. *Need for cognition and visualizers versus verbalizers* are two cognitive personality traits that influence consumer behavior. *p. 147*

Cognitive School. A philosophy of human motivation that believes all behavior is directed at goal achievement. Needs, past experiences, attitudes, and beliefs determine what actions a person will take. *p. 115*

Communication. The transmission of a message from a sender to a receiver by means of a signal of some sort sent through a communications channel (e.g., medium) of some sort. *p. 280*

Communication Feedback. The response given to a communicated message, whether a spoken reply, nonverbal communication, or some other variant. *p. 309*

Comparative Advertising. Advertising that explicitly names or otherwise identifies one or more competitors of the advertised brand for the purpose of claiming superiority, either on an overall basis or on selected product attributes. *p. 303*

Comparative Reference Group. A group whose norms serve as a benchmark for highly specific or narrowly defined types of behavior. (See also Normative Reference Group.) *p. 282*

Compatibility. The degree to which potential customers perceive a new product is consistent with their present needs, values, and practices. *p. 453*

Compensatory Decision Rule. A type of decision rule in which a consumer evaluates each brand in terms of each relevant attribute and then selects the brand with the highest weighted score. *p. 491*

Complaint Analysis. A process used to evaluate issues raised by unsatisfied customers. A good system should encourage customers to complain about unsatisfactory products and provide suggestions for improvement, as well as use "listening posts" to voice those concerns. *p. 63*

Complexity. The degree to which a new product is difficult to understand or use. *p. 454*

Composite-Variable Index. An index that combines a number of socioeconomic variables (such as education, income, occupation) to form one overall measure of social class standing. (See also Single-Variable Index.) *p. 340*

Compulsive Consumption. When buying becomes an addiction; consumers who are compulsive buyers are in some respects "out of control," and their actions may have damaging consequences to them and to those around them. *p. 151*

Concentrated Marketing. Targeting a product or service to a single market segment with a unique marketing mix (price, product, promotion, method of distribution). *p. 100*

Conjunctive Decision Rule. A noncompensatory decision rule in which consumers establish a minimally acceptable cutoff point for each attribute evaluated. Brands that fall below the cutoff point on any one attribute are eliminated from further consideration. *p. 491*

Consumer Behavior. The behavior that consumers display in searching for, purchasing, using, evaluating, and disposing of products, services, and ideas. *p. 23*

Consumer Decision Making. The process of making purchase decisions based on cognitive and emotional influences such as impulse, family, friends, advertisers, role models, moods, and situations that influence a purchase. *p. 36*

Consumer Decision Rules. Procedures adopted by consumers to reduce the complexity of making product and brand decisions *p. 491*

Consumer Dogmatism. A personality trait that measures how individuals react when presented with information that is unfamiliar or contradicts their beliefs. A highly dogmatic person will be defensive, whereas a low dogmatic person will keep an open mind. *p. 144*

Consumer Ethics. Moral rules that apply to consumers, such as the choice to return a used item for a refund, shoplift, and engage in software piracy, as well as the steps the company takes to counter these actions, such as charging restocking fees and limiting returns. *p. 531*

Consumer Ethnocentrism. A consumer's predisposition to accept or reject foreign-made products. *p. 140*

Consumer Fieldwork. Observational research by anthropologists of the behaviors of a small sample of people from a particular society. *p. 377*

Consumer-Generated Media. All ads that reach the consumer online and on any mobile communication devices such as PDAs, cell phones, and smartphones. *p. 297*

Consumer Imagery. Products and brands have symbolic value for individuals, who evaluate them on the basis of their consistency with their personal pictures of themselves. *p. 186*

Consumer Innovativeness. The degree to which consumers are receptive to new products, new services, or new practices. *p. 140*

Consumer Innovators. Those who are among the first to purchase a new product. *p. 141*

Consumer Involvement. The *degree of personal relevance* that the product or purchase holds for that consumer. High-involvement purchases are those that are very important to the consumer and provoke extensive problem solving and information processing. Low-involvement purchases are purchases that are not very important to the consumer, hold little relevance, and have little perceived risk, and, thus, provoke very limited information processing. *p. 229*

Consumer Materialism. A personality-like trait of individuals who regard possessions as particularly essential to their identities and lives. *p. 140*

Consumer Panel. A group of people who are paid to record their purchases and/or media viewing habits in diaries, which are then compiled and analyzed to determine trends. *p. 46*

Consumer Profile. Psychographic/demographic description of actual or proposed consumers for a specific product or service. *p. 295*

Consumer Research. The process, methodology and tools used to study and understand consumption-related behavior. *p. 27*

Consumer-Rooted Segmentation Bases. A means of identifying targeted consumers based on their physical, social, and psychological characteristics. *p. 76*

Consumer Socialization. The process, started in childhood, by which an individual learns the skills and attitudes relevant to consumer purchase behavior. *p. 323*

Consumption Process. A process consisting of three stages: the *input stage* establishes the consumption set and consuming style; the *process* of consuming and possessing, which includes using, possessing, collecting, and disposing of things; and the *output stage*, which includes changes in feelings, moods, attitudes, and behavior toward the product or service based on personal experience. *p. 476*

Consumption-Specific Segmentation Bases. A means of identifying targeted consumers based on their usage of certain products or established attitudes and preferences. *p. 88*

Content Analysis. A method for systematically analyzing the content of verbal and/or pictorial communication. The method is frequently used to determine prevailing social values of a society in a particular era under study. *p. 376*

Continuous Innovation. A new product entry that is an improved or modified version of an existing product rather than a totally new product. A continuous innovation has the least disruptive influence on established consumption patterns. *p. 451*

Controlled Experiment. A form of testing in which only one variable is manipulated while all others are kept constant, leading the tester to suggest any change in conditions is due to the changed variable and not something extraneous. *p. 55*

Core Values. Priorities and codes of conduct that both affects and reflects the character of American society. *p. 378*

Corrective Advertising. A form of retraction or clarification a company must issue when it makes false or misleading claims in its advertising. *p. 526*

Countersegmentation. A strategy in which a company combines two or more segments into a single segment to be targeted with an individually tailored product or promotion campaign. *p. 100*

Country-of-Origin Effects. The perception a consumer has of a product based on where it is manufactured, due to reputation or personal biases. *p. 428*

Covert, Masked, or Stealth Marketing. Marketing messages and promotional materials that appear to come from independent parties although, in fact, they are sent by marketers. *p. 523*

Cross-Cultural Consumer Analysis. Research to determine the extent to which consumers of two or more nations are similar in relation to specific consumption behavior. *p. 430*

Culture. The sum total of learned beliefs, values, and customs that serve to regulate the consumer behavior of members of a particular society. *p. 366*

Customer Lifetime Value Profile. A forecasted estimate of how much a given customer will spend at a given product or service provider over the customer's entire "stay" with that vendor. Such a profile is based on the collection and analysis of internal secondary data. *p. 44*

Customer Retention. Providing value to customers continuously so they will stay with the company rather than switch to a competitor. *p. 30*

Customer Satisfaction. An individual's perception of the performance of the product or service in relation to his or her expectations. *p. 29*

Customer Satisfaction Measurement. Quantitative and qualitative measures that gauge the level of customer satisfaction and its determinants. *p. 61*

Customer Satisfaction Survey. A tool used to measure how satisfied customers are with the relevant attributes of a company's product or service. *p. 61*

Customer Value. The ratio between the customer's perceived benefits and the resources used to obtain those benefits. *p. 29*

Deceptive Advertising. Marketing claims that mislead consumers in terms of a product's traits or performance. *p. 526*

Decoding. The process by which a receiver of a communication message interprets it. Such interpretation is influenced by the receiver's personal needs, traits, and prior experiences. *p. 290*

Defense Mechanisms. Methods by which people mentally redefine frustrating situations to protect their self-images and their self-esteem. *p. 112*

Defensive Attribution. A theory that suggests consumers are likely to accept credit for successful outcomes (internal attribution) and to blame other persons or products for failure (external attribution). *p. 273*

Demographics. Personal attributes of consumers such as a person's age, gender, ethnicity, and income which are objective and empirical, which are often used to classify consumers into distinct market segments. *p. 76*

Depth Interview. A lengthy and relatively unstructured interview designed to uncover a consumer's underlying attitudes and/or motivations. *p. 47*

Determined Detractors. Persistent critics of marketers who initiate bad publicity online. *p. 287*

Differential Decay. A theory that suggests the memory of a negative cue simply decays faster than the message itself, leaving behind the primary message content. *p. 290*

Differential Threshold. The minimal difference that can be detected between two stimuli. Also known as the *j.n.d. (just noticeable difference)*. (See also Weber's Law.) *p. 176*

Differentiated Marketing. Targeting a product or service to two or more segments, using a specifically tailored product, promotional appeal, price, and/or method of distribution for each. *p. 100*

Diffusion of Innovations. The framework for exploring the spread of consumer acceptance of new products throughout the social system. *p. 450*

Diffusion Process. The process by which the acceptance of an innovation is spread by communication to members of a social system over a period of time. *p. 450*

Discontinuous Innovation. A dramatically new product entry that requires the establishment of new consumption practices. *p. 451*

Disjunctive Rule. A noncompensatory decision rule in which consumers establish a minimally acceptable cutoff point for each relevant product attribute; any brand meeting or surpassing the cutoff point for any one attribute is considered an acceptable choice. *p. 492*

Door-in-the-Face Technique. A situation in which a large, costly, or high first request that is probably refused is followed by a second, more realistic, less costly request. *p. 273*

Downscale Consumers. Those potential buyers having annual household incomes of $40,000 or less. *p. 356*

Downward Mobility. Consumers who have a lower social class level than their parents in terms of the jobs they hold, their residences, level of disposable income, and savings. *p. 346*

Dynamically Continuous Innovation. A new product entry that is sufficiently innovative to have some disruptive effects on established consumption practices. *p. 451*

Ego-Defensive Function. A component of the functional approach to attitude-change that suggests that consumers want to protect their self-concepts from inner feelings of doubt. *p. 260*

Elaboration Likelihood Model (ELM). A theory that suggests that a person's level of involvement during message processing is a critical factor in determining which route to persuasion is likely to be effective. (See also Central and Peripheral Routes to Persuasion.) *p. 268*

E-mail Surveys. Questionnaires sent to target customers electronically through e-mail rather than traditional postal mail. *p. 57*

Emotional Motives. The selection of goals according to personal or subjective criteria (e.g., the desire for individuality, pride, fear, affection, status). *p. 110*

Encoding. The process by which the sender (or source) of a communication message selects and assigns words or visual images to represent the message's content. *p. 226*

Enculturation. The learning of the culture of one's own society. *p. 371*

E-referrals and Recommendations. An online marketing technique in which e-merchants offer links so consumers can send notices of certain products and offers to their friends. *p. 286*

European Union (EU). A group of 27 nations who eased trade restrictions among each other in hopes of pooling their resources and consumers, creating a single economic power. *p. 426*

Evaluation of Alternatives. A stage in the consumer *decision-making process* in which the consumer appraises the benefits to be derived from each of the product alternatives being considered. *p. 484*

Evoked Set. The specific brands a consumer considers in making a purchase choice in a particular product category. *p. 235*

E-WOM. Word of mouth advertising that takes place online. *p. 283*

Expected Self. How individuals expect to see themselves at some specified future time. *p. 164*

Experimentation. A research technique that evaluates how a change in a certain variable or combination of variables affects consumer behavior. *p. 55*

Exploitive Targeting. Unethical marketing directed to groups that are especially vulnerable to undue influence by advertising, such as children and persons of lesser education. *p. 516*

Exploratory Study. A small-scale study that identifies critical issues to include in a large-scale research study. *p. 43*

Exposure Effects. The number of consumers exposed to a message and how they react. *p. 310*

Extended Family. A household consisting of a husband, wife, offspring, and at least one other blood relative. *p. 320*

Extended Self. When a consumer uses self-altering products or services to conform to or take on the appearance of a particular type of person (e.g., a biker, a physician, a lawyer, a college professor). *p. 163*

Extensive Problem Solving. Decision making efforts by consumers who have no established criteria for evaluating a product category or specific brands in that category, or have not narrowed the number of brands to a manageable subset. *p. 478*

External Attributions. Attribution theory suggests that consumers are likely to credit their successes to outside sources (e.g., their graduate degrees or other persons). (See also Internal Attributions.) *p. 272*

Extrinsic Cues. Cues external to the product (e.g., price, store image, or brand image) that serve to influence the consumer's perception of a product's quality. *p. 195*

False of Misleading Advertising. Marketing claims that distort a product's effectiveness or suggest comparisons showing a brand's superiority over other brands that have not been verified. *p. 525*

Family. Two or more persons related by blood, marriage, or adoption who reside together. *p. 318*

Family Branding. The practice of marketing several company products under the same brand name. *p. 215*

Family Life Cycle (FLC). The progression through which a typical family passes determined on the basis of such demographics as marital status, age, and the absence or presence of children. *p. 80*

Field Observation. An anthropological measurement technique that focuses on observing behavior within a natural environment (often without the subjects' awareness). *p. 377*

Figure and Ground. A Gestalt principle of perceptual organization that focuses on contrast. *Figure* is usually perceived clearly because [in contrast to (back) *ground*] it appears to be well defined, solid, and in the forefront, while the *ground* is usually perceived as indefinite, hazy, and continuous. Music can be figure or (back) ground. *p. 182*

Focus Group. A qualitative research method in which about eight to ten persons participate in an unstructured group interview focused on a product or service concept. *p. 48*

Foot-in-the-Door Technique. A theory of attitude change that suggests individuals form attitudes that are consistent with their own prior behavior. *p. 273*

Formal Communications Source. A source that speaks on behalf of an organization—either a for-profit (commercial) or a not-for-profit organization. *p. 281*

Frequency Award Programs. A brand loyalty technique in which marketers reward consumers who consistently buy their products with special benefits. Frequent-flyer miles are a prime example. *p. 92*

Freudian Theory. A theory of personality and motivation developed by the psychoanalyst Sigmund Freud. (See Psychoanalytic Theory of Personality.) *p. 137*

Functional Approach. An attitude-change theory that classifies attitudes in terms of four functions: *utilitarian*, *ego-defensive*, *value-expressive*, and *knowledge* functions. *p. 260*

Gender Subcultures. Sex roles are an important cultural component and require products that are either exclusively or strongly associated with the members of one sex. *p. 417*

Generation X. Born between 1965 and 1979, this is a post baby-boomer segment (also referred to as *Xers* or *busters*). *p. 410*

Generation Y. The approximately 71 million Americans who were born between the years 1977 and 1994 (i.e., the children of baby boomers). Members of Generation Y (also known as "echo boomers" and the "millennium generation") can be divided into three subsegments: Gen Y adults (age 19–28), Gen Y teens (age 13–18), and Gen Y kids, or "tweens." *p. 410*

Generic Goals. The general classes or categories of goals that individuals select to fulfill their needs. (See also Product-Specific Goals.) *p. 107*

Geodemographic Clusters. A composite segmentation strategy that uses both geographic variables (zip codes, neighborhoods, or blocks) and demographic variables (e.g., income, occupation, value of residence) to identify target markets. *p. 347*

Geodemographics. A hybrid segmentation scheme based on the premise that people who live close to one another are likely to have similar tastes, preferences, lifestyles, and consumption habits. *p. 80*

Geographical and Regional Subcultures. The differences consumers from various parts of the country display in product selection and consumption due to their location and the area's traditions. *p. 400*

Gestalt Psychology. A German term meaning "pattern" or "configuration" that has come to represent various principles of perceptual organization. *p. 182*

Gifting Behavior. The process of gift exchange that takes place between a giver and a recipient. *p. 500*

Green Marketing. Advertising that promotes use of healthy, reusable, and ecofriendly products. *p. 529*

Global Strategy. Standardizing both product and communications programs when conducting business on a global basis. *p. 442*

Grouping. A concept of perceptual organization that proposes that individuals tend to group stimuli automatically so that they form a unified picture or impression. The perception of stimuli as groups or chunks of information, rather than as discrete bits of information, facilitates their memory and recall. *p. 182*

Halo Effect. A situation in which one feature is assumed to carry over to other features; for example, a man who looks you in the eye when he speaks is assumed to be trustworthy, fine, and noble. *p. 186*

Hemispheric Lateralization. Learning theory in which the basic premise is that the right and left hemispheres of the brain "specialize" in the kinds of information that they process. Also called split brain theory. *p. 231*

Heuristics. (See Consumer Decision Rules.) *p. 481*

Hispanic American Subculture. The largest American minority group, representing about 14 percent of the U.S. population. The three largest groups are Mexican Americans, Puerto Ricans, and Cubans. *p. 393*

Household. A social unit made up of the people living within a particular structure, who may or may not be related. *p. 318*

Husband-Dominated Decisions. Consumer choices generally made by the husband, either by tradition or knowledge. *p. 329*

Hybrid Segmentation. The use of several segmentation variables to more accurately define or "fine-tune" consumer segments. *p. 75*

Ideal Self-Image. How individuals would *like* to perceive themselves (as opposed to Actual Self-Image—the way they *do* perceive themselves). *p. 164*

Ideal Social Self-Image. How consumers would like others to see them. *p. 164*

Impersonal Communication. Communication directed to a large and diffused audience, with no direct communication between source and receiver. Also known as *mass communication*. *p. 281*

Index of Status Characteristics. A composite measure of social class that combines occupation, source of income (not amount), house type, and dwelling area into a single weighted index of social class standing. Also known as *Warner's ISC*. *p. 344*

Inept Set. Brands that a consumer excludes from purchase consideration. *p. 488*

Inert Set. Brands that a consumer is indifferent toward because they are perceived as having no particular advantage. *p. 488*

Informal Communication Source. Originally defined as a person whom the message receiver knows personally, such as a parent or friend who gives product information or advice, today it includes people who influence one's consumption via online social networks and other Web forums. *p. 281*

Information Overload. A situation in which the consumer is presented with too much product- or brand-related information. *p. 227*

Information Processing. A cognitive theory of human learning patterned after computer information processing that focuses on how information is stored in human memory and how it is retrieved. *p. 225*

Innate Needs. Physiological needs for food, water, air, clothing, shelter, and sex. Also known as *biogenic* or *primary needs*. *p. 106*

Inner-Directedness. Consumers who tend to rely on their own "inner" values or standards when evaluating new products and who are likely to be consumer innovators. *p. 144*

Institutional Advertising. Advertising designed to promote a favorable company image rather than specific products. *p. 287*

Instrumental Conditioning. A behavioral theory of learning based on a trial-and-error process, with habits formed as the result of positive experiences (reinforcement) resulting from specific behaviors. (Also known as operant conditioning.) *p. 212*

Intention-to-Buy Scales. A method of assessing the likelihood of a consumer purchasing a product or behaving in a certain way. *p. 251*

Interactive TV (iTV). A combination of TV programming and the interactivity of the Web, delivered to a TV, computer, or a mobile device. *p. 298*

Interference Effects. The greater the number of competitive ads in a product category, the lower the recall of brand claims in a specific ad. *p. 228*

Internal Attributions. Attribution theory suggests that some people attribute their success in performing certain tasks (e.g., using products) to their own skills. (See also External Attributions.) *p. 272*

Interpersonal Communication. Communication that occurs directly between two or more people by mail, by telephone, by e-mail, or in person. *p. 281*

Intrinsic Cues. Physical characteristics of the product (such as size, color, flavor, or aroma) that serve to influence the consumer's perceptions of product quality. *p. 195*

Joint (Equal or Syncratic) Decisions. Family purchase decisions in which the husband and wife are equally influential. Also known as *syncratic decisions*. *p. 329*

Just Noticeable Difference (j.n.d.). The minimal difference that can be detected between two stimuli. (See also Differential Threshold and Weber's Law.) *p. 176*

Knowledge Function. A component of the functional approach to attitude-change theory that suggests that consumers have a strong need to know and understand the people and products with which they come into contact. *p. 260*

Learning. The process by which individuals acquire the knowledge and experience they apply to future purchase and consumption behavior. *p. 208*

Levels of Aspiration. New and higher goals that individuals set for themselves. *p. 111*

Lexicographic Decision Rule. A noncompensatory decision rule in which consumers first rank product attributes in terms of their importance, then compare brands in terms of the attribute considered most important. If one brand scores higher than the other brands, it is selected; if not, the process is continued with the second ranked attribute, and so on. *p. 492*

Licensing. The use by manufacturers and retailers of well-known brands, celebrity or designer names (for a fee) to acquire instant recognition and status for their products. *p. 217*

Likert Scale. A popular measurement tool in which consumers rank their preference along a scale that varies from "agree" to "disagree," with various gradations between the extremes. *p. 61*

Limited Problem Solving. A limited search by a consumer for a product that will satisfy his or her basic criteria from among a selected group of brands. *p. 478*

Local Strategy. Customizing both product and communications programs by area or country when conducting business on a global basis. *p. 442*

Long-Term Store. In information-processing theory, the stage of real memory where information is organized, reorganized, and retained for relatively extended periods of time. *p. 225*

Looking-in Research. An online research method is which researchers enter several relevant key words related to a product or company into a search engine to evaluate online postings, blogs, and the like that provide insight into consumers' views on products. *p. 53*

Magazine Readership Survey. A consumer research survey conducted of magazine readers to provide magazine publishers and staff with feedback on their readers and their reading habits as they relate to that magazine. Marketing plans for advertisers are then based on that feedback. *p. 59*

Mail Surveys. Research questionnaires sent directly to consumers at their homes through the postal service. *p. 57*

Manufacturer's Image. The impression consumers have of a particular company in the marketplace. *p. 201*

Market Mavens. Individuals whose influence stems from a general knowledge and market expertise that lead to an early awareness of new products and services. *p. 292*

Market Segmentation. The process of dividing a potential market into distinct subsets of consumers and selecting one or more segments as a target market to be reached with a distinct marketing mix. *p. 28*

Market Targeting. The selection of one or more consumer segments the company wishes to pursue in its advertising. *p. 28*

Marketing Concept. A consumer-oriented philosophy that suggests that satisfaction of consumer needs provides the focus for product development and marketing strategy to enable the firm to meet its own organizational goals. *p. 26*

Marketing Ethics. Designing, packaging, pricing, advertising, and distributing products in such a way that negative consequences to consumers, employees, and society in general are avoided. *p. 516*

Marketing Mix. The unique configuration of the four basic marketing variables (product, promotion, price, and channels of distribution) that a marketing organization controls. *p. 28*

Marketplace Decision Difficulty (MPDD). An attribute depicting one's hardship in making buying decisions. *p. 78*

Maslow's Hierarchy of Needs. A theory of motivation that postulates that individuals strive to satisfy their needs according to a basic hierarchical structure, starting with physiological needs, then moving to safety needs, social needs, egoistic needs, and finally self-actualization needs. *p. 116*

Mass Marketing. Offering the same product and marketing mix to all consumers. *p. 70*

Mass Media. The traditional avenues advertisers have used to convey messages, generally classified as *print* (newspapers, magazines, billboards) and *broadcast* (radio, television). *p. 294*

Media Strategy. The placement of ads in the specific media read, viewed, or heard by each targeted audience, based on consumer profile. *p. 295*

Medium. A communication channel, generally classified as either *impersonal* (e.g., mass medium) and *interpersonal* (conversations between people). *p. 294*

Megabrands. Well-known brand names. *p. 236*

Membership Group. A group to which a person either belongs or would qualify for membership. *p. 282*

Message. Ideas to be conveyed through verbal (spoken or written) or nonverbal (a photograph, illustration, or symbol) communication. *p. 299*

Message Framing. Positively framed messages (those that specify benefits to be *gained* by using a product) are more persuasive than negatively framed messages (those that specify benefits *lost* by not using a product). *p. 301*

Microtargeting. (See Behavioral Targeting.) *p. 97*

Mixed Strategies. A marketing strategy that combines elements of the global and local marketing strategies, offering either a customized message and uniform product, or a uniform message and customized product. *p. 442*

Mobile Advertising. (See Consumer-Generated Media.) *p. 297*

Modeling. (See Observational Learning.) *p. 224*

Mood. An individual's subjectively perceived "feeling state." *p. 482*

Motivation. The driving force within individuals that impels them to action. *p. 106*

Motivational Researcher. Qualitative research designed to uncover consumers' subconscious or hidden motivations. The basic premise of motivational research is that consumers are not always aware of, or may not wish to reveal, the basic reasons underlying their actions. *p. 46*

Multiattribute Attitude Models. Attitude models that examine the composition of consumer attitudes in terms of selected product attributes or beliefs. *p. 251*

Multinational Strategies. Decisions that marketers make on how to reach all potential consumers of their products in countries throughout the world. *p. 442*

Multiple Selves. Consumers have different images of themselves in response to different situations and are quite likely to act differently with different people and in different situations. *p. 163*

Mystery Shoppers. Professional observers who pose as customers to provide a company with unbiased evaluations of their service personnel. *p. 61*

Narrowcast Messages. Addressable communications that are significantly more response measurable than traditional broadcast ads. *p. 297*

Narrowcasting. A marketing method that allows marketers to develop and deliver more customized messages to increasingly smaller market segments on an ongoing basis. *p. 34*

Narrow Categorizers. (see Broad versus narrow categorizers) *p. 202*

Nationality Subcultures. Nationality subcultures in a larger society in which members often retain a sense of identification and pride in the language and customs of their ancestors. *p. 393*

Need for Cognition. The personality trait that measures a person's craving for or enjoyment of thinking. *p. 147*

Need Recognition. The realization by the consumer that there is a difference between "what is" and "what should (or can) be." *p. 484*

Negative Reinforcement. An unpleasant or negative outcome that serves to encourage a specific behavior. (Not to be confused with punishment, which discourages repetition of a specific behavior.) *p. 221*

Neo-Freudian Theory. A school of psychology that stresses the fundamental role of social relationships in the formation and development of personality. *p. 137*

Neo-Pavlovian Conditioning. The creation of a strong association between the conditioned stimulus (CS) and the unconditioned stimulus (US) requiring (1) forward conditioning; (2) repeated pairings of the CS and the US; (3) a CS and US that logically belong together; (4) a CS that is novel and unfamiliar; and (5) a US that is biologically or symbolically salient. *p. 213*

New Media. A more dynamic communication technology, sometimes called alternative or nontraditional media, characterized by addressability, interactivity, and response measurability. *p. 294*

Noncompensatory Decision Rule. A type of consumer decision rule by which positive evaluation of a brand attribute does not compensate for (i.e., is not balanced against) a negative evaluation of the same brand on some other attribute. *p. 491*

Nonfamily Households. Men and/or women living alone or with another person as an unmarried couple. *p. 335*

Nonprobability Sample. The population under study has been predetermined in a nonrandom fashion on the basis of the researcher's judgment or decision to select a given number of respondents from a particular group. *p. 63*

Nontraditional Family. A living arrangement other than a man, wife, and their children; for example, single-parent homes, blended families, and homosexual couples. *p. 336*

Nonverbal Communication. Messages conveyed through some means other than speech or writing, such as body language, a picture, an illustration, or a symbol. *p. 299*

Normative Reference Group. A group that influences the general values or behavior of an individual. (See Comparative Reference Group.) *p. 281*

North American Free Trade Agreement (NAFTA). A trade association consisting of Canada, the United States, and Mexico that reduces trade restrictions between the countries in an effort to bolster marketing opportunities. *p. 426*

Nuclear Family. A household consisting of a husband and wife and at least one offspring. *p. 320*

Objective Measures. Selected fact-based demographic or socioeconomic variables (such as occupation, income, education level) that are used to classify individuals in terms of social class. *p. 340*

Observability. The ease with which a product's benefits or attributes can be observed, imagined, or described to potential consumers. *p. 454*

Observational Learning. A process by which individuals observe the behavior of others, remember it, and imitate it. Also known as *modeling*. *p. 224*

Observational Research. A form of consumer research that relies on observation of consumers in the process of buying and using products. *p. 54*

Older Consumers. Those customers who are approximately age 60 to 65 and older, which is expanding as a percentage of the market pool due to the declining birthrate, the aging of baby boomers, and advancements in medical care. *p. 413*

One-Sided Versus Two-Sided Messages. A one-sided message tells only the benefits of a product or service; a two-sided message also includes some negatives, thereby enhancing the credibility of the marketer. *p. 302*

Online or Internet-Based Surveys. Research method in which potential respondents are directed to a particular Web site to respond to marketing questions. *p. 57*

Operant Conditioning. (See Instrumental Conditioning.) *p. 212*

Opinion Leader. A person who informally gives product information and advice to others. *p. 282*

Opinion Leadership. The process by which one person (the *opinion leader*) informally influences the consumption actions or attitudes of others, who may be *opinion seekers* or *opinion recipients*. *p. 282*

Opinion Receiver. An individual who either actively seeks product information from others or receives unsolicited information. *p. 282*

Optimum Stimulation Levels (OSLs). Personality traits that measure the level or amount of novelty or complexity that individuals seek in their personal experiences. High OSL consumers tend to accept risky and novel products more readily than low OSL consumers. *p. 145*

Order Effects. An evaluation of how the order that advertisements are viewed affects how consumers respond to them; for example, TV commercials shown in the middle of a sequence are recalled less than those at the beginning or end. *p. 302*

Organizational Consumer. A business, government agency, or other institution (profit or nonprofit) that buys the goods, services, and/or equipment necessary for the organization to function. *p. 23*

Other-Directedness. Consumers who tend to look to others for direction and for approval. *p. 144*

"Ought-To" Self. Consists of traits or characteristics that an individual believes it is his or her duty or obligation to possess. *p. 164*

Outcome Dimension. In a comparison of consumers' expectations versus their perceptions of the actual product or service, the dimensions that focus on reliable delivery of the core service. *p. 198*

Out-of-home Media. Promotional tools that target mobile customers in more innovative, captivating, and interactive ways than through mass media. *p. 295*

Participant-Observers. Researchers who participate in the environment that they are studying without notifying those who are being observed. *p. 377*

Passive Learning. Without active involvement, individuals process and store right-brain (nonverbal, pictorial) information. *p. 232*

Penetration Policy. Setting a relatively low introductory price on a new product to discourage competition from entering the market. *p. 462*

Perceived Price. How a consumer perceives a price—as high, as low, or as fair. *p. 193*

Perceived Quality. Consumers often judge the quality of a product or service on the basis of a variety of informational cues that they associate with the product; some of these cues are intrinsic to the product or service; others are extrinsic, such as price, store image, service environment, brand image, and promotional messages. *p. 195*

Perceived Risk. The degree of uncertainty perceived by the consumer as to the consequences (outcome) of a specific purchase decision. *p. 201*

Perception. The process by which an individual selects, organizes, and interprets stimuli into a meaningful and coherent picture of the world. *p. 175*

Perceptual Blocking. The subconscious "screening out" of stimuli that are threatening or inconsistent with one's needs, values, beliefs, or attitudes. *p. 182*

Perceptual Defense. A subconscious screening by consumers of stimuli they find psychologically threatening or damaging. *p. 181*

Perceptual Mapping. A research technique that enables marketers to plot graphically consumers' perceptions concerning product attributes of specific brands. *p. 190*

Peripheral Route to Persuasion. (See Central and Peripheral Routes to Persuasion.) *p. 231*

Personal Consumer. The individual who buys goods and services for his or her own use, for household use, for the use of a family member, or for a friend. (Also referred to as the *Ultimate Consumer* or *End User*.) *p. 23*

Personal Interview Surveys. Face-to-face interviews, often held in a public place, between a researcher and potential consumers. *p. 56*

Personality. The inner psychological characteristics that both determine and reflect how a person responds to his or her environment. *p. 136*

Personality Traits. Attributes such as self-confidence, open mindedness, or being a high achiever that help psychologically categorize a consumer. *p. 76*

Persuasion Effects. Determination if the marketing message was correctly received, understood, and interpreted. *p. 310*

Physiological Measures. A way to track bodily responses to stimuli, in an effort to see which products generate the most positive response. *p. 311*

Physiological Observation. Research using a device that monitors respondents' patterns of information processing through physical signs, such as electronic eye cameras or electronic sensors. *p. 55*

Portable People Meters (PPMs). PDA-sized devices carried by individuals that will eventually be able to monitor all media programming and media exposures. *p. 45*

Positioning. Establishing a specific image for a brand in relation to competing brands. *p. 28*

Positive Reinforcement. A favorable outcome to a specific behavior that strengthens the likelihood that the behavior will be repeated. *p. 221*

Postpurchase Evaluation. An assessment of a product based on actual trial after purchase. *p. 497*

Prepurchase Search. A stage in the consumer decision-making process in which the consumer perceives a need and actively seeks out information concerning products that will help satisfy that need. *p. 484*

Price/Quality Relationship. The perception of price as an indicator of product quality (e.g., the higher the price, the higher the perceived quality of the product). *p. 198*

Primary Needs. (See Innate Needs.) *p. 106*

Primary Research. Original research undertaken by individual researchers or organizations to meet specific objectives. Collected information is called *primary data*. *p. 42*

PRIZM NE. A composite index of geographic and socioeconomic factors expressed in residential zip-code neighborhoods from which geodemographic consumer segments are formed. *p. 347*

Probability Sample. Respondents are selected in such a way that every member of the population studied has a known, nonzero chance of being selected. *p. 63*

Process Dimension. In a comparison of consumers' expectations versus their perceptions of the actual product or service, the dimensions that focus on how the core service is delivered and its tangible aspects. *p. 198*

Product Category Extensions. New products that are variations of existing products; for example, M&M introducing a gourmet version of its original candy. *p. 215*

Product Form Extensions. Introducing an existing product in a new form. For example, tablets of Tide detergent and Listerine Paks of Listerine mouthwash. *p. 215*

Product or Service Innovation. The creation and introduction of a new product or service into the market, which can be viewed from different classifications. The *firm-oriented approach* views the new product from the perspective of the company producing it. The *product-oriented approach* views the product in terms of the product's traits. The *market-oriented approach* looks at the new product in terms of its exposure to new consumers. The *consumer-oriented approach* considers a product new if it is new to them. *p. 450*

Product Line Extensions. A marketing strategy of adding related products to an already established brand (based on the Stimulus Generalization Theory). *p. 215*

Product Placement. A marketing technique in which a product is integrated into a TV show or film through its use by the characters, its integration as a plot point, or its association with a character, who may also be the product's spokesperson. *p. 182*

Product-Specific Goals. The specifically branded or labeled products that consumers select to fulfill their needs. (See also Generic Goals.) *p. 107*

Product Standardization. An orientation for assessing whether to use a global versus local marketing strategy concentrating on a high-tech to high-touch continuum. *p. 442*

Projective Techniques. A variety of disguised "tests" that contain ambiguous stimuli (e.g., incomplete sentences, untitled pictures, word-association tests) that help consumers express themselves and reveal their inner motivations. *p. 52*

Psychoanalytic Theory of Personality. A theory of motivation and personality that postulates that unconscious needs and drives, particularly sexual and other biological drives, are the basis of human motivation and personality. *p. 137*

Psychographics. A person's activities, interests, and opinions, which help form attitudes toward various issues; a lifestyle. *p. 76*

Psychological Noise. A barrier to message reception (i.e., competing advertising messages or distracting thoughts). *p. 293*

Publicity. When commercial or noncommercial messages appear in space or time that is not paid for and usually reserved for editorial messages. *p. 287*

Purchase Behavior. Behavior that involves two types of purchases: *trial purchases* (the exploratory phase in which consumers evaluate a product through direct use) and *repeat purchases*, which usually signify that the product meets with the consumer's approval and that the consumer is willing to use it again. *p. 497*

Qualitative Research. Research methods (e.g., interviews, focus groups, metaphor analysis, collage research, projective techniques) that are primarily used to obtain new ideas for promotional campaigns and products. *p. 42*

Quantitative Research. Research methods (e.g., experiments, survey techniques, observations) that enable researchers to understand the effects of various promotional inputs on the consumer, thus enabling marketers to predict consumer behavior. *p. 42*

Questionnaire. The primary data collection instrument, consisting of questions on a particular topic. *p. 58*

Racial Subcultures. Subgroups within a culture based on nationality or ethnicity. The major racial subcultures in the United States are Caucasian, Hispanic, African American, Asian American, and American Indian. *p. 402*

Rank-order Scale. Survey technique in which consumers rank items in order of preference on some criterion, such as overall quality or value for the money. *p. 61*

Rational Motives. Motives or goals based on economic or objective criteria, such as price, size, weight, or miles-per-gallon. *p. 110*

Recall Tests. (See Aided and Unaided Recall Tests.) *p. 234*

Recognition and Recall Tests. Tests conducted to determine whether consumers remember seeing an ad, the extent to which they have read it or seen it and can recall its content, their resulting attitudes toward the product and the brand, and their purchase intentions. *p. 234*

Recognition Tests. (See Aided and Unaided Recall Tests.) *p. 234*

Reference Group. A person or group that serves as a point of comparison (or reference) for an individual in the formation of either general or specific values, attitudes, or behavior. *p. 281*

Reference Prices. External or internal prices that a consumer uses as a basis for comparison in judging another price. *p. 194*

Rehearsal. The silent, mental repetition of material. *p. 226*

Relationship Marketing. Marketing aimed at creating strong, lasting relationships with a core group of customers by making them feel good about the company and by giving them some kind of personal connection to the business. *p. 223*

Relative Advantage. The degree to which potential customers perceive a new product as superior to existing substitutes. *p. 453*

Reliability. The degree to which a measurement instrument is consistent in what it measures. *p. 58*

Religious Subcultures. Groups classified by religious affiliation that may be targeted by marketers because of purchase decisions that are influenced by their religious identity. *p. 400*

Response-Measurable Messages. The ability to precisely and directly measure a receiver's response to a message. *p. 295*

Retail Store Image. Consumers' impressions of a business's products, prices, service, environment, and clientele, which influence their decisions whether or not to shop there. *p. 199*

Retrieval. The stage of information processing in which individuals recover information from long-term storage. *p. 227*

Ritual. A type of symbolic activity consisting of a series of steps (multiple behaviors) occurring in a fixed sequence and repeated over time. *p. 373*

Rokeach Value Survey. A self-administered inventory consisting of eighteen "terminal" values (i.e., personal goals) and eighteen "instrumental" values (i.e., ways of reaching personal goals). *p. 378*

Role. A pattern of behavior expected of an individual in a specific social position, such as mother, daughter, teacher, lawyer. One person may have a number of different roles, each of which is relevant in the context of specific social situations. *p. 163*

Routinized Response Behavior. A habitual purchase response based on predetermined criteria. *p. 478*

Sales Effects. Determination if an advertisement increased a product's sales. *p. 310*

Sample. A population subset used to estimate the characteristics of the entire population. *p. 63*

Screener Questionnaire. A questionnaire designed to ensure the appropriate individuals are invited to take part in a research study, and those not in the target market are not invited. *p. 48*

Secondary Data. Data that has been collected for reasons other than the specific research project at hand. *p. 44*

Secondary Needs. (See Acquired Needs.) *p. 106*

Selective Attention. Consumers exercise a great deal of selectivity in terms of the attention they give to commercial stimuli. They have a heightened awareness of stimuli that meet their needs or interests and minimal awareness of stimuli irrelevant to their needs. *p. 181*

Selective Exposure. Perception technique in which consumers actively seek out messages that they find pleasant or are sympathetic to, and actively avoid painful or threatening ones. *p. 181*

Self-Gifts. Gifts to oneself. *p. 500*

Self-Perception Theory. A theory that suggests that consumers develop attitudes by reflecting on their own behavior. *p. 272*

Semantic Differential Scale. A survey technique consisting of a series of bipolar adjectives (good/bad, like/dislike) anchored on an odd-numbered continuum. *p. 61*

Sensation. The immediate and direct response of the sensory organs to simple stimuli (e.g., taste, color, smell, brightness, loudness, feel). *p. 175*

Sensation Seeking (SS). A trait characterized by the need for varied, novel, and complex sensations and experience, and the willingness to take physical and social risks for the sake of such experience. *p. 146*

Sensory Adaptation. "Getting used to" certain sensations; becoming accommodated a certain level of stimulation. *p. 176*

Sensory Receptors. The human organs (eyes, ears, nose, mouth, skin) that receive sensory inputs. *p. 175*

Sensory Store. The place in which all sensory inputs are housed very briefly before passing into the short-term store. *p. 225*

Sex Roles. Traits and tendencies often associated with a particular gender; for example, masculine traits include aggressiveness and competitiveness, whereas feminine traits include neatness, tactfulness, gentleness, and talkativeness. *p. 417*

Shaping. Reinforcement performed before the desired consumer behavior actually takes place. *p. 224*

Short-Term Store. The stage of real memory in which information received from the sensory store for processing is retained briefly before passing into the long-term store or forgotten. *p. 225*

Single-Parent Family. Households consisting of only one parent and at least one child. *p. 320*

Single-Variable Index. The use of a single socioeconomic variable (such as income) to estimate an individual's relative social class. (See also Composite-Variable Index.) *p. 340*

Skimming Policy. Pricing policy in which marketers initially sell a product at a high price to consumers who are willing to pay top dollar for it, and then gradually lower the price to draw in additional buyers. *p. 462*

Sleeper Effect. The tendency for persuasive communications to lose the impact of source credibility over time (i.e., the influence of a message from a high credibility source tends to *decrease* over time; the influence of a message from a low credibility source tends to *increase* over time). (See also Source Amnesia.) *p. 290*

Social Class. The division of members of a society into a hierarchy of distinct status classes, so that members of each class have either higher or lower status than members of other classes. *p. 76*

Social Networks. Groups where people share information about themselves with others, generally those with similar interests. *p. 281*

Social Self-Image. How consumers feel others see them. *p. 164*

Social Status. The amount of status members of one social class have in comparison with members of other social classes. *p. 338*

Socialization Agent. A person or organization involved in passing along the basic values and behaviors of a group, mainly because they are in close proximity and control the means to reward and/or punish actions. *p. 325*

Socialization of Family Members. A process that includes imparting to children and other family members the basic values and modes of behavior consistent with the culture. *p. 323*

Societal Marketing Concept. A revision of the traditional marketing concept that suggests that marketers adhere to principles of social responsibility in the marketing of their goods and services; that is, they must endeavor to satisfy the needs and wants of their target markets in ways that preserve and enhance the well-being of consumers and society as a whole. *p. 27*

Sociocultural Values and Beliefs. Sociological and anthropological variables that provide a base for market segmentation. For measurement purposes, these factors are a consumer's abstract cognitions and can be measured via psychological tests. *p. 87*

Socioeconomic Status Score. A multivariable social class measure used by the United States Bureau of the Census that combines occupational status, family income, and educational attainment into a single measure of social class standing. *p. 344*

Source Amnesia. Phenomenon in which people forget the source of a message but remember the message itself; for example, knowing George Washington was the first U.S. president, but not knowing how that was learned. (See also Sleeper Effect.) *p. 290*

Source Credibility. The perceived honesty and objectivity of the source of the communication. *p. 287*

Stages in the Adoption Process. (See Adoption Process.) *p. 463*

Stereotypes. A series of beliefs about a person based on that person's race, gender, religion, or other traits. *p. 183*

Stimulus. Any unit of input to any of the senses. *p. 175*

Stimulus Discrimination. The ability to select a specific stimulus from among similar stimuli because of perceived differences. *p. 218*

Stimulus Generalization. The inability to perceive differences between slightly dissimilar stimuli. *p. 215*

Stimulus-Response Learning. The premise that observable responses to specific external stimuli signal that learning has taken place. (See also Behavioral Learning.) *p. 212*

Subcultural Interaction. Because consumers are simultaneously members of several subcultural groups, marketers must determine how consumer's specific subcultural memberships interact to influence the consumer's purchase decisions. *p. 420*

Subculture. A distinct cultural group that exists as an identifiable segment within a larger, more complex society. *p. 392*

Subjective Measures. A series of personal evaluations an individual uses to put himself or herself into a social class. *p. 340*

Subliminal Perception. Perception of stimuli received *below* the level of conscious awareness. *p. 178*

Substitute Goal. A goal that replaces an individual's primary goal when that goal cannot be achieved. *p. 112*

Symbol. Anything that stands for something else. *p. 372*

Symbolic Group. A group with which an individual identifies by adopting its values, attitudes, or behavior despite the unlikelihood of future membership. *p. 282*

Target Audience. The group of consumers marketers hope to reach with a specific message. *p. 290*

Targeting. The selection of a distinct market segment at which to direct a marketing strategy. *p. 72*

Telephone Interview Surveys. A research technique in which researchers call prospective consumers at home over the phone. *p. 56*

Test Marketing. Introducing a new product into a select area to see how the public responds prior to releasing it to a larger population. *p. 56*

Theory of Planned Behavior. An extension of the TRA model which includes an additional factor leading to intention—a customer's perception whether a behavior is within his or her control. *p. 254*

Theory-of-Reasoned-Action (TRA) Model. A comprehensive theory of the interrelationship among attitudes, intentions, and behavior. *p. 253*

Theory of Trying to Consume. Recasts the theory-of-reasoned-action model by replacing actual *behavior* with *trying to behave* (i.e., consume) as the variable to be explained and/or predicted. *p. 255*

Three Ps. Marketing elements—place, people, and products—considered when developing a marketing plan. *p. 443*

Traditional Family Life Cycle. A progression of stages through which many families pass. The five traditional *FLC* stages are

Bachelorhood, Honeymooners, Parenthood, Postparenthood, and Dissolution. *p. 332*

Trait Theory. A theory of personality that focuses on the measurement of specific psychological characteristics. *p. 137*

Trialability. The degree to which a new product is tried on a limited basis. *p. 454*

Tricomponent Attitude Model. An attitude model consisting of three parts: a cognitive (knowledge) component, an affective (feeling) component, and a conative (doing) component. *p. 249*

Trio of Needs. The basic human needs for power, affiliation, and achievement; each has a unique relevance to consumer motivation. *p. 121*

Truth-in-Advertising Laws. Legislation that protects consumers from false advertising claims. *p. 526*

Unmeasured Media. Refers to how organizations monitoring companies using new or nontraditional media have not yet developed a distinct means for computing the amount of money spent on each separate medium. *p. 295*

Upward Mobility. Movement upward in social-class standing from the social-class position into which the consumer was born. *p. 346*

Usage Rate. Segmentation that is based on the differences among *heavy, medium,* and *light users,* and *nonusers* of a specific product, service, or brand. *p. 88*

Usage Situation. Segmentation that is based on the idea that the occasion or situation often determines what consumers will purchase or consume (i.e., certain products for certain situations, special usage occasions). *p. 88*

Utilitarian Function. A component of the functional approach to attitude-change theory that suggests consumers hold certain attitudes partly because of the brand's utility. *p. 260*

Validity. The degree to which a measurement instrument accurately measures what it is designed to measure. *p. 58*

VALS. (See Values and Lifestyle System.) *p. 84*

Value-Expressive Function. A component of the functional approach to attitude-change theory that suggests that attitudes express consumers' general values, lifestyles, and outlook. *p. 260*

Values and Lifestyle System. A research service that tracks marketing-relevant shifts in the beliefs, values, and lifestyles of psychological segments of the American population. *p. 84*

Variety or Novelty Seeking. A personality trait similar to *OSL*, which measures a consumer's degree of variety seeking. *p. 146*

Verbal Communication. A message passed from sender to receiver through speech or writing. *p. 299*

Viral Marketing. The practice of encouraging individuals to pass on an e-mail message to others, thus creating the potential for exponential growth in the message's exposure and influence. *p. 285*

Virtual Personality or Self. A notion that provides an individual with the opportunity to "try on" different personalities or different identities, such as creating a fictitious personality in an online chat room. *p. 168*

Visualizers versus Verbalizers. The theory that some consumers (visualizers), due to their personality, respond better to highly visual advertising and/or advertising about visual products. In contrast, other consumers (verbalizers) respond better to advertising that offers detailed descriptions and/or promotes a product utilizing written or verbal information. *p. 147*

Weber's Law. A theory concerning the perceived differentiation between similar stimuli of varying intensities; that is, the stronger the initial stimulus, the greater the additional intensity needed for the second stimulus to be perceived as different. (See also Just Noticeable Difference.) *p. 176*

Webisodes. Short videos shown online featuring entertainment centered around a particular brand. *p. 299*

Wife-Dominated Decisions. Consumer choices generally made by the wife, either by tradition or knowledge. *p. 329*

Word-of-Mouth (WOM). Informal conversations between friends concerning products or services. *p. 281*

Working Women. Females who are employed outside the home. *p. 418*

World Brands. Products that are manufactured, packaged, and positioned the same way regardless of the country in which they are sold. *p. 438*

Zaltman Metaphor Elicitation Technique (ZMET). The first patented marketing research tool in the United States, which relies on visual images to assess consumers' thoughts about products, services, and marketing strategies. *p. 53*

Company Index

Note: Italicized page numbers indicate illustrations.

Name Index

Note: Italicized page numbers indicate illustrations.

T

U

Subject Index

Note: Italicized page numbers indicate illustrations.

清华会计学系列英文版教材

1. 管理会计（第 6 版）Management Accounting, 6/e

   Rajiv D. Banker, Robert S. Kaplan, S. Mark Young, Anthony A. Atkinson

2. 会计信息系统（第 11 版）Accounting Information Systems, 11/e

   George H. Bodnar, William S. Hopwood

3. 财务会计（第 10 版）Financial Accounting and GAP Annual Report, 10/e

   Walter T. Harrison, Charles T. Horngren

4. 会计学基础（第 11 版）Essentials of Accounting, 11/e

   Robert N. Anthony, Leslie Pearlman

5. 成本会计：管理的着重点（第 10 版）Cost Accounting: A Managerial Emphasis, 10/e

   Charles T. Horngren, George Foster, Srikant M. Datar

清华营销学系列英文版教材

1. 消费者行为学（第 10 版）Consumer Behavior, 10/e

   Leon G. Schiffman, Leslie Lazar Kanuk

2. 市场营销原理（第 15 版）Principles of Marketing, 15/e

   Philip Kotler, Gary Armstrong

3. 全球营销管理（第 7 版）Global Marketing Management, 7/e

   Warren J. Keegan

4. 营销调研精要（第 6 版）Essentials of Marketing Research, 6/e

   William G. Zikmund

5. 广告、促销与整合营销传播（第 5 版）Integrated Advertising, Promotion, and Marketing Communications, 5/e

   Kenneth E. Clow, Donald Baack

清华管理学系列英文版教材

1. 供应链管理：战略、规划与运作（第 5 版）Supply Chain Management: Strategy, Planning and Operations, 5/e

   Sunil Chopra, Peter Meindl

2. 公共关系实务（第 12 版）The Practice of Public Relations, 12/e

   Fraser P. Seitel

3. 管理学（第 11 版）Management, 11/e

   Stephen P. Robbins，Mary Coulter

4. 人力资源管理（第 11 版）Human Resource Management, 11/e

   Gary Dessler

5. 实用多元统计分析（第 6 版）Applied Multivariate Statistical Analysis, 6/e

   Richard A. Johnson, Dean W. Wichern

6. 物流学（第 1 版）Logistics, 1/e

David J. Bloomberg, Stephen B. LeMay, Joe B. Hanna

7. 管理技能开发（第 8 版）Developing Management Skills, 8/e

David A. Whetten, Kim S. Cameron

8. 罗宾斯 MBA 管理学（第 6 版）Supervision Today!, 6/e

Stephen P. Robbins, David A. DeCenzo

9. 战略管理基础（第 2 版）Fundamentals of Strategy, 2/e

Gerry Johnson, Richard Whittington, Kevan Scholes

10. 组织行为学（第 10 版）Behavior in Organizations, 10/e

Jerald Greenberg

11. 组织行为学（第 3 版）Essentials of Organizational Behaviour, 3/e

Laurie Mullins, Gill Christy

清华金融学系列英文版教材

1. 金融市场与金融机构（第 3 版）Financial Markets and Institutions, 3/e

Frederic S. Mishkin, Stanley G. Eakins

2. 期权、期货和其他衍生品（第 7 版）Options, Futures, and Other Derivatives，7/e

John C. Hull

3. 投资学（第 6 版）Investments, 6/e

William F. Sharpe, Gordon J. Alexander, Jeffery V. Bailey

4. 财务管理基础（第 13 版）Fundamentals of Financial Management, 13/e

James C. Van Horne, John M. Wachowicz, Jr.

5. 公司理财学基础：财务管理逻辑与实践（第 4 版）Foundations of Finance: The Logic and Practice of Financial Management, 4/e

Arthur J. Keown, John D. Martin, J. William Petty, David F. Scott, Jr.

清华经济学系列英文版教材

1. 微观经济学（第 7 版）Microeconomics, 7/e

Robert S. Pindyck, Daniel L. Rubinfeld

2. 宏观经济学（第 6 版）Macroeconomics, 6/e

Olivier Blanchard

3. 微观经济学原理（第 5 版）Principles of Microeconomics, 5/e

Robert H. Frank, Ben S. Bernanke

4. 宏观经济学原理（第 5 版）Principles of Macroeconomics, 5/e

Robert H. Frank, Ben S. Bernanke

5. 国际经济学：理论与政策（上册　国际贸易）（第 9 版）International Economics: Theory and Policy, 9/e

Paul R. Krugman, Maurice Obstfeld

6. 国际经济学：理论与政策（下册　国际金融）（第 9 版）International Economics: Theory and Policy, 9/e

   Paul R. Krugman, Maurice Obstfeld

7. 国际经济学基础 Introduction to International Economics

   Dominick Salvatore

8. 国际经济学（第 8 版）International Economics, 8/e

   Dominick Salvatore

9. 计量经济学导论：现代观点（第 5 版）Introductory Econometrics: A Modern Approach, 5/e

   Jeffrey M. Wooldridge

清华 MBA 核心课程英文版教材

1. 会计学：财务会计分册（第 9 版）Accounting: The Financial Chapters, 9/e

   Charles T. Horngren, Walter T. Harrison

2. 会计学：管理会计分册（第 9 版）Accounting: The Managerial Chapters, 9/e

   Charles T. Horngren, Walter T. Harrison

3. 组织行为学（第 14 版）Organizational Behavior, 14/e

   Stephen P. Robbins

4. 战略管理：概念与案例（第 13 版）Strategic Management: Concepts and Cases, 13/e

   Fred R. David

5. 营销管理（第 13 版）Marketing Management, 13/e

   Philip Kotler

6. 管理信息系统：管理数字化公司（第 12 版）Management Information Systems: Managing The Digital Firm, 12/e

   Kenneth C. Laudon, Jane P. Laudon

清华物流学系列英文版教材

1. 供应链管理原理：均衡方法（第 2 版）Principles of Supply Chain Management: A Balanced Approach,2/e

   Joel D. Wisner, G. Keong Leong, Keah-Choon Tan

2. 采购与供应链管理（第 4 版）Sourcing and Supply Chain Management, 4/e

   Robert Handfield, Robert Monczka, etc.

3. 采购与供应管理（第 15 版）Purchasing and Supply Management, 15/e

   P. Fraser Johnson, Anna E. Flynn

教学支持说明

尊敬的老师：

您好！

为了确保您及时有效地申请培生整体教学资源，请您务必完整填写如下表格，加盖学院的公章后传真给我们，我们将会在 2～3 个工作日内为您处理。

请填写所需教辅的开课信息：

采用教材			☐ 中文版 ☐ 英文版 ☐ 双语版
作　　者		出版社	
版　　次		ISBN	
课程时间	始于　　年　月　日	学生人数	
	止于　　年　月　日	学生年级	☐ 专科 ☐ 本科 1/2 年级 ☐ 研究生 ☐ 本科 3/4 年级

请填写您的个人信息：

学　　校			
院系/专业			
姓　　名		职　　称	☐助教 ☐讲师 ☐副教授 ☐教授
通信地址/邮编			
手　　机		电　　话	
传　　真			
official E-mail(必填) (eg:XXX@ ruc. edu. cn)		E-mail (eg:XXX@ 163. com)	
是否愿意接受我们定期的新书讯息通知：	☐ 是	☐ 否	

系/院主任：____________(签字)

(系/院办公室章)

____年____月____日

资源介绍：

—教材、常规教辅(PPT、教师手册、题库等)资源：请访问 www. pearsonhighered. com/educator； (免费)

—MyLabs / Mastering 系列在线平台：适合老师和学生共同使用；访问需要 Access Code； (付费)

清华大学出版社

北京市海淀区清华园学研大厦 B 座 509 室

邮编：100084

电话：8610-62770175-4506

传真：8610-62775511

E-mail：tupfuwu@ 163. com

Website：www. tup. com. cn

Pearson

Pearson Education Beijing Office

培生教育出版集团北京办事处

北京市东城区北三环东路 36 号北京环球贸易中心 D 座 1208 室

邮编：100013

电话：(8610)5735 5169

传真：(8610)5825 7961